Northern California

Northern Mountains
p333

North Coast & Redwoods
p218

Gold Country
p398

Lake Tahoe
p424

Napa & Sonoma Wine Country
p159

Yosemite & the Sierra Nevada
p460

San Francisco
p64

Marin County & the Bay Area
p108

Sacramento & Central Valley
p367

Central Coast
p274

Helena Smith, Brett Atkinson, Sara Benson, Alison Bing, Celeste Brash,

Nate Cavalieri, Michael Grosberg, Ashley Harrell, Josephine Quintero, John A Vlahides

Contents

ALAMO SQUARE PARK,
SAN FRANCISCO P82

/HAYK_SHALUNTS/SHUTTERSTOCK ©

SANDY L KIRRNER/GETTY IMAGES/FLICKR RF ©

YOSEMITE NATIONAL PARK
P461

Contents

SPECIAL FEATURES

Welcome to Northern California

With soaring peaks, vast coastline and the tallest of the world's trees, Northern California inspires all who visit to dream that much bigger.

Natural Splendor

Mother Nature puts on a spectacular show across Northern California. In the mighty Sierra Nevada Mountains, blue Lake Tahoe is so deep that if drained it would fill the state with 14 inches of water. Yosemite National Park is home to some of the world's highest waterfalls, and the tallest trees on the planet grow in Redwood National Park. Lassen Volcanic National Park showcases a bona fide volcano, while King's Canyon has gorges deeper than even the Grand Canyon. Across the Sierra's eastern escarpment, the mountains hang like curtains above the vast high deserts of the Great Basin.

Food & Drink

Expect to eat really well – this is a region at the forefront of American culinary trends. Everything grows here, from apple trees to Zinfandel grapes, and great food and wine are a collective fetish. You need not be fancy. Locals wax poetic about the humble burrito, or a platter of fresh cracked crab, plucked that day from the sea. Napa and Sonoma are the rural outposts of the Bay Area's dynamic and progressive food scene, with restaurants by celeb chefs, you-pick-'em orchards and artisanal dairy farms producing some of the highest-grade foods anywhere in the nation.

Weekend Escapes

Idyllic escapes are never far away here – just pick your theme. For road trips, it's hard to beat coastal drives up fog-shrouded Hwy 1 to Mendocino; or down the dramatic Pacific Coast Hwy to Big Sur, a thousand feet above the crashing surf. For history, head east to explore the foothills of the Sierra Nevada and Old West towns dating to the gold rush. For outdoor adventure, go up, up, up the mighty Sierra Nevada and hike granite domes and valleys made famous by John Muir. And for world-class art and culture, you need never leave San Francisco's city limits.

Big City, Little Towns

Whether it comes from the dramatic, Victorian-clad hills, the buzzing innovations of the culinary scene, or the eccentric, larger-than-life residents, there's an unmistakable energy crackling through San Francisco, beckoning visitors. Orbiting this cultural capital, Northern California's smaller cities and towns each hold their own unique appeal. There's the vibrant diversity of Oakland, the seaside elegance of Mendocino, and the sun-drenched idyll of Santa Cruz. Nevada City is the picture of a well-preserved and charming former gold-rush town, and even Sacramento, with its historic parks and agricultural bounty, will occasionally inspire a traveler to gasp with awe.

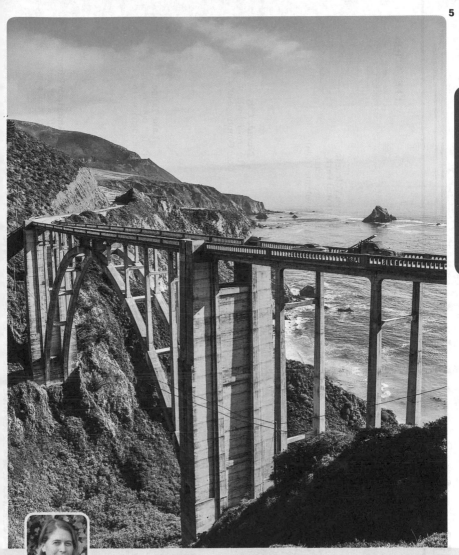

Why I Love Northern California

By Ashley Harrell, Writer

I'll never get over the feeling of crossing the Golden Gate Bridge, its massive red towers peeking above the fog, a swirl of ocean, sky and mountains framed by suspension cables in every direction. There are things I miss about SF: sunset hikes up Bernal Hill, sipping wine and playing Balderdash on a blanket in Dolores Park, the curiously slanting floors of my Chinatown apartment. But the storybook farmlands of Point Reyes made the deepest impression, and particularly one rancher I know there, who replaced a horse's lost eye with a ping-pong ball. Only in NorCal.

For more about our writers, see p576

Above: Bixby Bridge (p301)

Northern California

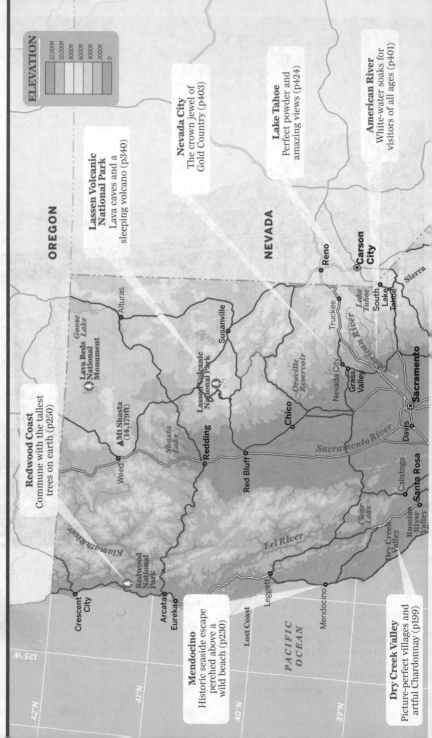

Redwood Coast
Commune with the tallest trees on earth (p250)

Lassen Volcanic National Park
Lava caves and a sleeping volcano (p340)

Nevada City
The crown jewel of Gold Country (p403)

Lake Tahoe
Perfect powder and amazing views (p424)

American River
White-water soaks for visitors of all ages (p401)

Mendocino
Historic seaside escape perched above a wild beach (p230)

Dry Creek Valley
Picture-perfect villages and artful Chardonnay (p199)

OREGON

NEVADA

ELEVATION

12,000ft
10,000ft
8000ft
6000ft
4000ft
2000ft
0

100 miles
200 km

Crescent City

Arcata
Eureka

Lost Coast

Mendocino

PACIFIC OCEAN

Leggett

Dry Creek Valley

Russian River Valley

Calistoga

Santa Rosa

Clear Lake

Eel River

Klamath River

Redwood National Park

Weed

▲Mt Shasta (14,179ft)

Shasta Lake

Lava Beds National Monument

Goose Lake

Alturas

Lassen Volcanic National Park

Redding

Red Bluff

Chico

Sacramento River

Davis

Sacramento

Susanville

Oroville Reservoir

Nevada City

Grass Valley

Truckee

Reno

Lake Tahoe

South Lake Tahoe

American River

Sierra

Carson City

42°N

41°N

40°N

39°N

125°W

Yosemite National Park
A wonderland of carved granite peaks and waterfalls (p461)

Highway 395
Jaw-dropping drive through the Sierra Nevada (p495)

Napa & Sonoma Valleys
America's most renowned wine region (p159)

San Francisco
Bold, urbane and irreverent (p64)

San Luis Obispo & Paso Robles
Rolling wine country that quietly rivals Napa (p320)

Northern California's
Top 25

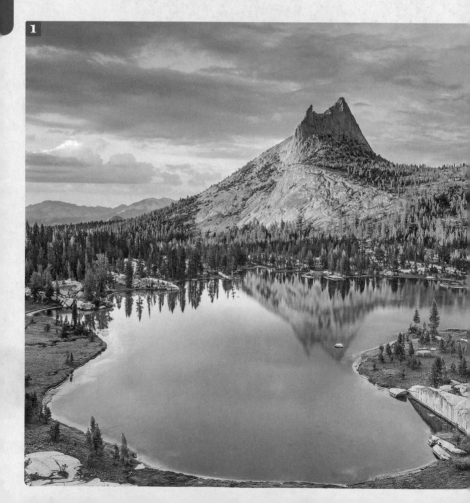

1

Yosemite National Park

1 Yosemite (p461) is arguably Northern California's greatest natural wonder. This beloved national park is gorgeous at any time, but especially so in spring, when several of the world's tallest waterfalls thunder and roar in the valley. Come summer, head up high to hike subalpine valleys ablaze with wildflowers, then cross the mile-high eastern escarpment and drop into vast desert landscapes where tumbleweeds blow. The leaves change colors in autumn, as the waterfalls start to dry up. In winter, snow blankets meadows, and jagged mountain peaks sparkle iridescent-white against an electric-blue sky.

San Francisco

2 SF (say Ess-Eff, not Frisco) is the gateway to Northern California. The views are iconic – clanging cable cars rattling up impossibly high hills, sunsets through the towers of the Golden Gate Bridge – and so is the culture, high art and low, with a Grammy-winning symphony, weird underground performance art, and America's most dynamic food scene. Nature holds a special place in SF (p64): keep your eye on the sky to spot flocks of wild green parrots, and head to the glittering blue bay to hear sea lions bark and bray. Bottom right: Golden Gate Bridge (p71)

Lassen Volcanic National Park

3 These days Mt Lassen volcano might be dormant, but its eruption a century ago created what's now Lassen Volcanic National Park (p340). Descend into the earth down a pitch-black lava tube, and explore bubbling thermal fields, where mud pots spew sulfur. This wildly alive geological landscape is visibly morphing itself into a new landscape. And it's remote: even at the peak of summer, it never feels crowded. Book ahead to stay at a classic dude ranch, and ride horseback into grassy meadows that fringe the high-mountain landscape.

Skiing Tahoe

4 Epic snowfall, warm sunshine and panoramic vistas of blue, blue Lake Tahoe (p424) make skiing in Northern California unlike skiing anywhere else. In a good year, these mountains receive some of the deepest snowpack on the continent, and an average 300 annual days of sunshine mean you can work on your tan while you perfect your carves. The terrain varies wildly, from Olympic-caliber steeps and rocky chutes, to ballroom groomers and gentle baby bunny slopes. Book a cozy cabin to snuggle fireside and watch icicles drip from the eaves outside.

LUCIILAD/GETTY IMAGES ©

SUCCESS'S IBC/GETTY IMAGES ©

Big Sur

5 Hwy 1 around Big Sur (p301) is the most famous stretch of highway in all of California. The road twists and turns a thousand feet above the vast blue Pacific, hugging the skirts of mile-high mountains. This is a drive that merits an upgraded rental car. Alas, passengers get the best views. Spend a night or two in a famous inn or cozy cottage, hike high peaks poking through the fog like islands in the sky, and take a late-night soak beneath the stars in seaside hot springs.

Napa & Sonoma Valleys

6 Napa and Sonoma (p159) not only produce America's best wines but are also stunningly beautiful areas to explore. Cruise hidden back roads by bicycle or convertible in search of that perfect bottle of wine; soak in thermal springs and bathe in mud at day spas; feast on dishes prepared by celebrity chefs; and bed down at a country inn. The pastoral landscape provides a lovely backdrop for hedonism – a patchwork of vineyards on oak-dotted hillsides, rising from serpentine rivers flanked by redwoods. Top right: Napa Valley (p162)

Mendocino

7 Perched atop a windswept headland surrounded on three sides by the Pacific, Mendocino (p230) is *the* romantic weekend getaway. A former whaling village taken over by artists in the 1960s, Mendo appears frozen in time, with century-old New England–style saltbox cottages you don't see elsewhere in California. Amble wooden sidewalks and peek into galleries and shops inside rose-covered cottages and weathered-wooden water towers. Leave time to kayak, watch for whales, chat up sophisticated bohemian locals, and drift asleep in a quiet country inn.

Point Reyes National Seashore

8 Only an hour from San Francisco, Point Reyes National Seashore (p127) juts 10 miles out to sea, a 1400ft-high peninsula atop an entirely different tectonic plate from the mainland. Its rugged natural beauty is dazzling. Seals colonize the rocky headlands, tide pools teem with life, grass-lands burst into color with spring flowers, and herds of tule elk roam high bluffs above the crashing surf. Descend 300 steps – 30 stories – from the bluff tops to the Pt Reyes Lighthouse for the best whale-watching in Northern California. Top: Tule elk bulls

Mono Lake

9 Spectacularly eerie Mono Lake (p501) sits on the floor of a vast high-mountain desert, surrounded by towering snow-covered peaks, its shores dense with pungent sagebrush. The ancient lake sprawls far and wide, with curious 'tufa' towers of calcium carbonate rising verti-cally from its salty black waters. Millions of migratory birds come to dive-bomb and feast on brine shrimp, and 80% of all the seagulls in California begin their lives here. The scale of things is enormous. Instead of hiking, consider kayaking.

JULIE VADER/SHUTTERSTOCK ©

DANIELLE KROMA/EYEEM/GETTY IMAGES ©

Highway 395

10 Hwy 395 (p495) (aka the Eastern Sierra Scenic Byway) is California's ultimate road trip (sorry Pacific Coast Hwy), a north–south route tracing the eastern escarpment of the mighty Sierra Nevadas, with offshoots to the highest and lowest points in the continental US. Expect to lose perspective on scale and distance as you drive beneath mountains rising nearly 3 miles high. Famous destinations include the back side of Yosemite National Park (summer only); eerie Mono Lake; Mt Whitney, the highest peak in the lower 48; and the rugged Alabama Hills, backdrop of old Hollywood Westerns.

Dry Creek Valley & Russian River Area

11 Know your geography: there are three Sonomas – the town, the valley, and the county. The latter's remote western and northern valleys are among the least known – and far less busy than famous Sonoma Valley – but they produce some incredible wines. Plan to sample topnotch Pinot Noir and Chardonnay in the foggy Russian River Valley (p197); and jammy Zinfandel in narrow and warm Dry Creek Valley (pictured, p199). During crush season in autumn, the leaves go red and gold, and the smell of fermenting fruit lingers on the breeze.

Rafting the American River

12 It's more than a little unfair that the American River (p401) trumps so many other white-water destinations in California – it's actually three rivers in one. All three branches – the North Fork, Middle Fork and South Fork – are ready-made for family outings. River expeditions can be short and sweet, or full-on adrenaline-packed multiday adventures. And on the way home, it's a quick detour to one of several classic Gold Country towns, such as Nevada City, where you can immerse yourself in history.

LUCKY-PHOTOGRAPHER/SHUTTERSTOCK ©

PIA BENZER/SHUTTERSTOCK ©

TRINETTE REED/GETTY IMAGES ©

Sequoia & Kings Canyon National Parks

13 This is a landscape of superlatives – a cleft in high mountains deeper than the Grand Canyon, and pristine backcountry wilderness that neighbors the highest peak in the continental United States, Mt Whitney (14,497ft). But it's the enormous trees that grab all the attention for being so unfathomably large and in charge – find the granddaddy of them all, General Sherman (p491), a giant sequoia thought to be the most massive tree on earth. Come wintertime, snow blankets the park: plan to snowshoe through the silent woods. Left: Sentinel, Sequoia National Park (p491)

San Luis Obispo & Paso Robles

14 Napa and Sonoma may be more famous, but the rolling golden hills around San Luis Obispo (p323) and Paso Robles (p320) cover three times the ground of Napa. And they produce remarkably great wines, similar in style to France's Rhône Valley. Booming craft-beer and urban-distillery scenes also offer compelling local flavors. The compact and appealing city of San Luis Obispo anchors the region, with a sophisticated dining scene providing a cosmopolitan counterpoint to the sleepy rural farms and wineries that sprawl everywhere outside town. Top right: San Luis Obispo (p323)

Hot Springs & Swimming Holes

15 You're traveling over the Yuba River Bridge on a blazing July day when, in the middle of nowhere, you pass a cluster of cars parked at the side of Hwy 49. Don't ask questions – just park, strip and plunge. And then there are the hot springs. On a chilly winter evening keep an eye out for bubbles in the undeveloped mud holes in the Eastern Sierra and by eerie Mono Lake. Or try an old-fashioned spa resort in Calistoga (pictured, p181), where the local specialty is a volcanic-ash mud bath.

Monterey

16 Monterey (p287) is home to the finest aquarium on the West Coast and the incredible marine reserve that is Monterey Bay. The former fishing and canning town, made famous by Steinbeck's *Cannery Row*, is now the Central Coast's most family-friendly destination. After you've gawked at all the finned aquarium critters, take the kids for saltwater taffy at Fisherman's Wharf, on a boat trip to spot whales, and to explore old forts, missions and historic adobes from California's Mexican and Spanish past. Top: Monterey Wharf & Marina

Klamath Basin National Wildlife Refuges

17 The Klamath Basin (p360) provides bird-watchers with a thrilling spectacle beneath the Pacific Flyway, the 'avian superhighway' of migrating north–south bird traffic. If whipping out high-powered binoculars to spot a semipalmated sandpiper doesn't quicken your pulse, take heart: birds are but a few of the awe-inspiring animals found everywhere in this remote northern mountain region. Head to the edges of Lava Beds National Monument and you'll encounter ever more wildlife, from vesper bats and mule deer (pictured), to flying squirrels and marmot.

KEN WOLTER/SHUTTERSTOCK ©

ALUKICH/GETTY IMAGES ©

The Redwood Coast

18 A few minutes craning your neck at the world's tallest trees (p264), contemplating what it means to be standing before a 2000-year-old living thing, and the day-to-day world feels far away. It is. Most people never make it to this northernmost edge of the state, but consider this: there's no other place on the globe where coast redwoods grow. And the primordial forest – lush with spiky prehistoric ferns and hot-pink azalea flowers – is as biologically complex as the rainforest. *Carpe diem*: brave the drive.

Mt Shasta

19 No other mountain in California stirs the imagination quite like Mt Shasta (p349). Its conical summit rises over 14,000ft from the sea-level Central Valley flatlands, and stays shrouded by snow many months of the year. Native tribes believed a god left heaven to live on its summit. John Muir said it made his 'blood turn to wine.' An early-20th-century explorer reported a city of mummies 11 miles below its surface. New Agers claim it's an energy vortex in the earth. Find your own metaphor on a hike to the summit.

MNSTUDIO/SHUTTERSTOCK ©

CHRISTOPHER BOSWELL/SHUTTERSTOCK ©

PETE NIESEN/SHUTTERSTOCK ©

ALEXANDER HOWARD/LONELY PLANET ©

Lost Coast

20 If you crave getting as far away as possible from the sound of civilization and internal combustion engines, you can't get further than the Lost Coast (p252), the longest stretch of undeveloped coastline in California. The King Range rises so abruptly from the Pacific Ocean – a mile nearly straight up – that building a road on its flanks proved impossible. The only way to reach this windswept foggy shore is to hike in. Along the way, spot roaming herds of Roosevelt elk, rusted-out shipwrecks, and wide-open vistas of the roaring sea.

Nevada City & Gold Country

21 Judging by a trip to the Gold Country's most famous town, you'd think that the forty-niners stormed California in search of antiques shops, ice-cream parlors, and frilly B&Bs. Nevada City (pictured, p403) may be the most famous, but it's not the only well-preserved town along winding Hwy 49, aka the Gold Country Hwy. Plan to visit Columbia State Historic Park for a glimpse of the Wild West, complete with swinging saloon doors; and detour from the main road to find Murphys, which looks like it always has (except for the horseless carriages).

Santa Cruz & Capitola

22 Though surfers, hippies, college students and left-wing activists would disagree, Santa Cruz (p276) feels more like Southern California than Northern. Blame geography: Santa Cruz faces south, not west, and gets drenched in sunshine. The beach is everybody's backyard. After exploring the park-like campus of USC, and shopping downtown for records and vintage clothing, hit the sand. No visit is complete without a trip to the famous Boardwalk and a ride aboard the bone-rattling Giant Dipper, a century-old wooden roller coaster and National Historic Landmark right on Main Beach (pictured, p277).

Muir Woods

23 Pictures don't do justice to Muir Woods National Monument (p123) – you simply can't appreciate the scale of the world's tallest trees until you're standing beneath them, watching fog swirl in the branches like evanescing ghosts. Muir Woods is tiny compared with northern redwood parks but it's just a half-day trip from San Francisco, providing a glimpse of the trees without the long drive. Get here first thing to beat crowds, and then make sure to ascend nearby Mt Tamalpais – by foot or car – for bird's-eye vistas of ocean and forest.

Guerneville

24 A perfect day in gay-friendly Guerneville (p205) begins with tasting earthy Pinots and green apple pie in the town's refurbished 1921 bank that recently became an adorable retail and gallery space. Next, float down the lazy Russian River with a few friends and a flask, then go play bingo with a bunch of indulgent, gender-bending nuns. If there's still time, get sweaty strolling among the world's tallest trees in Armstrong Redwoods State Natural Reserve and then cool off at one of R3 Hotel's clothing-optional pool parties.

Wilderness Camping

25 Nowhere else in the US has the majestic natural beauty Northern California does, making its campgrounds some of the country's most desirable. Whether it's the high-mountain forests of the Trinity Alps, the granite domes of Yosemite, the forgotten expanse of the Lost Coast, or lonely Angel Island (p120) right in San Francisco Bay, you'll find many breathtaking and beautiful places to sleep beneath the stars. For serious hiking, plan a backpacking trip along the epic Pacific Crest Trail, which runs all the way from Canada to Mexico. Bottom: Angel Island (p120)

Need to Know

For more information, see Survival Guide (p549)

Currency
US dollars ($)

Language
English

Visas
Visa information is highly subject to change. Double-check current visa requirements *before* coming to the USA on the State Department's US Visa website (https://travel.state.gov/content/visas/en.html).

Money
ATMs and banks widely available. Credit cards required for car and hotel reservations. Checks rarely accepted. Tipping is customary, not optional.

Cell Phones
Foreign GSM multiband phones will work in the USA. Prepaid cell phones are widely available. Coverage can be spotty in remote areas.

Time
Pacific Time Zone (GMT/UTC minus eight hours)

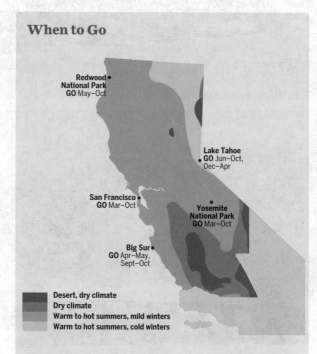

When to Go

Redwood
National Park
GO May–Oct

Lake Tahoe
GO Jun–Oct,
Dec–Apr

San Francisco
GO Mar–Oct

Yosemite
National Park
GO Mar–Oct

Big Sur
GO Apr–May,
Sept–Oct

Desert, dry climate
Dry climate
Warm to hot summers, mild winters
Warm to hot summers, cold winters

High Season
(Jun–Aug)

➡ Accommodations are at their most expensive; weekday rates are cheaper, especially at popular weekend destinations, such as Wine Country.

➡ During holiday weekends, prices for accommodations increase dramatically.

Shoulder
(Sep–Oct, Mar–May)

➡ Prices drop in fall and spring.

➡ Best time to visit the national parks, as they're less crowded and generally accessible, especially in autumn, before snow season.

Low Season
(Nov–Feb)

➡ Crowds vanish at national parks and in Wine Country, but not at ski towns.

➡ Prices and occupancy spike during holidays.

➡ Lake Tahoe has high-season pricing in wintertime (ski season); highest rates are around Christmastime.

Useful Websites

California Travel & Tourism Commission (www.visitcalifornia.com) Multilingual trip-planning guides.

SF Gate Travel (www.sfgate.com/travel) Travel features and Bay Area getaways.

Redwood Hikes (www.redwoodhikes.com) A guide to walking under old-growth redwood.

Lonely Planet (www.lonelyplanet.com/california) Destination information, hotel bookings, traveler forum and more.

California State Parks (www.parks.ca.gov) Outdoor activities and free e-guides.

Caltrans (www.dot.ca.gov) Highway information.

Important Numbers

Country code	☎1
International access code	☎011
Operator	☎0
Emergency (ambulance, fire & police)	☎911
Directory assistance (local)	☎411

Exchange Rates

Australia	A$1	$0.75
Canada	C$1	$0.74
Europe	€1	$1.12
Japan	¥100	$0.89
Mexico	MXN10	$0.54
New Zealand	NZ$	$0.70
UK	£1	$1.30

For current exchange rates see www.xe.com.

Daily Costs

Budget: Less than $100

➡ Burrito for dinner: $6–10

➡ Campsites: $20–40

➡ Hostels: $25–40

➡ Museum admission: free (once per month) to $10

➡ Public transit in San Francisco: $2.25; cable cars: $7

Midrange: $100–200

➡ Two-star motel room: $75–150

➡ Car rental: from $30 per day, plus insurance and gas

➡ Short taxi trip: $8–15, plus tip

Top End: More than $200

➡ Single-day rafting trip: $135

➡ Meal in top restaurant: $60–75, plus alcohol and tip

➡ Three-star lodging: from $150

Opening Hours

Standard opening hours:

Banks 9am to 5pm Monday to Thursday, to 6pm Friday, some 9am to 12:30pm Saturday

Bars 5pm to 2am daily (to midnight in rural areas)

Business hours (general) 9am to 5pm Monday to Friday

Nightclubs 9pm to 2am Thursday to Saturday

Post offices 9am to 5pm Monday to Friday, some 9am to noon Saturday

Restaurants 7am to 10:30am, 11:30am to 2:30pm and 5pm to 9:30pm daily, some later Friday and Saturday

Shops 10am to 6pm or 7pm Monday to Saturday, noon to 5pm Sunday (malls open later)

Arriving in Northern California

San Francisco International Airport BART to downtown ($8.95, 30 minutes). Door-to-door shuttles ($15 to $20, one hour); find shuttles upstairs at departures level. Taxis to downtown cost $40 to $55, plus 15% tip (30 to 50 minutes).

Oakland International Airport Trams ($6) connect airport with BART station; BART to downtown SF ($3.80, 25 minutes). Taxis to downtown SF cost about $65.

Sacramento International Airport Good for Wine Country, Yosemite, Gold Country and Sierra Nevada. Capitol Corridor (www.capitolcorridor.org) trains connect to the Bay Area (from $19); transfer to BART in Richmond.

Getting Around

A car is a nuisance in San Francisco, but a necessity everywhere else in Northern California.

Car Essential for travel at your own pace. Drive on the right. For highway information, contact Caltrans (www.dot.ca.gov).

Train Amtrak serves many cities in Northern California; uses connecting bus services from main train routes to lesser destinations. Read schedules carefully; look for bus icons to determine which routes are served by bus, not train.

Bus Greyhound serves major California cities, with limited service on the coast. Other companies, notably around San Francisco, serve the suburbs and parts of Wine Country.

Air Because of the state's size, consider flying between some cities (you'll need a rental car when you arrive, except in SF).

For much more on **getting around**, see p559

If You Like...

Majestic Scenery

Northern California has some of America's most spectacular natural lands. Make time for at least one national park.

Yosemite National Park High meadows and granite domes; this was conservationist John Muir's wonderland.

Lassen Volcanic National Park Discover alien lava fields, sulfuric mud pots and a snow-capped dormant volcano. (p340)

Redwood National and State Parks The world's tallest trees date from prehistory at this patchwork of parks. (p267)

Sequoia and Kings Canyon National Parks Stand agape beneath the world's most massive living things; hike into California's wildest canyon wilderness. (p486)

Marin Headlands Across the Golden Gate from San Francisco, eagles and hawks circle above dramatic cliffs; find hiking trails and hidden beaches. (p110)

Point Reyes National Seashore Driving the elk-studded hills of this super-green wonderland by the sea is the stuff of legends and fairy tales. (p127)

History

Gold Country Follow in the footsteps of Western pioneers and hardscrabble miners, or pan for real gold yourself. (p400)

Sutter's Fort State Historic Park The highest ground in Sacramento, this historic fort was California's first major settlement. (p370)

Alcatraz 'The Rock' – America's first military prison – rises just offshore from San Francisco. (p71)

Bodie State Historic Park California's creepiest, biggest ghost town, preserved in a state of arrested decay. (p497)

Manzanar National Historic Site Commemorates the Japanese Americans interned here during WWII. (p515)

Sonoma State Historic Park Offers multiple historic sites, some dating back to the 1820s when California still belonged to Mexico. (p188)

Small Towns

Ferndale With Victorian-era 'butterfat mansions,' this former dairy capital made the National Register of Historic Places. (p256)

Mendocino Tiny New England–style town, on a fog-shrouded rocky peninsula by the sea. (p230)

Angels Camp Twain wrote on jumping frogs here, and the place still buzzes with gold-rush history. (p418)

Weaverville Beneath the majestic Trinity Alps, this tiny berg has an ancient Chinese temple but no stoplights. (p362)

Boonville Great food, stylish lodging, a killer brewery and dynamic wineries make for a brilliant escape. (p243)

Nevada City Once brimming with gold prospectors, this well-preserved town now offers antique shops and charming B&Bs. (p403)

Lakes

Lake Tahoe Come summer to swim and sail; come wintertime to ski with a big blue view. (p424)

Shasta Lake Party with your friends on a houseboat, or find tranquility hiking endless miles of shoreline. (p339)

Eagle Lake Navigate gorgeous two-lane roads to the pristine surroundings of Cali's third-largest natural lake. (p347)

PLAN YOUR TRIP IF YOU LIKE...

Mono Lake Eerie towers of calcium carbonate abound – plan to kayak and bird-watch here, not swim. (p501)

Tenaya Lake California's prettiest, glittering blue lake is along the high-country summertime-only road through Yosemite. (p467)

Bass Lake A local Marin swimming hole perfect for a cool dip after the moderately strenuous, 3-mile hike. (p125)

Museums

de Young Museum A copper-skinned temple to global art in San Francisco's Golden Gate Park. (p78)

California Academy of Sciences San Francisco's natural-history museum and aquarium breathes 'green' in its eco-certified design, with a four-story rainforest and living roof. (p78)

California Museum Sacramento's modern-history museum highlights famous people and lesser-known tales from the state's past. (p369)

Laws Railroad Museum Old West aficionados love Bishop's original 1883 train depot and museum. (p512)

Charles M Schulz Museum An homage to the creator of Peanuts cartoons, who was a Santa Rosa resident. (p210)

Musée Mécanique Collection of gold-rush era penny arcade games and artifacts, located at Fisherman's Wharf. (p75)

Live Music

Fillmore Auditorium Built by Bill Graham in the '60s and advertising past shows by The Dead, The Doors, Radiohead and Adele. (p103)

Top: Bodie State Historic Park (p497)

Bottom: California Academy of Sciences (p78)

Yoshi's In Oakland's Jack London Sq, Yoshi's stages top talents in jazz and blues and serves delish Japanese food. (p136)

San Francisco Symphony Under the baton of famous conductor Michael Tilson Thomas, the SFS often wins Grammys. (p103)

Buck Owens' Crystal Palace Shine your boots and don pressed denim at the premier country-music venue in the Central Valley. (p395)

High Sierra Music Festival Top-notch folk and jam band festival in the middle of nowhere (read: no crowds). (p347)

Skinny Dippin'

Northern California has a remarkable variety of au naturel hot springs and swimming spots. These are but a few.

Orr Hot Springs Connect with your inner hippie, camp beneath the stars and soak in thermal waters, just hours from San Francisco. (p247)

Esalen Institute Big Sur's blissful retreat is spendy, but the memory of soaking in a bath on a ledge over the crashing Pacific will last a lifetime. (p305)

Finnish Country Sauna and Tubs Private open-air redwood tubs and a European coffee-house vibe make this a unique North Coast soak. (p261)

Baker Beach Most days you'll need a sweater, but when the sun's out, head to the northern end of San Francisco's principal clothing-optional beach. (p75)

R3 Hotel Best clothing-optional pool parties in all the land. (p206)

Mind-Bending Festivals

Northern California hosts some of the most wild, wacky and wonderful festivals in the nation. Not for the xenophobic, these festivals are a study in diversity.

Hardly Strictly Bluegrass San Francisco's best free music festival hosts three days of A-list folk, rock, bluegrass and country artists. (p90)

Reggae on the River In the heart of Humboldt County, this music event is all dreadlocks and Jamaican-influenced jams. (p252)

Burning Man A trippy art party that also happens to be the world's greatest experiment in culture and community. (p27)

San Francisco Pride Month The last Sunday in June, a million people descend upon San Francisco to celebrate Gay Pride Day. (p26)

Bay to Breakers May's zany, costumed Embarcadero to Ocean Beach race; joggers dressed as salmon run upstream. (p88)

Kinetic Grand Championship An elaborate, yearly sculpture race otherwise known as the triathlon of the art world. (p26)

Beautiful Coastline

Julia Pfeiffer Burns State Park This remote crescent-shaped beach is a stunner – and includes a waterfall that drains into the sea. (p304)

Point Reyes National Seashore Migrating whales, incredible birding, excellent hiking and kayaking on a pristine peninsula, an hour from San Francisco. (p127)

Redwood Coast Mysterious and majestic, this wild coast of big trees and brooding surf feels lost in time. (p264)

Sonoma Coast State Beach A series of rocky coves and sandy beaches reveal the awesome power of nature. (p223)

Big Sur This enchanting, rugged stretch of Hwy 1 wins for its cypress trees, rocky cliffs and striking ocean vistas. (p301)

Month by Month

January

Typically California's wettest month. Coastal regions go quiet. The hills turn green. Mountain ski resorts are packed on weekends, quiet on weekdays. Bay Area skies gray. Wine Country a bargain.

🎎 Chinese New Year

San Francisco's Chinatown (www.sanfrancisco chinatown.com/events/chinesenewyearparade. html) sounds like a war zone, as firecrackers announce the lunar new year with parades, lion dancers and street vendors. Late January, early February.

February

Rain up and down the coast, heavy snow in the mountains – ski season is in full swing. Beach towns and the Wine Country are quiet.

🏃 Wildlife-Watching

Don't let rain keep you indoors – February is prime time to spot whales migrating offshore, colonies of elephant seals mating and birthing, monarch butterflies roosting in the trees, and hundreds of bird species along the Pacific Flyway.

March

Following winter's rains, the entire state turns deep green, just for March – except the Sierra Nevada, which remains white. California poppies appear along the coast.

🎎 North Lake Tahoe SnowFest

Celebrating the peak of the winter season, this wild affair (http://tahoesnowfest. org) celebrates all things snow, with costume parties, ski competitions, parades and (of course) a snow queen contest.

🎎 Mendocino Coast Whale Festivals

As the northbound winter migration of gray whales peaks, Mendocino and Fort Bragg fill three weekends with food and wine tasting, art shows, marine-mammal educational exhibits and naturalist-guided walks and talks.

🍴 California Artisan Cheese Festival

The ultimate cheese party (www.artisancheesefestival. com), involving farm tours held far and wide, curious cheese courses and cheesemonger contests. Attendants can get involved in multi-course pairings matching cheese with beer, wine and cocktails, and the whole thing is done to promote 'an awareness of cheesemaking.'

🏃 World Naked Bike Ride

The increasingly popular San Francisco event is one of many taking place across the world in protest of our global economy's dependency on oil. The SF version gets super-naked, though. Bring sunscreen.

April

Shoulder season on the coast and mountains brings hotel deals – except during spring break, around Easter. Wildflower season peaks at lower elevations and Gold Country wildflowers bloom. Tahoe spring skiing is at its best – as are Yosemite's waterfalls.

✕ San Joaquin Asparagus Festival

A noteworthy celebration of stinky little green stalks. Where else on earth are you going to find asparagus ice cream? (p388)

✻ San Francisco International Film Festival

Since 1957, North America's longest-running film festival has been bringing independent-minded films to San Francisco, including provocative global premiers; late April, early May. (p88)

☆ Perpetual Indulgence in Dolores Park

On Easter Sunday, the Sisters of Perpetual Indulgence (Catholic drag queens) stage an Easter egg hunt, bonnet contest and the notorious Hunky Jesus Contest in San Francisco's Dolores Park.

✻ Redwood Coast Music Festival

This Dixieland celebration (http://www.rcmfest.org) held each April in Eureka has long focused on hot jazz, but over the years has expanded to other musical genres and a great many venues.

May

Weather warms statewide, dry season begins. Coastal fog forms as the sun's now-hot rays hit the icy Pacific.

Summer begins Memorial Day weekend – among the year's busiest weekends. Yosemite rangers install cables for climbers ascending Half Dome.

🏃 Kinetic Grand Championship

Over Memorial Day weekend, this 'triathlon of the art world' is a three-day, 38-mile race, from Arcata to Ferndale, of human-powered, self-propelled contraptions that defy definition. Competitors – all tinkerers and inventors – are hell-bent on outdoing one another. (p262)

✻ Healdsburg Future Farmers Country Fair

Sonoma County's très chic capital of gastronomy reverts to its agrarian roots for this country fair, featuring the future farmers' parade, when little children display baby animals and the whole town cheers. (p214)

June

School's out by the end of the month; family travel begins. Everywhere is busy. Coastal fog – 'June gloom' – thickens and spreads over San Francisco, drawn through the Golden Gate by the Central Valley's intense heat.

✻ Pride Month

Out and proud since 1970, San Francisco's big, bawdy celebrations take place throughout June, with costumed parades, coming-out parties, live music, DJs and more. It's one of the city's most joyful events. (p88)

July

At the peak of summer, the trails of Yosemite get crowded; the Central Valley gets blazingly hot. July 4 is summer's busiest weekend; towns host fairs and fireworks. Lake Tahoe's high season begins.

✻ California State Fair

A million people come to Sacramento's fairgrounds for two weeks in July to pet pigs and cheer horse races, browse blue ribbons, and sample California wines and microbrews. Special events – such as concerts and bull-riding – draw huge crowds. (p372)

☆ Reggae on the River

Come party with the 'Humboldt Nation' of hippies, Rastafarians, tree-huggers and other beloved NorCal eccentrics for two days of live reggae bands, arts and crafts, barbecue, juggling, unicycling, camping and swimming; mid-July. (p252)

✕ Gilroy Garlic Festival

A long-standing and massive three-day celebration of Gilroy's pungent claim to fame, held at Christmas Hill Park and involving live music on three stages, cooking demonstrations and various family activities.

August

Warm weather keeps Santa Cruz beaches crowded; non-south-facing coastal areas remain shrouded in fog three days out of four. Europeans throng San Francisco. Wildflowers peak in the High Sierra.

Strawberry Festival at Monterey Bay

The messy marquee event at this Watsonville festival is the pie-eating contest, but live music and tons of fruit keep families entertained. The berries are entirely local: Watsonville produces almost 90% of all the strawberries grown in the US. (p55)

Burning Man

Although Burning Man (https://burningman. org) happens in Nevada's Black Rock Desert, it began in San Francisco and draws tens of thousands of Northern Californians, who celebrate art's ephemeral nature, radical inclusion, self-reliance and self-expression. No commerce or advertising allowed. Make arrangements way ahead.

September

Summer's last hurrah is Labor Day weekend, when cities empty and parks get crowded. High Sierra aspens turn gold. School resumes. Fog clears at the coast; San Francisco warms. Wine Country begins its harvest.

☆ Monterey Jazz Festival

A roster of iconic artists and young jazz visionaries arrive to play one of the world's longest-running jazz festivals, featuring

outdoor concerts and more intimate indoor shows over a long weekend in mid-September. (p292)

October

Vineyard Festivals

California's wine regions celebrate their harvest with star-chef food-and-wine shindigs, grape-stomping 'crush' parties and barrel tastings; some events start in September.

Litquake

San Francisco's thrilling literary festival features readings, storytelling hours, workshops, author appearances, guided walking tours and a 'LitCrawl' between Mission district pubs. (p90)

Half Moon Bay Art & Pumpkin Festival

Pays homage to pumpkins, art, wine and community, not necessarily in that order. The event (http:// pumpkinfest.miramar events.com) has been held in the ostensible world pumpkin capital for more than 45 years.

November

Rain and snow begin to fall and ski season begins at the end of the month. The weeks between Thanksgiving and Christmas are cold and dark; nobody travels at this time, and hotel rates plummet.

Día de los Muertos

Mexican communities honor ancestors on November 2 with costumed parades, sugar skulls, graveyard picnics and candlelight processions. Join the colorful festivities in San Francisco's Mission District. (p90)

December

Hoards descend for skiing in Tahoe. Roads to Yosemite are closed in the winter, and rain can sometimes flood Wine Country. San Fran is lit up with holiday lights and music performances.

Great Dickens Christmas Fair

Over several winter weekends, San Francisco's Cow Palace is transformed into a scene out of Victorian London, where lamp-lit, treasure-filled shops line the street and vendors hawk their wares. The event (www.dickensfair. com) includes hundreds of costumed performers, along with music halls, pubs and dance floors.

Fairytale Winter Wonderland

Over two December weekends Sacramento hosts Fairytale Town, a celebration of all traditions winter throughout the world held in William Land Park. The town is aglow with twinkling lights and holiday decor, and populated with live entertainers, performers, artists and the like.

Itineraries

 1 WEEK San Francisco, Marin County & Wine Country

This classic NorCal itinerary explores San Francisco, then heads north up the rugged coast and inland to Wine Country.

San Francisco begs exploration – its hills, cable cars, glorious bay and dynamic culture are unique in the world. Wander hidden alleyways in Chinatown, see Beat-poet hangouts in North Beach and ascend Telegraph Hill beneath flocks of wild parrots. Head to Golden Gate Park for gorgeous gardens and thrilling museums, then make for the Mission District to find colorful murals and delicious tacos. Cross the Golden Gate Bridge to the **Marin Headlands** and hike cliffs rising straight from the Pacific. Or wander among redwoods – the world's tallest trees – at cathedral-like **Muir Woods National Monument**. For a full-day trip, go whale-watching on the rugged coast of **Point Reyes National Seashore**. Stay the night.

Explore Sonoma Coast State Beach, near **Bodega Bay**, then cut inland to tiny **Occidental** and Wine Country to spend another night. Recharge in thermal springs and mud baths in **Calistoga** before sampling famous California vintages in the surrounding Napa Valley. Grab a fancy meal in downtown **Napa** and return to San Francisco via **Sonoma** to explore historic sights between visits to wine-tasting rooms.

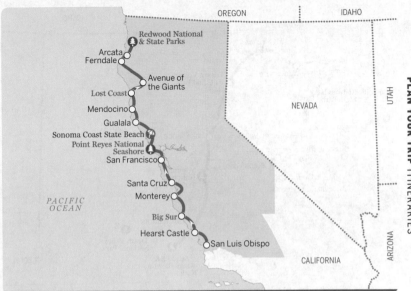

10 DAYS Up the Coast

The serpentine stretch of Hwy 1 (and Hwy 101) between San Luis Obispo and the Oregon border is among Northern California's most epic road trips, connecting cute beach towns, rugged coastline and majestic redwood forests.

Start with a delicious breakfast and a stroll among the cafes and boutiques of college town **San Luis Obispo** before heading for jaw-dropping **Hearst Castle** (reservations are essential). Here begins one of America's most famous and dramatic drives: the **Big Sur** coast, 1000ft above the Pacific and lush with cypress trees. Spend at least one night between Hearst Castle and Santa Cruz. Choose your adventure: a romantic hideaway in Big Sur, the West's best aquarium at **Monterey**, or a classic beachside amusement park, complete with boardwalk and bone-rattling wooden roller coaster, in **Santa Cruz**. Or combine them over several days.

Get an early start for **San Francisco**, the thrilling urban centerpiece of the trip. Spend at least two days exploring the City by the Bay, being sure to wander through the verdant Golden Gate Park and tap into Beat-poet culture in North Beach. Then continue north for a day to the stunningly scenic **Point Reyes National Seashore** and **Sonoma Coast State Beach**, where you can pick up baguettes and some incredible cheese and stop for picnicking, tide-pooling and whale-watching. Here the coast gets wild again, with windswept bluffs and nary a traffic light. Spend a couple of nights in a seaside cottage near **Gualala** and lollygag on hidden beaches; or book a B&B in moody **Mendocino** to gallery-hop, explore rocky headlands and fall asleep beside a toasty, crackling fire.

Hwy 1 cuts inland and joins four-lane Hwy 101 at the **Lost Coast**, the North Coast's premier backpacking destination. Leave the main highway to follow the parallel-running **Avenue of the Giants**, flanked by towering redwoods. Most people turn around after the Avenue, but to see the depth of the redwood forests, keep going north. Detour from the main road for lunch in the cute-as-a-button Victorian village of **Ferndale**, or the wildly progressive college town of **Arcata**. Spend two days exploring the magnificent ancient groves of **Redwood National and State Parks** before returning south.

3 WEEKS # Northern California Classics

To see Northern California's most spectacular scenery, plan to make a loop around the entire region. Begin with a dose of big-city culture in **San Francisco**. Get a taste of the California food scene at the Ferry Building market, then hop on a ferry to notorious Alcatraz. Plan to ride a cable car, wander the waterfront, and discover the spectacular gardens and museums of Golden Gate Park. Head north over the famous Golden Gate Bridge to **Marin County** and the windswept coastline of Point Reyes National Seashore. California's most famous grapes grow nearby in Wine Country – leave time to explore the over-the-top wineries of **Napa Valley** and historic **Sonoma**. If you've extra time, get lost on back roads in the **Russian River Valley**. Wine Country meets the boondocks in hidden **Anderson Valley**, on the way north to coastal **Mendocino**, a picture-perfect New England–like village on rocky Pacific headlands above the roaring surf.

Work your way north, past Leggett, where Hwy 1 cuts inland and joins Hwy 101; here begins the Redwood Coast, home to the world's tallest trees. In **Humboldt Redwoods State Park** drive beneath towering redwoods along the Avenue of the Giants. Stop for a night in conservative **Eureka**, with its pretty waterfront and candy-colored Victorians; or let your hair down with the college kids in Eureka's left-leaning neighbor, **Arcata**. Turn east on Hwy 299 for a mountainous scenic drive toward gold-rush-era **Weaverville**, skirting the lake-studded Trinity Alps. Head north on I-5 to gape at stunning **Mt Shasta**, then head southeast on Hwy 89 to **Lassen Volcanic National Park**, that hellishly beautiful volcanic landscape in the Cascade Range. Keep trucking southeast on Hwy 89 to **Lake Tahoe**, a four-season mountain resort. Spend a couple of nights. Afterward, cut south down the Eastern Sierra and Hwy 395 to the back-door entrance into **Yosemite National Park**, via summertime-only Tioga Rd.

If you've time, tack on a drive down spectacularly scenic Hwy 395, which passes between the highest and lowest points in the contiguous US: **Mt Whitney** and Death Valley. Otherwise, after a night or two in Yosemite Valley, head west and then south to check out **Sequoia and Kings Canyon National Parks**, where you can wander groves of giant sequoias – the world's most massive living things.

Top: Yosemite Falls
(p461), Yosemite
National Park

Bottom: Alamo Square
Park (p82), San
Francisco

California: Off the Beaten Track

LAVA BEDS NATIONAL MONUMENT

A geological wonderland of lava flows, spatter cones, shield volcanoes and craters. Strap on a helmet and clamber inside two dozen lava tubes. (p359)

AMADOR COUNTY WINE REGION

Explore one of California's oldest but least-known wine countries up in the Sierra Nevada foothills, where old Zinfandel grapevines thrive in mineral-rich soil. (p414)

BODIE STATE HISTORIC PARK

High above Mono Lake, this gold-rush-era mining camp has become a ghost town where 200 buildings stand eerily frozen in time. (p497)

SMITH RIVER NATIONAL RECREATION AREA

One of the state's last undammed river systems tumbles out of the Siskiyou Mountains, into Redwood National and State Parks. Plan to hike or raft. (p269)

LOST COAST

Tackle an epic backpacking route, take a day hike to Punta Gorda Lighthouse, or beachcomb in utterly remote Shelter Cove, an overnight escape. (p254)

COLEMAN VALLEY ROAD

One of NorCal's most scenic drives winds off the Bohemian Highway near wacky Occidental, climbs through forestland and by lush meadows, and delivers you to the roaring blue Pacific. (p207)

200 km
100 miles

OREGON

NEVADA

Alturas

Goose Lake

Eagle Lake

Susanville

Reno

Truckee

Carson City

Lake Tahoe

South Lake Tahoe

AMADOR COUNTY WINE REGION

Lassen Volcanic National Park

Lake Oroville

Chico

Nevada City

Sacramento

LAVA BEDS NATIONAL MONUMENT

Weed

Redding

Red Bluff

Sacramento River

Clear Lake

Calistoga

Occidental

Santa Rosa

SMITH RIVER RECREATION AREA

Crescent City

Arcata

Eureka

Leggett

Mendocino

Eel River

Russian R

LOST COAST

COLEMAN VALLEY ROAD

PACIFIC OCEAN

SACRAMENTO–SAN JOAQUIN RIVER DELTA

Dawdle lazily beside waterways and wildlife wetlands, taste farm bounty, and cruise one-stoplight towns with yesteryear saloons and colorful historical sites. (p376)

SAN FRANCISCO PENINSULA

In a rush to reach Monterey, many drivers skip seeing the coast between San Francisco and Santa Cruz, despite the many state beaches, parks and family farms that line the route. (p148)

PINNACLES NATIONAL PARK

On the way to nowhere, petite Pinnacles is worth a big detour for a chance to see endangered California condors soaring above spiring rock formations. (p319)

BODIE STATE HISTORIC PARK

ANCIENT BRISTLECONE PINE FOREST

Speeding along Hwy 395 between Mammoth Lakes and Lone Pine, drivers often miss the turn-off to the world's oldest trees – don't be one of them. (p514)

MINERAL KING VALLEY

Forget overcrowded Yosemite Valley. Head south to Sequoia National Park, where this wildflower-strewn basin shaped by glaciers beckons, with hiking trails to unspoiled alpine lakes. (p491)

Sonoma
Napa
San Francisco
SAN FRANCISCO PENINSULA
Santa Cruz
Monterey

SACRAMENTO–SAN JOAQUIN RIVER DELTA

Sierra Nevada

Yosemite National Park

Bishop

Kings Canyon National Park
Sierra Nevada
Sequoia National Park

Mono Lake

Death Valley National Park

Barstow

Mojave

San Joaquin River
Kings River

Fresno

MINERAL KING VALLEY

Bakersfield

PINNACLES NATIONAL PARK

Paso Robles
Morro Bay
San Luis Obispo

Santa Barbara

Channel Islands National Park

Plan Your Trip

Road Trips & Scenic Drives

With such incredibly dramatic scenery, Northern California is ready-made for road-tripping. Budget 50 miles per hour, except along popular coastal and high-mountain routes (such as Hwy 1 on the Big Sur Coast, or Tioga Rd across Yosemite's High Country), where traffic slows to half that. Confirm your rental has unlimited mileage – you'll need it!

Driving Time & Distances from San Francisco

The following don't account for rush-hour traffic, gas stops or detours.

Napa Valley 49 miles, 1¼ hours

Yosemite National Park 165 miles, 3½ hours

Redwood National Park 330 to 370 miles, six hours via inland Hwy 101, nine hours via coastal Hwy 1

Sequoia and Kings Canyon National Parks 265 miles, five hours

Point Reyes Lighthouse 60 miles, 1½ to two hours

South Lake Tahoe 188 miles, 3½ hours

Hearst Castle via Big Sur 213 miles, five hours via Hwy 1, four hours via Hwy 101 (add two hours during rush hours)

Sacramento 87 miles, 1½ hours

Nevada City 147 miles, 2½ hours

Bakersfield via I-5 283 miles, 4½ hours

Avenue of the Giants 225 miles, four hours

Oregon border via Hwy 1 375 to 426 miles, seven hours via inland Hwy 101, 10 hours via coastal Hwy 1

Big Sur

You'll recognize California's most famous coastal drive from countless car commercials. The two-lane road twists and turns atop 1000ft-high cliffs over the roiling blue Pacific, with dizzying views all the way from San Luis Obispo to Monterey. Prep for traffic: take it slow.

Why Go

Whether it's your first trip or your 50th, driving the Big Sur Coast inspires imagination like no other. Consider a convertible. Plan to stop near iconic Bixby Creek Bridge, the Point Sur Lighthouse, and at random bluffs, tide pools and rocky outcroppings that define this journey. Don't expect to find many sandy beaches – you're up too high.

This part of Northern California is as much state of mind as geographic location – since the late '40s it's been home to artists, writers and back-to-the-landers, but now it would take 10 artists to afford one house. Vigilant protection has preserved Big Sur's stunning nature, with zero highrise hotels or subdivisions. Cell-phone service? Forget it. You'll be lucky to coax a couple of 20-dollar bills from a dial-up ATM.

Road Trips & Scenic Drives

ROUTES

- Big Sur
- San Francisco to Mendocino
- The Golden Chain: Highway 49
- Avenue of the Giants & Redwood National Park
- Eastern Sierra Scenic Byway

When to Go

April, May, September and October – when skies are clearest. Summertime brings moody gray fog. Avoid during winter's heavy rains.

The Route

Although only 135 miles from San Luis Obispo to Monterey, it takes at least three hours, if not four. To lollygag and sightsee, budget a full day. North of Monterey, you can save time by cutting inland from Hwy 1 to faster-running Hwy 101 or I-280 – provided it's not rush hour, when Bay Area freeways jam.

Worthy Detour

Stop in Santa Cruz for a wild ride on the Giant Dipper, a historic wooden roller coaster on a classic seaside boardwalk, overlooking a sandy beach packed with sunbathers and surfers.

Time & Mileage

Distance: 135 miles
Time: at least three hours

Road Closures

In 2017 landslides and flooding plagued Hwy 1 along Big Sur's southern coast, which caused road closures, demolished the Pfeiffer Canyon Bridge and prompted numerous visitors to cancel their trips to the iconic destination. At the time of research, everything north of the bridge remained open and some lodgings and state parks in the area that had been shut were reopening. Remaining closures included Hwy 1 at Mud Creek (where a landslide buried the road in 40ft of debris), Andrew Molera State Park, Julia Pfeiffer Burns State Park, Ventana Big Sur and Nepenthe's Restaurant (which was only accepting guests who were staying at Post Ranch Inn). Before setting out on a road trip here, be sure to do your research on what's open and what's not.

San Francisco to Mendocino

Everyone rushes to drive the Big Sur coast, but the trip north is almost as scenic and gets far less traffic. The terrain is more varied, with table bluffs, pastureland, redwood forests and long rocky beaches. Hardly anyone en route to Mendocino takes Hwy 1 the entire way (instead favoring the faster Hwy 101 to Hwy 128), leaving the winding road largely empty from Bodega Bay to Mendocino. In the springtime, expect brilliant wildflowers, including hot-pink azaleas. November to March, gray whales migrate along the misty coast.

Why Go

The North Coast provides a lower perspective on the coast than Big Sur. Here the road runs right at water level for long stretches, with access to low bluffs jutting like fingers into the sea, and to wide-open beaches where rolling breakers crash against the driftwood trunks of fallen giant redwoods.

Just over the Golden Gate Bridge, nature immediately reveals itself – high bluffs and coastal hills rise straight from the sea. Follow Hwy 1 to the ancient redwood forests of Muir Woods, and over the mountains to Stinson Beach for long walks on the sand. Further north, the little village of Point Reyes Station has good eats and pretty B&Bs within easy reach of spectacular Point Reyes National Seashore. Add time to explore the windswept beaches and hike seaside bluff trails; in wintertime Point Reyes Lighthouse is the hands-down best place to spot whales anywhere in Northern California.

North of Point Reyes Station, the road hugs ocean-side bluffs, darting up and down, in and out, along the headlands and coves of Sonoma Coast State Beach, where you'll need a sweater, not a bikini, most days of summer. At Fort Ross State Historic Park, glimpse a re-created Russian Fort. Ascend Point Arena lighthouse – the tallest in California that you can ascend – to better understand the geography, then find wild and windy Manchester State Beach, where the San Andreas Fault juts out to sea. End in Mendocino, a little village of New England–style saltbox cottages on a flat-topped headland surrounded on three sides by the roaring Pacific. Spend the night in a romantic B&B.

When to Go

April and May are greenest; June to August are foggy three days out of four. In September and October the sun returns.

The Route

Take Hwy 101/Hwy 1 north across the Golden Gate Bridge; turn north on Hwy 1 all the way to Mendocino. For a quicker return to San Francisco, cut inland along Hwy 128, through the Anderson Valley, and connect with Hwy 101 at Cloverdale to shave an hour off the trip.

Worthy Detour

Fort Bragg, the former mill town just north of Mendocino, looks more like the rest of America, with shopping strips and traffic lights. But it also has the gorgeous Mendocino Coast Botanical Garden, where the flora of different climatic zones is represented in gardens terraced on cliffs above the Pacific.

Time & Mileage

Distance: 170 miles
Time: two to four days

Top: Redwood forest

Bottom: Bixby Bridge (p301)

The Golden Chain: Highway 49

That highway number is no coincidence: it commemorates the forty-niners who came to strike it rich during California's gold rush. The 300-some-mile road through the Sierra Nevada foothills connects historic towns leftover from the Wild West. Brush up on history, stop to taste wine, and maybe run some Class III white water. Further north, the road cuts inland and ascends the mountains along the Yuba River, where you can pan for gold or cool off at hidden swimming holes.

Why Go

An adventure along Hwy 49 traces the turf of gold-rushing forty-niners, who left behind a series of historic towns, some of which remain largely unchanged. The route hovers at an elevation of around 2500ft to 3500ft on the skirts of the mighty Sierra Nevada. When summer heat gets unbearable – as it often does in Gold Country – go white-water rafting on the American or Yuba Rivers, or take refuge in quaint history museums that showcase bizarre taxidermy and old mining equipment.

After gold came the railroads – get the story at Jamestown's Railtown 1897 State

20 GREAT TRIPS FROM THE BAY AREA

DESTINATION	APPROXIMATE DISTANCE & TIME FROM SAN FRANCISCO	GOOD FOR	BEST TIME TO GO
Arcata	280 miles, 5hr	Political radicals, college kids, redwood trees	Year-round
Bear Valley	180 miles, 4hr	Skiing, sledding, snowshoeing	Dec-Apr
Big Sur	150 miles, 3½hr	Picturesque coastline, amazing drive	Sep-Nov
Blossom Trail	200 miles, 3½hr	Blooming fruit trees, roadside farm stands, small towns	late Feb–mid-Mar
Gualala	155 miles, 3hr	B&Bs, beachcombing, whale-watching	Apr-Nov
Lake Tahoe	190 miles, 3½hr to Truckee	Swimming, boating, camping, hiking, casinos	Jun-Sep
Lake Tahoe ski resorts	186 miles, 4hr	Skiing, snowboarding, sledding, snowshoeing	Dec-Apr
Lost Coast	230 miles, 4½hr	Wilderness hiking, deserted beaches, sea lions	Jun-Oct
Mendocino	155 miles, 3½hr	Art, nature, wine tasting, B&Bs	Jun-Oct
Monterey	115 miles, 2½hr	Aquarium, boutiques, rugged coastline	Year-round
Mt Shasta	276 miles, 5hr	Climbing, camping, swimming, mysticism	Jul-Sep
Murphys	142 miles, 3hr	Old West town, wine tasting, caverns	Year-round
Nevada City	148 miles, 2½hr	Gold-rush town, wine tasting, swimming holes	May-Sep
Russian River Area	65 miles, 1½hr	Wine tasting, cycling, canoeing, coastline	Year-round
San Luis Obispo & Paso Robles	233 miles, 4hr	College town, rolling countryside, Hearst Castle, great wine	Sep-Nov
Santa Cruz	75 miles, 1½-2hr	Beaches, thrift-shopping, wine tasting, roller coasters	Jun-Oct
Sonoma Coast	45 miles, 1½hr	Misty coves, beachcombing, barking seals	Year-round
Sonoma Valley	45 miles, 1¼hr	History, wine tasting, small towns, hiking, cycling	Mar-Nov
Trinity Scenic Byway	217 miles, 4hr	Hiking, camping, mountain towns, scenic drives	Jun-Oct
Yosemite Valley	190 miles, 3½-4hr	Hiking, camping, snowshoeing, wildlife-watching	Year-round

Historic Park. At nearby Angels Camp, the wooden sidewalks and Old West storefront provide the backdrop for the famous annual jumping-frog competition, made famous by Mark Twain. Add a stop at Columbia State Historic Park, where costumed docents play out 19th-century life. No Gold Country trip would be complete without seeing where James Marshall discovered gold, at Marshall Gold Discovery State Historic Park.

At the drive's northern end, gas lamps line Nevada City, the largest, best-preserved Gold Country town, where historic storefronts house galleries, restaurants, saloons and ice-cream parlors. The gingerbread Victorians and Old West architecture look like a scene from beneath a Christmas tree. When it's hot, keep going north to the South Yuba Bridge to swim beneath giant white boulders where miners once panned for gold.

Bonus: Amador and El Dorado counties make pretty good wine. Head directly for heat-loving varietals, such as Zinfandel and Cabernet Sauvignon, which thrive in these rolling hills.

When to Go

Spring through fall. April and May are prettiest, with green grass and flowers. Summers are busy and hot: stick to the rivers. September and October are ideal, once the weather cools.

The Route

Start in Jamestown and follow Hwy 49, making detours to tiny old towns, such as Murphys, that were bypassed when the new highway was built. Continue all the way to Nevada City.

Time & Mileage

Distance: 127 miles
Time: one to two days

Avenue of the Giants & Redwood National Park

Driving beneath the canopy of the world's tallest trees is an experience like no other – cars look like tiny matchbox toys beneath the mighty giants. The 32-mile scenic route along the Avenue of the Giants

---

ODDITIES OF THE NORTHERN COAST

Giant Paul Bunyan A gargantuan lumberjack waves hello at Trees of Mystery. On weekends, Paul even wisecracks (via loudspeaker) at visitors ambling in the parking lot.

Drive-Thru Trees Conflicted conservationists navigate Chevys through the bellies of redwood. There are – count 'em – *three* opportunities along the North Coast.

California's Smallest Licensed Bar Order a martini on a cruise aboard the *Madaket*, America's oldest continuously operating passenger vessel, based in Eureka.

Confusion Hill (p251) Clapper-trap complex of slanting floors, skewed perspectives and corny delights – pure roadside Americana.

---

is the old two-lane highway, which parallels modern four-lane Hwy 101, through Humboldt Redwoods State Park. After the Avenue, continue north through Redwood National Park to Prairie Creek Redwoods State Park, where elk roam alongside the highway.

Why Go

Few road trips pack such a punch. The giant redwoods of Northern California are the largest trees in the world, some 2000 years old, and so thick in the trunk that it takes 15 people with arms outstretched to encircle one single tree. If you feel nothing in the face of such enormity, we suggest immediate counseling.

Begin the trip around Garberville, where right-wing loggers, left-wing hippies, pot farmers and back-to-the-landers coexist in a little main-street village. Heading north, take the first exit for the Avenue of the Giants – there are several – to commune with trees that were seedlings during the Roman Empire. The half-mile stroll through Founders' Grove provides a good glimpse. Head north along Hwy 101 to the Newton B Drury Scenic Pkwy (once again, the old two-lane highway, bypassed by the modern four-lane freeway), which winds through ancient groves at Prairie

Creek Redwoods State Park, and ends at the mouth of the Klamath River, where eagles and bears compete for salmon. The trip ends with a whimper in Crescent City, an otherwise nothing-special town, but a welcome sight after so many miles of driving through woods.

When to Go

April to October. For hiking, come May to September, when rangers re-open seasonal walking bridges that close during the rainy season. Contact Redwood National and State Parks for current details.

The Route

From Garberville look for signs to Phillipsville and the Avenue of the Giants/State Rte 254, which parallels Hwy 101. Rejoin Hwy 101 just south of Rio Dell, and follow it through Eureka and Arcata. Take exit 753 for the Newton B Drury Scenic Pkwy to Klamath, reconnecting with Hwy 101 toward Crescent City.

Worthy Detour

The entire village of Ferndale is listed on the National Register of Historic Places for its stunning Victorian mansions. It's 5 miles west of Hwy 101, just north of the Avenue of the Giants.

Time & Mileage

Distance: 155 miles
Time: two days

Eastern Sierra Scenic Byway

The mountains hang like curtains from heaven along US Hwy 395, which rivals Hwy 1 for the title of the state's most spectacular drive. The highway flanks the high-mountain deserts of the Great Basin, hugging the vertically rising eastern escarpment of the Sierra Nevada, passing the otherworldly tufa towers at Mono Lake, dense pine forests, crystalline alpine lakes, a Wild West ghost town and hidden hot springs.

Why Go

You'll lose all perspective on scale, size and distance as you drive this spectacular road along the backside of the Sierra Nevada. The mountains form a mile-high near-vertical wall, delineating the edge of the Great Basin's deserts from the escarpment of the High Sierra. The road passes near the highest and lowest points in the continental US (Mt Whitney and Death Valley, respectively), plus three national parks, including the back entrance to Yosemite (summer only).

Along the way, spur roads lead to Bodie State Historic Park, California's best ghost town; Mammoth Mountain, where you can ride a year-round gondola up an 11,000ft peak; the Ancient Bristlecone Pine Forest, location of the world's oldest living trees (one named Methuselah has lived over 4750 years); the Alabama Hills, backdrop of John Wayne Hollywood Westerns; and heartbreaking Manzanar National Historic Site, where 10,000 Japanese descendants were interned during WWII. To linger longer, spend time fly-fishing and hunting for hot springs.

When to Go

Unless you're skiing Mammoth Mountain, come during summer or fall, once summertime-only Tioga Rd/Hwy 120 opens over the mountains of Yosemite, usually July to October.

The Route

Connect with Hwy 395 east of Bakersfield, via CA 178, and travel north to reach CA 120 (summer only), west across Yosemite National Park; if it's closed for winter, continue north to year-round CA 88 to cross the mountains. Or do it in reverse.

Worthy Detour

Instead of ending at Yosemite, continue north to Lake Tahoe.

Time & Mileage

Distance: 300 miles (Bakersfield to Lee Vining)
Time: one to three days

Plan Your Trip

Northern California Camping & Outdoors

Mountains, rivers and vast wildernesses provide a majestic backdrop for Northern California's outdoor adventures. Hike among coastal wildflowers in spring, explore sub-alpine meadows in summer, mountain-bike through fiery fall foliage, and schuss through deep snow in winter. Surfers take note: Northern California was the birthplace of the wetsuit.

Camping

Northern California camping is among the best in America – what else would you expect of a state that covers both the highest and lowest places in the lower 48 states? Backcountry campers reap the biggest rewards – especially in the High Sierra, land of John Muir, where you can pitch a tent beside a hidden alpine lake, within view of jagged High Sierra peaks, and not see another soul. Car-campers and travelers in RVs (recreational vehicles) won't have that same solitude; California's state and national parks fill up every weekend in high season. Still, with such a diversity between the regional, state, county and federal campgrounds, there are campgrounds near and far to get you off the grid. Even RVs are (sometimes) accommodated at the super-basic (but often free!) national forest campgrounds. If you didn't bring a tent, you can rent or buy camping gear in most cities – find good deals at REI (www.rei.com) in San Francisco and Sacramento.

The Best of Northern California

Cycling Pacific Coast Hwy

Backpacking John Muir Trail and Mt Whitney

White-water rafting American River and Cherry Creek on the Upper Tuolumne River

Mountain biking Downieville and Marin County

Rock climbing Yosemite Valley

Whale-watching Bodega Bay, Point Reyes National Seashore and the Farallon Islands

Surfing Mavericks, Bolinas and Santa Cruz

Northern California's Best Places to Camp

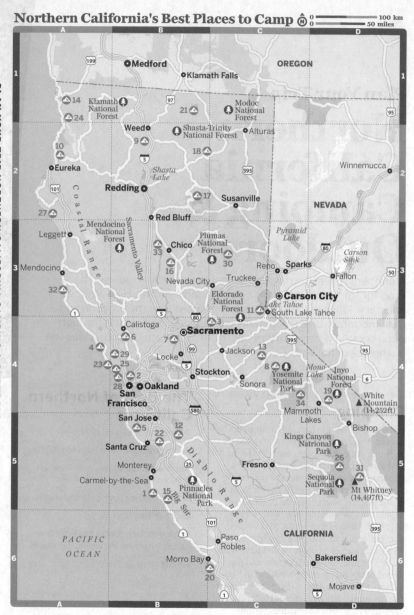

Camping Types & Amenities

Primitive campsites The cheapest; these rarely fill up. Usually have fire pits, picnic tables and access to drinking water and vault toilets. Most common in USFS-managed national forests and on Bureau of Land Management (BLM) land.

Developed campgrounds Typically found in state and national parks, with more amenities, including flush toilets, barbecue grills and occasionally

Northern California's Best Places to Camp

hot showers and a coin-op laundry. May need reservations.

RV hookups and dump stations Available at many privately owned campgrounds, but only a few public-lands campgrounds.

Private campgrounds Cater mainly to RVers. Offer hot showers, swimming pools, wi-fi and family camping cabins; tent sites may be few, exposed and uninviting. Typically more expensive than developed public campgrounds and usually not as nice.

Walk-in (environmental) sites More peace and privacy; a few public-lands campgrounds reserve these for long-distance hikers and cyclists.

Hiker/biker sites Along the coast the 'hiker/biker' sites are the best value for those traveling the slow way along Hwy 1. While occasionally crowded, they reward hikers and cyclists with excellent sites.

Seasons & Rates

Many campgrounds, especially in the mountains, are closed late fall through early spring. Actual opening dates depend on weather. Private campgrounds are sometimes open year-round, especially those nearest cities, beaches and major highways, but these often lack natural beauty.

Many public and private campgrounds accept reservations for all, or some, of their sites, but a few are strictly first-come, first-served. Overnight rates range from free for the most primitive campsites to $75 or more for pull-through RV sites with full hookups. The best deals are almost always with USFS campgrounds and in the national forests of the Northern Mountains. Check with a ranger station before setting up your tent, but an astonishing amount of land in the Plumas, Lassen, Mendocino, Modoc, Trinity and Shasta National

NO RESERVATIONS?

If you can't get reservations, call or show up to the campground between 10am and noon, when other campers are leaving. Don't be too choosy, or you may end up with nothing at all, especially during summer holidays. Park rangers, visitor centers and campground hosts can often tell you where spaces may still be available, if any; otherwise, ask about overflow camping and dispersed camping areas nearby. Note that in popular areas, like the stretch of Big Sur coast on Hwy 1, it's almost impossible to score quality last-minute campsites.

ADVANCE RESERVATIONS THAT ARE WORTH IT
....

Wright's Beach Campground (p224) Easy car-camping, right on a sandy stretch of the North Coast.

Angel Island State Park Campgrounds (p120) Stunning views of the San Francisco skyline from an island in the bay.

Yosemite Creek Campground (p476) Trailhead permits for popular backcountry camps fill months in advance.

Limekiln State Park Campground (p307) One of the best camping options on Big Sur, with only 24 sites.

Bothe-Napa Valley State Park Campground (p182) Shady camping near redwoods, gorgeous hiking and fantastic yurts.

Forests allows camping for no fee whatsoever. If you decide to go this route, always have a good supply of water on hand, and be prepared to haul out your waste.

Cycling & Mountain Biking

Strap on that helmet! Northern California is outstanding cycling territory for a leisurely spin along the coast, an adrenaline-fueled mountain ride or a multiday bike-touring adventure. Cycling season runs year-round in coastal areas, but expect cold rain in wintertime. The mountains are off limits, due to snow, late October through April.

Road Rules

➡ In national and state parks bicycles are usually limited to paved and dirt roads and are not allowed on trails or in designated wilderness areas.

➡ Most national forests and BLM lands are open to mountain bikers. Stay on established tracks and always yield to hikers and horseback riders.

Best Places to Cycle

➡ In the summer, Hwy 1 is a heavily traveled route for cycle tourism on the coast, especially the dizzying stretch through Big Sur.

➡ In Northern California's bike-friendly San Francisco, you can cruise through Golden Gate Park and over the Golden Gate Bridge, then hop on the ferry from Sausalito back across the bay.

➡ A new cycling path over the eastern span of the Bay Bridge runs between Oakland/Emeryville and Treasure Island.

➡ South along the Central Coast, the waterfront Monterey Peninsula Recreational Trail and the famously scenic 17-Mile Drive (p299) entice cyclists of all skill levels.

➡ NorCal's Wine Country offers some beautiful bike tours and wine tasting – just don't get too wobbly.

➡ Up north at Humboldt Redwoods State Park (p254), ride beneath the world's tallest trees on the winding Avenue of the Giants.

➡ In the Sierra Nevada, Yosemite National Park has mostly level, paved recreational paths through a glacier-carved valley overhung by waterfalls.

Best Mountain-Biking Areas

➡ Serious mountain bikers should prioritize a stop in Downieville, a little gold-rush town that offers an enormous downhill sweep.

➡ Just north of San Francisco, the Marin Headlands offers a bonanza of trails for fat-tire fans – nearby Mt Tamalpais (p121) is the sport's birthplace.

➡ Top-rated single-track rides near Lake Tahoe include Mr Toad's Wild Ride and the Flume Trail.

➡ Speed freaks also sing the praises of the Eastern Sierra's Mammoth Mountain, whose summer-only bike park beckons with 70 miles of dirt singletrack.

➡ More ski areas that open trails and chairlifts to mountain bikers can be found at some resorts at Lake Tahoe.

➡ State parks especially popular with mountain bikers include NorCal's **Prairie Creek Redwoods** (707-488-2039; www.parks.ca.gov; Newton B Drury Scenic Pkwy; 9am-5pm May-Sep, to 4pm Wed-Sun Oct-Apr), the Gold Country's Calaveras Big Trees (p419), Wilder Ranch outside Santa Cruz, Andrew Molera (p303) in Big Sur and San Luis Obispo's Montaña de Oro (p316).

Maps & Online Resources

Local bike shops can supply you with more cycling-route ideas, maps and advice.

California Association of Bicycling Organizations (www.cabobike.org) Offers free bicycle touring and freeway-access information.

California Bicycle Coalition (www.calbike.org) Links to free online cycling maps, bike-sharing programs and community bike shops.

Adventure Cycling Association (www.adventurecycling.org) Sells long-distance cycling route guides and touring maps, including the Pacific Coast Hwy (PCH).

League of American Bicyclists (www.bikeleague.org) Find bicycle specialty shops, local cycling clubs, group rides and other special events.

MTBR.com (www.mtbr.com) Online forums and reviews of mountain-biking trails in California.

Hiking

California's epic scenery and extensive parks provide many chances to hike, even in urban areas. No matter where you find yourself in California, you're never far from a trail. During spring, colorful wildflowers bloom on coastal hillsides; wildflower season in the Sierra happens in summer, after the snow melts. The deserts are best fall through spring, and the coastal forests and beaches are ideal year-round.

Best Places to Hike

For jaw-dropping scenery, head to national and state parks to choose from a staggering variety of trails, from easy nature walks negotiable by wheelchairs and strollers, to multiday backpacking routes through rugged wilderness.

Sierra Nevada In Yosemite, Sequoia and Kings Canyon National Parks, clamber toward waterfalls, wildflower meadows and alpine lakes, tackle mighty granite domes and peaks, or wander among the world's biggest trees – giant sequoias.

North Coast Redwood National and State Parks provide misty trails through groves of old-growth redwoods; or backpack the truly wild beaches of the challenging Lost Coast Trail.

San Francisco Bay Area Marin Headlands, Muir Woods, Mt Tamalpais, Point Reyes National Seashore and Big Basin Redwoods State Park,

all within a 90-minute drive of San Francisco, are crisscrossed by dozens of superb trails.

Northern Mountains Summiting Mt Shasta is a spiritually uplifting experience; Lassen Volcanic National Park is a bizarre, raw world of smoking fumaroles, cinder cones and craters.

Fees & Wilderness Permits

➡ Most California state parks charge a daily parking fee of $5 to $15; there's often no charge if you walk or cycle into these parks.

➡ National-park entry averages $10 to $20 per vehicle for seven consecutive days; some national parks are free.

➡ For unlimited admission to national parks, national forests and other federal recreation lands, buy an 'America the Beautiful' annual pass for $80.

➡ Often required for overnight backpackers and extended day hikes, wilderness permits are issued at ranger stations and park visitor centers. Daily quotas may be in effect during peak periods, usually late spring through early fall.

➡ Some wilderness permits may be reserved ahead of time, and very popular trails (like the ascent to the top of Half Dome or Mt Whitney) may sell out months in advance.

➡ Buy passes from USFS ranger stations and select local vendors, such as sporting-goods stores.

TAKE A (REALLY LONG) HIKE

Famous long-distance trails that wind through California include the 2650-mile **Pacific Crest National Scenic Trail** (PCT; www.pcta.org), which runs all the way from Mexico to Canada. Following portions of the PCT, the 211-mile **John Muir Trail** links Yosemite Valley and Mt Whitney via the Sierra Nevada high country. The lake and mountain views are likewise thrilling along the 165-mile **Tahoe Rim Trail** (www.tahoerimtrail.org), portions of which trace the footsteps of early pioneers and Native Americans.

Maps & Online Resources

Find bulletin boards showing basic trail maps and other information at most major trailheads in national, state and regional parks. For short, well-established hikes, the free trail maps handed out at visitor centers and ranger stations are usually sufficient. A more detailed, tear-proof topographical map may be necessary for longer backcountry hikes. Topo maps are sold at park bookstores, visitor centers, ranger stations and outdoor-gear shops including REI (www.rei.com). We especially like Tom Harrison (www.tomharrisonmaps.com) waterproof maps.

US Geological Survey (USGS; https://store. usgs.gov) Offers its topographic maps as free downloadable PDFs, or you can order print copies online.

Trails.com (www.trails.com) Lets you search for hundreds of multisport trails throughout California (trail overviews are free).

Coastwalk (www.coastwalk.org) Advocates for a long-distance trail along California's entire 1271-mile shoreline. Join a group hike, or volunteer to do beach cleanup or trail maintenance.

Leave No Trace Center (www.lnt.org) Learn how to minimize your impact on the environment while traipsing through the wilderness.

Rock Climbing

Climbers test their mettle on the granite monoliths, domes and boulders of Yosemite National Park, where climbing season runs April to October. Outfitters offer guided climbs and instruction.

Other prime spots for bouldering and rock climbing include Sequoia and Kings Canyon National Parks, south of Yosemite; around Bishop in the Eastern Sierra; outside Truckee, near Lake Tahoe; and at Pinnacles National Monument in central California.

SuperTopo (www.supertopo.com) is a one-stop shop for rock-climbing guidebooks, online forums, free topo maps and route descriptions across the state.

Beaches & Swimming

If you've come to Northern California expecting the idyllic scenes from a Beach Boys song, forget it. You'll get more use from a good sweater than a skimpy swimsuit. Northern California beaches are best for strolling, not swimming: the water is icy cold, with strong currents. If you must swim, bring or rent a wetsuit. The water

EVEN MORE IN THE OUTDOORS!

ACTIVITY	LOCATION	REGION
Bird-watching	Klamath Basin National Wildlife Refuges	Northern Mountains
	Mono Lake	Yosemite & the Sierra Nevada
	Marin Headlands	Marin County & the Bay Area
Caving	Lava Beds National Monument	Northern Mountains
	Crystal Cave	Yosemite & the Sierra Nevada
	Pinnacles National Monument	Central Coast
Fishing*	Shasta Lake	Northern Mountains
	Bodega Bay	North Coast & Redwoods
	Mammoth Lakes	Yosemite & the Sierra Nevada
Horseback riding	Yosemite National Park	Yosemite & the Sierra Nevada
	Wild Horse Sanctuary	Northern Mountains
	Point Reyes National Seashore	Marin County & the Bay Area
Kiteboarding & Windsurfing	San Francisco Bay	San Francisco
	Bodega Bay	North Coast & Redwoods
	Lake Tahoe	Lake Tahoe

*For fishing licenses, regulations and location information, consult the California Department of Fish & Game (www.dfg.ca.gov).

warms around Santa Barbara and points south.

The mind-bogglingly detailed *California Coastal Access Guide* (University of California Press, 2014) has comprehensive beach driving directions and maps.

Water quality varies from beach to beach, and day to day. Stay out of the ocean for at least three days after major rainstorms, due to toxic pollutants flushing out to sea through storm drains. For current water-safety conditions statewide, check the Beach Report Card (http://brc. healthebay.org).

Scuba Diving & Snorkeling

All along the coast, rock reefs, shipwrecks and kelp beds teem with sea creatures. If you've already got your PADI certification, you can rent one-tank dive outfits for $65 to $100, while two-tank boat dives cost over $100; reserve either at least a day in advance. Snorkel kits can be rented from most dive shops for around $15 to $40 per day. If you're going to be taking the plunge more than once or twice, it's probably worth buying your own mask and fins. Remember to not touch anything while you're out snorkeling, and don't snorkel alone. Sunblock can hurt reefs; choose a 'reef-safe' brand, or better yet, wear a UV-protection suit.

Best Scuba-Diving & Snorkeling Spots

➡ With national marine sanctuary protection, Monterey Bay offers world-renowned diving and snorkeling – but you'll need a wetsuit.

➡ Further south, Point Lobos State Natural Reserve (p298) is another gem for scuba divers (snorkeling prohibited); permit reservations are required.

➡ North of San Francisco, dive boats depart from Bodega Bay.

Sea Kayaking

Few water sports are as accessible and fun for groups as kayaking. Most outfitters offer a choice between sit-upon (open)

kayaks and sit-in (closed-hull) ones, the latter usually requiring some training before you head out. Kayak rentals average $40 to $70 per day, and you'll usually have a choice between single and tandem. A reputable outfitter will make sure you're aware of the tide schedule and wind conditions of your proposed route. Many also give lessons and lead guided paddles (from $50), including full-moon, sunset and sunrise trips. Try to make reservations at least a day ahead.

There are dozens of places to launch along the coast. If you're a beginner and the idea of kayaking on waves scares you, consider instead the calm water of Tomales Bay, in Point Reyes National Seashore, where you can spot incredible birds and leopard sharks as you paddle the placid bay.

Surfing

Surf's up! – well, for part of the year, at least. The most powerful swells arrive along the coast during late fall and winter. May and June are generally the flattest months, although they do bring warmer water. On the subject of temperature, don't believe all those images of hot blondes surfing in bikinis; without a wetsuit, you'll freeze your butt off, except maybe at the height of summer.

Crowds can be a problem at many surf spots, as can overly territorial surfers. Befriend a local surfer for an introduction before hitting the most famous waves. Sharks do inhabit California waters, but wattacks are extremely rare. Most happen in the 'Red Triangle' between Monterey on the Central Coast, Tomales Bay north of San Francisco and the offshore Farallon Islands.

Generally speaking, Northern California is better for beginners than for hard-core pros, who find greater challenges down south. There are notable exceptions: Santa Cruz' Steamers Lane, with glassy point breaks and rocky reef breaks, and Half Moon Bay's Mavericks (p156), world-famous for big-wave surfing. Mavericks tops 50ft when the most powerful winter swells arrive.

Best Breaks for Beginners

The best spots to learn to surf are at the beach breaks of long, shallow bays where waves are small and rolling, including the following:

Central Coast Santa Cruz, Cayucos

San Francisco Area Pacifica

North Coast Bolinas, Stinson Beach

Rentals & Lessons

➜ You'll find board rentals on just about every patch of sand where surfing is possible. Expect to pay about $25 per day for a board, with wetsuit rental another $15.

➜ Two-hour group lessons for beginners start at around $75 per person, while private, two-hour instruction costs over $100 per hour. If you're ready to jump in the deep end, many surf schools offer pricier weekend surf clinics and week-long 'surfari' camps.

➜ Stand-up paddle surfing (SUP) is easier to learn, and it's skyrocketing in popularity. You'll find similarly priced board-and-paddle rentals and lessons all along the coast.

Books, Maps & Online Resources

➜ Plan a coastal surfing adventure using Surfline (www.surfline.com), which details seasonal weather and water temperatures.

➜ Enlightened surfers can join up with Surfrider (www.surfrider.org), a nonprofit organization that seeks to protect the coastal environment.

White-Water Rafting

California has dozens of kick-ass rivers, which flow heavily in spring, then diminish as the snowpack disappears at higher elevation. Like ski season, rafting season depends entirely upon winter's snow depth. Paddling giant, ice-cold white-water rapids, ripping through sheer canyons, it can be a challenge to overcome fear. Sometimes it's all you can do to hang on for dear life. Too much for you? Fret not: beginner paddlers will find many places to develop their skills – in a safe environment – and in little time can become river rats.

California Whitewater Rafting (www.c-w-r.com) covers all of California's prime river-running spots, with links to outfitters and river-conservation groups. Most of the premier river runs are in the Sierra Nevada and the Gold Country, but the Northern Mountains also offer some rollicking rides, including on the Klamath, Trinity, Sacramento, Smith and California Salmon Rivers.

White-water trips are not without danger, and it's not unusual for participants to fall out of the raft in rough conditions. Serious injuries are rare, however, and most trips are without incident. No prior experience is needed for guided river trips up to Class III, but for Class IV you want to be healthy, active, in good shape and an excellent swimmer, plus have some paddling experience under your belt. As for Class V, you'd better know what the hell you're doing or stay away.

Seasons, Rates & Reservations

Commercial outfitters run a variety of trips, from short, inexpensive morning or afternoon floats to overnight outings and multiday expeditions. Expect to pay from $100 for a guided all-day trip. Reservations are recommended, especially for overnight trips.

The main river-running season is from April to August, although the exact months depend on which river you're rafting and how much snow accumulated during the preceding winter. During drought years, the season can end mid-summer. You'll either take a large raft, with a captain at the motor and a dozen or more passengers; or a small motorless raft, which seats only a half-dozen people, all of whom paddle. Be sure to inquire whether or not you will be expected to paddle.

Whale-Watching

During their annual migration, gray whales can be spotted off the California coast from December to April, while blue, humpback and sperm whales pass by in summer and fall. You can try your luck from the shore whale-watching at lighthouses, for example. This is free, but you're less likely to see whales and you'll be removed from the action.

CALIFORNIA'S BEST WHITE-WATER RAFTING

NAME	CLASS	SEASON	DESCRIPTION
American River	Class II-IV	Apr-Oct	The South Fork is ideal for families and rafting virgins looking to get their feet wet, while the more challenging Middle and North Forks carve through deep gorges in the Gold Country.
Kern River	Class II-V	Apr-Sep	Staged near Bakersfield, the Upper and Lower Forks offer some of the southern Sierra's best white water.
Kaweah River	Class IV+	Apr-Jul	After steeply dropping through Sequoia National Park, this fast, furious ride is for experienced paddlers craving hair-raising white water.
Kings River	Class III-IV	Apr-Jul	One of California's most powerful rivers cuts a groove deeper than the Grand Canyon; trips begin outside Kings Canyon National Park.
Merced River	Class III-IV	Apr-Jul	Starting outside Yosemite National Park, this canyon run is the Sierra's best one-day intermediate trip.
Stanislaus River	Class II-IV	Apr-Oct	In the Gold Country, the North Fork provides rafting trips for novices and the more adventure-minded.
Truckee River	Class II-IV	Apr-Aug	Near Lake Tahoe, this is a great beginners' run, with a white-water park for kayakers on the river in downtown Reno.
Tuolumne River	Class IV-V	Apr-Sep	Experienced paddlers may prefer a ferocious run on 'the T'; in summer, experts-only Cherry Creek is a legendary Sierra Nevada run.

➡ Just about every port town worth its sea salt offers whale-watching boat excursions, especially during winter. Bring binoculars!

➡ Half-day boat trips cost from $30 to $50, while all-day trips average $65 to $100; make reservations at least a day ahead.

➡ Better tour boats limit the number of people and have a trained naturalist or marine biologist on board. Ask before booking about the credentials of the person leading the tour.

➡ Some tour companies will let you go again for free if you don't spot any whales on your first trip.

➡ Choppy seas can be nauseating. To avoid seasickness, sit outside on the boat's second level – but not too close to the diesel fumes in back – and watch the horizon line. Crystallized ginger helps settle queasy stomachs. We've also had good success wearing motion-sickness pressure-point bracelets and taking Dramamine or Bonine.

Snow Sports

In a good snow year, the Sierra Nevada gets one of the deepest snowpacks in North America. Most resorts are above 6000ft elevation, with the best topping out over 10,000ft. This is the roof of California, and the scenery is breathtaking. However, powder days are rare. It's just too warm for fluffy dry snow – they call it 'Sierra cement' for a reason. But with an annual average of 300 sunny days, and midday temperatures above freezing, you can work on your tan while schussing down the slopes.

Seasons, Rates & Lessons

Ski season runs late November or early December until the end of April, depending on resorts' specific elevations and weather conditions. The higher the resort, the drier the snow and longer the season. The best months are typically January to March. All resorts have ski schools and equipment-rental facilities and offer a variety of lift tickets, including half-day and multiday. Prices vary wildly, from $25 to $95 per day for adults. Discounts for children, teens, students and seniors are usually available. 'Ski and stay' lodging packages offer good value, as do learn-to-ski packages geared toward families.

Best Places for Snow Sports

The triumvirate of California's top ski resorts is Mammoth Mountain, Squaw Valley and Heavenly Mountain. Mammoth is highest, Heavenly biggest, Squaw steepest.

The highest concentration of resorts is around Lake Tahoe, which is within four hours of San Francisco and manageable as a long day trip – but it's better to stay a night or two. Mammoth Mountain is seven hours from the Bay Area, making it more popular among Southern California skiers; it often stays open until June.

The highest-elevation resorts (read: drier snow) are Kirkwood, Mount Rose and Mammoth. For the best views of Lake Tahoe, choose Homewood, Heavenly or Diamond Peak. In a storm, the best-protected Tahoe resorts are Homewood and Northstar.

West of Donner Pass, near Truckee, a handful of tiny family resorts have prices half those of the big resorts. They're ideal for beginners, but may not open in bad snow years. Also nearby is Royal Gorge (p448), the largest cross-country resort in North America, but again, conditions depend on snowfall.

Skiing in Yosemite National Park, at Badger Pass (p471), is more novelty than sport, but lovely for beginners – and where else can you ski with a view of Half Dome? But low elevations and warm temps mean a short season. For another only-in-California winter wonderland, consider Sequoia and Kings Canyon National Parks, in the Southern Sierra, where you can tramp or cross-country among giant sequoia trees.

If you just want to play in the snow, California's family-friendly **sno-parks** (☏916-324-1222; www.ohv.parks.ca.gov/?page_id=1233; pass per day/year $5/25) offer sledding and snow play. To find them, visit the website.

Plan Your Trip
Travel with Children

Young travelers love Northern California. It's an adventurous destination, and it's also safe for family travel. Because of the coast's mild climate, you can cycle, hike or beachcomb February to November. In winter there's great skiing in Tahoe. And year-round, you'll find family-friendly museums and indoor entertainment galore in the region's cities.

Children's Highlights

Aquariums & Museums

San Francisco (p64) The Bay Area is a mind-bending classroom for kids, especially the hands-on Exploratorium, the multimedia Children's Creativity Museum and the eco-friendly California Academy of Sciences.

Chabot Space & Science Center (p132) Stargazers will go gaga over this kid-oriented science and technology center in the Oakland Hills.

Bay Area Discovery Museum (p113) Excellent hands-on museum in the Marin Headlands, with multilingual exhibits including a wave workshop, a small underwater tunnel and a large outdoor play area with a shipwreck.

Monterey Bay Aquarium (p287) Get acquainted with the denizens of the deep next door to the Central Coast's biggest marine sanctuary.

Seymour Marine Discovery Center (p276) Santa Cruz' university-run aquarium makes interactive science fun, with nearby tide pools for exploring at the beach.

Turtle Bay Exploration Park (p335) In Redding, this indoor-outdoor attraction combines an eco-museum with arboretum, botanical and butterfly gardens.

Best Regions for Kids

San Francisco & the Bay Area

In San Francisco, explore hands-on, whimsical science museums, hear the barking sea lions at Pier 39, traipse through Golden Gate Park and along that famous bridge, and make new friends at the city's many playgrounds.

Yosemite & the Sierra Nevada

Kids will gawk at Yosemite's waterfalls and granite domes and can hike through ancient groves of giant sequoias, the world's most massive living things. Mammoth Lakes is a four-seasons family adventure base camp, as are some of the resorts at Lake Tahoe, notably Squaw Valley, Heavenly and Northstar.

Gold Country

Young imaginations run wild in Gold Country, ignited by tall tales of rough-n-tumble forty-niners, gun-slinging bandits and treasure-hunters. Connect with the Wild West in historic towns such as Columbia State Historic Park and Nevada City. In late summer and fall, gather apples together at you-pick-'em orchards.

Lake Tahoe (p424)

Beaches

Central Coast (p274) Beach towns line the coast, from Pismo Beach all the way north to Santa Cruz, famous for its beachside boardwalk and pier.

Lake Tahoe (p424) In summer, it's California's favorite high-altitude beach escape, a sparkling jewel in the craggy Sierra Nevada mountains.

North Coast (p218) No swimming – the water is too rough – but plenty of chances for beachcombing, collecting shells and building sandcastles on uncrowded beaches. The giant driftwood trunks of redwood trees strewn on the sand are ready-made climbing structures.

Parks

Yosemite National Park (p461) The ultimate in Sierra Nevada scenery, with gushing waterfalls, alpine lakes, glacier-carved valleys and 2-mile-high peaks.

Golden Gate Park (p78) The giant green swath in the heart of San Francisco has grassy areas for lounging, strolling ice-cream vendors, a carousel, children's playgrounds, model boating and plenty of space to fly a kite.

Redwood National and State Parks (p267) On the fog-shrouded North Coast, a patchwork of nature reserves protect magnificent wildlife, beaches and the world's tallest trees.

Lassen Volcanic National Park (p340) An off-the-beaten-path destination in the Northern Mountains, with otherworldly volcanic scenery and lakeside camping and cabins.

Columbia State Historic Park (p421) Like a miniature gold-rush Disneyland, but with more authenticity and heart.

Planning

When to Go

Family travel is viable year-round in Northern California, but some family-centric attractions close during winter – check individual listings. Explore the coast from spring through fall. Once winter's rains arrive, consider a ski trip to the mountains.

Accommodations

Motels and hotels often have rooms with two beds or an extra sofa bed, ideal for families. Many hotels have roll-away beds or cots, sometimes for a surcharge. Most offer 'kids stay free' promotions, provided the kids are under 18 and traveling with their parents. Some B&Bs don't allow children; ask when booking.

Resorts may have drop-off day camps for kids or on-call babysitting services. At other hotels, the front-desk staff or concierge may be able to help you make babysitting arrangements, whereby the sitter comes to your hotel room. Make sure the sitter is licensed, bonded and fully insured.

Transportation

Airlines usually allow infants (up to age two) to fly for free, while older children requiring a seat of their own qualify for reduced fares. Children receive substantial discounts on Amtrak and Greyhound. In cars, any child under age eight must be buckled up in the back seat in a child or infant safety seat, unless they're over 4ft 9in tall, in which case they may ride in front with a seat belt.

Most car-rental agencies rent safety seats for about $10 per day or up to $80 per trip, but you must book them in advance. Hertz offers AAA members one free child seat. Take note: rest stops on freeways are few and far between, and gas stations and fast-food bathrooms are frequently icky.

A word of advice: don't pack your schedule too tightly. Navigating metro areas, such as San Francisco, and the winding back roads to Northern California's natural areas always takes longer than expected.

What to Pack

There are two magic words for traveling in Northern California: sunscreen and layers.

The first of these is always necessary, even where cool, high-altitude climates and overcast skies lull visitors into a false sense of security – the higher the elevation, the thinner the atmosphere, especially in the High Sierra. The second is an absolute

---

HOW OLD IS OLD ENOUGH?

Naturally some outdoor activities will be easier to master than others. Those as young as five can take part in paddling and skiing. Horseback riding is a good choice for kids aged seven and up, and there are plenty of pleasant hikes easy enough for little legs. Teens will love the challenge of rock climbing, white-water rafting and surfing.

---

must: a day that is blisteringly hot in the Gold Country can be chilly in the Sierra and downright bone-chilling on the coast. This is particularly true in San Francisco, where the weather changes fast.

For outdoor vacations, bring broken-in shoes and your own camping equipment. Alternatively, outdoors gear can be purchased or often rented from outdoor stores. But remember that brand-new hiking shoes often result in blisters, and setting up a new tent in the dark ain't easy.

If you forget some critical piece of equipment, Baby's Away (www.babysaway.com) rents cribs, strollers, car seats, high chairs, backpacks, beach gear and more.

Before You Go

➡ For all-round information and advice, check out Lonely Planet's *Travel with Children*.

➡ Lonelyplanet.com (www.lonelyplanet.com) lets you ask questions and get advice from other travelers on the Thorn Tree's 'Kids to Go' and 'USA' forums.

➡ California Travel & Tourism (www.visitcalifornia.com), the state's official visitor website, lists family-friendly attractions, activities and more – just search for 'Family Fun' and 'Events.'

➡ Family Travel Files (www.thefamilytravelfiles.com/locations/california) is an info-packed site with vacation-planning articles, tips and discounts.

Artichokes alla romana alla turca

Plan Your Trip
Eat & Drink Like a Local

At the vanguard of culinary invention, Northern California determines the way America eats – or will eat, eventually. Sustainable, local food trends originated in the Bay Area, and lately farmers and other artisanal producers are achieving superstar status. Deliciousness is available (almost) everywhere, provided you know where to look.

MEL MELCON/CONTRIBUTOR/GETTY IMAGES ©

The Year in Food

Northern California is an agricultural wonderland, with ideal climate and soil to produce much of the country's fruits, vegetables and nuts. No matter the season, you can bet there's plenty to harvest, and some kind of celebration going on involving the veritable cornucopia.

Spring (March–May)

Asparagus, artichokes, green garlic and fava beans are specific to these months, and the Gilroy Garlic Festival (p317) takes place in May.

Summer (June–August)

Time for eggplants, green beans and berries. Monterey Bay's **Strawberry festival** (www.celebratestrawberries.com; ☺early Aug) happens in August.

Fall (September–October)

Broccoli rabe, squash and Brussels sprouts are harvested, crush happens in Wine Country, along with many food and wine festivals.

Local Specialities

The City

Let's face it: your best meals will likely be in the cities of Northern California, which are blessed with fresh ingredients, a thriving (if cutthroat) scene of ethnic restaurants, and a large base of customers.

San Francisco has been the region's culinary capital since the gold rush, when the population boomed and the doors to Chinese noodle shops and French restaurants swung open just as quickly. And though SF remains home to a startling array of restaurants, and in 2015 *Bon Appetit* named San Francisco the country's best food city, in 2016 many Bay Area restaurants struggled and closed. In large part this was because food prices are up and rent is too damn high. Skyrocketing housing costs have meant that employees have to live further away from their places of work, and those brutal commutes are rarely sustainable. Hikes in minimum wage, particularly in Oakland, have also forced restaurant owners to scramble.

What this means for visitors is that prices are rising and restaurants may be closed one or more days a week due to staff shortages. A new spot with great reviews from the month before may have failed by the time your trip comes around. New places may tend toward 'fast casual,' with no table service, which cuts labor costs.

Despite all of this gloomy news, San Francisco of course remains an utterly delicious place to eat. Its signature dishes such as *cioppino* (Dungeness crab stew) and sourdough bread bowls have stood the test of time, and tasting menus continue to feature wild chanterelles found beneath California oaks, miner's lettuce from Berkeley hillsides and stinging nettles from SF backyards.

The Valley

From above, the Central Valley – America's most agriculturally rich region – looks like a green garden. As it should; it accounts for a sizable percentage of domestic produce. Hot, sunny, and watered with Sierra snowmelt, this area grows anything that isn't tropical, and produces millions of pounds of tomatoes, grapes, stone fruit, almonds and asparagus. Even though much valley turf is controlled by huge agribusiness conglomerates, it also hosts a growing number of farms dedicated to organic vegetables, dairy products and meat, whose goods often end up in discerning restaurants in Northern California. You'll be hard pressed to find fresher food – organic or not – than at the farm stands of the Central Valley.

The Coast

A thousand miles of Pacific coastline and scores of rushing rivers mean that the fruits of the waters are a staple of the California diet. In the winter, travelers tie on bibs at crab feeds on the coast; from spring through fall, local salmon is on the menu; and tourists obsess about clam chowder in a sourdough bowl year-round. Though most of the indigenous oysters are gone, you can still shuck fresh, briny ones at oyster farms near Point Reyes, on Tomales Bay. But remember to eat responsibly. Monterey Bay Aquarium (www.montereybayaquarium.org) publishes a 'Seafood Watch: West Coast' downloadable pocket guide that lists good, sustainably harvested seafood.

The Mountains

Nature smiles on the mountains, which are both rugged and lush, yielding mountain honey, wild blackberries, chanterelle mushrooms and other wild-crafted delicacies. At roadside inns, restaurants and saloons, the cuisine has a historical precedent to cater to the rugged appetites of miners who lacked the patience for agriculture or families for consolation, instead seeking out fast food, faster women and strong drink. Breweries and bordellos flourished; public health did not. But there were competing culinary forces at work in seasonal, local, wild-crafted Ohlone and Miwok cuisine. In addition to fishing, hunting game, and gathering wild mushrooms and berries, these indigenous Californians tended orchards and cultivated foods. Some of these traditions are still around today, even though mountain menus often are geared to hikers who are ready to indulge carnivorous inclinations.

From Farm to Table

Northern Californian 'locavores' fancy themselves on the sustainable-food vanguard, and they might be right.

The Queen of California Cuisine Alice Waters

Some revolutions start with a manifesto. But Alice Waters – chef, author and proprietor of now-famous Berkeley restaurant Chez Panisse – changed American diets with a menu. Back in 1971, diners at Chez Panisse lacked the terminology to describe the food they tasted. It would be years until terms such as 'California cuisine,' 'certified organic,' and 'locavore' (one who eats food grown locally) were coined.

Vineyard near Paso Robles (p320)

Waters' programs outside her restaurant – such as the Edible Schoolyard program, which encourages healthy food in public schools, and the Chez Panisse Foundation, which partnered with First Lady Michelle Obama's 'Let's Move!' campaign against childhood obesity – have made lasting impacts. Waters even helped plant a garden at the White House.

Seeds of Revolt

Waters was hardly alone, and the long-simmering reaction to the previous generation's rapid industrialization of food found particularly assertive expression in Northern California. Measured against the rest of the country, Californians are picky eaters indeed.

This spirit is most evident in the region's abundant farmers markets, which have affected the food economy by connecting families directly to farmers. The Bay Area hosts hundreds of farmers markets, many of which fill public spaces on weekends.

In addition to the standard veggies, markets offer sustainable meats, rare and heirloom varieties of vegetables, and foods picked at peak ripeness – often too delicate

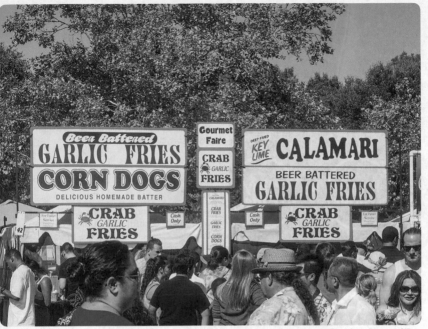

Gilroy Garlic Festival (p317)

for conventional packing and shipping. And the difference is apparent from the first bite.

Sustainable Dining

You don't have to have a kitchen to enjoy the fruits of Northern California. The region's delicious strengths are equally evident when you sit down to order at a restaurant. Eateries here are more dedicated to sustainable, organic, local ingredients than any other region of the US.

The connection between the rich soil and waters of Northern California and its elegant houses of fine dining is strong. Organic, local produce is almost a given; you'll also find rare treats such as sustainably farmed abalone (the prized dish of Native Americans), a winter harvest of wild mushrooms and line-caught trout.

Wine

California's wine producers are the best in America and among the best in the world. Far beyond Napa Valley, the wines of Northern California are well worth a day-long detour.

America's Vineyard

California might still be a Mexican province guzzling Australian wines but for one drunken night in Sonoma in 1846. Under the influence of local wine, a group of frontier rabble-rousers decided to seize the state government from Mexican authorities. California history and Sonoma's reputation for drink were made. One hundred and thirty years later, neighboring Napa Valley kicked off another revolution at the 1976 Paris Tasting, aka the 'World Cup of Wine,' when a Stag's Leap Cabernet Sauvignon and a beat home-*terroir* French favorites.

Napa, Sonoma, Santa Cruz and Mendocino counties continue to produce the state's most illustrious vintages. With an exceptional combination of coastal fog, sunny valleys, rocky hillsides and volcanic soils, Napa and Sonoma Valleys together mimic wine-growing regions across France and Italy. Precious bottom-land sells for up to $20,000 an acre in skinny, 30-mile-long Napa, where many wineries

Pliny the Elder beer, Russian River Brewing Co (p212)

Paso Robles One of the largest wine regions in the south, this area has all of the accolades of Napa's wineries, and easier access to the Pacific Ocean.

Lodi A quick trip from the Bay Area and the perfect detour on the way to LA, the country roads surrounding Lodi turn out excellent Zins, big Cabs and jammy Merlot.

Edna Valley In the gorgeous, rolling hills east of San Luis Obispo, Edna Valley wineries produce good Chardonnay, Pinot Noir, and earthy Syrah – consider bicycling between them.

Beer

Don't be surprised if ordering a Budweiser earns you a scornful look in these parts. Alongside excellent beer scenes in Colorado and Oregon, Northern California's craft breweries are a point of locals' hubris... especially after they've had a couple.

Some of the most famous labels are found in the region, but excellent, largely unknown microbreweries are also found in many small towns.

Like most of the small breweries of the western US, these breweries specialize in bold, hoppy India Pale Ales (IPAs) and creative Belgium-inspired fusions. Both of these have high alcohol content, so remember to take it slow.

NorCal's Best Breweries

Six Rivers Brewery (p263) Women-owned brewery with excellent beer and a great view.

North Coast Brewing Company (p238) Red Seal amber ale and aged Belgian-style brews.

Anderson Valley Brewing Company (p243) Play disc golf with amber ale or oatmeal stout in hand at this solar-powered Bavarian brewhouse.

Fieldwork Brewing Company (p144) Dog-friendly, industrial taproom with a tasting flight of IPAs and an outstanding Mexican hot chocolate stout.

Russian River Brewing Co (p212) This famous Santa Rosa brewery crafts a wildly popular double IPA, Pliny the Elder, plus top-grade sour beer aged in wine barrels.

Sierra Nevada Brewing Company (p381) Hordes gather at the birthplace of Sierra Nevada Pale Ale and Schwarber, a Chico-only black ale.

understandably stick to established, marketable Chardonnay and Cabernet Sauvignon. Neighboring Sonoma and Mendocino have complex microclimates, with morning fog cover to protect the thin-skinned, prized Pinot Noir grape.

But California's risk-taking attitude prevails even on prestigious Napa, Sonoma and Mendocino turf, with unconventional red blends and freak-factor Pinots with 'forest floor' flavors claiming top honors in industry mags and the Super Bowl of US wine competitions, the San Francisco Chronicle Wine Competition.

Other NorCal Wine Regions

Although a tour through Napa-Sonoma is the Holy Grail of American oenophiles, younger wine regions turn out quality vintages, served with a fraction of the attitude. These are some of our favorites.

Amador and El Dorado Counties With intense, earthy Zinfandels and zero pretense, Gold Country's wineries are the best for budget-conscious wine-lovers.

Top: Vineyard near
Paso Robles (p320)

Bottom: Sierra Nevada
Brewing Company
(p381)

SIERRA NEVADA
BREWING CO.

Regions at a Glance

Considering it's only half a state, Northern California is huge. To comprehend the geography, think of it as a giant bathtub, ringed by mountains. To the west, the Coastal Range rises straight from the Pacific Ocean, a wall unbroken except at the Golden Gate – mouth of San Francisco Bay. To the east, the Sierra Nevada makes another unbroken wall, only much higher, comprising the tallest peaks in the Continental US. To the north, the Cascade and Siskiyou Ranges bleed into Oregon. To the south, the Transverse Ranges anomalously run east–west, separating Northern California from Southern California – geographically, if not culturally. And in the middle – the floor of the bathtub – extends the vast sea-level Central Valley, which drains into San Francisco Bay. The dramatic scenery is in the hills and mountains.

San Francisco

Food
Culture
Museums

Markets

SF has glorious markets, especially the Ferry Building. This 19th-century ferry terminal was converted into a covered market and showcases the best of Northern California's small-batch food producers.

New Perspectives

Northern California's 'Left Coast' reputation rests on SF, where self expression is a high virtue. Freethinkers, techies, foodies and renegade artists set the city's creative tone, and pot smoke lingers on the breeze.

Arts & Sciences

SF loves its museums, and goes out of its way to flaunt them. Case in point: the glass-walled pier for the hands-on Exploratorium. Also, the living roof and indoor rainforest at the Academy of Sciences.

p64

Marin County & the Bay Area

Outdoors
Nature
Cities

Mountain Biking

Discover the birthplace of mountain biking at Mt Tamalpais, which rises from the Pacific. Trails reveal jaw-dropping vistas of the entire Bay Area.

Wildlife Spotting

Across the San Andreas Fault, Point Reyes National Seashore juts 10 miles to sea, with towering cliffs and spectacular vistas. Plan to hike high bluffs among wild elk, and keep a look out for rare birds and migrating whales.

Oakland & Berkeley

A revitalized Oakland offers diverse neighborhoods and a burgeoning food scene. Berkeley remains at the forefront of social change thanks to its university; check out the campus.

p108

Napa & Sonoma Wine Country

Wine
Food
Outdoors

Wineries

Napa is famous for Cabernet Sauvignon and side-by-side wineries. Sonoma County has more history, and retains its folksy roots. Lucky for you, they're neighbors: see both.

Farm-to-Table Dining

Napa's top-end restaurants are the rural outpost of San Francisco's dining scene, but the raw ingredients often come from Sonoma County, where you can tour farms and orchards.

Cycling & Canoeing

Sonoma County's back roads are made for cycling, with few cars and gorgeous scenery. The Russian River is ideal for kayaking, canoeing and even tubing.

p159

North Coast & Redwoods

Forests
Beaches
Towns

Redwood Trees

Redwood trees, the tallest trees on earth, rise like giants up and down the North Coast, the only place in the entire world that they grow. Plan on a six-hour drive from San Francisco, and a two-night stay.

State Beaches

The North Coast's wild and rugged beaches are shrouded in fog and littered with giant driftwood of fallen redwoods. Bring a warm sweater and plan to beachcomb, not swim.

Mendocino Coast

This wild stretch of coast, four hours from San Francisco, remains largely undeveloped, with side-by-side state parks and tiny towns built by whalers and loggers. Consider a romantic night in a cozy B&B.

p218

Central Coast

Wildlife
Beaches
Scenic Drives

Elephant Seals & Whales

Elephant seals breed along the Central Coast, splitting time between Año Nuevo State Park, near Santa Cruz, and Point Piedras Blancas, near Hearst Castle. To spot whales, board a cruise in Monterey.

Surfing

Learn to surf and try your new skill along the coast at the various surf breaks. Explore the history of the sport at Santa Cruz' tiny surfing museum.

Coastal Highway 1

The most famous drive in all of California – if not all of America – hugs the coastline north of San Simeon, atop 1000ft cliffs, to achingly beautiful Big Sur. Passengers get the best view southbound, drivers northbound.

p274

Northern Mountains

Mountains
Lakes
Landscape

Famous Peaks

Mount Shasta rises to over 11,000ft, drawing Native Americans, ice-axe-wielding alpinists, poets and painters. At Lassen Volcanic National Park, the otherworldly landscape includes a volcano and steaming vents from the earth's mantle.

Fishing & Boating

The wild lands of far northeastern California comprise spectacular lakes and reservoirs. Consider renting a houseboat and fishing pole, and fry your own trout for dinner.

Scenic Drives

Make a loop around the dramatic volcanic landscape of Lassen Volcanic National Park, and if time permits, also find the cute-as-a-button, lesser-known, gold-rush-era town of Weaverville.

p333

Sacramento & Central Valley

History
Culture
Gastronomy

History Parks

When early American settlers ventured west to California, they were aiming for Sutter's Fort in Sacramento, the otherwise-flat city's highest point. Today the fort is a state park.

Then & Now

Sacramento has fantastic museums, which focus on various periods in state history. Look for the exceptional California Museum and California State Railroad Museum.

Emerging Foodie Scene

As the prices at restaurants in other cities have spiraled out of control, Sacramento's Midtown and Tower Districts have seen a number of hip, affordable restaurants open up. Tables topped with farm-fresh ingredients spill onto the sidewalks in the summer.

p367

Gold Country

History
Culture
Outdoors

Gold Rush

Glimpse back in time at the 19th-century towns lining Hwy 49. Stop at Sutter's Mill to see where gold was first discovered. Consider an attempt at panning for gold with the kids.

Living-History Parks

The region has incredible outdoor history parks on both subjects – head directly to Jamestown and Columbia for the best examples.

White-Water Rafting

Gold Country is in the foothills of the mighty Sierra Nevada Mountains, which regularly get pummeled by deep snow. When the snow melts, the American River runs wild, producing incredible rapids you can experience firsthand on a single- or multiday rafting trip.

p398

Lake Tahoe

Adventure
Lakes
Romance

Skiing

Some of the deepest snow in America falls around Lake Tahoe, and the skiing and snowboarding are incredible at over a dozen resorts. And this being California, most days are sunny and it's never bitterly cold.

Swimming & Boating

Lake Tahoe is so deep that it never freezes over, but the surface temperature changes with the seasons. By July it's warm enough for splashing around, and boating is popular in the spring and fall.

Cabins & Campgrounds

Tahoe's dreamy accommodations, including cottages, knotty-pine cabins and campgrounds, tend to sit beneath towering pines on the lake's shore – they're ideal for a romantic weekend.

p424

Yosemite & the Sierra Nevada

Landscape
Wildlife
Adventure

Waterfalls & Granite

Yosemite's incredible waterfalls run heaviest in spring, roaring over rock and casting rainbows. Rising above, Yosemite's famous granite domes include Half Dome.

Flora & Fauna

Wildflowers carpet the valley in spring, the High Country in summer. You probably won't see a bear – provided you properly store food – but you will see incredible birds, deer and – if you're lucky – the elusive bighorn sheep.

Valley Walks

Many brilliant hiking trails originate in Yosemite Valley, including waterfall walks to Vernal and Nevada Falls, and the near-vertical ascent of famous Yosemite Falls. Follow the watercourses for maximum drama.

p460

On the Road

Northern Mountains p333

North Coast & Redwoods p218

Gold Country p398

Lake Tahoe p424

Napa & Sonoma Wine Country p159

Yosemite & the Sierra Nevada p460

San Francisco p64

Marin County & the Bay Area p108

Sacramento & Central Valley p367

Central Coast p274

San Francisco

POP 870,887

Best Places to Eat

➡ In Situ (p94)
➡ Benu (p94)
➡ La Taqueria (p98)
➡ Rich Table (p98)
➡ Cala (p98)
➡ Al's Place (p99)

Best Places to Sleep

➡ Hotel Drisco (p92)
➡ Argonaut Hotel (p92)
➡ Hotel Vitale (p90)
➡ Inn at the Presidio (p91)
➡ Hotel Bohème (p91)

Why Go?

Get to know the capital of weird from the inside out, from mural-lined alleyways named after poets to clothing-optional beaches on a former military base. But don't be too quick to dismiss San Francisco's wild ideas. Biotech, gay rights, personal computers, cable cars and organic fine dining were once considered outlandish too, before San Francisco introduced these underground ideas into the mainstream decades ago. San Francisco's morning fog erases the boundaries between land and ocean, reality and infinite possibility.

Rules are never strictly followed here. Golden Gate Bridge and Alcatraz are entirely optional – San Franciscans mostly admire them from afar – leaving you free to pursue inspiration through Golden Gate Park, past flamboyantly painted Victorian homes and through Mission galleries. Just don't be late for your sensational, sustainable dinner: in San Francisco, you can find happiness and eat it too.

When to Go
San Francisco

Jan–Mar Low-season rates, brisk but rarely cold days, and Lunar New Year parade fireworks.

May–Aug Farmers markets and festivals make up for high-season rates and chilly afternoon fog.

Sep–Nov Blue skies, free concerts, bargain hotel rates and flavor-bursting harvest cuisine.

San Francisco Highlights

1 Following your bliss through SF's mile-wide wild streak: **Golden Gate Park** (p84).

2 Seeing how real life is cooler than science fiction at the **Exploratorium** (p75).

3 Watching fog dance atop the deco towers of the **Golden Gate Bridge** (p71).

4 Plotting your escape from **Alcatraz** (p71), SF's notorious island prison.

5 Wandering through 150 years of California history in **Chinatown** (p76).

6 Coming out and celebrating LGBTQ history in

The Castro (p82), the center of the gay universe.

7 Climbing **Coit Tower** (p71), taking in the murals as you go before gazing at the panoramic views.

8 Grazing at **Ferry Building** (p67), SF's local, sustainable-food destination.

History

Oysters and acorn bread were prime dinner options in the Mexico-run Ohlone settlement of San Francisco circa 1848 – but a year and some gold nuggets later, Champagne and chow mein were served by the bucket. Gold found in nearby Sierra Nevada foothills turned a sleepy 800-person village into a port city of 100,000 prospectors, con artists and prostitutes, in addition to honest folk – good luck telling them apart in the city's 200 saloons.

Panic struck when Australia glutted the market with gold in 1854. Rioters burned waterfront 'Sydney-Town' before turning on SF's Chinese community, who from 1877 to 1945 were restricted to living and working in Chinatown by anti-Chinese exclusion laws. Chinese laborers were left with few employment options besides dangerous work building railroads for San Francisco's robber barons, who dynamited, mined and clear-cut their way across the Golden West, and built Nob Hill mansions above Chinatown.

But the city's grand ambitions came crashing down in 1906, when earthquake and fire reduced the city to rubble. Theater troupes and opera divas performed for free amid smoldering ruins, and reconstruction hummed along at an astounding rate of 15 buildings per day.

During WWII, soldiers accused of insubordination and homosexuality were dismissed in San Francisco, as though that would teach them a lesson. Instead San Francisco's counterculture thrived, with North Beach jazz and Beat poetry. When the Central Intelligence Agency (CIA) tested LSD on the willing volunteer and *One Flew Over the Cuckoo's Nest* author Ken Kesey, he slipped some into Kool-Aid and kicked off the psychedelic '60s.

The Summer of Love brought free food, love and music to the Haight, and pioneering gay activists in the Castro helped elect Harvey Milk as San Francisco supervisor – America's first out gay official. When San Francisco witnessed devastating losses from HIV/AIDS in the 1980s, the city rallied to become a global model for epidemic treatment and prevention.

San Francisco's unconventional thinking spawned the web in the 1990s, until the dot-com bubble burst in 2000. But risk-taking SF continues to float outlandish new ideas – social media, mobile apps, biotech. Congratulations: you're just in time for San Francisco's next wild ride.

⊙ Sights

⊙ Downtown, Civic Center & SoMa

★ San Francisco
Museum of Modern Art   MUSEUM
(SFMOMA; Map p68; ☑ 415-357-4000; www.sfmoma.org; 151 3rd St; adult/under 18yr/student $25/free/$19; ⊙ 10am-5pm Fri-Tue, to 9pm Thu, public spaces from 9am; ⦿; ☐ 5, 6, 7, 14, 19, 21, 31, 38, Ⓜ Montgomery, Ⓑ Montgomery) The expanded SFMOMA is a mind-boggling feat, tripled in size to accommodate a sprawling collection of modern masterworks and 19 concurrent exhibitions over 10 floors – but, then again, SFMOMA has defied limits ever since its 1935 founding. The museum was a visionary early investor in then-emerging art forms, including photography, installations, video, performance art, and (as befits a global technology hub) digital art and industrial design. Even during the Depression, SFMOMA envisioned a world of vivid possibilities, starting in San Francisco.

DON'T MISS...

Saloons The Barbary Coast is roaring back to life with historically researched whiskey cocktails and staggering gin concoctions in San Francisco's great Western-saloon revival.

Rooftop-garden cuisine SF chefs are raising the roof on hyperlocal fare with ingredients raised right upstairs: city-bee honey at Jardinière (p97), edible pansies at Coi (Map p74; ☑ 415-393-9000; www.coirestaurant.com; 373 Broadway; set menu $250; ⊙ 5:30-10pm Thu-Mon; ℗; ☐ 8, 10, 12, 30, 41, 45, ☐ Powell-Mason) ✿, herbs at farm:table (p93) and salad greens to feed the homeless at Glide Memorial (Map p68; ☑ 415-674-6090; www.glide.org; 330 Ellis St; ⊙ celebrations 9am & 11am Sun; ⦿; ☐ 38, Ⓜ Powell, Ⓑ Powell).

Green everything Recent reports rank San Francisco as the greenest city in North America, with its pioneering parklets, citywide composting laws and the USA's biggest stretch of urban greenery: Golden Gate Park (p78).

★**Asian Art Museum**   MUSEUM
(Map p68; ☑415-581-3500; www.asianart.org;
200 Larkin St; adult/student/child $15/10/free,
1st Sun of month free; ☉10am-5pm Tue, Wed &
Fri-Sun, to 9pm Thu; ❋; Ⓜ Civic Center, Ⓑ Civic
Center) Imaginations race from ancient Persian miniatures to cutting-edge Japanese
minimalism across three floors spanning
6000 years of Asian art. Besides the largest collection outside Asia – 18,000 works
– the museum offers excellent programs for
all ages, from shadow-puppet shows and
tea tastings with star chefs to mixers with
cross-cultural DJ mash-ups.

★**Contemporary Jewish Museum**   MUSEUM
(Map p68; ☑415-344-8800; www.thecjm.org; 736
Mission St; adult/student/child $14/12/free; after
5pm Thu $5; ☉11am-5pm Mon, Tue & Fri-Sun, to
8pm Thu; ❋; ☐14, 30, 45, Ⓑ Montgomery, Ⓜ Montgomery) That upended blue-steel box mirac-
ulously balancing on one corner isn't sculpture but the Yerba Buena Lane entry to the
Contemporary Jewish Museum – an institu-
tion that upends conventional ideas about
art and religion. Exhibits here are compelling explorations of Jewish ideals and visionaries, including writer Gertrude Stein,
rock promoter Bill Graham, cartoonist Roz
Chast and filmmaker Stanley Kubrick.

★**Luggage Store Gallery**   GALLERY
(Map p68; ☑415-255-5971; www.luggagestore
gallery.org; 1007 Market St; ☉noon-5pm Wed-Sat;
☐5, 6, 7, 21, 31, Ⓜ Civic Center, Ⓑ Civic Center)
Like a dandelion pushing through sidewalk
cracks, this plucky nonprofit gallery has
brought signs of life to one of the Tenderloin's toughest blocks for two decades. By
giving SF street artists a gallery platform,
the Luggage Store helped launch graffi-
ti-art star Barry McGee, muralist Rigo and
street photographer Cheryl Dunn. Find the
graffitied door and climb to the 2nd-floor
gallery, which rises above the street without losing sight of it.

★**SF Camerawork**   GALLERY
(Map p68; ☑415-487-1011; www.sfcamerawork.
org; 1011 Market St, 2nd fl; ☉noon-6pm Tue-Sat;
☐6, 7, 9, 21, Ⓑ Civic Center, Ⓜ Civic Center) 𝗙𝗥𝗘𝗘
Since 1974, this nonprofit art organization
has championed experimental photo-based
imagery beyond classic B&W prints and
casual digital snapshots. Since moving into
this spacious new Market St gallery, Camerawork's far-reaching exhibitions have exam-
ined memories of love and war in Southeast

BEFORE YOU GO

➡ Make reservations at top San
Francisco restaurants – some accept
early/late walk-ins, but not all do.

➡ Reserve Alcatraz tickets two to four
weeks ahead, especially for popular
night tours.

➡ Download SF-invented apps for ride
sharing (Lyft, Uber), home sharing
(Airbnb), restaurant booking (Yelp) and
audio walking tours (Detour) – all widely
used here.

Asia, taken imaginary holidays with slide
shows of vacation snapshots scavenged from
the San Francisco Dump and showcased SF-
based artist Sanaz Mazinani's mesmerizing
Islamic-inspired photo montages made of
tiny Trumps.

★**Ferry Building**   LANDMARK
(Map p68; ☑415-983-8030; www.ferrybuilding
marketplace.com; cnr Market St & the Embarcadero; ☉10am-7pm Mon-Fri, 8am-6pm Sat, 11am-
5pm Sun; ❋; ☐2, 6, 9, 14, 21, 31, Ⓜ Embarcadero,
Ⓑ Embarcadero) Hedonism is alive and well at
this transit hub turned gourmet emporium,
where foodies happily miss their ferries over
Sonoma oysters and bubbly, SF craft beer
and Marin-raised beef burgers, or locally
roasted coffee and just-baked cupcakes. Star
chefs are frequently spotted at the farmers
market (p95) that wraps around the building all year.

**Diego Rivera's Allegory
of California Fresco**   PUBLIC ART
(Map p68; www.sfcityguides.org/desc.html?
tour=96; 155 Sansome St; tours free; ☉tours by
reservation with SF City Guides 3pm 1st & 3rd Mon
of month; Ⓑ Montgomery, Ⓜ Montgomery) 𝗙𝗥𝗘𝗘
Hidden inside San Francisco's Stock Exchange tower is a priceless treasure: Diego
Rivera's 1930–31 *Allegory of California* fresco. Spanning a two-story stairwell between
the 10th and 11th floors, the fresco shows
California as a giant golden goddess offering farm-fresh produce, while gold miners
toil beneath her and oil refineries loom on
the horizon. Rivera's *Allegory* is glorious,
but cautionary – while Californian workers, inventors and dreamers go about their
business, the pressure gauge in the left-hand
corner is entering the red zone.

Downtown San Francisco & SoMa

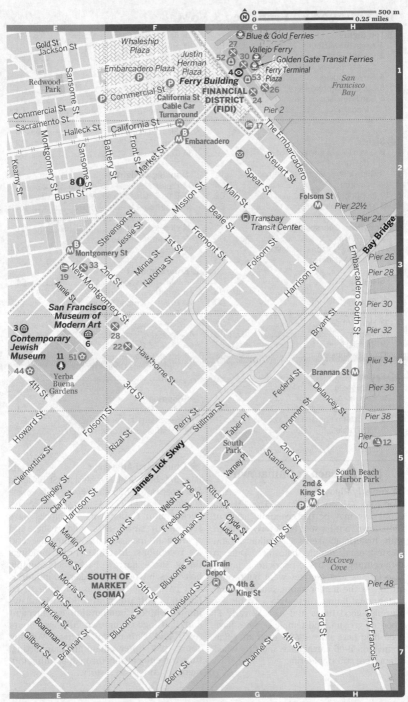

Downtown San Francisco & SoMa

◎ North Beach & Chinatown

★ Waverly Place   STREET

(Map p74; 🚌1, 30, 🚋California, Powell-Mason)
Grant Ave may be the economic heart of
Chinatown, but its soul is Waverly Pl, lined
with historic clinker-brick buildings and
flag-festooned temple balconies. Due to
19th-century race-based restrictions, family
associations and temples were built right
on top of the barber shops, laundries and
restaurants lining these two city blocks.
Through good times and bad, Waverly Pl
stood its ground, and temple services have
been held here since 1852 – even after San
Francisco's 1906 earthquake and fire, when
altars were still smoldering.

★ Chinatown Alleyways   AREA

(Map p74; btwn Grant Ave, Stockton St, California
St & Broadway; 🚌1, 30, 45, 🚋Powell-Hyde, Powell-
Mason, California) The 41 historic alleyways
packed into Chinatown's 22 blocks have
seen it all since 1849: gold rushes and
revolution, incense and opium, fire and
icy receptions. In clinker-brick buildings
lining these narrow backstreets, temple
balconies jut out over bakeries, laundries
and barbers – there was nowhere to go
but up in Chinatown after 1870, when laws
limited Chinese immigration, employment
and housing. Chinatown Alleyway Tours
(p87) and Chinatown Heritage Walking
Tours (p88) offer community-supporting,
time-traveling strolls through defining moments in American history.

⭐ **City Lights Books** CULTURAL CENTER
(Map p74; ☑415-362-8193; www.citylights.com; 261 Columbus Ave; ◷10am-midnight; 🖳; 🚌8, 10, 12, 30, 41, 45, 🚋Powell-Mason, Powell-Hyde) Free speech and free spirits have flourished here since 1957, when City Lights founder and poet Lawrence Ferlinghetti and manager Shigeyoshi Murao won a landmark ruling defending their right to publish Allen Ginsberg's magnificent epic poem *Howl*. Celebrate your freedom to read freely in the designated Poet's Chair upstairs overlooking Jack Kerouac Alley, load up on 'zines on the mezzanine and entertain radical ideas downstairs in the new Pedagogies of Resistance section.

⭐ **Coit Tower** PUBLIC ART
(Map p74; ☑415-249-0995; www.sfrecpark.org; Telegraph Hill Blvd; nonresident elevator fee adult/child $8/5; ◷10am-6pm Apr-Oct, to 5pm Nov-Mar; 🚌39) The exclamation mark on San Francisco's skyline is Coit Tower, with 360-degree views of downtown and wraparound 1930s Works Progress Administration (WPA) murals glorifying SF workers. Initially denounced as communist, the murals are now a national landmark. For a wild-parrot's panoramic view of San Francisco 210ft above the city, take the elevator to the tower's open-air platform. To glimpse seven recently restored murals up a hidden stairwell on the 2nd floor, join the 11am tour Wednesday or Saturday (free; donations welcome).

Beat Museum MUSEUM
(Map p74; ☑800-537-6822; www.kerouac.com; 540 Broadway; adult/student $8/5, walking tours $25; ◷museum 10am-7pm, walking tours 2-4pm Sat; 🚌8, 10, 12, 30, 41, 45, 🚋Powell-Mason) The closest you can get to the complete Beat experience without breaking a law. The 1000-plus artifacts in this museum's literary-ephemera collection include the sublime (the banned edition of Ginsberg's *Howl*, with the author's own annotations) and the ridiculous (those Kerouac bobblehead dolls are definite head-shakers). Downstairs, watch Beat-era films in ramshackle theater seats redolent with the odors of literary giants, pets and pot. Upstairs, pay your respects at shrines to individual Beat writers.

Chinese Historical Society of America MUSEUM
(CHSA; Map p74; ☑415-391-1188; www.chsa.org; 965 Clay St; adult/student/child $15/10/free; ◷noon-5pm Tue-Fri, 10am-4pm Sat & Sun; 🖳; 🚌1, 8, 30, 45, 🚋California, Powell-Mason, Powell-Hyde) **FREE** Picture what it was like to be Chinese in America during the gold rush, transcontinental railroad construction or Beat heyday in this 1932 landmark, built as Chinatown's YWCA by Julia Morgan (chief architect of Hearst Castle). CHSA historians unearth fascinating artifacts, from 1920s silk *qipao* dresses to Chinatown miniatures created by set designer Frank Wong. Exhibits reveal once-popular views of Chinatown, including the sensationalist opium-den exhibit at San Francisco's 1915 Panama-Pacific International Expo inviting fairgoers to 'Go Slumming' in Chinatown.

👁 **The Marina, Fisherman's Wharf & the Piers**

⭐ **Alcatraz** HISTORIC SITE
(Alcatraz Cruises ☑415-981-7625; www.nps.gov/alcatraz; tours adult/child 5-11yr day $37.25/23, night $44.25/26.50; ◷call center 8am-7pm, ferries depart Pier 33 half-hourly 8:45am-3:50pm, night tours 5:55pm & 6:30pm; 🖳) Alcatraz: for over 150 years, the name has given the innocent chills and the guilty cold sweats. Over the decades, it's been the nation's first military prison, a forbidding maximum-security penitentiary and disputed territory between Native American activists and the FBI. No wonder that first step you take onto 'the Rock' seems to cue ominous music: dunh-dunh-dunnnnh!

⭐ **Maritime National Historical Park** HISTORIC SITE
(Map p76; ☑415-447-5000; www.nps.gov/safr; 499 Jefferson St, Hyde St Pier; 7-day ticket adult/child $10/free; ◷9:30am-5pm Oct-May, to 5:30pm Jun-Sep; 🖳; 🚌19, 30, 47, 🚋Powell-Hyde, Ⓜ F) Four historic ships are floating museums

---

DON'T MISS

GOLDEN GATE BRIDGE

Hard to believe the Navy almost nixed SF's signature art-deco **landmark** (www.goldengatebridge.org/visitors; Hwy 1; northbound free, southbound $6.50-7.50; 🚌28, all Golden Gate Transit buses) by architects Gertrude and Irving Murrow and engineer Joseph B Strauss. Photographers, take your cue from Hitchcock: seen from **Fort Point** (p77), the 1937 bridge induces a thrilling case of vertigo. Fog aficionados prefer Marin's Vista Point, watching gusts billow through bridge cables. For the full effect, hike or bike the 2-mile span.

Alcatraz

A HALF-DAY TOUR

Book a ferry from Pier 33 and ride 1.5 miles across the bay to explore America's most notorious former prison. The trip itself is worth the money, providing stunning views of the city skyline. Once you've landed at the ❶ **Ferry Dock & Pier**, you begin the 580-yard walk to the top of the island and prison; if you need assistance to reach the top, there's a twice-hourly tram.

As you climb toward the ❷ **Guardhouse**, notice the island's steep slope; before it was a prison, Alcatraz was a fort. In the 1850s, the military quarried the rocky shores into near-vertical cliffs. Ships could then only dock at a single port, separated from the main buildings by a sally port (a drawbridge and moat in what became the guardhouse). Inside, peer through floor grates to see Alcatraz' original prison.

Volunteers tend the brilliant ❸ **Officer's Row Gardens** an orderly counterpoint to the overgrown rose bushes surrounding the burned-out shell of the ❹ **Warden's House**. At the top of the hill, by the front door of the ❺ **Main Cellhouse**, beautiful shots unfurl all around, including a view of the ❻ **Golden Gate Bridge**. Above the main door of the administration building, notice the ❼ **historic signs & graffiti**, before you step inside the dank, cold prison to find the ❽ **Frank Morris cell**, former home to Alcatraz' most notorious jail-breaker.

TOP TIPS

➜ Book at least one month prior for self-guided daytime visits, longer for ranger-led night tours. For info on garden tours, see www.alcatraz gardens.org.

➜ Be prepared to hike; a steep path ascends from the ferry landing to the cell block. Most people spend two to three hours on the island. You need only reserve for the outbound ferry; take any ferry back.

➜ There's no food (just water) but you can bring your own; picnicking is allowed at the ferry dock only. Dress in layers as weather changes fast and it's usually windy.

Historic Signs & Graffiti
During their 1969–71 occupation, Native Americans graffitied the water tower: 'Home of the Free Indian Land.' Above the cellhouse door, examine the eagle-and-flag crest to see how the red-and-white stripes were changed to spell 'Free.'

Warden's House
Fires destroyed the warden's house and other structures during the Indian Occupation. The government blamed the Native Americans; the Native Americans blamed agents provocateurs acting on behalf of the Nixon Administration to undermine public sympathy.

Parade Grounds

Officer's Row Gardens
In the 19th century soldiers imported topsoil to beautify the island with gardens. Well-trusted prisoners later gardened – Elliott Michener said it kept him sane. Historians, ornithologists and archaeologists choose today's plants.

Main Cellhouse
During the mid-20th century, the maximum-security prison housed the day's most notorious troublemakers, including Al Capone and Robert Stroud, the 'Birdman of Alcatraz' (who actually conducted his ornithology studies at Leavenworth).

View of Golden Gate Bridge
The Golden Gate Bridge stretches wide on the horizon. Best views are from atop the island at Eagle Plaza, near the cellhouse entrance, and at water level along the Agave Trail (September to January only).

Power House

Recreation Yard

Water Tower

Officers' Club

Lighthouse

Guard Tower

Guardhouse
Alcatraz' oldest building dates to 1857 and retains remnants of the original drawbridge and moat. During the Civil War the basement was transformed into a military dungeon – the genesis of Alcatraz as prison.

Frank Morris Cell
Peer into cell 138 on B-Block to see a recreation of the dummy's head that Frank Morris left in his bed as a decoy to aid his notorious – and successful – 1962 escape from Alcatraz.

Ferry Dock & Pier
A giant wall map helps you get your bearings. Inside nearby Bldg 64, short films and exhibits provide historical perspective on the prison and details about the Indian Occupation.

Chinatown & North Beach

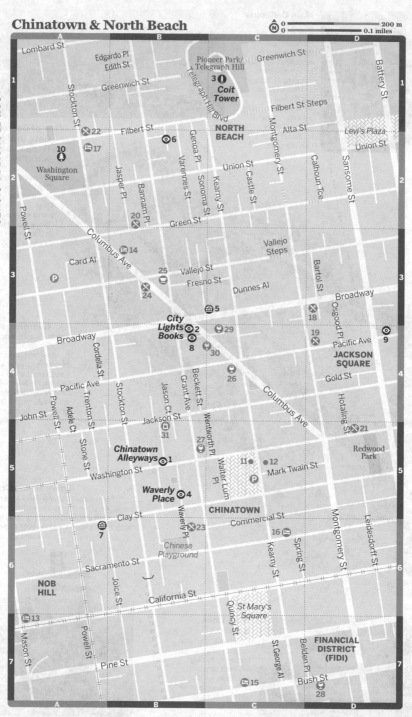

Chinatown & North Beach

at this maritime national park, Fisherman's Wharf's most authentic attraction. Moored along Hyde St Pier, standouts include the 1891 schooner *Alma*, which hosts guided sailing trips in summer; 1890 steamboat *Eureka*; paddlewheel tugboat *Eppleton Hall*; and iron-hulled *Balclutha*, which brought coal to San Francisco. It's free to walk the pier; pay only to board ships.

★ Baker Beach   BEACH
(Map p86; ☎10am-5pm 415-561-4323; www.nps.gov/prsf; ☉sunrise-sunset; ℗; ☒29, PresidiGo Shuttle) Picnic amid wind-sculpted pines, fish from craggy rocks or frolic nude at mile-long Baker Beach, with spectacular views of the Golden Gate. Crowds come weekends, especially on fog-free days; arrive early. For nude sunbathing (mostly straight girls and gay boys), head to the north. Families in clothing stick to the south, nearer parking. Mind the currents and the c-c-cold water.

★ Musée Mécanique   AMUSEMENT PARK
(Map p76; ☎415-346-2000; www.musee mechanique.org; Pier 45, Shed A; ☉10am-8pm; ♿; ☒47, ☒Powell-Mason, Powell-Hyde; Ⓜ E, F) A flashback to penny arcades, the Musée Mécanique houses a mind-blowing collection of vintage mechanical amusements. Sinister, freckle-faced Laughing Sal has creeped out kids for over a century, but don't let this manic mannequin deter you from the best

arcade west of Coney Island. A quarter lets you start brawls in Wild West saloons, peep at belly dancers through a vintage Mutoscope and even learn a cautionary tale about smoking opium.

★ Exploratorium   MUSEUM
(Map p76; ☎415-528-4444; www.exploratorium.edu; Pier 15; adult/child $30/20, 6-10pm Thu $15; ☉10am-5pm Tue-Sun, over 18yr only 6-10pm Thu; ℗♿; Ⓜ E, F) ⬤ Is there a science to skateboarding? Do toilets really flush counterclockwise in Australia? Find out things you'll wish you learned in school at San Francisco's hands-on science museum. Combining science with art and investigating human perception, the Exploratorium nudges you to question how you perceive the world around you. The setting is thrilling: a 9-acre, glass-walled pier jutting straight into San Francisco Bay, with large outdoor portions you can explore free of charge, 24 hours a day.

★ Crissy Field   PARK
(Map p76; ☎415-561-4700; www.crissyfield.org; 1199 East Beach; ℗; ☒30, PresidiGo Shuttle) War is for the birds at Crissy Field, a military airstrip turned waterfront nature preserve with knockout Golden Gate views. Where military aircraft once zoomed in for landings, bird-watchers now huddle in the silent rushes of a reclaimed tidal marsh. Joggers pound beachside trails and the only security

Fisherman's Wharf, The Marina & Russian Hill

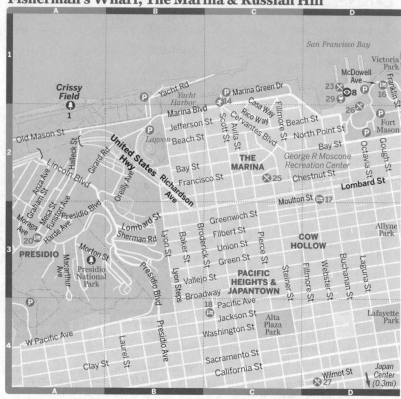

Fisherman's Wharf, The Marina & Russian Hill

alerts are raised by puppies suspiciously sniffing surfers. On foggy days, stop by the certified-green **Warming Hut** (Map p114; ☑415-561-3042; www.parksconservancy.org/visit/eat/warming-hut.html; 983 Marine Dr; items $4-9; ⊙9am-5pm; Ⓟ⧖; ⧆PresidiGo shuttle) ✎ to browse regional-nature books and warm up with fair-trade coffee.

Fort Mason Center
AREA

(Map p76; ☑415-345-7500; www.fortmason.org; cnr Marina Blvd & Laguna St; Ⓟ; ⧆22, 28, 30, 43, 47, 49) San Francisco takes subversive glee in turning military installations into venues for nature, fine dining and out-there experimental art. Evidence: Fort Mason, once a shipyard and embarkation point for WWII troops, now a vast cultural center and gathering place for events, drinking and eating. Wander the waterfront, keeping your eyes peeled for fascinating outdoor art-and-science installations designed by the Exploratorium (p75).

Fort Point
HISTORIC SITE

(Map p114; ☑415-556-1693; www.nps.gov/fopo; Marine Dr; ⊙10am-5pm Fri-Sun; Ⓟ; ⧆28) FREE This triple-decker, brick-walled US military fortress was completed in 1861, with 126 cannons, to protect the bay against certain invasion during the Civil War...or not, as it turned out. Without a single shot having been fired, Fort Point was abandoned in 1900. Alfred Hitchcock made it famous in his 1956 film *Vertigo* – this is where Kim Novak jumped into the bay. Now the fort showcases Civil War displays and knockout panoramic viewing decks of the bridge's underside.

Pier 39
PIER

(Map p76; ☑415-705-5500; www.pier39.com; cnr Beach St & the Embarcadero; Ⓟ⧖; ⧆47, ⧆Powell-Mason, ⓂE, F) The focal point of Fisherman's Wharf isn't the waning fishing fleet but the carousel, carnival-like attractions, shops and restaurants of Pier 39 – and, of course, the

GOLDEN GATE PARK

When San Franciscans refer to 'the park,' there's only one that gets the definite article. Everything they hold dear is in **Golden Gate Park** (Map p86; www.golden-gate-park.com; btwn Stanyan St & Great Hwy; 🅿️👤🐾; 🚌5, 7, 18, 21, 28, 29, 33, 44, Ⓜ️N) 🐾, including free spirits, free music, Frisbee and bison.

At the east end you can join year-round drum circles at **Hippie Hill**, sweater-clad athletes at the historic **Lawn Bowling Club**, toddlers clinging for dear life onto the 100-year-old carousel and meditators in the AIDS Memorial Grove. To the west, turtles paddle past model yachts at Spreckels Lake, offerings are made at pagan altars behind the baseball diamond and free concerts are held in the Polo Fields, site of 1967's hippie Human Be-In.

This scenery seems far-fetched now, but impossible when proposed in 1866. When New York's Central Park architect Frederick Law Olmsted balked at transforming 1017 acres of dunes into the world's largest developed park, San Francisco's green scheme fell to tenacious young civil engineer William Hammond Hall. He insisted that instead of casinos, resorts, race tracks and an igloo village, park features should include **botanical gardens** (Strybing Arboretum; Map p86; 📞415-661-1316; www.strybing.org; 1199 9th Ave; adult/child $8/2, before 9am daily & 2nd Tue of month free; 🕐7:30am-7pm Mar-Sep, to 6pm Oct–mid-Nov & Feb, to 5pm mid-Nov–Jan, last entry 1hr before closing, bookstore 10am-4pm; 👤; 🚌6, 7, 44, Ⓜ️N) 🐾, a dedicated **buffalo paddock** (Map p86; www.golden-gate-park.com/buffalo-paddock.html; 🕐sunrise-sunset; 🚌5, 21) **FREE** and waterfalls at **Stow Lake** (Map p86; www.sfrecpark.org; 🕐sunrise-sunset; 👤; 🚌7, 44, Ⓜ️N). Today the park offers 7.5 miles of bicycle trails, 12 miles of equestrian trails, an archery range, fly-casting pools, four soccer fields and 21 tennis courts. Sundays, when John F Kennedy Dr closes to traffic around 9th Ave, don't miss roller disco and lindy-hopping in the park. Other times, catch these park highlights:

de Young Museum (Map p86; 📞415-750-3600; http://deyoung.famsf.org; 50 Hagiwara Tea Garden Dr; adult/child $15/free, 1st Tue of month free; 🕐9:30am-5:15pm Tue-Sun, to 8:45pm Fri Apr-Nov; 👤; 🚌5, 7, 44, Ⓜ️N) Follow sculptor Andy Goldsworthy's artificial fault line in the sidewalk into Herzog & de Meuron's sleek, copper-clad building that's oxidizing green to blend into the park. Don't be fooled by the de Young's camouflaged exterior: shows here boldly broaden artistic horizons, from Oceanic ceremonial masks and trippy-hippie handmade fashion to James Turrell's domed *Skyspace* installation, built into a hill in the sculpture garden. Ticket includes free same-day entry to the **Legion of Honor** (Map p86; 📞415-750-3600; http://legionofhonor.famsf.org; 100 34th Ave; adult/child $15/free, discount with Muni ticket $2, 1st Tue of month free; 🕐9:30am-5:15pm Tue-Sun; 👤; 🚌1, 2, 18, 38); $2 discount with Muni ticket.

California Academy of Sciences (Map p86; 📞415-379-8000; www.calacademy.org; 55 Music Concourse Dr; adult/student/child $35/30/25; 🕐9:30am-5pm Mon-Sat, from 11am Sun; 🅿️👤; 🚌5, 6, 7, 21, 31, 33, 44, Ⓜ️N) Architect Renzo Piano's 2008 landmark LEED-certified green building houses 40,000 weird and wonderful animals in a four-story rainforest, split-level aquarium and planetarium all under a 'living roof' of California wildflowers. After the penguins nod off to sleep, the wild rumpus starts at the kids-only Penguins+Pajamas Sleepovers ($109 including snack and breakfast; ages five to 17, plus adult chaperones; 6pm to 8am) and the over-21 NightLife Thursdays ($15; 6pm to 10pm), when rainforest-themed cocktails encourage strange mating rituals among shy internet daters.

Japanese Tea Garden (Map p86; 📞415-752-1171; www.japaneseteagardensf.com; 75 Hagiwara Tea Garden Dr; adult/child $8/2, before 10am Mon, Wed & Fri free; 🕐9am-6pm Mar-Oct, to 4:45pm Nov-Feb; 🅿️👤; 🚌5, 7, 44, Ⓜ️N) Since 1894, this picturesque 5-acre garden has blushed with cherry blossoms in spring, flamed red with maple leaves in fall, and induced visitors to lose track of time in its meditative Zen Garden. The bonsai grove was cultivated by the Hagiwara family, who returned from WWII Japanese American internment camps to discover that many of their prized miniature evergreens had been sold – they spent decades recovering them. Visit the Tea House for tea and fortune cookies, introduced to the US right here.

Conservatory of Flowers (Map p86; 📞info 415-831-2090; www.conservatoryofflowers.org; 100 John F Kennedy Dr; adult/student/child $8/6/2, 1st Tue of month free; 🕐10am-4pm Tue-Sun; 👤; 🚌5, 7, 21, 33, Ⓜ️N) Flower power is alive and well at San Francisco's Conservatory of Flowers. This gloriously restored 1878 Victorian greenhouse is home to freaky outer-space orchids, contemplative floating lilies and creepy carnivorous plants gulping down insect lunches.

famous **sea lions** (Map p76; www.pier39.com; Pier 39, cnr Beach St & the Embarcadero; ☉24hr; 🚼; 🚌15, 37, 49, Ⓜ️E, F). Developed in the 1970s to revitalize tourism, the pier draws thousands of tourists daily, but it's really just a big outdoor shopping mall. On the plus side, its visitors center rents strollers, stores luggage and has free phone-charging stations.

USS Pampanito HISTORIC SITE
(Map p76; 🕿415-775-1943, tickets 855-384-6410; www.maritime.org/pamphome.htm; Pier 45; adult/child/family $20/10/45; ☉9am-8pm Thu-Tue, to 6pm Wed; 🚼; 🚌19, 30, 47, 🚋Powell-Hyde; Ⓜ️E, F) Explore a restored WWII submarine that survived six tours of duty while you listen to submariners' tales of stealth mode and sudden attacks in a riveting audio tour that makes surfacing afterwards a relief (caution, claustrophobes).

👁 Nob Hill, Russian Hill & Fillmore

★Lombard Street STREET
(Map p76; 🚋Powell-Hyde) You've seen the eight switchbacks of Lombard St's 900 block in a thousand photographs. The tourist board has dubbed it 'the world's crookedest street,' which is factually incorrect: Vermont St in Potrero Hill deserves that award, but Lombard is much more scenic, with its redbrick pavement and lovingly tended flowerbeds. It wasn't always so bent; before the arrival of the car it lunged straight down the hill.

★Cable Car Museum HISTORIC SITE
(Map p68; 🕿415 474 1887; www.cablecar museum.org; 1201 Mason St; donations appreciated; ☉10am-6pm Apr-Sep, to 5pm Oct-Mar; 🚼; 🚋Powell-Mason, Powell-Hyde) 🆓 Hear that whirring beneath the cable-car tracks? That's the sound of the cables that pull the cars, and they all connect inside the city's long-functioning cable-car barn. Grips, engines, braking mechanisms...if these warm your gearhead heart, you'll be besotted with the Cable Car Museum.

Huntington Park PARK
(Map p68; http://sfrecpark.org; California St, btwn Mason & Taylor Sts; 🚼; 🚌1, 🚋California) San Francisco's poshest park, Huntington's 1.3 acres mark the crest of Nob Hill. At the center rises the four-sided 'Fountain of the Tortoises,' a century-old recreation of a 400-year-old limestone fountain in Rome. If you're staying down the hill and don't have

a lot of time to explore, the park makes a perfect picnic destination – especially with kids, who love the little playground, kitted out with spongy-soft ground cover.

Vallejo Street Steps ARCHITECTURE
(Map p76; Vallejo St, btwn Mason & Jones Sts; 🚋Powell-Mason, Powell-Hyde) This glorious high staircase connects North Beach with Russian Hill – ideal for working off a pasta dinner. Ascend Vallejo toward Mason St; stairs rise toward Jones St, passing **Ina Coolbrith Park** (Map p76; cnr Vallejo & Taylor Sts; 🚌10, 12, 🚋Powell-Mason). Sit at the top for brilliant views of the Bay Bridge lights, then continue west to Polk St for nightlife.

Diego Rivera Gallery GALLERY
(Map p76; 🕿415-771-7020; www.sfai.edu; 800 Chestnut St; ☉9am-7pm; 🚌30, 🚋Powell-Mason) 🆓 Diego Rivera's 1931 *The Making of a Fresco Showing the Building of a City* is a trompe l'oeil fresco within a fresco, showing the artist himself, pausing to admire his work, as well as the work in progress that is San Francisco. The fresco covers an entire wall in the Diego Rivera Gallery at the San Francisco Art Institute. For a memorable San Francisco aspect, head to the terrace cafe for espresso and panoramic bay views.

👁 The Haight & Hayes Valley

Haight & Ashbury LANDMARK
(Map p86; 🚌6, 7, 33, 37, 43) This legendary intersection was the epicenter of the psychedelic '60s, and 'Hashbury' remains a countercul-ture magnet. On average Saturdays here you can sign Green Party petitions, commission a poem and hear Hare Krishna on keyboards and Bob Dylan on banjo. The clock overhead always reads 4:20 – better known in herbal circles as International Bong-Hit Time. A local clockmaker recently fixed the clock; within a week it was stuck again at 4:20.

Zen Center HISTORIC BUILDING
(Map p84; 🕿415-863-3136; http://sfzc.org; 300 Page St; ☉9:30am-12:30pm & 1:30-4pm Mon-Fri, 8:30am-noon Sat; 🚌6, 7, 21, 22) With its sunny courtyard and generous cased windows, this uplifting 1922 building is an interfaith landmark. Since 1969 it's been home to the largest Buddhist community outside Asia. Before she built Hearst Castle, Julia Morgan (California's first licensed woman architect) designed this Italianate brick structure to house the Emanu-El Sisterhood, a residence for low-income Jewish working women –

PACK-SHOT/SHUTTERSTOCK ©

San Francisco by Cable Car

Carnival rides can't compare to cable cars, San Francisco's vintage public transit. Novices slide into strangers' laps – cable cars were invented in 1873, long before seat belts – but regular commuters just grip the leather hand straps, lean back and enjoy the ride. On this trip, you'll master the San Francisco stance, and conquer SF hills without breaking a sweat.

At the ❶**Powell St Cable Car Turnaround** operators turn the car atop a revolving wooden platform and there's a vintage kiosk where you can buy an all-day Muni Passport for $21, instead of paying $7 per ride. Board the red-signed Powell-Hyde cable car, and begin your 338ft ascent up Nob Hill.

Nineteenth-century city planners were skeptical of inventor Andrew Hallidie's 'wire-rope railway' – but after more than a century of near-continuous operation, his wire-and-hemp cables have seldom broken. On the ❷**Powell-Hyde car**, you'll enjoy Bay views as you careen past flower-lined Lombard Street toward ❸**Fisherman's Wharf**. At the wharf you can see SF as sailors did, as you emerge from the submarine ❹**USS Pampanito** (p###). Witness Western saloon brawls in vintage arcade games at the ❺**Musée Mécanique** (p###) before hitching the Powell-Mason cable car to North Beach. Hop off to see Diego Rivera's 1931 cityscape in the ❻**Diego Rivera Gallery** (p###) at the San Francisco Art Institute, or follow your rumbling stomach directly to ❼**Liguria Bakery** (p###). Stroll through North Beach and Chinatown alleyways, or take the Powell-Mason line to time-travel through the ❽**Chinese Historical Society of America** (p###). Nearby, catch a ride on the city's oldest line: the California St cable car. The terminus is near the ❾**Ferry Building** (p###), where champagne-and-oyster happy hour awaits.

HOLBOX/SHUTTERSTOCK ©

Top: Powell-Mason cable car
Bottom: Powell-Hyde cable car

note the ironwork Stars of David on the 1st-floor loggia.

Today the Zen Center opens to the public for visits, meditation (see the website for a schedule), introductions to Zen practice (8:45am Saturdays) and other Zen workshops.

Alamo Square Park   PARK
(Map p84; www.sfparksalliance.org/our-parks/parks/alamo-square; cnr Hayes & Steiner Sts; ⊙sunrise-sunset; ⊞⚇; ☐5, 21, 22, 24) Hippie communes and Victorian bordellos, jazz greats and opera stars, earthquakes and Church of Satan services: these genteel 'Painted Lady' Victorian mansions have hosted them all since 1857, and survived elegantly intact. Pastel Postcard Row mansions along Alamo Sq's eastern side pale in comparison with the colorful characters along the northwestern end of this hilltop park. The northern side features Barbary Coast baroque mansions at their most bombastic, bedecked with fish-scale shingles and gingerbread trim dripping from peaked roofs.

⊙ The Castro & Noe Valley

★Castro Theatre   THEATER
(Map p84; ☑415-621-6120; www.castrotheatre.com; 429 Castro St; ⊙Tue-Sun; Ⓜ Castro St) The city's grandest movie palace opened in 1922. The Spanish-Moorish exterior yields to mishmash styles inside, from Italianate to Oriental. Ask nicely and staff may let you take a peek, or come for the nightly cult or classic films (p104), or one of the many film festivals – check calendars online. At evening shows, arrive early to hear the organist play before the curtain rises.

Barbie-Doll Window   PUBLIC ART
(Map p84; 4099 19th St; ☐24, Ⓜ Castro) No first-time loop through the Castro would be complete without a peek at the Barbie-Doll Window – better called the Billy-Doll Window, a gay spin-off of Barbie, notable for its shockingly huge penis. Dolls are dressed – well, some of them – in outrageous costumes and arranged in miniature protest lines, complete with signs. One of them says it best: 'It's Castro, Bitch.'

Harvey Milk & Jane Warner Plazas   SQUARE
(Map p84; cnr Market & Castro Sts; Ⓜ Castro St) A huge rainbow flag flaps above Castro and Market Sts, officially Harvey Milk Plaza. Look closer and spot a plaque honoring the man whose legacy is gay civic pride and political clout. Across Castro, by the F-train terminus, is Jane Warner Plaza, where ragtag oddballs and kids too young for the bars congregate at public tables and chairs.

⊙ The Mission, Dogpatch & Potrero Hill

★Anglim Gilbert Gallery   GALLERY
(☑415-528-7258; http://anglimgilbertgallery.com; 1275 Minnesota St, 2nd fl; ⊙11am-6pm Tue-Sat; ☐48, ☐T) FREE The Bay Area hits the big time here, with gallerist Ed Gilbert continuing Anglim's 30-year legacy of launching art movements from Beat assemblage to Bay Area conceptualists. Major gallery artists range from political provocateur Enrique Chagoya to sublime sculptor Deborah Butterfield, yet shows here maintain a hair-raising edge, such as an upraised fist pushed through gallery walls in David Huffman's *Panther*. Check the website for concurrent Anglim Gilbert shows at the gallery's downtown location at 14 Geary St.

★826 Valencia   CULTURAL CENTER
(Map p84; ☑415-642-5905; www.826valencia.org; 826 Valencia St; ⊙noon-6pm; ⊞; ☐14, 33, 49, Ⓑ16th St Mission, Ⓜ J) Avast, ye scurvy scalawags! If ye be shipwrecked without yer eye patch or McSweeney's literary anthology, lay down ye doubloons and claim yer booty at this here nonprofit Pirate Store. Below decks, kids be writing tall tales for dark nights a'sea, and ye can study writing movies and science fiction and suchlike, if that be yer dastardly inclination. Arrrr!

★Dolores Park   PARK
(Map p84; http://sfrecpark.org/destination/mission-dolores-park; Dolores St, btwn 18th & 20th Sts; ⊙6am-10pm; ⊞⚇; ☐14, 33, 49, Ⓑ16th St Mission, Ⓜ J) Semiprofessional tanning and taco picnics: welcome to San Francisco's sunny side. Dolores Park has something for everyone, from street ball and tennis to the Mayan-pyramid playground (sorry, kids: no blood sacrifices allowed). Political protests and other favorite local sports happen year-round, and there are free movie nights and mime troupe performances in summer. Climb to the upper southwestern corner for superb views of downtown, framed by palm trees.

⭐ **Balmy Alley** PUBLIC ART
(Map p84; ☑415-285-2287; www.precitaeyes.org; btwn 24th & 25th Sts; ☐10, 12, 14, 27, 48, Ⓑ24th St Mission) Inspired by Diego Rivera's 1930s San Francisco murals and provoked by US foreign policy in Central America, 1970s Mission *muralistas* (muralists) led by Mia Gonzalez set out to transform the political landscape, one mural-covered garage door at a time. Today, Balmy Alley murals span three decades, from an early memorial for El Salvador activist Archbishop Óscar Romero to a homage to Frida Kahlo, Georgia O'Keeffe and other trailblazing female modern artists.

⭐ **Creativity Explored** GALLERY
(Map p84; ☑415-863-2108; www.creativityexplored.org; 3245 16th St; donations welcome; ☉10am-3pm Mon-Wed & Fri, to 7pm Thu, noon-5pm Sat & Sun; ⛷; ☐14, 22, 33, 49, Ⓑ16th St Mission, ⓂJ) Brave new worlds are captured in celebrated artworks destined for museum retrospectives, international shows, and even Marc Jacobs handbags and CB2 pillowcases – all by local artists with developmental disabilities, who create at this nonprofit center. Intriguing themes range from monsters to Morse code, and openings are joyous celebrations with the artists, their families and rock-star fan base.

⭐ **Galería de la Raza** GALLERY
(Map p84; ☑415-826-8009; www.galeriadelaraza.org; 2857 24th St; donations welcome; ☉during exhibitions noon-6pm Wed-Sat; ⛷; ☐10, 14, 33, 48, 49, Ⓑ24th St Mission) Art never forgets its roots at this nonprofit that has showcased Latino art since 1970. Culture and community are constantly being redefined here, from contemporary Mexican photography and group shows exploring Latin gay culture

to performances capturing community responses to Mission gentrification. Outside is the Digital Mural Project, where, in place of the usual cigarette advertisements, a billboard features slogans like 'Abolish borders!' in English, Arabic and Spanish.

🏃 **Activities**
Cycling & Skating

Basically Free Bike Rentals CYCLING
(Map p76; ☑415-741-1196; www.sportsbasement.com/annex; 1196 Columbus Ave; half-/full-day bike rentals adult from $24/32, child $15/20; ☉9am-7pm Mon-Fri, 8am-7pm Sat & Sun; ⛷; ☐F, 30, 47, ☐Powell-Mason, Powell-Hyde) This quality bike-rental shop cleverly gives you the choice of paying for your rental or taking the cost as credit for purchases (valid for 72 hours) at sporting-goods store **Sports Basement** (☑415-437-0100; www.sportsbasement.com; 610 Old Mason St; ☉9am-9pm Mon-Fri, 8am-8pm Sat & Sun; ☐30, 43, PresidiGo Shuttle), in the Presidio en route to the Golden Gate Bridge. (If you buy too much to carry, Sports Basement staff will mount panniers or mail your stuff home.)

Blazing Saddles CYCLING
(Map p76; ☑415-202-8888; www.blazingsaddles.com/san-francisco; 2715 Hyde St; bicycle rental per hour $8-15, per day $32-88, electric bikes per day $48-88; ☉8am-8pm; ⛷; ☐Powell-Hyde) Blazing Saddles is tailored to visitors, with a main shop on Hyde St and six rental stands around Fisherman's Wharf, convenient for biking the Embarcadero or to the Golden Gate Bridge. It also rents electric bikes and offers a 24-hour return service – a big plus. Reserve online for a 20% discount; rental includes all extras (bungee cords, packs etc).

BAY BRIDGE

San Francisco's other landmark bridge was inspired by a madman. Joshua Norton lost his shirt and his mind in the Gold Rush before proclaiming himself 'Emperor of these United States and Protector of Mexico,' and ordering construction of a trans-bay bridge in 1872. Taxpayers took some convincing: the Bay Bridge was completed in 1936. But the eastern span collapsed in the 1989 Loma Prieta earthquake, taking 12 years and $6.4 billion to repair.

Emperor Norton's idea seemed not quite so bright anymore – until artist Leo Villareal installed 25,000 LED lights along the western span, mesmerizing commuters with a 1.8-mile-long light show that shimmers and pulses in patterns that never repeat. The show ran from dusk until 2am nightly from March 2013 through to March 2015 – but a crowdfunding campaign in collaboration with the State of California brought the installation back in January 2016, and now the lights are now set to twinkle indefinitely. For more, see www.thebaylights.org.

The Mission & The Castro

The Mission & The Castro

◉ Top Sights

◉ Sights

☺ Activities, Courses & Tours

🛏 Sleeping

✖ Eating

🍸 Drinking & Nightlife

✪ Entertainment

The Richmond, The Haight & Golden Gate Park

The Richmond, The Haight & Golden Gate Park

Golden Gate Park Bike & Skate CYCLING
(Map p86; ☑415-668-1117; www.goldengatepark
bikeandskate.com; 3038 Fulton St; skates per hour
$5-6, per day $20-24, bikes per hour $3-5, per day
$15-25, tandem bikes per hour/day $15/75, discs
$6/25; ☉10am-6pm Mon-Fri, to 7pm Sat & Sun;
☑; ☐5, 21, 31, 44) Besides bikes (for kids and
adults) and skates (four-wheeled and inline),
this rental shop just outside Golden Gate
Park rents disc putters and drivers for the
park's free Frisbee golf course. Bargain rates;
helmets included with rentals. Call ahead to
confirm it's open if the weather looks iffy.

Kayaking & Whale-Watching

★**Oceanic Society Expeditions** CRUISE
(Map p76; ☑ 415-256-9604; www.oceanicsociety.
org; 3950 Scott St; whale-watching trips per person $128; ☉ office 9am-5pm Mon-Fri, to 2pm Sat;
☐30) The Oceanic Society runs top-notch,
naturalist-led, ocean-going weekend boat
trips – sometimes to the Farallon Islands –
during both whale-migration seasons. Cruises depart from the yacht harbor and last all
day. Kids must be 10 years or older. Reservations required.

City Kayak KAYAKING
(Map p68; ☑ 415-294-1050, 888-966-0953; www.
citykayak.com; Pier 40, South Beach Harbor; kayak
rentals per hour $35-125, 3hr lesson & rental $49,
tours $59-75; ☉ rentals noon-3pm, return by 5pm
Thu-Mon; ☐30, 45, Ⓜ N, T) You haven't seen
San Francisco until you've seen it from the
water. Newbies to kayaking can take lessons
and paddle calm waters near the Bay Bridge;
experienced paddlers can rent kayaks to
brave currents near the Golden Gate (conditions permitting; get advice first). Sporty romantics: twilight tours past the Bay Bridge
lights are ideal for proposals. Check website
for details.

Spas

★**Kabuki Springs & Spa** SPA
(☑415-922-6000; www.kabukisprings.com; 1750
Geary Blvd; adult $25; ☉10am-9:45pm, co-ed Tue,
women only Wed, Fri & Sun, men only Mon, Thu
& Sat; ☐22, 38) This favorite urban retreat
recreates communal, clothing-optional Japanese baths. Salt-scrub in the steam room,
soak in the hot pool, then cold-plunge and
reheat in the sauna. Rinse and repeat. Silence is mandatory, fostering a meditative
mood – if you hear the gong, it means Shh-
hh! Men and women alternate days, except
on co-ed Tuesdays (bathing suits required
Tuesdays).

The look befits the location – slightly dated Japanese modern, with vaulted
lacquered-wood ceilings, tile mosaics and
low lighting. Plan on two hours minimum,
plus a 30- to 60-minute wait at peak times
(add your name to the waiting list, then go
next door to slurp noodles or shop; they'll
text you when your key is ready). Communal bathing is discounted with massage appointments; book ahead and come on the
gender-appropriate day.

𝒞 Tours & Courses

★**Chinatown Alleyway Tours** WALKING
(Map p74; ☑415-984-1478; www.chinatownal
leywaytours.org; Portsmouth Sq; adult/student
$26/16; ☉tours 11am Sat; ☑; ☐1, 8, 10, 12, 30, 41,
45, ☐California, Powell-Mason, Powell-Hyde) Teen-
age Chinatown residents guide you on two-
hour tours through backstreets that have
seen it all – Sun Yat-sen plotting China's revolution, forty-niners squandering fortunes
on opium, services held in temple ruins after the 1906 earthquake. Your presence here
helps the community remember its history
and shape its future – Chinatown Alleyway

Tours is a nonprofit youth-led program of the Chinatown Community Development Center.

Chinatown Heritage Walking Tours WALKING
(Map p74; ☑ 415-986-1822; www.cccsf.us; Chinese Culture Center, Hilton Hotel, 3rd fl, 750 Kearny St; group tour adult $25-30, student $15-20, private tour (1-4 people) $60; ☺ tours 10am, noon & 2pm Tue-Sat; 🚼; 🚇 1, 8, 10, 12, 30, 41, 45, 🚋 California, Powell-Mason, Powell-Hyde) These local-led tours pack discoveries into a kid-friendly, school-accredited program. One-hour Public Art walks explore Chinatown's history through its murals – including new Wentworth Alley murals. Two-hour Democracy Walks reveal Chinatown's role in US civil rights and international human-rights movements. Proceeds support the nonprofit Chinese Culture Center; book online or by phone three days ahead.

★**Precita Eyes**
Mission Mural Tours WALKING
(Map p84; ☑ 415-285-2287; www.precitaeyes.org; 2981 24th St; adult $15-20, child $3; 🚼; 🚇 12, 14, 48, 49, 🅱 24th St Mission) Muralists lead weekend walking tours covering 60 to 70 Mission murals within a six- to 10-block radius of mural-bedecked Balmy Alley (p83). Tours last 90 minutes to two hours and 15 minutes (for the more in-depth Classic Mural Walk). Proceeds fund mural upkeep at this community arts nonprofit.

★**Emperor Norton's**
Fantastic Time Machine WALKING
(Map p68; ☑ 415-644-8513; www.emperornortontour.com; $20; ☺ 11am & 2:30pm Thu & Sat, 11am Sun; 🚇 30, 38, 🅱 Powell St, 🅼 Powell St, 🚋 Powell-Mason, Powell-Hyde) Huzzah, San Francisco invented time-travel contraptions! They're called shoes, and you wear them to follow the self-appointed Emperor Norton (aka historian Joseph Amster) across 2 miles of the most dastardly, scheming, uplifting and urban-legendary terrain on Earth...or at least west of Berkeley. Sunday waterfront tours depart from the Ferry Building; all others depart from Union Sq's Dewey Monument. Cash only.

★**18 Reasons** COOKING
(Map p84; ☑ 415-568-2710; www.18reasons.org; 3674 18th St; classes & dining events $12-125; 🚼; 🚇 22, 33, 🅼 J) 🍴 Go gourmet at this Bi-Rite–affiliated community food nonprofit offering deliciously educational events: wine tastings, knife-skills and cheese-making workshops, and chef-led classes. Mingle with fellow foodies at family-friendly, $12 community suppers and multicourse winemaker dinners ($95 to $125). Check the website for bargain guest-chef pop-ups and low-cost classes with cookbook authors. Spots fill quickly for excellent hands-on cooking classes – book early.

🎊 Festivals & Events

Lunar New Year CULTURAL
(www.chineseparade.com; ☺ Feb) Chase the 200ft dragon, legions of lion dancers and frozen-smile runners-up for the Miss Chinatown title during Lunar New Year celebrations. Firecrackers and fierce troops of tiny-tot martial artists make this parade the highlight of San Francisco winters.

SF International Film Festival FILM
(www.sffs.org; ☺ Apr) The nation's oldest film festival is still looking stellar, featuring hundreds of films and directors, and plenty of star-studded premieres. Plan ahead for two weeks of screenings citywide, including showcases at the Castro Theatre (p104), Alamo Drafthouse (p104) and Roxie Cinema (p104).

SF Pride Celebration LGBT
(☺ Jun) A day isn't enough to do SF proud: June begins with the San Francisco LGBTQ Film Festival and goes out in style over the last weekend with Saturday's **Dyke March** (www.thedykemarch.org) to the Castro's Pink Party and the joyous, million-strong **Pride Parade** (www.sfpride.org; ☺ last Sun Jun) on Sunday.

Bay to Breakers SPORTS
(www.baytobreakers.com; race registration from $65; ☺ 3rd Sun May) Run costumed or in not much at all from the Embarcadero to Ocean Beach; joggers dressed as salmon run upstream.

San Francisco LGBTQ Film Festival FILM
(www.frameline.org; tickets $10-35; ☺ Jun) Here, queer and ready for a premiere since 1976, the San Francisco LGBTQ Film Festival is the oldest, biggest lesbian/gay/bisexual/transgender/queer film fest anywhere. Binge-watch up to 300 films from 30 countries over two weeks. If you can afford a festival pass, get one: pass holders can show up at the last minute and avoid the ubiquitous lines.

AIDS Walk San Francisco SPORTS
(http://sf.aidswalk.net/; ☺ 3rd Sun Jul) Until AIDS takes a hike, you can: this 10km fundraiser

City Walk
North Beach Beat

START CITY LIGHTS BOOKS
END LI PO
LENGTH 1.5 MILES; TWO HOURS

At **1 City Lights Books** (p71), home of Beat poetry and free speech, pick up something to inspire your journey into literary North Beach – Ferlinghetti's *San Francisco Poems* and Ginsberg's *Howl* make excellent company.

Head to **2 Caffe Trieste** (p100) for opera on the jukebox and potent espresso in the back booth, where Francis Ford Coppola allegedly drafted *The Godfather* screenplay.

At **3 Washington Square**, you'll spot parrots in the treetops and octogenarians in tai chi tiger stances on the lawn – pure poetry in motion. At the corner, **4 Liguria Bakery** (p94) will give you something to write home about: focaccia hot from a 100-year-old oven.

Peaceful **5 Bob Kaufman Alley** was named for the legendary street-corner poet, who broke a 12-year vow of silence that lasted until the Vietnam War ended, whereupon he finally walked into a North Beach cafe and recited his poem 'All Those Ships That Never Sailed': 'Today I bring them back/Huge and transitory/And let them sail/Forever.'

Dylan jam sessions erupt in the bookshop, Allen Ginsberg spouts poetry nude in backroom documentary screenings, and onlookers grin beatifically at it all. Welcome to the **6 Beat Museum** (p71), where visitors are all (to quote Ginsberg's *Howl*) 'angelheaded hipsters burning for the ancient heavenly connection.'

The obligatory literary bar crawl begins at **7 Specs** (p100) amid merchant-marine memorabilia, tall tales and pitchers of Anchor Steam. *On the Road* author Jack Kerouac once blew off Henry Miller to go on a bender across the street at **8 Vesuvio** (p100), until bartenders ejected him into the street now named for him: **9 Jack Kerouac Alley**. Note the words of Chinese poet Li Po embedded in the alley: 'In the company of friends, there is never enough wine.'

Follow the lead of Kerouac and Ginsberg and end your night under the laughing Buddha at **10 Li Po** (p100) – there may not be enough wine, but there's plenty of beer.

RESOURCES

SFGate (www.sfgate.com) *San Francisco Chronicle* news and event listings.

7x7 (www.7x7.com) Trend-spotting SF restaurants, bars and style.

Craigslist (http://sfbay.craigslist.org) SF-based source for jobs, dates and free junk.

Lonely Planet (www.lonelyplanet.com/san-francisco) Destination information, hotel bookings, traveler forum and more.

walk through Golden Gate Park benefits 43 AIDS organizations. Over three decades, $88 million has been raised to fight the pandemic and support those living with HIV.

Stern Grove Festival   MUSIC
(www.sterngrove.org) Music for free among the redwood and eucalyptus trees every summer since 1938. Stern Grove's 2pm Sunday concerts include hip-hop, world music and jazz, but the biggest events are performances by the SF Ballet, SF Symphony and SF Opera.

Hardly Strictly Bluegrass   MUSIC
(www.hardlystrictlybluegrass.com; ⊘Oct) The West goes wild for free bluegrass at Golden Gate Park, with three days of concerts by 100-plus bands and seven stages of headliners.

Litquake   LITERATURE
(www.litquake.org; ⊘2nd week Oct) Stranger-than-fiction literary events take place during SF's outlandish literary festival, with authors leading lunchtime story sessions and spilling trade secrets over drinks at the legendary Lit Crawl.

Día de los Muertos   FESTIVAL
(Day of the Dead; www.dayofthedeadsf.org; ⊘2 Nov) Zombie brides and Aztec dancers in feather regalia party to wake the dead on Día de los Muertos, paying their respects to the dead at altars along the Mission processional route.

🛏 Sleeping

🛏 Downtown, Civic Center & SoMa

★**Marker**   BOUTIQUE HOTEL **$$**
(Map p68; ☑844-736-2753, 415-292-0100; http://themarkersanfrancisco.com; 501 Geary St; r from $209; ❄@🕾🕿; ☐38, 🚋Powell-Hyde, Powell-

Mason) 🅟 Snazzy Marker gets details right, with guest-room decor in bold colors – lipstick-red lacquer, navy-blue velvet and shiny purple silk – and thoughtful amenities like high-thread-count sheets, ergonomic workspaces, digital-library access, multiple electrical outlets and ample space in drawers, closets and bathroom vanities. Extras include a spa with a Jacuzzi, a small gym, evening wine reception and bragging rights to stylish downtown digs.

★**Axiom**   BOUTIQUE HOTEL **$$**
(Map p68; ☑415-392-9466; www.axiomhotel.com; 28 Cyril Magnin St; d $189-342; @🕾🕿; 🚋Powell-Mason, Powell-Hyde, 🅱Powell, 🅜Powell) Of all the downtown SF hotels aiming for high-tech appeal, this one gets it right. The lobby is razzle-dazzle LED, marble and riveted steel, but the game room looks like a start-up HQ, with arcade games and foosball tables. Guest rooms have low-slung, gray-flannel couches, king platform beds, dedicated routers for high-speed wireless streaming to Apple/Google/Samsung devices, and Bluetooth-enabled everything.

Hotel Carlton   DESIGN HOTEL **$$**
(Map p68; ☑800-922-7586, 415-673-0242; www.hotelcarltonsf.com; 1075 Sutter St; r $269-309; @🕾🕿; ☐2, 3, 19, 38, 47, 49) 🅟 World travelers feel right at home at the Carlton amid Moroccan tea tables, Indian bedspreads, West African wax-print throw pillows and carbon-offsetting, LEED-certified initiatives (note the rooftop solar panels). It's not the most convenient location – 10 minutes from Union Sq – but offers good value for colorful, spotlessly clean rooms. The quietest rooms are those with the suffix -08 to -19.

★**Hotel Vitale**   BOUTIQUE HOTEL **$$$**
(Map p68; ☑415-278-3700, 888-890-8688; www.hotelvitale.com; 8 Mission St; r $385-675; ❄@🕾🕿; 🅜Embarcadero, 🅱Embarcadero) When your love interest or executive recruiter books you into the waterfront Vitale, you know it's serious. The office-tower exterior disguises a snazzy hotel with sleek, up-to-the-minute luxuries. Beds are dressed with silky-soft, 450-thread-count sheets, and there's an excellent on-site spa with two rooftop hot tubs. Rooms facing the bay offer spectacular Bay Bridge views, and Ferry Building dining awaits across the street.

★**Palace Hotel**   HOTEL **$$$**
(Map p68; ☑415-512-1111; www.sfpalace.com; 2 New Montgomery St; r from $300; ❄@🕾🖼🕿;

Ⓜ Montgomery, Ⓑ Montgomery) The 1906 landmark Palace remains a monument to turn-of-the-century grandeur, with 100-year-old Austrian-crystal chandeliers and Maxfield Parrish paintings. Cushy (if staid) accommodations cater to expense-account travelers, but prices drop at weekends. Even if you're not staying here, visit the opulent Garden Court to sip tea beneath a translucent glass ceiling. There's also a spa; kids love the big pool.

North Beach & Chinatown

Pacific Tradewinds Hostel HOSTEL $
(Map p74; ☎ 415-433-7970; www.san-francisco
-hostel.com; 680 Sacramento St; dm $35-45;
⊙ front desk 8am-midnight; ➔ @ 🛜; 🚇 1, 🚋 California, Ⓑ Montgomery) San Francisco's smartest all-dorm hostel has a blue-and-white nautical theme, a fully equipped kitchen (free peanut butter and jelly sandwiches all day!), spotless glass-brick showers, a laundry (free sock wash!), luggage storage and no lockout time. Bunks are bolted to the wall, so there's no bed-shaking when bunkmates roll. No elevator means hauling bags up three flights – but it's worth it. Great service; fun staff.

★ Hotel Boheme BOUTIQUE HOTEL $$
(Map p74; ☎ 415-433-9111; www.hotelboheme.com;
444 Columbus Ave; r $235–295; ➔ @ 🛜; 🚇 10, 12, 30, 41, 45) Eclectic, historic and unabashedly poetic, this quintessential North Beach boutique hotel has jazz-era color schemes, pagoda-print upholstery and photos from the Beat years on the walls. The vintage rooms are smallish, some face noisy Columbus Ave (quieter rooms are in back) and bathrooms are teensy, but novels beg to be written here – especially after bar crawls. No elevator or parking lot.

★ Orchard Garden Hotel BOUTIQUE HOTEL $$
(Map p74; ☎ 415-399-9807, 888-717-2881; www.
theorchardgardenhotel.com; 466 Bush St; r $207–
390; Ⓟ ➔ ✻ @ 🛜; 🚇 2, 3, 30, 45, Ⓑ Montgomery)
🍃 San Francisco's original LEED-certified, all-green-practices hotel uses sustainably grown wood, chemical-free cleaning products and recycled fabrics in its soothingly quiet rooms. Don't think you'll be trading comfort for conscience: rooms have unexpectedly luxe touches, like high-end down pillows, Egyptian-cotton sheets and organic bath products. Don't miss the sunny rooftop terrace – a sweet spot at day's end.

Washington Square Inn B&B $$
(Map p74; ☎ 415-981-4220, 800-388-0220;
www.wsisf.com; 1660 Stockton St; r $209-359;
@ 🛜; 🚇 30, 41, 45, 🚋 Powell-Mason) On leafy, sun-dappled Washington Sq, this restored 1910 inn offers European style, complete with wine-and-cheese receptions and continental breakfasts in bed. The tasteful rooms are styled with a few choice antiques, including carved wooden armoires. The least-expensive rooms don't leave much room for North Beach shopping, but this is a stellar location for people-watching, dining and exploring. No elevator.

The Marina, Fisherman's Wharf & the Piers

**★ HI San Francisco
Fisherman's Wharf** HOSTEL $
(Map p76; ☎ 415-771-7277; www.sfhostels.com; Fort
Mason, Bldg 240; dm $30-53, r $116-134; Ⓟ @ 🛜;
🚇 28, 30, 47, 49) Trading downtown convenience for a glorious park-like setting with million-dollar waterfront views, this hostel occupies a former army-hospital building, with bargain-priced private rooms and dorms (some co-ed) with four to 22 beds (avoid bunks one and two – they're by doorways). Huge kitchen. No curfew, but no heat during daytime: bring warm clothes. Limited free parking.

★ Inn at the Presidio HOTEL $$
(Map p76; ☎ 415-800-7356; www.innatthe
presidio.com; 42 Moraga Ave; r $295-380;
Ⓟ ➔ @ 🛜 ✻; 🚇 43, PresidiGo Shuttle) 🍃 Built in 1903 as bachelor quarters for army officers, this three-story, redbrick building in the Presidio was transformed in 2012 into a spiffy national-park lodge, styled with leather, linen and wood. Oversized rooms are plush, including feather beds with Egyptian-cotton sheets. Suites have gas fireplaces. Nature surrounds you, with hiking trailheads out back, but taxis downtown cost $25. Free parking.

Hotel Zephyr DESIGN HOTEL $$
(Map p76; ☎ 844-617-6555, 415-617-6565; www.
hotelzephyrsf.com; 250 Beach St; r $250-400;
Ⓟ ✻ @ 🛜; 🚇 8, 39, 47, 🚋 Powell-Mason, Ⓜ E, F) 🍃
Completely revamped in 2015, this vintage-1960s hotel surrounds a vast courtyard with fire pits and lounge chairs, modern art from nautical junk, and games like table tennis in a tube – reminders you're here to play, not work. Rooms are fresh and spiffy, with

up-to-date amenities, including smart TVs that link with your devices. Best rooms face the water. Parking costs $57.

Hotel del Sol
MOTEL $$

(Map p76; ☎877-433-5765, 415-921-5520; www. jdvhotels.com; 3100 Webster St; d $259-359; P❋@🗢❋❋; 🚌22, 28, 30, 43) 🅿 The spiffy, kid-friendly Marina District Hotel del Sol is a riot of color, with tropical-themed decor. This is a quiet, revamped 1950s motor lodge with a palm-lined central courtyard, and is one of the few San Francisco hotels with a heated outdoor pool. Family suites have trundle beds and board games. Free parking.

★Hotel Drisco
BOUTIQUE HOTEL $$$

(Map p76; ☎800-634-7277, 415-346-2880; www. hoteldrisco.com; 2901 Pacific Ave; r $338-475; @🗢; 🚌3, 24) The only hotel in Pacific Heights, a stately 1903 apartment-hotel tucked between mansions, stands high on the ridgeline. It's notable for its architecture, attentive service and chic rooms, with their elegantly austere decor, but the high-on-a-hill location is convenient only to the Marina; anywhere else requires a bus or taxi. Still, for a real boutique hotel, it's tops.

★Argonaut Hotel
BOUTIQUE HOTEL $$$

(Map p76; ☎800-790-1415, 415-563-0800; www. argonauthotel.com; 495 Jefferson St; r from $389; P❋❋@🗢❋; 🚌19, 47, 49, 🚋Powell-Hyde) 🅿 Fisherman's Wharf's top hotel was built as a cannery in 1908 and has century-old wooden beams and exposed-brick walls. Rooms sport an over-the-top nautical theme, with porthole-shaped mirrors and plush, deep-blue carpets. Though all rooms have the amenities of an upper-end hotel – ultra-comfy beds, iPod docks – some are tiny with limited sunlight. Parking is $59.

🛏 Nob Hill, Russian Hill & Fillmore

Golden Gate Hotel
HOTEL $$

(Map p68; ☎800-835-1118, 415-392-3702; www. goldengatehotel.com; 775 Bush St; r $215, without bath $145; @🗢; 🚌2, 3, 🚋Powell-Hyde, Powell-Mason) Like an old-fashioned *pension*, the Golden Gate has kindly owners and simple rooms with mismatched furniture, in a 1913 Edwardian hotel safely up the hill from the Tenderloin. Rooms are small, clean and comfortable, and most have private bathrooms (some with antique claw-foot bathtubs). Enormous croissants, homemade

cookies and a resident cat provide TLC after long days of sightseeing.

Petite Auberge
BOUTIQUE HOTEL $$

(Map p68; ☎800-365-3004, 415-928-6000; www. petiteaubergesf.com; 863 Bush St; r $270-410; 🗢; 🚌2, 3, 27) Petite Auberge feels like a French country inn, with floral-print fabrics, sunny-yellow colors and in-room gas fireplaces – it's among central SF's most charming midprice stays. Alas, several rooms are dark (especially tiny 22) and face an alley where rubbish collectors rattle cans early (request a quiet room). Breakfast and afternoon wine are served fireside in the cozy salon.

Queen Anne Hotel
B&B $$

(Map p76; ☎415-441-2828, 800-227-3970; www. queenanne.com; 1590 Sutter St; r $210-350; @🗢; 🚌2, 3) The Queen Anne occupies a lovely 1890 Victorian mansion, formerly a girls' boarding school, long on character and architectural charm. Though the chintz decor borders on twee, it matches the stately house. Rooms are comfy (some are tiny) and have a mishmash of antiques; some have romantic wood-burning fireplaces.

★Fairmont San Francisco
HOTEL $$$

(Map p74; ☎800-441-1414, 415-772-5000; www. fairmont.com; 950 Mason St; r from $329; P❋@🗢❋; 🚋California) Heads of state choose the Fairmont, whose magnificent lobby is decked out with crystal chandeliers, marble floors and towering yellow-marble columns. Notwithstanding the opulent presidential suite, rooms have traditional business-class furnishings and lack the finer details of top-end luxury hotels. Still, few addresses compare. For old-fashioned character, reserve in the original 1906 building; for jaw-dropping views, go for the tower.

🛏 The Castro & Noe Valley

★Parker Guest House
B&B $$

(Map p84; ☎888-520-7275, 415-621-3222; www. parkerguesthouse.com; 520 Church St; r $219-279, without bath $179-99; @🗢; 🚌33, Ⓜ J) The Castro's stateliest gay digs occupy two side-by-side Edwardian mansions. Details are elegant and formal, never froufrou. Rooms feel like they belong more to a swanky hotel than to a B&B, with super-comfortable beds and down duvets. Bathroom fixtures gleam. The garden is ideal for a lovers' tryst – as is the steam room. No elevator.

Beck's Motor Lodge MOTEL $$
(Map p84; ☑415-621-8212; www.becksmotor
lodge.com; 2222 Market St; r $189-279; P❋🖵;
MCastro St) This three-story motor-lodge
motel got a makeover in 2016 and its
rooms look colorful, sharp and clean.
Though technically not gay oriented,
its placement at the center of the Castro
makes it a de facto gay favorite. Bringing
kids isn't recommended, especially dur-
ing big gay events, when rooms book out
months ahead.

🛏 The Haight & Hayes Valley

Metro Hotel HOTEL $
(☑415-861-5364; www.metrohotelsf.com; 319
Divisadero St; r $107; @🖵; 🖵6, 24, 71) Trendy
Divisadero St offers boutiques and res-
taurants galore, and the Metro Hotel has
a prime position – some rooms overlook
the garden patio of top-notch Ragazza
Pizzeria. Rooms are cheap and clean, if
bland – if possible, get the one with the SF
mural. Some have two double beds; one
room sleeps six ($150). The hotel's handy
to the Haight and has 24-hour reception;
no elevator.

★ Chateau Tivoli B&B $$
(☑415-776-5462, 800-228-1647; www.chateau
tivoli.com; 1057 Steiner St; r $195-300, without
bath $150-200; 🖵; 🖵5, 22) The source of
neighborhood gossip since 1892, this gilded
and turreted mansion once hosted Isadora
Duncan, Mark Twain and (rumor has it) the
ghost of a Victorian opera diva – and now
you can be the Chateau Tivoli's guest. Nine
antique-filled rooms and suites set the scene
for romance; most have claw-foot bathtubs,
though two share a bathroom. No elevator;
no TVs.

Parsonage B&B $$
(Map p84; ☑415-863-3699; www.theparsonage.
com; 198 Haight St; r $220-280; @🖵; 🖵6, 71, MF)
With rooms named for San Francisco's grand
dames, this 23-room 1883 Italianate Victorian
retains gorgeous original details, including
rose-brass chandeliers and Carrara-marble
fireplaces. Spacious, airy rooms offer antique
beds with cushy SF-made McRoskey mat-
tresses; some rooms have wood-burning fire-
places. Take breakfast in the formal dining
room, and brandy and chocolates before bed.
Charming owners. There's even an elevator.

✖ Eating

✖ Downtown, Civic Center & SoMa

★ farm:table AMERICAN $
(Map p68; ☑415-292-7089; www.farmtablesf.
com; 754 Post St; dishes $6-9; ⊘7:30am-2pm
Tue-Fri, 8am-3pm Sat & Sun; 🖉; 🖵2, 3, 27, 38)
🍃 A ray of sunshine in the concrete heart
of the city, this plucky little storefront
showcases seasonal California organics in
just-baked breakfasts and farmstead-fresh
lunches. Check the menu on Twitter (@
farmtable) for today's homemade cereals,
savory tarts and game-changing toast –
mmmm, ginger peach and mascarpone on
whole-wheat sourdough. Tiny space, but
immaculate kitchen and great coffee. Cash
only.

Red Chilli NEPALI $
(Map p68; ☑415-931-3529; www.redchillisf.com;
522 Jones St; mains $8-11; ⊘11:30am-10:30pm;
🖵2, 3, 27, 38) Mt Everest is for amateurs –
gourmet adventurers brave the Tenderloin's
mean streets for Red Chilli's bargain butter
chicken, Kathmandu rolls (naan wraps) and
pickle-spice lamb *achar*. Can't decide? Get
rice-plate combos, but don't skip the *mo-
mos* (Nepalese dumplings). This family-run
storefront diner is welcoming, charmingly
kitschy and convenient before/after Bour-
bon & Branch (p99) cocktails – otherwise,
get delivery.

El Porteño Empanadas ARGENTINE $
(Map p68; ☑415-513-4529; www.elportenosf.com;
1 Ferry Bldg, cnr Market St & the Embarcadero; em-
panadas $4.50; ⊘9am-7pm Mon-Sat, 10am-5pm
Sun; 🖉🖐; ⓑEmbarcadero, MEmbarcadero) 🍃
Pocket change left over from farmers-market
shopping scores Argentine pocket pastries
packed with local flavor at El Porteño. Veg-
etarian versions like *acelga* (organic Swiss
chard and Gruyère) and *humita* (Brentwood
sweet corn and caramelized onions) are just
as mouthwatering as classic *jamon y que-
so* (prosciutto and fontina). Save room for
dulce de leche alfajores (cookies with gooey
caramel centers).

Sentinel SANDWICHES $
(Map p68; ☑415-284-9960; www.thesentinelsf.
com; 37 New Montgomery St; sandwiches $9-12;
⊘7:30am-2:30pm Mon-Fri; 🖵12, 14, MMont-
gomery, ⓑMontgomery) Rebel SF chef Dennis
Leary revolutionizes the humble sandwich

with top-notch seasonal ingredients: lamb gyros get radical with pesto and eggplant, and corned beef crosses borders with Swiss cheese and housemade Russian dressing. Check the website for daily menus and call in your order, or expect a 10-minute wait – sandwiches are made to order. Enjoy in nearby **Yerba Buena Gardens** (cnr 3rd & Mission Sts).

★**Cotogna** ITALIAN $$
(Map p74; ☎415-775-8508; www.cotognasf.com; 490 Pacific Ave; mains $19-35; ⊙11:30am-10:30pm Mon-Thu, to 11pm Fri & Sat, 5-9:30pm Sun; ☑; ☐10, 12) Chef-owner Michael Tusk racks up James Beard Awards for a quintessentially Italian culinary balancing act: he strikes ideal proportions among a few pristine flavors in rustic pastas, wood-fired pizzas and salt-crusted branzino. Reserve, especially for bargain $55 four-course Sunday suppers with $35 wine pairings – or plan a walk-in late lunch/early dinner. Top-value Italian wine list (most bottles are $55).

★**In Situ** CALIFORNIAN, INTERNATIONAL $$
(Map p68; ☎415-941-6050; http://insitu.sfmoma.org; SFMOMA, 151 3rd St; mains $14-34; ⊙11am-3:30pm Mon & Tue, 11am-3:30pm & 5-9pm Thu-Sun; ☐5, 6, 7, 14, 19, 21, 31, 38, Ⓑ Montgomery, Ⓜ Montgomery) The landmark gallery of modern cuisine attached to SFMOMA also showcases avant-garde masterpieces – but these ones you'll lick clean. Chef Corey Lee collaborates with star chefs worldwide, scrupulously recreating their signature dishes with California-grown ingredients so that you can enjoy Harald Wohlfahrt's impeccable anise-marinated salmon, Hiroshi Sasaki's decadent chicken thighs and Albert Adrià's gravity-defying cocoa-bubble cake in one unforgettable sitting.

★**Benu** CALIFORNIAN, FUSION $$$
(Map p68; ☎415-685-4860; www.benusf.com; 22 Hawthorne St; tasting menu $285; ⊙6-9pm seatings Tue-Sat; ☐10, 12, 14, 30, 45) SF has pioneered Asian fusion cuisine for 150 years, but the pan-Pacific innovation chef-owner Corey Lee brings to the plate is gasp-inducing: foie-gras soup dumplings – what?! Dungeness crab and truffle custard pack such outsize flavor into Lee's faux–shark's fin soup, you'll swear Jaws is in there. Benu dinners are investments, but don't miss star sommelier Yoon Ha's ingenious pairings ($185).

★**Kusakabe** SUSHI, JAPANESE $$$
(Map p74; ☎415-757-0155; http://kusakabe-sf.com; 584 Washington St; prix fixe $95; ⊙5-10pm, last seating 8:30pm; ☐8, 10, 12, 41) Trust chef Mitsunori Kusakabe's *omakase* (tasting menu). Sit at the counter while the chef adds a herbal hint to fatty tuna with the *inside* of a *shiso* leaf. After you devour the menu – mostly with your hands, 'to release flavors' – you can special-order Hokkaido sea urchin, which the chef perfumes with the *outside* of the *shiso* leaf. Soy sauce isn't provided – or missed.

North Beach & Chinatown

★**Golden Boy** PIZZA $
(Map p74; ☎415-982-9738; www.goldenboypizza.com; 542 Green St; slices $2.75-3.75; ⊙11:30am-11:30pm Sun-Thu, to 2:30am Fri & Sat; ☐8, 30, 39, 41, 45, ☐ Powell-Mason) Looking for the ultimate post-bar-crawl or morning-after slice? Here you're golden. Since 1978, second-generation Sodini family *pizzaioli* (pizza makers) have perfected Genovese-style focaccia-crust pizza, achieving that mystical balance between chewy and crunchy with the ideal amount of olive oil. Go for toppings like clam and garlic or pesto, and bliss out with hot slices and draft beer at the tin-shed counter.

★**Liguria Bakery** BAKERY $
(Map p74; ☎415-421-3786; 1700 Stockton St; focaccia $4-6; ⊙8am-1pm Tue-Fri, from 7am Sat; ☑Ⓕ; ☐8, 30, 39, 41, 45, ☐ Powell-Mason) Bleary-eyed art students and Italian grandmothers are in line by 8am for cinnamon-raisin focaccia hot out of the 100-year-old oven, leaving 9am dawdlers a choice of tomato or classic rosemary and garlic, and 11am stragglers out of luck. Take yours in waxed paper or boxed for picnics – but don't kid yourself that you're going to save some for later. Cash only.

★**Molinari** DELI $
(Map p74; ☎415-421-2337; www.molinarisalame.com; 373 Columbus Ave; sandwiches $10-13.50; ⊙9am-6pm Mon-Fri, to 5:30pm Sat; ☐8, 10, 12, 30, 39, 41, 45, ☐ Powell-Mason) Observe quasi-religious North Beach noontime rituals: enter Molinari, and grab a number and a crusty roll. When your number's called, wisecracking staff pile your roll with heavenly fixings: milky buffalo mozzarella, tangy sun-dried tomatoes, translucent sheets of prosciutto di Parma, slabs of

THE FERRY BUILDING

San Francisco's monument to food, the Ferry Building (p67) still doubles as a trans-bay transit hub – but with dining options like these, you may never leave.

Ferry Plaza Farmers Market (Map p68; ☑415-291-3276; www.cuesa.org; street food $3-12; ⊙10am-2pm Tue & Thu, from 8am Sat; ☑⬤;) The pride and joy of SF foodies, the Ferry Building market showcases 50 to 100 prime purveyors of California-grown, organic produce, pasture-raised meats and gourmet prepared foods at accessible prices. On Saturdays, join top chefs early for prime browsing, and stay for eclectic bayside picnics of Namu Korean tacos, RoliRoti porchetta, Dirty Girl tomatoes, Nicasio cheese samples, and Frog Hollow fruit turnovers.

Slanted Door (Map p68; ☑415-861-8032; www.slanteddoor.com; mains $18-42; ⊙11am-4:30pm & 5:30-10pm Mon-Sat, 11:30am-10pm Sun) Live the dream at this bayfront bistro, where California-fresh, Vietnamese-inspired dishes are served with sparkling waterfront views. Chinatown-raised chef-owner Charles Phan is a James Beard Award winner and a local hero for championing California-grown ingredients in signature dishes like garlicky grass-fed 'shaking beef' and Dungeness crab heaped atop cellophane noodles. Book weeks ahead, or settle for Out the Door takeout.

Hog Island Oyster Company (Map p68; ☑415-391-7117; www.hogislandoysters.com; 4 oysters $14; ⊙11am-9pm) Slurp the bounty of the North Bay with East Bay views at this local, sustainable oyster bar. Get them raw, grilled with chipotle-bourbon butter, or Rockefeller (cooked with spinach, Pernod and cream). Not the cheapest oysters in town, but consistently the best – with excellent wines. Stop by Hog Island's farmers-market stall 8am to 2pm Saturday for $2 oysters.

Mijita (Map p68; ☑415-399-0814; www.mijitasf.com; dishes $4-10; ⊙10am-7pm Mon-Thu, to 8pm Fri, 9am-8pm Sat, 9am-3pm Sun; ☑⬤) Jealous seagulls circle above your outdoor bayside table, eyeing your sustainable fish tacos and tangy jicama and grapefruit salad. James Beard Award–winning chef Traci Des Jardins honors her Mexican grandmother's cooking at this sunny taqueria – the Mexico City–style quesadilla is laced with *epazote* (Mayan herbs) and the *agua fresca* (fruit punch) is made from just-squeezed juice.

legendary house-cured salami, drizzles of olive oil and balsamic. Enjoy hot from the panini press at sidewalk tables.

★**Mister Jiu's** CHINESE $$
(Map p74; ☑415-857-9688; http://misterjius.com; 28 Waverly Pl; mains $14-45; ⊙5:30-10:30pm Tue-Sat; ☐30, ☐California) Ever since the gold rush, San Francisco has craved Chinese food, powerful cocktails and hyperlocal specialties – and Mister Jiu's satisfies on all counts. Build your own banquet of Chinese classics with California twists: chanterelle chow mein, Dungeness-crab rice noodles, quail and Mission-fig sticky rice. Cocktail pairings are equally inspired – try the jasmine-infused-gin Happiness ($13) with tea-smoked Sonoma-duck confit.

✖ The Marina, Fisherman's Wharf & the Piers

★**Off the Grid** FOOD TRUCK $
(Map p76; www.offthegridsf.com; Fort Mason Center, 2 Marina Blvd; items $6-14; ⊙5-10pm Fri Apr-Oct; ⬤; ☐22, 28) Spring through fall, some 30 food trucks circle their wagons at SF's largest mobile-gourmet hootenannies on Friday night at Fort Mason Center, and 11am to 4pm Sunday for **Picnic at the Presidio** on the Main Post lawn. Arrive early for the best selection and to minimize waits. Cash only.

Lucca Delicatessen DELI $
(Map p76; ☑415-921-7873; www.luccadeli.com; 2120 Chestnut St; sandwiches $9-12; ⊙9am-6pm; ☐28, 30, 43) Open since 1929, this classic Italian deli is an ideal spot to assemble picnics for Marina Green. Besides perfect prosciutto and salami, nutty cheeses and fruity

Chiantis, expect made-to-order sandwiches on fresh-baked Acme bread, including yummy meatball subs. There's hot homemade soup from 11am to 3pm.

★ **Greens** VEGETARIAN, CALIFORNIAN **$$**
(Map p114; ☑ 415-771-6222; www.greensrestaurant. com; Fort Mason Center, 2 Marina Blvd, Bldg A; mains lunch $16-19, dinner $20-28; ⊕ 11:45am-2:30pm & 5:30-9pm; ☑ ♿; ☐ 22, 28, 30, 43, 47, 49) ✿ Career carnivores won't realize there's zero meat in the hearty black-bean chili, or in Greens' other flavor-packed vegetarian dishes, made using ingredients from a Zen farm in Marin. And, oh, what views! The Golden Gate rises just outside the window-lined dining room. The on-site cafe serves to-go lunches, but for sit-down meals, including Sunday brunch, reservations are essential.

★ **Gary Danko** CALIFORNIAN **$$$**
(Map p76; ☑ 415-749-2060; www.garydanko.com; 800 North Point St; 3-/5-course menu $86/124; ⊕ 5:30-10pm; ☐ 19, 30, 47, ☐ Powell-Hyde) Gary Danko wins James Beard Awards for his impeccable Californian *haute cuisine*. Smoked-glass windows prevent passersby from tripping over their tongues at the exquisite presentations – roasted lobster with blood oranges, blushing duck breast with port-roasted grapes, lavish cheeses and trios of crèmes brûlées. Reservations a must.

✗ Nob Hill, Russian Hill & Fillmore

★ **Swan Oyster Depot** SEAFOOD **$$**
(Map p68; ☑ 415-673-1101; 1517 Polk St; dishes $10-25; ⊕ 10:30am-5:30pm Mon-Sat; ☐ 1, 19, 47, 49, ☐ California) Superior flavor without the superior attitude of typical seafood restaurants – Swan's downside is an inevitable wait for the few stools at its vintage lunch counter, but the upside of high turnover is incredibly fresh seafood.

Out the Door VIETNAMESE **$$**
(Map p76; ☑ 415-923 9575; www.outthedoors. com; 2232 Bush St; mains lunch $14-22, dinner $20-36; ⊕ 11am-2:30pm & 5:30-9:30pm Mon-Fri, 9am-2:30pm & 5:30-9:30pm Sat & Sun; ☐ 2, 3, 22) Offshoot of the famous Slanted Door (p95), this casual outpost jump-starts afternoon shopping with stellar Dungeness-crab noodles, five-spice chicken and rice plates and Vietnamese coffee. At dinner, rice

---

SAN FRANCISCO TREATS

Life is sweet in San Francisco, where chocolate bars were invented in the gold rush and velvet ropes keep ice-cream lines from getting ugly. Before you dismiss dessert, consider these temptations.

Tout Sweet (Map p68; ☑ 415-385-1679; www.toutsweetsf.com; Macy's, 3rd fl, cnr Geary & Stockton Sts; baked goods $2-8; ⊕ 11am-6pm Sun-Wed, to 8pm Thu-Sat; 📶 ♿; ☐ 2, 38, ☐ Powell-Mason, Powell-Hyde, ☐ Powell) Mango with Thai chili or peanut butter and jelly? Choosing your favorite California-French macaron isn't easy at Tout Sweet, where *Top Chef Just Desserts* champion Yigit Pura keeps outdoing his own inventions – he's like the love child of Julia Child and Steve Jobs. Chef Pura's sweet retreat on Macy's 3rd floor offers unbeatable views overlooking Union Sq, excellent teas and free wi-fi.

Craftsman & Wolves (Map p84; ☑ 415-913-7713; http://craftsman-wolves.com; 746 Valencia St; pastries $3-8; ⊕ 7am-6pm Mon-Fri, from 8am Sat & Sun; ☐ 14, 22, 33, 49, ☐ 16th St Mission, ☐ J) Breakfast routines are made to be broken by the infamous Rebel Within: a sausage-spiked Asiago-cheese muffin with a silken soft-boiled egg baked inside. SF's surest pick-me-up is a Highwire macchiato with *matcha* (green tea) cookies; a Thai coconut-curry scone enjoyed with pea soup and rosé is lunch perfected. Exquisite hazelnut cube-cakes and vanilla-violet cheesecakes are ideal for celebrating unbirthdays and imaginary holidays.

Humphry Slocombe (Map p84; ☑ 415-550-6971; www.humphryslocombe.com; 2790 Harrison St; ice creams $4-6; ⊕ 1-11pm Mon-Fri, from noon Sat & Sun; ♿; ☐ 12, 14, 49, ☐ 24th St Mission) Indie-rock organic ice cream may permanently spoil you for Top 40 flavors. Once 'Elvis: The Fat Years' (banana and peanut butter) and 'Hibiscus Beet Sorbet' have rocked your taste buds, cookie dough seems so basic – and ordinary sundaes can't compare to 'Secret Breakfast' (bourbon and cornflakes) and 'Blue Bottle Vietnamese Coffee' drizzled with hot fudge, California olive oil and sea salt.

plates and noodles are replaced with savory clay-pot meats and fish – an evening you won't soon forget. Make reservations.

★ La Folie
FRENCH $$$

(Map p76; ☑ 415-776-5577; www.lafolie.com; 2316 Polk St; 3-/4-/5-course menu $100/120/140; ◉ 5:30-10pm Tue-Sat; ☐ 19, 41, 45, 47) Casually sophisticated La Folie remains one of SF's top tables – even after 30 years. Its success lies in the French-born chef-owner's uncanny ability to balance formal and playful. He's a true artist, whose cooking references classical tradition but also nods to California sensibilities. The colorful flourishes on the plate are mirrored in the *très professionnel* staff. Book a week ahead.

★ Acquerello
CALIFORNIAN, ITALIAN $$$

(Map p68; ☑ 415-567-5432; www.acquerello. com; 1722 Sacramento St; 3-/4-/5-course menu $95/120/140; ◉ 5:30-9:30pm Tue-Sat; ☐ 1, 19, 47, 49, ☐ California) A converted chapel is a fitting location for a meal that'll turn Italian culinary purists into true believers in Cal-Italian cuisine. Chef Suzette Gresham's generous pastas and ingenious seasonal meat dishes include heavenly quail salad, devilish lobster *panzerotti* and venison loin chops. Suave *maître d'hôtel* Giancarlo Paterlini indulges every whim, even providing black-linen napkins if you're worried about lint.

★ Seven Hills
ITALIAN $$$

(Map p68; ☑ 415-775-1550; www.sevenhillssf.com; 1550 Hyde St; mains $19-31; ◉ 5:30-9:30pm Sun-Thu, to 10pm Fri & Sat; ☐ 10, 12, ☐ Powell-Hyde) Anthony Florian has studied with some of the great chefs of California and Italy, and he's an expert at taking several seasonal ingredients and making them shine. His short, market-driven menu features housemade pastas with elements such as rabbit and house-cured pancetta. The four mains showcase quality California meats. Tables are close in the elegant little storefront, but brilliant sound-canceling technology eliminates noise. Stellar service, too.

★ State Bird Provisions
CALIFORNIAN $$$

(☑ 415-795-1272; http://statebirdsf.com; 1529 Fillmore St; dishes $9-30; ◉ 5:30-10pm Sun-Thu, to 11pm Fri & Sat; ☐ 22, 38) Even before winning back-to-back James Beard Awards, State Bird attracted lines for 5:30pm seatings not seen since the Dead played neighboring Fillmore Auditorium. The draw is a thrilling play on dim sum, wildly inventive with seasonal-regional ingredients and esoteric flavors, like fennel pollen and garum. Plan to order multiple dishes. Book exactly 60 days ahead. The staff couldn't be lovelier.

✕ The Haight & Hayes Valley

★ Souvla
GREEK $

(Map p84; ☑ 415-400-5458; www.souvlasf.com; 517 Hayes St; sandwiches & salads $11-14; ◉ 11am-10pm; ☐ 5, 21, 47, 49, Ⓜ Van Ness) Ancient Greek philosophers didn't think too hard about lunch, and neither should you at Souvla. Get in line and make no-fail choices: pita or salad, wine or not. Instead of go-to gyros, try roast lamb atop kale with yogurt dressing, or tangy chicken salad with pickled onion and *mizithra* cheese. Go early/late for skylit communal seating, or head to **Patricia's Green** (Map p84; http://proxysf.net; cnr Octavia Blvd & Fell St; ☐ 5, 21) with takeout.

★ Brenda's Meat & Three
SOUTHERN US $

(☑ 415-926-8657; http://brendasmeatandthree. com; 919 Divisadero St; mains $8-15; ◉ 8am-10pm Wed-Mon; ☐ 5, 21, 24, 38) The name means one meaty main course plus three sides – though only superheroes finish ham steak with Creole red-eye gravy and exemplary grits, let alone cream biscuits and eggs. Chef Brenda Buenviaje's portions are defiantly Southern, which explains brunch lines of marathoners and partiers who forgot to eat last night. Arrive early, share sweet-potato pancakes, and pray for crawfish specials.

Three Twins Ice Cream
ICE CREAM $

(Map p84; ☑ 415-487-8946; www.threetwins icecream.com; 254 Fillmore St; cones $3-5.75; ◉ 3-10pm Mon, 2-10pm Tue-Thu, 2-11pm Fri, 1-11pm Sat, 1-10pm Sun; ⊞; ☐ 6, 7, 22, Ⓜ N) For local flavor, join the motley crowd of Lower Haighters lining up for extra-creamy organic ice cream in seasonal flavors. To guess who gets what, here's a cheat sheet: Wiggle bikers brake for dad's cardamom, foodie babies coo over lemon cookie, and stoned skaters feast on California clichés (two scoops, pistachios, olive oil, sea salt, caramel and whipped cream).

★ Jardinière
CALIFORNIAN $$

(Map p68; ☑ 415-861-5555; www.jardiniere.com; 300 Grove St; mains $20-36; ◉ 5-9pm Sun-Thu, to 10:30pm Fri & Sat; ☐ 5, 21, 47, 49, Ⓜ Van Ness) ✔ *Iron Chef* winner, *Top Chef Masters* finalist and James Beard Award–winner Traci Des Jardins champions sustainable, salacious California cuisine. She has a way with California's organic produce, sustainable meats, and seafood, slathering sturgeon with buttery chanterelles and lavishing root vegetables with truffles and honey from Jardinière's rooftop hives. Mondays bring $55 three-course dinners with wine pairings.

★**Rich Table**   CALIFORNIAN $$
(Map p68; ☏415-355-9085; http://richtablesf.com; 199 Gough St; mains $17-36; ☺5:30-10pm Sun-Thu, to 10:30pm Fri & Sat; ☐5, 6, 7, 21, 47, 49, Ⓜ Van Ness) ✐ Impossible cravings begin at Rich Table, inventor of porcini doughnuts, miso-marrow-stuffed pasta and fried-chicken madeleines with caviar. Married co-chefs and owners Sarah and Evan Rich playfully riff on seasonal California fare, freestyling with whimsical off-menu amuse-bouches like trippy beet marshmallows or the Dirty Hippie: nutty hemp atop silky goat-buttermilk *pannacotta*, as offbeat and entrancing as Hippie Hill drum circles.

★**Cala**   MEXICAN, CALIFORNIAN $$$
(Map p68; ☏415-660-7701; www.calarestaurant.com; 149 Fell St; ☺5-10pm Mon-Wed, to 11pm Thu-Sat, 11am-3pm Sun, taco bar 11am-2pm Mon-Fri; ☐6, 7, 21, 47, 49, Ⓜ Van Ness) Like discovering a long-lost twin, Cala's Mexico Norte cuisine is a revelation. San Francisco's Mexican-rancher roots are deeply honored here: silky bone-marrow salsa and fragrant heritage-corn tortillas grace a sweet potato slow-cooked in ashes. Brace yourself with mezcal margaritas for the ultimate California surf and turf: sea urchin with beef tongue. Original and unforgettable, even before Mayan-chocolate gelato with amaranth brittle.

✕ The Castro & Noe Valley

★**Poesia**   ITALIAN $$
(Map p84; ☏415-252-9325; http://poesiasf.com; 4072 18th St; mains $19-31; ☺5-10:30pm Mon-Sat, to 10pm Sun; Ⓜ Castro St) An all-Italian staff flirts with diners at this unpretentious 2nd-floor bistro with a sunny yellow interior and comfy banquettes good for lingering long after a hearty dinner. Expect dishes you don't typically see at American-Italian restaurants, with standout housemade pastas and a stellar *branzino* (sea bass) cooked in parchment. Fun fact: this is where Oprah ate when she visited the Castro.

★**Frances**   CALIFORNIAN $$$
(Map p84; ☏415-621-3870; www.frances-sf.com; 3870 17th St; mains $26-34; ☺5-10pm Sun & Tue-

Thu, to 10:30pm Fri & Sat; Ⓜ Castro St) Chef-owner Melissa Perello earned a Michelin star for fine dining, then ditched downtown to start this market-inspired neighborhood bistro. Daily menus showcase bright, seasonal flavors and luxurious textures: cloud-like sheep's-milk ricotta gnocchi with crunchy breadcrumbs and broccolini, grilled calamari with preserved Meyer lemon, and artisan wine served by the ounce, directly from Wine Country.

✕ The Mission, Dogpatch & Potrero Hill

★**La Taqueria**   MEXICAN $
(Map p84; ☏415-285-7117; 2889 Mission St; items $3-11; ☺11am-9pm Mon-Sat, to 8pm Sun; ♿; ☐12, 14, 48, 49, Ⓑ 24th St Mission) SF's definitive burrito has no saffron rice, spinach tortilla or mango salsa – just perfectly grilled meats, slow-cooked beans and tomatillo or mesquite salsa wrapped in a flour tortilla. They're purists at James Beard Award–winning La Taqueria. You'll pay extra to go without beans, because they add more meat – but spicy pickles and *crema* (sour cream) bring burrito bliss. Worth the wait, always.

★**Mitchell's Ice Cream**   ICE CREAM $
(☏415-648-2300; www.mitchellsicecream.com; 688 San Jose Ave; ice cream $3.50-6; ☺11am-11pm; ♿; ☐14, 49, Ⓑ 24th St Mission, Ⓜ J) When you see happy dances break out on Mission sidewalks, you must be getting close to Mitchell's. One glance at the day's flavors induces gleeful gluttony: classic Kahlua mocha cream, exotic tropical *macapuno* (young coconut)... or *both*?! Avocado and *ube* (purple yam) are acquired tastes, but they've been local favorites for generations – Mitchell's has kept fans coming back for seconds since 1953.

★**La Palma Mexicatessen**   MEXICAN $
(Map p84; ☏415-647-1500; www.lapalmasf.com; 2884 24th St; tamales, tacos & huarache $3-5; ☺8am-6pm Mon-Sat, to 5pm Sun; ✐♿; ☐12, 14, 27, 48, Ⓑ 24th St Mission) ✐ Follow the applause: that's the sound of organic tortilla-making in progress at La Palma. You've found the Mission mother lode of handmade tamales, *pupusas* (tortilla pockets) with potato and *chicharones* (pork crackling), *carnitas* (slow-roasted pork), *cotija* (Oaxacan cheese) and La Palma's own tangy tomatillo sauce. Get takeout, or bring a small army to finish that massive meal at sunny sidewalk tables.

★ **Al's Place** CALIFORNIAN $$
(☑415-416-6136; www.alsplacesf.com; 1499 Valencia St; share plates $15-19; ⊙5:30-10pm Wed-Sun; ☑; 🚇12, 14, 49, Ⓜ J, Ⓑ24th St Mission) ✎ The Golden State dazzles on Al's plates, featuring homegrown heirloom ingredients, pristine Pacific seafood, and grass-fed meat on the side. Painstaking preparation yields sun-drenched flavors and exquisite textures: crispy-skin cod with frothy preserved-lime dip, grilled peach melting into velvety foie gras. Dishes are half the size but thrice the flavor of mains elsewhere – get two or three, and you'll be California dreaming.

Foreign Cinema CALIFORNIAN $$$
(Map p84; ☑415-648-7600; www.foreigncinema. com; 2534 Mission St; mains $22-33; ⊙5:30-10pm Sun-Wed, to 11pm Thu-Sat, brunch 11am-2:30pm Sat & Sun; 🚇12, 14, 33, 48, 49, Ⓑ24th St Mission) ✎ Chef Gayle Pirie's acclaimed California classics such as velvety Pacific *poke* (marinated tuna) and crisp sesame fried chicken are the star attractions here – but subtitled films by Luis Buñuel and François Truffaut screening in the courtyard are mighty handy when conversation lags with first dates or in-laws. Get the red-carpet treatment with valet parking ($15) and a well-stocked oyster bar.

✖ **Golden Gate Park & the Avenues**

★ **Cinderella Russian Bakery** RUSSIAN $
(Map p86; ☑415-751-6723; www.cinderella bakery.com; 436 Balboa St; pastries $1.50-3.50, mains $7-13; ⊙7am-7pm; 🚼🐾; 🚇5, 21, 31, 33) Fog banks and cold wars are no match for the heartwarming powers of the Cinderella, serving treats like your *baba* used to make since 1953. Join SF's Russian community in Cinderella's new parklet near Golden Gate Park for scrumptious, just-baked egg-and-green-onion piroshki, hearty borscht and decadent dumplings – all at neighborly prices.

Revenge Pies DESSERTS $
(Map p86; www.revengepies.com; 1248 9th Ave; pies $5-8, picecreams $3-6; ⊙9am-9pm; 🚼; 🚇6, 7, 43, 44, Ⓜ N) Living well is only the second-best revenge – a face full of pecan Revenge Pie is far more satisfying. Here's the compensation for every skimpy à la mode serving you've endured: picecream (homemade frozen custard with flakes of buttery pie crust). The chocolate-almond Revenge Pie is a crowd-pleaser – but the key-lime picecream

could make, break and remake friendships. Inside San Franpsycho.

★ **Dragon Beaux** DIM SUM $
(Map p86; ☑415-333-8899; www.dragonbeaux. com; 5700 Geary Blvd; dumplings $4-9; ⊙11:30am-2:30pm & 5:30-10pm Mon-Thu, to 10:30pm Fri, 10am-3pm & 5:30-10pm Sat & Sun; 🚼; 🚇2, 38) Hong Kong meets Vegas at SF's most glamorous, decadent Cantonese restaurant. Say yes to cartloads of succulent roast meats – hello, duck and pork belly – and creative dumplings, especially XO dumplings with plump, brandy-laced shrimp in spinach wrappers. Expect premium teas, sharp service and impeccable Cantonese standards, including Chinese doughnuts, *har gow* (shrimp dumplings) and Chinese broccoli in oyster sauce.

🍷 **Drinking & Nightlife**

No matter what you're having, SF bars, cafes and clubs are here to oblige. But why stick to your usual, when there are California wines, Bay spirits, microbrews and local roasts to try? Adventurous drinking is abetted by local bartenders, who've been making good on gold-rush-saloon history. SF baristas take their cappuccino-foam drawings seriously and, around here, DJs invent their own software.

🍸 **Downtown, Civic Center & SoMa**

★ **Pagan Idol** LOUNGE
(Map p74; ☑415-985-6375; www.paganidol.com; 375 Bush St; ⊙4pm-1am Mon-Fri, 6pm-1:30am Sat; ⒷMontgomery, Ⓜ F, J, K, L, M) Volcanoes erupt inside Pagan Idol every half hour, or until there's a virgin sacrifice...what, no takers? Then order your island cocktail and brace for impact – these tiki drinks are no joke. Flirt with disaster over a Hemingway is Dead: rum, bitters and grapefruit, served in a skull. Book online to nab a hut for groups of four to six.

★ **Bourbon & Branch** BAR
(Map p68; ☑415-346-1735; www.bourbonand branch.com; 501 Jones St; ⊙6pm-2am; 🚇27, 38) 'Don't even think of asking for a cosmo' read the House Rules at this Prohibition-era speakeasy, recognizable by its deliciously misleading Anti-Saloon League sign. For award-winning cocktails in the liquored-up library, whisper the password ('books') to be ushered through the bookcase secret passageway. Reservations required for front-room booths and Wilson & Wilson Detective Agency, the

noir-themed speakeasy-within-a-speakeasy (password supplied with reservations).

★ Bar Agricole   BAR
(Map p84; ☑415-355-9400; www.baragricole. com; 355 11th St; ⊘5-11pm Mon-Thu, 5pm-12am Fri & Sat, 10am-2pm & 6-9pm Sun; ☐9, 12, 27, 47) ❂ Drink your way to a history degree with well-researched cocktails: Whiz Bang with house bitters, whiskey, vermouth and absinthe scores high, but El Presidente with white rum, farmhouse curaçao and California-pomegranate grenadine takes top honors. This overachiever wins James Beard Award nods for spirits and eco-savvy design, plus popular acclaim for $1 oysters and $5 aperitifs during happy hour (5pm to 6pm, Monday to Sunday).

North Beach & Chinatown

★ Comstock Saloon   BAR
(Map p74; ☑415-617-0071; www.comstock saloon.com; 155 Columbus Ave; ⊘4pm-midnight Sun-Mon, to 2am Tue-Thu & Sat, noon-2am Fri; ☐8, 10, 12, 30, 45, ☐Powell-Mason) Relieving yourself in the marble trough below the bar is no longer advisable – Emperor Norton is watching from above – but otherwise this 1907 Victorian saloon brings back the Barbary Coast's glory days with authentic pisco punch and martini-precursor Martinez (gin, vermouth, bitters, maraschino liqueur). Reserve booths or back-parlor seating to hear on nights when ragtime-jazz bands play.

★ Li Po   BAR
(Map p74; ☑415-982-0072; www.lipolounge.com; 916 Grant Ave; ⊘2pm-2am; ☐8, 30, 45, ☐Powell-Mason, Powell-Hyde) Beat a hasty retreat to red-vinyl booths where Allen Ginsberg and Jack Kerouac debated the meaning of life under a golden Buddha. Enter the 1937 faux-grotto doorway and dodge red lanterns to place your order: Tsingtao beer or a sweet, sneaky-strong Chinese mai tai made with *baijiu* (rice liquor). Brusque bartenders, basement bathrooms, cash only – a world-class dive bar.

★ Specs   BAR
(Specs Twelve Adler Museum Cafe; Map p74; ☑415-421-4112; 12 William Saroyan Pl; ⊘5pm-2am; ☐8, 10, 12, 30, 41, 45, ☐Powell-Mason) The walls here are plastered with merchant-marine memorabilia, and you'll be plastered too if you try to keep up with the salty characters holding court in back. Surrounded by seafaring mementos – including walrus genitalia over the bar – your order seems obvious: pitcher of Anchor Steam, coming right up. Cash only.

★ Caffe Trieste   CAFE
(Map p74; ☑415-392-6739; www.caffetrieste. com; 601 Vallejo St; ⊘6:30am-10pm Sun-Thu, to 11pm Fri & Sat; ☎; ☐8, 10, 12, 30, 41, 45) Poetry on bathroom walls, opera on the jukebox, live accordion jams and sightings of Beat poet-laureate Lawrence Ferlinghetti: this is North Beach at its best, since the 1950s. Linger over legendary espresso and scribble your screenplay under the Sardinian fishing mural just as young Francis Ford Coppola did. Perhaps you've heard of the movie: *The Godfather*. Cash only.

★ Vesuvio   BAR
(Map p74; ☑415-362-3370; www.vesuvio.com; 255 Columbus Ave; ⊘8am-2am; ☐8, 10, 12, 30, 41, 45, ☐Powell-Mason) Guy walks into a bar, roars and leaves. Without missing a beat, the bartender says to the next customer, 'Welcome to Vesuvio, honey – what can I get you?' Jack Kerouac blew off Henry Miller to go on a bender here and, after you've joined neighborhood characters on the stained-glass mezzanine for microbrews or Kerouacs (rum, tequila and OJ), you'll see why.

The Marina, Fisherman's Wharf & the Piers

★ Interval Bar & Cafe   BAR
(Map p76; www.theinterval.org; 2 Marina Blvd, Fort Mason Center, Bldg A; ⊘10am-midnight; ☐10, 22, 28, 30, 47, 49) Designed to stimulate discussion of philosophy and art, the Interval is a favorite spot in the Marina for cocktails and conversation. It's inside the Long Now Foundation, with floor-to-ceiling bookshelves, which contain the canon of Western lit, rising above a glorious 10,000-year clock – a fitting backdrop for a daiquiri, gimlet or aged Tom Collins, or single-origin coffee, tea and snacks.

★ Buena Vista Cafe   BAR
(Map p76; ☑415-474-5044; www.thebuenavista. com; 2765 Hyde St; ⊘9am-2am Mon-Fri, 8am-2am Sat & Sun; ☎; ☐19, 47, ☐Powell-Hyde) Warm your cockles with a prim little goblet of bitter-creamy Irish coffee, introduced to America at this destination bar that once served sailors and cannery workers. That old Victorian floor manages to hold up carousers and families alike, served community-style

SOMA GAY BARS

Sailors have cruised Polk St and Tenderloin gay/trans joints since the 1940s, Castro bars boomed in the 1970s and women into women have been hitting Mission dives since the '60s – but SoMa warehouses have been the biggest weekend gay scene for decades now. From leather bars and drag cabarets to full-time LGBTQ clubs, SoMa has it all. True, internet cruising has thinned the herd, many women still prefer the Mission and some nights are slow starters – but the following fixtures on the gay drinking scene pack at weekends.

Eagle Tavern (Map p84; www.sf-eagle.com; 398 12th St; $5-10; ⊘2pm-2am Mon-Fri, from noon Sat & Sun; ▣9, 12, 27, 47) Legendary leather bar with Sunday beer busts.

Oasis (Map p84; ✐415-795-3180; www.sfoasis.com; 298 11th St; tickets $15-35; ▣9, 12, 14, 47, �M Van Ness) SF's dedicated drag cabaret mounts outrageous shows, sometimes literally.

Lone Star Saloon (Map p84; ✐415-863-9999; http://lonestarsf.com; 1354 Harrison St; ⊘4pm-2am Mon-Thu, from 2pm Fri, from noon Sat & Sun; ▣9, 12, 27, 47) The original bear bar makes manly men warm and fuzzy at happy hour.

Stud (Map p68; www.studsf.com; 399 9th St; $5-8; ⊘noon-2am Tue, 5pm-3am Thu-Sat, 5pm-midnight Sun; ▣12, 19, 27, 47) The freaks come out at night for surreal, only-in-SF theme events.

Powerhouse (Map p68; ✐415-522-8689; www.powerhouse-sf.com; 1347 Folsom St; free-$10; ⊘4pm-2am; ▣9, 12, 27, 47) Major men-only back-patio action.

Hole in the Wall (Map p68; ✐415-431-4695; www.holeinthewallsaloon.com; 1369 Folsom St; ⊘2pm-2am Mon-Fri, noon-2am Sat & Sun; ▣9, 12, 47) Spiritual home to gay bikers and loudmouth punks.

Club OMG (Map p68; ✐415-896-6473; www.clubomgsf.com; 43 6th St; free-$10; ⊘5pm-2am Tue-Fri & Sun, 7pm-2am Sat; �M Powell, ⒷPowell) Dance in your skivvies on Skid Row.

---

at round tables overlooking the cable-car turnaround at Victoria Park.

Nob Hill, Russian Hill & Fillmore

★**Tonga Room**   LOUNGE
(Map p74; ✐reservations 415-772-5278; www.tonga room.com; Fairmont San Francisco, 950 Mason St; cover $5-7; ⊘5-11:30pm Sun, Wed & Thu, to 12:30am Fri & Sat; ▣1, ▣California, Powell-Mason, Powell-Hyde) Tonight's San Francisco weather: 100% chance of tropical rainstorms every 20 minutes, but only on the top-40 band playing on the island in the middle of the indoor pool – you're safe in your grass hut. For a more powerful hurricane, order one in a plastic co-conut. Who said tiki bars were dead? Come before 8pm to beat the cover charge.

Big 4   BAR
(Map p68; www.big4restaurant.com; 1075 California St; ⊘11:30am-midnight; ⏹; ▣1, ▣California) A classic for swank cocktails, the Big 4 is named for the railroad barons who once dominated Nob Hill society, and its decor pays tribute with opulence – oak-paneled walls, studded green leather and a big mahogany bar where you can order great martinis. Service isn't fab, but the room's lovely. Live piano on weekend evenings.

The Haight & Hayes Valley

★**Blue Bottle Coffee Kiosk**   CAFE
(Map p68; www.bluebottlecoffee.net; 315 Linden St; ⊘7am-6pm Mon-Sat, from 8am Sun; ⏹⏺; ▣5, 21, 47, 49, �M Van Ness) Don't mock SF's coffee geek-ery until you've tried the elixir emerging from this back-alley garage-door kiosk. The Bay Area's Blue Bottle built its reputation with microroasted organic coffee – especially Blue Bottle–invented, off-the-menu Gibraltar, the barista-favorite drink with foam and espresso poured together into the eponymous short glass. Expect a (short) wait and seats outside on creatively repurposed traffic curbs.

★**Riddler**   WINE BAR
(Map p84; www.theriddlersf.com; 528 Laguna St; ⊘4-10pm Tue-Thu & Sun, to 11pm Fri & Sat; ▣5, 6, 7, 21) Riddle me this: how can you ever thank the women in your life? As the Riddler's all-women sommelier-chef-investor team points out, champagne makes a fine start. Bubbles begin at $12 and include Veuve

Clicquot, the brand named after the woman who invented riddling, the process that gives champagne its unclouded sparkle.

★ Aub Zam Zam
BAR

(Map p86; ☑ 415-861-2545; 1633 Haight St; ☺ 3pm-2am Mon-Fri, 1pm-2am Sat & Sun; ☐ 6, 7, 22, 33, 43, Ⓜ N) Persian arches, *One Thousand and One Nights* murals, 1930s jazz on the jukebox and top-shelf cocktails at low-shelf prices have brought Bohemian bliss to Haight St since 1941. Legendary founder Bruno used to throw people out for ordering a vodka martini, but he was a softie in the end, bequeathing his beloved bar to regulars who had become friends. Cash only.

🍷 The Castro & Noe Valley

Swirl
WINE BAR

(Map p84; ☑ 415-864-2262; www.swirloncastro.com; 572 Castro St; ☺ 2-8pm Mon-Thu, 1-9pm Fri, noon-9pm Sat, to 8pm Sun; ☐ 33, ☐ F, Ⓜ K, L, M) Other Castro bars are niche driven, but this wine shop–bar has universal appeal: reliably delicious wine at fair prices in friendly company. Come as you are – pinstripes or leather, gay, straight or whatever – to toast freedom with sublime bubbly, or find liquid courage for sing-alongs at the Castro Theatre in flights of bold reds.

Blackbird
GAY

(Map p84; ☑ 415-503-0630; www.blackbirdbar.com; 2124 Market St; ☺ 3pm-2am Mon-Fri, from 2pm Sat & Sun; Ⓜ Church St) The Castro's first-choice lounge-bar draws an unpretentious mix of guys in tight T-shirts and their gal pals for seasonally changing cocktails made with bitters and tinctures, good wine and craft beer by the glass, billiards and – everyone's favorite bar amenity – the photo booth. Ideal on a Castro pub crawl, but crowded – and earsplittingly loud – at weekends.

Twin Peaks Tavern
GAY

(Map p84; ☑ 415-864-9470; www.twinpeakstavern.com; 401 Castro St; ☺ noon-2am Mon-Fri, from 8am Sat & Sun; Ⓜ Castro St) Don't call it the glass coffin. Show some respect: Twin Peaks was the world's first gay bar with windows open to the street. The jovial crowd skews (way) over 40, but they're not chicken hawks (or they wouldn't hang here) and they love it when happy kids show up to join the party.

🍷 The Mission, Dogpatch & Potrero Hill

★ %ABV
COCKTAIL BAR

(Map p84; ☑ 415-400-4748; www.abvsf.com; 3174 16th St; ☺ 2pm-2am; ☐ 14, 22, Ⓑ 16th St Mission, Ⓜ J) As kindred spirits will deduce from the name (the abbreviation for 'percent alcohol by volume'), this bar is backed by cocktail crafters who know their Rittenhouse rye from their Japanese malt whisky. Top-notch hooch is served promptly and without pretension, including excellent Cali wine and beer on tap and original historically inspired cocktails like the Sutro Swizzle (Armagnac, grapefruit shrub, maraschino liqueur).

★ Trick Dog
BAR

(Map p84; ☑ 415-471-2999; www.trickdogbar.com; 3010 20th St; ☺ 3pm-2am; ☐ 12, 14, 49) Drink adventurously with ingenious cocktails inspired by local obsessions: San Francisco muralists, Chinese diners or conspiracy theories. Every six months, Trick Dog adopts a new theme and the entire menu changes – proof that you can teach an old dog new tricks, and improve on classics like the Manhattan. Arrive early for bar stools or hit the mood-lit loft for high-concept bar bites.

★ Zeitgeist
BAR

(Map p84; ☑ 415-255-7505; www.zeitgeistsf.com; 199 Valencia St; ☺ 9am-2am; ☐ 14, 22, 49, Ⓑ 16th St Mission) You've got two seconds flat to order from tough-gal barkeeps used to putting macho bikers in their place – but with 48 beers on draft, you're spoiled for choice. Epic afternoons unfold in the graveled beer garden, with folks hanging out and smoking at long picnic tables. SF's longest happy hour lasts 9am to 8pm weekdays. Cash only; no photos (read: no evidence).

☆ Entertainment
Live Music
★ SFJAZZ Center
JAZZ

(Map p68; ☑ 866-920-5299; www.sfjazz.org; 201 Franklin St; tickets $25-120; ☒; ☐ 5, 6, 7, 21, 47, 49, Ⓜ Van Ness) ✎ Jazz legends and singular talents from Argentina to Yemen are showcased at North America's newest, largest jazz center. Hear fresh takes on classic jazz albums and poets riffing with jazz combos in the downstairs Joe Henderson Lab, and witness extraordinary main-stage collaborations ranging from Afro-Cuban All Stars to roots legends Emmylou Harris, Rosanne Cash and Lucinda Williams.

★Chapel LIVE MUSIC

(Map p84; ☑415-551-5157; www.thechapelsf. com; 777 Valencia St; cover $15-40; ☺bar 7pm-2am; ☐14, 33, Ⓜ J, Ⓑ 16th St Mission) Musical prayers are answered in a 1914 California arts-and-crafts landmark with heavenly acoustics. The 40ft roof is regularly raised by shows by New Orleans brass bands, folk-YEAH! Americana groups, legendary rockers like Peter Murphy and hip-hop icons such as Prince Paul. Many shows are all ages, except when comedians like W Kamau Bell test edgy material.

★Bottom of the Hill LIVE MUSIC

(☑415-621-4455; www.bottomofthehill.com; 1233 17th St; $5-20; ☺shows generally 9pm Tue-Sat; ☐10, 19, 22) The bottom of Potrero Hill tops the list for rocking out with punk legends the Avengers, Pansy Division and Nerf Herder and newcomers worth checking out for their names alone (Summer Salt, the Regrettes, Sorority Noise). The smokers' patio is covered in handbills and ruled by a cat that prefers music to people – totally punk rock. Anchor Steam on tap; cash only bar.

★Great American Music Hall LIVE MUSIC

(Map p68; ☑415-885-0750; www.gamh.com; 859 O'Farrell St; shows $20-45; ☺box office 10:30am-6pm Mon-Fri & show nights; ⛟; ☐19, 38, 47, 49) Everyone busts out their best sets at this opulent 1907 bordello turned all-ages venue – indie rockers like the Band Perry throw down, international legends such as Salif Keita grace the stage, and John Waters hosts Christmas extravaganzas. Pay $25 extra for dinner with prime balcony seating to watch shows comfortably, or rock out with the standing-room scrum downstairs.

Fillmore Auditorium LIVE MUSIC

(☑415-346-6000; http://thefillmore.com; 1805 Geary Blvd; tickets from $20; ☺box office 10am-3pm Sun, plus 30min before doors open to 10pm show nights; ☐22,38) Jimi Hendrix, Janis Joplin, the Doors – they all played the Fillmore. Now you might catch the Indigo Girls, Willie Nelson or Tracy Chapman in the historic 1250-capacity, standing-room-only theater (if you're polite and lead with the hip, you might squeeze up to the stage). Don't miss the priceless collection of psychedelic posters in the upstairs gallery.

Classical Music & Dance

★San Francisco Symphony CLASSICAL MUSIC

(Map p68; ☑box office 415-864-6000, rush-ticket hotline 415-503-5577; www.sfsymphony.org; Grove St, btwn Franklin St & Van Ness Ave; tickets $20-150; ☐21, 45, 47, Ⓜ Van Ness, Ⓑ Civic Center) From the moment conductor Michael Tilson Thomas bounces up on his toes and raises his baton, the audience is on the edge of their seats for another thunderous performance by the Grammy-winning SF Symphony. Don't miss signature concerts of Beethoven and Mahler, live symphony performances with such films as *Star Trek*, and creative collaborations with artists from Elvis Costello to Metallica.

★San Francisco Opera OPERA

(Map p68; ☑415-864-3330; www.sfopera.com; War Memorial Opera House, 301 Van Ness Ave; tickets $10-350; ☐21, 45, 47,49, Ⓑ Civic Center, Ⓜ Van Ness) Opera was SF's gold-rush soundtrack – and SF Opera rivals the Met, with world premieres of original works ranging from Stephen King's *Dolores Claiborne* to *Girls of the Golden West*, filmmaker Peter Sellars' collaboration with composer John Adams. Expect haute couture costumes and radical sets by painter David Hockney. Score $10 same-day standing-room tickets at 10am, check website for Opera Lab pop-ups.

San Francisco Ballet DANCE

(Map p68; ☑tickets 415-865-2000; www.sfballet. org; War Memorial Opera House, 301 Van Ness Ave; tickets $22-141; ☺ticket sales 10am-4pm Mon-Fri; ☐5, 21, 47, 49, Ⓜ Van Ness, Ⓑ Civic Center) The USA's oldest ballet company is looking sharp in more than 100 shows annually, from *The Nutcracker* (the US premiere was here) to modern originals. Performances are mostly at the War Memorial Opera House from January to May, and occasionally at the Yerba Buena Center for the Arts. Score $15-to-$20 same-day standing-room tickets at the box office (from noon Tuesday to Friday, 10am weekends).

Theater & Performing Arts

★American Conservatory Theater THEATER

(ACT; Map p68; ☑415-749-2228; www.act-sf.org; 405 Geary St; ☺box office 10am-6pm Mon, to curtain Tue-Sun; ☐8, 30, 38, 45, ☐Powell-Mason, Powell-Hyde, Ⓑ Powell, Ⓜ Powell) Breakthrough shows launch at this turn-of-the-century landmark, which has hosted ACT's productions of Tony Kushner's *Angels in America* and Robert Wilson's *Black Rider*, with William S Burroughs' libretto and music by Tom Waits. Major playwrights like Tom Stoppard, Dustin Lance Black, Eve Ensler and David Mamet premiere work here, while the ACT's new **Strand Theater** (Map p68; 415-749-2228; www.act-sf.org/home/box_office/strand. html; 1127 Market St; F, Civic Center, Civic Center) stages experimental works.

★**Oberlin Dance Collective** DANCE
(ODC; Map p84; box office 415-863-9834, classes 415-549-8519; www.odctheater.org; 3153 17th St; drop-in classes from $15, shows $20-50; 12, 14, 22, 33, 49, 16th St Mission) For 45 years, ODC has been redefining dance with risky, raw performances and the sheer joy of movement. ODC's season runs from September to December, but its stage presents year-round shows featuring local and international artists. ODC Dance Commons is a hub and hangout for the dance community, offering 200-plus classes a week, from flamenco to vogue; all ages and skill levels welcome.

**Yerba Buena
Center for the Arts** PERFORMING ARTS
(YBCA; Map p68; 415-978-2700; www.ybca. org; 700 Howard St; tickets free-$35; box office noon-6pm Sun, Tue & Wed, to 8pm Thu-Sat, galleries closed Mon & Tue; ; 14, Powell, Powell) Rock stars would be jealous of art stars at YBCA openings, which draw overflow crowds of art-school groupies with shows ranging from cyberpunk video art to hip-hop showdowns and Indian kathak–American tap-dance fusion freestyle. Most touring dance and jazz companies perform at YBCA's main theater (across the sidewalk from the gallery).

Cinema

★**Castro Theatre** CINEMA
(Map p84; 415-621-6120; www.castrotheatre. com; 429 Castro St; adult/child $11/8.50; Castro St) The Mighty Wurlitzer organ rises from the orchestra pit before evening performances and the audience cheers for the Great American Songbook, ending with: 'San Francisco open your Golden Gate/You let no stranger wait outside your door...' If there's a cult classic on the bill – say, *Whatever Happened to Baby Jane?* – expect participation. Otherwise, crowds are well behaved and rapt.

★**Alamo Drafthouse Cinema** CINEMA
(Map p84; 415-549-5959; https://drafthouse. com/sf; 2550 Mission St; tickets $9-20; ; 14,

24th St Mission) The landmark 1932 New Mission cinema, now restored to its original Timothy Pfleuger–designed art-deco glory, has a new mission: to upgrade dinner-and-a-movie dates. Staff deliver microbrews and tasty fare to plush banquette seats, so you don't miss a moment of the premieres, cult revivals (especially Music Mondays) or SF favorites from *Mrs Doubtfire* to *Dirty Harry* – often with filmmaker Q&As.

★**Roxie Cinema** CINEMA
(Map p84; 415-863-1087; www.roxie.com; 3117 16th St; regular screening/matinee $11/8; 14, 22, 33, 49, 16th St Mission) This vintage 1909 cinema is a neighborhood nonprofit with an international reputation for distributing documentaries and showing controversial films banned elsewhere. Tickets to film-festival premieres, rare revivals and raucous Oscars telecasts sell out – get tickets online – but if the main show's packed, discover riveting documentaries in teensy next-door Little Roxy instead. No ads, plus personal introductions to every film.

🔒 Shopping

Union Square is the city's principal shopping district, with flagship stores and department stores, including international chains. Downtown shopping-district borders are (roughly) Powell St (west), Sutter St (north), Kearny St (east) and Market St (south), where the **Westfield mall** (Map p68; www.westfield.com/sanfrancisco; 865 Market St; 10am-8:30pm Mon-Sat, 11am-7pm Sun; ; Powell-Mason, Powell-Hyde, Powell, Powell) sprawls. The epicenter of the Union Square shopping area is around Post St, near Grant Ave. Stockton St crosses Market St and becomes 4th St, flanked by flagship stores and **Metreon cinema and mall** (Map p68; 415-369-6201; www.amctheatres.com; 101 4th St; adult/child $14.49/11.49; 14, Powell, Powell). For boutique offerings, head toward **Jackson Sq** (Map p74; www.jacksonsquaresf.com; around Jackson & Montgomery Sts; Embarcadero, Embarcadero) and along Commercial St.

★**Recchiuti Chocolates** FOOD & DRINKS
(Map p68; 415-834-9494; www.recchiuticonfec tions.com; 1 Ferry Bldg, cnr Market St & the Embarcadero; 10am-7pm Mon-Fri, 8am-6pm Sat, 10am-5pm Sun; Embarcadero, Embarcadero) No San Franciscan can resist award-winning Recchiuti: Pacific Heights parts with old money for its *fleur de sel* caramels; Noe Valley's foodie kids prefer S'more Bites to the

campground variety; North Beach toasts to the red-wine-pairing chocolate box; and the Mission approves SF-landmark chocolates designed by Creativity Explored – proceeds benefit the Mission arts-education nonprofit for artists with developmental disabilities.

★**Heath Ceramics** HOMEWARES
(Map p68; ☑415-399-9284; www.heathceramics.com; 1 Ferry Bldg, cnr Market St & the Embarcadero; ☺10am-7pm Mon-Fri, 8am-6pm Sat, 11am-5pm Sun; Ⓜ Embarcadero, Ⓑ Embarcadero) Odds are your favorite SF meal was served on Heath Ceramics, Bay Area chefs' tableware of choice ever since Alice Waters started using Heath's modern, hand-thrown dishes at Chez Panisse. Heath's muted colors and streamlined, mid-century designs stay true to Edith Heath's originals c 1948. Pieces are priced for fine dining, except studio seconds, sold here at weekends.

★**Golden Gate
Fortune Cookie Company** FOOD & DRINKS
(Map p74; ☑415-781-3956; 56 Ross Alley; ☺9am-6pm; ☑8, 30, 45, ☑Powell-Mason, Powell-Hyde) Make a fortune at this bakery, where cookies are stamped from vintage presses – just as they were in 1909, when fortune cookies were invented for SF's Japanese Tea Garden (p78). Write your own fortunes for custom cookies (50¢ each), or get cookies with regular or risqué fortunes (pro tip: add 'in bed' to regular ones). Cash only; 50¢ tip for photos.

ⓘ Information

DANGERS & ANNOYANCES

Keep your city smarts and wits about you, especially at night in the Tenderloin, South of Market (SoMa) and the Mission.
➡ Avoid using your smart phone unnecessarily on the street – phone-snatching is a crime of opportunity and a problem in SF.
➡ The Bayview–Hunters Point neighborhood (south of Potrero Hill, along the water) is plagued by crime and violence and isn't suitable for wandering tourists.
➡ After dark, Mission Dolores Park, Buena Vista Park and the entry to Golden Gate Park at Haight and Stanyan Sts are used for drug deals and casual sex hookups.

EMERGENCY & MEDICAL SERVICES

Before traveling, contact your health-insurance provider to learn what medical care they will cover outside your hometown (or home country). Overseas visitors should acquire travel insurance that covers medical situations in the US, where nonemergency care for uninsured patients can be very expensive.

For nonemergency appointments at hospitals, you'll need proof of insurance, or credit card or cash. Even with insurance, you'll most likely have to pay up front for nonemergency care and then wrangle afterward with your insurance company to get reimbursed. San Francisco has excellent medical facilities, plus alternative medical practices and herbal apothecaries.

San Francisco General Hospital (Zuckerberg San Francisco General Hospital and Trauma Center; ☑emergency 415-206-8111, main hospital 415-206-8000; www.sfdph.org; 1001 Potrero Ave; ☺24hr; ☑9, 10, 33, 48) Best for serious trauma. Provides care to uninsured patients, including psychiatric care; no documentation required beyond ID.

University of California San Francisco Medical Center (☑415-476-1000; www.ucsfhealth.org; 505 Parnassus Ave; ☺24hr; ☑6, 7, 43, Ⓜ N) ER at leading university hospital.

Haight-Ashbury Free Clinic (HealthRIGHT 360; ☑415-746-1950; www.healthright360.org; 558 Clayton St; ☺by appointment 8:45am-noon & 1-5pm; ☑6, 7, 33, 37, 43, Ⓜ N) Provides substance abuse and mental health services by appointment.

San Francisco City Clinic (☑415-487-5500; www.sfcityclinic.org; 356 7th St; ☺8am-4pm Mon, Wed & Fri, 1-6pm Tue, 1-4pm Thu) Low-cost treatment for sexually transmitted diseases (STDs), including emergency contraception and post-exposure prevention (PEP) for HIV.

Drug & Alcohol Emergency Info Line (☑415-362-3400; www.sfsuicide.org)

Trauma Recovery & Rape Treatment Center (☑24hr hotline 415-206-8125, business hours 415-437-3000; www.traumarecoverycenter.org)

INTERNET ACCESS

Apple Store (☑415-392-0202; www.apple.com/retail/sanfrancisco; 300 Post St; ☺9am-9pm Mon-Sat, 10am-8pm Sun; ☎; ☑38, ☑Powell-Mason, Powell-Hyde, Ⓜ Powell) Free wi-fi and internet-terminal usage.

San Francisco Main Library (☑415-557-4400; www.sfpl.org; 100 Larkin St; ☺10am-6pm Mon & Sat, 9am-8pm Tue-Thu, noon-6pm Fri, noon-5pm Sun; ☎; Ⓜ Civic Center) Free 30-minute internet-terminal usage; spotty wi-fi access.

POST

Rincon Center Post Office (Map p68; ☑800-275-8777; www.usps.gov; 180 Steuart St; ☺7:30am-5pm Mon-Fri, 9am-2pm Sat; Ⓜ Embarcadero, Ⓑ Embarcadero) Postal services plus historic murals.

US Post Office (Map p68; ☎800-275-8777; www.usps.gov; Macy's, 170 O'Farrell St; ☺10am-5pm Mon-Sat; 🚋Powell-Mason, Powell-Hyde, Ⓜ Powell, Ⓑ Powell) Inside Macy's department store.

TOURIST INFORMATION

California Welcome Center (Map p76; ☎415-981-1280; www.visitcwc.com; Pier 39, 2nd fl; ☺9am-7pm; 🚌47, 🚋Powell-Mason, ⓂE, F) Handy resource for stroller and wheelchair rental, plus luggage storage, phone charging, and ideas for broader California travel.

San Francisco Visitor Information Center (Map p68; ☎415-391-2000; www.sftravel.com/visitor-information-center; lower level, Hallidie Plaza, cnr Market & Powell Sts; ☺9am-5pm Mon-Fri, to 3pm Sat & Sun, closed Sun Nov-Apr; 🚋Powell-Mason, Powell-Hyde, Ⓜ Powell, Ⓑ Powell) Provides practical multilingual information, sells transportation passes, publishes glossy maps and booklets, and provides interactive touch screens.

ℹ Getting There & Away

If you've unlimited time, consider taking the train, instead of driving or flying, to avoid traffic hassles and excess carbon emissions.

Flights, cars and tours can be booked online at lonelyplanet.com/bookings.

AIR

The Bay Area has three international airports: **San Francisco** (SFO; www.flysfo.com; S McDonnell Rd), **Oakland (OAK**; p137) and **San Jose (SJC**; p153). Direct flights from Los Angeles take 60 minutes; Chicago, four hours; Atlanta, five hours; New York, six hours. Factor in additional transit time – and cost – to reach San Francisco proper from Oakland or San Jose, and note that what you save in airfare you may wind up spending on ground transportation. However, if schedule is most important, note that SFO has more weather-related delays than OAK.

BUS

San Francisco's intercity hub is the Transbay Transit Center. From here you can catch the following buses:

AC Transit (p137) Buses to the East Bay.

Greyhound (☎800-231-2222; www.greyhound.com) Buses leave daily for Los Angeles ($39 to $90, eight to 12 hours), Truckee near Lake Tahoe ($35 to $46, 5½ hours) and other major destinations.

Megabus (p153) Low-cost bus service to San Francisco from Los Angeles, Sacramento and Reno.

SamTrans Southbound buses to Palo Alto and the Pacific coast.

TRAIN

Easy on the eyes and light on carbon emissions, train travel is a good way to visit the Bay Area and beyond.

Caltrain (www.caltrain.com; cnr 4th & King Sts) connects San Francisco with Silicon Valley hubs and San Jose.

Amtrak (☎800-872-7245; www.amtrakcalifornia.com) serves San Francisco via stations in Oakland and Emeryville (near Oakland), with free shuttle-bus connections to San Francisco's Ferry Building and Caltrain station, and Oakland's Jack London Sq. Amtrak offers rail passes good for seven days of travel in California within a 21-day period (from $159).

CAR & MOTORCYCLE

Major car-rental operators have offices at airports and downtown.

ℹ Getting Around

When San Franciscans aren't pressed for time, most walk, bike or ride Muni instead of taking a car or cab. Traffic is notoriously bad at rush hour, and parking is next to impossible in center-city neighborhoods. Avoid driving until it's time to leave town – or drive during off-peak hours.

For Bay Area transit options, departures and arrivals, call ☎511 or check www.511.org. A detailed *Muni Street & Transit Map* is available free online.

BART High-speed transit to East Bay, Mission St, SF airport and Millbrae, where it connects with Caltrain.

Cable cars Frequent, slow and scenic, from 6am to 12:30am daily. Single rides cost $7; for frequent use, get a Muni Passport ($21 per day).

Muni streetcar and bus Reasonably fast, but schedules vary wildly by line; infrequent after 9pm. Fares are $2.50.

Taxi Fares are about $2.75 per mile; meters start at $3.50. Add 15% to the fare as a tip ($1 minimum). For quickest service in San Francisco, download the Flywheel app for smart phones, which dispatches the nearest taxi.

TO/FROM THE AIRPORT

SamTrans (☎800-660-4287; www.samtrans.com) Express bus KX takes about 30 to 45 minutes to run from San Francisco International Airport to SF's **Transbay Transit Center** (Map p68; cnr Howard & Main Sts; 🚌5,38,41,71), and makes two stops in downtown SF (the last at the Transbay Transit Center).

Airport Express (☎800-327-2024; www.airportexpressinc.com) Runs a scheduled shuttle every hour from 5:30am to 12:30am between San Francisco International Airport and Sonoma ($34) and Marin ($26) counties.

BART

The fastest link between downtown and the Mission District also offers transit to SF airport (SFO; $8.95), Oakland ($3.45) and Berkeley ($4). Four of the system's five lines pass through SF before terminating at Daly City or SFO. Within SF, one-way fares start at $1.95.

BICYCLE

Contact the San Francisco Bicycle Coalition (p112) for maps, information and legal matters regarding bicyclists. Bike sharing is new in SF: racks for **Bay Area Bike Share** (☑855-480-2453; www.bayareabikeshare.com; 30-day membership $30) are located east of Van Ness Ave, and in the SoMa area; however, bikes come without helmets, and biking downtown without proper protection can be particularly dangerous. Bicycles can be taken on BART, but not aboard crowded trains, and never in the first car, nor in the first three cars during weekday rush hours; folded bikes are allowed in all cars at all times. On Amtrak, bikes can be checked as baggage for $5.

BOAT

With the revival of the Embarcadero and the reinvention of the Ferry Building as a gourmet dining destination, commuters and tourists alike are taking the scenic ferry across the bay.

Alcatraz

Alcatraz Cruises (Map p/6; ☑415-981-7625; www.alcatrazcruises.com; tours day adult/child/family $37.25/23/112.75, night adult/child $44.25/26.50; Ⓜ E, F) has ferries (reservations essential) departing Pier 33 for Alcatraz every half-hour from 8:45am to 3:50pm and at 5:55pm and 6:30pm for night tours.

East Bay

Blue & Gold Fleet Ferries (Map p68; ☑415-705-8200; www.blueandgoldfleet.com) operates from the Ferry Building, Pier 39 and Pier 41 at Fisherman's Wharf to Jack London Sq in Oakland (one way $6.65). During baseball season, a Giants ferry service runs directly from the landing at AT&T Park's Seals Plaza entrance to Oakland and Alameda. Ticket booths are located at the Ferry Building and Piers 39 and 41.

San Francisco Bay Ferry (p137) operates from both Pier 41 and the Ferry Building to Oakland/Alameda. Fares are $6.60.

Marin County

Golden Gate Transit Ferries (Map p68; ☑415-455-2000; www.goldengateferry.org; ⊘6am-9:30pm Mon-Fri, 10am-6pm Sat & Sun) runs regular ferry services from the Ferry Building to Larkspur and Sausalito (one way $11.75).

Transfers are available to Muni bus services and bicycles are permitted. Blue & Gold Fleet Ferries also operate to Tiburon or Sausalito (one way $11.50) from Pier 41.

Napa Valley

Get to Napa car free (weekdays only) via the **Vallejo Ferry** (Map p68; ☑707-643-3779, 877-643-3779; http://sanfranciscobayferry.com), with departures from the Ferry Building docks about every hour from 6:30am to 7pm weekdays and roughly every 90 minutes from 10am to 9pm on weekends; bikes are permitted. However, the connecting bus from the Vallejo Ferry Terminal – Napa Valley Vine bus 29 to downtown Napa, Yountville, St Helena or Calistoga – operates only on weekdays. Fares are $13.80.

CAR

If you can, avoid driving in San Francisco: heavy traffic is a given, street parking is harder to find than true love, and meter readers are ruthless.

MUNI

Muni (Municipal Transit Agency; ☑511; www.sfmta.com) Operates bus, streetcar and cable-car lines. Buses and streetcars are referred to interchangeably as Muni, but when streetcars run underground beneath Market St, they're called the Muni Metro. Some areas are better connected than others, but Muni spares you the costly hassle of driving and parking – and it's often faster than driving, especially along metro-streetcar lines J, K/T, L, M and N.

Muni stops are indicated by a street sign and/or a yellow-painted stripe on the nearest lamppost, with route numbers stamped on the yellow stripe; if there is no street sign or lamppost, look on the pavement for a yellow bar with a route number painted on it. Ignore yellow circles and Xs on the pavement, or bars that do not also have route numbers; these other markings tell electric-trolley drivers when to engage or disengage the throttle; they do not indicate bus stops.

TAXI

DeSoto Cab (☑415-970-1300; http://flywheeltaxi.com/)

Green Cab (☑415-626-4733; www.greencabsf.com) Fuel-efficient hybrids; worker-owned collective.

Homobiles (☑415-574-5023; www.homobiles.org) Get home safely with secure, reliable, donation-based transport for the GLBT community: drivers provide 24/7 taxi service – text for fastest service.

Luxor (☑415-282-4141; www.luxorcab.com)

Yellow Cab (☑415-333-3333; www.yellowcabsf.com)

Marin County & the Bay Area

Includes →

Best Places to Eat

→ Chez Panisse (p144)

→ Fish (p116)

→ Hog Island Oyster Company (p126)

→ Sunday Marin Farmers Market (p119)

→ Commis (p133)

Best Places to Sleep

→ Cavallo Point (p111)

→ Mountain Home Inn (p121)

→ HI Pigeon Point Lighthouse (p157)

→ Steep Ravine (p122)

Why Go?

The San Francisco Bay Area encompasses a bonanza of natural vistas and wildlife. Cross the Golden Gate Bridge into Marin County and visit wizened ancient redwoods body-blocking the sun and herds of elegant tule elk prancing along the bluffs of Tomales Bay. Gray whales show some fluke off the cape of the wind-scoured Point Reyes peninsula, while hawks surf the skies in the shaggy hills of the Marin Headlands.

On the cutting edge of intellectual thought, Stanford University – near the tech powerhouse of Silicon Valley and the University of California, Berkeley in the East Bay – draws academics and students from around the world. The city of Berkeley sparked the state's locavore food movement and continues to be at the forefront of environmental and left-leaning political causes. South of San Francisco, Hwy 1 traces miles of undeveloped coastline and sandy pocket beaches as it slowly winds south to Santa Cruz.

When to Go
Berkeley

Dec–Mar
Elephant-seal pupping season and gray-whale migration along the coast.

Mar–Apr
Wildflowers hit their peak on trails throughout the region.

Aug–Sep
Sunny days at the beaches, and farmers markets overflow with seasonal goodness.

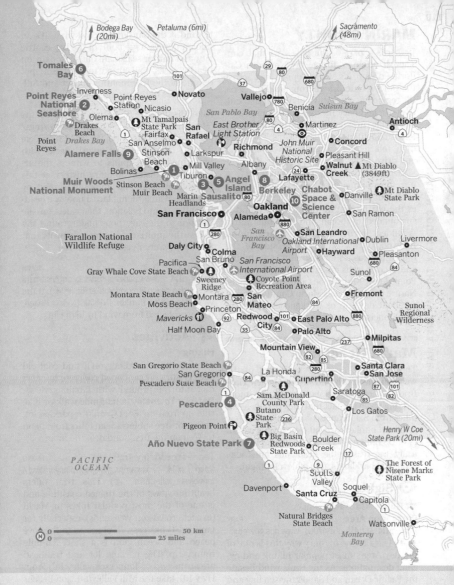

Marin County & the Bay Area Highlights

1 Gazing up at a majestic redwood canopy at **Muir Woods National Monument** (p123).

2 Spotting gray whales from the lighthouse at **Point Reyes National Seashore** (p127).

3 Ferrying over from San Francisco to bohemian **Sausalito** (p112) houseboats bobbing in the bay.

4 Touring the coastline along Hwy 1 to **Pescadero** (p156).

5 Hiking or cycling the **Angel Island** (p120) perimeter.

6 Kayaking past harbor seals in **Tomales Bay** (p128).

7 Spying on noisy elephant seals in **Año Nuevo State Park** (p157).

8 Hanging with hippies, students and passionate foodies in **Berkeley** (p138).

9 Cooling off at blissful Bass Lake, then trekking to **Alamere Falls** (p125).

10 Heading into the Oakland Hills to marvel at stars and planets in the **Chabot Space & Science Center** (p132).

MARIN COUNTY

If there's a part of the Bay Area that consciously attempts to live the Northern California dream, it's Marin County. Just across the Golden Gate Bridge from San Francisco, the region has a wealthy population that cultivates a laid-back lifestyle. Towns may look like idyllic rural hamlets, but the shops cater to cosmopolitan, expensive tastes. The 'common' folk here eat organic, vote Democrat and drive Teslas.

Geographically, Marin County is a near mirror image of San Francisco. It's a south-pointing peninsula that nearly touches the north-pointing tip of the city, and is surrounded by ocean and bay. But Marin is wilder, greener and more mountainous. Redwoods grow on the coast side of the hills, surf crashes against cliffs, and hiking and cycling trails crisscross blessedly scenic Point Reyes, Muir Woods and Mt Tamalpais. Nature is what makes Marin County such an excellent day trip or weekend escape from San Francisco.

Marin Headlands

The headlands rise majestically out of the water at the north end of the Golden Gate Bridge, their rugged beauty all the more striking given the fact that they're only a few miles from San Francisco's urban core. A few forts and bunkers are left over from a century of US military occupation – which is, ironically, the reason the headlands are today protected parklands, free of development.

◉ Sights

★ Golden Gate National Recreation Area
PARK

(Map p114; ☑ 415-561-4700; www.nps.gov/goga; P 🚲) FREE It's no mystery why this is one of the Bay Area's most popular hiking and cycling destinations. As the trails wind beside the Pacific Ocean and San Francisco Bay and through the Marin Headlands, they afford stunning views of the sea, the Golden Gate Bridge and the city of San Francisco.

★ Point Bonita Lighthouse
LIGHTHOUSE

(Map p114; ☑ 415-331-1540; www.nps.gov/goga/pobo.htm; ⊙ 12:30-3:30pm Sat-Mon; P) FREE This historical lighthouse is a breathtaking half-mile walk from a small parking area off Field Rd. From the tip of Point Bonita, you can see the distant Golden Gate Bridge and

beyond it the San Francisco skyline. It's an uncommon vantage point of the bay-centric city, and harbor seals haul out seasonally on nearby rocks. Call ahead to reserve a spot on one of the free monthly sunset and full-moon tours of the promontory.

Nike Missile Site SF-88
HISTORIC SITE

(Map p114; ☑ 415-331-1540; www.nps.gov/goga/nike-missile-site.htm; Field Rd; ⊙ 12:30-3:30pm Sat; P) FREE File past guard shacks with uniformed mannequins to witness the area's not-too-distant military history at this fascinating Cold War museum staffed by veterans. Watch them place a now-warhead-free missile into position, then ride a missile elevator to the cavernous underground silo to see the multikeyed launch controls that thankfully were never set in motion.

Rodeo Beach
BEACH

(Map p114; www.parksconservancy.org/visit/park sites/rodeo-beach.html; off Bunker Rd; P 🚲) At the western end of Bunker Rd sits Rodeo Beach, partly protected from wind by high cliffs.

🏃 Activities

Hiking

All along the coastline you'll find cool old battery sites – abandoned concrete bunkers dug into the ground with fabulous views. **Battery Townsley**, a half-mile walk or bike ride up from the **Fort Cronkite** parking lot, opens for free subterranean tours from noon to 4pm on the first Sunday of the month.

Tennessee Valley Trail
HIKING

(Map p114; www.nps.gov/goga/planyourvisit/tennessee_valley.htm; 🚲) This trail offers beautiful views of the rugged coastline and is one of the most popular hikes in Marin (expect crowds on weekends), especially for families. It has easy, level access to the cove beach and ocean, and is a short 3.5-mile round-trip. The parking lot and trailhead are at the end of Tennessee Valley Rd. From Hwy 101, take the Mill Valley/Stinson Beach/Hwy 1 exit, follow Shoreline Hwy and turn left on to Tennessee Valley Rd.

Coastal Trail
HIKING

(Map p114; www.nps.gov/goga/planyourvisit/hiking.htm) From nearby Rodeo Beach, the Coastal Trail meanders 3.5 miles inland, past abandoned military bunkers, to intersect the Tennessee Valley Trail. It then continues almost 3 miles along the blustery headlands all the way to Muir Beach (p123).

WHY IS IT SO FOGGY?

When the summer sun's rays warm the air over the chilly Pacific, fog forms and hovers offshore. To grasp how it moves inland requires an understanding of California's geography. The vast agricultural region in the state's interior, the Central Valley, is ringed by mountains like a giant bathtub. The only substantial sea-level break in these mountains occurs at the Golden Gate to the west, which happens to be the direction from which prevailing winds blow. As the inland valley heats up and the warm air rises, it creates a deficit of air at surface level, generating wind that gets sucked through the only opening it can find: the Golden Gate. It happens fast and it's unpredictable. Gusty wind is the only indication that the fog is about to roll in. But even this is inconsistent: there can be fog at the beaches south of the Golden Gate and sun a mile to the north. Hills block fog – especially at times of high atmospheric pressure, as often happens in summer. Because of this, weather forecasters speak of the Bay Area's 'microclimates.' In July it's not uncommon for inland areas to top 100°F (38°C), while the mercury at the coast barely reaches 70°F (21°C).

Mountain Biking

The Marin Headlands have some excellent mountain-biking routes and it's an exhilarating ride across the Golden Gate Bridge to reach them.

For a good 12-mile dirt loop, choose the **Coastal Trail** west from the fork of Conzelman and McCullough Rds, bumping and winding down to Bunker Rd where it meets **Bobcat Trail**, which joins **Marincello Trail** and descends steeply into the Tennessee Valley parking area. The **Old Springs Trail** and the **Miwok Trail** take you back to Bunker Rd a bit more gently than the Bobcat Trail, though any attempt to avoid at least a couple of hefty climbs is futile.

🛏 Sleeping

There's one deluxe lodge, a cozy youth hostel and four campgrounds in the headlands. **Hawk Camp, Bicentennial** and **Haypress** campgrounds are inland, with free camping; sites must be reserved through the Marin Headlands Visitor Center (p112). None have water available and two campgrounds require hiking (or cycling) in from the nearest parking lot.

Kirby Cove Campground CAMPGROUND $
(Map p114; ☏ reservations 877-444-6777; www. recreation.gov; Kirby Cove Rd; tent sites $25; ⊙ Apr-Nov; ℗) In a spectacular shady nook near the entrance to the bay, there's a small beach with the Golden Gate Bridge arching over the rocks nearby. At night you can watch the phantom shadows of cargo ships passing by (and sometimes be lulled to sleep by the dirge of a fog horn). Reserve far ahead.

HI Marin Headlands HOSTEL $
(Map p114; ☏ 415-331-2777; www.norcalhostels. org/marin; Fort Barry, Bldg 941; r with shared bath $105-135, dm $31-40; ⊙ reception 7:30am-11:30pm; ℗ 🖨 @ 🛜) 🌿 Wake up to grazing deer and dew on the ground at this Spartan 1907 military compound snuggled in the woods. It has comfortable beds and two well-stocked kitchens, and guests can gather round a fireplace in the common room, shoot pool or play Ping-Pong. Hiking trails beckon outside.

Cavallo Point LODGE $$$
(Map p114; ☏ 415-339-4700; www.cavallopoint. com; 601 Murray Circle; r from $399; ℗ 🖨 ✳ @ 🛜 🐾 🐾) 🌿 Spread over 45 acres of the Bay Area's most scenic parkland, Cavallo Point lodge flaunts an eco-conscious focus with a full-service spa, restaurant and bar, and easy access to outdoor activities. Choose from richly renovated rooms in the landmark Fort Baker officers' quarters or contemporary, stylish 'green' accommodations with exquisite bay views (including a turret of the Golden Gate Bridge).

🍴 Eating

Bring a picnic lunch, trail snacks and enough water with you, since there's nowhere to eat in the Marin Headlands except at Cavallo Point lodge and the children's museum, near Sausalito.

Murray Circle MODERN AMERICAN $$$
(Map p114; ☏ 415-339-4750; www.cavallopoint.com; 601 Murray Circle; dinner mains $25-36; ⊙ 7-11am & 11:30am-2pm Mon-Fri, 7am-2:30pm Sat & Sun, 5:30-9pm Sun-Thu, 5:30-10pm Fri & Sat; 🅿🍴) 🌿 At Cavallo Point lodge, dine on locally sourced

DON'T MISS

HIKING & CYCLING THE GOLDEN GATE BRIDGE

Walking or cycling across the Golden Gate Bridge to Sausalito is a fun way to avoid traffic, get some great ocean views and fresh air. Getting to Sausalito is a relatively easy journey, mostly flat or downhill when heading north from San Francisco. Cycling back isn't nearly as fun. The return trip involves a big climb out of Sausalito. Unless you want a work out, simply hop on a ferry back to SF.

The trip is about 4 miles from the south end of the bridge and takes less than an hour. Pedestrians have access to the bridge's east walkway between 5am and 9pm daily (until 6pm in winter). Cyclists generally use the west side, except on weekdays between 5am and 3:30pm, when they share the east side with pedestrians (who have the right-of-way). After 9pm (6pm in winter), cyclists can still cross the bridge on the east side through a security gate. Check the bridge website for changes.

For more ambitious cyclists, the Cal Park Hill Tunnel is a safe subterranean passage from Larkspur (another ferry terminus) to San Rafael.

More information and resources are available at the websites of the **San Francisco Bicycle Coalition** (☏ 415-431-2453; www.sfbike.org) and the **Marin County Bicycle Coalition** (MCBC; ☏ 415-456-3469; www.marinbike.org).

meats, seafood and produce – perhaps grass-fed organic beef burgers or Dungeness-crab BLT sandwiches – in a clubby dining room topped by a pressed-tin ceiling. Reservations recommended for dinner and weekend brunch.

ℹ Information

Information is available from the **Golden Gate National Recreation Area** (p110) and the **Marin Headlands Visitors Center** (Map p114; ☏ 415-331-1540; www.nps.gov/goga/marin-headlands.htm; Bunker Rd, Fort Barry; ⏰ 9:30am-4:30pm), in an old chapel off Bunker Rd near Fort Barry.

ℹ Getting There & Away

By car, take the Alexander Ave exit just after crossing north over the Golden Gate Bridge and dip left under the freeway. Conzelman Rd, to the right, takes you up along the bluffs; you can also take Bunker Rd, which leads to the headlands through a one-way tunnel. Arrive before 2pm on weekends to avoid traffic and parking congestion, or cycle over the bridge instead.

On Saturday, Sunday and holidays, **MUNI** (☏ 511, 415-701-2311; www.sfmta.com) bus 76X runs every 60 to 90 minutes from San Francisco's Financial District to the Marin Headlands Visitors Center, Rodeo Beach and the Nike missile site. Buses are equipped with bicycle racks.

Sausalito

Perfectly arranged on a secure little harbor on the bay, Sausalito is undeniably lovely. Named for the tiny willows that once populated the banks of its creeks, it's famous

for its colorful houseboats bobbing in the bay. Much of the well-heeled downtown has uninterrupted views of San Francisco and Angel Island, and due to the ridgeline at its back, fog generally skips it.

Sausalito is understandably a major tourist trap, jam-packed with souvenir shops and costly boutiques. It's the first town you encounter after crossing the Golden Gate Bridge from San Francisco, so daytime crowds turn up in droves and make parking difficult. Ferrying over from San Francisco makes for a more relaxing excursion.

The town sits on Richardson Bay, a smaller bay within San Francisco Bay. The commercial district is mainly one street, Bridgeway Blvd, which runs alongside the waterfront.

◎ Sights

★**Sausalito Houseboats**   ARCHITECTURE
(Map p114) Bohemia still thrives along the shoreline of Richardson Bay, where free spirits inhabit hundreds of quirky homes that bobble in the waves among the seabirds and seals. Structures range from psychedelic mural-splashed castles to dilapidated salt-sprayed shacks and immaculate three-story floating mansions. You can poke around the houseboat docks located off Bridgeway Blvd between Gate 5 and Gate 6½ Rds.

It's a tight-knit community, where residents tend sprawling dockside gardens and stop to chat on the creaky wooden boardwalks as they wheel their groceries home.

Etiquette tips for visitors: no smoking, no pets, no bicycles and no loud noise.

Bay Model Visitors Center   MUSEUM
(Map p114; 🗷415-332-3871; www.spn.usace. army.mil/missions/recreation/baymodelvisitor center.asp; 2100 Bridgeway Blvd; ⊙9am-4pm Tue-Sat, extended summer hours 10am-5pm Sat & Sun; ⏚🖕) FREE One of the coolest things in town, fascinating to both kids and adults, is the Army Corps of Engineers' solar-powered visitor center. Housed in one of the old (and cold!) Marinship warehouses, it's a 1.5-acre hydraulic model of San Francisco Bay and the delta region. Self-guided tours take you over and around it as the water flows.

Bay Area Discovery Museum   MUSEUM
(Map p114; 🗷415-339-3900; www.baykidsmuseum. org; 557 McReynolds Rd; $14, 1st Wed each month free; ⊙9am-4pm Tue-Fri, to 5pm Sat & Sun, also 9am-4pm some Mon; ⏚🖕) Below the north tower of the Golden Gate Bridge, at Fort Baker, this excellent hands-on activity museum is designed for children. Multilingual exhibits include a wave workshop, a small underwater tunnel and a large outdoor play area with a shipwreck to romp around. The museum's **Bean Sprouts Café** has healthy nibbles.

🏃 Activities

Sausalito is great for **bicycling**, whether for a leisurely ride around town, a trip across the Golden Gate Bridge or a longer-haul journey. From the ferry terminal, an easy option is to head south on Bridgeway Blvd, veering left on to East Rd toward the Bay Area Discovery Museum. Another nice route heads north along Bridgeway Blvd, then crosses under Hwy 101 to Mill Valley. At Blithedale Ave, you can veer east to Tiburon; a bike path parallels parts of Tiburon Blvd.

Sea Trek   KAYAKING, SUP
(Map p114; 🗷415-332-8494; www.seatrek.com; 2100 Bridgeway; kayak or SUP set per hour from $25, tours from $75; ⊙9am-5pm Mon-Fri, 8:30am-5pm Sat & Sun Apr-Oct, 9am-4pm daily Nov-Mar) On a sunny day, Richardson Bay is irresistible. Kayaks and stand up paddleboard (SUP) sets can be rented here. No experience is necessary, and lessons and group outings are also available. Guided kayaking excursions include full-moon and starlight tours and an adventurous crossing to Angel Island. May through October is the best time to paddle.

Sausalito Bike Rentals   BICYCLE RENTAL
(🗷415-331-2453, 415-332-8815; www.sausalito bikerentals.com; 34a Princess St; bicycle rental per hour from $15; ⊙9:30am-6:30pm; 🖕) Rents road, mountain, hybrid, tandem and electric bicycles by the hour or the day to explore the area.

🛌 Sleeping

Most of the lodgings in town charge a pretty penny, with a two-night minimum on weekends. On the outskirts of town, midrange chain motels and hotels line the Hwy 101 corridor.

Hotel Sausalito   HISTORIC HOTEL **$$**
(Map p114; 🗷415-332-0700; www.hotelsausalito. com; 16 El Portal St; r from $175; ⏚⊝❄🛱) Steps away from the ferry in the middle of downtown, this grand 1915 hotel has loads of period charm, paired with modern touches such as satellite TV, DVD player and MP3-player docking station. Each guest room is decorated in Mediterranean hues and some enjoy partial bay views. Parking is $20.

Inn Above Tide   BOUTIQUE HOTEL **$$$**
(Map p114; 🗷415-332-9535; www.innabovetide. com; 30 El Portal; r $405-695; ⏚⊝❄@🛱) Next to the ferry terminal, ensconce yourself in one of 31 modern and spacious rooms – most with private deck and wood-burning fireplace – that practically levitate over the water. There are envy-inducing bay views from your window; scan the horizon with the in-room binoculars. Free parking and loaner bicycles.

Gables Inn   INN **$$$**
(Map p114; 🗷415-289-1100; www.gablesinn sausalito.com; 62 Princess St; r $190-545; ⏚⊝@🛱) Tranquil and inviting, this inn has nine guest rooms in a historic 1869 home and six in a newer building. The more expensive rooms have Jacuzzi, fireplace and balcony with spectacular views, but even the smaller, cheaper rooms are stylish and tranquil. Evening wine and cheese included. Parking is $20.

🍴 Eating

Bridgeway Blvd is packed with moderately priced cafes, a few casual budget-priced options and many more expensive bay-view seafood restaurants.

Marin County

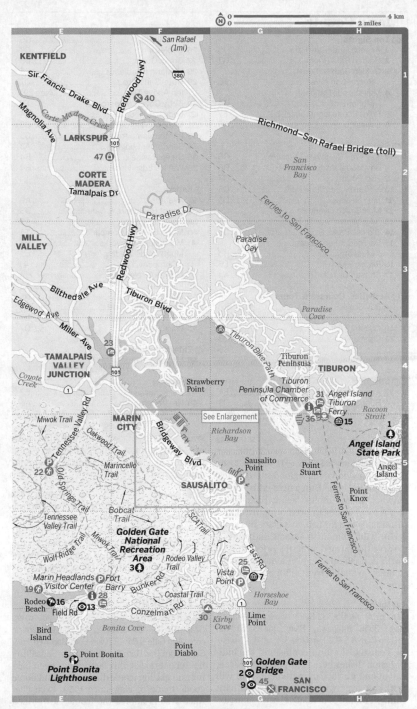

Marin County

★ **Fish** SEAFOOD $$
(Map p114; ☏ 415-331-3474; www.331fish.com;
350 Harbor Dr; mains $17-36; ⊙ 11:30am-8:30pm;
🖶) 🥢 Chow down on seafood sandwiches,
BBQ oysters or a Dungeness-crab roll at
redwood picnic tables facing Richardson
Bay. A local leader in promoting fresh and
sustainably caught fish, this place has won-
derful wild salmon in season and refuses
to serve the farmed stuff. It's pricey, but so
worth it. Cash only. Expect a queue. Limit-
ed menu available from 4:30pm to 5:30pm
daily.

Avatar's INDIAN $$
(Map p114; ☏ 415-332-8083; www.enjoyavatars.
com; 2656 Bridgeway Blvd; mains $13-20;
⊙ 11am-3pm & 5-9:30pm Mon-Sat; 🖉🖶) Boasting a cuisine of 'ethnic confusions,' the Indi-
an-fusion dishes here incorporate Mexican,
Italian and Caribbean ingredients and will
bowl you over with flavor and creativity.
Think Punjabi enchiladas with curried

sweet potato or spinach fettucine with
mild-curry tomato sauce. All diets (vegan,
gluten-free etc) are graciously accommodated.

Sushi Ran JAPANESE $$$
(Map p114; ☏ 415-332-3620; http://sushiran.com;
107 Caledonia St; shared dishes $5-38; ⊙ 11:45am-
2:30pm Mon-Fri, 5-10pm Sun-Thu, 5-11pm Fri & Sat)
Many Marin residents claim this place is the
best sushi spot around. If you didn't reserve
ahead, the wine and sake bar next door eases
the pain of the long wait for a table.

🛍 Shopping

Heath Ceramics HOMEWARES
(Map p114; ☏ 415-332-3732; www.heathceramics.
com; 400 Gate 5 Rd; ⊙ 10am-6pm Mon-Wed, Fri &
Sat, to 7pm Thu, 11am-6pm Sun) Near Sausalito's
houseboat docks, this factory has been bak-
ing and glazing iconic dinnerware and home
goods made of clay since 1959. Even chef
Alice Waters adores the iconic earth-toned

place settings, which show arts-and-crafts styling. The showroom discounts overstock and seconds. Reserve ahead for free factory tours on Fridays, Saturdays and Sundays.

ℹ Information

Sausalito Chamber of Commerce (Map p114; ☑ 415-331-1093; www.sausalito.org; foot of El Portal St; ⊙ 10am-4pm) offers local information at a visitor kiosk by the ferry terminal.

ℹ Getting There & Away

Driving to Sausalito from San Francisco, take the Alexander Ave exit (the first exit after the Golden Gate Bridge) and follow the signs into downtown. There are five municipal parking lots in town, each charging varying rates; you can get three hours of free parking in the lot at the foot of Locust St, off Bridgeway Blvd. Street parking (metered or free, but time-limited) is difficult to find.

The ferry is a fun and easy way to travel to Sausalito. **Golden Gate Ferry** (☑ 415-455-2000, ☑ 511; http://goldengateferry.org) operates to and from San Francisco's Ferry Building ($11.75, 25 to 30 minutes) several times daily. **Blue & Gold Fleet** (☑ 415-705-8200; www.blueandgoldfleet.com) sails to Sausalito several times daily from the Fisherman's Wharf area in San Francisco ($11.50, 30 to 55 minutes). Both ferries operate year-round and transport bicycles for no additional charge.

Golden Gate Transit (☑ 415-455-2000, ☑ 511; www.goldengatetransit.org) bus 30 runs hourly to Sausalito from downtown San Francisco ($4.75, 40 to 55 minutes). On weekends and holidays, **West Marin Stagecoach** (☑ 415-226-0825; www.marintransit.org/stage.html) route 61 ($2) extends to Sausalito, with at least a few departures for Pantoll Station in Mt Tamalpais State Park, Stinson Beach and Bolinas. The seasonal **Muir Woods Shuttle** (Route 66F; www.marintransit.org; round-trip adult/child $5/free) connects with San Francisco ferries arriving in Sausalito before 3pm.

Tiburon

At the end of a small peninsula pointing out into the center of the bay, Tiburon is blessed with gorgeous views. The name comes from the Spanish Punta de Tiburon (Shark Point). Take the ferry from San Francisco, browse the shops on Main St, grab a bite to eat and you've seen Tiburon. The town is also a jumping-off point for nearby Angel Island.

The central part of town is comprised of Tiburon Blvd, Juanita Lane and charming Main St. Main St, which is also known as Ark Row, is where the old houseboats have taken root on dry land and metamorphosed into classy shops and boutiques.

◉ Sights & Activities

Railroad & Ferry Depot Museum MUSEUM
(Map p114; ☑ 415-435-1853; http://landmarkssociety.com; 1920 Paradise Dr; suggested donation $5; ⊙ 1-4pm Wed-Sun Apr-Oct) Formerly the terminus for a 3000-person ferry to San Francisco and a railroad that once reached north to Ukiah, this late 19th-century building showcases a scale model of Tiburon's commercial hub, c 1900. The restored stationmaster's quarters can be visited upstairs.

Bay Cruises CRUISE
(Map p114; ☑ 415-435-2131; http://angelislandferry.com; 21 Main St; 90min cruise adult/child $20/10; ⊙ usually 6:30-8pm Fri & Sat mid-May–mid-Oct) The Angel Island Tiburon Ferry (p118) runs San Francisco Bay sunset cruises on weekend evenings in summer and fall. Reserve ahead and bring your own picnic dinner to enjoy outside on the deck.

🛏 Sleeping

Tiburon has only a couple of places to stay downtown. Midrange motels and chain hotels line Hwy 101.

Lodge at Tiburon HOTEL $$
(Map p114; ☑ 415-435-3133; www.lodgeattiburon.com; 1651 Tiburon Blvd; r from $225; 🅿 ⊛ ❋ @ 🤶 ⊠ 🐾) 🐾 Now a stylish and comfortable contemporary hotel, concrete hallways and staircases testify to the more basic motel it once was. The best value in town, it's a short stroll to anywhere – including the ferry – and there's a pool, DVD library, tavern, rental bikes, free parking and a rooftop deck with fireplace and heady Mt Tamalpais views.

Waters Edge Hotel BOUTIQUE HOTEL $$$
(Map p114; ☑ 415-789-5999; www.watersedgehotel.com; 25 Main St; r from $269; 🅿 ⊛ ❋ @ 🤶) 🐾 At this hotel, with its deck extending over the bay, tasteful rooms have an elegant minimalism that combines comfort and style. Rooms with rustic, high wood ceilings are quite romantic and all afford bay views. Complimentary bicycles and evening wine and cheese included. Parking is $15.

✕ Eating

Downtown, Tiburon Blvd and Main St offer several cafes and restaurants, mostly pricey and unsatisfying.

Sam's Anchor Cafe　　　　SEAFOOD $$
(Map p114; ✐ 415-435-4527; www.samscafe.com; 27 Main St; mains $13-25; ⏰ 11am-9:30pm Mon-Fri, from 9:30am Sat & Sun; ⊞) Sam's has been slinging seafood and burgers since 1920, and though the entrance looks like a shambling little shack, the area out back has fantastic waterfront views. On a warm afternoon, you can't beat a cocktail or a tasty plate of sautéed prawns on the deck.

❶ Information

Tiburon Peninsula Chamber of Commerce (Map p114; ✐ 415-435-5633; www.tiburon chamber.org; 96b Main St) provides area information.

❶ Getting There & Away

On Hwy 101, look for the off-ramp for Tiburon Blvd/E Blithedale Ave/Hwy 131. Drive about 4 miles east to downtown, where Tiburon Blvd intersects Main St.

Golden Gate Transit (p117) commuter bus 8 runs direct between San Francisco and Tiburon ($5.50, 60 to 80 minutes) once or twice on weekdays.

Blue & Gold Fleet (p117) sails several times daily from San Francisco's Pier 41 or 39 to Tiburon ($11.50, 30 to 50 minutes). Golden Gate Ferry (p117) connects San Francisco's Ferry Building with Tiburon ($11.50, 30 minutes) during weekday commuter hours only. You can transport bicycles for free on both ferry services.

In downtown Tiburon, the smaller **Angel Island Tiburon Ferry** (Map p114; ✐ 415-435-2131; http://angelislandferry.com; 21 Main St; round-trip adult/child/bicycle $15/13/1; ⊞) departs from a nearby dock.

Sir Francis Drake Boulevard & Around

The towns along and nearby the Sir Francis Drake Blvd corridor – including Larkspur, Corte Madera, Ross, San Anselmo and Fairfax – evoke charmed small-town life, even though things get busy around Hwy 101.

Starting from the eastern section in **Larkspur**, window-shop along Magnolia Ave or explore the redwoods in nearby **Baltimore Canyon**. On the east side of the freeway is the hulking mass of **San Quentin State Penitentiary**, California's oldest and most notorious prison, founded in 1852.

Take the bicycle and pedestrian bridge from the ferry terminal across the road to the **Marin Country Mart**, a shopping center with a excellent eateries and outdoor seating. One favorite is the **Marin Brewing Company** (Map p114; ✐ 415-461-4677; www. marinbrewing.com; 1809 Larkspur Landing Cirle, Larkspur; mains $11-15; ⏰ 11:30am-midnight Sun-Thu, to 1am Fri & Sat; ⊞) brewpub, where you can see the glassed-in kettles behind the bar. The head brewer, Arne Johnson, has won many awards, and the Mt Tam Pale Ale complements the menu of pizza, burgers and hearty sandwiches.

Just south, **Corte Madera** is home to one of the Bay Area's best bookstores, **Book Passage** (Map p114; ✐ 415-927-0960; www.bookpassage. com; 51 Tamal Vista Blvd; ⏰ 9am-9pm; 🛜), in the Marketplace shopping center. It has a strong travel section, and frequent readings.

West along Sir Francis Drake, **San Anselmo** is a cute downtown area along San Anselmo Ave. The attractive center of neighboring **Fairfax** has ample dining and shopping options, and cyclists congregate at **Gestalt Haus Fairfax** (✐ 415-721-7895; https://gestalthausoffairfax.com; 28 Bolinas Rd, Fairfax; ⏰ 11:30am-10pm Mon, to 11pm Tue, to midnight Wed & Thu, to 2am Fri & Sat, to 9pm Sun) for the indoor bicycle parking, board games, European draft beers and sausages.

Six miles east of Olema on Sir Francis Drake Blvd, **Samuel P Taylor State Park** (✐ 415-488-9897; www.parks.ca.gov; 8889 Sir Francis Drake Blvd, Lagunitas; per car $8; ⏰ 8am-sunset; P⊞) has beautiful, secluded campsites in redwood groves and a coveted handful of new five-person cabins with electricity and wood stoves. The park's also located on the paved **Cross Marin Trail**, with miles of creekside landscape to explore along a former railroad grade.

San Rafael

The oldest and largest town in Marin, San Rafael is slightly less upscale than most of its neighbors but doesn't lack atmosphere. It's a common stop for travelers on their way to Point Reyes. Two blocks south of the 19th-century Spanish Catholic mission that gives the town its name, San Rafael's main drag, 4th St, is lined with cafes and shops. If you follow it west out of downtown San Rafael, it meets Sir Francis Drake Blvd and continues west to the coast. Just north of San Rafael, Lucas Valley Rd heads west toward Nicasio, passing George Lucas' Skywalker Ranch.

◉ Sights

Marin County Civic Center ARCHITECTURE
(☑415-473-3762; www.marincounty.org/depts/cu/tours; 3501 Civic Center Dr; tour adult/child $10/5; ⊙10am-6pm Mon-Fri, guided tour 10:30am Wed; ℗) Although he didn't live to see it built, this was architect Frank Lloyd Wright's final commission. He designed the horizontal hilltop buildings to flow with the natural beauty of the county's landscape, with sky-blue roofs and sand-colored walls. Show up on Wednesday morning for a one-hour guided tour or access the prerecorded audioguide and self-guiding tour brochure online anytime.

China Camp State Park PARK
(☑415-456-0766; https://friendsofchinacamp.org; San Pedro Rd; per car $5; ⊙8am-sunset; ℗🚻) About 6 miles northeast of San Rafael, this is a pleasant place to stop for a picnic or short hike. From Hwy 101, take the N San Pedro Rd exit and continue east. A Chinese shrimp-fishing village once stood here and a small museum exhibits interesting artifacts from the 19th-century settlement.

🛏 Sleeping

Midrange motels and hotels hug Hwy 101 on the outskirts of town.

China Camp State Park Campground CAMPGROUND $
(☑reservations 800-444-7275; www.reserveamerica.com; 730 N San Pedro Rd; tent sites $35; ℗) Pretty waterfront park with 31 walk-in campsites. It has pleasant shade and coin-op hot showers.

✕ Eating

Downtown overflows with restaurants and cafes, all within walking distance of each other. Start exploring along 4th St.

★ Sunday Marin Farmers Market MARKET $
(☑415-472-6100; http://agriculturalinstitute.org; 3501 Civic Center Dr; ⊙8am-1pm Sun; ℗🚻) 🍴 Nowhere else in Marin County do as many farmers, ranchers, fishers and gourmet-food makers gather than at this Sunday-morning farmers market, happening rain or shine at the Marin Civic Center off Hwy 101. Browse the season's most luscious fruit, freshest vegetables, richest honey and cheeses, aromatic breads, colorful flowers and even handmade art, jewelry and crafts. With almost 200 vendors, it's the third-largest farmers market in California.

Sol Food PUERTO RICAN $$
(☑415-451-4765; www.solfoodrestaurant.com; 903 Lincoln Ave; mains $8-17; ⊙9am-midnight Sun-Thu, to 1am Fri & Sat) 🍴 Tangy ceiling fans, tropical plants and the pulse of Latin rhythms create a soothing atmosphere for delicious dishes such as a *jíbaro* sandwich with thinly sliced steak and other island-inspired meals concocted with plantains, organic veggies and free-range meats.

State Room CALIFORNIAN $$
(☑415-295-7929; http://stateroombrewery.com; 1132 4th St; mains $15-25; ⊙11:30am-10pm Sun & Tue-Wed, to midnight Thu-Sat) Wood-fired pizzas, fresh market salads and create-your-own burgers stacked hands high will sate your grumbling stomach at this downtown brewery, bar and kitchen. Serious cocktails and draft beers, ciders and barley wine on tap.

☆ Entertainment

Smith Rafael Film Center CINEMA
(☑415-454-1222; http://rafaelfilm.cafilm.org; 1118 4th St; tickets $8.50-11.25) Innovative art-house programming on three screens in state-of-the-art surroundings in a restored cinema.

ℹ Information

Marin Convention & Visitors Bureau (☑415-925-2060; www.visitmarin.org; 1 Mitchell Blvd; ⊙9am-5pm Mon-Fri) Provides tourist information for the entire county.

ℹ Getting There & Away

Several Golden Gate Transit (p117) buses operate between San Francisco and the San Rafael Transit Center at 3rd and Hetherton Sts ($6.75, one hour). From the transit center, local buses ($2) run by Golden Gate Transit and **Marin Transit** (☑415-455-2000, ☑511; www.marintransit.org) fan out across the county.

For ambitious cyclists, the Cal Park Hill Tunnel is a safe subterranean passage from Larkspur – a terminus for Golden Gate Ferry (p117) services from San Francisco – to San Rafael.

Mill Valley

Nestled under the redwoods at the base of Mt Tamalpais, tiny Mill Valley is one of the Bay Area's most picturesque hamlets. Mill

WORTH A TRIP

ANGEL ISLAND

Angel Island (Map p114; ☑ 415-435-5390; www.parks.ca.gov; ♿) FREE, in San Francisco Bay, has a mild climate with fresh bay breezes, which makes it pleasant for hiking and cycling. For a unique treat, picnic in a protected cove overlooking the surrounding cities. The island history is apparent in its unique buildings – it was a hunting and fishing ground for the Miwok people, served as a military base, an immigration station, a WWII Japanese internment camp and a Nike missile site. There are 12 miles of roads and trails around the island, including a hike to the summit of 781ft **Mt Livermore** (no bicycles) and a 5-mile perimeter trail.

The **Immigration Station** (USIS; ☑ 415-435-5537; www.aiisf.org/visit; adult/child $5/3, incl tour $7/5, cash only; ⊙ 11am-3pm Wed-Sun), which operated from 1910 to 1940, was the Ellis Island of the West Coast. But this facility was primarily a screening and detention center for Chinese immigrants, who were at that time restricted from entering the US under the **Chinese Exclusion Act**. Many detainees were cruelly held for long periods before ultimately being sent home. The mournful Chinese poetry etched into the barrack walls is a heartbreaking testament to their trials. The site is now a museum with excellent interpretive exhibits; tours include admission fees and can be reserved ahead or purchased on-site.

Sea Trek (p113) runs kayaking excursions around the island. You can rent bicycles (per hour/day $12.50/40) at **Ayala Cove**, and there are **tram tours** ($15) around the island. Tour schedules vary seasonally; go to www.angelisland.com for information.

You can camp on the island, and when the last ferry sails for the night, the place is your own – except for the very persistent raccoons. The dozen hike-, bicycle- or kayak-in **campsites** (☑ reservations 800-444-7275; www.reserveamerica.com; tent sites from $30) are usually reserved months in advance. Near the ferry dock, there's a cafe serving sandwiches and snacks.

Getting There & Away

All ferry tickets are sold on a first-come, first-served basis.

From San Francisco's Pier 41, take a **Blue & Gold Fleet** (p117) ferry (one-way adult/child $9/4.75). There are at least three or four daily sailings year-round.

From Tiburon, take the **Angel Island Tiburon Ferry** (p118), which runs daily from April to September (weekends only November to March). As you board, pay fares (one-way adult/child $9/4.75) by cash or check only.

Valley was originally a logging town, its name stemming from an 1830s sawmill – the first in the Bay Area to provide lumber. Though the 1892 Mill Valley Lumber Company still greets motorists on Miller Ave, the town is a vastly different place today, packed with wildly expensive homes, luxury cars and pricey boutiques.

Mill Valley once served as the starting point for the scenic railway that carried visitors up Mt Tamalpais. The tracks were removed in 1940 and today the Depot Bookstore & Cafe occupies the former rail station.

🏃 Activities

⭐ **Dipsea Trail**   HIKING
(Map p114; www.dipsea.org) A beloved though demanding hike, the 7-mile Dipsea Trail climbs over the coastal range and down to Stinson Beach, cutting through a corner of Muir Woods (p123). This classic trail starts at **Old Mill Park** (Map p114; ☑ 415-383-1370; www.cityofmillvalley.org; Throckmorton Ave & Cascade Dr; ⊙ dawn-dusk; ♿) with a climb up 676 steps in three separate flights, and includes a few more ups and downs before reaching the ocean.

The few slaloms between staircases aren't well-signed, but locals can point the way. West Marin Stagecoach (p117) route-61 buses run from Stinson Beach back to Mill Valley at least a few times every day, making it a doable one-way day hike. You can refill water bottles and grab a snack at **Muir Woods Trading Company** (Map p114; ☑ 415-388-7059; www.muirwoodstradingcompany.com; 1 Muir Woods Rd, Mill Valley; items $2-11; ⊙ 8am-5pm; ♿) 🍴 cafe, about a 2-mile hike from Mill Valley, or start or end the trail there instead.

✦ Festivals & Events

Mill Valley Film Festival　　　　　FILM
(📞415-383-5256; www.mvff.com; adult/child per film $15/10; ⊙Oct) In October look for an innovative, internationally regarded program of independent films screened in Mill Valley and San Rafael.

🛏 Sleeping

Lackluster midrange motels stand beside Hwy 101. Boutique hotels and inns shelter by the waterfront and on the forested hillsides around Mt Tamalpais.

Acqua Hotel　　　　BOUTIQUE HOTEL $$
(Map p114; 📞415-380-0400; www.marinhotels.com; 555 Redwood Hwy; r from $229; P🐾❄@📶🐾🐾) 🌿 With views of the bay and Mt Tamalpais, and a lobby with a welcoming fireplace, this boutique hotel doesn't lack for eye candy. Contemporary rooms are sleekly designed with beautiful fabrics and aromatherapy bath products. Perks include free loaner bikes for guests and a morning espresso bar and evening wine service.

Mountain Home Inn　　　　INN $$$
(Map p114; 📞415-381-9000; www.mtnhomeinn.com; 810 Panoramic Hwy; r $195-345; 🐾🐾) Set amid redwood, spruce and pine trees on a ridge of Mt Tamalpais, this retreat is both modern and rustic. The larger (more expensive) rooms are rugged beauties, with unfinished timbers forming columns from floor to ceiling, as though the forest is shooting up through the floor. Smaller rooms are cozy dens for two. The positioning of a good local trail map on each dresser makes it clear that it's a place to breathe and unwind. West Marin Stagecoach (p117) route 61 stops at the inn.

🍴 Eating

You'll find a handful of cafes and restaurants downtown.

Depot Bookstore & Cafe　　　　CAFE $
(Map p114; 📞415-383-2665; http://depotbook store.com; 87 Throckmorton Ave; mains $5-10; ⊙cafe 7am-7pm, bookstore from 8am; 🐾) Smack in the town center, Depot serves coffee and espresso drinks, sandwiches, soups and baked goods. The bookstore sells lots of local publications, including trail guides.

Mill Valley Beerworks　　　　GASTROPUB $$
(Map p114; 📞415-888-8218; www.millvalleybeer works.com; 173 Throckmorton Ave; dinner mains $18-30; ⊙5:30-9pm Sun & Mon, to 9:30pm Tue-

Thu, to 10:30pm Fri & Sat, also 11:30am-3pm Sat & Sun) 🌿 With hard-to-find bottled brews and a few of its own (from Fort Point Beer Company in San Francisco) among the dozen or so on tap, here beer-lovers can pair their favorites with the kitchen's delicious farm-to-table cooking. The unsigned seating is stark and stylish, with a pressed-tin wall and chalkboards above the bar.

ℹ Information

Mill Valley Chamber of Commerce (Map p114; 📞415-388-9700; www.enjoymillvalley.com; 85 Throckmorton Ave; ⊙10am-4pm Tue-Sat) Offers tourist information and maps.

ℹ Getting There & Away

From San Francisco or Sausalito, take Hwy 101 north to the Mill Valley/Stinson Beach/Hwy 1 exit. Follow Hwy 1/Shoreline Hwy to Almonte Blvd (which becomes Miller Ave), then follow Miller Ave into downtown Mill Valley.

From the north, take the E Blithedale Ave exit from Hwy 101, then head west into downtown Mill Valley.

Golden Gate Transit (p117) bus 4 runs directly from San Francisco to Mill Valley ($4.75, one hour, every 20 to 60 minutes) on weekdays. Marin Transit (p119) route 17 ($2, 30 minutes, every 30 to 60 minutes) connects Mill Valley with the Sausalito ferry terminal daily.

Mt Tamalpais State Park

Standing guard over Marin County, majestic Mt Tamalpais (Mt Tam) has breathtaking 360-degree views of ocean, bay and hills rolling into the distance. The rich, natural beauty of the 2572ft mountain and its surrounding area is inspiring – especially considering it lies within an hour's drive from one of the state's largest metropolitan areas.

Mt Tamalpais State Park (Map p114; 📞415-388-2070; www.parks.ca.gov; per car $8; ⊙7am-sunset; P🐾) 🌿 was formed in 1930, partly from land donated by congressman and naturalist William Kent (who also donated the land that became Muir Woods National Monument in 1907). Its 6300 acres are home to deer, foxes, bobcats and 60 miles of hiking and mountain-biking trails.

Mt Tam was a sacred place to the Coast Miwok people for thousands of years before the arrival of European and American settlers. By the late 19th century, San Franciscans were escaping the bustle of the city with all-day outings on the mountain, and in 1896 the 'world's crookedest railroad' (281 turns) was completed from Mill Valley to the summit. Though the railroad was closed in 1930, Old Railroad Grade is today one of Mt Tam's most popular and scenic hiking and cycling paths.

🏃 Activities

Panoramic Hwy climbs from Mill Valley through the park to Stinson Beach. From Pantoll Station, it's 4.2 miles by car to **East Peak Summit**; take Pantoll Rd and then panoramic Ridgecrest Blvd to the top. A 10-minute hike leads to a fire lookout at the very top and awesome sea-to-bay views.

Mountain Biking

Cyclists must stay on the fire roads (and off the single-track trails) and keep to speeds under 15mph. Rangers are prickly about these rules and a ticket can result in a steep fine.

The most popular ride is the Old Railroad Grade from Mill Valley to Mt Tam's East Peak. Alternatively, from just west of Pantoll Station, cyclists can take either the **Deer Park Fire Road**, which runs close to the Dipsea Trail through giant redwoods to the main entrance of Muir Woods, or the aptly named **Coast View Trail**, which joins Hwy 1 north of Muir Beach Overlook. Both options require a return to Mill Valley via Frank Valley/Muir Woods Rd, which climbs steadily (800ft) to Panoramic Hwy, then becomes Sequoia Valley Rd as it drops toward Mill Valley.

For more information on bicycle routes and rules, contact the Marin County Bicycle Coalition (p112); its *Marin Bicycle Map* ($10) is the gold standard for local cycling.

Old Railroad Grade   MOUNTAIN BIKING

For a sweaty, 6-mile, 2500ft climb, start in Mill Valley at the end of W Blithedale Ave and cycle up to East Peak. For a head start, begin part way up at the Mountain Home Inn instead and follow Gravity Car Rd to the Old Railroad Grade, an easy half-hour ride to the summit.

Hiking

The park map is a smart investment as there are a dozen worthwhile hiking trails, including to Cataract Falls.

From Pantoll Station, the **Steep Ravine Trail** follows a wooded creek on to the coast (about 2.1 miles each way). For a longer hike, veer right (northwest) after 1.5 miles on to the Dipsea Trail (p120), which meanders

through trees for 1 mile before ending at Stinson Beach. Grab some lunch, then walk north through town and follow signs for the **Matt Davis Trail**, which leads 2.7 miles back to Pantoll Station, making a good loop. The Matt Davis Trail continues on beyond Pantoll Station, wrapping gently around the mountain with superb views.

Cataract Falls & Alpine Lake   HIKING

(Map p114) A worthy hiking option on Mt Tam is the **Cataract Trail**, which runs along Cataract Creek. From the trailhead along Pantoll Rd, it's less than 3 miles to Alpine Lake. The last mile or so is a spectacular rooty staircase that descends alongside Cataract Falls, at its prettiest immediately after winter or spring rainfall.

🛏 Sleeping

★ Steep Ravine   CAMPGROUND, CABIN $

(Map p42; ✆ reservations 800-444-7275; www.reserveamerica.com; tent sites $25, cabins $100; ☉ Nov-Sep; 🅿) Just off Hwy 1, about 1 mile south of Stinson Beach, this jewel has seven primitive beachfront campsites and nine rustic five-person cabins with woodstoves overlooking the ocean. Both options book up far in advance; reservations can be made up to seven months ahead.

Bootjack Campground   CAMPGROUND $

(Map p114; ✆ info 415-388-2070; www.parks.ca.gov; Panoramic Hwy; tent sites $25; 🅿🐾) The 15 first-come, first-served walk-in campsites are right on two of the park's best hiking trails and adjacent to Redwood Creek, with open vistas to the south. It's 0.3 miles northeast of Pantoll Station.

Pantoll Campground   CAMPGROUND $

(Map p114; ✆ info 415-388-2070; www.parks.ca.gov; Panoramic Hwy; tent sites $25; 🅿🐾) From the parking lot it's only a 100yd walk or cycle to the campground, with 16 first-come, first-served woodsy tent sites, fire pits, picnic tables and potable water, but no showers.

☆ Entertainment

Mountain Theater   THEATER

(Cushing Memorial Amphitheater; Map p114; ✆ 415-383-1100; www.mountainplay.org; off Pantoll Rd; adult/child $40/25; ☉ late May–mid-Jun; ♿) Built by the Civilian Conservation Corps in the 1930s, the park's natural-stone, 3750-seat theater hosts the annual 'Mountain Play' series on weekend afternoons in late spring and early summer. Free shuttles run from Mill Valley; otherwise, parking is $15 to $20.

ℹ Information

Pantoll Station (Map p114; 📞415-388-2070; www.parks.ca.gov; 801 Panoramic Hwy; ⊙hours vary; 🛜) The park headquarters. Detailed park maps are sold here.

East Peak Visitor Center (Map p114; www.friendsofmttam.org; off Ridgecrest Blvd; ⊙11am-4pm Sat & Sun) Small center with nature and historical exhibits and a gift shop.

ℹ Getting There & Away

To reach Pantoll Station by car, take Hwy 1 to the Panoramic Hwy and look for the signs. Panoramic Hwy climbs from Mill Valley through the park, then winds downhill to Stinson Beach.

West Marin Stagecoach (p117) route 61 runs a few times daily on weekdays from Marin City via Mill Valley (more frequent weekend and holiday service from the Sausalito ferry terminal) to Pantoll Station ($2, 55 minutes).

Muir Woods National Monument

Walking through an awesome stand of the world's tallest trees is an experience to be had only in Northern California and a small part of southern Oregon. The old-growth redwoods at **Muir Woods** (Map p114; 📞415-388-2595; www.nps.gov/muwo; 1 Muir Woods Rd, Mill Valley; adult/child $10/free; ⊙8am-8pm mid-Mar–mid-Sep, to 7pm mid-Sep–early Oct, to 6pm Feb–mid-Mar & early Oct-early Nov, to 5pm early Nov-Jan; 🅿🚻) 🍴, just 12 miles north of the Golden Gate Bridge, make up the closest redwood stand to San Francisco. The trees were initially eyed by loggers, and Redwood Creek, as the area was known, seemed ideal for a dam. Those plans were halted when congressman and naturalist William Kent bought a section of Redwood Creek and, in 1907, donated 295 acres to the federal government. President Theodore Roosevelt made the site a national monument in 1908, the name honoring John Muir, naturalist and founder of environmental organization the Sierra Club.

Muir Woods can become quite crowded, especially on weekends. Try to come midweek, early in the morning or late in the afternoon, when tour buses are less of a problem. Even at busy times, a short hike will get you out of the densest crowds and onto trails with huge trees and stunning vistas. A lovely cafe, **Muir Woods Trading Company** (Map p114; 📞415-388-7059; www.muirwoodstradingcompany.com; items $2-11; ⊙8am-5pm; 🚻) 🍴 serves local and organic goodies and hot drinks that hit the spot on foggy days.

🏃 Activities

The 1-mile Main Trail Loop is a gentle walk alongside Redwood Creek to the 1000-year-old trees at **Cathedral Grove**; it returns via **Bohemian Grove**, where the tallest tree in the park stands 254ft high. The **Dipsea Trail** is a good 2-mile hike up to the top of aptly named Cardiac Hill.

You can also walk down into Muir Woods by taking trails from the Panoramic Hwy, such as the **Bootjack Trail** from the Bootjack picnic area, or from Mt Tamalpais' Pantoll Station campground, along the **Ben Johnson Trail**.

ℹ Getting There & Away

The parking lot is insanely full during busy periods, so consider taking the seasonal **Muir Woods Shuttle** (p117) from Sausalito, where ferries from San Francisco arrive.

To get there by car, drive north on Hwy 101, exit at Hwy 1 and continue north along Hwy 1/ Shoreline Hwy to the Panoramic Hwy (a right-hand fork). Follow that for about 1 mile to Four Corners, where you turn left on to Muir Woods Rd (there are plenty of signs).

Muir Beach

Muir Beach is a quiet hamlet with a pretty beach and superb views up and down the coast from an overlook just north of town. For visitors, it's a quick stop between visiting Muir Woods and Stinson Beach.

⊙ Sights

Muir Beach Overlook   VIEWPOINT
(Map p114; www.nps.gov/goga/planyourvisit/muirbeach.htm; Shoreline Hwy; 🅿) Just over a mile north of Pelican Inn (p124) along Hwy 1, there are superb coastal views from this overlook. During WWII scouts kept watch from the surrounding concrete lookouts for invading Japanese ships.

Muir Beach   BEACH
(Map p114; www.nps.gov/goga/planyourvisit/muirbeach.htm; off Pacific Way; 🅿🚻) 🍴 Restored wetlands, creeks, lagoons and sand dunes provide habitat for birds, California red-legged frogs and coho salmon. In winter you might spot monarch butterflies roosting in

a small grove of Monterey pines and migratory whales swimming offshore. The turnoff from Hwy 1 is next to the coast's longest row of mailboxes at Mile 5.7, just before Pelican Inn.

🛏 Sleeping & Eating

Most people visit Muir Beach on a day trip from San Francisco.

Green Gulch   LODGE $$
(Map p114; ☑ 415-383-3134; www.sfzc.org/green gulch; 1601 Shoreline Hwy; s $100-175, d $175-250, incl all meals; P☺@☎) ⏀ In the hills above Muir Beach, this Zen Buddhist retreat center's contemporary accommodations are restful. Delicious buffet-style vegetarian meals are included.

Pelican Inn   PUB FOOD $$$
(Map p114; ☑ 415-383-6000; www.pelicaninn.com; 10 Pacific Way; dinner mains $18-36; ☺ 8-11am Sat & Sun, 11:30am-3pm & 5:30-9pm daily; ⊞) The oh-so-English Pelican Inn is Muir Beach's only commercial establishment. Hikers, cyclists and families come for pub lunches inside its timbered restaurant and cozy bar, perfect for a pint, a game of darts and warming up beside the open fire. The food is nothing mind-blowing and the service is hit or miss, but the setting is magical. Upstairs are seven cozy rooms (from $225) with half-canopy beds.

Stinson Beach

Just 5 miles north of Muir Beach, Stinson Beach is positively buzzing on warm weekends. The town flanks Hwy 1 for about three blocks and is densely packed with galleries, shops, eateries and B&Bs. The beach is often blanketed with fog, and when the sun's shining it's blanketed with surfers, families and gawkers. There are views of Point Reyes and San Francisco on clear days, and the beach is long enough for an invigorating stroll.

⊙ Sights

Stinson Beach   BEACH
(Map p114; ☑ 415-868-0942; www.nps.gov/goga; off Hwy 1; ☺ from 9am daily, closing time varies seasonally; P⊞) Three-mile-long Stinson Beach is a popular surf spot, with swimming advised from late May to mid-September only. For updated weather and surf conditions call ☑ 415-868-1922. The beach is one block

west of Hwy 1. There's free parking but the lot often fills up before noon on sunny days.

Martin Griffin Preserve   WILDLIFE RESERVE
(☑ 415-868-9244; www.egret.org; 4900 Shoreline Hwy; suggested donation $20; ☺ hours vary; P⊞) ⏀ One of four regional Audubon Canyon Ranch preserves hides in the hills above Bolinas Lagoon. It's a major nesting ground for great blue herons and great egrets; viewing scopes are set up behind blinds where you can watch these magnificent birds congregate to nest and hatch their chicks in tall redwoods. At low tide, harbor seals often doze on sandbars in the lagoon. Confirm hours, which vary seasonally, before visiting. It's 3 miles north of Stinson Beach on Hwy 1.

🛏 Sleeping & Eating

Sandpiper Lodging   MOTEL, CABIN $$
(Map p114; ☑ 415-868-1632; www.sandpiperstin sonbeach.com; 1 Marine Way; r $165-180, cabins $220-250, cottages $350; P☺☎) Just off Hwy 1 and a quick stroll to the beach, these nine comfortable rooms, cabins and cottage all have gas fireplace and kitchenette, and are ensconced in a lush garden and picnic area. Two-night minimum stay on weekends and holidays between April and October.

Parkside   AMERICAN, BAKERY $$
(Map p114; ☑ 415-868-1272; www.parksidecafe. com; 43 Arenal Ave; mains $9-28; ☺ 7:30am-9pm, coffee bar from 6am; ☑⊞) ⏀ Famous for its hearty breakfasts and lunches, this cozy eatery next to the beach serves wood-fired pizzas and excellent coastal cuisine such as Tomales Bay oysters and king salmon at dinner, when reservations are recommended. Popular with beachgoers, hikers and cyclists, Parkside's outdoor snack bar serves burgers, fruit smoothies, baked goods and ice cream.

❶ Getting There & Away

By car from San Francisco, it's nearly an hour's drive, though on weekends plan for toe-tapping traffic delays.

West Marin Stagecoach (p117) route 61 runs a few daily minibuses ($2) from Marin City (one hour), with more frequent weekend and holiday services connecting with Sausalito ferries (75 minutes).

Bolinas

For a town that is so famously unexcited about tourism, Bolinas offers some fairly tempting attractions for the visitor. Known as Jugville during the gold-rush days, the sleepy beachside community is home to writers, musicians and fisherfolk, and deliberately hard to find. The highway department used to put signs up at the turnoff from Hwy 1; locals kept taking them down, so the highway department finally gave up.

◎ Sights & Activities

Palomarin Field Station   NATURE CENTER
(☑ 415-868-0655; www.pointblue.org; 999 Mesa Rd; ◷ sunrise-sunset; 🅿 ♿) 🏊 FREE Formerly Point Reyes Bird Observatory, Point Blue's Palomarin Field Station has bird-banding and netting demonstrations, an unstaffed visitor center and a nature trail. Banding demonstrations are held in the morning Tuesday to Sunday from May through late November, and on Wednesday, Saturday and Sunday the rest of the year. Show up between 8am and 11am for the best bird-watching.

★**Bass Lake & Alamere Falls Trail**   HIKING
(www.nps.gov/pore) At the end of Mesa Rd, the Palomarin parking lot accesses various hiking trails in the southern part of Point Reyes National Seashore (p127), including the easy (and popular) 3-mile trail to lovely **Bass Lake**. Continuing another 1.5 miles northwest, you'll reach an unmaintained trail to **Alamere Falls**, a fantastic flume plunging 50ft off a cliff and on to the beach.

A sweet inland spot buffered by tall trees, small Bass Lake is perfect for a swim on a toasty day. You can dive in wearing your birthday suit (or not), bring an inner tube to float about, or do a long lap all the way across.

Approaching Alamere Falls, sketchy beach access may make it more enjoyable to hike another 1.5 miles along the trail to Wildcat Beach, then backtrack a mile south on sand.

2 Mile Surf Shop   SURFING
(☑ 415-868-0264, surf report 415-868-2412; www.2milesurf.com; 22 Brighton Ave; ◷ 9am-6pm May-Oct, 10am-5pm Nov-Apr, closed Wed Jan-Mar) Surfing's popular in these parts, and this shop behind the post office rents boards and wet suits and also gives lessons.

Agate Beach County Park   BEACH
(www.marincounty.org; end of Elm Rd; ◷ dawn-dusk) Meander by tide pools along the coastline at Agate Beach, around the end of Duxbury Point. Collecting rocks, shells or marine life is prohibited.

🛏 Sleeping & Eating

Smiley's Saloon & Hotel   INN $$
(☑ 415-868-1311; http://smileyssaloon.com; 41 Wharf Rd; r $135-225; 🛜♿) A crusty old place dating to 1851, Smiley's has simple but decent rooms (no TV or phone), and last-minute weekday rates can be a bargain. The bar, which serves some food, has live bands on weekends and is frequented by plenty of salty dogs and grizzled deadheads.

Coast Cafe   AMERICAN $$
(☑ 415-868-2298; www.coastcafebolinas.com; 46 Wharf Rd; dinner mains $15-32; ◷ 11:30am-3pm & 5-8pm Tue-Thu, to 9pm Fri, 8am-3pm & 5-9pm Sat, to 8pm Sun; ♿) 🏊 The only 'real' restaurant in town. Everyone jockeys for outdoor seats among the flower boxes for fish-and-chips, barbecued oysters, or buttermilk pancakes with damn good coffee. Live music on Thursday and Sunday nights.

❶ Getting There & Away

By car, follow Hwy 1 north from Stinson Beach and turn west for Bolinas at the first road north of the lagoon. At the first stop sign, take another left on to Olema–Bolinas Rd and follow it 2 miles to town.

West Marin Stagecoach (p117) route 61 travels a few times daily from the Marin City transit hub (more frequent weekend and holiday service connects with the Sausalito ferry) to downtown Bolinas ($2).

Olema & Nicasio

Near the junction of Hwy 1 and Sir Francis Drake Blvd, Olema was the main settlement in west Marin in the 1860s. Back then, there was stagecoach service to San Rafael and *six* saloons. In 1875, when the railroad was built through Point Reyes Station instead of Olema, the town's importance began to fade.

About a 15-minute drive inland from Olema, at the geographic center of Marin County, is Nicasio, a tiny town with a low-key rural flavor.

The **Bolinas Ridge Trail** (www.nps.gov/goga/planyourvisit/bolinas.htm), a 12-mile series of ups and downs for hikers or bikers, starts about 1 mile west of Olema, on Sir Francis Drake Blvd. It has great views.

In the former Olema Inn, a creaky 1876 building, hyper-local **Sir & Star** (☑ 415-663-1034;

www.sirandstar.com; 10000 Sir Francis Drake Blvd, Olema; mains $20, Sat prix-fixe menu $85; ⊗5-9pm Wed-Sun; 🐕) 🍴 restaurant delights with Marin-sourced seasonal bounty such as Tomales Bay oysters, Dungeness crab and duck 'faux' gras. Reservations recommended.

A few minutes away in Nicasio, check out the **Nicasio Valley Cheese Company** (☑415-662-6200; http://nicasiocheese.com; 5300 Nicasio Valley Rd; ⊗10am-5pm), where you can get free tastings at one of Marin County's renowned cheese-making shops. Crafted on a ranch started by a Swiss immigrant family, these wheels of soft cheeses – such as the award-winning Foggy Morning *fromage blanc* – appear on chef's menus and at farmers markets around the Bay Area.

You can get a dose of local flavor at the tiny town's music venue, **Rancho Nicasio** (☑415-662-2219; www.ranchonicasio.com; 1 Old Rancheria Rd, Nicasio; tickets free-$25; ⊗show schedules vary), a rustic saloon that regularly attracts local and national blues, rock and country performers.

🛈 Getting There & Away

Olema is about 13 miles northwest of Stinson Beach via Hwy 1. Nicasio is at the west end of Lucas Valley Rd, 10 miles from Hwy 101.

West Marin Stagecoach (p117) Route 68 runs several times daily to Olema from the San Rafael Transit Center, stopping at Samuel P Taylor State Park.

Point Reyes Station

Though the railroad stopped coming through in 1933 and the town is small, Point Reyes Station is nevertheless the hub of western Marin County. Dominated by dairies and ranches, the region was invaded by artists in the 1960s. Today Main St is a diverting blend of art galleries, tourist shops, restaurants and cafes. The town has a rowdy saloon and the occasional smell of cattle on the afternoon breeze.

🛏 Sleeping & Eating

Cute little cottages, cabins and B&Bs are plentiful in and around Point Reyes. The **West Marin Chamber of Commerce** (☑415-663-9232; www.pointreyes.org) and the Point Reyes Lodging Association (www.ptreyes.com) have additional listings.

Windsong Cottage Guest Yurt YURT $$
(☑415-663-9695; www.windsongcottage.com; 25 McDonald Lane; d $195-230; 🅿😊🐕) A

wood-burning stove, private outdoor hot tub, comfy king bed and kitchen stocked with breakfast supplies make this round skylighted abode a slice of rural heaven.

Nick's Cove COTTAGE $$$
(☑415-663-1033; http://nickscove.com; 23240 Hwy 1, Marshall; cottages $250-850; 🅿😊🐕🍴) Fronting a peaceful cove at Tomales Bay, these water-view and waterfront vacation cottages are expensive, but oh-so romantic. Some have wood-burning fireplace, deep soaking tub, private deck and plasma TV. Two-night minimum stay on weekends and holidays. It's about a 20-minute drive north of Point Reyes Station.

★Hog Island Oyster Company SEAFOOD $
(☑415-663-9218; https://hogislandoysters.com; 20215 Hwy 1, Marshall; 12 oysters $13-16, picnic per person $5; ⊗shop 9am-5pm daily, picnic area from 10am, cafe 11am-5pm Fri-Mon) Ten miles north of Point Reyes Station you'll find the salty turnout for Hog Island Oyster Company. There's not much to see: just some picnic tables and BBQ grills, an outdoor cafe and a window selling the famously silky oysters and a few other provisions. A picnic at the farm is an unforgettable lunch – and popular, so make reservations (required).

Cowgirl Creamery at Tomales Bay Foods DELI $
(☑415-663-9335; www.cowgirlcreamery.com; 80 4th St; deli items $3-10; ⊗10am-6pm Wed-Sun; 🖉🖐) 🍴 An indoor deli and marketplace in an old barn sells farm-fresh picnic items, including gourmet cheeses and organic produce. Reserve in advance for an artisanal cheese-maker's demonstration and tasting ($5); watch the curd-making and cutting; then sample a half-dozen fresh and aged cheeses. The milk is local and organic, with vegetarian rennet in soft cheeses.

Bovine Bakery BAKERY $
(☑415-663-9420; www.bovinebakeryptreyes.com; 11315 Hwy 1; most items $2-6; ⊗6:30am-5pm Mon-Fri, 7am-5pm Sat, 7am-4pm Sun; 🖉🖐) 🍴 Don't leave town without sampling something buttery from this beloved country bakery. A sweet bear-claw pastry and organic coffee are a good way to kick off your morning.

Marshall Store SEAFOOD $$
(☑415-663-1339; www.themarshallstore.com; 19225 Hwy 1, Marshall; mains $11-20; ⊗10am-5pm Mon-Fri, to 6pm Sat & Sun, closes 1hr earlier Oct-Apr; 🖐) Catapulted to fame by peripatetic chef and

TV host Anthony Bourdain, this ramshackle country store lets you slurp down BBQ oysters at tables as your legs practically dangle in Tomales Bay. Smoked seafood plates and sandwiches aren't half bad either. It's a 15-minute drive north of Point Reyes Station.

❶ Getting There & Away

From Hwy 101 and San Rafael, it's about a 45-minute drive to Point Reyes Station. Driving the coast, it's less than 30 minutes from Bolinas. Hwy 1 becomes Main St in town, running right through the center.

West Marin Stagecoach (p117) route 68 runs to Point Reyes Station several times daily from the San Rafael Transit Center ($2, 75 minutes) via Bear Valley Visitor Center at Point Reyes National Seashore.

Inverness

The last outpost on your journey westward toward the tip of Point Reyes, this tiny town stretches out along the west side of Tomales Bay. Several great beaches are only a short drive away.

✖ Activities

★ **Blue Waters Kayaking**   KAYAKING
(☑ 415-669-2600; www.bluewaterskayaking.com; 12944 Sir Francis Drake Blvd; rentals/tours from $60/68; ☺ usually 9am-5pm, last rental 2pm; ⅏) Long-running outfit guides tours of Tomales Bay, or you can rent a kayak and paddle to secluded beaches and rocky crevices on your own; no experience necessary. Book ahead for full-moon and bioluminescence excursions.

☕ Sleeping

**Dancing Coyote Beach
Cottages**   COTTAGE $$$
(☑ 415-669-7200; www.dancingcoyotebeach.com; 12794 Sir Francis Drake Blvd; cottages $200-295; ℗☺☎❋) Serene and comfortable, these four modern cottages back right on to Tomales Bay, with skylights and decks extending the views in all directions. Full kitchens contain locally sourced breakfast foods, and fireplaces are stocked with firewood for foggy nights.

**Cottages at Point Reyes
Seashore**   COTTAGE $$
(☑ 415-669-7250;   www.cottagespointreyes. com; 13275 Sir Francis Drake Blvd; r $129-269; ℗☺☎❋❋) Hidden in the woods, this

family-friendly place offers contemporary kitchenette rooms in A-frame structures and a tennis court, hot tub, croquet, horseshoe pitches, barbecue grills and saltwater pool. There's also a large garden and private nature trail.

❶ Getting There & Away

From Hwy 1, Sir Francis Drake Blvd heads northwest straight into Inverness. West Marin Stagecoach (p117) route 68 from San Rafael ($2) makes several daily runs here via Olema and Point Reyes Station.

Point Reyes National Seashore

Windswept Point Reyes peninsula is a rough-hewn beauty that has always lured marine mammals and migratory birds as well as scores of shipwrecks. It was here in 1579 that Sir Francis Drake landed to repair his ship, the *Golden Hind*. During his five-week stay he mounted a brass plaque near the shore claiming this land for England. In 1595 the first of scores of ships lost in these waters went down. The *San Augustine* was a Spanish treasure ship out of Manila, laden with luxury goods – to this day bits of its cargo still wash up on shore. Despite modern navigatiosan, the dangerous waters here continue to claim the odd boat.

Point Reyes National Seashore (Map p42; ☑ 415-654-5100; www.nps.gov/pore; ℗⅏) ⚑**FREE** protects 110 sq miles of pristine ocean beaches and coastal wilderness and has excellent hiking and camping opportunities. Be sure to bring warm clothing, as even the sunniest days can quickly turn cold and foggy.

◉ Sights & Activities

For a curious view, follow the 0.6-mile **Earthquake Trail** from the picnic area opposite Bear Valley Visitor Center. The trail reaches a 16ft gap between the two halves of a once-connected fence line, a lasting testimonial to the power of the 1906 earthquake that was centered in this area. Another 0.8-mile trail leads from the visitor center around **Kule Loklo**, a reproduction of a Coast Miwok village.

Limantour Rd, off Bear Valley Rd about 1 mile north of Bear Valley Visitor Center, leads to **Limantour Beach**, where a 2-mile trail runs along Limantour Spit with Estero de Limantour on one side and Drakes

Bay on the other. The **Inverness Ridge Trail** heads from Limantour Rd for around 3 miles up to Mt Vision (1282ft), affording spectacular views of the entire national seashore. You can drive almost to the top of Mt Vision from the other side.

Northwest of the town of Inverness, Pierce Point Rd splits off to the right from Sir Francis Drake Blvd. The road lets you access two swimming beaches on Tomales Bay: seductively named **Heart's Desire**, in **Tomales Bay State Park** (☑415-669-1140; www.parks.ca.gov; 1100 Pierce Point Rd, Inverness; per car $8; ☺8am-sunset; P🚻), is accessible by car, while **Marshall Beach** requires a 1.2-mile hike from the parking area at the end of the road.

Pierce Point Rd continues to the huge windswept sand dunes at **Abbotts Lagoon**, full of peeping killdeer and other shorebirds. At the end of the road is historical Pierce Point Ranch, the trailhead for the 9.4-mile round-trip **Tomales Point Trail** through the **Tule Elk Reserve**. The plentiful elk are an amazing sight, standing with their big horns against the backdrop of Tomales Point, with Bodega Bay to the north, Tomales Bay to the east and the Pacific Ocean to the west.

Point Reyes Lighthouse   LIGHTHOUSE
(☑415-669-1534; www.nps.gov/pore; end of Sir Francis Drake Blvd; ☺10am-4:30pm Fri-Mon, lens room 2:30-4pm Fri-Mon; P🚻) **FREE** With wild terrain and ferocious winds, this spot feels like the end of the earth and offers the best whale-watching along the coast. The lighthouse sits below the headlands; to reach it you need to descend more than 300 stairs.

Five Brooks Ranch   HORSEBACK RIDING
(☑415-663-1570; www.fivebrooks.com; 8001 Shoreline Hwy, Olema; trail rides $40-180; 🚻) Explore the Point Reyes landscape on horseback with a trail ride. Take a slow amble through a pasture or ascend Inverness Ridge for views of the Olema Valley. If you can stay in the saddle for six hours, ride along the coastline to Alamere Falls (p125) via Wildcat Beach.

Chimney Rock   HIKING
(www.nps.gov/pore; off Sir Francis Drake Blvd) Not far from the lighthouse, Chimney Rock is a fine short hike, especially in spring when wildflowers are blossoming. During winter, a viewing area allows you to spy on an elephant-seal colony hauled out below the cliffs.

🛏 Sleeping

Wake up to deer nibbling under a blanket of fog at one of Point Reyes' very popular **backcountry campgrounds** (☑reservations 877-444-6777; www.recreation.gov; tent sites $20), or stay at the pastoral youth hostel. More inns, motels and B&Bs are found in nearby Inverness, off Sir Francis Drake Blvd.

HI Point Reyes   HOSTEL $
(☑415-663-8811; www.norcalhostels.org/reyes; 1390 Limantour Spit Rd; r with shared bath $105-130, dm $29-38; ☺reception 7:30-10:30am & 4:30-10pm; P🖨@) 🅿 Just off Limantour Rd, this rustic hostel has bunkhouses with warm and cozy front rooms, big-view windows and outdoor areas with hill vistas. A newer building with Leadership in Energy and Environmental Design (LEED) certification has four private rooms (two-night minimum stay on weekends) and a modern kitchen. It's in a beautiful secluded valley 2 miles from the ocean and surrounded by lovely hiking trails.

ℹ Information

At park headquarters, a mile west of Olema, **Bear Valley Visitor Center** (☑415-464-5100; www.nps.gov/pore; 1 Bear Valley Rd, Point Reyes Station; ☺10am-5pm Mon-Fri, 9am-5pm Sat & Sun; 🖨) has information and maps. You can also get information at the Point Reyes Lighthouse and the **Kenneth Patrick Center** (☑415-669-1250; www.nps.gov/pore; 1 Drakes Beach Rd; ☺9:30am-4:30pm Sat, Sun & holidays late Dec-late Mar or early Apr) at Drakes Beach.

ℹ Getting There & Away

By car you can get to Point Reyes a few different ways. The curviest is along Hwy 1, through Stinson Beach and Olema. More direct is to exit Hwy 101 in San Rafael and follow Sir Francis Drake Blvd all the way to the tip of Point Reyes. By either route, it's less than 1½ hours to Olema from San Francisco barring weekend and rush-hour traffic jams.

Just north of Olema, where Hwy 1 and Sir Francis Drake Blvd come together, is Bear Valley Rd; turn left to reach Bear Valley Visitor Center. If you're heading to the outermost reaches of Point Reyes, follow Sir Francis Drake Blvd north toward Point Reyes Station, turning left and heading out on to the peninsula (at least a 45-minute drive).

West Marin Stagecoach (p117) route 68 from San Rafael stops several times daily at the Bear Valley Visitor Center ($2, 70 minutes) before continuing to the town of Point Reyes Station.

EAST BAY

Berkeley and Oakland are what most San Franciscans think of as the East Bay, though the area includes numerous other suburbs that swoop up from the bayside flats into exclusive enclaves in the hills. Many residents of the 'West Bay' would like to think they needn't ever cross the Bay Bridge or take a Bay Area Rapid Transit (BART) train through an underwater tunnel. But a wealth of museums and historical sites, a world-famous university, excellent restaurants and bars, a creative arts scene, offbeat shopping, woodsy parks and better weather are just some of the attractions that lure travelers from San Francisco over to the sunny side of the Bay.

Oakland

Named for the grand oak trees that once lined its streets, Oakland is to San Francisco what Brooklyn is to Manhattan. To some degree a less expensive alternative to 'the city' across the Bay, this is often where people have moved to escape skyrocketing San Francisco housing costs. An ethnically diverse city, Oakland has a strong African American community and a long labor-union history. Urban farmers raise chickens in their backyard or occupy abandoned lots to start community gardens; families find more room to stretch out; and self-satisfied residents thumb their noses at San Francisco's fog while basking in sunny weather. For visitors, the city offers a handful of diverting museums and historical sites, a vibrant arts scene, innovative restaurants and bars, vintage and boutique shops, and outdoor recreation galore – down by the waterfront, around Lake Merritt and up in the forested hills.

◉ Sights & Activities

Oakland is full of historic buildings and a growing number of colorful businesses. With such easy access from San Francisco via BART or ferry, it's worth spending part of a day exploring here on foot or by bicycle.

◉ Downtown, Chinatown & Waterfront

Pedestrianized **City Center**, between Broadway and Clay St, 12th and 14th Sts, forms the heart of downtown Oakland. Nearby **City Hall** (Map p130; ☎ 510-444-2489; www. oaklandnet.com; Frank H Ogawa Plaza; ⊙9am-6pm Mon-Fri; Ⓑ12th St Oakland City Center) is a beautifully refurbished 1914 beaux-arts building.

Old Oakland, west of Broadway between 8th and 10th Sts, is lined with restored historic buildings dating from the late 19th century. The area has a lively restaurant and after-work scene, and a farmers market every Friday from 8am until 2pm.

East of Broadway and bustling with commerce, Oakland's Chinatown centers on Franklin and Webster Sts, as it has since the 1850s. Jack London Sq is on the waterfront further south.

Oakland Museum of California　MUSEUM (OMCA; Map p130; ☎ 510-318-8400; http://museumca.org; 1000 Oak St; adult/child $16/7, 1st Sun each month free; ⊙11am-5pm Wed-Thu, to 9pm Fri, 10am-6pm Sat & Sun; Ⓟ ⓘ; Ⓑ Lake Merritt) Near the southern end of Lake Merritt, this museum has rotating exhibitions on artistic and scientific themes, and permanent galleries dedicated to the state's diverse ecology and history, as well as California art. Admission is steeply discounted on Friday nights (after 5pm), when DJs, food trucks and free art workshops for kids make it a fun hangout.

◉ Uptown & Lake Merritt

North of downtown Oakland, the Uptown district contains many of the city's art-deco beauties, such as the Fox Theater (p135) and Paramount Theatre (p136), and a proliferating arts, restaurant and nightlife scene. The area stretches roughly between Telegraph and Broadway, bounded by Grand Ave to the north.

Follow Grand Ave east of Broadway and you'll run into the shores of Lake Merritt. Grand Ave (north of the lake) and Lakeshore Ave (east of the lake) are pedestrian-friendly streets for local shops, restaurants, cafes and bars.

Lake Merritt　LAKE (Map p130; ☎ 510-238-7275; www.oaklandnet.com; Ⓟ ⓘ; Ⓑ Lake Merritt) ⚤ An urban respite, Lake Merritt is a popular place to stroll or go running (a 3.5-mile paved path circles the lake), with bonsai and botanical gardens, a children's amusement park (p131), bird sanctuary, **boathouse** (Map p130; ☎ 510-238-2196; www.oaklandnet.com; 568 Bellevue Ave; boat rentals per hour $12-24, cash only; ⊙daily Mar-Oct, Sat & Sun only Nov-Feb; ⓘ; ▣ AC Transit 12) and **gondola rides** (Map p130; ☎ 510-663-6603; http://

Central Oakland

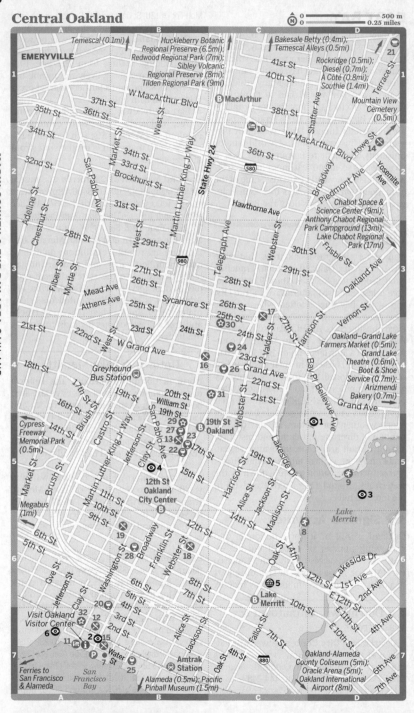

EMERYVILLE

Temescal (0.1mi)

Huckleberry Botanic
Regional Preserve (6.5mi);
Redwood Regional Park (7mi);
Sibley Volcanic
Regional Preserve (8mi);
Tilden Regional Park (9mi)

Bakesale Betty (0.4mi);
Temescal Alleys (0.5mi)

Rockridge (0.5mi);
Diesel (0.7mi);
À Côté (0.8mi);
Southie (1.4mi)

Mountain View
Cemetery
(0.5mi)

41st St
40th St

38th St

W MacArthur Blvd

MacArthur

10

14

36th St

State Hwy 24

580

Hawthorne Ave

Chabot Space &
Science Center (9mi);
Anthony Chabot Regional
Park Campground (13mi);
Lake Chabot Regional
Park (17mi)

35th St
37th St
36th St
34th St
33rd St
Brockhurst St

Market St
West St
San Pablo Ave

980

Piedmont Ave
Broadway
Webster St

31st St
28th St
27th St
26th St

30th St
29th St

Frisbie St
Oakland Ave

Vernon St

Adeline St
Chestnut St
Filbert St
Myrtle St

Mead Ave
Athens Ave
25th St
23rd St
24th St
Sycamore St
26th St
25th St
17
30

Telegraph Ave
24th St
Valdez St
27th St
Harrison St

Oakland–Grand Lake
Farmers Market (0.5mi);
Grand Lake
Theatre (0.6mi);
Boot & Shoe
Service (0.7mi);
Arizmendi
Bakery (0.7mi)

21st St
22nd St
West St
W Grand Ave

24
16
26

23rd Ave
Grand Ave
22nd St
21st St

Grand Ave

18th St
17th St
16th St
Brush St
19th St
Castro St
San Pablo Ave
20th St
William St
19th St
29
27
23
13
22
B 19th St
Oakland

31

Webster St
Harrison St
19th St
Lakeside Dr

1

Cypress
Freeway
Memorial Park
(0.5mi)

Market St
Brush St
14th St
Martin Luther King Jr Way
Jefferson St
Clay St
4
15th St

12th St
Oakland
City Center
B

Alice St
Jackson St
Madison St

9

3

Lake
Merritt

Megabus
(1mi)

11th St
10th St
9th St

19

Broadway
Franklin St
Webster St

12th St
14th St
Oak St

8

6th St
5th St
Gve St
Jefferson St
Clay St

28
18

8th St
7th St

6th St

Lakeside Dr

1st Ave

Washington St

20
32
12
2 15
11
6

3rd St
2nd St
Water St
7
25

Alice St
Jackson St
Fallon St

5
Lake
Merritt
B

Oak St
10th St

14th St
12th St
E 12th St
E 11th St
E 10th St
4th Ave

Oakland-Alameda
County Coliseum (5mi);
Oracle Arena (5mi);
Oakland International
Airport (8mi)

6th Ave
7th Ave
2nd Ave

Amtrak
Station

880

Ferries to
San Francisco
& Alameda

San
Francisco
Bay

Alameda (0.5mi); Pacific
Pinball Museum (1.5mi)

21

Terrace St
Shafter Ave
Howe St
Yosemite Ave

W MacArthur Blvd

Bay Pl
Bellevue Ave

Central Oakland

gondolaservizio.com; 1520 Lakeside Dr; 30/50min cruise $60/85; B Lake Merritt). The two main commercial streets skirting Lake Merritt are Grand Ave, running along the north shore, and Lakeshore Ave on the eastern edge of the lake.

Children's Fairyland AMUSEMENT PARK
(Map p130; ☎ 510-452-2259; http://fairyland.org; 699 Bellevue Ave; $10, child under 1yr free; ⊙ 10am-4pm Mon-Fri, to 5pm Sat & Sun Jun-Aug, off-season hours vary; P ⓗ; ⓠ AC Transit 12) Lakeside Park, on the northern side of Lake Merritt, includes this 10-acre kiddie attraction, which dates from 1950 and has a charming fairy-tale-themed train, carousel and mini Ferris wheel.

⊙ Jack London Square

Jack London Square SQUARE
(Map p130; ☎ 510-645-9292; www.jacklondonsquare.com; Broadway & Embarcadero; ⊙ 24hr, shop, restaurant & bar hours vary; P; ⓠ Broadway Shuttle) The area where writer and adventurer Jack London once raised hell now bears his name. The pretty waterfront location is worth a stroll, especially when the Sunday **farmers market** (Map p130; ☎ 415-291-3276; www.cuesa.org; ⊙ 10am-3pm Sun; ⓟⓗ) ✿ takes over, or get off your feet and kayak around the harbor. Contemporary redevelopment has added a cinema complex, condo development and popular restaurants and bars. A replica of Jack London's Yukon cab-

in stands at the eastern end of the square. Oddly, people throw coins inside as if it's a fountain.

Another interesting historical stop, adjacent to the tiny cabin, is Heinold's First & Last Chance Saloon (p135). Catch a ferry from San Francisco – a worthwhile excursion in itself – and you'll land just paces away.

USS Potomac SHIP
(Map p130; ☎ 510-627-1215; www.usspotomac.org; 540 Water St; adult/child $10/free; ⊙ tours 11am-2:30pm Wed, Fri & Sun; ⓠ Broadway Shuttle) Franklin D Roosevelt's 'floating White House,' the 165ft USS *Potomac,* is moored at Clay and Water Sts by the ferry dock, and is open for dockside tours. Two-hour cruises (adult/child $55/35) are scheduled several times a month from April through November (book far ahead).

⊙ Piedmont Ave, Temescal & Rockridge

North of downtown Oakland, Broadway becomes a lengthy strip of car dealerships called Auto Row. Detour a couple of blocks east to Piedmont Ave, wall-to-wall with vintage-clothing stores, coffeehouses, restaurants and an art-house cinema.

A half-dozen or so long blocks west of Broadway, Temescal wins the prize for being Oakland's artiest, hippest neighborhood.

Find unique shops, creative restaurants and happening bars on Telegraph Ave north of 40th St.

Rockridge, a lively, upscale neighborhood, is further north between Broadway and Telegraph Ave. College Ave is lined with upscale boutiques, a bookstore, pubs and cafes and quite a few fancy restaurants.

Mountain View Cemetery   CEMETERY
(☑ 510-658-2588; www.mountainviewcemetery. org; 5000 Piedmont Ave; ☉ 6:30am-7:30pm; 🅿 ; 🚊 AC Transit 12) At the northern end of Piedmont Ave, this is perhaps the most serene and lovely artificial landscape in the East Bay. Designed by Frederick Law Olmstead (the landscape architect of New York City's Central Park), it's great for walking and the views are stupendous.

◉ Oakland Hills

The large parks of the Oakland Hills are ideal for day hiking and challenging cycling, and the **East Bay Regional Parks** (☑ 888-327-2757; www.ebparks.org; per car free-$6; ☉ hours vary; 🚴🐾) *✿* manages more than 1200 miles of trails in 65 regional parks, preserves and recreation areas in the Alameda and Contra Costa Counties.

Off Hwy 24, **Robert Sibley Volcanic Regional Preserve** is the northernmost of the Oakland Hills parks. It has great views of the Bay Area from its **Round Top Peak** (1761ft). From Sibley, Skyline Blvd runs south past **Redwood Regional Park** and adjacent **Joaquin Miller Park** to **Anthony Chabot Regional Park**. A hike or mountain-bike ride through the groves and along the hilltops of any of these sizable parks will make you forget you're in an urban area. At the southern end of Chabot Park is the enormous **Lake Chabot**, with an easy trail along its shore, and canoes, kayaks and other boats for rent from the **Lake Chabot Marina** (☑ 510-247-2526; www.lakechabotrecreation. com; 17936 Lake Chabot Rd, Castro Valley; rentals/ tours from $23/45; ☉ 6am-6pm Mon-Thu, to 7pm Fri-Sun May-early Sep, off-season hours vary; 🚴).

★ Chabot Space & Science Center   MUSEUM
(☑ 510-336-7300; www.chabotspace.org; 10000 Skyline Blvd; adult/child $18/14; ☉ 10am-5pm Wed-Sun, also Tue Jun-Aug; 🅿🚴; 🚊 AC Transit 339) *✿* Stargazers will go gaga over this kid-oriented science and technology center in the Oakland Hills with loads of exhibits

on subjects such as space travel and eclipses, as well as cool planetarium shows. When the weather's good, check out the free Friday and Saturday evening viewings (7:30pm to 10:30pm) using a 20in refractor telescope.

Admission is just $5 on the first Friday evening of each month (6pm to 10pm), when the museum organizes hands-on activities, science demonstrations, movies and night hikes.

★✿ Festivals & Events

Oakland First Fridays   STREET CARNIVAL
(☑ 510-361-0615; http://oaklandfirstfridays.org; Telegraph Ave; entry by donation; ☉ 5-9:30pm 1st Fri each month; 👶; 🅱 19th St Oakland) A kinetic street festival takes place on the first Friday of the month, when a five-block stretch of Telegraph Ave closes to car traffic. Thousands of people turn out for food vendors, live music and performances.

🛏 Sleeping

Oakland has surprisingly few places to stay, apart from chain motels and hotels off the freeways, downtown and near the airport.

Anthony Chabot Regional Park   CAMPGROUND $
(☑ reservations888-327-2757;www.reserveamerica. com; end of Marciel Rd, Castro Valley; tent sites $25, RV sites with hookups $25-35; 🅿🚴) *✿* In the East Bay's forested hills, this 5000-acre park has 75 campsites open year-round and hot showers.

Inn at Temescal   MOTEL $$
(Map p130; ☑ 510-652-9800; www.innattemescal. com; 3720 Telegraph Ave; r from $129; 🅿➕✳🈁; 🅱 MacArthur) Though the location isn't lovely, it's a short walk to BART or Temescal's main strip. Recently renovated, the motel has exterior doors painted in avocado green and sunset orange. Clean-lined rooms come with pillow-top mattresses, wall-sized historic photos and retro accents. Expect some street noise.

Waterfront Hotel   BOUTIQUE HOTEL $$$
(Map p130; ☑ 510-836-3800; www.waterfronthotel oakland.com; 10 Washington St; r from $299; 🅿➕✳@🈁🏊🐾) Paddle-printed wallpaper and lamps fashioned from faux lanterns round out the playful nautical theme of this cheerful harborside hotel. A huge brass-topped fireplace warms the foyer, and comfy rooms include iPod docking stations and coffeemakers. Unless you're an avid

train-spotter, water-view rooms are preferred, as trains rattle by on the city side. Complimentary wine-and-cheese reception on weekdays. Parking is $30.

✖ Eating

Oakland's diverse eateries nearly rival those of foodie neighbor San Francisco. Take your pick of sophisticated restaurants run by top Bay Area chefs, neighborhood cafes, international kitchens or pop-up food trucks. Downtown, Old Oakland and Chinatown abound with budget-friendly local favorites. Uptown, Temescal and Rockridge attract culinary trend-spotters. West Oakland does soul food, while East Oakland has authentic taquerias.

✖ Uptown, Downtown & Jack London Square

Swan's Market   FOOD HALL $

(Map p130; ☑ 510-287-5353; http://swansmarket. com; 510 9th St; most mains $8-15; ☉ 9am-10pm Mon-Sat; ⊞; ᴮ 12th St Oakland City Center) Old Oakland's 100-year-old marketplace has been given new life with a gourmet food court, where the wooden tables are always full, day and night. Stop at Cosecha for Mexican fare, AS B-Dama for udon noodles and Japanese fried chicken, Delage sushi bar, the Cook & Her Farmer oyster bar and cafe, Rosamunde Sausage Grill or Miss Ollie's for Caribbean food.

Shandong Restaurant   CHINESE $

(Map p130; ☑ 510-839-2299; http://shandongoak land.com; 328 10th St; mains $7-13; ☉ 11am-3pm & 4-9pm Sun-Thu, to 9:30pm Fri & Sat; ⊞; ᴮ 12th St Oakland City Center) Not everything tastes so amazing at this crowded, family-friendly Chinatown restaurant, but that's OK because you're only here for two things: handmade sesame noodles and from-scratch pork dumplings. Expect a wait for a table.

Authentic Bagel Co   BAKERY, DELI $

(Map p130; ☑ 510-459-1201; www.abagelcompany. com; 463 2nd St; sandwiches $3-10; ☉ 7am-3pm; ☑⊞) Once upon a time two Jewish guys from Rhode Island set up shop near Jack London Sq. Today they make the Bay Area's best East Coast–style bagels while blasting Beastie Boys albums. Chow down on a 'Lox Monsta' (pumpernickel bagel with bacon, lox, avocado and cilantro curry) at sunny sidewalk tables.

Kingston 11   CARIBBEAN $$

(Map p130; ☑ 510-465-2558; http://kingstonn11eats.com; 2270 Telegraph Ave; mains $13-20; ☉ 11am-2pm & 5-10pm Tue-Fri, 5-10pm Sat, 11am-4pm Sun; ⊞; ᴮ 19th St Oakland) The wait will be worth it at this raucous Caribbean bar with a groovy soundtrack, where oxtail stew, salt-fish fritters, fried plantains and goat curry are succulent feasts. Swing by for 'Irie Hour' (5pm to 7pm Tuesday through Friday) to sip out-of-this-world cocktails such as the Rise Up (cold-brew coffee, coconut milk, spiced rum and Angostura bitters). Reservations recommended.

Mua   CALIFORNIAN $$

(Map p130; ☑ 510-238-1100; https://muaoakland.com; 2442a Webster St; shared plates $7-15, mains $21-35; ☉ 5:30-11pm Mon-Thu, to midnight Fri & Sat, 5-10pm Sun; ☑; ᴮ 19th St Oakland) A warehouse-sized space in Uptown, this social gathering spot is just as good for date night as it is for groups getting ready for a night out. Peruse the long, long menu of creative shared plates like quinoa-arugula salad with nectarines and goat's cheese or beef bone-marrow toast, with a 'Stormy Oaktown' cocktail or rosemary martini in hand. Reservations recommended.

Camber Uptown   THAI, LAOTIAN $$

(Map p130; ☑ 510-663-4560; http://camber oakland.com; 1707 Telegraph Ave; mains $10-20; ☉ 11:30am-2:30pm & 5-9:30pm Mon-Thu, 11:30am-11:30pm Fri, 5-11:30pm Sat; ☑; ᴮ 19th St Oakland) While you might find cheaper and more authentic Southeast Asian kitchens in Oakland's Chinatown, Camber can't be beaten for proximity to Uptown nightlife. Fusion dishes such as the 'bouncing beef' stir-fry and garlic-basil fish with sliced jalapeño peppers are popular with the young crowd sidling up to the bar.

✖ Piedmont Ave, Temescal & Rockridge

★ Commis   CALIFORNIAN $$$

(Map p130; ☑ 510-653-3902; http://commisres taurant.com; 3859 Piedmont Ave; 8-course dinner $149, with wine & beer pairings $229; ☉ 5:30-9:30pm Wed-Sat, 5-9pm Sun; ☐ AC Transit 51A) The East Bay's only Michelin-starred restaurant, the signless and discreet dining room counts a minimalist decor and some coveted counter real estate where patrons can watch chef James Syhabout and his team piece together creative and innovative dishes,

SUMMONING ALL PINBALL WIZARDS

Put down that video-game console, cast aside your latest phone app, and return to the bygone days of pinball play. Lose yourself in bells and flashing lights at **Pacific Pinball Museum** (☑510-769-1349; http://pacificpinball.org; 1510 Webster St, Alameda; all-day pass adult/child $20/10; ⊙11am-9pm Tue-Thu & Sun, to 10pm Fri & Sat; ☻; ☐AC Transit 51A), a pinball parlor with almost 100 games dating from the 1930s to the present, and vintage jukeboxes playing hits from the past. Take AC Transit bus 51A from downtown Oakland.

maybe Monterey Bay abalone, soy-milk custard with chanterelles or a perfectly ripe peach topped with oats, beeswax creme and marigolds. Reservations essential.

Bakesale Betty SANDWICHES, BAKERY $
(☑510-985-1213; www.bakesalebetty.com; 5098 Telegraph Ave; sandwiches $9; ⊙11am-2pm Tue-Sat; ☐AC Transit 6) Aussie expat Alison Barakat has patrons licking their lips and lining up out the door and down the block for heavenly strawberry shortcake and scrumptious fried-chicken sandwiches. Rolling pins dangle from the ceiling and blissed-out locals sit down at ironing-board sidewalk tables.

Southie SANDWICHES $
(☑510-654-0100; http://southieoakland.com; 6311 College Ave; mains $9-18; ⊙9am-9pm Mon-Sat, to 3pm Sun; ⒷRockridge) Wood Tavern's side venture steals the show with its gobstopping meatball and pork-belly sandwiches. This busy storefront eatery has only a few tightly squeezed-together tables, with a half-dozen wines and craft beers on tap. Finish off with passion-fruit–buttermilk *panna cotta* or a brownie ice-cream sandwich.

✕ Lake Merritt

★**Oakland–Grand Lake Farmers Market** MARKET $
(☑415-472-6100; https://agriculturalinstitute.org; Lake Park Ave, at Grand Ave; ⊙9am-2pm Sat; ☻☻; ☐AC Transit 12) ✔ A rival to San Francisco's Ferry Plaza Farmers Market, this bountiful weekly market hauls in bushels of fresh fruit, vegetables, seafood, ranched meats, artisanal cheese and baked goods from as far away as Marin County and the Central Valley. The northern side of the market is cheek-to-jowl with food trucks and hot-food vendors – don't skip the dim-sum tent.

Arizmendi Bakery BAKERY $
(☑510-268-8849; http://arizmendilakeshore.com; 3265 Lakeshore Ave; pizza slices $2.50; ⊙7am-8pm Tue-Sun; ☻; ☐AC Transit 12) ✔ Great for breakfast or lunch but beware: this bakery co-op is not for the weak-willed. Gourmet vegetarian pizza, chewy breads and gigantic scones, all baked fresh, are addictive.

Boot & Shoe Service PIZZA $$
(☑510-763-2668; www.bootandshoeservice.com; 3308 Grand Ave; pizzas $14-22; ⊙7am-noon & 5:30-10pm Tue-Thu, 7am-noon & 5-10:30pm Fri,10am-2pm & 5-10:30pm Sat, 10am-2pm & 5-10pm Sun; ☻; ☐AC Transit 12) ✔ The name plays off its former identity as a cobbler's shop, but the current patrons pack this brick-walled place for its wood-fired pizzas, original cocktails and creative antipasti made from sustainably sourced fresh ingredients.

Camino CALIFORNIAN $$$
(☑510-547-5035; www.caminorestaurant.com; 3917 Grand Ave; dinner mains $32-42; ⊙5:30-9:30pm Mon, Wed & Thu, to 10pm Fri, 10am-2pm & 5:30-10pm Sat, to 9:30pm Sun; ☻; ☐AC Transit 12) ✔ From the culinary imagination of chef Russell Moore (a Chez Panisse alum), Camino's short daily-changing menu showcases the best of local organic produce and meats, most cooked over an open fire in slow-food-meets-California-now style. The tables are of recycled old-growth redwood and the place buzzes with bon vivants buzzed on craft cocktails and European and California wines. Reservations essential.

🍷 Drinking & Nightlife

Oakland's busiest and hippest bars are in the Uptown district, just north of downtown and a short stumble from BART. You'll find eclectic watering holes near Jack London Sq and in Old Oakland. Students hang out in Rockridge, while a mix of locals gravitate to bars around Lake Merritt, along Piedmont Ave and on Temescal's main drag.

★**Blue Bottle Coffee Company** CAFE
(Map p130; ☑510-653-3394; http://bluebottle coffee.com; 4270 Broadway; ⊙7am-6pm; ☐AC Transit 51A) ✔ Blue Bottle's roomier cafe is inside the beautiful WC Morse Building, a 1920s truck showroom. Communal tables, lofty ceilings and minimalist white decor

invite sipping a Gibraltar – similar to a cortado (espresso with a dash of milk), but made with more milk – or a cold-brew iced coffee.

Drake's Dealership
BEER GARDEN

(Map p130; ☑ 510-568-2739; http://drinkdrakes.com/visit/dealership; 2325 Broadway; ☉ 11:30am-11pm Sun-Wed, to 1am Thu-Sat; ⚑ ☢; Ⓑ 19th St Oakland) East Bay craft brewer Drake's Brewing Company has transformed a humdrum Dodge dealership into a lively restaurant, bar and outdoor beer garden with fire pits that crackle on foggy nights. Order a pint of Black Robusto porter or Hopocalypse double IPA with a wood-oven-fired pizza. DJs spin Thursday to Saturday. Book ahead online for complimentary tours of the actual brewery, a short bus ride from San Leandro BART station.

Dogwood
COCKTAIL BAR

(Map p130; ☑ 510-444-6669; www.bardogwood.com; 1644 Telegraph Ave; ☉ 4pm-2am; Ⓑ 19th St Oakland) A hip, tattooed young crowd hobnobs inside this red-brick-walled bar on a busy corner of Uptown. Order a creative house cocktail or classic concoction such as the Brooklyn from mixologists behind the bar. Simple sandwiches and meat-and-cheese plates keep stomachs from growling.

Make Westing
COCKTAIL BAR

(Map p130; ☑ 510-251-1400; www.makewesting.com; 1741 Telegraph Ave; ☉ 4pm-2am; Ⓑ 19th St Oakland) On weekends, people pack this Uptown hot spot, named for a Jack London short story, for its indoor bocce courts and eclectic cocktails. Toss back a 'Garden Gimlet' (gin, cucumber, basil and lime) and satiate the munchies with cilantro-and-habañero-infused popcorn or a mason jar of homemade pickled beets.

Trappist
PUB

(Map p130; ☑ 510-238-8900; www.thetrappist.com; 460 8th St; ☉ noon-12:30am Sun-Thu, to 1:30am Fri & Sat; Ⓑ Oakland 12th St City Center) Busting out of its original brick-and-wood-paneled shoe box into a second storefront and outdoor back patio, this place specialises in Belgian ales. Two dozen drafts rotate through the taps, and tasty charcuterie and cheese boards, salads and grilled cheese sandwiches make it easy to linger.

Heinold's First & Last Chance Saloon
BAR

(Map p130; ☑ 510-839-6761; www.heinoldsfirstandlastchance.com; 48 Webster St; ☉ noon-11pm Sun-Thu, to 1am Fri & Sat; ☐ Broadway Shuttle) At this 1883 bar constructed from wood scavenged from an old whaling ship, you really have to hold on to your beer. Keeled to a severe slant during the 1906 earthquake, the building's tilt might make you feel self-conscious about stumbling before you even order. Its big claim to fame is that adventure writer Jack London was a regular patron.

Café Van Kleef
BAR

(Map p130; ☑ 510-763-7711; http://cafevankleef.com; 1621 Telegraph Ave; ☉ 4pm-2am Mon, from noon Tue-Fri, from 6pm Sat, from 7pm Sun; Ⓑ 19th St Oakland) Order a greyhound (with freshly squeezed grapefruit juice) and take a gander at the profusion of antique musical instruments, fake taxidermy heads, sprawling formal chandeliers and bizarro ephemera clinging to every surface possible. Quirky even *before* you get lit, it features live blues, jazz and the occasional rock band on weekends.

Luka's Taproom & Lounge
LOUNGE

(Map p130; ☑ 510-451-4677; www.lukasoakland.com; 2221 Broadway; ☉ 5:30-11pm Sun-Wed, to 1am Thu, to 2am Fri & Sat; Ⓑ 19th St Oakland) Go Uptown to get down. At this long-running restaurant and lounge, DJs spin a soulful mix of hip-hop, R&B and Latin grooves Thursday to Sunday nights (cover charge $5 to $10).

Beer Revolution
BAR

(Map p130; http://beer-revolution.com; 464 3rd St; ☉ noon-11pm Sun-Thu, to midnight Fri & Sat; ☐ Broadway Shuttle) With 50 beers on tap and hundreds more in bottles, there's a lifetime of discovery ahead, so kick back on the sunny deck or park yourself at that barrel table embedded with bottle caps. Bonuses include a punk-rock soundtrack played at conversation-friendly levels.

☆ Entertainment

Professional sports teams play at Oakland–Alameda County Coliseum and Oracle Arena off I-880 including Golden State Warriors (p136) (NBA basketball; moving to San Francisco in 2019), Oakland Raiders (p136) (NFL football; headed to Las Vegas in 2020) or Oakland A's (p136) (American League baseball; not leaving, phew). See www.coliseum.com for upcoming concerts and events. Most of Oakland's smaller live-music and performing-arts venues are Uptown.

★ Fox Theater
THEATER

(Map p130; ☑ 510-302-2250, tickets 800-745-3000; http://thefoxoakland.com; 1807 Telegraph

MARIN COUNTY & THE BAY AREA OAKLAND

Ave; tickets from $35; ⊘ hours vary; B 19th St Oakland) A phoenix arisen from the urban ashes, this restored 1928 art-deco stunner adds dazzle and neon lights to Telegraph Ave, where it's a cornerstone of the happening Uptown theater and nightlife district. Once a movie house, it's now a popular concert venue for edgy and independent Californian, national and international music acts. Buy tickets early, since many shows sell out.

★ **Golden State Warriors** BASKETBALL
(✍ tickets 888-479-4667; www.nba.com/warriors; 7000 Coliseum Way; tickets from $55; ⊘ Oct-Apr; ♠; B Coliseum) If it's hoops you must have, then it's the Warriors for you. Originally from Philadelphia, this team moved across the bay from San Francisco in 1971. Today they play at Oracle Arena (next to the Coliseum). The Warriors caused quite a commotion when they won the National Basketball Association (NBA) championship playoffs in 2015. Alas, they're moving back to San Francisco in 2019.

Paramount Theatre THEATER, CINEMA
(Map p130; ✍ 510-465-6400; www.paramountthe atre.com; 2025 Broadway; movie/concert tickets from $7/25; ⊘ hours vary; 🚇 19th St Oakland) This massive 1931 art-deco masterpiece shows classic films a few times each month and is also home to the Oakland Symphony (www.oaklandsymphony.org) and Oakland Ballet (http://oaklandballet.org). It periodically books big-name concerts and screens classic flicks. Guided tours ($5) are given at 10am on the first and third Saturdays of the month (no reservations).

Yoshi's JAZZ
(Map p130; ✍ 510-238-9200; www.yoshis.com; 510 Embarcadero W; from $20; ⊘ hours vary; 🚇 Broadway Shuttle) Yoshi's has a solid jazz calendar, with talent from around the world passing through on a near-nightly basis. It's also a Japanese restaurant, so if you enjoy a sushi dinner before the show, you'll be rewarded with reserved cabaret-style seating. Otherwise, resign yourself to limited high-top tables squeezed along the back walls of this intimate club.

Grand Lake Theatre CINEMA
(✍ 510-452-3556; www.renaissancerialto.com; 3200 Grand Ave; tickets $5-12.50; ⊘ hours vary; ♠; 🚇 AC Transit 12) Once a vaudeville theater and silent-movie house, this 1926 beauty near Lake Merritt lures you in with its huge corner marquee (which sometimes displays left-leaning political messages) and keeps you coming with a fun balcony and a Wurlitzer organ playing on weekends.

New Parkway Theater CINEMA
(Map p130; ✍ 510-658-7900; www.thenewpark way.com; 474 24th St; tickets $5-10; ⊘ hours vary; 🚇 AC Transit 6) This laid-back movie house, pub and community-events space shows second-run and throwback indie films. Reasonably priced beer, wine, sandwiches and pizza are delivered to your couch seat.

Oakland A's BASEBALL
(✍ 510-568-5600, tickets 877-493-2255; http:// oakland.athletics.mlb.com; 7000 Coliseum Way; tickets from $15; ⊘ Apr-Sep; ♠; B Coliseum) When the San Francisco Giants are away, the Oakland A's are usually home, which expands the possibilities for those desperate for a summer baseball fix. The A's most recent World Series pennant came at the Giants' expense in the quake-addled 1989 series, and they remain contenders. If you want to catch them in interleague play, get tickets early.

Oakland Raiders FOOTBALL
(✍ 510-864-5022, tickets 800-724-3377; www. raiders.com; 7000 Coliseum Way; tickets from $40; ⊘ Sep-Jan; B Coliseum) With three Super Bowl championships, the notorious bad boys of the National Footbal League (NFL) have had ups and downs over the years, but they still have the staunchest, rowdiest fans in the western US. The team ungratefully moved to Los Angeles for 12 years, but returned in 1995 to Oakland's open arms. They're leaving again for Las Vegas in 2020.

ℹ Information

MEDIA
Oakland's daily newspaper is the *Oakland Tribune* (www.insidebayarea.com/oaklandtribune). The free weekly *East Bay Express* (www.eastbay express.com) has good Oakland and Berkeley listings.

TOURIST INFORMATION
Visit Oakland Visitor Center (Map p130; ✍ 510-839-9000; www.visitoakland.com; 481 Water St; ⊘ 9am-5pm Mon-Fri, 10am-4pm Sat & Sun) At Jack London Sq.

ℹ Getting There & Away

AIR
Oakland International Airport is less crowded and sometimes cheaper to fly into than San Francisco International Airport (SFO) across

the bay. OAK airport is connected to Oakland, Berkeley and San Francisco by frequent BART trains.

BART

Within the Bay Area, the most convenient way to get to Oakland and back is by BART (Bay Area Rapid Transit; www.bart.gov). Trains run on a set schedule approximately every 10 to 20 minutes from around 4:30am to midnight on weekdays, 6am to midnight on Saturday and 8am to midnight on Sunday.

Downtown BART stations are on Broadway at 12th and 19th Sts; other Oakland stations are on the south side of Lake Merritt, close to Chinatown; near Temescal (MacArthur station) and in Rockridge.

To get to downtown Oakland, catch a Richmond or Pittsburg/Bay Point train. The fare to Oakland's 12th or 19th St stations from any BART station in downtown San Francisco is $3.45. Rockridge is on the Pittsburg/Bay Point line, while all Berkeley stops are on the Richmond line. To Lake Merritt or the Coliseum (for connections to Oakland's airport), catch a BART train heading toward Fremont or Dublin/ Pleasanton.

BUS

AC Transit (☏ 510-891-4777; www.actransit. org) runs convenient buses from San Francisco's Transbay Transit Center to downtown Oakland ($4.20, or $2.10 with purchase of $5 day pass valid on local East Bay buses). Scores of Transbay buses run during commute hours, but only the 'O' line runs both ways all day and on weekends.

After BART trains stop, late-night transportation between downtown San Francisco and downtown Oakland is with the AC Transit bus 800 line ($4.20), which runs hourly on weekdays and every 20 minutes on weekends.

Between downtown Berkeley and downtown Oakland, take fast and frequent AC Transit bus 6 along Telegraph Ave. Alternatively, take AC Transit bus 18 via Martin Luther King Jr Way and Shattuck Ave. The one way local bus fare for either is $2.10.

Greyhound operates direct buses from Oakland, including to Vallejo, San Jose, Santa Rosa, Sacramento and Los Angeles; its **bus station** (Map p130; ☏ 510-832-4730; 2103 San Pablo Ave; ⓑ 19th St Oakland) in downtown Oakland is seedy. Discount carrier **Megabus** (☏ 877-462-6342; http://us.megabus.com) has daily service to LA, Burbank and Anaheim, departing from outside the West Oakland BART station.

CAR & MOTORCYCLE

From San Francisco by car, cross the Bay Bridge and enter Oakland via one of two ways: I-580, which leads to I-980 heading to downtown

Oakland; or I-880, which curves through West Oakland and lets you off near the south end of Broadway. I-880 then continues to the Coliseum, Oakland International Airport and, eventually, San Jose. Driving back westbound from the East Bay to San Francisco, the bridge toll is $4 to $6, depending on the time and day of the week.

FERRY

From San Francisco's Ferry Building and Pier 41, **San Francisco Bay Ferry** (☏ 415-705-8291; http://sanfranciscobayferry.com) sails to Jack London Sq (one-way $6.60, 30 to 45 minutes) more frequently on weekdays than on weekends. Ferry tickets include a free transfer, which you can use on AC Transit buses.

TRAIN

Oakland is a regular stop for Amtrak trains operating up and down the coast. From Oakland's **Amtrak station** (245 2nd St; ⓑ Broadway Shuttle) at Jack London Sq, catch AC Transit bus 12 or the free Broadway Shuttle to downtown Oakland, or take a ferry across the bay to San Francisco.

Amtrak passengers with reservations on to San Francisco disembark at the **Emeryville Amtrak station** (5885 Horton St), one stop north of Oakland. From there, an Amtrak bus shuttles you to San Francisco's Ferry Building stop. Emeryville is also the terminus for Amtrak's daily California Zephyr train service to/from Chicago. The free **Emery Go Round** (☏ 510-451-3862; www.emerygoround.com) shuttle runs a weekday circuit including the Emeryville Amtrak and MacArthur BART stations.

ⓘ Getting Around

The best way to get around much of central Oakland is to walk, cycle or take public buses.

TO/FROM THE AIRPORT

Flying into **Oakland International Airport** (OAK; www.oaklandairport.com; 1 Airport Dr; ☏; ⓑ Oakland International Airport), car rentals are available from all the major agencies. Outside the terminal, free shuttle buses depart every 10 minutes for the airport's rental-car center.

BART is the easiest public transportation option. Opposite the terminal, catch a BART shuttle train to Coliseum Station, where you'll pay min the fare to your final destination when changing trains. BART trains run on weekdays between 4:30am until after midnight daily (from 6am on Saturday, 8am on Sunday).

SuperShuttle (☏ 800-258-3826; www.super shuttle.com) is one of many door-to-door shuttle services operating out of Oakland International Airport. One-way service to San Francisco destinations starts at around $60 for up to four people. East Bay service destinations are also served. Reserve ahead.

A taxi from Oakland International Airport to downtown Oakland costs about $40; to downtown San Francisco about $70.

BUS

AC Transit (p137) has a comprehensive bus network within Oakland. Local bus fares are $2.10; pay with cash (bring exact change) or a Clipper card (www.clippercard.com).

The free **Broadway Shuttle** (www.meetdown townoak.com/shuttle.php; ⊙7am-10pm Mon-Thu, to 1am Fri, 6pm-1am Sat) runs along Broadway between Jack London Sq and Lake Merritt, stopping at Old Oakland/Chinatown, downtown BART stations and the Uptown district. The lime-green buses arrive every 10 to 15 minutes.

Berkeley

Berkeley – the birthplace of the free-speech and disability-rights movements, and the home of the hallowed halls of the University of California, Berkeley (aka 'Cal') – is no bashful wallflower. A national hot spot of (mostly left-of-center) intellectual discourse and with one of the most vocal activist populations in the country, this infamous college town has an interesting mix of graying progressives and idealistic undergrads. It's easy to stereotype 'Beserkeley' for some of its recycle-or-else PC crankiness, but the city is often on the forefront of environmental and political issues that eventually go mainstream.

Berkeley is also home to a large South Asian community, as evidenced by an abundance of sari shops on University Ave and an unusually large number of Indian, Pakistani and Nepalese restaurants.

◉ Sights & Activities

◉ University of California, Berkeley

The Berkeley campus of the University of California (UCB, called 'Cal' by both students and locals) is the oldest university in the state. The decision to found the college was made in 1866, and the first students arrived in 1873. Today UCB has more than 35,000 students, more than 1500 professors and more Nobel laureates than you could point a particle accelerator at.

From Telegraph Ave, enter the campus via Sproul Plaza and Sather Gate, a center for people-watching, soapbox oration and pseudotribal drumming. Or you can enter from Center St and Oxford Lane, near the downtown BART station.

Campanile   LANDMARK
(Sather Tower; Map p140; ☑510-642-6000; http://campanile.berkeley.edu; adult/child $3/2; ⊙10am-3:45pm Mon-Fri, 10am-4:45pm Sat, to 1:30pm & 3-4:45pm Sun; ♿; ⒝ Downtown Berkeley) Officially called Sather Tower, the Campanile was modeled on St Mark's Basilica in Venice. The 307ft spire offers fine views of the Bay Area, and at the top you can stare up into the carillon of 61 bells, ranging from the size of a cereal bowl to that of a Volkswagen. Recitals take place on weekdays at 7:50am and at noon and 6pm Monday to Saturday, with a longer piece performed at 2pm on Sunday.

Sather Gate   GATE
(Map p140; ☑510-642-6000; www.berkeley.edu; Sather Rd; ⊙24hr; ⒜AC Transit 6, 51B) The frenetic energy buzzing from the university's Sather Gate on any given day is a mixture of youthful posthippies reminiscing about days before their time and fashion-conscious hipsters and punk rockers who sneer at tie-dyed nostalgia. Political activists still hand out leaflets here at the south entrance to campus.

Bancroft Library   LIBRARY
(Map p140; ☑510-642-3781; www.lib.berkeley.edu/libraries/bancroft-library; University Dr; ⊙archives 10am-4pm or 5pm Mon-Fri; ⒝ Downtown Berkeley) FREE The Bancroft houses, among other gems, the papers of Mark Twain, a copy of Shakespeare's folios and a diary from the Donner Party. Its small public exhibits of historical Californiana include the surprisingly small gold nugget that sparked the 1849 gold rush. Rotating temporary exhibits spotlight history and art, with pieces from the library's own collections. To register to use the library, you must present a current government or academic-issued photo ID. The registration desk is on your way in.

UC Berkeley Art Museum   MUSEUM
(BAMPFA; Map p140; ☑510-642-0808; www.bampfa.berkeley.edu; 2155 Center St; adult/child $12/free; ⊙11am-7pm Sun, Wed & Thu, to 9pm Fri & Sat; ⒝ Downtown Berkeley) With a stainless-steel exterior wrapping around a 1930s printing plant, the museum's new location holds multiple galleries showcasing a limited number of artworks, from ancient Chinese to cutting-edge contemporary. The complex also houses a bookstore, cafe and the much-loved Pacific Film Archive (p146).

Phoebe A Hearst Museum of Anthropology
MUSEUM

(Map p140; ☑510-642-3682; http://hearstmuseum.berkeley.edu; Bancroft Way, at College Ave; adult/child $6/free; ⊙11am-5pm Sun-Wed & Fri, to 8pm Thu, 10am-6pm Sat; ☐AC Transit 6, 51B) South of the Campanile in Kroeber Hall, this small museum includes exhibits from indigenous cultures around the world, including ancient Peruvian, Egyptian and African items. There's also a large collection highlighting Native Californian cultures.

UC Museum of Paleontology
MUSEUM

(Map p140; ☑510-642-1821; www.ucmp.berkeley.edu; Campanile Way; ⊙8am-10pm Mon-Thu, 8am-5pm Fri, 10am-5pm Sat, 1-10pm Sun; ☑Downtown Berkeley) FREE Housed in the ornate Valley Life Sciences Building (and primarily a research facility that's closed to the public), this museum has a number of fossil exhibits in the atrium, including a *Tyrannosaurus rex* skeleton.

Julia Morgan Theater
THEATER

(Map p140; ☑510-845-8542; http://tickets.berkeleyplayhouse.org; 2640 College Ave; ⊙not open to the public, except for performances; ☐AC Transit 51B) A beautifully understated, redwood-paneled 1910 theater, this performance space (formerly a church) was created by Bay Area architect Julia Morgan. She designed several landmark Bay Area buildings and, most famously, Hearst Castle on the Central Coast.

People's Park
PARK

(Map p140; 2556 Haste St; ⊙24hr; ☐AC Transit 6) This park, just east of Telegraph Ave, is a marker in local history as a political battleground between residents and the city and state government in the late 1960s. Occasional festivals do still happen here, but it's rather run-down and serves mostly as a gathering spot for Berkeley's homeless.

There's talk of redeveloping the park into university-student housing.

⊙ South of Campus

South of campus along College Ave is the **Elmwood District**, a charming nook of shops and restaurants that offers a calming alternative to the frenetic buzz around Telegraph Ave. Continue further south and you'll be in Rockridge, in the neighboring city of Oakland.

Telegraph Avenue
STREET

(Map p140; ⊙shop & restaurant hours vary; ℗; ☐AC Transit 6) Telegraph Ave has traditionally been the throbbing heart of studentville in Berkeley, the sidewalks crowded with undergrads, postdocs and youthful shoppers squeezing their way past throngs of vendors, buskers and panhandlers. Street stalls hawk everything from crystals to bumper stickers to self-published tracts. Several cafes and budget eateries cater to students.

First Church of Christ, Scientist
CHURCH

(Map p140; ☑510-845-7199; www.friendsoffirstchurch.org; 2619 Dwight Way; ⊙tour 12:15pm 1st Sun each month; ℗; ☐AC Transit 6) FREE Bernard Maybeck's impressive 1910 church uses concrete and wood in its blend of arts-and-crafts, Asian and Gothic influences. Maybeck was a professor of architecture at UC Berkeley and designed San Francisco's Palace of Fine Arts, plus many landmark homes in the Berkeley Hills.

Free 45-minute guided tours are given on the first Sunday of every month.

⊙ Downtown

Berkeley's downtown, centered on Shattuck Ave between University Ave and Dwight Way, has few traces of the city's tie-dyed reputation. Today it abounds with shops, restaurants and restored public buildings.

The nearby **arts district** revolves around the acclaimed thespian stomping grounds of the Berkeley Repertory Theatre and Aurora Theatre Company and live music at the historic Freight & Salvage Coffeehouse, all on Addison St.

⊙ North Berkeley & Albany

Not too far north of the university campus, North Berkeley is a neighborhood filled with lovely garden-front homes and parks. The popular **Gourmet Ghetto** stretches along Shattuck Ave north of University Ave for several blocks, anchored by acclaimed restaurant Chez Panisse (p144). Further northwest, **Solano Avenue**, which crosses from Berkeley into Albany, is lined with funky shops and family-friendly restaurants.

Berkeley Rose Garden
GARDENS

(☑510-981-6700; www.ci.berkeley.ca.us; 1200 Euclid Ave; ⊙dawn-dusk; ☐AC Transit 65) FREE In North Berkeley discover the Berkeley Rose Garden, with its eight terraces of colorful explosions. Here you'll find quiet benches

Central Berkeley

and a plethora of almost perpetually blooming roses arranged by hue. Across the street, **Cordornices Park** has a children's playground with a very fun concrete slide, about 40ft long.

👁 The Berkeley Hills

★ **Tilden Regional Park**   PARK
(📞 510-544-2747; www.ebparks.org/parks/tilden; ⏰ 5am-10pm; 🅿🚻🐾; 🚌 AC Transit 67) 🅿 **FREE**
This 2079-acre park, up in the hills east of town, is Berkeley's best. It has nearly 40 miles of hiking and multiuse trails of var-

ying difficulty, from paved paths to hilly scrambles, including part of the magnificent Bay Area Ridge Trail. There's also a miniature steam train ($3), a children's farm and environmental education center, a wonderfully wild-looking botanical garden and an 18-hole golf course. Lake Anza is good for picnics and from spring through fall you can swim ($3.50).

AC Transit bus 67 runs to the park on weekends and holidays from Downtown Berkeley BART station, but only stops at the park entrance on weekdays.

Central Berkeley

UC Botanical Garden at Berkeley GARDENS
(☏510-643-2755; http://botanicalgarden.berkeley.
edu; 200 Centennial Dr; adult/child $10/2; ⊘9am-
5pm, last entry 4:30pm, closed 1st Tue each month;
P⛽; 🚌Bear Transit H) 🍴 With 34 acres and
more than 10,000 types of plants, this garden in the hills above campus has one of the
most varied collections in the USA. Flora
from every continent except Antarctica are
lovingly tended here, with special emphasis
on Mediterranean species that grow in California, the Americas, the Mediterranean and
southern Africa.

On weekdays, catch the university's Bear
Transit H Line shuttle ($1) from campus.
Limited parking across the street from the
garden costs $1 per hour.

A nearby **fire trail** makes a woodsy walking loop around Strawberry Canyon, offering great views of town and the off-limits
Lawrence Berkeley National Laboratory.
Find the trailhead on the east side of Centennial Dr just southwest of the botanical
garden; you'll emerge near the Lawrence
Hall of Science.

Lawrence Hall of Science MUSEUM
(☏510-642-5132; www.lawrencehallofscience.org;
1 Centennial Dr; adult/child $12/10; ⊘10am-5pm
Wed-Sun, daily mid-Jun–early Sep; P⛽; 🚌AC
Transit 65) Near Grizzly Peak Blvd, this science hall is named after Ernest Lawrence,
who won the Nobel Prize for his invention

of the cyclotron particle accelerator. He was
a key member of the WWII Manhattan Project, and he's also the name behind the Lawrence Berkeley and Lawrence Livermore
national laboratories. The museum has
interactive but dated exhibits for kids and
adults (many closed weekdays) on subjects
ranging from earthquakes to nanotechnol-
ogy. Outside there's a 60ft model of a DNA
molecule.

From Downtown Berkeley BART station,
take AC Transit bus 65. From campus, catch
the university's Bear Transit H Line shuttle
($1). On-site parking costs $1 per hour.

⊙ West Berkeley

Adventure Playground PARK
(☏510-981-6720; www.cityofberkeley.info/adven
tureplayground; 160 University Ave; ⊘11am-5pm
mid-Jun–mid-Aug, Sat & Sun only rest of year; P⛽;
🚌AC Transit 81) 🆓 At the Berkeley Marina,
this is one of the coolest play spaces in the
Bay Area – a free outdoor park encouraging
creativity and cooperation where supervised
kids of any age can help build and paint
their own structures. There's an awesome
zipline too. Dress the tykes in play clothes,
because they *will* get dirty.

Berkeley Marina MARINA
(☏510-981-6740; www.ci.berkeley.ca.us; 201 University Ave; ⊘6am-10pm; P⛽🐾; 🚌AC Transit

81) At the west end of University Ave is the marina, frequented by squawking seagulls, silent types fishing from the pier and, especially on windy weekends, families flying colorful kites. It offers sweeping waterfront views from paved walking, cycling and running paths.

The marina was originally built in the late 19th century, then replaced by a ferry pier in the 1920s (its unusual length dictated by the bay's extreme shallowness).

Takara Sake　　　　　　　　　MUSEUM
(☑ 510-540-8250; www.takarasake.com; 708 Addison St; tasting fee $5-10; ☉ noon-6pm, last tasting 5:30pm; ☐ AC Transit 51B) Stop in to see the traditional wooden tools used for making sake and a short video of the brewing process. Tours of the factory aren't offered, but you can view elements of modern production and bottling through a window. Sake flights are poured in a spacious tasting room constructed with reclaimed wood and floor tiles fashioned from recycled glass.

🛏 Sleeping

Lodging rates spike during special university events such as graduation (mid-May) and home football games. A number of older, less expensive motels along University Ave can be handy during peak demand, as can chain motels and hotels off I-80 in Emeryville or Vallejo.

Graduate Berkeley　　　BOUTIQUE HOTEL $$
(Map p140; ☑ 510-845-8981; http://graduate berkeley.com; 2600 Durant Ave; r from $160; ⓟ➔❄@☎❄; ☐ AC Transit 51B) Located a block from campus, this classic 1928 hotel has been cheekily renovated to highlight the connection to the university. The lobby is adorned with embarrassing yearbook photos and a ceiling mobile of exam books, and smallish rooms have dictionary-covered shower curtains and bongs repurposed into bedside lamps. Parking is $20.

Berkeley City Club　　　HISTORIC HOTEL $$
(Map p140; ☑ 510-848-7800; www.berkeleycity club.com; 2315 Durant Ave; r/ste from $215; ⓟ➔@☎❄; ☐ AC Transit 51B) Designed by Julia Morgan (the architect of Hearst Castle), the 35 rooms and dazzling common areas of this refurbished 1929 historic landmark building (which is also a private club) feel like a glorious time warp into a more refined era. The hotel contains lush and serene Italianate courtyards, gardens and terraces and a stunning indoor pool. Parking is $20.

Elegant Old World rooms contain no TV, and those with numbers ending in 4 and 8 have to-die-for views of the bay and the Golden Gate Bridge.

Hotel Shattuck Plaza　　　　　HOTEL $$
(Map p140; ☑ 510-845-7300; www.hotelshattuck plaza.com; 2086 Allston Way; r from $200; ⓟ➔❄@☎; Ⓑ Downtown Berkeley) Following a $15-million renovation and greening of this 100-year-old downtown jewel, a foyer of red Italian glass lighting, flocked Victorian-style wallpaper – and yes, a peace sign tiled into the floor – leads to comfortable rooms with down comforters and an airy, columned restaurant serving all meals. Accommodations off Shattuck Ave are quietest, while cityscape rooms boast bay views.

Bancroft Hotel　　　　HISTORIC HOTEL $$
(Map p140; ☑ 510-549-1000; http://bancrofthotel. com; 2680 Bancroft Way; r $125-230; ⓟ➔@☎; ☐ AC Transit 51B) 🏠 A gorgeous 1928 arts-and-crafts building that was originally a women's club, the Bancroft is just across the street from campus and two blocks from Telegraph Ave (p139). It has 22 small, simply furnished rooms (some with lovely balconies) and a spectacular bay-view rooftop, though no elevator. Limited parking.

★ Claremont Resort & Spa　　　RESORT $$$
(☑ 510-843-3000; www.fairmont.com/claremont -berkeley; 41 Tunnel Rd; r from $240; ⓟ➔❄@☎❄❄) The East Bay's classy crème de la crème, this Fairmont-owned historic hotel is a glamorous white 1915 building with elegant restaurants, a fitness center, swimming pools, tennis courts and a full-service spa. The bay-view rooms are superb. It's located at the foot of the Berkeley Hills, off Hwy 13 (Tunnel Rd) near the Oakland border. Parking is $30.

🍴 Eating

Telegraph Ave is packed with cafes, pizza counters and cheap restaurants, and Berkeley's Little India runs along the University Ave corridor. Many more restaurants can be found along Shattuck Ave near the Downtown Berkeley BART station. The section of Shattuck Ave north of University Ave, nicknamed the 'Gourmet Ghetto,' is home to excellent restaurants and cafes for all budgets.

Downtown & Around Campus

KoJa Kitchen FUSION $

(Map p140; ☑510-962-5652; www.kojakitchen.com; 2395 Telegraph Ave; items $4-10; ☺11am-10pm; ☐AC Transit 51B) From food truck to a brick-and-mortar shop, this Korean-Japanese fusion eatery makes addictive short-rib and braised-pork sandwiches out of garlicky fried-rice buns, with kimchi-spiked waffle fries on the side. Order ahead, or expect a wait.

Smoke's Poutinerie FAST FOOD $

(Map p140; ☑510-540-7500; http://smokespoutinerie.com; 2518 Durant Ave; items $3-13; ☺11am-4am; ☐AC Transit 51B) Since California legalized recreational marijuana use, demand has only increased at this Canadian poutine shop, open till the wee hours. Get the classic Quebecois taste of cheese curds and gravy, or a wilder combination such as jerk chicken or veggie nacho.

Butcher's Son VEGAN, DELI $

(Map p140; ☑510-984-0818; www.thebutchersveganson.com; 1941 University Ave; mains $8-13; ☺11am-8pm Mon & Thu-Fri, to 3pm Tue & Wed, 9am-5pm Sat & Sun; ☑; ☐Downtown Berkeley) What could be more in tune with Berkeley's granola-crunchy, latter-day-hippie vibe than a vegan deli? Gorge yourself on imitation deli meats and cheeses that will scratch that itch for a fried mozzarella and meatball sandwich or hot turkey and roast beef on rye, all made without any animal products.

Cream ICE CREAM $

(Map p140; ☑510-649-1000; http://creamnation.com; 2399 Telegraph Ave; items $2-4; ☺noon-11pm Sun-Thu, to midnight Fri & Sat; ☑☐; ☐AC Transit 51B) With a line out the door, this corner shop smooshes together ice-cream sandwiches with creative flavors and freshly baked cookies. Otherwise, get an ice-cream sundae in a less exciting cup or cone.

North Berkeley Farmers Market MARKET $

(Map p140; ☑510-548-3333; www.ecologycenter.org; Shattuck Ave, at Rose St; ☺3-7pm Thu; ☑☐; ☐AC Transit 79) ☑ Pick up some organic produce or tasty prepared food at North Berkeley's weekly farmers market, operating year-round.

Ippuku JAPANESE $$

(Map p140; ☑510-665-1969; www.ippukuberkeley.com; 2130 Center St; shared plates $5-20; ☺5-10pm Tue-Thu, to 11pm Fri & Sat; ☐Downtown Berkeley) Japanese expats gush that Ippuku reminds them of *izakaya* (Japanese gastropubs) back in Tokyo. Choose from a menu of *yakitori* (skewered meats and vegetables) and handmade soba noodles as you settle in at one of the traditional tatami tables (no

---

WATERSPORTS ON THE BAY

As well as making for a lovely postcard or iconic snapshot, San Francisco Bay offers plenty of options for getting out on the water. Myriad outfitters provide equipment, lessons and guided tours.

California Canoe & Kayak (Map p130; ☑510-893-7833; www.calkayak.com; 409 Water St; kayak & SUP rentals per hour $25-50, tours from $50; ☺10am-6pm Mon-Fri, 9am-6pm Sat, 9am-5pm Sun; ☐Broadway Shuttle) Rents kayaks and stand up paddleboard (SUP) sets at Oakland's Jack London Sq. Book ahead for moonlight paddles along the waterfront.

Cal Adventures (☑510-642-4000, recorded info 510-642-7707; http://recsports.berkeley.edu/cal-adventures; 124 University Ave; rentals/classes from $20/45; ☺hours vary; ☐AC Transit 81) Run by the UC Aquatic Center at Berkeley Marina, it organizes sailing, windsurfing, SUP and sea-kayaking classes and rentals.

Cal Sailing Club (www.cal-sailing.org; 124 University Ave; 3-month membership $99; ☺noon-sunset Mon-Fri, from 9am Sat & Sun; ☐AC Transit 81) Membership-based, volunteer-run nonprofit that runs sailing and windsurfing programs at Berkeley Marina.

Boardsports California (☑415-385-1224; https://boardsportscalifornia.com; rentals/lessons from $25/49; ☺hours vary) Offers lessons and rentals for kiteboarding, windsurfing, SUP and kayaking, with locations at Alameda in the East Bay and Coyote Point Recreation Area in San Mateo, near San Francisco International Airport.

Sea Trek (p113) In Sausalito, this long-running outfitter has kayaks and SUP sets for rent and a fabulous array of tours, including bay crossings to Angel Island.

shoes, please) or cozy booth perches. Order *shōchū*, a distilled alcohol usually made from rice or barley. Reservations essential.

La Note
FRENCH $$

(Map p140; ☑ 510-843-1525; www.lanoterestaurant. com; 2377 Shattuck Ave; mains $10-25; ☺ breakfast & lunch 8am-2:30pm Mon-Fri, to 3pm Sat & Sun, dinner 6-10pm Thu-Sat; ⓑ Downtown Berkeley) A rustic country-French bistro downtown, La Note serves excellent breakfasts. Wake up to a big bowl of café au lait, paired with brioche *pain perdu* or lemon-gingerbread pancakes with poached pears. Anticipate a wait on weekends.

Gather
CALIFORNIAN $$

(Map p140; ☑ 510-809-0400; www.gatherrestaurant.com; 2200 Oxford St; dinner mains $16-30; ☺ 11:30am-2pm & 5-9pm Mon-Thu, 11:30-2pm & 5-10pm Fri, 10am-2pm & 5-10pm Sat, 10am-2pm & 5-9pm Sun; ☑; ⓑ Downtown Berkeley) ◢ When vegan foodies and passionate farm-to-table types dine out together, they often end up here. Inside a salvaged-wood interior punctuated by green vines streaking down over an open kitchen, dishes are created from locally sourced ingredients and sustainably raised meats. Reservations recommended.

✕ North Berkeley

Cheese Board Collective
PIZZA $

(Map p140; ☑ 510-549-3055; www.cheeseboardcollective.coop; 1504 & 1512 Shattuck Ave; slices/half-pizzas $2.75/11; ☺ shop 7am-1pm Mon, to 6pm Tue-Fri, to 5pm Sat, pizzeria 11:30am-3pm & 4:30-8pm Tue-Sat; ☑⊞; ⬚ AC Transit 7) Stop in to take stock of more than 300 cheeses available at this worker-owned business and scoop up some fresh bread to make a picnic lunch. Or sit down for a slice of the crispy veggie pizza just next door, where live music's often featured.

★ Chez Panisse
CALIFORNIAN $$$

(Map p140; ☑ cafe 510-548-5049, restaurant 510-548-5525; www.chezpanisse.com; 1517 Shattuck Ave; cafe dinner mains $22-35, restaurant prixfixe dinner $75-125; ☺ cafe 11:30am-2:45pm & 5-10:30pm Mon-Thu, 11:30am-3pm & 5-11:30pm Fri & Sat, restaurant seatings 5:30pm & 8pm Mon-Sat; ☑; ⬚ AC Transit 7) ◢ Foodies come to worship here at the church of Alice Waters, inventor of California cuisine. It's in a lovely arts-and-crafts house in Berkeley's 'Gourmet Ghetto,' and you can choose to pull out all the stops with a prix-fixe meal downstairs, or go less expensive and a tad less formal in the upstairs cafe. Reservations accepted one month ahead. The restaurant is as good and popular as it ever was, and despite its fame, the place has retained a welcoming atmosphere.

✕ West Berkeley

Vik's Chaat Corner
INDIAN $

(☑ 510-644-4412; www.vikschaatcorner.com; 2390 4th St; mains $6-12; ☺ 11am-6pm Mon-Thu, to 8pm Fri-Sun; ☑⊞; ⬚ AC Transit 80) Off in West Berkeley, this longtime, popular *chaat* house gets mobbed at lunchtime by regulars that include equal numbers of hungry office workers, students and Indian families. Order samosas or a puffy *bhature* (flatbread) with *chole* (chickpea curry), an *uttapam* (savory pancake) or one of many filling *dosas* (savory crepes). Colorful Indian sweets, sold by the piece or pound, are irresistible.

Bette's Oceanview Diner
AMERICAN $$

(☑ 510-644-3230; www.bettesdiner.com; 1807 4th St; mains $7-16; ☺ 6:30am-2:30pm Mon-Fri, to 4pm Sat & Sun; ⊞; ⬚ AC Transit 51B) ◢ This is a buzzing breakfast spot, especially on the weekends. It dishes up baked soufflé pancakes and German-style potato pancakes with applesauce, plus eggs and sandwiches. From-scratch baked goods and a nifty diner interior make it worth the wait.

⚱ Drinking & Nightlife

You'll never come up short of places to imbibe in Berkeley. Join students at bars and pubs scattered around downtown, on side streets near the university campus or along College Ave in Elmwood. Detour to industrial areas of West Berkeley to discover craft beers and a sake distillery (p142).

Fieldwork Brewing Company
BREWERY

(☑ 510-898-1203; http://fieldworkbrewing.com; 1160 6th St; ☺ 11am-10pm Sun-Thu, to 11pm Fri & Sat; ⬚ AC Transit 12) Come to this industrial brewery taproom at the edge of town for outstanding craft beer and sit down on the outdoor patio with a tasting flight of IPAs or a glass of rich Mexican hot chocolate stout. It's dog-friendly, and there are racks to hang your bicycle inside the front door. There's a short menu of Mexican-Californian food too.

Asha Tea House
CAFE

(Map p140; www.ashateahouse.com; 2086 University Ave; ☺ 11am-10pm Mon-Sat, to 8pm Sun; ☎; ⓑ Downtown Berkeley) ◢ Find your bliss in this industrial-modern tea shop, where acrylic prints of verdant tea plantations overhang the bar. Handcrafted Indian chai, Japanese matcha and Hong Kong–style milk tea star on a connoisseur's drinks menu.

Torpedo Room
BAR

(☑ 510-647-3439; www.sierranevada.com/brewery /california/torpedoroom; 2031 4th St; ⊘ noon-9pm Tue-Fri, from 11am Sat, noon-7pm Sun; ☐ AC Transit 51B) Sample a flight of tasting pours or order a pint from the 16 rotating drafts (including some rare small-batch beers) on tap at Sierra Nevada brewery's tasting room in West Berkeley.

Albatross
PUB

(☑ 510-843-2473; www.albatrosspub.com; 1822 San Pablo Ave; ⊘ 6pm-2am Sun-Tue, from 4:30pm Wed-Sat; ☐ AC Transit 51B) Berkeley's oldest pub is one of the most inviting and friendly in the city. Some serious darts are played here and board games get played around many of the worn-out tables. Sunday is trivia quiz night.

Jupiter
PUB

(Map p140; ☑ 510-843-8277; www.jupiterbeer.com; 2181 Shattuck Ave; ⊘ 11:30am-12:30am Mon-Thu, to 1:30am Fri, noon-1:30am Sat, noon-11:30pm Sun; Ⓑ Downtown Berkeley) This downtown pub has loads of regional microbrews, a beer garden, decent pizza and live bands most nights. Sit upstairs for a bird's-eye view of bustling Shattuck Ave.

Caffe Strada
CAFE

(Map p140; ☑ 510-843-5282; 2300 College Ave; ⊘ 6am-midnight; 🛜; ☐ AC Transit 51B) At this popular, student-saturated hangout with an inviting shaded patio, try the strong espressos or a sweet white-chocolate mocha.

☆ Entertainment

Berkeley's arts district, centered on Addison St between Milvia St and Shattuck Ave, anchors downtown's performing-arts scene.

Berkeley also has plenty of intimate live-music venues. Cover charges usually range from $5 to $20, and several venues are all-ages or 18-and-over.

Freight & Salvage Coffeehouse
LIVE MUSIC

(Map p140; ☑ 510-644-2020; www.thefreight.org; 2020 Addison St; tickets $5-45; ⊘ shows daily; 🛗) Ⓑ Downtown Berkeley) This legendary club has almost 50 years of history and is conveniently located in the downtown arts district. It features great traditional folk, country, bluegrass and world music and welcomes all ages, with half-price tickets for patrons under 21.

924 Gilman
LIVE MUSIC

(☑ 510-524-8180; www.924gilman.org; 924 Gilman St; tickets from $10; ⊘ Sat & Sun; ☐ AC Transit 12) This volunteer-run and booze-free all-ages space is a West Coast punk-rock institution. Check the online calendar for upcoming shows on weekend nights.

Ashkenaz
WORLD MUSIC, DANCE

(☑ 510-525-5054; www.ashkenaz.com; 1317 San Pablo Ave; free-$20; ⊘ hours vary; 🛗; ☐ AC Transit 52) Ashkenaz is a 'music and dance community center' attracting activists, hippies and fans of folk, swing, world music and more who love to dance (lessons offered).

La Peña Cultural Center
WORLD MUSIC

(☑ 510-849-2568; www.lapena.org; 3105 Shattuck Ave; free-$16; ⊘ hours vary; Ⓑ Ashby) This fun-loving, warmhearted community center presents dynamic dance classes and musical and visual arts events with a peace and justice bent. Look for a vibrant mural outside and the on-site Mexican cafe, perfect for grabbing drinks and a preshow bite.

Berkeley Repertory Theatre
THEATER

(Map p140; ☑ 510-647-2949; www.berkeleyrep. org; 2025 Addison St; tickets $40-100; ⊘ box office noon-7pm Tue-Sun; Ⓑ Downtown Berkeley) This highly respected company has produced bold versions of classical and modern plays since 1968. Most shows have half-price tickets for patrons under 30.

California Shakespeare Theater
THEATER

(☑ 510-548-9666; www.calshakes.org; 701 Heinz Ave; tickets $21-56; ⊘ late May-early Oct) Headquartered in Berkeley, with the fantastic outdoor Bruns Amphitheater east of the Berkeley Hills in Orinda, 'Cal Shakes' is a warm-weather tradition of alfresco Shakespeare and other classic productions.

Zellerbach Hall
PERFORMING ARTS

(Map p140; ☑ 510-642-9988; https://calperfor mances.org; off Bancroft Way; tickets from $10; ⊘ ticket office usually noon-5:30pm Tue-Fri, 1-5pm Sat & Sun; ☐ AC Transit 51B) At the south end of campus near Bancroft Way and Dana St, Zellerbach Hall features dance events, musical concerts and performances of all types by national and international touring artists. The on-site Cal Performances Ticket Office sells tickets.

Shotgun Players
THEATER

(☑ 510-841-6500; www.shotgunplayers.org; 1901 Ashby Ave; tickets $20-50; ⊘ hours vary; Ⓑ Downtown Berkeley) 🌱 Berkeley's solar-powered

WORTH A TRIP

EAST BROTHER LIGHT STATION

Most Bay Area residents have never heard of this speck of an island off the East Bay city of Richmond, and even fewer know that the **East Brother Light Station** (☑ 510-233-2385; www. ebls.org; 1900 Stenmark Dr, Richmond; d incl breakfast & dinner $295-415; ☺ Thu-Sun; ☻) is a five-room Victorian B&B. Spend the night in the romantic lighthouse or fog-signal building (the foghorn blares from October 1 to April 1). Access is by boat; reserve ahead.

Resident innkeepers serve afternoon hors d'oeuvres and champagne, and after dinner you can stroll around the breezy 0.75-acre islet and rummage through historical photos and artifacts.

theater company stages exciting and provocative works in an intimate space.

Aurora Theatre Company THEATER
(Map p140; ☑ 510-843-4822; www.auroratheatre. org; 2081 Addison St; tickets from $25; ☺ box office usually 1-4pm Tue-Fri; B Downtown Berkeley) Intimate downtown theater performs contemporary, thought-provoking plays staged with subtle aesthetics.

Pacific Film Archive CINEMA
(PFA; Map p140; ☑ 510-642-5249; www.bampfa. berkeley.edu; 2155 Center St; adult/child from $12/8; ☺ hours vary; ☷ ; B Downtown Berkeley) A world-renowned film center with an ever-changing schedule of international and classic films – cineastes should seek out this place. The spacious theater has seats comfy enough for hours-long movie marathons. Movie tickets include same-day admission to the UC Berkeley Art Museum (p138).

🔒 Shopping

Heading south of the university campus, Telegraph Ave caters mostly to students, hawking a steady dose of urban hippie gear, handmade sidewalk-vendor jewelry and head-shop paraphernalia. Audiophiles will swoon over the music stores.

Berkeley's other shopping corridors include College Ave in the Elmwood District (on the Oakland border), 4th St (north of University Ave) and Solano Ave (heading into Albany).

Amoeba Music MUSIC
(Map p140; ☑ 510-549-1125; www.amoeba.com; 2455 Telegraph Ave; ☺ 11am-8pm Sun-Thu, to 10pm Fri & Sat; ☷ AC Transit 51B) If you're a music junkie, you might plan on spending a few hours at the original Berkeley branch of Amoeba Music, packed with massive quantities of new and used CDs, DVDs, tapes and records (yes, lots of vinyl).

Down Home Music MUSIC
(☑ 510-525-2129; www.downhomemusic.com; 10341 San Pablo Ave, El Cerrito; ☺ 11am-7pm Tue-Sun; ☷ AC Transit 72) North of Berkeley, this world-class store for roots, blues, folk, country, jazz and world music is affiliated with the Arhoolie record label, which has been issuing landmark recordings since the early 1960s.

University Press Books BOOKS
(Map p140; ☑ 510-548-0585; www.universitypress books.com; 2430 Bancroft Way; ☺ 11am-7pm Mon-Fri, to 6pm Sat, noon-5pm Sun; ☷ AC Transit 51B) Across the street from campus, this academic and scholarly bookstore stocks works by UC Berkeley professors and other academic and museum publishers, with frequent author appearances.

REI SPORTS & OUTDOORS
(☑ 510-527-4140; www.rei.com; 1338 San Pablo Ave; ☺ 10am-9pm Mon-Fri, to 8pm Sat, to 7pm Sun; ☷ ; ☷ AC Transit 52) This large and busy co-op lures in active folks for camping and mountaineering rentals, sports clothing and all kinds of nifty outdoor gear.

North Face Outlet SPORTS & OUTDOORS
(☑ 510-526-3530; www.thenorthface.com; 1238 5th St; ☺ 10am-7pm Mon-Sat, 11am-5pm Sun; ☷ AC Transit 12) Discount store for the Bay Area–based brand of outdoor gear is just off Gilman St.

Fourth Street HOMEWARES, FASHION
(☑ 510-644-3002; www.fourthstreet.com; ☺ store hours vary; ☷ AC Transit 51B) Hidden within an industrial section near I-80, this three-block area offers shaded sidewalks for upscale shopping or just strolling, and a few good restaurants.

Moe's Books BOOKS
(Map p140; ☑ 510-849-2087; www.moesbooks. com; 2476 Telegraph Ave; ☺ 10am-10pm; ☷ AC Transit 51B) A long-standing local favorite, Moe's offers four floors of new, used and remaindered books for hours of browsing.

ℹ Information

MEDICAL SERVICES

Alta Bates Summit Medical Center, Ashby Campus (☑ 510-204-4444; www.sutterhealth. org; 2450 Ashby Ave; ⊗ 24hr; 🚊 AC Transit 6) offers 24-hour emergency services.

TOURIST INFORMATION

UC Berkeley Koret Visitor Center (Map p140; ☑ 510-642-5215; http://visit.berkeley. edu; 2227 Piedmont Ave; ⊗ 8:30am-4:30pm Mon-Fri, 9am-1pm Sat & Sun; 🚊 AC Transit 36) Campus maps anad information available at the new visitor center on Goldman Plaza at California Memorial Stadium (Map p140; ☑ 510-642-2730; www.californiamemorialstadium.com; 2227 Piedmont Ave; ⊗ hours vary; 🚹; 🚊 AC Transit 52). Free 90-minute campus walking tours usually start at 10am daily (advance reservations required).

Visit Berkeley (Map p140; ☑ 510-549-7040; www.visitberkeley.com; 2030 Addison St; ⊗ 9am-1pm & 2-5pm Mon Fri; 🅱 Downtown Berkeley) The helpful Berkeley Convention & Visitors Bureau prints a free visitors guide, also available online.

ℹ Getting There & Away

BART

To get to Berkeley, catch a Richmond-bound train to one of three BART (p137) stations: Ashby, Downtown Berkeley or North Berkeley. Fares between Berkeley and San Francisco cost $4.10 to $4.40, between Berkeley and downtown Oakland $1.95. After 8pm on weekdays, 6pm on Saturday and all day Sunday, there is no direct train service operating from San Francisco to Berkeley; instead, catch a Pittsburg/Bay Point train, then transfer at 19th St station in Oakland.

BUS

On AC Transit (p137), the F line leaves from the Transbay Transit Center in San Francisco for downtown Berkeley and the university campus approximately every half-hour ($4.20, 40 minutes). The Transbay bus fare is discounted to $2.10 if you also purchase a day pass ($5) valid on AC Transit's local East Bay bus routes.

Between downtown Berkeley and downtown Oakland, take fast and frequent AC Transit bus 6 along Telegraph Ave. Alternatively, take bus 18 via Martin Luther King Jr Way and Shattuck Ave. Bus 51B travels along University Ave past Downtown Berkeley BART station to the Berkeley Marina. All one-way local bus fares on AC Transit are $2.10.

CAR & MOTORCYCLE

From San Francisco, drive over the Bay Bridge and then follow either I-80 (for University Ave, Berkeley Marina, downtown Berkeley and the university campus) or Hwy 24 (for College Ave and the Berkeley Hills).

TRAIN

Amtrak does stop in Berkeley, but the platform is not staffed and direct connections are few. More convenient is Emeryville Amtrak station (p137), about 2 miles south.

To reach the Emeryville station from downtown Berkeley, take AC Transit bus F ($4.20) or ride BART to the MacArthur station ($1.95, five minutes) and then catch the free Emery Go Round (p137) shuttle bus.

ℹ Getting Around

Local buses, cycling and walking are the best ways to get around Berkeley.

BICYCLE

By Downtown Berkeley BART station, **Bike Station** (☑ 510-548-7433; http://bikehub.com/ bartbikestation; 2208 Shattuck Ave; per day/ week/month $35/95/200; ⊗ 7am-9pm Mon-Fri, 11am-7pm Sat) rents bicycles with a helmet and U-lock.

BUS

AC Transit (p137) operates local public buses in and around Berkeley. The one-way fare is $2.10; pay with cash (exact change required) or a Clipper card (www.clippercard.com).

The university's **Bear Transit** (☑ 510-643-7701; http://pt.berkeley.edu) runs a shuttle from Downtown Berkeley BART station to various points on campus. From Bear Transit's on-campus stop at Hearst Mining Circle, the H Line runs along Centennial Dr to the upper parts of the campus. For visitors, each ride costs $1 (bring cash).

CAR & MOTORCYCLE

Drivers should note that numerous barriers have been set up to prevent car traffic from traversing residential streets at high speeds, so zigzagging is necessary in some neighborhoods.

Downtown and near the university campus, pay-parking lots are well signed. Metered street-parking spots are rarely empty.

Mt Diablo State Park

Collecting a light dusting of snowflakes on the coldest days of winter, Mt Diablo (3849ft) is over 1200ft higher than Mt Tamalpais in Marin County. On a clear day (early on a winter morning is a good bet) the views from Diablo's summit are vast and sweeping. To the west you can see over the bay and out to the Farallon Islands; to the east you can look out over the Central Valley to the Sierra Nevada.

Most easily accessed from Danville or Walnut Creek, the **park** (☎ 925-837-2525; www.mdia.org; per vehicle $6-10; ⊙ 8am-sunset) is threaded by over 50 miles of hiking trails. You can also drive to the summit, where there's a visitor center.

🛏 Sleeping

**Mt Diablo State Park
Campgrounds**   CAMPGROUND $
(☎ reservations 800-444-7275; www.reserveameri ca.com; tent & RV sites $30) Of the park's three drive-in campgrounds, Juniper and Live Oak have showers. All campgrounds may be closed during high fire danger and water may be turned off throughout the park if water restrictions are in effect.

❶ Information

Summit Visitor Center (www.parks.ca.gov; ⊙ 10am-4pm) Mt Diablo State Park's small main visitor center.

John Muir National Historic Site

Naturalist John Muir's **former residence** (☎ 925-228-8860; www.nps.gov/jomu; 4202 Alhambra Ave, Martinez; ⊙ Muir Home 10am-5pm, Mt Wanda sunrise-sunset) **FREE** sits in a pastoral patch of farmland in bustling, modern Martinez. Though Muir wrote of sauntering the Sierra Nevada with a sack of tea and bread, it may be a shock for those familiar with the iconic Sierra Club founder's ascetic weather-beaten appearance that this house (built by his father-in-law) is a model of Victorian Italianate refinement, with a tower cupola, a daintily upholstered parlor and splashes of white lace.

Muir's 'scribble den' has been left as it was during his life, with crumbled papers overflowing from wire wastebaskets and dried-bread balls – his preferred snack – resting on the mantelpiece.

Acres of the family's fruit orchards still stand, and visitors can enjoy seasonal samples. The grounds include the 1849 Martinez Adobe, part of the ranch on which the house was built, and oak-speckled hiking trails on nearby Mt Wanda, named for one of Muir's daughters. Check the website for special campfire programs, wildflower walks and full-moon hikes. The park is just north of

Hwy 4. **County Connection** (☎ 925-676-7500; https://countyconnection.com) buses 16 and 98X from nearby Amtrak and BART stations stop here.

THE PENINSULA

South of San Francisco, squeezed tightly between the bay and the coastal foothills, a vast swath of suburbia continues toward San Jose. Dotted inside this area are Palo Alto, home of Stanford University, and Silicon Valley, the epicenter of the Bay Area's tech industry.

Don't bother looking for Silicon Valley on the map – you won't find it. Because silicon chips form the basis of modern microcomputers, and the Santa Clara Valley – stretching from Palo Alto through Mountain View, Sunnyvale and Cupertino to San Jose – is thought of as the birthplace of the microcomputer, it's nicknamed 'Silicon Valley.' It's hard to imagine that even after WWII this was still a wide expanse of orchards and farms.

Further west, the 70-mile stretch of coastal Hwy 1 from San Francisco to Santa Cruz is one of California's most bewitching oceanside drives. For the most part, it's winding, two-lane blacktop, passing beach after beach.

San Francisco to San Jose

South of the San Francisco peninsula, I-280 is the dividing line between the densely populated South Bay area and the rugged and lightly populated Pacific Coast. With sweeping views of hills and reservoirs, I-280 is a more scenic choice than Hwy 101, which runs through business parks. Unfortunately, these parallel north–south arteries are often both clogged with traffic.

A historic site where European explorers first set eyes on San Francisco Bay, **Sweeney Ridge** (www.nps.gov/goga/sweeney.htm; end of Sneath Lane, San Bruno) straddles a prime spot between Pacifica and San Bruno, and offers hikers unparalleled ocean and bay views. From I-280, exit at Sneath Lane and follow it 2 miles west until it dead ends at the trailhead.

Right on the bay at the northern edge of San Mateo, 4 miles south of San Francisco International Airport, is **Coyote Point Recreation Area** (☎ 650-573-2592; http://parks. smcgov.org; 1701 Coyote Point Dr, San Mateo; per car $6; ⊙ 8am-8pm Apr-Aug, to 6pm or 7pm Sep-Mar;

P 🚻), a popular park and windsurfing destination. The main attraction – formerly known as the Coyote Point Museum – is **CuriOdyssey** (🖉 650-342-7755; http://curiodyssey.org; adult/child $11/8; ⊙ 10am-5pm Tue-Sun; P 🚻), with innovative exhibits highlighting science and wildlife. Exit Hwy 101 at Coyote Point Dr.

Stanford University

Sprawled over 8200 leafy acres in Palo Alto, Stanford University (www.stanford.edu) was founded by Leland Stanford, one of the Central Pacific Railroad's 'Big Four' founders and a former governor of California. When the Stanfords' only child died of typhoid during a European tour in 1884, they decided to build a university in his memory. The campus was built on the site of the Stanfords' horse-breeding farm and, as a result, Stanford is still known as 'The Farm.'

⊙ Sights

Main Quad   PLAZA
(🖉 650-723-2560; http://visit.stanford.edu/plan/guides/visit.html; off Palm Dr) Auguste Rodin's *Burghers of Calais* bronze sculpture marks the entrance to Stanford University's Main Quad, an open plaza where the original 12 campus buildings, a mix of Romanesque and Mission Revival styles, were joined by Memorial Church in 1903. The church is noted for its beautiful mosaic-tiled frontage, stained-glass windows and five organs with more than 8000 pipes. Free guided tours of 'MemChu' are given at 2pm every Friday and 11:15am on the first Sunday of the month.

Hoover Tower   TOWER
(🖉 650-723-2560; http://visit.stanford.edu/plan/guides/hoover.html; adult/child $4/3; ⊙ 10am-4pm, last entry 3:30pm) A campus landmark at the east of the Main Quad, the 285ft-high Hoover Tower offers superb views. The tower houses a university library, offices and part of the right-wing Hoover Institution on War, Revolution & Peace (where Donald Rumsfeld caused a university-wide stir by accepting a position after he resigned as Secretary of Defense).

Cantor Arts Center   MUSEUM
(🖉 650-498-1480; http://museum.stanford.edu; 328 Lomita Dr; ⊙ 11am-5pm Wed & Fri-Mon, to 8pm Thu; P) FREE The Cantor Center for Visual Arts is a large museum originally dating from 1894. Its collection spans works from ancient civilizations to contemporary art, sculpture and photography, and rotating exhibits are eclectic in scope. Step outside into the Rodin and Papua New Guinea sculpture gardens.

ℹ️ Information

Stanford Visitor Center (🖉 650-723-2560; http://visit.stanford.edu; 295 Galvez St; ⊙ 8:30am-5pm Mon-Fri, 10am-5pm Sat & Sun) Offers free 70-minute walking tours of the campus at 11am and 3:15pm daily, except during academic breaks and some holidays. Special-interest tours also available.

MARIN COUNTY & THE BAY AREA SAN FRANCISCO TO SAN JOSE

NERD'S NIRVANA

Touted as the largest computer-history exhibition in the world, the **Computer History Museum** (🖉 650-810-1010; www.computerhistory.org; 1401 N Shoreline Blvd, Mountain View; adult $17.50, student & senior $13.50; ⊙ 10am-5pm Wed-Sun, to 8pm Fri; P) has rotating exhibits drawn from its 100,000-item collection. Artifacts range from the abacus to the iPod, including Cray-1 supercomputers, a Babbage Difference Engine (a Victorian-era automatic computing engine) and the first Google server.

Though there are no tours of the **Googleplex** (🖉 650-214-3308; www.google.com/about/company/facts/locations; 1600 Amphitheatre Pkwy, Mountain View; ⊙ store 10am-6:30pm Mon-Fri; P), visitors can stroll the campus and gawk at the public art on the leafy grounds, where scads of Googlers zoom about on primary-colored bicycles. Don't miss the 'dessert yard' outside Building 44, with lawn sculptures of Android operating systems (a cupcake! a donut! a robot!), and across the street, a toothy Tyrannosaurus rex festooned in pink flamingos next to the volleyball court.

At the Intel headquarters, the **Intel Museum** (🖉 408-765-5050; www.intel.com/museum; 2200 Mission College Blvd, Santa Clara; ⊙ usually 9am-6pm Mon-Fri, 10am-5pm Sat; P) FREE has displays on the birth and growth of the computer industry with special emphasis, not surprisingly, on microchips and Intel's involvement. Reserve ahead if you want to schedule a tour.

ℹ Getting There & Away

Stanford University's free public shuttle, **Marguerite** (📞650-723-9362; http://transportation. stanford.edu/marguerite), provides service from Caltrain's Palo Alto and California Ave stations to the campus, and has bicycle racks. Parking on campus is expensive and trying.

San Jose

Though culturally diverse and historic, San Jose has always been in San Francisco's shadow, awash in Silicon Valley's suburbia. Founded in 1777 as El Pueblo de San José de Guadalupe, San Jose is California's oldest Spanish civilian settlement. Its downtown is small and scarcely used for a city of its size, though it does bustle with 20-something clubgoers on weekends. Industrial parks, high-tech computer firms and look-alike housing developments have sprawled across the city's landscape, taking over where farms, ranches and open spaces once spread between the bay and the surrounding hills.

◉ Sights

History Park   HISTORIC BUILDING
(📞408-287-2290; http://historysanjose.org; 1650 Senter Rd; ◷noon-5pm Mon-Fri, 11am-5pm Sat & Sun, last entry 4:30pm; 🅿♿) FREE Historic buildings from all over San Jose have been brought together in this open-air history museum, southeast of the city center in Kelley Park. The centerpiece is a scaled-down replica of the 1881 **Electric Light Tower**. Other buildings include the 1880 **Pacific Hotel**, which has rotating art exhibits inside (closed Monday). The **Trolley Barn** restores historic trolley cars to operate on San Jose's light-rail line; on weekends you can ride a trolley along the park's own short line.

Tech Museum of Innovation   MUSEUM
(The Tech; 📞408-294-8324; www.thetech.org; 201 S Market St; adult/child $24/19, incl IMAX movie $29/23; ◷10am-5pm; ♿) Opposite Plaza de Cesar Chavez, San Jose's excellent technology museum examines subjects from robotics to space exploration, and genetics to virtual reality. The museum also includes an IMAX dome theater, which screens newly released films throughout the day.

MACLA   GALLERY
(Movimiento de Arte y Cultura Latino Americana; 📞408-998-2783; http://maclaarte.org; 510 S 1st St; ◷noon-7pm Wed & Thu, to 5pm Fri & Sat) FREE A cutting-edge gallery highlighting themes by both established and emerging Latino artists, MACLA is one of the Bay Area's best community arts spaces, with open-mike performances, live-music shows, experimental theater and well-curated, thought-provoking visual-arts exhibits.

Rosicrucian Egyptian Museum   MUSEUM
(📞408-947-3635; www.egyptianmuseum.org; 1660 Park Ave; adult/child $9/5; ◷9am-5pm Wed-Fri, 10am-6pm Sat & Sun; 🅿) West of downtown, this unusual and educational Egyptian museum is one of San Jose's more unusual attractions. Its extensive collection includes statues, household items and mummies; there's even a two-room, walk-through reproduction of an ancient subterranean tomb.

San Jose Museum of Art   MUSEUM
(📞408-271-6840; http://sjmusart.org; 110 S Market St; adult/child $10/5; ◷11am-5pm Tue-Sun) With a permanent collection of 20th-century works and imaginative changing exhibits, the city's central art museum is worth a quick look. The main building started life as the post office in 1892, was damaged by the 1906 earthquake and became an art gallery in 1933. A modern wing was added in 1991.

🛏 Sleeping

Budget and midrange motels and hotels cluster near freeways, especially Hwy 101 from south of San Francisco International Airport to San Jose. Upmarket hotels and motels and atmospheric lodges and inns cluster off Hwy 1 near the beaches, especially around Half Moon Bay. Off Hwy 1 is also where you'll find charming lighthouse hostels, campgrounds and cabins.

Hotel De Anza   HISTORIC HOTEL $$
(📞408-286-1000; www.destinationhotels.com/hotel-de-anza; 233 W Santa Clara St; r from $149; ☺❄@🛜🏊) Opened during the Jazz Age, this downtown hotel is a restored art-deco beauty that pays homage to the property's history. Guest rooms offer plush comforts (those facing south are a tad larger) and there's full concierge service. Complimentary midnight snacks, in-room espresso makers and a 24-hour fitness center seal the deal.

Hotel Valencia   BOUTIQUE HOTEL $$
(📞408-551-0010; www.hotelvalencia-santanarow. com; 355 Santana Row; r from $189; 🅿☺❄@🛜🏊)

WINCHESTER MYSTERY HOUSE

An odd structure purposefully commissioned to be so by the heir to the Winchester rifle fortune, this ridiculous Victorian **mansion** (☑ 408-247-2101; www.winchestermysteryhouse. com; 525 S Winchester Blvd; adult/child $36/26; ⊙ 9am-7pm, to 5pm early Sep-late May; Ⓟ) is filled with 160 rooms of various sizes and little utility, with dead-end hallways and a staircase that runs up to a ceiling all jammed together like a toddler playing architect. The standard hour-long guided mansion tour includes a self-guided romp through the gardens plus entry to an exhibition of guns and rifles.

Apparently, Sarah Winchester spent 38 years constructing this mammoth white elephant because the spirits of the people killed by Winchester rifles told her to. No expense was spared in the construction, the extreme results of which sprawl over 4 acres.

The house is west of central San Jose and just north of I-280, incongruously across the street from **Santana Row**, a shopping center.

A burbling lobby fountain and deep-red corridor carpeting set the tone for this tranquil 212-room contemporary hotel in the **Santana Row** (☑ 408-551-4611; www.santanarow.com; 377 Santana Row; ⊙ 10am-9pm Mon-Sat, 11am-7pm Sun; ⊛) shopping complex. In-room minibars and bathrobes and an outdoor pool and hot tub create a stylish oasis of contemporary design. Parking is $24.

Westin San Jose   HISTORIC HOTEL $$
(☑ 408-295-2000; www.westinsanjose.com; 302 S Market St; r from $149; Ⓟ ⊖ ❋ @ ⊗ ❖) Formerly the Sainte Claire, this atmospheric 1926 landmark hotel overlooking Plaza de Cesar Chavez has a gorgeous lobby with stretched-leather ceilings. Guest rooms are smallish, but have been remodeled. Parking is $39.

✖ Eating

San Jose is no culinary hub, but you'll find plenty of thronged restaurants downtown. Budget-friendly cafes are further east near the SJSU campus. For a more memorable meal, visit San Jose's historic Japantown, spread out along Jackson St east of 1st St, north of downtown.

Hukilau   FUSION $
(☑ 408-279-4888; www.dahukilau.com/sanjose; 230 Jackson St; mains $10-18; ⊙ 11am-2pm & 5-9pm Mon-Thu & Sun, 11am-2pm & 5-10pm Fri, 11am-2.30pm & 5-10pm Sat; ⊛) Incongruously located in San Jose's tiny Japantown, this fun Hawaii-themed bar puts together incredibly filling island-style plate meals (sesame chicken is da best) and *pupus* (snacks or appetizers) such as Spam *musubi* (block of rice with a slice of fried Spam on top, wrapped with a strip of nori) and bowls of *ahi poke* (raw-fish salad). Live Hawaiian music some weekend evenings.

San Pedro Square Market   FOOD HALL $
(www.sanpedrosquaremarket.com; 87 N San Pedro St; most mains $6-20; ⊙ usually 7am to 10pm-1am; ⊛ ⊛) Always busy, this indoor/outdoor marketplace downtown showcases a few shining local food stars such as Bray Butcher Block and Bistro, Pizza Bocca Lupo, Konjoe Burger Bar and Treatbot ice cream. All seating is first-come, first-served. Live music every Friday and Saturday evening and Sunday afternoon. Some vendors validate parking in the adjacent garage.

Tofoo Com Chay   VEGETARIAN, VIETNAMESE $
(☑ 408-286-6335; 388 E Santa Clara St; mains from $6.50; ⊙ 9am-9pm Mon-Fri, 10am-6pm Sat; ⊛) Conveniently located on the border of the San Jose State University campus. Students and vegetarians queue for the Vietnamese dishes such as the fake-meat pho and the heaped combo plates.

Back A Yard   CARIBBEAN $$
(☑ 408-294-8626; www.backayard.net/sanjose; 80 N Market St; mains $8-16; ⊙ 11am-2:30pm & 4:30-8:30pm Mon-Thu, 11am-9pm Fri, from noon Sat) Jamaican-jerk chicken, pork, salmon and tofu are the house specialties of this Caribbean-barbecue kitchen, which also fries catfish, snapper and shrimp, all hot and spicy. Look for beef oxtail and curried goat on the daily specials menu, and tropically colored murals on the red-brick walls.

Original Joe's   ITALIAN $$
(☑ 408-292-7030; www.originaljoes.com; 301 S 1st St; mains $10-33; ⊙ 11am-midnight) Waiters in bow ties flit about this busy 1950s San Jose landmark, serving standard Italian dishes to locals and conventioneers. The dining room is a curious but tasteful hodgepodge of '50s

brick, contemporary wood paneling and tall Asian vases. Expect a wait.

Arcadia
STEAK, SEAFOOD $$$

(☑ 408-278-4555; www.michaelmina.net/restaurants; 100 W San Carlos St; mains lunch $15-23, dinner $34-64; ⏱ 6:30am-2pm daily, 5:30-10pm Mon-Sat) This New American steakhouse restaurant in the Marriott Hotel is run by chef Michael Mina, one of San Francisco's celebrity chefs. It's not the daring, cutting-edge style Mina is known for, but it's slick, expensive and reasonably good.

Drinking & Nightlife

Original Gravity Public House
CRAFT BEER

(☑ 408-915-2337; www.originalgravitypub.com; 66 S 1st St; ⏱ 11:30am-10:30pm Sun-Wed, to midnight Thu-Sat) Squeeze inside this crowded yet friendly pub for beer geeks and the 'craft curious.' With nearly three dozen rotating taps of brews, including ciders and meads, as well as scores of bottles, you'll be confounded by choice. Consider your options while you nosh on housemade sausage, a grilled cheese sandwich or duck-fat poutine.

Paper Plane
COCKTAIL BAR

(☑ 408-713-2625; www.paperplanesj.com; 72 S 1st St; ⏱ 4:30pm-midnight Sun-Tue, to 2am Wed-Sat) Downtown at this industrial-chic watering hole with wall-sized, backlit shelves of liquor, tattooed bartenders willingly customize your drink if nothing on the menu of old-school classics and imaginative modern mixology tempts. Share a punch bowl and appetizers with friends.

B2 Coffee
COFFEE

(www.bellanocoffee.com; 170 W St John St; ⏱ 7am-7pm Mon-Fri, 8am-7pm Sat & Sun) Haute coffee-roaster Bellano has opened a branch inside downtown's San Pedro Square Market (p151), serving the same rich pour-over coffee, nitro cold brew and iced almond-milk lattes mixed with from-scratch vanilla syrup.

Haberdasher
COCKTAIL BAR

(☑ 408-792-7356; www.haberdashersj.com; 43 W San Salvador St; ⏱ 5pm-midnight Sun, Tue & Wed, to 1am Thu-Sat) A cool basement lounge, where sharply dressed bartenders artfully mix cocktails (including 'House Fittings' options), with some recipes dating to before Prohibition. It's a justifiably popular place but you can (and should) book ahead for a table Friday and Saturday nights to guarantee your spot.

Hedley Club
LOUNGE

(☑ 408-286-1000; www.destinationhotels.com/hotel-de-anza/dining/hedley-club-lounge; 233 W Santa Clara St; ⏱ hours vary) Inside the elegant 1931 Hotel De Anza, the Hedley Club is a good place for a quiet drink in swanky art-deco surroundings. Jazz combos play most nights.

☆ Entertainment

Avaya Stadium
SPECTATOR SPORT

(1123 Coleman Rd; ⏱ hours vary) Located near San Jose's airport, this is the home of the San Jose Earthquakes (☑ 408-556-7700; www.sjearthquakes.com), the city's professional soccer team (season runs from February through October).

SAN JOSE FOR CHILDREN

Children's Discovery Museum (☑ 408-298-5437; www.cdm.org; 180 Woz Way; $13, child under 1yr free; ⏱ 10am-5pm Tue-Sat, noon-5pm Sun; 👶) Downtown, this science and creativity museum has hands-on displays incorporating art, technology and the environment, with plenty of toys and cool play-and-learn areas for tots to school-aged children. The museum is on Woz Way, named after Steve Wozniak, cofounder of Apple.

California's Great America (☑ 408-988-1776; www.cagreatamerica.com; 4701 Great America Pkwy, Santa Clara; adult/child under 4ft $69/48; ⏱ Apr-Oct, hours vary; 👶) If you can handle the shameless product placements, kids love the roller coasters and other thrill rides. Online tickets cost much less than walk-up prices. Parking is $15 to $25, but the park is also accessible by public transportation.

Raging Waters (☑ 408-238-9900; www.rwsplash.com; 2333 S White Rd; adult/child under 4ft $39/29; ⏱ May-Sep, hours vary; 👶) A water park inside Lake Cunningham Regional Park, Raging Waters has fast waterslides, a wave pool and a nifty Pirate's Cove. Buy tickets online for discounts. Parking is $6 to $10.

SAP Center STADIUM
(☑408-287-9200; www.sapcenteratsanjose.com;
525 W Santa Clara St) The fanatically popular
San Jose Sharks (☑800-559-2333; www.nhl.
com/sharks), the city's professional hockey
team, plays at this massive glass-and-metal
stadium (formerly the HP Pavilion) from
September through April. Megaconcerts by
touring acts go on stage year-round.

California Theatre THEATER
(☑408-792-4111; http://sanjosetheaters.org/
theaters/california-theatre; 345 S 1st St; ☺hours
vary) The absolutely stunning Spanish Colonial interior of this landmark entertainment venue is cathedral-worthy. The theater
is home to Opera San Jose and Symphony
Silicon Valley.

ℹ Information

San Jose Convention & Visitors Bureau
(☑408-792-4511; www.sanjose.org; 408 Almaden Blvd; ☺9am-5pm Mon-Fri) Free visitor
information guides and maps online.
Santa Clara Valley Medical Center (☑408-
885-5000; www.scvmc.org; 751 S Bascom Ave;
☺24hr) 24-hour emergency services.

ℹ Getting There & Away

AIR
Four miles northwest of downtown between Hwy
101 and I-880, **Mineta San Jose International
Airport** (SJC; ☑408-392-3600; www.flysan
jose.com; 1701 Airport Blvd) has free wi-fi and
mostly domestic US flights from two terminals.

BART
To access the BART (p137) system in the East
Bay, VTA bus 181 runs between downtown San
Jose and the Fremont BART station ($4, 35 to 45
minutes, every 15 to 20 minutes).

BUS
Greyhound buses to Los Angeles ($21 to $84,
6½ to 10½ hours) leave from San Jose's **Diridon Station** (Diridon Transit Center; 65 Cahill
St). Discount carrier **Megabus** (☑877-462-
6342; http://us.megabus.com) offers daily
service between San Jose and Burbank, Los
Angeles or Anaheim ($5 to $44, six to seven
hours), with departures outside Diridon Station.

The **Santa Clara Valley Transportation Authority** (VTA; ☑408-321-2300, 800-894-9908;
www.vta.org) Hwy 17 Express bus plies a handy
route between Diridon Station and Santa Cruz
($7, 55 minutes, hourly).

CAR & MOTORCYCLE
San Jose is at the southern end of the San
Francisco Bay, about 40 miles from Oakland (via
I-880) or 50 miles from San Francisco (via Hwy
101 or I-280). Expect lots of traffic at all times
of day on Hwy 101 from San Francisco; although
I-280 is slightly longer, it's much prettier and
usually less congested. Heading south, Hwy 17
leads over the mountains to Santa Cruz.

TRAIN
A double-decker commuter rail service operating up and down the peninsula, **Caltrain**
(☑800-660-4287; www.caltrain.com) runs
between San Jose and San Francisco ($9.75, 65
to 85 minutes). Trains run hourly on weekends
and more frequently on weekdays. Bicycles may
be brought on designated cars only. San Jose's
terminal, **Diridon Station**, is just south of the
Alameda.

Diridon Station also is the terminal for Amtrak
trains serving Seattle, Los Angeles and Sacramento, as well as **Altamont Commuter Express**
(ACE; ☑800-411-7245; www.acerail.com) trains,
which run to Great America, Livermore and
Stockton.

VTA runs a free weekday shuttle (known as the
Downtown Area Shuttle or DASH) from Diridon
Station to downtown San Jose.

ℹ Getting Around

VTA buses run all over Silicon Valley. Fares for
VTA buses (except express lines) and light-rail
trains are $2 for a single ride (day pass $6).

From the airport, free VTA Airport Flyer shuttles (route 10) run every 10 to 15 minutes to the
Metro/Airport Light Rail station, where you can
catch light rail to downtown San Jose; shuttles
also go to the Santa Clara Caltrain station.

The main San Jose light-rail line runs north–
south from the city center. Heading south gets
you as far as Almaden and Santa Teresa. The
northern route runs to Japantown, the airport
and Tasman, where it connects with another line
that heads west past Great America to downtown Mountain View.

In San Jose, many downtown retailers offer
two-hour parking validation. Otherwise, city-
owned lots and garages downtown charge a $5
flat rate after 6pm on weekdays and all day on
weekends. Check www.sjdowntownparking.com
for details.

Pacifica & Devil's Slide

One of the real surprises of the Bay Area is
how fast the cityscape disappears along the
rugged and largely undeveloped coast. The
lazy beach town of Pacifica, just 15 miles
from downtown San Francisco, signals
the end of the urban sprawl. Most beaches
along Hwy 1 are buffeted by wild and unpredictable surf, making them better suited

to sunbathing (weather permitting) than swimming. Immediately south of Pacifica is the Devil's Slide, a gorgeous coastal cliff area now bypassed by a car tunnel.

Pacifica State Beach   BEACH
(Linda Mar Beach; ☑ 650-738-7381; www.parks.ca.gov; 5000 Pacific Coast Hwy; per car $5-9; ☺ 5am-dusk; P ♿) In Pacifica, collecting a suntan or catching a wave are the main attractions at popular Pacifica State Beach, as well as Rockaway Beach just north.

Nor-Cal Surf Shop   SURFING
(☑ 650-738-9283; 5440 Coast Hwy, Pedro Point Shopping Center; ☺ 9am-6pm Sun-Thu, to 7pm Fri, 8am-7pm Sat) Rents surfboards ($19 per day), wet suits ($16.50) and SUP sets ($45) next to Pacifica State Beach. Book ahead for surf lessons (from $95).

Devil's Slide Trail   HIKING
(☑ 650-355-8289; http://parks.smcgov.org/devils-slide-trail; Hwy 1; ☺ 8am-8pm Apr-Aug, closes earlier Sep-Mar; ♿) Hikers and cyclists cruise along the Devil's Slide Coastal Trail, a paved 1.3-mile section of the old highway. Heading south or north on Hwy 1, turn off before entering the tunnels into the trailhead parking lots.

Pacifica to Half Moon Bay

Other than a string of gorgeous, wild beaches along Hwy 1, there's little to stop for on the short, but distractingly scenic drive between Pacifica and Half Moon Bay. South of historic Point Montara Lighthouse, a hidden marine reserve protects natural tide pools and harbor seals.

Montara State Beach   STATE PARK
(☑ 650-726-8819; www.parks.ca.gov; Hwy 1; ☺ 8am-sunset; P ♿) FREE About 5 miles south of the town of Pacifica, this wide-open crescent is a local favorite for its pristine sand. Inland the park encompasses McNee Ranch, which has hiking and cycling trails aplenty, including a strenuous ascent to a panoramic viewpoint atop Montara Mountain (1898ft), a 7.6-mile round-trip from Hwy 1.

Ranch Corral de Tierra   PARK
(www.nps.gov/goga/rcdt.htm; off Hwy 1) FREE From the town of Montara, about 20 miles from San Francisco, trails climb from Montara State Beach to access the undeveloped 4000-acre park of Ranch Corral de Tierra, part of Golden Gate National Recreation Area.

Fitzgerald Marine Reserve   NATURE RESERVE
(☑ 650-728-3584; www.fitzgeraldreserve.org; 200 Nevada Ave, Moss Beach; ☺ 8am-8pm Apr-Aug, closes earlier Sep-Mar; P ♿) 🖉 FREE At Moss Beach, this marine reserve protects tide pools teeming with sea life. Walk out among the pools at low tide – wearing shoes that you can get wet – and explore the myriad crabs, sea stars, mollusks and rainbow-colored sea anemone. Note that it's illegal to remove any creatures, shells or even rocks from the marine reserve.

From Hwy 1, turn west on to Vermont Ave, which becomes Lake St and intersects Nevada Ave. SamTrans bus 17 stops along Hwy 1, only a five-minute walk or so from the reserve.

HI Point Montara Lighthouse   HOSTEL $
(☑ 650-728-7177; www.norcalhostels.org/montara; cnr Hwy 1 & 16th St, Montara; r with shared bath $83-128, dm $33-39; ☺ reception 7:30am-10:30pm; P ♻ @ 🛜) 🖉 Starting life as a fog station in 1875, Point Montara Lighthouse Hostel is adjacent to the current lighthouse, which dates from 1928. This very popular hostel has a living room, kitchen facilities and an international clientele. There are a few private rooms for couples or families. Reservations are a good idea anytime, but especially on weekends and in summer.

If you're not staying at the hostel, you can visit the lighthouse grounds between 9am and sunset daily (but check in at the front desk first). SamTrans bus 17 stops across the highway from the hostel.

Moss Beach Distillery   BAR
(☑ 650-728-5595; www.mossbeachdistillery.com; 140 Beach Way, Moss Beach; ☺ noon-9pm Mon-Sat, 11am-9pm Sun) Overlooking the cove where bootleggers used to unload Prohibition-era liquor, the restaurant's heated ocean-view deck is perfectly positioned to catch sunset. In fair weather it's the best place for miles around to have a leisurely cocktail, but head elsewhere for a meal if you're hungry.

Half Moon Bay

With its long coastline and mild weather, this area has always been prime real estate. When Spanish missionaries set up shop along the coast in the late 1700s, this had been indigenous Ohlone territory for thousands of years. Developed as a beach resort in the early 1900s, Half Moon Bay today is the main coastal town between San Francisco

SCENIC DRIVE: HIGHWAY 84

Inland from the Pacific, vast stretches of the peninsula's hills are protected in a patch-work of parks that, just like the coast, remain remarkably untouched despite huge urban populations only a short drive away.

Heading east from Hwy 1, about 10 miles south of Half Moon Bay (p154), Hwy 84 winds its way upward through thick stands of redwood trees, passing local and state parks and open-space preserves with hiking and mountain-biking opportunities. Allow at least an hour to make the 25-mile drive to Palo Alto without stopping.

A mile in from **San Gregorio State Beach** (☑650-726-8819; www.parks.ca.gov; Hwy 1, San Gregorio; per car $8; ⊘8am-sunset) on Hwy 1, kick off your shoes and stomp your feet to live bluegrass, Celtic and folk music on the weekends at the **San Gregorio General Store** (☑650-726-0565; www.sangregoriostore.com; 7615 Stage Rd, San Gregorio; ⊘store 10:30am-6pm Sun-Thu, to 7pm Fri, 10am-7pm Sat, to 6pm Sun). Check out the wooden bar singed by area branding irons.

Eight miles further east is the tiny township of **La Honda**, former home to *One Flew Over the Cuckoo's Nest* author Ken Kesey and the launching spot for his 1964 psyche-delic bus trip immortalized in Tom Wolfe's *The Electric Kool-Aid Acid Test*. Housed in a 19th-century blacksmith's shop, **Apple Jack's** (☑650-747-0331; 8790 Hwy 84; ⊘noon-2am) is a rustic, down-home country-and-western bar with motorcycles lined up in a row outside.

To stretch your legs in the redwoods, **Sam McDonald County Park** (☑650-879-0238; http://parks.smcgov.org/sam-mcdonald-park; 13435 Pescadero Creek Rd, Loma Mar; per car $6; ⊘8am-8pm Apr-Aug, closes earlier Sep-Mar; P ▮), 2 miles south of La Honda, has forested hiking trails and a secluded hike-to **cabin** (☑650-390-8411; www.sierraclub.org/loma-prieta/hikers-hut; per night adult $20-30, child $10; ⊘) ✑. From the park, it's a 20-minute winding drive downhill along Pescadero Creek Rd to visit the tiny farm town of Pescadero (p156), just inland from the coast.

Otherwise, backtrack to La Honda and continue north on Hwy 84, passing more nature preserves and viewpoints over Silicon Valley. Turn left on to Skyline Blvd to eat at **Alice's Restaurant** (☑650-851-0303; www.alicesrestaurant.com; 17288 Skyline Blvd, Woodside; mains $9-14; ⊘8am-8pm Sun-Thu, to 9pm Fri-Sat) inside an early 20th-century general store. It's not the same diner made famous by 1960s folk singer Arlo Guthrie, but it's still a popular stop for bikers, cyclists and Sunday drivers, especially for weekend brunch.

Keep following Hwy 84 as it corkscrews downhill, turning right on to Sand Hill Rd, which leads east to Stanford University (p149) and downtown Palo Alto.

(29 miles north) and Santa Cruz (49 miles south). Its long stretches of beach still attract rambling weekenders and die-hard surfers.

Half Moon Bay spreads out along Hwy 1/ Cabrillo Hwy, but despite development, it's still relatively small. Downtown, the main drag is a five-block stretch of Main St lined with art galleries, antiques shops, cafes and restaurants. For aquatic pursuits and seafood restaurants, detour to Pillar Point Harbor, about 4 miles northwest of downtown, off Hwy 1.

Sea Horse Ranch　　HORSEBACK RIDING
(☑650-726-9903; http://seahorseranch.org; 1828 Cabrillo Hwy; trail ride $60-90; ⊘hours vary; ▮) Just over a mile north of the Hwy 92 junction, Sea Horse Ranch offers daily horseback rides along the beach. Minimum age for riders is seven years; weight limits and clothing restrictions apply. Book ahead.

**Half Moon Bay
Kayak Co**　　WATER SPORTS, CYCLING
(☑650-773-6101; www.hmbkayak.com; 2 Johnson Pier; kayak or SUP set rental per hour/day $25/75, bicycle rental $25/50; ⊘9am-5pm Wed-Mon; ▮) When the bay is calm, get out on the water with Half Moon Bay Kayak Co, which rents kayaks, stand up paddle surfing (SUP) sets and bicycles too. Book ahead for harbor, sunset or full-moon tours or an adventurous kayak-fishing trip. Last walk-up rental is at 3:30pm.

Mavericks

SURFING

At the western end of Pillar Point is Mavericks, a serious surf break that attracts pro big-wave riders to battle its huge, steep and very dangerous waves. The invitational **Titans of Mavericks** (http://titansofmavericks. com/event) FREE surf contest, called on a few days' notice when the swells get huge, is held annually between November and March.

Half Moon Bay Art & Pumpkin Festival

FOOD, CULTURAL

([☎]650-726-9652; www.pumpkinfest.miramar events.com; Main St; ⊙mid-Oct; [♿]) FREE Pumpkins are a major deal around Half Moon Bay and the pre-Halloween harvest is celebrated with this annual festival. It kicks off with the World Championship Pumpkin Weigh-Off, where some bulbous beasts bust the scales at nearly 2000lb.

Half Moon Bay Brewing Company

PUB FOOD **$$**

([☎]650-728-2739; www.hmbbrewingco.com; 390 Capistrano Rd; mains $12-25; ⊙11:30am-9pm Mon-Thu, to 10pm Fri, 10am-10pm Sat, to 9pm Sun; [🛜][♿][🐾]) Chomp on seafood and burgers while you swill pints from a respectable menu of local brews and gaze out at the bay from a sheltered, heated outdoor patio. Live music some weekends.

❶ Getting There & Away

SamTrans bus 294 operates hourly between the Caltrain (p153) Hillsdale station in San Mateo and Half Moon Bay ($2.25, 45 minutes). From Half Moon Bay, SamTrans bus 17 heads up the coast to Moss Beach, Montara and Pacifica ($2.25, one hour) every hour or two daily, with limited weekday service south to Pescadero ($2.25, 25 minutes).

Pescadero

A foggy speck of coastal crossroads between Half Moon Bay and Santa Cruz, 160-year-old Pescadero is a close-knit rural town of sugar-lending neighbors and community pancake breakfasts. But on weekends the tiny downtown strains its seams with long-distance cyclists panting for carbohydrates and day-trippers dive-bombing in from the oceanfront highway. They're all drawn to the winter vistas of emerald-green hills parched to burlap brown in summer, the wild Pacific beaches populated by seals and pelicans, and the unbelievably fresh food from local farms and ranches. With its cornucopia of tide-pool coves and parks of sky-blotting redwood canopy, city dwellers come here to slow down and smell the sea breeze wafting over fields of bushy artichokes.

◉ Sights

Pigeon Point Light Station State Historic Park

LIGHTHOUSE

([☎]650-879-2120; www.parks.ca.gov; 210 Pigeon Point Rd; ⊙8am-sunset, visitor center 10am-4pm Thu-Mon; [P][♿]) A half-dozen miles south of Pescadero along the coast, the 115ft light station is one of the tallest lighthouses on the West Coast. The 1872 landmark had to close access to the upper tower when chunks of its cornice began to rain from the sky (future restorations are planned), but the beam still flashes brightly and the bluff is a prime though blustery spot to scan for breaching gray whales in winter. Half-hour guided history walks of the lighthouse grounds leave at 1pm (weather permitting) from the visitor center and bookstore.

Bean Hollow State Beach

BEACH

([☎]650-726-8819; www.parks.ca.gov; off Hwy 1; ⊙8am-sunset; [P][♿]) [🐾] FREE Pretty sand beaches speckle the coast, though one of the most interesting places to stop is Pebble Beach, a jewel less than 2 miles south of Pescadero Creek Rd (and part of Bean Hollow State Beach). The shore is awash with bite-sized eye candy of agate, jade and carnelian, and sandstone troughs are pockmarked by groovy honeycombed formations called tafoni.

Butano State Park

STATE PARK

([☎]650-879-2040; www.parks.ca.gov; 1500 Cloverdale Rd; per car $10; ⊙sunrise-sunset; [P][♿]) [🐾] Five miles south of Pescadero, bobcats and coyotes reside discreetly in this pretty park's 4600 acres of dense redwood canyon and uplands laced with hiking and mountain-biking trails and shady campsites. From Pescadero Creek Rd in downtown Pescadero, follow Cloverdale Rd south for 4 miles to the turnoff.

To take the scenic route back to Hwy 1, continue south on Cloverdale Rd, turning right on to Gazos Creek Rd and winding 2 more miles to the coast.

Pescadero State Beach & Marsh Natural Preserve

STATE PARK

([☎]650-726-8819; www.parks.ca.gov; off Hwy 1; per car $8; ⊙8am-sunset; [P][♿]) [🐾] Fifteen miles south of Half Moon Bay, this state beach and marshland preserve attract beachcombers and birders. Pull over and get out of the car to explore the marine-life-rich coastal tide pools on rocky outcroppings.

🛏 Sleeping & Eating

HI Pigeon Point Lighthouse HOSTEL $

(☑650-879-0633; www.norcalhostels.org/pigeon; 210 Pigeon Point Rd; r with shared bath from $82-186, dm $26-32; ☉reception 7:30am-10:30pm; ❓🖥@❓) ✎ Not your workaday youth hostel, this highly coveted coastside lodging is all about location. Book ahead and check in early to snag a spot in the outdoor hot tub ($8 per person per 30 minutes) and contemplate roaring waves as the lighthouse beacon races through a starburst sky. It's about 6 miles south of Pescadero.

Butano State Park Campground CAMPGROUND $

(☑reservations 800-444-7275; www.reserveamerica.com; 1500 Cloverdale Rd; tent & RV sites $35; ❓🐾) ✎ Shady campsites have picnic tables and fire pits, but the most serene spots are the walk-in, tent-only sites tucked back into the forest.

Costanoa CABIN, LODGE $$

(☑650-879-1100; www.costanoa.com; 2001 Rossi Rd; tent/cabin with shared bath from $100/200, lodge r from $200; ❓🖥❓) Even though this coastal resort, about 10 miles south of Pescadero, includes a **campground** (☑650-879-7302; http://koa.com/campgrounds/santa-cruz-north; tent/RV sites with hookups from $36/85; ❓❓🐾), no one can pull a straight face and declare they're actually roughing it here. Down bedding swaddles guests in canvas-sided tent bungalows and hard-sided Douglas-fir cabins. Chill-averse folks can use communal 'comfort stations' with 24-hour dry saunas, fireside patio seating, heated floors and hot showers.

Bland lodge rooms with private fireplaces and hot-tub access cater to those without such Spartan delusions. There's an expensive restaurant, bar and spa on-site. Bicycle rentals, yoga classes, horseback rides and guided bird-watching are available to guests only.

Pescadero Creek Inn INN $$

(☑650-879-1898; www.pescaderocreekinn.com; 393 Stage Rd; d $175-250; ❓🖥❓) ✎ Unwind in the private two-room cottage or one of the spotless Victorian rooms in a restored 100-year-old farmhouse with a tranquil creekside garden.

Duarte's Tavern AMERICAN $$

(☑650-879-0464; www.duartestavern.com; 202 Stage Rd; mains $8-39; ☉7am-8pm; 🖥) You'll rub shoulders with fancy-pants foodies, spandex-swathed cyclists and dusty cowboys at this casual, surprisingly unpretentious fourth-generation family restaurant. Duarte's is this town's culinary magnet, though some critics say it's resting on its laurels. Feast on crab cioppino and a half-and-half split of cream of artichoke and green-chili soups, then bring it home with a wedge of olallieberry pie. Except for the unfortunate lull of Prohibition, the wood-paneled bar has been hosting the locals and their honored guests since 1894. Reservations strongly recommended.

❶ Getting There & Away

By car, the town is 3 miles east of Hwy 1 on Pescadero Creek Rd, leading inland from Pescadero State Beach. On weekdays, **SamTrans** (☑511, 800-660-4287; www.samtrans.com) bus 17 runs twice a day to and from Half Moon Bay ($2.25, 25 minutes).

Año Nuevo State Park

Just over a dozen miles southeast of Pescadero State Beach, **Año Nuevo State Park** (☑park office 650-879-2025, recorded info 650-879-0227, tour reservations 800-444-4445; www.parks.ca.gov; 1 New Years Creek Rd; per car $10, 2½hr tour per person $7; ☉8:30am-sunset Apr-Nov, tours only Dec 15–Mar 31; ❓🖥) ✎ is home to the world's largest mainland breeding colonies of northern elephant seals. More raucous than a full-moon beach rave, thousands of boisterous animals party year-round on the dunes of Año Nuevo Point, their squeals and barks reaching fever pitch during the winter pupping season.

Northern elephant seals were just as fearless two centuries ago as they are today, but unfortunately, seal trappers were not as friendly as today's tourists. During the 19th century, northern elephant seals were driven to the edge of extinction. Only a handful survived around the Guadalupe Islands off the Mexican state of Baja California. With the availability of substitutes for seal oil and the conservationist attitudes of more recent times, northern elephant seals have come back, reappearing on the Southern

THE CULINARY COAST

Pescadero is renowned for Duarte's Tavern (p157), but loads of other tidbits are close by.

Arcangeli Grocery Company (Norm's Market; ☑650-879-0147; www.normsmarket.com; 287 Stage Rd; sandwiches $7-10; ☺10am-6pm; ☑ ⋔) Create a picnic with made-to-order deli sandwiches, homemade artichoke salsa and a chilled bottle of California wine. Don't go breezing out the door without nabbing a crusty loaf of the famous artichoke garlic herb bread, baked fresh almost hourly.

Harley Farms Goat Dairy (☑650-879-0480; http://harleyfarms.com; 250 North St; ☺10am-5pm Thu-Mon Apr-Dec, 11am-4pm Fri-Sun Jan-Mar; ☑ ⋔) Another local food treasure, here the split-level farm shop sells creamy artisanal goat's cheeses festooned with fruit, nuts and a rainbow of edible flowers, as well as goat's-milk bath and body products. Show up anytime to pat the heads of the goats out back, or reserve ahead for a weekend farm tour ($30) or dinner ($150) in the Victorian-era barn. The farm is less than a mile east of downtown: follow the cool wooden cutouts of the goat and the Wellington-shod girl with the faraway eyes.

Pie Ranch (☑650-879-9281; www.pieranch.org; 2080 Cabrillo Hwy; ☺noon-5pm Mon-Fri, 10am-5pm Sat & Sun; ⋔) Hit the brakes for this roadside farm stand in a wooden barn to pick up fresh produce, eggs and coffee, plus amazing fruit pies (which sell out fast). The historic pie-slice-shaped farm is a nonprofit dedicated to leadership development and food education for urban youth. Check the website for volunteer work days, farm tours, potluck dinners and barn dances. It's around 11 miles south of Pescadero Creek Rd.

Swanton Berry Farm Stand & U-Pick (☑650-469-8804; www.swantonberryfarm.com; 25 Swanton Rd, Davenport; ☺8am-8pm late May-early Sep, closes earlier rest of year; ☑ ⋔) Roll up your shirtsleeves and harvest some fruit at this organic pick-your-own farm south of Año Nuevo. It's a union outfit (operated by Cesar Chavez's United Farm Workers), with buckets of seasonal strawberries, olallieberries, blackberries and even kiwis ripe for the plucking. The farm stand sells baskets of ripe berries and berry shortcakes, pies and jams.

Bonnie Doon Vineyard Tasting Room (☑831-471-8031; www.bonnydoonvineyard.com; 450 Hwy 1, Davenport; tasting fee $10-20; ☺11am-5pm, to 6pm Fri & Sat late May-early Sep, closed Wed early Sep-Feb; ☑) In the sleepy village of Davenport, round out your palate with a wine flight in the roadside tasting room of Randall Grahm's acclaimed winery, where Edison lights and rough-hewed wooden tables entice you to sample Le Cigare Volant (yes, that's a flying cigar), a Rhône-style red blend and other bottles made with lesser-known grape varietals. The tasting room is about 10 miles northwest of Santa Cruz on Hwy 1.

California coast during the 1920s. They returned to Año Nuevo Beach in 1955.

In peak season, during the mating and birthing time from mid-December to end of March, visitors are only permitted access to the reserve on guided tours. For the busiest period, from mid-January to mid-February, it's recommended you book two months ahead. Although the park office can answer general questions, tours must be arranged through ReserveAmerica (http://anonuevo. reserveamerica.com).

The rest of the year, advance reservations aren't necessary, but visitor permits from the entrance station are required; arrive before 3pm in September, October or November or 3:30pm April to August. From the ranger station it's a 3- to 5-mile round-trip hike on sand; allow two to three hours. Dogs are not allowed on-site and no visitors are permitted during the first two weeks of December.

The park is less than 7 miles southeast of Pigeon Point or over 20 miles northwest of Santa Cruz.

Napa & Sonoma Wine Country

Best Places to Eat

➡ Handline (p202)

➡ Oxbow Public Market
(p169)

➡ Fremont Diner (p192)

➡ SingleThread (p216)

➡ Shed (p215)

Best Places to Sleep

➡ El Bonita (p176)

➡ Shanti Permaculture Farm
(p204)

➡ Hotel Healdsburg (p214)

➡ Windhaven Cottage (p191)

➡ Brannan Cottage Inn (p182)

Why Go?

America's premier viticulture region has earned its reputation among the world's best. Despite hype about Wine Country style, it's from the land that all Wine Country lore springs. Rolling hills, dotted with century-old oaks, turn the color of lion's fur under the summer sun and swaths of vineyards carpet hillsides as far as the eye can see. Where they end, redwood forests follow serpentine rivers to the sea.

There are over 900 wineries in Napa and Sonoma Counties, but it's quality, not quantity, that distinguishes the region – especially in Napa, which competes with France and doubles as an outpost of San Francisco's top-end culinary scene. Sonoma prides itself on agricultural diversity, with goat's-cheese farms, you-pick-'em orchards and roadside fruit stands. Plan to get lost on back roads, and, as you picnic atop sun-dappled hillsides, grab a hunk of earth and know firsthand the thing of greatest meaning in Wine Country.

When to Go
Napa

Jan Bright-yellow flowers carpet the valleys during the off-season; room rates plummet.

Apr–May Before summer holidays is the perfect time for touring, with long days and warm sun.

Sep–Oct 'Crush' time is peak season, when winemaking operations are in full force.

Napa & Sonoma Wine Country Highlights

1 Tasting California's biggest and boldest red wines and falling under their intoxicating spell in the **Napa Valley** (p162), then grabbing snacks downtown at Napa's Oxbow Public Market.

2 Feasting in Northern California's greatest food town, **Healdsburg** (p213). Then, wallet permitting, hitting up exciting new restaurant, SingleThread.

3 Submerging yourself in a volcanic-ash mud bath at a fabulous **Calistoga** (p186) hot-springs resort, then sleeping in a yurt in Bothe-Napa Valley State Park.

4 Getting lost on the winding and spectacular Coleman Valley Rd before arriving in the region's wackiest town, **Occidental** (p203) .

5 Floating in a canoe, kayak or tube down NorCal's

natural lazy **Russian River** (p197; put-ins available at Guerneville and Healdsburg), then hopping out and drinking some wine.

6 Picnicking in sun-dappled grass on the state's largest historic town square, **Sonoma Plaza** (p188)

7 Pedaling between wineries along pastoral and undulating West Dry Creek Rd in **Dry Creek Valley** (p199).

❶ Getting There & Getting Away

Napa and Sonoma Counties each have an eponymous city and valley. So Sonoma town is in Sonoma County, at the southern end of Sonoma Valley. The same goes for the city, county and valley of Napa.

From San Francisco, public transportation gets you to the valleys, but it's insufficient for vineyard-hopping. For public-transit information, dial 🖉 511, or look online at www.transit.511.org.

Both valleys are a 90-minute drive from San Francisco. Napa, further inland, has about 500 wineries and attracts the most visitors (expect heavy traffic on summer weekends). Sonoma County has more than 425 wineries and around 40 in Sonoma Valley, which is less commercial and less congested than Napa. If you have time to visit only one, for ease go with Sonoma.

AIR

Visitors fly into either **San Francisco International Airport** (☎650-821-8211; www.flysfo.com; 780 S Airport Blvd) or **Sacramento International Airport** (☎916-929-5411; http://sacramento.aero/smf; 6900 Airport Blvd); the drive from either to Napa Valley takes about 1½ hours. San Francisco is a more attractive destination but its airport is also far busier and more crowded than Sacramento's.

BOAT

Baylink Ferry (☎877-643-3779; www.sanfranciscobayferry.com) Downtown San Francisco to Vallejo (adult/child $13.80/6.90, 60 minutes); connect with Napa Valley Vine bus 29 (weekdays) or bus 11 (daily).

BUS

Evans Transportation (☎707-255-1559; www.evanstransportation.com) Shuttles ($40) to Napa from San Francisco and Oakland airports.

Golden Gate Transit (p117) Bus from San Francisco to Petaluma (adult/youth $11.75/5.75) and Santa Rosa (adult/youth $13/6.50); board at 1st and Mission Sts. Connects with Sonoma County Transit buses.

Greyhound (☎800-231-2222; www.greyhound.com) Buses run from San Francisco to Santa Rosa ($21 to $38).

Napa Valley Vine Operates local bus 10 daily from downtown Napa to Calistoga ($1.60); express bus 29 Monday to Friday from the Vallejo Ferry Terminal ($3.25) and El Cerrito del Norte Bay Area Rapid Transit (BART) station via Napa to Calistoga ($5.50); and local bus 11 daily from the Vallejo Ferry Terminal to downtown Napa ($1.60).

Sonoma County Airport Express (☎800-327-2024, 707-837-8700; www.airportexpressinc.com) Shuttles ($34) between Sonoma County Airport (Santa Rosa) and San Francisco and Oakland airports.

CAR & MOTORCYCLE

From San Francisco, take Hwy 101 north over the Golden Gate Bridge, then Hwy 37 east to Hwy 121 north; continue to the junction of Hwy 12/121. For Sonoma Valley, take Hwy 12 north; for Napa Valley, take Hwy 12/121 east. Plan 70 minutes in light traffic, two hours during the weekday commute.

Hwy 12/121 splits south of Napa: Hwy 121 turns north and joins with Hwy 29/St Helena Hwy; Hwy 12 merges with southbound Hwy 29 toward Vallejo. Hwy 29 backs up weekdays 3pm to 7pm, slowing returns to San Francisco.

From the East Bay (or downtown San Francisco), take I-80 east to Hwy 37 west (north of Vallejo), then northbound Hwy 29.

From Santa Rosa, take Hwy 12 east to access the northern end of Sonoma Valley. From Petaluma and Hwy 101, take Hwy 116 east.

TRAIN

Amtrak (☎800-872-7245; www.amtrak.com) trains travel to Martinez (south of Vallejo), with connecting buses to Napa (45 minutes), Santa Rosa (1¼ hours) and Healdsburg (1¾ hours). From San Francisco, **BART Trains** (☎415-989-2278; www.bart.gov) connecting to Richmond station can deliver you to Amtrak.

BART also runs from San Francisco to El Cerrito del Norte ($4.45, 30 minutes). **Napa Valley Vine** bus 29 runs weekdays from that same BART stop to Calistoga, via Napa ($5.50); on Saturdays take **SolTrans** (☎707-648-4666; www.soltransride.com; adult/youth $5/4) from BART to Vallejo ($5, 30 minutes), then connect with Napa Valley Vine bus 11 to Napa and Calistoga ($1.60); on Sundays, there's no connecting bus service from BART.

ⓘ Getting Around

You'll need a car or bike to winery-hop. Alternatively visit tasting rooms in downtown Napa or downtown Sonoma. For more information on touring Napa and Sonoma Wine Country by bicycle, see page p163.

BICYCLE

Touring Wine Country by bicycle is a fantastic experience. The majority of trails between wineries are flat and very approachable for beginners, however crossing between the Napa and Sonoma valleys is challenging with steep roads. It's best to stick to back roads, and we particularly recommend West Dry Creek Rd.

BUS

Sonoma County Transit (☎800-345-7433, 707-576-7433; http://sctransit.com) buses travel around Santa Rosa, Healdsburg, Sebastopol, Petaluma, Kenwood, Glen Ellen, Russian River towns, Sonoma Valley and Geyserville. Prices range from $1.50 to $4.80 depending on how many zones you pass through on your journey. Youth prices range from $1.25 to $4.55.

Napa Valley Vine (☎800-696-6443, 707-251-2800; www.ridethevine.com) local bus 10 runs daily from downtown Napa to Calistoga (adult/youth $1.60/1.10).

CAR & MOTORCYCLE

Napa Valley is 30 miles long and 5 miles across at its widest point (city of Napa) and 1 mile at its narrowest (Calistoga). Two roads run north-south: Hwy 29/St Helena Hwy and the more scenic Silverado Trail, a mile east. Drive up one, down the other.

The American Automobile Association ranks Napa Valley among America's most congested rural vacation destinations. Summer and fall weekend traffic is unbearable, especially on Hwy 29 between Napa and St Helena. Plan accordingly.

Cross-valley roads linking Silverado Trail with Hwy 29 – including Yountville, Oakville and Rutherford crossroads – are bucolic and get less traffic. For scenery, the Oakville Grade and rural Trinity Rd (which leads southwest to Hwy 12 in Sonoma Valley) are narrow, curvy and beautiful – but treacherous in rainstorms. Mt Veeder Rd leads through pristine countryside west of Yountville.

Note: police watch like hawks for traffic violators. *Don't drink and drive.*

There are a number of shortcuts between the Napa and Sonoma Valleys: from Oakville, take Oakville Grade to Trinity Rd; from St Helena, take Spring Mountain Rd into Calistoga Rd; from Calistoga, take Petrified Forest Rd to Calistoga Rd.

TRAIN

The **Napa Valley Wine Train** (p167) can take you from Napa to St Helena and back in a comfy, vintage dining car. An additional winery tour is optional. Trains depart from **Napa Valley Wine Train Depot** (http://winetrain.com/getting-here; 1275 McKinstry St) on McKinstry St near 1st St.

NAPA VALLEY

The birthplace of modern-day Wine Country is famous for regal Cabernet Sauvignons, château-like wineries and fabulous food. It attracts more than three million visitors a year, many planning to wine and dine themselves into a stupor, maybe get a massage, and sleep somewhere swell with fine linens and a heated pool.

The city of Napa anchors the valley, but the real work happens up-valley. And while Napa may not be as scenic as other stops, it has some noteworthy sights, among them Oxbow Public Market and the new cooking-school campus, CIA at Copia. The prettiest towns include St Helena, Yountville and Calistoga – the latter more famous for mud and water than wine.

History

A few decades ago, Napa was a quiet agricultural valley dense with orchards, its 5-by-35-mile strip peppered with stagecoach stops. Grapes had grown here since the gold rush, but juice-sucking phylloxera bugs, Prohibition and the Great Depression reduced 140 wineries in the 1890s to around 25 by the 1960s.

In 1968 Napa was declared the 'Napa Valley Agricultural Preserve,' effectively blocking future valley development for non-ag purposes. The law prohibited the subdivision of valley-floor land under 40 acres, which helped preserve the valley's natural beauty. But when Napa wines earned top honors at a 1976 blind tasting in Paris, the wine-drinking world noticed, land values skyrocketed and only the very rich could afford to build – hence so many architecturally jaw-dropping wineries. Independent, family-owned wineries still exist – we highlight a number of them – but much of Napa Valley is now owned by global conglomerates.

Napa Valley Wineries

Cab is king in Napa. No varietal captures imaginations like the fruit of the Cabernet Sauvignon vine – Bordeaux is the French equivalent – and no wine fetches a higher price. Napa farmers can't afford *not* to grow Cabernet, and Chardonnay, which flourishes in the calcium-rich soil of cooler areas of the valley, is second. Other varietals such as Merlot and Zinfandel also thrive here.

Napa's wines merit their reputation among the world's finest – complex, with luxurious finishes. Napa wineries sell many 'buy-and-hold' wines, versus Sonoma's 'drink-now' wines.

★**Hess Collection** WINERY, GALLERY
(☏707-255-1144; www.hesscollection.com; 4411 Redwood Rd, Napa; museum free, tasting $25 & $35, tours free; ◷10am-5:30pm, last tasting 5pm)
🖉 Art-lovers: don't miss Hess Collection, whose galleries display mixed-media and large-canvas works, including pieces by Francis Bacon and Robert Motherwell. In the elegant stone-walled tasting room, find well-known Cabernet Sauvignon and Chardonnay, but also try the Viognier. There's garden service in the warmer months, which is lovely, as Hess overlooks the valley. Make reservations and be prepared to drive a winding road. Bottles are $30 to $100. Public tour 10:30am.

TOURING NAPA & SONOMA WINE COUNTRY

Touring Wine Country by bicycle is unforgettable. Stick to back roads. We love pastoral West Dry Creek Rd, northwest of Healdsburg, in Sonoma County. Through Sonoma Valley, take Arnold Dr instead of Hwy 12; through Napa Valley, take the Silverado Trail instead of Hwy 29. Cycling between wineries isn't demanding – the valleys are mostly flat – but crossing between the Napa and Sonoma Valleys is intense, particularly via steep Oakville Grade and Trinity Rd (between Oakville and Glen Ellen). Bicycles, in boxes, can be checked on Greyhound buses (p161) for $30 to $40; bike boxes cost $10 (call ahead). You can transport bicycles on Golden Gate Transit (p117) buses.

Bicycle Tours & Rentals

Guided tours start around $90 per day including bikes, tastings and lunch. Daily rentals cost $25 to $85; make reservations.

Getaway Adventures (☑800-499-2453, 707-568-3040; http://getawayadventures.com; 5½hr tour $139-175) These great guided cycling tours visit wineries and other attractions, and include a picnic lunch. They depart from Napa and Calistoga.

Backroads (☑800-462-2848; www.backroads.com) All-inclusive, multiday guided biking and walking.

Calistoga Bike Shop (☑707-942-9687; http://calistogabikeshop.com; 1318 Lincoln Ave; bicycle rental from $28, guided tours from $149; ◷10am-6pm) Rents full-suspension mountain bikes, hybrids, road bikes and tandem models and provides reliable trail information. DIY touring packages ($110 per day) include free tastings and wine pickup.

Napa River Velo (☑707-258-8729; www.naparivervelo.com; 680 Main St, Napa; rentals per day $40-90; ◷10am-7pm Mon-Fri, 9am-6pm Sat, to 5pm Sun) Hourly, daily and weekly rentals in downtown Napa; reservations recommended.

Spoke Folk Cyclery (☑707-433-7171; www.spokefolk.com; 201 Center St; hybrid bicycle rental per hour/day from $14/38; ◷10am-6pm Mon-Fri, to 5pm Sat & Sun) Rents touring, racing and tandem bicycles that come with locks and helmets. Great service.

Sonoma Adventures (☑707-938-2080; www.sonoma-adventures.com; bicycle rental per day $30-65, tours $129-189, segway tours $129) Bicycle rentals and guided cycling tours of Sonoma Valley, Dry Creek Valley and Carneros. There's a minimum of two people for the Sonoma tours, four people for the Dry Creek Valley and Carneros tours.

Wine Country Bikes (Map p198; ☑707-473-0610; www.winecountrybikes.com; 61 Front St; rentals per day from $39, guided tours from $139; ◷9am-5pm) Rents bikes in downtown Healdsburg and guides multiday Sonoma County tours.

Napa Valley Bike Tours (☑707-944-2953; www.napavalleybiketours.com; 6500 Washington St, Yountville; bicycle rental per day $45-75, tours $109-124; ◷8:30am-5pm) Two-hour and daily rentals, as well as easy and moderately difficult tours starting in Yountville. Second location at the foot of the Vine Trail at 3259 California Blvd, you can rent in one location and drop off in the other for $10 extra.

Other Tours

Platypus Wine Tours (☑707-253-2723; www.platypustours.com; join-in tour per person $110) Billed as the anti-wine-snob tour, Platypus specializes in backroad vineyards and family-owned operations. There's a daily 'join-in' tour that takes in four wineries and a picnic lunch, and private tours with a dedicated driver. The Napa tours are the most popular, but Platypus also takes people to Sonoma, Russian River and Dry Creek Valleys.

Beyond the Label (☑707-363-4023; www.btlnv.com; per couple from $995) Personalized tours, including lunch at home with a vintner, guided by a knowledgeable Napa native.

Beau Wine Tours (Map p168; ☑707-938-8001, 800-387-2328; www.beauwinetours.com) Winery tours in sedans and stretch limos; charges a base rate of $65 to $205 per hour (four- to six-hour minimum), but expect to pay more for gas, tax and tip.

Magnum Tours (☑707-753-0088; www.magnumwinetours.com) Sedans and specialty limousines from $65 to $110 per hour (four-hour minimum, five hours Saturdays).

★ **Robert Sinskey Vineyards** WINERY
(☎707-944-9090; www.robertsinskey.com; 6320 Silverado Trail, Napa; bar tasting $40, seated food & wine pairings $70-175; ⏲10am-4:30pm; 🅿) 🦆
The fabulous hillside tasting room, constructed of stone, redwood and teak, resembles a small cathedral – fitting, given the sacred status here bestowed upon food and wine. It specializes in bright-acid organic Pinot Noir, plus exceptional aromatic white varietals, dry rosé and Bordeaux varietals such as Merlot and Cab Franc, all crafted for the dinner table.

Small bites accompany bar tastings, and seated food and wine experiences are curated by chef Maria Sinskey herself. Reserve ahead for sit-down tastings and culinary tours. Bottles $22 to $100.

★ **Frog's Leap** WINERY
(☎707-963-4704; www.frogsleap.com; 8815 Conn Creek Rd, Rutherford; tasting $20-25, incl tour $25; ⏲10am-4pm by appointment only; 🅿♿🦆) 🦆 Meandering paths wind through magical gardens and fruit-bearing orchards surrounding an 1884 barn and farmstead with cats and chickens. The vibe is casual and down-to-earth, with a major emphasis on *fun*. Sauvignon Blanc is its best-known wine but the Merlot merits attention. There's also a dry, restrained Cabernet, atypical of Napa.All grapes are organically farmed. Bottles cost $20 to $55.

★ **Tres Sabores** WINERY
(☎707-967-8027; www.tressabores.com; 1620 South Whitehall Lane, St Helena; tour & tasting $40; ⏲10:30am-3pm, by appointment; 📷) 🦆 At the valley's westernmost edge, where sloping vineyards meet wooded hillsides, Tres Sabores is a portal to old Napa – no fancy tasting room, no snobbery, just great wine in a spectacular setting. Bucking the Cabernet custom, Tres Sabores crafts elegantly structured, Burgundian-style Zinfandel and spritely Sauvignon Blanc, which the *New York Times* dubbed a top 10 of its kind in California. Reservations are essential.

Pride Mountain WINERY
(☎707-963-4949; www.pridewines.com; 4026 Spring Mountain Rd, St Helena; tasting & tour $20-30, summit experience $75; ⏲by appointment only)
High atop Spring Mountain, cult-favorite Pride straddles the Napa–Sonoma border and bottles vintages under both appellations. The well-structured Cabernet and heavy-hitting Merlot are the best-known wines but there's also an elegant Viognier (perfect with oysters) and standout Cab Franc, available only here. Picnicking is spectacular: choose Viewpoint for drop-dead vistas, or Ghost Winery for shade and the historic ruins of a 19th-century winery, but you must first reserve a tasting. Bottles cost $42 to $70.

Artesa WINERY
(☎707-254-2126; www.artesawinery.com; 1345 Henry Rd, Napa; tastings from $35, tour/glass $45/15; ⏲10am-5pm, last pour 4:30pm) Begin or end the day with a glass of bubbly or Pinot at Artesa, southwest of Napa. Built into a mountainside, the ultramodern Barcelona-style ar-

NAPA OR SONOMA?

Napa and Sonoma Valleys run parallel, separated by the narrow, imposing Mayacamas Mountains. The two couldn't be more different. It's easy to mock aggressively sophisticated Napa, its monuments to ego, trophy homes and trophy wives, $1000-a-night inns, $50-plus tastings and wine-snob visitors. Sonoma residents refer to Napa as 'the dark side'; still, its wines are some of the world's best. Constrained by geography, Napa stretches along a single valley, making it easy to visit. Drawbacks are high prices and heavy traffic, but there are more than 500 wineries, nearly side by side. And the valley is gorgeous.

There are three Sonomas: Sonoma town is in Sonoma Valley, which is in Sonoma County. Think of them as Russian dolls. Sonoma County is much more down-to-earth and politically left-leaning. Though it's becoming gentrified, Sonoma lacks Napa's chic factor (Healdsburg notwithstanding) and locals like it that way. The wines are more approachable, but the county's 400 or so wineries are spread out. If you're here on a weekend, head to Sonoma (County or Valley), which gets less traffic, but on a weekday, see Napa too. Ideally schedule two to four days: one for each valley and one or two additional days for western Sonoma County.

Spring and fall are the best times to visit. Summers are hot, dusty and crowded. Fall brings fine weather, harvest time and the 'crush,' the pressing of the grapes, but lodging prices skyrocket.

chitecture is stunning and you can't beat the top-of-the-world vistas over San Pablo Bay. Tours run at 11am and 2pm. Recent changes include a new winemaker and increased focus on wine and food pairings. Reservations recommended. Bottles cost $28 to $85.

Cade
WINERY

(☑ 707-965-2746; www.cadewinery.com; 360 Howell Mountain Rd S, Angwin; tasting & tour $80; ☺ by appointment only) 🖋 Ascend Mt Veeder for drop-dead vistas, 1800ft above the valley, at Napa's oh-so-swank, first-ever organically farmed, Leadership in Energy and Environmental Design (LEED) gold-certified winery, partly owned by former San Francisco mayor Gavin Newsom. Hawks ride thermals at eye level as you sample bright Sauvignon Blanc and luscious Cabernet Sauvignon that's more Bordelaise in style than Californian. Reservations required. Bottles cost $44 to $80.

Vincent Arroyo
WINERY

(☑ 707-942-6995; www.vincentarroyo.com; 2361 Greenwood Ave, Calistoga; ☺ by appointment) FREE The tasting room is a garage, where you may even meet Mr Arroyo, known for his all-estate-grown Petite Sirah and Cabernet Sauvignon. They're distributed nowhere else and are so consistently good that 75% of production is sold before it's bottled. Tastings are free, but appointments are required. Bottles are $21 to $65.

Long Meadow Ranch
FARM

(☑ 707-963-4555; www.longmeadowranch.com; 738 Main St, St Helena; tasting $25-40, chef's table $145; ☺ 11am-6pm) 🖋 Long Meadow stands out for olive-oil tastings ($5), plus good estate-grown Cabernet, Sauvignon Blanc, Chardonnay and Pinot Noir, served inside an 1874 farmhouse surrounded by lovely gardens. It also has a whiskey flight for $30; sells housemade products such as preserves, BBQ sauce and Bloody Mary mix; and hosts chef's tables (four- to five-course food and wine experiences) at lunch and dinner daily. Reservations for chef's table required. Bottles $20 to $50.

Twenty Rows
WINERY

(☑ 707-265-7750; www.twentyrows.com; 880 Vallejo St, Napa; tasting $20, glass $10; ☺ 11am-6pm Wed-Mon, by appointment Tue) This long-standing downtown Napa winery crafts light-on-the-palate Cabernet Sauvignon ($32 a bottle). Taste in a chilly garage with fun dudes who know their wines, or sip on the newly constructed back patio. Good Sauvignon Blanc.

❶ BOOKING APPOINTMENTS AT WINERIES

Because of strict county zoning laws, many Napa wineries cannot legally receive drop-in visitors; unless you've come strictly to buy, you'll have to call ahead. This is *not* the case with all wineries. We recommend booking one tasting, plus a lunch or dinner reservation, and planning your day around those appointments.

Hall
WINERY

(☑ 707-967-2626; www.hallwines.com; 401 St Helena Hwy, St Helena; tasting & tour from $40; ☺ 10am-5:30pm; 🅿 ♿) 🖋 Co-owned by Bill Clinton's former ambassador to Austria, Hall specializes in Cabernet Sauvignon, Sauvignon Blanc and Merlot, crafted in big-fruit California style. Its dramatic tasting room has a stand-up bar with 180-degree views of vineyards and mountains through floor-to-ceiling glass, and the glorious art collection includes a giant chrome rabbit leaping over the vines. Bottles cost $24 to $170.

Schramsberg
WINERY

(☑ 707-942-2414, 800-877-3623; www.schramsberg.com; 1400 Schramsberg Rd, off Peterson Dr; tour & tasting $70, tour & sparkling-wine tasting $95, reserve wine & cheese pairing $125; ☺ by appointment at 9:30am, 10am, 10:30am, 11:30am, noon, 1:30pm, & 2:30pm) Napa's second-oldest winery, Schramsberg makes some of California's best brut sparkling wines, and in 1972 was the first domestic wine served at the White House. Blanc de Blancs is the signature. The appointment-only tasting and tour (book well ahead) is expensive, but you'll sample all the *tête de cuvées*, not just the low-end wines. Tours include a walk through the caves; bring a sweater. Bottles cost $24 to $150.

Titus
WINERY

(☑ 707-963-3235; www.titusvineyards.com; 2971 Silverado Trail N, St Helena; tasting $20; ☺ by appointment; ♿ ♿) Formerly modest Titus has gone fancy of late, opening a modern tasting facility with windows for days, surrounded by 40 acres of vineyards. It's best to call ahead to sample the winery's good-value, fruit-forward Cabernet Sauvignon and old-vine Zinfandel – rare in Napa. Afterward, take your glass outside, and relax on the expansive patio. The tasting fee is waived with a purchase; bottles are $20 to $70.

Castello di Amorosa
WINERY, CASTLE

(☑707-967-6272; www.castellodiamorosa.com; 4045 Hwy 29, Calistoga; entry & tasting $25-35, incl guided tour $40-85; ☺9:30am-6pm Mar-Oct, to 5pm Nov-Feb; P🚗) It took 14 years to build this perfectly replicated, 13th-century Italian castle, complete with moat, hand-cut stone walls, ceiling frescoes by Italian artisans, Roman-style cross-vault brick catacombs, and a torture chamber with period equipment. You can taste without an appointment, but this is one tour worth taking. Oh, the wine? Some respectable Italian varietals, including a velvety Tuscan blend and a Merlot that goes great with pizza. Bottles are $20 to $98.

Darioush
WINERY

(☑707-257-2345; www.darioush.com; 4240 Silverado Trail, Napa; tasting from $40; ☺10:30am-5pm; P) Like a modern-day Persian palace, Darioush ranks high on the fabulosity scale, with towering columns, Le Corbusier furniture, Persian rugs and travertine walls. Though known for Cabernet Sauvignon, Darioush also bottles Chardonnay, Merlot and Shiraz, all made with 100% of their respective varietals. Call about wine-and-cheese pairings ($75). Bottles cost $40 to $95.

Mumm Napa
WINERY, GALLERY

(☑800-686-6272, 707-967-7700; www.mummnapa.com; 8445 Silverado Trail, Rutherford; tasting $20-50, tour $30, glass $12-15; ☺10am-6pm; P) Valley views are spectacular at Mumm, which makes respectable sparkling wines you can sample by the glass beneath a vine-yard-side pergola or seated on a vineyard-view terrace – ideal if you want to impress conservative parents-in-law. Dodge crowds by coming early, or paying $50 for the reserve-tasting Oak Terrace (reservations required). There's also a fabulous photography gallery featuring the work of Ansel Adams. Last seating is at 5:45pm.

Regusci
WINERY

(☑707-254-0403; www.regusciwinery.com; 5584 Silverado Trail, Napa; tasting $50, incl tour $60; ☺10am-5pm; P) One of Napa's oldest, Regusci dates to the late 1800s, with 160 acres of vineyards unfurling around a century-old stone winery that makes Bordeaux-style blends on the valley's quieter eastern side – good when traffic up-valley is bad. There's a lovely oak-shaded picnic area. Reservations required; tasting fee is waived with a purchase of $80 or more. Bottles cost $55 to $120.

Elizabeth Spencer
WINERY

(☑707-963-6067; www.elizabethspencerwinery.com; 1165 Rutherford Rd, Rutherford; tasting $25-60; ☺10am-6pm, last tasting 5:30pm) Check in at this 1872 former post-office building and indulge in tastings tableside in the outdoor garden courtyard at this inviting small winery. Featured are monster-sized Pinot Noir, a range of white-wine varietals including Sauvignon Blanc and Chenan Blanc, structured light-body Grenache and an array of Cabernet. Tastings are a relaxed affair; allow an hour for the alfresco experience. Bottles cost $35 to $250.

CALIFORNIA WILDFIRES

In mid-October 2017 – days before this book went to press – ten simultaneous massive wildfires ravaged Wine Country. Fueled by bone-dry vegetation and sometimes hurricane-force winds, they burned for two weeks, becoming the worst fires in California history. As of this writing, 42 people were dead, thousands homeless. Nearly 200,000 acres and 8500 structures had been destroyed. But no sooner had acrid smoke appeared everywhere than yard signs did, too, proclaiming 'The Love In the Air is Thicker than the Smoke.' Indeed, the stories of heartbreak and heroism astound; for a glimpse, search online for #sonomaproud, #napastrong, #sonomafire, #napafire, #atlasfire, #tubbsfire....

Remarkably, the principal destinations in this chapter – Napa and Sonoma Valleys – were largely spared at valley-floor level, even if the hills above were not. Despite the devastation, 2017 may prove good for wine: 90% of the grapes had already been harvested, and those still on the vine were Cabernet Sauvignon, which have thicker skins than Chardonnay or Sauvignon Blanc, and thus aren't as susceptible to 'smoke taint,' especially late in the season. Long-term effects on the vines are unknown.

You should absolutely plan to visit Wine Country – even if some of the countryside has temporarily lost its pastoral beauty. We've removed the listings we know to have burned, but do call ahead to anyplace you're determined to see especially parks and camp-grounds – to ensure full operation. *John A Vlahides, San Francisco, Oct 27, 2017*

Robert Mondavi WINERY
(☑707-226-1395, 888-766-6328; www.robertmon
daviwinery.com; 7801 Hwy 29, Oakville; tasting/tour
from $5/25; ◷10am-5pm, store to 6pm; 🅿🚻) 🄿
Tour buses flock to this corporate-owned
winery, but if you know nothing about wine
and can cope with crowds, the worthwhile
tours provide good insight into winemaking.
Definitely skip the charcuterie plate, but do
consider attending one of the glorious outdoor summer **concerts**; call for schedules.
Bottles cost $35 to $165.

Napa

The valley's workaday hub was once a
nothing-special city of storefronts, Victorian cottages and riverfront warehouses,
but booming real-estate values caused an
influx of new money that's transforming
downtown into a hub of arts and food.

Napa lies between Silverado Trail and
St Helena Hwy/Hwy 29. For downtown,
exit Hwy 29 at 1st St and drive east. Napa's
main drag, 1st St, is lined with shops and
restaurants.

◉ Sights

★**di Rosa** ARTS CENTER
(☑707-226-5991; www.dirosaart.org; 5200 Hwy 121;
$5, tours $12-15; ◷10am-4pm Wed-Sun; 🅿) West
of downtown, scrap-metal sculptures dot Carneros vineyards at the 217-acre di Rosa Art
+ Nature Preserve, a stunning collection of
Northern California art, displayed indoors in
galleries and outdoors in gardens by a giant
lake. Reservations recommended for tours.

★**Oxbow Public Market** MARKET
(Map p168; ☑707-226-6529; www.oxbowpublic
market.com; 610 & 644 1st St; ◷9am-9pm;
🅿🚻) 🄿 Showcasing all things culinary
(produce stalls, kitchen shops and everywhere something to taste), Oxbow is foodie
central with an emphasis on seasonal eating and sustainability. Some vendors and
restaurants open early or close late. Come
hungry.

CIA at Copia CENTER
(Map p168; ☑707-967-2500; www.ciaatcopia.
com; 500 1st St; ◷10:30am-9pm) The former
food museum beside Napa's famous Oxbow
Public Market has been revived as a center
of all things edible by the prestigious Culinary Institute of America. In its new life as
Copia, the 80,000-sq-ft campus offers wine

tastings, interactive cooking demos, an innovative restaurant, a massive fork statue
(composed of many thousands of smaller
forks) and more food-related features.

The eponymous **Restaurant at CIA Copia** takes a new approach to food service,
with cart-and-tray dishes traveling around
the dining room and chefs similarly on the
move, answering burning questions from
curious guests.

☞ Tours

Napa Valley Wine Train TOURS
(Map p168; ☑800-427-4124, 707-253-2111; http://
winetrain.com; 1275 McKinstry St; ticket incl dining from $146) A cushy, if touristy, way to see
Wine Country, the Wine Train offers three-
hour daily trips in vintage Pullman dining
cars, from Napa to St Helena and back, with
optional winery tours. It also offers six-hour
journeys visiting multiple wineries with
Napa Valley cuisine served between visits.

🛏 Sleeping

The digs here are decent, ranging from high-
end spa resorts to quiet inns to comfy chain
hotels but prices are high. On weekends and
over summer, when rates skyrocket, consider staying in Calistoga. Archer Hotel (https://
archerhotel.com/napa) and its Charlie Palm-
er Steakhouse are new to downtown, and
everybody is talking about them.

★**Carneros Resort & Spa** RESORT $$$
(☑888-400-9000, 707-299-4900; www.the-
carnerosresort.com; 4048 Sonoma Hwy; r from

Napa

Napa

$500; ✳ @ 🛜 🏊 🐕) Carneros Resort & Spa's contemporary aesthetic and retro small-town agricultural theme shatter the predictable Wine Country mold. The interiors of the semidetached, corrugated-metal cottages are snappy and chic, with cherry-wood floors, ultrasuede headboards, wood-burning fireplaces, heated-tile bathroom floors, giant tubs and indoor-outdoor showers.

Andaz Napa   HOTEL **$$$**
(Map p168; ☎ 707-687-1234; www.andaznapa.com; 1450 1st St; r from $270; P ❄ ✳ @ 🛜) Smack downtown, the Andaz was constructed in 2009 and feels like a big-city hotel, with

business-class-fancy rooms styled in sexy contemporary style. It's walking distance to restaurants and bars. There's an on-site terrace bar with fire pits and guests have access to an adjacent health club with indoor lap pool, sauna and gym.

Cottages of Napa Valley   BUNGALOW $$$

(🕿 707-252-7810; www.napacottages.com; 1012 Darns Lane; cottages $350-600; ❈ 🛜) Eight pristine cottages of quality construction – made for romantic hideaways, with extralong soaking tubs, indoor gas fireplaces and outdoor campfire pits – surround a big garden shaded by towering pines. Cottages 4 and 8 have private porches and swinging chairs. The only drawback is noise from traffic, but interiors are quiet.

Milliken Creek Inn   INN $$$

(🕿 707-255-1197; www.millikencreekinn.com; 1815 Silverado Trail; r $295-750; ❈ @ 🛜) Understatedly elegant Milliken Creek combines small-inn charm, fine-hotel service and B&B intimacy. Rooms are impeccably styled in English-colonial style and higher-end rooms have top-flight amenities, fireplace and ultrahigh-thread-count linen. Breakfast is delivered. Book a river-view room.

Blackbird Inn   B&B $$$

(Map p168; 🕿 707-226-2450, 888-567-9811; www.blackbirdinnnapa.com; 1755 1st St; r $250-285; ❈ 🛜) Gorgeous, eight-room arts-and-crafts-style B&B. Anticipate street noise.

Napa River Inn   HOTEL $$$

(Map p168; 🕿 707-251-8500, 877-251-8500; www.napariverinn.com; 500 Main St; r $300-600; ❈ @ 🛜 🐾) Beside the river in the 1884 Hatt Building, the inn has top-end rooms, Victoriana to modern, in three satellite buildings. Walkable distance to restaurants and bars. Dogs get special treatment.

Napa Winery Inn   HOTEL $$$

(🕿 707-257-7220; www.napawineryinn.com; 1998 Trower Ave; r Mon-Fri $179-279, Sat & Sun $229-350; ❈ @ 🛜 🐾 🐾) Request a remodeled room at this good-value hotel, north of downtown, decorated with Colonial-style furniture. It has a hot tub and good service. There are complimentary wine receptions each night: weekdays 5:30pm to 6:30pm, to 7pm weekends.

River Terrace Inn   HOTEL $$$

(🕿 707-320-9000; www.riverterraceinn.com; 1600 Soscol Ave; r $189-360; ❈ 🛜 🐾) Upmarket, business-class, chain-style hotel with shopping-mall-bland architecture fronting on the Napa River. The entire property was recently renovated, including a new restaurant and bar.

🍴 Eating

Deliciousness abounds, but it's going to cost you. Make reservations whenever possible, and cut costs by grabbing sandwiches from Soda Canyon Store for a picnic lunch.

★ Oxbow Public Market   MARKET $

(Map p168; 🕿 707-226-6529; www.oxbowpublicmarket.com; 610 & 644 1st St; items from $3; ⊙ 9am-9pm; 🛜 🚻) 🍴 Graze at this gourmet market and plug into the Northern California food scene. Standouts: **Hog Island Oyster Co**; comfort cooking at celeb-chef Todd Humphries' **Kitchen Door**; great Cal-Mexican tacos at **C Casa & Taco Lounge**; the India pale ales (IPAs) and sour beers at **Fieldwork Brewing Company**; espresso from **Ritual Coffee**; and **Three Twins** certified-organic ice cream.

Tuesday is locals' night (5pm to 8pm), with many discounts. Some stalls remain open to 9pm, even on Sundays, but many close earlier and some vendors open early in the morning.

Alexis Baking Company & Cafe   CAFE $

(Map p168; 🕿 707-258-1827; www.abcnapa.com; 1517 3rd St; mains $9-17; ⊙ 7am-3pm Mon-Fri, 7:30am-3pm Sat, 8am-2pm Sun; 🍴 🚻) Our fave spot for quality egg scrambles, granola, focaccia sandwiches, big cups of joe and boxed lunches to go.

Taqueria Maria   MEXICAN $

(Map p168; 🕿 707-257-6925; www.taqueriamariapa1.com; 640 3rd St; mains $8-15; ⊙ 8am-9pm Sun-Thu, to 9:30pm Fri & Sat; 🍴 🚻) Reliably good Mexican cooking that won't break the bank. Also serves breakfast.

Buttercream Bakery & Diner   DINER $

(🕿 707-255-6700; www.buttercreambakery.com; 2297 Jefferson St; breakfast $5-10, cakes $15-25; ⊙ bakery 5:30am-6pm Mon-Sat, to 4pm Sun, diner 5:30am-3pm Mon-Sat, to 2:30pm Sun) This retro-flashback pink-striped diner, favored by Napa's little old ladies, has all-day breakfasts and white-bread lunches, served by matrons in heavy eye shadow. Also famous for its champagne cakes.

Soda Canyon Store   DELI $

(🕿 707-252-0285; www.sodacanyonstore.com; 4006 Silverado Trail; ⊙ 6am-6pm Mon-Sat, 7am-5pm Sun) This roadside deli with shaded picnic area makes an easy stop while winery-hopping north of town.

Oenotri

ITALIAN $$

(Map p168; ☑707-252-1022; www.oenotri.com; 1425 1st St; brunch $13-15, dinner mains $18-34; ☺brunch 10am-3pm Sat & Sun, 5:30-9pm Sun-Thu, to 10pm Fri & Sat) ☞ Housemade *salumi* (cured meat) and pastas, and wood-fired Naples-style pizzas are the stars at always-busy Oenotri, which draws crowds for daily-changing, locally sourced, rustic-Italian cooking, served in a cavernous brick-walled space.

Pizza Azzuro

PIZZA $$

(Map p168; ☑707-255-5552; www.azzurropizzeria. com; 1260 Main St; mains $15-18; ☺11:30am-9:30pm Sun-Thu, to 10pm Fri & Sat; ☑☻) This Napa classic gets deafeningly loud, but it's worth bearing for tender-crusted pizzas, salad-topped 'manciata' bread, good Caesar salads and pastas.

Norman Rose Tavern

PUB FOOD $$

(Map p168; ☑707-258-1516; www.normanrosenapa. com; 1401 1st St; mains $10-24; ☺11:30am-9pm Sun-Thu, to 10pm Fri & Sat; ☻) This happening gastropub, styled with reclaimed wood and tufted-leather banquettes, is good for a burger and beer. Great fries and plenty of seasonal favorites. Full bar.

Bounty Hunter Wine Bar & Smokin' BBQ

BARBECUE $$

(Map p168; ☑707-226-3976; www.bountyhunter winebar.com; 975 1st St; mains $14-28; ☺11am-10pm Sun-Thu, to midnight Fri & Sat; ☻) Inside an 1888 grocery store, Bounty Hunter has an Old West vibe and superb barbecue, made with house-smoked meats. The standout 'beer-can chicken' is a whole chicken roasted over a can of Tecate. Libations include 40 local beers, 60 whiskeys and 400 wines (40 by the glass).

Angèle

FRENCH $$$

(Map p168; ☑707-252-8115; www.angelerestau rant.com; 540 Main St; lunch mains $14-27, dinner

---

A LOVELY SPOT FOR A PICNIC

Unlike Sonoma, there aren't many places to picnic legally in Napa. Here's a short list, in south–north order, but call ahead and remember to buy a bottle (or glass, if available) of your host's wine. If you don't finish it, California law forbids driving with an uncorked bottle in the car (keep it in the trunk).

➡ Regusci (p166)

➡ Napa Valley Museum (p172)

➡ Pride Mountain (p164)

$26-30; ☺11:30am-4pm & 5-9pm Sun-Thu, to 10pm Sat & Sun) Stalwart Angèle serves reliable provincial-French cooking – French onion soup, Nicoise salads and *croques messieurs* (gourmet toasted ham and cheese sandwiches) at lunch, cassoulet with duck confit at dinner – on a river-view deck or in the cozy dining room, both perfect for lingering with a good bottle of wine.

Bistro Don Giovanni

ITALIAN $$$

(☑707-224-3300; www.bistrodongiovanni.com; 4110 Howard Lane; mains $16-34; ☺11:30am-10pm Sun-Thu, to 11pm Fri & Sat) This long-running favorite roadhouse serves modern-Italian pastas, crispy pizzas and wood-roasted meats. Reservations essential. Weekends get packed. Request a vineyard-view table (good luck).

Torc

CALIFORNIAN $$$

(Map p168; ☑707-252-3292; www.torcnapa.com; 1140 Main St; mains $28-46, prix-fixe menu $46; ☺5-9:30pm Wed-Mon) Wildly popular Torc plays off the seasons with dynamic combinations of farm-fresh ingredients such as pork belly with satsuma-imo potato and choy raab, or artichoke velouté with wild mushrooms. Well-arranged for people-watching, the big stone dining room has an open-truss ceiling and pinewood tables that downplay formality. Reservations essential.

🍷 Drinking & Nightlife

There is no shortage of drinking establishments in the downtown area, including breweries, sports bars and wine-tasting rooms, which have proliferated in recent years.

Vintners' Collective

WINE BAR

(Map p168; ☑707-255-7150; www.vintnerscollective. com; 1245 Main St; tastings $10-40, private tastings $75 & $95; ☺11am-7pm) Ditch the car and chill in downtown Napa at this tasting bar inside a former 20th-century brothel. It represents 20-plus high-end boutique wineries that are too small to have their own tasting rooms. There are around 140 wines to try, and the pricier the tasting, the more sought-after the wine. The $75 and $95 tastings include artisanal cheese and charcuterie.

Tannery Bend Beerworks

BREWERY

(☑707-681-5774; http://tannerybendbeerworks. com; 101 S Coombs St; ☺noon-8pm Wed-Sun) What do you call a brewery smaller than micro? A Napa brewery stepped up to answer that question in 2017 and this nanobrewery produces just 15 gallons of beer per batch. The teeny tiny booze biz is a collaboration between a chef, a brewer and a restaurateur (same one who owns the fabulous Oenotri, p169). With their powers combined, they've created a few delicious and locally sourced Saisons and IPAs.

Carpe Diem Wine Bar WINE BAR
(Map p168; ☑707-224-0800; www.carpediem winebar.com; 1001 2nd St; ⊙4-9pm Mon-Thu, to 10pm Fri & Sat) This busy storefront wine bar and restaurant (mains $22–$48) makes inventive, flavorful small plates, from simple skewers and flatbreads to elaborate ostrich burgers, salumi platters and – wait for it – duck confit 'quack and cheese.'

Downtown Joe's SPORTS BAR, BREWERY
(Map p168; ☑707-258-2337; www.downtownjoes. com; 902 Main St, at 2nd St; ⊙8am-1am Mon & Tue, to 2am Wed-Sun; ☎) Live music Thursday to Sunday, TV sports nightly and a pet-friendly, riverfront patio. Often packed, usually messy.

Billco's Billiards & Darts SPORTS BAR
(Map p168; www.billcos.com; 1234 3rd St; ⊙noon-2am Mon-Sat, to midnight Sun) Dudes with beards swill craft beers and throw darts inside this lively pool hall.

☆ Entertainment

Silo's Jazz Club LIVE MUSIC
(Map p168; ☑707-251-5833; www.silosnapa.com; 530 Main St; cover varies; ⊙4-10pm Wed, 5-10pm Thu, 7-11pm Fri & Sat, varied hours Sun) A cabaret-style wine-and-beer bar, Silo's hosts free jazz on Wednesday, and varied music acts on Friday and Saturday nights. On Thursday it's good for drinks. Book ahead for weekends.

Uptown Theatre THEATER
(Map p168; ☑707-259-0123, ext 6; www.uptown theatrenapa.com; 1350 3rd St) Big-name acts play this restored 1937 theater.

🛍 Shopping

Napa Valley Olive Oil Mfg Co FOOD
(Map p168; ☑707-265-6866; 1331 1st St; ⊙10am-5:30pm) Sample 40 varieties of fine olive oil and vinegar at this downtown specialty-food boutique, which also carries fancy salts and local jam.

Betty's Girl WOMEN'S CLOTHING, VINTAGE
(Map p168; ☑707-254-7560; www.bettysgirlnapa. com; 968 Pearl St; ⊙by appointment) Expert couturier Kim Northrup fits women with fabulous vintage cocktail dresses and custom-made designs, altering and shipping for

---

ℹ SHIPPING IT HOME

Bodega Shipping Co (☑Napa 707-968-5462, Sonoma 707-343-1656; www.bodegashippingco.com) picks up wine in Napa and Sonoma Valleys, packages it, and ships nationwide via UPS and FedEx, with no hidden fees. Also ships to some international destinations, including the UK, Australia, Hong Kong and some countries in South America. For a case (12 bottles) budget $38 to $73; in summer add $10 to $20 for temperature-controlled shipping; for international shipments, budget a few hundred dollars, depending on destination. Call for a quote.

---

no additional charge. She also has an annex at 1320 2nd St.

Napa General Store GIFTS & SOUVENIRS
(Map p168; ☑707-259-0762; www.napageneral store.com; 540 Main St; ⊙8am-6pm) Finally, cutesy Wine Country souvenirs reasonably priced. The on-site **wine bar** is convenient for nonshopping spouses.

ℹ Information

INTERNET
Napa Library (☑707-253-4241; www.county ofnapa.org/library; 580 Coombs St; ⊙10am-9pm Mon-Thu, to 6pm Fri & Sat; ☎) Free internet access.

TOURIST INFORMATION
Napa Valley Welcome Center (Map p168; ☑707-251-5895, 855-847-6272; www.visitna pavalley.com; 600 Main St; ⊙9am-5pm; 🖥) Lodging assistance (call ☑707-251-9188 or ☑855-333-6272), wine-tasting passes, spa deals and comprehensive winery maps.

ℹ Getting There & Away

From San Francisco, public transportation can get you to Napa, but it's insufficient for vineyard-hopping. For public-transit information, dial ☑511, or look online at www.transit.511.org.

Downtown Napa is about an 80-minute drive from San Francisco.

ℹ Getting Around

Pedicabs park outside downtown restaurants – especially at the foot of Main St, near the Napa Valley Welcome Center – in summer. Car-sharing service Uber (www.uber.com) operates in Napa, but plans to hire an Uber can go awry in some areas due to spotty cell reception.

Yountville

This onetime stagecoach stop, 9 miles north of Napa, is now a fine-food destination playing to the haute bourgeoisie, with more Michelin stars per capita than any other American town. A stay in Yountville means drinking at dinner without having to drive afterward, as the town is walkable, but Napa and Calistoga make for livelier bases. Most businesses are on Washington St.

◉ Sights

Ma(i)sonry GALLERY, WINERY
(☑707-944-0889; www.maisonry.com; 6711 Washington St; ◷10:30am-4:30pm Sun-Thu, to 5:30pm Fri & Sat; P) Ma(i)sonry occupies a free-to-browse 1904 stone house and garden, transformed into a fussy winery-collective and gallery of pricey rustic-modern *meubles* (furniture) and art, some quite cool. Reservations recommended for wine tastings.

Napa Valley Museum MUSEUM
(☑707-944-0500; www.napavalleymuseum.org; 55 Presidents Circle; adult/child $7/2.50; ◷11am-4pm Wed-Sun; P) Yountville's modernist 40,000-sq-ft museum chronicles cultural history and showcases local paintings. Good picnicking outside. From town, it's across Hwy 29. Second Saturdays of the month are free.

Yountville Park PARK
(cnr Washington & Madison Sts; ◷6am-8pm) Good park for a picnic.

🛏 Sleeping

There are some lovely inns here and many are walking distance from the restaurants and shops. Budget travelers will not find suitable accommodations though.

Poetry Inn INN $$$
(☑707-944-0646; www.poetryinn.com; 6380 Silverado Trail; r $1100-1975; ❄🛜🏊) There's no better valley view than from this contemporary five-room inn, high on the hills east of Yountville. Decorated with posh restraint, rooms have private balcony, wood-burning fireplace, 1000-thread-count linen and enormous bath with indoor-outdoor shower. Bring a ring.

Petit Logis INN $$$
(☑877-944-2332, 707-944-2332; www.petitlogis.com; 6527 Yount St; r $145-325; ❄🛜) Simple, cozy and comfortable, this cedar-sided inn has five uniquely adorned rooms, each with jetted tub and gas fireplace.

✘ Eating

Make reservations or you may not eat. Yountville Park has picnic tables and barbecue grills. Find groceries across from the post office. There's a great taco truck parked in town.

Bouchon Bakery BAKERY $
(☑707-944-2253; www.bouchonbakery.com; 6528 Washington St; items from $3; ◷7am-7pm; ☑) Bouchon makes as-good-as-in-Paris French pastries and strong coffee. There's always a line and rarely a seat: get it to go.

Ottimo ITALIAN $
(☑707-944-0102; www.ottimo-nv.com; 6525 Washington St; pizzas $14, crescintines $8; ◷7am-6pm) Chef Michael Chiarello opened this Italian market, cafe and *mozzeria* in Yountville's V Marketplace across from his popular farm-to-table establishment Bottega in early 2017, and it quietly became a prime spot for industry folks and in-the-know tourists. Most delicious are the brick-oven pizzas and crescentines (panini-like sandwiches), along with samples of preserves (from Chiarello's family recipes) in the shop. Grab a table on the sunny outdoor patio and hit the espresso bar on your way out.

Tacos Garcia FAST FOOD $
(☑707-980-4896; 6764 Washington St; tacos $1.50; ◷11am-9pm) This beloved taco truck operates out of the parking lot in front of the dive bar Pancha's (p174), offering delicious tacos with fillings such as beef cheeks, *tripa* (fried intestine) and fried pork double-wrapped in a corn tortilla and topped with onion and cilantro.

Redd Wood ITALIAN $$
(☑707-299-5030; www.redd-wood.com; 6755 Washington St; pizzas $16-19, most mains $17-28; ◷11:30am-10pm Sun-Thu, to 11pm Fri & Sat) Celeb-chef Richard Reddington's casual Italian trattoria serves outstanding homemade pastas, *salumi* and tender-to-the-tooth pizzas from a wood-fired oven.

Addendum SOUTHERN US $$
(☑707-944-1565; www.adhocrestaurant.com/addendum; 6476 Washington St; box lunch $16.50; ◷11am-2pm Thu-Sat; 🅟) An offspring of parent restaurant Ad Hoc (p174), Thomas Keller's Addendum provides boxed lunches of finger-lickin' buttermilk-fried chicken, BBQ pork ribs and pulled-pork sandwiches, accompanied by Southern-style sides to go. It's simple and delicious.

Napa Valley South

NAPA & SONOMA WINE COUNTRY YOUNTVILLE

★ **French Laundry**   CALIFORNIAN **$$$**
(📋 707-944-2380; www.thomaskeller.com/tfl; 6640 Washington St; prix-fixe dinner $310; ⊘ seatings 11am-12:30pm Fri-Sun, 5-9pm daily) The pinnacle of California dining, Thomas Keller's French Laundry is epic, a high-wattage culinary experience on par with the world's best. Book one month ahead on the online app Tock, as tickets are released in groupings. This is the meal you can brag about the rest of your life.

★ **Ciccio**   ITALIAN **$$$**
(📋 707-945-1000; www.ciccionapavalley.com; 6770 Washington St; mains $25-32; ⊘ 5-9pm Wed-Sun) The small, frequently changing menu at this family-owned Italian place is dependent on the season and likely to include just a couple of veggies, pastas, meat options and four to six wood-fired pizzas. But wow! You cannot go wrong, especially if you're lucky enough to show up when whole sea bass and garlicky pea tendrils are available. There's a negroni bar and many delicious wines from the owner's Altamura Ranch, along with a prix-fixe chef's dinner (by limited reservation) that includes menu and off-menu favorites for visitors to choose from.

Bouchon   FRENCH **$$$**
(📋 707-944-8037; www.thomaskeller.com; 6354 Washington St; mains $19-59; ⊘ 11am-midnight Mon-Fri, from 10am Sat & Sun) Details at celeb-chef Thomas Keller's French brasserie are so impeccable – zinc bar to white-aproned waiters – you'd swear you were in Paris. Only the Bermuda-shorts-clad Americans look out of place. On the menu: oysters, onion soup, roasted chicken, trout with almonds, runny cheeses and perfect profiteroles.

Ad Hoc   CALIFORNIAN **$$$**
(📋 707-944-2487; www.adhocrestaurant.com; 6476 Washington St; prix-fixe dinner from $55; ⊘ 5-10pm Thu-Sat & Mon, 9am-1:30pm & 5-10pm Sun)

A winning formula by Thomas Keller, Yountville's culinary patriarch, Ad Hoc serves the master's favorite American home cooking in four family-style courses with no variations (dietary restrictions notwithstanding). The menu changes daily but regularly features pot roast, BBQ and fried chicken, which is also available (for takeout only) on weekends behind Ad Hoc at Keller's latest venture, Addendum (p172).

Mustards Grill   CALIFORNIAN **$$$**
(📋 707-944-2424; www.mustardsgrill.com; 7399 St Helena Hwy; mains $16-33; ⊘ 11:30am-9pm Mon-Thu, to 9:30pm Fri, 11am-9:30pm Sat & Sun; 🪑) The valley's original and always-packed roadhouse makes platters of crowd-pleasing, wood-fired, California comfort food: roasted meats, lamb shanks, pork chops, hearty salads and sandwiches.

Bistro Jeanty   FRENCH **$$$**
(📋 707-944-0103; www.bistrojeanty.com; 6510 Washington St; mains $21-34; ⊘ 11:30am-10:30pm) French bistros by classical definition serve comfort food to weary travelers and that's what French-born chef-owner Philippe Jeanty does here, with succulent cassoulet, coq au vin, *steak frites* (steak and chips), slow-roasted pork shoulder and scrumptious tomato soup.

🍷 Drinking & Nightlife

There are a couple of wine-tasting rooms in town where much of the day-drinking is done, while the smoky local dive Pancha's passes for nightlife.

Pancha's   BAR
(📋 707-944-2125; 6764 Washington St; ⊘ noon-2am) If you don't mind constant cigarette smoke, hang here and swill tequila with vineyard workers early in the night and waiters later. Cash only.

FLYING & BALLOONING

Wine Country is stunning from the air – a multihued tapestry of undulating hills, deep valleys and rambling vineyards. Make reservations.

The **Vintage Aircraft Company** (p191) flies over Sonoma in a vintage biplane with an awesome pilot who'll do loop-de-loops on request (add $50). Twenty-minute tours cost $175/270 for one/two adults.

Napa Valley's signature hot-air balloon flights leave early, around 6am or 7am, when the air is coolest; they usually include a champagne breakfast on landing. Adults pay about $200 to $250, and kids $150 to $175. Call **Balloons Above the Valley** (📋 707-253-2222, 800-464-6824; www.balloonrides.com; 603 California Blvd) or **Napa Valley Balloons** (📋 707-944-0228, 800-253-2224; www.napavalleyballoons.com; per person $239, 2-person private flight $2200), both in Yountville.

☆ Entertainment

Lincoln Theater THEATER
(☑box office 707-949-9900; www.lincolntheater. org; 100 California Dr) Various artists, including Napa Valley Symphony, play this 1200-seat theater.

🔒 Shopping

Finesse, the Store GIFTS & SOUVENIRS
(☑707-363-9552; www.finessethestore.com; 6540 Washington St; ⊘11am-6pm Thu-Mon) Thomas Keller disciples and fanatics can finally take a piece of the action home. The culinary guru's new gift and souvenir shop features items such as cookbooks, cookware, aprons and sauces.

ℹ Getting There & Away

For public-transit information, dial ☑ 511, or look online at www.transit.511.org. Yountville is about an 80-minute drive from San Francisco.

Oakville & Rutherford

It'd be easy to drive through Oakville and never know you'd missed it. Vineyards sprawl everywhere. Rutherford is slightly more conspicuous.

🛏 Sleeping & Eating

There aren't many places to stay here and those on a budget should steer clear. North in Calistoga and south in downtown Napa there are far more choices.

The two tiny towns have between them a couple of good markets and the lip-smacking Rutherford Grill, which is essentially a Houston's.

★Auberge du Soleil LUXURY HOTEL $$$
(☑800-348-5406, 707-963-1211; www.aubergedus oleil.com; 180 Rutherford Hill Rd, Rutherford; r $795-1500, ste $1525-5300; ❄🛜🏊) The top splurge for a no-holds-barred romantic weekend, Auberge's hillside cottages, some of which are brand new, are second to none. A meal in its **dining room** (breakfast mains $33, lunch $31 to $42, three-/four-/six-course prix-fixe dinner $115/130/150) is an iconic Napa experience: come for a fancy breakfast, lazy lunch or will-you-wear-my-ring dinner; valley views are mesmerizing – *don't* sit inside.

Make reservations; arrive before sunset.

Rancho Caymus HOTEL $$$
(☑800-845-1777, 707-963-1777; www.ranchocaymus. com; 1140 Rutherford Rd, Rutherford; r $400-800;

❄@🛜🏊) Styled after California's missions, this hacienda-like inn was closed for years before a recent comeback. The restored hotel features 25 large suites with oak-beamed wood ceilings, gas fireplaces and secluded patios. The steeper price reflects work put in to refurbish the entire property, including the relaxing spa, leafy courtyard and plunge pool.

Rutherford Grill AMERICAN $$
(☑707-963-1792; www.rutherfordgrill.com; 1180 Rutherford Rd, Rutherford; mains $15-38; ⊘11:30am-9:30pm Mon-Thu, to 10pm Fri, 11am-10pm Sat, to 9:30pm Sun) Yes, it's part of a chain (Houston's), but its bar at lunchtime provides a chance to rub shoulders with winemakers. The food is consistent – ribs, rotisserie chicken, good grilled artichokes – and there's no corkage, so bring that bottle you just bought.

St Helena

You'll know you're here when traffic halts. St Helena (ha-*lee*-na) is the Rodeo Dr of Napa. Fancy boutiques line the historic downtown's Main St (Hwy 29) and provide excellent window-shopping. Parking, however, is next-to-impossible on summer weekends. Tip: look behind the visitor center (p180).

◎ Sights

Robert Louis Stevenson Museum MUSEUM
(☑707-963-3757; http://stevensonmuseum.org; 1490 Library Lane; ⊘noon-4pm Tue-Sat; P) FREE This museum contains the largest displayed collection of Robert Louis Stevenson's belongings in the world. In 1880 the author – then sick, penniless and unknown – stayed in an abandoned bunkhouse at the old Silverado Mine on Mt St Helena with his wife, Fanny Osbourne; his novel the *Silverado Squatters* is based on his time there. Turn east off Hwy 29 at the Adams St traffic light and cross the railroad tracks.

Farmers Market MARKET
(☑707-486-2662; www.sthelenafarmersmkt.org; ⊘7:30am-noon Fri May-Oct) Meets at Crane Park, half a mile south of downtown.

🍃 Courses

Culinary Institute of America at Greystone COOKING
(☑707-967-1100; www.ciachef.edu/california; 2555 Main St; 🅿) Inside an 1889 stone château, this culinary-school campus houses a new

restaurant, a gadget- and cookbook-filled culinary shop, a bakery-cafe, weekend cooking demonstrations and wine-tasting classes. Cooking demonstrations are $25 and take place at 1:30pm Saturday and Sunday. Classes start at $95.

🛏 Sleeping

Most options in St Helena are pricey, particularly on weekends and during high season. The one reasonable option is El Bonita, but it fills up fast.

★ El Bonita   MOTEL $$
(☎800-541-3284, 707-963-3216; www.elbonita.com; 195 Main St; r $140-325; P🐕❄✳@🛜♨🐕) Book in advance to secure this sought-after motel, with up-to-date rooms (quietest are in back), attractive grounds, a heated pool, hot tub and sauna.

Las Alcobas   BOUTIQUE HOTEL $$$
(☎707-963-7000; www.lasalcobasnapavalley.com; 1915 Main St; r from $600-2500; ✳🛜♨) A newcomer with a sister property in Mexico City, this boutique has already secured its place among Napa Valley's finest stays. The plush, modern rooms offer both vineyard vista and proximity to some of the region's best dining, shopping and wine tasting. That's if you attempt to pry yourself from the delicious hotel-restaurant Acacia, heated pool and relaxing spa.

Meadowood   RESORT $$$
(☎707-963-3646, 877-963-3646; www.meadowood.com; 900 Meadowood Lane; r from $850; P🐕❄✳@🛜♨) Hidden in a wooded dell with towering pines and miles of hiking, Napa's grandest resort has cottages and rooms in satellite buildings surrounding a croquet lawn. We most like the hillside fireplace suites; lawn-view rooms lack privacy but are good for families. The vibe is Republican country club: wear linen and play *Great Gatsby*. Kids love the mammoth pool and there's also an adult pool.

Harvest Inn by Charlie Palmer   INN $$$
(☎800-950-8466, 707-963-9463; www.harvestinn.com; 1 Main St; r $449-899; ✳@🛜♨🐕) 🍳 A former estate, this 78-room resort has rooms in satellite buildings on sprawling manicured grounds. The reception and rooms were recently repainted and redecorated; vineyard-view rooms are loveliest (each has private hot tub). The grounds contain two heated pools and two hot tubs. The Harvest Table restaurant is delish, with ostentatious flaming cocktails and locally sourced, expertly prepared New American cuisine.

Wydown Hotel   BOUTIQUE HOTEL $$$
(☎707-963-5100; www.wydownhotel.com; 1424 Main St; r Sun-Thu $320-370, Fri & Sat $500-550; ✳🛜) Opened in 2012, this fashion-forward boutique hotel, with good service, sits smack downtown, its 12 oversized rooms smartly decorated with tufted velvet, distressed leather, subway-tile baths and California-king beds with white-on-white high-thread-count linens.

🍴 Eating

St Helena is packed with fabulous restaurants where you'll need reservations; alternatively, self-cater at the local market Sunshine Foods.

Napa Valley Olive Oil Mfg Co   MARKET $
(☎707-963-4173; www.oliveoilsainthelena.com; 835 Charter Oak Ave; ⊘8am-5:30pm) Before the advent of fancy-food stores, this ramshackle market introduced Napa to Italian delicacies: real prosciutto and salami, meaty olives, fresh bread, nutty cheeses and, of course, olive oil. Ask nicely and the owner will lend you a knife and a board to picnic at the rickety tables in the grass outside. Cash only.

Sunshine Foods   MARKET, DELI $
(☎707-963-7070; www.sunshinefoodsmarket.com; 1115 Main St; ⊘7:30am-8:30pm) Town's best grocery store; excellent deli.

Model Bakery   CAFE $
(☎707-963-8192; www.themodelbakery.com; 1357 Main St; dishes $8-10; ⊘6:30am-5pm Mon-Sat, 7am-5pm Sun) Good bakery with scones, muffins, salads, pizzas, sandwiches and exceptional coffee.

Cook St. Helena   ITALIAN $$
(☎707-963-7088; www.cooksthelena.com; 1310 Main St; lunch $14-23, dinner $18-26; ⊘11:30am-10pm Mon-Sat, 4-9pm Sun) Locals crowd this tiny storefront bistro, beloved for its earthy Cal-Italian cooking: homemade pasta and risotto, crispy sole and soft polenta. Expect a wait, even with reservations. Next door, the pizzeria Cook Tavern is under the same ownership and also a good choice.

Cindy's Backstreet Kitchen   MODERN AMERICAN $$
(☎707-963-1200; www.cindysbackstreetkitchen.com; 1327 Railroad Ave; mains $17-29; ⊘11:30am-9pm) 🍳 The inviting retro-homey decor complements the Cal-American comfort

WINE TASTING

The best way to discover the real Wine Country is to avoid factory wineries and visit family-owned boutique houses (producing fewer than 20,000 annual cases) and mid-sized houses (20,000 to 60,000 annual cases). Why does it matter? Think of it. If you were to attend two dinner parties, one for 10 people, one for 1000, which would have the better food? Small wineries maintain tighter control. Also, you won't easily find these wines elsewhere.

Tastings are called 'flights' and include four to six different wines. Napa wineries charge around $10 to $50. In Sonoma Valley, tastings cost about $5 to $20, often refundable with purchase. In Sonoma County, tastings are free or $5 to $10. You must be 21 to taste.

Do not drink and drive. The curvy roads are dangerous and police monitor traffic, especially on Napa's Hwy 29.

To avoid burnout, visit no more than three wineries per day. Most open daily 10am or 11am to 4pm or 5pm, but call ahead if your heart's set, or you absolutely want a tour, especially in Napa, where law requires that some wineries accept visitors only by appointment. If you're buying, ask if there's a wine club, which is free to join and provides discounts, but you'll have to agree to buy a certain amount annually.

food, such as avocado-and-papaya salad, a Chinatown duck burger and sautéed petrale sole. The bar makes a mean mojito.

Gott's Roadside
AMERICAN $$
(☏707-963-3486; http://gotts.com; 933 Main St; mains $8-16; ☺10am-10pm May-Sep, to 9pm Oct-Apr; ☻) ✐ Wiggle your toes in the grass and feast on quality burgers – beef, turkey, ahi or veggie – plus Cobb salads and fish tacos at this classic roadside drive-in. Avoid weekend waits by phoning ahead or ordering online. There's another at Oxbow Public Market (p169).

Market
MODERN AMERICAN $$
(☏707-963-3799; www.marketsthelena.com; 1347 Main St; mains $14-22; ☺11:30am-9pm Mon-Thu, to 10pm Fri & Sat, 10am-9pm Sun) ✐ We love Market's big portions of simple, fresh American cooking, including hearty salads of local produce and soul-satisfying mains such as buttermilk-fried chicken. The stone-walled dining room dates to the 19th century, as does the ornate backbar, where cocktails get muddled to order. Free corkage.

Restaurant at Meadowood
CALIFORNIAN $$$
(☏707-967-1205; www.meadowood.com; 900 Meadowood Lane; 12-course menu $275; ☺5:30-9:30pm Tue-Sat) If you couldn't score reservations at French Laundry, fear not: Meadowood – the valley's only other three-Michelin-star restaurant – has a slightly more sensibly priced menu, elegantly unfussy dining room and lavish haute cuisine that's not too esoteric. Auberge (p175) has better views, but Meadowood's food and service far surpass it.

Farmstead
MODERN AMERICAN $$$
(☏707-963-4555; www.longmeadowranch.com; 738 Main St; mains $22-31; ☺11:30am-9:30pm Mon-Thu, to 10pm Fri & Sat, 11am-9:30pm Sun; ☻) ✐ An enormous open-truss barn with big leather booths and rocking-chair porch, Farmstead draws an all-ages crowd and farms many of its own ingredients – including grass-fed beef and lamb – for an earthy menu highlighting wood-fired cooking.

Terra
CALIFORNIAN $$$
(☏707-963-8931; www.terrarestaurant.com; 1345 Railroad Ave; 4-/5-/6-course menu $78/93/105; ☺6-9pm Thu-Mon) Seamlessly blending Japanese, French and Italian culinary styles, Terra is one of Wine Country's top tables – the signature meal is broiled sake-marinated black cod with shrimp dumplings in shiso broth. The adjoining bar serves small bites without reservations, but the dining room's the thing.

Archetype
FUSION $$$
(☏707-968-9200; http://archetypenapa.com; 1429 Main St; dinner mains $25-37; ☺11am-2:30pm Wed & Thu, 9am-2:30pm Sat & Sun, 5:30-9pm Wed-Sun) In an architect-designed dining room that breaks the Wine Country mold, Archetype effortlessly melds Asian and Mediterranean techniques with the best of California farms and foraging. Savor anything from the oak wood-burning oven and grill, or show up for sweet weekend brunch on the sunny back patio. Happy-hour drinks and bites are a steal (from just $5).

Napa Valley North

0 — 2 km
0 — 1 mile

Calistoga (enlargement)

0 — 400 m
0 — 0.2 miles

CALISTOGA

Lake St
Washington St
Grant St
Lincoln Ave
Brannan
Cedar St
St Helena Hwy
Napa River
Washington St

Calistoga Visitors Center & Chamber of Commerce

Tubbs La
Grant St
Greenwood Ave
Lincoln Ave

Meadowlark Country House (0.3mi); Safari West (1mi); Petrified Forest (3.5mi); Santa Rosa (12mi); Guerneville (26mi)

CALISTOGA

See Calistoga Enlargement

Silverado Trail
Dunaweal La
St Helena Hwy

Bothe Napa Valley State Park

Larkmead
Silverado Trail

Santa Rosa (12mi)

St Helena Hwy

Napa River
29
128

Lodi La

Sanitarium Rd

Deer Park Rd

Spring Mountain Rd

ST HELENA

29

See St Helena Enlargement

Spring St
Pope St
Silverado Trail

St Helena (enlargement)

St Helena Hwy
Oak Ave
Spring St
Pope St

ST HELENA

0 — 200 m
0 — 0.1 miles

St Helena Welcome Center

Napa Valley North

Goose & Gander MODERN AMERICAN $$$
(☏ 707-967-8779; www.goosegander.com; 1245 Spring St; mains $19-39; ⊙ 11:30am-11pm Sun-Thu, to midnight Fri & Sat) Inside a converted arts-and-crafts house with cathedral ceiling and gorgeous woodwork, Goose & Gander has a clubby vibe conducive to drinking, excellent craft cocktails and an imaginative (sometimes heavy) menu with standouts such as the G&G burger. Consider the garden, although hard-drinking locals favor the basement pub.

Gatehouse Restaurant CALIFORNIAN $$$
(☏ 707-967-1010; www.ciarestaurantgroup.com/gatehouse-restaurant; 2555 Main St; 3-/4-course lunch $32/$42, dinner $39/$49; ⊙ 11:30am-1pm & 6-8:30pm Tue-Sat) Testing skills and knowledge they've picked up in culinary school, students serve prix-fixe meals at this elegant restaurant on the Culinary Institute of America's Greystone campus. Ingredients for many dishes come from CIA's farm and herb gardens.

🍷 Drinking & Nightlife

There's not a whole lot going on here after hours. Calistoga to the north offers a more vibrant bar scene.

🛍 Shopping

Main St is lined with high-end boutiques (think $100 socks), but some mom-and-pop shops remain.

Woodhouse Chocolates　　　　FOOD
(www.woodhousechocolate.com; 1367 Main St; ⊙11am-5:30pm) Woodhouse looks more like Tiffany than a candy shop, with housemade chocolates similarly priced, but their quality is beyond reproach.

Rabbit Rabbit Fair Trade　　HOMEWARES
(☑707-968-9182; www.rabbitrabbitfairtrade.com; 1327 Main St; ⊙11am-5pm Sun & Mon, 10am-5pm Tue-Thu, to 6pm Fri & Sat) 🖉 Handcrafted fairtrade goods including gifts, cards, toys, household items, accessories and other items.

Footcandy　　　　　　　　　SHOES
(☑707-963-2040; www.footcandyshoes.com/info/about; 1239 Main St; Manolo Blahnik pairs up to $1245; ⊙10am-6pm Mon-Sat, 10:30am-6pm Sun) A boutique shoe store that feels more like high-heel museum, with designer pairs from Christian Louboutin, Jimmy Choo and Manolo Blahnik.

Napa Soap Company　　　COSMETICS
(☑707-963-5010; www.napasoap.com; 655 Main St; ⊙10am-5:30pm) 🖉 Ecofriendly bath products, locally produced.

Lolo's Consignment　　　　VINTAGE
(☑707-963-7972; www.lolosconsignment.com; 1120 Main St; ⊙10am-4pm Mon, to 5:30pm Tue-Sat, 11am-4pm Sun) Groovy cheap dresses and cast-off cashmere.

Main Street Books　　　　　BOOKS
(☑707-963-1338; 1315 Main St; ⊙10am-5:30pm Mon-Sat, 11am-3pm Sun) Good used books.

ℹ️ Information

St Helena Welcome Center (☑707-963-4456; www.sthelena.com; 657 Main St; ⊙9am-5pm Mon-Fri, 10am-4pm Sat, 11am-5pm Sun) The visitor center has information and lodging assistance.

ℹ️ Getting There & Away

For public-transit information, dial ☑511, or look online at www.transit.511.org. St Helena is an 80-minute drive from San Francisco.

Calistoga & Around

Famed 19th-century author Robert Louis Stevenson said of Calistoga: 'the whole neighborhood of Mt St Helena is full of sulfur and boiling springs...Calistoga itself seems to repose on a mere film above a boiling, subterranean lake.' And indeed, it does. Calistoga is synonymous with mineral water bearing its name, bottled here since 1924, and its springs and geysers have earned it an appropriate nickname: 'Hot springs of the West.'

The least gentrified town in Napa Valley feels refreshingly simple, with an old-fashioned main street lined with quirky shops and diverse characters wandering the sidewalks. Bad hair? No problem. Fancy-pants St Helena couldn't feel further away. Many don't go this far north, but you should, if only for a spa visit to indulge in the local specialty: hot-mud baths, made with volcanic ash from nearby Mt St Helena.

⊙ Sights

Safari West　　　　　　　　　ZOO
(☑707-579-2551; www.safariwest.com; 3115 Porter Creek Rd; adult/child 4-12yr from $83/45; ⊙tours at 9am, 10am, 1pm, 2pm & 4pm; 🅿🖐) Giraffes in Wine Country? Whadya know. Safari West sprawls over 400 acres and protects wildebeests, zebras, cheetahs and other exotic animals, which mostly roam free. See them and some recently born giraffe and wildebeest babies on a guided 2½-hour safari in open-sided jeeps, which also includes a 30-minute hike; reservations required, no kids under four (unless you book a private wagon). Those feeling adventurous can stay overnight in nifty canvas-sided **tent cabins** (including breakfast $260 to $475) inside the preserve.

Bale Grist Mill State Historic Park　PARK
(☑707-963-2236; 3369 St Helena Hwy; adult/child $5/2; ⊙10am-4pm Sat & Sun; 🖐) This park features a 36ft-high water-powered mill wheel dating to 1846 – the largest still operating in North America; on Saturdays and Sundays (and sometimes Fridays, rarely Mondays) from 10am to 4pm, it grinds flour. In early October, look for living-history festival Old Mill Days.

Robert Louis Stevenson
State Park　　　　　　　STATE PARK
(☑707-942-4575; www.parks.ca.gov; 3801 Hwy 29; ⊙sunrise-sunset; 🅿) **FREE** At this undeveloped state park 8 miles north of Calistoga,

the long-extinct volcanic cone of Mt St Helena marks Napa Valley's end and often gets snow in winter. It's a strenuous 5-mile climb to the peak's 4343ft summit, but what a view – 200 miles on a clear winter's day. Check conditions before setting out. Also consider 2.2-mile one-way **Table Rock Trail** (go south from the summit trailhead parking area) for drop-dead valley views. No dogs allowed.

Olabisi Wines   WINERY
(☑707-942-4472; www.olabisiwines.com; 1226 Washington St; tasting $25; ☺11am-6pm) In downtown Calistoga, this newer tasting room run by a long-time winemaker specializes in extremely small-production wines produced with wild yeast. The big Cabs, floral Pinots and dry whites often sell out quickly, with the winery producing less than 1000 cases a year. Bottles cost $38 to $125. Tasting fee is waived with a purchase of three bottles.

Bothe-Napa Valley State Park   STATE PARK
(☑707-942-4575; 3801 St Helena Hwy; parking $8; ☺8am-sunset; ⊕) A mile-long trail leads from Bale Grist Mill State Historic Park to adjacent Bothe-Napa Valley State Park, where there's a swimming pool ($5) and camping, plus hiking through redwood groves. If you're two or more adults, go first to Bothe and pay $8, instead of the per-head charge at Bale Grist.

Sharpsteen Museum   MUSEUM
(☑707-942-5911; www.sharpsteenmuseum.org; 1311 Washington St; suggested donation $3; ☺11am-4pm; ⊕) FREE Across from the picturesque 1902 City Hall (originally an opera house), the Sharpsteen Museum was created by an ex-Disney animator (whose Oscar is on display) and houses a fantastic diorama of town in the 1860s, big Victorian dollhouse, full-size horse-drawn carriage and a restored cottage from entrepreneur Samuel Brannan's original resort. (The only Brannan cottage still at its original site is at 109 Wappo Ave).

Petrified Forest   FOREST
(☑707-942-6667; www.petrifiedforest.org; 4100 Petrified Forest Rd; adult/child 6-11yr/child 12-18yr $12/6/8; ☺10am-7pm late May-early Sep, to 6pm Apr-late May & early Sep-Oct, to 5pm Nov-Mar; ℗⊕) Three million years ago at this now roadside-Americana attraction, a volcanic eruption at Mt St Helena blew down a stand of redwoods. The trees fell in the same direction, away from the blast, and over the millennia the mighty giants' trunks turned to stone.

Discover them on short trails through the woods and stop by the monument that marks Robert Louis Stevenson's 1880 visit, which he described in the *Silverado Squatters*. Guided tours go at 11am, 1pm and 3pm.

🏃 Activities

Find biking information and rentals at Calistoga Bike Shop (p163).

Oat Hill Mine Trail   CYCLING, HIKING
(2082 Oat Hill Mine Rd) One of Northern California's most technically challenging trails, this draws hard-core mountain bikers and hikers. Less experienced walkers take heart: a moderately strenuous half-mile up from town, there's a bench with incredible valley views. The trailhead is at the intersection of Hwy 29 and Silverado Trail.

Spas
Calistoga is famous for hot-spring spas and mud-bath emporiums, where you're buried in hot mud and emerge feeling supple, detoxified and enlivened. (The mud is made with volcanic ash and peat; the higher the ash content, the better the bath.)

Packages take 60 to 90 minutes and cost $90 to $100. You start semisubmerged in hot mud, then soak in hot mineral water – a steam bath and blanket-wrap follow. A massage increases the cost to $130 or more.

Baths can be taken solo or, at some spas, as couples. Variations include thin, painted-on clay-mud wraps (called 'fango' baths, good for those uncomfortable sitting in mud), herbal wraps, seaweed baths and various massage treatments. Discount coupons are sometimes available from the visitors center (p185). Book ahead, especially on summer weekends. Reservations are essential everywhere. Most spas offer multi-treatment packages. Some offer discounted spa-lodging packages.

★ Indian Springs Spa   SPA
(☑707-709-2449; www.indianspringscalistoga.com; 1712 Lincoln Ave; ☺by appointment 9am-9pm) California's longest continually operating spa, and original Calistoga resort, has concrete mud tubs and mines its own ash. Treatments include use of the huge, hot-spring-fed pool. Great cucumber body lotion.

Dr Wilkinson's Hot Springs Resort   SPA
(☑707-942-4102; www.drwilkinson.com; 1507 Lincoln Ave; mud bath from $94; ☺by appointment 8:30am-3:45pm) For more than 60 years running, 'the doc' uses more peat in its mud.

Spa Solage SPA

(☑707-266-0825; www.solage.aubergeresorts. com/spa; 755 Silverado Trail; ◎by appointment 8am-8pm) Chichi, austere, top-end spa, with couples' rooms and a fango-mud bar for DIY paint-on treatments. Also has zero-gravity chairs for blanket wraps and sex-segregated clothing-optional mineral pools.

Golden Haven Hot Springs SPA

(☑707-942-8000; www.goldenhaven.com; 1713 Lake St; mud bath $99; ◎by appointment 8am-8pm) Old-school and unfussy; offers couples' mud baths and massage.

Calistoga Spa Hot Springs SPA

(☑707-942-6269, 866-822-5772; www.calisto-gaspa.com; 1006 Washington St; mud bath $99; ◎by appointment 9am-4pm Mon-Thu, to 7pm Fri-Sun) Traditional mud baths and massage at a motel complex with two huge swimming pools.

Mount View Spa SPA

(☑707-942-1500; www.mountviewhotel.com; 1457 Lincoln Ave; single/couple mud bath $90/110; ◎by appointment 8:30am-7pm) Traditional full-service, five-room spa, good for clean-hands gals who prefer a mineral bath infused with lighter mud.

🛏 Sleeping

From upscale hot-springs resorts to quaint country cottages, there must be a dozen good options in and around Calistoga. Budget travelers will love the yurts and campsites in Bothe-Napa Valley State Park.

Bothe-Napa Valley State Park Campground CAMPGROUND $

(Map p42; ☑800-444-7275; www.reserveamerica. com; 3801 Hwy 128; camping & RV sites $35, yurts $55-70, cabins $150-225; ⊛🐾) Three miles south of Calistoga, Bothe has shady camping near redwoods, coin-operated showers, and gorgeous hiking (p181). Sites 28 to 36 are most secluded.

EuroSpa & Inn MOTEL $$

(☑707-942-6829; www.eurospa.com; 1202 Pine St; r $169-325; ⊛🛜🏊) Immaculate single-story motel on a quiet side street, with extras such as gas-burning fireplaces, afternoon refreshments and small on-site spa. Excellent service, but tiny pool.

Dr Wilkinson's Motel & Hideaway Cottages MOTEL, COTTAGES $$

(☑707-942-4102; www.drwilkinson.com; 1507 Lincoln Ave; r $165-275, cottage $175-280; ⊛@🛜🏊) This good-value vintage-1950s motel has well-kept rooms facing a swimming-pool courtyard with hot tub, three pools (one indoors) and mud baths. Also rents simple, great-value stand-alone cottages with kitchen at the affiliated Hideaway Cottages, also with pool and hot tub.

Best Western Plus Stevenson Manor HOTEL $$

(☑800-528-1234, 707-942-1112; www.stevenson manor.com; 1830 Lincoln Ave; r weekday $179-209, weekend $299-329; ⊛@🛜🏊) This entry-level business-class hotel feels generic, but has good extras, including full hot breakfast. Upstairs rooms are quietest. New elevator and exercise room.

Calistoga Spa Hot Springs MOTEL $$

(☑866-822-5772, 707-942-6269; www.calistoga spa.com; 1006 Washington St; r $197-267; ⊛🛜🏊) Great for families who jam the place on weekends, this motel-resort has slightly scuffed generic rooms (request one that's been remodeled) with kitchenette, and fantastic pools: two full size, a kiddie pool with miniwaterfall and a huge adults-only Jacuzzi. Outside are barbecues and a snack bar.

Calistoga Inn INN $$

(☑707-942-4101; www.calistogainn.com; 1250 Lincoln Ave; r with shared bath $169-229, cottages $229-289; 🛜) Upstairs from a busy bar, this inn has 17 clean, basic rooms with shared bath, ideal for no-fuss bargain hunters. No TV and no elevator. Bring earplugs. A newer cottage contains its own bathroom, air-conditioning and TV.

★Brannan Cottage Inn BOUTIQUE HOTEL $$$

(☑707-942-4200; https://brannancottageinn.com; 109 Wappo Ave; r from $309; 🅿⊛🛜) Adorable, gingerbread-style Victorian cottage amid lush grounds that in the 1860s belonged to the town's favorite entrepreneur Samuel Brannan. Recently restored to preserve its old-timey character, the cottage is listed in the National Register of Historic Places and offers six uniquely adorned rooms featuring comfy, pillow-top mattresses and modern amenities. A concierge will help plan your trip.

Solage
RESORT $$$

(📞 707-226-0800, 866-942-7442; www.solage.aubergeresorts.com; 755 Silverado Trail; r $530-675, ste $835-1275; ❇🐾❄🐾) 🏊 Recently taken over by Auberge Resorts, Calistoga's top spa-hotel ups the style factor, with Cali-chic semidetached cottages and a glam pool surrounded by palm trees. Rooms are austere, with vaulted ceilings, zillion-thread-count linens and pebble-floor showers. Cruiser bikes included.

Indian Springs Resort
RESORT $$$

(📞 707-942-4913; www.indianspringscalistoga.com; 1712 Lincoln Ave; r/cottages from $269/349; P ❄ ❇🐾❄🐾) The definitive old-school Calistoga resort, Indian Springs has cottages facing a central lawn with palm trees, shuffleboard, bocce and hammocks – not unlike a vintage Florida resort. Some sleep four. There are also top-end, motel-style lodge rooms (adults only). Huge hot-springs-fed swimming pool. Also has Sam's Social Club (p184).

Meadowlark Country House
B&B $$$

(📞 707-942-5651; www.meadowlarkinn.com; 601 Petrified Forest Rd; r $245-450, ste $310-355; ❇🐾❄🐾) About a mile west of Calistoga, sitting on 20 lush acres, Meadowlark has homey rooms decorated in contemporary style, most with deck and Jacuzzi. Outside there's a hot tub, sauna and clothing-optional pool. The truth-telling innkeeper lives elsewhere, offers helpful advice, then vanishes when you want privacy. There's a fabulous cottage costing $450 for two and $640 for four. Gay friendly.

Cottage Grove Inn
BUNGALOW $$$

(📞 707-942-8400; www.cottagegrove.com; 1711 Lincoln Ave; cottages $275-450; ❇🐾❄) Romantic cottages for over-40s, with wood-burning fireplaces, two-person Jacuzzis and rocking-chair front porches.

Chelsea Garden Inn
B&B $$$

(📞 707-942-0948; www.chelseagardeninn.com; 1443 2nd St; r $195-350; ❇🐾❄🐾) On a quiet side street, this single-story inn has five floral-print rooms with private entrances, facing pretty gardens. Never mind the pool's rust spots.

Chateau De Vie
B&B $$$

(📞 707-942-6446, 877-558-2513; www.cdvnapavalley.com; 3250 Hwy 128; r $269-469; ❇🐾❄🐾) Surrounded by vineyards, with gorgeous views of Mt St Helena, CDV has five modern, elegantly decorated B&B rooms with top-end amenities and zero froufrou. Charming owners serve wine on the sun-dappled patio, then leave you alone. Hot tub, big pool. Gay friendly.

Chanric
B&B $$$

(📞 707-942-4535; www.thechanric.com; 1805 Foothill Blvd; r from $690; ❇🐾❄🐾) A converted Victorian near the road, this cushy B&B has small but smartly furnished rooms, plus many free extras including champagne on arrival and lavish three-course breakfasts. Gay friendly. No elevator.

Aurora Park Cottages
COTTAGE $$$

(📞 707-942-6733, 877-942-7700; www.aurorapark.com; 1807 Foothill Blvd; cottages $269-349, houses $399-899; ❇🐾) Six immaculately kept, sunny-yellow cottages – with polished-wood floors, feather beds and sundeck – stand in a row beside flowering gardens. There's also a pricier rental home with a full kitchen. Though close to the road, everything's quiet by night and the innkeeper couldn't be nicer.

Mount View Hotel & Spa
HISTORIC HOTEL $$$

(📞 707-942-6877; www.mountviewhotel.com; 1457 Lincoln Ave; r Mon-Fri $209-429, Sat & Sun $279-459; ❇🐾❄) Smack in the middle of town, this 1917 Mission Revival hotel is decorated in vaguely mod-Italian style at odds with the vintage building – rooms are clean and fresh-looking nonetheless. Gleaming bathrooms, on-site spa, year-round heated pool. No elevator.

Calistoga Motor Lodge & Spa
MOTEL $$$

(📞 707-942-0991; www.thesunburstcalistoga.com; 1880 Lincoln Ave; r $229-469; @🐾❄) This single-story 1950s motor lodge got a makeover in 2017, with mid-century-modern-led aesthetics, but it's basically still a drive-to-the-door motel with upscale furnishings and thin walls.

✖️ Eating

The dining scene in Calistoga isn't as uppity as the rest of the valley, but you can certainly procure a high-class meal at Calistoga Kitchen (p184), Solbar (p184) and the newly opened Sam's Social Club (p184). Many decent and affordable restaurants line Lincoln Ave.

Buster's Southern BBQ
BARBECUE $

(📞 707-942-5605; www.busterssouthernbbq.com; 1207 Foothill Blvd; dishes $8-12; ⏰10am-8pm

Mon-Sat, to 7pm Sun;) The sheriff dines at this indoor-outdoor barbecue joint, which serves smoky ribs, chicken, tri-tip steak and burgers, plus beer and wine. It closes early at dinnertime.

★ Calistoga Kitchen   CALIFORNIAN $$$

(☑ 707-942-6500;   www.calistogakitchen.com; 1107 Cedar St; mains lunch $12-36; dinner $20-36; ⊘ 5:30pm-close Thu, 11:30am-3pm & 5:30pm-close Fri & Sat, 9:30am-3pm Sun) A sparsely decorated cottage surrounded by a white picket fence, Calistoga Kitchen is especially good for lunch in the garden. The chef-owner favors simplicity, focusing on quality ingredients in a half-dozen changing dishes, such as a delicious braised rabbit. Reservations advised, especially for the patio.

Solbar   CALIFORNIAN $$$

(☑ 707-226-0860;   www.solage.aubergeresorts. com; 755 Silverado Trail N, Calistoga; lounge menu dishes $4-16, dinner mains $26-38; ⊘ 7am-11:30am, 11:45am-3pm & 5:30-9pm, to 9:30pm Fri & Sat) ✐ We like the Spartan ag-chic look of this Michelin-starred resort restaurant, the menu of which writing maximizes seasonal produce in elegant dishes, playfully composed. A chef from Italy had just been hired, but the crispy petrale sole tacos were as delectable as ever. The menu remains split for calorie-counters into light and hearty dishes. Reservations essential.

All Seasons Bistro   MODERN AMERICAN $$$

(☑ 707-942-9111;   www.allseasonsnapavalley.net; 1400 Lincoln Ave; mains lunch $12-18, dinner $16-27; ⊘ 11:30am-2:30pm & 5:30-9pm, hours vary) ✐ It looks like a white-tablecloth soda fountain, but All Seasons makes very fine meals, from a simple lasagna to composed dishes such as scallop, prawn, mussel and clam risotto. The salads are fresh and totally organic.

Sam's Social Club   AMERICAN $$$

(☑ 707-942-4969;   http://samssocialclub.com; 1712 Lincoln Ave; dinner mains $17-38; ⊘ 7:30am-9pm Mon-Wed, to 9:30pm Thu-Sun) Housed in the Indian Springs Resort (p183), this is Calistoga's fancy American restaurant that also brews its own beer. Colorful and expertly prepared dishes feature the freshest local ingredients, and the bacon-wrapped, Point Reyes Farmstead blue-cheese-stuffed dates are otherworldly. There's outdoor patio seating and a bright, comfortable dining room and bar. It's perfect for a relaxing feast post mud bath.

Calistoga Inn & Brewery   AMERICAN $$$

(☑ 707-942-4101; www.calistogainn.com; 1250 Lincoln Ave; dinner mains $15-38; ⊘ 11:30am-9:30pm Mon-Fri, from 11am Sat & Sun) Locals crowd the outdoor beer garden on Sundays. Midweek we prefer the country dining room's big oakwood tables – a homey spot for simple American cooking. Live music on summer weekends.

🍷 Drinking & Nightlife

There are a few hoppin' bars along Lincoln Ave and they'll often have live music on weekends.

Brannan's Grill   BAR

(☑ 707-942-2233;   www.brannanscalistoga.com; 1374 Lincoln Ave; ⊘ 11:30am-9pm) The mahogany bar at Calistoga's handsomest restaurant is great for martinis and microbrews, especially 7pm to 10pm Friday and Saturday, when there's live jazz.

Yo El Rey   CAFE

(www.yoelreyroasting.com; 1217 Washington St; ⊘ 6:30am-5:30pm) ✐ Hip kids favor this microroastery, which serves stellar small-batch, organic, fair-trade coffee.

Susie's Bar   BAR

(☑ 707-942-6710; 1365 Lincoln Ave; ⊘ noon-2am Mon-Fri, 10am-2am Sat & Sun) Turn your baseball cap sideways, swill beer and shoot pool to a soundtrack of classic rock.

Solbar   BAR

(☑ 707-226-0860;   www.solage.aubergeresorts. com; 755 Silverado Trail; ⊘ 11am-9pm, to 9:30pm Fri & Sat) Sip craft cocktails beside outdoor fireplaces and a pool surrounded with palm trees at this Napa-swank resort bar.

Hydro Grill   BAR

(☑ 707-942-9777; 1403 Lincoln Ave; ⊘ 8:30am-10:30pm Mon-Thu, to 11:30pm Fri-Sun) Live music plays on Sundays and one Saturday a month at this hoppin' corner bar-restaurant.

🛍 Shopping

Calistoga Pottery   CERAMICS

(☑ 707-942-0216; www.calistogapottery.com; 1001 Foothill Blvd; ⊘ 9am-5pm Mon-Sat) Artisanal pottery, hand-thrown on-site. Ask about the pots glazed with local grapevine ash.

Coperfield's Books   BOOKS

(☑ 707-942-1616; 1330 Lincoln Ave; ⊘ 10am-7pm Sun-Thu, to 8pm Fri & Sat) Indie bookshop, with local maps and guides.

ℹ️ Information

Calistoga Visitors Center & Chamber of Commerce (☎707-942-6333; www.visitcalistoga.com; 1133 Washington St; ☻9am-5pm) Lodging info, maps, pamphlets etc.

ℹ️ Getting There & Away

From San Francisco, public transportation can get you to Calistoga, though it's better to have your own wheels. For public-transit information, dial ☎511, or look online at www.transit.511.org.

Calistoga is about a 100-minute drive from San Francisco.

ℹ️ Getting Around

Hwys 128 and 29 split in Calistoga, where Hwy 29 turns east and becomes Lincoln Ave, continuing across Silverado Trail, toward Clear Lake. Hwy 128 continues north as Foothill Blvd.

SONOMA VALLEY

We have a soft spot for Sonoma's folksy ways. Unlike fancy Napa, nobody cares if you drive a clunker and vote Green. Locals call it 'Slow-noma.' Anchoring the bucolic 17-mile-long valley, the town of Sonoma makes a great jumping-off point for exploring Wine Country – it's an hour from San Francisco – and has a marvelous sense of place, with storied 19th-century historical sights surrounding the state's largest town square.

Halfway up-valley, tiny Glen Ellen (p194) is straight from a Norman Rockwell painting – in stark contrast to the valley's northernmost town, Santa Rosa (p210), the workaday urban center best known for traffic. If you have more than a day, explore Sonoma's quiet, rustic western side along the Russian River Valley, and continue to the sea.

Sonoma Valley Wineries

Rolling grass-covered hills rise from Sonoma Valley. Its 40-some wineries get less attention than Napa's, but many are equally good. If you love Zinfandel and Syrah, you're in for a treat.

Picnicking is allowed at Sonoma wineries. Get maps and discount coupons in the town of Sonoma or, if you're approaching from the south, the Sonoma Valley Visitors Bureau (p191) at Cornerstone Gardens.

Plan at least five hours to visit the valley from bottom to top.

OUTLET SHOPPING

Max out your credit cards on last season's closeouts.

Napa Premium Outlets (☎707-226-9876; www.premiumoutlets.com; 629 Factory Stores Dr; ☻10am-8pm Mon-Thu, to 9pm Fri & Sat, to 7pm Sun) A large shopping center with fifty stores west of downtown Napa..

Petaluma Village Premium Outlets (☎707-778-9300; www.premiumoutlets.com; 2200 Petaluma Blvd N, Petaluma; ☻10am-9pm) Sixty stores, Sonoma County.

Vacaville Premium Outlets (☎707-447-5755; www.premiumoutlets.com/vacaville; 321 Nut Tree Rd, Vacaville; ☻10am-9pm) One hundred and twenty stores, northeast of Wine Country on I-80.

★**Gundlach-Bundschu Winery** WINERY
(Map p186; ☎707-938-5277; www.gunbun.com; 2000 Denmark St, Sonoma; tasting $20-30, incl tour $30-60; ☻11am-5:30pm May-Oct, to 4:30pm Nov-Apr; ℗) 🍷 California's oldest family-run winery looks like a castle but has a down-to-earth vibe. Founded in 1858 by a Bavarian immigrant, its signatures are Gewürztraminer and Pinot Noir, but 'Gun-Bun' was the first American winery to produce 100% Merlot. Down a winding lane, it's a terrific bike-to winery with picnicking, hiking, a lake and frequent concerts, including a two-day folk-music festival in June. Tour the 1800-barrel cave by reservation only. Bottles are $20 to $50.

★**Bartholomew Park Winery** WINERY
(Map p186; ☎707-939-3026; www.bartpark.com; 1000 Vineyard Lane, Sonoma; tasting $15; ☻11am-4:30pm; ℗) 🍷 A great bike-to winery, Bartholomew Park occupies a 375-acre nature preserve with oak-shaded picnicking and valley-view hiking. The vineyards were originally cultivated in 1857 and now yield certified-organic, citrusy Sauvignon Blanc, Cabernet Sauvignon softer in style than Napa and lush Zinfandel. There's also a new collection of reserve wines and a new private tasting experience. Bottles are $27 to $48. Tasting fee is waived with bottle purchase.

St Francis Winery & Vineyards WINERY
(Map p186; ☎707-538-9463; www.stfranciswinery.com; 100 Pythian Rd at Hwy 12, Santa Rosa; tasting $15, wine & cheese pairing $25, wine & food pairing

$68; ⊙10am-5pm) The vineyards are scenic and all, but the real reason to visit St Francis is the much-lauded food-pairing experience. The mouthwatering, multicourse affair is hosted by amiable and informative wine experts and includes things such as braised Kurobuta pork with Okinawan sweet potatoes paired with Cab Franc, and American Wagyu strip loin and chanterelles paired with an old-vine Zin. Seatings at 11am, 1pm and 3pm, Thursday to Monday. Spots fill fast; book well in advance.

Robledo
WINERY

(Map p186; ☎707-939-6903; www.robledofamily winery.com; 21901 Bonness Rd, off Hwy 116; tasting $15-25; ⊙10am-5pm Mon-Sat, 11am-4pm Sun) Sonoma Valley's feel-good winery, Robledo was founded by a former migrant worker from Mexico who worked his way up to vineyard manager, then land owner, now vintner. His kids run the place. The wines – served at hand-carved Mexican furniture in a barn – include a nonoaked Sauvignon Blanc, spicy Cabernet and bright, fruit-forward Pinot Noir. Bottles cost $20 to $60. Appointments recommended for groups of six or more.

Little Vineyards
WINERY

(Map p186; ☎707-996-2750; www.littlevineyards. com; 15188 Sonoma Hwy, Glen Ellen; tasting $15; ⊙11am-4:30pm Thu-Mon; ⊕⊛) The name fits at this family-owned small-scale winery surrounded by grapes, with a lazy dog to greet you and a weathered, old-timey wooden bar, at which Jack London formerly drank (before it moved here). The big reds include Syrah, Petite Sirah, Zin, Cab and several delish blends. It also has a rosé and a Pinot Blanc. There's good picnicking on the vineyard-view terrace. Also rents a cottage in the vines. Bottles cost $20 to $50.

Homewood
WINERY

(Map p186; ☎707-996-6353; www.homewoodwin ery.com; 23120 Burndale Rd, Sonoma; tasting $10; ⊙10am-4pm; ℗) Barn cats dart about at this down-home winery with several different tasting areas and a $20 wine and chocolate pairing. The winemaker crafts standout Chardonnays and Roussannes, and an array of other whites, reds and late-harvest dessert wines. Bottles are $22 to $36; tasting fee waived with purchase.

Hawkes
TASTING ROOM

(Map p190; ☎707-938-7620; www.hawkeswine. com; 383 1st St W, Sonoma; tasting $15; ⊙11am-6pm Thu-Mon) When you're in downtown

Sonoma Valley

Sonoma and don't feel like fighting traffic, Hawke's refreshingly unfussy tasting room showcases meaty Cabernet Sauvignon from family-owned vineyards in Alexander Valley, never blended with other varietals. Bottles are $30 to $70; the tasting fee is waived with a purchase over $40.

Sonoma Valley

Benziger
WINERY

(Map p186; ☑ 888-490-2739, 707-935-3000; www.benziger.com; 1883 London Ranch Rd, Glen Ellen; tasting $20-40, tours $25-50; ⊙10am-5pm; P⊡) ✐ If you're new to wine, make Benziger your first stop for Sonoma's best crash course in winemaking. The worthwhile tour (11am–3:30pm; reservations recommended) includes an open-air tram ride (weather permitting) through biodynamic vineyards and a five-wine tasting. Great picnicking, excellent for families. The large-production wine is OK (head for the reserves); the tour's the thing. Bottles are $20 to $80.

Marimar Estate
WINERY

(☑ 707-823-4365; www.marimarestate.com; 11400 Graton Rd, Sebastopol; tasting $15; ⊙11am-5pm by appointment only; ☒) ✐ Middle-of-nowhere Marimar Estates specializes in all-organic Pinot – seven different kinds – and Spanish varietals. The hilltop tasting room has a knockout vineyard-view terrace, good for picnics. Also consider the guided tour, which includes a bottle ($95). Bottles are $49 to $59.

Cline Cellars
WINERY

(Map p186; ☑707-940-4030; www.clinecellars.com; 24737 Arnold Dr, Hwy 121; tasting free-$20; ⊙tasting room 10am-6pm, museum to 4pm) ✐ Balmy days are for pondside picnics and rainy ones for fireside tastings of old-vine Zinfandel and Mourvèdre inside an 1850s farmhouse. Stroll out back to the **California Mission Museum**, housing 1930s miniature replicas of California's original 21 Spanish Colonial missions.

Kunde
WINERY

(Map p186; ☑707-833-5501; www.kunde.com; 9825 Hwy 12, Kenwood; tasting $15-50, cave tours free; ⊙10:30am-5pm; P) ✐ This family-owned winery on a historic ranch has vineyards that are more than a century old. It offers mountaintop tastings with impressive valley views and seasonal guided hikes (advance reservations recommended), though you can also just stop for a tasting and a tour. Elegant, 100% estate-grown wines include crisp Chardonnay and unfussy red blends, all made sustainably. Bottles $17 to $100.

Loxton WINERY

(Map p186; ☑707-935-7221; www.loxtonwines.com; 11466 Dunbar Rd, Glen Ellen; tasting $10-20, walking tour $25; ☺11am-5pm) Say g'day to Chris the Aussie winemaker at Loxton, a no-frills winery with million-dollar views of the grapes you'll actually be tasting. The tasting room contains a small warehouse where racing cars were once designed, and there you can sample wonderful Syrah and Zinfandel; nonoaky, fruit-forward Chardonnay; and good port. Bottles cost $17 to $32.

Ravenswood Winery WINERY

(Map p186; ☑707-933-2332; www.ravenswoodwinery.com; 18701 Gehricke Rd, Sonoma; tasting $20-60, incl tour $25; ☺10am-4:30pm) With the slogan 'no wimpy wines,' this buzzing winery pours a full slate of estate Zinfandels. Novices welcome. Tours at 10:30am daily; reservations recommended.

Scribe WINERY

(Map p186; ☑707-939-1858; http://scribewinery.com; 2100 Denmark St, Sonoma; tasting $35, food pairing $65; ☺11:30am-4pm Thu-Mon, by appointment only) With Scribe, a new generation has found its place in Wine Country. Bantering groups of bespectacled, high-waisted-jeans-wearing millennials frequent this hip winery designed to resemble a French château, and at outdoor picnic tables they hold forth on the terroir-driven rosé of Pinot, the skin-fermented Chardonnay and the bold Cab. The food pairing is hit and miss.

BR Cohn WINERY

(Map p186; ☑707-938-4064, 800-330-4064; www.brcohn.com; 15000 Sonoma Hwy, Glen Ellen; tasting indoors $20, weekend patio tasting $30; ☺10am-5pm) Picnic like a rock star at always-busy BR Cohn. Its founder managed '70s superband the Doobie Brothers before moving on to make outstanding organic olive oils and fine wines. Although the winery has changed hands, it's still an excellent spot for tasting wine, slurping oysters (weekends only) and sampling olive oil in the gourmet shop. Bottles are $16 to $56.

Imagery Estate WINERY

(Map p186; ☑707-935-4515, 800-989-8890; www.imagerywinery.com; 14335 Sonoma Hwy, Glen Ellen; tasting $15; ☺10am-4:30pm Mon-Fri, to 5:30pm Sat & Sun; ⓟ🏍) 🍴 Imagery produces lesser-known varietals such as Legrain and Tannat, biodynamically grown, that you often can't buy anywhere else. Each bottle sports an artist-designed label, with originals on

display in the on-site gallery. Lovely gardens include a grassy picnic area with horseshoes, cornhole and bocce. Limited picnic supplies available. Bottles are $27 to $65. Kid and dog-friendly.

Sonoma & Around

Fancy boutiques may lately be replacing hardware stores, but Sonoma still retains an old-fashioned charm, thanks to the plaza – California's largest town square – and its surrounding frozen-in-time historic buildings. You can legally drink on the plaza – a rarity in California parks – but only between 11:30am and sunset.

Sonoma has a rich history. In 1846 it was the site of a second American revolution, this time against Mexico, when General Mariano Guadalupe Vallejo deported all foreigners from California, prompting outraged frontiersmen to occupy the Sonoma Presidio and declare independence. They dubbed California the Bear Flag Republic after the battle flag they'd fashioned.

The republic was short-lived. The Mexican-American War broke out a month later, and California was annexed by the US. The revolt gave California its flag, which remains emblazoned with the words 'California Republic' beneath a muscular brown bear. Vallejo was initially imprisoned but ultimately returned to Sonoma to play a major role in its development.

◉ Sights

★**Sonoma Plaza** SQUARE

(Map p190; btwn Napa, Spain & 1st Sts) Smack in the center of the plaza, the Mission Revival-style city hall, built 1906–08, has identical facades on four sides, reportedly because plaza businesses all demanded City Hall face their direction. At the plaza's northeast corner, the **Bear Flag Monument** (Map p190; Sonoma Plaza) marks Sonoma's moment of revolutionary glory. The **weekly farmers market** (5:30-8pm Tues Apr-Oct) showcases Sonoma's incredible produce.

Sonoma State Historic Park HISTORIC SITE

(Map p190; ☑707-938-9560; www.parks.ca.gov; adult/child $3/2; ☺10am-5pm) This park in Sonoma is comprised of multiple sites, most side by side. Founded in 1823, Mission San Francisco Solano anchors the plaza, and was the final California mission. Sonoma Barracks houses exhibits on 19th-century life.

A WINE COUNTRY PRIMER

When people talk about Sonoma, they're referring to the *whole* county, which unlike Napa, is huge. It extends all the way from the coast, up the Russian River Valley, into Sonoma Valley and eastward to Napa Valley; in the south it stretches from San Pablo Bay (an extension of San Francisco Bay) to Healdsburg in the north. It's essential to break Sonoma down by district.

West County refers to everything west of Hwy 101 and includes the Russian River Valley and the coast. Sonoma Valley stretches north–south along Hwy 12. In northern Sonoma County, Alexander Valley lies east of Healdsburg, and Dry Creek Valley lies north of Healdsburg. In the south, Carneros straddles the Sonoma–Napa border, north of San Pablo Bay. Each region has its own particular wines; what grows where depends upon the weather.

Inland valleys get hot; coastal regions stay cool. In West County and Carneros, nighttime fog blankets the vineyards. Burgundy-style wines do best, particularly Pinot Noir and Chardonnay. Further inland, Alexander, Sonoma and much of Dry Creek Valleys (as well as Napa Valley) are protected from fog. Here Bordeaux-style wines thrive, especially Cabernet Sauvignon, Sauvignon Blanc, Merlot and other heat-loving varieties. For California's famous Cabernets, head to Napa. Zinfandel and Rhône-style varieties such as Syrah and Viognier grow in both regions, warm and cool. In cooler climes, wines are lighter and more elegant; in warmer areas they are heavier and more rustic. As you explore, notice the bases of grapevines: the fatter they are, the older. 'Old vine' grapes yield color and complexity not found in grapes from younger vines.

Some basics: wineries and vineyards aren't the same. Grapes grow in a vineyard then get fermented at a winery. Wineries that grow their own grapes are called estates, as in 'estate-grown' or 'estate-bottled,' but estates also ferment grapes from other vineyards. When vintners speak of 'single-vineyard' or 'vineyard-designate' wines, they mean the grapes all originated from the same vineyard; this allows for tighter quality control. 'Single varietal' means all the grapes are the same variety (such as 100% Merlot) but may come from different vineyards. Reserves are the vintner's limited-production wines; they're usually available only at the winery.

Don't be afraid to ask questions. Vintners love to talk. If you don't know how to taste wine, or what to look for, ask the person behind the counter to help you discover what you like. Just remember to spit out the wine; the slightest buzz will diminish your capacity to taste.

For a handy-dandy reference on the road, pick up a copy of Karen MacNeil's *The Wine Bible* (2015, Workman Publishing) or Jancis Robinson's *The Oxford Companion to Wine* (2015, Oxford University Press) to carry in the car.

The 1886 Toscano Hotel lobby is beautifully preserved – peek inside. The 1852 Vallejo's Home (p191) lies a half-mile northwest. One ticket allows same-day admission to all, including **Petaluma Adobe State Park** (☎707-762-4871; www.petalumaadobe.com; 3325 Adobe Rd, Petaluma; adult/child $3/2; ⊙10am-5pm; P) at General Vallejo's former ranch, 15 miles away.

Mission San Francisco Solano
HISTORIC BUILDING
(Map p190; ☎707-938-9560; www.parks.ca.gov; 114 E Spain St; adult/child $3/2; ⊙10am-5pm) At Sonoma Plaza's northeast corner, the mission was built in 1823, partly to forestall Russians at Fort Ross from moving inland. This was the 21st and final California mission – the northernmost point on El Camino Real – and the only one built during the Mexican period (the rest were founded during the Spanish Colonial era). Five original rooms remain. The not-to-be-missed **chapel** dates to 1840.

Toscano Hotel
HISTORIC BUILDING
(Map p190; ☎707-938-9560; www.parks.ca.gov; 20 E Spain St; adult/child $3/2; ⊙10am-5pm) Toscano Hotel opened as a store and library in the 1850s, then became a hotel in 1886. Peek into the lobby and, except for the traffic outside, you'd swear you were peering back in time. Tours 1pm–4pm Saturday and Sunday.

Sonoma Barracks
HISTORIC BUILDING
(Map p190; ☎707-939-9420; www.parks.ca.gov; 20 E Spain St; adult/child $3/2; ⊙10am-5pm) The adobe Sonoma Barracks was built by Vallejo between 1834 and 1841 to house Mexican troops. Today, interpretive displays describe life during the Mexican and

Sonoma

Sonoma

American periods. The barracks became the capital of a rogue nation on June 9, 1846, when American settlers of varying sobriety surprised guards and declared an independent 'California Republc' [sic] with a homemade flag featuring a blotchy bear.

Bartholomew Park   PARK
(Map p186; ☏707-938-2244; www.bartholomew park.org; 1000 Vineyard Lane; ◷10am-4:30pm; 🅿🚻) FREE The top near-town outdoors destination is 375-acre Bartholomew Park, off Castle Rd, where you can picnic beneath gi-

ant oaks and hike 2 miles of trails, with hilltop vistas to San Francisco. The **Palladian Villa**, at the park's entrance, is a re-creation of Count Haraszthy's original Pompeian residence, open noon to 3pm Saturdays and Sundays. There's also a good **winery**, independently operated. Last entry is at 4:30pm.

Vallejo's Home　　　HISTORIC BUILDING
(Map p186; ☑707-938-9559; 363 3rd St W; adult/child $3/2; ⊙10am-5pm) A half-mile from the plaza, this lovely historical estate, also known as Lachryma Montis (Latin for 'Tears of the Mountain'), was built in the 1850s for General Vallejo and named for the on-site spring, which the Vallejo family made good money from by piping water to town. The Gothic-style American-Victorian home remained in the family until 1933, when the state of California purchased it, along with its original furnishings. A bicycle path leads to the house from downtown. Tours 1pm, 2pm and 3pm Saturday and Sunday.

Sonoma Valley Museum of Art　　MUSEUM
(Map p190; ☑707-939-7862; www.svma.org; 551 Broadway; adult/child 14-17yr/family $10/5/15; ⊙11am-5pm Wed-Sun) The 8000-sq-ft modern- and contemporary-art museum presents changing exhibitions by international and local artists, and focuses on building community around art.

Cornerstone Sonoma　　　GARDENS
(Map p186; ☑707-933-3010; www.cornerstone sonoma.com; 23570 Arnold Dr; ⊙10am-5pm, gardens to 4pm; P☑) FREE This roadside, Wine Country marketplace showcases 25 walk-through (in some cases edible) gardens, along with a bunch of innovative and adorable shops, wine-tasting parlors and on-site **Sonoma Valley Visitors Bureau** (Map p186; ☑707-996-1090; www.sonomavalley.com; 23570 Hwy 121, Cornerstone Gardens; ⊙10am-4pm). There's a good, if pricey, cafe, and an outdoor 'test kitchen.' Look for the enormous orange Adirondack chair at road's edge.

Activities

Many local inns provide bicycles.

Willow Stream Spa at Sonoma Mission Inn　　　SPA
(Map p186; ☑707-938-9000; www.fairmont.com/sonoma; 100 Boyes Blvd; ⊙9am-6pm Mon-Thu, to 8pm Fri-Sun) Few Wine Country spas compare with glitzy Sonoma Mission Inn. Purchasing a treatment or paying $89 (make reservations) allows use of three outdoor

and two indoor mineral pools, gym, sauna and herbal steam room at the Romanesque bathhouse. No under 18s.

Wine Country Cyclery　　　CYCLING
(Map p190; ☑707-966-6800; www.winecountry cyclery.com; 262 W Napa St; bicycle rental per day $30-75; ⊙10am-6pm) Offers hybrids, electric bikes, road bikes and even tandem bikes. Book ahead.

Sonoma Valley Cyclery　　　CYCLING
(Map p186; ☑707-935-3377; www.sonomacyclery.com; 20091 Broadway/Hwy 12; bikes per day from $30; ⊙10am-6pm Mon-Sat, to 4pm Sun; ☑) Sonoma is ideal for cycling – not too hilly – with multiple wineries near downtown. This place rents mountain bikes, road bikes and hybrids. Book ahead for weekends.

Vintage Aircraft Company　　SCENIC FLIGHTS
(Map p186; ☑707-938-2444; www.vintageaircraft.com; 23982 Arnold Dr, Sonoma; 20min flight 1/2 people $175/270) Scenic flights in biplanes, with an option to add aerobatic maneuvers.

Courses

Ramekins Sonoma Valley Culinary School　　　COOKING
(Map p190; ☑707-933-0450; www.ramekins.com; 450 W Spain St; ☑) Offers excellent demonstrations and hands-on classes for home chefs, covering things such as hors d'oeuvres and cheese-and-wine pairings. The school also hosts culinary tours of local farms and dinners with vintners and chefs.

Sleeping

There are lots of historic inns and romantic cottages suitable for a midrange budget, but those counting pennies will have better luck in Santa Rosa. Off-season rates plummet. Reserve ahead and ask about parking; some inns don't have lots.

★**Windhaven Cottage**　　COTTAGE $$
(Map p186; ☑707-938-2175, 707-483-1856; www.windhavencottage.com; 21700 Pearson Ave; cottages $165-175; ☑☑) Great-bargain Windhaven has two units: a hideaway cottage with vaulted wooden ceilings and fireplace, and a handsome 800-sq-ft studio. We prefer the romantic cottage. Both have hot tubs. Bicycles and barbecues sweeten the deal.

Sonoma Chalet　　　B&B $$
(Map p186; ☑800-938-3129, 707-938-3129; www.sonomachalet.com; 18935 5th St W; r $160-190, r with shared bath $150, cottages $210-235; P☑) On

a historic farmstead surrounded by rolling hills, rooms in this Swiss-chalet-style house are adorned with little balconies and country-style bric-a-brac. We love the garden hot tub and the freestanding cottages; Laura's has a wood-burning fireplace. Breakfast is served on a deck overlooking a nature preserve. No air-conditioning in rooms with shared bath. No phone, no internet.

Sonoma Creek Inn   MOTEL $$
(Map p186; ☑ 707-939-9463; www.sonomacreekinn. com; 239 Boyes Blvd; r Sun-Thu $155-195, Fri & Sat $205-240; ❄ 🕏 ❄) This cute-as-a-button motel has spotless, cheery, retro-Americana rooms, but it's not downtown. Valley wineries are a short drive. When available, last-minute bookings cost just $89.

Sonoma Hotel   HISTORIC HOTEL $$
(Map p190; ☑ 707-996-2996, 800-468-6016; www. sonomahotel.com; 110 W Spain St; r weekday $160-248, weekend $225-248, ste $308; ❄ ❄ 🕏) Long on charm, this good-value, vintage hotel was built in 1872 and is decorated with country-style willow-wood furnishings. It sits right on the plaza and its double-pane glass blocks the noise, but there's no elevator or parking lot.

El Dorado Hotel   BOUTIQUE HOTEL $$$
(Map p190; ☑ 707-996-3030; www.eldoradosonoma. com; 405 1st St W; r Sun-Thu $225-330, Fri & Sat $385-500; P ❄ ❄ 🕏 ❄) Stylish touches, such as high-end linens, justify rates and compensate for the rooms' compact size, as do private balconies, which overlook the plaza or rear courtyard (we prefer the plaza view, despite noise). No elevator.

El Pueblo Inn   MOTEL $$$
(Map p186; ☑ 707-996-3651, 800-900-8844; www. elpuebloinn.com; 896 W Napa St; r $189-384; ❄ @ 🕏 ❄) One mile west of downtown, family-owned El Pueblo has surprisingly cushy rooms with great beds. The big lawns and heated pool are perfect for kids; parents appreciate the 24-hour hot tub. Check the website for discounts.

Hidden Oak Inn   B&B $$$
(Map p190; ☑ 707-996-9863; www.hiddenoakinn. com; 214 E Napa St; r $255-315; ❄ 🕏 ❄) Three-room, 1914 arts-and-crafts B&B with lovely service.

MacArthur Place   INN $$$
(Map p186; ☑ 707-938-2929, 800-722-1866; www.macarthurplace.com; 29 E MacArthur St; r/ ste from $399/555; ❄ @ 🕏 ❄) Sonoma's top

full-service inn occupies a former estate with century-old gardens. There's also an attached steakhouse, spa, giant chess set on the lawn and a complimentary wine-and-cheese reception each night.

Sonoma's Best Guest Cottages   COTTAGE $$$
(Map p186; ☑ 707-933-0340; www.sonomasbest cottages.com; 1190 E Napa St; cottages $199-349, q $279-395; ❄ 🕏) Each of these four colorful, inviting cottages has a bedroom, living room, kitchen and barbecue, with comfy furniture, stereo, DVDs and bicycles. It's 1 mile east of the plaza, just behind a general store under the same ownership, featuring a deli, an espresso bar and a wine-tasting room.

✗ Eating

Sonoma takes a culinary backseat to many towns in Napa Valley and Healdsburg to the north, but has some decent restaurants on the plaza plus Fremont Diner, the best diner in Wine Country.

Angelo's Wine Country Deli   DELI $
(Map p186; ☑ 707-938-3688; 23400 Arnold Dr; sandwiches $7; ⊙ 9am-5pm) Look for the cow on the roof of this roadside deli south of town, a fave for fat sandwiches and home-made turkey and beef jerky (free samples!).

Pearl's Diner   DINER $
(Map p186; ☑ 707-996-1783; 561 5th St W; mains $7-10; ⊙ 7am-2:30pm; 🖶) Across from Safeway's west-facing wall, greasy-spoon Pearl's serves giant American breakfasts, including standout bacon and waffles with batter enriched by melted vanilla ice cream. More of a locals joint than a tourist spot.

Sonoma Market   DELI $
(Map p186; ☑ 707-996-3411; https://sonomamar ket.net; 500 W Napa St; sandwiches from $6; ⊙ 5am-9:30pm) Sonoma's best groceries and deli sandwiches.

★ Fremont Diner   AMERICAN, SOUTHERN $$
(Map p186; ☑ 707-938-7370; www.thefremontdiner. com; 2698 Fremont Dr; mains $9-22; ⊙ 8am-3pm Mon-Wed, to 9pm Thu-Sun; 🖶) 🖉 Lines snake out the door at peak times at this farm-to-table roadside diner. We prefer the indoor tables but will happily accept a picnic table to feast on buttermilk pancakes with home-made cinnamon-vanilla syrup, chicken and waffles, oyster po'boys, finger-licking barbecue and skillet-baked cornbread.Arrive early or late to beat queues, or call ahead within

an hour of your arrival to put your name on the wait list.

Della Santina's   ITALIAN $$
(Map p190; ☑ 707-935-0576; www.dellasantinas. com; 133 E Napa St; mains $14-26; ⏰ 11:30am-3pm & 5-9:30pm) The waiters have been here forever and the 'specials' rarely change, but Della Santina's Italian-American cooking – linguini pesto, veal parmigiana, rotisserie chickens – is consistently good and the brick courtyard is inviting on warm evenings.

Hopmonk Tavern   PUB FOOD $$
(Map p190; ☑ 707-935-9100; www.hopmonk.com; 691 Broadway; mains $11-23; ⏰ 11:30am-9pm Sun-Thu, to 10pm Fri & Sat) This happening gastropub and beer garden takes its brews seriously with over a dozen of its own and guest beers on tap, served in type-appropriate glassware. Live music Friday through Sunday, open mike on Wednesday starting at 8pm.

Taste of the Himalayas   INDIAN, NEPALESE $$
(Map p190; ☑ 707-996-1161; 464 1st St E; mains $10-20; ⏰ 11am-2:30 Tue-Sun, 5-10pm daily) Spicy curries, luscious lentil soup and sizzle-platter meats make a refreshing break from the usual French-Italian Wine Country fare.

Red Grape   ITALIAN $$
(Map p190; ☑ 707-996-4103; http://theredgrape. com; 529 1st St W; mains $12-20; ⏰ 11:30am-9pm; 🖐) A reliable spot for an easy meal, Red Grape serves good thin-crust pizzas and big salads in a cavernous, echoey space. Good for takeout too.

★ Cafe La Haye   CALIFORNIAN $$$
(Map p190; ☑ 707-935-5994; www.cafelahaye.com; 140 E Napa St; mains $19-25; ⏰ 5:30-9pm Tue-Sat) ✐ One of Sonoma's top tables for earthy New American cooking, La Haye only uses produce sourced from within 60 miles. Its dining room gets packed cheek-by-jowl and service can border on perfunctory, but the clean simplicity and flavor-packed cooking make it many foodies' first choice. Reserve well ahead.

Girl & the Fig   FRENCH $$$
(Map p190; ☑ 707-938-3634; www.thegirlandthefig. com; 110 W Spain St; mains $20-32; ⏰ 11:30am-10pm Mon-Thu, 11am-11pm Fri, 8am-11pm Sat, 10am-10pm Sun) For a festive evening, book a garden table at this French-provincial bistro, with good small plates ($14 to $16), including steamed mussels with matchstick fries or duck confit with lentils. Weekday three-course prix fixe

costs $42; add $12 for wine. Stellar cheeses. Reservations essential.

La Salette   PORTUGUESE $$$
(Map p190; ☑ 707-938-1927; www.lasalette-restaurant.com; 452 1st St E; mains lunch $12-25, dinner $22-32; ⏰ 11:30am-2:30pm & 5:30-9pm Mon-Fri, 11:30am-9pm Sat & Sun) ✐ Contemporary Portuguese cuisine is the focus at this just-off-the-plaza restaurant that serves excellent-value, proper sit-down meals, including a standout fisherman's stew. Make reservations.

El Dorado Kitchen   CALIFORNIAN $$$
(Map p190; ☑ 707-996-3030; http://eldorado sonoma.com/restaurant; 405 1st St W; mains lunch $15-24, dinner $21-31; ⏰ 8-11am, 11:30am-2:30pm & 5:30-9pm Mon-Thu, to 10pm Fri & Sat) ✐ The swank plazaside choice for contemporary California-Mediterranean cooking, El Dorado showcases seasonal-regional ingredients in dishes such as seafood paella, ahi tartare and housemade pasta, served in a see-and-be-seen dining room with a big community table at its center. The happening lounge serves good small plates ($11 to $22) and craft cocktails. Make reservations.

Harvest Moon Cafe   MODERN AMERICAN $$$
(Map p190; ☑ 707-933-8160; www.harvestmoon cafesonoma.com; 487 1st St W; mains $19-29; ⏰ 5:30-9pm Sun-Mon & Wed-Thu, to 9:30pm Sat & Sun) ✐ Inside a cozy 1836 adobe, this casual bistro uses local ingredients in its changing menu, with simple soul-satisfying dishes such as grilled Liberty Farm duck breast with dried cherry farro, cauliflower and saba sauce. Book the patio in warm weather.

🍷 Drinking & Nightlife

There's more of a late-night scene here than in other Sonoma Valley towns; **Steiner's** (Map p190; ☑ 707-996-3812; www.steinerstavern. com; 465 1st St W; ⏰ 6am-2am; 🗟) is pretty much the social hub.

Carneros Brewing Company   MICROBREWERY
(Map p186; ☑ 707-938-1880; www.carnerosbrew ing.com; 22985 Burndale Rd; ⏰ noon-5:30pm Wed-Mon) A family-owned microbrewery with seasonal craft beers and a mission-inspired tap room halfway between downtown Sonoma and Napa. On weekend afternoons the beer garden is a lively scene.

Prohibition Spirits Distillery   DISTILLERY
(Map p186; ☑ 707-933-7507; www.prohibition-spir its.com; 23570 Arnold Dr, Sunset Gardens at Cornerstone; ⏰ 10am-5pm) New at Cornerstone, this

WHAT'S CRUSH?

Crush is autumn harvest, the most atmospheric time of year, when the vine's leaves turn brilliant colors and you can smell fermenting fruit on the breeze. Farmers throw big parties for the vineyard workers to celebrate their work. Everyone wants to be here and room rates skyrocket. If you can afford it, visit in autumn. To score party invitations, join your favorite winery's wine club.

hip tasting room offers sips of a California version of Italian aperitifs limoncello, orangecello and grappa, along with tasty gins made with things such as cantaloupe and elderflower, and brandy distilled from prickly pear cacti.

Murphy's Irish Pub　　　　　　　PUB
(Map p190; ☑707-935-0660; www.sonomapub. com; 464 1st St E; ⊙11am-9pm) Don't ask for Bud – there are only *real* brews here. Good hand-cut fries and shepherd's pie. Live music Friday and Saturday evenings.

☆ Entertainment

Free jazz concerts happen on the plaza every second Tuesday of the month, June to September, 6pm to 8:30pm; arrive early and bring a picnic.

Sebastiani Theatre　　　　　　CINEMA
(Map p190; ☑707-996-2020; www.sebastianitheatre.com; 476 1st St E) The plaza's gorgeous 1934 Mission Revival cinema screens art-house and revival films, and sometimes live theater.

🛍 Shopping

Chateau Sonoma　　　　　　HOMEWARES
(Map p190; ☑707-935-8553; www.chateausonoma.com; 23588 Arnold Dr; ⊙10am-5pm) France meets Sonoma in one-of-a-kind gifts and arty home-decor store, which recently relocated to Cornerstone Sonoma.

Figone's Olive Oil　　　　　　　FOOD
(Map p190; ☑707-282-9092; www.figoneoliveoil. com; 483 1st St W; ⊙10am-6pm Sun-Thu, to 7pm Fri & Sat) Figone's presses its own extra-virgin olive oil and infuses some with flavors such as Meyer lemon, all free to sample.

Vella Cheese Co　　　　　　　　FOOD
(Map p190; ☑707-938-3232; www.vellacheese. com; 315 2nd St E; ⊙9:30am-6pm Mon-Fri, to 5pm Sat) Known for its jacks (made here since the 1930s), Vella specializes in dry-jack with a cocoa-powder-dusted rind. Also try Mezzo Secco, a cheese you can only find here. Staff will vacuum-pack for shipping.

Tiddle E Winks　　　　　　　　TOYS
(Map p190; ☑707-939-6933; www.tiddleewinks. com; 115 E Napa St; ⊙10:30am-5:30pm Mon-Sat, 11am-5pm Sun; ⊞) Vintage five-and-dime, with classic mid-20th-century toys.

ⓘ Information

Sonoma Valley Visitors Bureau (Map p190; ☑866-966-1090; www.sonomavalley.com; 453 1st St E; ⊙9am-5pm Mon-Sat, 10am-5pm Sun) Offers guides, maps, pamphlets, merchandise information on deals and events, and more. There's another at Cornerstone Sonoma (p191).

ⓘ Getting There & Away

Public transport is not a great idea but it can be done. Find out by dialing ☑511 or looking online at www.transit.511.org. Sonoma Valley is a 90-minute drive from San Francisco.

ⓘ Getting Around

Sonoma Hwy/Hwy 12 is lined with wineries and runs from Sonoma to Santa Rosa, then to western Sonoma County; Arnold Dr has less traffic (but few wineries) and runs parallel up the valley's western side to Glen Ellen. Plan at least five hours to visit the valley from bottom to top.

Glen Ellen & Kenwood

Sleepy Glen Ellen is a snapshot of old Sonoma, with white picket fences and tiny cottages beside a poplar-lined creek. When downtown Sonoma is jammed, you can wander quiet Glen Ellen and feel far away. It's ideal for a leg-stretching stopover between wineries or a romantic overnight – the nighttime sky blazes with stars. Glen Ellen's biggest daytime attractions are Jack London State Historic Park and Benziger winery (p187).

◎ Sights & Activites

Jack London State Historic Park　　PARK
(Map p186; ☑707-938-5216; www.jacklondonpark. com; 2400 London Ranch Rd, Glen Ellen; per car $10, cottage adult/child $4/2; ⊙9:30am-5pm; ℙⓟ) 🎗 Napa has Robert Louis Stevenson, but Sonoma has Jack London. This 1400-acre park frames that author's last years; don't miss the excellent on-site museum. Miles of **hiking trails** (some open to mountain bikes)

weave through oak-dotted woodlands, between 600ft and 2300ft elevations; an easy 2-mile loop meanders to **London Lake**, great for picnicking. On select summer evenings, the park transforms into a theater for 'Broadway Under the Stars.' Be alert for poison oak.

Changing occupations from Oakland fisher-man to Alaska gold prospector to Pacific yachtsman (and novelist on the side) London (1876–1916) ultimately took up farming. He bought 'Beauty Ranch' in 1905 and moved here in 1911. With his second wife, Charmian, he lived and wrote in a small cottage while his mansion, **Wolf House**, was under construction. On the eve of its completion in 1913, it burned down. The disaster devastated London, and although he toyed with rebuilding, he died before construction got underway. His widow, Charmian, built the **House of Happy Walls**, which has been preserved as a **museum** (open 10am to 5pm). It's a half-mile walk from there to the remains of Wolf House, passing London's grave along the way. Other paths wind around the farm to the cottage, open noon to 4pm, where he lived and worked.

Quarryhill Botanical Garden GARDENS
(Map p186; ☑707-996-3166; www.quarryhillbg.org; 12841 Hwy 12; adult/child 13-17yr $12/8; ⏱9am-4pm) Just when you thought the vineyards would stretch as far as the eye could see, out of nowhere comes a world-renowned botanical garden specializing in the flora of Asia. It's a treat to stroll the trails, observing specimens collected on yearly expeditions to countries throughout the Far East, and to relax near the pond, contemplating the artfully created woodland landscape.

Sugarloaf Ridge State Park PARK
(Map p186; ☑707-833-5712; www.sugarloafpark.org; 2605 Adobe Canyon Rd, Kenwood; per car $8; P 🐾) 🌿 There are 30 miles of fantastic hiking – when it's not blazingly hot. On clear days, **Bald Mountain** has drop-dead views to the sea, while the **Brushy Peaks Trail** peers into Napa Valley. Both are moderately strenuous; plan on a three-hour round-trip. Bikes and horses can use perimeter trails seasonally. There's a small but well-stocked visitor center.

Oak Hill Farm FARM
(Map p186; ☑707-996-6643; www.oakhillfarm.net; 15101 Sonoma Hwy, Glen Ellen; ⏱9am-3pm Sat May-Dec; P 🐾) 🌿 At the southern end of Glen Ellen, Oak Hill Farm contains acres upon acres of organic flowers and produce,

hemmed in by lovely steep oak and manzanita woodland. The farm's **Red Barn Store** is a historic dairy barn filled with handmade wreaths, herbs and organic goods reaped from the surrounding fields. Try the heirloom tomatoes, pumpkins and blue plums.

Triple Creek Horse Outfit HORSEBACK RIDING
(Map p186; ☑707-887-8700; www.triplecreek horseoutfit.com; 2400 London Ranch Rd; 60/90min rides $80/100; ⏱9am-5pm Mon-Sat) Explore Jack London State Park by horseback for vistas over Sonoma Valley. Reservations required.

Morton's Warm Springs SWIMMING
(Map p186; ☑707-833-5511; www.mortonswarm springs.com; 1651 Warm Springs Rd, Glen Ellen; adult/child $12/6; ⏱10am-6pm Tue-Sun Jun-Aug, Sat, Sun & holidays May & Sep; 🐾) This old-fashioned spring-fed geothermal-pool complex and family-friendly gathering place has two mineral pools, limited hiking, volleyball and BBQ facilities. From Sonoma Hwy in Kenwood, turn west on Warm Springs Rd.

🛏 Sleeping

Couples will not regret staying in the romantic cottages and inns of Glen Ellen. Kenwood has one high-end resort and an excellent campground.

Sugarloaf Ridge State Park CAMPGROUND $
(Map p42; ☑707-833-6084, 800-444-7275; www.reserveamerica.com; 2605 Adobe Canyon Rd, Kenwood; tent & RV sites $35; 🐾) Sonoma's nearest camping is north of Kenwood at this lovely hilltop park, with 48 drive-in sites, clean coin-operated showers and great hiking.

Beltane Ranch B&B $$
(Map p186; ☑707-833-4233; www.beltaneranch. com; 11775 Hwy 12, Glen Ellen; d $185-375; P 🐾 🐕 🖤) 🌿 Surrounded by horse pastures and vineyards, Beltane is a throwback to 19th-century Sonoma. The cheerful 1890s ranch house has double porches lined with swinging chairs and white wicker. Though it's technically a B&B, each country-Americana-style room and the cottage has a private entrance – nobody will make you pet the cat. No phone or TV means zero distraction from pastoral bliss.

Glen Ellen Cottages BUNGALOW $$
(☑707-996-1174; www.glenelleninn.com; 13670 Arnold Dr, Glen Ellen; cottages Sun-Thu $149-175, Fri & Sat $219-275; 🖤 🐕) Hidden behind Glen Ellen Inn (p196), these five creekside cottages are designed for romance, with oversized jetted tub, steam shower and gas fireplace.

Jack London Lodge   MOTEL $$

(✆707-938-8510; www.jacklondonlodge.com; 13740 Arnold Dr, Glen Ellen; r Mon-Fri $134, Sat & Sun $205; ❀☎⬛) An old-fashioned wood-sided motel with well-kept rooms decorated with antique repros, this is a weekday bargain. Outside there's a pool and hot tub; next door, a saloon. Two-night minimum during high-season weekends.

Gaige House Inn   INN $$$

(✆707-935-0237; www.gaige.com; 13540 Arnold Dr, Glen Ellen; d/ste from $275/345; P☀@ ☎⬛❀) Among the valley's most chic inns, Gaige has 23 rooms, five inside an 1890 house decked out in Euro-Asian style. Best are the Japanese-style 'Zen suites,' with requisite high-end bells and whistles, including freestanding tubs made from hollowed-out granite boulders. Fabulous.

Kenwood Inn & Spa   INN $$$

(Map p186; ✆707-833-1293, 800-353-6966; www. kenwoodinn.com; 10400 Sonoma Hwy, Kenwood; r $450-825; ❀@☎⬛) Lush gardens surround ivy-covered bungalows at this sexy 30-room inn, designed to resemble a Mediterranean château. Two hot tubs (one with a waterfall) and an on-site spa make it ideal for lovers, boring for singles. No kids. Book an upstairs balcony room.

✖ Eating

Italian and French establishments dominate the scene, but there are also a couple of good bakeries and a market for self-caterers. Jack London Village has some good options.

Garden Court Cafe & Bakery   CAFE $

(✆707-935-1565; www.gardencourtcafe.com; 13647 Arnold Dr, Glen Ellen; mains $9-12; ☺8:30am-2pm Wed, Thu & Mon, 8am-2pm Sat & Sun) Basic breakfasts, sandwiches and salads.

Fig Cafe & Winebar   FRENCH, CALIFORNIAN $$

(✆707-938-2130; www.thefigcafe.com; 13690 Arnold Dr, Glen Ellen; mains $12-24, 3-course dinner $36; ☺10am-2:30pm Sat & Sun, 5-9pm Sun-Thu, 5-9:30pm Fri & Sat) The earthy California-Provençal comfort food includes flash-fried calamari with spicy lemon aioli, fig and arugula salad and *steak frites*. Good wine prices and weekend brunch give reason to return. No reservations; complimentary corkage.

Mayo Winery Reserve   WINERY $$

(Map p186; ✆707-833-5504; www.mayofamilywinery.com; 9200 Sonoma Hwy, Kenwood; 7-course menu $50; ☺by appointment 10:30am-6:30pm) Feast on a seven-course small-plates menu paired with seven wines for $50 at this roadside wine-tasting room.

Cafe Citti   ITALIAN $$

(Map p186; ✆707-833-2690; www.cafecitti. com; 9049 Sonoma Hwy, Kenwood; mains $8-15; ☺11am-3:30pm & 5-8:30pm Sun-Thu, to 9pm Fri & Sat; 🍴) Locals favor this order-at-the-counter Italian-American deli, with standout roast chicken, and homemade gnocchi and ravioli. At lunchtime there's pizza and house-baked focaccia sandwiches.

Glen Ellen Inn   AMERICAN $$

(✆707-996-6409; www.glenelleninn.com; 13670 Arnold Dr, Glen Ellen; mains $16-25; ☺11:30am-9pm Thu-Tue, 5:30-9pm Wed) Oysters, martinis and grilled steaks. Lovely garden, full bar.

Glen Ellen Star   CALIFORNIAN, ITALIAN $$$

(✆707-343-1384; http://glenellenstar.com; 13648 Arnold Dr, Glen Ellen; pizzas $15-20, mains $24-50; ☺5:30-9pm Sun-Thu, to 9:30pm Fri & Sat; 🍴) ✿ Helmed by chef Ari Weiswasser, who once worked at Thomas Keller's French Laundry (p174), this petite Glen Ellen bistro shines a light on the best of Sonoma farms and ranches. Local, organic and seasonal ingredients star in dishes such as spring-lamb ragù, whole roasted fish with broccoli di cicco or golden beets with harissa crumble. Reservations recommended. Wednesdays are neighborhood nights, which means no corkage fee and a $35 two-course menu.

Aventine   ITALIAN $$$

(Map p186; ✆707-934-8911; http://glenellen.aventinehospitality.com; 14301 Arnold Dr, Glen Ellen; mains $14-28; ☺4:30-10pm Wed-Fri, 11am-10pm Sat & Sun) The Sonoma outpost of the popular San Francisco restaurant occupies an atmospheric former grist mill with a sun-dappled outdoor patio. It serves Italian-derived dishes, including house-special Aventino: mozzarella-stuffed meatball with pesto over polenta. Make reservations.

❶ Getting There & Away

Glen Ellen is an hour's drive north from San Francisco.

RUSSIAN RIVER AREA

Lesser-known western Sonoma County was formerly famous for its apple farms and vacation cottages. Lately vineyards are replacing orchards and the Russian River has taken its place among California's important wine appellations, especially for Pinot Noir.

'The River,' as locals call it, has long been a summer-weekend destination for Northern Californians who come to canoe, wander country lanes, taste wine, hike redwood forests and live at a lazy pace. In winter the river floods, and nobody's here. The Russian River begins in the mountains north of Ukiah, in Mendocino County, but the most visited sections lie southwest of Healdsburg, where the river cuts a serpentine course toward the sea.

Russian River Wineries

Sonoma County's wine-growing regions encompass several diverse areas, each famous for different reasons. Pick up the free, useful *Russian River Wine Road* map (www.wine road.com) from tourist-brochure racks.

Russian River Valley

Nighttime coastal fog drifts up the Russian River Valley, then usually clears by midday. Pinot Noir does beautifully, as does Chardonnay, which also grows in hotter regions, but prefers the longer 'hang time' of cooler climes. The highest concentration of wineries is along Westside Rd, between Guerneville and Healdsburg.

★**Macrostie**   WINERY
(Map p198; 707-473-9303; www.macrostiewin ery.com; 4605 Westside Rd; tasting $20-25, with tour $55; 11am-5pm Mon-Thu, 10am-5pm Fri-Sun) For its creamy and crisp Chardonnays and earthy Pinots, along with top-notch service and an elegant tasting room, Macrostie is the talk of Wine Country. The sit-down tastings are relaxed and highly personal, with gorgeous views of the vineyard. Visionary winemaker Heidi Bridenhagen holds the distinction of being the youngest female on the job in Sonoma Valley. Pair your tasting with a delicious charcuterie plate that includes three local cheeses, prosciutto, olives, almonds and dried fruit.

Hartford   WINERY
(Map p198; 800-588-0234; www.hartfordwines. com; 8075 Martinelli Rd, Forestville; tasting $15; 10am-4:30pm) Surprisingly upscale for West County, Hartford sits in a pastoral valley surrounded by redwood-forested hills, on one of the area's prettiest back roads. It specializes in fine single-vineyard Pinot (13 kinds), Chardonnay and Zinfandel from old-vine fruit. Umbrella-shaded picnic tables dot the garden. Bottles are $30 to $100; the tasting fee is waived with purchase.

J Winery   WINERY
(Map p198; 707-431-3646, 707-431-5430; www. jwine.com; 11447 Old Redwood Hwy; tasting/tour $20/30; 11am-5pm) J crafts crisp sparkling wines, among Sonoma's best, but it's pricey. Make an appointment and splurge on one of the seated food-and-wine-pairing experiences. The decadent 'bubble room' tasting includes five wines paired with five locally sourced dishes prepared by chef Carl Shelton ($110 per person). The alfresco 'terrace' tasting (April to November) is also a winner, with four wines paired with four small appetizers ($55). Bottles cost $24 to $75.

De La Montanya   WINERY
(Map p198; 707-433-3711; www.dlmwine.com; 999 Foreman Lane, Healdsburg; tasting $10; 11am-4:30pm;) This tiny winery, tucked amid vineyards, is known for 17 small-batch varieties made with estate-grown fruit. Viognier, Primitivo, Pinot and Cabernet are signatures; the 'summer white' and Gewürztraminer are great back-porch wines. Apple-shaded picnic area, bocce ball and horseshoes add to the fun. Bottles are $20 to $60 and the tasting fee is refundable with a purchase. Appointments suggested.

Landmark Vineyards at Hop Kiln Estate   WINERY
(Map p198; 707-433-6491; www.landmarkwine. com; 6050 Westside Rd; tasting $20; 10am-5pm) This photogenic historic landmark has a busy tasting room inside a former hop kiln; we especially like the Flocchini Chardonnay. You can build your own picnic with meats, cheeses and crackers for $40, and the winery provides wine glasses, baskets, blankets and cheese boards with knives.

Porter Creek   WINERY
(Map p198; 707-433-6321; www.porter creekvineyards.com; 8735 Westside Rd; tasting $15; 10:30am-4:30pm;) Inside a vintage-1920s garage, Porter Creek's tasting bar is a former bowling-alley lane. Porter is old-school Northern California, an early

Russian River Area

pioneer in biodynamic farming. High-acid, food-friendly Pinot Noir and Chardonnay are specialties, but there's old-vine Zinfandel and other Burgundian- and Rhône-style wines too. Tasting fee waived with purchase. Bottles cost $24 to $72.

Moshin
WINERY

(Map p198; ☎707-433-5499; www.moshinvineyards.com; 10295 Westside Rd; tasting $15, private tour & tasting by appointment only $30; ⊙11am-4:30pm; ℗) 🌿 Pinot Noir is a finicky grape that withers in sun and mildews in fog, yet it thrives in Russian River Valley, including

at solar-powered Moshin Vineyards. The winery also specializes in small-production Pinot Noir, Sauvignon Blanc, Chardonnay, Merlot, Petite Sirah and Zinfandel. Tasting fee waived with purchase.

Iron Horse
WINERY

(Map p198; ☎707-887-1507; www.ironhorsevineyards.com; 9786 Ross Station Rd, off Hwy 116, Sebastopol; tasting $25, incl tour $50; ⊙10am-4:30pm, last tasting 4pm; ℗) Atop a hill with drop-dead views over the county, Iron Horse is known for sparkling wines, which the White House often pours. The outdoor tasting room is refreshingly unfussy; when you're done with your wine, pour it in the grass. On Sundays from noon to 4pm, April through October, oysters, cheese and olive oil are served. Bottles cost $30 to $110. Reservations strongly recommended.

Korbel   WINERY
(Map p198; ☎707-824-7000; www.korbel.com; 13250 River Rd, Guerneville; ⊙10am-5pm; P) **FREE** Gorgeous rose gardens (April to October) and a stellar on-site deli make Korbel worth a stop for a free tasting, but the sparkling wine's just OK. Try the sparkling

wine you can't get elsewhere; the rouge is particularly good.

Gary Farrell   WINERY
(Map p198; ☎707-473-2909; www.garyfarrellwines.com; 10701 Westside Rd; tasting $35-75; ⊙10am-3pm Mon-Fri, by appointment; P) High on a hilltop overlooking the Russian River, Gary Farrell's tasting room sits perched among second-growth redwoods. The elegant Chardonnay and long-finish Pinot Noir, made by a big-name winemaker, score high marks for consistency. Bottles are $35 to $75.

Dry Creek Valley

Hemmed in by 2000ft-high mountains, Dry Creek Valley is relatively warm, ideal for Sauvignon Blanc and Zinfandel, and in some places Cabernet Sauvignon. It's west of Hwy 101, between Healdsburg and Lake Sonoma. Dry Creek Rd is the fast-moving main thoroughfare. Parallel-running West Dry Creek Road is an undulating country lane with no center stripe – one of Sonoma's great back roads, ideal for cycling.

Bella   WINERY
(Map p198; ☎707-473-9171; www.bellawinery.com; 9711 W Dry Creek Rd; tasting $15; ⊙11am-4:30pm; P) Atop the valley's north end, always-fun Bella has cool caves built into the hillside. The estate-grown grapes include 112-year-old vines from Alexander Valley. The focus is on big reds – Zinfandel and Syrah – but there's terrific rosé (good for barbecues) and late-harvest Zinfandel (great with brownies). The wonderful vibe and dynamic staff make Bella special. Bottles are $25 to $55.

Preston   WINERY
(Map p198; ☎707-433-3372; www.prestonvineyards.com; 9282 W Dry Creek Rd; tasting/tours $10/25; ⊙11am-4:30pm; P⚑) ✿ An early leader in organics and recently certified biodynamic, Lou Preston's 19th-century farm is old Sonoma. Weathered picket fencing frames the tasting room, with candy-colored walls and tongue-in-groove ceilings setting a country mood. The signature is citrusy Sauvignon Blanc, but try the Rhône varietals and small-lot wines: Carignane, Viognier, Cinsault and cult-favorite Barbera. Preston also bakes good bread and cold-presses its own olive oil; picnic in the shade of a walnut tree. Bottles are $22 to $40. Tours by appointment.Monday to Friday, there's bocce and a new farm store sells seasonal produce adjacent to the tasting room.

Family Wineries
WINERY

(Map p198; ☏888-433-6555; www.familywines. com; 4791 Dry Creek Rd; tasting $10; ⊘10:30am-4:30pm Mar-Dec, Thu-Mon Jan-Feb) Sample multiple varietals at this cooperative, which showcases six boutique wineries too small to have their own tasting rooms. Tasting fee is refundable with a purchase.

Truett Hurst
WINERY

(Map p198; ☏707-433-9545; www.truetthurst.com; 5610 Dry Creek Rd; tasting $10; ⊘10am-5pm; P) ✐ Pull up an Adirondack chair and picnic creekside at Truett Hurst, one of Dry Creek's biodynamic wineries. Sample terrific old-vine Zinfandel, standout Petite Sirah and Russian River Pinot Noir at the handsome contemporary tasting room, then meander through fragrant fruit and gardens to the creek, where salmon spawn in autumn. Another good winery, VML, now shares tasting-room space with Truett Hurst. Bottles are $20 to $53.

Unti Vineyards
WINERY

(Map p198; ☏707-433-5590; www.untivineyards. com; 4202 Dry Creek Rd; tasting $10; ⊘10am-4pm by appointment only; ☻) ✐ Inside a vineyard-view tasting room, Unti pours all estate-grown varietals – Châteauneuf-du-Pape–style Grenache, compelling Syrah and superb Sangiovese – favored by oenophiles for their structured tannins and concentrated fruit. If you love small-batch wines, don't miss Unti. Bottles are $20 to $50 and the tasting fee is refundable with a purchase.

Quivira
WINERY

(Map p198; ☏707-431-8333, 800-292-8339; www. quivirawine.com; 4900 W Dry Creek Rd; tasting $15-30, incl tour $40, tour & estate tasting by reservation only; ⊘11am-4pm, 10am-4:30pm Apr-Oct; P☻☻) ✐ Sunflowers, lavender, beehives and crowing roosters greet your arrival at this winery and biodynamic farm, with self-guided garden tours and a redwood grove beside the vines. Kids can giggle with pigs and chickens while you sample Rhône varietals, unusual blends and lip-smacking, award-winning Sauvignon Blanc. Bottles are $24 to $55.

Alexander Valley

Bucolic Alexander Valley flanks the Mayacamas Mountains, with postcard-perfect vistas and wide-open vineyards. Summers are hot, ideal for Cabernet Sauvignon, Merlot and warm-weather Chardonnays, but there are also fine Sauvignon Blancs and Zinfandels. For events info visit www.alexandervalley.org.

Hawkes
WINERY

(Map p198; ☏707-433-4295; www.hawkeswine. com; 6734 Hwy 128; tasting $15, barrel/vineyard tour $45/45; ⊘10am-5pm; P☻) Hawkes makes an easy stopover while you're exploring the valley, and offers private barrel tastings in which guests sample straight from the oak and order 'futures' from a new vintage before the wine is bottled or released to the market. The single-vineyard Cabernet Sauvignon is damn good, as is the Merlot; there's also a clean-and-crisp Chardonnay. Bottles are $30 to $75.

Francis Ford Coppola Winery
WINERY, MUSEUM

(Map p198; ☏707-857-1471; www.francisfordcoppola winery.com; 300 Via Archimedes, Geyserville; tasting $18-25; ⊘11am-6pm; P☻) ✐ The famous movie director's vineyard estate is a self-described 'wine wonderland.' Taking over historic Chateau Souverain, this hillside winery has a bit of everything: wine-tasting flights, a free museum of moviemaking memorabilia, a shameless gift shop and two modern Italian-American restaurants. Outside you'll find bocce courts by two **swimming pools** (Map p198; day pass adult/child $35/15; ⊘11am-6pm daily Jun-Sep, Fri-Sun Apr, May & Oct; ☻). The most satisfying tasting is the reserve flight ($25) upstairs. Bottles are $12 to $90. From 5pm to 9pm on Tuesdays, there's A Tavola, a multiple-course, family-style meal served by staff in elaborate costumes ($45).

Hanna
WINERY

(Map p198; ☏707-431-4310, 800-854-3987; www. hannawinery.com; 9280 Hwy 128; tasting $20-40; ⊘10am-4pm; P) Abutting oak-studded hills, Hanna's tasting room has lovely vineyard views and good picnicking. At the bar, find estate-grown Sauvignon Blanc, Malbec, Cabernet Sauvignon, Chardonnay and big-fruit Zinfandel. Sit-down wine-and-cheese tastings ($40) are available with advance reservations. Bottles cost $19 to $68.

Soda Rock Winery
WINERY

(Map p198; ☏707-433-3303; www.sodarockwin ery.com; 8015 CA 128; tasting $15; ⊘11am-5pm) Come to Soda Rock to behold Lord Snort, a 20,000lb metal boar sculpture displayed out front, and stay for the big Bordeaux varietals, including Cabernet Savignon, Cab Franc and Petit Verdot, along with a rare and juicy Primitivo. With a sky-high ceiling and dignified brick, the lovingly restored tasting room is a former general store that now doubles as an elegant event space. Bottles cost $18 to $41. Tasting fee waived with one bottle purchase.

Trentadue WINERY
(Map p198; ☎707-433-3104, 888-332-3032; www.trentadue.com; 19170 Geyserville Ave, Geyserville; tasting $10-15, tour $25; ☺10am-5pm; ☻) Specializes in ports (ruby, not tawny); the chocolate port makes a great gift. The tour is good fun and includes tastes of sparkling and still wine as guests are towed through the vineyards by a tractor. Tasting fee waived with four-bottle purchase or wine-club sign-up. Bottles $15 to $38.

Foley Sonoma WINERY
(Map p198; ☎707-433-1944; www.foleysonoma.com; 5110 Hwy 128; tasting $20, incl tour $40; ☺10am-5pm; ℗) ✐ Wow, what a view from the hilltop concrete-and-glass tasting room at Foley Sonoma. Winemaker Courtney Foley specializes in Bordeaux varietals and blends, along with Zinfandels and Pinots. An hour-long tour takes guests through the crush pad, barrel room and vineyard and finishes with a tasting. Bottles are $30 to $80.

Sebastopol

Grapes have replaced apples as the new cash crop, but Sebastopol's farm-town identity remains rooted in the apple – evidenced by the much-heralded summertime Gravenstein Apple Fair. The town center feels suburban because of traffic, but a hippie tinge gives it color. This is the refreshingly laid-back side of Wine Country and makes a good-value base for exploring the area.

◉ Sights

Around Sebastopol, look for family-friendly farms, gardens, animal sanctuaries and pick-your-own orchards. For a countywide list, check out the Sonoma County Farm Trails Guide (www.farmtrails.org).

★**Patrick Amiot Junk Art** GALLERY
(www.patrickamiot.com; Florence Ave; ℗ ♿) Prepare to gawk and giggle at the wacky Patrick Amiot sculptures gracing front yards along Florence Ave. Fashioned from recycled materials, a hot-rodding rat, a hectic waitress and a witch in midflight are a few of the oversized and demented lawn ornaments parading along the street. Keep an eye out and you'll notice more of these scattered throughout Sebastopol.

California Carnivores GARDENS
(☎707-824-0433; www.californiacarnivores.com; 2833 Old Gravenstein Hwy S; ☺10am-4pm Thu-Mon) Even vegans can't help admiring these incredible carnivorous plants (the largest collection in the US), including specimens from around the globe. Owner Peter D'Amato encourages visitors to BYOB (bring your own bugs) and watch as the plants devour them. He's also written a book with a perfect name, *The Savage Garden*.

Spirit Works Distillery DISTILLERY
(☎707-634-4793; www.spiritworksdistillery.com; 6790 McKinley St, 100, Barlow; tasting/tour $18/20; ☺11am-5pm Wed-Sun) ✐ A bracing alternative to wine tasting, Spirit Works crafts superb small-batch spirits – vodka, gin, sloe gin and (soon) whiskey – from organic California red-winter wheat. The distillery abides by a 'grain-to-glass' philosophy, with milling, mashing, fermenting and distilling all done on-site. Sample and buy in the warehouse. Tours (by reservation) happen Friday to Sunday at 5pm and finish with a tasting. Bottles are $27 to $36.

Barlow MARKET
(☎707-824-5600; www.thebarlow.net; cnr Sebastopol & Morris Sts; ☺hours vary; ℗ ♿) ✐ The Barlow occupies a former apple-processing plant, repurposed into a 12-acre village of food producers, artists, winemakers, coffee roasters, spirits distillers and indie restaurateurs, who showcase West County's culinary and artistic diversity. Wander shed to shed, sample everything from house-brewed beer to ice cream flash-frozen with liquid nitrogen and meet artisans in their workshops. Usually on Thursdays 4pm to 8pm, from May to October, the Barlow hosts a 'street fair,' with live music and local vendors.

Farmers Market MARKET
(www.sebastopolfarmmarket.org; cnr Petaluma & McKinley Aves; ☺10am-1:30pm Sun) Meets at the downtown plaza.

✩ Festivals & Events

Apple Blossom Festival CULTURAL
(www.appleblossomfest.com; ☺Apr) Live music, food, drink, wine, a parade and exhibits.

Gravenstein Apple Fair FOOD & DRINK
(www.gravensteinapplefair.com; ☺Aug) Arts, crafts, food, wine, brews, games, live entertainment and farm-life activities.

⛏ Sleeping

There are only a couple of hotels in Sebastopol, but staying here is convenient to Russian River Valley, the coast and Sonoma Valley.

Sebastopol Inn
MOTEL $$

(☑800-653-1082, 707-829-2500; www.sebastopol inn.com; 6751 Sebastopol Ave; r $119-388; ☀☎☾) We like this independent, *non*-cookie-cutter motel for its quiet, off-street location, usually reasonable rates and good-looking if basic rooms. Outside are grassy areas for kids and a hot tub.

✗ Eating

Sebastopol is a town of artists and locavores, and while its restaurant scene reflects those predilections, there are plenty of international options as well. Above all, the local produce and seafood is top-notch.

★ Handline
CALIFORNIAN $

(☑707-827-3744; www.handline.com; 935 Gravenstein Ave; mains $9-21; ☺11am-10pm) 🍴 Housed in a former Foster's Freeze, this highly anticipated seafood restaurant is over-the-counter casual but undeniably elegant. The stylish interior is defined by reclaimed wood and shoji-style paneling that opens to a tree-shaded patio. In a room designated the *tortilleria,* corn tortillas are hand-molded each day and topped with battered and fried rockfish, pickled onion and roasted summer squash. The oysters and ceviche are divine, and in a nod to the previous tenant there's organic Straus soft serve for dessert.

Slice of Life
VEGETARIAN $

(☑707-829-6627; www.thesliceoflife.com; 6970 McKinley St; mains under $10; ☺11am-9pm Tue-Fri, 9am-9pm Sat & Sun; ☝) 🍴 This good vegan-vegetarian kitchen doubles as a pizzeria and also offers plenty of Mexican dishes. Breakfast all day. Great smoothies.

Mom's Apple Pie
DESSERTS $

(☑707-823-8330; www.momsapplepieusa.com; 4550 Gravenstein Hwy N; whole pies $7-17; ☺10am-6pm; ☝☝) Pie's the thing at this roadside bakery – and yum, that flaky crust. Apple is predictably good, especially in autumn, but the blueberry is our fave, made better with vanilla ice cream.

Screamin' Mimi
ICE CREAM $

(☑707-823-5902; www.screaminmimisicecream. com; 6902 Sebastopol Ave; ☺11am-10pm) Delish homemade ice cream.

Pacific Market
MARKET $

(Pacific Market; ☑707-823-9735; www.pacificmkt. com; 550 Gravenstein Hwy N; ☺7am-9pm Mon-Sat, 8am-8pm Sun) Excellent for groceries and picnics; north of downtown.

Hopmonk Tavern
PUB FOOD $$

(☑707-829-7300; www.hopmonk.com; 230 Petaluma Ave; mains $12-23; ☺11:30am-9pm Mon-Thu, to 10pm Fri, 11am-10pm Sat & Sun; ☎) Inside a converted 1903 railroad station, Hopmonk's serves 76 varieties of beer – served in type-specific glassware – that pair with a good menu of burgers, fried calamari, charcuterie platters and salads.

Zazu Kitchen & Farm
AMERICAN $$$

(☑707-523-4814; http://zazukitchen.com; 6770 McKinley St, 150, Barlow; mains lunch $13-18, dinner $24-29; ☺5-10pm Mon & Wed, 3-10pm Thu, 11:30am-midnight Fri & Sat, 9am-10pm Sun) 🍴 We love the farm-to-table ethos of Zazu – it grows its own pigs and sources everything locally – but some dishes miss and the industrial-style space gets crazy loud. Still, it does excellent pizzas, salads, housemade *salumi,* pork and bacon. Good breakfasts too.

K&L Bistro
FRENCH $$$

(☑707-823-6614; www.klbistro.com; 119 S Main St; lunch $14-20, dinner $19-29; ☺11am-11pm) K&L serves earthy provincial Cal-French bistro cooking in a convivial bar-and-grill space with sidewalk patio. Expect classics such as mussels and french fries, and grilled steaks with red-wine reduction. Reservations essential.

🍷 Drinking & Nightlife

Nightlife isn't Sebastopol's strong suit, but there are a couple of great breweries and tastings rooms at the Barlow (p201).

Woodfour Brewing Co
BREWERY

(☑707-823-3144; www.woodfourbrewing.com; 6780 Depot St, Barlow; ☺noon-7pm Wed & Thu, to 8pm Fri & Sat, 11am-6pm Sun) 🍴 Woodfour's solar-powered brewery serves about a dozen housemade beers, light on alcohol and hops, plus several sours (high-acid beer). It also has an exceptionally good menu of small plates (designed to pair with beer), from simple snacks to refined, technique-driven dishes better than any we've had at a California brewery.

Taylor Maid Farms
CAFE

(☑707-634-7129; www.taylormaidfarms.com; 6790 McKinley St, Barlow; ☺6:30am-6pm Sun-Thu, to 7pm Fri, 7am-7pm Sat) 🍴 Choose your brew method (drip, press etc) at this third-wave coffeehouse that roasts its own organic beans. Seasonal drinks include lavender lattes.

Hardcore Espresso
CAFE

([707-823-7588; 81 Bloomfield Rd; ☺5am-7pm Mon-Fri, 6am-7pm Sat & Sun; 🖀) 🖉 Meet local hippies and artists over coffee and smoothies at this classic NorCal, off-the-grid, indoor-outdoor coffeehouse, south of downtown, that's essentially a corrugated-metal-roofed shack surrounded by umbrella tables.

🔒 Shopping

Antique shops line Gravenstein Hwy S toward Hwy 101.

Funk & Flash
CLOTHING

([707-829-1142; www.funkandflash.com; 228 S Main St; ☺11am-7pm) Disco-glam party clothes, inspired by Burning Man.

Midgley's Country Flea Market
MARKET

([707-823-7874; www.mfleamarket.com; 2200 Gravenstein Hwy S; ☺7:30am-4:30pm Sat, 6:30am-5:30pm Sun) The region's largest flea market.

Copperfield's Books
BOOKS

([707-823-2618; www.copperfields.net; 138 N Main St; ☺10am-7pm Mon-Sat, to 6pm Sun) Indie bookshop with literary events.

Beekind
FOOD, HOMEWARES

([707-824-2905; www.beekind.com; 921 Gravenstein Hwy S; ☺10am-6pm Mon-Sat, to 4pm Sun) 🖉 Local honey and beeswax candles.

Antique Society
ANTIQUES

([707-829-1733; www.antiquesociety.com; 2661 Gravenstein Hwy S; ☺10am-5pm) More than 125 antiques vendors under one roof.

Aubergine
VINTAGE

([707-827-3460; www.auberginevintageempori um.com; 755 Petaluma Ave; ☺10:30am-6pm) Vast vintage emporium, specializing in cast-off European thrift-shop clothing.

Sumbody
COSMETICS

([707-823-2053; www.sumbody.com; 118 N Main St; ☺10am-7pm Mon-Fri, to 8pm Sat, to 6pm Sun) Ecofriendly bath products made with all-natural ingredients. Also offers facials ($79) and massages ($80) at its small on-site spa.

Toyworks
TOYS

([707-829-2003; www.sonomatoyworks.com; 6940 Sebastopol Ave; ☺10am-6pm Mon-Sat, 11am-5pm Sun; 🖘) Indie toy seller with phenomenal selection of quality games for kids.

ℹ️ Information

Sebastopol Area Chamber of Commerce & Visitors Center ([877-828-4748, 707-823-3032; www.sebastopol.org; 265 S Main St; ☺10am-5pm Mon-Fri) Maps, information and exhibits.

ℹ️ Getting There & Away

For public-transit information, dial [511, or look online at www.transit.511.org.

Sebastopol is about an 80-minute drive north from San Francisco. Hwy 116 splits downtown; southbound traffic uses Main St, northbound traffic Petaluma Ave. North of town, it's called Gravenstein Hwy N and continues toward Guerneville; south of downtown, it's Gravenstein Hwy S, which heads toward Hwy 101 and Sonoma.

Occidental & Around

Our favorite West County town is a haven of artists, back-to-the-landers and counterculturalists. Historic 19th-century buildings line a single main street, easy to explore in an hour; continue north by car and you'll hit the Russian River in Monte Rio. At Christmastime, Bay Area families flock to Occidental to buy trees. The town decorates to the nines and there's weekend cookie-decorating and caroling at the Union Hotel's Bocce Ballroom.

⊙ Sights & Activities

Grove of the Old Trees
FOREST

([707-544-7284; www.landpaths.org; 17599 Fitzpatrick Lane; ☺dawn-dusk) FREE Outside Occidental and up on a ridge off Fitzpatrick Lane, Grove of the Old Trees is a peaceful, 28-acre forest of old-growth redwoods. The forest and its trails are managed by a local nonprofit.

Bohème Wines
WINERY

([707-874-3218; www.bohemewines.com; 3625 Main St; ☺3-5pm Thu & Fri, noon-6pm Sat & Sun) Drop in to this little tasting room in downtown Occidental for free swigs of dry Chardonnay, earthy Pinots and a big Syrah, all from the cooler climes. Bottles range from $39 to $49.

Occidental Bohemian Farmers Market
MARKET

([707-874-8478; www.occidentalfarmersmarket. com; 3611 Bohemian Hwy; ☺4pm-dusk Fri Jun-Oct; 🖘) 🖉 Meet the whole community at Occidental's detour-worthy farmers market, with musicians, craftspeople and – the star attraction – Gerard's Paella (www.gerardspa ella.com) of Food Network TV fame.

Osmosis
SPA

(☑ 707-823-8231; www.osmosis.com; 209 Bohemian Hwy, Freestone; packages from $219; ⊘ by appointment 9am-8pm) Tranquility prevails at this Japanese-inspired spa, which indulges patrons with dry-enzyme baths of aromatic cedar fibers paired with other treatments including outdoor massages and facials. The tea-and-meditation gardens are lovely. Make reservations.

Sonoma Canopy Tours
OUTDOORS

(☑ 888-494-7868; www.sonomacanopytours.com; 6250 Bohemian Hwy; adult $99-109, child $69) North of town, fly through the redwood canopy on seven interconnected ziplines, ending with an 80ft-rappel descent; reservations required.

🛏 Sleeping

Occidental offers a couple of historic inns and one fantastic farmstay.

★ Shanti Permaculture Farm
FARMSTAY $$

(☑ 707-874-2001; www.shantioccidental.com; Coleman Valley Rd; tent & RV sites $75, cottages & yurts $199-225) Tucked back in the redwoods on scenic Coleman Valley Rd, this is the ultimate NorCal farmstay. The knowledgeable Oregonian owner educates guests about ecofriendly agricultural concepts such as biochar and hugelkultur, and shows off her chickens, ducks, goats and enormous llama. While the operation feels somewhat rustic, it is impressively MacGyvered and the one-bedroom cottage is surprisingly posh.

Near the top of the 6-acre property, a wonderfully homey yurt offers comfort and seclusion, though the llama has been known to wander up the hill to stare through a window at sleeping guests. Continuing down the hill, private campsites are ensconced in the trees, and RVs are also welcome at the bottom of the hill, where a hookup is available for a fee. Delicious farm-to-table meals are available for $15 to $20.

Valley Ford Hotel
INN $$

(☑ 707-876-1983; www.vfordhotel.com; r $115-175) Surrounded by pastureland 8 miles southeast in Valley Ford, this 19th-century, seven-room inn has good beds, great rates and a terrific roadhouse bar and restaurant.

Inn at Occidental
INN $$$

(☑ 800-522-6324, 707-874-1047; www.innatoccidental.com; 3657 Church St; r $259-399; ❄) One of Sonoma's finest, this beautifully restored 18-room Victorian inn is filled with collectible antiques; rooms have gas fireplaces and cozy feather beds.

🍴 Eating & Drinking

Delicious meals and snacks abound for every budget, all in close proximity.

Wild Flour Bread
BAKERY $

(☑ 707-874-2938; www.wildflourbread.com; 140 Bohemian Hwy, Freestone; items from $3; ⊘ 8:30am-6:30pm Fri-Mon; 🐾) Organic brick-oven artisan breads, giant sticky buns and good coffee.

Howard Station Cafe
AMERICAN $

(☑ 707-874-2838; www.howardstationcafe.com; 3611 Bohemian Hwy; mains $8-14; ⊘ 7am-2:30pm Mon-Fri, to 3pm Sat & Sun; 🐾🥗) Big plates of comfort-food cooking and freshly squeezed juices. Cash only.

Bohemian Market
DELI $

(☑ 707-874-3312; 3633 Main St; ⊘ 8am-9pm, 7am-9pm Sat & Sun) Occidental's best grocery store has a good deli which prepares sandwiches from 10am to 7pm. There's also a coffee bar open daily until 1pm.

Hazel
CALIFORNIAN $$

(☑ 707-874-6003; www.restauranthazel.com; 3782 Bohemian Hwy; mains $15-32; ⊘ 5-9pm Wed-Sat, 10am-2pm & 5-9pm Sun) Occidental's newest restaurant is small, unassuming and serves absolutely delectable food. The menu only features a few starters, pizzas and mains but you cannot go wrong, particularly with the scallop ceviche (fresh mango, radishes, a delightful medley of oils and spices, delicate morsels of mollusk). Also great: fried brussels sprouts, braised pot roast and the strawberry-rhubarb crisp with vanilla ice cream.

Union Hotel
ITALIAN $$

(☑ 707-874-3555; www.unionhoteloccidental.com; 3703 Bohemian Hwy; meals $15-26; ⊘ 11am-9pm, bar to 2am; 🐾) Occidental has two old-school American-Italian restaurants that serve family-style meals. The Union is slightly better and serves a delicious, complimentary bruschetta with the purchase of any main. Monday nights mean $5 pizza or pasta in-house (adults only). On a sunny day you can't beat the patio for lunch, and there's also a bakery with freshly baked cookies for $1.

Barley & Hops
PUB

(☑ 707-874-9037; www.barleynhops.com; 3688 Bohemian Hwy; ⊘ 4-9pm Mon-Thu, 1-9:30pm Fri-Sun) Serving around 40 beers, sandwiches, burgers, giant salads and amazing bacon-cheddar fries. Mains $10-15.

🛍 Shopping

Hand Goods CERAMICS
(📞707-874-2161; www.handgoods.net; 3627 Main St; ⊙10am-6pm) Collective of ceramicists, potters, jewelers, fine artists and more.

❶ Getting There & Away

Occidental is about a two-hour drive from San Francisco. There's no good way to get here via public transportation.

Guerneville & Around

The Russian River's biggest vacation-resort town, Guerneville gets busy over summer weekends with party-hardy gay boys, sun-worshiping lesbians and long-haired, beer-drinking Harley riders, earning it the nickname 'Groin-ville.' Though the town is slowly gentrifying, it hasn't lost its honky-tonk vibe – fun-seeking crowds still come to canoe, hike and hammer cocktails poolside.

Downriver, some areas are sketchy (due to drugs). The local chamber of commerce has chased most of the tweakers from Main St in Guerneville, but if some off-the-beaten-path areas feel creepy – especially campgrounds – they probably are.

Four miles downriver, tiny Monte Rio has a sign over Hwy 116 declaring it 'Vacation Wonderland' – an overstatement, but the dog-friendly beach is a hit with families. Further west, idyllic Duncans Mills is home to a few dozen souls and has picture-ready historic buildings converted into cute shops. Upriver, east of Guerneville, Forestville is where farm country resumes.

◉ Sights & Activies

Look for sandy beaches and swimming holes along the river; there's good river access east of town at Sunset Beach. Fishing and watercraft outfitters operate mid-May to early October, after which winter rains dangerously swell the river. A **farmers market** (16290 5th St) meets downtown on Wednesdays, May through September, from 3pm to 7pm. On summer Saturdays, there's also one at **Monte Rio Beach**, 11am to 2pm.

Armstrong Redwoods State Natural Reserve FOREST
(📞info 707-869-2015, visitor center 707-869-2958; www.parks.ca.gov; 17000 Armstrong Woods Rd; per car $8; ⊙8am-1hr after sunset; 🅿🚻) 🌿 A magnificent redwood forest 2 miles north of Guerneville, this 805-acre reserve was saved from the saw by a 19th-century lumber magnate. Short interpretive trails lead into magical forests, with old-growth redwoods 30 stories high. Beyond lie 20 miles of back-country trails through oak woodlands in adjoining **Austin Creek State Recreation Area**, one of Sonoma County's last remaining wilderness areas. Walk or cycle in for free; pay only to park.

Sunset Beach BEACH
(📞707-433-1625; www.sonoma-county.org/parks; 11060 River Rd, Forestville; per car $7; ⊙7am-sunset) Nice park on the water featuring paddle sports and picnicking.

Burke's Canoe Trips CANOEING
(📞707-887-1222; www.burkescanoetrips.com; 8600 River Rd, Forestville; canoe/kayak rental incl shuttle $68/$45, cash only) You can't beat Burke's for a day on the river. Self-guided canoe and kayak trips include shuttle back to your car. Make reservations; plan for four hours. Camping in the riverside redwood grove is $10 per person.

Johnson's Beach WATER SPORTS
(📞707-869-2022; www.johnsonsbeach.com; 16215 &16217 First St; kayak & canoe rental per hour/day $15/40; ⊙10am-6pm summer only; 🚻) `FREE` Canoe, kayak and paddleboat rental available. Beer, wine, hot dogs and burgers are for sale. Beach admission is free though it's $5 to park and closed in poor weather. You can camp (p206) here.

R3 Hotel Pool SWIMMING
(Triple R; 📞707-869-8399; www.ther3hotel.com; 16390 4th St; ⊙9am-close) `FREE` The gay, adults-only, party-scene swimming pool at the R3 Hotel (p206) is free, provided you buy drinks. Bring your own towel. Bathing suits are mandatory, but only because state liquor-license laws require them.

Pee Wee Golf & Arcade GOLF, CYCLING
(📞707-869-9321; 16155 Drake Rd, at Hwy 116; 18/36 holes $8/12; ⊙11am-10pm Jun-Aug, to 5pm Sat & Sun May & Sep; 🚻) Flash back to 1948 at this impeccably kept retro-kitsch 36-hole miniature golf course, just south of the Hwy 116 bridge, with brilliantly painted obstacles, including T Rex and Yogi Bear. Bring your own cocktails. It also rents gas barbecue grills.

King's Sport & Tackle OUTDOORS
(📞707-869-2156; www.kingsrussianriver.com; 16258 Main St; ⊙8am-6pm May-Oct, hours vary Nov-Apr) *The* local source for fishing and river-condition information. Also rents kayaks

($45 to $65), stand up paddleboards (from $60) and fishing gear.

River Rider
CYCLING

(📞707-887-2453; www.riverridersrentals.com; half-/full-day rental from $35/45, delivery $20; ⊙7am-7pm) Delivers bicycles, along with wine-tasting passes on request; there are discounts for multiday rentals.

★ Festivals & Events

Naughty Nuns Bingo
LGBT

(www.rrsisters.org/bingo.html; 16255 1st St; 2 bingo cards & 5 raffle tickets $20; ⊙ doors 5:30pm, 2nd Sat of month) These fabulous themed bingo nights are put on by the Russian River Sisters of Perpetual Indulgence, an activist group of gender-bending performance artists who dress as ostentatious nuns.

Monte Rio Variety Show
MUSIC

(www.monterioshow.org; adult/child $30/15; ⊙Jul) Members of the elite, secretive Bohemian Grove (Google it) perform publicly, sometimes showcasing unannounced celebrities.

Lazy Bear Weekend
LGBT

(www.lazybearweekend.com; ⊙Aug) Read: heavy, furry gay men.

Russian River Jazz & Blues Festival
MUSIC

(www.russianriverfestivals.com; ⊙Sep) A day of jazz, followed by a day of blues, with occasional luminaries such as BB King.

🛏 Sleeping

Guerneville has lovely resorts, inns and cottages, but few budget sleeps apart from campgrounds; prices drop midweek. For weekends and holidays, book ahead. Also, because the river sometimes floods, some lodgings have cold linoleum floors: pack slippers.

🛏 Guerneville

Bullfrog Pond Campground
CAMPGROUND $

(📞707-869-2015; www.stewardscr.org; sites reserved/nonreserved $35/25; 🐾) Reached via a steep road from Armstrong Redwoods State Natural Reserve (p205), 4 miles from the entrance kiosk, Bullfrog Pond has forested campsites with cold water and primitive hike-in and equestrian backcountry campsites. Reserve via www.hipcamp.com or by phone.

Johnson's Beach Resort
CABIN, CAMPGROUND $

(📞707-869-2022; www.johnsonsbeach.com; 16241 1st St; tent sites $40, cabins $145-165) On the

river in Guerneville, Johnson's (p205) has rustic but clean, thin-walled cabins on stilts; all have kitchen. There's camping too, but no RVs. Credit card only.

Schoolhouse Canyon Campground
CAMPGROUND $

(📞707-869-2311; www.schoolhousecanyon.com; 12600 River Rd; tent sites for 2 people & a car $40; 🐾) Two miles east of Guerneville, Schoolhouse's well-tended sites lie beneath tall trees across the main road from the river. Coin-operated hot showers, clean bathrooms, quiet by night. Cash only.

Guerneville Lodge
CAMPGROUND $

(📞707-869-0102; www.guernevillelodge.com; 15905 River Rd; tent sites $40) The prettiest place to camp in downtown Guerneville is behind this retreat-center lodge on sprawling grassy lawns fronting the river. Amenities: hot clean showers, big campsites, refrigerator access, fire pits with grills. When available, lodge rooms cost $199.

R3 Hotel
RESORT $$

(Triple R; 📞707-869-8399; www.ther3hotel.com; 16390 4th St; r $125-299; 🛜🏊) Ground zero for party-hardy gay lads and lesbians, Triple R (as it's known) has plain-Jane, motel-style rooms surrounding a bar and pool deck that get so crowded on summer weekends that management won't allow guests to bring pets because 'they get hurt' (actual quote). Come for the scene, not for quiet (light sleepers: bring earplugs). Midweek it's mellow, wintertime dead.

Boon Hotel + Spa
BOUTIQUE HOTEL $$

(📞707-869-2721; www.boonhotels.com; 14711 Armstrong Woods Rd; tents $175-225, r $225-425; 🅿🐾🛜🏊) 🚭 Rooms surround a swimming-pool courtyard (with Jacuzzi) at this 14-room adults-only resort, gussied up in minimalist modern style. The look is austere but fresh, with organic-cotton linens and spacious rooms; most have wood-burning fireplaces. Between Memorial Day and Labor Day, 'glamping tents' and an Airstream trailer are also available. It's a 15-minute walk north of downtown.

Highlands Resort
CABIN, CAMPGROUND $$

(📞707-869-0333; www.highlandsresort.com; 14000 Woodland Dr; tent sites $40-60, r $95-180, cabins $130-215; 🛜🏊) Guerneville's mellowest gay (and straight-friendly) resort sits on a wooded hillside, walkable distance to town, and has simply furnished rooms, little

SCENIC DRIVE: COLEMAN VALLEY ROAD

Wine Country's most scenic drive isn't through the grapes, but along these 10 miles of winding West County byway, from Occidental to the sea. It's best late morning, after the fog has cleared. Drive west, not east, with the sun behind you and the ocean ahead. First you'll pass through redwood forests and lush valleys where Douglas firs stand draped in sphagnum moss – an eerie sight in the fog. The real beauty shots lie further ahead, when the road ascends 1000ft hills, dotted with gnarled oaks and craggy rock formations, with the vast blue Pacific unfurling below. The road ends at coastal Hwy 1, where you can explore Sonoma Coast State Beach (p223), then turn left and find your way to the tiny town of Bodega (not Bodega Bay) to see locales where Hitchcock shot his 1963 classic, *The Birds*.

cottages with porches and good camping. The large pool is clothing-optional (weekday/weekend day use $10/15).

Fern Grove Cottages CABIN **$$**
(☑707-869-8105; www.ferngrove.com; 16650 River Rd; cabins $159-249, with kitchen $229-299; @�()☎) Downtown Guerneville's cheeriest resort, Fern Grove has vintage-1930s pine-paneled cabins tucked beneath redwoods and surrounded by lush flowering gardens. Some have Jacuzzi and fireplace. The pool uses salt, not chlorine; there are concierge services and breakfast includes homemade granola.

★ **Applewood Inn** INN **$$$**
(☑707-869-9093; www.applewoodinn.com; 13555 Hwy 116; r $250-500; ☀@☎☎) A hideaway estate on a wooded hilltop south of town, cushy Applewood has marvelous 1920s-era detail, with dark wood and heavy furniture that echo the forest. Some rooms have Jacuzzi and couples' shower; some have fireplace. Amenities include a small spa and two heated pools, but the best perk is the coupon for complimentary tastings at more than 100 wineries. At the time of writing, the hotel's new Italian restaurant was about to open.

Santa Nella House B&B **$$$**
(☑707-869-9488; www.santanellahouse.com; 12130 Hwy 116; r $205-249; @☎☎) All five spotless rooms at this 1871 Victorian, south of town, have wood-burning fireplace and frilly Victorian furnishings. Upstairs rooms are biggest. Outside there's a hot tub and sauna. Best for travelers who appreciate the B&B aesthetic.

Forestville

Farmhouse Inn INN **$$$**
(Map p198; ☑707-887-3300, 800-464-6642; www.farmhouseinn.com; 7871 River Rd; r $695-1495; ☀@☎☎) Think love nest. The area's premier

inn was recently renovated and offers spacious rooms and cottages, styled with cushy amenities such as saunas, steam showers and wood-burning fireplaces. Small on-site spa and top-notch restaurant (Farmhouse Inn restaurant on p208). Check in early to maximize time.

Raford Inn B&B **$$$**
(☑707-887-9573, 800-887-9503; http://rafordinn.com; 10630 Wohler Rd; r $225-275; ☀@☎) 🍴 We love this 1880 Victorian B&B's secluded hilltop location, surrounded by tall palms and rambling vineyards. Rooms are big and airy, with lace and antiques; some have fireplace. And wow, those sunset views.

Monte Rio

Village Inn INN **$$**
(☑707-865-2304; www.villageinn-ca.com; 20822 River Blvd; r $145-250; ☎) 🍴 This cute, old-fashioned, 11-room inn perches beneath towering trees, right on the river. Some rooms have river views; all have fridge and microwave. No elevator.

Rio Villa Beach Resort INN **$$**
(☑707-865-1143, 877-746-8455; www.riovilla.com; 20292 Hwy 116; r with kitchen $190-205, without $160-165; ☀☎☎) Landscaping is lush at this small riverside resort with excellent sun exposure (you see redwoods, but you're not under them). Rooms are well-kept but simple (request a quiet room, not by the road); the emphasis is on the outdoors, evident by the large riverside terrace, outdoor fireplace and barbecues. Some air-conditioning.

Highland Dell INN **$$**
(☑707-865-2300; www.highlanddell.com; 21050 River Blvd; r $109-179; ☺Apr-Nov; ☀☎☎) 🍴 Built in 1906 in grand lodge style, redone in 2007, the inn fronts right on to the river. Above the giant dining room are 12 bright, fresh-looking

rooms with comfy beds. No elevator. Doubles as an event center.

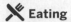 Eating

Staying downtown means you can walk to restaurants and bars. From deli sandwiches to farm-to-table feasts to Korean-diner grub, there are plenty of good options.

Guerneville

Big Bottom Market
MARKET, CAFE **$**

(☑707-604-7295; www.bigbottommarket.com; 16228 Main St; sandwiches $11-15; ☺8am-5pm Wed-Mon) ✐ Gourmet deli and wine shop with coffee, delicious pastries and grab-and-go picnic supplies. Supposedly the home of Oprah's favorite biscuit.

Taqueria La Tapatia
MEXICAN **$**

(☑707-869-1821; 16632 Main St; mains $7-14; ☺4-9pm Tue-Sun) Reasonable choice for traditional Mexican.

Garden Grill
BARBECUE **$**

(☑707-869-3922; www.gardengrillbbq.com; 17132 Hwy 116, Guerneewood Park; mains $6-12; ☺8am-3pm) One mile west of Guerneville, this roadhouse barbecue joint, with redwood-shaded patio, serves good house-smoked meats but the fries could be better.

Food for Humans
MARKET **$**

(☑707-869-3612; 16385 1st St; ☺9am-8pm; ☑) ✐ Organic groceries; better alternative than neighboring Safeway.

Dick Blomster's Korean Diner
KOREAN, AMERICAN **$$**

(☑707-896-8006; 16236 Main St; mains breakfast & lunch $8.50-12.50, dinner $15-20; ☺8am-2pm & 5-9pm Sun-Thu, to 10pm Fri & Sat) By day a vintage-1940s coffee shop, by night a Korean-American diner with full bar, Dick Blomster's serves playfully tongue-in-cheek dishes, including fried peanut butter and jelly sandwiches and 'the other KFC – Korean fried crack': fried chicken with sugary-sweet brown sauce, which sure hits the spot after a night of drinking.

Seaside Metal Oyster Bar
SEAFOOD **$$**

(☑707-604-7250; http://seasidemetal.com; 16222 Main St; dishes $8-18; ☺5-9pm Wed, Thu & Sun, to 10pm Fri & Sat) Unexpectedly urban for Guerneville, this storefront raw bar is an offshoot of San Francisco's Bar Crudo – one of the city's best – and showcases oysters, clams, shrimp and exquisitely prepared raw-fish dishes. There's limited hot food, but it's overwrought: stick to raw. Reservations recommended.

Boon Eat + Drink
CALIFORNIAN **$$$**

(☑707-869-0780; http://eatatboon.com; 16248 Main St; mains lunch $15-18, dinner $15-26; ☺11am-3pm Thu-Tue, 5-9pm Sun-Thu, to 10pm Fri & Sat; ☑) Locally sourced ingredients inform the seasonal, Cali-smart cooking at this tiny, always-packed, New American bistro, with cheek-by-jowl tables that fill every night. Serves local wine and craft beer. Show up early or expect to wait.

Forestville

Canneti Roadhouse
ITALIAN **$$**

(Map p198; ☑707-887-2232; http://cannetirestaurant.com; 6675 Front St; mains lunch $12-24, dinner $16-38; ☺5:30-9pm Tue-Wed, 11:30am-3pm & 5:30-9pm Thu-Sat, 11am-8:30pm Sun) ✐ A Tuscan-born chef makes bona fide *cucina Italiana* using quality ingredients from local farms at this austere restaurant in downtown Forestville, worth the 15-minute drive from Guerneville. The menu ranges from simple brick-oven pizzas to an all-Tuscan, five-course tasting menu ($65, dinner only). When it's warm, sit on the patio beneath a giant redwood. Make reservations. Thursdays, three-course dinners cost $40.

★ Backyard
CALIFORNIAN **$$$**

(☑707-820-8445; www.backyardforestville.com; 6566 Front St; mains lunch & brunch $10-22, dinner mains $21-28; ☺11am-9pm Mon & Thu, to 9:30pm Fri, 9am-9:30pm Sat, to 8:30pm Sun) This relaxing, alfresco spot gets every fruit, vegetable and animal from local farmers or fishers and the chef knows just what to do with all of it. California-inspired dishes are simple and delicious; the steak, piquillo-pepper and duck-egg hash was perhaps the world's most perfect brunch. The coffee and artisanal doughnut holes are winners.

Oh, and don't start a meal with anything other than the house pickle plate, which comes with the most delightful array of pickled, seasonal vegetables (often including cauliflower and asparagus) and house-fermented kimchi.

Farmhouse Inn
MODERN AMERICAN **$$$**

(☑707-695-1495; www.farmhouseinn.com; 7871 River Rd; 3-/4-course dinner $99/115; ☺5:30-8:30pm Thu-Mon) ✐ Special-occasion worthy, Michelin-starred Farmhouse changes its seasonal Euro-Cal menu daily, using locally raised, organic ingredients such as Sonoma lamb, wild halibut and rabbit – the latter is the house specialty. The wine pairings are exquisite, but detractors call the whole thing precious. Reservations required.

Monte Rio

Rio Café   FAST FOOD $

(707-865-4190; www.riocafetake2.com; 20396 Bohemian Hwy; sandwiches $4-12; ⊙8am-8pm Wed-Sun summer, noon-7pm Fri-Sun winter;) Gourmet burgers, hot dogs and grilled sandwiches, along with breakfast options and lots of veggie choices, behind the Rio Theater. Beer and wine also served.

Village Inn   AMERICAN $$$

(707-865-2304; www.villageinn-ca.com; 20822 River Blvd; mains $19-26; ⊙5-8pm Wed-Sun) The straightforward steaks-and-seafood menu is basic American and doesn't distract from the wonderful river views. Great local wine list, full bar.

Duncans Mills

Cape Fear Cafe   AMERICAN $$

(707-865-9246; 25191 Main St; mains lunch $9-15, dinner $15-25; ⊙10am-9pm Mon-Fri, to 9pm Sat & Sun) A country-Americana diner in a 19th-century grange, Cape Fear is visually charming, but it's erratic – except at weekend brunch when the kitchen makes excellent Benedicts. Good stopover en route to the coast.

♦ Drinking & Nightlife

Stumptown Brewery is the town's after-hours social hub, but there are plenty of good opportunities for day-drinking – particularly at the wineries and while floating down the river in summer.

Rainbow Cattle Company   GAY

(www.queersteer.com; 16220 Main St; ⊙noon-2am) This stalwart gay watering hole has pinball and shuffleboard. Tuesdays are big, with a donation-based buffet, silent auction, raffle and a percentage of sales going to various causes.

Sophie's Cellars   WINE BAR

(707-865-1122; www.sophiescellars.com; 25179 Main St/Hwy 116; glasses $7-15; ⊙11am-5pm Thu, Sat & Sun, to 7pm Fri) The perfect stopover between river and coast, Sophie's rural wine bar pours glasses and tastes of local wine, and carries cheese, salami and a well-curated selection of bottles. Friday's

'locals happy hour' (4pm to 7pm) brings hors d'oeuvres, drink specials and a big crowd.

Stumptown Brewery   BREWERY

(Map p198; www.stumptown.com; 15045 River Rd; ⊙11am-midnight Sun-Thu, to 2am Fri & Sat) Guerneville's best straight bar, 1 mile east of downtown, is gay friendly and has a foot-stompin' jukebox, billiards, riverside beer garden and several homemade brews. Pretty good pub grub includes house-smoked barbecue.

☆ Entertainment

Rio Nido Roadhouse   LIVE MUSIC

(Map p198; 707-869-0821; www.rionidoroadhouse.com; 14540 Canyon Two, off River Rd, Rio Nido) Raucous roadhouse bar, 4 miles east of Guerneville, with eclectic lineup of live bands. Shows start 6pm Saturday and sometimes Friday and Sunday too; check website. There's also a pool open 11am to 6pm daily, to 5pm on Saturday and water aerobics is offered. The pool was being renovated at the time of writing.

Rio Theater   CINEMA

(707-865-0913, 707-520-4075; www.riotheater.com; 20396 Bohemian Hwy, Monte Rio; $10-12;) Dinner and a movie take on new meaning at this vintage-WWII Quonset hut converted to a cinema in 1950. In 2014 they finally added heat, but still supply blankets. Only in Monte Rio. Shows nightly (and sometimes Sunday afternoons), but call ahead, especially off-season.

Main Street Bistro   CABARET

(707-869-0501; www.mainststation.com; 16280 Main St; ⊙4-11pm Mon-Thu, noon-11pm Fri-Sun;) Hosts live acoustic-only jazz, blues and cabaret nightly in summer (weekends in winter). Families are welcome as the cabaret doubles as an American-Italian restaurant (stick to pizza).

♦ Shopping

Eight miles west of Guerneville, tiny Duncans Mills has good shopping in a handful of side-by-side businesses within weathered 19th-century cottages.

★ Guerneville Bank Club   FOOD

(707- 666-9411; www.guernevillebankclub.com; 16290 Main St; ⊙11am-9pm Sun-Thu, to 10pm Fri & Sat) After 30 years of abandonment, this beautifully restored 1921 bank building now contains stuff more valuable than money:

art, wine, ice cream and pie. The new collective retail and art-gallery space houses small businesses such as Chile Pies Banking Company (go for the Mexican Chocolate Pecan) and Nimble Finn's Ice Cream, which sells organic dairy products, jams, cakes etc. There's a small wine-tasting room and the old vault has been converted into a photo booth adorned in murals.

Pig Alley   JEWELRY
(📌707-865-2698; www.pigalleyshop.com; 25193 Main St; ⊗10am-5pm Mon-Fri, 9:30am-5:30pm Sat & Sun) Vast selection of hand-crafted American-made jewelry, notable for gorgeous earrings.

Mr Trombly's Tea & Table   FOOD & DRINKS
(📌707-865-9610; www.mrtromblystea.com; 25185 Main St; ⊗10am-5pm Sun-Thu, to 5:30pm Fri & Sat) Different kinds of tea and teapots, plus quality kitchen gadgets and well-priced tableware.

❶ Information

Russian River Chamber of Commerce & Visitors Center (Map p198; 📌707-869-9000; www.russianriver.com; 16209 1st St; ⊗10am-5pm Mon-Sat, plus to 3pm Sun May-Oct) Information and lodging referrals.

❶ Getting There & Away

Public transit isn't a great option, but to check bus routes dial 📌511, or look online at www.transit.511.org. The drive from San Francisco takes about two hours.

Santa Rosa

Wine Country's biggest city and the Sonoma County seat, Santa Rosa claims two famous native sons – a world-renowned cartoonist and a celebrated horticulturalist – whose legacies include museums and gardens that'll keep you busy for an afternoon. Otherwise, there isn't much to do, unless you need your car fixed or you're here in July during the **Sonoma County Fair** (www.sonomacountyfair.com), at the fairgrounds on Bennett Valley Rd.

Beyond that, Santa Rosa is mostly known for traffic and suburban sprawl, though the downtown's redwood trees make for some impressive landscaping.

Orientation

The main shopping stretch is 4th St, which abruptly ends at Hwy 101, but reemerges across the freeway at historic Railroad Sq. Downtown parking garages (75¢ per hour, $8 maximum) are cheaper than street parking. East of town, 4th St becomes Hwy 12 into Sonoma Valley.

◉ Sights & Activities

Charles M Schulz Museum   MUSEUM
(📌707-579-4452; www.schulzmuseum.org; 2301 Hardies Lane; adult/child $12/5; ⊗11am-5pm Mon & Wed-Fri, 10am-5pm Sat & Sun; 🅿🚼) Charles Schulz, creator of *Peanuts* cartoons and Santa Rosa resident, was born in 1922, published his first drawing in 1937, introduced Snoopy and Charlie Brown in 1950 and produced *Peanuts* cartoons until his death in 2000. This modern museum honors his legacy with a Snoopy labyrinth, *Peanuts*-related art and a re-creation of Schulz' studio. Skip Snoopy's Gallery gift shop; the museum has the good stuff.

Farmers Market   MARKET
(www.wednesdaynightmarket.org; Old Courthouse Sq; ⊗5-8:30pm Wed mid-May–Aug) Sonoma County's largest farmers market. A second smaller market meets year-round, 9am to 1pm, Wednesdays and Saturdays at Santa Rosa Veterans Building.

Luther Burbank Home & Gardens   GARDENS
(📌707-524-5445; www.lutherburbank.org; 204 Santa Rosa Ave; grounds free, tour adult/child $10/5; ⊗gardens 8am-dusk, museum 10am-4pm Tue-Sun Apr-Oct) Pioneering horticulturist Luther Burbank (1849–1926) developed many hybrid plant species, including the Shasta daisy, here at his 19th-century, Greek-revival home. Guided tours 10am-3:30pm Tuesday-Sunday April-October. The extensive gardens are lovely. The house and adjacent **Carriage Museum** have displays on Burbank's life and work, or you can take a self-guided cellphone tour of the grounds for free.

Epicenter   CENTER
(Map p198; 📌707-708-3742; www.visitepicenter.com; 3215 Coffey Lane; ⊗11am-midnight Sun-Thu, to 2am Fri & Sat) An entertainment complex with restaurants, bars, bowling, an arcade and a trampoline park.

Children's Museum of Sonoma County   SCIENCE CENTER
(📌707-546-4069; www.cmosc.org; 1835 Steele Lane; $12; ⊗9am-4pm Mon & Wed-Sat, 11am-4pm Sun; 🚼) Geared to children 10 and under, this happy learning center inspires discovery, exploration and creativity with hands-on indoor

and outdoor exhibits focused on nature and science. Picnicking welcome. No adults without kids.

Redwood Empire Ice Arena SKATING
(📞707-546-7147; www.snoopyshomeice.com; 1667 West Steele Lane; incl skates $5-13; ⊘ hours vary; 🏄) This skating rink was formerly owned and deeply loved by *Peanuts* cartoon creator Charles Schulz. It's open most afternoons (call for schedules). Bring a sweater.

🛏 Sleeping

Chain hotels abound, in addition to a couple of historic inns and a decent campground. In general, Santa Rosa offers reasonably priced accommodations and easy access to Sonoma County and Valley.

Spring Lake Park CAMPGROUND $
(📞707-539-8092, reservations 707-565-2267; www.sonomacountyparks.org; 5585 Newanga Ave; sites $32; ⊘ campground May-Sep, weekends only Oct-Apr; 🐾) 🍴 Lovely lakeside park, 4 miles from downtown; make reservations online ($8.50 fee) or by phone 10am to 3pm weekdays. The park is open year-round, with lake swimming (complete with a floating playground) in summer. Take 4th St eastbound, turn right on Farmer's Lane, pass the first Hoen St and turn left on the second Hoen St, then left on Newanga Ave.

Hillside Inn MOTEL $
(📞707-546-9353; www.hillside-inn.com; 2901 4th St; s/d $78/86; 🛜🐾) Santa Rosa's best-value motel, Hillside is close to Sonoma Valley; add $4 for kitchens. Furnishings are dated and service peculiar, but everything is scrupulously maintained. Adjoins an excellent breakfast cafe.

Sandman INN $$
(📞707-293-2100; www.sandmansantarosa.com; 3421 Cleveland Ave; r $120-300; 🐾@🛜🐾) Once Santa Rosa's best budget choice, Sandman has been revamped by new owners to feature a Southwestern aesthetic, quirky vintage furnishings and a hot bar replete with bamboo sofas and poolside cocktail window. The pool's heated and there's a hot tub.

Hotel La Rose HISTORIC HOTEL $$
(📞707-579-3200; www.hotellarose.com; 308 Wilson St; r Mon-Fri $149-199, Sat & Sun $209-269; 🐾🛜) 🍴 At Railroad Sq, Hotel La Rose has rooms in a well-kept historic 1907 brick hotel and across the street in a 1980s-built 'carriage house,' which feels like a small condo

complex with boxy, spacious rooms. All are decorated in out-of-fashion pastels but have excellent beds with quality linens and down duvets; some have jetted tubs.

Vintners Inn INN $$$
(Map p198; 📞707-575-7350, 800-421-2584; www.vintnersinn.com; 4350 Barnes Rd; r $245-495; 🐾@🛜) 🍴 Surrounded by 92 acres of vineyards north of town (near River Rd), Vintner's Inn caters to the gated-community crowd with business-class amenities. Complimentary wine tastings in the lobby at 5pm on Fridays. Check for last-minute specials.

Flamingo Conference Resort & Spa HOTEL $$
(📞707-545-8530, 800-848-8300; www.flamingoresort.com; 2777 4th St; r $179-299; 🐾@🛜🐾🐾) 🍴 Sprawling over 11 acres, this mid-century modern hotel doubles as a conference center. Rooms are business-class generic, but the pool is gigantic – and kept at 82ºF (28ºC) year-round. Kids love it. On-site health club and gym. Prices double on summer weekends.

Best Western Garden Inn MOTEL $$
(📞707-546-4031; www.thegardeninn.com; 1500 Santa Rosa Ave; r Mon-Fri $119-139, Sat & Sun $199-229; 🐾@🛜🐾🐾) Recently renovated motel, south of downtown, with two pools and a hot tub. Rear rooms open to grassy gardens, but you may hear kids in the pool; book up front for quiet. The street gets seedy by night but the hotel is secure, clean and comfortable.

Best Western Wine Country Inn & Suites HOTEL $$
(📞707-545-9000; www.winecountryhotel.com; 870 Hopper Ave; r $135-140, Sat & Sun $180-220; 🐾@🛜🐾🐾) 🍴 Pretty standard midrange chain hotel, off Cleveland Ave. There's a pool and some rooms have Jacuzzi.

🍴 Eating

Santa Rosa's culinary star is on the rise, with a solid selection of long-time international and farm-to-table restaurants and plenty of ambitious openings to keep things interesting.

Criminal Baking Co BAKERY $
(📞707-888-3546; www.criminalbaking.com; 463 Sebastopol Ave; baked goods $1-5; ⊘ 7:30am-4pm Mon-Fri, 8am-4pm Sat & Sun) A superior Santa Rosa bakery, with delicious vegan banana-walnut cookies, three-cheese knishes and supernutritious lunches such

as the 'warrior bowl,' which comes with spinach, quinoa, potatoes, artichokes, bacon and goat's cheese. Don't miss the lavender lemonade.

Taqueria Las Palmas
MEXICAN $

(☑ 707-546-3091; 415 Santa Rosa Ave; dishes $4-11; ⊙9am-9pm; ☑) For Mexican, this is the real deal, with standout *carnitas* (barbecued pork), homemade salsas and veggie burritos.

Jeffrey's Hillside Cafe
AMERICAN $

(☑ 707-546-6317; www.jeffreyshillsidecafe.com; 2901 4th St; dishes $9-13; ⊙7am-2pm; ☑) ☑ East of downtown, near Sonoma Valley, chef-owned Jeffrey's is excellent for breakfast or brunch before wine tasting.

Tasca Tasca
TAPAS $$

(Map p190; ☑ 707-996-8272; www.tascatasca. com; 122 W Napa St; 3/5/7 items $15/24/32; ⊙noon-midnight) Specializing in Portuguese and Mediterranean fare, this new tapas tavern in food-obsessed downtown Sonoma holds its own. Try the authentic *caldo verde* (Portugal's national soup), along with one of the fabulous cheeses and the inventive Dungeness-crab empanadas with chipotle mayo. Wash everything down with the house-red sangria, made with passion fruit.

Yeti
NEPALI $$

(☑ 707-521-9608; www.yeticuisine.com; 190 Farmers Lane; mains lunch $12-17, dinner $18-25; ⊙11:30am-2pm & 5-9:30pm) This places serves up spectacular Indian and Nepali dishes, and offers a brunch smorgasbord every Saturday and Sunday with spicy curries, *saag paneer* (spinach and paneer curry) and tikka masala (with both meat and veggie options).

OLIVE-OIL TASTING

When you weary of wine tasting, pop by one of the following olive-oil makers and dip some crusty bread – it's free. Harvest and pressing happen in November.

➡ BR Cohn (p188)
➡ Napa Valley Olive Oil Mfg Co (p171)
➡ Long Meadow Ranch (p165)
➡ Figone's Olive Oil (p194)

Naked Pig
CAFE $$

(☑ 707-978-3231; 435 Santa Rosa Ave; mains $11-14; ⊙8am-3pm Wed-Sun) ☑ This tiny cafe in a former bus depot makes everything from scratch and serves simple-delicious, farm-to-table breakfasts and lunches at communal tables.

Rosso Pizzeria & Wine Bar
PIZZA $$

(☑ 707-546-6317; www.rossopizzeria.com; 53 Montgomery Dr, Creekside Shopping Center; pizzas $13-17; ⊙11:30am-10pm; ☑) ☑ Fantastic wood-fired pizzas, inventive salads and standout wines make Rosso worth seeking out.

★ Flower + Bone
INTERNATIONAL $$$

(☑ 707-708-8529; www.flowerandbonerestaurant. com; 640 5th St; mezes $11-18, 6-course prix fixe $67; ⊙11am-3pm Wed, 6-9pm Thu-Sat) From the foraging, pickling, preserving Santa Rosa couple behind the Naked Pig comes Flower + Bone. The cuisine is inspired by ancient cooking techniques, including bone broths, pasture-raised meat and housemade hooch. The prix-fixe menu, also known as 'the full story,' is epic, with everything from foraged weeds to Polish dumplings. Dessert involves a gold-dusted truffle.

Spinster Sisters
CALIFORNIAN $$$

(☑ 707-528-7100; www.thespinstersisters.com; 401 South A St; mains lunch $10-16, dinner $23-26; ⊙8am-2:30pm Mon, to 9pm Tue-Thu, to 10pm Fri, 9am-10pm Sat, to 2:30pm Sun) ☑ At Santa Rosa's culinary vanguard, this casual market-driven restaurant makes its own bagels, cheese and charcuterie meats. The diverse tapas-like small plates ($7 to $14) pair well with the extensive wine list.

🍷 Drinking & Nightlife

There are a few decent pubs and bars around town, but Russian River Brewing Co is the social hub of Santa Rosa, drawing visitors from all over Northern California for its double IPA.

★ Russian River Brewing Co
BREWERY

(☑ 707-545-2337; www.russianriverbrewing.com; 729 4th St; ⊙11am-midnight) Santa Rosa's justly famous brewery crafts a wildly popular double IPA called Pliny the Elder, plus top-grade sour beer aged in wine barrels. Good pizza and pub grub too.

A'Roma Roasters CAFE
(⏩ 707-576-7765; www.aromaroasters.com; 95 5th St, Railroad Sq; ⊙ 6am-11pm Mon-Thu, to midnight Fri, 7am-midnight Sat, to 10pm Sun; ⓦ) Town's hippest cafe serves no booze, but hosts acoustic music Saturday evenings.

ℹ Information

MEDICAL SERVICES

Santa Rosa Memorial Hospital (⏩ 707-525-5300; www.stjoesonoma.org; 1165 Montgomery Dr; ⊙ 24hr) Wide range of health services; houses the region's trauma center.

TOURIST INFORMATION

California Welcome Center & Santa Rosa Visitors Bureau (⏩ 707-577-8674, 800-404-7673; www.visitsantarosa.com; 9 4th St; ⊙ 9am-5pm) Same-day lodging assistance. At Railroad Sq, west of Hwy 101; take downtown exit from Hwy 12 or 101.

ℹ Getting There & Away

Sonoma County Airport Express (p161) runs shuttles ($34) between Sonoma County Airport (Santa Rosa) and San Francisco and Oakland airports.

Golden Gate Transit (p117) buses run between San Francisco and Santa Rosa (adult/youth $13/6.50); board at 1st and Mission Sts in San Fran.

Greyhound (p161) buses run from San Francisco to Santa Rosa ($21 to $38).

Healdsburg & Around

Once a sleepy ag town best known for its Future Farmers of America parade, Healdsburg has emerged as northern Sonoma County's culinary capital. Foodie-scenester restaurants and cafes, wine-tasting rooms and fancy boutiques line Healdsburg Plaza, the town's sun-dappled central square (bordered by Healdsburg Ave and Center, Matheson and Plaza Sts).

Traffic grinds to a halt on summer weekends, when second-home-owners and tourists jam downtown. Old-timers aren't happy with the Napa-style gentrification but at least Healdsburg retains its historic look, if not its once-quiet summers. It's best visited weekdays – stroll tree-lined streets, sample locavore cooking and soak up the NorCal flavor.

⊙ Sights

Tasting rooms surround the plaza.

Saturday Market MARKET
(www.healdsburgfarmersmarket.org; ⊙ 9am-noon Sat May-Dec) Healdsburg's downtown farmers market.

Wednesday Market MARKET
(⏩ 707-824-8717; cnr Vine & North Sts; ⊙ 3:30-6pm Wed Jun-Nov) Healdsburg's weekday farmers market.

Locals Tasting Room TASTING ROOM
(⏩ 707-857-4900; www.tastelocalwines.com; Geyserville Ave & Hwy 128; ⊙ 11am-6pm) **FREE** Eight miles north of Healdsburg, tiny Geyserville is home to this indie tasting room, which represents 10 small-production wineries with free tastings.

Healdsburg Public Library LIBRARY
(⏩ 707-433-3772; www.sonomalibrary.org; cnr Piper & Center Sts; ⊙ 10am-9pm Mon & Wed, to 6pm Tue, Thu & Fri, to 4pm Sat) Wine Country's leading oenology-reference library.

Healdsburg Veterans Memorial Beach BEACH
(Map p198; ⏩ 707-433-1625; www.sonomacounty parks.org; 13839 Old Redwood Hwy; per car $7; ⊙ 7am-30min before sunset; P ♿) You can swim at this in-town beach between July and early September – lifeguards are on duty summer weekends. The fastidious can confirm current water quality online (www.sonoma-county. org/health/services/freshwater.asp).

Healdsburg Museum MUSEUM
(⏩ 707-431-3325; www.healdsburgmuseum.org; 221 Matheson St; donation requested; ⊙ 11am-4pm Wed-Sun) Rotating exhibits include compelling installations on northern Sonoma County history, with an emphasis on Healdsburg. Pick up the walking-tour pamphlet.

♣ Activities

After you've walked around the plaza, there isn't much to do in town. Go wine tasting in Dry Creek Valley or Russian River Valley. Bicycling on winding W Dry Creek Rd is brilliant, as is paddling the Russian River, which runs through town. Rent bikes from Spoke Folk Cyclery (p163).

NAPA & SONOMA WINE COUNTRY HEALDSBURG & AROUND

River's Edge Kayak & Canoe Trips
KAYAKING, CANOEING

(☎707-433-7247; www.riversedgekayakandcanoe.com; 13840 Healdsburg Ave; kayak/canoe rental & shuttle from $50/100) Rents hard-sided canoes and kayaks (single and double) for self-guided river tours that include a shuttle.

Russian River Adventures
CANOEING

(☎707-433-5599, 800-280-7627; www.russianriveradventures.com; 20 Healdsburg Ave; half-day canoe rental & shuttle adult/child from $45/25;) Paddle a secluded stretch of river in quiet inflatable canoes, stopping for rope swings, swimming holes, beaches and bird-watching. This ecotourism outfit points you in the right direction and shuttles you back at day's end. Or they'll guide your kids downriver while you go wine tasting (guides $125 per day). Reservations required.

☞ Tours

Getaway Adventures
CYCLING, KAYAKING

(☎800-499-2453; www.getawayadventures.com; tours 1-day $139-175, multiday $899-2500) Guides a variety of hiking, biking and kayaking tours in Dry Creek Valley, varying in length and difficulty. For example, a one-day tour might include spectacular morning vineyard cycling in Dry Creek Valley, followed by lunch and optional kayaking on Russian River.

✎ Courses

Relish Culinary Adventures
COOKING

(☎707-431-9999; www.relishculinary.com; 14 Matheson St; ⊘by appointment) Plug into the locavore food scene with culinary day trips, demo-kitchen classes or winemaker dinners.

✯ Festivals & Events

Russian River Wine Road Barrel Tasting
WINE

(www.wineroad.com; ⊘Mar) Sample wine, directly from the cask, before it's bottled or released for sale.

Future Farmers Parade
CULTURAL

(www.healdsburgfair.org; ⊘May) The whole town shows up for this classic-Americana farm parade, which kicks off a country fair.

Wine & Food Affair
FOOD & DRINK

(www.wineroad.com/events/wine-food-affair; ⊘Nov) Special food and wine pairings at over 100 wineries.

🛏 Sleeping

Healdsburg is expensive: demand exceeds supply. Rates drop winter to spring, but not significantly. Guerneville is much less expensive and just 20 minutes away. Most Healdsburg inns are within walking distance of the plaza; several B&Bs are in surrounding countryside. Find motels at Hwy 101's Dry Creek exit.

Cloverdale Wine Country KOA
CAMPGROUND $

(☎707-894-3337, 800-562-4042; www.winecountrykoa.com; 1166 Asti Ridge Rd, Cloverdale; tent/RV sites from $50/65, 1-/2-bedroom cabins $85/95;) Six miles from central Cloverdale (exit 520) off Hwy 101; hot showers, pool, hot tub, laundry, paddleboats and bicycles.

L&M Motel
MOTEL $$

(☎707-433-6528; www.landmmotel.com; 70 Healdsburg Ave; r $175-195; P❉❆🐾⊛) This simple, clean, old-fashioned motel with big lawns and barbecue grills is great for families. There's an indoor swimming pool, Jacuzzi and dry cedar sauna too. Breakfast included. Winter rates plummet.

Geyserville Inn
MOTEL $$

(☎877-857-4343, 707-857-4343; www.geyservilleinn.com; 21714 Geyserville Ave, Geyserville; r Mon-Fri $160-205, Sat & Sun $269-315; P❉❆🐾⊛) Eight miles north of Healdsburg, this immaculately kept upmarket motel is surrounded by vineyards. Rooms have unexpectedly smart furnishings and quality extras such as feather pillows. Request a remodeled room. There's a solar-heated pool and a hot tub.

Best Western Dry Creek
MOTEL $$

(☎707-433-0300; www.drycreekinn.com; 198 Dry Creek Rd; r Mon-Wed $143-198, Thu-Sun $187-239; ❉@❆⊛) This generic midrange motel has good service and an outdoor hot tub. New rooms have jetted tubs and gas fireplaces.

★Hotel Healdsburg
HOTEL $$$

(☎707-431-2800; www.hotelhealdsburg.com; 25 Matheson St; r from $499; ❉@❆⊛) Smack on the plaza, the fashion-forward HH has a coolly minimalist style of concrete and velvet, with requisite top-end amenities, including sumptuous beds and extradeep tubs. There's a full-service spa. The restaurant, **Dry Creek Kitchen**, is run by celeb-chef Charlie Palmer.

Madrona Manor HISTORIC HOTEL **$$$**
(📞 800-258-4003, 707-433-4231; www.madrona manor.com; 1001 Westside Rd; r Mon-Fri $255-655; ❄️🛜🏊) The first choice of lovers of country inns and stately manor homes, the regal 1881 Madrona Manor exudes Victorian elegance. Surrounded by 8 acres of woods and gorgeous century-old gardens, the hilltop mansion is decked out with many original furnishings. A mile west of downtown, it's convenient to Westside Rd wineries.

Belle de Jour Inn B&B **$$$**
(📞 707-431-9777; www.belledejourinn.com; 16276 Healdsburg Ave; r $225-295, ste $355; ❄️🛜) Charming Belle de Jour's sunny, uncluttered rooms have American-country furnishings, with extras such as private entrances, sun-dried sheets and jetted tubs. The manicured gardens are ready-made for a moonlight tryst.

Camellia Inn B&B **$$$**
(📞 707-433-8182, 800-727-8182; www.camelliainn. com; 211 North St; r $159-395; ❄️🛜🏊) Elegantly furnished 1869 mansion, with (among others) a rare-for-Healdsburg budget room ($159), plus a two-bed family room ($269). There are no TVs, but iPads are provided. Also, the innkeeper is really nice.

Healdsburg Inn on the Plaza INN **$$$**
(📞 800-431-8663, 707-433-6991; www.healds burginn.com; 112 Matheson St; r $295-460; ❄️🛜) The spiffy, clean-lined rooms, conservatively styled in khaki and beige, feel bourgeois summer-house casual, with fine linen and gas fireplace; some have jetted double tub. The plaza-front location explains the price.

H2 Hotel HOTEL **$$$**
(📞 707-431-2202; www.h2hotel.com; 219 Healdsburg Ave; r Mon-Fri $269-389, Sat & Sun $399-699; 🅿️❄️🍴@🛜🏊) ✈ Little sister to Hotel Healdsburg, H2 has the same angular concrete style, but was built LEED-gold-certified from the ground up, with a living roof, reclaimed everything and fresh-looking rooms with bamboo floors and organic-cotton linens. Also has a heated saltwater pool and free bikes. Waters, snacks and espresso are complimentary.

Haydon Street Inn B&B **$$$**
(📞 707-433-5228; www.haydon.com; 321 Haydon St; r $210-350, cottages $425-450; ❄️🛜) Two-story Queen Anne with big front porch and separate cottage.

Honor Mansion INN **$$$**
(📞 707-433-4277, 800-554-4667; www.honorman sion.com; 891 Grove St; r $450-695; ❄️🛜🏊) Elegant 1883 Victorian mansion with spectacular resort-like grounds, cushy rooms and great service.

✖ Eating

Healdsburg is the gastronomic capital of Sonoma County. Your hardest decision will be choosing where to eat. Reservations essential.

★ Shed CAFE **$$**
(📞 707-431-7433; www.healdsburgshed.com; 25 North St; dinner mains $15-30; ⏰ 8am-9pm Wed-Mon, to 6pm Tue; 🍴) ✈ At the vanguard of locavore eating, the Shed integrates food at all stages of production, milling its own locally sourced grain flours, fermenting vinegars and kombucha from local fruit and growing its own produce. It comprises a cafe with wood-fired dishes, a fermentation bar with home-grown shrubs, a coffee bar with stellar pastries and a market with prepared-to-go foods.

Reason enough to visit Healdsburg, the Shed is not a restaurant per se, but a dynamic multiuse culinary center, like a modern-day grange built of glass, nudging diners to see through what they're eating and take an active role in the future of food. Events, such as movie nights, biodynamic cannabis panel discussions and sushi-making workshops, are held upstairs.

Costeaux French Bakery & Cafe CAFE **$$**
(📞 707-433-1913; www.costeaux.com; 417 Healdsburg Ave; mains $10-13; ⏰ cafe 7am-3pm Mon-Sat, to 1pm Sun, bakery to 4pm Mon-Thu, to 5pm Sat & Sun; 🛜) This cavernous bakery-cafe is good for an easy lunch of salads and sandwiches on house-baked bread, plus all-day breakfast dishes including omelets and scrambles.

Diavola ITALIAN, CALIFORNIAN **$$**
(📞 707-814-0111; www.diavolapizzera.com; 21021 Geyserville Ave, Geyserville; mains $16-29; ⏰ 11:30am-9pm; 🍴) ✈ Ideal for lunch while wine tasting in Alexander Valley, Diavola makes outstanding *salumi* and thin-crust pizzas, served in an Old West, brick-walled space, loud enough to drown out the kids.

Healdsburg Bar & Grill PUB FOOD **$$**
(📞 707-433-3333; www.healdsburgbarandgrill.com; 245 Healdsburg Ave; mains $11-23; ⏰ 11am-9pm Mon-Fri, 9am-9pm Sat & Sun) *Top Chef Masters* winner Doug Keane's gastropub is perfect when you're famished but don't want to fuss. Expect simple classics – mac 'n' cheese,

pulled-pork sandwiches, top-end burgers and truffle-parmesan fries. At breakfast, look for homemade waffles and English muffins fresh from Costeaux Bakery. Sit in the garden.

★ Madrona Manor
CALIFORNIAN $$$

(☑ 707-433-4231, 800-258-4003; www.madrona manor.com; 1001 Westside Rd; 11-course menu $165; ☺ 6-9pm Wed-Sun) 🍴 You'd be hard-pressed to find a lovelier place to propose than this retro-formal Victorian mansion's garden-view verandah – though there's nothing old-fashioned about the artful haute cuisine: the kitchen churns its own butter, each course comes with a different variety of just-baked bread, courses include items such as Monterey abalone and Hokkaido-scallop crudo, and there's frozen lemon verbena for dessert. Reserve a presunset table.

★ SingleThread Farm-Restaurant-Inn
JAPANESE $$$

(☑ 707-723-4646; www.singlethreadfarms.com; 131 North St; tasting menu per person $293; ☺ 5:30-11pm Tue-Sun) The most ambitious project in Northern California is SingleThread, a world-class restaurant and, secondarily, an inn, where *omotenashi* (warm hospitality in Japanese) reigns and dishes from an 11-course tasting menu are prepared in handmade Japanese *donabe* (earthenware pots). The cuisine is California-Japanese and guests book tickets in advance, offering up their preferences and dietary restrictions, and the chef abides.

On arrival, guests are taken to a roof to enjoy sparkling wine, canapes and 360-degree views of the countryside before sitting down to feast. The sleek space features its own fermentation tank, which local winemakers use to craft a new vintage each year, along with a boutique **hotel** offering five sumptuous rooms starting at $800 a night. Down the road, the owners have a 5-acre organic garden where they farm specialized Japanese produce, hens and flowers.

Valette
CALIFORNIAN $$$

(☑ 707-473-0946; www.valettehealdsburg.com; 344 Center St; 'trust me' tasting menu per course $15, minimum 4 courses; ☺ 5:30-9:30pm) If you're looking to impress somebody, Healdsburg residents suggest Valette. The sleek American restaurant is regularly packed with suits and fancy ladies making a show of swirling their local wine (corkage fee is only $20) and ordering the multicourse 'trust me' tasting menu, where the gifted chef asks what you're into then decides what to feed you.

The scallop dish, which is baked within a squid-inked puffy pastry and bathed in caviar-studded champagne beurre blanc, is otherworldly.

Barndiva
CALIFORNIAN $$$

(☑ 707-431-0100; www.barndiva.com; 231 Center St; mains lunch $16-24, dinner $28-38; ☺ noon-2:30pm & 5:30-9pm Wed-Sat, from 11am Sun) 🍴 Impeccable seasonal-regional cooking, happening bar, beautiful garden, but service sometimes misses.

Bravas Bar de Tapas
TAPAS $$$

(☑ 707-433-7700; www.starkrestaurants.com/stark-restaurant/bravas-bar-de-tapas; 420 Center St; tapas $7-16, family-style large plates $28-74; ☺ 11:30am-9pm Sun-Thu, to 10pm Fri & Sat) This beloved tapas restaurant is part of the distinguished Stark restaurant chain and serves up Spanish cuisine, including the ever-popular paella, on small and large plates to share. The back patio is particularly lovely on a warm evening and the vast menu includes everything from crispy pig ears to duck-meatball sliders. Good sangria too.

Mateo's Cocina Latina
FUSION $$$

(☑ 707-433-1520; www.mateoscocinalatina.com; 214 Healdsburg Ave; mains lunch $12-19, dinner $14-35; ☺ 11am-9pm Wed-Sun) 🍴 Here the upmarket Yucatan-inspired cooking at lunch and the California-French fusion dishes in the evening integrate fine technique and all-local ingredients for standout dishes, such as daily beef cuts and *cochinita pibil* (a pork dish cooked with annatto seed), whose subtle flavors shine through the spice. The full bar showcases rare tequilas and mescals. Make reservations; request a garden table.

Self-Catering

Downtown Bakery & Creamery
BAKERY $

(☑ 707-431-2719; 308a Center St; ☺ 6am-5:30pm Mon-Fri, 7am-5:30pm Sat, 7am-4pm Sun) Healdsburg's classic bakery makes perfect breakfast pastries and specialty breads.

Noble Folk Ice Cream & Pie Bar
DESSERTS $

(☑ 707-395-4426; www.thenoblefolk.com; 116 Matheson St; items $3-6; ☺ noon-9pm; 🖼) 🍴 Hand-crafted ice cream and classic American pie, made with top-quality, all-local ingredients.

Moustache Baked Goods
BAKERY $

(☑ 707-395-4111; www.moustachebakedgoods.com; 381 Healdsburg Ave; cupcakes $3.50;

11am-7pm) Incredible locavore small-batch sweets (some gluten-free), including scrumptious cupcakes in unusual combos such as maple-bacon (available seasonally).

Shelton's Natural Foods Market MARKET, DELI $

(707-431-0530; www.sheltonsmarket.com; 428 Center St; 8am-8pm) Indie alternative for groceries and picnic supplies; reasonably priced.

Jimtown Store DELI, MARKET $$

(707-433-1212; www.jimtown.com; 6706 Hwy 128; sandwiches $8-13; 7am-3pm Sun, Mon & Wed-Fri, 7:30am-4pm Sat) One of our favorite Alexander Valley stopovers, Jimtown is great for picnic supplies and sandwiches spread with housemade condiments.

Oakville Grocery DELI $$

(707-433-3200; www.oakvillegrocery.com; 124 Matheson St; sandwiches $10-15; 5am-5pm) Fancy sandwiches and grab-and-go gourmet picnics. It's pricey, but the plaza-view fireside terrace is ever so fun for scouting Botox blonds, while nibbling cheese and sipping vino.

🍷 Drinking & Nightlife

Healdsburg is not a party town, but there are some good craft breweries and a new cocktail bar that stays open on weekends till (gasp!) 2am.

Bear Republic Brewing Company BREWERY

(707-433-2337; www.bearrepublic.com; 345 Healdsburg Ave; 11am-9:30pm Sun-Thu, to 10pm Fri & Sat) Bear Republic features hand-crafted award-winning ales, non award-winning pub grub, weekly trivia and monthly comedy nights.

Duke's Spirited Cocktails COCKTAIL BAR

(707-431-1060; www.healdsburgcottages.com; 111 Plaza St; 4pm-midnight Sun-Thu, 4pm-2am Fri, 2pm-2am Sat) The town's new cocktail bar is as popular for its crafty libations as it is for staying open beyond midnight on weekends, which is pretty much unheard of in Healdsburg. Also the drinks have really cute names such as 'Unicorn Tears' and 'Mr Bojangles.'

Flying Goat Coffee CAFE

(www.flyinggoatcoffee.com; 324 Center St; 7am-7pm) See ya later, Starbucks. Flying Goat is what coffee should be – fair-trade and house-roasted – and locals line up for it every morning.

☆ Entertainment

In summer free summer concerts take place each Tuesday afternoon in the plaza.

Raven Performing Arts Theater THEATER

(707-433-6335; www.ravenfilmcenter.com; 115 North St) Hosts concerts, events and first-run art-house films.

🛍 Shopping

One World GIFTS & SOUVENIRS

(707-473-0880; www.oneworldfairtrade.net; 104 Matheson St; 10am-6pm, to 5:30pm Sun) Household goods with a global outlook: alpaca shawls to Vietnamese trivets to cashmere shawls from Tibet, sourced from fair-trade collectives in 58 countries.

Copperfield's Books BOOKS

(707-433-9270; www.copperfieldsbooks.com; 104 Matheson St; 9am-7pm Sun-Thu, to 8pm Fri & Sat) Good general-interest books.

Options Gallery CRAFTS, JEWELRY

(707-431-8861; www.optionsgallery.com; 126 Matheson St; 10:30am-5:30pm Mon-Sat, 11am-4pm Sun) Gifts, crafts and jewelry by local artists, including lovely earrings.

Gardener GARDENS

(707-431-1063; www.thegardener.com; 516 Dry Creek Rd; 10am-5pm) Garden-shop lovers: don't miss this rural beauty.

Levin & Company BOOKS, MUSIC

(707-433-1118; 306 Center St; 9am-9pm Mon-Sat, 10am-6pm Sun) Fiction and CDs; co-op art gallery.

ℹ Information

Healdsburg Chamber of Commerce & Visitors Bureau (Map p198; 800-648-9922, 707-433-6935; www.healdsburg.com; 217 Healdsburg Ave; 10am-4pm Mon-Fri, to 3pm Sat & Sun) A block south of the plaza. Has winery maps and information on ballooning, golf, tennis, spas and nearby farms; 24-hour walk-up booth.

ℹ Getting There & Away

Sonoma County Transit (p161) buses travel around Healdsburg and connect it to neighboring cities, with prices ranging from $1.50 to $4.80 depending on how many zones you pass through on your journey. Youth prices range from $1.25 to $4.55.

Healdsburg is about an 80-minute drive north from San Francisco.

North Coast & Redwoods

Best Places to Eat

➡ Saw Shop Bistro (p242)
➡ Brick & Fire (p253)
➡ Saucy Ukiah (p246)
➡ Taka's Japanese Grill (p237)
➡ Fishetarian Fish Market (p222)

Best Places to Sleep

➡ Alegria (p233)
➡ Philo Apple Farm Guest Cottages (p245)
➡ Bay Hill Mansion (p222)
➡ Elk Cove Inn & Spa (p230)
➡ Didjeridoo Dreamtime Inn (p232)

Why Go?

This is not the legendary California of the Beach Boys' song – there are no palm-flanked beaches and very few surfboards. The jagged edge of the continent is wild, scenic and even slightly foreboding, where spectral fog and an outsider spirit have fostered the world's tallest trees, most potent weed and a string of idiosyncratic two-stoplight towns. Explore hidden coves with a blanket and a bottle of local wine, scan the horizon for migrating whales and retreat at night to fire-warmed Victorians. As you travel further north, find valleys of redwood, wide rivers and mossy, overgrown forests. Expect cooler, damper weather too. Befitting this dramatic clash of land and water are its unlikely mélange of residents: timber barons and tree huggers, pot farmers and radicals of every political persuasion.

When to Go
Eureka

Jun–Jul The driest season in the Redwoods is spectacular for day hikes and big views.

Aug–Oct Warm weather and clear skies are the best for hiking the Lost Coast.

Dec–Apr Whales migrate off the coast. In early spring look for mothers and calves.

North Coast & Redwoods Highlights

1 Hiking along meandering trails of **Redwood National Park** (p267), flanked by virgin redwood forests that will give you a crick in your neck.

2 Climbing to the top of historic **Point Arena Lighthouse** (p228) for sweeping views over the extraordinary coastline.

3 Admiring the dazzle of plants and flowers at the coast-side **Mendocino Coast Botanical Gardens** (p236).

4 Sipping the samplers at brewpub **Six Rivers Brewery** (p263) near Arcata; one of the best in Northern California.

5 Indulging in some all-American roadside kitsch along Hwy 101 at **Trees of Mystery** (p270).

6 Discovering the life of early settlers via the excellent **Mendocino County Museum** (p249) in Willits.

7 Enjoying the wonderful retro experience of a drive-in movie at the classic **Lakeport Auto Movies** (p243) in Clearlake.

❶ Getting Around

Although Hwy 1 is popular with cyclists and there are bus connections, you will almost certainly need a car to explore this region. Those headed to the far north and on a schedule should take Hwy 101, the faster, inland route, and then cut over to the coast. Windy Hwy 1 hugs the coast, then cuts inland and ends at Leggett, where it joins Hwy 101. Neither Amtrak nor Greyhound serve cities on coastal Hwy 1.

AIR

Arcata-Eureka Airport (p260) is located north of McKinleyville on the North Coast, signposted west of Hwy 101. **Alaska Airlines** (☑1-800-252-722; www.alaskaair.com), **Penair** (www.penair.com), Delta, American Airlines and United Airlines are the main carriers to operate national flights to/from here but fares tend to be high. Flights come and go from several major Californian cities, including Los Angeles, San Francisco, Sacramento and San Diego. There are also regular flights from other US cities, including New York, Denver, Phoenix and Portland (Oregon).

In the far north of the region, Crescent City is home to the tiny Del Norte County Regional Airport (p272). Alaska Airlines and Penair are the main carriers to serve this airport. Most flights contact with the nearby hubs of Arcata-Eureka Airport and Portland Airport in Oregon, from where there are connecting flights to US cities further afield.

BUS

Brave souls willing to piece together bus travel through the region will face a time-consuming headache, but connections are possible to most (but certainly not all!) towns in the region. **Greyhound** (☑800-231-2222; www.greyhound.com; ☎) runs buses between San Francisco and Ukiah ($44, three hours, daily), Willits ($44, 3½ hours, daily), Rio Dell (near Fortuna; $57, six hours, daily), Eureka ($57, 6¾ hours, daily) and Arcata ($57, seven hours, daily).

The **Mendocino Transit Authority** (MTA; ☑800-696-4682, 707-462-1422; www.mendocinotransit.org; 241 Plant Rd, Ukiah; most 1-way fares $1.50-6) operates bus 65, which travels between Fort Bragg, Willits, Ukiah and Santa Rosa daily, with an afternoon return ($26.25, three hours, four daily). Bus 95 runs between Point Arena and Santa Rosa via Jenner, Bodega Bay and Sebastopol ($8.25, 3¼ hours, daily). Bus 75 heads north every weekday from Gualala to the Navarro River junction at Hwy 128, then runs inland through the Anderson Valley to Ukiah, returning in the afternoon ($6.75, 2½ hours, daily). The North Coast route 60 goes north between Navarro River junction and Albion, Little River, Mendocino and Fort Bragg, Monday to Friday ($2.25, 1½ hours, two daily).

North of Mendocino County, the **Redwood Transit System** (☑707-443-0826; www.redwoodtransit.org) operates buses ($3) Monday through Saturday between Scotia and Trinidad (2½ hours), stopping en route at Eureka (1¼ hours) and Arcata (1½ hours). **Redwood Coast Transit** (☑707-464-9314; www.redwoodcoasttransit.org) runs buses Monday to Saturday between Crescent City, Klamath ($1.50, one hour, three daily) and Arcata ($30, two hours, three daily), with numerous stops along the way.

TRAIN

Amtrak (☑800-872-7245; www.amtrakcalifornia.com) operates the Coast Starlight between Los Angeles and Seattle. From LA, Amtrak buses connect to several North Coast towns, including Leggett ($87, 11 hours, two daily) and Garberville ($87, 11½ hours, two daily).

COASTAL HIGHWAY 1

Down south it's called the 'PCH,' or Pacific Coast Hwy, but North Coast locals simply call it 'Hwy 1.' However you label it, get ready for a fabulous coastal drive, which cuts a winding course on isolated cliffs high above the crashing surf. Compared to the famous Big Sur coast, the serpentine stretch of Hwy 1 up the North Coast is more challenging, more remote and more *real*, passing farms, fishing towns and hidden beaches. Drivers use roadside pullouts to scan the hazy Pacific horizon for migrating whales and explore a coastline dotted with rock formations that are relentlessly pounded by the surf. The drive between Bodega Bay and Fort Bragg takes four hours of daylight driving without stops. At night in the fog, it takes steely nerves and much, much longer. The most popular destination is the cliffside charmer of Mendocino.

Considering their proximity to the Bay Area, Sonoma and Mendocino Counties remain unspoiled, and the austere coastal bluffs are some of the most spectacular in the country. But the trip north gets more rewarding and remote with every mile. By the time Hwy 1 cuts inland to join Hwy 101, the land along the Pacific – called the Lost Coast – offers the state's best-preserved natural gifts.

Coastal accommodations (including campgrounds) can fill from Memorial Day to Labor Day (late May to early September) and on fall weekends, and often require two-night stays, so reserve ahead. There is a good choice of places to lay your head along the highway, although the budget conscious may find a definite lack of chain motels in these parts.

Bodega Bay

Bodega Bay is the first pearl in a string of sleepy fishing towns that line the North Coast and was the setting of Hitchcock's terrifying 1963 avian psycho-horror flick *The Birds*. The skies are free from bloodthirsty gulls today (though you'd best keep an eye on the picnic); it's Bay Area weekenders who descend en masse for extraordinary beaches, tide pools, whale-watching, fishing, surfing and seafood. Mostly a few restaurants, hotels and shops on both sides of Hwy 1, the downtown is not made for strolling, but it is a great base for exploring the endless nearby coves of the Sonoma Coast State Beach. Hwy 1 runs through town and along the east side of Bodega Bay. On the west side, a peninsula resembling a crooked finger juts out to sea, forming the entrance to Bodega Harbor.

◉ Sights & Activities

Surfing, beachcombing and sportfishing are the main activities here – the latter requires advance booking. From December to April, the fishing boats host whale-watching trips, which are also good to book ahead. Just about everyone in town sells kites, which are great for flying at Bodega Head. The excellent **Farm Trails** (www.farmtrails.org) guide at the Sonoma Coast Visitor Center has suggestions for tours of local ranches, orchards, farms and apiaries.

Bodega Head   VIEWPOINT
(Bay Flat Rd) At the peninsula's tip, Bodega Head rises 265ft above sea level. It's great for whale-watching. Landlubbers enjoy hiking above the surf, where several good trails include a 3.75-mile trek to Bodega Dunes Campground and a 2.2-mile walk to Salmon Creek Ranch. Head west from Hwy 1 onto Eastshore Rd, then turn right at the stop sign onto Bay Flat Rd.

Ren Brown Collection Gallery   GALLERY
(☎707-875-2922; www.renbrown.com; 1781 Hwy 1; ⊙10am-5pm Wed-Sun) The renowned collection of modern Japanese prints and California works at this small gallery is a tranquil escape from the elements. Check out the Japanese garden at the back.

Bodega Marine Laboratory & Reserve   SCIENCE CENTER
(☎707-875-2211; www.bml.ucdavis.edu; 2099 Westshore Rd; ⊙2-4pm Fri; P) FREE Run by University of California (UC) Davis, this spectacularly diverse teaching and research reserve surrounds the research lab, which has studied Bodega Bay since the 1920s. The 263-acre reserve hosts many marine environments, including rocky intertidal coastal areas, mudflats and sand flats, salt marsh, sand dunes and freshwater wetlands. On most Friday afternoons docents give tours of the lab and surrounds.

Chanslor Ranch   HORSEBACK RIDING
(☎707-875-3333, 707-875-2721; www.horsenaround trailrides.com; 2660 N Hwy 1; rides from $125; ⊙10am-5pm; ⚫) Just north of town, this friendly outfit leads horseback expeditions along the coastline and the rolling inland hills. Ron, the trip leader, is an amiable, sun-weathered cowboy straight from central casting; he recommends taking the Salmon Creek ride or calling ahead for weather-permitting moonlight rides. The 90-minute beach rides are justifiably popular.

BLOODTHIRSTY BIRDS OF BODEGA BAY

Bodega Bay has the enduring claim to fame as the setting for Alfred Hitchcock's *The Birds*. Although special effects radically altered the actual layout of the town, you still get a good feel for the supposed site of the farm owned by Mitch Brenner (played by Rod Taylor). The once-cozy Tides Wharf & Restaurant (p223), where much avian-caused havoc occurs in the movie, is still there but since 1962 it has been transformed into a vast restaurant complex. Venture 5 miles inland to the tiny town of Bodega and you'll find two icons from the film: the schoolhouse and the church. Both stand just as they did in the movie – a crow overhead may make the hair rise on your neck.

Coincidentally, right after production of *The Birds* began, a real-life bird attack occurred in Capitola, the sleepy seaside town south of Santa Cruz. Thousands of seagulls ran amok, destroying property and attacking people.

Bodega Bay
Sportfishing Center FISHING, WHALE-WATCHING
(☏707-875-3495; www.bodegacharters.com; 1410b Bay Flat Rd; fishing trips $135, whale-watching adult/child $50/35; ⚓) Beside the Sandpiper Cafe, this outfit organizes full-day fishing trips and three-hour whale-watching excursions. It also sells bait, tackle and fishing licenses. Call ahead to ask about recent sightings.

Bodega Bay Surf Shack SURFING
(☏707-875-3944; www.bodegabaysurf.com; 1400 N Hwy 1, Pelican Plaza; surfboard/SUP/kayak/bike rental from $17/40/45/16) If you want to get on the water, this easygoing one-stop shop has all kinds of rentals, lessons and good local information. It also rents bikes for landlubbers.

🎊 Festivals & Events

Bodega Bay Fishermen's Festival CULTURAL
(www.bbfishfest.org; ⊙Apr) At the end of April, this festival culminates in a blessing of the fleet, a flamboyant parade of vessels, an arts-and-crafts fair, kite-flying and feasting.

Bodega Seafood, Art & Wine Festival FOOD & DRINK
(www.winecountryfestivals.com; 16855 Bodega Hwy, Watt's Ranch; ⊙10am-6pm Sat, to 5pm Sun late Aug; ⚓) Held over a weekend in late August, this festival of food and drink brings together the best beer- and wine-makers of the area, tons of seafood and activities for kids. It takes place in the town of Bodega.

🛏 Sleeping

There's a wide spread of options – RV and tent camping, quaint motels, B&Bs and fancy hotels. Several have lovely views of the bay and all fill up early during peak seasons and at weekends. Campers should consider heading just north of town to the state-operated sites.

Doran Regional Park CAMPGROUND $
(www.parks.sonomacounty.ca.gov; 201 Doran Park Rd; tent sites $7, RV sites without hookups $32; ⊙7am-sunset; 🅿⚓) Watch for the sign if you are approaching town from the south. There are a few campsites here and easy access to the protected 2-mile Doran Beach, which has a boat launch and picnic areas.

Westside Regional Park CAMPGROUND $
(www.parks.sonomacounty.ca.gov; 2400 Westshore Rd; tent sites $7, RV sites without hookups $32; ⊙7am-sunset) This park caters mainly for RVs and boaters. It has windy exposures, beaches, hot showers, fishing and boat ramps.

Chanslor Guest Ranch RANCH $$
(☏707-875-2721; www.chanslorranch.com; 2660 Hwy 1; campsites $50, r from $144) A mile north of town, this working horse ranch has rooms and options for upscale camping. Wildlife programs and guided horse tours make this one sweet place, with sweeping vistas across open grasslands to the sea.

★ **Bay Hill Mansion** B&B $$$
(☏877-468-1588; www.bayhillmansion.com; 3919 Bay Hill Rd; d $279-299; 🅿🌐☏⚓❄) A luxe B&B in a spacious, modern mansion. The decor is tasteful and the cleanliness and comfort standards are some of the best we've ever seen. Get a private yoga class or massage, then the helpful hosts, Kirtis and Kristopher, can direct you to the area's best spots. Views overlook trees with just a peek at the bay.

The daily breakfast is more like a brunch, with a vast selection of delicious fare on offer. Other perks include a complimentary bottle of wine on arrival, cocktails at dusk and Nespresso machines in all rooms.

Bodega Bay Lodge & Spa LODGE $$$
(☏707-875-3525; www.bodegabaylodge.com; Doran Beach Rd; r $190-470; 🅿🌐@☏⚓) Bodega's plushest option, this small oceanfront resort has an ocean-view swimming pool, a golf course, a Jacuzzi and a state-of-the-art fitness club. In the evenings it hosts wine tastings. The more expensive rooms have commanding views, but all have balconies. The other pluses on-site include Bodega Bay's best spa and Drakes restaurant, which is the fanciest dining in town.

🍴 Eating & Drinking

For the old-fashioned thrill of seafood by the docks, there are several options where you can enjoy sea views, along with a simple menu of clam chowder, fried fish and coleslaw. There are also fish and produce markets in town where self-caterers can pick up supplies, and a fair range of other eateries specializing in everything from fast-food hotdogs to Tex-Mex and super-sophisticated offerings.

★ **Fishetarian Fish Market** CALIFORNIAN $
(☏707-480-9037; www.fishetarianfishmarket.com; 599 Hwy 1; mains from $12; ⊙11am-6pm Mon-Thu & Sun, to 7pm Fri & Sat; 🅿🚻⚓) A fish market,

deli and great place to eat with reggae as the soundtrack, an outdoor deck near the water and an expansive menu that includes colorful and imaginative organic salads, fried tofu (or calamari) with homemade fries, oysters, fish tacos, crab cakes and a fine clam chowder. Also serves craft beers on tap and decadent desserts.

Spud Point Crab Company   SEAFOOD $
(☑707-875-9472; www.spudpointcrab.com; 1860 Westshore Rd; mains $6.75-12; ☺9am-5pm; ℗🚻) In the classic tradition of dockside crab shacks, Spud Point serves salty-sweet crab sandwiches and *real* clam chowder (that consistently wins local culinary prizes). You can also buy a crab to take home if you fancy. Eat at picnic tables overlooking the marina. Take Bay Flat Rd to get here.

Lucas Wharf Restaurant & Bar   SEAFOOD $$
(☑707-875-3522; www.lucaswharfrestaurant. com; 595 Hwy 1; mains $9-28; ☺11:30am-9pm Mon-Fri, 11am-9:30pm Sat & Sun; ℗🚻) Located right on the water, this place specializes in sophisticated seafood options, with ingredients such as roasted cherry tomatoes accompanying dishes like Dungeness crab cakes and popcorn shrimp. Founded by a family of commercial fishers, the restaurant originated as a fish market, which is now next door, together with an upmarket deli. In other words, these folks know their seafood and you can guarantee it is flapping fresh.

Tides Wharf & Restaurant   SEAFOOD $$
(☑707-875-3652; www.innatthetides.com; 835 Hwy 1; breakfast $9-24, lunch $17-30, dinner $25-38; ☺7:30am-9:30pm Mon-Thu, 7:30am-10pm Fri, 7am-10pm Sat, 7am-9:30pm Sun; ℗🚻) Enjoy a stunning view of the bay and an upscale atmosphere. Seafood is the emphasis here, but pasta and meat dishes are also available. The black-and-white pics of the Hitchcock days add to the atmosphere and, if you're lucky, you may spy seals and dolphins from the vast picture window. The desserts are outstanding.

Terrapin Creek Cafe & Restaurant   CALIFORNIAN $$
(☑707-875-2700; www.terrapincreekcafe.com; 1580 Eastshore Dr; lunch mains $12-19, dinner mains $23-30; ☺11am-2:30pm & 4:30-9pm Thu-Sun; ℗🌲🍷) 🍴 This upscale restaurant is run by a husband-wife team who espouse the slow-food movement and serve local dishes sourced from the surrounding area.

Comfort-food offerings such as black cod roasted in lemongrass and coconut broth are artfully executed, while the Dungeness crab salad is fresh, briny and perfect. Jazz and warm light complete the atmosphere.

Drakes   CALIFORNIAN $$$
(☑888-875-2250; www.drakesbodegabay.com; 103 Hwy 1, Bodega Bay Lodge & Spa; mains $25-28, appetizers $8-17; ☺7am-10pm; ℗🍷) This fancy spot offers a choice of dining experiences. The Drakes Sonoma Coast Kitchen offers breakfast and dinner, the latter concentrating on such classics as pan-seared duck breast and Black Angus rib-eye steak with accompaniments like orange and almond relish and Parmesan mash. The Fireside Lounge offers a relaxed setting for lighter bites, including Pacific oysters and garlic fries.

Gourmet Au Bay   WINE BAR
(☑707-875-9875; www.gourmetaubay.com; 1412 Bay Flat Rd; ☺11am-6pm Thu-Tue; 🍷) This sophisticated wine bar moved to larger premises in 2017 and now offers sophisticated snacks to accompany your tipple. Head to the spacious deck where you can enjoy a salty breeze along with your wine tasting.

ⓘ Information

Sonoma Coast Visitor Center (☑707-875-3866; www.bodegabay.com; 850 Hwy 1; ☺9am-5pm Mon-Thu & Sat, to 6pm Fri, 10am-5pm Sun) Opposite the Tides Wharf. Stop by for the best help on the coast and for a copy of the *North Coaster,* a small-press indie newspaper of essays and brilliant insights on local culture.

Sonoma Coast State Beach

Stretching 17 miles north from Bodega Head to Vista Trail, 4 miles north of Jenner, the glorious Sonoma Coast State Beach is actually a series of beaches separated by several beautiful rocky headlands. Some beaches are tiny, hidden in little coves, while others stretch far and wide. Most of the beaches are connected by vista-studded coastal hiking trails that wind along the bluffs. Bring binoculars and your camera – the views are stunning, with rock outcrops, mini islands, inlets and shifting tides. During summer there can be morning fog, which generally burns off by midday. Exploring this area makes an excellent day-long adventure, but facilities are zero, so bring water and food, as well as a fully charged cell phone, in case of emergency. Also note that the surf is often too treacherous to wade, so keep a close eye on children.

◉ Sights & Activities

Schoolhouse Beach
BEACH
(btwn Bodega Bay & Jenner; P) A very pleasant beach with parking (but no other facilities); can be prone to riptides so swimmers should take care.

Goat Rock
BEACH
(5400-5900 N Hwy 1, Jenner; P) Famous for its colony of harbor seals, lazing in the sun at the mouth of the Russian River. Noted for its mystical-looking rock archway, as well.

Duncan's Landing
BEACH
(6947 Cliff Ave, Bodega Bay; P) Small boats unload near this rocky headland in the morning. A good place to spot wildflowers in the spring.

Shell Beach
BEACH
(Shell Beach Rd, Jenner; P) Just south of the small town of Jenner, a boardwalk and trail leads out to a stretch perfect for tide-pooling and beachcombing.

Salmon Creek Beach
BEACH
(3095 Hwy 1, Bodega Bay; P) Situated around a lagoon, with 2 miles of hiking and good waves for surfing.

Portuguese Beach
BEACH
(btwn Bodega Bay & Jenner; P) Very easy to access; sheltered coves between rocky outcroppings.

⌂ Sleeping

Unless you are willing to hammer down tent pegs (and even that is increasingly restricted; most camping is for day-use only), you will need to base yourself in Bodega Bay or Jenner. This is no real hardship, however, as both are just a few miles away either to the south or the north.

Wright's Beach Campground
CAMPGROUND $
(☑ 800-444-7275;   www.reserveamerica.com; 7095 Hwy 1; tent & RV sites $35, day use $8; P) Of the precious few parks that allow camping along Sonoma Coast State Beach, this is the best, even though sites lack privacy and there are no hot showers. There are just 27 sites but they can be booked six months in advance, and numbers one to 12 are right on the beach. There are BBQ pits for day use and it's a perfect launch for sea kayakers.

Bodega Dunes
CAMPGROUND $
(☑ 800-444-7275; www.reserveamerica.com; 3095 Hwy 1, Ranch Rd, Bodega Bay; tent & RV sites $35, day use $8; P) The largest campground in the Sonoma Coast State Beach system of parks with close to 100 sites; it is also closest to Bodega Bay, so it gets a lot of use. Sites are in high dunes and have hot showers, but be warned – the foghorn sounds all night.

Jenner

Perched on the hills looking out to the Pacific and above the mouth of the Russian River, tiny Jenner offers access to the coast and the Russian River wine region. A **harbor-seal colony** sits at the river's mouth and pups are born here from March to August. There are restrictions about getting too close to the chubby, adorable pups – handling them can be dangerous and cause the pups to be abandoned by their mothers. Volunteers answer questions along the roped-off area where day-trippers can look on at a distance. The best way to see them is by kayak, and most of the year you will find **Water Treks Ecotours** (☑ 707-865-2249; www.watertreks.com; kayak rental from $30; ☺ hours vary) renting kayaks on the highway. Heading north on Hwy 1 you will begin driving on one of the most beautiful, windy stretches of California highway. You'll also probably lose cell-phone service – possibly a blessing.

⌂ Sleeping & Eating

River's End Inn
COTTAGE $$
(☑ 707-865-2484;   www.ilovesunsets.com;   11048 Hwy 1; cottages $169-279; P ☺) Run by the same folk who own the superb River's End Restaurant, these ocean-view cottages are wood-paneled and have no TVs, wi-fi or phones, but many do come with fireplaces, breezy decks and breathtaking ocean views, complete with harbor seals. Children under 12 years old not recommended.

★ Café Aquatica
CAFE $
(☑ 707-865-2251; 10439 Hwy 1; pastries & sandwiches $4-10; ☺ 8am-5pm; �) This is the kind of North Coast coffee shop you've been dreaming of: fresh pastries, fog-lifting organic coffee and chatty locals. The expansive view of the Russian River from the patio and gypsy sea-hut decor make it hard to leave, especially at weekends when a strumming

guitarist adds to the California dreamin' ambience.

River's End Restaurant   CALIFORNIAN $$$
([☎]707-865-2484; www.ilovesunsets.com; 11048 Hwy 1; lunch mains $15-26, dinner mains $26-42; [⊙]noon-3:30pm & 5-9pm Fri-Mon; [P][🛜]) Unwind in style at this picture-perfect restaurant, perched on a cliff overlooking the river's mouth and a grand sweep of the Pacific Ocean. It serves world-class meals at world-class prices, but the real reward is the view.

Fort Ross State Historic Park

A curious glimpse into Tsarist Russia's exploration of the California coast, the salt-washed buildings of **Fort Ross State Historic Park** ([☎]707-847-3437; www.fortross.org; 19005 Hwy 1; per car $8; [⊙]10am-4:30pm) offer a fascinating insight into the pre-American Wild West. It's a quiet, picturesque place with a riveting past. If you pass by on a weekday when the fort is closed (due to budget cuts), you still may be able to walk down and have a peek inside if a school group is there.

In March 1812, a group of 25 Russians and 80 Alaskans (including members of the Kodiak and Aleutian tribes) built a wooden fort here, near a Kashaya Pomo village. The southernmost outpost of the 19th-century Russian fur trade on America's Pacific Coast, Fort Ross was established as a base for sea-otter hunting operations and trade with Alta California, and for growing crops for Russian settlements in Alaska. The Russians dedicated the fort in August 1812 and occupied it until 1842, when it was abandoned because the sea-otter population had been decimated and agricultural production had never taken off.

Fort Ross State Historic Park, an accurate reconstruction of the fort, is 11 miles north of Jenner on a beautiful point. The original buildings were sold, dismantled and carried off to Sutter's Fort during the gold rush. The visitor center has a great museum with historical displays and an excellent bookshop on Californian and Russian history. Ask about hikes to the Russian cemetery.

On Fort Ross Heritage Day, the last Saturday in July, costumed volunteers bring the fort's history to life; check www.parks.ca.gov or call the visitor center for other special events.

🛏 Sleeping

Stillwater Cove Regional Park   CAMPGROUND $
([☑]reservations 707-565-2267; www.sonoma-county.org/parks; 22455 N Hwy 1; tent & RV sites $28; [P]) Two miles north of Timber Cove, this park has hot showers and hiking under Monterey pines. Sites 1, 2, 4, 6, 9 and 10 have ocean views.

Timber Cove Inn   INN $$$
([☑]707-847-3231; www.timbercoveinn.com; 21780 N Hwy 1; r $230-350; [P][🍴][🛜]) A dramatic and quirky '60s-modern seaside inn that has been refurbished into a luxury lodge. The rustic architectural shell is stunning, and a duet of tinkling piano and crackling fire fills the vast open-plan lobby. Rooms have fireplaces and balconies or terraces. Prices vary according to the views. The Coast Kitchen restaurant offers a menu of well-prepared Californian cuisine.

Even those who don't bunk here should wander agape in the shadow of Benny Bufano's 93ft peace statue, a spectacular totem on the edge of the sea.

Salt Point State Park

Stunning 6000-acre **Salt Point State Park** ([☑]707-847-3221; www.parks.ca.gov; 25050 Hwy 1; per car $8; [⊙]park sunrise-sunset, visitor center 10am-3pm Sat & Sun Apr-Oct; [P]) has sandstone cliffs that drop dramatically into the kelp-strewn sea and hiking trails that crisscross windswept prairies and wooded hills, connecting pygmy forests and coastal coves rich with tidepools. The 6-mile-wide park is bisected by the **San Andreas Fault** – the rock on the east side is vastly different from that on the west. Check out the eerily beautiful tafonis (honeycombed-sandstone formations) near Gerstle Cove. For a good roadside photo op, there's a pullout at mile marker 45.

Though many of the day-use areas have been closed off due to budget cuts, trails lead off Hwy 1 pullouts to views of the pristine coastline. The platform overlooking Sentinel Rock is just a short stroll from the Fisk Mill Cove parking lot at the park's north end. Further south, seals laze at **Gerstle Cove Marine Reserve**, one of California's first underwater parks. Tread lightly around tidepools and don't lift the rocks: even a glimpse of sunlight can kill some critters. If you're here between April and June, you must see **Kruse Rhododendron State Reserve**.

Growing abundantly in the forest's filtered light, magnificent, pink rhododendrons reach heights of over 30ft, making them the tallest species in the world; turn east from Hwy 1 onto Kruse Ranch Rd and follow the signs. Be sure to walk the short Rhododendron Loop Trail.

Sleeping

★ Ocean Cove Lodge Bar & Grill MOTEL $
(☑ 707-847-3158; www.oceancovelodge.com; 23255 Hwy 1; r from $89; ➌✳🕾) Just a few minutes south of Salt Point State Park is Ocean Cove Lodge Bar & Grill, a godsend for those on a budget. It's just a basic motel but the location is fabulous, with uninterrupted ocean views (and whale-watching) beyond the sweeping lawns and hot tub. There's a surprisingly good American-style restaurant on the premises. The owner prides himself on the homemade cinnamon rolls made daily with an added hit of chili.

Salt Point State Park Campgrounds CAMPGROUND $
(☑ 800-444-7275; www.reserveamerica.com; Salt Point State Park; tent/RV sites $25/35; ℗) Two campgrounds, Woodside and Gerstle Cove, both signposted off Hwy 1, have sites with cold water. Inland Woodside (closed December to March) is well protected by Monterey pines. Gerstle Cove's trees burned over a decade ago and have only grown halfway back, giving the gnarled, blackened trunks a ghostly look when the fog twirls between the branches.

Sea Ranch

Though not without its fans, the exclusive community of Sea Ranch is a sort of weather-beaten Stepford-by-the-Sea. The ritzy subdivision that sprawls 10 miles along the coast is connected with a well-watched network of private roads, with hiking trails leading to the sea and along the bluffs. Approved for construction prior to the existence of the watchdog Coastal Commission, the community was a precursor to the concept of 'slow growth,' with strict zoning laws requiring that houses be constructed of only weathered wood. Though there are some pleasant short-term rentals here, don't break any community rules – like throwing wild parties – or security will come knockin'. For supplies and gasoline, go to Gualala. North of the Sea Ranch Lodge, you'll find the iconic nondenominational chapel; an extraordinary contemporary building surrounded by meadows of grazing cattle.

◎ Sights

Stengel Beach BEACH
(Hwy 1, Mile 53.96; ⊘ 6am-sunset May-Sep, from 8am Oct-Apr; ℗🖰) One of a handful of idyllic beaches on this stretch of coastline, Stengel has a large, free car park and a short access trail lined by cypress trees that takes you to a wooden staircase leading to the beach.

Walk-On Beach BEACH
(Hwy 1, Mile 56.53; parking per day $7; ⊘ 6am-sunset May-Sep, from 8am Oct-Apr; ℗) A short trail passes through a large grove of cypress trees leading to a staircase down to the pristine quarter-mile beach; note that there is also wheelchair access. Walkers can follow the stunning Bluff Top Trail from here, which leads north to Gualala Point Regional Park.

Shell Beach BEACH
(Hwy 1, Mile 55.24; parking per day $7; ⊘ 6am-sunset May-Sep, from 8am Oct-Apr; ℗🖰) A lovely beach comprising two sandy coves divided by a rocky headland. You can park just south of Whale Bone Reach Rd from where there is an approximately 2-mile access trail to the beach via pine trees and meadows. Note that there are no facilities, aside from toilets at the car park.

Sleeping

Depending on the season, it can be surprisingly affordable to rent a house in Sea Ranch. There are several agencies that can assist you in finding a place, including **Rams Head Realty & Rentals** (☑ 707-884-1427; www.ramshead.com; 309000 Hwy 1; ⊘ 9am-6pm) and **Sea Ranch Rentals** (☑ 707-884-4235; www.searanchrentals.com; 39200 Hwy 1; ⊘ 9am-6pm), both located in the center of nearby Gualala.

Sea Ranch Lodge HOTEL $$$
(☑ 707-785-2371; www.searanchlodge.com; 60 Sea Walk Dr; r $199-369; ℗🕾) A marvel of '60s-modern California architecture, timber clad Sea Ranch has spacious, minimalist rooms, many with dramatic views of the ocean; some have hot tubs and fireplaces. On the downside, Sea Ranch lodge is starting to look just a little bit dated and readers have complained about a lack of insulation which can be a problem with noisy neighbors.

Gualala & Anchor Bay

Located at the mouth of the Gualala River on the Pacific Coast, Gualala (pronounced by most locals as 'Wah-la-la') is a Native American Pomo name meaning 'where the waters flow down'. It is northern Sonoma coast's hub for a weekend getaway as it sits squarely in the middle of the 'Banana Belt,' an area known for unusually sunny weather. Founded as a prosperous lumber town in the 1860s, the downtown stretches along Hwy 1 with a bustling commercial district that has a great grocery store and some cute, slightly upscale shops.

Just north, quiet Anchor Bay is the destination of choice for many visitors seeking a tranquil stay, as it is home to some exceptional accommodation choices with a string of secluded, hard-to-find beaches situated just to the north. Both Gualala and Anchor Bay are excellent jumping-off points for exploring the surrounding area.

◉ Sights & Activities

Seven miles north of Anchor Bay, pull off at mile marker 11.41 for **Schooner Gulch**. A trail into the forest leads down cliffs to a sandy beach with tide pools. Bear right at the fork in the trail to reach iconic **Bowling Ball Beach**, where low tide reveals rows of big, round rocks resembling bowling balls. Consult tide tables for Arena Cove. The forecast low tide must be lower than +1.5ft on the tide chart for the rocks to be visible.

Gualala Arts Center ARTS CENTER
(☑ 707-884-1138; www.gualalaarts.org; 46501 Old State Hwy, Gualala; ☻9am-4pm Mon-Fri, noon-4pm Sat & Sun; ℗) Inland along Old State Hwy, at the south end of town, and beautifully built entirely by volunteers, this center hosts changing exhibitions, organizes the **Art in the Redwoods Festival** in late August, holds a range of art classes and has loads of info on local art.

🛏 Sleeping & Eating

Of the two towns, Gualala has more services than Anchor Bay, including places to stay, and is a more practical hub for exploring – there is a bunch of good motels, plus campgrounds and a handful of inns and B&Bs.

Gualala Point Regional Park CAMPGROUND $
(☑ 707-567-2267; http://parks.sonomacounty. ca.gov; 42401 Hwy 1, Gualala; tent & RV sites $35; ℗) Shaded by a stand of redwoods and fragrant California bay laurel trees, a short trail connects this creek-side campground to the windswept beach. The quality of sites, including several secluded hike-in spots, makes it the best drive-in camping on this part of the coast.

Gualala River Redwood Park CAMPGROUND $
(☑ 707-884-3533; www.gualalapark.com; Gualala Rd, Gualala; day use $6, tent/RV sites $42/49; ℗) Another excellent Sonoma County Park. Located inland from the Old State Hwy, you can camp and do short hikes along the Gualala River.

★St Orres Inn INN $$
(☑ 707-884-3303; www.saintorres.com; 36601 Hwy 1, Gualala; B&B $95-135, cottages $140-445; ℗☻⊛⊛) Famous for its striking Russian-inspired architecture: dramatic rough-hewn timbers, stained glass and burnished-copper domes, there's no place quite like St Orres. On the property's fairytale-like, wild mushroom–strewn 90 acres, hand-built cottages range from rustic to luxurious. The inn's fine restaurant is worth the splurge, with inspired California cuisine in one of the coast's most romantic rooms.

North Coast Country Inn B&B $$
(☑ 707-884-4537; www.northcoastcountryinn.com; 34591 S Hwy 1, Anchor Bay; r $185-235; ℗☻⊛⊛) Perched on an inland hillside beneath towering trees and surrounded by lovely gardens, the perks of this adorable place begin with the gregarious owner and a hot tub. The six spacious, country-style rooms are decorated with lovely prints and boast exposed beams, fireplaces, board games and private entrances.

★Mar Vista Cottages CABIN $$$
(☑ 707-884-3522; www.marvistamendocino.com; 35101 Hwy 1, Anchor Bay; cottages $190-310; ℗☻⊛⊛) ⊘ These elegantly renovated 1930s fishing cabins offer a simple, stylish seaside escape with a vanguard commitment to sustainability. The harmonious environment is the result of pitch-perfect details: linens are line-dried over lavender, guests browse the organic vegetable garden to harvest their own dinner and chickens cluck around the grounds laying the next morning's breakfast. It often requires two-night stays.

Trinks
CAFE $

(☑707-884-1713; www.trinkscafe.com; 39140 Hwy 1, Gualala; snacks & sandwiches $10-15; ⏱7am-4pm Mon-Tue, Fri & Sat, to 8pm Wed & Thu, 8am-4pm Sun; P 🛜) Tucked into the corner of a strip of shops with a seaview terrace, the overstuffed sandwiches are great value here. Be sure to leave room for a slice of fresh fruit pie; there are generally at least four to select from. Lightweights can opt for quiche and salad, while vegetarians will rejoice over the hearty veg-filled lentil bowl.

Anchor Bay Village Market
MARKET $

(☑707-884-4245; 35513 S Hwy 1, Anchor Bay; ⏱8am-7pm Mon-Sat, to 6pm Sun; P) This grocery store specializes in organic produce and products, with a superb range including baked goods and deli items.

❶ Information

Redwood Coast Visitors Center (☑707-884-1080; www.redwoodcoastchamber.com; 39150 Hwy 1, Shoreline Hwy, Gualala; ⏱noon-5pm Thu, Fri & Sun, from 11am Sat) A well-stocked tourist office with plenty of information on the area, including a free local map.

Point Arena

This laid-back little town of less than 450 residents combines creature comforts with relaxed, eclectic California living and is the first town up the coast where the majority of residents don't seem to be retired Bay Area refugees, but are rather a young, creative bunch who tout organic food, support their local theater and sell their fair share of dream catchers. The main street is part of scenic Hwy 1, with a small harbor at one end and a clutch of small arty shops, cafes and restaurants housed in pretty Victorian-era buildings running through the center of town. Peruse the shops and restaurants then follow the sign leading to the lighthouse at the north end of Main St, or head to the docks a mile west of town at Arena Cove and watch surfers mingle with fisherfolk and locals.

◉ Sights

★ Point Arena Lighthouse
LIGHTHOUSE

(☑707-882-2809; www.pointarenalighthouse.com; 45500 Lighthouse Rd; adult/child $7.50/1; ⏱10am-3:30pm mid-Sep–mid-May, to 4:30pm mid-May–mid-Sep; P) This 1908 lighthouse (the tallest on the US West Coast) stands 10 stories high and is the only lighthouse in California you can ascend. Check in at the museum, then climb 145 steps to the top and see the Fresnel lens and the jaw-dropping view. You can stay on-site. The turnoff is 2 miles northwest of town off Hwy 1.

Stornetta Public Lands
NATURE RESERVE

(Lighthouse Rd; P) For fabulous bird-watching, hiking on terraced rock past sea caves and access to hidden coves, head 1 mile down Lighthouse Rd from Hwy 1 and look for the Bureau of Land Management (BLM) signs on the left indicating these 1132-acre public lands. The best, most dramatic walking trail leads along the coast and also begins on Lighthouse Rd from a small parking area about a quarter-mile before the lighthouse parking area.

🛏 Sleeping

Point Arena Lighthouse Lodging
RENTAL HOUSE $$

(☑707-882-2809; www.pointarenalighthouse.com; 45500 Lighthouse Rd; houses $150-250; P♿🛜) True lighthouse buffs should look into staying at the plain, three-bedroom, kitchen-equipped former coast-guard homes at the lighthouse. They're quiet, windswept retreats.

Wharf Master's Inn
HOTEL $$

(☑707-882-3171; www.wharfmasters.com; 785 Iversen Ave; r $129-259; P♿🛜🐾) This is a cluster of comfortable, spacious rooms on a cliff overlooking fishing boats and a stilt pier. Recently reformed, they are eminently comfortable; several sporting four-poster beds. Most of the rooms have private balconies with uninterrupted sea views.

✖ Eating & Drinking

Franny's Cup & Saucer
BAKERY $

(☑707-882-2500; www.frannyscupandsaucer.com; 213 Main St; cakes from $2; ⏱8am-4pm Wed-Sat) The cutest patisserie on this stretch of coast is run by Franny and her mother, Barbara (a veteran of Chez Panisse in Berkeley). The fresh berry tarts and creative housemade chocolates seem too beautiful to eat, until you take the first bite and immediately want to order another. Once a month they pull out all the stops for a farmhouse dinner ($28).

Arena Market
ORGANIC, DELI $

(☑707-882-3663; www.arenaorganics.org; 185 Main St; soup $6.50, sandwiches $8; ⏱7am-7pm Mon-Sat, 8am-6pm Sun; P🛜) ✦ The deli at this fully stocked organic co-op makes excellent to-go veg and gluten-free options, including sandwiches, with ingredients generally sourced from local farms. The serve-yourself soup is delicious; you can enjoy it at one of the tables out front.

Uneda CALIFORNIAN **$$**
(☑ 707-882-3800; www.unedaeat.com; 206 Main St; mains $16-25; ☺ 5:30-8:30pm Wed-Sat) The owners are serious about food, they travel the world sourcing recipes and have a catering business as well as a food truck. The menu changes nightly depending on what is fresh in the market that day, but is always healthy and imaginative. There are just nine tables so reserve ahead of time. Cash only.

215 Main BAR
(www.facebook.com/215Main; 215 Main St; ☺ 2pm-2am Tue-Sun) Head to this open, renovated historic building to drink local beer and wine. There's jazz on the weekends.

☆ Entertainment

Arena Theater CINEMA
(☑ 707-882-3020; www.arenatheater.org; 214 Main St) Shows mainstream, foreign and art films in a beautifully restored movie house. Sue, the ticket seller, has been in that booth for 40 years. Got a question about Point Arena? Ask Sue.

Manchester

Follow Hwy 1 north beyond Point Arena, through gorgeous rolling fields dropping down from the hills to the blue ocean, and a turnoff leads to **Manchester State Beach**, a long, wild stretch of sand. If you visit from October to April, you may spy gray and humpback whales during their annual migration. Part of the protected **Manchester State Park** (☑ 707-882-2463; www.parks.gov.ca; Kinney Rd; tent sites $25-35; ℗), a 111-acre camping park, the area around here is remote and beautiful, with grazing land for sheep and cattle further inland and two freshwater streams noted for their salmon and steelhead (anglers take note). The population hovers around the 200 mark so there is not much here in terms of shops and facilities (only one grocery store), but it's a quick 7-mile drive east to Point Arena with its shops, restaurants and appealing places to stay.

Based inland around 8 miles to the north and actually closer to Elk, **Ross Ranch**

TOP WHALE-WATCHING SPOTS

Watch for spouts, sounding and breaching whales and pods. Anywhere coastal will do, but the following are some of the North Coast's best:

➡ Bodega Head (p221)

➡ Mendocino Headlands State Park (p232)

➡ Jug Handle State Natural Reserve (p235)

➡ MacKerricher State Park (p238)

➡ Shelter Cove (p254) & Lost Coast (p252)

➡ Trinidad Head Trail (p265)

➡ Klamath River Overlook (p270)

(☑ 707-877-1834; www.rossranch.biz; 28300 Philo Greenwood Rd; rides $50-60; 🐎) organizes two-hour rides along Manchester Beach or in nearby woodlands and forest for groups of up to 10.

Toward the ocean, **Mendocino Coast KOA** (☑ 707-882-2375; www.manchesterbeach koa.com; 44300 Kinney Rd; tent/RV sites from $32/65, cabins $75-85; ℗ 🐕) is an impressive private campground with tightly packed campsites beneath enormous Monterey pines, a cooking pavilion, hot showers, a hot tub, bicycles and a community campfire area. The cabins are a great option for families who want to get the camping experience without roughing it.

Elk

Itty-bitty Elk is famous for its stunning cliff-top views of 'sea stacks,' towering rock formations jutting out of the water. Otherwise, it's one of the cutest yet gentrified-looking villages before Mendocino. There is *nothing* to do after dinner, so bring a book if you're a night owl. And you can forget about the cell phone, too; reception here is nonexistent. Elk's visitor center (p230) has exhibits on the town's logging past. At the southern end of town, **Greenwood State Beach** sits where Greenwood Creek meets the sea and marks the spot where ships used to stop when carrying timber to San Francisco and China. There are some excellent walks along the cliffs offering dramatic ocean views combined with dense woods.

🛏 Sleeping & Eating

★ Elk Cove Inn & Spa ⠀⠀⠀⠀INN $$$
(☎800-725-2967; www.elkcoveinn.com; 6300 S Hwy 1; r $100-375, cottages $275-355; P😊🐾📶❄) Several upmarket B&Bs take advantage of the views but you simply can't beat those from Elk Cove Inn & Spa, located on a bluff with steps leading down to the drift-wood-strewn beach below. Prices in the wide selection of rooms and cottages include breakfast, wine, champagne and cocktails, plus you can relax even further at the deluxe spa.

Elk Store ⠀⠀⠀⠀DELI $
(☎707-877-3544; 6101 Hwy 1, Shoreline Hwy; sandwiches from $9; ⊙9am-6pm) Make a stop here for gourmet foods, gifts, Mendocino County wines and a great deli menu with build-your-own sandwiches, burritos, bagels and wraps, and an awesomely good clam chowder.

Queenie's Roadhouse Cafe ⠀⠀CAFE $
(☎707-877-3285; 6061 S Hwy 1, Shoreline Hwy; mains $6-10; ⊙8am-3pm Thu-Mon; 🐾) Everyone swears by this excellent, retro-chic classic diner for a creative range of breakfast (try the wild-rice waffles) and lunch treats, including a great burger and Reuben sandwich.

ℹ Information

Elk Visitor Center (☎707-937-5804; www.mendoparks.org/greenwood-state-beach-elk-ca/; Greenwood State Beach; ⊙11am-1pm Sat & Sun mid-Mar–Oct; 🐾) This small visitor center-cum-museum provides information about the region and also has a photographic display about the history of Elk (formerly known as Greenwood) as a lumber town in the late 1800s.

Van Damme State Park

Three miles south of Mendocino, this sprawling 1831-acre **park** (☎707-937-5804; www.parks.ca.gov; 8001 N Hwy 1, Little River; per car $8; ⊙8am-9pm; P) draws beachcombers, divers and kayakers to its easy-access beach, and hikers to its pygmy forest. The latter is a unique and precious place, where acidic soil and an impenetrable layer of hardpan have created a miniature forest of decades-old trees. The visitor center has nature exhibits and programs.

You can reach the forest on the moderate 3.5-mile **Fern Canyon Scenic Trail**, which crosses back and forth over Little River and

past the Cabbage Patch, a bog of skunk cabbage that's rich with wildlife.

Two pretty **campgrounds** (☎800-444-7275; www.reserveamerica.com; 8001 Hwy 1, Little River; tent/RV sites $25/35; P🐾) are excellent for family car camping. They both have hot showers: one is just off Hwy 1, the other is in a highland meadow, which has lots of space for kids to run around. Nine environmental campsites (tent sites $25) lie just a 1¼-mile hike up Fern Canyon; there's untreated creek water.

For sea-cave kayaking tours contact **Kayak Mendocino** (☎707-937-0700; www.kayakmendocino.com, 8001 N Hwy 1, Little River; adult/child $60/40; ⊙tours 9am, 11:30am & 2pm).

Mendocino

Leading out to a gorgeous headland, Mendocino is the North Coast's salt-washed perfect village, with B&Bs surrounded by rose gardens, white-picket fences and New England–style redwood water towers. Bay Area weekenders walk along the headland among berry bramble and wildflowers, where cypress trees stand over dizzying cliffs. The town itself is full of cute shops – no chains – and has earned the nickname 'Spendocino,' for its upscale goods.

Built by transplanted New Englanders in the 1850s, Mendocino thrived late into the 19th century, with ships transporting redwood timber from here to San Francisco. The mills shut down in the 1930s, and the town was rediscovered in the 1950s by artists and bohemians. Today the culturally savvy, politically aware, well-traveled citizens welcome visitors, but eschew corporate interlopers – don't look for a Big Mac or Starbucks. To avoid crowds, come midweek or in the low season, when the vibe is mellower – and prices more reasonable.

◎ Sights

Mendocino is lined with all kinds of interesting galleries, which hold openings on the second Saturday of each month from 5pm to 8pm.

Kwan Tai Temple ⠀⠀⠀⠀TEMPLE
(Map p231; ☎707-937-5123; www.kwantaitemple.org; 45160 Albion St; ⊙by appointment) Peering in the window of this 1852 temple reveals an old altar dedicated to the Chinese god of war. Tours are available by appointment and provide a fascinating insight into the

Mendocino

0 — 200 m
0 — 0.1 miles

Mendocino

history of the area's Chinese American immigrants, dating from the mid-19th century when they worked in the lumber industry.

Point Cabrillo Light Station   LIGHTHOUSE
(☎707-937-6123; www.pointcabrillo.org; 45300 Lighthouse Rd; ☉park sunrise-sunset, lighthouse 11am-4pm) **FREE** Restored in 1909, this stout lighthouse stands on a 300-acre wildlife preserve north of town, between Russian Gulch and Caspar Beach. Guided walks of the preserve leave at 11am on Sundays from May to September. You can also stay in the lighthouse keeper's house and cottages.

Kelley House Museum   MUSEUM
(Map p231; ☎707-937-5791; www.mendocino history.org; 45007 Albion St; $2; ☉11am-3pm Thu-Tue Jun-Sep, Fri-Mon Oct-May) Check out the research library and changing exhibits on

early California and Mendocino. The 1861 museum hosts seasonal, two-hour walking tours for $10; call for times.

Mendocino Art Center   GALLERY

(Map p231; ☑707-937-5818; www.mendocinoart center.org; 45200 Little Lake St; ⊙10am-5pm Apr-Oct, to 4pm Tue-Sat Nov-Mar) FREE Behind a yard of twisting iron sculpture, the city's art center takes up a whole tree-filled block, hosting exhibitions, the 81-seat Helen Schonei Theatre and nationally renowned art classes. This is also where to pick up the *Mendocino Arts Showcase* brochure, a quarterly publication listing all the happenings and festivals in town.

🏃 Activities

Wine tours, whale-watching, shopping, hiking, cycling: there's more to do in the area than a thousand long weekends could accomplish. For navigable river and ocean kayaking, launch from tiny Albion, which hugs the north side of the Albion River mouth, 5 miles south of Mendocino.

Catch a Canoe & Bicycles, Too!   CANOEING, CYCLING

(☑707-937-0273; www.catchacanoe.com; 44850 Comptche-Ukiah Rd, Stanford Inn by the Sea; 3hr kayak, canoe or bicycle rental adult/child $28/14; ⊙9am-5pm; ♠) This friendly outfit rents bikes, kayaks and canoes (including redwood outriggers) for trips up the 8-mile Big River tidal estuary. Northern California's longest undeveloped estuary has no highways or buildings, only beaches, forests, marshes, streams, abundant wildlife and historic logging sites. Bring a picnic and a camera to enjoy the ramshackle remnants of century-old train trestles and majestic blue herons.

Mendocino Headlands State Park   HIKING

(Map p231; ☑707-937-5804; www.parks.ca.gov; Ford St) FREE Mendocino Headlands State Park surrounds the village, where trails crisscross bluffs and rocky coves. Ask at the visitor center (p235) about guided weekend walks, including spring wildflower explorations and whale-watching jaunts.

✷ Festivals & Events

For a complete list of Mendocino's many festivals, check with the visitor center or www.gomendo.com.

Mendocino Whale Festival   WILDLIFE

(www.mendowhale.com; ⊙early Mar) Wine and chowder tastings, whale-watching and plenty of live music.

Mendocino Music Festival   MUSIC

(www.mendocinomusic.com; ⊙mid-Jul; ♠) Enjoy orchestral and chamber music concerts on the headlands, children's matinees and open rehearsals.

Mendocino Wine & Mushroom Festival   FOOD & DRINK

(www.mendocino.com; ⊙early Nov) Includes guided mushroom tours and symposia.

🛏 Sleeping

Standards are high in stylish Mendocino and so are prices; two-day minimums often crop up on weekends. Fort Bragg, 10 miles north, has cheaper lodgings. All B&B rates include breakfast; only a few places have TVs. For a range of cottages and B&Bs, contact **Mendocino Coast Reservations** (Map p231; ☑707-937-5033; www.mendocinovacations. com; 45084 Little Lake St; ⊙9am-5pm).

Russian Gulch State Park   CAMPGROUND $

(☑reservations 800-444-7275; www.reserve america.com; tent & RV sites $35; Ⓟ) In a wooded canyon 2 miles north of town, with secluded drive-in sites, hot showers, a small waterfall and the Devil's Punch Bowl (a collapsed sea arch).

★Didjeridoo Dreamtime Inn   B&B $$

(Map p231; ☑707-937-6200; www.didjeridoo inn.com; 44860 Main St; r $112-160; ♠♥♠) One of the town's more economical choices, rooms here are all different yet share the same homey, unpretentious atmosphere with tasteful artwork, antiques and parquet flooring. Several rooms have en suites, and a couple have mini hot tubs. The breakfast spread is excellent and on Sunday you are treated to some soothing live music. The front garden is a lovely place to sit.

MacCallum House Inn   B&B $$

(Map p231; ☑707-937-0289; www.maccallum house.com; 45020 Albion St; r & cottages from $149, water-tower ste $259-359; Ⓟ♥@♠♠) ♦ One of the finest B&B options in town with gardens in a riot of color. There are cheerful cottages, and a modern luxury home, but the most memorable space is within one of Mendocino's iconic, historic water towers – living quarters fill the ground floor, a sauna is on the 2nd and there's a view of the coast from the top.

Andiron Seaside Inn & Cabins   CABIN $$

(☎707-937-1543; http://theandiron.com; 6051 N Hwy 1, Little River; d $109-299; 🅿🖨🛜🐾) 🖋 Styled with hip vintage decor, this cluster of 1950s roadside cottages is a refreshingly playful option amid the cabbage-rose and lace aesthetic of Mendocino. Each cabin houses two rooms with complementing themes: 'Read' has old books, comfy vintage chairs and retro eyeglasses, while the adjoining 'Write' features a huge chalkboard and a ribbon typewriter.

Lighthouse Inn at Point Cabrillo   B&B $$

(☎707-937-6124; www.pointcabrillo.org; Point Cabrillo Dr; cottages from $132, houses from $450; 🅿🖨🛜🐾) On 300 acres, in the shadow of Point Cabrillo lighthouse, the stately lightkeeper's and assistant lightkeeper's houses, together with the staff's two turn-of-the-century cottages have been revamped into vacation rentals. All options have verandas and lush period decor but are not very private.

Packard House   B&B $$

(Map p231; ☎707-937-2677; www.packardhouse. com; 45170 Little Lake St; r $175-225; 🅿🖨🛜) Decked out in contemporary style, this place is Mendocino's most chic and sleek B&B choice, with beautiful fabrics, colorful minimalist paintings and limestone bathrooms.

⭐ Alegria   B&B $$$

(Map p231; ☎707-937-5150; www.oceanfront magic.com; 44781 Main St; r $239-299; 🖨🛜) A perfect romantic hideaway, beds have views over the coast, decks have ocean views and all rooms have wood-burning fireplaces; outside, a gorgeous path leads to a big, amber-gray beach. Ever-so-friendly innkeepers whip up amazing breakfasts served in the sea-view dining area. Less-expensive rooms are available across the street at bright and simple Raku House (Map p231; ☎800-780-7905; 998 Main St; r $109-139; 🅿🖨🛜).

⭐ Stanford Inn by the Sea   INN $$$

(☎707-937-5615; www.stanfordinn.com; 44850 Comptche-Ukiah Rd; r $211-299; 🖨@🛜🐕🏊) 🖋 This masterpiece of a lodge standing on 10 lush acres has wood-burning fireplaces, knotty-pine walls, original art, stereos and top-quality mattresses in every room. Take a stroll in the organic gardens, where they har-

vest food for the excellent on-site restaurant, and a dip in the solarium-enclosed pool and hot tub, and it's a sublime getaway.

Brewery Gulch Inn   B&B $$$

(☎707-937-4752; www.brewerygulchinn.com; 9401 N Hwy 1; d $245-495; 🖨🛜) 🖋 Just south of Mendocino, this bright, woodsy place has 10 modern rooms (all with flat-screen televisions, gas fireplaces and spa bathtubs), and guests enjoy touches like feather beds and leather reading chairs. The hosts pour heavily at the complimentary wine hour and leave out sweets for midnight snacking. Made-to-order breakfast is served in a small dining room overlooking the distant water.

Glendeven   B&B $$$

(☎707-937-0083; www.glendeven.com; 8205 Hwy 1, Shoreline Hwy; r $216-280; 🅿🖨🛜) 🖋 This historic 1860s estate 2 miles south of town has organic gardens, grazing llamas (with daily feedings at dusk), chickens for those breakfast eggs, forest and oceanside trails and a wine bar serving only Mendocino wines – and that's just the start. Romantic rooms have neutral tones, soothing decor, fireplaces and top-notch linens. Farm-to-table dinners are available at the bistro.

🍴 Eating

With quality to rival Napa Valley, the influx of Bay Area weekenders has fostered an excellent dining scene that enthusiastically espouses organic, sustainable principles. Make reservations. Gathering picnic supplies is easy at Harvest Market (p235) organic grocery store (with deli) and the farmers market (Map p231; cnr Howard & Main St; ⏰noon-2pm Fri May-Oct).

Tote Fête Deli & Burger Grill   BURGERS $

(Map p231; ☎707-937-3383; 10450 Lansing St; burgers $9-15, mains $12-15; ⏰11:30am-7:30pm Mon, Tue & Thu-Sat, to 5pm Sun) Dine in or take away at this serious burger place with its all-natural, grass-fed beef and 11 choices, including veggie and portobello-mushroom options. Also on the menu are seafood dishes, such as fish tacos, calamari and coconut shrimp, plus steaks, gourmet salads and sandwiches. The atmosphere is laid back; this is not the place for a romantic dinner.

Frankie's   PIZZA $

(Map p231; ☎707-937-2436; www.frankies mendocino.com; cnr Ukiah & Lansing Sts; pizza $13-16; ⏰11am-9pm; 🚸) 🖋 There is no Sicilian-style simplicity to these pizzas, they are pure Californian with piled-high organic ingredients such as cremini mushrooms, Canadian bacon, roasted red peppers and pineapple (not combined, fortunately). It also serves healthy fare such as quinoa kale cakes and gluten-free falafel, plus soups, salads and Fort Bragg's famous Cowlick's ice cream.

Flow
CALIFORNIAN $$

(Map p231; ☑707-937-3569; www.mendocino flow.com; 45040 Main St; mains $14-20; ⊙8am-10pm; ☎☑) Run by the Mendocino Cafe, this very busy place has the best views of the ocean in town from its 2nd-story perch. Brunch is a specialty as are Mexican-inspired small plates, artisan pizzas and a sublime local Dungeness crab chowder. Gluten-free and vegan options are available.

Ledford House
MEDITERRANEAN $$

(☑707-937-0282; www.ledfordhouse.com; 3000 N Hwy 1, Albion; mains $14-30; ⊙5-8pm Wed-Sun; ℗) Watch the water pound the rocks and the sun set out of the Mendocino hubbub (8 miles south) at this friendly Cal-Med bistro. Try the cassoulet or the gnocchi. It's a local hangout and gets hoppin' with live jazz most nights.

Patterson's Pub
PUB FOOD $$

(Map p231; www.pattersonspub.com; 10485 Lansing St; mains $13-16; ⊙10am-midnight, food to 11pm) If you pull into town late and hungry, you'll thank your lucky stars for this place; it serves quality pub grub – fish and chips, burgers and dinner salads – with cold beer. The only traditional Irish pub ambience spoiler is the plethora of flat-screen TVs. A busy brunch is served on Saturday and Sunday mornings from 10am to 2pm.

★Café Beaujolais
CALIFORNIAN $$$

(Map p231; ☑707-937-5614; www.cafebeaujolais. com; 961 Ukiah St; lunch mains $10-18, dinner mains $23-38; ⊙11:30am-2:30pm Wed-Sun, dinner from 5:30pm daily; ℗) ✔ Mendocino's iconic, beloved country-Cal–French restaurant occupies an 1893 farmhouse restyled into a monochromatic urban-chic dining room, perfect for holding hands by candlelight. The refined, inspired cooking draws diners from San Francisco, who make this the centerpiece of their trip. The locally sourced menu changes with the seasons, but the Petaluma duck confit is a gourmand's delight.

955 Ukiah Street
CALIFORNIAN $$$

(Map p231; ☑707-937-1955; www.955restaurant. com; 955 Ukiah St; mains $18-37; ⊙from 6pm Thu-Sun) One of those semi-secret institutions, the menu here changes with what's available locally. When we visited, that meant wondrous things such as a roasted cauliflower, feta and caramelized-onion appetizer. The dimly lit, bohemian setting overlooks rambling gardens. Check the website for the excellent-value, three-course meal with wine for $25 every Thursday, and other events.

Don't miss the paintings by Emmy Lou Packard, who lived round the corner during the '60s and was famously both a communist and an assistant to Mexican painter and muralist, Diego Rivera.

MacCallum House Restaurant
CALIFORNIAN $$$

(Map p231; ☑707-937-0289; www.maccallum house.com; 45020 Albion St; cafe dishes $12-18, mains $25-42; ⊙8:15-10am Sat & Sun, plus 5:30-9pm daily; ℗) ✔ Sit on the veranda or fireside for a romantic dinner of all-organic game, fish or risotto primavera. Chef Alan Kantor makes *everything* from scratch and his commitment to sustainability and organic ingredients is nearly as visionary as his menu. The cafe menu, served at the Grey Whale Bar, is one of Mendocino's few four-star bargains.

Ravens
CALIFORNIAN $$$

(☑707-937-5615; www.ravensrestaurant.com; Stanford Inn by the Sea, Comptche-Ukiah Rd; breakfast $11-15, mains $24-30; ⊙8am-10pm; ℗☑) ✔ Ravens brings haute-contemporary concepts to a completely vegetarian and vegan menu. Produce comes from the idyllic organic gardens of the Stanford Inn by the Sea (p233) and the bold menu takes on everything from sea-palm strudel and portabella sliders to decadent (guilt-free) desserts.

🍸 Drinking & Nightlife

Have cocktails at the **Mendocino Hotel** (Map p231; ☑707-937-0511; www.mendocinohotel.com; 45080 Main St; ℗☺☎) or the Grey Whale Bar at the MacCallum House Inn (p232). For boisterousness and beer head straight to Patterson's Pub.

Dick's Place
BAR

(Map p231; ☑707-937-6010; 45080 Main St; ⊙11:30am-2am) A bit out of place among the fancy-pants shops downtown, but an excellent spot to check out the *other* Mendocino and do shots with rowdy locals. And don't miss the retro experience of dropping 50¢ in the jukebox to hear that favorite tune.

🔒 Shopping

Mendocino's walkable streets are great for shopping, and the ban on chain stores ensures unique, often upscale gifts. There are many small galleries in town where one-of-a-kind artwork is for sale.

Twist CLOTHING
(Map p231; ☑707-937-1717; www.mendocino twist.com; 45140 Main St; ☺11am-5pm Mon-Fri, 10:30am-5:30pm Sat & Sun) 🍴 Twist stocks eco-friendly, natural-fiber clothing and lots of locally made clothing and toys.

Mendocino Chocolate Company CHOCOLATE
(Map p231; ☑800-722-1107; www.mendocino-chocolate.com; 10466 Lansing St; ☺10am-5:30pm) This company has been around for 30 years in Fort Bragg, so it know its cocoa beans. This newer second outlet adds a sweet touch to Mendocino's shopping scene. Check out the exquisite handmade seashells in marbled white, milk and dark chocolate.

Harvest Market FOOD & DRINK
(Map p231; ☑707-937-5879; www.harvestmarket. com; 10501 Lansing St; ☺7:30am-10pm) 🍴 The town's biggest grocery store has legit organic credentials, an excellent cold-food bar and great cheese and meat.

Village Toy Store TOYS
(Map p231; ☑707-937-4633; www.mendotoystore. com; 10450 Lansing St; ☺10am-6pm) Get a kite or browse the old-world selection of wooden toys and games that you won't find in the chains – hardly anything requires batteries.

Gallery Bookshop BOOKS
(Map p231; ☑707-937-2665; www.gallerybook shop.com; 319 Kasten St; ☺9:30am-6pm) Stocks a great selection of books on local topics, titles from California's small presses and specialized outdoor guides.

Out of This World SPORTS & OUTDOORS
(Map p231; ☑707-937-3335; www.outofthis worldshop.com; 45100 Main St; ☺10am-5:30pm) Birders, astronomy buffs and science geeks head directly to this telescope, binocular and science-toy shop.

ℹ️ Information

Ford House Museum & Visitor Center (Map p231; ☑707-537-5397; www.mendoparks.org; 45035 Main St; ☺11am-4pm) Enjoy maps, books, information and exhibits, including a scale model of 1890 Mendocino, plus a historical setting with original Victorian-period furniture and decor.

Jug Handle State Reserve

Between Mendocino and Fort Bragg, Jug Handle (☑707-937-5804; www.parks.ca.gov; Hwy 1, Caspar; ☺sunrise-sunset; P 🚻) 🍴 FREE preserves an **ecological staircase** that you can view on a 5-mile (round-trip) self-guided nature trail. The reserve is also a good spot to stroll the headlands, whale-watch or lounge on the beach; you can pick up a printed guide detailing the area's geology, flora and fauna from the parking lot. Note that it's easy to miss the entrance; watch for the turnoff, just north of Caspar.

Five wave-cut terraces ascend in steps from the seashore, each 100ft and 100,000 years removed from the previous one, and each with its own distinct geology and vegetation. One of the terraces has a **pygmy forest**, similar to the better known example at Van Damme State Park, 9 miles south.

Jug Handle Creek Farm & Nature Center (☑707-964-4630; www.jughandlecreek farm.com; 15501 N Hwy 1; tent sites $14, r & cabins adult/student $45/38; ☺9am-8pm; P🚻🐾) is a nonprofit 39-acre farm with rustic cabins and hostel rooms in a 19th-century farmhouse. Call ahead about work-stay discounts. Drive 5 miles north of Mendocino to Caspar; the farm is on the east side of Hwy 1. Take the second driveway after Fern Creek Rd.

Fort Bragg

In the past, Fort Bragg was Mendocino's ugly stepsister, home to a lumber mill, a scrappy downtown and blue-collar locals who gave a cold welcome to outsiders. Since the mill closure in 2002, the town has started to reinvent itself, slowly warming to a tourism-based economy, with the downtown continuing to develop as a wonderfully unpretentious alternative to Mendocino (even if the southern end of town is hideous). Unlike the *entire* franchise-free 180-mile stretch of Coastal Hwy 1 between here and the Golden Gate, in Fort Bragg you can get a

Big Mac, grande latte or any of a number of chain-store products whose buildings blight the landscape. Don't fret. In downtown you'll find better hamburgers and coffee, old-school architecture and residents eager to show off their little town.

By car, twisting Hwy 20 provides the main access to Fort Bragg from the east, and most facilities are near Main St, a 2-mile stretch of Hwy 1. The Mendocino Transit Authority (p220) operates bus 65, which travels between Fort Bragg, Willits, Ukiah and Santa Rosa daily, with an afternoon return ($23, three hours, four daily). Monday to Friday, the North Coast route 60 goes north between Navarro River junction and Albion, Little River, Mendocino and Fort Bragg ($2.25, 1½ hours, two daily).

⊙ Sights & Activities

Fort Bragg has the same banner North Coast activities as Mendocino – beachcombing, surfing, hiking – but basing yourself here is much cheaper and arguably less quaint and pretentious. The wharf lies at Noyo Harbor – the mouth of the Noyo River – south of downtown. Here you can find whale-watching cruises and deep-sea fishing trips.

★ Mendocino Coast Botanical Gardens   GARDENS
(☑707-964-4352; www.gardenbythesea.org; 18220 N Hwy 1; adult/child/senior $14/5/10; ☺9am-5pm Mar-Oct, to 4pm Nov-Feb; P) 🐾 This gem of Northern California displays native flora, rhododendrons and heritage roses. The succulent display alone is amazing and the organic garden is harvested by volunteers to feed area residents in need. The serpentine paths wander along 47 seafront acres south of town. Primary trails are wheelchair accessible.

Northcoast Artists Gallery   GALLERY
(www.northcoastartists.org; 362 N Main St; ☺10am-6pm) An excellent local arts cooperative where 20 full-time members work in photography, glass, woodworking, jewelry, painting, sculpture, textiles and printmaking. Openings are on the first Friday of the month. Visit www.mendocino.com for a comprehensive list of galleries throughout Mendocino County.

Glass Beach   BEACH
(Elm St) Named for (what's left of) the sea-polished glass in the sand, remnants of its days as a city dump, this beach is now part of MacKerricher State Park (p238). Take the headlands trail from Elm St, off Main St, but leave the glass – visitors are not supposed to pocket souvenirs.

Triangle Tattoo & Museum   MUSEUM
(☑707-964-8814; www.triangletattoo.com; 356b N Main St; ☺noon-7pm) FREE This one-off museum has an excellent exhibition of international tattoo art and explains the history in various cultures. You can also get a tattoo done here if you fancy.

★ Skunk Train   HISTORIC TRAIN
(☑707-964-6371; www.skunktrain.com; 100 W Laurel St; adult/child $84/42; ☺9am-3pm; 👶) Fort Bragg's pride and joy, the vintage train got its nickname in 1925 for its stinky gas-powered steam engines, but today the historic steam and diesel locomotives are odorless. Passing through redwood-forested mountains, along rivers, over bridges and through deep mountain tunnels, the trains run from both Fort Bragg and Willits (p249) to the midway point of Northspur, where they turn around.

If you want to go to Willits, plan to spend the night. The depot is downtown at the foot of Laurel St, one block west of Main St.

All-Aboard Adventures   FISHING, WHALE-WATCHING
(☑707-964-1881; www.allaboardadventures.com; 32400 N Harbor Dr; fishing trips $80, whale-watching $40) Captain Tim leads five-hour crabbing and salmon-fishing trips and two-hour whale-watching explorations during the whale migration.

☆☆ Festivals & Events

Fort Bragg Whale Festival   WILDLIFE
(www.mendowhale.com; ☺Mar) Held on the third weekend in March, with microbrew tastings, crafts fairs and whale-watching trips.

Paul Bunyan Days   CARNIVAL
(www.paulbunyandays.com; ☺Sep) Held on Labor Day weekend in September, celebrate California's logging history with a logging show, square dancing, parade and fair.

🛏 Sleeping

Fort Bragg's lodging is cheaper than Mendocino's, but most of the motels along noisy Hwy 1 don't have air-conditioning, so you'll hear traffic through your windows. The best of the motel bunch is **Colombi Motel**

(☑707-964-5773; www.colombimotel.com; 647 E Oak St; 1-/2-bedroom units with kitchenette from $80/85; ☻☎), which is in town. Most B&Bs do not have TVs and they all include breakfast.

Country Inn
B&B $$

(☑707-964-3737; www.beourguests.com; 632 N Main St; r $125-170; P☻☎☒) This gingerbread-trimmed B&B in the middle of town is an excellent way to dodge the chain motels for a good-value stay. The lovely family hosts are welcoming and easygoing and can offer good local tips. Breakfast can be delivered to your room and at night you can soak in a hot tub out back. There is a minimum two-night stay at weekends.

Grey Whale Inn
B&B $$

(☑707-964-0640; www.greywhaleinn.com; 615 N Main St; r $110-172; P☻☎) Situated in a historic (some say haunted!) building and former hospital on the north side of town (walking distance from downtown and glass beach), this comfortable, family-run inn has simple, straightforward rooms that are good value for families. Expect a warm welcome, especially from Sweetpea, the resident cat.

Shoreline Cottages
MOTEL, COTTAGE $$

(☑707-964-2977; www.shoreline-cottage.com; 18725 Hwy 1; d $129-149; P☻☎☒) Low-key, four-person rooms and cottages with kitchens surround a central, tree-filled lawn. The family rooms are a good bargain, and suites feature modern artwork and clean sight lines. All rooms have microwaves, cable TV, snacks and access to a library of DVDs, plus there's a communal hot tub.

Weller House Inn
B&B $$$

(☑707-964-4415; www.wellerhouse.com; 524 Stewart St; r $200-310; P☻☎) Rooms in this beautifully restored 1886 mansion have down comforters, underfloor heating, good mattresses and fine linens. The water tower is the tallest structure in town – and it has a hot tub at the top! Breakfast is in the massive redwood ballroom.

✗ Eating

Similar to the lodging scene, the food in Fort Bragg is less spendy than Mendocino, but there are a number of truly excellent options, mainly located on or around Main St. Self-caterers should try the farmers market (p238) downtown or the **Harvest Market** (☑707-964-7000; cnr Hwys 1 & 20; ☺5am-11pm) for the best groceries.

★ Taka's Japanese Grill
JAPANESE $

(☑707-964-5204; 250 N Main St; mains $10.50-17; ☺11:30am-3pm & 4:30-9pm; P) Although it may look fairly run of the mill, this is an exceptional Japanese restaurant. The owner is a former grader at the Tokyo fish market so the quality is tops and he makes a weekly run to San Francisco to source freshly imported seafood. Sushi, teriyaki dishes, noodle soups and pan-fried noodles with salmon, beef or chicken are just a few of the options.

Los Gallitos
MEXICAN $

(☑707-964-4519; 130 S Main St; burritos $5.50-6.50; ☺11am-8pm Mon-Sat, from 10am Sun) A packed hole-in-the-wall that serves the best Mexican on the coast. Chips are homemade, the guacamole is chunky and the dishes, from the fresh fish tacos to homemade pork tamales and generous soups, are consistently flavorful and well beyond the standard glob of refried beans. It's located across the parking lot from the CVS.

Cowlick's Handmade Ice Cream
ICE CREAM $

(☑707-962-9271; www.cowlicksicecream.com; 250b N Main St; scoops from $1.85; ☺11am-9pm) Just great ice cream in fun flavors, from classics such as mocha almond fudge to the very unusual, such as candy cap mushroom (tastes like maple syrup but better), ginger or blackberry chocolate chunk. The sorbets (try the grapefruit Campari) are also delish.

Headlands Coffeehouse
CAFE $

(☑707-964-1987; www.headlandscoffeehouse. com; 120 E Laurel St; mains $4-8; ☺7am-10pm Mon-Sat, to 7pm Sun; ☎☒) The town's best cafe is in the middle of the historic downtown, with high ceilings and lots of atmosphere. The menu gets raves for the Belgian waffles, homemade soups, veggie-friendly salads, panini and lasagna.

Silver's at the Wharf
CALIFORNIAN $

(☑707-964-4283; www.silversatthewharf.com; 32260 N Harbor Dr; mains $10-15; ☺11am-9:30pm; P☒) Given its position, overlooking the docks, you would expect this to be a swanky oysters-and-champagne sort of place. Far from it. The decor is stuck in the '60s and the cuisine is well prepared but solidly traditional, with a vast selection that includes pasta, rib-eye steak, Mexican fare and seafood, such as Pacific

NORTH COAST BEER TOUR

The craft breweries of the North Coast don't mess around – bold hop profiles, Belgian-style ales and smooth lagers are regional specialties, and they're produced with style. Some breweries are better than others, but the following tour makes for an excellent long weekend of beer tasting in the region.

Anderson Valley Brewing Company (p243), Boonville

North Coast Brewing Company (p238), Fort Bragg

Six Rivers Brewery (p263), near Arcata

Eel River Brewing (p256), Fortuna

Bay shrimp and calamari steak. Ideal for families.

Farmers Market   MARKET $
(cnr E Laurel & N Franklin Sts; ⊙3:30-6pm Wed May-Oct) This is an above-average farmers market with an excellent array of fresh produce, plus breads, preserves and locally produced cheese.

★**Piaci Pub & Pizzeria**   ITALIAN $$
(☑707-961-1133; www.piacipizza.com; 120 W Redwood Ave; mains $8-20; ⊙11am-9:30pm Mon-Thu, to 10pm Fri & Sat, 4-9:30pm Sun) Fort Bragg's must-visit pizzeria is known for its sophisticated wood-fired, brick-oven pizzas as much as for its long list of microbrews. Try the 'Gustoso' – with chèvre, pesto and seasonal pears, all carefully orchestrated on a thin crust. It's tiny, loud and fun, with much more of a bar atmosphere than a restaurant. Expect to wait at peak times.

North Coast Brewing Company   AMERICAN $$
(☑707-964-2739; www.northcoastbrewing.com; 455 N Main St; mains $17-25; ⊙restaurant 4-10pm Sun-Thu, to 11pm Fri & Sat, bar from 2pm daily; 🐾) Though thick, rare slabs of steak and a list of specials demonstrate that they take the food as seriously as the bevvies, it's the burgers and garlic fries that soak up the fantastic selection of handcrafted brews. A great stop for serious beer lovers.

★**Cucina Verona**   ITALIAN $$$
(☑707-964-6844; www.cucinaverona.com; 124 E Laurel St; mains $26-30; ⊙9am-9pm) A real-deal Italian restaurant with no-fail traditional dishes, plus a few with a Californian tweak, such as butternut-squash lasagne and artichoke bruschetta. The atmosphere is as comforting as the cuisine, with dim lighting, a warm color scheme and unobtrusive live music most evenings. There is an extensive microbrewery selection on offer, as well as local and imported wines.

☆ Entertainment

Gloriana Musical Theater   THEATER
(Eagles Hall Theater; ☑707-964-7469; www.gloriana.org; 210 N Corry St; tickets from $12; ⊙hours vary) Since 1976 this company has been staging high-standard musical theater and operettas.

🛍 Shopping

There's plenty of window-shopping in Fort Bragg's compact downtown, including a string of antique shops along Franklin St.

Fractalize Eco Boutique   FASHION & ACCESSORIES
(☑707-672-2208; www.fractalizeecoboutique.com; 107 E Laurel St; ⊙11am-5pm Wed-Sun) Sells a fabulous array of women's fashions in rich earth colors made with all-natural fabrics, including hemp and bamboo.

Outdoor Store   SPORTS & OUTDOORS
(☑707-964-1407; www.mendooutdoors.com; 247 N Main St; ⊙10am-5:30pm Mon-Sat, to 5pm Sun) If you're planning on camping on the coast or exploring the Lost Coast, this is the best outfitter in the region, stocking detailed maps of the region's wilderness areas, fuel for stoves and high-quality gear.

ℹ Information

Fort Bragg-Mendocino Coast Chamber of Commerce (☑707-961-6300; www.mendocinocoast.com; 332 S Main St; ⊙10am-5pm Mon-Fri, to 3pm Sat; 🐾) The chamber of commerce has lots of helpful information about this stretch of coast and what's on. Its online guide is also worth checking out.

MacKerricher State Park

Three miles north of Fort Bragg, the **MacKerricher State Park** (☑707-964-9112; www.parks.ca.gov) preserves 9 miles of pristine rocky headlands, sandy beaches, dunes and tidepools.

The visitor center sits next to the whale skeleton at the park entrance. Hike the

Coastal Trail along dark-sand beaches and see rare and endangered plant species. **Lake Cleone** is a 30-acre freshwater lake stocked with trout and visited by over 90 species of birds. At nearby **Laguna Point** an interpretive boardwalk (accessible to visitors with disabilities) overlooks harbor seals and, from December to April, migrating whales. **Ricochet Ridge Ranch** (☑707-964-7669; www.horse-vacation.com; 24201 N Hwy 1; per hr/day $60/330; ☺9am-6:30pm) offers horseback-riding trips through redwoods or along the beach.

Just north of the park is **Pacific Star Winery** (☑707-964-1155; www.pacificstarwinery.com; 33000 Hwy 1; tastings $5; ☺noon-5pm Thu-Mon), in a dramatic, rub-your-eyes-in-disbelief-beautiful location on a bluff over the sea. The wines don't get pros excited but they are very drinkable, the owners are friendly and you're encouraged to picnic at one of the many coast-side tables, stroll some of the short coastal trails along the cliffs and generally enjoy yourself (which isn't hard).

Popular **campgrounds** (☑800-444-2725; www.reserveamerica.com; tent & RV sites $35), nestled in pine forest, have hot showers and water; the first-choice reservable tent sites are numbers 21 to 59. Ten superb, secluded walk-in tent sites (numbers 1 to 10) are first-come, first-served.

Westport

If sleepy Westport feels like the peaceful edge of nowhere, that's because it is. The last hamlet before the Lost Coast, on a twisting 15-mile drive north of Fort Bragg, it is the last town before Hwy 1 veers inland on the 22-mile ascent to meet Hwy 101 in Leggett. The population here is around 60 and the town today consists of little more than a couple of choice places to stay, a fine pub, a small grocer and deli, and a couple of gas pumps. Westport dates from 1877 when it was called Beall's Landing after a (long-gone) timber loading facility built by Samuel Beall, the town's first white settler.

Head 1.5 miles north of town for the ruggedly beautiful **Westport-Union Landing State Beach** (☑707-937-5804; 40501 Hwy 1; tent sites $25; P⊞), which extends for 3 miles on coastal bluffs. A rough hiking trail leaves the primitive campground and passes by tidepools and streams, accessible at low tide.

🛏 Sleeping & Eating

Westport Inn　　　　　　　　　INN $
(☑707-964-5135; www.westportinnca.com; 37040 Hwy 1, Shoreline Hwy; r from $80; P⊖🐾) Dating from the 1970s, this simple place to stay has beach access and recently refurbished, pleasant rooms with fresh flowers and nice art work. The owner is charming and can provide meals on request.

★**Westport Hotel & Old Abalone Pub**　　　　　　INN $$
(☑877-964-3688; www.westporthotel.us; 38921 Hwy 1, Shoreline Hwy; r $150-245; P⊖🛜) Westport Hotel & Old Abalone Pub is quiet enough to have a motto that brags 'You've finally found nowhere.' The rooms are sumptuous – feather duvets, hardwood furniture, plush carpeting – with excellent views. The classy historic pub downstairs is the only option for dinner, so be thankful it's a delicious sampling of whimsical California fusions and hearty, expertly presented pub food.

Howard Creek Ranch　　　　CABIN $$
(☑707-964-6725; www.howardcreekranch.com; 40501 N Hwy 1, Shoreline Hwy; r $90-198, cabins $105-198; P⊖🛜🐾) Howard Creek Ranch, sitting on 60 stunning acres of forest and farmland abutting the wilderness, has accommodations in an 1880s farmhouse or a few cabins including a carriage barn, whose way-cool redwood rooms have been expertly handcrafted by the owner. Rates include full breakfast. Bring hiking boots, not high heels.

ALONG HIGHWAY 101

To get into the most remote and wild parts of the North Coast on the quick, eschew winding Hwy 1 for inland Hwy 101, which runs north from San Francisco as a freeway, then as a two- or four-lane highway north of Sonoma County, occasionally pausing under the traffic lights of small towns.

Know that escaping the Bay Area at rush hour (weekdays between 4pm and 7pm) ain't easy. You might sit bumper-to-bumper through Santa Rosa or Willits, where trucks bound for the coast turn onto Hwy 20.

Although Hwy 101 may not look as enticing as the coastal route, it's faster and less winding, leaving you time along the way to detour into Sonoma and Mendocino Counties' wine regions (Mendocino claims to be the greenest wine region in the country), explore pastoral Anderson Valley, splash about Clear Lake or soak at hot-springs resorts outside Ukiah – time well spent indeed!

Hopland

Apparently using the most solar power per capita in the world, Hopland flaunts its eco-geek, green-living ways at every turn with more organic produce available than you can shake a carrot stick at, plus a sustainable-living demonstration site, complete with a bio-fuel pump that recycles vegetable oil from local restaurants! Hops were first grown here in 1866, but Prohibition brought the industry temporarily to a halt. Today, with its location as a gateway to Mendocino County's wine country, booze drives Hopland's economy again, with wine tasting the primary draw. Most of the tasting rooms are conveniently located right on Hwy 101, which runs through the center of town, and are generally small, boutique-style operations offering an enjoyable personalized experience.

◉ Sights

For an excellent weekend trip, use Hopland as a base for exploring the regional wineries. More information about the constantly growing roster of wineries is available at www.destinationhopland.com. Find a map to the wine region at www.visitmendocino.com.

Brutocao Cellars TASTING ROOM
(☑800-433-3689; www.brutocaocellars.com; 13500 S Hwy 101; ☉10am-5pm; ℗) FREE Located in a former 1920s schoolhouse in central Hopland, this fourth-generation family-owned winery has bocce courts, bold red wines and chocolate – a perfect combo. There is also, refreshingly, no charge for wine tasting here (although there is generally a limit to how much tippling you can do!). The gift shop specializes in gourmet goodies, great for gifts.

Real Goods Solar Living Center MUSEUM
(☑707-742-2460; www.solarliving.org; 13771 S Hwy 101; self-guided tour free, guided tour per person/family $3/5, wine tasting $5; ☉center 9am-6pm daily, tours 11am & 3pm Sat & Sun Apr-Oct; ℗⊞) ✐ This progressive, futuristic 12-acre campus is largely responsible for

the area's bold green initiatives. The Real Goods Store, run by the same company that sold the first solar panel in the US in 1978, is an impressive straw-bale-house showroom. You can also enjoy an exhibition on permaculture and a demonstration of solar-powered water systems. Plus, on the off chance your car runs on bio-diesel, you can fill up your tank here.

Graziano Family of Wines WINERY
(☑707-744-8466; www.grazianofamilyofwines.com; 13251 S Hwy 101; ☉10am-5pm; ℗) FREE The Italian Graziano family is one of the oldest grape-growing families in Mendocino County and specializies in 'Cal-Ital' wines – including Primitivo, Dolcetto, Barbera and Sangiovese – at some great prices. Wine tasting is complimentary.

Saracina Vineyards WINERY
(☑707-670-0199; www.saracina.com; 11684 S Hwy 101; tasting & tour $15; ☉11am-5pm; ℗) ✐ The highlight of a tour here is the descent into the cool caves. Sensuous whites are all bio-dynamically and sustainably farmed.

🛏 Sleeping & Eating

Piazza de Campovida INN $$
(☑707-744-1977; www.piazzadecampovida.com; 13441 S Hwy 101; ste $185-220; ℗⊞🐾) Modern Californian meets Italian at this very comfortable inn where all of the spacious suites have Jacuzzis, fireplaces and private balconies. The homey taverna and pizzeria in front have big tables for communal dining and fantastic artisanal pizzas, craft beer and wine.

Burger My Way BURGERS $
(☑707-744-8762; 13600 Mountain House Rd, 76 Gas Station; burgers $6-8; ☉8am-9pm; ℗⊞) Look beyond the surroundings (this place is attached to a gas station) and instead concentrate on the quality of burgers, with some 17 varieties, including vegetarian, turkey and salmon. The fries are hand cut and crispy and there are non-burger options too, including a selection of Mexican dishes, sandwiches and salads. But it's the burgers that will have you salivating...

Bluebird Cafe DINER $
(☑707-744-1633; 13340 S Hwy 101; breakfast $11-13, lunch mains $10-15; ☉7am-2pm Mon-Thu, to 7pm Fri-Sun; ⊞) This classic American diner serves hearty breakfasts and homemade pie (the summer selection of peach-blueberry pie is dreamy). For a more

exciting culinary adventure, try the wild-game burgers, such as elk, with a bite of horseradish.

Clear Lake

With over 100 miles of shoreline and 68 square miles of surface area, Clear Lake is the largest naturally occurring freshwater lake in California (Tahoe is bigger, but crosses the Nevada state line). In summer the warm water thrives with algae, giving it a murky green appearance and creating a fabulous habitat for fish, especially bass and catfish, so you can expect plenty of anglers here, particularly on weekends. Mt Konocti, a 4200ft-tall dormant volcano, lords over the scene. The lake is ringed by small, tasteful resorts with places to stay, dine and kick back enjoying the lake views. You can also rent boats, kayaks, paddleboards and just about anything else that floats on the water at one of several marinas. On a more somber note, the area was devastated by fire in the summer of 2015 with Middletown, in particular, being badly affected; a vigorous rebuilding program continues.

Locals refer to the northwest portion as 'upper lake' and the southeast portion as 'lower lake.' Likeable and well-serviced **Lakeport** (population 4695) sits on the

northwest shore, a 45-minute drive east of Hopland along Hwy 175 (off Hwy 101); tiny, Old West style **Kelseyville** (population 3353) is 7 miles south. **Clearlake**, off the southeastern shore, is the biggest town.

Hwy 20 links the relatively bland northshore hamlets of **Nice** (the northernmost town) and **Lucerne**, 4 miles southeast. **Middletown**, a cute village, lies 20 miles south of Clearlake at the junction of Hwys 175 and 29, 40 minutes north of Calistoga.

◉ Sights

Clear Lake State Park   STATE PARK
(☑707-279-2267, 707-279-4293; www.clearlake statepark.org; 5300 Soda Bay Rd, Kelseyville; per car $8; ☺sunrise-sunset; 🅿🐾) Four miles from Kelseyville, on the lake's southern shore, this park is idyllic and gorgeous, with hiking trails, fishing, boating and camping. The bird-watching is extraordinary. The visitor center has natural history and cultural diorama exhibits.

🛏 Sleeping & Eating

For the greatest range of places to stay, head to Lakeport, where most accommodations are conveniently located on and around Main St. Be sure to make reservations ahead on weekends and during summer, when people flock to the cool water. There

---

TOP CLEAR LAKE WINERIES

These four wineries are the best; some offer tours by appointment.

Kaz Winery (☑707-833-2536; www.kazwinery.com; 1435 Big Valley Rd, Lakeport; tasting $5-10; ☺11am-5pm Sat or by appointment; 🅿) A cult favorite, supercool Kaz is about blends: whatever is in the organic vineyards goes into the wine – and they're blended at crush, not during fermentation. Expect lesser-known varietals like Tannat and Lenoir, and worthwhile cabernet-merlot blends. Bottles cost $26 to $45.

Brassfield Estate (☑707-998-1895; www.brassfieldestate.com; 10915 High Valley Rd, Clearlake Oaks; tasting $5; ☺11am-5pm May-Nov, from noon Dec-Apr; 🅿) Remote, stunning Tuscan villa in the unique High Valley appellation surrounded by magnificent landscaped gardens.

Wildhurst (☑707-279-4302; www.wildhurst.com; 3855 Main St, Kelseyville; ☺10am-5pm; 🅿) Looking like a Western movie set, downtown Kelseyville is where family-owned winery tasting rooms such as Wildhurst (tasting free) rustle beside hardware stores, soda fountains and cafes.

Langtry Estate Vineyards (☑707-995-7521; www.langtryestate.com; 21000 Butts Canyon Rd, Middletown; tasting $5, tours from $60; ☺11am-5pm; 🅿) This winery has a stunning location on a hilltop overlooking the lake with picnic tables available for anyone who wants to pack a lunch. Visitors can opt for a wine tasting of six wines, a tasting plus tour, a vineyard tour or a historical tour that includes a wine tasting with appetizers at the nearby Lillie Langry mansion; the famous late actress owned the vineyard and house from 1888 until 1906.

are several campsites close to the lake, although be aware that they can flood if there are heavy rains, so always check in advance. For the budget conscious, Lakeport also has the most affordable options.

Clearlake

Visto del Lago Lakehouse CABIN $$
(707-356-9721; www.vdlresort.com; 14103 Lakeshore Dr, Clearlake; cottages $75-179; P🐕😊🛜) Located right on the main road, so handy for shops and restaurants, these clean-as-a-whistle cottages are a delight. Sizes and facilities vary greatly, but all have well-equipped kitchenettes and are comfortably furnished. Other options may include hot tubs, fireplaces and Netflix; one cabin even has its own pool table. There is an outside Jacuzzi, swing chair and barbecue right on the lake.

Lakeport & Kelseyville

There are a number of motels along the main drags in Kelseyville and Lakeport, but if you want fresh air, Clear Lake State Park has four **campgrounds** (800-444-7275; www.reserveamerica.com; State Park Rd; tent & RV sites $35; 🕐year round; P🚻🐕) with showers. The weekly **farmers market** (www.clearlakefarmersmarket.com/; Hwy 29 & Thomas Dr; 🕐8:30am-noon Sat Jun-Oct) is in Kelseyville.

★Lakeport English Inn B&B $$
(707-263-4317; www.lakeportenglishinn.com; 675 N Main St, Lakeport; r $185-210, cottages $210; P🐕😊🛜) The finest B&B at Clear Lake is an 1875 Carpenter Gothic with 10 impeccably furnished rooms, styled with a nod to the English countryside and with such quaint names as the Prince of Wales or (wait for it) Roll in the Hay. Weekends take high tea (nonguests welcome by reservation), with scones and real Devonshire cream.

★Angelina's Bakery & Espresso CAFE $
(707-263-0391; www.angelinas365.com; 365 N Main St, Lakeport; sandwiches from $5; 🕐7am-5pm Mon-Fri, 8am-2pm Sat; 🛜) The best baked goodies in Clear Lake, especially the giant decadent muffins and gooey cinnamon rolls. Also makes sandwiches to order and serves savory pastries. The coffee is the real McCoy, with a caffeine kick that should set you up for the day.

Park Place AMERICAN $
(707-263-0444; www.parkplacelakeport.com; 50 3rd St, Lakeport; mains $7-11; 🕐11am-9pm Tue-Sun, to 3pm Mon; P) Simple but right on the waterfront, come to this bright and completely unpretentious eatery for basics like pasta, burgers and pizza made from sustainable, local produce at great prices. A local favorite.

Studebaker's Coffee House DELI $
(707-279-8871; 3990 Main St, Kelseyville; sandwiches from $6; 🕐6am-4pm Mon-Fri, 7am-4pm Sat, 7am-2pm Sun) A friendly, old-style diner with plenty of character, from black-and-white checker linoleum floors to old photos on the wall. Great sandwiches, including vegetarian options, plus Mexican fare such as quesadillas and burritos; the coffee's good too.

★Saw Shop Bistro CALIFORNIAN $$
(707-278-0129; www.sawshopbistro.com; 3825 Main St, Kelseyville; small plates $10-16, mains $15-26; 🕐11:30am-10pm Tue-Sat; 🛜) The best restaurant in Lake County serves a California-cuisine menu of wild salmon and rack of lamb, as well as a small-plates menu of sushi, lobster tacos, Kobe-beef burgers and flatbread pizzas. Laid-back atmosphere, too. Reservations recommended.

Northshore

Tallman Hotel HISTORIC HOTEL $$
(information 707-275-2244, reservations 707-275-2245; www.tallmanhotel.com; 9550 Main St, Upper Lake; r $185-265; P🐕🚻🛜) 🍴 The centerpiece may be the smartly renovated historic hotel – tile bathrooms, warm lighting, thick linens – but the rest of the property's lodging, including the shady garden, walled-in swimming pool, brick patios and porches, exudes timeless elegance. Some garden rooms come with outdoor Japanese soaking tubs heated by an energy-efficient geothermal-solar system.

Featherbed Railroad Co HOTEL $$
(707-274-8378; www.featherbedrailroad.com; 2870 Lakeshore Blvd, Nice; cabooses $175-220; 😊🚻🐕) A treat for train buffs and kids, Featherbed has 10 comfy, real cabooses on a grassy lawn. Some of the cabooses straddle the border between kitschy and tacky (the 'Easy Rider' has a Harley-Davidson headboard and a mirrored ceiling), but they're great fun if you keep a sense of humor. There's a tiny beach across the road.

Sea Breeze Resort COTTAGE $$

(☎707-998-3327; www.seabreezeresort.net; 9595 Harbor Dr, Glenhaven; cottages $125-180; ☺Apr-Oct; P🐾❄️🛜) Just south of Lucerne on a small peninsula, lush green gardens surround seven spotless lakeside cottages. All but one have full kitchens.

Drinking & Nightlife

Library Park, in Lakeport, has free lakeside Friday-evening summer concerts, with blues and rockabilly tunes to appeal to road-trippers.

Kelsey Creek Brewing BREWERY

(☎707-279-2311; www.kelseycreekbrewing.com; 3945 Main St, Kelseyville; ☺2-8pm Mon-Fri, noon-8pm Sat, noon-6pm Sun) A 'hop'-ping fun local's scene with excellent craft beer, peanut shells on the floor and a bring-your-own-food, bring-your-dog kind of laid-back vibe.

☆ Entertainment

Lakeport Auto Movies CINEMA

(www.lakeportautomovies.com; 52 Soda Bay Rd, Lakeport; 1/2/3 people per car $10/18/25; ☺Fri & Sat Apr-Sep; 👶) Lakeport is home to one of the few surviving and wonderfully nostalgic drive-in movie theaters, with showings on Friday and Saturday nights.

ℹ Information

Lake County Visitor Information Center

(☎800-525-3743; www.lakecounty.com; 255 N Forbes St, Lakeport; ☺9am-5pm Mon-Sat, noon-4pm Sun) Has complete information and an excellent website, which allows potential visitors to narrow their focus by interests.

ℹ Getting Around

Lake Transit (☎707-994-3334, 707-263-3334; www.laketransit.org; 9240 Highway 53, Lower Lake) Operates weekday routes between Middletown, Calistoga and St Helena ($5, 35 minutes, three daily). Buses serve Ukiah ($8, two hours, four daily), from Clearlake via Lakeport ($5, 1¼ hours, seven daily). Since piecing together routes and times can be difficult, it's best to phone ahead.

Anderson Valley

A one-time redwood-logging community, rolling hills surround pocket-size Anderson Valley, more famous today for the apple orchards, vineyards, pastures and its general air of tranquility. Visitors come primarily to winery-hop; the winery scene here has been compared to the Napa Valley some 30 years ago. Most of the wineries are clustered between Boonville and Navarro, but you'll also find good hiking and cycling in the hills and the chance to escape civilization (although weekends can get busy with San Franciscans escaping the clamor of the city). Other things to check out include the craft breweries and the farmstead cheeses; look for signs on the roadside. Cheese is also sold at several of the vineyards and agreeably available for tasting along with the wine. Traveling through the valley is the most common route to Mendocino and Fort Bragg from San Francisco.

Boonville (population 1488) and **Philo** (population 349) are the valley's principal towns. From Ukiah, winding Hwy 253 heads 20 miles south to Boonville. Equally scenic Hwy 128 twists and turns 60 miles between Cloverdale on Hwy 101, south of Hopland, and Albion on coastal Hwy 1.

◉ Sights & Activities

Philo Apple Farm FARM

(☎707-895-2333; www.philoapplefarm.com; 18501 Greenwood Rd, Philo; ☺10am-5pm; P👶) 🍎 For the best fruit, skip the obvious roadside stands and head to this gorgeous farm for organic preserves, chutneys, heirloom apples and pears, as well as a tasteful array of homeware and furniture. For overnight guests, the farm also hosts **cooking classes**. You can make a weekend out of it by staying in one of the Philo Apple Farm Guest Cottages (p245).

Anderson Valley Brewing Company BREWERY

(☎707-895-2337; www.avbc.com; 17700 Hwy 253, Boonville; tasting from $2, tours & disc-golf course free; ☺11am-6pm Sat-Thu, to 7pm Fri; P👶) 🍎 East of the Hwy 128 crossroads, this solar-powered brewery crafts award-winning beers in a Bavarian-style brewhouse. You can also toss around a Frisbee on the **disc-golf course** while enjoying the brews, but, be warned, the sun can take its toll. Tours leave at 1:30pm daily (no reservations).

Anderson Valley Historical Society Museum MUSEUM

(☎707-895-3207; www.andersonvalleymuseum.org; 12340 Hwy 128, Boonville; ☺1-4pm Sat & Sun Feb-Nov; P) 🆓 Situated in a tastefully renovated red schoolhouse west of Boonville, this museum displays historical artifacts, including an interesting display centered on the Pomos (an indigenous Native American tribe who once populated this region and were famed for their beautiful woven baskets). You can examine the works here, ranging from 4ft-to-5ft storage baskets to tiny intricate examples barely the size of a finger tip.

✦✦ Festivals & Events

Pinot Noir Festival
WINE

(☎707-895-9463; www.avwines.com; Goldeneye Winery, Philo; ⊙May) One of Anderson Valley's many wine celebrations; held over four days toward the end of May.

Sierra Nevada World Music Festival
MUSIC

(www.snwmf.com; Mendocino County Fairgrounds, 14400 Hwy 128, Boonville; ⊙mid-Jun) In the middle of June, over three days, the sounds of reggae and roots fill the air, co-mingling with the scent of Mendocino County's *other* cash crop.

Mendocino County Fair & Apple Show
FAIR

(www.mendocountyfair.com; Mendocino County Fairgrounds, 14400 Hwy 128, Boonville; adult/child $9/6; ⊙mid-Sep; ⊛) A county classic autumnal fair with wine tasting, a rodeo and lively parades.

⛏ Sleeping

Overall the accommodation options are in the midrange to high-end categories, catering to San Franciscan weekenders seeking a self-pampering break with wine tasting, vineyard views and Egyptian-cotton sheets thrown in. If you are looking for somewhere more family and budget friendly, there are some excellent campsites in the valley, some with cabin accommodation available. The Anderson Valley Chamber of Commerce can advise on places to stay throughout the region.

Hendy Woods State Park
CAMPGROUND $

(☎707-937-5804, reservations 800-444-7275; www.reserveamerica.com; Hwy 128; tent & RV sites $40, cabins $60; ℗) Bordered by the Navarro River on Hwy 128, west of Philo, this lovely park has hiking, picnicking and a forested campground with hot showers.

Other Place
COTTAGE $$

(Sheep Dung Properties; ☎707-895-3979; www.sheepdung.com; 14655 CA-128, Boonville; cottages $190-350; ℗⊖⊛⊙) Located outside of town on a ridge with blissful panoramic and vineyard views, the 500 acres of ranch land here surround private, fully equipped hilltop cottages. The owners also hire out a cottage in downtown Boonville that shares access to the ranch with its picturesque views and walking trails.

★ Boonville Hotel
BOUTIQUE HOTEL $$$

(☎707-895-2210; www.boonvillehotel.com; 14050 Hwy 128, Boonville; d $295-365; ℗⊖⊛⊙) Decked out in a contemporary American country feel with sea-grass flooring, pastel colors and fine linens, this historic hotel's rooms and suites are safe for urbanites who refuse to abandon style just because they've gone to the country. The rooms are all different and there are agreeable extras, including hammocks and fireplaces.

TOP ANDERSON VALLEY WINERIES

The valley's cool nights yield high-acid, fruit-forward, food-friendly wines. Pinot Noir, Chardonnay and dry Gewürztraminer flourish. Most wineries (www.avwines.com) sit outside Philo. Many are family-owned and offer free tastings; some give tours. The following are particularly noteworthy:

Navarro Vineyards (☎707-895-3686; www.navarrowine.com; 5601 Hwy 128, Philo; ⊙8am-6pm Mon-Fri, to 5pm Sat & Sun; ℗) The best option around with award-winning Pinot Noir and dry Gewürztraminer; has twice-daily free tours (reservations accepted) and picnicking facilities.

Husch Vineyards (☎707-462-5370; www.huschvineyards.com; 4400 Hwy 128, Philo; ⊙10am-6pm, to 5pm Nov-Mar; ℗) The oldest vineyard in the valley serves exquisite tastings inside a rose-covered cottage.

Bink Wines (☎707-895-2940; www.binkwines.com; 9000 Hwy 128, Philo; ⊙11am-5pm Wed-Mon; ℗) This winery produces small-batch artisanal wines that get rave reviews. Bink is located within the Med-style Madrones complex, which houses a total of four local vintners, as well as a hotel, restaurant and gift shop.

★Philo Apple Farm Guest Cottages
COTTAGE $$$

(☑707-895-2333; www.philoapplefarm.com; 18501 Greenwood Rd, Philo; d $250-300; P➘) ⬧ Set within the orchard, guests of bucolic Philo Apple Farm (p243) choose from four exquisite cottages, each built with reclaimed materials. With bright, airy spaces, polished plank floors, simple furnishings and views of the surrounding trees, each one is an absolute dream.

Red Door cottage is a favorite because of the bathroom – you can soak in the slipper tub, or shower on the private deck under the open sky. The cottages often get booked with participants of the farm's cooking classes, so book well in advance. For a swim, the Navarro River is within walking distance.

Madrones
HOTEL $$$

(☑707-895-2955; www.themadrones.com; 9000 Hwy 128, Philo; r $175-350; P➘➘) Tucked off the back of the Madrones Mediterranean-inspired complex that includes a restaurant and the wonderful Bink Wines tasting room, the spacious 'guest quarters' here are modern-country-luxe, with a tinge of Tuscany. Above all, they are eminently comfortable with plush furnishings, marshmallow-soft pillows, soft carpeting and a soothing color scheme.

✕ Eating

Boonville restaurants seem to open and close as they please, so expect hours to vary based on season and whims. There are several places along Hwy 128 which can supply a picnic with fancy local cheese and fresh bread. Locally grown produce is the norm in these parts, so you can expect organic seasonal veg and a pleasing lack of fast-food options. Nope, gourmet burgers don't count.

Paysanne
ICE CREAM $

(☑707-895-2210; www.sweetpaysanne.com; 14111 Hwy 128, Boonville; ice cream from $2.50; ⊙10am-6pm Sun-Thu; ⬧⬧) Boonville's fantastic sweets shop serves the innovative flavors of Three Twins Ice Cream, whose delightful choices include Lemon Cookie and Strawberry Je Ne Sais Quoi (which has a hint of balsamic vinegar); it's the best ice cream to be found in the Anderson Valley according to the locals – and they know best.

Boonville General Store
DELI $

(☑707-895-9477; 17810 Farrer Lane, Boonville; dishes $7-14; ⊙7:30am-3pm Mon-Thu, 7:30am-3pm & 5:30-8pm Fri, 8:30am-3pm Sat & Sun; P⬧) ⬧ Opposite the Boonville Hotel, this superb deli is good to stock up for picnics, offering gourmet sandwiches on homemade bread, thin-crust pizzas and organic cheeses. It also serves hearty homemade soups if you feel like grabbing a pew, as well as scrumptious breakfasts. Organic produce is used as far as possible and there are plenty of vegetarian options.

★Table 128
CALIFORNIAN $$

(☑707-895-2210; www.boonvillehotel.com; 14050 Hwy 128, Boonville; lunch mains $10-14, dinner mains $19-31; ⊙6-8pm Thu-Mon Apr–mid-Jun, from 4:30pm mid-Jun–mid-Oct; P➘) Food-savvy travelers love the constantly changing New American menu here, featuring simple dishes done well, like Alaskan turbot, grilled local lamb, and cheesecake. The family-style service makes dinner a free-wheeling, elegant social affair, with big farm tables and soft lighting. It's got great wines, craft beers, scotch and cocktails.

❶ Information

Anderson Valley Chamber of Commerce
(☑707-895-2379; www.andersonvalley chamber.com; 9800 Hwy 128, Boonville; ⊙9am-5pm Mon-Fri) Has tourist information and a complete schedule of annual events, plus can also advise on places to stay, including campsites.

Ukiah

As the county seat and Mendocino's largest city, Ukiah is mostly a utilitarian stop for travelers to refuel the car and get a bite. But, if you have to stop here for the night, you could do much worse: the town is a friendly place that's gentrifying. There is a plethora of cookie-cutter hotel chains, some cheaper mid-century motels and a handful of very good dining options. The coolest attractions, a pair of thermal springs and a sprawling campus for Buddhist studies complete with 10,000 golden Buddha statues, lie outside the city limits. There are also some excellent wineries and tasting rooms within easy access from the center; the helpful **Chamber of Commerce** (☑707-462-4705; www.gomendo.com; 200 S School St; ⊙9am-5pm Mon-Fri) can point you in the right direction. Ukiah has a pleasant, walkable shopping district along School St near the courthouse, where you can find some idiosyncratic small shops and larger chains.

◉ Sights

Grace Hudson Museum & Sun House
MUSEUM

(🖉707-467-2836; www.gracehudsonmuseum. org; 431 S Main St; $4; ⊙10am-4:30pm Wed-Sat, from noon Sun) One block east of State St, the collection's mainstays are paintings by Grace Hudson (1865–1937). Her sensitive depictions of Pomo people and other indigenous groups complement the ethnological work and Native American baskets collected by her husband, John Hudson. The lovely 1911 Sun House, adjacent to the museum, was the former Hudson home and is typical of the arts-and-crafts style of that era; docent-guided tours are available.

✷ Festivals & Events

Redwood Empire Fair
FAIR

(🖉707-462-3884; www.redwoodempirefair.com; 1055 N State St; ⊙Jun & Aug; ⚑) There are two major fairs held here: the Redwood Empire Spring Fair, held over a weekend in early June, and the Redwood Empire Fair, held over a weekend in early August. Both have loads of events, ranging from quilt exhibitions to garden expos.

Ukiah Country PumpkinFest
CULTURAL

(www.cityofukiah.com; ⊙late Oct; ⚑) In late October, with an arts-and-crafts fair, children's carnival and a fiddle contest.

🛏 Sleeping

Hampton Inn
MOTEL $$

(🖉707-462-6555; www.hamptoninn3.hilton.com; 1160 Airport Park Blvd; r $125-175; ▣❈✿❀) The best of the chain gang in Ukiah, with a whiff of a Hilton about it (Hampton is now part of the Hilton portfolio). Expect excellent amenities, including a fitness center and comprehensive offerings for the business bunch. The recently updated rooms may still be hotel-chain bland but are comfortable, carpeted and spacious.

✗ Eating

It'd be a crime to eat the fast-food junk located off the highway; Ukiah has a burgeoning food scene that pairs nicely with the surrounding wine country.

★ Schat's Bakery & Cafe
CAFE $

(🖉707-462-1670; www.schats.com; 113 W Perkins St; lunch mains $5-8, dinner mains $8-14; ⊙5:30am-6pm Mon-Fri, to 5pm Sat) Founded by Dutch bakers, Schat's makes a dazzling array of chewy, dense breads, sandwiches, wraps, big salads, dee-lish hot mains, full breakfasts and homemade pastries.

Kilkenny Kitchen
CAFE $

(🖉707-462-2814; www.kilkennykitchen.com; 1093 S Dora St; sandwiches $8; ⊙10am-3pm Mon-Fri; ✦⚑) Tucked into a neighborhood south of downtown, county workers love this chipper yellow place for the fresh rotation of daily soups and sandwich specials (a recent visit on a blazing-hot day found a heavenly, cold spinach and dill soup). The salads – like the cranberry, spinach with pecans and feta cheese – are also fantastic, and there's a kid's menu.

★ Saucy Ukiah
PIZZA $$

(🖉707-462-7007; www.saucyukiah.com; 108 W Standley St; pizzas $14-19, mains $13-19; ⊙11:30am-9pm Mon-Thu, to 10pm Fri, noon-10pm Sat) Yes there are arty pizzas with toppings like organic fennel pollen and almond basil pesto but there are also amazing soups, salads, pastas and starters – Nana's meatballs are to die for and the 'kicking' minestrone lives up to its name. The small-town ambience is mildly chic but fun and informal at the same time.

Oco Time
JAPANESE $$

(🖉707-462-2422; www.ocotime.com; 111 W Church St; lunch mains $7-10, dinner mains $8-19; ⊙11:15am-2:30pm Tue-Fri, 5:30-8:30pm Mon-Sat; ✦) Shoulder your way through the locals to get Ukiah's best sushi, noodle bowls and oco (a delicious combo of seaweed, grilled cabbage, egg and noodles). The 'Peace Café' has a great vibe, friendly staff and interesting special rolls. Downside? The place gets mobbed, so reservations are a good idea.

Patrona
MODERN AMERICAN $$

(🖉707-462-9181; www.patronarestaurant.com; 130 W Standley St; lunch mains $10-16, dinner mains $15-34; ⊙11am-9pm Sun-Thu, to 10pm Fri & Sat) 🌿 Foodies flock to excellent Patrona for earthy, flavor-packed, seasonal and regional organic cooking in super stylish surrounds. The unfussy menu includes dishes such as roasted chicken, brined-and-roasted pork chops and housemade pasta, as well as local wines. Reservations recommended at weekends.

Ukiah Garden Cafe CALIFORNIAN **$$**
(☑707-462-1221; 1090 S State St; mains $17-
24; ⊙11am-9pm Tue-Fri, from 4pm Mon & Sat;
📶) Meat lovers will be swooning at the
top-quality steaks, roast prime rib and lamb
and pork chops here. The chicken dishes
are also winners but vegetarians will have
to stick to the appetizers: think homemade
fried mozzarella sticks or crispy zucchini
with a creamy dip.

Himalayan Cafe NEPALI **$$**
(☑707-467-9900; www.thehimalayancafe.com; 1639
S State St; mains $15-18; ⊙5-9pm Mon,11am-3pm
Tue-Sat) South of downtown, find delicately
spiced Nepalese cooking – think tandoori
breads and curries, including plenty of vegetarian options. Some Sundays there's a Nepalese buffet at 4pm.

Drinking & Nightlife

Dive bars and scruffy cocktail lounges line
State St, especially to the north of town.
For a wider and marginally classier selection, head to S State St and the surrounding
streets.

Black Oak Coffee Roasters CAFE
(☑866-390-1427; www.blackoakcoffee.com; 476
N State St; ⊙6:30am-6pm Mon-Fri, 7am-5pm Sat
& Sun; 🛜) A big modern coffee house that
roasts its own beans with some interesting
and delicious choices such as a *café borgia
latté* with artisan chocolate and orange essence or, for tea lovers, a *matcha chia* milk-
shake. Light breakfasts and lunches are also
on offer.

❶ Information

Army Corps of Engineers (☑707-462-7581;
www.spn.usace.army.mil/mendocino; 1160
Lake Mendocino Dr; ⊙8am-4pm Mon-Fri
May-Sep) The visitor center here can provide
information about Lake Mendocino, including
hiking and biking trails, as well as boating and
campsites.

Bureau of Land Management (☑707-
468-4000; www.blm.gov; 2550 N State St;
⊙10am-5pm Mon-Fri) Maps and information
on backcountry camping, hiking and biking in
wilderness areas.

❶ Getting Around

Mendocino Transit Authority (☑707-462-
1422; www.mendocinotransit.org; 241 Plant
Rd) The Mendocino Transit Authority runs a
sparse bus service covering major towns in the
Mendocino region.

Around Ukiah

Vichy Springs Resort

This **spa resort** (☑707-462-9515; www.vichy
springs.com; 2605 Vichy Springs Rd; s $175-235, d
$235-285, ste s/d $255/315, cottages from $325;
📶😊❄🛜🐾) offers a tranquil retreat with
a choice of rooms and suites in a historic
1870s inn with a shared terrace overlooking
sweeping lawns. The cottages are airy and
light with floral fabrics and light pine decor
and a fully equipped kitchen. Guests can enjoy the spa facilities as well as hiking trails
on the 700-acre property.

Vichy is the oldest continuously operating mineral-springs spa in California. The
water's composition perfectly matches that
of its famous namesake in Vichy, France. A
century ago, Mark Twain, Jack London and
Robert Louis Stevenson traveled here for the
water's restorative properties, which amelio-
rate everything from arthritis to poison oak.

Today, the historic resort has the only
warm-water, naturally carbonated mineral
baths in North America. Unlike others, Vichy requires swimsuits (rentals $3). Day use
(for guests and non-guests) costs $35 for two
hours, $65 for a full day.

Facilities include a swimming pool, outdoor mineral hot tub, 14 indoor and outdoor
tubs with natural 100°F (38°C) waters, and
a grotto for sipping the effervescent waters.
Massages and facials are available. The resort's hiking trails lead to a 40ft waterfall, an
old cinnabar mine and 1100ft peaks – great
for sunset views.

Orr Hot Springs

A soak in the thermal waters of the rustic
Orr Hot Springs resort (☑707-462-6277;
www.orrhotsprings.org; 13201 Orr Springs Rd;
day-use adult/child $30/25; ⊙by appointment
10am-10pm) is heavenly. While it's not for
the bashful, the clothing-optional resort is
beloved by locals, back-to-the-land hipsters,
backpackers and liberal-minded tourists.
Still, you don't have to let it all hang out. Enjoy the private tubs, a sauna, a spring-fed,
rock-bottomed swimming pool, steam room,
massage and magical gardens. Soaking in
the rooftop stargazing tubs on a clear night
is magical. Make reservations.

You can stay here in one of the elegantly
rustic **accommodations** (☑707-462-6277;
www.orrhotsprings.org; 13201 Orr Springs Rd; tent

site per adult/child $70/25, r & yurt $210, cottages $280; P⊝≋). Accommodations include use of the spa and communal kitchen, while some share bathrooms; cottages have their own kitchens. There are also six yurts tucked into the woods here, offering total privacy.

Orr Hot Springs can be tricky to find. Drive south on Hwy 101 and take exit 551 for N State St. Turn left and head approximately a quarter mile north, turning left onto Orr Springs Rd. Follow the paved road over the hills for approximately 12 miles until you reach the signposted hot springs.

Ukiah Wineries

You'll notice the acres of grapes stretching out in every direction on your way into town. Winemakers around Ukiah enjoy many of the same climatic conditions that made Napa so famous. Pick up a wineries map from the Ukiah Chamber of Commerce (p245). Tasting fees are generally around $5.

Nelson Family Vineyards WINERY
(☏707-462-3755; www.nelsonfamilyvineyards. com; 550 Nelson Ranch Rd; ⊙10am-5pm; P⊞) Just north of Ukiah, this winery, vineyard and pear, olive and Christmas-tree farm with wondrous views over the valley is a great place to picnic (in a redwood grove), make friends and sip not-too-sweet Chardonnay and luscious red blends. Just one aside – it is a popular venue for weddings, which can affect visits by the public.

Parducci Wine Cellars WINERY
(☏707-463-5357; www.parducci.com; 501 Parducci Rd; wine tasting $5; ⊙10am-5pm; P) ✿ Sustainably grown, harvested and produced, 'America's Greenest Winery' offers affordable, bold, earthy reds. The tasting room, lined in brick with low ceilings and soft lights, is a perfect little cave-like environment to get out of the summer heat, sip wine and chat about sustainability practices. Or head for the terrace overlooking the vineyards and organic gardens, complete with contented chickens.

Montgomery Woods State Natural Reserve

Two miles west of Orr Hot Springs, this 2743-acre reserve (☏707-937-5804; www. parks.ca.gov; 15825 Orr Springs Rd; P) ✿ FREE

protects five old-growth virgin redwood groves, which are some of the best groves within a day's drive from San Francisco. A 2-mile loop trail, starting near the picnic tables and toilets, crosses the creek, winding through the serene groves. It's out of the way, so visitors are likely to have it mostly to themselves.

The trees here are impressive – some are up to 14ft in diameter – but remember to admire them from the trail, both to protect the root systems of the trees and to protect yourself from poison oak, which is all over the park.

City of Ten Thousand Buddhas

The showpiece at the **City of Ten Thousand Buddhas** (☏707-462-0939; www.cttbusa.org; 4951 Bodhi Way; ⊙8am-6pm; P) is the beautiful temple with its 10,000 golden Buddha statues. Elsewhere enjoy pretty courtyards, lush landscaping and decorative peacocks. This Buddhist monastery and college is home to both nuns and monks and runs courses on Buddhism; check the website for more information. There is an interesting gift shop with souvenirs as well as literature on Buddhism.

The excellent **Jyun Kang Vegetarian Restaurant** (4951 Bodhi Way; mains $8-12; ⊙11:30am-3pm Wed-Mon; ✐) will have vegetarians (and vegas) swooning over the superb Asian-influenced dishes.

Willits

Twenty miles north of Ukiah, Willits mixes NorCal dropouts with loggers and ranchers (the high school has a bull-riding team). Lamp posts on the main drag are decorated with cowboys and similar, while the heart of the place has a small-town atmosphere with an appealing clutch of idiosyncratic small shops and some solid eating choices.

Though ranching, timber and manufacturing may be its mainstays, tie-dye and gray ponytails are de rigueur. For visitors, Willits has a couple of claims to fame: it is the eastern terminus of the Skunk Train and is also home to the oldest continuous rodeo in California. Willits Frontier Days & Rodeo, held annually here in July, attracts bucking bronco fans from all over the US. Fort Bragg is about 35 miles away on the coast; allow an hour to navigate twisty Hwy 20.

◉ Sights & Activities

Ten miles north of Willits, Hwy 162/Covelo Rd makes for a superb drive following the route of the Northwestern Pacific Railroad along the Eel River and through the **Mendocino National Forest**. The trip is only about 30 miles, but plan on taking at least an hour on the winding road, passing exquisite river canyons and rolling hills. Eventually, you'll reach **Covelo**, known for its unusual round valley.

★**Mendocino County Museum**　　MUSEUM
(☑707-459-2736; www.mendocinomuseum.org; 400 E Commercial St; adult/child $4/1; ☺10am-4:30pm Wed-Sun; ℗) Among the best community museums in this half of the state, this puts the lives of early settlers in excellent historical context – much drawn from old letters – and there's an entire 1920s soda fountain and barber shop inside. You could spend an hour perusing Pomo and Yuki basketry and artifacts, or reading about local scandals and countercultural movements.

Outside, the **Roots of Motive Power** (www.rootsofmotivepower.com) exhibit occasionally demonstrates steam logging and machinery.

Ridgewood Ranch　　HISTORIC SITE
(☑reservations 707-459-7910; www.seabiscuit heritage.org; 16200 Hwy 101; group/private tours $25/40; ☺9:30am 1st & 3rd Sat May-Oct) Willits' most famous resident was the horse Seabiscuit, who grew up here. Three-hour tours for eight or more people are available by reservation and there are other events listed on the website; private tours are also available. Docent-led nature tours of the surrounding natural area are free with advance reservations.

Skunk Train　　HISTORIC TRAIN
(☑707-964-6371; www.skunktrain.com; E Commercial St; adult/child $54/34) This heritage railroad has its depot on E Commercial St, three blocks east of Hwy 101. Trains run between Willits and Fort Bragg (p236), passing through some lush redwood country en route.

**Jackson Demonstration
State Forest**　　HIKING
(www.stateparks.com; Fort Bragg-Willits Rd) Fifteen miles west of Willits on Hwy 20, the forest offers day-use recreational activities, including hiking trails and mountain-biking. You can also camp here. A demonstration forest is so named as it is used for forestry education, research and sustainable felling techniques. Seek out the Chamberlain Creek Waterfall on the Chamberlain Creek Trail and Camellia Trail if you can. These beautiful falls are situated in a lush canyon surrounded by redwoods and ferns.

✯ Festivals & Events

Willits Frontier Days & Rodeo　　RODEO
(www.willitsfrontierdays.com; adult/child $15/5; ☺early Jul) Dating from 1926, Willits has the oldest continuous rodeo in California, occurring in the first week in July.

🛏 Sleeping

Quality accommodations are pretty sparse here. Some of the in-town motels – and there seems to be about a hundred of them – are dumps, so absolutely check out the room before checking in. Ask about Skunk Train packages. For only the most desperate campers, there are a couple of crowded, loud RV parks on the edges of town.

★**Old West Inn**　　MOTEL $
(☑707-459-4201; www.theoldwestinn.com; 1221 S Main St; r $79; ℗☻✳☎) The facade looks like a mock up of an Old West main street and each room has a theme, from the 'Stable' to the 'Barber Shop.' The decor is simple and comfy with just enough imagination to make it interesting. Besides that this is the cleanest, friendliest and most highly recommended place in town.

Baechtel Creek Inn & Spa　　BOUTIQUE HOTEL $$
(☑707-459-9063; www.baechtelcreekinn.com; 101 Gregory Lane; d $125-165; ℗☻✳☎☀☻) As Willits' only upscale option, this place draws an interesting mix: Japanese bus tours, business travelers and wine-trippers. The standard rooms are nothing too flashy, but they have top-notch linens, iPod docks and tasteful art. Custom rooms come with local wine and more space. The immaculate pool and lovely egg breakfast on the patio are perks.

✕ Eating

La Siciliana　　ITALIAN $
(☑707-459-5626; www.lasicilianawillits.com; 1611 S Main St; mains $11-13; ☺11am-9pm Tue-Sun; ♨) The *sugo* (sauce) is pure Sicilian, the pesto is rich with basil and pine nuts, the olive oil is extra virgin and the pizza crust is crisp and thin. There is no dreaded ping of the microwave and everything is freshly made

in-house. That said, the prices are low and the atmosphere no-fuss and family friendly.

Aztec Grill MEXICAN $
(781 S Main St; burritos $5-8; ⊘5am-9pm) Yes this is in the Chevron Gas Station, but the unanimous vote from locals is that this is, hands down, the best Mexican food in town. Cheap too.

Loose Caboose Cafe SANDWICHES $
(☑707-459-1434; www.loosecaboosewillits.com; 10 Wood St; sandwiches $7-11; ⊘7:30am-3pm) People tend to get a bit flushed when talking about the sandwiches at the Loose Caboose, which gets jammed at lunch. The Reuben and Sante Fe chicken sandwiches are two savory delights. Look for a ramshackle entrance complete with a historic rail crossing sign.

Adam's Restaurant CALIFORNIAN $$$
(☑707-409-4378; 50 N Main St; mains $22-27; ⊘5-9pm Tue-Sun; 🐾) Willits' swankiest address is known for its crab cakes and special occasion-worthy mains like big New York steaks, lamb osso buco or cajun chicken pasta, perhaps finished off with a blueberry crème brûlée. The ambience is simple and the service stellar. Check out its Facebook page.

Drinking & Nightlife

The main street through town is home to a couple of cafes, as well as a pub with regular live music and a dimly-lit bar (or two).

Shanachie Pub PUB
(☑707-459-9194; 50 N Main St; ⊘3pm-1am Mon-Sat) This is a friendly little garden-side dive with tons on tap and regular live music.

☆ Entertainment

Willits Community Theatre THEATER
(☑707-459-0895; www.willitstheatre.org; 37 W Van Lane; ⊘hours vary) Stages award-winning plays, poetry readings and comedy.

Shopping

JD Redhouse & Co CLOTHING, HOMEWARES
(☑707-459-1214; www.jdredhouse.com; 212 S Main St; ⊘9am-6pm Mon-Fri, from 10am Sat & Sun) Family-owned and operated, this central mercantile is a good reflection of Willits itself, balancing cowboy essentials – boots and grain, tools and denim – with treats for the weekend tourist. The Cowlick's counter (with excellent Mendocino-made ice cream)

is a good place to cool off when the heat on the sidewalk gets intense.

Mariposa Market FOOD & DRINK
(☑707-459-9630; www.mariposamarket.com; 600 S Main St; ⊘8am-7pm Mon-Fri, from 9am Sat & Sun) Willits' natural-food grocery market has plenty of organic fresh fruit and veg, plus a juice bar and baked-goods section.

SOUTHERN REDWOOD COAST

There's some real magic in the loamy soil and misty air 'beyond the redwood curtain'; it yields the tallest trees and most potent herb on the planet. North of Fort Bragg, Bay Area weekenders and antique-stuffed B&Bs give way to lumber wars, pot farmers and an army of carved bears. The 'growing' culture here is palpable and the huge profit it brings to the region has evident cultural side effects – an omnipresent population of transients who work the harvests, a chilling respect for 'No Trespassing' signs and a political culture that is an uneasy balance between gun-toting libertarians, ultra-left progressives and typical college-town chaos. Nevertheless, the reason to visit is to soak in the magnificent landscape, which runs through a number of pristine, ancient redwood forests.

ⓘ Information

Redwood Coast Heritage Trails (www.redwoods.info) gives a nuanced slant on the region, with itineraries based around lighthouses, Native American culture, the timber and rail industries, and maritime life.

Leggett

Leggett marks the redwood country's beginning and Hwy 1's end. There's not much going on here, aside from a single gas station, a grocery store, a small restaurant and a post office, however, fear not, there is plenty to do and see close by.

Visit 1000-acre **Standish-Hickey State Recreation Area** (☑707-925-6482; www.parks.ca.gov; 69350 Hwy 101; per car $8; 🚗), 1.5 miles to the north, for picnicking, swimming and fishing in the Eel River and hiking trails among virgin and second-growth redwoods.

Chandelier Drive-Thru Tree Park (☎707-925-6464; www.drivethrutree.com; 67402 Drive Thru Tree Rd; per car $5; ☉8:30am-9pm Jun-Aug, closes earlier Sep-May; P🚻) has 200 private acres of virgin redwoods with picnicking and nature walks. And yes, there's a redwood with a square hole carved out, which cars can drive through. Only in America.

The 1949 tourist trap of **Confusion Hill** (☎707-925-6456; www.confusionhill.com; 75001 N Hwy 101; Gravity House adult/child $5/4; ☉9am-6pm May-Sep, 10am-5pm Oct-Apr; 🚻) is an enduring curiosity and the most elaborate of the old-fashioned stops that line the route north.

Richardson Grove State Park

Fifteen miles to the north of Leggett, and bisected by the Eel River, serene **Richardson Grove** (☎707-247-3318; www.parks.ca.gov; 1600 Hwy 101, Garberville; per car $8) occupies 1400 acres of virgin forest. Many trees are over 1000 years old and 300ft tall, but there aren't many hiking trails. In winter, there's good fishing for silver and king salmon. For the last few years, CalTrans has been considering widening the road through Richardson Grove, which has sparked an intense protest.

The **visitor center** (☉9am-2pm May-Sep) sells books inside a 1930s lodge, which often has a fire going during cool weather. The park is primarily a **campground** (☎reservations 800-444-7275; www.reserveamerica.com; 1600 Hwy 101; tent & RV sites $35; P), with three separate areas and hot showers; some remain open year-round. Summeronly Oak Flat on the east side of the river is shady and has a sandy beach.

Garberville

The main supply center for southern Humboldt County is the primary jumping-off point for both the Lost Coast, to the west, and the Avenue of the Giants, to the north. There's an uneasy relationship between the old-guard loggers and the hippies, many of whom came in the 1970s to grow sinsemilla (potent, seedless marijuana) after the feds chased them out of Santa Cruz. More recently there has also been a troubling number of homeless on the streets, especially during the warm summer months. Reggae

Southern Redwood Coast

fans note that there is a popular music festival here in July attracting some top names in the genre. Two miles west, Garberville's ragtag sister, Redway, has fewer services. Garberville is about four hours north of San Francisco, one hour south of Eureka.

✦ Festivals & Events

The **Mateel Community Center** (www. mateel.org), in Redway, is the nerve center for many of the area's long-running annual festivals, which celebrate everything from hemp to miming.

**Harley-Davidson
Redwood Run**   MOTORCYCLE RALLY
(www.redwoodrun.com; ☺mid-Jun) The redwoods rumble with the sound of hundreds of shiny bikes in mid-June.

Reggae on the River   MUSIC
(www.reggaeontheriver.com; 657 Hwy 101; ☺mid-Jul) In mid-July, this fest draws huge crowds for reggae, world music, arts-and-craft fairs, camping and swimming in the river.

🛏 Sleeping

Humboldt Redwoods Inn   MOTEL $
(☑707-923-2451; www.humboldtredwoodsinn. com; 987 Redwood Dr; r $65-110; P🐾❄🛜🏊) A reliable low-budget option with spacious rooms, although they could do with a lick of paint. That said, the inn has the added plus of a pool.

★Benbow Historic Inn   HISTORIC HOTEL $$$
(☑707-923-2124; www.benbowinn.com; 445 Lake Benbow Dr, Garberville; d $175-475; P🐾❄🛜🏊🐕) This inn is a monument to 1920s rustic elegance; the Redwood Empire's first luxury resort is a national historic landmark. Hollywood's elite once frolicked in the Tudor-style resort's lobby, where you can play chess by the crackling fire, and enjoy complimentary afternoon tea and scones. Note that the inn is currently undergoing a massive expansion project.

Rooms have top-quality beds, antique furniture and crystal sherry decanters (including complimentary sherry). The window-lined **dining room** (breakfast and lunch $10 to $15, dinner mains $22 to $32) serves excellent meals; the rib eye earns rave reviews.

✖ Eating

Expect a small but varied choice of eateries, including some healthy options, as well as Mexican and down-home USA. Just about all the restaurants and cafes are located on Redwood Dr running through the center of town and essentially part of Hwy 101.

Woodrose Café   BREAKFAST, AMERICAN $
(☑707-923-3191; www.woodrosecafe.com; 911 Redwood Dr; mains $9-18; ☺8am-2pm; 🍴🥗) 🌱 Garberville's beloved cafe serves organic omelets, veggie scrambles and buckwheat pancakes with *real* maple syrup in a cozy room. Lunch brings crunchy salads, sandwiches with all-natural meats and good burritos. Plenty of gluten-free options.

Bon Bistro & Bakery   BAKERY $
(☑707-923-2509; 867 Redwood Dr; sandwiches from $5; ☺7am-3pm Mon-Fri, 8am-2pm Sat & Sun) At the southern, quieter end of town backed by lofty trees, this cozy spot has a cottage feel with its warm wood paneling and lacy curtains. Enjoy freshly baked breads, bagels and sandwiches with such tasty, unusual fillings as cashew chicken.

Cecil's New Orleans Bistro   CAJUN $$
(☑707-923-7007; www.garbervillebistro.com; 733 Redwood Dr; mains $18-28; ☺5-9pm Thu-Mon) This 2nd-story eatery overlooks Main St and serves ambitious dishes that may have minted the California-Cajun style. Start with fried green tomatoes before launching into the smoked-boar gumbo. Check the website for music events.

ℹ Information

Find out what's really happening by tuning in to amazing community radio KMUD FM91 (www. kmud.org).
Garberville-Redway Area Chamber of Commerce (☑707-923-2613; www.garberville.org; 784 Redwood Dr; ☺10am-4pm daily May-Aug, 10am-4pm Mon-Fri Sep-Apr) Located inside the Redwood Drive Center, with plenty of information about the town including where to stay and what is on.

Lost Coast

The North Coast's superlative backpacking destination is a mystifying coastal stretch where narrow dirt trails ascend rugged coastal peaks. Here you'll find volcanic beaches of black sand and ethereal mist hovering above the roaring surf as majestic Roosevelt elk graze the forests. The King Range boldly rises 4000ft within 3 miles of the coast between where Hwy 1 cuts inland north of Westport to just south of Ferndale. The coast became 'lost' when the state's highway system deemed the region impassable in the early 20th century. The area north of the King Range is more accessible, if less dramatic.

In autumn, the weather is clear and cool. Wildflowers bloom from April through May and gray whales migrate from December through April. The warmest, driest months are June to August, but days are foggy. Note the weather can quickly change.

Aside from a few one-horse villages, Shelter Cove is the only option for services.

ℹ Information

The area is a patchwork of government-owned land and private property; visit the **Bureau of Land Management** (BLM; ☑ 707-825-2300, 707-986-5400; www.blm.gov; 768 Shelter Cove Rd; ⊙ 8am-4:30pm Mon-Sat Sep-May, 8am-4:30pm Mon-Fri Jun-Aug) office for information, permits and maps. There are few circuitous routes for hikers, and rangers can advise on reliable (if expensive) shuttle services in the area.

For information about the flora and fauna stop by the **Needle Rock Visitor Center** (☑ 707-986-7711; www.parks.ca.gov; Bear Harbor Rd; per car $6; ⊙ hours vary).

A few words of caution: lots of weed is grown around here and it's wise to stay on trail and to respect 'no trespassing' signs, lest you find yourself at the business end of someone's right to bear arms. And pot farmers don't pose the only threat: you'll want to check for ticks (Lyme disease is common) and keep food in bear-proof containers, which are required for camping.

Sinkyone Wilderness State Park

Named for the Sinkyone people who once lived here, this 7367-acre wilderness extends south of Shelter Cove along pristine coastline. The **Lost Coast Trail** passes through here for 22 miles, from Whale Gulch south to Usal Beach Campground. It takes at least three days to walk as it meanders along high ridges, providing bird's-eye views down to deserted beaches and the crashing surf (side trails descend to water level).

To get to Sinkyone, drive west from Garberville and Redway on Briceland-Thorn Rd, 21 miles through Whitethorn to Four Corners. Turn left (south) and continue for 3.5 miles down a very rugged road to the ranch house; it takes 1½ hours.

North of the **Usal Beach Campground** (☑ 707-247-3318; www.parks.ca.gov; tent sites $25; Ⓟ), Usal Rd (County Rd 431) is much rougher and recommended only if you have a high-clearance 4WD and a chainsaw. Seriously.

King Range National Conservation Area

Stretching over 35 miles of virgin coastline, with ridge after ridge of mountainous terrain plunging to the surf, the 60,000-acre area tops out at namesake King's Peak (4087ft). The wettest spot in California, the range receives over 120in – and sometimes as much as 240in – of annual rainfall, causing frequent landslides; in winter, snow falls on the ridges. (By contrast, nearby sea-level Shelter Cove gets only 69in of rain and no snow.) Two thirds of the area is awaiting wilderness designation. Note that for overnight hikes, you will need a backcountry-use permit, which can be obtained from the Bureau of Land Management.

Fire restrictions begin July 1 and last until the first soaking rain, usually in November. During this time, there are no campfires allowed outside developed campgrounds.

North of the King Range

Though it's less of an adventure, you can reach the Lost Coast's northern section year-round via paved, narrow Mattole Rd.

HIKING THE LOST COAST

The best way to see the Lost Coast is to hike, and the best hiking is through the southern regions within the Sinkyone and Kings Range wilderness areas. Some of the best trails start from Mattole Campground, just south of Petrolia, which is on the northern border of the Kings Range. It's at the ocean end of Lighthouse Rd, 4 miles from Mattole Rd (sometimes marked as Hwy 211), southeast of Petrolia.

Both Wailaki and Nadelos have developed **campgrounds** (tent sites $8) with toilets and water. There are another four developed campgrounds around the range, with toilets but no water (except Honeydew, which has purable creek water). There are multiple primitive walk-in sites. You'll need a bear canister and backcountry permit, both available from the Bureau of Land Management (p253).

Plan on three hours to navigate the sinuous 68 miles from Ferndale in the north to the coast at Cape Mendocino, then inland to Humboldt Redwoods State Park and Hwy 101. Don't expect redwoods: the vegetation is grassland and pasture. It's beautiful in spots – lined with sweeping vistas and wildflowers that are prettiest in spring.

You'll pass two tiny settlements, both 19th-century stage-coach stops. **Petrolia** has an all-in-one store that rents bear canisters, and sells supplies for the trail, good beer and gasoline. **Honeydew** also has a general store. The drive is enjoyable, but the Lost Coast's wild, spectacular scenery lies further south in the more remote regions.

Shelter Cove

The only sizable community on the Lost Coast, Shelter Cove is surrounded by the King Range National Conservation Area and abuts a large south-facing cove. It's a tiny seaside subdivision with an airstrip in the middle – indeed, many visitors are private pilots. Fifty years ago, Southern California swindlers subdivided the land, built the airstrip and flew in potential investors, fast-talking them into buying seaside land for retirement. But they didn't tell buyers that a steep, winding, one-lane dirt road provided the *only* access and that the seaside plots were eroding into the sea. Today, the large number of 'For Sale' plaques are a sobering sign of the times.

Today, there's still only one route, but now it's paved. Cell phones barely work here: this is a good place to disappear. A short drive brings you to the stunning Black Sands Beach stretching for miles northward.

🛏 Sleeping

Oceanfront Inn INN $$
(☏707-986-7002; www.sheltercoveoceanfrontinn. com; 10 Seal Ct; r $180-235, ste $250; P⊖ 🛜) The recently renovated big, bright rooms here all have private balconies, fridges, microwaves, coffeemakers and phenomenal sea views, and the owners provide a basket of goodies; provisions are pretty scarce in this town. There is one suite complete with a full kitchen (minimum two-night stay). The nine-hole golf course across the street is within putting distance of the sea. The on-site Cove Restaurant is one of the top dining options in town.

Inn of the Lost Coast INN $$
(☏707-986-7521; www.innofthelostcoast.com; 205 Wave Dr, Shelter Cove; r from $225, ste from $240; P⊖🛜♨) Shelter Cove's most family-friendly hotel has a choice of rooms and suites; the latter including options with a full kitchen, private hot tub and sauna and/ or fireplace. The double rooms are spacious, with picture windows to maximize the breathtaking ocean views; most have private balconies.

Downstairs the Delgada Pizzeria & Bakery serves decent pizza, while the Fish Tank Cafe is a good stop for coffee, pastries and sandwiches.

Tides Inn HOTEL $$
(☏707-986-7900; www.sheltercovetidesinn.com; 59 Surf Pt; r $170, ste $195-390; P⊖🛜) Perched above tide pools teeming with starfish and sea urchins, the squeaky-clean rooms here offer excellent views (go for the mini suites on the 3rd floor with their fireplaces and full kitchens). The suite options are good for families, and kids are greeted warmly with an activity kit by the innkeeper.

Spy Glass Inn INN $$$
(☏707-986-4030; www.spyglassinnsheltercove. com; 118 Dolphin Dr; ste $345-375; P⊖🛜) Up on a hill a short walk from town, the four luxurious suites here all have sea-view Jacuzzi tubs, full kitchens, private decks and windows lit up by the expansive shoreline beyond. Note that there is a minimum two-night stay at weekends.

🍴 Eating

Shelter Cove General Store SUPERMARKET $
(☏707-986-7733; 7272 Shelter Cove Rd) For those who are self-catering, Shelter Cove General Store is 2 miles beyond town. Get groceries and gasoline here.

Cove Restaurant AMERICAN $$
(☏707-986-1197; www.sheltercoveoceanfrontinn. com; 10 Seal Ct; mains $10-44; ⊙5-9pm Thu-Sun; P) The first-choice place to eat, located at the Oceanfront Inn, this restaurant has everything from artichoke-mushroom lasagna to New York steaks.

Humboldt Redwoods State Park & Avenue of the Giants

Don't miss this magical drive through California's largest redwood park, **Humboldt Redwoods State Park** (☏707-946-2409;

www.parks.ca.gov; Hwy 101; P ♿) ✔ FREE, which covers 53,000 acres – 17,000 of which are old-growth – and contains some of the world's most magnificent trees. It also boasts three-quarters of the world's tallest 100 trees. Tree huggers take note: these groves rival (and some say surpass) those in Redwood National Park, which is a long drive further north, although the landscapes here are less diverse.

Exit Hwy 101 when you see the 'Avenue of the Giants' sign, take this smaller alternative to the interstate; it's an incredible, 32-mile, two-lane stretch. You'll find free driving guides at roadside signboards at both the avenue's southern entrance, 6 miles north of Garberville, near Phillipsville, and at the northern entrance, south of Scotia, at Pepperwood; there are access points off Hwy 101.

Three miles north, the **California Federation of Women's Clubs Grove** is home to an interesting four-sided hearth designed by renowned San Franciscan architect Julia Morgan in 1931 to commemorate 'the untouched nature of the forest.'

Primeval **Rockefeller Forest**, 4.5 miles west of the avenue via Mattole Rd, appears as it did a century ago. It's the world's largest contiguous old-growth redwood forest, and contains about 20% of all such remaining trees. Walk the 2.5-mile Big Trees Loop (note that at the time of research a footbridge had been taken out and you'll have to walk across a fallen tree to cross the river where the trail starts). You quickly walk out of sight of cars and feel like you have fallen into the time of dinosaurs.

In **Founders Grove**, north of the visitor center, the Dyerville Giant was knocked over in 1991 by another falling tree. A walk along its gargantuan 370ft length, with its wide trunk towering above, helps you appreciate how huge these ancient trees are.

The park has over 100 miles of trails for hiking, mountain biking and horseback riding. Easy walks include short nature trails in Founders Grove, Rockefeller Forest and **Drury-Chaney Loop Trail** (with berry picking in summer). Challenging treks include the popular **Grasshopper Peak Trail**, south of the visitor center, which climbs to the 3379ft fire lookout.

Humboldt Redwoods
State Park Campgrounds   CAMPGROUND $
(☑ information 707-946-2263, reservations 800-444-7275; www.reserveamerica.com; tent & RV sites $20-35; P 🐾) The park runs three seasonal campgrounds with hot showers, one environmental camp, a hike/bike camp and primitive trail camps. Of the developed spots, Burlington Campground is beside the visitor center and near a number of trailheads; Hidden Springs Campground is 5 miles south along Avenue of the Giants; and Albee Creek Campground is on Mattole Rd past Rockefeller Forest.

Miranda Gardens Resort   RESORT $$
(☑ 707-943-3011; www.mirandagardens.com; 6766 Avenue of the Giants, Miranda; cottages $125-300; P 🐾 ❄ ♿) The best indoor stay along the avenue. The cozy, dark, slightly rustic cottages have redwood paneling, some with fireplaces and kitchens, and are spotlessly clean. The grounds – replete with outdoor Ping Pong, a seasonal swimming pool and a play area for kids amid swaying redwoods – have wholesome appeal for families.

Riverbend Cellars   WINERY $$
(☑ 707-943-9907; www.riverbendcellars.com; 12990 Avenue of the Giants, Myers Flat; ☉ noon-6pm) For something a bit posh, pull over here. The El Centauro red – named for Pancho Villa – is an excellent estate-grown blend.

🛈 Information

Humboldt Redwoods Visitor Center (☑ 707-946-2263; www.humboldtredwoods.org; Avenue of the Giants; ☉ 9am-5pm Apr-Oct, 10am-4pm Nov-Mar) Located 2 miles south of Weott, a volunteer-staffed visitor center shows videos (three in total), sells maps and also has a small exhibition center about the local flora and fauna.

Scotia

For years, Scotia was California's last 'company town,' entirely owned and operated by the Pacific Lumber Company, which built cookie-cut houses and had an open contempt for long-haired outsiders who liked to get between their saws and the big trees. The company went belly up in 2006, sold the mill to another redwood company and, though the town still has a creepy *Twilight Zone* vibe, you no longer have to operate by the company's posted 'Code of Conduct.'

As you drive along Hwy 101 and see what appears to be a never-ending redwood forest, understand that this 'forest' sometimes consists of trees only a few rows deep – called a 'beauty strip' – a carefully crafted illusion for tourists. Most old-growth trees have been cut.

There are dingy diners and a couple of bars in Rio Dell, across the river. Back in the day, this is where the debauchery happened: because it wasn't a company town, Rio Dell had bars and hookers. In 1969 the freeway bypassed the town and it withered. Upon entering the town from the north, there is a Hoby's Market and Deli located in the Scotia Center (a small shopping center).

The best reason to pull off here is the **Eel River Brewing Company Taproom & Grill** (☑702-725-2739; http://eelriverbrewing. com; 1777 Alamar Way, Fortuna; ⊙11am-11pm) ✎, where a breezy beer garden and excellent burgers ($11 to $15) accompany all-organic brews.

Ferndale

The North Coast's most charming town is stuffed with impeccable Victorians – known locally as 'butterfat palaces' because of the dairy wealth that built them. There are so many, in fact, that the entire place is a state and federal historical landmark. Dairy farmers built the town in the 19th century and it's still run by the 'milk mafia': you're not a local till you've lived here 40 years. A stroll down Main St offers a taste of super wholesome, small-town America, from galleries to old-world emporiums and soda fountains. Although Ferndale relies on tourism, it has avoided becoming a tourist trap and has no chain stores. Though a lovely place to spend a summer night, folk close the shutters early in winter and it may be hard to find a bite to eat late evening time, let alone a pint of something frothy.

◉ Sights

Fern Cottage   HISTORIC BUILDING
(☑707-786-4835; www.ferncottage.org; 2121 Centerville Rd; group tours per person $10; ⊙11am-3pm Thu-Sat) This 1866 Carpenter Gothic grew to a 32-room mansion. Only one family ever lived here, so the interior is completely, and charmingly, preserved. Tours are held at 11am, noon and 2pm.

✹ Festivals & Events

This wee town has a packed social calendar, especially in the summer. If you're planning a visit, check the events page at www. victorianferndale.com.

Tour of the Unknown Coast   SPORTS
(www.tuccycle.org; ⊙May) A challenging one-day event in late May, in which participants in the 100-mile bicycle race climb nearly 10,000ft. Widely recognized as being California's toughest cycle race.

Humboldt County Fair   FAIR
(www.humboldtcountyfair.org; Humboldt County Fairgrounds; ⊙mid-Aug) Held in mid-August, the longest-running county fair in California.

🛌 Sleeping & Eating

Victorian Inn   HISTORIC HOTEL **$$**
(☑707-786-4949; www.victorianvillageinn.com; 400 Ocean Ave; r $125-250; ☻☎) The bright, sunny rooms inside this venerable, two-story former bank building (1890) are comfortably furnished with thick carpeting, period-style wallpaper, good linens and antiques.

Shaw House   B&B **$$**
(☑707-786-9958; www.shawhouse.com; 703 Main St; r $129-175, ste $225-275; ☻☎☎) Shaw House, an emblematic 'butterfat palace,' was the first permanent structure in Ferndale, completed by founding father Seth Shaw in 1866. Today, it's California's oldest B&B, set back on extensive grounds. Original details remain, including painted wooden ceilings. Most of the rooms have private entrances, and three have private balconies overlooking the large garden with its magnificent shady trees and suitably situated benches.

Hotel Ivanhoe   HISTORIC HOTEL **$$**
(☑707-786-9000; www.ivanhoe-hotel.com; 315 Main St; r $95-145; ☻☎) Ferndale's oldest hostelry opened in 1875. It has four antique-laden rooms and an Old West–style, 2nd-floor gallery, perfect for morning coffee. The adjoining saloon with dark wood and lots of brass is an atmospheric place for a nightcap, while the adjacent restaurant is a reliable choice for a meal.

★**Gingerbread Mansion**   B&B **$$$**
(☑707-786-4000; www.gingerbread-mansion.com; 400 Berding St; r $175-495; P☻☎) This is the cream of dairyland elegance, an 1898 Queen Anne–Eastlake that's unsurprisingly the town's most photographed building. And the inside is no less extravagant, with each room having its own unique (and complex) mix of floral wallpaper, patterned carpeting, grand antique furniture and perhaps a fireplace, wall fresco, stained-glass window or Greek statue thrown in for kicks.

✗ Eating

★ Lost Coast Cafe   VEGETARIAN $
(☑707-786-5330; 468 Main St; mains $7-10; ⊘10:30am-4pm Thu-Mon; ✐) Step into a homey kitchen, where the soups, sandwiches, salads and baked goods are easily the best vegetarian choices north of Fort Bragg. The owner, Mario, is a wonderful, friendly character and passionate about his cooking and Ferndale. Organic coffee is on the house. Cash only.

Humboldt Sweets   BAKERY $
(☑707-786-4683; 614 Main St; scones $5; ⊘8am-5pm Fri-Sun) This cute-as-a-button small place is recommended for coffee and cake; favorites include coconut cream and carrot. Or opt for one of the giant buttery scones, including jalapeño, and cheddar cheese with spring onions. It also makes its own truffles and toffees for the ultimate sugar rush.

No Brand Burger Stand   BURGERS $
(☑707-786-9474; 989 Milton Ave; burgers $7; ⊘11am-4pm; ℗) Hiding near the entrance to town by an industrial building, this hole-in-the-wall turns out a juicy jalapeño double cheeseburger that ranks easily as the North Coast's best burger. The shakes – so thick your cheeks hurt from pulling on the straw – are about the only other thing on the menu.

Farmhouse on Main
Restaurant   CALIFORNIAN $$
(☑707-786-9222; 460 Main St; mains $18-23; ⊘11am-2pm & 5-9pm Thu-Sun; 🎅) This light-filled dining space is one of Ferndale's latest culinary hits with a menu of no-fuss favorites like rib-eye steak, pork cutlets, lamb shanks and braised beef served with appetizing sides such as a creamy polenta. Lightweights can opt for the salads and homemade soups, plus housemade artisan breads, quiches and similar.

☆ Entertainment

Ferndale Repertory Theatre   THEATER
(☑707-786-5483; www.ferndale-rep.org; 447 Main St) This top-shelf community company produces excellent contemporary theater in the historic Hart Theatre Building.

🔒 Shopping

Main St is a great place to shop. Look for the handful of secondhand stores selling vintage cowboy boots and used designer jeans at reasonable prices.

Blacksmith Shop & Gallery   METAL GOODS
(☑707-786-4216; www.ferndaleblacksmith.com; 455 & 491 Main St; ⊘9:30am-5pm) From wrought-iron art to sculpture and jewelry, this is the largest collection of contemporary blacksmithing in the US. Note that there are two venues here: the shop and the gallery, two doors apart, and it is well worth checking them both out.

Ferndale Arts Gallery   ARTS & CRAFTS
(☑707-786-9634; www.ferndaleartgallery.com; 580 Main St; ⊘10am-5pm) This artists' co-operative runs a large gallery space selling prints, paintings, pottery, photography and greeting cards that showcase local artists from Humboldt County.

Humboldt Bay National Wildlife Refuge

This pristine **wildlife refuge** (☑707-733-5406; www.fws.gov/refuge/humboldt_bay; 1020 Ranch Rd, Loleta; ⊘8am-5pm; ℗⛓) 🗲FREE protects wetland habitats for more than 200 species of birds migrating annually along the Pacific Flyway. Between the fall and early spring, when Aleutian geese descend en masse to the area, more than 25,000 geese might be seen in a cackling gaggle outside the visitor center.

The peak season for waterbirds and raptors runs September to March; for black brant geese and migratory shorebirds it's mid-March to late April. Gulls, terns, cormorants, pelicans, egrets and herons come year-round. Look for harbor seals offshore; bring binoculars. If it's open, drive out South Jetty Rd to the mouth of Humboldt Bay for a stunning perspective.

Pick up a map from the **Richard J Guadagno Headquarters & Visitor Center**. Exit Hwy 101 at Hookton Rd, 11 miles south of Eureka, turn north along the frontage road, on the freeway's west side. In April, look for the Godwit Days festival, a celebration of the spring bird migration.

Eureka

One hour north of Garberville, on the edge of the giant Humboldt Bay, lies Eureka, the largest bay north of San Francisco. With a strip-mall sprawl surrounding a lovely historic downtown, it wears its role as the county seat a bit clumsily. Despite a diverse and interesting community of artists, writers, pagans and other free-thinkers, Eureka's wild side slips out only occasionally – the Redwood Coast Jazz Festival has events all over town, and summer concerts rock out the F Street Pier – but mostly, Eureka goes to bed early. Make for Old Town, a small historic district with good shopping and a revitalized waterfront. For nightlife, head to Eureka's livelier sister up the road, Arcata.

Eureka was a major logging town in the late 19th century, and Victorian lumber-baron mansions dot the town; an impressive 16% or so of the city's Old Town buildings have been catalogued as important historical structures.

Sights

The free *Eureka Visitors Map*, available at tourist offices, details walking tours and scenic drives, focusing on architecture and history. **Old Town**, along 2nd and 3rd Sts from C St to M St, was once down-and-out, but has been refurbished into a buzzing pedestrian district. The F Street Plaza and Boardwalk runs along the waterfront at the foot of F St. Gallery openings fall on the first Saturday of every month.

Romano Gabriel Wooden Sculpture Garden   GARDENS
(315 2nd St) The coolest thing to gawk at downtown is this collection of whimsical outsider art that's enclosed by aging glass. For 30 years, wooden characters in Gabriel's front yard delighted locals. After he died in 1977, the city moved the collection here.

Morris Graves Museum of Art   MUSEUM
(☑707-442-0278; www.humboldtarts.org; 636 F St; $5; ⊙noon-5pm Wed-Sun; ⊕) Across Hwy 101, this excellent museum shows rotating Californian artists and hosts performances inside the 1904 **Carnegie library**, the state's first public library. If you are around for a while it also hosts art workshops and classes for adults and kids.

Sequoia Park   PARK
(☑707-441-4263; www.sequoiaparkzoo.net; 3414 W St; park free, zoo adult/child $5/3; ⊙zoo 10am-5pm May-Sep, 10am-5pm Tue-Sun Oct-Apr; ⓟ⊕) A 77-acre old-growth redwood grove is a surprising green gem in the middle of a residential neighborhood. It has biking and hiking trails, a children's playground and picnic areas, and a small **zoo**, the oldest in California.

Kinetic Museum Eureka   MUSEUM
(☑707-786-3443; http://kineticgrandchampionship.com/kinetic-museum-eureka; 518 A St; admission by donation; ⊙2:15-6:30pm Fri-Sun, also 6-9pm 1st Sat of month; ⊕) Come see the fanciful, astounding, human-powered contraptions used in the annual Kinetic Grand Championship (p262) race from Arcata to Ferndale. Shaped like giant fish and UFOs, these colorful piles of junk propel racers over roads, water and marsh during the May event.

🏃 Activities

Harbor Cruise   CRUISE
(Madaket Cruises; ☑707-445-1910; www.humboldtbaymaritimemuseum.com; 1st St; narrated cruises adult/child $22/18; ⊙1pm, 2:30pm & 4pm Wed-Sat, 1pm & 2:30pm Sun-Tue mid-May–mid-Oct; ⊕) Board the 1910 *Madaket*, the USA's oldest continuously operating passenger vessel, and learn the history of Humboldt Bay. Docked at the foot of C St, it originally ferried mill workers and passengers until the Samoa Bridge opened in 1971. The $10 sunset cocktail cruise serves from the smallest licensed bar in the state, and there's also a 75-minute wildlife cruise.

**Hum-Boats Sail,
Canoe & Kayak Center**   BOATING
(☑707-443-5157; www.humboats.com; 601 Startare Dr; kayak tours from $55; ⊙9am-5pm Mon-Fri, to 6pm Sat & Sun Apr-Oct, to 2:30pm Nov-Mar) At Woodley Island Marina, this outfit rents kayaks and sailboats, offering lessons, tours, charters, sunset sails and full-moon paddles.

Tours

**Blue Ox Millworks
& Historic Park**   HISTORIC BUILDING
(☑707-444-3437; www.blueoxmill.com; 1 X St; adult/child 6-12yr $10/5; ⊙9am-5pm Mon-Fri year-round, plus 9am-4pm Sat Apr-Nov; ⊕) One of only a few of its kind in the US, here antique tools and mills are used to produce authentic gingerbread trim for Victorian buildings. One-hour self-guided tours take you through the mill and historical buildings, including a blacksmith shop and 19th-century skid camp. Kids love the oxen. Be sure to leave time to peruse the gift shop.

🛏 Sleeping

Every brand of chain hotel is along Hwy 101. Room rates run high midsummer; you can sometimes find cheaper options in Arcata, to the north, or Fortuna, to the south. There is also a handful of motels that cost from $55 to $100 and have no air-conditioning; choose places set back from the road. The cheapest options are south of downtown on the suburban strip.

Inn at 2nd & C
HISTORIC HOTEL $$

(📞707-444-3344; www.theinnat2ndandc.com; 139 2nd St; r from $129, ste from $209; ♻️🐾) Formerly the Eagle House Inn, but reopened under new ownership in May 2017, this glorious Victorian hotel has been tastefully restored to combine Victorian-era decor with every possible modern amenity. The magnificent turn-of-the-century ballroom is used for everything from theater performances to special events. There is also a yoga studio and spa room. Breakfast, tea and complimentary cocktails are additional perks.

Although the hotel is non-smoking, the owners have thoughtfully designated an outside secluded area for smokers (with a bay view, no less!).

Cornelius Daly Inn
B&B $$

(📞707-445-3638; www.dalyinn.com; 1125 H St; r with/without bathroom $185/130; ♻️) This impeccably maintained 1905 Colonial Revival mansion has individually decorated rooms with turn-of-the-20th-century European and American antiques. Guest parlors are trimmed with rare woods; outside are century-old flowering trees. The breakfasts reflect co-owner Donna's culinary skills with such gourmet offerings as apple-stuffed French toast.

Eureka Inn
HISTORIC HOTEL $$

(📞707-497-6903; www.eurekainn.com; cnr 7th & F Sts; r from $119; ♻️🐾) This majestic and enormous historic hotel with its mock Tudor frontage has been renovated. The style is cozy, in an early-20th-century-lodge, vaguely Wild West sort of way, the staff are extremely friendly and there's a decent bar and restaurant on the premises.

Carter House Inns
B&B $$$

(📞707-444-8062; www.carterhouse.com; 301 L St; r $184-384; 🅿️♻️🐾) Constructed in period style, this aesthetically remodeled hotel is a Victorian lookalike. Rooms have all modern amenities and top-quality linens; suites have in-room Jacuzzis and marble fireplaces. The same owners operate four other sumptuously decorated lodgings: a single-level house, two honeymoon hideaway cottages and a replica of an 1880s San Francisco mansion, which the owner built himself, entirely by hand.

✖️ Eating

You won't go hungry in this town, and health-conscious folk are particularly well catered to with two excellent natural-food grocery stores – **North Coast Co-op** (📞707-443-6027; www.northcoast.coop; cnr 4th & B Sts; ⏰6am-9pm) and **Eureka Natural Foods** (📞707-442-6325; www.eurekanaturalfoods.com; 1626 Broadway St; ⏰7am-9pm Mon-Sat, 8am-8pm Sun) – and two weekly farmers markets – one **street market** (cnr 2nd & F Sts; ⏰10am-1pm Tue Jun-Oct) and one at the **Henderson Center** (📞707-445-3101; 2800 F St; ⏰10am-1pm Thu Jun-Oct). The vibrant dining scene is focused in the Old Town district and has an excellent array of foodie options and price categories.

★Cafe Nooner
MEDITERRANEAN $

(📞707-443-4663; www.cafenooner.com; 409 Opera Alley; mains $10-14; ⏰11am-4pm Sun-Wed, to 8pm Thu-Sat; 🚼) Exuding a cozy bistro-style ambience with red-and-white checkered tablecloths and jaunty murals, this perennially popular restaurant serves natural, organic and Med-inspired cuisine with choices that include a Greek-style *meze* platter, plus kebabs, salads and soups. There's a healthy kid's menu, as well.

Ramone's Bakery & Cafe
BAKERY, DELI $

(📞707-443-6027; www.ramonesbakery.com; 2297 Harrison Ave; mains $6-10; ⏰7am-6pm Mon-Sat, 8am-4pm Sun; 🐾) Come here for delicious cakes, tarts, pies and pastries, as well as baguette sandwiches and salads; there are four other branches in town.

★Brick & Fire
CALIFORNIAN $$

(📞707-268-8959; www.brickandfirebistro.com; 1630 F St, Eureka; dinner mains $14-23; ⏰11:30am-9pm Mon & Wed-Fri, 5-9pm Sat & Sun; 🐾) Eureka's best restaurant is in an intimate, warm-hued, bohemian-tinged setting that is almost always busy. Choose from thin-crust pizzas, delicious salads (try the pear and blue cheese) and an ever-changing selection of appetizers and mains that highlight local produce and wild mushrooms. There's a weighty wine list and servers are well-versed in pairings.

Kyoto
JAPANESE $$

(📞707-443-7777; 320 F St; sushi $4-6, mains $15-27; ⏰11:30am-3pm & 5:30-9:30pm Wed-Sat) Renowned as the best sushi in Humboldt

NORTH COAST & REDWOODS EUREKA

County, dine in a tiny, packed room, where conversation with the neighboring table is inevitable. A menu of sushi and sashimi is rounded out by grilled scallops and fern-tip salad. North Coast travelers who absolutely need sushi should phone ahead for a reservation.

Jack's
SEAFOOD $$

(☑707-273-5273; www.jacksseafoodeureka.com; 4 C St; mains $16-24; ⊘11am-9pm; ⓟ🅿🛜🛗) Grab a pew by the large picture window overlooking the birds, the boats and Humboldt Bay. The seafood menu here includes all the classics, like steamer clams in a white wine broth and Dungeness crab cakes. Oysters are served three ways: smokey, traditional and raw. There are several pasta dishes, as well, and the salads are huge.

★ Restaurant 301
CALIFORNIAN $$$

(☑707-444-8062; www.carterhouse.com; 301 L St; mains $24-40; ⊘5-8:30pm) 🍴 Part of the excellent Carter House Inn, Eureka's top table, romantic, sophisticated 301 serves a contemporary Californian menu, using produce from its organic gardens (tours available). The five-course tasting menu ($62, with wine pairings $107) is a good way to taste local seasonal food in its finest presentation.

🍷 Drinking & Nightlife

Eureka has some fine old bars and pubs, including live music venues, mainly located in and around the historic center. The annual jazz festival attracts some top musicians and also includes blues concerts (unfortunately the Blues on the Bay annual festival has been suspended in recent years).

Old Town Coffee & Chocolates
CAFE

(☑707-445-8600; www.oldtowncoffeeeureka.com; 211 F St; ⊘7am-9pm; 🛜🛗) You'll smell roasting coffee blocks before you see this place. It's a local hangout in a historic building and has board games, local art on the wall and baked goods that include savory choices like bagels with hummus, and wraps.

Speakeasy
BAR

(☑707-444-2244; 411 Opera Alley; ⊘4-11pm Sun-Thu, to 2am Fri & Sat) Squeeze in with the locals at this New Orleans–inspired bar with regular live blues and an infectious convivial atmosphere.

2 Doors Down
WINE BAR

(☑707-268-8959; www.2doorsdownwinebar.com; 1626 F St; ⊘4:40-9:30pm Wed-Mon) Wonderfully cozy and inviting, this Victorian-feeling wine bar lets you create your own flights and will open any bottle on their list of 80-plus wines if you're getting two or more glasses from it. Plenty of snacks are available for order from Brick & Fire (p259) a couple of doors down.

Shanty
BAR

(☑707-444-2053; 213 3rd St; ⊘noon-2am; 🛜) The coolest spot in town is grungy and fun. Play pool, Donkey Kong, Ms Pac-Man or Ping-Pong, or kick it on the back patio with local 20- and 30-something hipsters.

☆ Entertainment

Morris Graves Museum of Art
PERFORMING ARTS

(☑707-442-0278; www.humboldtarts.org; 636 F St; suggested donation $5) Hosts performing-arts events between September and May, usually on Saturday evenings and Sunday afternoons, but sometimes on other days as well.

🛍 Shopping

Eureka's streets lie on a grid: numbered streets cross lettered streets. For the best window-shopping, head to the 300, 400 and 500 blocks of 2nd St, between D and G Sts. The town's low rents and cool old spaces harbor lots of indie boutiques.

ℹ Information

Eureka Chamber of Commerce (☑707-442-3738; www.eurekachamber.com; 2112 Broadway; ⊘8:30am-5pm Mon-Fri; 🛜) The main visitor information center is on Hwy 101.

ℹ Getting There & Around

Arcata-Eureka Airport (Humboldt County Airport; ☑707-839-5401; www.humboldtgov.org/1396/Aviation; 3561 Boeing Ave) The Arcata-Eureka Airport (ACV) is located north of McKinleyville on the North Coast, signposted west of Hwy 101 and with regular services to major cities in California and Oregon, as well as further afield. Several carriers operate from this airport including Penair (p220), United Airlines, Delta, American Airlines, United Airlines and Alaska Airlines (p220), though prices tend to be high.

Eureka Transit Service (☑707-443-0826; www.eurekatransit.org; Humboldt Transit Authority, 133 V St; single fare $1.70) Runs four routes throughout Eureka: the red, gold, green and purple routes. Fares may be paid on the bus and day or monthly passes are also available.

Samoa Peninsula

Grassy dunes and windswept beaches extend along the half-mile-wide, 7-mile long Samoa Peninsula. Stretches of it are spectacular, particularly the dunes, which are part of a 34-mile-long dune system – the largest in Northern California – and the wildlife viewing is excellent.

At the peninsula's south end, **Samoa Dunes Recreation Area** (☑707-825-2300; www.blm.gov; ⊘sunrise-sunset; Ⓟ) FREE is good for picnicking and fishing. For wildlife, head to **Mad River Slough & Dunes**; from Arcata, take Samoa Blvd west for 3 miles, then turn right at Young St, the Manila turnoff. Park at the community center lot, from where a trail passes mudflats, salt marsh and tidal channels. There are over 200 species of birds: migrating waterfowl in spring and fall, songbirds in spring and summer, shorebirds in fall and winter, and waders year-round.

These undisturbed dunes reach heights of over 80ft. Because of the environment's fragility, access is by guided tour only. **Friends of the Dunes** (www.friendsofthedunes.org) leads free guided walks.

The **Samoa Cookhouse** (☑707-442-1659; www.samoacookhouse.net; 908 Vance Ave; all-you-can eat meals per adult $13 17, child $5 9; ⊘7am-3pm & 5-8pm; Ⓟ☷) is the dining hall of an 1893 lumber camp. Hikers, hippies and lumberjacks get stuffed while sharing long, red-checked oilcloth-covered tables. There is no menu but you can guarantee that anything you order will be freshly made that day. Think fried chicken, pork ribs and bumper breakfasts. Vegetarians should call ahead.

Arcata

The North Coast's most progressive town, Arcata surrounds a tidy central square that fills with college students, campers, transients and tourists. Sure, it occasionally reeks of patchouli and its politics lean far left, but its earnest embrace of sustainability has fostered some of the most progressive civic action in America. Here, garbage trucks run on biodiesel, recycling gets picked up by tandem bicycle, wastewater gets filtered clean in marshlands and almost every street has a bike lane. Predictably enough, organic products and produce are the norm, art-and-craft markets are rampant and vegans are well catered to.

Founded in 1850 as a base for lumber camps, today Arcata is defined as a magnet for 20-somethings looking to expand their minds: either at Humboldt State University (HSU), and/or on the local highly potent marijuana. Since a 1996 state proposition legalized marijuana for medical purposes, the economy of the region has become inexorably tied to the crop.

◎ Sights

Around Arcata Plaza are two National Historic Landmarks: the 1857 **Jacoby's Storehouse** (☑707-826-2426; www.facebook.com/pages/Jacoby-Storehouse; Arcata Plaza; ⊘hours vary) and the 1915 **Hotel Arcata** (☑707-826-0217; www.hotelarcata.com; 708 9th St). Another great historic building is the 1914 **Minor Theatre** (☑707-822-3456; www.minortheatre.com; 1013 10th St; ⊘hours vary), which some local historians claim is the oldest theater in the US built specifically for showing films.

Arcata Marsh & Wildlife Sanctuary　WILDLIFE RESERVE
(www.cityofarcata.org; Klopp Lake) On the shores of Humboldt Bay, this sanctuary has 5 miles of walking trails and outstanding birding. The **Redwood Region Audubon Society** (☑707-826-7031; www.rras.org; donation welcome) offers guided walks on Saturdays at 8:30am, rain or shine, from the parking lot at I St's south end. Friends of Arcata Marsh offer guided tours Saturdays at 2pm from the Arcata Marsh Interpretive Center (p264).

Humboldt State University　UNIVERSITY
(HSU; ☑707-826-3011; www.humboldt.edu; 1 Harpst Dr; Ⓟ) ◈ The university on the northeastern side of town holds the Campus Center for Appropriate Technology (CCAT; www.ccathsu.com), a world leader in developing sustainable technologies. On Tuesday at 10am and Friday at 3pm you can take a tour of CCAT's house, a converted residence that uses only 4% of the energy of a comparably sized dwelling.

☆ Activities

Finnish Country Sauna and Tubs　SPA
(☑707-822-2228; http://cafemokkaarcata.com; 495 J St; per 30min adult/child $9.75/2; ⊘noon-11pm Sun-Thu, to 1am Fri & Sat; ☷) Like some kind of Euro-crunchy bohemian dream, these private, open-air redwood hot tubs and sauna are situated around a small frog pond. The staff is easygoing, and the facility

is relaxing, simple and clean. Reserve ahead, especially on weekends.

HSU Center Activities OUTDOORS

(☑707-826-3357; www.humboldt.edu/center activities; Humboldt State University, 1 Harpst Dr; ⏰10am-4pm Mon-Fri) An office on the 2nd floor of the University Center, beside the campus clock tower, sponsors myriad workshops, outings and sporting-gear rentals; non-students welcome.

★ Festivals & Events

Kinetic Grand Championship ART, SPORTS

(☑707-786-3443; www.kineticgrandchampionship. com; ⏰late May; 🖐) 🏁 Arcata's most famous event is held Memorial Day weekend: people on amazing self-propelled contraptions travel 42 miles from Arcata to Ferndale over a period of three days.

Arcata Bay Oyster Festival FOOD & DRINK

(www.oysterfestival.net; 8th St; ⏰mid-Jun) A magical celebration of oysters and beer held on a Saturday in mid-June.

North Country Fair FAIR

(www.sameoldpeople.org; Arcata Plaza; ⏰Sep) A fun September street fair, where bands with names like the Fickle Hillbillies jam.

🛏 Sleeping

Arcata has affordable but limited lodgings. A cluster of hotels – Comfort Inn, Hampton Inn etc – is just north of town, off Hwy 101's Giuntoli Lane. There's cheap camping further north at Clam Beach. One of the best situated hotels is the old fashioned **Hotel Arcata** (☑707-826-0217; www.hotelarcata.com; 708 9th St; r $97-167; 🅿🖐🛜🐾), right on the city's main square.

Fairwinds Motel MOTEL $

(☑707-822-4824; www.fairwindsmotelarcata.com; 1674 G St; s $70-75, d $80-90; 🛜) Serviceable rooms in a standard-issue motel, with some noise from Hwy 101. It's more expensive than the chain motels but has the advantage of being in town and also having an adjacent, reasonable (in price and quality) restaurant.

Lady Anne Inn INN $$

(☑707-822-2797; www.ladyanneinn.com; 902 14th St; r $115-220; 🅿🖐🛜) Dating from 1983, this eco inn is owned by the former mayor of Arcata, so he knows a fair bit about the town. The front garden is a dazzle of roses and native flowers and, while the rooms all differ, they continue the floral theme with decorative wallpaper and pastel paintwork. Dark wood antiques complete the look.

A couple of rooms have a claw-foot tub in the bedroom.

Arcata Stay ACCOMMODATION SERVICES $$

(☑707-822-0935; www.arcatastay.com; 814 13th St; apt from $169; ⏰11am-5pm) A network of excellent and centrally situated apartments, B&Bs and cottage rentals. There is a two-night minimum and prices go down the longer you stay.

🍴 Eating

Great food abounds in restaurants throughout Arcata, almost all casual and most promoting organic produce and ingredients; vegetarians and vegans will have no problem in this town.

There are fantastic farmers markets, at the **Arcata Plaza** (www.humfarm.org; btwn 8th & 9th Sts; ⏰9am-2pm Sat Apr-Nov, from 10am Dec-Mar) and in the parking lot of Wildberries Market. Just a few blocks north of downtown, there is a cluster of the town's best restaurants on G St, near Hwy 101.

Slice of Humboldt Pie CALIFORNIAN $

(☑707-630-5100; 828 I St; pies $4.50-7.50; ⏰11am-10pm Mon-Thu, to 11pm Fri & Sat) Pies and cider are the mainstays here, ranging from chicken pot pie to cottage, steak and mushroom and savory *empanadas*, including chicken coconut curry and Thai chicken with satay sauce. Sweet pastry treats include peanut-butter fudge and traditional apple, while the ciders cover imports and local varieties. The decor is pure industrial chic with exposed pipes and soft gray paintwork.

T's Cafe CAFE $

(☑707-826-2133; 860 10th St; breakfast $8-13; ⏰7am-2pm; 🛜) Housed in a wonderful early-20th-century mansion, try and grab the table on the front porch if you can. Inside, two cavernous rooms with mismatched furniture, local art, books, toys and magazines provide an informal kickback space for enjoying delicious breakfast classics such as eggs with corned beef hash, stuffed French toast and the specialty: seven choices of eggs Benedict.

Cafe Brio CAFE $

(☑707-822-5922; www.cafebrioarcata.com; 791 G St; mains $12-15; ⏰7am-5pm Mon, Tue & Thu, to 6pm Wed, to 9pm Fri & Sat) Occupying an ace

THE ECONOMICS OF THE HUMBOLDT HERB

With an estimated one-fifth of Humboldt County's population farming its world-famous weed, a good chunk of the economy here has run, for decades, as bank-less, tax-evading and cash only – but it's also been prosperous enough to strongly support many local businesses. Back in the 1990s farmers could expect to get around $6000 a pound for their crops but since medical marijuana has become legal the price has dropped radically, to just above $1000 per pound. In November 2016 a further law was passed legalizing recreational cannabis use in the state, which some feel may lead to prices plummeting still further and the possibility of large farms and corporations putting the small farmers out of business.

position on the corner of this central square, the patisserie here serves sumptuous cakes, breakfasts are delish and the lunch salads, sandwiches and pies are a notch above the norm. There is also a coffee-cum-wine-bar for suppin'.

Japhy's Soup & Noodles NOODLES $
(☑707-826-2594; www.japhys.com; 1563 G St; mains $7.50-9; ⊗11:30am-8pm Mon-Fri) Big salads, tasty coconut curry, cold noodle salads with a vast choice of sauces and homemade soups – and cheap!

★**Folie Douce** MODERN AMERICAN $$$
(☑707-822-1042; www.foliedoucearcata.com; 1551 G St; dinner mains $28-37, pizzas $17-24; ⊗11am-2pm Mon, 11am-2pm & 5:30-9pm Tue-Thu, 11am 2pm & 5:30-10pm Fri & Sat) 🍷 Just a slip of a place, but with an enormous reputation. The short but inventive menu features seasonally inspired bistro cooking, from Asian to Mediterranean, with an emphasis on local organics. Wood-fired pizzas are renowned and desserts are pretty special, as well. A slice of artichoke-heart cheesecake perhaps? Dinner reservations essential.

🍷 Drinking & Nightlife

Dive bars and cocktail lounges line the plaza's northern side. Arcata is awash with coffeehouses and brewpubs.

★**Six Rivers Brewery** MICROBREWERY
(☑707-839-7580; www.sixriversbrewery.com; 1300 Central Ave, McKinleyville; ⊗11:30am-11:30pm Sun & Tue-Thu, to 12:30am Fri & Sat, from 4pm Mon) One of the first female-owned breweries in California, the 'brew with a view' kills it in every category: great beer, amazing community vibe, occasional live music and delicious hot wings. The spicy chili-pepper ale is amazing. At first glance the menu might seem like ho-hum pub grub, but portions

are fresh and huge. They also make a helluva pizza.

Redwood Curtain Brewing Company MICROBREWERY
(☑707-826-7222; www.redwoodcurtainbrewing. com; 550 S G St; ⊗noon-11pm Sun-Tue, to midnight Wed-Sat) This tiny gem of a brewery has a varied collection of rave-worthy craft ales and live music or DJs some nights. Plus it offers free wheat thins and goldfish crackers to munch on.

Cafe Mokka CAFE
(☑707-822-2228; www.cafemokkaarcata.com; cnr 5th & J Sts; ⊗noon-11pm Sun-Thu, to 1am Fri & Sat) Bohos head to this cafe at Finnish Country Sauna & Tubs (p261) for a mellow, old-world vibe, good coffee drinks and homemade cookies.

Humboldt Brews BAR
(☑707-826-2739; www.humbrews.com; 856 10th St; ⊗11:30am-midnight Sat-Thu, to 2am Fri) This popular dimly-lit beer house has a huge range of carefully selected beer taps, fish tacos, buffalo wings and for veggies, smoked tofu (pub grub $11 to $13). Regular live music and a pool table add to the entertainment.

☆ Entertainment

Center Arts PERFORMING ARTS
(☑tickets 707-826-3928; www.humboldt.edu/ centerarts; Humboldt State University, 1 Harpst Dr; ⊗hours vary) Hosts events on campus and you'd be amazed at who shows up. The place to buy tickets is at the University Ticket Office in the HSY Bookstore on the 3rd floor of the University Center.

Arcata Theatre CINEMA
(☑707-822-1220; www.arcatatheater.com; 1036 G St) An exquisite remodeling has revived this classic movie house, which shows art films,

NORTH COAST & REDWOODS ARCATA

Northern Redwood Coast

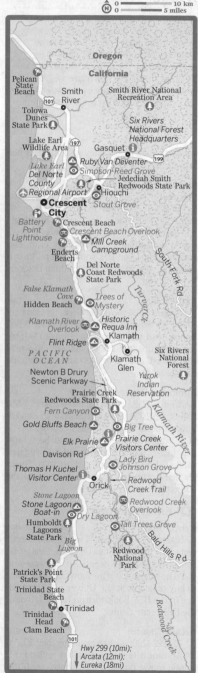

rock documentaries, silent films and more. Plus, it serves beer.

❶ Information

Arcata Marsh Interpretive Center (☎707-826-2359; www.humboldt.edu/arcatamarsh; 569 South G St; ⊗9am-5pm Tue-Sun, from 1pm Mon; ⊞) Staffed by the Friends of Arcata Marsh (FOAM), who give free guided tours on Saturday afternoons.

California Welcome Center (☎707-822-3619; www.arcatachamber.com; ⊗9am-5pm) At the junction of Hwys 299 and 101; has area info.

❶ Getting There & Around

Alaska Airlines, Penair, Delta, American Airlines and United Airlines are the main carriers to operate national flights to/from the Arcata-Eureka Airport (p260) but fares tend to be high. Flights come and go from several major Californian cities, including Los Angeles, San Francisco, Sacramento and San Diego. There are also regular flights from other US cities, including New York, Denver, Phoenix and Portland (Oregon).

Greyhound (p220) serves Arcata from San Francisco ($57, seven hours, daily). Redwood Transit System (p220) serves Arcata and Eureka on the Trinidad–Scotia routes Monday to Saturday ($3, 2½ hours).

Arcata city buses stop at the **Arcata & Mad River Transit Center** (☎707-825-8934; www.arcatatransit.org; 925 E St at 9th St). For shared rides, read the bulletin board at the North Coast Co-op.

Life Cycle Bike Shop (☎707-822-7755; www.lifecyclearcata.com; 1593 G St; per day $25; ⊗9am-6pm Mon-Sat) rents, services and sells bicycles.

Only in Arcata: borrow a bike from **Library Bike** (www.arcata.com/greenbikes; 865 8th St; deposit $20; ⊗hours vary). They're beaters, but they ride.

NORTHERN REDWOOD COAST

Congratulations, traveler, you've reached the middle of nowhere, or at least the top of the middle of nowhere. Here, the trees are so large that the tiny towns along the road seem even smaller. The scenery is pure drama: cliffs and rocks, native lore, legendary salmon runs, mammoth trees, wild elk and RVing retirees. Leave time to dawdle and bask in the haunting natural grandeur of it all and, even though there are scores of mid-century motels, try and make an effort to sleep outdoors if possible. Then, as you gaze skywards, ponder the fact that giant redwoods once covered some 5000 square miles of coast here, before the brutal mass logging that took place around the turn of the 20th century (apparently some 95% of the trees were felled). Fortunately, conservation measures are now firmly in place to protect these magnificent trees that can live for thousands of years.

Trinidad

Cheery, tiny Trinidad perches prettily on the side of the ocean, combining upscale mid-century homes with a mellow surfer vibe. Somehow it feels a bit off-the-beaten-path even though tourism augments fishing to keep the economy going. Trinidad is also a big hit with ornithologists; it's home to one of the most diverse seabird colonies in California. The town gained its name when Spanish sea captains arrived on Trinity Sunday in 1775 and named the area La Santisima Trinidad (the Holy Trinity); later it was the site of bloody battles and raids against the local Native Americans during the Civil War. Around this period, it also experienced a boom, becoming an important port for miners. If you can, check out the superb beaches and rocky coves and stop for a seafood meal overlooking the water.

◉ Sights & Activities

Trinidad is small: approach via Hwy 101 or from the north via Patrick's Point Dr (which becomes Scenic Dr further south). To reach town, take Main St.

The free town map at the information kiosk (p266) shows several fantastic hiking trails, most notably the **Trinidad Head Trail** with superb coastal views and excellent for **whale-watching** (December to April). Stroll along an exceptionally beautiful cove at **Trinidad State Beach**; take Main St and bear right at Stagecoach, then take the second turn left (the first is a picnic area) into the small lot.

Scenic Dr twists south along coastal bluffs, passing tiny coves with views back toward the bay. It peters out before reaching the broad expanses of **Luffenholtz Beach** (accessible via the staircase) and serene white-sand **Moonstone Beach**. Exit Hwy 101 at 6th Ave/Westhaven to get there.

Further south Moonstone becomes **Clam Beach County Park**.

Surfing is good year-round, but potentially dangerous: unless you know how to judge conditions and get yourself out of trouble – there are no lifeguards here – surf in better-protected Crescent City.

**HSU Telonicher
Marine Laboratory**   AQUARIUM
(☑ 707-826-3671; www.humboldt.edu/marinelab; 570 Ewing St; $1; ⊗ 9am-4:30pm Mon-Fri year-round, plus 10am-5pm Sat & Sun mid-Sep–mid-May; ℙ ♿)
🖉 Near Edwards St, this marine lab has a touch tank, several aquariums (look for the giant Pacific octopus), an enormous whale jaw and a cool 3D map of the ocean floor. You can join a naturalist on **tide-pooling expeditions** (per person $3, minimum $20). All tours are by appointment only so call ahead and be sure to ask about conditions.

🛏 Sleeping

Most of the inns and motels line Patrick's Point Dr, north of town, and are family owned and welcoming, with fabulous ocean views. In the center, choices are limited to a cute B&B which gets booked up fast at weekends. **Trinidad Retreats** (www.trinidadretreats.com) and **Redwood Coast Vacation Rentals** (www.redwoodcoast vacationrentals.com) can also help you find a bed for the night.

View Crest Lodge   LODGE $$
(☑ 707-677-3393; www.viewcrestlodge.com; 3415 Patrick's Point Dr; 1- & 2-bedroom cottages $95-240; ℙ ♿ ⊚) On a hill above the ocean on the inland side, these well-maintained, modern and terrific-value cottages all have ocean views and added extras like fireplaces and hot tubs. They range from one to two bedroom and breakfast is included in the price.

Trinidad Inn   INN $$
(☑ 707-677-3349; www.trinidadinn.com; 1170 Patrick's Point Dr; r $100-245; ℙ ♿ ⊚ ❄) Sparklingly clean and attractively decorated rooms fill this upmarket, gray-shingled motel under tall trees. The accommodations vary considerably; some rooms have sitting rooms, fireplaces and fully equipped kitchens, others are straightforward double rooms with a TV and desk.

★Lost Whale Inn   B&B $$$
(☑ 707-677-3425; www.lostwhaleinn.com; 3452 Patrick's Point Dr; r $199-325, ste $408-750;

P ⊖ 🗟) Perched atop a grassy cliff, high above crashing waves and braying sea lions, this spacious, modern, light-filled B&B has stunning views out to the sea. The lovely gardens have a 24-hour hot tub and other perks include the superb breakfast and complimentary tea that is served at 4pm. The owner is Portuguese and family antiques feature in every room.

Turtle Rocks Oceanfront Inn
B&B $$$

(📞 707-677-3707; www.turtlerocksinn.com; 3392 Patrick's Point Dr; r $295-335; P ⊖ 🗟) Enjoy truly stunning sea vistas from every room at this plush, modern place on three peaceful, windswept acres. Rooms are spacious with terraces; number 3 comes particularly recommended with its warm blue decor. A complimentary buffet is served from 3pm to 6pm.

Trinidad Bay B&B
B&B $$$

(📞 707-677-0840; www.trinidadbaybnb.com; 560 Edwards St; r $200-350; P ⊖ 🗟) Opposite the lighthouse, this light-filled Cape Cod–style home overlooks the harbor and Trinidad Head. Breakfast may be delivered to your uniquely styled room and in the afternoon the house fills with the scent of freshly baked cookies. The Trinity Alps room has a kitchenette and is well set up for families.

🍴 Eating

Trinidad is home to superb beaches and hideaway coves where packing a picnic is always a tempting option (thankfully the town has a solid choice of delis and supermarkets). Trinidad State Beach also has excellent picnicking facilities. The restaurants here are, unsurprisingly, centered on seafood and fish; several have coastal views to enhance that ocean-inspired dining experience.

Katy's Smokehouse & Fishmarket
SEAFOOD $

(www.katyssmokehouse.com; 740 Edwards St; ⊙ 9am-6pm) 🐟 Makes its own chemical-free and amazingly delicious smoked and canned fish, using line-caught, sushi-grade seafood; the tuna has been voted number one in the US, no less. There's no restaurant, just grab some for a picnic.

Beachcomber Café
CAFE $

(📞 707-677-0106; 363 Trinity St; breakfast from $4; ⊙ 7am-4pm Mon-Fri, 8am-4pm Sat & Sun; 🗟 📶) Head here for the best breakfast in these parts, ranging from a hearty bowl of organic black beans with avocado and poached egg

to moist and delicious homemade muffins. Also has plenty of newspapers and mags to peruse. Bring your own cup if you want a drink to go.

Lighthouse Café
CALIFORNIAN $

(📞 707-677-0390; 355 Main St; mains $6-9; ⊙ 11am-7pm Tue-Sun; 📶) 🐟 Across from the Chevron, this fun little arty joint makes good food fast, using mostly organic ingredients – try the creative soups, fish and chips with hand-cut fries, local grass-fed beef burgers and homemade ice cream. Order at the counter and then sit inside or out.

Larrupin Cafe
CALIFORNIAN $$$

(📞 707-677-0230; www.thelarrupin.com; 1658 Patrick's Point Dr; mains $22-42; ⊙ 5-9pm Tue-Sun; P) Everybody loves Larrupin, where Moroccan rugs, chocolate-brown walls, gravity-defying floral arrangements and deep-burgundy Oriental carpets create a moody atmosphere perfect for a lovers' tryst. On the menu, expect consistently good mesquite-grilled seafood and meats – the smoked beef brisket is amazing. In the summer, book a table on the garden patio for live music some nights.

❶ Information

Information Kiosk (www.trinidadcalif.com; cnr Patrick's Point Dr & Main St; ⊙ 11am-5pm Jun-Sep, shorter hours Oct-May) Just west of the freeway. Pick up the pamphlet *Discover Trinidad* from here – it has an excellent map.

Trinidad Chamber of Commerce (📞 707-667-1610; www.trinidadcalif.com) Information on the web, but no visitor center.

Patrick's Point State Park

Coastal bluffs jut out to sea at this 640-acre state park, where sandy beaches abut rocky headlands. Easy access to dramatic coastline makes this is a great bet for families, but any age will find a feast for the senses as they climb rock formations, search for breaching whales, carefully navigate tide pools and listen to barking sea lions and singing birds.

Sumêg is an authentic reproduction of a Yurok village, with hand-hewn redwood buildings where Native Americans gather for traditional ceremonies. In the native plant garden you'll find species for making traditional baskets and medicines.

On Agate Beach look for stray bits of jade and sea-polished agate. Follow the signs to tide pools. The 2-mile Rim Trail, an old

Yurok trail around the bluffs, circles the point with access to huge rocky outcrops. Don't miss Wedding Rock, one of the park's most romantic spots. Other trails lead around unusual formations like Ceremonial Rock and Lookout Rock.

The park's three well-tended **campgrounds** (🖉information 707-677-3570, reservations 800-444-7275; www.reserveamerica.com; 4150 Patrick's Point Dr; tent/RV sites $35/45; P🐾) have coin-operated showers and clean bathrooms. Penn Creek and Abalone campgrounds are more sheltered than Agate Beach.

Humboldt Lagoons State Park

Stretching out for miles along the coast, Humboldt Lagoons has long, sandy beaches and a string of coastal lagoons. **Big Lagoon** and the even prettier **Stone Lagoon** are both excellent for kayaking and bird-watching. Sunsets are spectacular, with no artificial structures in sight. Picnic at Stone Lagoon's north end. The Stone Lagoon Visitor Center, on Hwy 101, has closed due to staffing shortages, but there's a toilet and a bulletin board displaying information.

A mile north, **Freshwater Lagoon** is also great for birding. South of Stone Lagoon, tiny **Dry Lagoon** (a freshwater marsh) has a fantastic day hike and good agate hunting. Park at Dry Lagoon's picnic area and hike north on the unmarked trail to Stone Lagoon; the trail skirts the southwestern shore and ends up at the ocean, passing through woods and marshland rich with wildlife. Mostly flat, it's about 2.5 miles one way – and nobody takes it because it's unmarked.

You will have to sleep under canvas in these parts. All campsites are first-come, first-served. The park runs two **environmental campgrounds** (tent sites $20; ☺Apr-Oct; P); bring water. Stone Lagoon has six boat-in environmental campsites.

Humboldt County Parks also operates a lovely cypress-grove picnic area and campground: the **Big Lagoon County Park Campground** (🖉707-445-7651; http://co.humboldt.ca.us; off Hwy 101; tent sites $20; P🐾) beside Big Lagoon, a mile off Hwy 101, with flush toilets and cold water, but no showers.

Redwood National & State Parks

This richly forested region can be a little confusing regarding which park is where and what they all offer. The main parks in this jigsaw of mighty redwoods are: the Redwood National Park; Prairie Creek Redwoods State Park; Del Norte Coast Redwoods State Park and Jedediah Smith Redwoods State Park (famed for being a backdrop in the original *Star Wars* movie). Interspersed among the parks are a number of small towns, while to the south lies Orick (population 650), which offers a few storefronts, a gas station and an excellent visitor center. All the parks are an International Biosphere Reserve and World Heritage Site, yet they remain little visited when compared to their southern brethren, like the Sequoia National Park. It is worth contemplating that some of these trees have been standing here for time immemorial, predating the Roman Empire by over 500 years. Prepare to be impressed.

Redwood National Park

This park is the southernmost of a patchwork of state and federally administered lands under the umbrella of **Redwood National & State Parks** (🖉707-465-7335; www.nps.gov/redw; Hwy 101, Orick; P👣) 🏷**FREE**. After picking up a map at the **visitor center**, you'll have a suite of choices for hiking. A few miles north along Hwy 101, a

---

THE ENDANGERED MARBLED MURRELET

Notice how undeveloped the Redwood National and State Parks have remained? Thank the marbled murrelet, a small white and brown-black auk that nests in old-growth conifers. Loss of nesting territory due to logging has severely depleted the bird's numbers but Redwood National Park scientists have discovered that corvid predators (ravens, jays etc) are also to blame. Because corvids are attracted to food scraps left by visitors, the number of snacking, picnicking or camping humans in the park greatly affects predation on the marbled murrelet. Restrictions on development to prevent food scraps and thus protect the birds are so strict that it's nearly impossible to build anything new.

trip inland on Bald Hills Rd will take you to Lady Bird Johnson Grove, with its 1-mile, kid-friendly loop trail, or get you lost in the secluded serenity of Tall Trees Grove.

To protect the Tall Trees Grove, a limited number of cars per day are allowed access; get permits at the visitor center. This can be a half-day trip itself, but you're well rewarded after the challenging approach (a 6-mile rumble on an old logging road behind a locked gate, then a moderately strenuous 4-mile round-trip hike). Another recommended hike is to Trillium Falls – a 2½-mile trail leading to a small waterfall, accessed from Davidson Rd at Elk Meadow.

Note that during the winter, several foot bridges crossing the Redwood Creek are removed due to the high waters. If you are hiking at this time of year, be sure to check with a ranger regarding the current situation before striding out.

Elk Meadow Cabins   CABIN $$$
(☑ 866-733-9637; www.redwoodadventures.com; 7 Valley Green Camp Rd, Orick; cabins $239-289; P 🐾 🞉) These spotless and bright cabins with equipped kitchens and all the mod-cons are in a perfect mid-parks location – they're great if you're traveling in a group and the most comfy choice even if you're not. Expect to see elk on the lawn in the mornings. Cabins sleep six to eight people and there's an additional $65 cleaning fee.

❶ Information

Unlike most national parks, there are no fees and no highway entrance stations at Redwood National Park, so it's imperative to pick up the free map at the park headquarters in Crescent City (p272) or at the information center in Orick. Rangers here issue permits to visit Tall Trees Grove and loan bear-proof containers for back-packers.

For in-depth redwood ecology, buy the excellent official park handbook. The **Redwood Parks Association** (www.redwoodparksassociation. org) provides good information on its website, including detailed descriptions of all the park hikes.

Prairie Creek Redwoods State Park

Famous for some of the world's best virgin redwood groves and unspoiled coastline, this 14,000-acre **section** (www.parks.ca.gov; Newton B Drury Scenic Pkwy; per car $8; P 🖈) 🌿 of Redwood National & State Parks has

spectacular scenic drives and 70 miles of mainly shady hiking trails, many of which are excellent for children. Kids of all ages will enjoy the magnificent herd of elk here, which can generally be spied grazing at the Elk Prairie, signposted from the highway; the best times to be sure of seeing the elk are early morning and around sunset.

There are 28 **mountain-biking** and **hiking trails** through the park, from simple to strenuous. Only a few of these will appeal to hard-core hikers, who should take on the Del Norte Coast Redwoods. A few easy nature trails start near the visitor center, including Revelation Trail and Elk Prairie Trail. Stroll the recently reforested logging road on the Ah-Pah Interpretive Trail at the park's north end. The most challenging hike in this corner of the park is the spectacular 11.5-mile Coastal Trail which goes through primordial redwoods and is part of the California Coastal Trail (www.californiacoastaltrail.info).

Just past the Gold Bluffs Beach Campground the road deadends at Fern Canyon, the second busiest spot in the park, where 60ft fern-covered sheer-rock walls are so unusual that they were used in scenes from Steven Spielberg's *Jurassic Park 2: The Lost World*, as well as *Return of the Jedi*. This is one of the most photographed spots on the North Coast – damp and lush, all emerald green – and totally worth getting your toes wet to see.

Newton B Drury Scenic Parkway   DRIVING
(Hwy 101, Orick; 🖈) Just north of Orick is the turnoff for the 8-mile parkway, which runs parallel to Hwy 101 through untouched ancient redwood forests. This is a not-to-miss short detour off the freeway where you can view the magnificence of these trees. Numerous trails branch off from roadside pull-outs, including family-friendly options and trails that fit ADA (American Disabilities Act) requirements, such as Big Tree Wayside and Revelation Trail.

★ Gold Bluffs Beach   CAMPGROUND $
(tent sites $35) This gorgeous campground sits between 100ft cliffs and wide-open ocean, but there are some windbreaks and solar-heated showers. Look for sites up the cliff under the trees. No reservations.

Elk Prairie Campground   CAMPGROUND $
(☑ reservations 800-444-7275; www.reserve america.com; Prairie Creek Rd; tent & RV sites $35; P 🞉) Elk roam this popular campground,

SMITH RIVER NATIONAL RECREATION AREA

West of Jedediah Smith Redwoods State Park, the Smith River, the state's last remaining undammed waterway, runs right beside Hwy 199. Originating high in the Siskiyou Mountains, its serpentine course cuts through deep canyons beneath thick forests. Chinook salmon (October to December) and steelhead trout (December to April) annually migrate up its clear waters. Camp (there are four developed campgrounds), hike (75 miles of trails), raft (145 miles of navigable white water) and kayak here, but check regulations if you want to fish. Stop by the **Six Rivers National Forest Headquarters** (☑707-457-3131; www.fs.fed.us/r5/sixrivers; 10600 Hwy 199, Gasquet; ⊗8am-4:30pm daily May-Sep, 8am-4:30pm Mon-Fri Oct-Apr) to get your bearings. Pick up pamphlets for the **Darlingtonia Trail** and **Myrtle Creek Botanical Area**, both easy jaunts into the woods, where you can see rare plants and learn about the area's geology.

where you can sleep under redwoods or at the prairie's edge. There are hot showers, some hike-in sites and a shallow creek to splash in. Sites one to seven and 69 to 76 are on grassy prairies and get full sun; sites eight to 68 are wooded. To camp in a mixed redwood forest, book sites 20 to 27.

Del Norte Coast Redwoods State Park

Marked by steep canyons and dense woods north of Klamath, half the 6400 acres of this **park** (☑707-465-7335; www.parks.ca.gov; Mill Creek Rd; per car $8; P) 🖋 are virgin redwood forest, crisscrossed by 15 miles of hiking trails, some of which pass by branches of Mill Creek (bring your fishing rod). The park also fronts 8 miles of rugged coastline.

Hwy 1 winds in from the coast at dramatic Wilson Beach, and traverses the dense forest, with groves stretching as far as you can see. Picnic on the sand at False Klamath Cove. Heading north, tall trees cling precipitously to canyon walls that drop to the rocky, timber-strewn coastline. Unfortunately, it is impossible to hike to the water – as of April 2017, the trail bridge located 1.75 miles in from the parking lot on Damnation Creek Trail was closed until further notice.

Serious hikers will be most greatly rewarded by the Damnation Creek Trail. It's only 4 miles long, but the 1100-ft elevation change and cliff-side red-wood makes it the park's best hike. The unmarked trailhead starts from a parking area off Hwy 101 at Mile 16.

Crescent Beach Overlook and picnic area has superb wintertime whale-watching. At the park's north end,

watch the surf pound at Crescent Beach, just south of Crescent City via Enderts Beach Rd.

Mill Creek Campground (☑reservations 800-444-7275; www.reserveamerica.com; Mill Creek Rd; tent & RV sites $35; ⊗mid-May–Oct; P) has hot showers and 145 sites in a redwood grove, 2 miles east of Hwy 101 and 7 miles south of Crescent City. Sites 1-74 are woodsier; sites 75-145 sunnier. Hike-in sites are prettiest.

Pick up maps and inquire about guided walks at the Crescent City Information Center (p272) or the **Thomas H Kuchel Visitor Center** (☑707-465-7765; www.nps.gov/redw; Hwy 101, Orick; ⊗9am-5pm Apr-Oct, to 4pm Nov-Mar; 🐾) in Orick.

Jedediah Smith Redwoods State Park

The northernmost park, Jedediah Smith is 9 miles northeast of Crescent City (via Hwy 101 north to Hwy 199 east). The redwood stands are so thick that few trails penetrate the park, but the outstanding 11-mile **Howland Hill Rd scenic drive** cuts through otherwise inaccessible areas (take Hwy 199 to South Fork Rd; turn right after crossing two bridges). It's a rough road, impassable for RVs, but if you can't hike, it's the best way to see the forest.

Stop for a stroll under enormous trees in **Simpson-Reed Grove**. There's a swimming hole and picnic area near the park entrance. An easy half-mile trail, departing from the far side of the campground, crosses the Smith River via a summer-only footbridge, leading to Stout Grove, the park's most famous grove. The visitor center sells hiking maps and nature guides.

Klamath

Giant metal-cast golden bears stand sentry at the bridge across the Klamath River, announcing Klamath, one of the tiny settlements that break up Redwood National & State Parks between Prairie Creek Redwoods State Park and Del Norte Coast Redwoods State Park. With a gas station/market, diner and a casino, Klamath is basically a wide spot in the road with some seriously great roadside kitsch at its edges. The Yurok Tribal Headquarters is in the town center and the entire settlement and much of the surrounding area is the tribe's ancestral land. The Yuroks are the largest group of Native Americans in the state of California.

Klamath is roughly an hour north of Eureka and is popular with hikers, campers and anglers; the river is famed for its wild freshwater salmon and is one of California's last free-flowing rivers after a proposal to build a dam here was thwarted in 1994.

⊙ Sights & Activities

The mouth of the **Klamath River** is a dramatic sight. Marine, riparian, forest and meadow ecological zones all converge and the birding is exceptional. For the best views, head north of town to Requa Rd and the **Klamath River Overlook** and picnic on high bluffs above driftwood-strewn beaches. On a clear day, this is one of the most spectacular viewpoints on the North Coast, and one of the best whale-watching spots in California (this is one of the mammal's first feeding stops as they come south from Alaska). For a good hike, head north along the Coastal Trail. You'll have the sand to yourself at **Hidden Beach**; access the trail at the northern end of Motel Trees.

Just south of the river, on Hwy 101, the scenic **Coastal Drive**, a narrow, winding country road, traces extremely high cliffs over the ocean. Due to erosion a 3.3-mile section of the 9.5-mile loop (between Carruther's Cove trailhead and the intersection of the Coastal Drive with Alder Camp Rd) has been closed to motor traffic since 2011, but it's still walkable.

🛏 Sleeping

Woodsy Klamath is cheaper than Crescent City, but there aren't as many places to eat or buy groceries, and there's nothing to do at night but play cards. There are ample private RV parks in the area.

Flint Ridge Campground　CAMPGROUND
(☑707-464-6101) FREE Four miles from the Klamath River Bridge via Coastal Dr, this tent-only, hike-in campground sits among a wild, overgrown meadow of ferns and moss. It's a 10-minute walk (half a mile) east, uphill from the parking area. There's no water, plenty of bear sightings (bear boxes on-site) and you have to pack out trash. But, hey, it's free.

Ravenwood Motel　MOTEL $
(☑707-482-5911;　www.ravenwoodmotel.com; 131 Klamath Blvd; r/ste with kitchen $95/140; P🐾📶) The spotlessly clean rooms are individually decorated with furnishings and flair you'd expect in a city hotel, not a small-town motel. The same could be said of the surrounding attractions – there is a casino virtually next door!

★**Historic Requa Inn**　HISTORIC HOTEL $$
(☑707-482-1425; www.requainn.com; 451 Requa Rd; r $119-199; P🐾📶) 🍽 A woodsy country lodge on bluffs overlooking the mouth of the Klamath, the creaky and bright 1914 Requa Inn is a North Coast favorite and – even better – it's a carbon-neutral facility. Many of the charming, old-timey Americana rooms have mesmerizing views over the misty river, as does the dining room, which serves locally sourced, organic New American cuisine.

TREES OF MYSTERY

It's hard to miss the giant statues of Paul Bunyan and Babe the Blue Ox towering over the parking lot at **Trees of Mystery** (☑707-482-2251; www.treesofmystery.net; 15500 Hwy 101; museum free, gondola adult/child $16/8; ⊙8:30am-6:30pm Jun-Aug, 9am-6pm Sep & Oct, 9:30am-4:30pm Nov-May; P👶), a shameless tourist trap with a gondola running through the redwood canopy and a fun 'Tall Tales Forest' where chainsaw sculptures tell the tale of Paul Bunyan. It's perfect for families. The surprisingly wonderful **End of the Trail Museum** located behind the gift shop has an outstanding collection of Native American arts and artifacts, and it's free.

Crescent City

Crescent City is California's last big town north of Arcata. Founded as a thriving seaport and supply center for inland gold mines in the mid-19th century, the town's history was quite literally washed away in 1964, when half the town was swallowed by a tsunami. Of course, it was rebuilt (though mostly with the utilitarian ugliness of ticky-tacky buildings), but its marina was devastated by effects of the 2011 Japan earthquake and tsunami, when the city was evacuated. The economy depends heavily on shrimp and crab fishing, hotel tax and on Pelican Bay maximum-security prison, just north of town, which adds tension to the air and lots of cops to the streets.

Hwy 101 splits into two parallel one-way streets, with the southbound traffic on L St, northbound on M St. To see the major sights, turn west on Front St toward the lighthouse. Downtown is along 3rd St.

◉ Sights

If you're in town in August, the **Del Norte County Fair** features a rodeo, and lots of characters.

North Coast Marine
Mammal Center
SCIENCE CENTER
(☏707-465-6265; www.northcoastmmc.org; 424 Howe Dr; ◷10am-5pm; ♿) ✎ Just east of Battery Point, this is the ecologically minded foil to the garish Ocean World. The clinic treats injured seals, sea lions and dolphins and releases them back into the wild. There is an interesting gift shop.

Battery Point Lighthouse
LIGHTHOUSE
(☏707-467-3089; www.delnortehistory.org; South A St; adult/child $3/1; ◷10am-4pm Wed-Sun Apr-Sep) The 1856 lighthouse still operates on a tiny, rocky island that you can easily reach at low tide. You can also get a tour of the on-site museum for $3. Note that the listed hours are subject to change due to tides and weather.

Beachfront Park
PARK
(Howe Dr; P♿) Between B and H Sts, this park has a harborside beach with no large waves, making it perfect for little ones. Further east on Howe Dr, near J St, you'll come to **Kidtown**, with slides and swings and a make-believe castle.

🛏 Sleeping

Most people stop here for one night while traveling; motels are overpriced, but you'll pass a slew of good midrange hotels on the main arteries leading into and out of town, and you will generally have no problem finding a room, whatever the season. The county operates two excellent first-come, first-served campgrounds just outside of town and a couple of B&Bs have more recently opened up in town.

Curly Redwood Lodge
MOTEL $
(☏707-464-2137; www.curlyredwoodlodge.com; 701 Hwy 101 S; r $79-107; P♿❄🐾) The motel is a marvel: it's entirely built and paneled from a single curly redwood tree that measured over 18ft thick in diameter. Progressively restored and polished into a gem of mid-20th-century kitsch, the inn is like stepping into a time capsule and a delight for retro junkies. Rooms are clean, large and comfortable (request one away from the road).

Florence Keller Park
CAMPGROUND $
(☏707-464-7230; www.co.del-norte.ca.us; 3400 Cunningham Lane; tent sites $10; P) County-run Florence Keller Park has 50 sites in a beautiful grove of young redwoods (take Hwy 101 north to Elk Valley Cross Rd and follow the signs). There are limited facilities at this campground: toilets, but no showers.

Bay View Inn
HOTEL $
(☏800-742-8439; www.ccbvi.com; 310 Hwy 101 S; s/d $55/99; P♿🐾) Bright, modern, updated rooms with microwaves and refrigerators fill this centrally located, independent hotel. It may seem a bit like a better-than-average highway-exit chain, but colorful bedspreads and warm hosts add necessary homespun appeal. The rooms upstairs in the back have views of the lighthouse and the harbor.

Anna Wulf Bed & Breakfast
B&B $$
(☏707-464-5340; www.annawulfhousebedand breakfast.com; 622 J St; r/ste $100/150; P♿🐾) Nice, Victorian-style B&B built in 1896. It's not as frilly inside as the lavender exterior would predict. The Honeymoon Suite has an inviting clawfoot tub. Check-out time is civilized (noon) – refreshing in these parts.

★ Scopa at the Sea
B&B $$$
(☏541-944-4156; www.scopaproperties.com; 344 N Pebble Beach Dr; r from $250; P♿🐾) The Cape Cod–style architecture twinned with deluxe contemporary decor make this a

good option for those weary of motel chains. Furnished in warm earth colors with a design eye for detail, the en suites have tubs, as well as showers, while the front terrace is ideally placed for whale-watching. The breakfast highlights are the homemade breads and pastries made by innkeeper Deborah.

✗ Eating

Crescent City has plenty of restaurants, including a large number of fast-food options located on Hwy 101. For fresh seafood, there are a couple of aptly located restaurants near the water that specialize in fresh shrimp and crab. There is an excellent farmers market held every Saturday from June to October at the Del Norte County Fairgrounds.

Good Harvest Cafe   AMERICAN $
(☑707-465-6028; 575 Hwy 101 S; mains $7-16; ⊘7:30am-9pm Mon-Sat, from 8am Sun; ☑⊞) This popular family owned cafe is in a spacious location across from the harbor. It's got a bit of everything – all pretty good – from soups and sandwiches to full meals and smoothies. Fine beers, a crackling fire and loads of vegetarian options make this among the best dining spots in town.

North Coast Ocean Sports & Grill   GRILL $
(☑707-465-1465; www.northcoastoceansportsandgrill.com; 110 Anchor Way; mains $11-15; ⊘11am-8pm; P⊞) A young, informal vibe, a no-frills sound menu of seafood, burgers and salads and exceptional ice cream mean this place is always packed out, especially in summer when folk spill out onto the front deck across from the ocean. It also rents out surf boards, kayaks and bikes.

Enoteca   ITALIAN, AMERICAN $
(960 3rd St; mains $7-12; ⊘11am-7pm Mon-Wed & Sat, to 8pm Thu, to 10pm Fri; ☎) Stop in for salads, pasta, sandwiches or jazz on Friday nights. Hands down the most happening place downtown.

Chart Room   SEAFOOD $$
(☑707-464-5993; www.ccchartroom.com; 130 Anchor Way; dinner mains $10-28; ⊘7am-7pm Wed-Thu & Sun, to 8pm Fri & Sat, 11am-4pm Tue; P⊞) At the tip of the South Harbor pier, this joint is renowned far and wide for its fish and chips: batter-caked golden beauties that deliver on their reputation. It's often a hive of families, retirees, Harley riders and fisherfolk, so grab a beer at the small bar and wait for a table. Other rec-

ommendations include the creamy clam chowder.

ⓘ Information

Crescent City Information Center (☑707-465-7335; www.nps.gov/redw; 1111 2nd St; ⊘9am-5pm Apr-Oct, to 4pm Nov-Mar) On the corner of K St; you'll find rangers here and information about all four parks under its jurisdiction.

Crescent City-Del Norte Chamber of Commerce (☑707-464-3174; www.exploredelnorte.com; 1001 Front St; ⊘9am-5pm daily May-Aug, 9am-5pm Mon-Fri Sep-Apr) A helpful office that can provide local information, as well as a map.

ⓘ Getting There & Around

Alaska Airlines (p220) and Penair (p220) fly into tiny **Del Norte County Regional Airport** (CEC; ☑707-464-7288; www.flycrescentcity.com; 250 Dale Rupert Rd, Crescent City; ⊘5am-7:30pm), located 3 miles northwest of town. There are frequent flights to Eureka as well as Portland, Redding and North Bend in Oregon.

Redwood Coast Transit (p220) serves Crescent City with local buses ($1), and runs buses Monday to Saturday to Klamath ($1.50, one hour, three daily) and Arcata ($30, two hours, three daily), with stops in between. Have the exact fare, the driver carries no change.

Drivers may experience delays on Hwy 101 between Klamath and Crescent City as corrosion continues to affect the highway, particularly after heavy rains.

Tolowa Dunes State Park & Lake Earl Wildlife Area

Two miles north of Crescent City, this **state park and wildlife area** (☑707-464-6101, ext 5112; Kellogg Rd; ⊘sunrise-sunset) encompasses 10,000 acres of wetlands, dunes, meadows and two lakes – **Lake Earl** and **Lake Tolowa**. This major stopover on the Pacific Flyway route brings over 250 species of birds here. Listen for the whistling, warbling chorus. On land, look for coyotes and deer, angle for trout, or hike or ride 20 miles of trails; at sea, spot whales, seals and sea lions.

The park and wildlife area are a patchwork of lands administered by California State Parks and the Department of Fish and Game (DFG). The DFG focuses on single-species management, hunting and fishing; the State Parks' focus is on ecodiversity and recreation. You might be hiking a vast expanse of pristine dunes, then suddenly hear a shotgun or a whining 4WD. Strict regulations limit where and when you can hunt and drive; trails are clearly marked.

To get here from Crescent City, take Northcrest Dr north off of Hwy 101, which becomes Lake Earl Dr. Turn left on Lower Lake Rd to Kellogg Rd, which leads to the park.

Pelican State Beach

The northernmost beach in California and the most northern spot on the California Coastal Trail, never-crowded **Pelican State Beach** (✆707-464-6101, ext 5151; Gilbert Way, Hwy 101; P) occupies 5 coastal acres just south of the Oregon border. There are no facilities and due to its easy-to-miss access, this beach has been described as the loneliest beach in California, but it's great for walking, beachcombing and kite flying; pick one up at one of the kite specialty shops just over the border in Oregon.

The beach is around 2 miles east of Pelican Bay State Prison; the only so-called super maximum security facility in California and a world away, one imagines, from the tranquility of this beautiful unspoiled beach.

Clifford Kamph
Memorial Park   CAMPGROUND $
(✆707-464-7230; 15100 Hwy 101; tent sites $10) Pitch a tent by the ocean (no windbreaks) at Clifford Kamph Memorial Park; no RVs. It's a steal for the beachside location and, even though sites are exposed in a grassy area and there isn't much privacy, all have BBQs.

Casa Rubio   BOUTIQUE HOTEL $$
(✆707-487-4313; www.casarubio.com; 17285 Crissey Rd; r $98-178; P ♿ 🐾 🛜 🐕) The best reason to visit Pelican State Beach is to stay at secluded, charming Casa Rubio, where three of the four ocean-view rooms have kitchens. Surrounded by tropical gardens, a short path leads directly to the beach.

Central Coast

Best Places to Eat

➡ Assembly (p282)

➡ Ember (p332)

➡ Foremost Wine Co (p326)

➡ Thomas Hill Organics (p324)

➡ La Cosecha Bar & Restaurant (p321)

Best Places to Sleep

➡ Post Ranch Inn (p306)

➡ Jabberwock (p292)

➡ Cass House Inn (p313)

➡ Avila La Fonda (p329)

➡ Summerwood Inn (p321)

Why Go?

Too often forgotten or dismissed as 'flyover' country between San Francisco and LA, this fairy-tale stretch of California coast is packed with wild beaches, misty redwood forests where hot springs hide, and rolling golden hills of fertile vineyards and farm fields.

Coastal Hwy 1 pulls out all the stops, scenery-wise. Flower-power Santa Cruz and the historic port town of Monterey are gateways to the rugged wilderness of the bohemian Big Sur coast. It's an epic journey snaking down to vainglorious Hearst Castle, past lighthouses and edgy cliffs atop which endangered condors soar.

Get acquainted with California's agricultural heartland along inland Hwy 101, called El Camino Real (the King's Highway) by Spanish conquistadors and Franciscan friars. Colonial missions still line the route, which passes through Paso Robles' flourishing wine and craft-beer country. Then soothe your nature-loving soul in collegiate San Luis Obispo, ringed by sunny beach towns and volcanic peaks.

When to Go
Santa Cruz

Apr–May Balmy temperatures, but fewer tourists than summer; wildflowers bloom.

Jul–Aug Fog disappears as ocean waters warm up for beach season.

Sep–Oct Sunny blue skies, smaller crowds and wine-country harvest festivals.

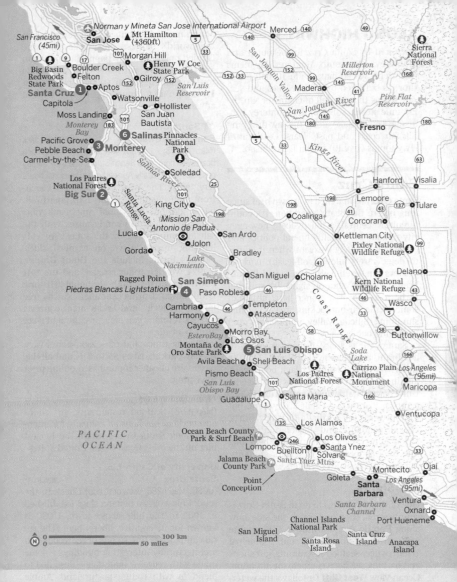

Central Coast Highlights

① Learning to surf, and scaring yourself silly on the Giant Dipper along the famed beach boardwalk in **Santa Cruz** (p276).

② Cruising Hwy 1, where the sky touches the sea along the rocky coastline of mystical **Big Sur** (p301).

③ Being mesmerized by aquatic denizens of the 'indoor ocean' at the superb aquarium in **Monterey** (p287).

④ Marveling at the jawdropping grandiosity of Hearst Castle in **San Simeon** (p309) after meeting the neighbors: ginormous elephant seals.

⑤ Chilling out in easygoing college town **San Luis Obispo** (p323), surrounded by beaches, vineyards and mountains.

⑥ Exploring **Salinas** (p317) and the blue-collar world of Nobel Prize–winning, down-to-earth novelist John Steinbeck.

ALONG HIGHWAY 1

Anchored by Santa Cruz to the north and Monterey to the south, Monterey Bay teems with richly varied marine life. Its half-moon shore is bordered by wild beaches and seaside towns that are full of character. On the 125-mile stretch south of the Monterey Peninsula, you'll snake along the jaw-dropping Big Sur coast and past Hearst Castle until Hwy 1 joins Hwy 101 in San Luis Obispo.

Santa Cruz

Santa Cruz has marched to its own beat since long before the Beat Generation. It's counterculture central, a touchy-feely, new-agey city famous for its leftie-liberal politics and easygoing ideology – except when it comes to dogs (rarely allowed off-leash), parking (meters run seven days a week) and Republicans (allegedly shot on sight). It's still cool to be a hippie or a stoner here, although some of the far-out-looking freaks are just slumming Silicon Valley millionaires and trust-fund babies.

Santa Cruz is a city of madcap fun, with a vibrant but chaotic downtown. On the waterfront is the famous beach boardwalk, and in the hills redwood groves embrace the University of California, Santa Cruz (UCSC) campus. Plan at least half a day here, but to appreciate the aesthetic of jangly skirts, crystal pendants and Rastafarian dreadlocks, stay longer and plunge headlong into the rich local brew of surfers, students, punks and eccentric characters.

◉ Sights

One of the best things to do in Santa Cruz is simply stroll, shop and watch the sideshow along **Pacific Ave** downtown. A 15-minute walk away is the beach and Municipal Wharf, where seafood restaurants, gift shops and barking sea lions compete for attention. Ocean-view **West Cliff Dr** follows the waterfront southwest of the wharf, paralleled by a paved recreational path.

★ Seymour Marine
Discovery Center   MUSEUM
(Map p286; ☑ 831-459-3800; http://seymourcenter. ucsc.edu; 100 Shaffer Rd; adult/child 3-16yr $8/6; ◎10am-5pm Tue-Sun; ℗⚓) ✎ By Natural Bridges State Beach, this kids' educational center is part of UCSC's Long Marine Laboratory. Interactive natural-science exhibits include tidal touch pools and

aquariums, while outside you can gawk at the world's largest blue-whale skeleton. Guided one-hour tours happen at 1pm, 2pm and 3pm daily, with a special 30-minute tour for families with younger children at 11am; sign up for tours in person an hour in advance (no reservations).

★ Santa Cruz
Beach Boardwalk   AMUSEMENT PARK
(Map p278; ☑ 831-423-5590; www.beach boardwalk.com; 400 Beach St; per ride $4-7, all-day pass $37-82; ◎ daily Apr-early Sep, seasonal hours vary; ℗⚓) The West Coast's oldest beachfront amusement park, this 1907 boardwalk has a glorious old-school Americana vibe. The smell of cotton candy mixes with the salt air, punctuated by the squeals of kids hanging upside down on carnival rides. Famous thrills include the **Giant Dipper**, a 1924 wooden roller coaster, and the 1911 **Looff carousel**, both National Historic Landmarks. During summer, catch free midweek movies and Friday-night concerts by rock veterans you may have thought were already dead.

Closing times and off-season hours vary. All-day parking costs $5 to $15, and all-day passes are cheaper if purchased online prior to visiting.

Municipal Wharf   LANDMARK
(Map p278) Seafood restaurants, gift shops and barking sea lions all compete for attention along Santa Cruz's wharf, the longest pier on the West Coast of the United States.

University of California,
Santa Cruz   UNIVERSITY
(UCSC; Map p286; www.ucsc.edu) Check it: the school mascot is a banana slug! Established in 1965 in the hills above town, UCSC is known for its creative, liberal bent. The rural campus has fine stands of redwoods and architecturally interesting buildings – some made with recycled materials – designed to blend in with rolling pastureland. Amble around the peaceful **arboretum** (Map p286; ☑ 831-502-2998; www.arboretum.ucsc.edu; cnr High St & Arboretum Rd; adult/child 6-17yr $5/2, free 1st Tue of each month; ◎9am-5pm) and picturesquely decaying 19th-century structures from Cowell Ranch, upon which the campus was built.

Museum of Art & History   MUSEUM
(Map p278; ☑ 831-429-1964; www.santacruzmah. org; McPherson Center, 705 Front St; adult/child 12-17yr $10/8, free 1st Fri of each month; ◎11am-5pm

TOP SANTA CRUZ BEACHES

Sun-kissed Santa Cruz has warmer beaches than San Francisco or Monterey. *Baywatch* it isn't, but 29 miles of coastline reveal a few Hawaii-worthy beaches, craggy coves, some primo surf spots and big sandy stretches where your kids will have a blast. Fog may ruin many a summer morning; it often burns off by the afternoon.

West Cliff Dr is lined with scramble-down-to coves and plentiful parking. If you don't want sand in your shoes, park yourself on a bench and watch enormous pelicans dive for fish. You'll find bathrooms and showers at the lighthouse parking lot.

Locals favor less-trampled East Cliff Dr beaches, which are bigger and more protected from the wind, meaning calmer waters. Except at a small metered lot at 26th Ave, parking is by permit only on weekends (buy a $8 per-day permit at 9th Ave).

Main Beach (Map p278) *The* scene in Santa Cruz, with a huge sandy stretch, volleyball courts and swarms of people. Park on E Cliff Dr and walk across the *Lost Boys* trestle to the beach boardwalk (p276).

Its Beach (Map p286; 🐾) The only official off-leash beach for dogs (before 10am and after 4pm) in Santa Cruz is just west of the lighthouse. The field across the street is another good romping ground.

Natural Bridges State Beach (Map p286; 📞831-423-4609; www.parks.ca.gov; 2531 W Cliff Dr; per car $10; ⊗8am-sunset; 🅿🚼) Best for sunsets, this family favorite has lots of sand, tide pools and monarch butterflies from mid-October through mid-February. It's at the far western end of W Cliff Dr.

Seacliff State Beach (📞831-685-6442; www.parks.ca.gov; State Park Rd, Aptos; per car $10; ⊗8am-sunset) Seacliff State Beach harbors a 'cement boat,' a quixotic freighter built of concrete that floated OK, but ended up here as a coastal fishing pier. During huge storms in February 2017, the boat actually broke apart but remains *in situ*.

Manresa State Beach (📞831-724-3750; www.parks.ca.gov; San Andreas Rd, Watsonville; per car $10; ⊗8am-sunset) Near Watsonville, the La Selva Beach exit off Hwy 1 leads here to this sparsely populated beach.

Moran Lake County Park (Map p286; F Cliff Dr; ⊗8am-sunset) With a good surf break and bathrooms, this pretty all-around sandy spot is further east of 26th Ave off E Cliff Dr.

Cowell's Beach (Map p278) Popular Santa Cruz surfing beach off W Cliff Dr.

Sunset State Beach (📞831-763-7062; www.parks.ca.gov; San Andreas Rd, Watsonville; per car $10; ⊗8am-sunset) The La Selva Beach exit off Hwy 1, near Watsonville, brings you here, where you can have miles of sand and surf almost all to yourself.

Tue-Thu & Sat & Sun, to 9pm Fri) In Santa Cruz's downtown, rotating displays by contemporary California artists and exhibits that dive into local history are worth a quick look. Recent renovations include an adjacent courtyard with cafes and restaurants.

Sanctuary Exploration Center MUSEUM (Map p278; 📞831-421-9993; www.montereybay. noaa.gov; 35 Pacific Ave; ⊗10am-5pm Wed-Sun; 🚼) 🆓 Operated by the Monterey Bay National Marine Sanctuary, this educational museum near the beach boardwalk is an interactive multimedia experience that teaches kids and adults about the bay's marine treasures, watershed conservation and high-tech underwater exploration for scientific research.

Santa Cruz Surfing Museum MUSEUM (Map p286; 📞831-420-6289; www.santacruz surfingmuseum.org; 701 W Cliff Dr; by donation; ⊗10am-5pm Wed-Mon Jul 4-early Sep, noon-4pm Thu-Mon early Sep-Jul 3; 🚼) A mile southwest of the wharf along the coast, this tiny museum inside an old lighthouse is packed with memorabilia, including vintage redwood surfboards. Fittingly, Lighthouse Point overlooks two popular surf breaks.

Mystery Spot LANDMARK (📞831-423-8897; www.mysteryspot.com; 465 Mystery Spot Rd; $8; ⊗10am-4pm Mon-Fri, to 5pm Sat & Sun Sep-May, 10am-6pm Mon-Fri, 9am-7pm Sat & Sun Jun-Aug; 🅿🚼) A kitschy, old-fashioned tourist trap, Santa Cruz's Mystery Spot has scarcely changed since it opened in 1940. On

Santa Cruz

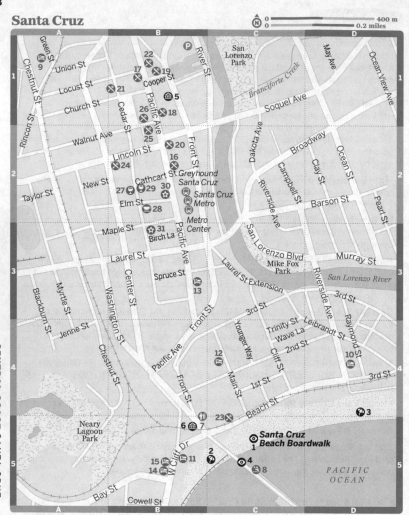

CENTRAL COAST SANTA CRUZ

a steeply sloping hillside, compasses seem to point crazily, mysterious forces push you around and buildings lean at silly angles. Make reservations, or risk getting stuck waiting for a tour. It's about 4 miles northeast of downtown: take Water St to Market St north and continue on Branciforte Dr into the hills. Parking costs $5. Don't forget your bumper sticker!

Santa Cruz Museum of Natural History   MUSEUM

(Map p286; ☏831-420-6115; www.santacruz museum.org; 1305 E Cliff Dr; adult/child under 18yr $4/free, free 1st Fri of each month; ☉11am-

4pm Tue-Fri & 10am-5pm Sat-Sun; ⚐) The collections at this pint-sized museum include stuffed-animal mounts, Native Californian cultural artifacts and a touch-friendly tide pool that shows off sea critters living by the beach right across the street.

🏃 Activities

★ Santa Cruz Food Tour   FOOD

(☏866-736-6343; www.santacruzfoodtour.com; per person $59; ☉2:30-6pm Fri & Sat) Combining Afghan flavors, a farm-to-table bistro, vegan cupcakes and artisan ice cream, these highly recommended walking tours

Santa Cruz

also come with a healthy serving of local knowledge and interesting insights into Santa Cruz history, culture and architecture. Sign up for a tour when you first arrive in town to get your bearings in the tastiest way possible.

Slow Adventure WALKING
(☎831-332-7923; www.slowadventure.us; per person $1495; ☻Apr-Oct) 🍴 Well-traveled Santa Cruz local Margaret Leonard arranges self-guided walking adventures around Monterey Bay. The full itinerary from Santa Cruz to Monterey takes six days and five nights, covering from 40 to 50 miles in total, and overnighting in very comfortable ocean-view accommodations along the way. Luggage is transferred independently, and highlights include birdlife, marine mammals and superb coastal views. Shorter four-day/three-night coastal adventures to the north and south of Santa Cruz are also available (per person $995 to $1095).

DeLaveaga Disc Golf Club GOLF
(Map p286; www.facebook.com/groups/Dela DDGC; Upper Park Rd; 👪) FREE Touring pros and families with kids toss discs across this challenging hillside layout that peaks at Hole No 27, nicknamed 'Top of the World.' It's a couple of miles northeast of downtown Santa Cruz, off Branciforte Dr.

SUP Shack WATER SPORTS
(Map p286; ☎831-464-7467; www.supshacksanta cruz.com; 2214 E Cliff Dr; rental/lessons from $20/59) Based in the calm waters of Santa Cruz Harbor, SUP Shack offers paddleboarding lessons and rentals. Kayaks and body boards are also available for rental.

Surfing
Year-round, water temperatures average under 60°F, meaning that without a wetsuit, body parts quickly turn blue. Surfing is incredibly popular, especially at experts-only **Steamer Lane** and beginners' Cowell's (p277), both off W Cliff Dr. Other favorite surf spots include **Pleasure Point Beach**, on E Cliff Dr toward Capitola, and Manresa State Beach (p277) off Hwy 1 southbound.

O'Neill Surf Shop SURFING
(Map p286; ☎831-475-4151; www.oneill.com; 1115 41st Ave; wetsuit/surfboard rental from $15/25; ☻9am-8pm Mon-Fri, from 8am Sat & Sun) Head east toward Pleasure Point to worship at this internationally renowned surfboard-maker's flagship store, with branches on the beach boardwalk and downtown.

Richard Schmidt Surf School SURFING
(Map p286; ☎831-423-0928; www.richard schmidt.com; 849 Almar Ave; 2hr group/1hr private lesson $90/120; 👪) Award-winning,

time-tested surf school can get you out there, all equipment included. Summer surf camps hook adults and kids alike.

Cowell's Beach Surf Shop
SURFING
(Map p278; ☑831-427-2355; www.cowellssurf shop.com; 30 Front St; 2hr group lesson $90; ☺8am-6pm, to 5pm Nov-Mar; 🖐) Rent surf-boards, boogie boards, wetsuits and other beach gear near the wharf, where veteran staff offer local tips and lessons.

Kayaking
Kayaking lets you discover the craggy coast-line and kelp beds where sea otters float.

Kayak Connection
WATER SPORTS
(Map p286; ☑831-479-1121; www.kayakconnection. com; Santa Cruz Harbor, 413 Lake Ave; kayak rent-al/tour from $35/50; ☺10am-5pm Mon, Wed & Fri, 9am-5pm Sat-Sun; 🖐) Rents kayaks and offers lessons and tours, including whale-watching, sunrise, sunset and full-moon trips. Also rents stand-up paddle boarding (SUP) sets (from $35), wetsuits ($10) and boogie boards ($10).

Venture Quest
KAYAKING
(Map p278; ☑831-427-2267, 831-425-8445; www. kayaksantacruz.com; Municipal Wharf; kayak rental/ tour from $35/56; ☺10am-7pm Mon-Fri, from 9am Sat & Sun late May–late Sep, hours vary late Sep–mid-May) Convenient rentals on the wharf, plus whale-watching and coastal sea-cave tours, moonlight paddles and kayak-sailing trips. Book ahead for kayak-surfing lessons.

Whale-Watching & Fishing
Winter whale-watching trips run from December through April, though there's plenty of marine life to see on a summer bay cruise.

Many fishing trips depart from Santa Cruz's wharf, where a few shops rent fishing tackle and poles, if you're keen to join locals waiting patiently for a bite.

Stagnaro's
BOATING
(Map p286; ☑info 831-427-0230, reservations 888-237-7084; www.stagnaros.com; 1718 Brom-mer St; adult/child under 14yr cruise from $22/15, whale-watching tour from $50/36) Longstanding tour operator offers scenic and sunset cruises around Monterey Bay during spring and summer, and whale-watching tours year-round.

🎉 Festivals & Events

Woodies on the Wharf
CULTURAL
(www.santacruzwoodies.com; ☺late June) Classic-car show features vintage surf-style station wagons on Santa Cruz's Municipal Wharf (p276).

Open Studio Art Tour
ART
(www.firstfridaysantacruz.com) Step inside local artists' creative workshops over three weekends in October. The arts council also sponsors 'First Friday' art exhibitions on the first Friday of each month, including access to artists' ateliers at the heritage Tannery Arts Center located just north of downtown.

🛏 Sleeping
Santa Cruz does not have enough beds to satisfy demand: expect high prices at peak times for nothing-special rooms. Places near the beach boardwalk (p276) range from friendly to frightening. For a decent motel, cruise Ocean St inland or Mission St (Hwy 1). Several new hotels scheduled to open from late 2017 will improve the city's accommodations options. Contact the visitor center (p284) for details.

HI Santa Cruz Hostel
HOSTEL $
(Map p278; ☑831-423-8304; www.hi-santacruz. org; 321 Main St; dm $28-31, r $85-140, all with shared bath; ☺check in 5-10pm; @🛜) Budget overnighters dig this cute hostel at the century-old Carmelita Cottages surrounded by flowering gardens, just two blocks from the beach. Cons: midnight curfew, daytime lockout (11am to 5pm) and three-night maximum stay. Reservations are essential. Street parking costs $2.

California State Park Campgrounds
CAMPGROUND $
(☑reservations 800-444-7275; www.reserveamerica. com; tent & RV sites $35-65) Book well ahead to camp at state beaches off Hwy 1 south of Santa Cruz or up in the foggy Santa Cruz Mountains off Hwy 9. Family-friendly campgrounds include Henry Cowell Redwoods State Park in Felton and New Brighton State Beach in Capitola.

★ Adobe on Green B&B
B&B $$
(Map p278; ☑831-469-9866; www.adobeongreen. com; 103 Green St; r $179; P🐾🛜) 🍃 Peace and quiet are the mantras at this place, a short walk from Pacific Ave. The hosts are practically invisible, but their thoughtful touches are everywhere, from boutique-hotel amenities in spacious, stylish and solar-powered rooms to breakfast spreads from their organic gardens.

Carousel Beach Inn
MOTEL $$
(Map p278; ☑831-425-7090; www.carousel-beach -inn.com; 110 Riverside Ave; r $159-229; P🛜) Colorful decor and bright artwork feature

at this recently renovated motel that is the closest accommodations to the attractions of the Santa Cruz boardwalk. Prices surge in summer, but it's worth checking online for off-peak and seasonal discounts.

Seaway Inn
MOTEL **$$**
(Map p278; ☑831-471-9004; www.seawayinn. com; 176 W Cliff Dr; r $139-150; P☕�➲🛜) Good value and welcoming accommodations just a short walk uphill from the Santa Cruz Municipal Wharf. Try and stay on a weekday as prices surge on weekends.

Hotel Paradox
HOTEL **$$**
(Map p286; ☑831-425-7100; www.thehotelparadox. com; 611 Ocean St; r from $229; @🛜🏊) This downtown boutique hotel brings the great outdoors inside, with nature prints on the walls, textured wood panels and earth-toned furnishings. Relax in a cabana by the pool or next to an outdoor fire pit. Weekday rates can be reasonable, but summer weekends are ridiculously high-priced. Parking is $10.

Mission Inn
MOTEL **$$**
(Map p286; ☑831-425-5455; www.mission-inn. com; 2250 Mission St; r $139-179; ❄🛜) Perfectly serviceable two-story motel with a garden courtyard, hot tub and complimentary continental breakfast. It's on busy Hwy 1 near the UCSC campus, away from the beach.

Pelican Point Inn
INN **$$**
(Map p286; ☑831-475-3381; www.pelicanpoint innsantacruz.com; 21345 E Cliff Dr; ste $139-229; P☕🛜🏊) Ideal for families, these roomy apartments near a kid-friendly beach come with everything you'll need for a lazy vacation, including kitchenettes. Weekly rates available. Pet fee $25.

Pacific Blue Inn
B&B **$$$**
(Map p278; ☑831-600-8880; www.pacificblueinn. com; 636 Pacific Ave; r $189-289; P☕🛜🏊) ❧ This downtown courtyard B&B is an eco-conscious gem, with water-saving fixtures and renewable and recycled building materials. Refreshingly elemental rooms have pillowtop beds, electric fireplaces and flat-screen TVs with DVD players. Free parking and loaner bikes. Pet fee $50.

Babbling Brook Inn
B&B **$$$**
(Map p286; ☑831-427-2437; www.babblingbrookinn. com; 1025 Laurel St; r $229-329; 🛜) Built around a running stream with meandering gardens, the inn has cozy rooms decorated in French-provincial style. Most have gas fireplaces, some have Jacuzzis and all have featherbeds. There's afternoon wine and hors d'oeuvres, plus a full breakfast.

Dream Inn
HOTEL **$$$**
(Map p278; ☑831-426-4330; www.dreaminn santacruz.com; 175 W Cliff Dr; r $279-576; P☕❄❋ @🛜🏊) Overlooking the wharf from a hillside perch, this chic hotel offers some of Santa Cruz's most stylish accommodations. Newly renovated rooms all have ocean views, while the beach and the revamped swimming pool area are just steps away. Don't miss having an end-of-day cocktail in the Jack O'Neill Lounge, named after Santa Cruz's iconic pioneer of surfing culture.

West Cliff Inn
INN **$$$**
(Map p278; ☑831-457-2200; www.westcliffinn. com; 174 W Cliff Dr; r $210-425; P🛜) In a classy Victorian house west of the wharf, this boutique inn's quaint rooms mix seagrass wicker, dark wood and jaunty striped curtains. The most romantic suites have gas fireplaces and let you spy on the breaking surf. Rates include a breakfast buffet and afternoon wine, tea and snacks.

🍴 Eating

Downtown Santa Cruz is packed with casual cafes. If you're looking for seafood, wander the wharf's takeout counter joints. Mission St, near UCSC, and 41st Ave offer cheaper eats.

★ Penny Ice Creamery
ICE CREAM **$**
(Map p278; ☑831-204-2523; www.thepenny icecreamery.com; 913 Cedar St; snacks $3-5; ☺noon-11pm; 🚻) ❧ With a cult following, this artisan ice-cream shop crafts zany flavors such as bourbon-candied ginger, lemon-verbena-blueberry and ricotta apricot all from scratch using local, organic and wild-harvested ingredients. Even plain old vanilla is special: it's made using Thomas Jefferson's original recipe. Also at a **downtown kiosk** (Map p278; 1520 Pacific Ave; snacks $3-5; ☺noon-6pm; 🚻) ❧ and near **Pleasure Point** (Map p286; 820 41st Ave; snacks $3-5; ☺noon-9pm Sun-Thu, to 10pm Fri & Sat; 🚻) ❧.

★ Santa Cruz Farmers Market
MARKET **$**
(Map p278; ☑831-454-0566; www.santacruz farmersmarket.org; cnr Lincoln & Center Sts; ☺1:30-6:30pm Wed; 🚼🚻) ❧ Organic produce, baked goods and arts-and-crafts and food booths all give you an authentic taste of the local vibe. Shorter fall and winter hours.

Akira
JAPANESE $

(Map p286; 📞831-600-7093; www.akirasantacruz. com; 1222 Soquel Ave; sushi & sashimi $10-15; ⏰11am-11pm; 📶) 🐾 Head northeast of downtown Santa Cruz to Soquel Ave's restaurant strip for Akira's modern take on sushi, sashimi and other Japanese flavors. Combining sake, craft brews and a surf-town ambience, Akira's menu harnesses briny-fresh tuna, salmon, eel and shellfish for a huge variety of sushi. Bento boxes for lunch ($10 to $14) are good value, and there's a wide range of vegetarian options.

Buttercup Cakes
CAFE $

(Map p278; 📞831-466-0373; www.facebook.com/ scbuttercupcakes; 1141 Pacific Ave; snacks from $3; ⏰10am-9pm; 📶) 🐾 Vegan and organic ingredients all feature, but there's absolutely no trade-off in flavor with Buttercup's cupcakes and desserts. The downtown location is a handy coffee stop, too.

Walnut Ave Cafe
BREAKFAST $

(Map p278; 📞831-457-2804; www.walnutavenue cafe.com; 106 Walnut Ave; mains $9-12; ⏰7am-3pm Mon-Fri, 8am-4pm Sat & Sun; 📶♿🐕) Line up at this clean, well-lit breakfast spot for fluffy Belgian waffles, blackened ahi tuna eggs benny, Mexican huevos rancheros with pulled pork and all kinds of veggie scrambles. Lunch brings less-exciting sandwiches, salads and soups. Dogs are welcome on the outdoor patio.

New Leaf Community Market
SUPERMARKET $

(Map p278; 📞831-425-1793; www.newleaf.com; 1134 Pacific Ave; ⏰8am-9pm; 📶) 🐾 Organic and local produce, natural-foods groceries and deli take-out meals in the middle of downtown Santa Cruz.

Picnic Basket
DELI $

(Map p278; 📞831-427-9946; www.facebook.com/ pg/thepicnicbasketsc; 125 Beach St; snacks $6-11; ⏰7am-9pm; 📶♿) Across the street from the beach boardwalk, this locavorian kitchen puts together creative sandwiches such as beet with lemony couscous or 'fancy pants' grilled cheese with fruit chutney, plus homemade soups, breakfast burritos and baked goods. Service can be standoffish, but icecream treats are sweet. It's open shorter hours in the off season.

★Assembly
CALIFORNIAN $$

(Map p278; 📞831-824-6100; www.assembly. restaurant; 1108 Pacific Ave; brunch & lunch $12-16, dinner mains $22-28; ⏰11:30am-9pm Mon & Wed-Thu, to 10pm Fri, 10am-10pm Sat-Sun; 📶) 🐾 Farm-to-table and proudly regional flavors feature at this excellent bistro in downtown Santa Cruz. Assembly's Californian vibe belies real culinary nous in the kitchen, and the seasonal menu could include dishes such as chicken breast with crispy pancetta or a truffle-laced asparagus risotto. Don't miss trying the Scotch olives and meatballs with a tasting flight of local craft beers.

Soif
BISTRO $$

(Map p278; 📞831-423-2020; www.soifwine.com; 105 Walnut Ave; small plates $5-17, mains $19-25; ⏰5-9pm Sun-Thu, to 10pm Fri & Sat; 📶) 🐾 Following a recent makeover, one of Santa Cruz's more established restaurants is now better than ever, and the chic and cosmopolitan decor showcases a stunning wine list – including tasting flights ($20.50) of local Santa Cruz varietals – and a well-curated menu with standouts like slow-roasted pork and scallops wrapped in bacon. Wine-matching suggestions are available for all dishes.

An on-site **wine shop** (noon-8pm Tue-Sun, 5-8pm Mon) also features many Californian wines.

Jaguar
MEXICAN $$

(Map p286; 📞831-600-7428; www.jaguarrestaurant inc.com; 1116 Soquel Ave; mains $14-22; ⏰5-10pm Thu-Tue) 🐾 Regional Mexican flavors feature at this bricks-and-mortar expansion of a popular long-standing Santa Cruz food stall. A strong adherence to organic ingredients shines in dishes like a delicious chicken mole (a Mexican dish with a rich spicy sauce), and a delicate ceviche packed with fresh seafood. Wines from local Santa Cruz vineyards partner well with the robust flavors.

Bantam
CALIFORNIAN, ITALIAN $$

(Map p286; 📞831-420-0101; www.bantam1010. com; 1010 Fair Ave; shared plates $11-23, pizza $11-20; ⏰5-9pm Mon-Thu, to 9:30pm Fri-Sat; 📶) Another opening in the up-and-coming dining scene in Santa Cruz's West End, Bantam's versatile space is often packed with SC locals enjoying wood-fired pizza, a savvy cocktail, the wine and craft-beer list, and moreish shared plates including squid, meatballs and pork belly. No reservations, but the informal and easygoing ambience means tables are turned over fairly promptly.

Laili
AFGHANI $$

(Map p278; 📞831-423-4545; www.lailirestaurant. com; 101b Cooper St; mains $14-26; ⏰11:30am-2:30pm & 5-9pm Tue-Sun; 📶) A chic downtown

TOP SANTA CRUZ BREWERIES & BEER BARS

We asked Derek Wolfgram, home brewer and local beer columnist, to share a few of his favorite places for a pint:

Boulder Creek Brewery Outpost (☑ 831-338-7882; www.facebook.com/bouldercreek brewery; 13101 Hwy 9, Boulder Creek; ☺ noon-9pm) High up in the mountains in the village of Boulder Creek, these guys brew amber 'Redwood Ale' and 'Dragon's Breath' American IPA. After a fire in 2016, they've relocated just across the road to this pop-up location while they rebuild.

Sante Adairius Rustic Ales (Map p286; ☑ 831-462-1227; www.rusticales.com; 103 Kennedy Dr; ☺ 3-8pm Tue-Thu, from noon Fri-Sun) Off Hwy 1 east of Santa Cruz, Belgian-inspired and barrel-aged beers are a beer geek's dream.

Discretion Brewing (Map p286; ☑ 831-316-0662; www.discretionbrewing.com; 2703 41st Ave, Soquel; ☺ 11:30am-9pm; ☒) Rye IPA, English ales and traditional Belgian and German brews are always on tap, off Hwy 1. The raffish beer garden is dog-friendly, and ramen noodles and risotto both come with a proudly Californian farm-to-table accent.

Santa Cruz Mountain Brewing (Map p286; ☑ 831-425-4900; www.scmbrew.com; 402 Ingalls St, Ingalls St Courtyard; ☺ 11:30am-10pm; ☒) An essential part of the eating and drinking scene in the Ingalls St Courtyard on Santa Cruz's Westside, Santa Cruz Mountain Brewing is a rustic spot to combine brews and a burger. Crowd into the compact tasting room or share an outside table with friendly locals and their well-behaved canine pals. Our favorite beer is the robust Devout Scout.

From Friday to Sunday, adjacent urban wine-tasting rooms are also open, often offering live music.

Santa Cruz Ale Works (Map p286; ☑ 831-425-1182; www.santacruzaleworks.com; 150 Du Bois St; ☺ 11am-6pm; ☒) Hefeweizen and 'Dark Night' oatmeal stout are commendable at this dog-friendly brewpub with a deli. The beers are good, but the location in an office park lacks ambience.

dining oasis, family-owned Laili invites diners in with an elegant high-ceilinged dining room and garden patio. Share apricot-chicken flatbread, tart pomegranate eggplant, roasted cauliflower with saffron, succulent lamb kebabs and more. Reservations for dinner advised.

Engfer Pizza Works PIZZA **$$**
(Map p286; ☑ 831-429-1856; www.engferpizza works.com; 537 Seabright Ave; pizzas $11-27; ☺ 4-9:30pm Tue-Sun; ☑ ☒) Detour to find this old factory, where wood-fired oven pizzas are made from scratch with love – the no-name specialty is like a giant salad on roasted bread. Play Ping-Pong and down craft beers from local breweries while you wait. Try the Hot Hawaiian pizza with a Santa Cruz Ale Works Hefeweizen.

El Palomar MEXICAN **$$**
(Map p278; ☑ 831-425-7575; www.elpalomar santacruz.com/; 1336 Pacific Ave; mains $10-22; ☺ 11:30am-10pm Mon-Fri, 10am-10pm Sat-Sun; ☒) Always packed and consistently good (if not great), El Palomar serves tasty Mexican

staples – try the ceviches – and fruity margaritas. Tortillas are made fresh by charming women in the covered courtyard.

🍷 Drinking & Nightlife

Santa Cruz's downtown overflows with bars, lounges and coffee shops. Heading west on Mission St (Hwy 1), craft breweries and wine-tasting rooms fill the raffish industrial ambience of the Smith St and Ingalls St courtyards.

Lupulo Craft Beer House CRAFT BEER
(Map p278; ☑ 831-454-8306; www.lupulosc.com; 233 Cathcart St; ☺ 11:30am-10pm Sun-Thu, to 11:30pm Fri-Sat) Named after the Spanish word for hops, Lupulo Craft Beer House is an essential downtown destination for traveling beer fans. Modern decor combines with an ever-changing taplist – often including seasonal brews from local California breweries – and good bar snacks such as empanadas, tacos and charcuterie plates. Almost 400 bottled and canned beers create delicious panic for the indecisive drinker.

If you're a fan of hard-to-find Belgian beers, you'll be in hoppy heaven.

515
COCKTAIL BAR

(Map p278; ☑831-425-5051; www.515santacruz. com; 515 Cedar St; ☺5pm-late Mon-Fri, 10am-late Sat-Sun) Superior cocktails and eclectic food feature at this cosmopolitan spot near Santa Cruz's main drag. Settle into a huge armchair amid vintage-chic decor and enjoy cocktails based on the American classics – think Sazeracs, Negronis and Whisky Sours – or a cold craft brew from the well-curated tap list. 515 is open to 1:30am from Friday to Saturday.

Verve Coffee Roasters
CAFE

(Map p278; ☑831-600-7784; www.vervecoffee.com; 1540 Pacific Ave; ☺6:30am-9pm; ☎) To sip finely roasted artisan espresso or a cup of rich pourover coffee, join the surfers and hipsters at this industrial-zen cafe. Single-origin brews and house blends rule. it's been so successful around their home patch that it's also opened satellite cafes in Los Angeles and Tokyo.

West End Tap & Kitchen
CRAFT BEER

(Map p286; ☑831-471-8115; www.westendtap.com; 334d Ingalls St, Ingalls St Courtyard; ☺11:30am-9:30pm Sun-Thu, to 10pm Fri-Sat) Another recent opening amid the gathering of brewpubs, cafes and wine-tasting rooms in the Ingalls St Courtyard, West End Tap & Kitchen combines beers from Hermitage Brewing in San Jose – often including zingy sour beers – and a full menu including Mediterranean-style flatbreads and hearty steaks, pasta and burgers. Try Hermitage's Ale of the Imp 8% Imperial IPA.

Caffe Pergolesi
CAFE

(Map p278; ☑831-426-1775; www.theperg.com; 418 Cedar St; ☺11am-9pm Mon-Sat, 11am-8pm Sun; ☎) Discuss conspiracy theories over stalwart coffee, tea or beer at this landmark Victorian house with a big ol' tree-shaded veranda. There's live music some evenings.

☆ Entertainment

Free tabloid *Good Times* (http://goodtimes. sc/) covers the music, arts and nightlife scenes in Santa Cruz.

Kuumbwa Jazz Center
LIVE MUSIC

(Map p278; ☑831-427-2227; www.kuumbwajazz. org; 320 Cedar St; admission varies by gig) Hosting jazz luminaries since 1975, this nonprofit theater is for serious jazz cats snapping their fingers for famous-name performers in an electrically intimate room.

Moe's Alley
LIVE MUSIC

(Map p286; ☑831-479-1854; www.moesalley.com; 1535 Commercial Way; admission varies by gig) In a way-out industrial wasteland, this joint puts on live sounds almost every night: jazz, blues, reggae, roots, salsa and acoustic world-music jams.

Catalyst
LIVE MUSIC

(Map p278; ☑831-423-1338; www.catalystclub. com; 1011 Pacific Ave; admission varies by gig) Over the years, this stage for local bands has seen big-time national acts perform, from Queens of the Stone Age to Snoop Dogg. Expect loads of punk attitude and look forward to gigs ranging from classic reggae acts to the occasional Ned Flanders–inspired thrash-metal band (c'mon down Okilly Dokilly...).

🛍 Shopping

Stroll Pacific Ave and downtown side streets to find Santa Cruz's one-of-a-kind, locally owned boutiques. For vintage clothing and surf shops, amble 41st Ave around Portola Dr.

Bookshop Santa Cruz
BOOKS

(Map p278; ☑831-423-0900; www.bookshop santacruz.com; 1520 Pacific Ave; ☺9am-10pm Sun-Thu, to 11pm Fri & Sat) Vast selection of new books, a few used ones, popular and unusual magazines, and 'Keep Santa Cruz Weird' bumper stickers.

Donnelly Fine Chocolates
FOOD

(Map p286; ☑831-458-4214; www.donnelly chocolates.com; 1509 Mission St; ☺10:30am-6pm Tue-Fri, from noon Sat & Sun) The Willy Wonka of Santa Cruz makes stratospherically priced chocolates on par with the big city. Try the cardamom or chipotle truffles. Pricey, but worth it we reckon.

ℹ Information

Public Library (☑831-427-7707; www. santacruzpl.org; 224 Church St; ☺10am-7pm Mon-Thu, 10am-5pm Fri & Sat, 1-5pm Sun; ☎) Free wi-fi and public internet terminals for California public-library cardholders (out-of-state visitors $10).

Santa Cruz Post Office (Map p286; ☑800-275-8777; www.usps.com; 850 Front St; ☺9am-5pm Mon-Fri)

Santa Cruz Visitor Center (Map p286; ☑831-425-1234; www.santacruzca.org; 303 Water St; ☺9am-noon & 1-4pm Mon-Fri, 11am-3pm Sat & Sun) Free public internet terminal, plus maps and brochures.

❶ Getting There & Around

Greyhound Santa Cruz (Map p278; ☎800-231-2222; www.greyhound.com; Metro Center, 920 Pacific Ave) Greyhound has a few daily buses to San Francisco, Salinas, Santa Barbara and Los Angeles.

Santa Cruz Airport Shuttles (☎831-421-9883; www.santacruzshuttles.com) Santa Cruz Airport Shuttles runs shared shuttles to/from the airports at San Jose ($50), San Francisco ($80) and Oakland ($80), with a $5 cash discount; the second passenger pays $10.

Santa Cruz Metro (Map p278; ☎831-425-8600; www.scmtd.com; 920 Pacific Ave; single-ride/day pass $2/6) Local and regional buses converge on downtown's Metro Center. Destinations include San Jose, Capitola and Watsonville.

Santa Cruz Trolley (www.santacruztrolley.com; per ride 25¢) From late May through early September, the trolley shuttles between downtown and the beach from 11am until 9pm daily.

Around Santa Cruz

Santa Cruz Mountains

Winding between Santa Cruz and Silicon Valley, Hwy 9 is a 40-mile backwoods byway through the Santa Cruz Mountains, passing tiny towns, towering redwood forests and fog-kissed vineyards. The Santa Cruz Mountains Winegrowers Association (www.scmwa.com) publishes a free winery map, available at tasting rooms, including those that have opened more convenient tasting rooms in Santa Cruz.

Heading north from Santa Cruz, it's 7 miles to **Felton**, where there is forest ziplining adventures and also hiking in the **Henry Cowell Redwoods State Park** (☎info 831-335-4598, reservations 800-444-7275; www.parks.ca.gov; 101 N Big Trees Park Rd; entry per car $10, campsites $35; ☉sunrise-sunset; 🅿♿) 🌲. Also in Felton is the pioneer-era fun and spectacle of **Roaring Camp Railroads** (☎831-335-4484; www.roaringcamp.com; 5401 Graham Hill Rd; adult/child 2-12yr from $29/22, parking $8; ♿). Seven miles further north on Hwy 9, stop in **Boulder Creek** for a bite and a cold beer at Boulder Creek Brewery Outpost (p283).

Follow Hwy 236 northwest for a further nine twisting miles from Boulder Creek to **Big Basin Redwoods State Park** (Map p42; ☎831-338-8860; www.parks.ca.gov; 21600 Big Basin Way; entry per car $10, campsites $35; ☉sunrise-sunset; 🅿♿) 🌲 for excellent hiking. A 12.5-mile

one-way section of the **Skyline to the Sea Trail** ends at Waddell Beach, almost 20 miles northwest of Santa Cruz on Hwy 1. On weekends between mid-March and mid-December, you can usually ride **Santa Cruz Metro** (☎831-425-8600; www.scmtd.com) bus 35A up to Big Basin in the morning and get picked up by bus 40 at the beach in the afternoon.

Capitola

Six miles east of Santa Cruz, the diminutive beach town of Capitola nestles quaintly between ocean bluffs. Show up for mid-September's **Capitola Art & Wine Festival**, or the famous **Begonia Festival** (www.begoniafestival.com), held over Labor Day weekend, with floral floats along Soquel Creek.

By the beach, downtown is laid out for strolling, where cute shops and touristy restaurants inhabit seaside houses. Drop by family-friendly **Capitola Beach Company** (Map p286; ☎831-462-5222; www.capitolabeachcompany.com; 131 Monterey Ave; surfboard/SUP rental from $12/20, surfing & SUP lessons from $85; ☉10am-6pm) or **Capitola Surf & Paddle** (Map p286; ☎831-435-6503; www.capitolasurfandpaddle.com; 208 San Jose Ave; surfboard/SUP rental from $10/20, surfing & SUP lessons $65-75; ☉10am-6pm) to rent water-sports gear or, if you book ahead, take surfing and stand up paddleboarding lessons.

Catch an organic, fair-trade java buzz at **Mr Toots Coffeehouse** (Map p286; ☎831 475 3679; www.facebook.com/MrTootsCoffeehouse; 2nd fl, 231 Esplanade; ☉7am-10pm; 🛜) 🍴, which has an art gallery, live music and ocean-view deck. Head inland to **Gayle's Bakery & Rosticceria** (Map p286; ☎831-462-1200; www.gaylesbakery.com; 504 Bay Ave; dishes $4-11; ☉6:30am-8:30pm; ♿), which has a deli to stock up for a beach picnic. A few miles east in Aptos, **Aptos St BBQ** (☎831-662-1721; www.aptosstbbq.com; 8059 Aptos St; mains $10-32; ☉11am-9pm) pairs smoked tri-tip beef and pulled pork with California craft beers and live music.

The **Capitola Chamber of Commerce** (Map p286; ☎800-474-6522; www.capitolachamber.com; 716G Capitola Ave; ☉10am-4pm) offers travel tips. Driving downtown can be a nightmare in summer and on weekends; use the parking lot behind City Hall, off Capitola Ave by Riverview Dr.

Moss Landing & Elkhorn Slough

Hwy 1 swings back toward the coast at Moss Landing, just south of the Santa Cruz County line, almost 20 miles north of Monterey.

Around Santa Cruz

Around Santa Cruz

From the working fishing harbor, **Sanctuary Cruises** (ℐinfo 831-917-1042, tickets 888-394-7810; www.sanctuarycruises.com; 7881 Sandholdt Rd; tours $45-55; ⊕) ℐ operates whale-watching and dolphin-spotting cruises year-round aboard biodiesel-fueled boats (reservations are essential). Devour dock-fresh seafood at warehouse-sized **Phil's Fish**

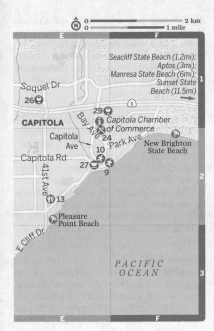

Seacliff State Beach (1.2mi);
Aptos (3mi);
Manresa State Beach (6mi);
Sunset State
Beach (11.5mi)

Soquel Dr

26

29

CAPITOLA

Capitola Chamber
of Commerce

Capitola
Ave

Bay Ave

Park Ave

New Brighton
State Beach

Capitola Rd

24

10

27

9

41st Ave

13

Pleasure
Point Beach

E Cliff Dr

*PACIFIC
OCEAN*

Market (☎831-633-2152; www.philsfishmarket. com; 7600 Sandholdt Rd; mains $10-26; ⊙10am-9pm; 🖽) or, after browsing the antiques shops, lunch at **Haute Enchilada** (☎831-633-5483; www.hauteenchilada.com; 7902 Moss Landing Rd; mains $13-26; ⊙11am-9pm) 🌱, an inspired Mexican restaurant inside an art gallery.

On the eastern side of Hwy 1, **Elkhorn Slough National Estuarine Research Reserve** (☎831-728-2822; www.elkhornslough.org; 1700 Elkhorn Rd, Watsonville; adult/child under 16yr $4/free; ⊙9am-5pm Wed-Sun; 🅿🖽) 🌱 is popular with bird-watchers and hikers, and can also be explored by cruising on an electric boat with **Whisper Charters** (☎800-979-3370; www.whispercharters.com; 2370 Hwy 1, Moss Landing; 2hr tour adult/child under 12yr $49/39; 🖽) 🌱. Kayaking and SUP are also fantastic ways to see the slough, though not on a windy day or when the tides are against you. Reserve ahead for kayak or SUP rentals, guided tours and paddling instruction with **Kayak Connection** (☎831-724-5692; www. kayakconnection.com; 2370 Hwy 1, Moss Landing; kayak & SUP rental from $35, tours adult/child from $50/40; ⊙9am-5pm; 🖽) 🌱 or **Monterey Bay Kayaks** (☎831-373-5357; www.montereybaykayaks.com; 2390 Hwy 1, Moss Landing; kayak & SUP rental/tour from $30/55; 🖽) 🌱.

Around 10 miles north of Moss Landing on the edge of **Watsonville** are a couple of interesting shops to stop at en route north or south.

Monterey

Working-class Monterey is all about the sea. What draws many visitors is a world-class aquarium overlooking **Monterey Bay National Marine Sanctuary**, which protects dense kelp forests and a sublime variety of marine life, including seals and sea lions, dolphins and whales. The city itself possesses the best-preserved historical evidence of California's Spanish and Mexican periods, with many restored adobe buildings. An afternoon's wander through downtown's historic quarter promises to be more edifying than time spent in the tourist ghettos of Fisherman's Wharf and Cannery Row.

◉ Sights

★**Monterey Bay Aquarium**   AQUARIUM
(Map p290; 🖳info 831-648-4800, tickets 866-963-9645; www.montereybayaquarium.org; 886 Cannery Row; adult/child 3-12yr/youth 13-17yr $50/30/40; ⊙10am-6pm; 🖽) 🌱 Monterey's most mesmerizing experience is its enormous aquarium, built on the former site of the city's largest sardine cannery. All kinds of aquatic creatures are featured, from kid-tolerant sea stars and slimy sea slugs to animated sea otters and surprisingly nimble 800lb tuna. The aquarium is much more than an impressive collection of glass tanks – thoughtful placards underscore the bay's cultural and historical contexts.

Every minute, up to 2000 gallons of seawater are pumped into the three-story **kelp forest**, re-creating as closely as possible the natural conditions you see out the windows to the east. The large fish of prey are at their charismatic best during mealtimes; divers hand-feed at 11am. More entertaining are the sea otters, which may be seen basking in the **Great Tide Pool** outside the aquarium, where they are readied for reintroduction to the wild.

Even new-agey music and the occasional infinity-mirror illusion don't detract from the astounding beauty of jellyfish in the **Jellies Gallery**. To see marine creatures – including hammerhead sharks, ocean sunfish and green sea turtles – that outweigh kids many times over, ponder the awesome

Open Sea tank. Upstairs and downstairs you'll find **touch pools**, where you can get close to sea cucumbers, bat rays and tide-pool creatures. Younger kids love the **Splash Zone**, with interactive bilingual exhibits in English and Spanish, and penguin feedings at 10:30am and 3pm.

To avoid long lines in summer and on weekends and holidays, buy tickets in advance. A visit can easily become a full-day affair, so get your hand stamped and break for lunch. Metered on-street parking is limited. Parking lots offering daily rates are plentiful just uphill from Cannery Row.

★ Monterey State Historic Park
HISTORIC SITE

(Map p290; ✏ info 831-649-7118; www.parks. ca.gov) FREE Old Monterey is home to an extraordinary assemblage of 19th-century brick and adobe buildings, administered as Monterey State Historic Park, and all found along a 2-mile self-guided walking tour portentously called the 'Path of History.' You can inspect dozens of buildings, many with charming gardens; expect some to be open while others aren't, according to a capricious schedule dictated by unfortunate state-park budget cutbacks.

➡ Pacific House

(Map p290; ✏831-649-7118; www.parks.ca.gov; 20 Custom House Plaza; walking tour adult/child $5/ free; ⊙10am-4pm, closed Mon-Wed Nov-Mar; ⛪) Find out what's currently open at Monterey State Historic Park, grab a free map and buy tickets for guided walking tours inside this 1847 adobe building, where fascinatingly in-depth exhibits cover the state's early Spanish, Mexican and American eras. Walking tours run at 10:30am, 12:30pm & 2pm Thursday to Sunday.

Nearby are some of the state park's historical highlights, including an **old whaling station** (Map p290; ⊙10am-2pm Tue-Fri) and **California's first theater** (Map p290). A 10-minute walk south is the **old Monterey jail** (Map p290; ✏831-646-5640; www.monterey. org; Dutra St; ⊙10am-4pm) FREE featured in John Steinbeck's novel *Tortilla Flat*.

➡ Custom House

(Map p290; ✏831-649-7111; www.parks.ca.gov; Custom House Plaza; ⊙10am-4pm; ⛪) FREE In 1822, a newly independent Mexico ended the Spanish trade monopoly and stipulated that any traders bringing goods to Alta (Upper) California must first unload their cargoes here for duty to be assessed. In 1846, when the US flag was raised over the Custom House, *voilà*! California was formally annexed from Mexico. Restored to its 1840s appearance, today this adobe building displays an exotic selection of goods that traders once brought to exchange for California cowhides.

➡ Stevenson House

(Map p290; ✏831-649-7118; www.parks.ca.gov; 530 Houston St; ⊙10am-4pm Thu-Sun) FREE Scottish writer Robert Louis Stevenson came to Monterey in 1879 to court his wife-to-be, Fanny Van de Grift Osbourne. This building, then the French Hotel, was where he stayed while reputedly devising his novel *Treasure Island*. The boarding-house rooms were primitive and Stevenson was still a penniless unknown. At the time of writing, the house was only open for private tours.

Cannery Row
HISTORIC SITE

(Map p290; ⛪) John Steinbeck's novel *Cannery Row* immortalized the sardine-canning business that was Monterey's lifeblood for the first half of the 20th century. A bronze **bust** of the Pulitzer Prize–winning writer sits at the bottom of Prescott Ave, just steps from the unabashedly touristy experience that the famous row has devolved into. The historical **Cannery Workers Shacks** (Map p290) at the base of flowery Bruce Ariss Way provide a sobering reminder of the hard lives led by Filipino, Japanese, Spanish and other immigrant laborers.

Back in Steinbeck's day, Cannery Row was a hardscrabble, working-class melting pot, which the novelist described as 'a poem, a stink, a grating noise, a quality of light, a tone, a habit, a nostalgia, a dream.' Sadly, there's precious little evidence of that era now, as overfishing and climatic changes caused the sardine industry's collapse in the 1950s.

Dali17
GALLERY

(Map p290; ✏831-372-2608; www.dali17.com; 5 Custom House Plaza, Museum of Monterey; adult/ child $20/10; ⊙10am-5pm Sun-Thu, 10am-7pm Fri-Sat) Escaping WWII in Europe, Spanish surrealist artist Salvador Dalí lived and worked in the Monterey and Carmel area in the 1940s. Comprising over 300 Dalí etchings, mixed media, lithographs and sculptures, this permanent exhibition in the Museum of Monterey is named after Carmel's 17-Mile Drive (p299), where the artist lived at Pebble Beach from 1943 to 1948.

Monterey Museum of Art   MUSEUM

(MMA; www.montereyart.org; adult/child $10/
free; ⊙11am-5pm Thu-Mon) Downtown, **MMA
Pacific Street** (Map p290; ☑831-372-5477;
559 Pacific St; adult/child $10/free; ⊙11am-5pm
Thu-Mon, to 8pm 1st Fri of month; P⛅) is particularly strong in California contemporary
art and modern landscape painters and
photographers, including Ansel Adams and
Edward Weston. Southeast of downtown,
MMA La Mirada (Map p290; ☑831-372-3689;
720 Via Mirada), a silent-film star's villa, has
humble adobe origins that are exquisitely
concealed. It is now only used for special
museum events, and not generally open to
the public. Check the website to see if anything is scheduled.

Royal Presidio Chapel
& Heritage Center Museum   CHURCH

(Map p290; ☑831-373-2628; www.sancarlos
cathedral.org; 500 Church St; donations accepted;
⊙10am-noon Wed, to 3pm Fri, to 2pm Sat, 1-3pm
Sun, also 10am-noon & 1:15-3:15pm 2nd & 4th Mon
of month; P⛅) Built of sandstone in 1794,
this graceful chapel is California's oldest
continuously functioning parish and first
stone building. The original 1770 mission
church stood here before being moved to
Carmel. As Monterey expanded under Mexican rule in the 1820s, older buildings were
gradually destroyed, leaving behind this National Historic Landmark as the strongest
reminder of the defeated Spanish colonial
presence. On-site docents are happy to provide tours during opening hours.

🏃 Activities

Like its larger namesake in San Francisco,
Monterey's **Fisherman's Wharf** is a tacky
tourist trap, but also a jumping-off point for
deep-sea fishing trips and whale-watching
cruises. A short walk east at workaday **Municipal Wharf 2**, fishing boats bob and sway
in the bay.

Dennis the Menace Park   PLAYGROUND

(Map p290; www.monterey.org; 777 Pearl St;
⊙10am-dusk, closed Tue Sep-May; ⛅) FREE
The brainchild of Hank Ketcham, the creator of the classic *Dennis the Menace* comic
strip, this ain't your standard dumbed-down
playground suffocated by Big Brother's safety regulations. With lightning-fast slides, a
hedge maze, a suspension bridge and towering climbing walls, even some adults can't
resist playing here.

Whale-Watching

You can spot whales off the coast of Monterey Bay year-round. The season for blue
and humpback whales runs from April to
early December, while gray whales pass by
from mid-December through March. Tour
boats depart from Fisherman's Wharf and
Moss Landing (p286). Reserve trips at least
a day in advance; be prepared for a bumpy,
cold ride.

Monterey Whale Watching   BOATING

(Map p290; ☑831-372-2203; www.monterey
whalewatching.com; 96 Fisherman's Wharf; 2½hr
tour adult/child 5-11yr $45/35) Several daily de-
partures; no children under age five or preg-
nant women allowed.

Monterey Bay Whale Watch   BOATING

(Map p290; ☑831-375-4658; www.montereybay
whalewatch.com; 84 Fisherman's Wharf; 3hr tour
adult/child 4-12yr from $44/29; ⛅) Morning and
afternoon departures; young children and
well-behaved dogs are welcome on board.

Diving & Snorkeling

Monterey Bay offers world-renowned diving
and snorkeling, including off **Lovers Point**
in Pacific Grove and at Point Lobos State
Natural Reserve (p298) south of Carmel-by-
the-Sea. You'll want a wetsuit year-round.
In summer, upwelling currents carry cold
water from the deep canyon below the bay,
sending a rich supply of nutrients up toward
the surface level to feed the bay's diverse marine life. These frigid currents also account
for the bay's chilly water temperatures and
the summer fog that blankets the peninsula.

Aquarius Dive Shop   DIVING

(☑831-375-1933; www.aquariusdivers.com; 2040
Del Monte Ave; snorkel/scuba-gear rental $35/65,
dive tours from $65; ⊙9am-6pm Mon-Fri, 7am-
6pm Sat-Sun) Talk to this five-star PADI operation for gear rentals, classes and guided
dives into Monterey Bay.

Monterey Bay Dive Charters   DIVING

(☑831-383-9276; www.mbdcscuba.com; scuba-
gear rental $75, shore/boat dives from $65/85)
Arrange shore or boat dives and rent a
full scuba kit with wetsuit from this well-
reviewed outfitter.

Kayaking & Surfing

Monterey Bay Kayaks   KAYAKING

(Map p290; ☑831-373-5357; www.montereybay
kayaks.com; 693 Del Monte Ave; kayak or SUP set
rental per day from $35, tours from $45; ⊙8:30am-
5pm, extended hours in summer) Rents kayaks

Monterey

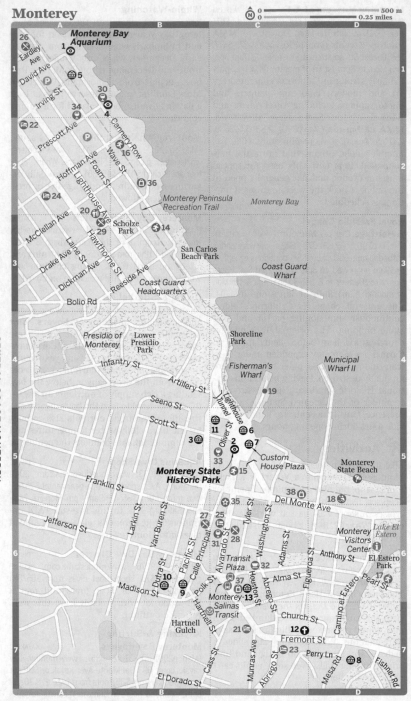

Monterey Bay Aquarium

1

26
Eardley Ave
David Ave
Irving St
5
P
30
34
4
Cannery Row
22
Prescott Ave
P
16
Wave St
36
Hoffman Ave
Foam St
Lighthouse Ave
24
20
29
Scholze Park
14
McClellan Ave
Laine St
Hawthorne St
Drake Ave
Dickman Ave
Reeside Ave
Bolio Rd

Monterey Peninsula Recreation Trail

Monterey Bay

San Carlos Beach Park

Coast Guard Wharf

Coast Guard Headquarters

Presidio of Monterey
Lower Presidio Park
Infantry St
Shoreline Park

Fisherman's Wharf

Municipal Wharf II

Artillery St
Seeno St
Scott St
11
3
2
33
15
6
7
19
Lighthouse Tunnel
Oliver St
Custom House Plaza

Monterey State Historic Park

Monterey State Beach

Franklin St
Jefferson St
Larkin St
Van Buren St
Pacific St
35
27
25
28
31
Calle Principal
Alvarado St
Tyler St
Washington St
Del Monte Ave
38
18
Monterey Visitors Center
Lake El Estero
El Estero Park
Anthony St
Adams St
Alma St
Figueroa St
17
Pearl St

Transit Plaza
32
10
9
Madison St
Dutra St
Polk St
Houston St
37
13
Monterey-Salinas Transit
Abrego St
Church St
12
Fremont St
Hartnell Gulch
Hartnell St
21
23
Perry Ln
Mesa Rd
8
Cass St
Munras Ave
Abrego St
Camino el Estero
Fishnet Rd
El Dorado St

Monterey

◎ Top Sights	
1 Monterey Bay Aquarium	A1
2 Monterey State Historic Park	C5

◎ Sights	
3 California's First Theater	B5
4 Cannery Row	A1
5 Cannery Workers Shacks	A1
6 Custom House	C5
7 Dali17	C5
8 Monterey Museum of Art – La Mirada	D7
9 Monterey Museum of Art – Pacific Street	B6
10 Old Monterey Jail	B6
11 Old Whaling Station	C5
Pacific House	(see 2)
12 Royal Presidio Chapel & Heritage Center Museum	C7
13 Stevenson House	C6

◎ Activities, Courses & Tours	
14 Adventures by the Sea	B3
15 Adventures by the Sea	C5
Bay Bikes	(see 32)
16 Bay Bikes	B2
17 Dennis the Menace Park	D6
18 Monterey Bay Kayaks	D5
Monterey Bay Whale Watch	(see 19)
19 Monterey Whale Watching	C4
20 Sunshine Freestyle Surf & Sport	A2

◎ Sleeping	
21 Casa Munras	C7
22 HI Monterey Hostel	A2
23 Hotel Abrego	C7
24 Jabberwock	A2
25 Monterey Hotel	C6

◎ Eating	
26 First Awakenings	A1
27 Montrio Bistro	B6
28 Old Monterey Marketplace	C6
29 Zab Zab	A3

◎ Drinking & Nightlife	
30 A Taste of Monterey	A1
31 Alvarado Street Brewery	C6
32 East Village Coffee Lounge	C6
33 Peter B's Brewpub	C5
34 Sardine Factory Lounge	A1

◎ Entertainment	
35 Osio Cinema	C5
Sly McFly's Fueling Station	(see 30)

◎ Shopping	
36 Monterey Peninsula Art Foundation Gallery	B2
37 Old Capitol Books	C6
38 Wharf Marketplace	C5

CENTRAL COAST MONTEREY

and SUP equipment, offers paddling lessons and leads guided tours of Monterey Bay, including full-moon and sunrise trips.

Sunshine Freestyle Surf & Sport SURFING
(Map p290; ☑831-375-5015; www.facebook.com/SunshineFreestyle; 443 Lighthouse Ave; surfboard/wetsuit/body board rental from $20/10/7; ⊙10am-6pm Mon-Sat, 11am-5pm Sun) Monterey's oldest surf shop rents and sells all the surfing gear you'll need.

Cycling & Mountain Biking

Along an old railway line, the **Monterey Peninsula Recreational Trail** travels for 18 car-free miles along the waterfront, passing Cannery Row en route to Lovers Point in Pacific Grove. Road-cycling enthusiasts can make the round trip to Carmel along the 17-Mile Drive (p299). Mountain-bikers head to **Fort Ord National Monument** to pedal over 80 miles of single-track and fire roads; the **Sea Otter Classic** (www.seaotterclassic. com) races there in mid-April.

Adventures by the Sea CYCLING, KAYAKING
(Map p290; ☑831-372-1807; www.adventuresbythesea.com; 299 Cannery Row; rental per day kay-ak or bicycle $35, SUP set $50, kayak tours from $60; ⊙9am-5pm, to 8pm in summer; ⓐ) Beach cruisers, electric bikes and water-sports gear rentals and tours available at multiple locations on Cannery Row and **downtown** (Map p290; 210 Alvarado St; ⊙9am-5pm, to 8pm in summer; ⓐ).

Bay Bikes CYCLING
(Map p290; ☑831-655-2453; www.baybikes.com; 585 Cannery Row; bicycle rental per hour/day from $9/36, tours from $70; ⊙9am-5pm Sun-Thu, to 6pm Fri, to 6:30pm Sat; ⓐ) Cruiser, tandem, hybrid and road-bike rentals near the aquarium and also **downtown** (Map p290; 486 Washington St; ⊙10am-5pm Sun-Mon, 10am-6pm Tue-Fri, 9am-6pm Sat; ⓐ). Check out its handy free maps detailing local bike routes. Tours taking in Cannery Row, Pacific Grove or local wine-tasting are also available.

🎉 Festivals & Events

Castroville Artichoke Food & Wine Festival FOOD & DRINK
(☑831-633-2465; www.artichokefestival.org; ⊙late May/early Jun) Head 15 miles north of Monterey for 3D 'agro art' sculptures, cooking

demos, a farmers market and field tours. A recent addition is a wine-and-beer garden with tasty beverages from around the region.

Monterey County Fair CARNIVAL, FOOD

(www.montereycountyfair.com; ⊙ late Aug & early Sep) Old-fashioned fun, carnival rides, horse-back riding and livestock competitions, wine tasting and live music.

★ Monterey Jazz Festival MUSIC

(www.montereyjazzfestival.org; ⊙ mid-Sep) One of the world's longest-running jazz festivals (since 1958) showcases big-name headliners over a long spring weekend.

🛏 Sleeping

Book ahead for special events, on weekends and in summer. To avoid the tourist conges-tion and jacked-up prices of Cannery Row, look to Pacific Grove. Cheaper motels line Munras Ave, south of downtown, and N Fre-mont St, east of Hwy 1.

HI Monterey Hostel HOSTEL $

(Map p290; ☑831-649-0375; www.montereyhostel. org; 778 Hawthorne St; with shared bath dm $30-40; ⊙check in 4-10pm; @☎) Four blocks from Can-nery Row and the aquarium, this simple, clean hostel houses single-sex and mixed dorms, as well as private rooms accommodating up to five people (check online for rates). Budget backpackers stuff themselves silly with make-your-own-pancake breakfasts. Reservations strongly recommended. Take MST bus 1 from downtown's Transit Plaza (p294).

Veterans Memorial Park Campground CAMPGROUND $

(Map p296; ☑831-646-3865; www.monterey. org; Veterans Memorial Park; tent & RV sites $30) Tucked into the forest, this municipal camp-ground has 40 grassy, non-reservable sites near a nature preserve's hiking trails. Amen-ities include coin-op hot showers, flush toi-lets, drinking water and barbecue fire pits. Three-night maximum stay.

Inn by the Bay MOTEL $$

(Map p296; ☑831-372-5409; www.innbythebay monterey.com; 936 Munras Ave; d from $110; P☺☎) An easy walk downhill to downtown Monterey, Inn on the Bay is the quiet achiev-er along the Munras Ave motel strip. Recent renovations have modernized the interiors, there are flat-screen TVs in the rooms, and a location set back from the street means it is uniformly quiet. A young, switched-on team

at reception offer plenty of tips for enjoying Monterey and around.

Hotel Abrego BOUTIQUE HOTEL $$

(Map p290; ☑831-372-7551; www.hotelabrego.com; 755 Abrego St; r from $144; ☎≋) At this down-town Monterey boutique hotel, most of the spacious, clean-lined contemporary rooms have gas fireplaces and chaise longues. Work out in the fitness studio, take a dip in the recently redeveloped outdoor pool or warm up in the hot tub. A new fire pit is a cozy addition for cooler Monterey evenings.

Casa Munras BOUTIQUE HOTEL $$

(Map p290; ☑831-375-2411; www.hotelcasamunras. com; 700 Munras Ave; r from $140; P☺@☎≋☀) Built around an adobe hacienda once owned by a 19th-century Spanish colonial don, chic modern rooms come with lofty beds and some have gas fireplaces, all inside two-storey motel-esque buildings. Splash in a heated outdoor pool, unwind at the tapas bar or take a sea-salt scrub in the tiny spa. Pet fee $50.

Monterey Hotel HISTORIC HOTEL $$

(Map p290; ☑831-375-3184; www.montereyhotel. com; 406 Alvarado St; r $131-275; ☎) In the heart of downtown and a short walk from Fisherman's Wharf, this 1904 edifice harbors five-dozen smallish but renovated rooms and suites with Victorian-styled furniture and plantation shutters. No elevator. A re-cently added boutique spa offers massage and beauty treatments.

★ Jabberwock B&B $$$

(Map p290; ☑831-372-4777; www.jabberwockinn. com; 598 Laine St; r $249-339; @☎) Barely visible through a shroud of foliage, this 1911 arts-and-crafts house hums a playful *Alice in Wonderland* tune through seven im-maculate rooms, a few with fireplaces and Jacuzzis. Over afternoon tea and cookies or evening wine and hors d'oeuvres, ask the ge-nial hosts about the house's many salvaged architectural elements. Weekends are more expensive and have a two-night minimum.

Also available is Tumtum Tree, a stand-alone cottage cradled by Monterey Cypress trees, and accommodating up to four guests.

Sanctuary Beach Resort HOTEL $$$

(☑831-883-9478; www.thesanctuarybeachresort. com; 3295 Dunes Dr, Marina; r from $260; ❄@☀ ≋☀) Be lulled to sleep by the surf at this low-lying retreat hidden in the sand dunes north of Monterey. Reached via golf carts, townhouses harbor petite rooms with gas fireplaces and binoculars for whale-watching. Sunset bonfires bring out s'mores. The beach is an off-limits nature preserve, but there are public beaches and walking trails nearby. Pet fee $50.

✖ Eating

Uphill from Monterey's Cannery Row, Lighthouse Ave features casual, budget-friendly eateries including Hawaiian barbecue and Thai flavors, through to sushi and Middle Eastern kebabs. Downtown around Alvarado St also features cafes and pub dining.

Zab Zab   NORTHERN THAI $

(Map p290; ☑831-747-2225; www.zabzabmonterey. com; 401 Lighthouse Ave; mains $11-15; ☺11am-2:30pm & 5-9pm Tue-Fri, noon-9pm Sat-Sun; ☑) Our pick of Lighthouse Ave's ethnic eateries, Zab Zab channels the robust flavors of northeast Thailand. The bijou cottage interior is perfect in cooler weather, but during summer the best spot is on the deck surrounded by a pleasantly overgrown garden. For fans of authentic Thai heat, go for the Kai Yang grilled chicken. Lunch boxes ($11 to $13) are good value.

Tricycle Pizza   PIZZA $

(Map p296; www.tricyclepizza.com; 899 Lighthouse Ave; pizza $11-13; ☺3-9pm Wed-Fri, noon-9pm Sat) One of Monterey's favorite food trucks has graduated to a bricks-and-mortar location along Lighthouse Ave. Tricycle's crusty wood-fired pizza is still cooked in the original truck on-site, but there's now the option of takeout or dining in a hip, industrial space nearby. Try the sausage and mushroom with organic oregano, wood-fired mushrooms and fennel sausage.

Old Monterey Marketplace   MARKET $

(Map p290; www.oldmonterey.org; Alvarado St, btwn Del Monte Ave & Pearl St; ☺4-7pm Tue Sep-May, to 8pm Jun-Aug; ☻) ✔ Rain or shine, head downtown on Tuesdays for farm-fresh fruit and veggies, artisan cheeses, international food stalls and a scrumptious 'baker's alley.'

First Awakenings   AMERICAN $

(Map p290; ☑831-372-1125; www.firstawakenings. net; American Tin Cannery, 125 Oceanview Blvd; mains $9-13; ☺7am-2pm Mon-Fri, to 2:30pm Sat & Sun; ☻) Sweet and savory, all-American breakfasts and lunches and bottomless pitchers of coffee merrily weigh down outdoor tables at this cafe uphill from the aquarium. Try the unusual 'bluegerm' pancakes or a spicy Sonoran frittata.

Monterey's Fish House   SEAFOOD $$

(☑831-373-4647; www.montereyfishhouse.com; 2114 Del Monte Ave; mains $11-25; ☺11:30am-2:30pm Mon-Fri & 5-9:30pm daily) Watched over by photos of Sicilian fishermen, dig into oak-grilled or blackened swordfish, barbecued oysters or, for those stout of heart, the Mexican squid steak. Reservations are essential (it's *so* crowded), but the vibe is island-casual: Hawaiian shirts seem to be de rigueur for men.

Montrio Bistro   CALIFORNIAN $$$

(Map p290; ☑831-648-8880; www.montrio.com; 414 Calle Principal; shared plates $12-30, mains $25-44; ☺4:30-10pm Sun-Thu, to 11pm Fri & Sat) ✔ Inside a 1910 firehouse, Montrio combines leather walls and iron trellises, and the tables have butcher paper and crayons for kids. The eclectic seasonal menu mixes local, organic fare with Californian, Asian and European flair, including tapas-style shared plates and mini desserts. Well-priced bar snacks and happy-hour prices from 4:30pm daily are a fine end-of-the-day option.

⬤ Drinking & Nightlife

Prowl downtown Monterey's Alvarado St, touristy Cannery Row and locals-only Lighthouse Ave for watering holes.

★ Alvarado Street Brewery   CRAFT BEER

(Map p290; ☑831-655-2337; www.alvaradostreet brewery.com; 426 Alvarado St; ☺11:30am-10pm Sun-Wed, to 11pm Thu-Sat) Vintage beer advertising punctuates Alvarado Street's brick walls, but that's the only concession to earlier days at this excellent craft-beer pub. Innovative brews harness new hop strains, sour and barrel-aged beers regularly fill the taps, and superior bar food includes Thai-curry mussels and truffle-crawfish mac 'n' cheese. In summer, adjourn to the alfresco beer garden out back.

Peter B's Brewpub   BREWERY

(Map p290; ☑831-649-2699; www.facebook.com/ PeterBsBrewpub; 2 Portola Plaza; ☺11am-11pm Sun-Thu, to midnight Fri-Sat) Often heaving with locals and tourists, Peter B's combines huge meals – the burgers are really good value – with a solid array of craft beers brewed on-site. Students crowd in to watch live sports on big-screen TVs, while visiting beer buffs work their way through beer sampling trays. Peter B's seasonal one-off brews are always worth trying.

A Taste of Monterey   WINE BAR

(Map p290; www.atasteofmonterey.com; 700 Cannery Row; tasting flights $14-22; ☺11am-6pm

Sun-Thu, to 8pm Fri-Sat) Sample medal-winning Monterey County wines from as far away as the Santa Lucia Highlands while soaking up dreamy sea views, then peruse thoughtful exhibits on barrel-making and cork production. Shared plates, including crab cakes and smoked salmon, provide a tasty reason to linger.

Sardine Factory Lounge   LOUNGE
(Map p290; ☑831-373-3775; www.sardinefactory. com; 701 Wave St; ⊘5pm-midnight) The leg-endary restaurant's fireplace lounge pours wines by the glass, delivers filling appetiz-ers to your table and has a live piano player most nights.

East Village Coffee Lounge   CAFE, LOUNGE
(Map p290; ☑831-373-5601; www.facebook.com/ eastvillagemonterey; 498 Washington St; ⊘6am-10pm Mon-Fri, from 7am Sat & Sun; 🛜) Downtown Monterey coffee shop on a busy corner brews with fair-trade, organic beans. At night, it pulls off a big-city lounge vibe with film, open-mike and live-music nights and an all-important booze license. Check the Facebook page for event listings.

☆ Entertainment

For comprehensive entertainment listings, browse the free tabloid *Monterey County Weekly* (www.montereycountyweekly.com).

Osio Cinema   CINEMA
(Map p290; ☑831-644-8171; http://osiotheater. com; 350 Alvarado St; adult $10, before 6pm $7; 🛜) Downtown Monterey cinema screens indie dramas, cutting-edge documentaries and offbeat Hollywood films. Drop by its Cafe Lumiere for locally roasted coffee, loose-leaf tea, decadent cheesecake and wi-fi.

Sly McFly's Fueling Station   LIVE MUSIC
(Map p290; ☑831-649-8050; www.slymcflys monterey.com; 700 Cannery Row; ⊘11:30am-midnight Sun-Thu, to 2am Fri & Sat) Waterfront dive showcases live local blues, jazz and rock bands nightly after 8:30pm or 9pm. Skip the food, though.

🛍 Shopping

Cannery Row is jammed with claptrap shops, while downtown Monterey's side streets hide more one-of-a-kind finds.

Wharf Marketplace   FOOD & DRINKS
(Map p290; ☑831-649-1116; www.thewharf marketplace.com; 290 Figueroa St; ⊘7am-7pm) 🍴

Inside an old railway station, this gourmet-food emporium carries bountiful farm goodness, artisanal products and wine from Monterey County and beyond. It's a good spot for a leisurely breakfast, too.

Monterey Peninsula
Art Foundation Gallery   ART
(Map p290; ☑831-655-1267; www.mpaf.org; 425 Cannery Row; ⊘11am-5pm) Taking over a cozy sea-view house, more than 30 local artists sell plein-air paintings and sketches along-side contemporary works in all media.

Old Capitol Books   BOOKS
(Map p290; ☑831-333-0383; www.oldcapitolbooks. com; 559 Tyler St; ⊘10am-6pm Wed-Mon, to 7pm Tue) Tall shelves of new, used and antiquar-ian books, including rare first editions, California titles and John Steinbeck's works.

ⓘ Information

Doctors on Duty (☑831-649-0770; www. doctorsonduty.com; 501 Lighthouse Ave; ⊘8am-8pm Mon-Sat, to 6pm Sun) Walk-in, non-emergency medical clinic.

Monterey Public Library (☑831-646-3933; www.monterey.org/library; 625 Pacific St; ⊘noon-8pm Mon-Wed, 10am-6pm Thu-Sat, 1-5pm Sun; 🛜) Free wi-fi and public internet terminals.

Monterey Visitors Center (Map p290; ☑831-657-6400; www.seemonterey.com; 401 Camino el Estero; ⊘9am-6pm Mon-Sat, to 5pm Sun, closes 1hr earlier Nov-Mar) Free tourist bro-chures and accommodations booking service; ask for a *Monterey County Literary & Film Map.*

Post Office (Map p290; ☑800-275-8777; www.usps.com; 565 Hartnell St; ⊘8:30am-5pm Mon-Fri, 10am-2pm Sat) Located just south of downtown Monterey.

ⓘ Getting There & Away

Monterey is 43 miles south of Santa Cruz and 177 miles north of San Luis Obispo.

AIR
A few miles east of downtown off Hwy 68, **Monterey Regional Airport** (☑831-648-7000; www. montereyairport.com; 200 Fred Kane Dr) has flights with United (LA, San Francisco), Amer-ican (Phoenix), Alaska (San Diego and LA) and Allegiant Air (Las Vegas). A taxi from downtown is around $20 (10 minutes), and to get here by public transport, catch buses 7, 56 or 93 ($2.50) from Monterey's **Transit Plaza** (Map p290; cnr Pearl & Alvarado Sts).

The **Monterey Airbus** (☑831-373-7777; www. montereyairbus.com; 🛜) shuttle service links Monterey with international airports in San Jose

($40, 1½ hours) and San Francisco ($50, 2½ hours) almost a dozen times daily; book online for discounts.

BUS

Monterey-Salinas Transit (MST; Map p290; 888-678-2871; www.mst.org; Jules Simmoneau Plaza; single-ride fares $1.50-3.50, day pass $10) operates local and regional buses; routes converge on downtown's Transit Plaza, including routes to Pacific Grove, Carmel and Big Sur. From late May until early September, MST's free trolley loops around downtown, Fisherman's Wharf and Cannery Row between 10am and 7pm or 8pm daily.

Pacific Grove

Founded as a tranquil Methodist summer retreat in 1875, Pacific Grove (or PG) maintained its quaint, holier-than-thou attitude well into the 20th century. The selling of liquor was illegal up until 1969, making it California's last 'dry' town. Today, leafy streets are lined by stately Victorian homes and a charming, compact downtown orbits Lighthouse Ave.

⊙ Sights & Activities

Pacific Grove's aptly named **Ocean View Blvd** affords views from Lovers Point Park west to Point Pinos, where it becomes **Sunset Dr**, offering tempting turnouts where you can stroll by pounding surf, rocky outcrops and teeming tide pools all the way to Asilomar State Beach. This seaside route is great for cycling, too – some say it rivals the famous 17-Mile Drive for beauty and, even better, it's free.

Asilomar State Beach　　　　BEACH
(Map p296; Sunset Dr) Negotiate a 1-mile trail boardwalk through rugged sand dunes. Note this beach is known for riptides and unpredictable surf, and care must be taken when swimming here.

Point Pinos Lighthouse　　　LIGHTHOUSE
(Map p296; 831-648-3176; www.pointpinoslighthouse.org; 80 Asilomar Ave; suggested donation adult/child 6-12yr $4/2; ⊙1-4pm Thu-Mon) The West Coast's oldest continuously operating lighthouse has been warning ships off the hazardous tip of the Monterey Peninsula since 1855. Inside are modest exhibits on the lighthouse's history and, alas, its failures – local shipwrecks.

Monarch Grove Sanctuary　　　PARK
(Map p296; www.cityofpacificgrove.org/visiting; 250 Ridge Rd; ⊙dawn-dusk; ♿) ⚑**FREE** Between November and February, over 25,000 migratory monarch butterflies cluster in this thicket of tall eucalyptus trees, secreted inland. During peak season, volunteer guides answer all of your questions between noon and 3pm, weather permitting.

Pacific Grove Golf Links　　　GOLF
(Map p296; 831-648-5775; www.playpacificgrove.com; 77 Asilomar Blvd; green fees $43-64) Can't afford to play at famous Pebble Beach? This historic 18-hole municipal course, where deer freely range, has impressive sea views, and it's a lot easier (not to mention cheaper) to book a tee time here.

🛏 Sleeping

Antique-filled B&Bs have taken over many stately Victorian homes around downtown Pacific Grove and by the beach. Motels cluster at the peninsula's western end, off Lighthouse and Asilomar Aves.

Asilomar Conference Grounds　LODGE $$
(Map p296; 831-372-8016; www.visitasilomar.com; 800 Asilomar Ave; r from $188; @🔊🐾) This state-park lodge sprawls by sand dunes in pine forest. Skip ho-hum motel rooms and opt for historic houses designed by early-20th-century architect Julia Morgan (of Hearst Castle fame) – the thin-walled, hardwood-floored rooms may be small, but they share a fireplace lounge. Head to the lodge lobby for Ping-Pong, pool tables and wi-fi. Bike rentals available.

Sunset Inn　　　　　　　　MOTEL $$
(Map p296; 831-375-3529; www.gosunsetinn.com; 133 Asilomar Blvd; r $99-235; 🐾) At this small motor lodge near the golf course and the beach, attentive staff hand out keys to crisply redesigned rooms that have hardwood floors, king-sized beds with cheery floral-print comforters and sometimes a hot tub and a fireplace.

🍴 Eating

Downtown PG teems with European-style bakeries, coffee shops and neighborhood cafes.

Jeninni Kitchen & Wine Bar　MEDITERRANEAN $$
(Map p296; 831-920-2662; www.jeninni.com; 542 Lighthouse Ave; mains $18-32; ⊙4pm-late Thu-Tue, 9:30am-1:30pm Sun) Happy-hour

Monterey Peninsula

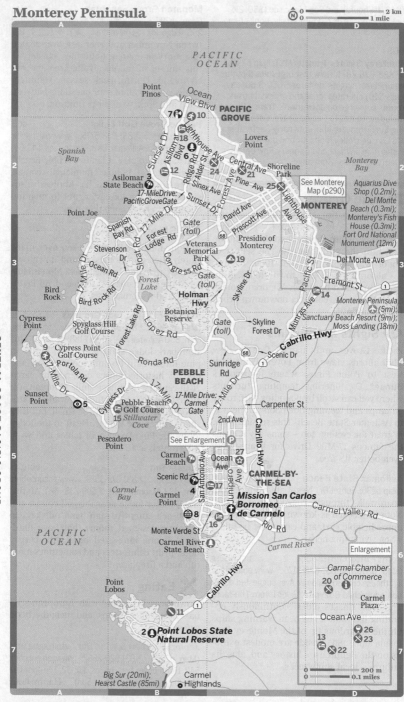

Monterey Peninsula

snacks from 4pm to 6pm segue to dinner at this bistro featuring the flavors of the Med. Housemade charcuterie and shared plates, such as crispy octopus, create a convivial ambience, while larger mains featuring venison, duck or lamb partner well with an informed wine list. On balmy summer nights, dine on the front patio watching Pacific Grove's passing parade.

Passionfish   SEAFOOD $$$
(Map p296; ☎831-655-3311; www.passionfish.net; 701 Lighthouse Ave; mains $21-42; ◎5-9pm Sun-Thu, to 10pm Fri & Sat; 🖋) 🍴 Fresh, sustainable seafood is artfully presented in any number of inventive ways, and a seasonally inspired menu also carries slow-cooked meats and vegetarian dishes spotlighting local farms. The earth-tone decor is spare, with tables squeezed conversationally close together. An ambitious world-ranging wine list is priced near retail, and there are as many Chinese teas as wines by the glass.

Reservations strongly recommended.

 Drinking & Nightlife

Pacific Grove is largely a daytime destination, so make the short journey to Monterey for better after-dark action.

 Information

Pacific Grove Chamber of Commerce (Map p296; ☎831-373-3304; www.pacificgrove.

org; 584 Central Ave; ◎9:30am-5pm Mon-Fri, 10am-3pm Sat)

🛈 Getting There & Around

MST (p295) bus 1 connects downtown Monterey and Cannery Row with Pacific Grove, continuing to Asilomar ($2.50, 15 minutes, every 30 to 60 minutes).

Carmel-by-the-Sea

With borderline fanatical devotion to its canine citizens, quaint Carmel has the well-manicured feel of a country club. Watch the parade of behatted ladies toting fancy-label shopping bags to lunch and dapper gents driving top-down convertibles along Ocean Ave, the village's slow-mo main drag.

Founded as a seaside resort in the 1880s – fairly odd, given that its beach is often blanketed in fog – Carmel quickly attracted famous artists and writers, such as Sinclair Lewis and Jack London, and their hangers-on. Artistic flavor survives in over 100 galleries that line downtown's immaculate streets, but sky-high property values have long obliterated any salt-of-the-earth bohemia.

Dating from the 1920s, Comstock cottages, with their characteristic stone chimneys and pitched gable roofs, still dot the town, making it look vaguely reminiscent of the English countryside. Even payphones, garbage cans and newspaper vending boxes are quaintly shingled.

◉ Sights & Activities

Escape downtown Carmel's harried shopping streets and stroll tree-lined neighborhoods on the lookout for domiciles charming and peculiar. The Hansel and Gretel houses on Torres St, between 5th and 6th Avenues, are just how you'd imagine them. Another eye-catching house in the shape of a ship, made from local river rocks and salvaged ship parts, is on Guadalupe St near 6th Ave.

★ Point Lobos
State Natural Reserve   STATE PARK
(Map p296; ☑831-624-4909; www.pointlobos.org; Hwy 1; per car $10; ☺8am-7pm, to 5pm early Nov–mid-Mar; P ☀) ❂ They bark, they bathe and they're fun to watch – sea lions are the stars here at Punta de los Lobos Marinos (Point of the Sea Wolves), almost 4 miles south of Carmel, where a dramatically rocky coastline offers excellent tide-pooling. The full perimeter hike is 6 miles, but shorter walks take in wild scenery too, including **Bird Island**, shady cypress groves, the historical **Whaler's Cabin** and the **Devil's Cauldron**, a whirlpool that gets splashy at high tide.

The kelp forest at Whalers Cove is popular with snorkelers and scuba divers. Don't skip paying the entry fee by parking outside the park gates on the highway shoulder – California's state parks are chronically underfunded and need your help.

➡ Whalers Cove
(Map p296) Without donning a wetsuit, you can still get an idea of the underwater terrain with a 3D model located by the parking lot. Reserve snorkeling, scuba-diving, kayaking and SUP permits ($10 to $30) up to two months in advance online.

★ Mission San Carlos
Borromeo de Carmelo   CHURCH
(Map p296; ☑831-624-1271; www.carmelmission. org; 3080 Rio Rd; adult/child 7-17yr $6.50/2; ☺9:30am-7pm; ☀) Monterey's original mission was established by Franciscan friar Junípero Serra in 1770, but poor soil and the corrupting influence of Spanish soldiers forced the move to Carmel two years later. Today this is one of California's most strikingly beautiful missions, an oasis of solemnity bathed in flowering gardens. The mission's adobe chapel was later replaced

with an arched basilica made of stone quarried in the Santa Lucia Mountains. Museum exhibits are scattered throughout the meditative complex.

The spartan cell attributed to Serra looks like something out of *The Good, the Bad and the Ugly*, while a separate chapel houses his memorial tomb.

Don't overlook the gravestone of 'Old Gabriel,' a Native American convert whom Serra baptized, and whose dates put him at 151 years old when he died. People say he smoked like a chimney and outlived seven wives. There's a lesson in there somewhere.

Tor House   HISTORIC BUILDING
(Map p296; ☑844-285-0244; www.torhouse. org; 26304 Ocean View Ave; adult/child 12-17yr $12/7; ☺tours hourly 10am-3pm Fri & Sat) Even if you've never heard of 20th-century poet Robinson Jeffers, a pilgrimage to this house built with his own hands offers fascinating insights into both the man and the bohemian ethos of Old Carmel. A porthole in the Celtic-inspired **Hawk Tower** reputedly came from the wrecked ship that carried Napoleon from Elba. The only way to visit the property is to reserve a tour (children under 12 years old not allowed), although the tower can be glimpsed from the street.

Carmel Beach City Park   BEACH
(Map p296; off Scenic Rd; ☀☀) Not always sunny, Carmel Beach is a gorgeous blanket of white sand, where pampered pups excitedly run off-leash. South of 10th Ave, bonfires crackle after sunset (until 10pm Monday through Thursday only).

✰ Festivals & Events

Pebble Beach Food & Wine   FOOD & DRINK
(☑866-907-3663; www.pbfw.com) Excellent four-day gastronomy-focused festival sponsored by the prestigious *Food & Wine* magazine. Held in mid- to late-April.

Carmel International Film Festival   FILM
(www.carmelfilmfest.com; ☺mid-Oct) Live music and over 100 independent film screenings. Animation, documentaries, features and short films are all covered.

🛏 Sleeping

Shockingly overpriced boutique hotels, inns and B&Bs fill up quickly in Carmel-by-the-Sea, especially in summer. Ask the chamber of commerce (p301) about last-minute deals.

For better-value lodgings, head north to Monterey.

Mission Ranch
INN $$

(Map p296; ☑831-624-6436; www.missionranch carmel.com; 26270 Dolores St; r $140-340; ☎) If woolly sheep grazing on green fields by the beach doesn't convince you to stay here, maybe knowing that Hollywood icon Clint Eastwood restored this historic ranch will. Accommodations are shabby-chic, even a tad rustic.

Sea View Inn
B&B $$

(Map p296; ☑831-624-8778; www.seaviewinn carmel.com; El Camino Real, btwn 11th & 12th Aves; r $145-295; ☎) Retreat from downtown Carmel's hustle to fireside nooks tailor-made for reading. The cheapest rooms with slanted ceilings are short on cat-swinging space. Rates include afternoon wine and noshes on the front porch.

Lodge at Pebble Beach
RESORT $$$

(Map p296; ☑831-624-3811; www.pebblebeach. com; 1700 17-Mile Drive; r from $815; ❋@☎☒) The luxurious Lodge at Pebble Beach includes a spa and designer shops where the most demanding of tastes are catered to. Even if you're not a trust-fund baby, you can still soak up the rich atmosphere in the resort's art-filled public spaces and bay views from the cocktail lounge.

Cypress Inn
BOUTIQUE HOTEL $$$

(Map p296; ☑831-624-3871; www.cypress-inn. com; cnr Lincoln St & 7th Ave; r/ste from $279/499; P☺☎☒) Done up in Spanish Colonial style, this 1929 inn is co-owned by movie star Doris Day. Airy terracotta hallways with colorful tiles give it a Mediterranean feel, while sunny rooms face the courtyard. Pet fee $30.

🍴 Eating

Carmel's dining scene has traditionally been more about old-world atmosphere, but a few recent openings have added a more modern, cosmopolitan sheen.

Cultura Comida y Bebida
MEXICAN $$

(Map p296; ☑831-250-7005; www.culturacarmel. com; Dolores St btwn 5th & 6th Aves; mains $19-32; ⊙11:30am-midnight Thu-Sun, 5pm-midnight Mon-Tue) Located near art galleries in a brick-lined courtyard, Cultura Comida y Bebida is a relaxed bar and eatery inspired by the food of Oaxaca in Mexico. Pull up a seat at the elegant bar and sample a vertical tasting of mezcal, or partner Monterey squid tostadas

---

17-MILE DRIVE

What to See

Pacific Grove and Carmel are linked by the spectacularly scenic, if overhyped, **17-Mile Drive** (Map p296; www.pebblebeach.com; per car/bicycle $10/free), which meanders through Pebble Beach, a wealthy private resort. It's no chore staying within the 25mph limit – every curve in the road reveals another postcard vista, especially when wildflowers are in bloom. Cycling the drive is enormously popular: try to do it during the week, when traffic isn't as heavy, and ride with the flow of traffic from north to south.

Using the self-guided touring map you'll receive at the toll gate, you can pick out landmarks such as **Spanish Bay**, where explorer Gaspar de Portolá dropped anchor in 1769; treacherously rocky **Point Joe**, which was often mistaken for the entrance to Monterey Bay and thus became the site of shipwrecks; and **Bird Rock**, also a haven for harbor seals and sea lions. The pièce de résistance is the trademarked **Lone Cypress** (Map p296), which has perched on a seaward rock for possibly more than 250 years.

Besides the coastal scenery, star attractions at Pebble Beach include world-famous golf courses, where a celebrity and pro tournament happens every February. The luxurious **Lodge at Pebble Beach** (p299) has a spa and designer shops.

The Route

Operated as a toll road by the Pebble Beach Company, the 17-Mile Drive is open from sunrise to sunset. The toll can be refunded later as a discount on a $30 minimum food purchase at local restaurants.

Time & Mileage

There are five separate gates for the 17-Mile Drive; how far you drive and how long you take is up to you. To take advantage of the most scenery, enter on Sunset Dr in Pacific Grove and exit onto San Antonio Ave in Carmel-by-the-Sea.

CARMEL VALLEY

Where sun-kissed vineyards rustle beside farm fields, Carmel Valley is a peaceful side trip, just a 20-minute drive east of Hwy 1 along eastbound Carmel Valley Rd. At organic **Earthbound Farm Stand** (☑805-625-6219; www.ebfarm.com; 7250 Carmel Valley Rd; ⊘8am-6:30pm Mon-Sat, 9am-6pm Sun; ⓕ) ⌀, sample homemade soups and salads or harvest your own herbs from the garden. Several wineries further east offer tastings – don't miss the Pinot Noir bottled by **Boekenoogen** (Map p302; ☑831-659-4215; www.boekenoogen wines.com; 24 W Carmel Valley Rd; tasting flights $10-15; ⊘11am-5pm; ⓟ). Afterwards, stretch your legs in the village of Carmel Valley, chock-a-block with genteel shops and bistros.

Corkscrew Cafe (Map p302; ☑831- 659-8888; www.corkscrewcafe.com; 55 W Carmel Valley Rd; mains $15-26; ⊘noon-9pm Wed-Mon) Just possibly Carmel Valley's coziest eatery, the Corkscrew Cafe combines a rustic wine-country vibe and a Mediterranean-influenced menu – think wood-fired salmon, pizza, and mushroom and lamb pasta – with a stellar local wine list. Relax into a Carmel Valley evening under the market umbrellas in the pleasant garden, and don't leave without checking out the quirky corkscrew museum.

Valley Greens Gallery (Map p302; ☑831-620-2985; www.valleygreensgallery.com; 16e E Carmel Valley Rd; 4-beer tasting flights $12; ⊘3-9pm Mon-Tue, 3-10pm Wed-Thu, 1-11pm Fri-Sat, 1-9pm Sun) One part funky art gallery and two parts craft-beer bar, Valley Greens is a stand-out destination amid Carmel Valley's laid-back main drag. Four rotating beer taps deliver some real surprises from smaller Californian breweries, old-school reggae and foosball tables create a fun ambience, and open-mike night from 6pm on Tuesdays is always worth catching.

and oak-roasted trout with cilantro, lime and garlic with Californian and French wines.

Mundaka
TAPAS $$

(Map p296; ☑831-624-7400; www.mundakacarmel. com; San Carlos St, btwn Ocean & 7th Aves; small plates $8-15; ⊘5-9pm Sun-Thu, to 10pm Fri-Sat) This stone courtyard hideaway is a svelte escape from Carmel's stuffy 'newly wed and nearly dead' crowd. Taste Spanish tapas and housemade sangria while world beats spin. Partner the garlic prawns or grilled octopus with a chilled glass of local wine.

La Bicyclette
FRENCH, ITALIAN $$

(Map p296; ☑831-622-9899; www.labicyclette restaurant.com; cnr Dolores St & 7th Ave; dinner mains $18-31; ⊘8am-10pm) ⌀ Rustic European comfort food using seasonal local ingredients packs canoodling couples into this bistro, with an open kitchen baking wood-fired-oven pizzas. Excellent local wines by the glass. It's also a top spot for a breakfast or lunch.

🍸 Drinking & Entertainment

Winery tasting rooms dot Carmel's compact and well-kept centre, and the best option for late-night drinks is the cool and energetic scene at Barmel.

Barmel
WINE BAR

(Map p296; ☑831-626-2095; www.facebook.com/ BarmelByTheSea; San Carlos St, btwn Ocean & 7th Aves; ⊘2pm-2am Mon-Fri, 1pm-2am Sat-Sun) Shaking up Carmel's conservative image and adding a dash of after-dark fun is this cool little Spanish-themed courtyard bar. There's live music from 7pm to 9pm from Thursday to Saturday, robust cocktails and an energetic, younger vibe.

Scheid Vineyards
WINE BAR

(Map p296; ☑831-656-9463; www.scheidvineyards. com; San Carlos St, at 7th Ave; tasting flights $10-20; ⊘noon-7pm Sun-Thu, to 8pm Fri & Sat) Pop into Scheid Vineyards' wine-tasting room to sip a prodigious range of grape varietals, all grown in Monterey County. Red wine varietals including Merlot, Pinot Noir and Cabernet Sauvignon are local stars.

Forest Theater
THEATER

(Map p296; ☑box office 831-622-0100; www. foresttheatercarmel.org; cnr Mountain View Ave & Santa Rita St) At this 1910 venue, community-theater musicals, dramas and comedies as well as film screenings take place under the stars by flickering fire pits.

ℹ Information

Carmel Chamber of Commerce (Map p296; ☑ 831-624-2522; www.carmelcalifornia.org; San Carlos St, btwn 5th & 6th Aves; ⊘ 10am-5pm)

ℹ Getting There & Away

Carmel is about 5 miles south of Monterey via Hwy 1. There's free parking (no time limit) in a **municipal lot** (Map p296; cnr 3rd & Junípero Sts) behind the Vista Lobos building.

MST (☑ 888-678-2871; www.mst.org) 'Grapevine Express' bus 24 ($2.50, hourly) connects Monterey's Transit Plaza with downtown Carmel, the mission and Carmel Valley. Bus 22 ($3.50) stops in downtown Carmel and at the mission en route to/from Point Lobos and Big Sur three times daily between late May and early September, and twice daily on Saturday and Sunday only the rest of the year.

Big Sur

Big Sur is more a state of mind than a place to pinpoint on a map, and when the sun goes down, the moon and the stars are the area's natural streetlights. (That's if summer's fog hasn't extinguished them.) Raw beauty and an intense maritime energy characterize this land shoehorned between the Santa Lucia Range and the Pacific Ocean, and a first glimpse of the craggy, unspoiled coastline is a special moment.

In the 1950s and '60s, Big Sur – named by Spanish settlers living on the Monterey Peninsula, who referred to the wilderness as *el país grande del sur* ('the big country to the south') – became a retreat for artists and writers, including Henry Miller and Beat Generation visionaries such as Lawrence Ferlinghetti. Today Big Sur attracts self-proclaimed artists, new-age mystics, latter-day hippies and city slickers seeking to unplug and reflect more deeply on this emerald-green edge of the continent.

◎ Sights

At Big Sur's state parks, your parking fee ($10) receipt is valid for same-day entry to all except Limekiln. Please don't skip paying the entry fee by parking illegally outside the parks along Hwy 1 – California's state parks have suffered severe budget cutbacks, and every dollar helps.

Garrapata State Park   PARK
(Map p302; ☑ 831-624-4909; www.parks.ca.gov; off Hwy 1; ⊕) FREE Over 4 miles south of Point Lobos on Hwy 1, pull over to hike coastal headlands, where you might spot whales cruising by offshore during winter, or into canyons of wildflowers and redwood trees. *Garrapata* is Spanish for 'tick,' of which there are many in the canyon and woods, so wearing long sleeves and pants is smart. Leashed dogs are allowed on the beach only.

Bixby Bridge   LANDMARK
(Map p302) Less than 15 miles south of Carmel, this landmark spanning Rainbow Canyon is one of the world's highest single-span bridges. Completed in 1932, it was built by prisoners eager to lop time off their sentences. There's a perfect photo-op pull-off on the bridge's north side. Before Bixby Bridge was constructed, travelers had to trek inland on what's now called the **Old Coast Rd**, a rough dirt route that reconnects after 11 miles with Hwy 1 near Andrew Molera State Park. When the weather is dry enough, the old road is usually navigable by 4WD or a mountain bike.

CENTRAL COAST BIG SUR

ℹ HIGHWAY 1 ROAD CLOSURES

At the time of writing, temporary road closures have shuttered a 23 mile stretch along Hwy 1 through Big Sur. To the north, the Pfeiffer Canyon Bridge has been condemned after the eroding hillside undermined the support columns. In the southern part of the region, mudslides have covered the road at Mud Creek, significantly changing the landscape and making the area inaccessible via car. The Pfeiffer Canyon Bridge is scheduled to reopen in September 2017. However, the California Department of Transportation has a larger challenge with the landslides. A plan was put forward in August 2017 to realign the highway across the landslide, but the enormous undertaking had no set date of completion at that time.

Until the road reopens, travelers can detour around Big Sur on Hwy 101 (p316). You'll miss out on some coastal views, but between stunning views of the California countryside, quaint towns and world-class wine tasting, it's a detour worth taking on its own merit.

Big Sur

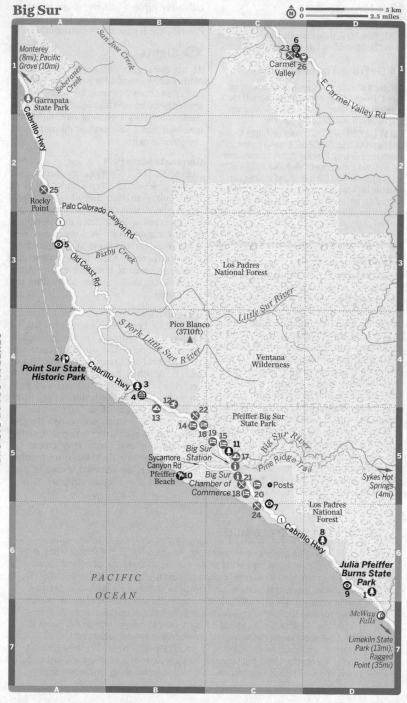

★ **Point Sur State Historic Park** LIGHTHOUSE
(Map p302; ☏ 831-625-4419; www.pointsur.org; off Hwy 1; adult/child 6-17yr from $12/5; ⊙ tours usually at 1pm Wed, 10am Sat & Sun Oct-Mar; 10am & 2pm Wed & Sat, 10am Sun Apr-Sep, also 10am Thu Jul & Aug) FREE A little over 6 miles south of Bixby Bridge (p301), Point Sur rises like a velvety green fortress out of the sea. It looks like an island, but is actually connected to land by a sandbar. Atop the volcanic rock sits an 1889 stone light station, which was staffed until 1974. During three-hour guided tours, ocean views and tales of the lighthouse keepers' family lives are engrossing. Meet your tour guide at the locked farm gate 0.25-miles north of Point Sur Naval Facility.

Special monthly moonlight tours are given between April and September. Call ahead to confirm all tour schedules. Show up early because space is limited (no reservations; some credit cards accepted).

Andrew Molera State Park STATE PARK
(Map p302; ☏ 831-667-2315; www.parks.ca.gov; Hwy 1; per car $10; ⊙ 30min before sunrise-30min after sunset; 🅿🚻) 🏊 Named after the farmer who first planted artichokes in California, this oft-overlooked park is a trail-laced pastiche of grassy meadows, ocean bluffs and rugged sandy beaches offering excellent wildlife watching. Look for the entrance just over 8 miles south of Bixby Bridge.

South of the parking lot, you can learn all about endangered California condors and long-term species recovery and monitoring programs inside the **Big Sur Discovery Center** (Map p302; ☏ 831-624-1202; www.ventanaws.org/discovery_center; ⊙ 10am-4pm Sat & Sun late May–early Sep; 🅿🚻) 🏊 FREE.

From the main parking lot, a short walk along the beach-bound trail passes through a first-come-first-serve campground, from where a gentle spur trail leads to the 1861 redwood **Cooper Cabin**, Big Sur's oldest building. Keep hiking on the main trail out toward a wild beach where the Big Sur River runs into the ocean; condors may be spotted circling overhead and migrating whales sometimes cruise by offshore.

Pfeiffer Big Sur State Park PARK
(Map p302; ☏ 831-667-2315; www.parks.ca.gov; 47225 Hwy 1; per car $10; ⊙ 30min before sunrise-30min after sunset; 🅿🚻) 🏊 Named after Big Sur's first European settlers who arrived in 1869, this is Big Sur's largest state park, where hiking trails loop through stately redwood groves. The most popular hike – to 60ft-high **Pfeiffer Falls**, a delicate cascade hidden in the forest, which usually runs from December to May – is a 2-mile round-trip. Built in the 1930s by the Civilian Conservation Corps (CCC), rustic **Big Sur Lodge** (Map p302; ☏ 831-667-3100; www.bigsurlodge.com; 47225 Hwy 1; d $309-439; 🅿❄🛜📶)

stands near the park entrance, about 13 miles south of Bixby Bridge (p301).

★ **Julia Pfeiffer Burns State Park**   PARK
(☑831-667-2315; www.parks.ca.gov; Hwy 1; per car $10; ☉30min before sunrise-30min after sunset; 🅿🏕) 🏊 If you're chasing waterfalls, swing into this state park named for a Big Sur pioneer. From the parking lot, the 1.3-mile round-trip **Overlook Trail** rushes downhill toward the ocean, passing through a tunnel underneath Hwy 1. Everyone comes to photograph 80ft-high **McWay Falls**, which tumbles year-round over granite cliffs and freefalls into the sea – or the beach, depending on the tide. The park entrance is on the east side of Hwy 1, about 8 miles south of Nepenthe restaurant (p307). McWay Falls is the classic Big Sur postcard shot, with tree-topped rocks jutting above a golden beach next to swirling blue pools and crashing white surf. From trailside benches, you might spot migrating whales during winter.

Pfeiffer Beach   BEACH
(Map p42; ☑831-667-2315; www.fs.usda.gov/lpnf; end of Sycamore Canyon Rd; per car $10; ☉9am-8pm; 🅿🏕🐕) This phenomenal, crescent-shaped and dog-friendly beach is known for its huge double-rock formation, through which waves crash with life-affirming power. It's often windy, and the surf is too dangerous for swimming. But dig down into the wet sand – it's purple! That's because manganese garnet washes down from the craggy hillsides above. To get here from Hwy 1, make a sharp right onto Sycamore Canyon Rd, marked by a small yellow sign that says 'narrow road' at the top. From the turnoff, which is a half-mile south of Big Sur Station on the ocean side of Hwy 1, it's two narrow, twisting miles down to the beach (RVs and trailers prohibited).

Henry Miller Memorial Library   ARTS CENTER
(Map p302; ☑831-667-2574; www.henrymiller.org; 48603 Hwy 1; donations accepted; ☉10am-5pm) **FREE** Novelist Henry Miller was a Big Sur denizen from 1944 to 1962. More of a beatnik memorial, alt-cultural venue and bookshop, this community gathering spot was never Miller's home. The house belonged to Miller's friend, painter Emil White, until his death and is now run by a nonprofit group. Stop by to browse and hang out on the front deck. It's 0.4 miles south of Nepenthe restaurant (p307).

Inside are copies of all of Miller's written works, many of his paintings and a collection of Big Sur and Beat Generation material, including copies of the top 100 books Miller said most influenced him. Check the online calendar for upcoming events.

Partington Cove   BEACH
(off Hwy 1) **FREE** This is a raw, breathtaking spot where crashing surf salts your skin. On the steep, half-mile dirt hike down to the cove, you'll cross a cool bridge and go through an even cooler tunnel. The cove's water is unbelievably aqua and within it grow tangled kelp forests. Look for the unmarked trailhead turnoff inside a hairpin turn on the ocean side of Hwy 1, about 6 miles south of Nepenthe restaurant (p307) and 2 miles north of Julia Pfeiffer Burns State Park.

The trail starts just beyond the locked vehicle gate. There's no real beach access and ocean swimming isn't safe, but some people scamper on the rocks and look for tide pools as waves splash ominously. Originally used for loading freight, Partington Cove allegedly became a landing spot for Prohibition-era bootleggers.

Limekiln State Park   PARK
(☑831-434-1996; www.parks.ca.gov; 63025 Hwy 1; per car $10; ☉8am-sunset) Two miles south of Lucia, this park gets its name from the four remaining wood-fired kilns originally built here in the 1880s to smelt quarried limestone into powder, a key ingredient in cement building construction from Monterey to San Francisco. Tragically, pioneers chopped down most of the steep canyon's old-growth redwoods to fuel the kilns' fires. A 1-mile round-trip trail leads through a redwood grove to the historic site, passing a creekside spur trail to a delightful 100ft-high waterfall.

Los Padres National Forest   FOREST
(☑805-968-6640; www.fs.usda.gov/lpnf; Hwy 1, almost opp Plaskett Creek Campground; 🐕) The tortuously winding 40-mile stretch of Hwy 1 south of Lucia to Hearst Castle is sparsely populated, rugged and remote, mostly running through national forest lands. Around 5 miles south of Kirk Creek Campground (p307) and Nacimiento-Fergusson Rd, almost opposite Plaskett Creek Campground (p307), is **Sand Dollar Beach** (http://campone.com; Hwy 1; per car $10, free with local USFS campground fee; ☉9am-8pm; 🐕). From the picnic area, it's a five-minute walk to southern Big Sur's longest sandy

VENTANA WILDERNESS

The 240,000-acre Ventana Wilderness is Big Sur's wild backcountry. It lies within the northern Los Padres National Forest, which straddles the Santa Lucia Range running parallel to the coast. Most of this wilderness is covered with oak and chaparral, though canyons cut by the Big Sur and Little Sur Rivers support virgin stands of coast redwoods and the rare endemic Santa Lucia fir, which grows on steep, rocky slopes too.

Now regenerating after devastating wildfires in 2008, Ventana Wilderness is popular with adventurous backpackers. A much-trammeled overnight destination is Sykes Hot Springs, natural 100°F (35°C) mineral pools framed by redwoods. It's a moderately strenuous 10-mile, one-way hike along the Pine Ridge Trail, starting from Big Sur Station (p308), where you can get free campfire permits and pay for overnight trailhead parking ($5). Don't expect solitude on weekends during peak season (April through September) and always follow Leave No Trace (www.lnt.org) principles.

beach, a crescent-shaped strip of sand protected from winds by high bluffs. Nearby is **Jade Cove** (http://campone.com; Hwy 1; ☉sunrise-sunset; ☒) FREE and it's a short drive south to Salmon Creek Falls.

Heading south before leaving Lucia, make sure you've got at least enough fuel in the tank to reach the expensive gas stations at Gorda, about 11 miles south of Limekiln State Park, or Ragged Point, another 12 miles further south.

Ragged Point   LANDMARK
(19019 Hwy 1) Your last – or first – taste of Big Sur's rocky grandeur comes at this craggy cliff outcropping with fabulous views of the coastline in both directions, about 15 miles north of Hearst Castle (p310). Once part of the Hearst empire, it's now taken over by a sprawling, ho-hum lodge with a pricey gas station. Heading south, the land grows increasingly wind-swept as Hwy 1 rolls gently down to the water's edge.

Salmon Creek Falls   WATERFALL
(www.fs.usda.gov/lpnf; Hwy 1; P☒☒) FREE Take a short hike to splash around in the pools at the base of this double-drop waterfall, tucked uphill in a forested canyon. The falls usually run from December through May, and the trail is dog-friendly. In a hairpin turn of Hwy 1, the roadside turnoff is marked only by a small brown trailhead sign, about 8 miles south of Gorda.

🏃 Activities

Esalen Hot Springs   HOT SPRINGS
(☎831-667-3047; www.esalen.org; 55000 Hwy 1; per person $30; ☉by reservation) At the private **Esalen Institute** (☎831-667-3000),

clothing-optional baths fed by a natural hot spring sit on a ledge above the ocean. We're confident you'll never take another dip that compares scenery-wise, especially on stormy winter nights. Only two small outdoor pools perch directly over the waves, so once you've stripped and taken a quick shower, head outside immediately. Credit cards only.

Advance reservations are required. The signposted entrance is on Hwy 1, about 3 miles south of Julia Pfeiffer Burns State Park (p304).

Molera Horseback Tours   HORSEBACK RIDING
(Map p302; ☎831-625-5486; www.molerahorseback tours.com; Hwy 1; per person $58-96; 🖐) Across Hwy 1 from Andrew Molera State Park (p303), Molera offers guided trail rides on the beach and through redwood forest. Walk-ins and novices are welcome; children must be at least six years old, with most rides recommended for ages 12 and up.

🛏 Sleeping

With few exceptions, Big Sur's lodgings do not have TVs and rarely have telephones. This is where you come to escape the world. There aren't a lot of rooms overall, so demand often exceeds supply and prices can be steep. Bigger price tags don't necessarily buy you more amenities either. In summer and on weekends, reservations are essential everywhere, from campgrounds to deluxe resorts.

Ripplewood Resort   CABIN $$
(Map p302; ☎831-667-2242; www.ripplewood resort.com; 47047 Hwy 1; cabins $140-250; ☺🛜) North of Pfeiffer Big Sur State Park (p303), Ripplewood has gotten behind fiscal equality by charging the same rates year-round.

Throwback Americana cabins mostly have kitchens and sometimes even wood-burning fireplaces. Quiet riverside cabins are surrounded by redwoods, but roadside cabins can be noisy. Wi-fi in restaurant only.

★ Post Ranch Inn
RESORT $$$

(Map p302; ☑ 831-667-2200; www.postranchinn.com; 47900 Hwy 1; d from $925; P ➷ ❋ @ ☎ ☎) The last word in luxurious coastal getaways, the exclusive Post Ranch pampers demanding guests with slate spa tubs, wood-burning fireplaces, private decks and walking sticks for coastal hikes. Ocean-view rooms celebrate the sea, while treehouses lack views and have a bit of sway. Paddle around the clifftop infinity pool after a shamanic-healing session or yoga class in the spa. No children allowed.

Panoramic sea-view Sierra Mar restaurant requires reservations for lunch and dinner; the gourmet breakfast buffet is served to guests only.

Ventana Inn & Spa
RESORT $$$

(Map p302; ☑ 831-667-2331; www.ventanainn.com; 48123 Hwy 1; d from $596; ☎ ☎) ✈ Almost at odds with Big Sur's hippie-alternative vibe, Ventana injects a little soul into its deluxe digs. Honeymooning couples and paparazzi-fleeing celebs pad from tai chi class to the Japanese baths and outdoor pools (one is famously clothing-optional), or hole up all day next to the wood-burning fireplace in their own private villa, hot-tub suite or ocean-view cottage.

Treebones Resort
CABIN $$$

(☑ 877-424-4787; www.treebonesresort.com; 71895 Hwy 1; campsites $95, d with shared bath from $320; ➷ ☎ ☎) Don't let the word 're-sort' throw you. Yes, it has an ocean-view hot tub, heated pool and massage treatments. But a unique woven 'human nest' and canvas-sided yurts with polished pine floors, quilt-covered beds, sink vanities and redwood decks are more like glamping, with little privacy. Communal bathrooms and showers are a short stroll away. Wi-fi in main lodge only.

Basic walk-in campsites (no vehicle access) are also available. Children must be at least six years old. Look for the signposted turnoff a mile north of Gorda, at the southern end of Big Sur.

Glen Oaks Motel
MOTEL, CABIN $$$

(Map p302; ☑ 831-667-2105; www.glenoaksbigsur.com; 47080 Hwy 1; d $300-475; P ➷ ☎) ✈ At this 1950s redwood-and-adobe motor lodge, rustic rooms and cabins seem effortlessly chic. Dramatically transformed by eco-conscious design, snug romantic hideaway rooms all have gas fireplaces. Woodsy cabins in a redwood grove have kitchenettes and share outdoor fire pits, or retreat to the one-bedroom house with a full kitchen.

Public Campgrounds

Camping is currently available at four of Big Sur's state parks and two United States Forest Service (USFS) campgrounds along Hwy 1.

CALIFORNIA'S COMEBACK CONDORS

When it comes to endangered species, one of the state's biggest success stories is the California condor (*Gymnogyps californianus*). These gigantic, prehistoric birds weigh over 20lb with a wingspan of up to 10ft, letting them fly great distances in search of carrion. They're easily recognized by their naked pink head and large white patches on the underside of each wing.

This big bird became so rare that in 1987 there were only 27 left in the world, and all were removed from the wild to special captive-breeding facilities. Read the whole gripping story in journalist John Moir's book *Return of the Condor: The Race to Save Our Largest Bird from Extinction*.

There are over 400 California condors alive today, with increasing numbers of captive birds being released back into the wild. It's hoped they will begin breeding naturally, although it's an uphill battle. Wild condors are still dying of lead poisoning caused by hunters' bullets in the game carcasses that the birds feed on.

The Big Sur coast and Pinnacles National Park (p319) offer excellent opportunities to view this majestic bird. In Big Sur, the Ventana Wildlife Society (www.ventanaws.org) occasionally leads two-hour guided condor-watching tours ($50) using radio telemetry to track the birds; for sign-up details, check the website or ask at the Big Sur Discovery Center (p303).

Big Sur Campground & Cabins
CABIN, CAMPGROUND $$

(Map p302; ☑831-667-2322; www.bigsurcamp. com; 47000 Hwy 1; tent/RV sites from $63/73, cabins $175-430; P☯) On the Big Sur River and shaded by redwoods, cozy cabins sport full kitchens and fireplaces, while canvas-sided tent cabins share bathroom facilities. The riverside campground, where neighboring sites have little privacy, is popular with RVs. There are hot showers and a coin-op laundry, playground and general store.

Pfeiffer Big Sur State Park Campground
CAMPGROUND $

(Map p302; ☑reservations 800-444-7275; www. reserveamerica.com; 47225 Hwy 1; tent & RV sites $35-50; P☯) Best for novice campers and families with young kids, here over 200 campsites nestle in a redwood-shaded valley. Facilities include drinking water, fire pits and coin-op hot showers and laundry.

Julia Pfeiffer Burns State Park Campground
CAMPGROUND $

(Map p42; ☑831-667-2315; www.parks.ca.gov; Hwy 1; tent sites $30) Two small walk-in campsites sit up on a semi-shaded ocean bluff, with fire pits and vault toilets but no water. All campers must check in first at Pfeiffer Big Sur State Park (p303), 11 miles north.

Andrew Molera State Park Campground
CAMPGROUND $

(Map p42; www.parks.ca.gov; Hwy 1; tent sites $25) Two-dozen primitive tent sites (no reservations) in a grassy meadow come with fire pits and drinking water, but no ocean views. The campground is a 0.3-mile walk from the parking lot.

Limekiln State Park Campground
CAMPGROUND $

(Map p42; ☑805-434-1996; www.parks.ca.gov; 63025 Hwy 1; tent & RV sites $35; ☯) In southern Big Sur, this quiet state park has two-dozen campsites huddled under a bridge next to the ocean. Drinking water, fire pits and coin-op hot showers are available.

USFS Kirk Creek Campground
CAMPGROUND $

(☑reservations 877-444-6777; www.recreation. gov; Hwy 1; tent & RV sites $35) Over 30 exposed ocean-view blufftop campsites cluster close together, nearly 2 miles south of Limekiln State Park (p304).

USFS Plaskett Creek Campground
CAMPGROUND $

(Map p42; ☑reservations 877-477-6777; www.rec reation.gov; Hwy 1; tent & RV sites $35) Nearly 40 spacious, shady campsites with drinking water and vault toilets circle a forested meadow near Sand Dollar Beach (p305) in southern Big Sur.

✖ Eating

Like Big Sur's lodgings, some restaurants and cafes alongside Hwy 1 can be overpriced and underwhelming, but stellar views at some locations do offset any mediocrity.

Big Sur Roadhouse
CALIFORNIAN $

(Map p302; ☑831-667-2370; www.bigsurroadhouse. com; 47080 Hwy 1; snacks & mains $7-15; ⊗8am-2:30pm; 🐾) This modern roadhouse glows with color-splashed artwork and an outdoor fire pit. At riverside tables, fork into upscale California-inspired pub grub like spicy wings, pork sliders and gourmet burgers, with craft beer on tap. It's also a top spot for coffee and cake.

Big Sur Deli & General Store
DELI $

(Map p302; ☑831-667-2225; www.bigsurdeli.com; 47520 Hwy 1; snacks $2-12; ⊗7am-8pm) With the most reasonable prices in Big Sur, this family-owned deli slices custom-made sandwiches and piles up tortillas with carne asada, pork *carnitas*, veggies or beans and cheese. The small market carries camping food, snacks, beer and wine.

Rocky Point
CALIFORNIAN, SEAFOOD $$

(Map p302; ☑831-624-2933; www.rockypoint restaurant.com; 36700 Hwy 1; mains $18-36; ⊗11:30am-8pm Thu-Tue) Come for the hillside ocean-view terrace, where cocktails and Californian wines are served all day long, and the steak and seafood menu includes on-the-road treats like scallops, paella and crab cakes. The spectacularly located restaurant is 2.5 miles north of Bixby Bridge (p301).

Nepenthe
CALIFORNIAN $$$

(Map p302; ☑831-667-2345; www.nepenthebig sur.com; 48510 Hwy 1; mains $18-50; ⊗11:30am-4:30pm & 5-10pm; 🐾🚻) Nepenthe comes from a Greek word meaning 'isle of no sorrow,' and indeed, it's hard to feel blue while sitting by the fire pit on this aerial terrace. Just-okay California cuisine (try the renowned Ambrosia burger) takes a backseat to the views and Nepenthe's history – Orson Welles and Rita Hayworth briefly owned a cabin here in the 1940s. Reservations essential.

ⓘ DRIVING HIGHWAY 1

Driving this narrow two-lane highway through Big Sur and beyond is very slow going. Allow about three hours to cover the distance between the Monterey Peninsula and San Luis Obispo, much more if you want to explore the coast. Traveling after dark can be risky and more to the point, it's futile, because you'll miss out on the seascapes. Watch out for cyclists and make use of signposted roadside pullouts to let faster-moving traffic pass.

Downstairs, cheaper but still expensive Café Kevah delivers coffee, baked goods, light brunches and head-spinning ocean views on its outdoor deck (closed during winter and bad weather).

Big Sur Bakery & Restaurant CALIFORNIAN $$$
(Map p302; ☑831-667-0520; www.bigsurbakery. com; 47540 Hwy 1; bakery items $3-14, mains $20-36; ☺bakery from 8am daily, restaurant 9:30am-2pm Mon-Fri, 10am-2:30pm Sat & Sun, 5:30pm-late Wed-Sat) Behind the Shell station, this warmly lit, funky house has seasonally changing menus, on which wood-fired pizzas share space with rustic dishes like grilled swordfish or wood-roasted chicken. Fronted by a pretty patio, the bakery makes addictive cinnamon buns and super-stuffed sandwiches. Expect longish waits and standoffish service. Dinner reservations are essential.

Big Sur River Inn AMERICAN $$$
(Map p302; ☑831-667-2700; www.bigsurriverinn. com; 46840 Hwy 1; breakfast & lunch $15-20, dinner $15-40; ☺8am-9pm; 🛜🐾) Woodsy restaurant with a deck, overlooking a creek teeming with throaty frogs. The food is standard American (seafood, grilled meats and pastas, plus vegetarian options), but diner-style breakfasts and lunches such as berry pancakes and BLT sandwiches satisfy. Rooms (starting at $150), a general store, and gas are also available.

🍷 Drinking & Entertainment

Californian craft beers are a Big Sur highlight at the Big Sur Taphouse and the Maiden Publick House, while there are excellent wine lists at clifftop restaurants with rugged Pacific Ocean vistas.

Big Sur Taphouse BAR
(Map p302; ☑831-667-2225; www.bigsur taphouse.com; 47520 Hwy 1; ☺noon-10pm Mon-Fri, 10am-midnight Sat, to 10pm Sun; 🛜) Down California craft beers and regional wines on the back deck or by the fireplace inside this high-ceilinged wooden bar with board games, sports on the TVs and pub grub from the next-door deli.

Maiden Publick House PUB
(Map p302; ☑831-667-2355; Village Center Shops, Hwy 1; ☺3pm-2am Mon-Thu, from 1pm Fri & from 11am Sat-Sun) Just south of the Big Sur River Inn, this dive has an encyclopedic beer bible and motley local musicians jamming, mostly on weekends. Sixteen rotating taps and three pages of bottled brews create havoc for the indecisive drinker.

**Henry Miller
Memorial Library** PERFORMING ARTS
(Map p302; ☑831-667-2574; www.henrymiller. org; 48603 Hwy 1; ☺10am-5pm & longer hours for specific events; 🛜) Just south of Nepenthe (p307), this nonprofit alternative space hosts a bohemian carnival of live-music concerts, author readings, open-mike nights and indie-film screenings outdoors, especially during summer.

ⓘ Information

Visitors often wander into businesses along Hwy 1 and ask, 'How much further to Big Sur?' In fact, there is no town of Big Sur as such, though you may see the name on maps. Commercial activity is concentrated along the stretch north of Pfeiffer Big Sur State Park. Sometimes called 'the Village,' this is where you'll find most of the lodgings, restaurants and shops.

Big Sur Chamber of Commerce (Map p302; ☑831-667-2100; www.bigsurcalifornia.org; Hwy 1; ☺9am-1pm Mon, Wed & Fri)

Big Sur Station (Map p302; ☑831-667-2315; www.bigsurcalifornia.org/contact.html; 47555 Hwy 1; ☺9am-4pm) About 1.5 miles south of Pfeiffer Big Sur State Park, this multiagency ranger station has information and maps for state parks, the Los Padres National Forest and Ventana Wilderness. The location is also one of the spots along Big Sur where there is more reliable cellphone coverage.

ⓘ Getting There & Around

Big Sur is best explored by car, since you'll be itching to stop frequently and take in the rugged beauty and vistas that reveal themselves after every hairpin turn. Even if your driving skills are up to these narrow switchbacks, others' aren't:

expect to average 35mph or less along the route. Parts of Hwy 1 are battle-scarred, evidence of a continual struggle to keep them open after landslides and washouts. Check current highway conditions with CalTrans (☑800-427-7623; www.dot.ca.gov) and fill up your gas tank beforehand.

MST (☑888-678-2871; www.mst.org) bus 22 ($3.50, 1¼ hours) travels from Monterey via Carmel and Point Lobos as far south as Nepenthe restaurant (p307), stopping en route at Andrew Molera State Park (p303) and the Big Sur River Inn. Buses run three times daily between late May and early September, and twice daily on Saturdays and Sundays only the rest of the year.

Point Piedras Blancas

Many lighthouses still stand along California's coast, but few offer such a historically evocative seascape. Federally designated an outstanding natural area, the jutting, windblown grounds of this 1875 **light station** (☑805-927-7361; www.piedrasblancas.gov; off Hwy 1; tours adult/child 6-17yr $10/5; ⊙tours 9:45am Mon-Tue & Thu-Sat mid-Jun–Aug, 9:45am Tue, Thu & Sat Sep–mid-Jun) have been replanted with native flora. Everything looks much the way it did when the first lighthouse keepers helped ships find safe harbor at San Simeon Bay. Guided tours meet at the old Piedras Blancas Motel, 1.5 miles north of the lighthouse gate on Hwy 1. No reservations are taken; call ahead to check tour schedules.

At a signposted vista point, around 4.5 miles north of Hearst Castle, you can observe a colony of northern elephant seals bigger than the one at Año Nuevo State Reserve near Santa Cruz. During peak winter season, about 18,000 seals seek shelter in the coves and beaches along this stretch of coast. On sunny days the seals usually 'lie around like banana slugs,' in the words of one volunteer. Interpretive panels along a beach boardwalk and blue-jacketed Friends of the Elephant Seal (www.elephantseal.org) guides demystify the behavior of these giant beasts.

Mission San Antonio De Padua

Remote and evocative, this historical mission sits in the Valley of the Oaks, once part of the sprawling Hearst Ranch landholdings and now inside the boundaries of the US Army's Fort Hunter Liggett. Around the grounds, you can inspect the remains of a grist mill and irrigation system with aqueducts. It's seldom crowded, and you may have this vast site all to yourself, except during Mission Days in late April and La Fiesta on the second Sunday of June.

The mission was founded in 1771 by Franciscan priest Junípero Serra. Built with Native Californian labor, the church has been restored to its early-19th-century appearance, with a wooden pulpit, canopied altar and decorative flourishes on whitewashed walls. A creaky door leads to a cloistered garden anchored by a fountain. The museum has a small collection of utilitarian items such as an olive press and a weaving loom once used in the mission's workshops.

You may be asked for photo ID and proof of your vehicle's registration at a nearby military checkpoint. From the north, take the Jolon Rd exit off Hwy 101 before King City and follow Jolon Rd (County Rte G14) about 18 miles south to Mission Rd. From the south, take the Jolon Rd (County Rte G18) exit off Hwy 101 and drive 22 miles northwest to Mission Rd.

San Simeon

Little San Simeon Bay sprang to life as a whaling station in 1852, by which time California sea otters had been hunted almost to extinction by Russian fur traders. Shoreline whaling was practiced to catch gray whales migrating between Alaskan feeding grounds and birthing waters in Baja California. In 1865 Senator George Hearst purchased 45,000 acres of ranch land and established a small settlement beside the sea. Designed by architect Julia Morgan, the historic 19th-century houses today are rented to employees of the Hearst Corporation's 82,000-acre free-range cattle ranch.

⊙ Sights & Activities

William Randolph Hearst Memorial State Beach BEACH (www.parks.ca.gov; Hwy 1; ⊙dawn-dusk) FREE Across from Hearst Castle (p310), this bayfront beach is a pleasantly sandy stretch punctuated by rock outcroppings, kelp forests, a wooden pier (fishing permitted) and picnic areas with barbecue grills.

Kayak Outfitters KAYAKING (☑805-927-1787; www.kayakcambria.com; Hwy 1; single/double kayak rentals from $20/40, tours

$50-110; ⊙10am-4pm or later mid-Jun–early Sep, call for off-season hours) Right on San Simeon's beach, you can rent sea kayaks, wetsuits, stand-up paddle boarding (SUP) sets, bodyboards and surfboards, or take a kayak-fishing trip or a guided paddle around San Simeon Cove. Sea kayaking along the famed Moonstone Beach south at Cambria is another excellent option.

🛏 Sleeping & Eating

Modern San Simeon is nothing more than a strip of unexciting motels and lackluster restaurants. There are better-value places to stay and eat in Cambria and beach towns further south, such as Cayucos and Morro Bay.

Hearst San Simeon
State Park Campground   CAMPGROUND $
(⌨reservations   800-444-7275;   www.reserve america.com; Hwy 1; tent & RV sites $25) About 5 miles south of Hearst Castle are two state-park campgrounds: **San Simeon Creek**, with coin-op hot showers and flush toilets; and undeveloped **Washburn**, located along a dirt road. Drinking water is available at both.

Morgan   MOTEL $$
(⌨805-927-3828; www.hotel-morgan.com; 9135 Hearst Dr; r from $179; 🛜🌊🐾) Although rates are high for these revamped motel-style accommodations, the oceanfront setting makes up for a lot, as do gas fireplaces in deluxe rooms. Complimentary continental breakfast and board games to borrow. Pet fee $25.

Sebastian's   AMERICAN $
(⌨805-927-3307; www.facebook.com/Sebastians SanSimeon; 442 SLO–San Simeon Rd; mains $9-14; ⊙11am-4pm Tue-Sun) Down a side road across Hwy 1 from Hearst Castle, this tiny historic market sells cold drinks, Hearst Ranch beef burgers, giant deli sandwiches and salads for beach picnics at San Simeon Cove. Hearst Ranch Winery tastings are available at the copper-top bar.

Hearst Castle

Perched high on a hill, **Hearst Castle** (⌨info 805-927-2020, reservations 800-444-4445; www.hearstcastle.org; 750 Hearst Castle Rd; tours) is a wondrous, historic, over-the-top homage to material excess. The estate sprawls across acres of lushly landscaped gardens, accentuated by shimmering pools and fountains, statues from ancient Greece and Moorish Spain and the ruins of what was in Hearst's day the world's largest private zoo (look for zebras grazing on the hillsides of neighboring Hearst Ranch). To see anything of this historic monument, you have to take a tour (try to book ahead).

The most important thing to know about William Randolph Hearst (1863–1951) is that he did not live like Citizen Kane. Not that Hearst wasn't bombastic, conniving and larger than life, but the moody recluse of Orson Welles' movie? Definitely not. Hearst also didn't call his 165-room estate a castle, preferring its official name, La Cuesta Encantada ('The Enchanted Hill'), or more often calling it simply 'the ranch.'

EYEING ELEPHANT SEALS

The elephant seals that visit coastal California each year follow a precise calendar. In November and December, bulls (adult males) return to their colony's favorite California beaches and start the ritual struggles to assert superiority. Only the largest, strongest and most aggressive 'alpha' males gather a harem of females. In January and February, adult females, already pregnant from last year's beach antics, give birth to pups and soon mate with the dominant males, who promptly depart on their next feeding migration. The bulls' motto is 'love 'em and leave 'em.'

At birth an elephant seal pup weighs about 75lb; while being fed by its mother, it puts on about 10lb a day. Female seals leave the beach in March, abandoning their offspring. For up to two months the young seals, now known as 'weaners,' lounge around in groups, gradually learning to swim, first in tidal pools, then in the ocean. The weaners depart by May, having lost 20% to 30% of their weight during a prolonged fast.

Between June and October, elephant seals of all ages and both sexes return in smaller numbers to the beaches to molt. Always observe elephant seals from a safe distance (minimum 25ft) and do not approach or otherwise harass these unpredictable wild animals, who surprisingly can move faster on the sand than you can!

From the 1920s into the '40s, Hearst and Marion Davies, his longtime mistress (Hearst's wife refused to grant him a divorce), entertained a steady stream of the era's biggest movers and shakers. Invitations were highly coveted, but Hearst had his quirks – he despised drunkenness, and guests were forbidden to speak of death.

California's first licensed woman architect Julia Morgan based the main building, Casa Grande, on the design of a Spanish cathedral, and over the decades she catered to Hearst's every design whim, deftly integrating the spoils of his fabled European shopping sprees, including artifacts from antiquity and pieces of medieval monasteries.

Much like Hearst's construction budget, the castle will devour as much of your time and money as you let it. In peak summer months, show up early enough and you might be able to get a same-day tour ticket, but it's always better to make reservations in advance.

Tours (adult/child 5-12yr from $25/12; daily except Thanksgiving, Christmas & New Year's Day, closing time varies) usually depart starting at 9am daily, with the last leaving the visitor center for the 10-minute ride to the hilltop by 4pm (later in summer). There are three main tours: the guided portion of each lasts about an hour, after which you're free to wander the gardens and terraces and soak up the views. Best of all are Christmas holiday and springtime evening tours, featuring living-history re-enactors who escort you back in time to the castle's 1930s heyday. For holiday and evening tours, book at least two weeks to a month beforehand.

Dress in plenty of layers: gloomy fog at the sea-level visitor center can turn into sunny skies at the castle's hilltop location, and vice versa. At the visitor center, a five-story-high theater shows a 40-minute historical film (free admission included with daytime tour tickets) about the castle and the Hearst family. Other facilities are geared for industrial-sized mobs of visitors. Before you leave, take a moment to visit the often-overlooked museum area at the back of the center.

RTA (☑805-541-2228; www.slorta.org) bus 15 makes a few daily round-trips to Hearst Castle via Cambria and Cayucos from Morro Bay ($23, 55 minutes), where you can transfer to bus 12 to San Luis Obispo.

Note that at the time of writing the famed Neptune Pool had been emptied for repairs, and restoration was expected to be completed by early- to mid-2018.

Cambria

With a whopping dose of natural beauty, the coastal idyll of Cambria is a lone pearl cast along the coast. Built on lands that once belonged to Mission San Miguel, one of the village's first nicknames was Slabtown, after the rough pieces of wood that pioneer buildings were constructed from. Today, just like at neighboring Hearst Castle, money is no object in this wealthy community, whose motto 'Pines by the Sea' is affixed to the back of BMWs that toodle around town.

◉ Sights & Activites

Although its milky-white moonstones are long gone, Moonstone Beach still attracts romantics to its oceanfront boardwalk and truly picturesque rocky shoreline. For more solitude, take the Windsor Blvd exit off Hwy 1 and drive down to where the road dead-ends, then follow a 2-mile round-trip blufftop hiking trail across Fiscalini Ranch Preserve.

A 10-minute drive south of Cambria, past the Hwy 46 turnoff to Pasa Robles' wine country, tiny Harmony (population 18) is an easygoing slice of Americana where an 1865 creamery houses artists' workshops, and a charming winery sits on a nearby hillside. A few miles further south there's good hiking at **Harmony Headlands State Park** (www.parks.ca.gov; Hwy 1; ⊙6am-sunset) FREE.

🛏 Sleeping

Cambria's choicest motels and hotels line Moonstone Beach Dr, while quaint B&Bs cluster around the village.

Bridge Street Inn GUESTHOUSE $
(☑805-215-0724; www.bsicambria.com; 4314 Bridge St; r $50-90, vans $30; ☎) Inside a 19th-century parsonage and surrounded by a pleasant garden, this European-style guesthouse has a quaint, raffish charm. There's a communal kitchen and five rooms with shared bathroom facilities, and the BBQ area is well-used by international guests. One additional room has a separate toilet and washbasin. There's parking outside for one smaller campervan, but you'll need to book ahead.

Van guests can use the kitchen, bathroom and lounge facilities, and also jump on Bridge Street's wi-fi network.

Blue Dolphin Inn
MOTEL $$

(☑ 805-927-3300; www.cambriainns.com; 6470 Moonstone Beach Dr; r from $188; 🛜🐾) This sand-colored, two-story, slat-sided building may not look as upscale as other oceanfront motels, but rooms have romantic fireplaces, pillowtop mattresses and to-go breakfast picnics to take to the beach. Pet fee $25.

Fogcatcher Inn
HOTEL $$$

(☑ 805-927-1400; www.fogcatcherinn.com; 6400 Moonstone Beach Dr; r from $204; 🛜🏊🐾) Moonstone Beach Dr hotels are nearly identical, but this one stands out with its pool and hot tub. Faux English Tudor–style cottages harboring quietly luxurious modern rooms, some with fireplaces and ocean views. Pet fee $75.

✖ Eating & Drinking

It's a short walk between cutesy cafes and interesting restaurants in Cambria's East Village.

Linn's Easy as Pie Cafe
AMERICAN $

(☑ 805-927-0371; www.linnsfruitbin.com; 4251 Bridge St; dishes $6-12; ⊙10am-7pm Mon-Thu, to 8m Fri-Sat; 🖍) If you don't have time to visit Linn's original farm stand on Santa Rosa Creek Rd (a 20-minute drive east via Main St), you can fork into its famous olallieberry pie at this take-out counter that delivers soups, salads, sandwiches and comfort fare such as chicken pot pie to a sunny deck.

Robin's
INTERNATIONAL $$

(☑ 805-927-5007; www.robinsrestaurant.com; 4095 Burton Dr; lunch $13-19, dinner $24-33; ⊙11am-9pm Sun-Thu, to 9:30pm Fri-Sat; 🖍) Global flavors from Asia and India feature on the wide-ranging menu at Robin's. Relax under the shaded arbor canopy in the rustic courtyard and graze on Indian flatbreads or Vietnamese spring rolls, or tuck into surprising lamb-curry burritos. A stellar wine list is equally cosmopolitan, with labels from Australia, New Zealand, Spain and France complementing Californian favorites.

Harmony Cellars
BAR

(☑ 805-927-1625; www.harmonycellars.com; 3255 Harmony Valley Rd, Harmony; tasting fee $7; ⊙10am-5pm, to 5:30pm Jul & Aug) This popular hillside winery is strong on robust reds including Syrah, Cabernet Sauvignon and Zin-

fandel, and cheese and charcuterie platters ($30 to $48, must be ordered 24 hours in advance) are also available.

927 Beer Company
CRAFT BEER

(☑ 805-203-5265.; www.927beer.com; 821 Cornwall St; ⊙noon-7pm Mon-Sat, to 6pm Sun) Enlivened by colorful music posters – 927's friendly owner is a big fan of Pearl Jam – this nano-brewery tucked away behind Main St in the West Village features a relaxed neighborhood tasting room that's a real hit with locals and their canine companions. Our favorite brews are the Mudhoney Oatmeal Stout and the zesty Belgian-style Saison.

❶ Information

Cambria Chamber of Commerce (☑ 805-927-3624; www.cambriachamber.org; 767 Main St; ⊙9am-5pm Mon-Fri, noon-4pm Sat & Sun) Staffed by a friendly crew ready to dispense maps and information.

❶ Getting There & Away

Cambria is 140 miles south of Monterey and 39 miles north of San Luis Obispo. From San Luis Obispo, RTA (p327) bus 15 makes a few daily trips from Morro Bay via Cayucos to Cambria ($3, 35 minutes), stopping along Main St and Moonstone Beach Dr. Most buses continue north to Hearst Castle (p310).

Cayucos

With its historic storefronts housing antiques shops and eateries, the main drag of amiable, slow-paced Cayucos recalls an Old West frontier town. Just one block west of Ocean Ave, surf's up by the recently renovated pier.

⊙ Sights & Activities

Fronting a broad white-sand beach, Cayucos' long wooden pier is popular with fishers. It's also a sheltered spot for beginner surfers.

Estero Bluffs State Park
PARK

(☑ 805-772-7434; www.parks.ca.gov; Hwy 1; ⊙sunrise-sunset) FREE Ramble along coastal grasslands and pocket beaches at this small state park, accessed from unmarked roadside pulloffs north of Cayucos. Look among the scenic sea stacks to spot harbor seals hauled out on tide-splashed rocks.

Good Clean Fun
WATER SPORTS

(☑ 805-995-1993; www.goodcleanfuncalifornia.com; 136 Ocean Front Ln; group surfing lesson or kayak tour from $75) By the beach, this friendly surf shop has all kinds of rental gear – wetsuits, body boards, surfboards, SUP sets and kayaks. Book in advance for surfing lessons and kayak (or kayak-fishing) tours.

Cayucos Surf Company SURFING
(☑805-995-1000;www.facebook.com/CayucosSurf; 95 Cayucos Dr; 1hr private/2hr group lesson $90/100; ☺10am-5pm Sun-Thu, to 6pm Fri & Sat) Near the pier, this landmark local surf shop rents surfboards, body boards and wetsuits. Call ahead for learn-to-surf lessons.

🛏 Sleeping

Cayucos doesn't lack for motels or beach-front inns. If there's no vacancy or prices look too high, head 6 miles south to Morro Bay (p314).

Shoreline Inn on the Beach HOTEL $$
(☑805-995-3681; www.cayucosshorelineinn.com; 1 N Ocean Ave; r $159-249; 🐾) There are few beachside lodgings on Hwy 1 where you can listen to the surf from your balcony for such a reasonable price tag. Standard-issue rooms are spacious and perked up by sea-foam painted walls. It's also dog-friendly (pet fee $35).

Seaside Motel MOTEL $$
(☑805-995-3809; www.seasidemotel.com; 42 S Ocean Ave; d $80-170; 🐱) Expect a superwarm welcome from the hands-on owners of this vintage motel with a pretty garden featuring Cape Cod chairs and ocean views. Country-kitsch rooms may be on the small side, though some have kitchenettes. Cross your fingers for quiet neighbors.

★Cass House Inn INN $$$
(☑805-995-3669; www.casshousecayucos.com; 222 N Ocean Ave; d $265-345; ☺❄🐱) Inside a charmingly renovated 1867 Victorian inn, five boutique rooms beckon, some with ocean views, deep-soaking tubs and antique fireplaces to ward off chilly coastal fog. All rooms have plush beds, flat-screen TVs with DVD players and tasteful, romantic accents. The best eating and drinking in town is most pleasantly on-site.

🍴 Eating & Drinking

The versatile dining scene at Cacuyos stretches from excellent barbecue and fish tacos to fine dining in a heritage inn.

Brown Butter Cookie Co BAKERY $
(☑805-995-2076; www.brownbuttercookies.com; 98 N Ocean Ave; snacks from $2.50; ☺9am-6pm; 🍴) Seriously addictive cookies are baked in all sorts of flavors including almond, citrus, cocoa, coconut-lime and original butter. Buy a bagful to provide tasty sustenance as you negotiate a stroll along Cayucos' recently restored 1872 pier.

Ruddell's Smokehouse SEAFOOD $
(☑805-995-5028; www.smokerjim.com; 101 D St; dishes $4-13; ☺11am-6pm; 🍴🐱) 'Smoker Jim' transforms fresh-off-the-boat seafood into succulently smoked slabs, sandwiches topped with spicy mustard and fish tacos slathered in a unique apple-celery relish. Squeeze yourself in the door to order. Dogs are allowed at the sidewalk tables. If you're lucky, you might chance upon the Ruddell's food truck on summer weekends at craft breweries around the region.

Cass House Grill CALIFORNIAN, FRENCH $$
(☑805-995-1014; www.casshousecayucos.com; Cass House Inn, 222 N Ocean Ave; mains $13-32; ☺11am-3pm & 4-8:30pm Thu-Sun mid-Sep–late May, plus Wed during summer) 🍴 The Grill's wood-fired oven is harnessed for pizza, empanadas and grilled prawn and lamb, and a lighter touch is evident in roast salmon and a delicate fettucine crammed with seasonal produce. Many of the ingredients are sourced locally and from Cass House's own gardens, and the wine and beer list both offer Californian provenance. See www.casshousecayucosevents.com for special winemaker dinners.

The adjacent Cass House Bakery is open from 7am Thursday to Sunday for coffee, scones and muffins.

Schooners Wharf BAR
(www.schoonerswharf.com; 171 N Ocean Ave; ☺11am-midnight) Come for drinks on the ocean-view deck, rather than the fried seafood. The cocktails are punchy and there's an OK selection of draft beers from central Californian breweries. Vistas of Cayucos' heritage pier come free of charge.

ⓘ Getting There & Away

Cayucos is 15 miles south of Cambria and 19 miles north of San Luis Obispo. **RTA** (☑805-541-2228; www.slorta.org) bus 15 travels three to five times daily from Morro Bay ($2, 15 minutes) to Cayucos, continuing north to Cambria ($2, 20 minutes) and Hearst Castle ($2, 35 minutes).

Morro Bay

Home to a commercial fishing fleet, Morro Bay's biggest claim to fame is Morro Rock, a volcanic peak jutting dramatically from the ocean floor. It's one of the Nine Sisters, a 21-million-year-old chain of rocks stretching all the way south to San Luis Obispo. The town's less boast-worthy landmark comes courtesy of the power plant, whose three cigarette-shaped smokestacks mar the bay views. Along this humble, working-class stretch of coast you'll find fantastic opportunities for kayaking, hiking and camping.

◉ Sights & Activities

This town harbors natural riches that are easily worth a half-day's exploration. The bay itself is a deep inlet separated from the ocean by a 5-mile-long sand spit. South of Morro Rock is the **Embarcadero**, a small waterfront boulevard jam-packed with souvenir shops and eateries.

Morro Rock LANDMARK
Chumash tribespeople are the only people legally allowed to climb this volcanic rock, now the protected nesting ground of peregrine falcons. You can laze at the small beach on the rock's north side, but you can't drive all the way around it. Instead, rent a kayak to paddle the giant estuary, inhabited by two-dozen threatened and endangered species, including brown pelicans, snowy plovers and sea otters.

Morro Bay Skateboard Museum MUSEUM
(☑ 805-610-3565; www.mbskate.com; Embarcadero, Marina Sq; donations appreciated; ☺ noon-5pm Mon-Wed & Fri, from 10am Sat-Sun; ☝) With exhibits, posters and more than 200 skateboards from the 1930s to the 21st century, this excellent privately operated museum is essential for anyone who's ever fallen under the spell of zipping along on four urethane wheels. Look forward to damn fine souvenir T-shirts and merchandise, too.

Morro Bay Whale Watching WHALE WATCHING
(☑ 805-772-9463; www.morrobaywhalewatching.com; 699 Embarcadero; adult/child/student $45/35/40; ☺ tours 9am & 12:30pm; ☝) Humpback whales visit the Morro Bay area from May to October, and then from December to May more than 20,000 gray whales pass by on their annual migration. Other species often seen include minke whales, dolphins, porpoises, sea lions and sea otters. Bring along binoculars for coastal and pelagic birdlife. Excursions take place on an open catamaran, so dress warmly. Tours only depart with a minimum of six passengers.

Kayak Shack WATER SPORTS
(☑ 805-772-8796; www.morrobaykayakshack.com; 10 State Park Rd; kayak/SUP rental from $14/16; ☺ usually 9am-4pm late May-Jun, to 5pm Jul-early Sep, 9am-4pm Fri-Sun mid-Sep–late May) No one gets you out on the water faster than this laid-back kayak, canoe and SUP rental spot by the marina in Morro Bay State Park. A no-frills DIY operation, this is a calmer place to start paddling than the Embarcadero. Guided kayak tours are also offered in conjunction with Central Coast Outdoors.

☞ Tours

Sub-Sea Tours BOATING
(☑ 805-772-9463; www.subseatours.com; 699 Embarcadero; 45min tour adult/child 3-12yr $18/10; ☺ hourly departures usually 11am-5pm; ☝) For pint-sized views of kelp forests and schools of fish, take the kids on a spin around the bay in a yellow semi-submersible with underwater viewing windows. Departures may be limited to twice daily outside of the peak season.

Central Coast Outdoors TOURS
(☑ 805-528-1080; www.centralcoastoutdoors.com; tours $65-150) Leads kayaking tours (including sunset and full-moon paddles), guided hikes and cycling trips along the coast and to Paso Robles and Edna Valley vineyards.

✽✥ Festivals & Events

Morro Bay Winter Bird Festival OUTDOORS
(☑ 805-234-1170; www.morrobaybirdfestival.org; ☺ Jan) Bird-watchers flock here for guided hikes, kayaking tours and naturalist-led field trips, during which over 200 species can be spotted along the Pacific Flyway.

⏟ Sleeping

Dozens of motels cluster along Hwy 1 and around Harbor and Main Sts, between downtown Morro Bay and the Embarcadero.

California
State Park Campgrounds CAMPGROUND $
(☑ reservations 800-444-7275; www.reserveamerica.com; tent & RV sites $25-50; ☝) In **Morro Bay State Park**, over 240 campsites are fringed by eucalyptus and cypress trees; amenities include coin-op hot showers and an RV dump station.

At the north end of town off Hwy 1, **Morro Strand State Beach** (☑ reservations 800-444-7275; www.reserveamerica.com; tent & RV sites $25-50) has 75 simpler oceanfront campsites.

456 Embarcadero Inn & Suites HOTEL $$
(☑ 805-772-2700; www.embarcaderoinn.com; 456 Embarcadero; r from $200; P ☎) Located at the quieter southern end of the Embarcadero, this recently renovated property features 33 chic and spacious rooms, some with excellent views of the estuary and Morro Rock. Decor is more modern than at a few other local accommodation spots, and online midweek discounts are good value. Ease into the Jacuzzi after an afternoon's kayaking.

Pleasant Inn Motel MOTEL $$
(☑ 805-772-8521; www.pleasantinnmotel.com; 235 Harbor St; r $169-229; ☎ ☒) Two blocks uphill from the Embarcadero, this spiffy motel has nautical-esque rooms (some with compact kitchens) sporting sailboat photos on the walls, open-beam wooden ceilings and blue-and-white rugs underfoot. A recent renovation makes it one of the most welcoming places in town, and the team at reception have plenty of good restaurant advice. Pet fee $25.

Beach Bungalow Inn & Suites MOTEL $$
(☑ 805-772-9700; www.morrobaybeachbungalow.com; 1050 Morro Ave; d $180-230; P ☺ ☎ ☒) This butter-yellow motor court's chic, contemporary rooms are dressed up with hardwood floors, plush rugs, pillowtop mattresses and down comforters for foggy nights. Cape Cod chairs circle a compact fire pit in the middle of the complex. Complimentary breakfasts are delivered to guests' rooms and the pet fee is $30.

★**Anderson Inn** INN $$$
(☑ 805-772-3434; www.andersoninnmorrobay.com; 897 Embarcadero; d $269-349; ☎) Like a small boutique hotel, this waterfront inn has just a handful of spacious, soothingly earth-toned rooms. If you're lucky, you'll get a gas fireplace, spa tub and harbor views. The friendly owners infuse the whole property with an easygoing Californian cool. Weekday rates offer the best value.

✖ **Eating**

Predictably touristy seafood shacks line the Embarcadero, and a few other worthwhile eateries are scattered around Morro Bay.

Flavor Factory BURGERS $
(☑ 805-772-4040; www.facebook.com/FlavorFactoryMB; 420 Quintana Rd; soup & burgers $9-13; ☺ 11am-8pm Fri-Tue) ✔ Superlative gourmet burgers make this place located in a compact shopping mall worth seeking out. Classics like beef and bacon share the menu with ritzy combos with blue cheese or stuffed green chillies, and the concise list of six rotating craft beers is equally surprising. Even the seasonal soups and salad bar crammed with local produce prepared on-site are winners.

Giovanni's Fish Market & Galley SEAFOOD $
(☑ 877-521-4467; www.giovannisfishmarket.com; 1001 Front St; mains $5-15; ☺ market 9am-6pm, restaurant from 11am; ☎) At this family-run joint on the Embarcadero, folks line up for batter-fried fish and chips and killer garlic fries. You'll have to dodge beggar birds on the outdoor deck. Inside there's a market with all the fixin's for a beach campground fish-fry.

The Galley Seafood Grill & Bar SEAFOOD $$$
(☑ 805-772-7777; www.galleymorrobay.com; 899 Embarcadero; mains $24-48; ☺ 11:30-10pm) Our pick of Morro Bay's Embarcadero restaurants, The Galley combines an absolute waterfront location and expert renditions of classic American dishes with a briny touch of the ocean. There's definitely nothing groundbreaking about the menu, but when you're hankering for crab cakes and fresh oysters, or perfectly grilled fish and a glass of white wine, this is where to come.

🍸 **Drinking & Nightlife**

Explore the Embarcadero for good wine and craft beer, or head up the hill to Morro Bay's Main St for live music and the occasional DJ.

★**Libertine Pub** PUB
(☑ 805-772-0700; www.libertinebrewing.com; 801 Embarcadero; ☺ noon-11pm Mon-Thu, 11am-11pm Fri-Sat, 10am-10pm Sun) Stroll down to the Embarcadero for barrel-aged and sour beers from one of California's most interesting breweries. Lots more excellent American craft beers are on the 48 taps, and entertainment comes from the bartenders spinning vintage vinyl, or occasional live gigs. Taster glasses make it easy for the traveling beer geek to dive in and explore some very special brews.

The Siren   LOUNGE

(☑805-772-8478; www.thesirenmorrobay.com; 900 Main St; ⊙11am-2am Tue-Sat, from 9am Sun) A laidback spot for a quiet drink or game of pool during the week, The Siren is transformed into a rockin' live-music venue on Friday and Saturday nights. Beats range from blues and Americana through to indie rock and reggae, and crowding onto the dance floor is definitely encouraged after a few nine-buck cocktails or tasty craft brews.

ℹ Information

Morro Bay Visitor Center (☎805-225-1633; www.morrobay.org; 695 Harbor St; ⊙10am-5pm) Located a few blocks uphill from the Embarcadero, in the less touristy downtown area.

ℹ Getting There & Away

Morro Bay is 142 miles south of Monterey and 13 miles northwest of San Luis Obispo. From San Luis Obispo, **RTA** (☎805-541-2228; www.slorta. org) bus 12 travels hourly on weekdays and a few times daily on weekends along Hwy 1 to Morro Bay ($2.50, 25 minutes). Three to five times daily, bus 15 heads north to Cayucos ($2, 15 minutes), Cambria ($2, 35 minutes) and Hearst Castle ($2, 55 minutes).

From late May through early October, a **trolley** (single ride $1, day pass $3) loops around the waterfront, downtown and north Morro Bay, operating varying hours (no service Tuesday to Thursday).

Montaña de Oro State Park

In spring the hillsides are blanketed by bright California native poppies, wild mustard and other wildflowers, giving this **park** (Map p42; ☎805-528-0513; www.parks.ca.gov; 3550 Pecho Valley Rd, Los Osos; ⊙6am-10pm; [P][🚻]) 🆓 its Spanish name, meaning 'mountain of gold.'

Wind-tossed coastal bluffs with wild, wide-open sea views make it a favorite spot with hikers, mountain bikers and horseback riders. The northern half of the park features sand dunes and an ancient marine terrace visible due to seismic uplifting.

Once used by smugglers, **Spooner's Cove** is now a postcard-perfect sandy beach and picnic area. If you go tidepooling, avoid disturbing the marine creatures and never remove them from their aquatic homes. You can hike along the grassy ocean bluffs, or drive uphill past the visitor center inside a historic ranch house to the start of the exhilarating 7-mile loop trail tackling **Valencia Peak** (1346ft) and **Oats Peak** (1347ft).

🛏 Sleeping

Montaña de Oro State Park Campground   CAMPGROUND $

(☑reservations800-444-7275;www.reserveamerica. com; Montaña de Oro State Park; tent & RV sites $25) Tucked into a small canyon, this minimally developed campground has pleasantly cool drive-up and environmental walk-in sites. Limited amenities include vault toilets, drinking water and fire pits.

ℹ Getting There & Away

To reach Montaña de Oro State Park by private car from the north, exit Hwy 1 in Morro Bay at South Bay Blvd; after 4 miles, turn right onto Los Osos Valley Rd (which runs into Pecho Valley Rd) for 6 miles. From the south, exit Hwy 101 in San Luis Obispo at Los Osos Valley Rd, then drive northwest for around 16 miles.

ALONG HIGHWAY 101

Driving inland along Hwy 101 is a quicker way to travel between the Bay Area and Southern California. Although it lacks the striking scenery of coastal Hwy 1, the historic El Camino Real (King's Highway), established by Spanish conquistadors and missionaries, has a beauty of its own. Along the way are plenty of sights worth stopping for – from oak-dappled golden hills and ghostly missions to jaw-dropping sights in Pinnacles National Park and sprawling wineries.

San Juan Bautista

In atmospheric old San Juan Bautista, where you can practically hear the whispers of the past, California's 15th mission is fronted by the state's only remaining original Spanish plaza. In 1876 the railroad bypassed the town, which has been a sleepy backwater ever since. Along 3rd St, evocative historic buildings mostly shelter antiques shops and petite garden restaurants. Hark! That cock you hear crowing is one of the town's roosters, which are allowed by tradition to stroll the streets at will.

CENTRAL COAST MONTAÑA DE ORO STATE PARK

◉ Sights

Mission San Juan Bautista   CHURCH
(☏ 831-623-4528; www.oldmissionsjb.org; 406 2nd
St; adult/child 5-17yr $4/2; ⊙ 9:30am-4:30pm;
🚻) Founded in 1797, this mission claims
the largest church among California's original 21 missions. Unknowingly built directly
atop the San Andreas Fault, the mission has
been rocked by earthquakes. Bells hanging
in the tower today include chimes that were
salvaged after the 1906 San Francisco earthquake toppled the original mission. Scenes
from Alfred Hitchcock's thriller *Vertigo*
were shot here, although the bell tower in
the movie's climactic scene was just a special
effect.

Below the mission cemetery, you can spy
a section of El Camino Real, the Spanish
colonial road built to link California's first
missions.

**San Juan Bautista
State Historic Park**   PARK
(☏ 831-623-4881; www.parks.ca.gov; 2nd St, btwn
Mariposa & Washington Sts; museum adult/child
$3/free; ⊙ 10am-4:30pm) Buildings around
the old Spanish plaza opposite the mission
anchor this small historical park. Cavernous **stables** hint at San Juan Bautista in its
1860s heyday as a stagecoach stop. The 1858
Plaza Hotel, which started life as a single-
story adobe building, now houses a little
historical **museum**. Next door to the hotel,
the **Castro-Breen Adobe** once belonged to
Mexican general and governor José Castro.
In 1848 it was bought by the Breen family,
survivors of the Donner Party disaster.

🛏 Sleeping & Eating

San Juan Bautista features a few B&Bs but is
conveniently visited as a day trip from Santa
Cruz or Monterey.

**Fremont Peak
State Park Campground**   CAMPGROUND $
(☏ reservations 800-444-7275; www.reserveamerica.
com; San Juan Canyon Rd; tent & RV sites $25) A
pretty but primitive 25-site campground
with vault toilets (no water) is shaded by
oak trees on a hilltop with distant views of
Monterey Bay.

Vertigo Coffee   CAFE $
(☏ 831-623-9533; www.facebook.com/vertigocoffee;
81 4th St; dishes $4-12; ⊙ 7am-7pm Tue-Fri, from
8am Sat & Sun) Rich espresso and pour-over
brews, wood-fired pizzas and garden salads
make this coffee-roaster's shop a real find.

Rotating exhibitions from local artists often
fill the whitewashed walls, and seven taps
of craft beer feature surprising brews from
around the central Californian coast. Ask if
anything from Brewery Twenty Five based in
nearby Hollister is available.

ⓘ Getting There & Away

San Juan Bautista is on Hwy 156, a few miles
east of Hwy 101, about a 20-minute drive south
of Gilroy. Public transport is very limited, and
the town is best visited with your own transport.
Further south, Hwy 101 enters the sun-dappled
eucalyptus grove that James Stewart and Kim
Novak drove through in *Vertigo*.

Gilroy

About 30 miles south of San Jose, the
self-proclaimed 'garlic capital of the world'
hosts the jam-packed **Gilroy Garlic Festival**
(www.gilroygarlicfestival.com) over the last full
weekend in July. Show up for the chow –
garlic fries, garlic ice cream and more – and
cooking contests under the blazing-hot sun.

Unusual **Gilroy Gardens** (☏ 408-840-
7100; www.gilroygardens.org; 3050 Hecker Pass
Hwy; adult/child 3-10yr $50/40; ⊙ 11am-5pm
Mon-Fri early Jun–mid-Aug, plus 10am-6pm Sat
& Sun early Apr-Nov; 🚻) is a nonprofit family-oriented theme park focused on food
and plants. You've got to really love flowers, fruit and veggies to get your money's
worth, though. Most rides such as the
'Mushroom Swing' are tame. Buy tickets
online to save. From Hwy 101, follow Hwy
152 west; parking is $12.

Heading east on Hwy 152 toward I-5 **Casa
de Fruta** (☏ 408-842-7282; www.casadefruta.
com; 10021 Pacheco Pass Hwy, Hollister; per ride
$2.50-4; ⊙ seasonal hours vary; 🚻) FREE is a
commercialized farm stand with an old-
fashioned carousel and choo-choo train
rides for youngsters.

Salinas

Best known as the birthplace of John Steinbeck and nicknamed the 'Salad Bowl of the
World,' Salinas is a working-class agricultural
center with down-and-out streets. It makes
a thought-provoking contrast with the afflu-
ence of the Monterey Peninsula, a fact of life
that helped shape Steinbeck's novel *East of
Eden*. Historic downtown stretches along
Main St, with the National Steinbeck Center
capping off its northern end.

◉ Sights

★ National Steinbeck Center
MUSEUM

(☏831-775-4721; www.steinbeck.org; 1 Main St; adult/child 6-17yr $13/7; ⊘10am-5pm; ♠) This museum will interest almost anyone, even if you don't know anything about Salinas' Nobel Prize–winning native son, John Steinbeck (1902–68), a Stanford University dropout. Tough, funny and brash, he portrayed the troubled spirit of rural, working-class Americans in novels like *The Grapes of Wrath*. Interactive exhibits and short video clips chronicle the writer's life and works in an engaging way. Gems include Rocinante, the camper in which Steinbeck traveled around the USA while researching *Travels with Charley*.

Take a moment and listen to Steinbeck's Nobel acceptance speech – it's grace and power combined.

Steinbeck House
HISTORIC BUILDING

(☏831-424-2735; www.steinbeckhouse.com; 132 Central Ave; ⊘restaurant 11:30am-2pm Tue-Sat, gift shop to 3pm) Steinbeck was born and spent much of his boyhood in this house, four blocks west of the museum. It's now a twee lunch cafe, which we're not sure he'd approve of. Guided tours are given on select summer Sundays; check online for details.

✯ Festivals & Events

Steinbeck Festival
CULTURAL

(www.steinbeck.org; ⊘early May) This three-day festival features films, lectures, live music and guided bus and walking tours.

California Rodeo Salinas
RODEO

(www.carodeo.com; ⊘late Jul) Bull riding, calf roping, cowboy poetry and carnival rides.

California International Airshow
OUTDOORS

(www.salinasairshow.com; ⊘late Sep) Professional stunt flying and vintage and military aircraft take wing.

⊨ Sleeping

Salinas has plenty of motels off Hwy 101, including at the Market St exit.

Laurel Inn
MOTEL $

(☏831-449-2474; www.laurelinnsalinas.com; 801 W Laurel Dr; r from $95; P✳☞≋) If chain motels don't do it for you, this sprawling, family-owned cheapie has cozy rooms that are nevertheless spacious.

✖ Eating

Cafes and restaurants feature in downtown Salinas, and at the time of research, spacious heritage buildings near the National Steinbeck Center were being repurposed to house new eating and drinking openings. Let us know what you discover.

First Awakenings
AMERICAN $

(☏831-784-1125; www.firstawakenings.net; 171 Main St; mains $8-13; ⊘7am-2pm; ♠) Fork into diner-style breakfasts of fruity pancakes, crepes and egg skillets, or turn up later in the day for handcrafted sandwiches and market-fresh salads. Try the Sonoran frittata, an open-faced omelet crammed with spicy chorizo.

Giorgio's at 201
MEDITERRANEAN, PIZZA $$

(☏831-800-7573; www.201complex.com; 201 Main St; mains $15-37; ⊘4-9pm Mon-Thu, to 11pm Fri-Sat, 10am-3pm Sun) In a stately, high-ceilinged former bank, Giorgio's at 201 is the lead address in an expanding if compact enclave of restaurants and terrace cafes. Drop in for excellent pizza, pasta and Mediterranean cuisine – with occasional diversions into Asian flavors – and then check out what new eating, drinking or live-music destinations have been added since we last visited.

♟ Drinking & Nightlife

Downtown Salinas has a compact selection of good pubs and bars, and the Alvarado Street Brewery & Tasting Room is definitely worth the short journey from central Salinas for craft-beer fans.

Farmers Union Pour House
CRAFT BEER

(☏831-975-4890; www.facebook.com/FarmersUnionPourHouse; 217 Main St; ⊘2-10pm Tue-Thu & Sun, to midnight Fri-Sat) Brick-lined walls and wooden floors combine with a thoroughly modern big screen displaying the 24 different beers on tap. Food options include cheese and charcuterie boards, or you can order pizza and full meals from the separate restaurant next door. Up to 15 Californian wines are also available.

Alvarado Street Brewery & Tasting Room
CRAFT BEER

(☏831-800-3332; www.alvaradostreetbrewery.com/salinas-brewery; 1315 Dayton St; ⊘3-8pm Tue-Fri, from 1pm Sat-Sun) This Salinas offshoot of the Monterey-based craft brewery is another excellent recent addition to the growing beer scene around Salinas.

Location-wise, it's in an industrial park around 3 miles south of downtown. Ask if the stonking 10.5% Triple IPA is on tap.

ℹ Information

Salinas 411 (☑ 831-594-1799; www.salinas411. org; 222 Main St; ◷11am-8pm)

ℹ Getting There & Away

Salinas is 106 miles south of San Francisco and 126 miles north of San Luis Obispo.

Amtrak (☑ 800-872-7245; www.amtrak.com; 11 Station Pl) runs daily *Coast Starlight* trains north to Oakland ($18, three hours) and south to Paso Robles ($20, two hours), San Luis Obispo ($28, 3¼ hours), Santa Barbara ($41, 6¼ hours) and LA ($58, 9¼ hours).

Greyhound (☑ 800-231-2222; www.greyhound. com; Station Pl) has a few daily buses north to Santa Cruz ($16, 65 minutes) and San Francisco ($21, 3½ to five hours), and south to Santa Barbara ($40, 4¾ hours). Buses depart from the Salinas railway station.

From the nearby **Salinas Transit Center** (110 Salinas St), **MST** (☑ 888-678-2871; www.mst. org) bus 20 goes to Monterey ($3.50, one hour, every 30 to 60 minutes).

Pinnacles National Park

Named for the towering spires that rise abruptly out of the chaparral-covered hills east of Salinas Valley, this off-the-beaten-path park protects the remains of an ancient volcano. The best time to visit **Pinnacles National Park** (☑ 831-389-4486; www.nps.gov/pinn; per car $15; P ♿) ♥ is during spring or fall; summer heat is extreme.

◎ Sights & Activites

Besides rock climbing (for route information, visit www.pinnacles.org), the park's biggest attractions are its two talus caves, formed by piles of boulders. **Balconies Cave** is almost always open for exploration. Scrambling through it is not an exercise recommended for claustrophobes, as it's pitch-black inside, making a flashlight essential. Be prepared to get lost a bit too. The cave is found along a 2.5-mile hiking loop from the west entrance. Nearer the east entrance, **Bear Gulch Cave** is closed seasonally, so as not to disturb a resident colony of Townsend's big-eared bats.

To really appreciate Pinnacles' stark beauty, you need to hike. Moderate loops of varying lengths and difficulty ascend into the High Peaks and include thrillingly narrow clifftop sections. In the early morning or late afternoon, you may spot endangered California condors soaring overhead. Get an early start to tackle the 9-mile round-trip trail to the top of **Chalone Peak**, granting panoramic views.

Rangers lead guided full-moon hikes and star-gazing programs on some weekend nights, usually in spring or fall. Reservations are required: call ☑ 831-389-4485 in advance or check for last-minute vacancies at the visitor center.

🍴 Sleeping & Eating

The **Pinnacles Campground Store** (☑ 831-389-4538; ◷ 3-4pm Mon-Thu, noon-6pm Fri, 9am-6pm Sat & Sun) sells water, drinks and basic snacks and supplies, but you're best to stock up for self-catering in supermarkets in King City or Salinas.

Pinnacles National Park Campground   CAMPGROUND $ (☑ 877-444-6777; www.recreation.gov; tent/RV sites $23/36; ♿ ♨) On the park's east side, this popular family-oriented campground has over 130 sites (some with shade), drinking water, coin-op hot showers, fire pits and an outdoor pool (usually closed from October to March).

ℹ Information

Pinnacles National Park Visitor Center (☑ 831-389-4485; ◷ 9:30am-5pm daily, to 8pm Fri late Mar-early Sep) Information, maps and books are available on the park's east side from the small NPS visitor center inside the campground store.

ℹ Getting There & Away

There is no road connecting the two sides of Pinnacles National Park. To reach the less-developed **west entrance** (◷7:30am-8pm), exit Hwy 101 at Soledad and follow Hwy 146 northeast for 14 miles. The **east entrance** (◷24hr), where you'll find the visitor center and campground, is accessed via lonely Hwy 25 in San Benito County, southeast of Hollister and northeast of King City.

San Miguel

Founded in 1797, **Mission San Miguel Arcángel** (☑ 805-467-3256; www.mission sanmiguel.org; 775 Mission St; adult/child 5-17yr $3/2; ◷10am-4:30pm) suffered heartbreaking damage during a 2003 earthquake.

Although repairs are still underway, the church, cemetery, museum and gardens are open. An enormous cactus out front was planted during the early days of the mission.

Hungry? Look for a couple of no-name Mexican delis, where the limited options include massive shrimp burritos.

Paso Robles

In northern San Luis Obispo County, Paso Robles is the heart of a historic agricultural region where grapes are now the biggest money-making crop. Scores of wineries along Hwy 46 produce a brave new world of more-than-respectable bottles. The Mediterranean climate and laidback lifestyle is yielding other bounties as well, and olive oil, craft beer and artisan distilleries are growing in popularity. Paso's historic downtown centers on Park and 12th Sts, where boutique shops and wine-tasting rooms await.

◉ Sights & Activities

Around Paso Robles, you could spend days wandering country back roads off Hwy 46, running east and west of Hwy 101. Most wineries have tasting rooms and a few offer vineyard tours. For dozens more wineries and olive-oil farms to visit, browse www.pasowine.com.

Studios on the Park   GALLERY
(☑805-238-9800;   www.studiosonthepark.org; 1130 Pine St; ☺noon-4pm Mon-Wed, to 6pm Thu & Sun, to 9pm Fri-Sat) Artists from around the Central Coast work and display their art at this collection of open studios on the eastern edge of Paso Robles' town square. Up to 15 different artists work from six studios, and other facilities include art galleries and an excellent fine art shop. Check the website for always-interesting special exhibitions and what interactive classes are scheduled.

◉ Eastside

J Lohr Vineyards & Wines   WINERY
(☑805-239-8900; www.jlohr.com; 6169 Airport Rd; tastings free-$10; ☺10am-5pm) A Central Coast wine pioneer, J Lohr owns vineyards in Napa Valley, Monterey's Santa Lucia Highlands and Paso's pastoral countryside. Knowledgeable staff guide you through a far-reaching wine list.

Tobin James Cellars   WINERY
(☑805-239-2204; www.tobinjames.com; 8950 Union Rd; ☺10am-6pm) Anti-serious Old West saloon pours bold reds, including an outlaw 'Ballistic' Zinfandel and 'Liquid Love' dessert wine. No tasting fee.

Eberle Winery   WINERY
(☑805-238-9607; www.eberlewinery.com; 3810 E Hwy 46; tastings free-$10; ☺10am-5pm) Offers lofty vineyard views and tours of its wine caves every half-hour from 10:30am to 5pm. Sociable tastings run the gamut of white and red varietals and Rhône blends.

◉ Westside

Tablas Creek Vineyard   WINERY
(☑805-237-1231; www.tablascreek.com; 9339 Adelaida Rd; tastings from $10; ☺10am-5pm) ◢ Breathe easy at this organic estate vineyard reached via a pretty winding drive up into the hills. Known for Rhône varietals, the signature blends also rate highly. Free tours at 10:30am and 2pm daily (reservations necessary).

Castoro Cellars   WINERY
(☑805-238-0725; www.castorocellars.com; 1315 N Bethel Rd; tasting fee $5; ☺10am-5:30pm) Husband-and-wife team produces 'dam fine wine' (the mascot is a beaver, get it?), including from custom-crushed and organic grapes. Outdoor vineyard concerts happen during summer.

Thacher Winery   WINERY
(☑805-237-0087; www.thacherwinery.com; 8355 Vineyard Rd; tastings $10; ☺11am-5pm Thu-Mon) Breathe deeply as you drive up the dirt road to this historic ranch that makes memorable Rhône blends – 'Controlled Chaos' is a perennial fave.

✯✯ Festivals & Events

Wine Festival   WINE, FOOD
(www.pasowine.com; ☺mid-May) Oenophiles come for Paso's premier Wine Festival in mid-May, but the Vintage Paso weekend, focusing on Zinfandel wines, in mid-March and the Harvest Wine Weekend in mid-October are just as much fun.

California Mid-State Fair   CARNIVAL, MUSIC
(www.midstatefair.com; ☺mid-Jul) Twelve days of live rock and country-and-western concerts, farm exhibits, carnival rides and a rodeo draw huge crowds.

🛏 Sleeping

Adelaide Inn
MOTEL **$$**

(☎ 805-238-2770; www.adelaideinn.com; 1215 Ysabel Ave; r $104-161; ❄ @ 🛜 🐾) Fresh-baked cookies, muffins for breakfast, mini golf and a fitness room keep families happy at this motel just off Hwy 101.

⭐ Summerwood Inn
B&B **$$$**

(☎ 805-227-1111; www.summerwoodwine.com; 2175 Arbor Rd; d from $300; 🖥 🛜) 🍴 Along Hwy 46 within an easy drive of dozens of wineries, this gorgeous inn renovated in cool neutral tones mixes vintage and modern elements. Each of the nine rooms is named after a wine varietal and has a gas fireplace and balcony overlooking the vineyards. Indulge with the chef's gourmet breakfast, afternoon hors d'oeuvres and evening desserts.

⭐ Hotel Cheval
BOUTIQUE HOTEL **$$$**

(☎ 805-226-9995; www.hotelcheval.com; 1021 Pine St; d $330-475; 🖥 🛜) Near downtown Paso Robles, this European-style boutique hotel has 16 rooms arrayed around a sheltered inner courtyard. Spacious guest accommodation features flat-screen TVs and fireplaces, and rates include breakfast. Stylish shared spaces incorporate a library – decked out with sumptuous leather couches – and the Pony Bar, serving Californian wines, and featuring live music from 5pm on Friday and Saturday. Rates are around $60 cheaper on weekdays.

Inn Paradiso
B&B **$$$**

(☎ 805-239-2800; www.innparadiso.com; 975 Mojave Ln; ste $395-425; 🛜 🐾) An intimate B&B pulls off no-fuss luxury with four suites decorated with art and antiques, and perhaps a fireplace, a deep soaking tub, a canopy king-sized bed or French balcony doors. Breakfast generously overflows with local and organic produce. Pet fee $50.

🍴 Eating

⭐ La Cosecha Bar & Restaurant
LATIN AMERICAN, SPANISH **$$**

(☎ 805-237-0019; www.lacosechabr.com; 835 12th St; pizza $14-15, mains $21-30) The Honduran heritage of chef and owner Santos MacDonal shines through at this cosmopolitan bar and bistro translating from Spanish into 'the harvest.' That means a strong focus on local and seasonal produce crafted into dishes with a Latin American and Iberian flair. Combine one of Paso's best wine and beer lists with delicate Ecuadorian shrimp, paella or wood-fired pizza.

Check the website for regular dinner events partnering with local winemakers.

The Hatch Rotisserie & Bar
AMERICAN **$$**

(☎ 805-221-5727; www.hatchpasorobles.com; 835 13th St; mains $15-23; ⊙ 3-9pm Mon-Wed, to 10pm Thu, to 11pm Fri-Sat) Wood-fired treats in this heritage location combining shimmering chandeliers and rustic bricks include grilled octopus, rotisserie chicken and creamy bone marrow, and a sly sophistication is added to American comfort food including shrimp and grits and buttermilk fried chicken. Regular smoked-meat specials, craft beer and cocktails, and Paso Robles wine on tap all make The Hatch an essential destination.

Artisan
CALIFORNIAN **$$$**

(☎ 805-237-8084; www.artisanpasorobles.com; 843 12th St; shared plates $14-16, mains $17-36; ⊙ 4:30pm-9pm Mon-Thu, to 10pm Fri-Sat, 10am-2:30pm & 4:30-9pm Sun) 🍴 Chef Chris Kobayashi often ducks out of the kitchen just to make sure you're loving his impeccable contemporary renditions of modern American cuisine, featuring sustainably farmed meats, wild-caught seafood and artisan California cheeses. Impressive wine, beer and cocktail menus. Reservations essential.

🍸 Drinking & Nightlife

Paso Robles is home to several excellent craft breweries, and the up-and-coming Tin City area south of the city also features cider bars, urban distilleries and wine-tasting rooms.

⭐ Tin City Cider Co
CIDER

(☎ 805-293-6349; www.tincitycider.com; 3005a Limestone Way, Tin City; tastings $12; ⊙ 1-7pm Tue-Thu, 1-8pm Fri, 11am-6pm Sat-Sun) Joining the tangle of breweries, distilleries and wine-tasting rooms in Paso Robles' Tin City neighborhood, Tin City Cider's thoroughly modern tasting room showcases tart and tangy tipples crafted from apples. Their standard range is crisp and refreshing, and more complex flavors underpin innovative variations fermented with Belgian brewers yeast, enlivened with passionfruit, or aged in bourbon barrels or French oak.

Silva Brewing
CRAFT BEER

(☎ 805-369-2337; www.silvabrewing.com; 525 Pine St; ⊙ 2-7pm Wed-Fri, noon-5pm Sat-Sun) Chuck Silva is US brewing aristocracy – he was

DON'T MISS

JAMES DEAN MEMORIAL

In Cholame, about 25 miles east of Paso Robles via Hwy 46, there's a memorial near the spot where *Rebel Without a Cause* star James Dean fatally crashed his Porsche on September 30, 1955, at the age of 24. Ironically, the actor had recently filmed a public-safety campaign TV spot, in which he said, 'The road is no place to race your car. It's real murder. Remember, drive safely. The life you save might be mine.'

Look for the shiny stainless-steel memorial wrapped around an oak tree outside the truck-stop Jack Ranch Cafe, which has old photographs and movie-star memorabilia inside.

previously with Green Flash Brewing in San Diego – and now he's crafting his own brews in a compact space in Paso Robles. Look forward to bold, hop-forward styles and also Belgian-influenced beers. Just through an adjoining door (literally!) is a separate craft-beer pub, so make a night of it.

Wine Shine   DISTILLERY

(805-286-4453; www.wineshine.com; 3064 Limestone Way, Tin City; 1-5pm Fri-Sun) Grape juice sourced from Paso Robles wineries is the versatile basis for the innovative spirits crafted by Wine Shine. Sample brandies tinged with mango, ginger or cinnamon and aged in oak barrels, or try Wine Shine's Manhattan Project whiskey that is a tribute to the classic days of American cocktails.

BarrelHouse Brewing Co   BREWERY

(805-296-1128; www.barrelhousebrewing.com; 3055 Limestone Way, Tin City; 2-8pm Wed-Thu, 11am-9pm Fri & Sat, to 8pm Sun) Detour south of downtown, where locals chill in the outdoor beer garden with ales, stouts, zingy sour beers and fruity Belgian-style brews. Live bands frequently play, and most evenings there's a local food truck in attendance. Make an afternoon of it.

Brewery tours run on a first-come, first-served basis at 3pm from Friday to Sunday. You'll need to wear closed-toe shoes for safety regulations.

Re:Find Distillery   DISTILLERY

(805-239-9456; www.refinddistillery.com; 2725 Adelaida Rd; 11am-5pm) Paso Robles' first micro-distillery makes crisp botanical brandy (gin) and also whiskey and flavored vodkas. Scores of lemons were being zested when we dropped by. Try all the spirits in the rustic and rural tasting room, and ask how the plans are going to open an urban tasting room in Paso Robles' iconic Fox Theater on the edge of downtown.

For more on the Paso Robles distillery scene see www.pasoroblesdistillerytrail.com, and download a touring map listing 10 different distilleries.

Shopping

Around Paso Robles' downtown square, side streets are full of wine-country boutiques.

Pasolivo   FOOD & DRINKS

(805-227-0186; www.pasolivo.com; 8530 Vineyard Dr; 11am-5pm) Located on a pleasantly winding back road in Paso Robles wine country, Pasolivo's olive-oil tasting room features bold and earthy oils flavored with basil, citrus and rosemary. The laid-back ranch-style surroundings make a pleasant break from wine-tasting, and the attached shop sells excellent artisan foods and olive oil–based soaps and beauty products.

Paso Robles General Store   FOOD, GIFTS

(805-226-5757; www.generalstorepr.com; 841 12th St; 10am-7pm) Stock up on picnic provisions such as California-made pistachio butter, fresh local baguettes, fruit jams and more, plus home goods like lavender soap. Many of the products are locally sourced, organic and sustainable. Also an excellent source of gifts and homewares.

Information

Paso Robles Chamber of Commerce (805-238-0506; www.travelpaso.com; 1225 Park St; 8:30am-5pm Mon-Fri, 9am-5pm Sat, 10am-2pm Sun)

Geting There & Away

From an unstaffed **Amtrak station** (800-872-7245; www.amtrak.com; 800 Pine St), daily *Coast Starlight* trains head north to Salinas ($20, two hours) and Oakland ($32, 4¾ hours) and south to Santa Barbara ($29, 4¼ hours) and LA ($43, 7½ hours). Several daily Thruway buses link to more-frequent regional trains, including the *Pacific Surfliner*.

RTA (805-541-2228; www.slorta.org) bus 9 travels between San Luis Obispo and Paso Robles ($3, 70 minutes) hourly Monday to Friday, and a few times daily on weekends.

San Luis Obispo

Almost midway between LA and San Francisco, at the junction of Hwys 101 and 1, San Luis Obispo is a popular overnight stop for road-trippers. With no must-see attractions, SLO might not seem to warrant much of your time. Even so, this low-key town has an enviably high quality of life – in fact, it has been named America's happiest city. CalPoly university students inject a healthy dose of hubbub into the city's streets, bars and cafes throughout the school year. Nestled at the base of the Santa Lucia foothills, SLO is just a grape's throw from Edna Valley wineries, too.

◉ Sights

San Luis Obispo Creek, once used to irrigate mission orchards, flows through downtown. Uphill from Higuera St, **Mission Plaza** is a shady oasis with restored adobe buildings and fountains overlooking the creek. Look for the **Moon Tree**, a coast redwood grown from a seed that journeyed on board *Apollo 14*'s lunar mission.

Mission San Luis Obispo de Tolosa   CHURCH
(Map p325; ☑805-543-6850; www.missionsanluis obispo.org; 751 Palm St; suggested donation $5; ☺9am-5pm late Mar-Oct, to 4pm Nov–mid-Mar; ⊕) Those satisfyingly reverberatory bells heard around downtown emanate from this active parish dating from 1772. The fifth California mission founded by Padre Junípero Serra, it was named for a 13th-century French saint. The modest **church** has an unusual L-shape and whitewashed walls decorated with Stations of the Cross. An adjacent building contains an old-fashioned **museum** about daily life during the Chumash tribal and Spanish colonial periods. Interesting guided tours of the mission take place most days at 1:15pm.

San Luis Obispo Museum of Art   MUSEUM
(Map p325; ☑805-543-8562; www.sloma.org; 1010 Broad St; ☺11am-5pm, closed Tue early Sep-early Jul) FREE By the creek, this small gallery showcases the work of local painters, sculptors, printmakers and fine-art photographers, as well as traveling California art exhibitions.

⚡ Activities & Tours

For hiking with ocean views, head to Montaña de Oro State Park (p316), not far away from San Luis Obispo.

Margarita Adventures   ZIPLINING, KAYAKING
(☑805-438-3120; www.margarita-adventures.com; 22719 El Camino Real, Santa Margarita; adult/child zip-line tour $119/89; ☺8am-4:30pm Thu-Tue; ⊕) Whoosh down five zip lines across the vineyards beneath the Santa Lucia Mountains at this historic ranch, about a 10-mile drive northeast of SLO via Hwy 101. Reservations are required and trips leave from Margarita Adventures' office in the main street of sleepy Margarita. Ziplining experiences are ten bucks cheaper from Monday to Friday.

Hop On Beer Tours   FOOD & DRINK
(☑855-554-6766; www.hoponbeertours.com; per person $30) Jump aboard these sociable minibus tours to explore the San Luis Obispo and Paso Robles craft-beer scenes. Tours visit up to four different breweries. Check the website for timings of Social Tours open to the public – usually on Friday, Saturday or Sunday nights, two to four times per month – as Hop On also runs private tours.

Tours depart from downtown San Luis Obispo. Note that beer needs to be purchased separately.

⚜ Festivals & Events

SLO International Film Festival   FILM
(www.slofilmfest.org; ☺mid-Mar) This annual six-day celebration of film has been a mainstay of the SLO cultural calendar since 1993. Events and screenings are held around the greater San Luis Obispo County area, including in Paso Robles and Pismo Beach.

Concerts in the Plaza   MUSIC, FOOD
(www.downtownslo.com; ☺Fri nights, Jun-Sep) Downtown's Mission Plaza rocks out with local bands and food vendors.

⛏ Sleeping

Motels cluster off Hwy 101 in San Luis Obispo, especially off Monterey St northeast of downtown and around Santa Rosa St (Hwy 1). A slew of interesting new openings has increased the range of accommodation in town.

HI Hostel Obispo   HOSTEL $
(Map p325; ☑805-544-4678; www.hostelobispo. com; 1617 Santa Rosa St; dm $32-39, r from $65, all with shared bath; ☺check in 4:30-10pm; @�) On a tree-lined street near SLO's train station, this solar-empowered, avocado-colored hostel inhabits a converted Victorian, which gives it a bit of a B&B feel. Amenities include a kitchen, bike rentals (from $10 per day)

and complimentary sourdough pancakes and coffee for breakfast. BYOT (bring your own towel).

The Butler
DESIGN HOTEL $$

(Map p325; ☑ 805-548-1884; www.thebutlerhotel. com; 1511 Monterey St; r $229-249; ❀ 🛜) Just six stylish rooms fill this unique property that used to be an automotive workshop. There's definitely no grease and grime now evident in the rooms decked out with colorful artwork and featuring stellar bathrooms. Shared spaces include a lounge with design books, a record player (including plenty of vintage jazz vinyl), and a compact kitchen with drinks and snacks available.

Note that guest access is via a key code and there are no hotel staff resident at the property.

San Luis Creek Lodge
HOTEL $$

(☑ 805-541-1122; www.sanluiscreeklodge.com; 1941 Monterey St; r $159-229; ❀ @ 🛜) Rubbing shoulders with neighboring motels, this boutique inn has fresh, spacious rooms with divine beds (and some have gas fireplaces and jetted tubs) inside three whimsically mismatched buildings built in Tudor, California arts-and-crafts, and Southern plantation styles. DVDs, chess sets and board games are free to borrow.

Madonna Inn
HOTEL $$

(☑ 805-543 3000; www.madonnainn.com; 100 Madonna Rd; r $209-329; ❀ @ 🛜 🛋) The fantastically campy Madonna Inn is a garish confection visible from Hwy 101. Japanese tourists, vacationing Midwesterners and irony-loving hipsters adore the 110 themed rooms – including Yosemite Rock, Caveman and hot-pink Floral Fantasy (check out photos online). The urinal in the men's room is a bizarre waterfall. But the best reason to stop here? Old-fashioned cookies from the storybook bakery.

SLO Brew Lofts
APARTMENT $$$

(Map p325; ☑ 805-543-1843; www.slobrew.com; 738 Higuera St; apts from $250; 🛜) Located above a brewpub and live-music venue, SLO Brew Lofts offer a unique urban stay in downtown. Apartments range from one to three bedrooms – the lofts are suitable for families or friends – and stylish decor is partnered by cool touches like a refrigerator stocked with SLO Brew's fine products, and record players with stacks of vintage vinyl. Expect some noise from downstairs, especially on weekends.

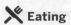 Eating

Downtown SLO has several excellent restaurants, befitting the area's farm-to-fork focus and wine-country heritage.

★ San Luis Obispo Farmers Market
MARKET $

(Map p325; ☑ 805-541-0286; www.downtownslo. com; Higuera St; ⊙ 6-9pm Thu; 🚗 🍴) 🍃 The county's biggest and best weekly farmers market turns downtown SLO's Higuera St into a giant street party, with smokin' barbecues, overflowing fruit and veggie stands, live music and free sidewalk entertainment, from salvation peddlers to wackadoodle political activists. Rain cancels it.

★ Thomas Hill Organics
BISTRO $$

(Map p325; ☑ 805-457-1616; www.thomashill organics.com; 858 Monterey St; mains $22-40; ⊙ 11am-late Mon-Sat, from 10am Sun; 🚗) 🍃 More contemporary than its original namesake eatery in Paso Robles, Thomas Hill's San Luis Obispo opening presents seasonal menus amid a stylish combination of chandeliers and whitewashed walls. Secure a spot at the bar and combine Central Coast wines with a delicate salad of beets, burrata and pistachios, or devour a sausage-and-mushroom pizza with a zingy draft cider. For Sunday brunch and on warm summer evenings, the outside patio is the place to be.

Guiseppe's Cucina Rustica
ITALIAN $$

(Map p325; ☑ 805-541-9922; www.giuseppes restaurant.com; 849 Monterey St; pizza & sandwiches $13-16, mains $21-36; ⊙ 11:30am-11pm) 🍃 Visit Guiseppe's for a leisurely downtown lunch dining on excellent salads, pizza and antipasti, or to grab a take-out meatball or Caprese sandwich from the deli counter out the front. Out the back, the facade of the heritage Sensheimer Brothers building looks over a shaded courtyard that's equally suited to long dinners of slow-roasted chicken and SLO County wines.

Luna Red
FUSION $$

(Map p325; ☑ 805-540-5243; www.lunaredslo.com; 1023 Chorro St; shared plates $6-20, mains $20-39; ⊙ 11:30am-9:30pm Mon-Thu, to midnight Fri, 9am-11:30pm Sat, to 9pm Sun; 🚗) 🍃 Local bounty from the land and sea, artisan cheeses and farmers-market produce pervade the chef's Californian, Asian and Mediterranean small-plates menu. Cocktails and glowing lanterns enhance a sophisticated ambience indoors, or

San Luis Obispo

San Luis Obispo

◎ Sights
1 Mission San Luis Obispo de Tolosa	A3
2 San Luis Obispo Museum of Art	A3

⊜ Sleeping
3 HI Hostel Obispo	D4
4 SLO Brew Lofts	B3
5 The Butler	D1

⊗ Eating
6 Foremost Wine Co	A4
7 Guiseppe's Cucina Rustica	B3
8 Luna Red	B3
9 Novo	A3
10 San Luis Obispo Farmers Market	B3
11 Thomas Hill Organics	B3

⊙ Drinking & Nightlife
12 Kreuzberg	A4
13 Libertine Brewing Company	B4
14 Luis Wine Bar	C3
SLO Brew	(see 4)

✪ Entertainment
15 Palm Theatre	B3

⊕ Shopping
16 Hands Gallery	B3
17 The Mountain Air	B4

linger over brunch on the mission-view garden patio. Reservations recommended.

Novo   FUSION $$
(Map p325; ☎805-543-3986; www.novorestaurant.com; 726 Higuera St; mains $18-36; ⊙11am-9pm Mon-Thu, to 1am Fri & Sat, 10am-9pm Sun) ✐ Novo spins out moreish European, Latin and Asian-inspired tapas with an artistic eye towards classy presentation. Pick from dozens of international beers, wines or sakes, then savor the view from tables on the

creekside deck. Reservations essential. It's a top spot for a leisurely Sunday brunch, too.

★ Foremost Wine Co
BISTRO $$$

(Map p325; ☑805-439-3410; www.foremostslo. com; 570 Higuera St; mains $24-32; ⊙4-10pm Tue-Sat, 10am-2pm Sun; ☑) ◢ Ease into the warehouse interior softened by rustic tables crafted from repurposed timber, and experience some of San Luis Obispo's best farm-to-table dining. Intensely seasonal menus and regular wine-matching events showcase the absolute best of the region. Ask if the lamb biryani or crispy potato tacos are available, and don't leave without browsing the on-site wine shop.

Drinking & Nightlife

Downtown in SLO, Higuera St is littered with college-student-jammed bars, and for craft-beer fans there is plenty to look forward to.

Libertine Brewing Company
CRAFT BEER

(Map p325; ☑805-548-2337; www.libertinebrewing. com; 1234 Broad St; ⊙11am-10pm Sun-Thu, to 11pm Fri-Sat) Barrel-aged and sour beers are the standout brews at this recent opening on the edge of downtown SLO. Saisions, kettle sours, goses and grisettes all appeal to the traveling beer geek, but the ambience is still welcoming and inclusive. When we visited, the finishing touches were being added to a spacious dining hall and live-music venue.

SLO Brew
BAR

(Map p325; ☑805-543-1843; www.slobrew.com; 736 Higuera St; ⊙11:30am-2am Tue-Sat, to midnight Sun-Mon) SLO Brew's versatile setup incorporates an on-site brewery with good pub meals – combine the Red Reggae wheat beer with the Yard Bird roast-chicken pizza – and it's also a rocking live-music venue with regular gigs. Past performers have included The Strokes and Lee 'Scratch' Perry, so it's definitely worth checking out who's playing.

Tap It Brewing
BREWERY

(☑805-545-7702; www.tapitbrewing.com; 675 Clarion St; ⊙noon-6pm Sun, to 7pm Tue, to 8pm Wed, to 10pm Thu-Sat) Head out toward the airport to this upstart brewery's tap room, where cacti grow inside an old Jeep and live bands sometimes rock on the patio. Order up a beer-tasting rack, chill with the brewery's regular posse of visiting hounds, and look forward to being surprised by Tap It's always interesting seasonal brews.

Luis Wine Bar
WINE BAR

(Map p325; ☑805-762-4747; www.luiswinebar. com; 1021 Higuera St; ⊙3-11pm Sun-Thu, to midnight Fri-Sat) Evincing style and sophistication, this downtown wine bar has wide-open seating, a strong craft-beer list of more than 70 brews, and small plates including cheese and charcuterie platters. Welcome to an urbane but unpretentious alternative to SLO's more raucous student-heavy bars and pubs.

Kreuzberg
CAFE

(Map p325; ☑805-439-2060; www.kreuzberg california.com; 685 Higuera St; ⊙cafe 7:30am-10pm daily, lounge 6-11pm Wed-Sat; ☎) ◢ This shabby-chic coffeehouse and roaster has earned a fervent following with its comfy couches, sprawling bookshelves and local art. Look forward to occasional live music partnered with craft beer and comfort food – think gourmet burgers, mac 'n' cheese and parmesan-risotto balls – in the adjacent lounge from Wednesday to Saturday.

☆ Entertainment

Sunset Drive-In
CINEMA

(☑805-544-4475; www.facebook.com/sunsetdrivein; 255 Elks Ln; adult/child 5-11yr $9/4; ⊕) Recline your seat, put your feet up on the dash and munch on bottomless bags of popcorn at this classic Americana drive-in. Sticking around for the second feature (usually a B-list Hollywood blockbuster) doesn't cost extra. It's about 2 miles southwest of downtown SLO off Higuera St.

Palm Theatre
CINEMA

(Map p325; ☑805-541-5161; www.thepalmtheatre. com; 817 Palm St; tickets $5-9) ◢ This small-scale movie house showing foreign and indie flicks just happens to be the USA's first solar-powered cinema. Seats are a bargain $5 on Mondays. Look for the SLO International Film Festival (p323) in March.

Shopping

For shopping fans to San Luis Obispo, downtown Higuera and Marsh Sts, along with all of the arcades and cross streets in between, are full of unique boutiques.

Hands Gallery
ARTS & CRAFTS

(Map p325; ☑805-543-1921; www.handsgallery. com; 777 Higuera St; ⊙10am-6pm Mon-Wed, to 8pm Thu-Sat, 11am-5pm Sun) Brightly lit downtown shop sells vibrant contemporary pieces by California artisans, including jewelry, fiber arts, sculptures, ceramics and blown glass.

The Mountain Air
SPORTS & OUTDOORS

(Map p325; ☑805-543-1676; www.themountainair. com; 667 Marsh St; ⊙10am-6pm Mon-Sat, to 8pm Thu, 11am-4pm Sun) At this local outdoor outfitter, pick up anything from campstove fuel and tents to brand-name clothing and hiking boots.

❶ Information

San Luis Obispo Visitor Center (Map p325; ☑805-781-2777; www.visitslo.com; 895 Monterey St; ⊙10am-5pm Sun-Wed, to 7pm Thu-Sat)

Mission San Luis Obispo Post Office (Map p325; ☑800-275-8777; www.usps.com; 893 Marsh St; ⊙10am-5pm Mon-Fri, to 2pm Sat) Centrally located in downtown SLO.

San Luis Obispo Library (☑805-781-5991; www.slolibrary.org; 995 Palm St; ⊙10am-5pm Wed-Sat, to 8pm Tue; 🛜) Free wi-fi and public internet terminals.

French Hospital (☑805-543-5353; www. frenchmedicalcenter.org; 1911 Johnson Ave; ⊙24hr) Emergency-room services.

❶ Getting There & Away

Amtrak (☑800-872-7245; www.amtrak.com; 1011 Railroad Ave) runs daily Seattle–LA *Coast Starlight* and twice-daily SLO–San Diego *Pacific Surfliner* trains. Both routes head south to Santa Barbara ($35, 2¾ hours) and Los Angeles ($57, 5½ hours). The *Coast Starlight* connects north via Paso Robles to Salinas ($28, 3 hours) and Oakland ($41, six hours). Several daily Thruway buses link to more regional trains.

Off Broad St, over 3 miles southeast of downtown, **San Luis Obispo County Regional Airport** (☑805-781-5205; www.sloairport.com; 903 Airport Dr) has scheduled flights with United (San Francisco and LA), American Airlines (Phoenix) and Alaska Airlines (Seattle). A new four-gate terminal opened at the airport in 2017.

There's no public bus transport to the airport and a taxi from downtown is around $18.

San Luis Obispo Regional Transit Authority (RTA; Map p325; ☑805-541-2228; www.slorta. org; single-ride fares $1.50-3, day pass $5) operates daily county-wide buses with limited weekend services. All buses are equipped with bicycle racks. Lines converge on downtown's **transit center** (Map p325; cnr Palm & Osos Sts).

Avila Beach

Quaint, sunny Avila Beach lures crowds with its strand of golden sand and a shiny seafront commercial district of restaurants, cafes and shops. Explore the arcades behind Front St for art galleries and winery tasting rooms. Two miles west of downtown, Port San Luis is a working fishing harbor with a rickety old pier.

◉ Sights & Activities

For a lazy summer day at Avila Beach, you can rent beach chairs and umbrellas, surfboards, boogie boards and wetsuits underneath **Avila Pier**, off downtown's waterfront promenade. Over by the port, the beach has bonfire pits and the barking of sea lions accompanies your stroll atop **Harford Pier**, one of the Central Coast's most authentic fishing piers.

★**Point San Luis Lighthouse**
LIGHTHOUSE

(Map p328; ☑guided hike reservations 805-528-8758, trolley tour reservations 805-540-5771; www. pointsanluislighthouse.org; lighthouse $5, incl trolley tour adult/child 3-12yr $20/15; ⊙guided hikes 8:45am-1pm Wed & Sat, trolley tours noon & 1pm Wed & Sat) Just getting to this scenic 1890 lighthouse, overshadowed by Diablo Canyon nuclear power plant, is an adventure. The cheapest way to reach the lighthouse is via a rocky, crumbling, 3.75-mile round-trip hiking trail, for which guided-hike reservations are required. If you'd rather take it easy and ride out to the lighthouse, join an afternoon trolley tour (reservations also required). Inside the lighthouse you can inspect an original Fresnel lens and authentic Victorian-period furnishings.

The **Pecho Coast Trail** to the lighthouse is open only for guided hikes led by Pacific Gas & Electric (PG&E) docents, weather permitting. These guided hikes are free; children under nine years old are not allowed. Make reservations online at least two weeks in advance and bring plenty of water.

Avila Valley Barn
FARM

(Map p328; ☑805-595-2816; www.avilavalleybarn. com; 560 Avila Beach Dr; ⊙9am-6pm mid-Mar–late Dec, to 5pm Thu-Mon Jan–mid-Mar; 🐾) At this rural farmstand and pick-your-own berry farm, park alongside the sheep and goat pens, lick an ice-cream cone, then grab a basket and walk out into the fields to harvest jammy olallieberries in late spring and early summer, mid-summer peaches and nectarines, or autumn apples and pumpkins. During summer, the kids can jump aboard tractor rides or pony rides.

CENTRAL COAST AVILA BEACH

San Luis Obispo Bay

0 ——————— 2 km
0 ——————— 1 mile

PORT SAN LUIS

1 *Point San Luis Lighthouse*

Harford Pier

Avila Beach Dr

Avila Beach Golf Resort

Point San Luis

Calpoly Pier

Avila Pier

See Avila Beach Enlargement

AVILA BEACH

6

San Luis Obispo (6mi)

San Luis Bay Dr

2

4

Avila Beach Rd

San Luis Obispo Ck

San Luis Obispo Bay

Avila Beach

Avila Beach Dr

15 8 7

1st St

Front St

San Luis Obispo Bay

12

0 ——————— 200 m
0 ——————— 0.1 miles

Shell Beach Rd

101
1

PACIFIC OCEAN

5

SHELL BEACH

Ocean Blvd

Price St

9

Price St

Pismo Beach

PACIFIC OCEAN

Dolliver St

16

14

Main St

13

18

Pomeroy Ave

Cypress St

Price St

17

Hinds Ave

11

Pismo Pier

Pismo Beach Visitors Information Center

Stimson Ave

0 ——————— 500 m
0 ——————— 0.25 miles

Pismo Pier

See Pismo Beach Enlargement

PISMO BEACH

Pismo State Beach

10

3

Pacific Blvd

4th St

Atlantic City Ave

101

Guadalupe (16mi)

Ember (1.5mi)

San Luis Obispo Bay

Sycamore Mineral Springs   SPA
(Map p328; ☎805-595-7302; www.sycamore springs.com; 1215 Avila Beach Dr; 1hr per person $15-20; ⊗8am-midnight) Make time for a therapeutic soak in one of these private redwood hot tubs discreetly laddered up a woodsy hillside. Call in advance for reservations, especially during summer and after dark on weekends. Last reservation time is 10:30pm.

Avila Hot Springs   HOT SPRINGS
(Map p328; ☎805-595-2359; www.avilahotsprings. com; 250 Avila Beach Dr; adult/child under 16yr $12/10; ⊗8am-9pm Sun-Tue & Thu, to 10pm Wed, Fri & Sat; ⊙) Slightly sulfuric, lukewarm public swimming pool has kiddie waterslides that are usually open from noon to 5pm on Saturday and Sunday.

⊨ Sleeping

Accommodation in Avila Beach ranges from simple RV parking to a very comfortable boutique hotel.

★ Avila La Fonda   INN $$$
(Map p328; ☎805-595-1700; www.avilalafonda. com; 101 San Miguel St; d from $269; @⊙) Downtown, this small boutique hotel is a harmonious mix of Mexican and Spanish colonial styles, with hand-painted tiles, stained-glass windows, wrought iron and rich wood. Gather around the fireplace for nightly wine and hors d'oeuvres. Complimentary beach gear to borrow for guests.

Avila Lighthouse Suites   HOTEL $$$
(Map p328; ☎805-627-1900; www.avilalighthouse suites.com; 550 Front St; ste from $359; ❋@⊙⊠) Any closer to the ocean and your bed would actually be sitting on the sand. With families

in mind, this apartment-style hotel offers suites and villas with kitchenettes. But it's the giant heated outdoor pool, Ping-Pong tables, putting green and life-sized checkers board that keep kids amused. Ask about steep off-season discounts. Reception is off First St.

✗ Eating & Drinking

Avila's Front St promenade features cafes and upscale restaurants. At Port San Luis, Harford Pier is home to seafood shops that sell fresh catch right off the boats.

Avila Beach Farmers Market   MARKET $
(Map p328; ☎805-801-1349; www.facebook.com/ AvilaBeachFarmersMarket; Front St; ⊗4-8pm Fri early Apr-late Sep) ⊘ With local farmers, food booths and rockin' live music, this outdoor street party takes over downtown's oceanfront promenade weekly from spring to fall.

PierFront Wine & Brew   WINE BAR
(Map p328; ☎805-439-3400; www.pierfrontwine andbrew.com; 480 Front St; ⊗noon-7pm Sun-Thu, to 9pm Fri-Sat; ⊙⊗) Californian craft beers and West Coast wines come with a side order of stellar sunset views of Avila's pier at this recent opening. Relax on a comfortable sofa in the eclectic interior or secure a sun-dappled spot under market umbrellas on the compact patio. Well-behaved dogs are welcomed as regulars, and PierFront's concise food menu includes flatbreads and cheese boards.

ⓘ Getting There & Away

Avila is around 10 miles south of San Luis Obispo and 8 miles northwest of Pismo Beach.

Between 10am and 4pm on Saturdays and Sundays from late March until mid-October, a free **trolley** (SCT; ☑ 805-781-4472; www.slorta. org) loops from Pismo Beach around downtown Avila Beach to Port San Luis; from early June to early September, extended hours are 10am to 6pm Thursday through Sunday. There's no public transportation offered between mid-October and late March.

Pismo Beach

Backed by a wooden pier that stretches toward the setting sun, Pismo Beach is where James Dean once trysted with Pier Angeli. Fronted by an invitingly wide, sandy beach, this 1950s-retro town feels like somewhere straight out of *Rebel Without a Cause* or *American Graffiti*. If you're looking for a sand-and-surf respite from coastal road tripping, break your journey here.

Pismo likes to call itself the 'Clam Capital of the World,' but these days the beach is pretty much clammed out. You'll have better luck catching something fishy off the pier, where you can rent rods. To rent a wetsuit, body board or surfboard, cruise nearby surf shops.

◉ Sights & Activities

Pismo Beach

Monarch Butterfly Grove   PARK
(Map p328; ☑805-773-5301; www.monarch butterfly.org; Hwy 1; ☺sunrise-sunset; 🅙) ⸜ FREE
From November through February, over 25,000 black-and-orange monarchs make their winter home here. Forming dense clusters in the tops of eucalyptus trees, they might easily be mistaken for leaves. Between 10am and 4pm during the roosting season, volunteers can tell you all about the insects' incredible journey, which outlasts any single generation of butterflies. Look for a gravel parking pull-out on the ocean side of Pacific Blvd (Hwy 1), just south of Pismo State Beach's **North Beach Campground** (399 S Dolliver St; tent & RV sites $40; 🅙).

Central Coast Kayaks   KAYAKING
(Map p328; ☑ 805-773-3500; www.centralcoast kayaks.com; 1879 Shell Beach Rd, Shell Beach; kayak or SUP set rental $20-25, classes $60-75, tours $60-120; ☺ 9am-4:30pm Mon-Tue & Thu-Fri, to 5pm Sat-Sun) Paddle out among sea otters and seals and through mesmerizing sea caves, rock grottos, arches and kelp forests. Wetsuits, paddle jackets and booties available (small surcharge applies) with kayak rentals.

✵ Festivals & Events

Wine, Waves & Beyond   CULTURAL, FOOD
(www.winewavesandbeyond.com; ☺ early Jun) Surfing competitions, surf-themed movies, wine tasting and a big bash on the beach with live music and food.

Clam Festival   FOOD & DRINK
(www.pismochamber.com; ☺ mid-Oct) Celebrate the formerly abundant and still tasty mollusc with a clam dig, chowder cookoff, food vendors and live music.

⛏ Sleeping

Pismo Beach has dozens of motels, but rooms fill up quickly and prices skyrocket in summer, especially on weekends. Resorts and hotels roost on cliffs north of town via Price St and Shell Beach Rd, while motels cluster near the beach and along Hwy 101.

Pismo Lighthouse Suites   HOTEL $$
(Map p328; ☑ 805-773-2411; www.pismolighthouse suites.com; 2411 Price St; ste from $239; 🅿 😟 🛜 🐾🐾) With everything a vacationing family needs – from kitchenettes to a life-sized outdoor chessboard, a putting green, table tennis and badminton courts – this contemporary all-suites hotel right on the beach is hard to tear yourself away from. Ask about off-season discounts and check out the onsite spa services. Pet fee $50.

Sandcastle Inn   HOTEL $$$
(Map p328; ☑ 805-773-2422; www.sandcastleinn. com; 100 Stimson Ave; r $305; 🛜) Many of these Eastern Seaboard–styled rooms are mere steps from the sand. The top-floor ocean-view patio is perfect for cracking open a bottle of wine at sunset or after dark by the fireplace.

✗ Eating

Good restaurants – including cheaper seafood joints – feature in downtown Pismo Beach, especially along Price St, and the nearby adjoining town of Arroyo Grande also has good eating.

Doc Burnstein's Ice Cream Lab   ICE CREAM $
(☑805-474-4068; www.docburnsteins.com; 114 W Branch St, Arroyo Grande; snacks $4-12; ☺11am-9:30pm Sun-Thu, to 10:30pm Fri & Sat, reduced hours in winter; 🅙) In Pismo's neighboring Arroyo Grande, Doc's scoops up fantastical flavors like Merlot raspberry truffle and the 'Elvis Special' (peanut butter with banana swirls). Live ice-cream lab shows start at

SCENIC DRIVE: HWY 1 SOUTH OF PISMO BEACH

What to See

Hwy 1 ends its fling with Hwy 101 at Pismo Beach, veering off toward the coast. Some truly wild, hidden beaches beckon along this back-door route to Santa Barbara.

Guadalupe Dunes

You almost expect to have to dodge tumbleweeds as you drive into the agricultural town of Guadalupe. Five miles further west at **Rancho Guadalupe Dunes Preserve** (www.countyofsb.org/parks/day-use/rancho-guadalupe-dunes.sbc; off Hwy 166; ⊙7am-sunset; Ⓟ) **FREE**, enormous Egyptian-esque film sets from Cecil B DeMille's 1923 Hollywood epic *The Ten Commandments* still lie buried in the sand. Learn more about the 'Lost City of DeMille,' the ecology of North America's largest coastal dunes, and the mystical Dunites who lived here during the 1930s back at downtown Guadalupe's small **Dunes Center** (☑805-343-2455; www.dunescenter.org; 1055 Guadalupe St; adult/child $5/free; ⊙10am-4pm Wed-Sun) museum.

Surf & Ocean Beaches

These wind-whipped beaches, one surf beach with a lonely Amtrak train whistlestop platform station, cozy up to the Vandenberg Air Force Base. On the 10-mile drive west of Lompoc and Hwy 1 (take Hwy 246/W Ocean Ave), you'll pass odd-looking structures supporting spy and commercial satellite launches. Between March and September, both Surf Beach and **Ocean Beach** (www.countyofsb.org/parks/day-use/ocean-beach.sbc; Ocean Park Rd, off Hwy 246; ⊙8am-sunset Oct-Feb) **FREE** may be closed to protect endangered Snowy Plovers during their nesting season.

Jalama Beach

Leaving Hwy 1 about 5 miles east of Lompoc, Jalama Rd follows 14 miles of twisting tarmac across ranch- and farmlands before arriving at utterly isolated **Jalama Beach County Park** (☑recorded info 805-736-3616; www.countyofsb.org/parks/jalama; Jalama Beach Rd, Lompoc; per car $10). To stay overnight, reserve a cabin in advance or arrive by 8am to get on the waiting list for a campsite in the crazily popular **campground** (☑805-568-2460; www.countyofsb.org/parks/jalama.sbc; 9999 Jalama Rd, Lompoc; tent/RV sites from $25/40, cabins $120-220; Ⓟ🐾) – look for the 'campground full' sign back near Hwy 1 to avoid a wasted trip. There is a local general store selling basics, but it's recommended to bring your food and drink supplies.

The Route

Heading south of Pismo Beach, Hwy 1 slowly winds along, passing through Guadalupe and Lompoc, where you can detour to **La Purísima Mission State Historic Park** (☑805-733-3713; www.lapurisimamission.org; 2295 Purísima Rd, Lompoc; per car $6; ⊙9am-5pm, tours at 1pm Wed-Sun & public holidays Sep-Jun, daily Jul & Aug; Ⓟ🐾) 🐾. Past Lompoc, Hwy 1 curves east to rejoin Hwy 101 south of Santa Barbara's wine country, near Gaviota.

Time & Mileage

With all of the detours described above, it's a 165-mile drive from Pismo Beach to Santa Barbara. The drive takes at least 3½ hours without any stops or traffic delays.

7pm sharp on Wednesday. From Hwy 101 southbound, exit at Grand Ave.

Frutiland La Casa Del Sabor　　　MEXICAN $$
(☑805-541-3663; www.facebook.com/frutiland. frutiland; 803 E Grand Ave, Arroyo Grande; mains $8-14; ⊙10am-6pm) Oversized, overstuffed Mexican *tortas* (sandwiches) will feed two, and there are two dozen varieties to choose

from. Or order a platter of blue-corn-tortilla fish tacos with a mango or papaya *agua fresca* (fruit drink). To find this taco shack in Arroyo Grande, exit Hwy 101 southbound at Halcyon Rd.

Cracked Crab　　　SEAFOOD $$
(Map p328; ☑805-773-2722; www.crackedcrab. com; 751 Price St; mains $16-59; ⊙11am-9pm Sun-

Thu, to 10pm Fri & Sat; 🖟) Fresh seafood and regional wines are the staples at this super-casual, family-owned grill. When the famous bucket o'seafood, full of flying bits of fish, Cajun sausage, red potatoes and cob corn, gets dumped on your butcher-paper-covered table, make sure you're wearing one of those silly-looking plastic bibs. No reservations, but the wait is worth it.

★ **Ember**   CALIFORNIAN **$$$**
(☑805-474-7700; www.emberwoodfire.com; 1200 E Grand Ave, Arroyo Grande; shared dishes $12-26, mains $26-36; ☉4-9pm Wed-Thu & Sun, to 10pm Fri & Sat) 🍴 Chef Brian Collins, who once cooked at Alice Waters' revered Chez Panisse, has returned to his roots in SLO County. Out of this heart-warming restaurant's wood-burning oven come savory flatbreads, artfully charred squid and hearty red-wine-smoked short ribs. No reservations, so show up at 4pm or after 7:30pm, or be prepared for a very long wait for a table.

Sociable seating in the bar, where you can order off the full menu, is first-come, first-served. Look forward to being surprised with a different seasonal menu each month. The restaurant is west of Hwy 101 (southbound exit Halcyon Rd) in Arroyo Grande.

Oyster Loft   CALIFORNIAN, SEAFOOD **$$$**
(Map p328; ☑805-295-5104; www.oysterloft.com; 101 Pomeroy Ave; mains $20-45; ☉5-9pm Sun-Thu & to 10pm Fri-Sat) Delve into the appetizers menu – including crab cakes or orange-glazed octopus – or kick off with tuna tataki or fresh oysters from the crudo raw bar. Mains including pan-fried halibut are still seafood-heavy, but do venture successfully into steaks and chicken. Look forward to excellent views of the surf and the Pismo Beach pier from the restaurant's elevated position. Reservations recommended although walk-in diners can sit at the bar.

🍸 Drinking & Nightlife

Pismo Beach has a standout craft-beer bar, and downtown Arroyo Grande along W Branch St has welcoming pubs, bistros and wine-tasting rooms.

The Boardroom   BAR
(Map p328; ☑805-295-6222; www.theboardroompismobeach.com; 160 Hinds Ave; ☉2-10pm Mon-Wed, noon-10pm Sun & Thu, noon-1am Fri-Sat; 🛜) An exemplary range of craft beers – mainly from the West Coast of the US – combines with knowledgeable and friendly bartenders at this easygoing bar with a surfing ambience. Get to know the locals over a game of darts, maximize your travel budget during happy hour from 4pm to 6pm, and fill up on pizza, salads and panini.

Taste of the Valleys   WINE BAR
(Map p328; ☑805-773-8466; www.pismowineshop.com; 911 Price St; ☉noon-9pm Mon-Sat & to 8pm Sun) Inside a wine shop stacked floor to ceiling with hand-picked vintages from around California and beyond, ask for a taste of anything they've got open, or sample from a quite astounding list of more than 1000 wines poured by the glass.

☆ Entertainment

Pismo Bowl   BOWLING
(Map p328; ☑805-773 2482; www.pismobeachbowl.com; 277 Pomeroy Ave; game per person $4.25, shoe rental $3.25; ☉noon-10pm Sun-Thu, to midnight Fri & Sat; 🖟) Epitomizing Pismo Beach's retro vibe, this old-fashioned bowling alley is just a short walk uphill from the pier. Blacklight 'cosmic' and karaoke bowling rule Friday and Saturday nights.

ℹ Information

Pismo Beach Visitors Information Center
(Map p328; ☑805-773-4382; www.classiccalifornia.com; 581 Dolliver St; ☉9am-5pm Mon-Fri, 10am-2pm Sat) Free maps and brochures. A smaller kiosk on the pier is open from 11am to 4pm on Sunday.

ℹ Getting There & Around

Hourly from Monday to Friday, and a few times daily on weekends, **RTA** (☑805-541-2228; www.slorta.org) bus 10 links San Luis Obispo with Pismo's Premium Outlets mall ($2, 30 minutes), a mile from the beach, before continuing to downtown Arroyo Grande ($1.50, 15 minutes).

Northern Mountains

Best Places to Eat

➡ Red Onion Grill (p346)

➡ Café Maddalena (p357)

➡ Cafe at Indian Creek (p363)

➡ Pangaea Cafe & Pub (p348)

➡ Etna Brewing Company (p366)

Best Places to Sleep

➡ McCloud River Mercantile Hotel (p358)

➡ Holiday Harbor Resort (p340)

➡ Quincy Courtyard Suites (p348)

➡ Shasta MountInn (p353)

➡ Feather River Canyon Campgrounds (p348)

Why Go?

'Hidden California' gets bandied around fairly casually, but here you have an entire corner of the state that does seem forgotten. The coast and foggy redwood groves are far away, so prepare yourself for something completely different: vast expanses of wilderness – some 24,000 protected acres – divided by rivers and streams, dotted with cobalt lakes, horse ranches and alpine peaks; further east is a stretch of shrubby, high desert cut with amber gorges, caves and dramatic light that is a photographer's dream. Much of it doesn't look the way people envision California – the topography more resembles the older mountains of the Rockies than the relatively young granite Yosemite. The towns are tiny but friendly, with few comforts; come to get lost in vast remoteness. Even the two principal attractions, Mt Shasta and Lassen Volcanic National Park, remain uncrowded (and sometimes snow-covered) at the peak of the summer.

When to Go

Lassen Volcanic National Park

Jul–Sep Warm weather and snow-free passes are ideal for backcountry camping.

Oct–Nov & Apr–May Shoulder seasons; scattered showers and snow at the high elevations.

Nov–Jan Skiing Mt Shasta is the main draw. Prices drop outside ski areas.

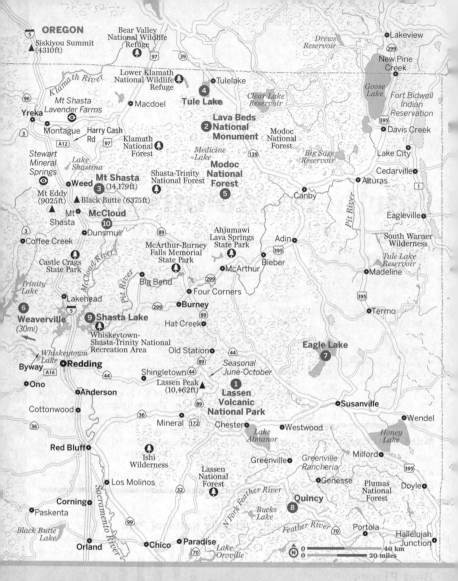

Northern Mountains Highlights

1 Gaping at geothermal spectacles in **Lassen Volcanic National Park** (p340).

2 Exploring deep caves and examining ancient petroglyphs at **Lava Beds National Monument** (p359).

3 Hiking and skiing **Mt Shasta** (p350), NorCal's most majestic mountain.

4 Looking overhead at the bird superhighway at **Tule Lake** (p360).

5 Getting lost in **Modoc National Forest** (p361), California's most remote national forest.

6 Enjoying the small-town charm of **Weaverville** (p362)

and wading in the trout-filled water nearby.

7 Camping along the shores of remote **Eagle Lake** (p347).

8 Chilling out in the mountain town of **Quincy** (p347).

9 Floating with a dozen pals on a **Shasta Lake** (p339) houseboat.

REDDING & AROUND

North of Red Bluff the dusty central corridor along I-5 starts to give way to panoramic mountain ranges on either side. Redding is the last major outpost before the small towns of the far north, and the surrounding lakes make for easy day trips or overnight camps. If you get off the highway – way off – this can be an exceptionally rewarding area of the state to explore.

Redding

Originally called Poverty Flats during the gold rush for its lack of wealth, Redding today has a whole lot of tasteless new money – malls, big-box stores and large housing developments surround its core. A tourist destination it is not, though it is the major gateway city to the northeast corner of the state and a useful spot for restocking before long jaunts into the wilderness. Recent constructions like the Sundial Bridge and Turtle Bay Exploration Park are enticing lures and worth a visit...but not a long one. A surge of good eating and drinking spots makes it an excellent pit stop for a meal if you're taking a long road trip on I-5. Downtown is bordered by the Sacramento River to the north and east. Major thoroughfares are Pine and Market Sts and there's often lots of traffic.

⊙ Sights & Activities

★**Sundial Bridge**   BRIDGE
(Map p336; http://turtlebay.org/sundialbridge) Resembling a beached cruise ship, the shimmering-white 2004 Sundial Bridge spans the river and is one of Redding's marquee attractions, providing an excellent photo op. The glass-deck pedestrian overpass connects the Turtle Bay Exploration Park to the north bank of the Sacramento River and was designed by renowned Spanish architect Santiago Calatrava.

The bridge/partially working sundial attracts visitors from around the world, who come to marvel at this unique feat of engineering artistry. It is accessed from the park and connects to the Sacramento River Trail system. The surrounding river scenery is beautiful.

Turtle Bay Exploration Park   MUSEUM, GARDENS
(Map p336; ☑ 800-887-8532; www.turtlebay.org; 844 Sundial Bridge Dr; adult/child $16/12, after 3:30pm $11/7; ⊙ 9am-5pm Mon-Sat, from 10am Sun, closes 1hr earlier Nov–mid-Mar; ☑) Situated on 300 meandering acres, this is an artistic, cultural and scientific center for visitors of all ages, with an emphasis on the Sacramento River watershed. The complex houses art and natural-science museums, with fun interactive exhibits. There are also extensive arboretum gardens, a butterfly house and a 22,000-gallon, walk-through river aquarium full of regional aquatic life (yes, including turtles).

The on-site Café at Turtle Bay (p337) serves hot and cold drinks.

Courthouse Museum   MUSEUM
(☑ 530-243-8194; www.parks.ca.gov; 15312 CA 299; $2; ⊙ 10am-5pm Thu-Sun; ☑) This building was the courthouse for over 30 years in the late 1800s and now houses a fun and informative museum and visitor center.

Redding Trails   HIKING, CYCLING
(Map p336; www.reddingtrails.com) Eighty miles of trails loop through parks, along rivers and up hills for strolling, hiking and mountain biking. Check the website for maps or pick up the pamphlet at almost any hotel. The star is the Sacramento River Trail, which meanders along the river all the way to Shasta Dam. There are several access points, including the Sundial Bridge.

Waterworks Park   WATER PARK
(www.waterworkspark.com; 151 N Boulder Dr; day pass adult/child $23/19; ⊙ usually late May-Sep) Redding gets really hot, and although most hotels and motels have pools, you'll have more fun splashing around at this water park, including on the four-story-high, cliff-steep Avalanche, a simulated white-water river, giant waterslides, plus a 'Lazy Lagoon' and kiddie pool. Great for kids or kidlike adults.

🛏 Sleeping

Redding's many motels and hotels (most large chains are represented and have swimming pools) huddle around noisy thoroughfares. A couple of rows lie close to the I-5 at the southern end of town: just west of the freeway close to the Cypress Ave exit on Bechelli Lane, and on the east side of the freeway on Hilltop Dr. Aim for the ones on less busy N Market St.

Apples' Riverhouse B&B   B&B $$
(Map p336; ☑ 530-243-8440; www.applesriverhouse.com; 201 Mora Ct; r $105-120; 🕙) Just steps from the Sacramento River Trail, this

Redding

modern, ranch-style home has three comfortable upstairs rooms, two with decks. It's a bit suburban, but it's the best independent stay in Redding. In the evening the sociable hosts invite you for cheese and wine. Bikes are yours to borrow and the proximity to the trail is inviting.

Tiffany House B&B Inn B&B **$$**
(☑530-244-3225; www.tiffanyhousebb.com; 1510 Barbara Rd; r $125-170; ☎✈) In a quiet cul-de-sac, a mile north of the river, this Victorian cottage has an expansive garden with sweeping views. Cozy rooms are packed with antiques, rosebuds and ruffles. Affable hosts make a big yummy to-do over breakfast.

✗ Eating

While it's certainly not a foodie hub, Redding has some surprisingly good places to eat, including for those on a budget.

Ma Der Ma Der Sap House & Grill LAOTIAN **$**
(Map p336; ☑530-691-4194; 1718 Placer St; ⊙11am-7pm Mon-Sat) Try the 'Sappritto,' a Laotian-inspired burrito with meat, eggs, veggies, sticky rice and a choice of hot sauce. Or go with pad thai, Lao-sausage tacos, cheesesteak sub or Lao-style wings. Sap means delicious in Lao and we agree. Everything from the hot sauces to the sausage are housemade daily. Call for to-go orders or eat in.

Wilda's Grill HOT DOGS, VEGETARIAN **$**
(1712 Churn Creek Rd; mains $6-7; ⊙11am-6pm Mon-Fri; ☑) The combo sounds weird but it works: big, excellent hot dogs with toppings from roasted garlic to homemade chili or blue cheese – or go vegetarian with outrageously delicious falafel or the much-lauded Buddha Bowl, made from rice, veggies and yummy, spicy sauces. Expect a line at peak hours. The mini-mall location lacks pizazz but it's very convenient from I-5.

Redding

Vintage Wine Bar & Restaurant
CALIFORNIAN $$

(Map p336; ☑530-229-9449; www.vintageredding. com; 1790 Market St; mains $13-28; ☺5-9pm Tue-Sat) Go here to try the region's best wines (and many more beyond) alongside unpretentious yet classy food and live entertainment most nights. Ask the staff to pair a wine or wine flight with your meal.

Cafe Paradisio
MEDITERRANEAN $$

(Map p336; ☑530-215-3499; www.cafeparadisio. com; 1270 Yuba St; mains lunch $6-12, dinner $10-32; ☺5-9pm Mon, Wed & Thu, to 10pm Fri & Sat, ☑) Take Mediterranean food and give it a bit of Asian flair and you have the comforting fare of this casual and friendly little nook. Start with the baked brie platter then continue with salmon with coconut curry or three-cheese lasagne. The portions are huge and there are lots of vegetarian choices.

Carnegie's
CALIFORNIAN $$

(Map p336; ☑530 246 2926; 1600 Oregon St; mains $12; ☺10am-3pm Mon & Tue, to 11pm Wed-Fri; ☑) This hip and homey, split-level cafe serves up healthy food: big fresh salads, garlicky prawns and pasta, and homemade tomato soup. There's a good selection of beer and wine too. Friday nights get a little rowdy, and there can be a wait.

Moonstone Bistro
CALIFORNIAN $$$

(☑530-241-3663; www.moonstonebistro.com; 3425 Placer St; mains lunch $13-22, dinner $23-44; ☺11am-9pm Tue-Thu, to 10pm Fri & Sat, 10am-2pm Sun; ☑) ◢ Organic, local, free range, line-caught, you name it, if the word is associated with sustainable food, you can use it to describe this place. Try the fish tacos at lunch and the hickory-smoked pork chops with

adobo chilies for dinner, but don't skip dessert – the chocolate soufflé in particular is to die for. Top it off with a microbrew.

Jack's Grill
STEAK $$$

(Map p336; ☑530-241-9705; www.jacksgrillredding. com; 1743 California St; mains $17-42; ☺restaurant 5-11pm, bar 4-11:30pm Mon-Sat) This funky little old-time place doesn't look so inviting – the windows are blacked out and it's dark as a crypt inside – but its popularity with locals starts with its stubborn ain't-broke-don't-fix-it ethos and ends with its steak – a big, thick, charbroiled decadence.

Regulars start lining up for dinner at 4pm, when cocktail hour begins. There are no reservations, so it easily takes an hour to get a seat.

🍷 Drinking & Entertainment

Café at Turtle Bay
CAFE

(Map p336; 844 Arboretum Dr; coffee from $1.50; ☺8:30am-5pm Mon-Sat, from 9:30am Sun) Cafe in the Turtle Bay Museum Store serving hot and cold drinks and light snacks.

Alehouse Pub
PUB

(☑530-221-7990; www.reddingalehouse.com; 2181 Hilltop Dr; ☺3pm-midnight Mon-Thu, to 1:30am Fri & Sat, 11am-5pm Sun) Too bad for fans of the cheap stuff, this local pub keeps a selection of highly hopped beers on tap and sells T-shirts emblazoned with 'No Crap on Tap.' It's a fun local place that gets packed after Redding's young professionals get out of work.

Cascade Theatre
LIVE MUSIC

(Map p336; ☑530-243-8877; www.cascadetheatre. org; 1733 Market St) Try to catch some live music downtown at this refurbished 1935 art deco theater. Usually it hosts second-tier

GETTING CRAFTY & DRAFTY IN REDDING

Redding has never gotten much praise for its food-and-beverage scene but that may be changing. Four new craft breweries, all making their own very unique brews, have opened in the last few years, giving folks more of a reason to veer off I-5 to stay a night or more. **Woody's Brewing Co.** (Map p336; ☑530-768-1034; www.woodysbrewing.biz; 1257 Oregon St; bar snacks from $3, meals $12-14; ☺11am-10pm Tue-Thu, to 11pm Fri & Sat, to 9pm Sun) and **Fall River Brewing** (☑530-605-0230; www.fallriverbrewing.com; 1030 E Cypress Ave D; ☺3-10pm Mon-Thu, noon-midnight Fri & Sat, to 8pm Sun) were the two earliest, serving the more classic styles of beer, while the new **Final Draft Brewing Company** (Map p336; ☑530-338-1198; www.finaldraftbrewingcompany.com; 1600 California St; ☺11am-10pm Sun-Thu, to 11pm Fri & Sat) offers barrel-aged, sour beers and more. **Wildcard Brewing Company** (Map p336; ☑530-255-8582; www.wildcardbrewingco.com; 1321 Butte St; ☺2-9pm Sun-Thu, to 10pm Fri & Sat) is the happy in-betweener with a little of everything and a convivial downtown location.

national acts, but if nothing else, take a peek inside; this is a neon-lit gem.

ℹ Information

California Welcome Center (☑530-365-1180; www.shastacascade.org; 1699 Hwy 273, Anderson; ☺9am-6pm Mon-Sat, from 10am Sun) About 10 miles south of Redding, in Anderson's Prime Outlets Mall. It's an easy stop for northbound travelers, who are likely to pass it on the I-5 approach. It stocks maps for hiking and guides to outdoor activities, and the website has an excellent trip-planning section for the region.

Redding Visitors Bureau (Map p336; ☑530-225-4100; www.visitredding.com; 777 Auditorium Dr; ☺9am-6pm Mon-Fri, 10am-5pm Sat) Near Turtle Bay Exploration Park.

Shasta-Trinity National Forest Headquarters (☑530-226-2500; 3644 Avtech Pkwy; ☺8am-4:30pm Mon-Fri) South of town, in the USDA Service Center near the airport. Has maps and free camping permits for all seven national forests in Northern California.

ℹ Getting There & Away

Redding Municipal Airport (RDD; http://ci.redding.ca.us/transeng/airports/rma.htm; 6751 Woodrum Circle) is 9.5 miles southeast of the city, just off Airport Rd. United Express flies to San Francisco.

The **Amtrak station** (www.amtrak.com; 1620 Yuba St), one block west of the Downtown Redding Mall, is not staffed. For the *Coast Starlight* service, make advance reservations by phone or via the website, then pay the conductor when you board the train. Amtrak travels once daily to Oakland ($44, six hours), Sacramento ($27, four hours) and Dunsmuir ($23, 1¾ hours).

The **Greyhound bus station** (Map p336; 1321 Butte St), adjacent to the Downtown Redding

Mall, never closes. Destinations include San Francisco ($40, 8½ hours, four daily) and Weed ($16, 1½ hours, three daily). The Redding Area Bus Authority (RABA; www.rabaride.com) has a dozen city routes operating until around 6pm Monday to Saturday. Fares start at $1.50 (exact change only).

Around Redding

Shasta State Historic Park

On Hwy 299, 6 miles west of Redding, this **state historic park** (☑520-243-8194; www.parks.ca.gov; 15312 CA 299; museum entry adult/child $3/2; ☺10am-5pm Thu-Sun) preserves the ruins of an 1850s gold rush mining town called Shasta – not to be confused with Mt Shasta City. When the gold rush was at its heady height, everything and everyone passed through this Shasta. But when the railroad bypassed it to set up in Poverty Flats (present-day Redding), poor Shasta lost its raison d'être.

An 1861 courthouse contains the excellent museum, the best in this part of the state. With its amazing gun collection, spooky holograms in the basement and gallows out back, it's a thrill ride. Pick up walking-tour pamphlets from the information desk and follow trails to the beautiful Catholic cemetery, brewery ruins and many other historic sites.

Whiskeytown Lake

Sparkling **Whiskeytown Lake** (☑530-242-3400; www.nps.gov/whis; off Hwy 299, Whiskeytown; 7-day pass per car $10; ℙ☼) takes its name from an old mining camp. When the lake was created in the 1960s by the construction of a 263ft dam, designed for power generation and Central Valley irrigation, the few remaining buildings of old Whiskeytown were moved and the camp was submerged. Today, the lake's serene 36 miles of forested shoreline is a perfect place to camp while enjoying nonmotorized water sports.

The **visitors center** (📞 530-246-1225; www.nps.gov/whis; Hwy 299 at JFK Memorial Dr, Whiskeytown; ⏰10am-4pm) has knowledgeable staff that can answer your questions about the area. Look for ranger-led interpretive programs and guided walks. The hike from the visitors center to roaring **Whiskeytown Falls** (3.4 miles round-trip) follows a former logging road and is a good quick trip.

On the western side of the lake, the **Tower House Historic District** contains the El Dorado mine ruins and the pioneer Camden House, open for summer tours. In winter it's an atmospheric place to explore.

On the southern shore of the lake, Brandy Creek is ideal for swimming. Just off Hwy 299, on the northern edge of the lake, Oak Bottom Marina rents boats.

The nice but tightly packed **Oak Bottom Campground** (📞800-365-2267; www.whiskeytownmarinas.com; tent/RV sites $24/21; 🐾) is near the shore of Whiskeytown Lake. There's a parking lot for tent campers and you have to walk in a short distance to the campsites.

Shasta Lake

About 15 minutes north of Redding, Shasta Lake (www.shastalake.com) was created in the 1940s when Shasta Dam flooded towns, railways and 90% of the local Wintu tribal lands to make the largest reservoir in California. Today it's home to the state's biggest population of nesting bald eagles. Surrounded by hiking trails and campgrounds, the lake gets packed in summer. The lake is also home to more than 20 different kinds of fish, including rainbow trout.

⊙ Sights & Activities

The lake is known as the 'houseboat capital of the world,' and is very popular with boaters of all kinds. **Packer's Bay** is the best area for leg-stretcher hikes with easy access off the I-5 (follow the Packer's Bay signs), but the prettiest trail (outside of summer months when the lack of shade can make it intensely hot) is the 7.5-mile loop of the **Clikapudi Trail**, which is also popular with

mountain bikers and horse-back riders. To get there, follow Bear Mountain Rd several miles until it dead-ends.

Lake Shasta Caverns   CAVE
(📞530-238-2341, 800-795-2283; www.lakeshastacaverns.com; 20359 Shasta Caverns Rd, Lakehead; 2hr tour adult/child 3-15yr $26/15; ⏰tours every 30min 9am-4pm late May-early Sep, hourly 9am-3pm Apr-late May & early-late Sep,10am, noon & 2pm Oct-Mar; 🅿️♿) High in the limestone megaliths at the north end of the lake hide these impressive caves. Tours through the many chambers dripping with massive formations operate daily and include a boat ride across Lake Shasta. Bring a sweater as the temperature inside is 58°F (14°C) year-round. With over 600 stairs, a decent level of fitness is required.

To get there, take the Shasta Caverns Rd exit from I-5, about 15 miles north of Redding, and follow the signs for 1.5 miles.

Shasta Dam   DAM
(📞530-275-4463; www.usbr.gov/mp/ncao/shasta-dam.html; 16349 Shasta Dam Blvd; ⏰visitor center 8am-5pm, tours 9am, 11am & 3pm; 🅿️♿) **FREE** On scale with the enormous natural features of the area, this colossal, 15-million-ton concrete dam is second only in size to Grand Coolie Dam in Washington state and second In height only to Hoover Dam in Nevada. The dam is located at the south end of the lake on Shasta Dam Blvd.

Built between 1938 and 1945, its 487ft spillway is nearly three times as high as Niagara Falls. Woody Guthrie wrote 'This Land Is Your Land' while he was here entertaining dam workers. The **Shasta Dam visitors center** offers fascinating free guided tours daily of the structure's rumbling interior – but skip the movie.

🛏 Sleeping & Eating

Hike-in camping and recreational vehicle (RV) parks are sprinkled around the

---

DETOUR AROUND THE I-5 DOLDRUMS

A good alternative for travelers heading north and south on I-5 is to drive along Hwy 3 through the Scott Valley, which rewards with world-class views of the Trinity Alps. Compared to rushing along the dull highway, this scenic detour will add an additional half-day of driving.

lakeshore, and houseboats are wildly popular. Most houseboats require a two-night minimum stay. Reserve as far in advance as possible, especially in summer. Houseboats usually sleep 10 to 16 adults and cost $1600 to $8400 per week. RV parks are often crowded and lack shade, but they have on-site restaurants. For exploring the area on a day trip, stay in Redding.

Holiday Harbor Resort
HOUSEBOATS, CAMPGROUND $

(☑530-238-2383; www.lakeshasta.com; Holiday Harbor Rd; tent & RV sites $42.50, houseboat per 2 nights from $975; 🛜🐾) Primarily an RV campground, it also rents houseboats (note that off-season rates are almost 50% lower) and the busy marina offers parasailing and fishing-boat rentals. A little **cafe** (☑530-238-2383; www.lakeshasta.com/service/the-harbor-cafe; 20061 Shasta Caverns Rd; meals around $10; ⊙8am-3pm Memorial Day-Labor Day) sits lakefront. It's off Shasta Caverns Rd, next to the lake.

Antlers RV Park & Campground
CAMPGROUND, CABINS $

(☑530-238-2322; www.shastalakevacations.com; 20679 Antlers Rd; tent & RV sites $32-45, trailer rentals $88-105; 🛜🐾🐾) East of I-5 in Lakehead, at the north end of the lake, this very popular, family-oriented campground has cabins, a country store and a marina renting watercraft and houseboats.

Lakeshore Inn & RV
CAMPGROUND $

(☑530-238-2003; www.shastacamping.com; 20483 Lakeshore Dr; RV sites $25-40, cabins from $100; 🛜🐾) On the western side of I-5, this lakeside vacation park has a restaurant and tavern, horseshoes and basic cabins.

US Forest Service Campgrounds
CAMPGROUND $

(☑info 530-275-1587, reservations 877-444-6777; www.recreation.gov; tent sites free-$35; 🅿🐾) About half of the campgrounds around Shasta Lake are open year-round. The lake's

---

KNOW ABOUT THE SNOW

Lassen Volcanic National Park has a very short season from around the beginning of June to the beginning of September. Lower elevations open up earlier but you can expect many services to be shut between October and May. That said, the winter is an incredibly peaceful time to visit as long as the roads are open!

---

many fingers have a huge range of camping, with lake and mountain views, and some of them are very remote. Free boat-in sites are first-come, first-served – sites without boat launches will be far less busy.

Dispersed camping outside organized campgrounds requires a campfire permit, available free from any USFS office.

MT LASSEN REGION

The dramatic crags, volcanic formations and alpine lakes of Lassen Volcanic National Park seem surprisingly untrammeled when you consider they are only a few hours from the Bay Area. Snowed in through most of winter, the park blossoms in late spring. While it is only 50 miles from Redding, and thus close enough to be enjoyed on a day trip, to really do it justice you'll want to invest a few days exploring the area along its scenic, winding roads. From Lassen Volcanic National Park you can take one of two very picturesque routes: Hwy 36, which heads east past Chester, Lake Almanor and historic Susanville; or Hwy 89, which leads southeast to the cozy mountain town of Quincy.

Lassen Volcanic National Park

The dry, smoldering, treeless terrain within this 106,000-acre **national park** (☑530-595-4480; www.nps.gov/lavo; 38050 Hwy 36 E, Mineral; 7-day entry per car mid-Apr–Nov $20, Dec–mid-Apr $10; 🅿🖼) 🥾 stands in stunning contrast to the cool, green conifer forest that surrounds it. That's the summer; in winter tons of snow ensure you won't get too far inside its borders. Still, entering the park from the southwest entrance is to suddenly step into another world. The lavascape offers a fascinating glimpse into the earth's fiery core. In a fuming display the terrain is marked by roiling hot springs, steamy mud pots, noxious sulfur vents, fumaroles, lava flows, cinder cones, craters and crater lakes.

In earlier times the region was a summer encampment and meeting point for Native American tribes, namely the Atsugewi, Yana, Yahi and Maidu. They hunted deer and gathered plants for basketmaking here. Some indigenous people still live nearby and work closely with the park to help educate visitors on their ancient history and contemporary culture.

DRIVING TOUR: THE LASSEN SCENIC BYWAY

Even in the peak of summer, you'll have the Lassen Scenic Byway mostly to yourself. The long loop though Northern California wilderness skirts the edge of Lassen Volcanic National Park and circles Lassen Peak, one of the largest dormant volcanoes on the planet. It mostly covers the big green patches on the map: expansive areas perfect for hiking, fishing, camping or just getting lost. This is a place where few people venture, and those who do come back with stories.

The launching point for this big loop could be either Redding or Sacramento, but there are few comforts for travelers along this course. The only cities in this neck of the woods – little places like Chester and Susanville – aren't all that exciting on their own; they're mostly just places to gas up, buy some beef jerky and enjoy the week's only hot meal. But the banner attractions are visible in every direction – the ominous, dormant volcanic peak of Lassen, the windswept high plains and the seemingly endless wilderness of the Lassen and Plumas National Forests.

This loop is formed by Hwy 36, Hwy 44 and Hwy 89. (You can see the map and some of the highlights at www.byways.org/explore/byways/2195.) It's best to do the drive between late June and mid-October. During other times of the year some of these roads close due to snow.

⊙ Sights & Activities

Lassen Peak, the world's largest plug-dome volcano, rises 2000ft over the surrounding landscape to 10,457ft above sea level. Classified as an active volcano, its most recent eruption was in 1917, when it spewed a giant cloud of smoke, steam and ash 7 miles into the atmosphere. The national park (p340) was created the following year to protect the newly formed landscape. Some areas destroyed by the blast, including the aptly named **Devastated Area** northeast of the peak, are recovering impressively.

Hwy 89, the road through the park, wraps around Lassen Peak on three sides and provides access to dramatic geothermal formations, pure lakes, gorgeous picnic areas and remote hiking trails.

In total, the park has 150 miles of **hiking trails**, including a 17-mile section of the **Pacific Crest Trail**. Experienced hikers can attack the **Lassen Peak Trail**; it takes at least 4½ hours to make the 5-mile round-trip but the first 1.3 miles up to the Grandview viewpoint is suitable for families. The 360-degree view from the top is stunning, even if the weather is a bit hazy. Early in the season you'll need snow and ice-climbing equipment to reach the summit. Near the Kom Yah-mah-nee visitor facility, a gentler 2.3-mile trail leads through meadows and forest to **Mill Creek Falls**. Further north on Hwy 89 you'll recognize the roadside **sulfur works** by its bubbling mud pots, hissing steam vent, fountains and fumaroles. At **Bumpass Hell** a moderate 1.5-mile trail and boardwalk leads to an active geothermal area, with bizarrely colored pools and billowing clouds of steam.

The road and trails wind through cinder cones, lava and lush alpine glades, with views of Juniper Lake, Snag Lake and the plains beyond. Most of the lakes at higher elevations remain partially and beautifully frozen in summer. Leave time to fish, swim or boat on **Manzanita Lake**, a slightly lower emerald gem near the northern entrance.

🛏 Sleeping & Eating

From the north on Hwy 89, you won't see many gas/food/lodgings signs after Mt Shasta City. Aside from the eight developed **campgrounds** (☑ 518-885-3639, reservations 877-444-6777; www.recreation.gov; tent & RV sites $12-24; [P]) in the park, there are many more in the surrounding Lassen National Forest. The nearest hotels and motels are in Chester, which accesses the south entrance of the park. There are some basic services near the split of Hwy 89 and Hwy 44, in the north.

There are a few basic places to eat in the small towns surrounding the park but for the most part you'll want to pack provisions.

🛏 North Entrance of the Park

Manzanita Lake Camping Cabins   CABIN $
(☑ May-Oct 530-335-7557, Nov-Apr 530-840-6140; www.lassenrecreation.com; Hwy 89, near Manzanita Lake; cabins $71-95; [P] ⊕) These recently built log cabins enjoy a lovely position on one of

Lassen Volcanic National Park

Old Station (15mi);
Hat Creek (25mi);
Mt Shasta (95mi)

Shingletown (20mi);
Redding (50mi)

North
Entrance
Station

Manzanita Lake Visitors
Center & Loomis Museum

Manzanita
Lake

Manzanita Lake
Campground &
Camping Cabins

Lassen
National
Forest

Crags

Reflection
Lake

Seasonal
June-October

Hot Rock
(6145ft)

Chaos Crags
(8503ft)

Crescent
Crater▲
(8645ft)

Eagle
Peak
(9222ft)

▲ Lassen Peak
(10,457ft)

Shadow
Lake

Badger
Mountain
(7127ft)

Prospect Peak
(8338ft)▲

Badger Flat

Lassen
Volcanic
National Park

Cluster
Lakes

Fairfield
Peak
(7272ft)

Hat Mountain
(7695ft)▲

Twin
Lakes

Rainbow
Lake

Ranger
Station

Summit Lake
North

Summit Lake
South

Crater Butte
(7267ft)
▲

Horseshoe
Lake

Mt Diller
(9087ft)
▲

Lake
Helen

Bumpass
Mtn
▲(8753ft)

Kings Creek

Pilot Mtn
(7175ft)
▲

Brokeoff Mtn
(9235ft)▲

Sulfur
Works

Bumpass
Hell

Drakesbad
Guest Ranch

Warner
Valley

Saddle Mtn
(7638ft)
▲

Kom Yah-mah-nee
Visitor Facility

Mill Creek
Falls

Twin
Meadows

Hot Springs Creek

Ranger
Station

Southwest
Entrance
Station

Mt Conard
(8204ft)

Seasonal
June-October

Sifford
Mountain
(7408ft)

Terminal
Geyser

Lassen's lakes, and they come in one- and two-bedroom options and slightly more basic eight-bunk configurations, which are a bargain for groups. They all have bear boxes, propane heaters and fire rings, but no bedding, electricity or running water. Shared bathrooms and coin-op hot showers are nearby.

Those who want to get a small taste of Lassen's more rustic comforts can call ahead to arrange a 'Camper's Amenity Package,' which includes basic supplies for a night under the stars (starting at $100, it includes a s'mores kit).

Manzanita Lake Campground CAMPGROUND $
(☑ reservations 877-444-6777; www.recreation.gov; tent & RV sites $15-24; 🐾) The biggest camping area in these parts has lake access, views of Lassen, and 179 sites with fire rings, picnic tables and bear boxes. There's a store, hot showers and kayak rentals here as well.

**Hat Creek Resort
& RV Park** CABIN, CAMPGROUND $
(☑ 530-335-7121; www.hatcreekresortrv.com; 12533 Hwy 44/89, Old Station; tent sites from $25, RV sites with/without hookups from $38/17, yurts $69-149, r $69-229, cabins $89-299; 🐾🐾) Outside the park, Old Station makes a decent stop before entering and is an OK choice. It sits along a fast-moving, trout-stocked creek. Some simple motel rooms and cabins have full kitchens. Stock up at the convenience store and deli, then eat on a picnic table by the river.

🛏 South Entrance of the Park

Mt Lassen/Shingletown KOA CAMPGROUND $
(☑ 530-474-3133; www.koa.com; 7749 KOA Rd; tent sites $39, RV sites from $69, cabins $71-169; ⊙ mid-Mar–Nov; 🐾🐾🐾) Enjoy all the standard Kampgrounds of America (KOA) amenities: a playground, a deli and laundry facilities.

are repeat visitors, use the hot-springs-fed swimming pool or go horseback riding. Except in the main lodge, there's no electricity (the kerosene lamps and campfires give things a lovely glow). Rates include country-style meals (vegetarian options available) and campfire barbecues every Wednesday.

This is one of the few places in the region to book up solidly, so make advance reservations as soon as possible.

ⓘ Information

Whether you enter at the north or southwest entrance, you'll be given a free map with general information.

Kom Yah-mah-nee Visitor Facility (☏530-595-4480; www.nps.gov/lavo; ◷9am-5pm, closed Mon & Tue Nov-Mar; 🖱) About half a mile north of the park's southwest entrance, this handsome center is certified at the highest standard by the US Green Building Council. Inside there are educational exhibits (including a cool topographical volcano), a bookstore, an auditorium, a gift shop and a restaurant. Visitor information and maps available.

Manzanita Lake Visitors Center & Loomis Museum (☏530-595-4480; ◷9am-5pm Jun-Sep) Just past the entrance-fee station at the park's northern boundary, you can see exhibits and an orientation video inside this museum. During summer, rangers and volunteers lead programs on geology, wildlife, astronomy and local culture. Visitor information and maps available.

Park Headquarters (☏530-595-4444; www.nps.gov/lavo; 38050 Hwy 36; ◷8am-4:30pm daily Jun-Sep, 8am-4:30pm Mon-Fri Oct-May) About a mile west of the tiny town of Mineral, it's the nearest stop for refueling and supplies.

ⓘ Getting There & Away

There's virtually no way to visit this park without a car, though all the two-lane roads around the park and the ample free national-forest camping options make for excellent, if fairly serious, cycle touring.

The park has two entrances. The northern entrance, at Manzanita Lake, is 50 miles east of Redding via Hwy 44. The southwest entrance is on Hwy 89, about 5 miles north of the junction with Hwy 36. From this junction it is 5 miles west on Hwy 36 to Mineral and 44 miles west to Red Bluff. Heading east on Hwy 36, Chester is 25 miles away and Susanville about 60 miles. Quincy is 65 miles southeast from the junction on Hwy 89.

It's off Hwy 44 in Shingletown, about 20 miles west of the park.

Village at Childs Meadow　　　CABIN $
(☏530-595-3383; www.thevillageatchildsmeadow. com; 41500 E Hwy 36, Mill Creek; tent/RV sites from $25/35, tiny homes $110-185; 🛜) Rustic, run-down 'tiny homes' – some of them more like permanently parked RV trailers – sit at the edge of a spectacularly lush mountain meadow 9 miles outside the park's southwest entrance. Don't expect the Ritz; it's an old-fashioned, fittingly grungy, mountain-resort experience, but it's very close to the park. Expect some changes as it's under new management.

Drakesbad Guest Ranch　　　RESORT $$$
(☏530-529-1512, ext 120; www.drakesbad.com; Warner Valley Rd; r per person $147-199; ◷Jun-early Oct; 🐎) Seventeen miles northwest of Chester, this fabulously secluded place lies inside the park's boundary. Guests, many of whom

WORTH A TRIP

WILD HORSE SANCTUARY

Since 1978 the **Wild Horse Sanctuary** (☑530-335-2241; www.wildhorsesanctuary. com; 5796 Wilson Hill Rd, Shingletown; free; ⊙10am-4pm Wed & Sat) FREE has been sheltering horses and burros that would otherwise have been destroyed. You can visit its humble visitor center on Wednesdays and Saturdays to see these lovely animals or even volunteer for a day, with advance arrangement. To see them on the open plains, take a two- to three-day weekend pack trip in spring or summer (from $435 per person). Shingletown lies 20 miles to the west of Lassen Volcanic National Park.

Lassen National Forest

The vast Lassen National Forest (www.fs.fed. us/r5/lassen) surrounding Lassen Peak and Lassen Volcanic National Park is so big that it's hard to comprehend: it covers 1.2 million acres (1875 sq miles) of wilderness in an area called the Crossroads, where the granite Sierra, volcanic Cascades, Modoc Plateau and Central Valley meet. It's largely unspoiled land, though if you wander too far off the byways surrounding the park, you'll certainly see evidence of logging and mining operations that still happen within its borders.

The Lassen National Forest supervisor's office is in Susanville. Other ranger offices include **Eagle Lake Ranger District** (☑530-257-4188; 477-050 Eagle Lake Rd, Susanville), **Hat Creek Ranger District** (☑530-336-5521; 43225 E Hwy 299, Fall River Mills; ⊙Mon-Fri) and **Almanor Ranger District** (☑530-258-2141; www.fs.usda.gov; 900 CA 36, Chester; ⊙8am-4:30pm Mon-Fri), about a mile west of Chester.

Lake Almanor Area

Calm, turquoise Lake Almanor lies south of Lassen Volcanic National Park via Hwys 89 and 36. This man-made lake is a crystalline example of California's sometimes awkward conservation and land-management policy: the lake was created by the now-defunct Great Western Power Company and is now ostensibly owned by the Pacific Gas & Electric Company. The lake is surrounded by lush meadows and tall evergreens and was once little-visited. Now, a 3000-acre ski

resort sits on the hills above, with properties continually being developed near its shore and power boats zipping across its surface. The northeastern section in particular has become particularly ritzy and there are even a few gated communities. On the rugged southern end you'll find miles with nothing but pine trees.

The main town near the lake, Chester (population 2144, elevation 4528ft), isn't a looker. Though you could whiz right by and dismiss it as a few blocks of nondescript roadside storefronts, this little community, while outwardly drab, has a fledgling art scene hidden along the back roads for those willing to explore. It also offers some comfy places to stay but none as exciting or woodsy as you'll find along the lake.

🏃 Activities

You can rent boats and water-sports equipment at many places around the lake.

Bodfish Bicycles & Quiet Mountain Sports   CYCLING, OUTDOORS
(☑530-258-2338; www.bodfishbicycles.com; 149 Main St, Chester; bicycle rental per hour/day $10/33; ⊙10am-5pm Tue-Sat, noon-4pm Sun, shorter off-season hours) This outfit rents bicycles, cross-country skis and snowshoes, and sells canoes and kayaks. It's a great source of mountain-biking and bicycle-touring advice. If you want just a taste of the lovely rides possible in this part of the state, make this a priority stop.

Coppervale Ski Hill   SKIING
(www.lassencollege.edu; Westwood; day passes $20-25; ⊙1-4:30pm Tue & Thu, 9:30am-4pm Sat & Sun) Run by Lassen Community College, this little place caters to downhill and cross-country skiers as well as snowboarders. There are eight trails and 740ft of vertical drop.

🛏 Sleeping & Eating

The best sleeping options for campers are in the surrounding national forest.

🛏 Chester

Along Chester's main drag you'll find a scattering of 1950s-style inns and a few chain lodgings (the nicest of which is the fairly overpriced Best Western Rose Quartz Inn). Many of these places keep seasonal hours, and when you live in a place where it can snow in mid-June, the season is short.

St Bernard Lodge
B&B $$

(☎530-258-3382; www.stbernardlodge.com; 44801 E Hwy 36, Mill Creek; d without bath from $99; ☎) Located 10 miles west of Chester, this old-world charmer has seven B&B rooms with views to the mountains and forest. All have knotty-pine paneling and quilted bedspreads. There are stables where those traveling with a horse can board them and have access to the nearby network of Lassen's trails. The tavern is good too, serving meaty American-style fare.

Bidwell House B&B
B&B $$

(☎530-258-3338; www.bidwellhouse.com; 1 Main St; r $125-260, without bath $80-115, cottage $185-285; ☎) Set back from the street, this historic summer home of pioneers John and Annie Bidwell is packed with antiques. The classic accommodations come with all the modern amenities (including a spa in some rooms) – no roughing it here. Enjoy goodies like a three-course breakfast, home-baked cookies and afternoon sherry.

🛏 Around the Lake

Book ahead for lakefront lodgings in summer. There are restaurants at the resorts.

PG&E Recreational Area Campgrounds
CAMPGROUND $

(☎916-386-5164; http://recreation.pge.com; tent & RV sites $14-22; ☉May-Sep; 🅿🐾) A favorite for tents and RVs, Rocky Point Campground is right on the lake, with some sites basically on the beach. For something more remote,

try Cool Springs Campground or Ponderosa Flat Campground, both at Butt Reservoir near the lake's south shore, at the end of Prattville Butt Reservoir Rd.

These campgrounds lie within the surrounding Lassen and Plumas National Forests on the lake's southwest shore. Sites tend to be more tranquil than the RV-centric private campgrounds that are right on the water.

Lake Almanor Campgrounds
CAMPGROUND $

(☎877-444-6777; www.recreation.gov; tent sites $15-18, RV sites $29-33) Large wooded campground on the lake. While RVs can camp here, there are no hookups.

North Shore Campground
CABINS, CAMPGROUND $

(☎530-258-3376; www.northshorecampground. com; 541 Catfish Beach Rd; tent sites $36, RV sites $45-56, pop-up trailer $89, cabins $119-269; ☎) Two miles east of Chester on Hwy 36, these expansive, forested grounds stretch for a mile along the water, and get filled up with mostly RVs. Ranch-style cabins have kitchens and are great for families. This place is fine if you want to spend all your time water-skiing on the lake, but those seeking the solitude of nature should look elsewhere.

Knotty Pine Resort & Marina
CABIN $$

(☎530-596-3348; www.knottypine.net; 430 Peninsula Dr; r $165, 2-bedroom cabins with kitchen $180; ☎🐾🐾) This full-service lakeside alternative, 7 miles east of Chester, has simple cabins and rents boats, kayaks and canoes.

LASSEN NATIONAL FOREST HIKES

The forest has some serious hikes, with 460 miles of trails, ranging from the brutally challenging (120 miles of the **Pacific Crest Trail**) to ambitious day hikes (the 12-mile Spencer Meadows National Recreation Trail), to just-want-to-stretch-the-legs-a-little trails (the 3.5-mile Heart Lake National Recreation Trail). Near the intersection of Hwys 44 and 89, visitors to the area will find one of the most spectacular features of the forest, the pitch-black 600yd **Subway Cave** lava tube. Other points of interest include the 1.5-mile volcanic **Spattercone Crest Trail**, **Willow Lake** and **Crater Lake**, 7684ft **Antelope Peak** and the 900ft-high, 14-mile-long **Hat Creek Rim** escarpment.

For those seeking to get far off the beaten trail, the forest has three wilderness areas. Two high-elevation wilderness areas are the **Caribou Wilderness** and the **Thousand Lakes Wilderness**, best visited from mid-June to mid-October. The **Ishi Wilderness** (named after Ishi, the last surviving member of the Yahi people, who walked out of this wilderness in 1911), at a much lower elevation in the Central Valley foothills east of Red Bluff, is more comfortable in spring and fall, as summer temperatures often climb to over 100°F (37°C). It harbors California's largest migratory deer herd, which can be upwards of 20,000 head.

★**Cravings** AMERICAN **$**
(☑530-258-2229; 278 Main St; mains $5-13; ☺7am-2pm Thu-Tue; 🛜🅿) You will get cravings for this place once you're gone. Think fresh, all homemade classics like crispy waffles or rustic Reuben sandwiches made to big-city-worthy standards. They make their own delectable pastries and pump out quality espresso while keeping small-town smiles. The new historic-building location includes a dedicated cafe, bookstore and creekside dining. Gluten-free and vegetarian friendly.

Tantardino's ITALIAN **$$**
(☑530-596-3902; www.tantardinos.com; 401 Ponderosa Dr, Lake Almanor Peninsula; mains $16-20, pizzas $12-26; ☺11:30am-9pm Tue-Sat) This is the locals' favorite place to eat in the region hands down – even folks from Susanville drive the 32 miles to get here, with pleasure, for the excellent Sicillian-style lasagna, yummy pizzas and meatball or caprese sandwiches at lunchtime. It's lively, friendly and you can eat and imbibe outside in summer. Reserve ahead for dinner.

★**Red Onion Grill** MODERN AMERICAN **$$$**
(☑530-258-1800; www.redoniongrill.com; 303 Peninsula Dr, Westwood; mains $12-36; ☺11am-9pm, shorter hours Oct-Apr) Head here for the finest dining on the lake with upscale New American, Italian-influenced cuisine (like the simply prepared shrimp scampi), and bar food that's executed with real panache. The setting is casual and fun, made all the more warm by the wine list.

❶ Information

Get information about lodging and recreation around the lake, in Lassen National Forest and in Lassen Volcanic National Park at **Chester & Lake Almanor Chamber of Commerce** (☑530-258-2426; www.chester-lakealmanor.com; 529 Main St, Chester; ☺9am-4pm Mon-Fri)

❶ Getting There & Away

Plumas Transit (☑530-283-2538; www.plumastransit.com; fares $1-4) runs buses to Quincy with connections to Redding, while **Lassen Rural bus** (☑530-252-7433; www.lassentransportation.com; fares $1-4) runs to/from Susanville.

Susanville

Though it sits on a lovely high desert plateau, the Lassen County seat isn't much of a charmer; it's a resupply post with a Wal-Mart,

a few stop lights and two prisons. Although not a tourist destination in itself, it provides good services for travelers passing through. It lies 35 miles east of Lake Almanor and 85 miles northwest of Reno – and is home to a couple of modest historic sites. The best event in town is the **Lassen County Fair** (☑530-251-8900; www.lassencountyfair.org; $6; ☺Jul), which swings into gear in July.

The restored **Susanville Railroad Depot**, south of Main St, off Weatherlow St, sits beside the terminus of the Bizz Johnson Trail.

The town's oldest building, **Roop's Fort** (1853), is named after Susanville's founder, Isaac Roop. The fort was a trading post on the Nobles Trail, a California emigrant route. The town itself was named after Roop's daughter, Susan.

Beside Roops Fort is the friendly **Lassen Historical Museum** (☑530-257-3292; 75 N Weatherlow St; admission by donation; ☺hours vary, closed Sun), which has well-presented displays of clothing and memorabilia from the area, which are worth a 20-minute visit.

The **Railroad Depot Visitors Center** (☑530-257-3252; 601 Richmond Rd; ☺10am-4pm May-Oct) rents bicycles and has brochures on mountain-biking trails in the area.

Motels along Main St average $65 to $90 per night. **High Country Inn** (☑530-257-3450; www.high-country-inn.com; 3015 Riverside Dr; r $87-159; 🛜🅿) is the best of these. For more character, try **Roseberry House B&B** (☑530-257-5675; www.roseberryhouse.com; 609 North St; r/ste $125/150; 🛜). This sweet 1902 Victorian house is two blocks north of Main St. Striking dark-wood antique headboards and armoires combine with rosebuds and frill. There are nice little touches, like bath salts and candy dishes. In the morning expect homemade muffins and jam as part of the full breakfast.

To eat, head to **Lassen Ale Works** (☑530-257-7666; www.lassenaleworks.com; 724 Main St; mains $9-21; ☺4-10pm Mon, 11am-10pm Tue-Thu, 11am-11pm Fri & Sat). In the renovated c 1862 Pioneer Saloon, this place looks like nothing from the outside but opens up to a big and bustling space. It's known for it's fish-and-chips but everything from steaks to Reuben sandwiches are fresh and as good as the service. Try one of the seven signature brews like the Pioneer Porter or Almanor Amber.

For local information about the town visit the **Lassen County Chamber of Commerce** (☑530-257-4323; www.lassencountychamber.org; 84 N Lassen St; ☺9am-4pm Mon-Fri), while the

Lassen National Forest supervisor's office (📞530-257-2151; 2550 Riverside Dr; ⊙8am-4:30pm Mon-Fri) has maps and recreation information for getting into the surrounding wilds.

SageStage(📞530-233-6410;www.sagestage.com) runs buses to Redding via Alturas ($18) and south to Reno ($22). **Susanville City Buses** (📞530-252-7433) makes a circuit around town (fare $2).

Eagle Lake

Those who have the time to get all the way out to Eagle Lake, California's second-largest natural lake, are rewarded with a stunningly blue jewel on the high plateau. From late spring until fall this lovely lake, about 15 miles northwest of Susanville, attracts a smattering of visitors who come to cool off, swim, fish, boat and camp. On the south shore, you'll find a pristine 5-mile **recreational trail** and several busy **campgrounds** (📞information 530-257-4188, reservations 877-444-6777; www.recreation.gov; tent/RV sites from $20/30) administered by Lassen National Forest and the **Bureau of Land Management** (BLM; 📞530-257-0456; 2550 Riverside Dr, Susanville). **Eagle Lake Marina** (📞877-444-6777; www.eaglelakerecreationarea.com), close by, has shower and laundry facilities, and can help you get out onto the lake with a fishing license.

Eagle Lake RV Park (📞530-825-3133; www.eaglelakeandrv.com; 687-125 Palmetto Way; tent/RV sites $25/36.50, cabins $37-100; 🖥️🐾), on the western shore, and **Eagle Lake Resort** (📞530-251-6770; www.eaglelakerv.com; Stones Landing; RV sites $33; 🖥️🐾), on the quieter northern shore, both rent boats.

Quincy

Idyllic Quincy is one of the northern mountains' three mountain communities, which teeter on the edge of becoming an incorporated town (the other two are Burney, in Shasta County, and Weaverville). Nestled in a high valley in the northern Sierra, southeast of Lassen Volcanic National Park via Hwy 89, it's a lovely little place, endowed with just enough edge by the student population of the local Feather River College. Nearby Feather River, Plumas National Forest, Tahoe National Forest and their oodles of open space make Quincy an excellent base from which to explore.

In town, Hwy 70/89 splits into two one-way streets, with traffic on Main St heading east, and traffic on Lawrence St heading west. Jackson St runs parallel to Main St, one block south, and is another main artery. Just about everything you need is on or close to these three streets, making up Quincy's low-key commercial district.

◉ Sights & Activities

Pick up free hiking-, biking- and driving-tour pamphlets from the Plumas National Forest Headquarters (p349) to guide you through the gorgeous surrounding **American Valley**. The **Feather River Scenic Byway** (Hwy 70) leads into the Sierra. In summer the icy waters of county-namesake **Feather River** (*plumas* is Spanish for 'feathers') are excellent for swimming, kayaking, fishing and floating in old inner tubes. The area is also a wonderland of winter activities, especially at Bucks Lake.

Plumas County Museum   MUSEUM
(📞530-283-6320; www.plumasmuseum.org; 500 Jackson St, at Coburn St; adult/child $2/1; ⊙9am-4:30pm Tue-Sat, 10am-3pm Sun; 🅿️🐾) In the block behind the courthouse, this multifloor county museum has flowering gardens, as well as hundreds of historical photos and relics from the county's pioneer and Maidu days, its early mining and timber industries, and construction of the Western Pacific Railroad. For the price, it's definitely worth the stop.

Plumas County Courthouse   HISTORIC BUILDING
(www.plumascourt.ca.gov; 520 Main St) Pop into the 1921 Plumas County Courthouse, at the west end of Main St, to see enormous interior marble posts and staircases, and a 1-ton bronze-and-glass chandelier in the lobby.

Big Daddy's Guide Service   FISHING
(📞530-283-4103; www.bigdaddyfishing.com; trips per person from $175) Captain Bryan Roccucci is Big Daddy, the best-known fishing guide in Northeast California. He knows the lakes well and leads trips for all levels.

🎉 Festivals & Events

⭐**High Sierra Music Festival**   MUSIC
(www.highsierramusic.com; ⊙Jul) On the first weekend in July, quiet Quincy is host to this blowout festival, renowned statewide. The four-day extravaganza brings a five-stage smorgasbord of art and music from a spectrum of cultural corners (indie rock, classic

blues, folk and jazz). Past acts include Thievery Corporation, Lauryn Hill, Primus, Ben Harper and Neko Case.

Sure, a curmudgeonly local might call it the Hippie Fest, but it's pretty tame in comparison to some of Northern California's true fringe festivals. If you plan to attend, reserve a room or campsite a couple of months in advance. For those who don't want to camp in nearby national-forest land, Susanville, one hour away, will have the largest number of rooms.

🛏 Sleeping

Ranchito Motel
MOTEL $
(☏ 530-286-2265; www.ranchitomotel.com; 2020 E Main St; r from $79; 🖤) With antique timber pillars, white-painted brick walls, old barn-style doors and the occasional wagon wheel for decoration, this friendly motel (in the eastern half of town) definitely has a Mexican ranch feel. Inside, rooms are modern, freshly painted and very comfortable for the price. The motel offers plenty more choices on the wooded land that extends back a few acres.

Pine Hill Motel
MOTEL $
(☏ 530-283-1670; www.pinehillmotel.com; 42075 Hwy 70; s/d/cabins from $70/75/150; 🌼🖤) A mile west of downtown Quincy, this little hotel is fronted by a manicured, flower-bedecked lawn dotted with white tables and chairs. The units are nothing fancy, but they're clean and in a constant state of renovation. Each is equipped with microwave, coffeemaker and refrigerator; some cabins have full kitchens.

Feather River Canyon Campgrounds
CAMPGROUND $
(☏ reservations 877-444-6777; www.fs.usda.gov; tent & RV sites $25) Area campgrounds are administered through the Mt Hough Ranger District Office (p349). They are in a cluster along the north fork of the Feather River west of Quincy – five are no-fee, but also have no piped water. All are first-come, first-served.

★ Quincy Courtyard Suites
APARTMENT $$
(☏ 530-283-1401; www.quincycourtyardsuites.com; 436 Main St; apt $129-169; 🅿🖤) Staying in this beautifully renovated 1908 Clinch building, overlooking the small main drag of Quincy's downtown, feels just right, like renting the village's cutest apartment. The warmly decorated rooms are modern – no

fussy clutter – and apartments have spacious, modern kitchens, claw-foot tubs and gas fireplaces.

Ada's Place
B&B $$
(☏ 530-283-1954; www.adasplace.com; 562 Jackson St; cottages $110-145; 🖤) Even though it feels like a B&B, it's a bit of a misnomer. Without breakfast, Ada's is just an excellent B. No problem, as each of the three brightly painted garden units has a full kitchen. Ada's Cottage is worth the slight extra charge, as its skylights offer an open feel. It's very quiet and private, yet right in town.

Greenhorn Guest Ranch
RANCH $$$
(☏ 800-334-6939; www.greenhornranch.com; 2116 Greenhorn Ranch Rd; per person per day incl trail rides from $260; ⊙May-Oct; 🖤🖤🖤) Not a 'dude' ranch but rather a 'guest' ranch: instead of shoveling stalls, guests are pampered with mountain-trail rides, riding lessons, even rodeo practice. Or you can just fish, hike, square-dance and attend evening bonfires, cookouts and frog races – think of it as a cowboy version of the getaway resort in *Dirty Dancing*.

Before you raise an eyebrow at the price, note that meals and riding are all included.

🍴 Eating & Drinking

★ Pangaea Cafe & Pub
CAFE $
(☏ 530-283-0426; www.pangaeapub.com; 461 W Main St; mains $10-13; ⊙11:30am-8:30pm Mon-Fri; 🖤🖤🖤) 🍴 Like a stranger you feel you've met before, this earthy spot feels warmly familiar, all the more lovable when you consider its commitment to serving local produce. Choose from regional beef burgers, salmon sushi, a slew of panini sandwiches (many veggie), burritos and rice bowls. It's hopping with locals drinking craft brews, kids running around and lots of hugging.

Farmers Market
MARKET $
(www.quincyfarmersmarket.org; 530 W Main St; ⊙4:30-7:30pm Thu mid-Jul–mid-Sep) Everything from fruits and veggies to handmade soaps, crafts and more. Enjoy it all to live music.

Patti's Thunder Café
BREAKFAST $
(☏ 530-283-3300; 557 Lawrence St; mains $9-16; ⊙7am-2pm; 🍴) Homey and hip, this is the best place in town for breakfast, and the vine-shaded patio is a lovely way to start the day. The menu has plenty of meaty or vegetarian options and portions are huge. Try the 'vegetaters' (roasted veg and potatoes smothered in cheese). The restaurant

is a no-cell-phone zone so bring a friend or a book.

Sweet Lorraine's
CALIFORNIAN $$

(384 Main St; mains $18-24; ⊙11:30am-2pm Mon-Fri, 5-8pm Tue-Sat) On a warm day – or, better yet, evening – the patio here is especially sweet. The menu features basic Californian cuisine (ribs, pork chops, half a roast chicken, soups and salads) and the ambience is woodsy and local. Finish things off with the delicious whiskey bread pudding.

Moon's
ITALIAN $$

(☑530-283-0765; www.moons-restaurant.com; 497 Lawrence St; mains $13-24; ⊙daily Jun-Oct, 5-9pm Tue-Sun Nov-May) Follow the aroma of garlic to this welcoming little chalet with a charming ambience. Dig into choice steaks and Italian-American classics, including excellent pizza and rich lasagna.

Drunk Brush
WINE BAR

(www.facebook.com/TheDrunkBrush; 438 Main St; ⊙2-7pm Mon-Wed, to 10pm Thu & Fri, to 8pm Sat) A sweet little courtyard wine bar that pours 25 wines and a few beers. Sample delicious appetizer pairings in a welcoming, arty atmosphere and sometimes to live music.

ⓘ Information

Mt Hough Ranger District Office (☑530-283-0555; 39696 Hwy 70; ⊙8am-4:30pm Mon-Fri) Five miles northwest of town. Has maps and outdoors information.

Plumas National Forest Headquarters (☑530-283-2050; 159 Lawrence St; ⊙8am-4:30pm Mon-Fri) For maps and outdoors information.

Bucks Lake

This clear mountain lake is cherished by locals in the know. Surrounded by pine forests, it's excellent for swimming, fishing and boating. It's about 17 miles southwest of Quincy, via the white-knuckle roads of Bucks Lake Rd (Hwy 119). The region is lined with beautiful **hiking trails**, including the **Pacific Crest Trail**, which passes through the adjoining 21,000-acre Bucks Lake Wilderness in the northwestern part of Plumas National Forest. In winter, the last 3 miles of Bucks Lake Rd are closed by snow, making it ideal for cross-country skiers.

Bucks Lake Lodge (☑530-283-2262; www.buckslakelodge.com; 16525 Bucks Lake Rd; d $99-109, cabins $119-195; 🖥🐾) is right on the lakeshore and its restaurant is popular with locals. **Haskins Valley Inn** (☑530-283-9667; www.haskinsvalleyinn.com; 1305 Haskins Circle; r $129-149; 🖥) is actually a B&B just across the street from the lake, with cozily overstuffed furnishings, woodsy paintings, Jacuzzis, fireplaces and a deck.

Five first-come, first-served campgrounds (p347) are open from June to September. Get a map at the Plumas National Forest Headquarters (p349) or Mt Hough Ranger District Office (p349), both in Quincy.

Aside from the lodge and B&B, you'll need to bring your own grub to this rustic area.

MT SHASTA REGION

'Lonely as God, and white as a winter moon,' wrote poet Joaquin Miller about this lovely mountain. The sight of it is so awe-inspiring that the new-age claims about its power as an 'energy vortex' sound plausible even after a first glimpse.

There are a million ways to explore the mountain and surrounding Shasta-Trinity National Forest – take scenic drives or get out and hike, mountain bike, raft, ski or snowshoe. At Mt Shasta's base sit three excellent little towns: Dunsmuir, Mt Shasta City and McCloud. Each has a distinct personality, but all hold a wild-mountain sensibility and first-rate amenities. Find the snaggle-toothed peaks of Castle Crags just 6 miles west of Dunsmuir.

A long drive northeast of Mt Shasta and a world away is eerily beautiful Lava Beds National Monument, a blistered badland of petrified rock. The contrasting wetlands of Klamath Basin National Wildlife Refuges lie just west.

Many services and some roads close in winter so summer is a far easier time to visit. However, winter is a peaceful and beautiful time to come here.

Mt Shasta

'When I first caught sight of it I was 50 miles away and afoot, alone and weary. Yet all my blood turned to wine, and I have not been weary since,' wrote naturalist John Muir of Mt Shasta in 1874. Mt Shasta's beauty is intoxicating, and the closer you get to her the headier you begin to feel. Dominating the landscape, the mountain is visible for more than 100 miles from many parts of Northern

Mt Shasta Area

California and southern Oregon. Though not California's highest peak (at 14,162ft it ranks fifth), Mt Shasta is especially magnificent because it rises alone on the horizon, unrivaled by other mountains.

Mt Shasta is part of the vast volcanic Cascade chain that includes Lassen Peak to the south and Mt Rainier to the north in Washington state. Thermal hot springs indicate that Mt Shasta is dormant, not extinct. The last eruption was about 200 years ago.

History

The story of the first settlers here is a sadly familiar one: European fur trappers arrived in the area in the 1820s, encountering several Native American tribes, including the Shasta, Karuk, Klamath, Modoc, Wintu and Pit River people. By 1851, hordes of Gold Rush miners had arrived and steamrolled the place, destroying the tribes' traditional life and nearly causing their extinction.

Later, the newly completed railroad began to import workers and export timber for the booming lumber industry. And since Mt Shasta City (called Sisson at the time) was the only non-dry town around, it became *the* bawdy, good-time hangout for lumberjacks.

The lumberjacks have now been replaced by middle-aged mystics and outdoor-sports enthusiasts. While the slopes have immediate appeal for explorers, spiritual seekers are attracted to the peak's reported cosmic properties. In 1987, about 5000 believers from around the world convened here for the Harmonic Convergence, a communal meditation for peace. Reverence for the mountain is nothing new; for centuries Native Americans have honored the mountain as sacred, considering it to be no less than the Great Spirit's wigwam.

◉ Sights & Activities

◉ The Mountain

You'll come across views of **Mt Shasta** (☑ 530-926-4511; www.fs.fed.us/r5/shastatrinity; Everitt Memorial Hwy; P ♿) ✐ either peaking over a ridge or completely dominating the landscape, from the Oregon border and even into the east toward Tule Lake. The mountain has two cones: the main cone has a crater about 200yd across, and the younger, shorter cone on the western flank, called Shastina, has a crater about half a mile wide.

You can drive almost the whole way up the mountain via the Everitt Memorial Hwy (Hwy A10) and see exquisite views at any time of year. Simply head east on Lake St from downtown Mt Shasta City, then turn left onto Washington Dr and keep going. **Bunny Flat** (6860ft), which has a trailhead for Horse Camp and the Avalanche Gulch summit route, is a busy place with parking spaces, information signboards and a toilet.

The section of highway beyond Bunny Flat is only open from about mid-June to October, depending on snow, but if it's clear, it's worth the trouble. This road leads to **Lower Panther Meadow**, where trails connect the campground to a Wintu sacred spring, in the upper meadows near the **Old Ski Bowl** (7800ft) parking area. Shortly thereafter is the highlight of the drive, **Everitt Vista Point** (7900ft), where a short interpretive walk from the parking lot leads to a stone-walled outcrop affording exceptional views of Lassen Peak to the south, the Mt Eddy and Marble Mountains to the west and the whole Strawberry Valley below.

Climbing the summit is best done between May and September, preferably in spring and early summer, when there's still enough soft snow on the southern flank to make footholds easier on the nontechnical route. Although the elements are occasionally volatile and the winds are incredibly strong, the round-trip could conceivably be done in one day with 12 or more hours of solid hiking. A more enjoyable trip takes at least two days with one night on the mountain. How long it actually takes depends on the route selected, the physical condition of the climbers and weather conditions (for weather information, call the recorded message of the Forest Service Mt Shasta climbing advisory on 530-926-9613).

The hike to the summit from Bunny Flat follows the **Avalanche Gulch Route**. Although it is only about 7 miles, the vertical climb is more than 7000ft, so acclimatizing to the elevation is important – even hearty hikers will be short of breath. Additionally, this route requires crampons, an ice axe and a helmet, all of which can be rented locally. Rock slides, while rare, are also a hazard. If you want to make the climb without gear, the only option is the **Clear Creek Route** to the top, which leaves from the east side of the mountain. In late summer, this route is usually manageable in hiking boots, though there's still loose scree, and it should be done as an overnight hike. Novices should contact the Mt Shasta Ranger Station (p354) for a list of available guides.

There's a charge to climb beyond 10,000ft: a three-day summit pass costs $25; an annual pass is $30. Contact the ranger station for details. You must obtain a free wilderness permit any time you go into the wilderness, whether on the mountain or in the surrounding area.

Mt Shasta Ski Park SNOW SPORTS
(📱 snow reports 530-926-8686; www.skipark.com; full-day weekend lift tickets adult/child $58/32; ⏰9am-9pm Thu-Sat, to 4pm Sun-Tue) On the south slope of Mt Shasta, off Hwy 89 heading toward McCloud, this winter skiing and snowboarding park opens depending on snowfall. The park has a 1435ft vertical drop, 32 alpine runs and 18 miles of cross-country trails. These are all good for beginner and intermediate skiers, and are a less crowded alternative to the slopes around Lake Tahoe.

Rentals, instruction and weekly specials are available; lift tickets are cheapest on weekdays. It's Northern California's largest night-skiing operation. There are lots of inexpensive options for skiing half a day or just at night, when hitting the slopes and taking in a full moon can be enchanting.

In summer the park occasionally hosts mountain-biking events.

👁 The Lakes

There are a number of pristine mountain lakes near Mt Shasta. Some of them are accessible only by dirt roads or hiking trails and are great for getting away from it all.

The closest lake to Mt Shasta City is lovely **Lake Siskiyou** (also the largest), 2.5 miles southwest on Old Stage Rd, where you can peer into **Box Canyon Dam**, a 200ft-deep chasm. Another 7 miles up in the mountains, southwest of Lake Siskiyou on Castle Lake Rd, lies **Castle Lake**, an unspoiled gem surrounded by granite formations and pine forest. Swimming, fishing, picnicking and free camping are popular in summer; in winter folks ice-skate on the lake. **Lake Shastina**, about 15 miles northwest of town, off Hwy 97, is another beauty.

Mt Shasta City

Comfortable and practical Mt Shasta City glows in the shadow of the white pyramid of Mt Shasta. The downtown is charming; you can spend hours poking around galleries and boutiques. Orienting yourself is easy with the mountain looming over the east side of town and you may get a kink in your neck from admiring it. The downtown area is a few blocks east of I-5. Take the Central Mt Shasta exit, then drive east on Lake St past the visitor center, up to the town's main intersection at Mt Shasta Blvd, the principal drag.

👁 Sights & Activities

To head out hiking on your own, first stop by the ranger station or the visitors center for excellent free trail guides, including several access points along the **Pacific Crest Trail**. Gorgeous **Black Butte**, a striking, treeless, black volcanic cone, rises almost 6436ft. The 2.5-mile trail to the top takes at least 2½ hours for the round-trip. It's steep and rocky in many places, and there is no shade or water, so don't hike on a hot summer day. Wear good, thick-soled shoes or hiking boots and bring plenty of water. If you want an easier amble, try the 10-mile **Sisson-Callahan National Recreation Trail**, a partially paved trail that affords great views of Mt Shasta and the jagged Castle Crags, following a historic route established in the mid-1800s by prospectors, trappers and cattle ranchers to connect the mining town of Callahan with the town of Sisson, now called Mt Shasta City.

Mt Shasta City Park
& Sacramento River Headwaters PARK
(http://msrec.org; Nixon Rd) FREE Off Mt Shasta Blvd, about a mile north of downtown, the headwaters of the Sacramento River gurgle up from the ground in a large, cool spring. It's about as pure as water can get – so bring a bottle and have a drink. The park also has walking trails, picnic spots, sports fields and courts, and a children's playground.

Sisson Museum MUSEUM
(http://mtshastamuseum.com; 1 Old Stage Rd; suggested donation $1; ⊘10am-4pm Jun-Sep, 1-4pm Fri-Sun Oct-Dec & Apr-May) A half-mile west of the freeway, this former hatchery headquarters is full of curious mountaineering artifacts and old pictures. The changing exhibitions highlight history – geological and human – but also occasionally showcase local artists. Next door, the oldest operating hatchery in the West maintains outdoor ponds teeming with rainbow trout that will eventually be released into lakes and rivers.

Siskiyou Ice Rink SKATING
(www.siskiyourink.org; cnr Rockfellow & Adams Drs; adult/child $10/7; ⊘9am-7:15pm Mon-Thu, to 9pm Fri & Sat, 8am-5pm Sun Dec-Mar) East of downtown, the immense outdoor skating rink is open to ice-skaters in winter and has lessons available.

River Dancers Rafting & Kayaking RAFTING
(☑530-925-0237; www.riverdancers.com; 705 Kenneth Way; half-day trips from $78) Excellent outfit run by active environmentalists who guide one- to five-day white-water-rafting excursions down the area's rivers: the Klamath, Sacramento, Salmon, Trinity and Scott. Chose from half-day to multiday adventures.

Shasta Mountain Guides OUTDOORS
(☑530-926-3117; http://shastaguides.com; 2-day climbs from $625 per person) Offers two-day guided climbs of Mt Shasta between April and September, with all gear and meals included. The experienced mountaineers have operated in Shasta for 30 years.

Courses

Mt Shasta Mountaineering
School ADVENTURE SPORTS
(www.swsmtns.com; 210a E Lake St; 2-day summit climbs $600) Conducts clinics and courses for serious climbers, or those looking to get serious on Mt Shasta.

Tours

Note that hiking Mt Shasta doesn't require an operator, but those wanting one have plenty of options; ask at the visitor center.

Shasta Vortex
 Adventures OUTDOORS, MEDITATION
(☑530-926-4326; www.shastavortex.com; 400 Chestnut St) For a uniquely Mt Shasta outdoor experience, Shasta Vortex offers low-impact trips accented with the spiritual quest as much as the physical journey. The focus of the trips includes guided meditation and an exploration of the mountain's metaphysical power. Full-day tours for two people cost $474; larger groups get a slight discount.

Sleeping

Shasta has it all, from free rustic camping to plush boutique B&Bs. If you're intent on staying at the upper end of the spectrum, make reservations well in advance, especially on weekends and holidays and during ski season.

Many modest motels stretch along S Mt Shasta Blvd (costing $60 to $140 depending on how recently they were remodeled). Most offer discount ski packages in winter and lower midweek rates year-round.

★**Historic Lookout**
& Cabin Rentals CABIN $
(☑information 530-994-2184, reservations 877-444-6777; www.fs.usda.gov/stnf; q $75; ⊘May/Jun–mid-Oct; ☺) What better way to rough it in style than to bunk down in a fire lookout on forested slopes? Built from the 1920s to '40s, cabins come with cots, tables and chairs, have panoramic views and can accommodate four people. Details about Little Mt Hoffman, Girard Creek and other lookouts can all be found on the national forest website.

Note that these cabins have become *very* popular and you'll need to reserve far in advance.

Panther Meadows
CAMPGROUND $

(www.fs.usda.gov; tent sites free; ⊙ usually Jul-Nov) Ten walk-in tent sites (no drinking water) sit at the timberline, right at the base of the mountain. They're a few miles up the mountain from other options, but are still easily accessible from Everitt Memorial Hwy. No reservations; arrive early to secure a site.

Swiss Holiday Lodge
MOTEL $

(☑ 530-926-3446; www.swissholidaylodge.com; 2400 S Mt Shasta Blvd; r $66-110; P ⊜ ❄ 🛜 🐾 🐕) Run by a friendly family and a small, energetic dog; you get a peek of the mountain from the back windows of these clean, well-priced rooms.

McBride Springs
CAMPGROUND $

(tent sites $10; ⊙ Memorial Day-late Oct, depending on weather) Easily accessible from Everitt Memorial Hwy, this campground has running water and pit toilets, but no showers. It's near mile marker 4, at an elevation of 5000ft. It's no beauty – a recent root disease killed many of the white fir trees that shaded the sites – but it's convenient. Arrive early in the morning to secure a spot (no reservations).

Lake Siskiyou Beach & Camp
CAMPGROUND $

(☑ 888-926-2618; www.lakesiskiyouresort.com; 4239 WA Barr Rd; tent/RV sites from $20/29, cabins $107-152; 🛜 🐕) Tucked away on the shore of Lake Siskiyou, this sprawling place has a summer-camp feel (there's an arcade and an ice-cream stand). Hardly rustic, it has a swimming beach, and kayak, canoe, fishing-boat and paddle-boat rentals. Lots of amenities make it a good option for families on an RV trip.

Horse Camp
HUT $

(www.sierraclubfoundation.org; per person with/without tent $5/3) This 1923 alpine lodge run by the Sierra Club is a 2-mile hike uphill from Bunny Flat, at 8000ft. The stone construction and natural setting are lovely. Caretakers staff the hut from May to September only.

★ Shasta MountInn
B&B $$

(☑ 530-926-1810; www.shastamountinn.com; 203 Birch St; r $150-175; P ⊜ 🛜) Only antique on the outside, this bright Victorian 1904 farmhouse is all relaxed minimalism, bold colors and graceful decor on the inside. Each airy room has a great bed and exquisite views of the luminous mountain. Enjoy the expansive garden, wraparound deck, outdoor hot tub and sauna. Not relaxed enough yet? Chill on the perfectly placed porch swings.

Mt Shasta Resort
RESORT $$

(☑ 530-926-3030; www.mountshastaresort.com; 1000 Siskiyou Lake Blvd; r from $119, 1-/2-bedroom chalets from $179/239; 🐾 🛜 🐕) Divinely situated away from town, this upscale golf resort and spa has arts-and-crafts-style chalets nestled in the woods around the shores of Lake Siskiyou. They're a bit soulless, but they're immaculate, and each has a kitchen and gas fireplace. Basic lodge rooms are near the golf course, which boasts some challenging greens and amazing views of the mountain.

The restaurant has excellent views and serves Californian cuisine with a large selection of steaks.

Strawberry Valley Inn
B&B $$

(☑ 530-926-2052; 1142 S Mt Shasta Blvd; d $109-169; 🛜) The understated rooms surround a garden courtyard, allowing you to enjoy the intimate feel of a B&B without the pressure of having to chat with the darling newlyweds around the breakfast table. A continental breakfast is included and guests can use the kitchen.

Dream Inn
B&B $$

(☑ 530-926-1536; www.dreaminnmtshastacity.com; 326 Chestnut St; r without bath $80-160, ste $120-160; 🛜 🐕) Made up of two houses in the center of town: one is a meticulously kept Victorian cottage stuffed with fussy knick-knacks; the other a Spanish-style two-story building with chunky, raw-wood furniture and no clutter. A rose garden with a koi pond joins the two properties. A good-sized breakfast is included. Excellent midtown location.

Finlandia Motel
MOTEL $$

(☑ 530-926-5596; www.finlandiamotel.com; 1612 S Mt Shasta Blvd; r $65-120, with kitchen $115-200) An excellent deal, the standard rooms are... standard – clean and simple. The suites get a little chalet flair with vaulted pine ceilings and mountain views. There's an outdoor hot tub and the Finnish sauna is available by appointment.

✖ Eating & Drinking

Trendy restaurants and cafes here come and go with the snowmelt, but there are still some tried-and-true places, favored by locals and visitors alike. For more options head 6 miles south to Dunsmuir, an unexpected hot spot for great food. A **farmers market** (p354) sets up on Mt Shasta Blvd during summer.

Poncho & Lefkowitz
MEXICAN, INTERNATIONAL $

(401 S Mt Shasta Blvd; meals $4-9; ⊙ 11am-4pm Tue-Sat; 🖋) Surrounded by a picnic table or three, this classy, wood-sided food cart turns out juicy Polish sausage, bratwurst and hot dogs, and big plates of nachos, tamales and burritos (including vegetarian options). It's a good bet for food on the go.

Berryvale Grocery
MARKET, CAFE $

(📞 530-926-1576; www.berryvale.com; 305 S Mt Shasta Blvd; cafe items from $5; ⊙ store 8am-8pm, cafe to 7pm; 🖋🖥) 🖋 This market sells groceries and organic produce to health-conscious eaters. The excellent cafe serves good coffee, fresh juices and an array of tasty – mostly veggie – salads, sandwiches and wraps.

Farmers Market
MARKET $

(www.mtshastafarmersmarket.com; 400 block of N Mt Shasta Blvd; ⊙ 3:30-6pm Mon mid-May–mid-Oct) Stock up on farm-fresh produce or graze the stalls of delicious tamales, bakery goods, pastas and more.

Mount Shasta Pastry
BAKERY $

(📞 530-926-9944; www.mountshastapastry.com; 610 S Mt Shasta Blvd; mains $5-11; ⊙ 7am-4pm Mon-Fri, to 1pm Sat & Sun, closed Mon & Tue Oct-May; 🖋🖥) Walk in hungry and you'll be plagued with an existential breakfast crisis: the feta spinach quiche or the Tuscan scramble? The flaky croissants or a divine apricot turnover? It also serves terrific sandwiches, gourmet pizza, Peet's coffee and mimosas.

Lily's
CALIFORNIAN $$

(www.lilysrestaurant.com; 1013 S Mt Shasta Blvd; mains breakfast & lunch $10-17, dinner $14-28; ⊙ 8am-2pm & 5-9pm; 🖋🖥) Enjoy quality Californian cuisine – Asian- and Mediterranean-touched salads, fresh sandwiches and all kinds of veg options – in a cute, white, clapboard house. Outdoor tables overhung by flowering trellises are almost always full, especially for breakfast. A Shasta classic, you can now expect vegan and gluten-free options.

Andaman Healthy Thai Cuisine
THAI $$

(📞 530-926-5288; 313 N Mt Shasta Blvd; mains $12-22; ⊙ 11am-9pm Mon, Tue, Thu & Fri, from 4pm Sat & Sun) The food is pretty good, but the kitchen and the staff can't keep up with the crowds. It also serves burgers if you're traveling with fussy folk.

Seven Suns Coffee & Cafe
CAFE

(1011 S Mt Shasta Blvd; ⊙ 5:30am-7pm; 📱) This snug little hangout serves organic, locally roasted coffee, light meals (around $10) and is consistently busy. There's live acoustic music some evenings.

🛍 Shopping

Looking for an imported African hand drum, some prayer flags or a nice crystal? You've come to the right place. The downtown shopping district has a handful of cute little boutiques to indulge a little shopping for the spiritual seeker.

Fifth Season Sports
SPORTS & OUTDOORS

(📞 530-926-3606; http://thefifthseason.com; 300 N Mt Shasta Blvd; ⊙ 9am-6pm Mon-Fri, from 8am Sat, 10am-5pm Sun) A favorite outdoor store in Shasta, this place rents camping, mountain-climbing and backpacking gear and has staff familiar with the mountain. It also rents skis, snowshoes and snowboards.

ℹ Information

Mt Shasta Ranger Station (📞 530-926-4511; www.fs.usda.gov/stnf; 204 W Alma St; ⊙ 8am-4:30pm Mon-Fri) One block west of Mt Shasta Blvd. Issues wilderness and mountain-climbing permits, good advice, weather reports and all you need for exploring the area. It also sells topographic maps.

Mt Shasta Visitors Center (📞 530-926-4865; www.mtshastachamber.com; 300 Pine St; ⊙ 9am-4:30pm) Detailed information on recreation and lodging across Siskiyou County.

ℹ Getting There & Away

Greyhound (www.greyhound.com) buses heading north and south on I-5 stop at the **depot** (628 S Weed Blvd) in Weed, 8 miles north on I-5. Services include Redding ($15, one hour and 20 minutes, three daily), Sacramento ($40, 5½ hours, three daily) and San Francisco ($50, 10½ hours, two or three times daily).

The **STAGE bus** (📞 530-842-8295; www.co.siskiyou.ca.us; 914 Pine St; fares $2.50-8) includes Mt Shasta City in its local I-5 corridor route (fares $2.50 to $8, depending on distance), which also serves McCloud, Dunsmuir, Weed and Yreka several times each weekday. Other buses connect at Yreka.

Dunsmuir

In 1886 Canadian coal baron Alexander Dunsmuir came to Pusher (named after the 'pusher' train engines) and was so enchanted that he promised the people a fountain if they would rename the town after him. The fountain stands in the park today. Stop

WEED & STEWART MINERAL SPRINGS

Just outside Weed, **Stewart Mineral Springs** (☑530-938-2222; http://stewartmineral springs.com; 4617 Stewart Springs Rd, Weed; sauna/mineral baths $18/30; ☉10am-6pm Thu-Sun, from noon Mon) is a popular clothing-optional hangout on the banks of a mountain stream. Henry Stewart founded these springs in 1875 after Native Americans revived him from a near-death experience. He attributed his recovery to the properties of the mineral waters, said to draw toxins from the body.

Today you can soak in a private claw-foot tub or steam in the dry-wood sauna. Other perks include massage, meditation, a Native American sweat lodge and a riverside sun-bathing deck. Call ahead to be sure there's availability. Dining and **accommodations** (tent & RV sites $35, tipis $45, d $80-120; ℙ☻) are on-site. To reach the springs, go 10 miles north of Mt Shasta City on I-5, past Weed to the Edgewood exit, then turn left at Stewart Springs Rd and follow the signs.

While in the area, tickle your nose at **Mt Shasta Lavender Farms** (☑530-926-2651; www.mtshastalavenderfarms.com; 9706 Harry Cash Rd, Montague; ☉9am-4pm mid-Jun–early Aug; ℙ), or drink up the tasty porter at the **Mt Shasta Brewing Company Alehouse** (☑530-938-2394; www.weedales.com; 360 College Ave, Weed; mains $11-18; ☉11am-9pm or 10pm).

there for a drink; it could easily be – as locals claim – 'the best water on earth.'

This town has survived avalanche, fire, flood, even a toxic railroad spill in 1991. Long since cleaned up, the river has been restored to pristine levels and the community has a plucky spirit, though today a number of empty storefronts attest to the community's greatest challenge: the Global Economic Crisis.

Still, it's home to a spirited set of artists, naturalists, urban refugees and native Dunsmuirians, who are rightly proud of the fish-stocked rivers around their little community. Its downtown streets – once a bawdy gold rush district – hold cafes, restaurants and galleries.

◉ Sights & Activities

The Dunsmuir Chamber of Commerce (p357) stocks maps of **cycling trails** and **swimming holes** on the Upper Sacramento River.

Dunsmuir City Park   PARK
(www.dunsmuirparks.org; ☉dawn-dusk) FREE
As you follow winding Dunsmuir Ave north over the freeway, look for this park with its local native **botanical gardens** and a vintage **steam engine** in front. A forest path from the riverside gardens leads to a small waterfall, but **Mossbrae Falls** are the larger and more spectacular of Dunsmuir's waterfalls.

It's actually illegal to walk to the falls since the trail is partially on the railroad tracks and a woman was hit by a train here in 2011. Still, plenty of people go. Be extremely careful of trains as you walk by the tracks – the river's sound can make it impossible to hear them coming and to escape a train you'll have to run for it or jump in the river. Park by the railroad tracks (there's no sign), then walk north along the right-hand side of the tracks for a half hour until you reach a railroad bridge built in 1901. Back-tracking slightly from the bridge, you'll find a little path going down through the trees to the river and the falls. The community is discussing making a safer trail, so ask around.

California Theater   HISTORIC BUILDING
(5741 Dunsmuir Ave) At downtown's north end stands what was the town's pride. This once-glamorous venue was being restored to its original glory, then the work stopped. First opened in 1926, the theater hosted stars such as Clark Gable, Carole Lombard and the Marx Brothers. Today the very sporadic lineup includes second-run films, musical performances and yoga classes.

🛏 Sleeping

Dunsmuir Lodge   MOTEL $
(☑530-235-2884; www.dunsmuirlodge.net; 6604 Dunsmuir Ave; r $59-153; ☎☀) Toward the south entrance of town, the simple but tastefully renovated rooms have hardwood floors, big chunky blond-wood bed frames and tiled baths. A grassy communal picnic area overlooks the canyon slope. It's a peaceful little place and very good value.

Cave Springs
MOTEL, CABIN $

(📞530-235-2721; www.cavesprings.com; 4727 Dunsmuir Ave; r/cabins from $75/89; ❄️🛜🏊) These creekside cabins seem unchanged since the 1920s, even though the interiors were recently updated. They are rustic – *very* rustic – but their location, nestled on a piney crag above the Sacramento River, is lovely and ideal for anglers. At night the sound of rushing water mingles with the haunting whistle of trains.

The motel rooms are bland, but they're up to modern standards and have more amenities than the cabins.

Dunsmuir Inn & Suites
MOTEL $

(📞530-235-4395; www.dunsmuirinn.com; 5400 Dunsmuir Ave; r $79-159; ❄️🛜) Straightforward, immaculately clean motel rooms make a good, no-fuss option. Great location in the main part of town.

Railroad Park Resort
INN, CAMPGROUND $$

(📞530-235-4440; www.rrpark.com; 100 Railroad Park Rd; tent/RV sites from $29/37, d $135-165; ❄️🛜🏊🐕) About 2 miles south of town, off I-5, visitors can spend the night inside refitted vintage railroad cars and cabooses. The grounds are fun for kids, who can run around the engines and plunge in a centrally situated pool. The deluxe boxcars are furnished with antiques and claw-foot tubs, although the cabooses are simpler and a bit less expensive.

You get tremendous views of Castle Crags, a peaceful creekside setting and tall pines shading the adjoining campground. In 2017 it came under enthusiastic new ownership.

✕ Eating

★ Dunsmuir Brewery Works
PUB FOOD $

(📞530-235-1900; www.dunsmuirbreweryworks. com; 5701 Dunsmuir Ave; mains $9-13; ⏱️11am-10pm May-Sep, to 9pm Tue-Sun Oct-Apr; 🛜) It's hard to describe this little microbrew pub without veering into hyperbole. Start with the beer: the crisp ales and porter are perfectly balanced and the India Pale Ale (IPA) is apparently pretty good too, because patrons are always drinking it dry. Soak it up with awesome bar food: a warm potato salad, bratwurst, or a thick Angus or perfect veggie nut burger.

The atmosphere, with a buzzing patio and aw-shucks staff, completes a perfect picture.

Cornerstone Bakery & Café
CAFE $

(5759 Dunsmuir Ave; mains $6-15; ⏱️8am-2pm Thu-Mon; 🌱) Smack in the middle of town, this homey place serves strong coffee, espresso and friendly service. It's more of a diner than a bakery and the offerings – basic to creative omelettes, French toast and some fun specials like chai sweet-potato waffles – are consistently delicious. The baked goods, including gooey cinnamon rolls, are often warm from the oven.

Yaks
AMERICAN $

(www.yaks.com; 4917 Dunsmuir Ave; mains $8-19; ⏱️11am-9pm Mon-Sat, to 8pm Sun; 🛜) Hiding under the Hitching Post sign just off I-5, this is the lplace to come to blow your diet. Breakfast means Cuban pepper-steak hash or perhaps home-baked cinnamon-roll French toast with your choice of house syrups like Baileys-and-bourbon. Lunch offers a huge range of burgers (try the one with the house-roasted coffee rub). There's also a take-out counter.

Wheelhouse
CAFE $

(📞530-235-0754; 5841 Sacramento Ave; mains $7-12; ⏱️7am-3pm Wed-Sun, to 8pm Fri & Sat; 🛜🌱) This casual, high-ceilinged, brick-walled hangout (formerly the Brown Trout Gallery & Dogwood Diner and originally the town mercantile) serves organic, healthy yet hefty and delicious New American–style breakfasts. If you're not feeling like bacon and eggs, try the Zephyr, ciabatta bread in a custard batter, grilled and topped with pineapple, brown sugar and brandied caramel syrup.

★ Café Maddalena
EUROPEAN, NORTH AFRICAN $$

(📞530-235-2725; www.cafemaddalena.com; 5801 Sacramento Ave; mains $15-26; ⏱️5-9pm Thu-Sun Feb-Dec) Simple and elegant, this cafe put Dunsmuir on the foodie map. The menu was designed by chef Bret LaMott (of Trinity Cafe fame) and changes seasonally to feature dishes from southern Europe and northern Africa. Some highlights include pan-roasted king salmon with basil cream, wild mushroom soup or sautéed rabbit with carrots and morel sauce.

The wine bar is stocked with rare Mediterranean labels, including a great selection of Spanish varietals.

Railroad Park Dinner House
CALIFORNIAN $$

(📞530-235-4440; www.rrpark.com; Railroad Park Resort, 100 Railroad Park Rd; mains $15-30; ⏱️5-9pm Fri & Sat Apr, 5-9pm Wed-Sun May-Oct) Set inside a vintage railroad car with views of Castle Crags, this popular restaurant-bar offers trainloads of dining-car ambience and Californian cuisine. Prime-rib specials are on Friday and Saturdays. A new chef started in 2017 so expect some surprises.

Sengthongs THAI, VIETNAMESE $$
(☑530-235-4770; http://sengthongs.com; 5855 Dunsmuir Ave; mains $17-27; ⊙4:30-8:30pm Thu-Sun) This funky joint serves up sizzling Thai, Lao and Vietnamese food and books first-rate jazz, reggae, salsa or blues some nights. Many dishes are simply heaping bowls of noodles, though the meat dishes – flavored with ginger, scallions and spices – are more complex and uniformly delicious. It's a Dunsmuir classic.

Information

Dunsmuir Chamber of Commerce (☑530-235-2177; www.dunsmuir.com; 5915 Dunsmuir Ave, Suite 100; ⊙10am-3:30pm Tue-Sat) Free maps, walking-guide pamphlets and excellent information on outdoor activities.

❶ Getting There & Away

Amtrak Station (www.amtrak.com; 5750 Sacramento Ave) Dunsmuir's Amtrak station is the railroad hub for the region and bus connections are available to the surrounding towns.

STAGE Bus (☑530-842-8295) This local bus service covers the Shasta region, including Shasta City and Weed.

Castle Crags State Park

The stars of this glorious state park (☑530-235-2684; www.parks.ca.gov; per car $8; ⊙sunrise-sunset) alongside Castle Crags Wilderness Area are its soaring spires of ancient granite formed some 225 million years ago, with elevations ranging from 2000ft along the Sacramento River to more than 6500ft at the peaks. The crags are similar to the granite formations of the eastern Sierra. Castle Dome resembles Yosemite's famous Half Dome.

Rangers at the park entrance station have information and maps covering nearly 28 miles of hiking trails. There's also fishing in the Sacramento River at the picnic area on the opposite side of I-5.

If you drive past the campground, you'll reach Vista Point, near the start of the strenuous 2.7-mile Crags Trail, which rises through the forest past the Indian Springs spur trail, then clambers up to the base of Castle Dome. You're rewarded with unsurpassed views of Mt Shasta, especially if you scramble the last 100yd or so up into the rocky saddle gap. The park also has gentle nature trails and 8 miles of the Pacific Crest Trail, which passes through the park at the base of the crags.

You can camp anywhere in the Shasta-Trinity National Forest surrounding the park if you get a free campfire permit, issued at park offices. At the time of writing, the future of this state park was uncertain because of budget issues.

The campground (☑reservations 800-444-7275; www.reserveamerica.com; tent & RV sites $15-30) is one of the nicer public campgrounds in this area, and very easily accessible from the highway. It has running water, hot showers and three spots that can accommodate RVs but have no hookups. Sites are shady, but suffer from traffic noise.

McCloud

This tiny, historic mill town sits at the foot of the south slope of Mt Shasta, and is an alternative to staying in Mt Shasta City. Quiet streets retain a simple, easygoing charm. It's the closest settlement to Mt Shasta Board & Ski Park and is surrounded by abundant natural beauty. Hidden in the woods upriver are woodsy getaways for the Western aristocracy, including mansions owned by the Hearst and Levi Strauss estates.

◉ Sights & Activities

The McCloud River Loop, a gorgeous, 6-mile, partially paved road along the Upper McCloud River, begins at Fowlers Camp, 5.5 miles east of town on Hwy 89, and re-emerges about 11 miles east of McCloud. Along the loop, turn off at Three Falls for a pretty trail that passes...yep, three lovely falls and a riparian habitat for bird-watching in the Bigelow Meadow. The loop can easily be done by car, bicycle or on foot, and has five first-come, first-served campgrounds.

Other good hiking trails include the Squaw Valley Creek Trail (not to be confused with the ski area near Lake Tahoe), an easy 5-mile loop trail south of town, with options for swimming, fishing and picnicking. Also south of town, Ah-Di-Na is the remains of a Native American settlement and historic homestead once owned by the William Randolph Hearst family. Sections of the Pacific Crest Trail are accessible from

Ah-Di-Na Campground, off Squaw Valley Rd, and also up near Bartle Gap, offering head-spinning views.

Fishing and swimming are popular on remote **Lake McCloud** reservoir, 9 miles south of town on Squaw Valley Rd, which is signposted in town as Southern. You can also go fishing on the Upper McCloud River (stocked with trout) and at the Squaw Valley Creek.

McCloud Mercantile　　　HISTORIC BUILDING
(www.mccloudmercantile.com; 222-245 Main St) The huge McCloud Mercantile anchors the downtown. There's a hotel (p358) upstairs and it hosts a couple of restaurants that warrant a longer stay, but those just passing through can get a bag of licorice at the old-world candy counter or browse the main floor. The collection of dry goods is very Nor-Cal: Woolrich blankets, handmade soap and interesting gifts for the gardener, outdoors person or chef.

Historical Museum　　　MUSEUM
(530-964-2604; 320 Main St; 11am-3pm Mon-Sat, 1-3pm Sun May-Sep) FREE The tiny historical museum sits opposite the McCloud Chamber of Commerce and could use a bit of organization – it has the feel of a cluttered, messy thrift store – but tucked in the nooks and crannies are plenty of worthwhile curiosities from the town's past.

Sleeping & Eating

Lodging in McCloud is excellent and reservations are recommended. For camping, the McCloud Ranger District Office (p359) has information on the half-dozen campgrounds nearby. Fowlers Camp is the most popular. The campgrounds have a range of facilities, from primitive (no running water and no fee) to developed (hot showers and fees of up to $15 per site). Ask about nearby fire-lookout cabins for rent for amazing, remote views of the area.

McCloud's eating options are few. For more variety, make the 10-mile trip over to Mt Shasta City.

Stoney Brook Inn　　　B&B $
(530-964-2300; www.stoneybrookinn.com; 309 W Colombero Dr; d $94, s/d without bath $53/79, ste with kitchen $99-156;) Smack in the middle of town, under a stand of pines, this alternative B&B also sponsors group retreats. Creature comforts include an outdoor hot tub, a sauna, a Native American sweat

lodge and massage by appointment. Downstairs rooms are nicest. Vegetarian breakfast available.

McCloud Dance Country RV Park　　　CAMPGROUND $
(530-964-2252; www.mccloudrvpark.com; 480 Hwy 89, at Southern Ave; tent sites $30, RV sites $39-46, cabins $140-175;) Chock-full of RVs, with campsites under the trees and a small creek, this is a good option for families. The view of the mountain is breathtaking and there's a large, grassy picnic ground. Cabins are basic but clean.

★**McCloud River Mercantile Hotel**　　INN $$
(530-964-2330; www.mccloudmercantile.com; 241 Main St; r $129-250;) Stroll upstairs to the 2nd floor of McCloud's central Mercantile Hotel and try not to fall in love; it's all high ceilings, exposed brick and a perfect marriage of preservationist class and modern panache. Antique-furnished rooms have open floor plans. Guests are greeted with fresh flowers and can drift to sleep on feather beds after soaking in claw-foot tubs.

One of the best hotels in the northern mountains.

McCloud Hotel　　　HISTORIC HOTEL $$
(530-964-2822; www.mccloudhotel.com; 408 Main St; r $145-255;) Regal, butter-yellow and a whole block long, this grand hotel opened in 1916 and has been a destination for Shasta's visitors ever since. The elegant historic landmark has been restored to a luxurious standard and Sage, the on-site restaurant, serves the most upscale meals in town. Many rooms have Jacuzzis; one room is accessible for travelers with disabilities.

McCloud River Inn　　　B&B $$
(530-964-2130; www.mccloudriverinn.com; 325 Lawndale Ct; r $99-199;) Rooms in this rambling, quaint Victorian are fabulously big – the bathrooms alone could sleep two. In the morning look out for the frittatas; in the evening have a bottle of wine delivered to your room. There's also an on-site day spa. The relaxed and familial atmosphere guarantees that it books up quickly.

White Mountain Cafe　　　AMERICAN $
(530-964-2005; 241 Main St; mains from $8; 8am-4pm Wed-Sun, to 2pm Oct-May) In the window-lined corner of the Mercantile, this old-fashioned yet classy diner serves classic American breakfasts, hot or cold sandwiches, burgers and shakes. The 'Not the Dolly

Varden' is an excellent vegetarian sandwich with roasted zucchini, red peppers and garlic aioli.

Drinking & Entertainment

Siskiyou Brew Works   BREWERY
(☑530-925-5894; 110 Squaw Valley Rd; ⊙4-8pm Wed-Sun) In a not-obvious spot in the McCloud Dairy Barn just off Hwy 89, this rustic little spot churns out the town's first craft beers and decent, heavily topped pizzas. Get a beer sampler to find your favorite.

★McCloud Dance Country   DANCE
(www.mcclouddancecountry.com; cnr Broadway & Pine Sts; packages from $299 per couple) Dust it up on the 5000-sq-ft maple dance floor in the 1906 Broadway Ballroom. Square dancing, round dancing, ballroom dancing – they do it all. Multiday packages include lessons and evening dances. It's a worthwhile centerpiece to a weekend getaway. Visit the website to see what's on and to sign up.

❶ Information

McCloud Chamber of Commerce (☑530-964-3113; www.mccloudchamber.com; 205 Quincy St; ⊙10am-4pm Mon-Fri) Has basic info and friendly staff.

McCloud Ranger District Office (☑530-964-2184, 2019 Forest Rd; ⊙8am-4:30pm Mon-Sat summer, 8am-4:30pm Mon-Fri rest of year) A quarter-mile east of town. Detailed information on camping, hiking and recreation.

McArthur-Burney Falls Memorial State Park & Around

This beautiful **state park** (☑530-335-2777; www.parks.ca.gov; Hwy 89, Burney; per car $8; P♿) 🍴 lies southeast of McCloud, near the crossroads of Hwys 89 and 299 from Redding. Fed by a spring, the splashing 129ft-tall waterfalls flow at the same temperature, 42°F (6°C), year-round. Rangers are quick to point out that it might not be California's highest waterfall, but it may be the most beautiful (Teddy Roosevelt considered it the eighth wonder of the world). Clear, lava-filtered water surges over the top and also from springs in the waterfall's face.

Hiking trails include a portion of the **Pacific Crest Trail**, which continues north to Castle Crags State Park. The 1.3-mile **Burney Falls Trail** is the one you shouldn't miss.

Upgraded with guardrails, it's an easy loop for families and allows close-up views of water rushing right out of the rock. You can **camp** (☑information 530-335-2777, summer reservations 800-444-7275; www.reserveamerica.com; off Hwy 89, Burney; tent & RV sites $35, cabins $83-105; P🐾) here.

A visit to nearby **Ahjumawi Lava Springs State Park** (☑530-335-2777; www.parks.ca.gov; ⊙sunrise-sunset) 🍴 comes with serious bragging rights as the abundant springs, aquamarine bays and islets, and jagged flows of black basalt lava are truly off the beaten path, and can be reached only by boat. After you paddle out, the hikes are glorious: there are basalt outcroppings, lava tubes, cold springs bubbling and all kinds of volcanic features.

Lava Beds National Monument

A wild landscape of charred volcanic rock and rolling hills, this remote **national monument** (☑530-667-8113; www.nps.gov/labe; 1 Indian Well HQ, Tulelake; 7-day entry per car $15; P♿) 🍴 is reason enough to visit the region. Off Hwy 139, immediately south of Tule Lake National Wildlife Refuge, it's a truly remarkable 72-sq-mile landscape of volcanic features – lava flows, craters, cinder cones, spatter cones, shield volcanoes and amazing lava tubes.

Lava tubes are formed when the surface of hot, spreading lava cools and hardens upon exposure to cold air. The lava inside is thus insulated and stays molten, flowing away to leave an empty tube of solidified lava. Nearly 400 such tubular caves have been found in the monument, and many more are expected to be discovered. Approximately two dozen are currently open for exploration by visitors.

On the south side of the park, the **visitors center** (☑530-667-8113; www.nps.gov/labe; Tulelake; ⊙8am-6pm late May-early Sep, to 5pm mid-Sep–mid-May) has free maps, activity books for kids, and information about the monument and its volcanic features and history.

From the visitors center rangers loan mediocre flashlights (and rent helmets and kneepads in the summer season only) for cave exploration and lead summer interpretive programs, including campfire talks and guided cave walks. To explore the caves it's essential you use a high-powered flashlight, wear good shoes and long sleeves (lava is sharp), and do not go alone.

Near the visitors center, a short, one-way **Cave Loop** drive provides access to many lava-tube caves. **Mushpot Cave**, the one nearest the visitors center, has lighting and information signs and is beautiful, besides being a good introductory hike. There are a number of caves that are a bit more challenging, including Labyrinth, Hercules Leg, Golden Dome and Blue Grotto. Each one of these caves has an interesting history – visitors used to ice skate by lantern light in the bottom of Merrill Cave, and when Ovls Cave was discovered, it was littered with bighorn sheep skulls. There are good brochures with details about each cave available from the visitors center. We found Sunshine Cave and Symbol Bridge Cave (the latter is reached via an easy 0.8-mile hike) to be particularly interesting. Rangers are stern with their warnings for new cavers, though, so be sure to check in with the visitors center before exploring to avoid harming the fragile geological and biological resources in the park.

The tall black cone of **Schonchin Butte** (5253ft) has a magnificent outlook accessed via a steep 1-mile hiking trail. Once you reach the top, you can visit the fire-lookout staff between June and September. **Mammoth Crater** is the source of most of the area's lava flows.

The weathered Modoc **petroglyphs** at the base of a high cliff at the far northeastern end of the monument, called Petroglyph Point, are thousands of years old, but unfortunately the cliffside is now sheltered behind a cyclone fence because of vandalism. There's also a short trail at the top of the hill that offers amazing views over the plains and Lower Klamath Lake. At the visitors center, be sure to take the leaflet explaining the origin of the petroglyphs and their probable meaning. Look for the hundreds of nests in holes high up in the cliff face, which provide shelter for birds that sojourn at the wildlife refuges nearby.

Also at the north end of the monument, be sure to go to the labyrinthine landscape of **Captain Jack's Stronghold**, the Modoc Indians' very effective ancient wartime defense area. A brochure will guide you through the breathtaking Stronghold Trail.

Forty-three first-come first-served sites are available at **Indian Well Campground** (www.nps.gov/labe/planyourvisit/campgrounds. htm; tent & RV sites $10; ⊗) 0.5 miles from

the Lava Beds National Monument Visitors Center. Each has a picnic table and a fire ring and there are communal flush toilets and sinks. It's legal to collect dead wood for fires in the nearby Modoc National Forest.

Klamath Basin National Wildlife Refuges

Of the six stunning national wildlife refuges in this group, Tule Lake and Clear Lake refuges are wholly within California, Lower Klamath refuge straddles the California–Oregon border, and the Upper Klamath, Klamath Marsh and Bear Valley refuges are across the border in Oregon. Bear Valley and Clear Lake (not to be confused with the Clear Lake just east of Ukiah) are closed to the public to protect their delicate habitats, but the rest are open during daylight hours.

These refuges provide habitats for a stunning array of birds migrating along the Pacific Flyway. Some stop over only briefly; others stay longer to mate, make nests and raise their young. The refuges are always packed with birds, but during the spring and fall migrations, populations can rise into the hundreds of thousands.

The **Klamath Basin National Wildlife Refuge Complex Visitor Center** (⬚530-667-2231; www.klamathbasinrefuges.fws.gov; 4009 Hill Rd, Tulelake; ⊗8am-4:30pm Mon-Fri, 9am-4pm Sat & Sun) sits on the west side of the Tule Lake refuge, about 5 miles west of Hwy 139, near the town of Tule Lake. Follow the signs from Hwy 139 or from Lava Beds National Monument. The center has an interesting video program, as well as maps, information on recent bird sightings and updates on road conditions. It rents photo blinds. Be sure to pick up the excellent, free *Klamath Basin Birding* Trail brochure for detailed lookouts, maps, color photos and a species checklist.

The spring migration peaks during March, and in some years more than a million birds fill the skies. In April and May the songbirds, waterfowl and shorebirds arrive, some to stay and nest, others to build up their energy before they continue north. In summer ducks, Canada geese and many other water birds are raised here. The fall migration peaks in early November. In and around February, the area hosts the largest wintering concentration of bald eagles in the lower 48 states, with 1000 in residence. The eagles prey on migrating geese, and yes, seeing an eagle catch and eat a goose is very dramatic. The Tule Lake and Lower Klamath refuges are by far the best places to see eagles and other raptors.

The Lower Klamath and Tule Lake refuges attract the largest numbers of birds year-round, and **auto trails** (driving routes) have been set up; a free pamphlet from the visitor center shows the routes. Self-guided canoe trails have been established in three of the refuges. Those in the Tule Lake and Klamath Marsh refuges are usually open from July 1 to September 30; no canoe rentals are available. Canoe trails in the Upper Klamath refuge are open year-round. Here, canoes can be rented at **Rocky Point Resort** (☑541-356-2287; 28121 Rocky Point Rd, Klamath Falls, OR; canoe & kayak rental per hour/half-day/day $20/45/60; ☺Apr-Oct; ♿☀), on the west side of Upper Klamath Lake.

Camp at nearby Lava Beds National Monument. Alternatively, a couple of RV parks and budget motels cluster along Hwy 139 near the tiny town of Tulelake (4035ft), including the friendly **Ellis Motel** (☑530-667-5242; 2238 Hwy 139; d with/without kitchen $95/75; ☎) and **Fe's B&B** (☑877-478-0184; www.fesbandb.com; 660 Main St; s/d without bath $70/80; ☎). **Wild Goose Lodge** (☑541-331-2701; www.wildgoosemotel.com; 105 E Court Dr, Merrill, OR; RV sites/r/cabins $30/57/115, ♿☀☎) – a good-value, locally owned motel with country charm – is the best option near Lava Beds National Monument outside of Klamath Falls. Klamath Falls, OR, 29 miles from Tulelake, is the closest real town, and there are lots of lodging options there.

Modoc National Forest

This enormous national forest (www.fs.usda.gov/modoc) covers almost two million spectacular, remote acres of California's northeastern corner. Fourteen miles south of Lava Beds National Monument, on the western edge of the forest, **Medicine Lake** is a stunning crater lake in a caldera (collapsed volcano), surrounded by pine forest, volcanic formations and campgrounds. The enormous volcano that formed the lake is the largest in area in California. When it erupted it ejected pumice followed by flows of obsidian, as can be seen at **Little Glass Mountain**, east of the lake.

Pick up the *Medicine Lake Highlands: Self-Guided Roadside Geology Tour* pamphlet from the McCloud ranger district

office to find and learn about the glass flows, pumice deposits, lava tubes and cinder cones throughout the area. Roads are closed by snow from around mid-November to mid-June, but the area is still popular for winter sports, and accessible by cross-country skiing and snowshoeing.

Congratulations are in order for travelers who make it all the way to the **Warner Mountains**. This spur of the Cascade Range in the east of the Modoc National Forest is probably the least visited range in California. With extremely changeable weather, it's also not so hospitable; there have been snowstorms here in every season of the year. The range divides into the North Warners and South Warners at **Cedar Pass** (elevation 6305ft), east of Alturas. Remote **Cedar Pass Snow Park** (☑530-233-3323; www.facebook.com/NCCPSP/; all-day pass $20; ☺10am-4pm Sat, Sun & holidays during ski season) offers downhill and cross-country skiing. The majestic **South Warner Wilderness** contains 77 miles of hiking and riding trails. The best time to use them is from July to mid-October.

Maps, campfire permits and information are all available at the **Modoc National Forest supervisor's headquarters** (☑530-233-5811; 800 W 12th St; ☺8am-5pm Mon-Fri) in Alturas.

If you are heading east into Nevada from the forest, you'll pass through **Alturas**, the pancake-flat, eerily quiet seat of Modoc County. The town was founded by the Dorris family in 1874 as a supply point for travelers, and it serves the same function today, providing basic services, motels and family-style restaurants.

WEST OF I-5

The wilderness west of I-5 is right in the sweet spot: here are some of the most rugged towns and seductive wilderness areas in the entire state of California – just difficult enough to reach to discourage big crowds. The Trinity Scenic Byway (Hwy 299) winds spectacularly along the Trinity River and beneath towering cliffs as it makes its way from the plains of Redding to the coastal redwood forests around Arcata. It provides a chance to cut through some of the northern mountains' most pristine wilderness and passes through the vibrant gold rush town of Weaverville.

Heavenly Hwy 3 (a highly recommended – although slower and windier – alternative route to I-5) heads north from Weaverville. This mountain byway transports you through the Trinity Alps – a stunning granite range dotted with azure alpine lakes – past the shores of Lewiston and Trinity Lakes, over the Scott Mountains and finally into emerald, mountain-rimmed Scott Valley. Rough-and-ready Yreka awaits you at the end of the line.

Weaverville

In 1941 a journalist asked James Hilton, the British author of Lost Horizon: 'In all your wanderings, what's the closest you've found to a real-life Shangri-La?' Hilton's response? 'A little town in northern California. A little town called Weaverville.'

Cute as a button, Weaverville's streets are lined with flower boxes in the summer and banks of snow in the winter. The seat of Trinity County, it sits amid an endless tract of mountain and forest. At almost 3300 sq miles, the county is roughly the size of Delaware plus Rhode Island, yet has a population of only 13,500 and not one freeway.

This gem of a town is on the National Register of Historic Places and has a laid-back, bohemian feel (thanks in part to the back-to-landers and marijuana-growing subculture). You can spend the day here strolling around the quaint storefronts and visiting art galleries or hit the great outdoors.

◉ Sights & Activities

There are 40 miles of hiking and mountain-biking trails in the Weaverville Basin Trail System, or you can cast a line along the Trinity River, Trinity Lake or Lewiston Lake for steelhead, salmon and trout.

★ Weaverville Joss House
State Historic Park
HISTORIC BUILDING

(☑530-623-5284; www.parks.ca.gov; 630 Main St; tour adult/child $4/2; ☉tours hourly 10am-4pm Thu-Sun; ℙ) The walls here actually talk – they're papered inside with 150-year-old donation ledgers from the once-thriving Chinese community, the immigrants who built Northern California's infrastructure, a rich culture that has all but disappeared. It's a surprise that the oldest continuously used Chinese temple in California (and an exceptionally beautiful one at that), dating from 1874, is in Weaverville.

The blue-and-gold Taoist shrine contains an ornate altar, more than 3000 years old, which was brought here from China. The adjoining schoolhouse was the first to teach Chinese students in California. It's rare to see a Chinese temple with all of the ancient features so well preserved.

Alpen Cellars
WINERY

(☑530-266-9513; www.alpencellars.com; East Fork Rd, Trinity Center; ☉10am-4pm summer, by appointment Oct-May) Jaunt over to little-known, utterly picturesque Alpen Cellars. Specializing in Riesling, Gewürztraminer, Chardonnay and Pinot Noir, the vineyard is open for tours, tastings and picnicking on idyllic riverside grounds.

To get there from Weaverville, take Hwy 3 for about 35 miles to the north end of Trinity Lake (5 miles past Trinity Center), then turn right on East Side Rd; 8 miles further, head left on East Fork Rd and continue for 2 miles.

JJ Jackson Memorial Museum & Trinity
County Historical Park
MUSEUM

(www.trinitymuseum.org; 508 Main St; donation requested; ☉10am-5pm daily May-Oct, noon-4pm daily Apr & Nov-Dec 24, noon-4pm Tue & Sat Dec 26-Mar) Next door to the Joss House you'll find gold-mining and cultural exhibits, plus vintage machinery, memorabilia, an old miner's cabin and a blacksmith shop.

Highland Art Center
GALLERY

(www.highlandartcenter.org; 691 Main St; ☉10am-5pm Mon-Sat, 11am-4pm Sun) Stroll through this large central gallery showcasing local artists.

Coffee Creek Ranch
FISHING, HIKING

(☑530-266-3343; www.coffeecreekranch.com; 4310 Coffee Creek Rd, Coffee Creek; all-inclusive per-person rates per day from $329; ➢) In Trinity Center, these guys run a dude ranch and lead fishing and fully outfitted pack trips into the Trinity Alps Wilderness.

⊨ Sleeping

There are a few basic motels at the edge of town in addition to the inn and hotel. The ranger station (p363) has information on many USFS campgrounds in the area, especially around Trinity Lake. Commercial RV parks, some with tent sites, dot Hwy 299.

Red Hill Motel & Cabins
MOTEL $

(☑530-623-4331; www.redhillresorts.com; 116 Red Hill Rd; d $52, cabins with/without kitchen $68/56;

🛜🖥) This very quiet and rustic motel is tucked under ponderosa pines at the west end of town, just off Main St, next to the library. It's a set of red wooden cabins built in the 1940s and they're equipped with kitchenettes and minifridges. The rooms are simple and good value. It sometimes fills with visiting groups, so book ahead.

Whitmore Inn   HISTORIC HOTEL $$
(📞530-623-2509; www.whitmoreinn.com; 761 Main St; r $100-165; ❄🛜) Settle into plush, cozy rooms in this downtown Victorian with a wraparound deck and abundant gardens. One room is accessible for travelers with disabilities. Only kids over five years old are welcome.

Weaverville Hotel   HISTORIC HOTEL $$
(📞800-750-8957, 530-623-2222; www.weaverville hotel.com; 481 Main St; r $110-390; 🅿♿❄🛜) Play like you're in the Old West at this upscale hotel and historic landmark, refurbished in grand Victorian style. It's luxurious but not stuffy, and the very gracious owners take great care in looking after you. Guests may use the local gym, and a $10 credit at local restaurants is included in the rates. Kids under 12 years are not allowed.

🍴 Eating

Downtown Weaverville caters to all, from hungry hikers to foodies. There's also a fantastic **farmers market** (www.weaverville tailgate.org; 691 Main St; ⊘4-7pm Wed May-Oct), which takes over Main St in the warmer months. In winter the tourist season dries up and opening hours can be hit or miss.

Trinideli   DELI $
(📞530-623-5856; www.trinideli.com; 201 Trinity Lakes Blvd; sandwiches $6-10; ⊘6:30am-4pm Mon-Fri, 10am-3pm Sat; 🖐) Cheerful staff prepare decadent sandwiches stuffed with fresh goodness. The 1.5lb 'Trinideli' with four types of meat and three types of cheese will fill the ravenous, while simple turkey and ham standards explode with fresh veggies and tons of flavor. Breakfast burritos are perfect for a quick prehike fill up.

Mountain Marketplace   MARKET $
(📞530-623-2656; 222 S Main St; ⊘9am-6pm Mon-Fri, 10am-5pm Sat; 🖐) Stock up on natural foods or hit its juice bar and vegetarian deli.

★ Cafe at Indian Creek   CALIFORNIAN $$
(📞530-623-1951; www.thecafeatindiancreek.com; 59741 Highway 299 W, Douglas City; mains $14-28; ⊘5-9pm Tue-Sun) About 8 miles south of Weaverville, this unlikely spot in a roadside lodge serves up the area's finest meals. Try anything with elk, the gnocchi is superb and there's a wine list to match. It also serves a much-lauded brunch on summer weekends.

La Grange Cafe   CALIFORNIAN $$
(📞530-623-5325; 520 Main St; mains $15-28; ⊘11am-9pm Tue-Sat) For years this has been Weaverville's more upscale offering, specializing in American favorites from burgers and steaks to ribs and grilled salmon. It's a homey, friendly place that's gone through management changes in the past few years and is still finding its new feet. You may not eat your most memorable meal here but expect it to be plenty tasty.

🍸 Drinking & Entertainment

Mamma Llama   CAFE
(www.mammallama.com; 490 Main St; breakfasts & sandwiches $3.50-8; ⊘6am-6pm Mon-Fri, 7am-6pm Sat, 7am-3pm Sun; 🛜) A local institution, this coffeehouse is a roomy and relaxed chill spot. The espresso is well made, there's a selection of comic books and CDs, and there are couches for lounging. The small menu does breakfasts, wraps and sandwiches, and there's microbrew beer available by the bottle. Live folk music (often including a hand drum) takes over occasionally.

Red House   CAFE
(📞530-623-1635; 218 S Miner St; ⊘6:30am-5:30pm Mon-Fri, 7:30am-1pm Sat) 🥗 This airy, light and bamboo-bedecked spot serves a wide selection of teas, light snacks (soups from $3) and organic, fair-trade, shade-grown coffee. The daily food specials include a delicious chicken-and-rice soup on Mondays. If you're in a hurry (rare in Weaverville), there's a drive-through window.

Trinity Theatre   CINEMA
(www.trinitytheatre.us; 310 Main St; adult/child $8.50/7) This newly renovated and inviting theater plays first-run movies.

ℹ Information

Trinity County Chamber of Commerce
(📞530-623-6101; www.trinitycounty.com; 215 Main St; ⊘10am-4pm) Knowledgeable, friendly staff with lots of useful information.
Weaverville Ranger Station (📞530-623-2121; www.fs.usda.gov/stnf; 360 Main St; ⊘8am-4:30pm Mon-Fri) A homey little office with maps, information and permits for all lakes,

national forests and wilderness areas in and near Trinity County.

ℹ️ Getting There & Away

A local **Trinity Transit** (☎ 530-623-5438; www.trinitytransit.org; fares from $1) bus makes a Weaverville–Lewiston loop via Hwy 299 and Hwy 3 from Monday to Friday. Another one runs between Weaverville and Hayfork, a small town about 30 miles to the southwest on Hwy 3.

Lewiston Lake

Adorable Lewiston is little more than a collection of rickety historic buildings beside a crossroad, 26 miles west of Redding. It's right beside the Trinity River, and the locals here are in tune with the environment – they know fishing spots on the rivers and lakes, where to hike and how to get around.

The lake is about 1.5 miles north of town and is a serene alternative to the other area lakes because of its 10mph boat speed limit. Migrating bird species sojourn here – early in the evening you may see ospreys and bald eagles diving for fish. The **Trinity River Fish Hatchery** (☎ 530-778-3931; www.wildlife.ca.gov/Fishing/Hatcheries/Trinity-River; 1000 Hatchery Rd; ⊙ 7am-3pm) FREE traps juvenile salmon and steelhead and holds them until they are ready to be released into the river. The only marina on the lake, **Pine Cove Marina** (www.pine-cove-marina.com; 9435 Trinity Dam Blvd), has free information about the lake and its wildlife, boat and canoe rentals, potluck dinners and guided off-road tours.

🛏️ Sleeping & Eating

Several commercial campgrounds dot the rim of the lake. For information on USFS campgrounds, contact the ranger station in Weaverville. Two of these campgrounds are on the lake: the wooded **Mary Smith** (☎ 877-444-6777; www.fs.usda.gov/recarea/stnf/recarea/?recid=6489; tent sites $11; ⊙ May-Sep), which is more private; and the sunny **Ackerman** (☎ 877-444-6777; www.fs.usda.gov; tent sites $13), which has more grassy space for families. If there's no host, both have self-registration options. There are also all kinds of RV parks, cabins for rent and motels in Lewiston.

⭐ **Lewiston Hotel**   HISTORIC HOTEL $
(☎ 530-778-3823; www.lewistonhotel.biz; 125 Deadwood Rd; r without bath $65; 🅿️ ❄️ 🛜) This 1862 rambling, ramshackle hotel has small,

rustic rooms with quilts, historic photos and river views – all have tons of character but none have attached bathrooms. Ask (or don't ask) for the room haunted by George. Explore the building to find giant stuffed moose heads, old girly calendars, rusty saws and so much more.

On-site are a friendly locals' bar, a dance-hall and a restaurant (with sporadic opening hours, especially in winter) that specializes in prime rib. Call to book a room.

Old Lewiston Bridge RV Resort   CAMPGROUND $
(☎ 530-778-3894; www.lewistonbridgerv.com; 8460 Rush Creek Rd, at Turnpike Rd; tent/RV sites $15/30, trailers $65; 🐕) A pleasant place to park the RV, with campsites beside the river bridge. It also rents travel trailers that sleep four people (bed linens not included).

Lakeview Terrace Resort   CABIN, CAMPGROUND $
(☎ 530-778-3803; www.lakeviewterraceresort.com; 9001 Trinity Dam Rd; RV sites $32, cabins $85-165; ❄️ 🛜 🐕 🏊) Five miles north of Lewiston, this is a woodsy Club Med, and rents boats.

Old Lewiston Inn B&B   B&B $$
(☎ 530-778-3385; www.theoldlewistoninn.com; 71 Deadwood Rd; r $125; ❄️ 🛜 🐕) The prettiest place in town and right beside the river, this B&B is in an 1875 house and serves country-style breakfasts. Enjoy the hot tub, or ask about all-inclusive fly-fishing packages. There's one two-bedroom suite, which is great for families.

🛍️ Shopping

Country Peddler   ANTIQUES
(4 Deadwood Rd; ⊙ hours vary) Impossible to miss, this funky old barn welcomes you with rusty vintage gas pumps (no gas) and beckons you inside for a simply wondrous collections of junk and treasures.

Trinity Lake

Placid Trinity Lake, California's third-largest reservoir, sits beneath dramatic snowcapped alps north of Lewiston Lake. In the off season it is serenely quiet, but it attracts multitudes in the summer, who come for swimming, fishing and other water sports. Most of the campgrounds, RV parks, motels, boat rentals and restaurants line the west side of the lake.

Spreading over 22 acres on the shores of Trinity Lake, **Pinewood Cove Resort**

(☑530-286-2201; www.pinewoodcove.com; 45110 Hwy 3; tent/RV sites $29/46, cabins $98-158; ⊙May 1-Oct 1; ❀) offers quality camping, cabins and marina facilities.

Klamath & Siskiyou Mountains

A dense conglomeration of rugged coastal mountains gives this region the nickname 'the Klamath Knot.' Coastal, temperate rainforest gives way to moist inland forest, creating an immense diversity of habitats for many species, some found nowhere else in the world. Around 3500 native plants live here. Local fauna includes the northern spotted owl, the bald eagle, the tailed frog, several species of Pacific salmon and carnivores like the wolverine and the mountain lion. One theory for the extraordinary biodiversity of this area is that it escaped extensive glaciation during recent ice ages. This may have given species refuge and longer stretches of relatively favorable conditions during which to adapt.

The region also includes the largest concentration of wild and scenic rivers in the US: the Salmon, Smith, Trinity, Eel and Klamath, to name a few. The fall color change is magnificent.

Five main wilderness areas dot the Klamath Knot. The **Marble Mountain Wilderness** in the north is marked by high rugged mountains, valleys and lakes, all sprinkled with colorful geological formations of marble and granite, and a huge array of flora. The **Russian Wilderness** is 8000 acres of high peaks and isolated, beautiful mountain lakes. The **Trinity Alps Wilderness**, west of Hwy 3, is one of the area's most lovely regions for hiking and backcountry camping, and has more than 600 miles of trails that cross passes over its granite peaks and head along its deep alpine lakes. The **Yolla Bolly-Middle Eel Wilderness** in the south is less visited, despite its proximity to the Bay Area, and so affords spectacular, secluded backcountry experiences. The **Siskiyou Wilderness**, closest to the coast, rises to heights of 7300ft, from where you can see the ocean. An extensive trail system crisscrosses the wilderness, but it is difficult to make loops.

The **Trinity Scenic Byway** (Hwy 299) follows the rushing **Trinity River** to the Pacific coast and is dotted with lodges, RV parks and blink-and-you'll-miss-'em burgs.

There's river rafting at Willow Creek, 55 miles west of Weaverville. **Bigfoot Rafting Company** (☑530-629-2263; www.bigfootrafting.com; 31221 State Hwy 299, Junction City; half-/full-day trips per person $69/89) leads guided trips and also rents rafts and kayaks (from $69 per day).

Scott Valley

North of Trinity Lake, Hwy 3 climbs along the gorgeous eastern flank of the Trinity Alps Wilderness to Scott Mountain Summit (5401ft) and then drops gracefully down into verdant Scott Valley, a bucolic agricultural area nestled between towering mountains. There are good opportunities for hiking, cycling and mountain biking, or taking horse trips to mountain lakes. For a bit of history, pick up the *Trinity Heritage Scenic Byway* brochure from the Weaverville ranger station (p363) before taking this world-class drive.

Etna (population 711), toward the north end of the valley, is known by its residents as 'California's Last Great Place,' and they might be right. Folks are uncommonly friendly, birdsong is more prevalent than road noise and if you're in town in summer and see lots of dirty people with backpacks, these are hard-core hikers taking a break from the nearby **Pacific Crest Trail** – Etna is a favorite pit stop.

Beyond Etna, **Fort Jones** (population 839) is just 18 miles from Yreka. The **visitors center** (☑530-468-5442; 11943 Main St; ⊙10am-5pm Tue-Sat, noon-4pm Sun) sits at the back of the Guild Shop mercantile. Down the street, a small **museum** (☑530-468-2444; www.fortjonesmuseum.com; 11913 Main St; donation requested; ⊙10am-4pm Mon-Fri, 11am-3pm Sat Memorial Day-Labor Day) houses Native American artifacts.

There are a few places to stay in the valley, from family-run motels to bucolic B&Bs. The clean, family-run **Motel Etna** (☑530-467-5338; www.theetnahotel.com; 317 Collier Way; s/d/tw $64/74/84; ❀ 🛜), on the outskirts of town, is a favorite with Pacific Crest Trail hikers and a good choice for anyone on a budget. The storybook-perfect 1877 mansion **Alderbrook Manor B&B** (☑530-467-3917; www.alderbrookmanor.com; 836 Sawyers Bar Rd; r $135, without bathroom $120, dm $35; 🛜❀) has a handful of pretty and bright antique-decorated rooms and a hikers' hut with dorm beds.

People talk about the **Etna Brewing Company** (www.etnabrew.com; 131 Callahan St; brewery tours free; ☺noon-8pm Wed-Sat) from Redding to Yreka. Don't miss a stop for a meal and one of its beers on tap if you're in Etna.

Yreka

Inland California's northernmost town, Yreka (wy-*ree*-kah) was once a booming gold rush settlement and has the gorgeous turn-of-the-century architecture to prove it. Most travelers only pass through en route to Oregon, but the new-age-tinged yet authentically Wild West–feeling historic downtown makes a good spot to stretch, eat and refuel before heading out into the hinterlands of the Scott Valley or the northeastern California wilderness.

◉ Sights & Activities

Siskiyou County Museum MUSEUM
(☑530-572-1099; www.siskiyoucountyhistorical society.org; 910 S Main St; adult/child $3/1; ☺9am-3pm Tue-Sat) Several blocks south of Yreka's downtown grid, this exceptionally well-curated museum brings together pioneer and Native American history. The native basketry collection is particularly impressive. An outdoor section contains historic buildings brought from around the county.

**Siskiyou County
Courthouse** HISTORIC BUILDING
(☑530-842-0199; www.siskiyou.courts.ca.gov; 311 4th St; ☺8am-noon & 1-4pm Mon-Fri) This hulking downtown building was built in 1857 and has a collection of gold nuggets, flakes and dust in the foyer.

Yreka Creek Greenway WALKING, CYCLING
(www.yrekagreenway.org) Behind the museum, the Yreka Creek Greenway has walking and cycling paths winding through the trees.

⌖ Sleeping & Eating

Motels, motels and more motels: budget travelers can do lots of comparison shopping along Yreka's Main St for mid-century motels galore. Klamath National Forest runs several campgrounds; the supervisor's office (p366) has information. RV parks cluster on the edge of town.

Klamath Motor Lodge MOTEL $
(☑530-842-2751; www.klamathmotorlodge.net; 1111 S Main St; s/d from $51/60; ☏☒) Folks at

this motel are especially friendly, the rooms are clean and – bonus for those headed in from the wilderness – it has an on-site laundry. Of all the motels in Yreka, this is tops. Book by phone for better rates than you'll find online.

Nature's Kitchen HEALTH FOOD, BAKERY $
(☑530-842-1136; 412 S Main St; dishes $8-14; ☺8am-5pm Mon-Sat; ☏) Friendly and quirky natural-foods store and bakery, serving healthy and tasty vegetarian and nonvegetarian dishes, fresh juices and good espresso. The adjoining store has all kinds of fairies, crazy socks, herbal supplements and new-agey trinkets.

Klander's Deli DELI $
(☑530-842-3806; 211 S Oregon St; sandwiches $6-9; ☺9am-3pm Mon-Fri) Local to the core, this deli's long list of yummy sandwiches is named after regulars. Bob is a favorite, named for the first owner and stacked with ham, turkey, roast beef and Swiss cheese.

▼ Drinking & Nightlife

Etna Brewery & Taphouse BREWERY
(☑530-841-0370; www.etnabrew.com; 231 W Miner St; mains $9-12; ☺11am-9pm Tue-Sat) Serving delicious Etna brews on tap, come here for the beer more than the ambience or food (mostly burgers).

❶ Information

Klamath National Forest Supervisor's Office
(☑530-842-6131; www.fs.usda.gov/klamath; 1711 S Main St; ☺8am-4:30pm Mon-Fri) Has the lowdown on recreation and camping.

Yreka Chamber of Commerce (☑530-842-1649; www.yrekachamber.com; 117 W Miner St; ☺9am-5pm, with seasonal variations; ☏) Has information about Yreka and surrounding areas.

❶ Getting There & Away

STAGE buses (☑530-842-8295; www.co.siskiyou.ca.us; fares $1.75-6) run throughout the region from a few different stops in Yreka. There are several daily services on weekdays along the I-5 corridor to Weed, Mt Shasta, McCloud and Dunsmuir. Other buses depart daily for Fort Jones (25 minutes), Greenview (35 minutes) and Etna (45 minutes) in the Scott Valley. On Monday and Friday only, buses go out to Klamath River (40 minutes) and Happy Camp (two hours).

Sacramento & Central Valley

Why Go?

The Central Valley is visible from space – a vast expanse of green between the Sierra Nevada and Pacific Ocean. The area is divided in two parts: the Sacramento Valley in the north and the San Joaquin Valley in the south. For millennia, the rivers cutting through these valleys flooded seasonally, creating extremely fertile soil. Today, those waterways are tamed by mighty public works projects that support massive agricultural endeavors. Half the produce in the US is grown in these valleys – including almost every almond, olive and bulb of garlic.

Like the birds that commute overhead, most travelers are just passing through – zipping along the highway to more popular parts of the state. But those who linger are rewarded with stately Victorian-era mansions, uniquely scenic byways and quirky small towns.

Best Places to Eat

➡ Empress Tavern (p375)

➡ Noriega's (p395)

➡ Towne House Restaurant (p386)

➡ Shubert's Ice Cream & Candy (p382)

Best Places to Sleep

➡ Padre Hotel (p394)

➡ Citizen Hotel (p373)

➡ Greens Hotel (p373)

When to Go

Sacramento

°C/°F **Temp**   **Rainfall** inches/mm

Feb–Mar Stop for pie and hot cider in the valley's technicolor Blossom Trail orchards.	**Nov–Feb** Catch the spectacular return of millions of migratory waterfowl in Sacramento.	**May–Sep** The peak of harvest time brings farmers markets and food festivals aplenty.

Sacramento & Central Valley Highlights

❶ Strolling between **breweries in Sacramento** (p375), the self-proclaimed mecca of beer.

❷ Driving bumper cars, eating fried Twinkies and checking out blue-ribbon livestock at the **California State Fair** (p372).

❸ Uncorking the region's emerging fine-wine scene in **Lodi** (p387).

❹ Tasting the valley's bounty in Sacramento's abundant **farmers markets** (p373).

❺ Sipping cold beer and listening to country music in **Buck Owens' Crystal Palace** (p395), Bakersfield.

❻ Rushing down world-class rapids on the mighty **Kern River** (p396).

SACRAMENTO VALLEY

The labyrinth of waterways making up the Sacramento–San Joaquin River Delta feeds San Francisco Bay and divides the Central Valley in half, with the Sacramento Valley in the north and the San Joaquin Valley in the south.

The Sacramento River, California's largest, rushes out of the northern mountains from Shasta Lake before hitting the Sacramento Valley basin above Red Bluff. It snakes south across grassy plains and orchards before skirting the state capital, fanning across the Delta and draining into San Francisco Bay. The valley is most beautiful in the bloom of spring. The shaded gardens and stately homes of Sacramento and its progressive neighbor, Davis, offer friendly respites from the blistering summer sun. If you're driving through the region on the way to one of California's marquee attractions, make time for a pit stop in Sacramento, which has a surprisingly vibrant food and beer scene.

Sacramento

Sacramento is a city of contrasts. It's a former cow town where state legislators' SUVs go bumper-to-bumper with farmers' muddy, half ton pickups at rush hour. It has sprawling suburbs, but also new lofts and upscale boutiques squeezed between aging mid-century storefronts.

The people of 'Sac' are a resourceful lot that have fostered small but thriving food, art and nightlife scenes. They rightfully crow about **Second Saturday**, the monthly Midtown gallery hop that is the symbol of the city's cultural awakening. Their ubiquitous farmers markets, farm-to-fork fare and craft beers are another point of pride.

History

The history of the state is contained in this city. Paleo-era peoples fished the rivers and thrived before colonists arrived. By the 1800s, the native communities were largely wiped out by colonizers. Control changed from Spanish to Mexican to American hands, when in 1847, a Swiss named John Sutter came seeking fortune. Recognizing the strategic importance of the major rivers, Sutter built an outpost and raised a militia. Soon the outpost became a safe haven for traders, and Sutter expanded his business operations in all directions.

It was at his lumber mill near Coloma that something glittered in the river in 1848. Eureka! Gold rushers stampeded to the trading post, which was eventually christened 'Sacramento.' Though plagued by fires and relentless flooding, the riverfront settlement prospered and became the state capital in 1850.

After the discovery of gold, a quarter of a million Chinese people arrived in California, often traveling through Sacramento. Although many were indentured servants who traded passage to the US in return for years of labor, they developed a thriving Chinatown and left an indelible mark on the region. These communities literally built the infrastructure of the city – as well as the levees and roads in the surrounding valley.

Chinese also built much of the Transcontinental Railroad, though you won't see any among the faces of the 'Big Four' – Leland Stanford, Mark Hopkins, Collis P Huntington and Charles Crocker. These wealthy men founded Central Pacific Railroad, which began construction here in 1863, and connected to the Union Pacific in Promontory, UT, in 1869.

◉ Sights

Sacramento is roughly halfway between San Francisco and Lake Tahoe. The city is boxed in by four main highways: Hwy 99, which is the best route through the Central Valley; I-5, which runs along its west side; I-80 skirts downtown on the city's northern edge, heading west to the Bay Area and east to Reno; and Hwy 50 runs along downtown's southern edge (where it's also called Business Route 80) before heading east to Tahoe.

In the middle is the Grid, where numbered streets run from north–south and lettered streets run east–west (Capitol Ave replaces M). One-way J St is a main drag east from Downtown to Midtown.

◉ The Grid

It's easy finding sights along the Grid, but everything is spread out.

★ **California Museum**　　　　MUSEUM
(Map p370; ☏ 916-653-0650; www.californiamuseum.org; 1020 O St; adult/child $9/6.50; ◷ 10am-5pm Tue-Sat, from noon Sun; ☞) This modern museum is home to the California Hall of Fame and so the only place to simultaneously encounter César Chávez, Mark Zuckerberg and Amelia Earhart. The *California Indians*

Downtown Sacramento

exhibit is a highlight, with artifacts and oral histories of more than 10 tribes.

★ **California State Capitol**   HISTORIC BUILDING
(Map p370; ☎916-324-0333; http://capitolmuseum.ca.gov; 1315 10th St; ⊗8am-5pm Mon-Fri, from 9am Sat & Sun; 🚹) **FREE** The gleaming dome of the California State Capitol is Sacramento's most recognizable structure. A painting of Arnold Schwarzenegger in a suit hangs in the West Wing along with the other governors' portraits. Some will find Capitol Park, the 40 acres of gardens and memorials surrounding the building more interesting than what's inside. Tours run hourly until 4pm.

**Sutter's Fort
State Historic Park**   HISTORIC SITE
(Map p370; www.suttersfort.org; 2701 L St; adult/child $5/3; ⊗10am-5pm) Originally built by John Sutter, this park was once the only trace of white settlement for hundreds of miles. Reserve a couple hours to stroll within its

walls, where furniture, medical equipment and a blacksmith shop are straight out of the 1850s.

State Indian Museum   MUSEUM
(Map p370; www.parks.ca.gov; 2618 K St; adult/child $5/3; ⊗10am-5pm) It's with some irony that the Indian Museum sits in the shadow of Sutter's Fort. The excellent exhibits and tribal handicrafts on display – including the intricately woven and feathered baskets of the Pomo – are traces of cultures nearly stamped out by the fervor Sutter ignited.

◉ Old Sacramento

This historic river port by Downtown remains the city's stalwart tourist draw. The aroma of saltwater taffy and restored buildings give Old Sac the vibe of a second-rate Frontierland, but it's good for a stroll on summer evenings, when boomers on Harleys rumble through the brick streets, and

Downtown Sacramento

tourists and natty legislative aides stroll the promenade. California's largest concentration of buildings on the National Register of Historic Places is here. Most now peddle Gold Rush trinkets and fudge. There are a few quality attractions, but the restaurant scene is a bust – head to Midtown. Right at the edge of Midtown is the gleaming new Golden 1 Center (p371), home to the Sacramento Kings.

★ **Golden 1 Center**   STADIUM
(Map p370; ☏916-701-5400; www.golden1center. com; 500 David J Stern Walk; 🚼) 🌿 Welcome to the arena of the future. This gleaming home to the Sacramento Kings is one of the most advanced sports facilities in the country. Made with the highest sustainability standard, it's built from local materials, powered by solar and cooled by five-story airplane hangar doors that swing open to capture the pleasant Delta breeze.

The building is also pushing the envelope of interactivity, with a free app that allows fans to monitor bathroom lines, order concessions (which follow a farm-to-fork philosophy, of course) and watch replays of the action on the court.

DON'T MISS

CALIFORNIA STATE FAIR

For two weeks in late July, the **California State Fair** (☑ 916-263-3247; www.castatefair.org/home; 1600 Exposition Blvd; adult/child $12/8; ☺ Jul; ⓘ) fills the Cal Expo, east of I-80 on the north side of the American River, with a small city of cows and carnival rides. It's likely the only place on earth where you can plant a redwood tree, watch a pig give birth, ride a roller coaster, catch some barrel racing and taste exquisite Napa vintages within one (exhausting) afternoon. Make time to see some of the auctions ($500 for a dozen eggs!) and the interactive agricultural exhibits run by the University of California Davis. Hotels near Cal Expo run regular shuttles to the event.

Crocker Art Museum   MUSEUM
(Map p370; ☑ 916-808-7000; https://crockerartmuseum.org; 216 O St; adult/child $10/5; ☺ 10am-5pm Tue, Wed & Fri-Sun, to 9pm Thu) Housed in the ornate Victorian mansion (and sprawling additions) of a railroad baron, this museum has striking architecture and an excellent collection. Works by California painters and European masters hang beside an enthusiastically curated collection of contemporary art.

California State Railroad Museum   MUSEUM
(Map p370; ☑ 916-323-9280; www.csrmf.org; 125 I St; adult/child $10/5, train ride $12/6; ☺ 10am-5pm; ⓟⓘ) Train buffs will delight in this incredible collection of vintage locomotives (even if history buffs will question the candy-coated presentation about the plight of workers who built the rails). You can also hop aboard a restored passenger train from the Sacramento Southern Railroad for a 45-minute jaunt along the river.

Weather permitting, train rides run hourly from 11am to 4pm on weekends from April to September and on select dates in October, November and December.

K Street Mall   PLAZA
(Map p370; www.kstreetmall.com) Known by locals as 'The Kay,' this formerly blighted neighborhood is undergoing a major redevelopment effort that has transformed it into a weekend hot spot. The pedestrian mall draws a party on weekends.

Sacramento History Museum   MUSEUM
(Map p370; www.historicoldsac.org/museum; 101 I St; adult/child $6/4, Underground Tour Mar-Dec $15/10; ☺ 10am-5pm; ⓘ) Exhibits, stories and artifacts of some of Sacramento's most fascinating citizens, though much of the information is focused on the Gold Rush. Get tickets here for the **Underground Tour**, a 45-minute look at what's under Old Sac's streets.

⊙ Tower District

South of Midtown, at the corner of Broadway and 16th St, the Tower District is dominated by Tower Theatre (p376), a beautiful 1938 art-deco movie palace that's easy to spot on the way into town. From the theater, head east on Broadway to a stretch of the city's most eclectic and affordable eateries. The **Tower Records** chain started here in 1960 and closed in 2006, a digital music casualty, but the original neon sign survives.

Activities

American River Parkway   OUTDOORS
(www.arpf.org; north bank of American River) The American River Parkway is a natural treasure. This massive urban park stretches along the north bank of the American River for over 20 miles, skirting one of the most extensive riparian habitats in the continental US.

The park's network of trails and picnic areas is easily accessed from Old Sacramento by taking Front St north until it becomes Jiboom St and crosses the river, or by taking the Jiboom St exit off I-5/Hwy 99.

The parkway includes a nice walking/running/bicycling path called the Jedediah Smith National Recreation Trail that's accessible from Old Sacramento at the end of J St. You can rent bicycles at the waterfront (per day $25).

City Bicycle Works   CYCLING
(Map p370; www.citybicycleworks.com; 2419 K St; per hour/day from $5/20; ☺ 10am-7pm Mon-Fri, to 6pm Sat, 11am-5pm Sun) The perfect spot to get a bike for cruising the amazing American River Parkway (p372) for a couple of hours. Road bikes and cruisers are in good condition and the staff is enthusiastic and helpful.

ⓒ Tours

Sacramento Beer Tour   BREWERY
(☑ 916-852-5466; www.sacramentobrewtour.com; 1751 Enterprise Blvd, West Sacramento) These

tours offer a fun, safe way to taste breweries around the city. Perfectly suited for larger groups, they offer a pick-up and drop-off service, and have great relationships with local beer makers. A three-brewery tour is led by a certified beer cicerone. It takes five hours and includes private tours, taster flights and local brews.

Sac Brew Bike
BREWERY
(Map p370; ☑916-952-7973; www.sacbrewbike.com; tours depart from 1519 19th St; 15-person tour from $350, individual pricing available) You can pedal your way between the city's best breweries on the multi-peddler 'Brew Bike.' You can join a mixed tour with random beer-and-bike loving strangers for about $20 per person, but tours are ideal for groups. The whole bike accommodates 15 people and two-hour tours start at $300. Rates increase on the weekends.

🎊 Festivals & Events

★ Second Saturday
CULTURAL
(www.2ndsaturdaysacramento.com) Look no further for evidence of Sacramento's cultural revival. Galleries and shops in Midtown draw crowds to the streets on the second Saturday of each month for open-air music, openings and cultural events.

Sacramento Central Farmers Market
FOOD & DRINK
(www.california-grown.com; cnr 8th & W St, under Hwy 80 overpass; ☉8am-noon Sun;) You're never far from a mind-blowing farmers market in Sacramento. They're hosted all year round and every day of the week in the summer and fall. Most will have food trucks and street performers.

Gold Rush Days
CULTURAL
(www.sacramentogoldrushdays.com; ☉Sep;) Old Sacramento comes alive in early September with horse races, historic costumes, music and kids' events. You can even pan for gold.

🛏 Sleeping

The capital is a magnet for business travelers, so Sacramento doesn't lack hotels. Many have good deals during legislative recesses. Unless you're in town for something at Cal Expo, stay Downtown or Midtown, where there's plenty to do within walking distance. If you're into kitschy motor lodges from the 1950s, cross the river into West Sac for the last-standing members of Motel Row on Rte 40.

HI Sacramento Hostel
HOSTEL $
(Map p370; ☑916-443-1691; http://norcalhostels.org/sac; 925 H St; dm $30-33, r from $86, without bath from $58; ☉reception 2-10:30pm;) In a grand Victorian mansion, this hostel offers impressive trimmings at rock-bottom prices. It's within walking distance of the capitol, Old Sac and the train station, and has a piano in the parlor and large dining room. It attracts an international crowd often open to sharing a ride to San Francisco or Lake Tahoe.

★ Citizen Hotel
BOUTIQUE HOTEL $$
(Map p370; ☑916-442-2700, 877-829-2429; www.thecitizenhotel.com; 926 J St; r from $180;) After an elegant, ultra-hip upgrade, this long-vacant 1927 beaux-arts tower became Downtown's coolest place to stay. The details are spot-on: luxe linens, wide-striped wallpaper and a roof-top patio with a great view of the city. There's an upscale farm-to-fork restaurant (Map p370; ☑916-492-4450; www.grangesacramento.com; mains $19-39; ☉6:30-10:30am, 11:30am-2pm & 5:30-10pm Mon-Thu, to 11pm Fri, 8am-2pm & 5:30-11pm Sat, to 10pm Sun;) on the ground floor.

Greens Hotel
BOUTIQUE HOTEL $$
(www.thegreenshotel.com; 1700 Del Paso Blvd.; r from $127;) This stylishly updated mid-century motel is one of Sacramento's hippest places to stay. Even though the neighborhood is a bit rough around the edges, the Greens' secure parking, pool and spacious grounds make it an ideal place for families to stop en route to or from Tahoe. The chic rooms are also classy enough for a romantic getaway.

Delta King
B&B $$
(Map p370; ☑800-825-5464, 916-444-5464; www.deltaking.com; 1000 Front St; d from $145;) It's a kitschy treat to sleep aboard the *Delta King*, a 1927 paddle wheeler docked on the river in Old Sacramento. It lights up like a Christmas tree at night.

Amber House
B&B $$
(Map p370; ☑800-755-6526, 916-444-8085; www.amberhouse.com; 1315 22nd St; r $199-279;) This Dutch Colonial home in Midtown has been transformed into a B&B, where rooms have Jacuzzis, fireplaces and lots of frill. The Mozart and Vivaldi rooms have private balconies perfect for enjoying breakfast.

DON'T MISS

THE GREAT MIGRATION

The Sacramento Valley serves as a rest stop for countless migrating species that arrive in such great numbers they are a spectacle even without binoculars.

October to February Four million waterbirds winter in the warm tules (marshes) on their way along the Great Pacific Flyway. Tours available at **Sacramento National Wildlife Refuge** (p380).

October to January Endangered chinook and steelhead fight their way upstream to spawn. Spot them along the **American River Parkway** (p372) and the **Nimbus Fish Hatchery** (☎916-358-2884; www.dfg.ca.gov; 2001 Nimbus Rd, Gold River; ◷9am-3pm) **FREE**.

March to June Cabbage white, painted lady and Western tiger swallowtail butterflies come to party. Their offspring will gorge and then grow wings to fly north. **Sacramento National Wildlife Refuge** (p380) has details.

June to August Hundreds of thousands of Mexican free-tailed bats shelter under the Yolo Causeway. Tours (www.yolobasin.org) catch them alighting at twilight.

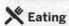 Eating

Skip the overpriced fare in Old Sacramento or by the capitol and head Midtown or to the Tower District. A cruise up J St or Broadway passes a number of hip, affordable restaurants where tables spill onto the sidewalks in the summer. Many source farm-fresh ingredients.

Shoki II Ramen House　　　　JAPANESE $
(Map p370; ☎916-441-0011; www.shokiramenhouse.com; 1201 R St; mains $8-16; ◷11am-10pm Mon-Fri, from noon Sat, 11am-8pm Sun) Like its tiny original location on 24th St, this cozy ramen house under the direction of Yasushi Ueyama makes amazing housemade noodles that live up to the motto of 'a bowl of dreams.' The fresh spinach, grass-fed beef and shiitake are organic and local.

Gunther's　　　　ICE CREAM $
(☎916-457-6646; www.gunthersicecream.com; 2801 Franklin Blvd; sundaes $4; ◷10am-10pm; ◉) Look for 'Jugglin Joe' – a cheerful, ice-cream-slinging neon giant – towering above this 1940s soda fountain. Gunther's makes its own ice cream and frozen novelties.

La Bonne Soupe Cafe　　　　DELI $
(Map p370; ☎916-492-9506; 920 8th St; items $5-8; ◷11am-3pm Mon-Sat) Divine soup and sandwiches assembled with such care that the line of Downtown lunchers snakes out the door. If you're in a hurry, skip it. This humble lunch counter is focused on quality that predates drive-through haste.

Andy Nguyen's　　　　VIETNAMESE, VEGETARIAN $
(Map p370; www.andynguyenvegetarian.com; 2007 Broadway; mains $9-15; ◷11:30am-9pm Sun-Thu,

to 9:30pm Fri & Sat; ◪) ◗ This tranquil vegetarian Buddhist diner serves steaming clay pots and curries. The Peaceful Existence Clay Pot – which includes a 'chicken' drumstick with a little wooden bone – lives up to its divine name.

Tank House BBQ and Bar　　　　BARBECUE $
(Map p370; www.tankhousebbq.com; 1925 J St; pork butt sando $10; ◷11:30am-2am Mon-Fri, from 11am Sat & Sun) The classy roadhouse vibe suits this historic railway stop, where you can get passable BBQ and soak in the mix of local characters, families and wayward tourists. Sidle up to the bar to order and start a tab. The smoker goes all day, so if you sit outside, position upwind.

Tower Cafe　　　　BREAKFAST $
(Map p370; ☎916-441-0222; www.towercafe.com; 1518 Broadway; mains $7-18; ◷8am-midnight Sun-Thu, to midnight Fri & Sat) Best bet for big ol' breakfasts – custardy French toast, chorizo sausage with eggs – at a 1938 art-deco movie theater.

Localis　　　　BRUNCH $$
(Map p370; ☎916-737-7699; www.localissacramento.com; 2031 S St.; ◷5-9pm Tue-Thu, to 10pm Fri & Sat, 10am-2pm Sun) The 'hyper-seasonal' menu includes the city's best fancy brunch (the lamb benedict is a decadent delight) and artfully prepared comfort food, all served in a sunny atrium.

Waterboy　　　　CALIFORNIAN $$
(Map p370; ☎916-498-9891; www.waterboy restaurant.com; 2000 Capitol Ave; mains $13-29; ◷11:30am-2:30pm Mon-Fri, 5-9:30pm Sun-Thu, to 10:30pm Fri & Sat) The wicker and palm in the windowed dining room offer a preview

of the chef's style – a French-Italian spin on Central Valley ingredients. The day's catch is always stellar.

Lucca   ITALIAN $$
(Map p370; www.luccarestaurant.com; 1615 J St; mains $13-20; ⊙11:30am-10pm Mon-Thu, to 11pm Fri, noon-11pm Sat, 4-9pm Sun) Within a stroll of the convention center is this quality Italian eatery. Parmesan frites with truffle aioli are the way to start.

★ Empress Tavern   NEW AMERICAN $$$
(Map p370; ☑916-662-7694; www.empresstavern. com; 1013 K St; mains $13-40; ⊙11:30am-9pm Mon-Thu, to 10pm Fri, 5-10pm Sat) In the catacombs under the historic Crest Theater, this gorgeous restaurant hosts a menu of creative, meat-focused dishes (including family-style options like the falling-off-the-bone lamb osso buco). The space itself is just as impressive as the food; the arched brick ceilings and glittering bar feel like a speakeasy supper club from a bygone era.

Kitchen Restaurant   CALIFORNIAN $$$
(☑916-568-7171; www.thekitchenrestaurant.com; 2225 Hurley Way; prix-fixe dinner $125; ⊙5-10pm Wed-Sun) Husband-and-wife team Randall Selland and Nancy Zimmer's cozy dining room in the northeast 'burbs is the pinnacle of Sacramento's food experience. Their demonstration dinners focus on — what else? — local, seasonal, organic food, immaculately prepared before your eyes. Reservations are essential.

Mulvaney's B&L   MODERN AMERICAN $$$
(Map p370; ☑916-441-6022; www.mulvaneysbl. com; 1215 19th St; dinner mains $33-45; ⊙11:30am-2:30pm & 5-10pm Tue-Fri, 5-10pm Sat) ✐ With effortless class and obsessive commitment to seasonality, this converted 19th-century firehouse offers delicate pastas (such as a fresh lamb tortellini) and grilled local meats on a menu that changes daily. As one of the area's farm-to-table pioneers, it's also deeply invested in community programs and sustainable food production.

🍷 Drinking & Nightlife

Sacramento has a split personality when it comes to drinking – upscale joints where hipster bartenders shake cocktails, and sans-bullshit dive bars with vintage neons and menus that begin and end with a-shot-ana-beer. Both options dot the Grid. If you're looking to party, head to the K Street Mall (p372), which has booming clubs and great restaurants.

Temple Coffee Roasters   COFFEE
(Map p370; www.templecoffee.com; 1010 9th St; ⊙6am-11pm; 🕏) ✐ Hip young patrons nurse organic free-trade coffee and chai morning to night in this steel and concrete space.

Mercantile Saloon   GAY
(Map p370; ☑916-447-0792; 1928 L St; ⊙10am-2am) Down an alley in a yellow Victorian, stiff drinks go for less than $5. Personal space is nil in this rowdy dive. Start here

---

SACTOWN BEER HEAVEN

In the past few years, Sacramento has developed one of California's best craft beer scenes. A number of excellent breweries is clustered on the Grid, and some of the most promising newer spots are just a bit further afield. If you want to taste all that Sacramento has to offer, sign up for one of the fun, safe guided trips from **Sacramento Beer Tour** (p372) or pedal your way from one brewery to the next on a 15-person human-powered contraption from **Sac Brew Bike** (p373). If you're going it alone, these are some of our favorites.

Fieldwork Brewing Company (Map p370; ☑916-329-8367; www.fieldworkbrewing.com; 1805 Capitol Ave; ⊙11am-9pm Sun-Thu, to 11pm Fri & Sat)

Big Stump Brew Company (Map p370; ☑916-668-7433; www.bigstumpbrewco.com; 1716 L St; ⊙3-10pm Mon-Wed, to 11pm Thu, noon-midnight Fri & Sat, noon-10pm Sun)

Rubicon Brewing Company (Map p370; www.rubiconbrewing.com; 2004 Capitol Ave; ⊙11am-11:30pm Mon-Thu, to 12:30am Fri & Sat, to 10pm Sun)

Sactown Union Brewery (☑916-917-5555; www.sactownunion.com; 1210 66th St; ⊙4-10pm Mon-Thu, 2-11pm Fri, noon-11pm Sat, to 8pm Sun)

Track 7 Brewing (www.track7brewing.com; 3747 W Pacific Ave, Suite F; ⊙3-9pm Mon-Thu, from noon Fri-Sun) before touring the four-block radius of gay bars and clubs that locals call 'Lavender Heights.'

58 Degrees and Holding Co WINE BAR
(Map p370; www.58degrees.com; 1217 18th St; ⊙11am-10pm Mon, Wed & Thu, to 11pm Fri & Sat, to 9pm Sun) A wide selection of California and European reds and a refined bistro menu make this a favorite for young professionals on the prowl.

Old Tavern Bar & Grill PUB
(Map p370; 1510 20th St; ⊙6pm-2am) This friendly dive stands out from Sac's many workaday joints with its huge beer selection, tall pours and 1980s-loaded jukebox.

☆ Entertainment

Pick up a copy of the free weekly *Sacramento News & Review* (www.newsandreview. com) for a list of current happenings around town.

Harlow's LIVE MUSIC
(Map p370; www.harlows.com; 2708 J St; ⊙7pm-midnight) Quality jazz, R&B and the occasional salsa or indie act in a classy joint. Just beware of the potent martinis.

California Musical Theatre PERFORMING ARTS
(Map p370; www.californiamusicaltheatre.com; 1419 H St) This top-notch company holds court at the Community Center Theater and the Wells Fargo Pavilion in town.

Crest Theatre CINEMA
(Map p370; www.thecrest.com; 1013 K St) A classic old movie house that's been restored to its 1949 splendor. Hosts indie and foreign films and the annual **Trash Film Orgy** (trashfilmorgy.com) on Saturdays in July and August.

Old Ironsides LIVE MUSIC
(Map p370; www.theoldironsides.com; 1901 10th St; cover $5-10; ⊙8am-2am Tue-Fri & Sun, from 6pm Sat) The tiny back room of this cool dive hosts some of the best indie bands that come through town.

Tower Theatre CINEMA
(Map p370; ☑916-442-4700; www.ReadingCinemas US.com; 2508 Landpark Dr) Classic, foreign and indie films screen at this historic movie house with a digital upgrade.

Sacramento River Cats BASEBALL
(Map p370; www.milb.com; Raley Field, 400 Ballpark Dr; tickets $8-60; ⊙Apr-Sep) Sacramento's

minor-league baseball team plays across the river at Raley Field, with views of the art-deco Tower Bridge.

ℹ Information

Convention & Visitors Bureau (Map p370; www.visitsacramento.com; 1608 I St; ⊙8am-5pm Mon-Fri) Local information, including event and bus schedules.

Sacramento Visitor Center (Map p370; ☑916-442-7644; www.visitsacramento.com; 1002 2nd St; ⊙10am-5pm) A great local resource that's well-equipped with information and suggestions for travelers.

ℹ Getting There & Away

At the intersection of major highways, you'll likely pass through Sacramento en route to other California destinations. The **Sacramento International Airport** (SMF; www.sacramento. aero/smf; 6900 Airport Blvd) is one of the nearest options for those traveling to Yosemite National Park.

Sacramento–San Joaquin River Delta

The Sacramento Delta is a sprawling web of waterways and one-stoplight towns plucked out of the 1930s. On weekends, locals gun powerboats on glassy waterways and cruise winding levy roads. This wetland area encompasses a huge swath of the state – from the San Francisco Bay to Sacramento, and all the way south to Stockton. Here the Sacramento and San Joaquin Rivers converge to drain into the San Francisco Bay. If you have the time to smell the grassy delta breezes on the slow route between San Francisco and Sacramento, travel the iron bridges of winding Hwy 160. You'll lazily make your way past rice fields, vast orchards, sandy swimming banks and little towns with long histories.

The region's best-known winery, **Bogle** (☑916-744-1092; www.boglewinery.com; 37783 Country Rd 144, Clarksburg; ⊙10am-5pm Mon-Fri, from 11am Sat & Sun; ℗) ✔ FREE, is a few miles southwest of Clarksburg via County Rds 141 and 144. It's set among vineyards on a sixth-generation family farm.

Old Sugar Mill (☑916-744-1615; www. oldsugarmill.com; 35265 Willow Ave, Clarksburg; ⊙11am-5pm; ℗ ♿) FREE is the hub of a thriving community of local winemakers. A jazz combo echoes through the space to complement wines of the Carvalho family, who own

THE DELTA DETOUR

Locke (☏916-776-1661; www.locketown.com; 13920 Main St, Walnut Grove; tours adult/student $5/3; ☺visitors center noon-4pm Tue & Fri, 11am-3pm Sat & Sun) is the most fascinating of the Sacramento Delta towns, founded by Chinese laborers who also built the levees that ended perpetual flooding and allowed agriculture to flourish here. After a malicious fire wiped out the settlement in 1912, a group of community leaders approached land baron George Locke for a leasehold; at the time, California didn't allow people of Chinese descent to own property. Locke became the only freestanding town built and managed by Chinese people in the US, most of whom spoke the Chungsan dialect of Cantonese. Tucked below the levee, Locke's main street feels like a ghost town these days, but the weather-beaten buildings are protected on the National Register of Historic Places.

The colorful **Dai Loy Museum** (☏916-776-1661; www.locke-foundation.org; 13951 Main St, Locke; donations appreciated; ☺noon-4pm Fri-Sun; ♿), housing dusty *pai gow* tables and an antique safe, is the main stop. Nearby is **Al's Place** (☏916-776-1800; 13943 Main St, Walnut Grove; mains $7-21; ☺11am-9pm), a saloon that's been pouring since 1915 and serves peanut-butter-slathered Texas toast. Below are creaking floorboards; above, the ceiling's covered in crusty dollar bills and more than one pair of erstwhile undies.

Hwy 160 also passes through Isleton, so-called Crawdad Town USA, whose main street has more shops, restaurants, bars and buildings that reflect the region's Chinese heritage. Isleton's Cajun Festival, at the end of June, draws folks from across the state, but you can get very lively crawdads year round at **Bob's Bait Shop** (☏916-777-6666; http://themasterbaiter.tripod.com; 302 2nd St, Isleton; ☺6am-noon Tue-Wed, to 5pm Thu-Sat, to 3pm Sun).

Further west on Hwy 160 you'll see signs for the Delta Loop, a drive that passes boater bars and marinas where you can rent something to take on the water. At the end is the **Brannan Island State Recreation Area** (☏916-777-6671; www.parks.ca.gov; 17645 Hwy 160, Rio Vista; per car $10; ☺sunrise-sunset; ♿), which has boat-in, drive-in and walk-in campsites.

In the 1930s the Bureau of Reclamation issued an aggressive water-redirection program – the Central Valley and California State Water Projects – that dammed California's major rivers and directed 75% of their supply through the Central Valley for agriculture and Southern California. The siphoning affected the delta, its wetlands and estuaries, and sparked debate. Learn about the area's unique legacy by bus or on a self-guided tour with **Delta Heartbeat Tours** (☏916-776-4010; www.deltaheartbeattours.com; Deckhands Marina, 14090 Hwy 160, Walnut Grove), which also has leads on boat rides. If you have a car, taste the fruits of the delta on the **Delta Grown Farm Trail** (☏916-775-1166; www.sacriverdeltagrown.org).

---

this custom crushing facility. The wines of the Clarksburg region have developed a lot over the last decade, benefiting from the blazing sun and cool delta breezes.

Brannan Island State Park Recreation Area Campgrounds (☏800-444-7275; www.reserveamerica.com; 17645 Hwy 160, Rio Vista; tent & RV sites $31-49, cabin $56; ♿) is a tidy facility in a protected wetland marsh that provides drive-in and walk-in campsites. There's a hike-in log cabin with electricity that sleeps four; bring sleeping bags.

In nearby Isleton, **Rogelio's** (☏916-777-5878; www.rogelios.net; 34 Main St, Isleton; mains $8-15; ☺4-8pm Wed & Thu, from noon Fri-Sun) makes the most of the delta's multiethnic history, serving a mash-up of Mexican and Chinese dishes, with a few Italian and American standards mixed in. But nothing beats the carnitas chow mein.

Davis

Bicycles whir through the streets of Davis, a vibrant oasis of culture, food and progressive politics. Much of the energy comes from the students who flock to the University of California, Davis (UCD), which boasts one of the nation's leading viticulture departments. Bikes outnumber cars two-to-one (it has more bikes per capita than any other American city) and students make up half the population. It's a fun and free-spirited place that makes an excellent pit stop when traveling in or out of the Bay Area.

Strolling the downtown grid, you'll pass family-operated businesses (city council has forbidden any store over 50,000 sq ft – sorry, Wal-Mart), public art projects and affordable international restaurants.

I-80 skirts the south edge of town, and you can reach downtown via the Richards Blvd exit. UCD is southwest of downtown, bordered by A St, 1st St and Russell Blvd.

◉ Sights & Activities

UC Davis Arboretum PARK
(http://arboretum.ucdavis.edu; 1 Shields Ave; 🚗) FREE With well-marked botanical collections, picnic grounds and family tours, the 100-acre 'Arb' is a treasure. Follow the peaceful 3.5-mile loop along one of the state's oldest reservoirs, dug in the 1860s.

Pence Gallery GALLERY
(www.pencegallery.org; 212 D St; ⊙11:30am-5pm Tue-Sun) This community gallery exhibits contemporary art and hosts classes, lectures and films. It offers a free reception 6pm to 9pm on the second Friday of each month.

Davis Transmedia Art Walk WALKING
(http://davisartwalk.com; 🚗) FREE This two-hour walking tour winds through Davis' public art collection, mostly clustered on D and G Sts. There's a free smartphone app with audio and interactive media. If you're low-tech, get a map at the Yolo County Visitors Bureau (p379) or **John Natsoulas Center for the Arts** (www.natsoulas.com; 521 1st St; ⊙11am-5pm Wed & Thu, to 9pm Fri, noon-5pm Sat & Sun) FREE.

🛏 Sleeping

Hotel rates are stable until graduation or special campus events, when they skyrocket and sell out fast. Worse, the trains that roll through the town will infuriate a light sleeper. For a utilitarian (if bland) stay, look for chains along the highway.

University Park Inn & Suites HOTEL $$
(☎844-277-4752; www.universityparkinn.com; 1111 Richards Blvd; r $149-200; 🅿 🌸 @ 🛜 🐕 🐾) Right off the highway, this independent hotel isn't the Ritz but it's clean, serves breakfast and offers free bikes for guests. Rates double in June.

Aggie Inn HOTEL $$
(☎530-756-0352; www.aggieinn.com; 245 1st St; r from $139; 🌸 🛜) Across from UCD's east entrance, the Aggie is neat, modern and unassuming. Cottages are not much more than regular rooms with kitchenettes and Jacuzzis.

Eating

College students love to eat and drink cheaply, and downtown has no short supply of lively spots for a quick plate of Pad Thai or slice of pizza. The Davis farmers market (p378) is incredible, and features food vendors, picnic supplies and buskers. More excellent self-catering options can be found at the **Davis Food Co-op** (http://davisfood.coop; 620 G St; ⊙7am-10pm).

★Davis Farmers Market MARKET $
(www.davisfarmersmarket.org; cnr 4th & C Sts; ⊙8am-1pm Sat year-round, 4:30-8:30pm Wed Mar-Oct.) With more than 150 vendors and an awe-inspiring selection of local produce, meat, flowers and baked goods, this is the vibrant heart of Davis. It's justly considered among the best farmers markets in the nation.

On Wednesday evenings in summer, browse for provisions for a dreamy dinner picnic in the park.

Sam's Mediterranean Cuisine MIDDLE EASTERN $
(☎530-758-2855; 301 B St; shawarma $6.99; ⊙11:30am-7:30pm Mon-Fri, from noon Sat) Delicious and cheap shawarma (get the beef with tangy yogurt and chili sauce) makes this little spot a university institution. Cash only.

Burgers and Brew PUB FOOD $
(☎530-750-3603; www.burgersandbrew.com; 403 3rd St; burgers $10; 🚗) It's all in the name; the brilliantly simple formula of this buzzing brewpub makes it a charming local favorite. The 30 craft beers on tap include the best of the region and a delicious house IPA. When you're a few deep, the 'Beast Mode Fries' (caramelized onions, cheese, and spicy sauce) are a fantastic idea.

Woodstock's PIZZA $
(www.woodstocksdavis.com; 219 G St; slice $3.50, pizzas $8-28; ⊙11am-1am Mon-Wed, to 2am Thu-Sat, to midnight Sun; 🚗) The most popular pizza joint in town serves slices at lunch and gets boisterous at happy hour. Besides the usual combos, it has a fun selection of gourmet pizzas. (Sriracha, bacon, pineapple and green onions? Yes, please.)

Woodstock's also hosts some weekly events that are popular when the students are in town, including a trivia night, live rock bands and an open mike.

Davis Noodle City   ASIAN $

(129 E St; mains $7-10; ⊕11am-9:30pm Mon-Sat, to 8:30pm Sun) Students and locals tuck into wooden booths at this cozy spot to slurp up thick homemade noodles, fresh dumplings and scallion pancakes.

Delta of Venus Cafe & Pub   CAFE $

(www.deltaofvenus.org; 122b St; mains $7-11; ⊕7:30am-10pm, hours vary seasonally; 🎵) This converted Arts and Crafts bungalow has a social, shaded front patio, delicious home-made granola, and tons of vegetarian and vegan options. At dinner, Chef Iwaca turns out fantastic Caribbean dishes while indie and folk songwriters add ambience. In the warm months, the cafe stays open late and sometimes has live music, but in winter it closes earlier.

🍸 Drinking & Nightlife

During the school year, downtown bars lure students with every trick in the book – drink specials, open mike nights, karaoke and trivia. In the summer, things are a bit quieter, but the downtown grid is the place to wander if you're thirsty.

Three Mile Brewing Company   MICROBREWERY

(📞 530-564-4351; www.threemilebrewing.com; 231 G St, Suite 3; ⊕3-10pm Thu-Fri, noon-10pm Sat, to 8pm Sun; 🎵) This welcome upstart micro-brew has a fantastic flight of crisp, hoppy beer made from local ingredients. Get a taster of four 5oz sips for $7. The list is always changing, but if you're lucky, it will have the smoky Big Deal Scotch on tap, which is made from peated malt.

Davis Beer Shoppe   BEER HALL

(📞 530-756-5212; 211 G St; bottle from $3; ⊕11am-11pm Mon-Wed, to 12:30am Thu-Sat, to 9pm Sun) This mellow beer hall and shop stocks 650 varieties of craft beer, bottled and on tap, import and brewed down the block. Pull any bottle from the back, or order one of its daily changing draft flights. BYO food.

☆ Entertainment

The college has fostered a thriving cultural scene – bulletin boards around town will announce readings and performances galore. For tickets and information to UC Davis' arts events, call the Mondavi Center (p379). For athletic events, call the **UC Davis Athletic Ticket office** (📞530-752-2471; http://campus recreation.ucdavis.edu; Aggie Stadium, off La Rue Rd).

Mondavi Center for
the Performing Arts   CONCERT VENUE

(www.mondaviarts.org; 1 Shields Ave) Major theater, music, dance and other performances take place at this state-of-the-art venue on the UCD campus.

Varsity Theatre   FILM

(www.davisvarsity.net; 616 2nd St) Davis' beloved art house movie theater has discerning programming and occasional Q&As with filmmakers.

❶ Information

The exhaustive www.daviswiki.org is fascinating.
Yolo County Visitors Bureau (📞530-297-1900; www.visityolo.com; 132 E St, Suite 200; ⊕8:30am-4:30pm Mon-Fri) Free bike maps, travel brochures and transit info.

❶ Getting There & Away

Amtrak (📞530-758-4220; 840 2nd St) Davis' station is on the southern edge of downtown. Trains connect with Sacramento ($9, 26 minutes) or San Francisco ($31, two hours) throughout the day.
Yolobus (📞530-666-2877; ⊕5am-11pm) Routes 42A and B ($2.25) loop between Davis and the Sacramento International Airport. The route also connects Davis with Woodland and Downtown Sacramento.

TULE FOG

As thick as the proverbial pea soup, tule (too-lee) fog causes chain collisions each year on area roads. In 2007, more than 100 cars and big rigs collided on a stretch of Hwy 99. At its worst, these dense, immobile clouds can limit visibility up to a foot.

Tule fog, named after a marsh grass common here, is thickest from November to March, when cold mountain air settles on the warm valley floor and condenses. The fog burns off for a few afternoon hours, just long enough for the ground to warm again and perpetuate the cycle.

If you find yourself driving in fog, turn on your low beams, give other cars extra distance and maintain an easy, constant speed. Avoid passing.

ℹ Getting Around

Unitrans (☑ 530-752-2877; http://unitrans. ucdavis.edu; one-way $1) If you're not biking, this student-run outfit shuttles people around town and campus in red double-deckers.

Ken's Bike, Ski, Board (www.kensbikeski.com; 650 G St; ⊘ 9am-8pm Mon-Fri, to 7pm Sat, noon-5pm Sun) Rents basic bikes (from $21 per day), as well as serious road and mountain bikes.

Oroville

North of Sacramento's bustle, the quiet town of Oroville has seen quite a reversal. In the mid-19th century the lust for gold brought a crush of white settlers, who drove out the native community. Today, crowds still seek riches – in the thriving tribal casinos on the outskirts of town. Aside from slots, the local economy relies on tourists headed to the rugged northern reaches of the Sierra Nevada.

Oroville's most enduring attraction, aside from the nearby lake, is an excellent museum established by descendants of a long-dispersed Chinese community. Oroville's other historic attractions revolve around the gold rush.

Hwys 162 and 70 head northeast from Oroville into the mountains and on to Quincy. Hwy 70 snakes along the magnificent **Feather River Canyon**, an especially captivating drive in autumn.

OROVILLE DAM CRISIS

In February 2017, Oroville made national headlines when a dam east of town threatened catastrophe. After heavy rains, several flood control measures failed and the swollen waters of Lake Oroville – California's second-largest reservoir and the water source for farms of the Central Valley and 23 million people – threatened disaster. In a chaotic evacuation, 188,000 people were given just an hour to leave their homes, while news helicopters live streamed the traffic jam. The dam held, but the crisis caused millions in damage and added another hot-button issue to the complex debate about California's water management, climate change and crumbling infrastructure.

◉ Sights & Activities

Lake Oroville State Recreation Area   LAKE
(☑ 530-538-2219; www.parks.ca.gov; 917 Kelly Ridge Rd; ⊘ park 8am-8pm, visitor center 9am-5pm; 🅿♿) This artificial lake was formed by the USA's tallest earth-filled dam, rising 770ft above the Feather River. There are boat-in, floating campsites available. The lake's **visitor center** (☑ 530-538-2219; www. parks.ca.gov; 917 Kelly Ridge Rd; ⊘ 9am-5pm) has exhibits on the California State Water Project and local tribe history, plus a viewing tower and loads of recreational information.

The area surrounding Lake Oroville is also full of hiking trails, and a favorite is the 7-mile round-trip walk to 640ft Feather Falls. The Brad Freeman Bicycle Trail is a 41-mile, off-road loop that takes cyclists to the top of 770ft Oroville Dam, then follows the Feather River back to the Thermalito Forebay and Afterbay storage reservoirs, east of Hwy 70. The ride is mostly flat, but the dam ascent is steep. Get a free map of the ride from the Oroville Area Chamber of Commerce (p381). The Forebay Aquatic Center (p380) rents non-motorized watercraft to get out on the water.

Chinese Temple
& Museum Complex   MUSEUM
(☑ 530-538-2496; 1500 Broderick St; adult/child $3/free; ⊘ noon-4pm; 🅿) This restored temple and museum offers a fascinating glimpse into Oroville's Chinese legacy and is well worth exploring. Built in 1863, it served the Chinese community, which built the area's levees and at its peak numbered 10,000. Inside is an unrivaled collection of 19th-century stage finery, religious **shrines** and a small **garden** with fine Qing-era relics.

Sacramento National
Wildlife Refuge   BIRDWATCHING
(www.fws.gov; $6; ⊘ 1hr before sunset-1hr after sunset) Serious bird-watchers sojourn here in winter, when millions of migratory waterfowl are spectacular. The visitor center (p381) is off I-5 near Willows; a splendid 6-mile driving trail and walking trails are open daily. The peak season to see birds is between October and late February, with the largest skein of geese arriving in December and January.

Forebay Aquatic Center   BOATING
(www.forebayaquaticcenter.com; 930 Garden Dr; kayaks per day from $40; ⊘ 10am-6pm Wed-Sun May-Sep) A pair of docks and a beach for easy water access for canoeing, kayaking, rowing,

pedal boats, hydro bikes, paddle boarding or just swimming in a motor-boat free area of the Thermalito Forebay. Rentals and lessons available.

🛏 Sleeping

★ Lake Oroville State Recreation Area Campground
CAMPGROUND $

(🖉information 530-538-2219, reservations 800-444-7275; www.reserveamerica.com; tent & RV sites $20-45; P) Drive-in campgrounds aren't the most rustic choice, but there are good primitive campsites if you're willing to hike or – perhaps the coolest feature of the park – boat. There's a cove of floating platform sites (per night $175).

🍷 Drinking & Nightlife

Keg Room
BAR

(🖉530-534-1394; 3035 Oro Dam Blvd E; ⊘7am-2am) Our favorite of Oroville's no-frills watering holes serves very cold beer and spicy Bloody Marys and has a shuffleboard table.

ℹ Information

For road conditions, phone 800-427-7623.

Feather River Ranger District (Plumas National Forest; 🖉530-534-6500; www.fs.usda.gov; 875 Mitchell Ave; ⊘8am-4:30pm Mon-Fri) This US Forest Service (USFS) office has maps and brochures

Oroville Area Chamber of Commerce (www.orovillechamber.net; 1789 Montgomery St) A source for free biking and trail maps and other area activities.

Sacramento National Wildlife Refuge Visitor Center (🖉530-934-2801; 752 County Rd, Willows; ⊘9am-4pm, closed Mon Nov-Feb, closed Sat & Sun Mar-Oct) An Audubon Society bookstore and exhibits on all things birds at this well-run visitor center. Pick up maps for self-guided wetland walks here.

ℹ Getting There & Away

Although **Greyhound buses** (🖉800-231-2222; www.greyhound.com; 420 Richards Blvd) stop near the **Valero gas station** (🖉530-533-2328; 555 Oro Dam Blvd E) a few blocks east of Hwy 70, a car is far and away the simplest and most cost effective way to reach the area. There are two buses daily between Oroville and Sacramento ($20, 1½ hours).

Chico

With its huge population of students, Chico has the wild energy of a college kegger during the school year, and a lazy, lethargic hangover during the summer. An oak-shaded downtown and university makes it one of Sacramento Valley's more attractive hubs, where folks mingle late in the restaurants and bars, which open onto patios when it's warm.

Though Chico wilts in the heat during summer, the swimming holes in Bidwell Park offer an escape, as does floating down the gentle Sacramento River. The brews of the Sierra Nevada Brewing Company, near downtown, are another of Chico's refreshing blessings.

It's ironic a town so widely celebrated for its beer was founded by John Bidwell, a California pioneer who made a bid for US president with the Prohibitionist party. In 1868, Bidwell and his philanthropist wife, Annie Ellicott Kennedy Bidwell, moved to the mansion that is now the Bidwell Mansion State Historic Park.

◉ Sights

Nearly all the sights are downtown, west of Hwy 99, easily reached via Hwy 32 (8th St). Main St and Broadway are the central downtown streets; from there, Park Ave stretches south and the tree-lined Esplanade heads north.

Sierra Nevada Brewing Company
BREWERY

(🖉530-899-4776; www.sierranevada.com; 1075 E 20th St; brewery tour free, Beer Geek tour $45; ⊘tours 11am-4pm Sun-Thu, to 5:30pm Fri & Sat) 🍺 Hordes of beer fans gather at the birthplace of the nationally distributed Sierra Nevada Pale Ale and Schwarber, a Chico-only black ale. You can also stock up on eccentric 'Beer Camp' collaborations, short-run craft beers brewed by über-beer nerds at invitation-only seminars. Free brewhouse tours are given regularly.

Chico Creek Nature Center
SCIENCE CENTER

(www.bidwellpark.org; 1968 E 8th St; suggested donation adult/child $4/2; ⊘11am-4pm Wed-Sun; 🚹) If you plan on spending the afternoon in Bidwell Park, stop here first for displays on local plants and animals and excellent hands-on science programs for families. The exhibit hall is closed on Wednesdays.

Chico State University
UNIVERSITY

Ask for a free map of the Chico State University campus, or about campus events and tours at the **CSU Information Center** (🖉530-898-4636; www.csuchico.edu; cnr 2nd & Normal Sts; ⊘7am-11pm Mon-Thu, to 10pm

Fri, 11am-10pm Sat, noon-11pm Sun school year), on the main floor of Bell Memorial Union. The attractive campus is infused with floral sweetness in spring, and there's a rose garden and several stately Romanesque buildings at its center.

Bidwell Mansion State Historic Park   HISTORIC BUILDING

(☑ 530-895-6144; www.parks.ca.gov; 525 Esplanade; adult/child $6/3; ⊘ noon-5pm Mon, 11am-5pm Sat & Sun) 🍂 Chico's most prominent landmark, the opulent Victorian home was built for Chico's founders, John and Annie Bidwell. The 26-room mansion was built between 1865 and 1868. It hosted many US presidents and John Muir, who was a personal friend of Annie. Tours start every hour from 11am to 4pm.

Honey Run Covered Bridge   HISTORIC SITE

(www.honeyruncoveredbridge.com; parking $3) The historic 1894 bridge is an unusual style this side of the country and a favorite spot for engagement photos. Take the Skyway exit off Hwy 99 on the southern outskirts of Chico, head east and go left on Honey Run-Humbug Rd. The bridge is in a small park 5 miles up the road.

🏃 Activities

In summer you can cool off by tubing the Sacramento. Inner tubes can be rented at grocery stores and other shops along Nord Ave (Hwy 32) for $7 to $12. Tubers enter at the Irvine Finch Launch Ramp on Hwy 32, a few miles west of Chico, and come out at Washout Beach, off River Rd.

Bidwell Park   SWIMMING

(www.bidwellpark.org) Growing out of downtown, the 3670-acre Bidwell Park is the nation's third-largest municipal park. It stretches 10 miles northwest along Chico Creek with lush groves and miles of trails. The upper part of the park is an untamed oasis. Several classic movies have been shot here, including parts of *Gone with the Wind* and *The Adventures of Robin Hood*.

The park is full of swimming spots. You'll find pools at One-Mile and Five-Mile recreation areas and swimming holes (including Bear Hole, Salmon Hole and Brown Hole) in Upper Bidwell Park, north of Manzanita Ave. Don't be surprised if some opt to swim au naturel.

Adventure Outing   OUTDOORS

(☑ 530-898-4011; www.aschico.com/adventure-outings; Bell Memorial Union basement, 2nd & Chestnut Sts; life jackets $4-8; ⊘ 9am-5pm Mon-Fri) The CSU-student-run outfitter rents equipment like life jackets, rafts and even coolers at very reasonable prices by the weekend or week. It also leads popular trips further afield.

🎊 Festivals & Events

With the students out of town, family-friendly outdoor events take over each summer. The Thursday Night Market fills several blocks of Broadway from April to September. At **City Plaza** (www.downtownchico.com; W 4th & Broadway Sts), you'll find free Friday night concerts starting in May.

🛏 Sleeping

There's plenty of decent independent motels with swimming pools, some of them along the shaded Esplanade north of downtown. Chico State's graduation and homecoming mania (May and October, respectively) send prices skyward.

Hotel Diamond (☑ 866-993-3100; www.hoteldiamondchico.com; 220 W 4th St; r $150-399; ❄ @ 🛜) is the most luxurious place to lay your head in Chico, with high thread counts and attentive room service. The Diamond Suite, with its spacious top-floor balcony, is a-*maz*-ing. There's also a swanky piano bar and top-notch restaurant, Two Twenty, downstairs.

🍴 Eating

Downtown Chico is packed with fun places to eat, many of them catering to a student budget. The outdoor farmers market (p382) draws from the plentiful surrounding valley.

Shubert's Ice Cream & Candy   ICE CREAM $

(www.shuberts.com; 178 E 7th St; ⊘ 9:30am-10pm Mon-Fri, from 11am Sat & Sun) Five generations of Shuberts have produced delicious homemade ice cream, chocolates and confections for more than 75 years at this beloved pastel-colored Chico landmark. The flavors change with the season; consider yourself lucky to get the boysenberry sundaes in the spring.

Chico Certified Farmers Market   MARKET $

(☑ 530-893-3276; www.chicofarmersmarket.com; Chico Municipal parking lot, 305 Wall St; ⊘ 7:30am-1pm Sat May-Sep) Rain or shine, this excellent open-air market brings in the best from the valley, artisanal baked goods and coffee.

El Paisa Taco Truck
MEXICAN $

(cnr 8th & Pine Sts; mains $1.50-5; ⊙11am-8pm) Debate about which of Chico's taco trucks is best can quickly lead to fisticuffs, but the smoky carnitas tacos served at this mobile kitchen are a dream.

Sin of Cortez
CAFE $

(www.sinofcortez.com; 2290 Esplanade; mains $6-16; ⊙7am-2pm; ⚑) The service won't win awards for speed, but this local favorite draws both vegetarian and omnivorous mobs with its burly breakfast plates. Order anything with the soy chorizo.

Sierra Nevada
Taproom & Restaurant
PUB FOOD $$

(www.sierranevada.com; 1075 E 20th St; mains $10-32; ⊙11am-9pm Sun-Thu, to 10pm Fri & Sat; ⚑) What's on tap is the main draw at the on-site restaurant of the Sierra Nevada Brewery Company (p381). This genuine Chico destination is great for downing brews but lacks ambience – the huge, loud dining room is basically a cafeteria. Still, it has better-than-average pub food and superbly fresh ales and lagers, some not available elsewhere.

Red Tavern
AMERICAN $$

(www.redtavern.com; 1250 Esplanade; mains $17-28; ⊙from 5pm Tue-Sat, 10am-2pm Sun) ⚑ The Red Tavern is one of Chico's favorite fine-dining experiences, with a sophisticated menu that uses local, seasonal and organic ingredients. On Sundays, it offers a delicious brunch and family-style dinners.

Celestino's Live from
New York Pizza
PIZZA $$

(101 Salem St; pizzas from $14; ⊙10:30am-10pm Sun-Thu, to 11pm Fri & Sat) A convincing imitation of 'real' New York pizza, it serves thin-crust pizzas and playful variations like the meaty Godfather. There's a budget slice-n-a-soda lunch for $4.75.

Leon Bistro
CALIFORNIAN $$$

(www.leonbistro.com; 817 Main St; mains $18-35; ⊙from 5pm Wed-Sat) When the most ordinary thing on the menu is a wagyu beef burger with bacon-onion marmalade, you know you're in for something nice. Chef Ann Leon cooked in several fine kitchens before opening her namesake restaurant, a go-to among Chico tastemakers. She regularly shares her skills in cooking classes.

5th Street Steakhouse
AMERICAN $$$

(www.5thstreetsteakhouse.com; 345 W 5th St; steaks from $26; ⊙11:30am-2:30pm Fri, from 4:30pm daily) This is where college kids take their visiting parents. It features crisp white tablecloths, steaks tender enough to cut with a reproachful look, and occasional live jazz loud enough to drown out any disapproval.

🍷 Drinking & Nightlife

Given Chico's party-school rep, you won't be thirsty. There's a strip of bars on Main St if you want to go hopping.

Naked Lounge
COFFEE

(☑530-895-0676; www.nakedcoffee.net; 118 W 2nd St; ⊙6:30am-8pm; 🖥) With excellent coffee, mellow music and a choice selection of beer on tap, this inviting downtown cafe is perfect for an easygoing morning.

Madison Bear Garden
BAR

(www.madisonbeargarden.com; 316 W 2nd St; ⊙11am-1:45am Mon-Sat, from 10am Sun; 🖥) This spacious brick building with adjoining big beer garden isn't only the most reliable scene in Chico – it's an institution. The walls are loaded with kitsch, and students pack the place for big burgers and cold pints.

Panama Bar & Cafe
BAR

(www.panamabarcafeinchico.com; 177 E 2nd St; iced tea from $3; ⊙11:30am-1:30am Tue-Sat, 11am-9pm Sun) The house specializes in 31 variations of Long Island iced teas (most of which are around $3), so brace yourself. The only way to take in alcohol any faster would be by IV drip. There are several adjoining dance clubs which get packed on the weekends.

☆ Entertainment

For entertainment options, pick up the free weekly *Chico News & Review* (www.newsandreview.com). For theater, films, concerts, art exhibits and other cultural events at the CSU campus, contact the **CSU Box Office** (☑530-898-6333; www.csuchico.edu; Sierra Hall, cnr 3rd & Chestnut; ⊙11am-6pm Mon-Fri) or the CSU Information Center (p381).

Pageant Theatre
CINEMA

(www.pageantchico.com; 351 E 6th St; tickets $8) Screens international and alternative films. Monday is 'cheap skate night,' with all seats just $4.

1078 Gallery
PERFORMING ARTS

(☑530-343-1973; www.1078gallery.org; 820 Broadway; ⊙12:30-5:30pm) Chico's contemporary gallery exhibits artworks, and hosts boundary-pushing literary readings, music and theater.

ℹ Information

Chico Chamber of Commerce & Visitor Center (☎800-852-8570, 530-891-5556; www.chicochamber.com; 441 Main St; ☺10am-4pm Mon-Fri) Local information including bike maps.

ℹ Getting There & Around

Greyhound (www.greyhound.com) buses stop multiple times a day at the **Amtrak station** (www.amtrak.com; 450 Orange St) heading to San Francisco ($48, six hours 40 minutes), Reno ($57, 10 hours), Los Angeles ($65, 11 hours) and points between. The platform is unattended so purchase tickets in advance or from the driver.

Amtrak trains on the *Coast Starlight* line depart Chico in the middle of the night for Redding ($20, one hour) and Sacramento ($26, 2½ hours). Amtrak's connecting buses travel through the region as well, but require booking a connecting train.

B-Line (Butte Regional Transit; ☎530-342-0221; www.blinetransit.com; W 2nd St at Salem; adult/child $1.40/1) handles all buses throughout Butte County, and can get you around Chico and down to Oroville in 50 minutes.

Car is the easiest way to get around, but Chico is one of the best biking towns in the country. Rent from **Campus Bicycles** (www.campusbicycles.com; 330 Main St; rental half/full day $20/35).

Red Bluff

The smoldering streets of Red Bluff – one of California's hottest towns due to the hot-air trap of the Shasta Cascades – aren't much of a draw on their own. But a glimpse toward the mountainous horizon reveals what brings most travelers this way.

Peter Lassen laid out the town site in 1847 and it grew into a key port along the Sacramento River. Now it's a pit stop on the way to the national park that bears his name.

Cowboy culture is alive and well here. Catch it in action the third weekend of April at the **Red Bluff Round-Up** (www.redbluffroundup.com; tickets $10-27), a major rodeo event dating back to 1918, or in any of the dive bars where the jukeboxes are stocked with country and plenty of cowboys belly up to the bar. You can also stock up on your own Western wear from one of several historic storefronts in the business district.

◉ Sights & Activities

Red Bluff Recreation Area PARK
(www.fs.usda.gov) On the east bank of the Sacramento River this sprawling park of meadows has interpretive trails, bicycle paths, boat ramps, a wildlife-viewing area with excellent bird-watching, and a salmon and steelhead ladder (most active July to September).

William B Ide Adobe State Historic Park HISTORIC SITE
(☎530-529-8599; 21659 Adobe Rd; per car $6; ☺10am-4pm Fri-Sun) Set on a beautiful, shaded piece of land overlooking a languorous section of the Sacramento River, this park preserves the original one-room adobe house, old forge and grounds of pioneer William B Ide, who 'fought' in the 1846 Bear Flag Revolt at Sonoma. He became president of the California Bear Republic, which lasted 25 days.

Head about a mile north on Main St, turn east onto Adobe Rd and go another mile, following the signs.

Sacramento River Discovery Center SCIENCE CENTER
(www.sacramentoriverdiscoverycenter.com; 1000 Sale Lane; admission by donation; ☺11am-3pm Tue-Sat; ⊞) This kid-friendly center has exhibits on the river and the Diversion Dam just outside its doors, which has been permanently opened to allow endangered chinook and green and white sturgeon to migrate. Though the fish aren't visible, up to 120 species of birds are. Bird walks along the 4.2 miles of wheelchair-accessible trails start the first Saturday of each month at 8am.

🛏 Sleeping & Eating

Sycamore Grove Camping Area CAMPGROUND $
(☎530-824-5196; www.recreation.gov; tent/RV sites $16/30) Beside the river in the Red Bluff Recreation Area is this quiet USFS campground. Campsites for tents and RVs are first-come, first-served, and offer new, shared showers and flush toilets. You can reserve a large group campground, Camp Discovery, which has basic screened-in cabins that must be booked as a block ($175 for all 11 cabins per night).

Los Mariachis MEXICAN $
(www.redblufflosmariachis.com; 604 S Main St; mains $5-14; ☺9am-9pm Mon-Fri, to 9:30pm Sat & Sun; ⊞) This bright, family-run Mexican

spot overlooks the central junction of Red Bluff. It has great salsa and *molcajetes* (meat or seafood stew, served in a stone bowl) big enough to satisfy hungry campers.

From The Hearth CAFE **$**
(☑530-727-0616; www.fthcafe.com; 638 Washington St; sandwiches $7-10; ☺7am-9pm Mon-Sat, to 6pm Sun) Pastries and expert coffee drinks in the morning, crispy panini on just-baked bread for lunch and dinner. Everything is very fresh, colorful and made-to-order. This sophisticated, no-fuss cafe is a dream for travelers who want to get a quick bite and get back on the road.

Thai House THAI **$**
(www.newthaihouse.com; 248 S Main St; mains $5-14; ☺11am-3pm & 4-8:30pm Mon-Fri, 11am-8:30pm Sat, from noon Sun; P❋☑) ◢ A remarkably solid Thai restaurant with excellent curries and soups.

� Drinking & Nightlife

Cedar Crest Brewing BREWERY
(615 Main St; ☺11am-8pm Mon-Thu, to 10pm Fri & Sat, noon-5pm Sun) Situated inside a local specialty food spot called Enjoy The Store, this young craft brewery (Red Bluff's first!) pours floral IPAs and a delicious Dark Matter Porter. The surrounding store is a great spot to stock up on fancy snacks, such as local cheese, olives and nuts.

E's Locker Room BAR
(☑530-527-4600; 1075 Lakeside Dr; ☺4-9:30pm Tue-Thu, to 10pm Fri & Sat, 3-9pm Sun) Framed photos of local legends and sports heroes clutter the walls of this friendly, casual Red Bluff watering hole. Take your pint out to the big porch out back, overlooking a lazy bend of the Sacramento River.

ℹ Information

Red Bluff Chamber of Commerce (☑530-527-6220; www.redbluffchamber.com; 100 Main St; ☺8:30am-4pm Mon, to 5pm Tue-Thu, to 4:30pm Fri) To get your bearings and a stack of brochures, find this white building just south of downtown.

ℹ Getting There & Away

Most visitors pull into Red Bluff to take a break from the busy I-5. By highway, the town is three hours north of San Francisco and 15 minutes north of Sacramento. **Amtrak** (www.amtrak.com; cnr Rio & Walnut Sts) and **Greyhound** (www.greyhound.com; 22700 Antelope Blvd) connect it with other California cities via bus.

SAN JOAQUIN VALLEY

The southern half of California's Central Valley – named for the San Joaquin River – sprawls from Stockton to the turbine-covered Tehachapi Mountains, southeast of Bakersfield. Everything stretches to the horizon in straight lines – railroad tracks, two-lane blacktop and long irrigation channels.

The tiny towns scattering the region retain their Main St Americana appeal while slowly embracing the influence of the Latino labor force.

This is a place of seismic, often contentious, development. Arrivals from the coastal cities have resulted in unchecked sprawl. What were once actual ranches and vineyards are now nostalgically named developments: a big-box shopping complex named Indian Ranch, a tidy row of McMansions named Vineyard Estates. More green lawns appear as the irrigation systems drain dry. Water rights is *the* issue on everyone's minds.

Lodi

Although Lodi was once the 'Watermelon capital of the world,' today, full-bodied wine rules this patch of the valley. Breezes from the Sacramento River Delta soothe the area's hot vineyards, where some of the world's oldest Zinfandel vines grow. Lodi's diverse soil is sometimes rocky, sometimes fine sandy loam, giving its grapes a range of distinctive characteristics that allow for experimentation with some less common varietals.

Lodi also hosts a slew of festivals dedicated to their famous export, including the **Wine & Chocolate Weekend** in February and **ZinFest** in May.

◉ Sights

Jessie's Grove at Olde Ice House Cellars WINERY
(☑209-368-0880; www.jessiesgrovewinery.com; 27 E Locust St; tasting $5; ☺noon-5pm Fri & Sat, from 1pm Sun; P) Several wineries have opened tasting rooms within a few blocks of one another downtown, including Jessie's Grove, which pours Zinfandel, Chardonnay, Merlot and more inside a historical ice house by the railroad tracks, north of the Lodi Arch.

Micke Grove Regional Park & Zoo ZOO
(☑209-331-2010; www.mgzoo.com; 11793 N Micke Grove Rd; adult/child $5/3, parking $5; ☺10am-

5pm; 🚻) For the seriously underage, Lodi's Micke Grove Regional Park and Zoo is a good stop, with a water play area, hissing cockroaches and some barking sea lions. There are also kiddie rides in a section called Fun Town. The park also houses an exceptional **Japanese Garden** (www.sjparks. com; 11793 N Micke Grove Rd; ⊙9am-2pm Mon-Thu, to 1pm Fri-Sun) FREE.

🛏 Sleeping & Eating

Wine & Roses   HOTEL $$
(📳209-334-6988; http://winerose.com; 2505 W Turner Rd; r $179-240, ste from $335; P🅿❄ @🛜🐾) Surrounded by a vast rose garden, this is the most luxurious offering to spring up amid Lodi's vineyards. Tasteful and romantic, the rooms have slate bathrooms, high-quality toiletries and lots of square footage. There's an acclaimed restaurant (p386) and spa too.

Dancing Fox Winery
& Bakery   AMERICAN, BAKERY $
(📳209-366-2634; www.dancingfoxwinery.com; 203 S School St; mains from $11; ⊙7:30am-9pm Tue-Sat, 9am-3pm Sun) Everything here celebrates grapes – from the Lewis Family Estate's own wines to the bread cultures created from the vineyard's petite sirah grapes. The best selections from the overly broad menu involve the wood-burning oven.

Farm Cafe   AMERICAN $
(📳206-368-7384; www.michaeldavidwinery.com; 4580 W Hwy 12; mains $7-14; ⊙7:30am-3pm; 🚻) On the outskirts of town at Michael David Winery, this farmstand cafe slings big breakfast plates of fluffy omelets with country potatoes, cinnamon pancakes and homemade breads with strawberry jam.

Towne House Restaurant   CALIFORNIAN $$$
(📳209-371-6160; www.loditownehouse.com; 2505 W Turner Rd; mains $20-55; ⊙7-10:30am, 11am-2pm & from 5pm Mon-Fri, 8am-2pm & from 5pm Sat & Sun) The bright, crisply designed on-site restaurant of Wine & Roses draws on locally sourced ingredients in an elegant preparation. There's often live jazz in the evening in the adjoining lounge, which pours cocktails and a selection of local wines.

🍷 Drinking & Nightlife

Blend Ultra Lounge   COCKTAIL BAR
(www.blendlodi.com; 115 S School St, Suite 13; ⊙5-9pm Wed, to 2am Thu-Sat, 1-6pm Sun) Patrons sip colorful cocktails while bathed in blue neon at this (almost) swanky lounge. When the Giants are on, it takes on the vibe of a (almost) swanky sports bar. It also serves tapas and good burgers (mains $11 to $22).

🛍 Shopping

Cheese Central   FOOD
(www.cheesecentrallodi.com; 11 N School St; ⊙10am-6pm Mon-Sat, 1-5pm Sun) Ask Cindy the cheesemonger for thoughtful pairings with Lodi wines. If you want to make a weekend out of Lodi's wine region, try one of the cooking classes.

Stockton

Stockton has had its share of ups and downs – including recent challenges with the housing crisis and large civic debt – but the downtown and waterfront redevelopment is one of the valley's more promising grassroots efforts. In the summer, when festivals take over the Weber Point Events Center (p387), Stockton makes for a fun detour.

The city has an interesting past that is just under the surface of its checkered

---

WATER WARS

Through the elaborate politics and machinery of water management, this once-arid region ranks among the most agriculturally productive places in the world, though the profits often go to agribusiness shareholders, not the increasingly disenfranchised family farmer. The region's water issue became dire in 2015, when a severe drought parched the region, bringing usage restrictions and heated debate. In 2016, things settled down when an extremely rainy winter brought deep snow to the Sierra Nevada and refilled the reservoirs. But the increasingly noticeable impact of climate change and population growth aren't going away, and water will continue to be a divisive issue in these communities. Plenty of roadside signs along Hwy 99 emblazoned with bold-font political slogans about the water crisis will keep the issue on travelers' minds as well.

TOP LODI WINERIES

Lodi's underrated wineries make an fun escape from the Bay Area, and the quality of grapes will delight true oenophiles. This is the source of many master blenders' secret weapons.

The region is easily accessed from I-5 or Hwy 99 and just as easy to navigate, as roads are well marked. For maps, check the **Lodi Wine & Visitor Center** (☑209-367-4727; www.lodiwine.com; 2545 W Turner Rd; ☻10am-5pm).

Jessie's Grove (www.jessiesgrovewinery.com; 1973 W Turner Rd; ☻noon-5pm) With its summer concert series and very long history, this is an anchor of Lodi wine producers. There's a new **tasting room** (p385) downtown on E Locust St.

Harney Lane (www.harneylane.com; 9010 E Harney Lane; tasting $5; ☻11am-5pm Thu-Mon) A sweet family outfit that's been around Lodi forever; their Tempranillo is an overachiever. Tasting fee refunded with purchase.

d'Art (www.dartwines.com; 13299 N Curry Ave; tasting $5; ☻noon-5pm Thu-Mon) Helen and Dave Dart's bold Cabernet Sauvignon is as fun and inviting as the tasting room. Tasting fee refunded with purchase.

LangeTwins (www.langetwins.com; 1525 East Jahant Rd, Acampo; tasting $5-10; ☻11am-4pm Thu-Sun) The Viognier and reserve blends are worth the 7-mile drive north of town to this state-of-the-art steel-and-redwood winery.

Riaza Wines (www.riazawines.com; 20 W Elm St; ☻1-6pm Fri & Sat, to 5pm Sun) The downtown tasting room pours Spanish varietals that only recently were discovered to grow like mad in the Lodi sun.

Jeremy Wine Co (www.jeremywineco.com; 6 W Pine St; ☻1-5pm Wed-Sun) Friendly folk in this brass- and wood-fitted tasting room downtown pour a bright fruit-forward Sangiovese.

Michael David (☑209-368-7384; www.michaeldavidwinery.com; 4580 W Hwy 12; tasting $5-10; ☻10am-5pm; P) These brothers have built an enthusiastic following with their oaky, fruity wines. Their renowned Zinfandel, '7 Deadly Zins,' is a standout. The cafe and farmstand make this tasting room a perfect lunch stop. Tasting fee refunded with purchase; last entry is at 4:30pm.

facades. It is a major inland port and was once the main supply hub for gold rushers. During WWII it became a major center of American shipbuilding, and remains home to a few maritime transportation facilities.

A block east of Weber Point, the **Department of Tourism** (☑209-938-1555; www.visitstockton.org; 125 Bridge Pl; ☻9am-5pm Mon-Fri) has complete information about the goings-on in town.

◉ Sights & Activities

★Wat Dhammararam

Buddhist Temple   BUDDHIST TEMPLE
(☑209-943-2883; www.watdhammararam buddhist.org; 3732 Carpenter Rd) **FREE** With elaborate grounds, brightly painted statues and a 50ft reclining Buddha, this is a vibrant home to the area's Cambodian population. The celebration of the Cambodian New Year

in mid-April draws thousands of people who celebrate with music, dance and an amazing pot-luck lunch.

Weber Point Events Center   LANDMARK
(www.stocktongov.com; 221 N Center St) Downtown on the McLeod Lake waterfront, the modern white edifice standing in the middle of a grassy park looking rather like a pile of sailboats is the Weber Point Events Center and marks the center of the action. This is also the site of the huge April San Joaquin Asparagus Festival (p388), a series of open-air concerts, and fountains where squealing kids cool off.

Banner Island Ballpark   STADIUM
(☑209-644-1900; www.stocktonports.com; 404 W Fremont St) The beautiful Banner Island Ballpark is where the minor-league Stockton Ports play ball April to September.

DON'T MISS

SAN JOAQUIN ASPARAGUS FESTIVAL

Of all the Central Valley food celebrations, perhaps none pay such creative respect to the main ingredient as the **San Joaquin Asparagus Festival** (www.asparagusfest.com; N Center St, btwn Oak St & W Weber Av; adult/child $13/free; ⊙ Apr), which brings together more than 500 vendors to serve these green stalks – more than 10 tons of them! – every way imaginable. It sprouts along the waterfront at the end of April.

Haggin Museum MUSEUM
(www.hagginmuseum.org; 1201 N Pershing Ave; adult/child $8/5; ⊙ 1:30-5pm Wed-Fri, noon-5pm Sat & Sun) This city gem houses a 26ft boat by Stockton's own Stephens Bros company, and an excellent collection of American landscape and 'Golden Age' paintings.

Opportunity Cruises CRUISE
(www.opportunitycruises.com; Stockton Marina, 445 W Weber Ave; cruises with/without meal $55/37) Cruises around the Sacramento Delta in open-sided river boats depart from the Marina.

🛏 Sleeping & Eating

University Plaza Waterfront Hotel HOTEL $$
(☎ 209-944-1140; www.universityplazawaterfront hotel.com; 110 W Fremont St; r from $125; 🛜) If you're spending the night here, the best option is University Plaza Waterfront Hotel, where business travelers mingle with University of the Pacific students and the mayor, who all live in the lofts on the upper floors. The very modern building overlooking the harbor and historic park, unlike the highway chains, is walkable from other locations in the city center.

Open-Air Asian and Farmers Market MARKET $
(200 E Washington St; ⊙ 5:30-11am Sat) You can find fresh fish and a huge variety of Asian vegetables each Saturday, under the elevated freeway.

Papa Urb's Grill FILIPINO $
(☎ 209-227-8144; www.papaurbsgrill.com; 331 E Weber Ave; mains $5-10; ⊙ 10am-7:30pm Mon-Fri, from 11am Sat, 11am-4pm Sun) Filipino flavors drive the menu of fusion fast food at this

bright cafe: there's adobo and *longanisa* (Filipino pork sausage) in many of the typically Mexican presentations. If you want to expand your horizons, go for the *sisig* fries, a savory mess of pork, cheese and tangy cilantro dipping sauce.

Smitty's Wings & Things CHICKEN $
(☎ 209-227-7479; 946 Acacia St; mains $9-15; ⊙ noon-7pm Tue-Thu, to 8pm Fri & Sat) This checker-tiled neighborhood wing joint is run by a former NFL player and his wife, who turn out perfectly crispy wings (which were recently featured on the Food Network) and pizzas. They have specials every day and a selection of cold beer on tap. The sauces for the wings are all amazing, but we love the tingling spice of the 'damn hot' and garlic chili.

On Lok Sam CANTONESE $$
(www.newonlocksam.com; 333 S Sutter St; mains $10-25; ⊙ 11am-9pm) Venture south of the Crosstown Freeway (Hwy 4) to (New) On Lok Sam, established in 1895 in the center of Stockton's lively Chinese settlement. The garlic chicken and spicy, deep-fried green beans are delicious.

🍷 Drinking & Nightlife

Abbey Trappist Pub CRAFT BEER
(www.abbeystockton.com; 2353 Pacific Ave. Suite B; ⊙ 4-10pm Tue-Wed, to 11:30pm Thu, to 1am Fri, 11am-1am Sat) The beer menu is deep at this excellent local favorite, which also boasts a raucous trivia night and quality European pub food, such as the sausage plate, Scotch eggs and frog legs with spicy remoulade.

AVE on the Mile BAR
(www.aveonthemile.com; 2333 Pacific Ave.; ⊙ 3:30pm-midnight Tue-Thu, to 1am Fri, 4:30pm-1am Sat, 10am-2pm Sun) Exposed brick and a glittering wall of bottles make this the most elegant option on the block. It has a full menu of upscale pub food and Sunday brunch comes with bottomless mimosas.

❶ Getting There & Away

By train, boat or car, Stockton is easy to reach; it sits between I-5 and Hwy 99. You can also take Amtrak's San Joaquin line or the regional **Altamont Commuter Express** (☎ 800-411-7245; www.acerail.com; 949 East Channel St; one-way tickets $6-$14.50) from the **Robert J Cabral Station** (☎ 800-872-7245; 949 East Channel St), or float from the downtown marina to the Sacramento–San Joaquin River Delta.

Modesto

Cruising was banned in Modesto in 1993, but the town still touts itself as the 'cruising capital of the world.' The pastime's notoriety stems mostly from homegrown George Lucas' 1973 film *American Graffiti*. You'll still see hot rods and flashy wheels around town, but they no longer clog thoroughfares on Friday nights.

This is a good spot for getting off the dusty highway. Old oaks arch over the city's streets and you can eat well and stretch your legs in the compact downtown. The **Ernest & Julio Gallo Winery**, makers of America's best-selling jug wines, is one of the town's biggest businesses.

Classic car shows and rock and roll fill the streets every June for **Graffiti Summer** (www.visitmodesto.com; ⊙Jun). Amid all the 1950s charm, the sparkling Gallo Center for the Arts (p389) brings huge acts to the valley. For details, check the **Modesto Convention & Visitors Bureau** (✆888-640-8467; www.visitmodesto.com; 1150 9th St; ⊙8am-5pm Mon-Fri).

✖ Eating & Drinking

Thailand Restaurant   THAI **$**
(✆209-544-0505; 950 10th St, Suite 17; mains $9-15; ⊙10:30am-9pm Mon-Fri, from 11am Sat; ⊘)
Go immediately for the spicy noodles and green papaya salad at this friendly, spotless Thai restaurant.

Brighter Side   SANDWICHES **$**
(www.brighter-side.com; 1125 K St, cnr 13th & K Sts; sandwiches $5-6; ⊙11am-3:30pm Mon-Fri; ⊘)
An earthy little sandwich shop housed in a wood-shingled, former gas station, serves up sandwiches such as the Larry (Polish sausage, mushrooms, green onions on rye) or the veggie Christine on the sunny patio.

A&W Drive-In   AMERICAN **$**
(www.awrestaurants.com; 1404 G St, cnr 14th & G Sts; cheeseburger $3, float $4; ⊙10am-9pm, to 8pm Oct-Mar) A vintage burger stand (part of a chain founded in nearby Lodi), where roller-skating carhops and classic cars on display move a lot of root beer floats. George Lucas supposedly cruised here as a youth.

Commonwealth   AMERICAN **$$**
(✆209-248-7451; www.commonwealthmodesto.com; 1022 11th St; mains $11-30; ⊙11am-10pm Mon-Wed, to midnight Thu-Fri, 9am-midnight Sat, 9am-9pm Sun) Elegant without being stuffy, there's a great selection of local wine and indulgent sandwiches at this downtown spot (try the M80, which joins jalapeño fried chicken and thick bacon). In the morning, it serves picture-perfect waffles.

Tiki Cocktail Lounge   GAY & LESBIAN
(✆209-577-9969; 932 McHenry Ave; ⊙5pm-2am) Campy decor, friendly bartenders and an indoor fire pit give this gay hangout lots of cozy atmosphere.

☆ Entertainment

Gallo Center for the Arts   PERFORMING ARTS
(✆209-338-2100; www.galloarts.org; 1000 I St; ⊙10am-6pm Mon-Fri, from noon Sat) This huge, state-of-the-art performing arts complex in downtown Modesto brings great musical, dance and theater acts to town.

State Theatre   THEATER
(www.thestate.org; 1307 J St) This historic theater has stood here since 1934 and continues to put on films and live music.

Merced

You can jog over to Yosemite from many of the small towns in this part of the valley, but this is a convenient staging area, right on Hwy 140. The machine of progress has not been kind to Merced, as it suffers more than its share of strip malls. Still, you'll find tree-lined streets, historic Victorian homes and a magnificent 1875 courthouse at the city's core. The downtown business district is a work in progress, with 1930s movie theaters, antique stores and a few casual eateries undergoing constant renovation.

Merced is right in the midst of a population makeover, thanks to the newest University of California campus, opened in 2005. UC Merced's first freshman class numbered just 1000 students, but the school continues to grow with a diverse student body and has begun to dramatically shape the city.

At the **Castle Air Museum** (✆209-723-2178; www.castleairmuseum.org; 5050 Santa Fe Dr, Atwater; adult/child $15/10; ⊙10am-4pm), aerospace buffs will enjoy strolling down the rows of vintage military aircraft, ranging from pre-WWII to the present, on former Air Force base grounds. Military mechanics volunteer their time restoring these planes and are often on-site to answer questions.

The museum recently acquired a gigantic Douglas RA-3 Skywarrior, a reconnaissance bomber with a wingspan of 72ft. It is the largest, heaviest jet to ever land on an aircraft carrier. More than 1200 wing bolts had to be unscrewed just to move it to the museum.

🛏 Sleeping

HI Merced Home Hostel
HOSTEL $

(🖉 209-725-0407; www.hiusa.org; dm $20-23; ⊙ reception 5:30-10pm) A night in this six-bed homestay in the northeast part of town feels like staying with your long-lost Aunt Jan and Uncle Larry, the kind of folks happy to lend advice about Yosemite at the kitchen table. Beds fill quickly and must be reserved in advance (call between 5:30pm and 10pm). They can shuttle you to/from the bus and train stations.

Hooper House Bear Creek Inn
B&B $$

(🖉 209-723-3991; www.hooperhouse.com; 575 W North Bear Creek Dr; r $139-169; ❉ 🐾 🤶) In a grand old Colonial-style mansion, Hooper House Bear Creek Inn is a leisurely retreat. Rooms are large and beautifully furnished with hardwood furniture, soft beds and tiled bathrooms. A full breakfast is included, which you can have sent to your room.

🍴 Eating & Drinking

Little Oven Pizza
PIZZA $

(www.littleovenmerced.com; 433 W Main St; slices $3-4; ⊙ 11:30am-9pm Tue-Thu, to 11pm Fri, 4-11pm Sat; 🤶) Turning out picture-perfect, New York–style thin crust, this tidy downtown spot offers daily specials and makes a quick, cheap option. The Pesto Bango – a pesto, garlic and mushroom combination – is delicious. Like everything else on the menu, the ingredients are sourced from the Central Valley.

New Thai Cuisine
THAI $

(🖉 209-726-1048; 909 W 16th St; mains $10-19; ⊙ 11am-8pm) Hardly the fanciest digs in town – just four bare walls and a few tables – but this downtown Thai restaurant makes an excellent combination pho soup, sweet-and-savory honey sesame wings and a nice duck curry.

Branding Iron
STEAK $$

(www.thebrandingiron-merced.com; 640 W 16th St; mains lunch $9-11, dinner $10-27; ⊙ 11:30am-2pm Mon-Fri, 5-10pm Sun-Thu, to 9:30pm Fri & Sat) The Branding Iron roadhouse, a favorite of ranchers in the area, has been spruced up

a bit for the tour buses, but locals still dig the hearty steak platters and Western atmosphere. Presiding over the dining room is 'Old Blue,' a massive stuffed bull's head from a local dairy farm.

17th Street Public House
BAR

(🖉 209-354-4449; www.17thstpub.com; 315 W Main St; noon-10pm Sun-Wed, to midnight Thu-Fri) This haven for serious beer drinkers has an excellent and often-updated rotation of taps and a huge selection of bottles.

ℹ Getting There & Away

YARTS (Yosemite Area Regional Transportation System; 🖉 209-388-9589; www.yarts.com) buses depart three (winter) to five (summer) times daily for Yosemite Valley from several Merced locations, including the **Merced Transpo Center** (www.mercedthebus.com; cnr 16th & N Sts) and the **Amtrak station** (www.amtrak.com; 324 W 24th St, cnr 24th & K Sts). The trip takes about 2½ hours and stops include Mariposa, Midpines and the Yosemite Bug Lodge & Hostel. Round-trip adult/child costs $26/20 and includes park entry (quite a bargain!). There's limited space for bicycles, so show up early if you have one.

Greyhound (710 W 16th St) also operates from the Transpo Center (Los Angeles $20, 6½ hours, four times daily).

Fresno

Smack in the arid center of the state, Fresno is the biggest city in the Central Valley. It's hardly scenic, but it is beautifully situated, just an hour's drive from four national parks (Yosemite, Sierra, Kings Canyon and Sequoia), making it the ideal last stop for expeditions.

In recent years, Fresno's agriculture-based economy has suffered from catastrophic droughts and plummeting food prices. A local farm movement in the area seeks to revolutionize food production through organic, sustainable practices and fair wages. Fresno's proximity to these progressive farms has fostered a food renaissance. The produce and meat is the freshest you'll find anywhere. Fresno? Oh, Fresyes.

Like many valley towns, Fresno is home to diverse Hmong, Mexican, Chinese and Basque communities, which arrived in successive waves. The longstanding Armenian community is famously represented by author and playwright William Saroyan, who was born, lived and died in this city he loved.

◉ Sights & Activities

One of the most bustling parts of town is the Tower District, north of downtown, an oasis of gay-friendly bars, book and record stores, music clubs and a handful of stylish restaurants. Many of the historic buildings are along the Santa Fe railroad tracks and downtown, including the 1894 **Fresno Water Tower** and the 1928 **Pantages (Warnors) Theatre**. The crowds gather at the sprawling **Convention Center** and **Chukchansi Park**, home of Fresno's Triple-A baseball team, the Grizzlies.

Downtown lies between Divisadero St, Hwy 41 and Hwy 99. Two miles north, the Tower District sits around the corner of E Olive and N Fulton Aves.

Forestiere Underground Gardens   GARDENS
(☑559-271-0734; www.undergroundgardens. info; 5021 W Shaw Ave; adult/child $17/8; ⊘tours 10am-4pm hourly Wed-Sun May-Sep, reduced hours Oct-Apr) If you see only one thing in Fresno, make it this intriguing historic landmark, two blocks east of Hwy 99. The gardens were built by Sicilian immigrant Baldassare Forestiere, who dug out some 70 acres beneath the hardpan soil to plant citrus trees, starting in 1906. This utterly fantastical accomplishment took 40 years to complete.

Roeding Park   PARK
(www.fresno.gov; 890 W Belmont Ave; per vehicle $5; ⊘6am-10pm Apr-Oct, to 7pm Nov-Mar) Just east of Hwy 99, this large and shady park is home to the small **Fresno Chaffee Zoo** (☑559-498-5910; www.fresnochaffeezoo.org; 894 W Belmont Ave; adult/child $10/5.50; ⊘9am-6pm; ⊕). Adjacent to it are **Storyland** (☑559-264-2235; www.storylandplayland.com; 890 W Belmont Ave; adult/child $5/3.50; ⊘10am-4pm Sat & Sun; ⊕), a kitschy children's fairy-tale world dating from 1962, and the freshly remodeled **Playland** (www.storylandplayland.com; 890 W Belmont Ave; adult/child $5/3.50; ⊘10am-4pm Wed-Sun; ⊕), which has kiddie rides and games.

Fresno Art Museum   MUSEUM
(☑559-441-4221; www.fresnoartmuseum.org; 2233 N 1st St; adult/child $10/5; ⊘11am-5pm Thu-Sun; ⊕) This museum has rotating exhibits of contemporary art – including work by local artists – that are among the most intriguing in the valley.

Woodward Park   PARK
(www.fresno.gov; 7775 Friant Rd; per vehicle $5; ⊘6am-10pm Apr-Oct, to 7pm Nov-Mar) The city's largest park has 300 acres of barbecue facilities, lakes and ponds, a **Japanese garden** (adult/child $5/1), and a huge amphitheater for Shakespeare and other performances. A 6-mile network of bike trails connects to the **Lewis S Eaton Trail**, which runs 22 miles from the northeast corner along Friant Rd to Friant Dam.

🛏 Sleeping & Eating

Fresno has room to grow when it comes to world-class accommodations, but those using it as a launch pad for visiting Sequoia and Kings Canyon National Parks have plenty of options in the cluster of chains near the airport or a couple of high-rise offerings downtown.

For food, the best stuff is scattered around town – making this, most definitely, a driving town. Trendy eateries and breweries are in the Tower District and hidden among abandoned storefronts downtown. Food trucks circle up every Thursday accompanied by live music in front of Fresno Brewing Company. For fantastic raw ingredients, Fresno's excellent farmers markets are abundant all year round.

Piccadilly Inn Shaw   HOTEL $$
(☑559-348-5520; www.picadillyinn.com; 2305 W Shaw Ave; r $89-159; ☷@🛜☷) This is Fresno's nicest option, with a lovely pool, big rooms and tons of amenities. Ask for a room with a fireplace to cuddle by in winter.

Rocket Dog Gourmet Brats & Brew   BREW PUB $
(☑559-283-8096; www.rocketdogbratsandbrew. com; 88 E Shaw Ave; hot dogs $8; ⊘11am-9pm Sun-Thu, to 10pm Fri) Sure, something like 'Hansel's Heaven' – a bratwurst served on a pretzel roll and covered in mac 'n' cheese – isn't health food, but this excellent, ultra-efficient brewpub is the perfect highway pit stop if you're on the way in or out of Yosemite and not counting calories. It has a long list of excellent, elaborate hot dogs and local beer on tap.

Sam's Italian Deli & Market   DELI $
(www.samsitaliandeli.com; 2415 N 1st St; mains $5-9; ⊘9am-6pm Mon-Sat) This Italian market and deli is the real deal, stacking up the 'New Yorker' pastrami and some mean prosciutto and mozzarella.

Fresno Farmers Market   MARKET $
(☑559-222-0182; www.vineyardfarmersmarket. com; ⊘3-6pm Wed, 7am-noon Sat) Local booths

serve the freshest seasonal food from surrounding farms.

CartHop FAST FOOD $
(http://carthopfresno.com; Fulton Mall; ⊙10am-2pm Thu) Every Thursday, a fleet of independent food trucks from around the valley park on the Fulton Mall, serving grab-and-go lunch options from every corner of the globe.

☆ Entertainment

Tower Theatre for the
Performing Arts PERFORMING ARTS
(www.towertheatrefresno.com; 815 E Olive Ave) In the center of Fresno's hippest neighborhood, it's hard to miss the neon deco palace that opens its stage to touring rock and jazz acts and seasonal cultural events.

ⓘ Information

Fresno/Clovis Convention & Visitors Bureau
(☑800-788-0836, 559-981-5500; www.playfresno.org; 1550 E Shaw Ave, Suite 101; ⊙8am-5pm Mon-Fri) Visitor information in a nondescript office complex. Brochures are also stocked in the Water Tower and airport. Its website is a good place to look for comprehensive listings about local farmers markets and events.

ⓘ Getting There & Around

Amtrak (Santa Fe station; ☑559-486-7651; 2650 Tulare St; ⊙5:30am-9:45pm) The most scenic way to travel these parts, the San Joaquin service stops in a white Mission

building smack in downtown Fresno on its way to other tourist destinations, including Yosemite ($40, four hours, twice daily) and San Francisco ($55, four hours).

Fresno Area Express (FAX; ☑559-621-7433; www.fresno.gov; one-way $1.25) The local service that has daily buses to the Tower District (bus 22 or 28) and Forestiere Underground Gardens (bus 20) from the downtown transit center at Van Ness Ave and Fresno St.

Fresno Yosemite International Airport (FAT; www.flyfresno.com; 5175 E Clinton Way) In the Central Valley.

Greyhound (☑559-268-1829; 1033 H St) Stops downtown near the Chukchansi ballpark. Multiple regular/express rides daily to Los Angeles ($24, four hours) and San Francisco ($20, five hours).

Visalia

Its agricultural prosperity and well-maintained downtown make Visalia one of the valley's convenient stops en route to Sequoia and Kings Canyon National Parks or the Sierra Peaks. Bypassed a century ago by the railroad, the city is 5 miles east of Hwy 99, along Hwy 198. Its downtown has old-town charm and makes for a nice stroll.

The original Victorian and Arts-and-Crafts–style homes in Visalia are architectural gems worth viewing on foot. Maps for many **self-guided tours** are available via the website of the **Visalia Convention & Visitor's Bureau** (☑559-334-0141; www.visitvisalia.org; 303 E Acequia Ave; ⊙8am-5pm Mon-Fri).

The main draw in the area is the **Kaweah Oak Preserve** (www.sequoiariverlands.org; 29979 Rd 182, Exeter; donation adult/child $3/1; ⊙8am-sunset), about 7 miles east of town. With 324 acres of majestic oak trees, it is a gorgeous setting for easy hikes. From Hwy 198, turn north onto Rd 182; the park is about a half mile along on your left.

🛏 Sleeping & Eating

Lamp Liter Motel MOTEL $
(☑559-732-4511; www.lampliter.net; 3300 W Mineral King Ave; r $75-125; ❄@☎☎) It could be a run-of-the-mill two-story courtyard motel, but this family-owned establishment surprises with its spotlessly clean, if dated, rooms and country cottages facing an outdoor pool. The Sequoia Shuttle stops here.

DOWN ON THE FARM

There's no better way to get a taste of this agricultural region than on its farms. Many offer tours and seasonal opportunities to pick your own. Central Valley visitor's bureaus can point you to popular stops. Here are a few family farms paving the way with progressive practices.

➡ **Page River Bottom Farms** (☑559-638-3124; 17780 E Vino Ave, Reedley; ⊙8am-5pm Mon-Sat)

➡ **Organic Pastures** (www.organicpastures.com; 7221 S Jameson Ave; ⊙8am-5pm Mon-Fri)

➡ **T&D Willey Farm** (☑559-673-9058; www.tdwilleyfarms.com; 13886 Road 20, Madera)

Spalding House B&B $
([☎]559-739-7877; www.thespaldinghouse.com; 631 N Encina St; s/d $85/95; [❄][☎]) Built by a lumber baron, this atmospheric 1901 Colonial Revival–style home offers three cozy guest suites with private sitting areas and gorgeous details, such as mosaic-tiled bathrooms, a stained-glass ceiling or a sleigh bed.

Char-Cu-Te-Rie CAFE $
([☎]559-733-7902; www.char-cu-te-rie.com; 211 W Main St; mains $6-9; [☺]8am-3pm) Truffled eggs on brioche French toast, sourdough sandwiches spread with goat cheese and sweet figs, maple-bacon popcorn, date and Nutella ice-cream shakes and artisan coffee are just a few of the treats at this downtown storefront.

Visalia Farmers Market – Downtown MARKET $
(www.visaliafarmersmarket.com; cnr E Main & N Church Sts; [☺]5-8pm Thu mid-Mar–Sep; [✈]) Fresh fruits and veggies sold downtown.

Brewbakers Brewing Company AMERICAN $
([☎]559-627-2739; www.brewbakersbrewingco.com; 219 E Main St; mains $8-18; [☺]11:30am-10pm; [☎]) Always jam-packed, Brewbakers beckons thirsty hikers with house-made sodas and craft beers. A huge menu of burgers, pizzas, pastas and salads promises more than it delivers, but it's a great place to refuel after a few days in the mountains.

☆ Entertainment

Visalia Fox Theatre CINEMA, LIVE MUSIC
([☎]559-625-1369; www.foxvisalia.org; 300 W Main St) A 1930s 'talkie' movie palace, the Fox has a stunning East Indian temple–themed interior and occasionally hosts film screenings, live music concerts, stand-up comedy and special events.

Cellar Door LIVE MUSIC
([☎]559-636-9463; www.cellardoor101.com; 101 W Main St; [☺]from 6pm Tue, Thu-Sat) Serving pizza, wine and live music in a subterranean club on Main St. The events are all over the place – a Metallica cover band one night, salsa dancing the next – but there's always something going on.

🔒 Shopping

Big 5 Sporting Goods SPORTS & OUTDOORS
([☎]559-625-5934; www.big5sportinggoods. com; 1430 S Mooney Blvd; [☺]10am-9pm Mon-Fri, 9am-9pm Sat, 9:30am-8pm Sun) Stock up on camping, fishing and outdoor-sports equipment here, less than a mile south of Hwy 198.

🛈 Getting There & Around

Visalia's transit options, including direct access to **Sequoia National Park** (p486), all funnel through the **Visalia Transit Center** (www.ci.visalia.ca.us; 425 E Oak Ave). **Amtrak** ([☎]800-872-7245; www.amtrak.com) shuttles run between the Transit Center and Hanford station a half hour away by reservation only (use local buses as an alternative). From Hanford, you can connect to all other Amtrak routes in the state, including the *San Joaquin*, which travels north to Sacramento ($32, four hours, two direct daily) or south to Bakersfield ($22.50, 1½ hours, six daily).

The convenient, bike-rack equipped **Sequoia Shuttle** ([☎]877-287-4453; www.sequoiashuttle. com; round-trip incl park entry fee $15; [☺]late May-late Sep) picks up from major hotels and takes two hours to reach the **Giant Forest Museum** (p491) in Sequoia National Park. The **Visalia Towne Trolley** (425 East Oak Ave; ticket 25¢; [☺]7:30am-5:30pm Mon-Wed, to 11pm Thu-Fri, 9:30am-11pm Sat) hits most downtown sights over two circuits.

Bakersfield

Nearing Bakersfield, the landscape has evidence of California's *other* gold rush: rusting rigs alongside the route burrow into Southern California's vast oil fields. Black gold was discovered here in the late 1800s, and Kern County, the southernmost along Hwy 99, still pumps more than some OPEC countries.

This is the setting of Upton Sinclair's *Oil!*, which was adapted into the 2007 Academy Award–winning film, *There Will Be Blood*. In the 1930s the oil attracted a stream of 'Okies' – farmers who migrated out of the Great Plains – to work the derricks. The children of these tough-as-nails roughnecks put the 'western' in country and western by creating the 'Bakersfield Sound' in the mid-1950s, with heroes Buck Owens and Merle Haggard waving a defiant middle finger at the silky Nashville establishment.

Downtown Bakersfield is making moves to fancy-up, evident in the upbeat mix of restored buildings and new restaurants, theaters and clubs.

◉ Sights

The Kern River flows along Bakersfield's northern edge, separating it from its blue-collar neighbor, Oildale, and a host of oil fields. Truxtun and Chester Aves are the main downtown thoroughfares. Though currently suffering from some neglect, Old Town Kern, located east of downtown around Baker and Sumner Sts, still has character underneath the decay. **Bakersfield Historic Preservation Commission** (which you can find with a quick search of www.bakersfieldcity.us) has downloadable maps of walking tours covering Old Town Kern and Bakersfield's historic downtown.

Cesar E Chavez National Monument
HISTORIC SITE

(☑ 661-823-6134; www.chavezfoundation.org; 29700 Woodford-Tehachapi Rd, Keene; $3; ⊙ 10am-4pm) This newly designated national monument, Nuestra Señora Reina de la Paz, is the national headquarters of the United Farmworkers of America and was the home of civil rights leader César Chávez from 1971 until his death in 1993. On view are exhibits on Chávez's work, his office and grave. Keene is 27 miles southeast of Bakersfield down Hwy 58.

Chávez was born near Yuma, AZ, in 1927, and was 11 when his family lost their farm and became migrant farm workers in California. At 14, he left school to labor in the fields. Eventually, he became a champion of nonviolent social change, negotiating for better wages and access to water and bathrooms in the fields. His work resulted in numerous precedents, including the first union contracts requiring safe use of pesticides and the abolition of short-handled tools that had crippled generations of farm workers.

Kern County Museum
MUSEUM

(www.kcmuseum.org; 3801 Chester Ave; adult $10, child $7-9; ⊙ 10am-5pm Tue-Sat, from noon Sun; P 🚻) 🎫 This museum brings local history to life with a pioneer village of more than 50 restored and replicated buildings (including Merle Haggard's childhood home) and courtyard with beautifully restored vintage neon signs. The main structure has a large (and fairly disturbing) display of taxidermy wildlife and pristine memorabilia from Bakersfield's musical heyday.

Five & Dime Antique Mall
LANDMARK

(☑ 661-321-0061; Woolworth Bldg, 1400 19th St; ⊙ 10am-5pm Mon-Sat, from noon Sun) Three stories hold vintage wares that date back to at least the same era as the Woolworth building they're housed in. Try to go when the diner (p394) is open.

🛏 Sleeping & Eating

Chain motels sprout like weeds off the highways near Bakersfield. Old-school budget motels, starting from about $50, line Union Ave south heading south from Hwy 178, but can be a little seedy.

★ Padre Hotel
BOUTIQUE HOTEL $$

(☑ 661-427-4900; www.thepadrehotel.com; 1702 18th St; r $119-229, ste from $459) A stylish update revived this exceptional historic hotel, adding an upscale restaurant and two bars that instantly became *the* places for cocktails in Bakersfield. The service is excellent and the rooms have lavish details: thick mattresses, plush sheets and designer furniture. The two themed suites – the 'Oil Baron' and 'Farmer's Daughter' – have playful decor and showers for two.

Cafe Smitten
CAFE $

(www.cafesmitten.com; 909 18th St; mains $9-11; ⊙ 6:30am-7pm Mon-Thu, to 9pm Fri, 8:30am-9pm Sat) This bright cafe in the heart of downtown has a great vibe, serving lighter fare, such as a savory 'avocado smash' sandwich, and buttery pastries. It has excellent coffee drinks and a sunny patio that attracts a fun crowd for after-work drinks.

Luigi's
ITALIAN $

(www.shopluigis.com; 725 E 19th St; mains $7.75-11.95; ⊙ 11am-2:30pm Tue-Sat; 🅿) Lined with black-and-white photos of sporting legends, this amazing lunch spot has been around for over 100 years. The stuffed chicken melts in your mouth and the excellent bakery turns out soft, buttery rolls and an exceedingly rich Butterfinger Pie. The adjacent bar and deli stay open until 4pm.

Dewar's Candy Shop
ICE CREAM $

(☑ 661-322-0933; 1120 Eye St; sundaes from $4.50; ⊙ 10am-9pm Mon-Sun; 🚻) Perched on the pink stools at the counter, families dig into homemade ice cream with ingredients sourced from surrounding farms since 1930. Dreamy flavors like lemon flake and cotton candy change seasonally.

Woolworth Diner
DINER $

(☑ 661-321-0061; Five & Dime Antique Mall, 1400 19th St; burgers $5.95; ⊙ 11am-4pm Mon-Sat, noon-4pm Sun) The soda jerks flip fantastic cheeseburgers and pour thick shakes at the store's original soda counter, buffed to its former glory.

WORTH A TRIP: WEEDPATCH CAMP

In the Depression era, more than a million poor, white laborers from the Dust Bowl states in the South and the Great Plains arrived in the Central Valley with dreams of opportunity. Branded 'Okies' by the locals (whether from Oklahoma or not), the majority found only more hardship in the Golden State.

Weedpatch Camp (Arvin Farm Labor Center; ☑ 661-832-1299; 8701 Sunset Blvd, Bakersfield; ☉ by appointment) is one of about 16 Farm Security Administration camps built in the US during the 1930s to aid migrant workers, and today it is the only one with original buildings still standing (as of press time, they were undergoing renovation). A reporter named John Steinbeck researched the people in this camp and their lives inspired *The Grapes of Wrath*. Nearby tract housing still shelters migrant workers for the six-month grape harvest.

From Bakersfield, take Hwy 58 east to Weedpatch Hwy; head south for about 7 miles, past Lamont; then turn left on Sunset Blvd, driving another half mile. Look for the 'Arvin Farm Labor Center' sign on your right. The **Dust Bowl Festival** is a free celebration of Okie history held here the third Saturday of October.

★ **Noriega's** BASQUE $$
(☑ 661-322-8419; www.noriegahotel.com; 525 Sumner St; breakfast $10, lunch $17, dinner $22; ☉ 7am-9am, from noon, from 7pm Tue-Sun) Surly Basque gentlemen pass the communal wine carafes at Bakersfield's family-style Basque institution. The fixed menu includes a procession of dishes leading to silky oxtail stew, ribs and amazing garlic fried chicken (check online for the day's menu). The magical ambience and the food earned a prestigious James Beard award. Reserve in advance, seating hours are strict.

The Mark AMERICAN $$
(☑ 661-322-7665; www.atthemark.com; 1623 19th St; mains from $17; ☉ 11am-10pm Mon-Fri, 4pm-11:30pm Sat, 7:30-11:30pm Sun) One of downtown Bakersfield's swanky spots has red banquettes and big-city classics such as cioppino and pistachio-crusted lamb chops.

Wool Growers BASQUE $$
(☑ 661-327-9584; www.woolgrowers.net; 620 E 19th St; lunch $15, dinner mains $18-32; ☉ 11:30am-2pm & 6-9pm Mon-Sat) A simple Basque eating hall loaded with character. You can order the nine – yes nine – sides without a main dish, or loosen your belt and get it all.

🍷 Drinking & Nightlife

Dionysus Brewing Company BREWERY
(☑ 661-833-6000; www.dionysusbrewing.com; 6201 Schirra Ct, Suite 13; ☉ 4-9pm Mon-Fri, from noon Sat, 11am-5pm Sun) Craft beer nerds should go out of their way for a snifter at this exceptional small brewery. It specializes in adventurous sour beers, but has something for every palette, from the Super Funkadelic sour aged with fresh guava and pomegranate to the crisp, clean Berliner Weisse.

Temblor Brewing Company BREWERY
(☑ 661-489-4855; www.temblorbrewing.com; 3200 Buck Owens Blvd; ☎) Housed in a cavernous, sleekly renovated industrial space, this brewpub is a welcome newcomer to Bakersfield's nightlife. It serves quality flatbreads with fresh ingredients and main dishes ($9 to $15), and excellent beer, including a refreshing Belgian with a hint of blood orange. It's particularly fun here when it hosts comedy and live music.

☆ Entertainment

★ **Buck Owens' Crystal Palace** LIVE MUSIC
(☑ 661-328-7560; www.buckowens.com; 2800 Buck Owens Blvd) For fans of the Bakersfield Sound, this is the first stop – just look for the huge neon homage to Buck's famous red, white and blue guitar. Part museum, honky-tonk and steakhouse (dinner from 5pm, brunch 9:30am to 2pm Sunday), it has top-drawer country acts nearly nightly. Locals in snap-button shirts, shiny boots and pressed jeans tear up the dance floor.

Trout's & the Blackboard Stage LIVE MUSIC
(www.therockwellopry.webs.com; 805 N Chester Ave at Decatur St, Oildale; ☉ 11am-late Mon-Sat) The legendary Trout's, north of town, is the only remaining honky-tonk in these parts, hobbling along after half a century as a testament to hell-raisin' days past. Hundreds of old guitars hang from the ceiling of this ramshackle dive, while Bakersfield legends and their disciples take the stage.

Bakersfield Music Hall of Fame ARTS CENTER
(☑661-864-1701; www.bakersfieldmusichalloffame.
com; 2230 Q St; ⊙10am-6pm Mon-Fri) Housing
a small theater, recording studios and displays on local legends, this space celebrates
past icons and fosters new talent. Check the
schedule for local up-and-comers, who take
the state-of-the-art stage and are quite a bit
more civilized than the rowdy honky-tonks
that made this town famous.

ℹ Information

**Greater Bakersfield Convention & Visitors
Bureau** (☑661-852-7282; www.bakersfieldcvb.
org; 515 Truxtun Ave; ⊙8am-5pm Mon-Fri) A
spacious building with maps and brochures.

ℹ Transport

Airport Valet Express (☑661-363-5000;
www.airportvaletexpress.com; 201 New Stine,
Suite 120; one-way/round-trip $49/89; ⊙to
LAX 3am, 8am, 5pm) Star-spangled buses
travel between Bakersfield (from the north side
of the San Joaquin Valley College campus) and
LAX (2½ hours, three daily). Book in advance
for a sizable discount.

Amtrak Station (☑800-872-7245; 601 Truxtun
Ave at S St) Trains travel north from here to
Sacramento ($45 to $65, five hours, two direct
trains). Buses head to LA, but fares must be
purchased in combination with a train ticket.

Golden Empire Transit (GET; www.getbus.org;
Transit Center, 1830 Golden State Ave; fares
from $1.25) The efficient local bus system's
Route 22 runs north on Chester Ave to the
Kern County Museum (p394) and Oildale (22
minutes).

Greyhound (☑661-327-5617; 1820 18th St at G
St) Cheap rides from downtown Bakersfield to
Los Angeles ($9, two hours).

Kern River Area

A half-century ago, Kern River originated
on the slopes of Mt Whitney and journeyed
close to 170 miles before finally settling into
the Central Valley. Now, after its wild descent from the high country – 60ft per mile
– the Kern is dammed in several places and
almost entirely tapped for agricultural use.

Its pristine upper reaches, declared wild
and scenic by the Secretary of the Interior,
is nicknamed 'Killer Kern' for its occasionally lethal force and makes for world-class
rafting.

There are two USFS Ranger Stations in
the area, one in **Kernville** (☑760-376-3781;
www.fs.usda.gov; ⊙8am-4:30pm Mon-Fri) and
another in **Lake Isabella** (☑760-379-5646;
⊙8am-4:30pm Mon-Fri). Both have hiking and
camping information, maps and wilderness
permits.

🏃 Activities

This part of the state is all about white water, and rafting is the banner attraction. The
town of **Lake Isabella** is a dreary strip of
local businesses on the south end of the lake,
but Hwy 155 runs north to **Kernville**, a cute
little town straddling the Kern River that
is *the* hub for local water sports. While the
lake is popular for cooling off, note that the
river's currents can be extremely dangerous.

The Upper Kern and Forks of the Kern
(both sections of the river north of Kernville)
yield Class IV and V rapids during spring
runoff and offer some of the most awe-inspiring white-water trips in the country.
You'll need experience before tackling these
sections, though there are still opportunities
for novices. Below Lake Isabella, the Kern is
tamer and steadier.

Currently seven rafting companies are licensed to operate out of Kernville; all offer
competitive prices and run trips from May
to August, depending on conditions. Excursions include popular one-hour runs (from
$40) and day-long Lower Kern trips (from
$120) and multiday Wild Forks of the Kern
experiences (from $600). Walk-ins are wel-
come and experience is not necessary. Kids
ages six and up can usually participate.

Kern River Outfitters RAFTING
(☑800-323-4234; www.kernrafting.com; 6602
Wofford Heights Blvd, Wofford Heights; ⊙8:30am-
5:30pm Mon-Fri) Offers the staple menu of
trips plus an adults-only Pub & Grub trip,
which includes beer tastings from the Kern
River Brewery.

Mountain & River Adventures RAFTING
(☑800-861-6553, 760-376-6553; www.mtnriver.
com; 11113 Kernville Rd) Besides rafting, this
outfit offers combo–kayak and rafting,
mountain-biking and winter excursions. It
also has a campground right on the banks
of the Kern.

Sierra South RAFTING
(☑760-376-3745, 800-457-2082; www.sierrasouth.
com; 11300 Kernville Rd) Rafting or for something calmer, paddle boarding, on Lake
Isabella.

A LITTLE SWEDEN IN THE VALLEY

The quiet hamlet of Kingsburg has a vibrant ethnic heritage. Around 1873, when it was established as a rail stop called 'Kings River Switch,' two Swedes arrived. Their country-men soon followed, and by 1921, 94% of Kingsburg's residents, as it had become known, were of Swedish heritage. Today, the Swedish past mixes with more recent Mexican im-migrants who drive the agricultural economy.

Draper St, the main drag, is decked out in Swedish Dala horses and crests of Swedish regions. Inside the cutesy Tudor buildings are gift shops and little bakeries stocked with buttery pastries. Diane at **Diane's Village Bakery & Cafe** (☑559-897-7460; Kingsburg Village Mall, 1332 Draper St; mains under $8.25; ☺8am-2:30pm Mon-Sat) cooks with her grandmother's recipes. Pick up Nordic decor and insight on the town from June, town icon and proprietor of **Svensk Butik** (☑559-897-5119; 1465 Draper St; ☺9am-5pm Mon-Sat). Sure, the town plays up its heritage for the crowds, but there is genuine pride in every 'Valkommen!'

The town has gone through pains to preserve its oldest structures. Under the cof-fee-pot water tower, the **city jail** (www.kingsburghistoricalpark.org; 1400 Marion St; ☺24hr) ` FREE ` is a quick stop. On the east end of town, a general store, schoolhouse and windmill, as well as artifacts and farm equipment, make up **Kingsburg Historical Park** (www.kingsburghistoricalpark.org; 2321 Sierra St; ☺1-4pm Fri).

Good times to visit are during the holiday explosion that is the Santa Lucia Festival (first Saturday of December) and the Swedish Festival (parades, maypole dancing and a real smorgasbord) in May. The Chamber of Commerce keeps a calendar.

Whitewater Voyages　RAFTING
(☑660-376-8806, 800-400-7238; www.whitewatervoyages.com; 11006 Kernville Rd) The first out-fitter to dare guide clients down the entire Wild and Scenic Forks of the Kern back in 1980.

🛌 Sleeping

USFS Campgrounds　CAMPGROUND $
(☑877-444-6777; www.fs.usda.gov; developed/undeveloped tent sites $24/20) These camp-grounds line the 10-mile stretch between Lake Isabella and Kernville, and several more lie north of Kernville on Mountain Hwy 99. There are seven in total, mostly undeveloped. Rangers recommend the Fair-view and Limestone (marked on the map) for their seclusion. Campgrounds without running water and electricity are free.

Whispering Pines Lodge　B&B $$
(☑760-376-3733; www.pineskernville.com; 13745 Sierra Way; r $189-219, house incl breakfast $359; ▣) This secluded B&B, blending rustic char-acter with luxurious comfort, is just north of town. Rooms with kitchens book up quickly in the summer.

🍷 Drinking & Nightlife

Kern River Brewing Company　BREWERY
(☑760-376-2337; www.kernriverbrewing.com; 13415 Sierra Hwy, Kernville; ☺11am-10pm Sun-Thu, to 11pm Fri & Sat) An excellent hub for local rafting guides and outdoor types, this brew-ery has a rotation of excellent seasonal beers. The Isabella Blonde is light and refreshing when the weather is sweltering. It also has a reliably tasty menu with pulled pork tacos, fish and chips, and fancy burgers.

Gold Country

Best Places to Eat

➡ New Moon Cafe (p405)
➡ Argonaut Farm to Fork Cafe (p411)
➡ La Cocina de Oro Taqueria (p408)
➡ Taste (p415)
➡ Ike's Quarter Cafe (p404)

Best Places to Sleep

➡ Outside Inn (p404)
➡ Lure Resort (p408)
➡ Camino Hotel (p412)
➡ Imperial Hotel (p415)
➡ Victoria Inn (p420)

Why Go?

Hollywood draws the dreamers and Silicon Valley lures fortune-hunters, but this isn't the first time droves of aspiring young folk have streamed into the Golden State. After a sparkle in the American River caught James Marshall's eye in 1848, more than 300,000 prospectors from America and abroad started digging for gold in the Sierra foothills. Soon California entered statehood with the official motto 'Eureka' solidifying its place as the land of opportunity.

The miner forty-niners are gone, but a ride along Hwy 49 through sleepy hill towns, past clapboard saloons and oak-lined byways is a journey back to the wild ride that was modern California's founding: umpteen historical markers tell tales of gold rush violence and banditry. Many travelers hardly hit the brakes while rushing between California's coasts and mountains, but those who do are rewarded with a taste of the helter-skelter era that kick-started the heartbeat of this state.

When to Go

Nevada City

°C/°F Temp
40/104 —
30/86 —
20/68 —
10/50 —
0/32 —
-10/14 —
J F M A M J J A S O N D

Rainfall inches/mm
— 12/300
— 10/250
— 8/200
— 6/150
— 4/100
— 2/50
— 0

Apr–May Pan for gold after the snowmelt washes the treasure into Jamestown's hills.

Jul As temperatures rise to scorching, plunge into a refreshing South Yuba swimming hole.

Sep–Nov When crisp, heritage apples are ripe for the picking, head to Apple Hill's sprawling ranches.

Gold Country Highlights

1 Witnessing the birthplace of modern California at **Marshall Gold Discovery State Historic Park** (p411).

2 Rumbling down the premier single-track bike trails above **Downieville** (p407).

3 Tasting wines made from grapes grown in the **Plymouth** (p414) hills.

4 Stepping back in time in the living history of **Columbia State Historic Park** (p421), the 'Gem of the Southern Mines.'

5 Wandering the historic streets of **Nevada City** (p403), Gold Country's relaxing jewel of a town.

6 Riding the white-water **American River** (p410).

7 Discovering rock art created by the Miwoks who once thrived near **Indian Grinding Rock State Historic Park** (p416).

8 Traveling down **Highway 49** (p409) through El Dorado and Amador counties in pursuit of antiques and ice cream.

NEVADA COUNTY & NORTHERN GOLD COUNTRY

The forty-niners hit it big in Nevada County – the richest score in the region known as the Mother Lode – and their wealth built one of the most picturesque and well-preserved boomtowns, Nevada City. Get out of town and you'll find lovely, remote wilderness areas, a clutch of historic parks and fascinating remnants of the long-gone miners, including a ghost town. This is also a magnet for adrenaline junkies looking to race down singletracks on mountain bikes or plunge into swimming holes that are remote enough for skinny-dipping.

Auburn

Look for the big man: a 45-ton effigy of French gold panner Claude Chana marks your arrival in Placer County's Gold Country. Its hallmarks are all here – ice-cream shops, strollable historic districts and antiques. A major stop on the Central Pacific's transcontinental route, Auburn still welcomes trains on the Union Pacific's main line to the east and is a popular stop for those rushing along I-80 between the Bay Area and Lake Tahoe. You'll have to venture along Hwy 49 for a deeper taste of Gold Country, but those who want just a sample will enjoy this accessible town.

⊙ Sights & Activities

The fact that Auburn is sometimes called the 'Endurance Sport Capital of the World' will give you a sense of how good the area is for cycling, trail running and other heart-pounding activities. See www.auburnendurancecapital.com for events.

Placer County Museum MUSEUM
(www.placer.ca.gov; 101 Maple St; ⊙10am-4pm) FREE The 1st floor of the domed 1898 Placer County Courthouse has Native American artifacts and displays of Auburn's transportation heritage, including a classic 1877 stage coach. It's the easiest museum to visit and gives a good overview of area history; there's also the glitter of the museum's gold collection with huge chunks of unrefined gold on display.

Hour-long walking tours of the town leave from the museum at 10am each Saturday.

Bernhard Museum Complex MUSEUM
(291 Auburn-Folsom Rd; entry by donation; ⊙11am-4pm Tue-Sun) This museum, built in 1851 as the Traveler's Rest Hotel, exhibits depictions of typical 19th-century-farm family life. Volunteers in period garb show you around, and the concept is that the family has just left the house.

Gold Country Museum MUSEUM
(1273 High St; ⊙11am-4pm Tue-Sun; 🚻) FREE Toward the back of the fairgrounds, the Gold Country Museum includes a reconstructed mine and gold panning, both great for kids.

Joss House MUSEUM
(☑530-823-0373; 200 Sacramento St; entry by donation; ⊙10am-4pm 1st Sat of month) Built by the Yue family in the 1920s, this clapboard residence stands on 'Chinese Hill,' one of many Chinese communities established during the gold rush. After a 'mysterious' fire ripped through the settlement, the family converted their home into a public space for worship, seasonal boarders and a school.

Grandson Richard is on hand to tell the story, and show you the house shrine and rudimentary kitchen.

🛏 Sleeping

Most visitors will want to head north to Nevada City or south to Placerville to find a more enticing spot to stay: Auburn is very much a gateway town. For an affordable place to sleep, look to the highway exits where there's every brand of chain hotel.

Powers Mansion Inn B&B $$
(☑916-425-9360; www.powersmansioninn.com; 195 Harrison Ave; r $129; 🖥) An unabashedly chintzy option, with much Victoriana – floral drapes, wrought-iron beds and claw-foot baths – as well as Jacuzzis and satellite TV. The rambling mansion was built in 1884 by gold-mining magnate Harold T Power. You can play games in the parlor and enjoy anecdotes courtesy of the friendly, voluble owner.

🍴 Eating & Drinking

Lincoln Way toward the Chamber of Commerce (p401) has several restaurants popular with locals, and there's plenty of sunny outdoor eating right off the highway around Sacramento St.

Ikedas DINER $
(www.ikedas.com; 13500 Lincoln Way; sandwiches $6-9; ⊙11am-7pm Mon-Thu, 10am-8pm Fri-Sun; 🚗) If you're cruising this part of the state

without time to explore, the best pit stop is this expanded farm stand – now a diner/market – off I-80 a few miles north of downtown. Thick, grass-fed beef or tofu burgers, homemade sweet and savory pies and the seasonal fresh-peach shake are deliriously good.

Katrina's BREAKFAST $
(www.katrinascafe.com; 456 Grass Valley Hwy; mains $10-15; ⊘7am-2:30pm Wed-Sat, to 2pm Sun) Lemon yogurt or banana nut pancakes, great omelets and all manner of hot sandwiches dished up in a homey atmosphere.

Auburn Alehouse BREWERY
(www.auburnalehouse.com; 289 Washington St; mains $8-21; ⊘11am-10pm Mon & Tue, to 11pm Wed & Thu, to midnight Fri, 9am-midnight Sat, 9am-10pm Sun) One of those rare brewpubs with both excellent craft beer *and* food; patrons dig into burgers, sweet-potato fries, 'adult mac 'n' cheese' and sweet-and-savory salads. The beer sampler is a great deal, as Auburn brings home tons of medals for its ales and pilsners, and the setting, with swirly stucco and a pressed-metal ceiling, is impressive.

ℹ Information

Auburn Area Chamber of Commerce (☑530-885-5616; www.auburnchamber.net; 1103 High St; ⊘10am-4pm Tue-Fri) In the Southern Pacific railroad depot at the north end of Lincoln Way, it has lots of useful local info and a monument to the Transcontinental Railroad nearby.

Auburn State Recreation Area Office (☑530-885-4527; 501 El Dorado St; ⊘9am-4pm Mon-Fri) Information on sights and outdoor activities in the area.

California Welcome Center (Placer County Visitors Center; ☑530-887-2111; www.visitplacer.com; 1103 High St; ⊘9am-4:30pm Mon-Sat, 11am-4pm Sun) Great information on Gold Country and eastward.

ℹ Getting There & Away

Amtrak (☑800-872-7245; www.amtrak.com; 277 Nevada St) runs one train a day along the Capital Corridor route (http://capitolcorridor.org) linking Auburn with Sacramento ($16, one hour); other destinations require connecting with Thruway buses. There is also one train daily east to Reno ($62, eight hours; requires a change).

Amtrak's *California Zephyr* stops in Auburn on its daily run between the Bay Area and Chicago via Reno and Denver (to San Francisco takes three hours and costs $39).

SUCTION DREDGING FOR GOLD

Floating down Gold Country's waterways, you may see someone trying to strike it rich with a suction dredge – a vacuum that sucks up the river bed and the gold in it. This method of prospecting was banned in California in 2009 for its destructive side effects, including disturbing riparian habitat and stirring up toxic quicksilver, the mercury that the forty-niners used to extract gold from ore.

The **Gold Country Stage Bus Service** (☑888-660-7433; www.goldcountrystage.com; adult $1.50-3, child free) links Auburn, including its Amtrak station, with Grass Valley and Nevada City five times a day on weekdays (limited service on Saturdays). Kids and bikes ride free. **Placer County Transit** (☑530-885-2877; www.placer.ca.gov/transit; 11460 F Ave; fare $2.50) also runs bus services in the Auburn area.

Auburn State Recreation Area

This is a park (☑530-885-4527; www.parks.ca.gov; per car $10; ⊘7am-sunset) of deep gorges cut by the rushing waters of the North and Middle Forks of the American River, which converge below a bridge on Hwy 49, 4 miles south of Auburn. In early spring, when waters are high, this is immensely popular for white-water rafting, as the rivers are Class II to V runs. Late summer, calmer waters allow for sunning and swimming, especially around the confluence. Numerous trails are shared by hikers, mountain bikers and horses.

One of the most popular hikes is the **Western States Trail**, which connects Auburn State Recreation Area to **Folsom Lake State Recreation Area** and Folsom Lake. It's the site of the **Western States 100-Mile Endurance Run** (www.wser.org), and the **Tevis Cup** (www.teviscup.org), an endurance race on horseback. The **Quarry Trail** takes a level path from Hwy 49, just south of the bridge, along the Middle Fork of the American. Several side trails reach the river.

The best tours of the American, Tuolumne and Stanislaus rivers are offered spring through fall by the family-run **All-Outdoors California Whitewater Rafting** (☑925-932-

8993; www.aorafting.com; 1250 Pine St, Walnut Creek; trips from $108). Its single- and multi-day wilderness rafting excursions include breaks for hiking among the boulders and historically significant sights in the canyons. Meals are provided (the burrito lunch might be worth the trip alone). Check online for discounts.

For **camping** (campsites $25-35), there are basic sites on a sweeping bend of the Middle Fork at the blackberry-dotted Ford's Bar that are accessible only by a 2-mile hike from Rucky-A-Chucky Rd, or a half-day raft. Required permits for these sites are available from the Auburn State Recreation Area Office (p401).

Grass Valley

From the margins, Grass Valley is the ugly utilitarian sister to Nevada City, a place to stock up on supplies and get an oil change, not necessarily vacation. But there are treasures if you dig, including a dense cluster of Victorian and art-deco buildings, some great independent boutiques and cafes, and a few surprisingly rowdy bars.

TRIBAL HISTORY IN GOLD COUNTRY

A few dedicated museums tell part of the stories of the Miwok, Maidu, Konkow, Monache, Nisenan, Tubatulabal, Washo and Foothill Yokuts – the people who called this region home, way before the rush for gold.

➜ **Maidu Museum & Historical Site** (www.roseville.ca.us; 1970 Johnson Ranch Dr, Roseville; adult/child $4.50/4; ⊙ 9am-4pm Mon-Fri, to 1pm Sat, plus 6:30-8:30pm every 3rd Sat) is built on the edge of an ancient Maidu village, occupied for over 3000 years.

➜ The roundhouse museum in **Indian Grinding Rock State Historic Park** (p416) has a variety of artifacts representing different tribes of the area. The limestone outcrop outside is dimpled with mortar holes for grinding acorns.

➜ The **State Indian Museum** (p370) in Sacramento features the most varied collections, with a redwood canoe and extraordinary beaded garments.

Historic Mill and W Main Sts mark the town center. E Main St leads north to modern shopping centers and mini-malls and into Nevada City. On Thursday nights in late June through August, Mill St closes to traffic to serve up farmstead food, arts and crafts and music. On the town's outskirts are some of the state's oldest shaft mines. Being the first to exploit lode-mining (tunneling to find veins of gold in hard rock) rather than placer techniques (sifting debris carried by waterways), these were among the most profitable claims.

◉ Sights

Empire Mine State Historic Park　　HISTORIC SITE
(☑530-273-8522; www.empiremine.org; 10791 Empire St; adult/child $7/3; ⊙10am-5pm; P🚻) Atop 367 miles of mine shafts tunneling almost a vertical mile beneath the surface, Gold Country's best-preserved gold-quartz-mining operation is worth a solid half-day's exploration. From 1850 to 1956 the miners here, mostly Cornish, produced 5.8 million ounces of gold (worth about $8 billion today). The visitor center has maps and leads guided tours (schedules vary).

It's very well worth paying to enter the mine yard, littered with mining equipment and buildings constructed from waste rock, and to view the main shaft's claustrophobic entry, next to the head frame (a tall structure used to haul ore and people from underground). Nearby is the English-manor-style cottage and rose garden of the Bourn family, who originally owned the mine; though this now appears incongruously idyllic, the noise of the mining activity must have been deafening.

Hiking the trails that meander past abandoned mines and equipment is free. Trailheads are located at the parking lots behind the visitor center and Penn Gate to its west.

North Star Mining Museum　　MUSEUM
(Powerhouse & Pelton Wheel Museum; www.nevadacountyhistory.org; 10933 Allison Ranch Rd; entry by donation; ⊙11am-5pm Tue-Sat, noon-4pm Sun May-Oct) A museum for those who ache when they see machinery set aside to rust. The engineering-minded docents here have polished and oiled their extensive collection of 19th-century mining equipment to a shine. See stamp mills, dredges, dynamite packing machines, Cornish pumps and the

largest Pelton wheel ever constructed in action.

The grassy banks of the creek that once powered the North Star mine are perfect for a picnic.

🛏 Sleeping & Eating

The menus around here don't vary much but the quality is good. There are several good brunch spots and bars around downtown, and every imaginable chain among the strip malls by the highway.

Holbrooke Hotel HISTORIC HOTEL $$
(☎530-273-1353; www.holbrooke.com; 212 W Main St; r $129-179, ste $249; ❀ 🗢) The register in this 1862 hotel boasts the signatures of Mark Twain and President Ulysses S Grant; rooms are aging but neat. The restaurant (mains $11 to $22) serves casual fare in the ornate dining room or on the shaded patio, but the best tables overlook the Main St action. Weekday rates drop by 15% to 30%.

There's live music in the saloon bar every night except Monday, with a regular slot for Celtic bands on a Sunday. Beware the haunted loo downstairs from reception.

Cousin Jack Pasties BAKERY $
(100 S Auburn St; meals $5.25-9; ⊙10:30am-6pm Mon-Sat, 11am-5pm Sun; ⚐) Cousin Jack and his kin have been serving flaky pasties – a meat-and-potato-stuffed pastry beloved by Cornish miners – for five generations. The pies – Basque lamb, pot roast and several vegetarian options – are all made from local ingredients. Anyone homesick for other British fare can buy Bramley pies, Bakewell tarts and Marmite here.

Lazy Dog Ice Cream ICE CREAM $
(www.spotlazydog.com; 111 Mill St; ice-cream bars $4; ⊙10am-9pm Sun-Thu, to 10pm Fri & Sat) This colorful ice-cream and candy shop explodes with sugar in all its forms. Besides scoops, there are hand-dipped bars, chocolates and old-timey candies from 'juicy wax sticks' to swirly suckers.

Tofanelli's ITALIAN $$
(☎530-272-1468; www.tofanellis.com; 302 W Main St; mains $8-23; ⊙8am-9pm) Hugely popular with locals in the know, this creative restaurant has everything from salads to hearty steaks and seasonal specials such as summer squash ravioli. Portions are burly and the patio is a treat.

☆ Entertainment

Center for the Arts ARTS CENTER
(☎530-274-8384; http://thecenterforthearts.org; 314 W Main St) Grass Valley punches above its weight with this excellent arts center. The varied program includes local and international music, dance, visual arts, comedy and literary events.

ℹ Information

Greater Grass Valley Visitor Center (☎530-273-4667; www.grassvalleychamber.com; 128 Main St; ⊙10am-5pm Mon-Fri, to 3pm Sat & Sun; 🖥) In the thick of the historical sights stands this brick livery stable, which is stocked with maps and brochures covering the county and more. There's a very comprehensive walking-tour map.

ℹ Getting There & Away

Transit in Grass Valley is by **Gold Country Stage Bus Service** (☎888-660-7433; www.goldcountrystage.com; 13083 John Bauer Ave), which links to Nevada City hourly from 7am to 6pm weekdays, 8am to 4pm Saturday. Fares are $1.50 to $3 for adults. Kids and bikes ride free. Check the website for connections to Auburn and schedule changes.

Amtrak (p401) bus connections are in Colfax, 12 miles south.

Nevada City

Nevada City knows it's charming, but it doesn't like to brag. The shops sell prayer flags and chia smoothies, while the drinking holes sling all manner of liquid enlightenment. The person browsing the history museum with you is just as liable to be a crusty old-timer, a road-weary backpacker or a mystical folk artist. In the midst of all that are the requisite Victorian and gold rush tourist attractions – an elegantly restored town center and frilly B&Bs.

This is the gateway to Tahoe National Forest, but linger a few days to experience some inviting NorCal culture. The theater companies, alternative film houses, bookstores and venues put on shows almost every night; tune into radical local radio station kvmr.org at 89.5FM to catch the vibe and hear what's on.

Nevada City's strollable streets are especially lively in summer. In December the snow blanket and twinkling lights are something from a storybook.

◉ Sights

The main attraction is the town itself – its restored buildings, all brick and wrought-iron trimmings, wear their history proudly. There are intriguing (if pricey) boutiques, galleries and places for food and drink everywhere, all with exhaustive posted histories.

Firehouse No 1 Museum   MUSEUM
(☑530-265-3937; www.nevadacountyhistory. org; 214 Main St; by donation; ⊗1-4pm Tue-Sun May-Oct, by appointment Nov-Apr) This small, painstakingly curated museum is run by the Nevada County Historical Society from a unique white wooden building with a tall bell tower. From stunning Nisenan baskets to preserved Victorian bridal wear, its collections tell the story of the local people. The prize exhibits are relics from the Chinese settlers who often built but seldom profited from the mines.

By 1880, miners of Chinese origin constituted more than a fifth of all engaged in the industry and were nearly exclusively subject to a hefty Foreign Miners' License Tax. The Chinese altar was saved by a local merchant who hid the pieces around town to keep it from marauders.

Nevada City Winery   WINERY
(☑530-265-9463; http://ncwinery.com; 321 Spring St; ⊗tasting room noon-5pm Sun-Thu, to 6pm Fri & Sat) This popular winery excels with Syrah and Zinfandel varietals, which you can savor while touring the production facility in the old Miners' Foundry Garage. It's a good place to get information on touring all of the surrounding wine region.

🛏 Sleeping

Weekends, Nevada City fills up with urban refugees who inevitably weigh themselves down with real-estate brochures. There are B&Bs everywhere. The cheapest options are the National Forest campgrounds, just outside town in any direction.

★Outside Inn   INN, COTTAGE $$
(☑530-265-2233; http://outsideinn.com; 575 E Broad St; d $79-210; ⓟ⊜❄☎☀☀) The best option for active explorers, this is an unusually friendly and fun inn, with 12 rooms and three cottages maintained by staff who love the outdoors. Some rooms have a patio overlooking a small creek; all have nice quilts and access to BBQ grills. It's a 10-minute walk from downtown and there's a small unheated outdoor pool.

★Two Room Inn   APARTMENT $$
(☑415-891-9022; http://tworoominn.com; 431 Broad St; d from $125) Nevada City isn't short on pretty buildings, but this is one of the most enchanting: a two-room cottage with a Hansel and Gretel vibe, latticed stained-glass windows and a redwood interior. The upstairs master bedroom has a pitched wooden roof; an alcove converts into a second bedroom. Located in the heart of town, this little gem has all the mod cons.

★Broad Street Inn   INN $$
(☑530-265-2239; www.broadstreetinn.com; 517 W Broad St; r $119-134; ❄☎☀) 🅿 This six-room inn in the heart of town is a favorite because it keeps things simple. (No weird old dolls, no yellowing lace doilies.) The good-value rooms are modern, brightly but soothingly furnished and elegant. No breakfast served.

National Hotel   HISTORIC HOTEL $$
(☑530-265-4551; www.thenationalhotel.com; 211 Broad St; r $80-140; ⓟ⊜) This historic 1850s hotel in the heart of downtown claims to be the oldest continuously operating hotel west of the Rocky Mountains and its unreconstructed charm supports this. Most of the rooms are en suite, but don't come here if you're looking for home comforts, as it's pretty spartan.

✗ Eating

In a town of holistic thinkers, it's no surprise most menus emphasize organic and seasonal ingredients. The options are mostly clustered in a three-block radius on Commercial and Broad Sts.

★Ike's Quarter Cafe   CREOLE, BREAKFAST $
(☑530-265-6138; www.ikesquartercafe.com; 401 Commercial St; mains $11-15; ⊗8am-3pm Thu-Mon; ☑🔸) 🅿 Right out of New Orleans' Garden District, Ike's serves splendid brunch fare with a sassy charm. Sit outside under the cherry tree or in the cluttered, funky interior. There's eggs Sardou, jambalaya, vegetarian po'boy sandwiches and more. It's an excellent place to get 'Hangtown Fry' – a cornmeal-crusted mess of oysters, bacon, caramelized onions and spinach.

Vegan and gluten-free options are available, including gluten-free cornbread.

Sopa Thai   THAI $
(☑530-470-0101; www.sopathai.net; 312 Commercial St; mains $10-15; ⊗11am-3pm & 5-9:30pm Mon-Fri, noon-9:30pm Sat & Sun) Huge quantities

of delicious mango red curry, steamed mussels and spring rolls in the region's best and most popular Thai restaurant. The rugged red-brick interior is furnished with imported carvings, silks and lanterns, and the patio seating in back makes for a busy scene midday. The $10.95 lunch special is great value.

Three Forks Bakery & Brewing Co   CAFE $
(☑530-470-8333; www.threeforksnc.com; 211 Commercial St; pizzas $10-15, cakes $4-5 per slice; ◷7am-10pm Mon, Wed & Thu, 7am-11pm Fri, 8am-11pm Sat, 8am-10pm Sun) An open-plan modern place, open all day and serving cakes, pizzas and beer brewed on site. It has a generic feel compared to some of the quirky options in town, but it's functional, fast and friendly.

Treats   DESSERTS $
(http://treatsnevadacity.com; 110 York St; items $3.50-5; ◷1-9pm Mon-Sat, 1-8pm Sun; ⊞) It's a crowded contest for Gold Country's best ice-cream shop, but this cute little spot – the brilliant second career of avuncular scooper Bob Wright – wins in a walk. Many flavors are sourced from ripe local produce like the River Hill Red sorbet (sweet red peppers and strawberry), mint chip and pear ginger.

★ New Moon Cafe   CALIFORNIAN $$$
(☑530-265-6399; www.thenewmooncafe.com; 203 York St; dinner mains $23-38; ◷11:30am-2pm Tue-Fri, 5-8:30pm Tue-Sun) ⌀ Pure elegance, Peter Selaya's organic- and local-ingredient menu changes with the seasons. If you visit during spring or summer, go for the line-caught fish or the house-made, moon-shaped fresh ravioli. The wine list is excellent.

🍷 Drinking & Entertainment

This little village has a vibrant arts scene, with two theater-cinemas and an ambitious arts center. The entertainment section of the *Union* newspaper (www.theunion.com) comes out on Thursday, and lists what's going on throughout the county. Bar-hopping in Nevada City is a delight, with friendly bar staff and locals, and delectable local brews to sample.

Crazy Horse Saloon Grill   BAR
(☑530-265-4000; http://crazyhorsenc.com; 230 Commercial St; ◷11:30am-1:30am) A fantastic town-center saloon with a long convivial bar where you can eat burgers and nachos, shoot the breeze with the friendly staff, then hit the dance floor. The little raised stage, wreathed in lanterns, hosts almost nightly live music, with jazz, funk, indie pop and rock, plus DJ nights.

★ Miners Foundry   ARTS CENTER
(☑530-265-5040; http://minersfoundry.org; 325 Spring St; ◷10am-5pm, plus evenings for events) As the name suggests, this was once an industrial building, constructed in 1856 and used to manufacture Pelton wheels. It has been brilliantly converted into an eclectic arts center, hosting music workshops, youth theater, dance classes and gigs.

★ Magic Theatre   CINEMA
(www.themagictheatre.com; 107 Argall Way) This beloved and adorably quirky theater screens a matchless lineup of unusual films and is about a mile south of downtown Nevada City. It serves bowls of fresh popcorn, coffee in real mugs and hot brownies. At the time of writing the owners were about to renovate and add a new screen, with a promise to keep the charm intact.

Nevada Theatre   THEATER, CINEMA
(www.nevadatheatre.com; 401 Broad St) This brick fortress is one of California's first theaters (1865) and has welcomed the likes of Jack London, Emma Nevada and Mark Twain to its stage. Now it's home to a number of small, top-notch theater companies and an off-beat indie film series.

ℹ️ Information

Nevada City Chamber of Commerce (☑530-265-2692; www.nevadacitychamber.com; 132 Main St; ◷9am-5pm Mon-Fri, 11am-4pm Sat, 11am-3pm Sun) Ideally located at the east end of Commercial St, this has two welcome traveler comforts – expert local advice and public toilets right next door.

Tahoe National Forest Headquarters (☑530-265-4531; www.fs.usda.gov/tahoe; 631 Coyote St; ◷8am-4:30pm Mon-Fri) A useful and friendly resource for trail and campground information, covering the area from here to Lake Tahoe. It sells topographical maps.

ℹ️ Getting There & Away

Nevada City is served by the **Gold Country Stage Bus Service** (☑530-477-0103; www.goldcountrystage.com; fares $1.50-3), which links it with Grass Valley (adult $1.50, 30 minutes) hourly from 6:30am to 5:30pm weekdays and 7:30am to 4:30pm Saturdays. Kids and bikes ride free. Check the website for connections to Auburn and schedule changes.

Amtrak (p401) bus connections are in Colfax, 15 miles south.

LOCAL KNOWLEDGE

SWIMMING HOLE 101

Gold Country's rivers carved out precious metals as well as emerald pools perfect for late-summer dips.

On the South Yuba River, 8 miles northeast of Nevada City on Bloomfield Rd, under the **Edwards Crossing** bridge is a lively, popular pool. Just a mile hike downstream you'll find the scenic cascade of waterfalls known as **Mountain Dog**, perfect for a more secluded skinny dip.

For an even more remote spot, head to the Stanislaus River, to Parrots Ferry Rd 7 miles south of Murphys, and then turn north on Camp Nine Rd. Near the end, where the river splits, a half-mile hike up the right fork will lead you to **Camp Nine**, a peaceful, limestone-bordered pool and beach.

Some keys to swimming hole usage: always test rope swings and currents before jumping in. Never dive. Pack in your supplies and pack out your trash. No glass. And always stay at least 100yd from the water when nature calls.

South Yuba River State Park

Cool off with a dip at **South Yuba River State Park** (✆530-432-2546; www.parks.ca.gov; 17660 Pleasant Valley Rd, Penn Valley; ☉park sunrise-sunset, visitor center 11am-4pm May-Sep, to 3pm Thu-Sun Oct-Apr; 🅿🚼🐾) **FREE**, which has popular swimming holes and hiking trails. It's near Bridgeport, which has the USA's longest covered wooden bridge (temporarily closed for restoration at the time of research), a 30-minute drive northwest of Nevada City or Grass Valley.

This area has a growing network of trails, including the wheelchair-accessible Independence Trail, which starts from the south side of the South Yuba River bridge on Hwy 49 and continues for a couple of miles with canyon overlooks. June is the best time, when the rivers are rushing and the wildflowers are out.

The longest, single-span, wood-truss covered bridge in the USA, all 251ft of it, crosses the South Yuba River at Bridgeport (not to be confused with the Eastern Sierra town of the same name). It's easy to spend a whole day hiking and swimming in this wild area, where crowds can be left behind with little effort. The Buttermilk Bend Trail skirts the South Yuba for 1.4 miles, offering river access and bountiful wildflowers around April.

Maps and park information are available from the state park headquarters in Bridgeport, or from the Tahoe National Forest Headquarters (p405) in Nevada City. The South Yuba River Park Association (www.southyubariverstatepark.org) is another great resource.

Malakoff Diggins State Historic Park

An otherworldly testament to the mechanical determination of the gold hunt, **Malakoff Diggins** (✆530-265-2740; 23579 N Bloomfield Rd; per car $8; ☉sunrise-sunset) is a place to get lost on fern-lined trails and take in the raw beauty of a landscape recovering from brutal hydraulic mining. There is a mesmerizing ghost town here, with a barber shop, ice-cream parlor and saloon, abandoned and now frozen in time. Join a tour of the town at the **museum** (✆530-265-2740; http://malakoffdigginsstatepark.org; 23579 North Bloomfield Rd; ☉9am-5pm, tours 1:30pm Fri-Sun May-Sep) or stay at the **campground** (✆800-444-7275; www.reserveamerica.com; North Bloomfield Rd; tent sites $35, cabins $40; ☉May-Sep) or in one of three humble miners' cabins.

California's largest hydraulic mine left behind massive gold and crimson cliffs and small mountains of tailings, which were carved from the land by mighty streams of water. The forestland has recovered since the legal battles between mine owners and downstream farmers shut down the mine in 1884, and makes for a pleasant hike.

In 1852, a French miner named Anthony Chabot channeled the Yuba through a canvas hose to blast away at the bedrock. To reach the veins of gold inside, miners eventually carved a canyon 600ft deep. To speed up the sorting process, they mixed the slurry of gravel with quicksilver (mercury) to recover the gold, and then washed all the leftovers into the Yuba River. When a few decades later, 20ft high glaciers of tailings and toxic waste choked the rivers and caused deadly flooding, farmers and miners collided in the courtroom. In 1884, the

Sawyer Decision set a critical precedent: a profitable industry can be stopped for the public good. No longer able to reap profits by dumping in the Yuba, most fortune hunters moved on. North Bloomfield, the mining community at the center of Malakoff's operation, is the eerie ghost town that stands within the park's limits.

Tours of the town – which had a population of 1229 back in 1880 – provide the chance to see some impressive gold nuggets. The 1-mile Diggins Loop Trail is the quickest way to get a glimpse of the scarred moonscape.

Access Tyler-Foote Crossing Rd, the turnoff for the park, 10 miles northwest of Nevada City on Hwy 49.

North Yuba River

The northernmost segment of Hwy 49 follows the North Yuba River through some stunning, remote parts of the Sierra Nevada, known for a tough, short season of white water and great fly-fishing. An entire lifetime outdoors could hardly cover the trail network that hikers, mountain bikers and skiers blaze every season. In summer, snow remains at the highest elevations and many places have roaring fireplaces year-round. The best source of trail and camping information is the **Yuba River Ranger Station** (☑530-288-3231; 15924 Hwy 49, Camptonville; ⊙8am-4:30pm Mon-Fri).

Downieville

Downieville, the biggest town in remote Sierra County (though that's not saying much), is located at the junction of the North Yuba and Downie Rivers. With a reputation that quietly rivals Moab, UT (before it got big), this is one of the premier places for mountain-bike riding in the US, and a staging area for true wilderness adventures.

As with most gold rush towns, it wasn't always fun and games: the first justice of the peace was the local barkeep, and a placard tells the story of the racist mob that hanged a Chicana named Josefa on the town bridge in 1851, the only recorded lynching of a woman in California. The town retains a grisly affection for frontier justice and its ghosts; a reconstructed gallows is across the river, by the civic building.

🏃 Activities

The mountains and rivers in these parts beg to be explored in summer. Favorite hikes include the **Sierra Buttes Fire Lookout**, a moderate 6 miler that joins the **Pacific Crest Trail** before a 1500ft elevation gain to epic views from the lookout tower, and **North Yuba Trail**, 12 miles along the canyon ridge, starting behind the courthouse in town. There are many more options. Pick up maps and a shuttle ride from the local outfitters.

Downieville Downhill MOUNTAIN BIKING (www.downievilleclassic.com) This world-class mountain biking trail shoots riders over the Sierra Buttes and a molar-rattling 4000ft down into Downieville. There are plenty of other scenic biking trails to explore, including **Chimney Rock**, **Empire Creek** and **Rattlesnake Creek**, but this route is the reason why pro-riders arrive in August for the **Downieville Classic**, a mix of cross-country and downhill racing and revelry.

Local outfitters run hourly shuttles to the start.

Yuba Expeditions MOUNTAIN BIKING (☑530-289-3010; www.yubaexpeditions.com; 208 Main St; bike rentals $80-100, shuttle $20; ⊙shuttles 9am-5pm May-Oct, reserve Nov-Apr) Yuba Expeditions is run by Sierra Buttes Trail Stewardship, a nonprofit in the center of the trail-bike scene. Non-bikers will find it helpful with maps and general trail advice.

Downieville Outfitters MOUNTAIN BIKING (☑530-289-0155; www.downievilleoutfitters.com; 114 Main St; bike rental per day $65, shuttle $20; ⊙8:30am-5pm Mon-Thu, 8am-6pm Fri-Sun, shuttles May-Oct) A good option for trail information, bike rental and shuttles in Downieville.

🎉 Festivals & Events

Downieville Mountain Brewfest BEER (www.downievillebrewfest.com; ⊙Aug)This August event is focused around the consumption of craft beer, but it also involves fabulous food vendors, live music and lots of fresh Downieville air.

🛏 Sleeping & Eating

In downtown Downieville, the soft roar of the rapids lull saddle-sore bikers to sleep in several small B&Bs. More secluded options are along Hwy 49 east of town.

Tahoe National Forest Campgrounds CAMPGROUND $
(☑information 530-994-3401, reservations 877-444-6777; www.recreation.gov; tent & RV sites $24; ☺May-Sep; P⛺) West of town on Hwy 49 are a string of beautiful campsites. Most have vault toilets, running water and reservable sites along the North Yuba River. Of these, the prettiest is Fiddlecreek, which has tent-only sites right on the river.

★ **Lure Resort** CABIN, CAMPGROUND $$
(☑530-289-3465; www.lureresort.com; 100 Lure Bridge Lane; camping cabins $80, housekeeping cabins $180-290; 🛜⛺) A great option if you want to come with biking buddies or a family, this circle of tidy, modernized log cabins is along a sublime stretch of river open to fly fishing with big lawns for the kids to play on. The basic camping cabins, which are BYO sleeping bag and have shared bathrooms, sleep four tightly.

Riverside Inn HOTEL $$
(☑530-289-1000; www.downieville.us; 206 Commercial St; r $95-125, ste $180-190; P⊜🛜⛺) There is a secluded, rustic charm to these 11 stove-warmed rooms and a suite overlooking the river near the heart of Downieville. About half have kitchens and all have balconies for enjoying the river. The delightful innkeepers share excellent information about hiking and biking in the area, and in winter lend snowshoes.

Carriage House Inn INN $$
(☑530-289-3573; www.downievillecarriagehouse.com; 110 Commercial St; r $95-195; 🛜⛺) This renovated homey inn has country-style charms, which include decks with rockers and river views. Rooms have wing-backed chairs and wrought-iron beds; two rooms share a shower.

★ **La Cocina de Oro Taqueria** MEXICAN $
(☑530-289-9584; 322 Main St; tacos from $2.50, burritos $10; ☺11am-8pm Thu-Sat, to 5pm Sun Apr-Dec; ☑) Chef-owner Feather Ortiz uses herbs and peppers from her garden and sources everything else from local growers to make the freshest food around. The burritos are the size of Chihuahuas. No credit cards.

Sierra City & The Lakes Basin

Sierra City is the primary supply station for people headed to the **Sierra Buttes**, a rugged, rocky shock of mountains that are probably the closest thing to the Alps you'll find in California without hoisting a backpack. It's also the last supply point for people headed into the fishing paradise of the Lakes Basin. There's information about lodging and area activities at www.sierracity.com.

There's just one main drag in town, and that's the Golden Chain Hwy (Hwy 49). All commerce happens here. The hotels often have the best restaurants – when they're open. Winter time is quiet.

◉ Sights & Activities

There's a vast network of trails, including access to the famed **Pacific Crest Trail**. The Sierra Country Store (p409) is about the only consistently open place in town, and it welcomes Pacific Crest Trail refugees with its laundromat and deli.

To reach the Sierra Buttes, and many lakes and streams nearby, take Gold Lake Hwy north from Hwy 49 at Bassetts, 9 miles northeast of Sierra City. An excellent hiking trail leads 1.1 miles to **Haskell Peak** (8107ft), where you can see from the Sierra Buttes right to Mt Shasta and beyond. To reach the trailhead, turn right from Gold Lake Hwy at Haskell Peak Rd (Forest Rd 9) and follow it for 8.5 miles to the marked parking lot.

Sierra City's local museum, the **Kentucky Mine** (☑530-862-1310; www.sierracountyhistory.org; 100 Kentucky Mine Rd; museum $1, tour adult/child $7/3.50; ☺10am-4pm Wed-Sun late May-early Sep; P⛏), is a worthy stop that introduces the famed 'Golden Chain Hwy' (California's Hwy 49). Its gold mine and stamp mill are just northeast of town.

🛏 Sleeping & Eating

This is very much outdoorsy terrain, and the campsites are excellent. The cheapest sleeps are in the USFS campgrounds east from Sierra City along Hwy 49. Wild Plum, Sierra, Chapman Creek and Yuba Pass all have vault toilets and running water (Sierra has river water only), and first-come, first-served sites. If you're not bringing your tent, Buttes Resort is the best option.

Salmon Creek Campground CAMPGROUND $
(☑information 530-994-3401, reservations 877-444-6777; www.recreation.gov; Gold Lake Hwy, Calpine; tent & RV sites $24; ☺mid-May–late Sep; P⛺) With dramatic views of the Sierra Buttes, this USFS campground in the Tahoe National Forest is 2 miles north of Bassetts

GOING FOR THE GOLD

California's gold rush started in 1848 when James Marshall was inspecting the fatefully sited lumber mill he was building for John Sutter near present-day Coloma. He saw a sparkle in the mill's tailrace water and pulled out a tiny nugget. Marshall hightailed it to Sacramento and consulted Sutter, who tested the gold by methods described in an encyclopedia. Sutter still wanted to finish his mill so he made a deal with his laborers, allowing them to keep gold they found after-hours if they kept working. Before long, word of the find leaked out.

Sam Brannan was among those who went to Coloma to investigate the rumors shortly after Marshall's find. After finding 6oz of gold in one afternoon, he paraded through San Francisco's streets proclaiming, 'Gold on the American River!' Then he snapped up every piece of mining equipment – from handkerchiefs to shovels – in the area. When gold seekers needed equipment for their adventure, Brannan sold them goods at a 100% markup and was a rich man before the gold seekers even reached the foothills.

The mill's construction was finished in the spring of 1848 when the first wave of miners arrived from San Francisco. Only a few months later, the cities were depleted of able-bodied men, while towns near the 'diggins,' as the mines were called, swelled to thousands. News of the gold rush spread around the world, and by 1849 more than 60,000 people (who became widely known as forty-niners) rushed into California. Everyone was looking for the mother lode: the mythical deposit believed to be the source of all the gold washing into the streams and riverbeds.

Most prospectors didn't stick around after the initial diggings petered out; gold-extraction processes became increasingly equipment-dependent and environmentally disastrous, culminating in the practice of hydraulic mining, by which miners drained lakes and rivers to power their water cannons and blast away entire hillsides. The most extreme example was the still-stark moonscape created at the **Malakoff Diggins** (p406). People downstream were inundated by the muck and floods and finally sued in 1884. The Sawyer court held the environmental cost was too great to justify the miners staying in business.

on Gold Lake Hwy, off Hwy 49. It has vault toilets, running water and sites for tents and RVs, but no hookups.

Sites 16 and 20 are separated from the rest by a creek.

Wild Plum Campground　　CAMPGROUND $
(✆530-993-1410; tent sites $18) Of the handful of camping areas east of Sierra City, this is the most scenic, along a rushing stretch of the river. The facilities – vault toilets and 47 first-come, first-served sites – are basic but clean.

★Buttes Resort　　CABIN, LODGE $$
(✆530-862-1170; www.buttesresort.com; 230 Main St; d $95-160; P❄) In the heart of Sierra City, the small Buttes Resort occupies a lovely spot overlooking the river and is a favorite with hikers looking to recharge. Most cabins have a private deck and barbecue, and some have full kitchens. You can borrow games from the wilderness-loving owners and there's a wood-lined communal area with a pool table.

Red Moose　　CAFE $
(✆530-862-1024; www.redmoosecafe.com; 224 Main St; ⊙7:30am-2pm, closed Tue) This rugged old-school wooden building on the main street houses a great little cafe, with an unlikely specialty in the British favorite fish and chips. It also serves big breakfast scrambles, burritos and burgers.

🛍 Shopping

Sierra Country Store　　MARKET
(✆530-862-1560; www.sierracountrystore.com; 213 Main St; ⊙8am-8pm May-Sep, 10am-6pm Oct-Apr; 🛜) A welcome sight for Pacific Crest Trail (PCT) hikers and anyone else needing a laundromat, deli, groceries, ATM and wi-fi.

EL DORADO & AMADOR COUNTIES

In the heart of the pine- and oak-covered Sierra foothills, this is where gold was first discovered – Spanish-speaking settlers named El Dorado County after a mythical city of riches.

Today, SUVs en route to South Lake Tahoe pull off Hwy 50 to find a rolling hillside dotted with the historic towns, sun-soaked terraces and fertile soil of one of California's burgeoning wine-growing regions. If you make the stop, don't leave without tasting a glass of regional Zinfandel, which, like the locals, is packed with earthy attitude and regional character. It's also worth the detour to pause at the shore where a glint of gold caught James Marshall's eye.

Coloma-Lotus Valley

Coloma-Lotus Valley surrounds Sutter's Mill (the site of California's first gold discovery) and Marshall Gold Discovery State Historic Park (p411). It is also a great launching pad for rafting operations. The South Fork of the American River gets the most traffic, since it features exciting rapids but is still manageable. Adrenaline junkies who have never rafted before should try the Middle Fork.

🏃 Activities

Half-day rafting trips usually begin at **Chili Bar** and end close to the Marshall Gold Discovery State Historic Park (p411). Full-day trips put in at the **Coloma Bridge** and take out at **Salmon Falls**, near Folsom Lake. The half-day options start in Class III rapids and are action-packed (full-day trips start out slowly, then build up to Class IV as a climax). Full-day trips include a lavish lunch. The season usually runs from May to mid-October, depending on water levels. Prices are generally lower on weekdays.

Don't want to get wet? Watch people navigate the **Troublemaker Rapids**, upstream from the bridge near Sutter's Mill in the state park.

Monroe Ridge Trail   WALKING
This 3-mile hike follows a steep route from Coloma. Take High St from the town center, then Marshall Park Way, winding through oak woodland to the Marshall Monument, via James Marshall's rugged cabin and an 1865 Catholic church and pioneer cemetery. You then join the Monroe Ridge Trail, which leads along the ridge, looping back down into Coloma.

Whitewater Connection   RAFTING
(☑ 530-622-6446; www.whitewaterconnection. com; half-day trips $95-115, full-day $129-149; ☻ Apr-Oct) Whitewater Connection is typical of the area's operators, with knowledgeable guides and excellent food.

Bekeart's Gun Shop   OUTDOORS
(329 Hwy 49, Coloma; per person $7; ☻ 10am-3pm Sat & Sun; 🔹) Panning for gold is always popular at Bekeart's Gun Shop, across the street from the Gold Discovery Museum & Visitor Center (p411). It's sometimes open on weekdays.

🛏 Sleeping & Eating

Unless you want to camp, for which you're very well served here, it's best to head south to Placerville, or get a cheap motel bed around Auburn.

American River Resort   CAMPGROUND, CABIN $
(☑ 530-622-6700; www.americanriverresort.com; 6019 New River Rd; tent & RV sites $25-50, cabins $185-280; 🛜 🐾) A quarter mile off Hwy 49, just south of the Marshall Gold Discovery State Historic Park (p411), this site is more built-up than other area campgrounds. There's a small convenience store, free wifi, a playground, fishing pond and pool. The sites are basic, but some are right on the river. The most spacious and pretty oak-shaded sites are 14 to 29.

Coloma Club Cafe & Saloon   AMERICAN $
(☑ 530-626-6390; http://colomaclub.com; 7171 Hwy 49, Coloma; mains from $9; ☻ restaurant 6:30am-9pm, bar 10am-2am; 🛜) The patio at this rowdy old saloon comes alive with guides and river rats when the water is high. It hosts bands and DJ nights on summer weekends.

Cafe Mahjaic   AMERICAN, INTERNATIONAL $$
(Lotus Inn; ☑ 530-622-9587; www.cafemahjaic. com; 1006 Lotus Rd, Lotus; mains $17-23; ☻ from 5pm Wed-Sun; 🛜) House-baked breads and organic meats, with a sophisticated menu and Japanese and Mexican influences in the cooking. The four-course prix fixe for $35 is a great deal. The owners also run the three-room Lotus Inn (rooms $109 to $139), tucked in the brick house behind the restaurant.

ℹ Getting There & Away

Hwy 49 runs right through the heart of Coloma. Boaters can use the **Coloma Shuttle** (p411), which serves the South Fork of the American River.

Coloma Shuttle (☑530-303-2404; https://colomashuttle.com; River Park Village, 7308 Suite F; daily membership fee $10) A van that connects local campsites to rafting spots on the river, with a trailer rigged up for boats and gear.

Marshall Gold Discovery State Historic Park

This **state park** (☑530-622-3470; www.parks.ca.gov; Hwy 49, Coloma; per car $8; ☺8am-8pm late May-early Sep, to 5pm early Sep-late May; P🚻⛲) comprises a fascinating collection of buildings in a bucolic riverside setting at the site of James Marshall's riot-inducing discovery. Buy your ticket at the **museum** (☑530-622-6198; http://marshallgold.com; 310 Back St, Coloma; free with park entry, guided tour adult/child $3/2; ☺10am-4pm, guided tours 11am & 1pm year-round; P🚻) to display on the dashboard, return to the museum for some background, then explore a replica of **Sutter's Mill**, mosey round the blacksmith's and Chinese store and even try panning for gold.

Compared to the stampede of gun-toting, hill-blasting, hell-raising settlers that populate tall tales along Hwy 49, the Marshall Gold Discovery State Historic Park is a place of tranquility, with two tragic protagonists in John Sutter and James Marshall.

Sutter, who had a fort in Sacramento, partnered with Marshall to build a sawmill on this swift stretch of the American River in 1847. It was Marshall who discovered gold here on January 24, 1848, and though the men tried to keep their findings secret, prospectors from around the world stampeded into town. In one of the ironies of the gold rush, the men who made this discovery died nearly penniless. In another, many of the new immigrants who arrived seeking fortune were indentured, taxed and bamboozled out of anything they found. Meanwhile, as the site museum stresses, the world of the local Native American Nisenan tribespeople was collapsing due to disease and displacement.

In the rare moments when there aren't a million schoolkids running around, the pastoral park by the river makes for a solemn stroll. A trail leads, via displays on panning and hydraulic mining and past the 1860 **Wah Hop Chinese Store**, to the spot on the bank of the wide American River where

Marshall found gold and started the revolutionary birth of the 'Golden State.'

On a hill overlooking the park is the **James Marshall Monument**, where he was buried in 1885, a ward of the state. You can drive the circuit but it's much better to meander up to the monument on foot, and then continue on the Monroe Ridge Trail for views of the town and the river.

Panning for gold ($7, free if you have your own equipment) is popular. From 10am to 3pm in the summer, or by request, you get a quick training session and 45 minutes to pan.

Coloma Resort (☑530-621-2267; www.colomaresort.com; 6921 Mt Murphy Rd; tent & RV sites $48-65, cabins & on-site RVs $95-375; 🛜⛲) is a long-established riverside campground with the feel of a summer camp and a good choice for RVs. It comes with wi-fi and a full range of activities: scavenger hunts, a rock wall, karaoke and face-painting. There's a range of accommodations, from camping to cabins and a country cottage.

Truly delicious soups, sandwiches, baked goods and coffee from well-known Sacramento and local purveyors find their way to **Argonaut Farm to Fork Cafe** (☑530-626-7345; www.argonautcafe.com; 331 Hwy 49, Coloma; items $3-10; ☺8am-4pm; 🛜🅿🚻). Crowds of schoolkids waiting for gelato can slow things down.

Placerville

Placerville is a great little place to explore while traveling between Sacramento and Tahoe on Hwy 50. It has a thriving and well-preserved downtown with antique shops and bars, and local wags who cherish the wild reputation of 'Hangtown' – a name earned when a handful of men swung from the gallows in the mid-1800s. Among the many awesome local legends is 'Snowshoe' John A Thompson, a postal carrier who regularly delivered 80lb of mail on skis from Placerville over the Sierras to Carson Valley during the winter.

Placerville has always been a travelers' town: it was originally a destination for fortune hunters who reached California by following the South Fork of the American River. In 1857 the first stagecoach to cross the Sierra Nevada linked Placerville to Nevada's Carson Valley, which eventually became part of the nation's first transcontinental stagecoach route.

PLACERVILLE WINERIES

The Placerville region's high heat and rocky soil produces excellent wines, which frequently appear on California menus. Oenophiles could spend a long afternoon rambling through the welcoming vineyards of El Dorado County alone (though a full weekend of tasting could be had if it was coupled with adjoining Amador County). Details can be found at the **El Dorado Winery Association** (☑800-306-3956; www.eldorado wines.org) or **Wine Smith** (p413), a local shop with just about everything grown in the area.

Some noteworthy wineries, all north of Hwy 50, include **Lava Cap Winery** (☑530-621-0175; www.lavacap.com; 2221 Fruit Ridge Rd; tasting fee free-$5; ☺10am-5pm; P), which has an on-hand deli for picnic supplies, and **Boeger Winery** (p412) with its 1872 fieldstone building and blacksmith.

◉ Sights

Main St is the heart of downtown Placerville and runs parallel to Hwy 50 between Canal St and Cedar Ravine Rd. Hwy 49 meets Main St at the west edge of downtown. Looking like a movie set, most buildings along Main St are false fronts and sturdy brick structures from the 1850s, dominated by the spindly **Bell Tower**, a relic from 1856 that once rallied volunteer firemen.

★ El Dorado County Historical Museum
MUSEUM
(http://museum.edcgov.us; 104 Placerville Dr; entry by donation; ☺10am-4pm Wed-Sun) On the El Dorado County Fairgrounds west of downtown (exit north on Placerville Dr from Hwy 50), is this complex of restored buildings, mining equipment and re-created businesses telling the story of old 'Hangtown.' There are displays on the pony express, wanted posters and wagons, a reconstructed old-time grocery and luxurious silk gowns.

Hangtown's Gold Bug Park & Mine
HISTORIC SITE
(☑530-642-5207; www.goldbugpark.org; 2635 Gold Bug Lane; adult/child $7/4; ☺10am-4pm Apr-Oct, from noon Sat & Sun Nov-Mar; P🚼) About 1 mile north of town via Bedford Ave, this historical park stands on the site of four

mining claims that yielded gold from 1849 to 1888. You can descend into the Gold Bug Mine with a self-guided audio tour, do some gem panning ($2 per hour) or just explore the grounds and picnic area for free.

Boeger Winery
WINERY
(☑530-622-8094; www.boegerwinery.com; 1709 Carson Rd; tasting $5-15; ☺10am-5pm; P) Amid vineyards that were planted in the gold rush era, relegated to producing sacramental wine for the local church during Prohibition, and then restored in the 1970s, this historic winery pours a mind-boggling number of varietals, but the flagship wine is Barbera. The place was first settled by an Italian in 1872, and the rugged homestead he built looks straight out of Tuscany.

🛏 Sleeping

There are some wonderful historic accommodations here, and chain motels can be found at either end of the center of Placerville along Hwy 50.

★ Camino Hotel
B&B $
(☑530-644-1800; www.caminohotel.com; 4103 Carson Rd, Camino; r $60-125) A former lumberjack bunkhouse that's every bit as creaky as you'd hope but with rooms that have been redone. The rates are a steal, especially on weekdays, and room 4 is perfect for families with two rooms adjoined by a central sitting room. Breakfast is made to order. A great spot to hunker down while touring Apple Hill's (p417) farms.

National 9 Inn
MOTEL $
(☑530-622-3884; www.national9inns.com; 1500 Broadway; r $50-89; ✳🛜) This mid-century motel, recently renovated by a young couple, is the best bargain in Placerville, even if it lies at the lonely north end of town. The building's exterior is ho-hum, but the rooms are sparkling with refrigerators, microwaves and remodeled baths. It's a great option for travelers who want a clean, no-frills stay and want to support independent businesses.

Cary House Hotel
HISTORIC HOTEL $$
(☑530-622-4271; www.caryhouse.com; 300 Main St; r from $121; ✳@🛜) This historic hotel in the middle of downtown Placerville has a large, comfortable lobby with backlit stained glass depicting scenes from the region's history. Once a major staging stop, it has updated rooms (some with kitchenettes) with period decor. Ask for a room

overlooking the courtyard to avoid street noise, or try room 212, a rumored supernatural haunt.

Seasons Bed & Breakfast   B&B $$
(📞530-626-4420; www.theseasons.net; 2934 Bedford Ave; r $90-190; 🛜) Stay near the heart of Placerville at this leafy inn, built as a stamp mill in 1859. A creek runs through the lush garden; you stay in little wooden cottages in the grounds or in an art-deco-themed room in the main house. The owner serves excellent homemade continental breakfasts.

🍴 Eating

Z-Pie   AMERICAN $
(3182 Center St; pies $7.25-7.95; ⊘11am-9pm) With its whimsical take on the all-American comfort-food staple, this casual stop stuffs flaky, butter-crusted pot pies with a gourmet flourish (steak Cabernet! Thai chicken! tomatillo stew!). California beers are on tap. The four-beer sampler ($8) is ideal for the indecisive.

Sweetie Pie's   BREAKFAST $
(www.sweetiepies.biz; 577 Main St; mains $5-12; ⊘6:30am-3pm Mon-Fri, 7am-3pm Sat, 7am-1pm Sun) Ski bunnies and bums fill this diner and bakery counter on the weekends en route to Tahoe, filling up with egg dishes and top-notch homemade baked goods including heavenly cinnamon rolls. Breakfast is the specialty, with an array of omelets, waffles, scrambles and pancakes, but it also does a capable lunch.

Farm Table Restaurant   MEDITERRANEAN $$
(📞530 295 8140; https://ourfarmtable.com; 311 Main St; sandwiches from $8, mains from $14; ⊘11am-5pm Mon, 11am-8pm Wed, 11am-9pm Thu-Sat, 9am-5pm Sun; 🍴) A lovely deli-style place dishing up well-cooked farm-fresh food with a Mediterranean feel, alongside homespun fare such as rabbit pot pie. It specializes in charcuterie and preserving, and has plenty of gluten-free and veggie options on the menu too.

Heyday Café   CAFE $$
(www.heydaycafe.com; 325 Main St; mains $9-25; ⊘11am-9pm Tue-Thu, to 10pm Fri & Sat, to 8pm Sun) Fresh and well-executed, the menu here leans toward simple Italian comfort food including pizza, made all the more comfortable by the wood-and-brick interior. The wine list is long on area vineyards. Locals rave about lunch.

🍷 Drinking & Entertainment

Liar's Bench   BAR
(📞530-622-0494; 255 Main St; ⊘8am-1am) The Liar's Bench survives as the town's classic watering hole under a neon martini sign that beckons after dark. Karaoke nights, a pool table and darts provide entertainment.

★Cozmic Café   LIVE MUSIC
(📞530-642-8481; http://ourcoz.com; 594 Main St; ⊘cafe 7am-8pm Tue-Sun, pub 6pm-midnight Thu-Sun; 🛜📶) Located in the historic Placerville Soda Works building attached to a mine shaft: ask staff if you can have a peek. The upstairs hall is a fantastic venue for high-quality homespun gigs, including a Thursday open mike night, while the feel-good cafe spotlights organic, vegetarian and healthy fare plus fresh-fruit smoothies. There's a good selection of wine and craft beer.

🛍 Shopping

★Hangtown Antiques   ANTIQUES
(452 Main St; ⊘11:30am-6pm Mon, Thu & Sun, to 10pm Fri & Sat) Specialists in kitsch and highly collectible Americana, with Hawaiian shirts, alternative vinyl, guitars, ukuleles and even pinball machines. In their words: 'no dishes, no dollies.'

Wine Smith   WINE
(📞530-622-0516; www.thewinesmith.com; 346 Main St; ⊘11am-8pm Mon-Sat, from noon Sun) The Placerville wine shop that specializes in local vintages – and beers too. It pairs wines with beer and chocolate for tasting sessions.

Placerville Hardware   HOMEWARES
(📞530-622-1151; 441 Main St; ⊘8am-6pm Mon-Sat, 9am-5pm Sun) The 1852 building, an anchor of Placerville's main drag, is the oldest continuously operating hardware store west of the Mississippi and a place to pick up a brochure for a self-guided tour of the town. The store has a smattering of Gold Country bric-a-brac but most of what clutters the place are bona-fide dry goods, like hammers and buckets.

Bookery   BOOKS
(326 Main St; ⊘10am-5:30pm Mon-Thu, to 7pm Fri & Sat, to 4pm Sun) A great used-book store to stock up on vacation reading, including Americana and travel and music books.

DON'T MISS

AMADOR COUNTY WINE REGION

Amador County might be an underdog among California's winemaking regions, but a thriving circuit of family wineries, gold rush history and local characters make for excellent imbibing without a whiff of pretension. The region lays claim to the oldest Zinfandel vines in the United States and the surrounding country has a lot in common with this celebrated variety – bold, richly colored, earthy and constantly surprising.

The region has two tiny towns, Plymouth and Amador City. Start in Amador and follow Hwy 49 north through the blip known as Drytown, continue on Hwy 49 to Plymouth, and then follow Shenandoah Rd northeast, which takes you past rolling hills of neatly pruned vines. Most hosts are exceedingly welcoming and helpful, offering free tastes and information on their operations. In July, 38 wineries throw an annual 10-day tasting extravaganza.

Maps are available at the wineries, and from the Amador Vintners Association (www.amadorwine.com).

Deaver Vineyards (☑ 209-245-4099; www.deavervineyards.com; 12455 Steiner Rd, Plymouth; tasting fee $5; ⊙10:30am-5pm; Ⓟ) A true family affair going back 150 years, where nearly everyone pouring has the last name on the bottles.

Drytown Cellars (☑ 209-245-3500; www.drytowncellars.com; 16030 Hwy 49, Drytown; ⊙11am-5pm; Ⓟ) This is one of the most fun tasting rooms in Amador County, thanks to vintner Allen Kreutzer, a gregarious host, and his array of big reds. At the time of research, there was no tasting fee.

Sobon Estate (www.sobonwine.com; 14430 Shenandoah Rd, Plymouth; ⊙10am-5pm) Founded in 1977, this is an environmentally conscious family-run estate.

Wilderotter Vineyard (☑ 209-245-6016; www.wilderottervineyard.com; 19890 Shenandoah School Rd, Plymouth; tasting fee $10; ⊙10:30am-5pm; Ⓟ) As if the fine rosé and award-winning Sauvignon Blanc weren't enough, here tastings are paired with complimentary artisanal cheeses.

Amador 360 Wine Collective (www.amador360.com; 18950 Hwy 49, Plymouth; ⊙11am-6pm) Run by the couple that organizes Amador's annual Barbera extravaganza (http://barberafestival.com), this expansive shop reserves special billing to boutique vintners who otherwise would not offer tastings.

❶ Information

El Dorado County Visitors Authority (Chamber of Commerce; ☑ 530-621-5885; http://visit-eldorado.com; 542 Main St; ⊙9am-5pm Mon-Fri) Maps and local information on everything from farm trails to films, breweries and Tahoe.

❶ Getting There & Away

Amtrak (☑ 877-974-3322; www.capitolcorridor.org; Mosquito Rd) Runs several buses daily to Sacramento ($20, 1½ hours), though some require train connections to points further along the Capital Corridor route.

El Dorado Transit (☑ 530-642-5383; www.eldoradotransit.com; 6565 Commerce Way, Diamond Springs; adult/child $1.50/75¢) Operates hourly weekday commuter links between 7am and 4pm to every corner of town out of the Placerville Station Transfer Center (2984 Mosquito Rd), a charming covered bus stop with benches and restrooms. It's about

half a mile from downtown, on the north side of Hwy 50.

Plymouth & Amador City

Two small, sunny villages make equally good bases for exploring Amador County's wine region. The first, Plymouth, is where the region's gold rush history is evident in its original name, Pokerville. Few card sharks haunt the slumbering town today; it wakes late when the tiny main street fills with the smell of barbecue, a few strolling tourists and the odd rumble of a motorcycle posse.

Six miles to the south, Amador City was once home to the Keystone Mine – one of the most prolific gold producers in California – but the town lay deserted from 1942 (when the mine closed) until the 1950s, when a family from Sacramento bought the dilapidated buildings and converted them into antique shops.

⊙ Sights

Chew Kee Store Museum
MUSEUM
(www.fiddletown.info; Fiddletown; entry by donation; ⊙noon-4pm Sat Apr-Oct) Remnants of the bygone era are just outside of Plymouth. The Chew Kee Store Museum, 6 miles east in Fiddletown, is an old herbal shop that once served railroad workers. The dusty collection of artifacts frozen in time are objets d'art.

Amador Whitney Museum
MUSEUM
(✒209-267-5250; www.amador-city.com; Main St, Amador City; ⊙noon-4pm Fri-Sun) FREE This rugged little 1860s building looks like something straight out of a John Ford movie, and houses a replica schoolhouse scene and the obligatory mine shaft.

⊨ Sleeping & Eating

★Imperial Hotel
B&B $$
(✒209-267-9172; www.imperialamador.com; 14202 Hwy 49, Amador City; r $110-155, ste $125-195; ❋☂) Built in 1879, this is one of the area's most inventive updates to the typical antique-cluttered hotel, with sleek art-deco touches accenting the warm red brick, a genteel bar and a very good, seasonally minded restaurant (dinner mains $14 to $30). On weekends and holidays, expect a two-night minimum.

★Taste
CALIFORNIAN $$$
(✒209-245-3463; www.restauranttaste.com; 9402 Main St, Plymouth; small plates $5-16, dinner mains $24-41; ⊙11:30am-2pm Fri-Sun, 5-9pm Mon, Tue, Thu & Fri, from 4:30pm Sat & Sun) Book a table at Taste, where excellent Amador County wines are paired with a fine menu of California-style cooking (big on meat and game). There's open seating in the wine bar.

⛻ Drinking & Nightlife

Drytown Club
BAR
(15950 Hwy 49, Drytown; ⊙noon-midnight Wed-Fri, to 2am Sat, to 9pm Sun) Tired of wine? Hit the Drytown Club, the local rowdy roadhouse with a Wild West vibe. The bands on weekends are bluesy, boozy and sometimes brilliant: the Doghouse Blues Band plays every Sunday at 4:40pm.

Sutter Creek

Perch on the balcony of one of the gracefully restored buildings on this particularly scenic Main St and view Sutter Creek, a gem of a Gold Country town with raised, arcade sidewalks and high-balconied buildings with false fronts that are perfect examples of California's 19th-century architecture. This is a good option for staying the night when visiting Amador and El Dorado County wineries.

Begin the visit at volunteer-operated Sutter Creek Visitors Center (p416) to collect a walking-tour map of historic traces left by Cornish, Yugoslavian and Italian arrivals, or pick up the excellent, free driving-tour guide to local gold mines.

⊙ Sights

Monteverde General Store
HISTORIC BUILDING
(✒209-267-0493; www.suttercreek.org; 11 Randolph St; entry by donation; ⊙by appointment) This building goes back in time to when the general store was the center of the town's social and economic life, represented by the chairs that circle the pot-belly stove and the detailed historic scale. Senior docents lead tours by appointment. If you're lucky, sometimes the building is open on weekends.

Knight Foundry
MINE
(www.knightfoundry.org; 81 Eureka St) In its prime, Sutter Creek was Gold Country's main supply center for all things forged. Three foundries operating in 1873 made pans and rock crushers, but only this one operated until 1996 – it was the last water-powered foundry and machine shop in the US. At the time of research, the interior was closed to visitors, with plans in the works to reopen.

⊨ Sleeping

Eureka Street Inn
B&B $$
(✒209-267-5500; www.eurekastreetinn.com; 55 Eureka St; r $145; ❋☂) Each of the four rooms in this 1914 arts-and-crafts-style home has unique decor and gas fireplaces. Once the home of a wealthy stagecoach operator, the inn is on a quiet side street.

Hotel Sutter
HOTEL $$
(✒209-267-0242; www.hotelsutter.com; 53 Main St; r $115-175; P❋☂) There was some controversy when they started gutting the beloved American Exchange, which had stood

in repose for more than 150 years. The bricks and facade may be the only things left, but the modern rooms (some with en-suite bathrooms), very fine restaurant (mains $24 to $32) and cool cellar bar seem to have quelled the protest.

Sutter Creek Inn B&B $$
(☑209-267-5606; www.suttercreekinn.com; 75 Main St; r $120-210; ❄) The 17 rooms and cottages here vary in decor and amenities (antiques, fireplaces, sunny patios). All have private bathrooms. Guests can snooze in the hammock by the gardens or curl up with a book on a comfy chair on the sprawling lawn.

Hanford House Inn B&B $$
(☑209-267-0747; www.hanfordhouse.com; 61 Hanford St; d $145-245; P❄❄@❄❄) Nod off on platform beds in contemporary rooms or fireplace cottage suites. Chef-prepared breakfasts are harvested from the inn's garden, freshly baked goods appear every afternoon and evening brings wine tasting.

✕ Eating

Sutter Creek Ice Cream Emporium SWEETS $
(☑209-267-0543; 51 Main St; ☺11am-6pm Thu-Sun) This sweet shop gets downright enchanting when town icon Stevens Price takes to the 1919 Milton piano and plays ragtime. The former proprietor still stops by in between organizing the Sutter Creek Ragtime Festival each August. Order ice-cream sodas, floats, sundaes or splits.

Gold Dust Pizza PIZZA $
(20 Eureka St; pizzas $14; ☺11am-9pm, closed Mon winter; ❄) Crisp, crusty pizza and pitchers of beer make this a favorite; it's the perfect place to hang out and chat to the locals. Combinations like the BBQ pizza put it over the top; you can order (huge) whole pizzas, or opt for slices.

Sutter Creek Cheese Shoppe MARKET $
(☑209-267-5457; www.suttercreekcheese.com; 33b Main St; ☺10am-5pm) A stop for cheeses from California and beyond. Call ahead for a picnic box of cheese, a baguette and even a little cutting board and knife to enjoy on your winery hop.

☆ Entertainment

Sutter Creek Theatre PERFORMING ARTS
(☑916-425-0077; www.suttercreektheater.com; 44 Main St; tickets $15-40) One of several excellent Gold Country arts venues, the theater has nearly a 100-year-long history of presenting live drama, but nowadays schedules mostly musical concerts, as well as films and other cultural events.

❶ Information

Sutter Creek Visitors Center (☑209-267-1344; www.suttercreek.org; 71a Main St; ☺10am-6pm) Volunteers stand by with maps, information and souvenirs. The printed walking tour through historic downtown is also available online.

Volcano

One of the fading plaques in Volcano, 12 miles upstream from Sutter Creek, tellingly calls it a place of 'quiet history.' Even though the little L-shaped village on the bank of Sutter Creek yielded tons of gold and a Civil War battle, today it slumbers away in remote solitude. Only a smattering of patinated bronze monuments and some characterfully battered buildings attest to Volcano's lively past.

Large sandstone rocks line Sutter Creek, which skirts the center of town. The rocks, now flanked by picnic tables, were blasted from surrounding hills by hydraulic mining before being scraped clean of their gold. The process had dire environmental consequences, but generated miners nearly $100 of booty a day.

◉ Sights & Activities

★Indian Grinding Rock State Historic Park HISTORIC SITE
(Chaw'se; ☑209-296-7488; www.parks.ca.gov; 14881 Pine Grove-Volcano Rd; per car $8; ☺museum 11am-4pm) Two miles southwest of Volcano, this sacred area for the local Miwok comprises a museum in a traditional wooden roundhouse, a village site, a limestone outcrop covered with petroglyphs – 363 originals and a few modern additions – and over 1000 mortar holes called *chaw'se*, used for grinding acorns and seeds into meal.

During the last weekend of September, the time of the acorn harvest, the Big Time festival at the site features crafts, dances and games. Look out for the wonderful feathered dance capes in the museum.

Daffodil Hill FARM
(☑209-296-7048; 18310 Rams Horn Grade; donations accepted; ☺10am-4pm mid-Mar–mid-Apr)

This hilltop farm, 2 miles northeast of Volcano, is blanketed with more than 300,000 daffodil blooms in the spring. The McLaughlin and Ryan families have operated the farm since 1887 and keep hyacinths, tulips, violets, lilacs and the occasional peacock among the daffodils.

Black Chasm Cavern CAVE
(☑ 888-762-2837; www.caverntours.com; 15701 Pioneer Volcano Rd, Pine Grove; adult/child $17.50/9.50; ☺ 9am-5pm mid-May–early Sep, 10am-4pm early Sep–mid-May; ℗ ♿) Less than 1 mile east of Volcano, this National Natural Landmark has the whiff of a tourist trap, but one look at the array of helictite crystals – rare clusters that grow horizontally – makes the crowd more sufferable. Guides for the one-hour tours are all experienced cavers.

🛏 Sleeping & Eating

Union Inn HISTORIC HOTEL $$
(☑ 209-296-7711; www.volcanounion.com; 21375 Consolation St; r $130-150; ℗ ♻ ❄ 🛜) The more comfortable of the two historic hotels in Volcano: there are four lovingly updated rooms with crooked floors, two with street-facing balconies. Flat-screen TVs and modern touches are a bit incongruous in the old building, but it's a cozy place to stay. The on-site Union Pub (p417) has the best food in town, and a lovely patio garden.

St George Hotel HISTORIC HOTEL $$
(☑ 209-296-4458; www.stgeorgevolcano.com; 16104 Main St; r $79-209) Up the crooked stairs of this charming galleried hotel are 20 rooms that vary in size and amenity (most have shared bathrooms) and are free of clutter. The restaurant (open for dinner Thursday to Sunday and brunch Sunday) has a menu anchored by steak. Hang out in the saloon and try to spot the rumored ghosts.

Union Pub PUB FOOD $$
(☑ 209-296-7711; www.volcanounion.com; 21375 Consolation St; mains $10-30; ☺ 5-8pm Mon & Thu, to 9pm Fri, noon-9pm Sat, noon-8pm Sun) The Union Inn's (p417) pub has a superb menu of big burgers, salads and steaks, plus an array of local wines and beers.

☆ Entertainment

Volcano Theatre Company PERFORMING ARTS
(☑ 209-419-0744; www.volcanotheatre.org; 16121 Main St; tickets adult/child $16/11; ☺ Sat & Sun Apr-Nov) On weekends between April and November, this highly regarded company

WORTH A TRIP

APPLE HILL

In 1860, a miner planted a Rhode Island Greening apple tree on a hill and with it established the foundation for bountiful Apple Hill, a 20-sq-mile area east of Placerville and north of Hwy 50 where there are more than 60 orchards. Apple growers sell directly to the public, usually from August to December, and some let you pick your own. Other fruits and Christmas trees are available during different seasons.

Maps of Apple Hill are available online through the **Apple Hill Association** (☑ 530-644-7692; www.applehill.com; 2461 Larsen Dr, Camino), or use the El Dorado **Farm Trails Guide** (http://visit-eldorado.com).

A great place to hunker down while touring the farms is the **Camino Hotel** (p412).

produces live dramas in an outdoor amphitheater and in the tiny 1856 Cobblestone Theater.

🔒 Shopping

Country Store FOOD & DRINKS
(☑ 209-296-4459; 16146 Main St; ☺ 10am-6pm Mon Sat, 11am-5pm Sun) In continuous use since 1852, this fantastically atmospheric and authentic old store has creaky floorboards, a long wooden counter and inbuilt stools, and shelves groaning with tins and bottles. The shopkeeper whips up canned beef sandwiches and hamburgers in the small cafe.

Jackson

Jackson has some historic buildings and a small downtown, but it ain't much to look at. It stands at the junction of Hwy 49 and Hwy 88, which turns east from Hwy 49 here and heads over the Sierra Nevada near the Kirkwood ski resort.

⊙ Sights

Kennedy Gold Mine HISTORIC SITE
(☑ 209-223-9542; http://kennedygoldmine.com; 12594 Kennedy Mine Rd; adult/child $10/6) You can't miss the ominous steel headframe of the mine from the road, rising to 125ft. Its pulleys lifted ore and miners from the

bowels of the earth. Guided tours last about 90 minutes and take you past the stamp, gold recovery mill and massive tailing wheels. The parking lot is off North Main St.

On-site **Kennedy Tailing Wheels Park** has marvelous examples of engineering and craftsmanship – four iron and wood wheels, 58ft in diameter, that transported tailings from neighboring Eureka Mine over two low hills. Once the deepest mine in the area, this is now a peaceful park good for a stroll. Be sure to climb to the top of the hill behind the wheels to see the impounding dam.

Mokelumne Hill   HISTORIC SITE
(www.mokehill.org) The somewhat undiscovered settlement of Mokelumne Hill is 7 miles south of Jackson just off Hwy 49. Settled by French trappers in the early 1840s, it's a good place to see historic buildings without the common glut of antique stores and gift shops. Stay at the old-style Hotel Leger (p418) if you want to soak up the peace and quiet.

🛏 Sleeping & Eating

Hotel Leger   HERITAGE HOTEL $
(☑209-286-1401; www.hotelleger.com; 8304 Main St, Mokelumne Hill; r $85) A grand and pleasingly old-fashioned place with an impressive galleried frontage and pretty decent food in the restaurant, plus characterful creaky floorboards and a stuck-in-time saloon bar. Get a room on the street side for a view of the picturesque little hillside town of Mokelumne Hill.

National Hotel   HISTORIC HOTEL $$
(☑209-223-0500; www.national-hotel.com; 2 Water St; r $140-160) Jackson's historic hotel has had a serious upgrade from the gold rush era. While the restored building retains its historical details, all rooms are newly refurbished with luxurious details like gas fireplaces and heated floors. The top-notch steakhouse and bar downstairs complete the picture.

Mel's & Faye's Diner   AMERICAN $
(http://melandfayes.homestead.com; 31 N Hwy 49; meals $7-12; ⊙10am-11pm Sun-Thu, to 2am Fri & Sat) A local institution near Hwy 88 that dates back to 1956: there's a takeout window but it's not meant for quick stops. Take a seat on the bottle-green leather benches for solid diner fare that includes huge breakfasts, classic burgers (try the chili-soaked 'Miner'), luscious milkshakes

and – to balance the grease binge – a decent salad bar.

ℹ Information

Amador County Chamber of Commerce (☑209-223-0350; www.amadorcountychamber.com; 115 Main St; ⊙8am-4pm Mon-Fri, 10am-2pm Sat & Sun) Stop off on Main St to pick up information about sights and stays.

ℹ Getting There & Away

The only way to easily travel through this area is with your own wheels. By car, Jackson is 2½ hours from San Francisco and just over one hour to the ski resorts of South Lake Tahoe.

Placer County runs its bus system out of Jackson, but good luck catching a bus – they're few and far between. **Amador Transit** (☑209-267-9395; http://amadortransit.com; 115 Valley View Way; fares $1-3; ⊙ Mon-Fri) is a bit better. It makes a weekday connection through Sutter Creek to Sacramento ($1, one hour) and, if you have enough patience, you can connect to Calaveras County and southern Gold Country.

CALAVERAS COUNTY & SOUTH GOLD COUNTRY

The southern region of Gold Country is hot as blazes in the summer, so cruising through its historic gold rush hubs will demand more than one stop for ice cream. The tall tales of yesteryear come alive here through the region's famous former residents: author Mark Twain, who got his start writing about a jumping frog contest in Calaveras County, and Joaquin Murrieta, a controversial symbol of the lawlessness of the frontier era who somehow seems to have frequented every old bar and hotel in the area.

Angels Camp

On the southern stretch of Hwy 49 one figure looms over all others: literary giant Mark Twain, who got his first big break with the story of *The Celebrated Jumping Frog of Calaveras County*, written and set in Angels Camp. There are differing claims as to when or where Twain heard this tale, but Angels Camp makes the most of it. There are gentlemanly Twain impersonators and statues, and bronze frogs on Main St honoring the champions of the past 80 years, as well as the **Jumping Frog Jubilee** (www.frogtown.org; 2465 Gun Club Rd; from $8; ⊙May; 🐸) on the third weekend in May (in conjunction with the county fair and something of a Harley rally). Look for the plaque of Rosie the Ribeter, who set an impressive 21ft record in 1986. Today the town is an attractive mix of buildings from the gold rush to art-deco periods.

It's perhaps not the greatest natural beauty, but Moaning Cavern, 7 miles east of Angels Camp, does have the most thrills. Visitors can rappel 165ft to the bottom ($72). A pile of bones discovered here are some of the oldest human remains in the US. There's also above-ground zip lines and a self-guided nature walk. Winter events like caroling utilize cave acoustics.

Strung out along Hwy 49 are a number of motels, including the simple **Jumping Frog** (☑209-736-2191; 330 Murphys Grade Rd; d $70; ❄❤).

For food, the class act in downtown Angels Camp is **Crusco's** (www.cruscos.com; 1240 S Main St; mains $14-26; ☺11am-3pm & 5-9pm Thu-Mon), which puts out a serious, authentic northern Italian menu. The owners regularly hit Italy for more recipes, like the Polenta Antonella (creamy cornmeal with chicken and mushroom sauce).

There are a couple of bars in town, but your best bet for a night out here is the wonderful restored art-deco **cinema** (☑209-736-2472; www.cinemawest.com; Angels 6 Theatres, 1228 S Main St; tickets $9.25).

Calaveras Transit (☑209-754-4450; http://transit.calaverasgov.us; 750 Industrial Way, San Andreas; fare $2) operates the most reliable public transportation system in the region from the Government Center in downtown San Andreas. Use it to connect to Angels Camp ($2, 30 minutes, several times daily) and other surrounding towns. You can catch it mid-route – just flag it down. To connect via public transportation to the rest of California, you have to catch Route 1 to San Andreas, switch to Route 3 to Mokelumne Hill and finally transfer to Amador Transit (p418).

Murphys

With its white picket fences and old-world charm, Murphys is one of the more scenic towns along the southern stretch of Gold Country, befitting its nickname as 'Queen of the Sierra.' It lies 8 miles east of Hwy 49 on Murphys Grade Rd, and is named for Daniel and John Murphy, who founded a trading post and mining operation on Murphy

CALAVERAS BIG TREES STATE PARK

Calaveras Big Trees State Park (☑209-795-2334; www.parks.ca.gov; 1170 Hwy 4, Arnold; per car $10; ☺sunrise-sunset; ℗❤) Home to giant sequoia trees that reach as high as 250ft with trunk diameters of over 25ft, these leftovers from the Mesozoic era are thought to weigh upwards of 2000 tons, or close to 10 blue whales. The giants are distributed in two large groves, one easily seen on the **North Grove Trail**, a 1.5-mile self-guided loop, near the park entrance. On the more remote **South Grove Trail**, it's a 5-mile round-trip hike to **Agassiz Tree**, the park's largest specimen.

Camping (☑reservations 800-444-7275; www.reserveamerica.com; off Hwy 4; tent & RV sites $25-35, cabins $165-185; ℗) is popular and reservations essential. North Grove Campground is near the park entrance; less crowded is Oak Hollow Campground, 4 miles further on the park's main road. Most atmospheric are the hike-in environmental sites. Store food and toiletries in the provided bear lockers at all times.

Creek in 1848. They employed the struggling local Miwok and Yokut people as laborers. While some settlers continued to persecute the tribes, John eventually married Pokela, a chieftain's daughter.

The town's Main St is refined, with tons of wine-tasting rooms, boutiques, galleries and good strolling. For information and a town overview, look to www.visitmurphys.com.

⊙ Sights & Activities

Ironstone Vineyards   WINERY
(www.ironstonevineyards.com; 1894 Six Mile Rd; tasting fee $5; ☺11am-5pm; ❤) ✹ The unusually family-friendly atmosphere makes the wine feel secondary at Ironstone. There's a natural spring waterfall, a mechanical pipe organ, frequent exhibits by local artists, and blooming grounds. By the deli, the museum displays the world's largest crystalline gold leaf specimen (it weighs 44lb and was found in Jamestown in 1992). The enormous tasting room accommodates crowds.

Murphys Old Timers Museum MUSEUM
(www.murphysoldtimersmuseum.com; 470 Main St; donation requested; ⏰noon-4pm Fri-Sun) The name is a good hint that this place approaches history with a humorous touch. Housed in an 1856 building, it has an inscrutable tintype of the outlaw Joaquin Murrieta and the entertaining 'Wall of Comparative Ovations.' Guided tours of town leave from the museum every Saturday at 10am.

California Cavern CAVING
(✆209-736-2708; www.caverntours.com; adult/child $14.95/7.95; ⏰10am-5pm Apr-Oct; 🅿) In Cave City, 12 winding miles north of Murphys (take Main St to Sheep Ranch Rd to Cave City Rd), is a natural cavern, which John Muir described as 'graceful flowing folds deeply placketed like stiff silken drapery.' Regular tours take 60 to 90 minutes.

🛏 Sleeping

Most accommodations in Murphys are top-end B&Bs. For the same price, there are some attractive rental cottages (p420) just off Main St, or check nearby Angels Camp or Arnold for cheaper alternatives.

⭐Victoria Inn B&B $$
(✆209-728-8933; www.victoriainn-murphys.com; 402 Main St; r $135-320, cottages from $295; 🅿🐾🌐) This newly built B&B has glamorous rooms with claw-foot slipper tubs, sleigh beds and balconies. Some rooms have wood-burning stoves and balconies overlooking the courtyard fountain. The common spaces, like the long verandah for enjoying tapas and wine from the **restaurant and bar** (✆209-728-0107; http://

vrestaurantandbar-murphys.com; 402 Main St; mains $11-32; ⏰bistro 11:30am-8:30pm, restaurant from 5:30pm Wed-Sun), have chic, modern country appeal.

Murphys Vacation Rentals COTTAGE $$
(✆209-736-9372; www.murphysvacationrentals.com; 549 S Algiers St; cottages $140-245) For the same price as a frilly B&B, picturesque cottages clustered just off Main St are available for rent. The charming Church St cottage has two bedrooms that sleep four and feels like the set of a 1950s TV show. Cleaning fee extra.

Murphys Historic Hotel INN $$
(✆209-728-3444; www.murphyshotel.com; 457 Main St; d $130-205, with shared bath $95-215; 🅿🐾) Since 1856, this hotel has been an anchor on Main St. A must-stop on the Mark-Twain-slept-here tour, the original structure is a little rough around the edges. The adjoining buildings have bland, modern rooms that cost more. Make your way down to the dining room for fried chicken ($21) at dinner.

🍴 Eating

Firewood AMERICAN, PIZZA $
(✆209-728-3248; www.firewoodeats.com; 420 Main St; mains $8-15; ⏰11am-9pm Sun-Thu, to 9:30pm Fri & Sat; 🅵) A rarity in a town with so much historical frill, Firewood's exposed-concrete walls and corrugated metal offer a minimalist respite. When the weather's nice, the front wall is opened for alfresco dining. There are wines by the glass, half a dozen beers on tap and basic pub fare, but the wood-fired pizzas are the hallmark.

Grounds MODERN AMERICAN $$
(✆209-728-8663; www.groundsrestaurant.com; 402 Main St; dinner mains $17-26; ⏰7am-3pm Mon & Tue, to 8:30pm Wed-Sun; 🍴) This casually elegant cafe does everything competently – expert breakfast foods, a roster of light lunch mains and weekend dinners of steak and fresh fish. Iced herbal tea and fresh vegetarian options are key when temperatures outside rise. Opening hours vary.

Alchemy Market & Cafe CALIFORNIAN $$
(✆209-728-0700; www.alchemymarket.com; 191 Main St; mains $13-25; ⏰11am-8pm Mon, Tue, Thu & Fri, from 10:30am Sat & Sun) The stellar cafe menu here has a long wine list and many dishes, from parsley truffle fries to iron-skillet mussels, all great for sharing on the

---

GOLD COUNTY'S BEST CAVES

➤ **California Cavern** (p420) in Murphys, marveled at by John Muir, offers a wide variety of tours and lengthy adventure trips.

➤ **Moaning Cavern** (✆209-736-2708; www.caverntours.com; 5350 Moaning Cave Rd, Vallecito; adult/child $17.50/9.50; ⏰10am-5pm) in Angels Camp has the deepest cave rappelling in California and an above-ground zip line.

➤ **Black Chasm** (p417) in Volcano features a quiet self-guided Zen Garden walk above ground and rare helictite crystals below.

patio. Live jazz every Tuesday from 5:30pm to 8pm.

Columbia

More than any other place in Gold Country, Columbia blurs the lines between present and past with a carefully preserved gold rush town – complete with volunteers in period dress – at the center of a modern community. In 1850 Columbia was founded over the 'Gem of the Southern Mines,' and as much as $150 million in gold was found here. The center of the town (run by the state parks system) looks almost exactly as it did in its heyday. On the fringe of these blocks are homes and businesses that blend in so well it's hard to tell what's park and what's not.

Docents lead free hour-long tours weekends at 11am from the Columbia Museum (p421).

◉ Sights

Columbia State Historic Park   HISTORIC SITE
(☑209-588-9128; www.parks.ca.gov; Main St; ⊙most businesses 10am-5pm; P⊕) **FREE** The so-called 'Gem of the Southern Mines' is like a miniature Gold Rush Disneyland, but with more authenticity and heart. Four blocks of town have been preserved, where volunteers perambulate in 19th-century dress and demonstrate gold panning. The blacksmith's shop, theater, hotels and saloon are all carefully framed windows into California's past. The yesteryear illusion of Main St is shaken only a bit by fudge shops and the occasional banjo-picker or play-acting forty-niner whose cell phone rings.

Columbia Museum   HISTORIC SITE
(☑209-532-3184; www.parks.ca.gov; cnr Main & State Sts; ⊙10am-5pm Apr-Sep, to 4pm Oct-Mar) **FREE** Looking rather like dinosaur bones, limestone and granite boulders are noticeable around town. These were washed out of the surrounding hills by hydraulic mining and scraped clean by prospectors. There's a fascinating explanation of this technique at this renovated museum inside Knapp's Store.

🛏 Sleeping & Eating

Fallon Hotel   HISTORIC HOTEL $
(☑information 209-532-1470, reservations 800-444-7275; www.reserveamerica.com; 11175 Washington St; r $50-115; ❋⑤) The historic Fallon Hotel hosts the most professional theater troupe in the region, the Sierra Repertory Theatre (p421). The (apparently haunted) building is done out in period style, with floral wallpaper, glass lanterns and gleaming wooden furnishings.

Cottages   COTTAGE $$
(☑information 209-532-1479, reservations 800-444-7275; www.reserveamerica.com; 1-/2-/3-bedroom cottage $127/149/171; P⊕) A cozy alternative to staying in a hotel are these cottages, two at the end of Main St, and the largest with three bedrooms on Columbia St.

City Hotel   HISTORIC HOTEL $$
(☑information 209-532-1479, reservations 800-444-7275; www.reserveamerica.com; 22768 Main St; r $85-115; P⊕❋⑤) Among a handful of restored Victorian hotels in the area, City Hotel is the most elegant, with rooms that overlook a shady stretch of Main St. Adjoining the on-site restaurant Christopher's at the City Hotel (mains $10 to $30), What Cheer Saloon is an atmospheric Gold Country joint with oil paintings of lusty ladies and striped wallpaper.

☆ Entertainment

Sierra Repertory Theatre   THEATER
(☑209-532-3120; www.sierrarep.org; 11175 Washington St) This theater mixes up Shakespeare, musicals, farce and popular revues.

Sonora & Jamestown

Settled in 1848 by miners from Sonora, Mexico, this area was once a cosmopolitan center of commerce and culture with parks, elaborate saloons and the Southern Mines' largest concentration of gamblers and gold. Racial unrest drove the Mexican settlers out and their European immigrant usurpers got rich on the Big Bonanza Mine, where Sonora High School now stands. That single mine yielded 12 tons of gold in two years (including a 28lb nugget).

Today, people en route to Yosemite National Park use Sonora as a staging post. The historic center is so well preserved that it's a frequent backdrop in films.

Smaller Jamestown is 3 miles south of Sonora, just south of the Hwy 49/108 junction. Founded around the time of Tuolumne County's first gold strike in 1848, today the place limps along on tourism and antiques. It has its charm but is only a few blocks long.

◉ Sights & Activities

Sonora is a base for **white-water rafting**: the Upper Tuolumne River is known for Class IV and V rapids and its population of golden eagles and red-tailed hawks, while the Stanislaus River is more accessible with Class III rapids. **Sierra Mac River Trips** (☎209-591-8027; www.sierramac.com; 27890 Hwy 120, Groveland; trips from $269) and All-Outdoors (p401) both have good reputations and run trips of one day or more on multiple rivers.

Tuolumne County Museum   MUSEUM
(www.tchistory.org; 158 W Bradford St, Sonora; ⊙10am-4pm Mon-Fri, to 3:30pm Sat) FREE In the former 1857 Tuolumne County Jail, you'll find this great little museum with a fortune's worth of gold on display in the form of nuggets and gold-bearing quartz. Each of the former jail cells takes on a different theme, one of which is the little-told story of African Americans during the gold rush.

The museum also explores the story of former slave William Suggs, who set up a leather harness business, built a mansion in the town and successfully campaigned to overturn segregation in local schools.

Railtown 1897
State Historic Park   STATE PARK
(☎209-984-3953; www.railtown1897.org; 10501 Reservoir Rd, Jamestown; adult/child $5/3, incl train ride $15/10; ⊙9:30am-4:30pm Apr-Oct, 10am-3pm Nov-Mar, train rides 10:30am-3pm Sat & Sun Apr-Oct; Ⓟ🚻) Five blocks east of Jamestown's Main St, this 26-acre collection of trains and railroad equipment is the photogenic sister to Sacramento's rail museum. It's served as a backdrop for countless films and TV shows including *Back to the Future III*, *Unforgiven* and *High Noon*. On some weekends and holidays, you can ride the narrow-gauge railroad that once transported ore, lumber and miners.

California Gold Panning Lessons   OUTDOORS
(☎209-694-6768; www.gold-panning-california. com; 17712 Harvard Mine Rd, Jamestown; sluicing & panning specials per 2hr from $180; ⊙9am-3pm Jun-Oct, or by appointment) Miner John and his crew provide boots and all needed equipment for a genuine experience panning at Woods Creek and beyond. Be warned: real prospecting involves lots of digging. A couple of hours in, you'll have gold fever, a blister or both. Take a right onto Harvard Mine Rd and drive to the parking lot with a 'Gold Panning' sign. Best to call ahead.

🛏 Sleeping & Eating

★Bradford Place Inn   B&B $$
(☎209-536-6075; www.bradfordplaceinn.com; 56 W Bradford St, Sonora; r $145-265; ❄@�🅰️) Gorgeous gardens and inviting porch seats surround this four-room B&B, which emphasizes green living. With a two-person claw-foot tub, the Bradford Suite is the definitive, romantic B&B experience. Breakfast can be served on the verandah: try the crème brûlée French toast or the filling Mother Lode Skillet.

Gunn House Hotel   HISTORIC HOTEL $$
(☎209-532-3421; www.gunnhousehotel.com; 286 S Washington St, Sonora; r $84-140; Ⓟ❄🅰️🏊) For a lovable alternative to Gold Country's cookie-cut chains, this historic hotel hits the sweet spot. Rooms feature period decor and guests take to rocking chairs on the wide porches in the evening. A nice pool and a breakfast buffet also make it a hit with families.

★Legends Books, Antiques
& Old-Fashioned Soda Fountain   CAFE $
(☎209-532-8120; 131 S Washington St, Sonora; ⊙11am-5pm) The place to sip sarsaparilla, snack on a Polish dog or share a scoop of huckleberry ice cream at a 26ft-long mahogany bar here since 1850. Then browse antiques and books downstairs in the old tunnel miners used to secret their stash directly into the former bank; there's even an in-house stream downstairs.

Lighthouse Deli & Ice Cream Shop   DELI $
(www.thelighthousedeli.com; 28 S Washington St, Sonora; sandwiches $8-9; ⊙8am-4pm Mon-Sat) The flavors of N'Awlins make this unassuming deli an unexpected delight. The muffeletta – a toasted piece of Cajun paradise that's stacked high with ham, salami, cheese and olive tapenade – is the best sandwich within 100 miles.

🍺 Drinking & Entertainment

The free and widely available weekend supplement of the *Union Democrat* comes out on Thursday and lists movies, music, performance art and events for Tuolumne County.

Iron Horse Lounge   BAR
(☎209-532-4482; 97 S Washington St, Sonora; beer $3-6; ⊙8:30am-2am) Sonora's classic and

fairly rugged hangout in the center of town. Bottles glitter like gold on the backlit bar.

Sierra Repertory Theatre   PERFORMING ARTS
(☑ 209-532-3120; www.sierrarep.com; 13891 Hwy 108, Sonora; tickets adult $26-32, child $18) Located in a restored tin warehouse in East Sonora, close to the Junction Shopping Center. This critically acclaimed company also performs in the Fallon Hotel (p421) in Columbia.

🛍 Shopping

Sierra Nevada
Adventure Company   SPORTS & OUTDOORS
(www.snacattack.com; 173 S Washington St, Sonora; ☺ 10am-6pm) This flagship is stocked with maps and has equipment for rent and sale. There's also friendly advice from passionate guides with knowledge of ways to get outdoors in the area.

ⓘ Information

Mi-Wuk Ranger District Office (☑ 209-586-3234; 24695 State Hwy 108; ☺ 8am-4:30pm Mon-Fri) For information and permits for the Stanislaus National Forest up in the Sierra Nevada on Hwy 108.

Tuolumne County Visitors Bureau (☑ 20 9-533-4420; www.yosemitegoldcountry.com; 193 S Washington St, Sonora; ☺ 9am-6pm daily

Jun-Sep, Mon-Sat Oct-May) More so than other brochure-jammed chamber of commerce joints, the staff here offer helpful trip-planning advice throughout Gold Country as well as Yosemite National Park and Stanislaus National Forest.

ⓘ Getting There & Away

Hwy 108 is the main access road here, and it links up with I-5, 55 miles west near Stockton. A summer-only entrance to Yosemite National Park lies 60 scenic miles south on Hwy 120.

A limited service is provided weekdays by **Tuolumne County Transit** (☑ 209-532-0404; www.tuolumnecountytransit.com; 48 Yaney Ave, Sonora; fare $1.50; ☺ Mon-Fri) buses, which make a circuit from Sonora hourly from 7am to 7:46pm; they also stop in Columbia and Jamestown less frequently.

Gleaming green **trolleys** (☑ 209-532-0404; www.tuolumnecountytransit.com; Washington St, Sonora; adult/child $1.50/free; ☺ 11am-9pm Sat, to 4pm Sun mid-May–early Sep) link the sights in Columbia, Sonora and Jamestown.

YARTS (☑ 209-388-9589; www.yarts.com; adult/child return $25/18, one-way $13/9) For Yosemite visitors staying in the Sonora area, YARTS operates two round-trip buses connecting downtown Sonora, Jamestown's Main St and Yosemite from June 14 to September 1. There is just one round-trip bus in May and September. Ask nicely to be dropped off at unscheduled stops in Yosemite.

Lake Tahoe

Best Places to Eat

➜ Moody's Bistro & Lounge (p451)

➜ Cafe Fiore (p438)

➜ Fire Sign Cafe (p443)

➜ Fat Cat (p445)

➜ Old Granite Street Eatery (p458)

Best Places to Sleep

➜ Cedar House Sport Hotel (p450)

➜ Hostel Tahoe (p453)

➜ PlumpJack Squaw Valley Inn (p447)

➜ Deerfield Lodge at Heavenly (p435)

➜ Sorensen's (p435)

Why Go?

Shimmering in myriad shades of blue and green, Lake Tahoe is the USA's second-deepest lake and, at 6255ft high, it is also one of the highest-elevation lakes in the country. Driving around the spellbinding 72-mile scenic shoreline will give you quite a workout behind the wheel. Generally, the north shore is quiet and upscale; the west shore, rugged and old-timey; the east shore, undeveloped; the south shore, busy and tacky, with aging motels and flashy casinos; and nearby Reno, the biggest little city in the region.

The horned peaks surrounding the lake, which straddles the California–Nevada state line, are year-round destinations. The sun shines on Tahoe three out of every four days. Swimming, boating, kayaking, windsurfing, stand up paddle surfing (SUP) and other water sports take over in summer, as do hiking, camping and wilderness backpacking adventures. Winter brings bundles of snow, perfect for hitting Tahoe's top-tier ski and snowboard resorts.

When to Go

South Lake Tahoe

Jul & Aug Beach season; wildflowers bloom, and hiking and mountain-biking trails open.

Sep & Oct Cooler temperatures, colorful foliage and fewer tourists after Labor Day.

Dec–Mar Snow sports galore at resorts; storms bring hazardous roads.

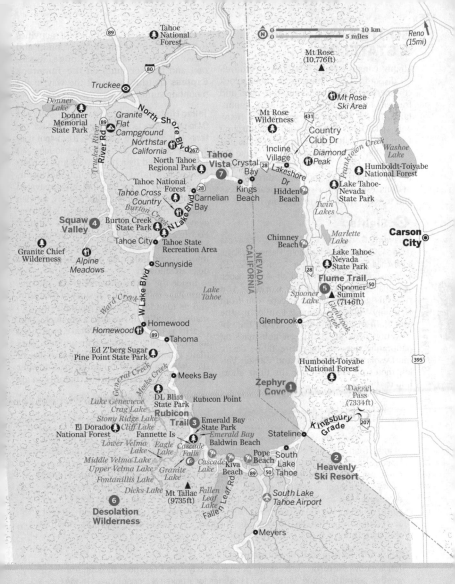

Lake Tahoe Highlights

1 Surveying the shimmering expanse of Lake Tahoe from a kayak or from the sandy beach at **Zephyr Cove** (p431).

2 Swooshing down the vertiginous double-black-diamond runs of **Heavenly** (p427) ski resort.

3 Trekking **Rubicon Trail** (p440) from Vikingsholm Castle on sparkling Emerald Bay to DL Bliss State Park.

4 Swimming in an outdoor lagoon or ice-skating above 8000ft atop the cable-car line in **Squaw Valley** (p446).

5 Thundering down **Flume Trail** (p455) on a mountain bike to tranquil Spooner Lake.

6 Escaping summer crowds with an overnight backpack to alpine lakes and high-country meadows in the **Desolation Wilderness** (p436).

7 Cozying up with your family around a lakefront beach fire pit or inside a comfortable cabin at **Tahoe Vista** (p452) on the no-fuss northern shore.

SOUTH LAKE TAHOE & STATELINE

Highly congested and arguably overdeveloped, South Lake Tahoe is a chockablock commercial strip bordering the lake and framed by picture-perfect alpine mountains. At the foot of the world-class Heavenly (p427) mountain resort, and buzzing from the gambling tables in the casinos just across the border in Stateline, NV, Lake Tahoe's south shore draws visitors with a cornucopia of activities, lodging and restaurant options, especially for summer beach access and tons of powdery winter snow.

◎ Sights

Heavenly Gondola   CABLE CAR
(Map p430; www.skiheavenly.com; Heavenly Village; adult/child 5-12yr/youth13-18yr from $45/27/37; ⊙10am-5pm Jun-Aug, reduced off-season hours; 🚇) Soar to the top of the world as you ride this gondola, which sweeps you from Heavenly Village to some 2.4 miles up the mountain in just 12 minutes. From the observation deck at 9123ft, get gobsmacking panoramic views of the entire Tahoe Basin, the Desolation Wilderness and Carson Valley, then jump back on for the final, short hop to the top.

From here there's a range of activities to enjoy (climbing, zip-lining, tubing) and decent eating (**Tamarack Lodge** restaurant and bar), or jump on the **Tamarack Express** chairlift to get all the way to the mountain summit.

Tallac Historic Site   HISTORIC SITE
(Map p430; www.tahoeheritage.org; Tallac Rd; optional tour adult/child $10/5; ⊙10am-4pm daily mid-Jun–Sep, Fri & Sat late May–mid-Jun; 🚇) **FREE** Sheltered by a pine grove and bordering a wide, sandy beach, this national historic site sits on the archaeologically excavated grounds of the former Tallac Resort, a swish vacation retreat for San Francisco's high society around the turn of the 20th century. Feel free to just amble or cycle around the breezy forested grounds, today transformed into a community arts hub, where leashed dogs are allowed.

Inside the 1921 **Baldwin Estate**, the museum has exhibits on the history of the resort and its founder, Elias 'Lucky' Baldwin, who made a bundle off Nevada's Comstock Lode. Nearby is the 1894 **Pope Estate**, now used for art exhibits and open for guided tours (daily except Wednesday). The boathouse of the **Valhalla Estate** functions as a theater venue. The 1923 **Grand Hall** contains an art

---

SKIING IN TAHOE

Lake Tahoe has phenomenal skiing, with thousands of acres of the white stuff beckoning at more than a dozen resorts. Winter-sports complexes range from the giant, jet-set slopes of **Squaw Valley** (p446), **Heavenly** (p427) and **Northstar** (p449), to the no-less-enticing insider playgrounds like **Sugar Bowl** (p449) and **Homewood** (p442). Tahoe's simply got a hill for everybody, from kids to kamikazes. Ski season generally runs November to April, although it can start as early as October and last until the last storm whips through in May or even June. All resorts have ski schools, equipment rental and other facilities; check their websites for snow conditions, weather reports and free ski-season shuttle buses from area lodgings.

Downhill Skiing & Snowboarding

Tahoe's downhill resorts are usually open every day from December through April, weather permitting. See Winter Sports listings for Truckee & Donner Lake, Tahoe City and South Lake Tahoe & Stateline. All of these resorts rent equipment and have places to warm up slope side and grab a quick bite or après-ski beer. Most offer group ski and snowboard lessons for adults and children (a surcharge applies,but usually no reservations are required).

Cross-Country Skiing & Snowshoeing

Tahoe's cross-country ski resorts are usually open daily from December through March, and sometimes into April. See Winter Sports listings for Truckee & Donner Lake, Tahoe City and South Lake Tahoe & Stateline. Most rent equipment and offer lessons; reservations typically aren't taken for either, so show up early in the morning for the best availability.

gallery and gift shop. In summer concerts, plays and other cultural events happen here, most notably the three-decade-old Valhalla Festival of Arts, Music & Film (p434).

The parking lot is about 3 miles north of the 'Y' junction of Hwys 89 and 50.

Lake Tahoe Historical Society Museum
MUSEUM

(Map p430; ☑ 530-541-5458; 3058 Lake Tahoe Blvd; ⊙ usually 11am-3pm Sat & Sun) **FREE** This small but interesting museum displays artifacts from Tahoe's pioneer past, including Washoe tribal baskets, vintage black-and-white films, hoary mining memorabilia and a model of a classic Lake Tahoe steamship. On summer Saturday afternoons, join a volunteer-led tour of the restored 1930s cabin out back.

🏃 Activities

Tahoe Treetop Adventure Park
ADVENTURE SPORTS

(Map p428; ☑ 530-581-7563; www.tahoetreetop. com; 725 Granlibakken Rd, off Hwy 89; adult/child 5-12yr $55/45; ⊙ 10am-5:30pm Sat & Sun Jan-late May, 9am-7:30pm daily late May-Aug, reduced hours Sep-Dec; ♿) At the Granlibakken (p445) resort, take a 2½-hour monkey-like romp between tree platforms connected by zip lines and swinging bridges. Various courses are geared to everyone from little kids (no more than 10ft off the ground) to daredevils (two 100ft zip lines and one that's 300ft). Reserve ahead.

Winter Sports

★ Heavenly
SNOW SPORTS

(Map p430; ☑ 775-586-7000; www.skiheavenly. com; 4080 Lake Tahoe Blvd; adult/child 5-12yr/youth 13-18yr $135/79/113; ⊙ 9am-4pm Mon-Fri, from 8:30am Sat, Sun & holidays; ♿) The 'mother' of all Tahoe mountains boasts the most acreage, the longest run (5.5 miles), great tree-skiing and the biggest vertical drop around. Follow the sun by skiing on the Nevada side in the morning, moving to the California side in the afternoon. Views of the lake and the high desert are heavenly indeed.

Two terrain parks won't strand snowboarders of any skill level, with the High Roller for experts only. Stats: 28 lifts, 3500 vertical feet, 97 runs.

Tahoe Ski Areas

Sierra-at-Tahoe
SNOW SPORTS

(☑ 530-659-7453; www.sierraattahoe.com; 1111 Sierra-at-Tahoe-Rd, off Hwy 50, Twin Bridges; adult/child 5-12yr/youth 13-22yr $90/30/83; ⊙ 9am-4pm Mon-Fri, 8:30am-4pm Sat, Sun & holidays; ♿) About 18 miles southwest of South Lake Tahoe, this is snowboarding central, with five raging terrain parks and a 17ft-high superpipe. A great beginners' run meanders gently for 2.5 miles from the summit, but there are also gnarly steeps and chutes for speed demons.

Kirkwood
SNOW SPORTS

(☑ 209-258-6000; www.kirkwood.com; 1501 Kirkwood Meadows Dr, off Hwy 88, Kirkwood; adult/child 5-12yr/youth 13-18yr $96/65/80; ⊙ 9am-4pm) Off-the-beaten-path Kirkwood, set in a high-elevation valley, gets great snow and holds it longer than almost any other Tahoe resort. It has stellar tree-skiing, gullies, chutes and terrain parks, and is the only Tahoe resort with backcountry runs accessible by snowcats. Novice out-of-bounds skiers should sign up in advance for backcountry safety-skills clinics.

It's 35 miles southwest of South Lake Tahoe via Hwy 89; ski-season shuttles are available (from $15). Stats: 15 lifts, 2000 vertical feet, 72 runs.

Lake Tahoe

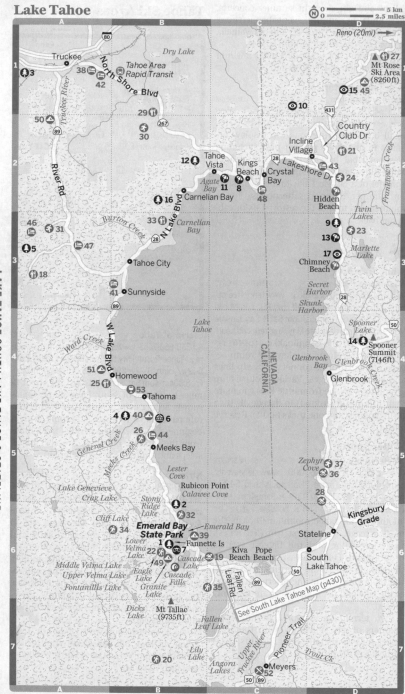

Lake Tahoe

LAKE TAHOE SOUTH LAKE TAHOE & STATELINE

Hiking

Many miles of summer hiking trails start from the top of the Heavenly Gondola (p426), many with mesmerizing lake views. On the Nevada side of the state line, **Lam Watah Nature Trail** meanders for just over a mile each way across United States Forest Service (USFS) land, winding underneath pine trees and beside meadows and ponds, on its way between Hwy 50 and Nevada Beach, starting from the community park off Kahle Dr.

Several easy kid- and dog-friendly hikes begin near the USFS Taylor Creek Visitor Center (p440) off Hwy 89. The mile-long, mostly flat **Rainbow Trail** loops around a creekside meadow, with educational panels about ecology and wildlife along the way. On the opposite side of Hwy 89, the gentle, rolling 1-mile **Moraine Trail** follows the shoreline of Fallen Leaf Lake; free trailhead parking is available near campsite No 75. Up at cooler elevations, the mile-long round-trip to **Angora Lakes** is another popular trek with kids, especially because it ends

South Land Tahoe

Nevada Beach (1.3mi);
Zephyr Cove (3mi)

STATELINE 35

5

Lake Tahoe
Visitors
Authority

28

23

Stateline
Transit
Center

24

Explore
Tahoe

16 17

29

1

Heavenly
Village Way

8

Keller Rd

State Line Ave

27

Cedar Ave

Pine Blvd

Park Ave

Friday Ave

Wildwood Ave

50

Lakeshore Blvd

**HEAVENLY
VILLAGE**

12

Forest Ave

25

Ski Run Blvd

20

7

Needle Peak Rd

Spruce Ave

41

15

Glenwood Way

El Dorado National
Forest

Heavenly Valley Creek

Pioneer Trail

40 14

9

37

4

South Lake Tahoe
State Recreation Area

26 33

42

Fremont Ave

Johnson Blvd

Al Tahoe Blvd

Bijou
Community
Park

6

38

19

2

Rufus Allen
Blvd

College
Dr

31

Martin Ave

Black Bart Ave

Lakeview Ave

Los Angeles Ave

Lake Tahoe

Trout Creek

36

USDA Lake
Tahoe Basin
Management Unit

O'Malley Dr

50

**SOUTH
LAKE
TAHOE**

Truckee Marsh

13

Tahoe Keys Blvd

Lake Tahoe Blvd

**TAHOE
VALLEY**

Tahoe
Valley
Center

Upper Truckee River

**TAHOE
KEYS**

Venice Dr

Dunlap Dr

43

South Y
Transit Center

32

The Y

34

D St

89

50

30

11th St

Julie Ave

15th St

13th St

10th St

Pope Beach Rd

Emerald Bay Rd

22

Lake Tahoe Blvd

Julie Ave

Jameson
Beach Rd

11

18

89

Truckee Marsh

El Dorado
National
Forest

4

USFS Taylor
Creek Visitor
Center

10

39

3

Baldwin
Beach (1mi);
Emerald Bay (3mi)

21

Fallen Leaf Lake Rd

N

0   1 miles
0   2 km

South Lake Tahoe

by a sandy swimming beach and a summer snack bar selling ice-cream treats. You'll find the trailhead on Angora Ridge Rd, off Tahoe Mountain Rd, accessed from Hwy 89.

For longer and more strenuous day hikes to alpine lakes and meadows, several major trailheads provide easy access to the evocatively named Desolation Wilderness (p436): Echo Lakes (south of town); Glen Alpine (near Lily Lake, south of Fallen Leaf Lake), to visit a historic tourist resort and waterfall; and Tallac (p436) (opposite the entrance to Baldwin Beach). The latter two trailheads also lead to the peak of Mt Tallac (9735ft), a strenuous 10- to 12-mile day hike. Self-serve wilderness permits for day hikers only are freely available at trailheads; overnight backpacking permits are subject to quotas.

Beaches & Swimming

On the California side, the nicest strands are **Pope Beach** (Map p430; per car $7), **Kiva Beach** (Map p430) and **Baldwin Beach** (Map p428; per car $7), each with picnic tables and barbecue grills; Kiva offers free parking and allows leashed dogs too. They're all found along Emerald Bay Rd (Hwy 89), running west and east of Tallac Historic Site (p426). Nearby, **Fallen Leaf Lake**, where scenes from the Hollywood flicks *The Bodyguard* and *City of Angels* were filmed, is also good for summer swims. **El Dorado Beach** (Map p430) is a free public beach in town, just off Lake Tahoe Blvd.

Many folks prefer to head over to Stateline and keep driving north 2 miles to pretty **Nevada Beach** (Map p428; per car $7), where the wind really picks up in the afternoons,

ℹ TOP WAYS TO SKI TAHOE FOR LESS MONEY

Midweek and half-day afternoon discounts on lift tickets are usually available, but expect higher prices on weekends and holidays. Lift-ticket rates go up incrementally almost every year too. Parents should ask about the interchangeable 'Parent Predicament' lift tickets offered by some resorts, which let one parent ski while the other one hangs with the kids, then switch off later.

The **Bay Area Ski Bus** (☑925-680-4386; www.bayareaskibus.com) allows you to leave the headache of driving I-80 to others. Round-trips start at $109 including lift tickets, with various add-on packages available. Pick-up locations include San Francisco and Sacramento.

In San Francisco, **Sports Basement** (https://shop.sportsbasement.com) sells deeply discounted lift tickets and has the best deals on multiday rental equipment because it doesn't charge for pickup or drop-off days.

Handy money-saving websites:

Ski Lake Tahoe (www.skilaketahoe.com) Portal for the seven biggest Tahoe resorts, with deals covering all.

Sliding on the Cheap (www.slidingonthecheap.com) Homegrown website listing discounts and deals on lift tickets.

or always-busy **Zephyr Cove** (Map p428; ☑775-589-4901; www.zephyrcove.com; 760 Hwy 50; per car $10; ♿), which has rustic resort and marina facilities along its sandy mile-long shoreline.

Boating & Water Sports

Ski Run Boat Company (Map p430; ☑530-544-0200; www.tahoesports.com; 900 Ski Run Blvd; parasailing $55-80), at the **Ski Run Marina** (Map p430; ☑530-544-9500; 900 Ski Run Blvd), and **Tahoe Keys Boat & Charter Rentals** (Map p430; ☑530-544-8888; www.tahoesports.com; 2435 Venice Dr; per hour $110-235), at the **Tahoe Keys Marina** (Map p430; ☑530-541-2155; www.tahoekeysmarina.net; 2435 Venice Dr E), both rent motorized powerboats, pontoons, sailboats and Jet Skis (rentals $110 to $235 per hour), as well as human-powered kayaks, canoes, hydro bikes, paddleboats and paddleboard sets (per hour $25 to $35). If you want to go parasailing up to 1200ft above Lake Tahoe's waves, the Ski Run Marina branch can hook you up (rides $55 to $80).

Kayak Tahoe KAYAKING, WATER SPORTS
(Map p430; ☑530-544-2011; www.kayaktahoe.com; 3411 Lake Tahoe Blvd; kayak single/double 1hr $25/35, 1 day $65/85, lessons & tours from $40; ⊗9am-5pm Jun-Sep) Rent a kayak or stand up paddleboard, take a lesson or sign up for a guided tour, including sunset cove paddles, trips to Emerald Bay and explorations of the Upper Truckee River estuary and the eastern shore. Five seasonal locations at **Timber**

Cove Marina (Map p430; ☑530-544-2942; 3411 Lake Tahoe Blvd), Vikingsholm (Emerald Bay) and Baldwin, Pope and Nevada Beaches.

Zephyr Cove Resort & Marina WATER SPORTS
(Map p428; ☑775-589-4901; www.zephyrcove.com; 760 Hwy 50, NV; ⊗9am-5pm) Rents powerboats, pedal boats, wave runners, Jet Skis, canoes, kayaks and stand up paddleboards; also offers single and tandem parasailing flights.

**Camp Richardson
Resort Marina** WATER SPORTS
(Map p430; ☑530-542-6570; www.camprichardson.com; 1900 Jameson Beach Rd; ⊗kayaks, paddleboats & paddleboards per 1hr $25) Rents powerboats, paddleboats, water skis, kayaks and SUP gear.

Mountain Biking

For expert mountain bikers, the classic **Mr Toad's Wild Ride**, with its steep downhill sections and banked turns reminiscent of a Disneyland theme-park ride, should prove sufficiently challenging. Usually open from June until October, the one-way trail along Saxon Creek starts off Hwy 89 south of town near Grass Lake and Luther Pass.

Intermediate mountain bikers should steer toward the mostly single-track **Powerline Trail**, which traverses ravines and creeks. You can pick up the trail off Ski Run Blvd near the Heavenly (p427) resort, from the western end of Saddle Rd. For a more leisurely outing over mostly level terrain, you can pedal around scenic **Fallen Leaf Lake**.

Anyone with good lungs might try the **Angora Lakes Trail**, which is steep but technically easy and rewards you with sweeping views of Mt Tallac and Fallen Leaf Lake. It starts further east, off Angora Ridge and Tahoe Mountain Ridge Rds.

For shuttle service and mountain-bike rentals for Mr Toad's Wild Ride, the Tahoe Rim Trail (p441) and other downhill adventures, as well as family friendly tours, talk to **Wanna Ride** (☑ 775-588-5800; www.wannaridetahoe.com; ☺ 8am-4pm Tue-Sat). For mountain-biking trail conditions, race schedules, volunteer days and other special events, contact the Tahoe Area Mountain Biking Association (www.tamba.org).

Cycling

The **South Lake Tahoe Bike Path** is a level, leisurely ride suitable for anyone. It heads west from El Dorado Beach (p431), eventually connecting with the **Pope-Baldwin Bike Path** past Camp Richardson (p435), Tallac Historic Site (p426) and the USFS Taylor Creek Visitor Center (p440). Visitor centers carry the excellent Lake Tahoe bike route map, available online from the Lake Tahoe Bicycle Coalition (www.tahoebike.org), which has an info-packed website for cycling enthusiasts. **Anderson's Bike Rental** (☑ 530-541-0500; www.laketahoebikerental.com; 645 Emerald Bay Rd/Hwy 89; per hour $10; ⓐ) rents hybrid bikes with helmets.

Golf

Edgewood Tahoe Golf Course GOLF
(Map p430; ☑ 775-588-3566; www.edgewood-tahoe.com/golf; 100 Lake Pkwy, Stateline, NV; green fee $110-260) Stunning lakeside scenery is a major distraction at this challenging championship 18-hole course designed by George Fazio, a favorite for celebrity golf tournaments. Tee-time reservations are required; cart and club rentals available.

Bijou Golf Course GOLF
(Map p430; ☑ 530-542-6097; www.cityofslt.us; 3464 Fairway Ave; green fee $18, club/cart rental $15/5; ☺ mid-Apr–Oct) So you don't know your putter from your nine iron? That's OK at this laid-back, no-reservations municipal course with views of Heavenly Mountain. Built in the 1920s, it's got just nine holes, which you can play twice around.

Horseback Riding

Both **Camp Richardson Corral & Pack Station** (Map p430; ☑ 530-541-3113; www.camp richardsoncorral.com; Emerald Bay Rd/Hwy 89; trail rides $50-168; ⓐ) and **Zephyr Cove Stables** (Map p428; ☑ 775-588-5664; www.zephyrcove stable.com; Hwy 50, NV; trail rides $40-80; ⓐ), about 4 miles north of Stateline casinos, offer daily horseback rides in summer, varying from one-hour kid-friendly trips through the forest, to extended treks with meadow and lake views (reservations required).

☞ Tours

Lake Tahoe Balloons BALLOONING
(Map p430; ☑ 530-544-1221; www.laketahoe balloons.com; per person $299) From May through October (weather permitting), you can cruise on a catamaran launched from Tahoe Keys Marina (p432), then clamber aboard a hot-air balloon launched right from the boat's upper deck. The lake and Sierra Nevada mountain views may take away what little breath you have left up at 10,000ft. Reservations required.

Woodwind Cruises CRUISE
(Map p428; ☑ 775-588-3000; www.tahoecruises.com; 760 Hwy 50, NV, Zephyr Cove Marina; 1hr cruise adult/child 2-12yr from $49/18) Sunset champagne and happy-hour floats aboard this sailing catamaran are the perfect way to chill after a sunny afternoon lazing on the beach. Five daily departures during summer; reservations recommended.

Lake Tahoe Cruises CRUISE
(Map p430; ☑ 800-238-2463; www.zephyrcove.com; 900 Ski Run Blvd; adult/child from $55/20; ⓐ) Two paddle wheelers ply Lake Tahoe's 'big blue' year-round with a variety of sightseeing, drinking, dining and dancing

LAKE TAHOE SOUTH LAKE TAHOE & STATELINE

SNOWSHOEING UNDER THE STARS

A crisp quiet night with a blazing glow across the lake. What could be more magical than a full-moon snowshoe tour? Reserve ahead, as ramblings at these places are very popular:

➜ **Ed Z'Berg Sugar Pine Point State Park** (p442)

➜ **Squaw Valley** (p446)

➜ **Tahoe Donner** (p449)

➜ **Northstar California** (p449)

➜ **Kirkwood** (p427)

cruises, including a narrated two-hour daytime trip to Emerald Bay. The *Tahoe Queen* leaves from Ski Run Marina (p432) – summer parking fee $8 – in town, while the MS *Dixie II* is based at Zephyr Cove Resort & Marina (p432) on the eastern shore in Nevada.

Action Watersports   BOATING
(Map p430; ☎530-544-5387; www.action-watersports.com; 3411 Lake Tahoe Blvd, Timber Cove Marina; adult/child under 13yr $69/35) In a hurry to get to Emerald Cove? Wanna avoid those near-constant traffic jams on Hwy 89? Jump on board the *Tahoe Thunder* speedboat, which zips across the lake – watch out, though, you'll get wet! Also offers parasailing rides (from $75).

🎊 Festivals & Events

Valhalla Festival of Arts,
Music & Film   CULTURAL
(☎530-541-4975; www.valhallatahoe.com; ☺Jun-Aug) A summerlong cultural bonanza of music and theater held at a 1930s Nordic hall.

Sleeping

🛏 South Lake Tahoe

South Lake Tahoe has a bazillion choices. Lodging options line Lake Tahoe Blvd (Hwy 50) between Stateline and Ski Run Blvd. Further west, closer to the intersection of Hwys 50 and 89, a string of budget motels ranges from adequate to inexcusable. For ski condos and rooms near the slopes, contact Heavenly (p427).

Fallen Leaf Campground   CAMPGROUND $
(Map p430; ☎info 530-544-0426, reservations 877-444-6777; www.recreation.gov; 2165 Fallen Leaf Lake Rd; tent & RV sites $33-35, yurts $84; ☺mid-May–mid-Oct; 🖥) Near the north shore of stunning Fallen Leaf Lake, this is one of the biggest and most popular campgrounds on the south shore, with pay showers and approximately 200 wooded sites and six canvas-sided yurts that can sleep a family of five (bring your own sleeping bags).

Big Pines Mountain House   MOTEL $
(Map p430; ☎530-541-5155; www.thebigpines.com; 4083 Cedar Ave; r $50-129, pet fee $15;

SOUTH LAKE TAHOE FOR CHILDREN

With oodles of outdoor activities, families will never run out of mountains to explore and beaches to dig. If the kids start to get fractious though, try one of these local favorites to mix things up a little.

Major ski resorts such as **Heavenly** (p427) and **Kirkwood** (p427) around South Lake Tahoe, and **Squaw Valley** (p446) and **Northstar California** (p449) near Truckee, offer sledding hills for the kiddos, some with tubing rentals and thrilling rope tows. Smaller ski mountains including **Sierra-at-Tahoe** (p427) outside South Lake Tahoe, and **Boreal** (p449), **Soda Springs** (p449) and **Tahoe Donner** (p449), all near Truckee, also offer child-friendly slopes.

To avoid the crowds, bring your own sleds to designated local snow-play areas at **North Tahoe Regional Park** (p452) in Tahoe Vista on the north shore, or to Nevada's **Incline Village** (p454), **Tahoe Meadows** (p454) off the Mt Rose Hwy (Hwy 431) or **Spooner Summit** on Hwy 50, all along the east shore. Back in California, DIY **Sno-Parks** (☎916-324-1222; www.parks.ca.gov; pass per day/year $5/25) are found along Hwy 89 at **Blackwood Canyon**, 3 miles south of Tahoe City on the west shore, and **Taylor Creek**, just north of Camp Richardson at South Lake Tahoe. Coming from Sacramento or the San Francisco Bay Area, two Sno-Parks are along I-80 at **Yuba Gap** (exit 161) and **Donner Summit** (exit 176 Castle Peak/Boreal Ridge Rd); their parking lots often fill by 11am on winter weekends. Buy required Sno-Park parking passes online or at local shops.

For private groomed sledding and tubing hills, swing by **Hansen's Resort** (Map p430; ☎530-544-3361; www.hansensresort.com; 1360 Ski Run Blvd; per person incl rental per hour $15; ☺9am-5pm) in South Lake Tahoe or **Adventure Mountain** (☎530-577-4352; www.adventuremountaintahoe.com; 21200 Hwy 50; per car $20, tube/2-person sled rental per day $20/10; ☺10am-4:30pm Mon-Fri, 9am-4:30pm Sat, Sun & holidays), south of town at Echo Summit.

ℹ NAVIGATING SOUTH TAHOE TRAFFIC

South Lake Tahoe's main east–west thoroughfare is a 5-mile stretch of Hwy 50 called Lake Tahoe Blvd. Most hotels and businesses hover around the California–Nevada state line and Heavenly Village. Casinos are located in Stateline, which is officially a separate city.

West of town, Hwy 50 runs into Hwy 89 at the 'Y' junction. Heavy snowfall sometimes closes Hwy 89 north of the **Tallac Historic Site** (p426). The section of Hwy 89 between South Lake Tahoe and Emerald Bay is also known as Emerald Bay Rd.

Traffic all along Hwy 50 between the 'Y' junction and Heavenly Village gets jammed around lunchtime and again by 5pm Monday to Friday in both summer and winter, but Sunday afternoons, when skiers head back down the mountain, are the worst.

An alternate, less crowded route through town is Pioneer Trail, which branches east off the Hwy 89/50 junction (south of the 'Y') and reconnects with Hwy 50 at Stateline.

❄ @ 🌐 🌊 🐾) Choose from over 70 comfortable rooms in various sizes – some with blissful mountain views – and in summertime, stroll to the private beach nearby or take a dip in the heated pool. Gas fireplaces cozy up the king kitchenette rooms.

Camp Richardson Resort CABIN, CAMPGROUND $
(Map p430; ☑ 530-541-1801; www.camprichardson. com; 1900 Jameson Beach Rd; tent sites from $35, RV sites with partial/full hookups from $40/45, r $95-215, cabins $125-263; 🌐) Removed from downtown's strip-mall aesthetic, this sprawling family camp is a hectic place offering seasonal camping (expect marauding bears all night long!), forested cabins rented by the week in summer, and so-so beachside hotel rooms. Sports-gear and bicycle rentals are available, and there's a popular ice-cream parlor across the road. Wi-fi in lobby only.

Blue Lake Inn MOTEL $
(Map p430; ☑ 530-544-6459; www.thebluelakeinn. com; 944 Friday Ave; r $89-104, pet fee $15; ❄ 🌐 🌊 🐾) A good-value choice near the Heavenly Gondola (p426), these ample motel rooms have the core amenities: microwave, refrigerator, coffeemaker and flat-screen TV, plus a hot tub and outdoor pool.

Campground by the Lake CAMPGROUND $
(Map p430; ☑ 530-542-6096; www.cityofslt.us; 1150 Rufus Allen Blvd; tent & RV sites with/without hookups from $40/29, cabins $49-80; ☉ Apr-Oct; 🌐 🐾) Highway noise can be an around-the-clock irritant, though proximity to the city pool and ice rink make this wooded in-town campground with an RV dump station a decent choice. Basic sleeping-platform cabins are available between Memorial Day (late May) and Labor Day (early September).

★ Sorensen's CHALET $$
(☑ 800-423-9949; www.sorensensresort.com; 14255 Hwy 88; r $135-195) A truly delightful option in the Hope Valley, with snug pine cottages and cabins, decked out with fairy lights and hammocks. There's a wealth of activities, including skiing, fishing and hiking. Magical in the snow, but just as lovely in summer. Bird-watching and stargazing events are held. The on-site cafe serves seasonal fish, steaks and salads.

Deerfield Lodge at Heavenly BOUTIQUE HOTEL $$
(Map p430; ☑ 530-544-3337; www.tahoedeerfield lodge.com; 1200 Ski Run Blvd; r/ste from $179/229, pet fee $25; ❄ 🌐) A small boutique hotel close to Heavenly ski resort, Deerfield has a dozen intimate rooms and spacious suites that each have a patio or balcony facing the green courtyard, along with a whirlpool tub, flickering gas fireplace and amusing coat racks crafted from skis and snowboards.

There's complimentary wine in the lobby, s'mores to be made over the fire pit, and barbecue grills appear in summer.

Alder Inn MOTEL $$
(Map p430; ☑ 530-544-4485; www.alderinn.com; 1072 Ski Run Blvd; r $89-149; 🅿 🌊 🌐 🐾) Even better than staying at your best friend's house by the lake, this hospitable inn on the Heavenly ski-shuttle route charms with color schemes that really pop, pillow-top mattresses, organic bath goodies, mini-refrigerators, microwaves and flat-screen TVs. Dip your toes in the kidney-shaped pool in summer.

HIKING & BACKPACKING THE DESOLATION WILDERNESS

Sculpted by powerful glaciers aeons ago, this relatively compact **wilderness area** (Map p428; www.fs.usda.gov/detail/eldorado/specialplaces/?cid=fsbdev7_019062) spreads south and west of Lake Tahoe and is the most popular in the Sierra Nevada. It's a 100-sq-mile wonderland of polished granite peaks, deep-blue alpine lakes, glacier-carved valleys and pine forests that thin quickly at the higher elevations. In summer wildflowers nudge out from between the rocks.

All this splendor makes for some exquisite backcountry exploration. Six major trailheads provide access from the Lake Tahoe side: Glen Alpine, **Tallac** (Map p428; Mt Tallac Rd B trailhead), Echo Lakes (near Echo Summit on Hwy 50), **Bayview** (Map p428), **Eagle Falls** (p440) and **Meeks Bay** (Map p428). Tallac and Eagle Falls get the most traffic, but solitude comes quickly once you've scampered past the day hikers.

Wilderness permits are required year-round for both day and overnight explorations. Day hikers can self-register at the trailheads, but overnight permits must be either reserved online (fee $6) at www.recreation.gov and printed at home, or picked up in person at one of the three USFS offices in South Lake Tahoe and Pollack Pines. Permits cost $5 per person for one night, $10 per person for two or more nights.

Quotas are in effect from late May through the end of September. Over half of the permits for the season may be reserved online, usually starting in late March or April; the other permits are available on a first-arrival basis on the day of entry only.

Bear-proof canisters are strongly advised in all wilderness areas (hanging your food in trees will not work – these bears are too smart!). Borrow canisters for free from the USFS offices. Bring bug repellent as the mosquitoes can be merciless. Wood fires are a no-no, but portable stoves are OK. Dogs must be leashed at *all* times.

Fireside Lodge INN $$
(Map p430; ☏ 530-544-5515; www.tahoefireside lodge.com; 515 Emerald Bay Rd/Hwy 89; d $149-219, pet fee $25; ☎ ❄) This woodsy cabin B&B wholeheartedly welcomes families, with free bikes, kayaks and snowshoes to borrow and evening s'mores and wine and cheese. Kitchenette rooms and suites have river-rock gas fireplaces, cozy patchwork quilts and pioneer-themed touches like wagon wheels or vintage skis.

Heavenly Valley Lodge B&B $$
(Map p430; ☏ 530-564-1500; www.heavenlyvalley lodge.com; 1261 Ski Run Blvd; d $145-255, pet fee $25; ☎ ❄) Located along the Heavenly shuttle route, this family-run place perfects the balance of old Tahoe – all-fireplace rooms of knotty pine and river rock – and great amenities, like DVD players and a huge movie library, a fire-pit patio and afternoon happy hour. Some kitchenette units.

Basecamp Hotel BOUTIQUE HOTEL $$
(Map p430; ☏ 530-208-0180; www.basecamphotels. com; 4143 Cedar Ave; d $109-229, 8-person bunk room $209-299, pet fee $40; ☎ ❄) ☑ Recycled wood, original nature-themed canvases and artsy artifacts gussy up this stylish former motel. Lucky couples can rough it in the 'Great Indoors' room with a tented bed and faux campfire, and families can overnight in spacious bunk-bed rooms. A rooftop hot tub, beer and wine bar, and communal dinner nights sweeten the deal.

Timber Lodge HOTEL $$
(Map p430; ☏ 530-542-6600; www.marriott.com; 4100 Lake Tahoe Blvd; r $150-230, ste from $230; ❄ @ ☎ ❄) Don't let the Marriott chain-gang brand put you off this modern ski lodge with an enviable position, where you can watch the Heavenly Gondola (p426) whoosh by outside your window. Cookie-cutter hotel rooms have kitchenettes, while apartment-style 'vacation villa' suites come with full kitchens, gas fireplaces and deep soaking tubs for après-ski warm-ups.

Paradice Inn MOTEL $$
(Map p430; ☏ 530-544-6800; www.paradicemotel tahoe.com; 953 Park Ave; r $150-220; ❄ ☎) Harried travelers will appreciate the fabulous hospitality (turndown service!) at this small two-story motel. Step outside your minimalist room bordered by flower baskets, then stroll across the street to the Heavenly Gondola (p426). Families should ask about the two-bedroom suites.

Spruce Grove Cabins CABIN $$
(Map p430; 530-544-0549; www.sprucegrove
tahoe.com; 3599-3605 Spruce Ave; 4-/6-person
cabins $169/215, cleaning fee $30, refundable pet
deposit $100; 🐾📶) Away from the Heavenly
hubbub, these tidy, private cabins are fenced
off on a quiet residential street. The vintage
look of the kitchen-equipped cabins, from
knotty pine walls to the stone-bordered gas
fireplaces, will make you feel like you're stay-
ing lakeside. Let your dogs cavort in the yard
while you swing in the hammock or soak in
outdoor hot tubs.

Inn by the Lake HOTEL $$
(Map p430; 530-542-0330; www.innbythelake.
com; 3300 Lake Tahoe Blvd; r $180-300, pet fee
$20; ❄@📶🐾📶) Rooms here are rather
nondescript, although a bilevel outdoor hot
tub, spa suites with kitchens, and bicycles
and snowshoes to borrow are nifty. Rooms
out back are cheaper and quieter, but then
you'll miss the lake views.

Landing HOTEL $$$
(Map p430; 855-700-5263; www.thelandingtahoe.
com; 4104 Lakeshore Blvd; d/ste from $319/619,
pet fee $100; ❄@📶🐾📶) South Lake's newest
and most luxurious lakeside resort dazzles
with an in-house spa, marble bathrooms
with toilet night lights and heated seats, Ke-
urig coffeemakers, a private beach and the
swank Jimmy's restaurant. Each room has
a fireplace seating arrangement, and other
perks include a complimentary town shuttle,
a year-round outdoor pool and nightly wine
tasting.

🛏 Stateline, NV
At Nevada's high-rise casinos, prices rise and
fall like a gambler's luck. In winter ask about
ski-and-stay packages.

Nevada Beach Campground CAMPGROUND $
(Map p428; 775-588-5562, reservations 877-
444-6777; www.recreation.gov; off Hwy 50; tent &
RV sites $32-38; ⊙mid-May–mid-Oct; 🐾) Bed
down on a carpet of pine needles at this tidy
lakeside campground, about 3 miles north
of Stateline, where 48 sites are nestled amid
pines. Leashed dogs are allowed at camp-
sites, but not the beach.

Harrah's CASINO HOTEL $$
(Map p430; 775-588-6611; https://caesars.com/
harrahs-tahoe; 15 Hwy 50; r $85-369; ❄@📶📶)
Clad in an oddly tasteful forest-green facade, this buzzing casino hotel is Stateline's

top contender. Let yourself be swallowed
up by even standard 'luxury' rooms, which
each have two bathrooms with telephones,
or spring for a luxury suite with panoramic
lake-vista windows. For more eye-popping
views, snag a window table at one of Har-
rah's upper-floor restaurants.

MontBleu CASINO HOTEL $$
(Map p430; 775-588-3515; www.montbleuresort.
com; 55 Hwy 50; r $70-210, ste from $240;
❄@📶🐾📶) The public areas may sport uber-
cool modern boutique decor, but hallways
are seriously dim. Remodeled rooms have
fluffy duvets and art-deco-esque accents,
and some of the marble-accented bathrooms
sport hedonistic circular tubs. Rooms above
the 5th floor are best, and those in the pre-
miere category have lake views. Unwind in
the lavish indoor-pool lagoon, accented by a
rockscape and mini waterfalls.

Harvey's CASINO HOTEL $$
(Map p430; 775-588-2411; www.harveystahoe.
com; 18 Hwy 50; r $80-229, pet fee $75;
❄@📶🐾📶) Harvey's was South Lake Ta-
hoe's first casino, and with 740 rooms, is also
its biggest. Mountain Tower rooms have fancy marble bathrooms and oodles of space,
but renovated Lake Tower rooms are more
chic and design-savvy. The heated outdoor
pool is open year-round, for beach and snow
bunnies alike. Wi-fi costs $11 daily.

🍴 Eating
For late-night cravings, each of the big casinos in Stateline has a 24-hour coffee shop for
hangover-helper and night-owl breakfasts.
If you're just looking for filling pub grub or
après-ski appetizers and cocktails, most bars
and cafes also serve just-OK food, some with
waterfront views and live music too.

Sprouts VEGETARIAN $
(Map p430; www.sproutscafetahoe.com; 3123
Harrison Ave; mains $7-10; ⊙8am-9pm; 🐾🏠)
Cheerful chatter greets you at this energetic, mostly organic cafe that gets extra kudos
for its smoothies. A healthy menu will have
you noshing happily on satisfying soups, rice
bowls, sandwiches, burrito wraps, tempeh
burgers and fresh salads.

Sugar Pine Bakery BAKERY $
(Map p430; http://sugarpinecakery.com; 3564
Lake Tahoe Blvd; pastries $1-5; ⊙8am-5pm Tue-
Sat, to 4pm Sun) Organic crunchy baguettes,
ooey-gooey cinnamon rolls, fruit tarts and
choco-chunk cookies.

Cork & More DELI $

(Map p430; www.thecorkandmore.com; 1032 Al Tahoe Blvd; sandwiches $5-10; ⊙10am-7pm) Specialty foods, gourmet deli (sandwiches, soups, salads) and picnic baskets to go.

Ernie's Coffee Shop DINER $

(Map p430; ✆530-541-2161; http://erniescoffee shop.com; 1207 Hwy 50; mains $8-14; ⊙6am-2pm; ☝) A sun-filled local institution, Ernie's dishes out filling three-egg omelets, hearty biscuits with gravy, fruity and nutty waffles and bottomless cups of locally roasted coffee. Breakfast is served all day.

Burger Lounge FAST FOOD $

(Map p430; ✆530-542-2010; 717 Emerald Bay Rd; dishes $4-10; ⊙10am-8pm Jun-Sep, 11am-7pm Thu-Mon Oct-May; ☝) You can't miss that giant beer mug standing outside a shingled cabin. Step inside for the south shore's tastiest burgers, including the crazy 'Jiffy burger' (with peanut butter and cheddar cheese), the zingy pesto fries or the knockout ice-cream shakes.

★Cafe Fiore ITALIAN $$

(Map p430; ✆530-541-2908; www.cafefiore.com; 1169 Ski Run Blvd; mains $18-34; ⊙5:30-9pm) Serving upscale Italian without pretension, this tiny romantic eatery pairs succulent pasta, seafood and meats with an award-winning 300-vintage wine list. Swoon over the veal scaloppine, homemade white-chocolate ice cream and near-perfect garlic bread. With only seven tables (a baker's dozen in summer when the candlelit outdoor patio opens), reservations are essential.

Freshie's FUSION $$

(Map p430; ✆530-542-3630; www.freshiestahoe. com; 3330 Lake Tahoe Blvd; mains $14-28; ⊙11:30am-9pm; ☝) From vegans to seafood-lovers, everybody should be able to find a favorite on the extensive menu at this Hawaiian fusion joint with sunset upper-deck views. Most of the produce is local and organic, and the blackened fish tacos are South Lake Tahoe's best. Check the webcam to see if there's a wait.

Off the Hook SUSHI $$

(Map p430; www.offthehooksushi.com; 2660 Lake Tahoe Blvd; mains $14-23; ⊙5-10pm) Sushi, so far from the ocean? Yup. Locals keep on coming back to this dynamite little sushi shack, where you can feast on bento boxes and *nigiri* (oblong-shaped sushi) combos, or

big steaming bowls of floury udon noodles and pan-fried halibut steaks off the Japanese, Hawaiian and Californian menu.

Latin Soul LATIN AMERICAN $$

(Map p430; ✆775-588-7777; www.lakesideinn.com; 168 Hwy 50, Stateline, NV; mains $9-28; ⊙8am-11pm) For something completely different, steal away to this little casino kitchen with a big, bold menu of spicy south-of-the-border flavors: Argentinean churrasco-grilled steak, Veracruz shrimp ceviche, goat *birria* (stew) and outrageously mixed mojitos.

Blue Angel Cafe CALIFORNIAN $$

(Map p430; ✆530-544-6544; www.theblueangel cafe.com; 1132 Ski Run Blvd; lunch $11-16, dinner $12-25; ⊙11am-9pm; ☝☝☝☝) Inside a cute wooden house on the way uphill to ski at Heavenly (p427), this modern international-inspired kitchen churns out seafood, club sandwiches, elaborate salads, pastas and flank steaks to stuff your belly. Turn up for happy hour or the rotating lunch and dinner specials.

Getaway Cafe AMERICAN $$

(Map p428; www.getawaycafe.com; 3140 Hwy 50, Meyers; mains breakfast & lunch $8-13, dinner $10-19; ⊙11am-10pm Mon-Thu, to 11pm Fri & Sat, 8:30am-10pm Sun; ☝) On the outskirts of town, just south of the agriculture inspection checkpoint, this place really lives up to its name; avoid the weekend crowds here. Friendly waitstaff sling heaped-up buffalo chicken salads, barbecue burgers, chiles rellenos, coconut-encrusted French toast and more.

Lake Tahoe Pizza Co PIZZA $$

(Map p430; ✆530-544-1919; www.laketahoepizzaco. com; 1168 Emerald Bay Rd/Hwy 89; pizzas $11-23; ⊙4-9:30pm; ☝) Since the '70s, this classic pizza parlor has been hand rolling its house-made dough (cornmeal or whole wheat, anyone?), then piling the pizzas with crafty combos such as the meaty 'Barnyard Massacre' or vegan 'Green Giant.'

✖ Self-Catering

Grass Roots Natural Foods FOOD & DRINKS

(Map p430; http://grassrootstahoe.com; 2030 Dunlap Dr; ⊙9am-8pm) ✔ This store sells a wealth of organic produce, lifestyle products and grocery goods, as well as sandwiches and fresh pizzas.

Safeway SUPERMARKET $

(Map p430; www.safeway.com; 1020 Johnson Blvd; ◷24hr) Standard supermarket fare, with an in-house deli and bakery.

Drinking & Entertainment

The siren song of blackjack and slot machines calls the masses over to Stateline, NV. Published on Thursdays, the free alt-weekly newspaper *Reno News & Review* (www.newsreview.com/reno) has comprehensive Stateline entertainment and events listings. For what's going on around South Lake Tahoe, pick up a copy of the free weekly *Lake Tahoe Action*, published by the *Tahoe Daily Tribune* (www.tahoedaily tribune.com).

Beacon Bar & Grill BAR

(Map p430; www.camprichardson.com; 1900 Jameson Beach Rd, Camp Richardson Resort; ◷11am-10pm) Imagine all of Lake Tahoe is your very own front yard when you and your buddies sprawl across this big wraparound wooden deck. If you want to get schnockered, order the signature Rum Runner cocktail. Bands rock here in summer.

Boathouse on the Pier BAR

(Map p430; 3411 Lake Tahoe Blvd; ◷11am-9pm, extended hours Jun-Sep) On the lake behind the Beach Retreat complex, this upstairs and upscale restaurant at the Timber Cove marina is the perfect spot for sunset cocktails, with outdoor tables to feel the summer breeze.

MacDuffs Pub PUB

(Map p430; www.macduffspub.com; 1041 Fremont Ave; ◷11:30am-9:30pm) With excellent beers rotating on tap, a dartboard on the wall, and fish-and-chips and shepherd's pie (as well as gourmet burgers and wood-fired pizzas) on the menu, this dark and bustling gastropub wouldn't look out of place in Edinburgh. Sports fans and beer drinkers, step right up.

Brewery at Lake Tahoe BREWERY

(Map p430; www.brewerylaketahoe.com; 3542 Lake Tahoe Blvd; ◷11am-10:30pm) This crazy-popular brewpub pumps its signature Bad Ass Ale into grateful local patrons, who may sniff at bright-eyed out-of-towners. The barbecue is dynamite and a roadside patio opens in summer. Don't leave without a bumper sticker!

Opal Ultra Lounge CLUB

(Map p430; ☑775-586-2000; www.montbleuresort. com; 55 Hwy 50, MontBleu, Stateline, NV; cover free-$10; ◷10pm-4am Wed-Sat) With DJ booths and go-go dancers, this Top 40 and electro dance club draws a young party crowd that enjoys getting their bodies painted in-house. Ladies may get in free before midnight. On summer Sunday nights, hit up the casino's poolside DJ parties. Dress to impress.

Stateline Brewery BREWERY

(Map p430; www.statelinebrewery.com; 4118 Lake Tahoe Blvd; ◷11am-9pm Sun-Thu, to 10:30pm Fri & Sat) Seat yourself by the shiny industrial brewing vats at this subterranean eating and drinking spot. German- and American-style ales taste mighty good after a day of sunning yourself on the lakeshore or skiing Heavenly (p427) (the gondola swings nearby).

Improv COMEDY

(Map p430; www.caesars.com/harveys-tahoe; 18 Hwy 50, Stateline, NV; tickets $25-30; ◷usually 9pm Wed, Fri & Sun, 8:30pm & 10:30pm Sat) Catch up-and-coming stand-up comedians doing their funny shtick at the intimate cabaret theater inside Harvey's (p437) old-school casino.

Information

Barton Memorial Hospital (☑530-541-3420; www.bartonhealth.org; 2170 South Ave; ◷24hr) Around-the-clock emergency room. Barton's urgent-care clinic is inside the Stateline Medical Center at 155 Hwy 50, Stateline, NV.

Explore Tahoe (Map p430; ☑530-542-4637; www.cityofslt.us; 4114 Lake Tahoe Blvd, Heavenly Village Transit Center; ◷9am-5pm) Find information on transport and recreation at **Heavenly** (p427).

Lake Tahoe Visitors Authority (Map p430; ☑800-288-2463; www.tahoesouth.com; 169 Hwy 50, Stateline, NV; ◷9am-5pm Mon-Fri) A full range of tourist information.

South Lake Tahoe Library (☑530-573-3185; www.eldoradolibrary.org/tahoe.htm; 1000 Rufus Allen Blvd; ◷10am-8pm Tue & Wed, to 5pm Thu-Sat; 🛜) First-come, first-served free internet terminals.

Tahoe Urgent Care (☑530-553-4319; www. tahoeurgentcare.com; 2130 Lake Tahoe Blvd; ◷8am-6pm) Walk-in medical clinic for nonemergencies.

USDA Lake Tahoe Basin Management Unit (Map p430; ☑530-543-2600; www.fs.usda. gov/ltbmu; 35 College Dr; ◷8am-4:30pm Mon-Fri) Find out about camping and outdoor options, plus acquire permits for wilderness trips.

LAKE TAHOE SOUTH LAKE TAHOE & STATELINE

USFS Taylor Creek Visitor Center (Map p430; ☑ 530-543-2674; www.fs.usda.gov/ltbmu; Visitor Center Rd, off Hwy 89; ⊗ 8am-5pm late May-Sep, to 4pm Oct) Outdoor information, wilderness permits and daily ranger-led walks and talks during July and August.

ⓘ Getting There & Away

From Reno-Tahoe International Airport, **South Tahoe Airporter** (☑ 775-325-8944; www.southtahoeexpress.com; adult/child 4-12yr $30/17) operates several daily shuttle buses to Stateline casinos; the journey takes from 75 minutes up to two hours.

Amtrak (☑ 800-872-7245; www.amtrak.com) has a daily Thruway bus service between Sacramento and South Lake Tahoe ($34, 2½ hours), stopping at the **South Y Transit Center** (p440).

ⓘ Getting Around

South Lake Tahoe's main transportation hubs are the **South Y Transit Center** (Map p430; 1000 Emerald Bay Rd/Hwy 89), just south of the 'Y' intersection of Hwys 50 and 89; and the more central **Stateline Transit Center** (Map p430; 4114 Lake Tahoe Blvd).

BlueGO (☑ 530-541-7149; www.tahoetransportation.org/transit; single/day pass $2/5) local buses operate year-round from 6am to 11pm daily, stopping all along Hwy 50 between the two transit centers.

On summer weekends, BlueGO's **Emerald Bay Trolley** (☑ 531-541-7149; www.tahoetransportation.org; fare $2; 👶) heads north from the South Y Transit Center to the Vikingsholm and Eagle Falls parking lot at Emerald Bay, but confirm the schedule as it changes from year to year. During winter ski season, BlueGO provides free and frequent shuttle service from Stateline and South Lake Tahoe to all **Heavenly** (p427) base operations every 30 minutes from stops along Hwy 50, Ski Run Blvd and Pioneer Trail.

LAKE TAHOE WESTERN SHORE

Lake Tahoe's densely forested western shore, between Emerald Bay and Tahoe City, is idyllic. Hwy 89 sinuously wends past gorgeous state parks with swimming beaches, hiking trails, pine-shaded campgrounds and historic mansions. Several trailheads also access the rugged splendor of the Desolation Wilderness (p436).

All campgrounds and many businesses shut down between November and May. Hwy 89 often closes after snowfall for plowing or due to imminent avalanche danger. Once you drive its tortuous slopeside curves, you'll understand why. The further south you are, the more of a roller coaster it is, no matter the season – so grip that steering wheel!

Emerald Bay State Park

Sheer granite cliffs and a jagged shoreline hem in glacier-carved **Emerald Bay** (Map p428; ☑ 530-541-6498; www.parks.ca.gov), a teardrop cove that will have you digging for your camera. Its most captivating aspect is the water, which changes from cloverleaf green to light jade depending on the angle of the sun.

⊙ Sights

You'll spy panoramic pullouts all along Hwy 89, including at **Inspiration Point** (Map p428), opposite USFS Bayview Campground. Just south, the road shoulder evaporates on both sides of a steep drop-off, revealing a postcard-perfect view of Emerald Bay to the north and Cascade Lake to the south.

Fannette Island, an uninhabited granite speck, is Lake Tahoe's only island. It holds the vandalized remains of a tiny 1920s teahouse belonging to heiress Lora Knight, who would occasionally motorboat guests to the island from **Vikingsholm Castle** (Map p428; http://vikingsholm.com; tour adult/child 7-17yr $10/8; ⊗ 10:30am-3:30pm or 4pm late May–Sep; 👶), her Scandinavian-style mansion on the bay. The focal point of the state park, Vikingsholm Castle is a rare example of ancient Scandinavian-style architecture. Completed in 1929, it has trippy design elements aplenty, including sod-covered roofs that sprout wildflowers in late spring. The mansion is reached by a steep 1-mile trail, which also leads to a visitor center.

🏃 Activities

Hiking

Vikingsholm Castle is the southern terminus of the famous **Rubicon Trail** (Map p428).

Two popular trailheads lead into the Desolation Wilderness. From the Eagle Falls parking lot ($5), the **Eagle Falls Trail** (Map p428) travels one steep mile to Eagle Lake, crossing by Eagle Falls along the way. This scenic short hike often gets choked with visitors, but crowds disappear quickly as the trail continues up to the Tahoe Rim Trail and Velma, Dicks and Fontanillis Lakes (up to 10 miles round-trip). From the back of USFS Bayview Campground, it's a steep 1-mile climb to glacial Granite Lake or a moderate 1.5-mile round-trip to Cascade Falls, which rushes with snowmelt in early summer.

Boating
Fannette Island is accessible by boat, except during Canada goose nesting season (typically February to mid-June). Rent boats at Meeks Bay (p441) or South Lake Tahoe; from the latter, you can also catch narrated bay cruises or speedboat tours.

Scuba Diving
Divers prepared for chilly high-altitude plunges can explore sunken barges, a submerged rockslide and artifacts at a historic dumping ground at the unique Underwater State Parks of Emerald Bay and DL Bliss State Park. Reno-based Sierra Diving Center (www.sierradive.com) and Adventure Scuba Center (www.renoscuba.com) offer classes and trips.

🛏 Sleeping

Eagle Point Campground CAMPGROUND $
(Map p428; 📞530-525-7277, reservations 800-444-7275; www.reserveamerica.com; Hwy 89; tent & RV sites $38; ☉mid-Jun–early Sep) With over 90 sites perched on the tip of Eagle Point, this state-park campground provides flush toilets, hot pay showers, beach access and bay views. Another 20 scattered sites are reserved for boat-in campers.

USFS Bayview Campground CAMPGROUND $
(Map p428; Hwy 89; tent & RV sites $15; ☉Jun-Sep; 🐾) This rustic, nay, primitive forest-service campground has 13 no-reservation sites and vault toilets, but its potable water supplies are often exhausted sometime in July. It's opposite Inspiration Point (p440).

DL Bliss State Park
DL Bliss State Park (Map p428; 📞530-525-7277; www.parks.ca.gov; per car $10; ☉late May–Sep; 🅿🚻) 🏊 has the western shore's nicest beaches at Lester Beach and Calawee Cove. A short nature trail leads to the Balancing Rock, a giant chunk of granite perched on a rocky pedestal. Pick up information from the visitor center by the park entrance.

Near Calawee Cove is the northern terminus of the scenic one-way Rubicon Trail. The park's campground (Map p428; 📞800-

444-7275; www.reserveamerica.com; tent & RV sites $35-45, hike-and-bike sites $7; ☉mid-May–Sep; 🐾) has 145 sites, including some coveted spots near the beach, along with flush toilets, hot pay showers, picnic tables, fire rings and an RV dump station.

The small visitor parking lot at Calawee Cove usually fills up by 10am, in which case it's a 2-mile walk from the park entrance to the beach. Alternatively, ask park staff at the entrance station about closer access points to Rubicon Trail.

Meeks Bay
With a wide sweep of shoreline, sleek and shallow Meeks Bay has warm water by Tahoe standards and is fringed by a beautiful, but busy, sandy beach. West of the highway, north of the fire station, is a trailhead for the Desolation Wilderness.

A mostly level, shaded path parallels Meeks Creek before heading steeply uphill through the forest to Lake Genevieve (9 miles round-trip), Crag Lake (10 miles round-trip) and other backcountry ponds, all surrounded by scenic Sierra peaks.

🛏 Sleeping & Eating

USFS Meeks Bay Campground CAMPGROUND $
(Map p428; 📞530-525-4733, reservations 877-444-6777; www.recreation.gov; tent & RV sites $27-29; ☉mid-May–mid-Oct) This developed campground offers 36 reservable sites along the beach, along with flush toilets, picnic tables and fire rings. For pay showers, head to Meeks Bay Resort (p441) next door.

Meeks Bay Resort CABIN, CAMPGROUND $$
(Map p428; 📞530-525-6946; www.meeksbayresort.com; 7941 Emerald Bay Rd/Hwy 89; tent/RV sites with full hookups $30/50, cabins $125-400; ☉May-Oct) The Washoe tribe offers various lodging options (cabins require minimum

LAKE TAHOE WESTERN SHORE

stays) plus kayak, canoe and paddleboat rentals. If you're hungry, swing by the waterfront grill or small market, which stocks limited groceries and camping, fishing and beach gear, as well as Native American crafts and cultural books.

Ed Z'berg Sugar Pine Point State Park

Ed Z'berg Sugar Pine Point State Park (Map p428; ☑530-525-7982; www.parks.ca.gov; per car $10) occupies a promontory blanketed by a fragrant mix of pine, juniper, aspen and fir. It has a swimming beach, hiking trails and abundant fishing in General Creek. A paved bike path travels north to Tahoe City and Squaw Valley. In winter, 12 miles of groomed cross-country trails await inside the park; book ahead for ranger-guided full-moon snowshoe tours. In summer the park offers kayak and hiking tours through the Sierra State Parks Foundation (www.sierrastateparks.org).

Historic sights include the modest 1872 cabin of William 'General' Phipps, an early Tahoe settler, and the considerably grander 1903 Queen Anne–style Hellman-Ehrman Mansion (Map p428; tours adult/youth 7-17yr $10/8; ⊙10:30am-3:30pm mid-Jun–Sep).

The park's secluded General Creek Campground (Map p428; ☑800-444-7275; www.reserveamerica.com; tent & RV sites $25-35; ⊙late May–mid-Sep) has 120 fairly spacious, pine-shaded sites, plus flush toilets and hot pay showers; a dozen sites stay open year-round (but without showers).

Tahoma

A blink-and-you'll-miss-it lakeside outpost, Tahoma has a post office and a handful of places to stay and eat. Within striking distance of Tahoe City, Tahoma offers a more secluded base for outdoor enthusiasts.

If you don't want to camp, the best option is Tahoma Meadows B&B Cottages (☑530-525-1553; www.tahomameadows.com; 6821 W Lake Blvd; cottages $119-239, pet fee $20; P☺☎☒), set in a pine grove.

You can booze all day long at Chamber's Landing (Map p428; ☑530-525-9190; 6400 W Lake Blvd; ⊙noon-8pm Jun-Sep) if you so desire.

Homewood

This quiet and very alpine-looking resort hamlet (Map p428; ☑530-525-2992; www.skihomewood.com; 5145 Westlake Blvd, off Hwy 89; adult/child 5-12yr/youth 13-19yr $83/35/65; ⊙9am-4pm; ☒) is popular with summertime boaters and, in winter, skiers and snowboarders. West Shore Sports (☑530-525-9920; www.westshoresports.com; 5395 W Lake Blvd; ⊙8am-5pm) rents out all the winter and summer gear you'll need.

🛏 Sleeping & Eating

USFS Kaspian Campground   CAMPGROUND $
(Map p428; ☑877-444-6777; www.recreation.gov; tent sites $20; ⊙mid-May–mid-Oct) The closest campground is this nine-site, tent-only spot set among ponderosa and fir trees; amenities include flush toilets, picnic tables and fire rings.

West Shore Inn   INN $$$
(☑530-525-5200; www.westshorecafe.com; 5160 W Lake Blvd; r/ste from $199/349; ☒☎) Oriental rugs and arts-and-crafts decor give this luxurious six-room inn a classic, aged ambience, and the lake's so close you feel like you could dive in. It's an upscale mountain lodge where crisp, modern suites feel decadent, and each has a fireplace and lake-view balcony. Rates include complimentary use of bicycles, kayaks and stand up paddleboards.

West Shore Café   CALIFORNIAN $$
(☑530-525-5200; www.westshorecafe.com; 5160 W Lake Blvd; mains $12-33; ⊙11am-9:30pm mid-Jun–Sep, 5-9:30pm Oct–mid-Jun) At the West Shore Inn's (p442) cozy destination restaurant, chef Mike Davis whips up worthy meals using fresh produce and ranched meats, from juicy burgers to Arctic char with spaghetti squash and hedgehog mushrooms. Dinner reservations recommended.

Sunnyside

Sunnyside is a lakeshore hamlet that may be just a dot on the map, but it has a couple of detour-worthy restaurants. To work off all that dang-good eating, rent a bicycle from an outpost of West Shore Sports (☑530-583-9920; www.westshoresports.com; 1785 W Lake Blvd), where you can get the scoop on all sorts of local outdoor information. You can pedal all the way north to Tahoe City along the paved bike path, or rent a stand up paddling set and hit the popular local beaches.

Sleeping & Eating

Sunnyside Lodge
INN $$

(☑530-583-7200; www.sunnysidetahoe.com; 1850 W Lake Blvd; d $150-380, pet fee $35; 🛜🐾) This recently upgraded lodge features modern rooms with new bathrooms, pillow-top mattresses and flat-screen TVs, afternoon tea and cookies, and a guests-only sitting room overlooking the lake. The less expensive 'garden view' rooms lack good lake views. Note that there's lots of activity from the restaurant, and boat dock and marina next door.

★ Fire Sign Cafe
AMERICAN $

(www.firesigncafe.com; 1785 W Lake Blvd; mains $7-13; ⊘7am-3pm; 🍴🚻) For breakfast, everyone heads to the friendly Fire Sign for down-home omelets, blueberry pancakes, eggs Benedict with smoked salmon, fresh made-from-scratch pastries and other carbo-loading bombs, plus organic coffee. In summer, hit the outdoor patio. Lines are usually very long, so get here early.

Spoon
AMERICAN $

(☑530-581-5400; www.spoontakeout.com; 1785 W Lake Blvd; mains $9.50-15; ⊘3-9pm, closed Tue & Wed Oct-May; 🚻) Call ahead for takeout, or squeeze yourselves into the cozy upstairs dining room at this little slat-sided cabin by the side of the highway. Barbecue tri-tip beef sandwiches, roasted veggies, soups, baked pastas and chicken enchiladas are the comfort-food staples, with brownies and ice cream for dessert.

Sunnyside Restaurant
CALIFORNIAN $$

(☑530-583-7200; www.sunnysidetahoe.com; 1850 W Lake Blvd; mains lunch $10-13, dinner $16-35) Classic and innovative contemporary takes on steak and seafood – think porterhouse pork with cherry chutney or roasted chicken with braised fennel – pervade this lakeside dining room. In summer you'll probably have more fun doing lunch – or drinks with the signature zucchini sticks and a piece of hula pie – on the huge lakefront deck.

❶ Getting There & Around

Tahoe Area Rapid Transit (TART; Map p428; ☑530-550-1212; www.laketahoetransit. com; 10183 Truckee Airport Rd; single/day pass $2/4) buses can take you to and from Sunnyside.

TAHOE CITY

The western shore's commercial hub, Tahoe City straddles the junction of Hwys 89 and 28, making it almost inevitable that you'll find yourself breezing through here at least once during your round-the-lake sojourn. The town is handy for grabbing food and supplies and renting sports gear. It's also the closest lake town to Squaw Valley. The main drag, N Lake Blvd, is chockablock with outdoor outfitters, touristy shops and cafes.

◉ Sights

Gatekeeper's Museum & Marion Steinbach Indian Basket Museum
MUSEUM

(☑530-583-1762; www.northtahoemuseums.org; 130 W Lake Blvd/Hwy 89; adult/child under 13yr $5/ free; ⊘10am-5pm daily late May-Sep, 11am-4pm Fri & Sat Oct-Apr) In a reconstructed log cabin close to town, this museum has a small but fascinating collection of Tahoe memorabilia, including Olympics history and relics from the early steamboat era and tourism explosion around the lake. In the museum's newer wing, uncover an exquisite array of Native American baskets collected from over 85 indigenous California tribes.

Fanny Bridge
BRIDGE

Just south of the always-jammed Hwy 89/28 traffic stoplight junction, the Truckee River flows through dam floodgates and passes beneath this bridge, cutely named for the most prominent feature of people leaning over the railings to look at fish (in American slang, 'fanny' means your rear end). The side facing the lake displays historical photos and hydrological facts.

Watson Cabin
MUSEUM

(☑530-583-8717; www.northtahoemuseums.org; 560 N Lake Tahoe Blvd; adult/child under 13yr $2/ free; ⊘noon-4pm Thu-Sun mid-Jun–early Sep) A few blocks east of Fanny Bridge (p443) over the Truckee River, this well-preserved 1908 settlers' cabin made from hand-hewn logs is one of the town's oldest buildings, built overlooking the beach.

Commons Beach
PARK

(400 N Lake Blvd) Commons Beach is a small, attractive park with sandy and grassy areas, picnic tables, barbecue grills, a climbing rock and playground, as well as free summer concerts (www.concertsatcommonsbeach. com) and outdoor movie nights. Leashed dogs welcome.

🏃 Activities

Winter Sports

Alpine Meadows SNOW SPORTS

(Map p428; ☑530-452-4356; www.skialpine.com; 2600 Alpine Meadows Rd, off Hwy 89; adult/child under 13yr/youth 13-22yr $124/75/109; ⊘9am-4pm) Though now owned by neighboring Squaw (tickets are good at both resorts and a free shuttle connects them), Alpine remains a no-nonsense resort with challenging terrain and without the fancy village, attitude or crowds. It gets more snow than Squaw and it's the most backcountry-friendly resort around. Boarders jib down the mountain in a terrain park designed by Eric Rosenwald.

Also look for the supersmart and adorable ski-patrol dogs. The turnoff is 4 miles northwest of Tahoe City. Stats: 13 lifts, 1800 vertical feet, over 100 runs.

Tahoe Cross Country SKIING

(Map p428; ☑530-583-5475; www.tahoexc.org; 925 Country Club Dr, off N Lake Blvd/Hwy 28; adult/child under 12yr/youth 13-17yr $24/free/20; ⊘8:30am-5pm; 🖨🐕) Run by the nonprofit Tahoe Cross Country Ski Education Association, this center, about 3 miles north of Tahoe City, has 40 miles of groomed tracks (23 trails) that wind through lovely forest, suitable for all skill levels. Group lessons come with good-value equipment-rental packages; half-day and twilight trail-pass discounts are also available.

Ask about free skate clinics and beginners' cross-country midweek lessons.

Dogs are allowed on three trails.

Tahoe City is within easy reach of a half dozen downhill and cross-country skiing and snowboarding resorts.

Tahoe Dave's OUTDOORS

(☑530-583-0400,530-583-6415;www.tahoedaves. com; 590 N Lake Tahoe Blvd; ski & snowboard rentals per day from $32) The main regional outfitter, with additional branches at Squaw Valley, Kings Beach and Truckee (rentals can be returned to any shop); reservations accepted.

River Rafting

Truckee River Raft Rentals RAFTING

(☑530-583-0123; www.truckeeriverraft.com; 185 River Rd; adult/child 6-12yr $30/25; ⊘8:30am-3:30pm Jun-Sep; 🖨) The Truckee River here is gentle and wide as it flows northwest from the lake – perfect for novice paddlers. This outfit rents rafts for the 5-mile float from Tahoe City to the River Ranch Lodge (p445), including transportation back to town. Reservations strongly advised.

Hiking

Explore the fabulous trails of the **Granite Chief Wilderness** (Map p428) north and west of Tahoe City. For maps and trailhead directions, stop by the visitor center. Recommended day hikes include the moderately strenuous **Five Lakes Trail** (over 4 miles round-trip), which starts from Alpine Meadows Rd off Hwy 89 heading toward Squaw Valley, and the easy trek to **Paige Meadows**, leading onto the Tahoe Rim Trail (p441). Paige Meadows is also good terrain for novice mountain bikers and snowshoeing. Wilderness permits are not required, even for overnight trips, but free campfire permits are needed, even for gas stoves. Leashed dogs are allowed on these trails.

Cycling

The paved 4-mile **Truckee River Bike Trail** runs from Tahoe City toward Squaw Valley, while the multi-use **West Shore Bike Path** heads 9 miles south to Ed Z'berg Sugar Pine Point State Park (p442), including highway-shoulder and residential-street sections. Both are fairly easy rides, but expect crowds on summer weekends. The whole family can rent bicycles from any of several shops along N Lake Blvd. Park and head out from the **64 Acres Park** trailhead behind the Tahoe City Transit Center (p446). The excellent bike-trail map of Lake Tahoe Bicycle Coalition (www.tahoebike.org) is available on its website.

🛏 Sleeping

If you show up without reservations, dingy, last-resort budget motels are along N Lake Blvd. For camping, head north to USFS campgrounds off Hwy 89 or south along Hwy 89 to state parks and small towns along the lake's western shore.

USFS William Kent

Campground CAMPGROUND $

(☑877-444-6777; www.recreation.gov; Hwy 89; tent & RV sites $27-29; ⊘mid-May–mid-Oct) About 2 miles south of Tahoe City, this roadside campground offers over 85 nicely shaded but cramped sites that often fill up. Amenities include flush toilets, picnic tables and fire rings, along with swimming-beach access.

Mother Nature's Inn
INN $$

(☑530-581-4278; www.mothernaturesinn.com; 551 N Lake Blvd; r $65-155, pet fee $15; 🖥🐾) Right in town behind the Cabin Fever knickknack boutique, this good-value option offers quiet motel-style rooms with a tidy country look, fridges and coffeemaker, eclectic furniture and comfy pillow-top mattresses. It's within walking distance of Commons Beach.

Granlibakken
LODGE $$

(Map p428; ☑530-583-4242; www.granlibakken. com; 725 Granlibakken Rd, off Hwy 89; r/ste from $150/242, 1-/2-/3-bedroom town house from $330/409/516; 🖥🐾) Sleep old-school at this cross-country ski area and kitschy wedding and conference venue. Basic lodge rooms are spacious, but time-share town houses with kitchens, fireplaces and lofts can be a decent deal for families and groups. Amenities include tennis courts, a full spa, year-round outdoor pool and hot tub, and winter shuttle service to Homewood (p442).

Pepper Tree Inn
MOTEL $$

(☑530-583-3711; www.peppertreetahoe.com; 645 N Lake Blvd; r $96-199; 🖥🐾) The tallest building in town, this somberly painted establishment redeems itself with some bird's-eye lake views. Fairly comfortable modern rooms with that familiar log-cabin decor each have a microwave and mini-refrigerator. Top-floor rooms with hot tubs are most in demand.

🍴 Eating

★ Fat Cat
CALIFORNIAN $

(www.tahoefatcat.com; 599 N Lake Blvd; mains $9-17; ☺11am-9pm, bar to 2am; 🖥) This casual, family run restaurant with local art splashed on the walls does it all: from-scratch soups, heaped salads, sandwiches, incredible burgers, pasta bowls and plenty of fried munchies for friends to share. Look for live indie music on Friday and Saturday nights.

Tahoe House Bakery
BAKERY $

(www.tahoe-house.com; 625 W Lake Blvd; items $2-10; ☺6am-6pm; 🖥) Before you take off down the western shore for a bike ride or hike, drop by this mom-and-pop shop that opened in the 1970s. Their motto: 'While you sleep, we loaf.' Sweet cookies, European pastries, fresh-baked deli sandwiches and homemade salads and soups will keep you going all afternoon on the trail.

New Moon Natural Foods
DELI, HEALTH FOOD $

(505 W Lake Blvd; mains $6-12; ☺9am-8pm Mon-Sat, 10am-7pm Sun; 🖥) 🍃 A tiny but well-stocked natural-foods store, its gem of a deli concocts scrumptious ethnic food to go, all packaged in biodegradable and compostable containers. Try the fish tacos or Thai salad with organic greens and spicy peanut sauce.

Dam Cafe
CAFE $

(55 W Lake Blvd; mains $6-11; ☺6am-3pm) This cute cottage is right by the Truckee River dam and Fanny Bridge (p443); stash your bikes in the racks outside and walk inside for a breakfast burrito, ice-cream fruit smoothie or pick-me-up espresso.

Syd's Bagelry & Espresso
CAFE $

(550 N Lake Blvd; items $2-8.50; ☺7am-5pm; 🖥) A handy spot on the main drag that serves bagels and locally roasted coffee, plus smoothies and breakfast burritos made with organic produce.

★ Dockside 700
Wine Bar & Grill
AMERICAN $$

(☑530-581-0303; www.dockside700.com; 700 N Lake Blvd; lunch $10-17, dinner $14-32; ☺11:30am-8pm Mon-Thu, to 9pm Fri-Sun; 🖥🐾) On a lazy summer afternoon, grab a table on the back deck that overlooks the boats bobbing at Tahoe City Marina. Barbecue chicken, ribs and steak light a fire under dinner (reservations advised), alongside seafood pastas and pizzas.

Rosie's Cafe
DINER $$

(www.rosiescafe.com; 571 N Lake Blvd; breakfast & lunch $7-14, dinner $14-20; ☺7:30am-9:30pm; 🖥) With antique skis, shiny bikes and lots of pointy antlers belonging to stuffed wildlife mounted on the walls, this quirky place serves breakfast until 2:30pm. The all-American hodgepodge menu with items such as Yankee pot roast is all right, but the convivial atmosphere is a winner.

River Ranch Lodge
MODERN AMERICAN $$

(Map p428; ☑530-583-4264; http://riverranch lodge.com; Hwy 89 at Alpine Meadows Rd; mains patio & cafe $8-13, restaurant $22-30; ☺lunch Jun-Sep, dinner year-round, call for seasonal hours) This stone-built riverside dining room is a popular stop, drawing rafters and bikers to its patio for summer barbecue lunches.

LAKE TAHOE TAHOE CITY

☻ Drinking & Nightlife

There's an unpretentious and enjoyable nightlife scene here, with several restaurants joining in the fun by staging live music.

Tahoe Mountain Brewing Co   BREWERY
(www.tahoebrewing.com; 475 N Lake Blvd; ⏰11:30am-10pm) Brewed in nearby Truckee, the Sugar Pine Porter, barrel-aged sours and award-winning Paddleboard Pale Ale here pair splendidly with sweet-potato fries, burgers and other pub grub on the outdoor lake-facing patio.

Bridgetender Tavern & Grill   PUB
(www.tahoebridgetender.com; 65 W Lake Blvd; ⏰11am-11pm, to midnight Fri & Sat) Après-ski crowds gather for beer, burgers and chili-cheese or garlic waffle fries at this woodsy bar (mains $8 to $14). In summer, grab a seat on the open-air patio.

ℹ Information

Tahoe City Downtown Association (www.visittahoecity.org; 425 N Lake Blvd; ⏰9am-5pm Mon-Thu) Tourist information and online events calendar.

Tahoe City Library (☑530-583-3382; 740 N Lake Blvd, Boatworks Mall; ⏰10am-5pm Tue & Thu, 11am-6pm Wed & Fri, 10am-2pm Sat; 📶) Free wi-fi and walk-in internet terminals.

Tahoe City Visitors Information Center (☑530-581-6900; www.gotahoenorth.com; 100 N Lake Blvd; ⏰9am-5pm) At the Hwy 89/28 split.

Truckee Tahoe Medical Group (☑530-581-8864, ext 3; www.ttmg.net; 925 N Lake Blvd, Trading Post Center; ⏰9am-6pm Mon-Sat year-round, also 10am-5pm Sun Jul-early Sep) Walk-in clinic for nonemergencies.

ℹ Getting There & Away

Just south of the Hwy 28/89 split, the modern new **Tahoe City Transit Center** (www.nextbus.com/tahoe; 870 Cabin Creek Rd, off Hwy 89) is the main bus terminal, with a comfy waiting room. Behind it you'll find trailhead parking for the **Tahoe Rim Trail** (p441) and various bike-path routes. Regular buses connect the town with other spots on the lake.

SQUAW VALLEY

The nirvana of the north shore, Squaw Valley played host to the 1960 Olympic Winter Games and still ranks among the world's top ski resorts. The stunning setting amid granite peaks, though, makes it a superb destination in any season, and this deluxe family-friendly resort stays almost as busy in summer as in winter.

◉ Sights & Activities

Much summertime action centers on 8200ft **High Camp** (☑800-403-0206; http://squawalpine.com; cable car adult/child 5-12yr/youth 13-22yr $39/15/25, all-access pass $46/19/38; ⏰11am-4:30pm; ▣), reached by a cable car, and offering swimming, disc golf, tennis and ice/roller-skating. Other activities down below include a ropes course with zip lines, a climbing wall, mini-golf and a bungee trampoline, all operated by **Squaw Valley Adventure Center** (Map p428; ☑530-583-7673; www.squawadventure.com). Golfers tee off at the **Resort at Squaw Creek Golf Course** (Map p428; ☑530-583-6300; www.squawcreek.com; green fee incl cart $59-99).

Several hiking trails radiate out from High Camp, or try the lovely, moderate **Shirley Lake Trail** (round-trip 5 miles), which follows a sprightly creek to waterfalls, granite boulders and abundant wildflowers. It starts at the mountain base, near the end of Squaw Peak Rd, behind the cable-car building. Leashed dogs are allowed.

★ **Squaw Valley**   SNOW SPORTS
(Map p428; ☑530-452-4331; www.squaw.com; 1960 Squaw Valley Rd, off Hwy 89, Olympic Valley; adult/child 5-12yr/youth 13-22yr $124/75/109; ⏰9am-4pm Mon-Fri, from 8:30am Sat, Sun & holidays; 📶) Few ski hounds can resist the siren call of this megasized, world-class, see-and-be-seen resort that hosted the 1960 Winter Olympic Games. Hard-core skiers thrill to white-knuckle cornices, chutes and bowls, while beginners practice their turns in a separate area on the upper mountain. There's also a great après-ski scene, and relatively short chairlift waits.

The valley turnoff is 5 miles northwest of Tahoe City. Stats: 29 lifts, 2850 vertical feet, over 170 runs.

Olympic Museum   MUSEUM
(☑800-403-0206; http://squawalpine.com; High Camp; entry incl with cable car adult/child 5-12yr/youth 13-22yr $39/15/25; ⏰11am-4pm Sat & Sun) A fun retro exploration of the 1960 Olympics, featuring a film and much memorabilia. Located at High Camp (p446).

✦ Festivals & Events

WinterWonderGrass Tahoe MUSIC
(www.winterwondergrasstahoe.com; ☺Mar) Book
early for this great little outdoor festival
of bluegrass and acoustic roots music, the
stage encircled by the snow and pines of
Squaw Valley. It's a family-oriented event,
with an ethos of sustainability.

🛏 Sleeping & Eating

There are some premier accommodations
here, with boutique options as well as more
rugged places.

River Ranch Lodge INN $$
(Map p428; ☑530-583-4264; www.riverranchlodge.
com; Hwy 89 at Alpine Meadows Rd; r $115-190;
🛰🐾) Though there's some noise from traf-
fic outside and the bar downstairs, request
a river-facing room so you can drift off to
dreamland as the Truckee River tumbles
below your window. Rooms bulge with
lodgepole-pine furniture; those upstairs have
wistful balconies. Pet-friendly rooms availa-
ble in summer only.

**★ PlumpJack
Squaw Valley Inn** BOUTIQUE HOTEL $$$
(Map p428; ☑530-583-1576; www.plumpjack
squawvalleyinn.com; 1920 Squaw Valley Rd, Olympic Valley; r summer $205-385, winter $340-645;
🏧@🛰🐾) Bed down at this artsy bou-
tique hotel in the village, where every room
has mountain views and extracomfort fac-
tors like plush terry-cloth robes and slippers.
Ski-in, ski-out access doesn't hurt either, but
a $150 pet fee will. The chic **PlumpJack
Cafe**, with its crisp linens and plush ban-
quettes, serves seasonally inspired California cuisine with ace wines.

Le Chamois & Loft Bar PIZZA, PUB FOOD $
(Map p428; www.squawchamois.com; 1970 Squaw
Valley Rd; mains $7-17; ☺11am-6pm Mon-Fri, to
8pm Sat & Sun, bar open to 9pm or 10pm; 🐾🐾)
For a social bite after shedding your bind-
ings, this slopeside favorite is handily positioned between the cable-car building and
the rental shop. Slide on over to devour a hot
sammy or pizza and a beer with eye-pleasing
mountain views.

ℹ Getting There & Away

The village at Squaw Valley, at the base of the
mountain cable car, is about a 20-minute drive
from Tahoe City or Truckee via Hwy 89 (turn off
at Squaw Valley Rd).

Tahoe Area Rapid Transit (p443) buses between Truckee and Tahoe City, Kings Beach and
Crystal Bay stop at Squaw Valley every hour
or so between 6am and 5pm daily, with a free
morning ski shuttle from December to April.

TRUCKEE &
DONNER LAKE

Cradled by mountains and the Tahoe National Forest, Truckee is a thriving town
steeped in Old West history. It was put on
the map by the railroad, grew rich on logging and ice harvesting, and even had its
brush with Hollywood during the 1924 film-
ing of Charlie Chaplin's *The Gold Rush*. Today tourism fills much of the city's coffers,
thanks to a well-preserved historical downtown and its proximity to Lake Tahoe and
no fewer than six downhill and four cross-
country ski resorts.

◉ Sights

The aura of the Old West still lingers over
Truckee's teensy one-horse downtown,
where railroad workers and lumberjacks
once milled about in raucous saloons, bawdy
brothels and shady gambling halls. Most of
the late 19th-century buildings now contain
restaurants and upscale boutiques. **Donner
Memorial State Park** (p447) and **Donner
Lake** (www.donnerlakemarina.com; P🐾), a busy
recreational hub, are 3 miles further west.

Donner Memorial State Park STATE PARK
(Map p428; ☑530-582-7892; www.parks.ca.gov;
Donner Pass Rd; per car $8; ☺10am-5pm; P🐾)
At the eastern end of Donner Lake (p447),
this state-run park occupies one of the sites
where the doomed Donner Party (p448)
got trapped during the fateful winter of
1846. Though its history is gruesome, the
park is gorgeous and has a sandy beach,
picnic tables, hiking trails and wintertime
cross-country skiing and snowshoeing. The
entry fee includes admission to the **visitor
center**, which has fascinating, if macabre,
historical exhibits and a 25-minute film
reenacting the Donner Party's horrific plight.

There are also displays about the Chinese workers who turned from gold mining
to building California's railways. Outside,
the **Pioneer Monument** has a 22ft pedes-
tal – the exact depth of the snow piles that
horrendous winter. A short trail leads to a
memorial at one family's cabin site.

THE DOOMED DONNER PARTY

In the 19th century, tens of thousands of people migrated west along the Overland Trail with dreams of a better life in California. Among them was the ill-fated Donner Party.

When the families of George and Jacob Donner and their friend James Reed departed Springfield, IL, in April 1846 with six wagons and a herd of livestock, they intended to make the arduous journey as comfortable as possible. But the going was slow and, when other pioneers told them about a shortcut that would save 200 miles, they jumped at the chance.

However, there was no road for the wagons in the Wasatch Mountains, and most of the livestock succumbed under the merciless heat of the Great Salt Lake Desert. Arguments and fights broke out. James Reed killed a man, was kicked out of the group and left to trundle off to California alone. By the time the party reached the eastern foot of the Sierra Nevada, near present-day Reno, morale and food supplies were running dangerously low.

To restore their livestock's energy and stock up on provisions, the emigrants decided to rest here for a few days. But an exceptionally fierce winter came early, quickly rendering what later came to be called Donner Pass impassable and forcing the pioneers to build basic shelter near today's Donner Lake. They had food to last a month and the fervent hope that the weather would clear by then. It didn't.

Snow fell for weeks, reaching a depth of 22ft. Hunting and fishing became impossible. In mid-December a small group of 15 made a desperate attempt to cross the pass. They quickly became disoriented and had to ride out a three-day storm that killed a number of them. One month later, less than half of the original group staggered into Sutter's Fort near Sacramento, having survived on one deer and their dead friends.

By the time the first rescue party arrived at Donner Lake in late February, the trapped pioneers were still surviving – barely – on boiled ox hides. The rescuers themselves fell into difficulty, and when the second rescue party, led by the banished James Reed, made it through in March, evidence of cannibalism was everywhere. Journals and reports tell of 'half-crazed people living in absolute filth, with naked, half-eaten bodies strewn about the cabins.' Many were too weak to travel.

When the last rescue party arrived in mid-April, only a sole survivor, Lewis Keseberg, was there to greet them. The rescuers found George Donner's body cleansed and wrapped in a sheet, but no sign of Tasmen Donner, George's wife. Keseberg admitted to surviving on the flesh of the dead, but denied charges that he had killed Tasmen for fresh meat. He spent the rest of his life trying to clear his name.

In the end, only 47 of the 89 members of the Donner Party survived. They settled in California, their lives forever changed by the harrowing winter at Donner Lake.

Old Jail   HISTORIC BUILDING
(www.truckeehistory.org; 10142 Jiboom St, cnr Spring St; suggested donation $2; ⊘11am-4pm Sat & Sun late May & mid-Jun–mid-Sep) Continuously in use until the 1960s, this 1875 redbrick building is filled with relics from the wild days of yore. George 'Machine Gun' Kelly was reportedly once held here for shoplifting at a local variety store, and 'Baby Face' Nelson and 'Ma' Spinelli and her gang did time too.

🏃 Activities

Northstar Mountain
Bike Park   MOUNTAIN BIKING
(Map p428; www.northstarcalifornia.com; 5001 Northstar Dr, off Hwy 267; lift ticket adult/child 9-12yr $55/35; ⊘Jun-Sep) Sure, there's great cross-country here, but the downhill at this lift-serviced ski resort brings on the adren-aline with lots of intermediate and expert singletrack and fire roads. Over 100 miles of trails; bikes and body-armor rental available.

Back Country   OUTDOORS
(☑530-582-0909; www.thebackcountry.net; 11400 Donner Pass Rd; ⊘8am-6pm, call ahead in winter & spring) Rents bicycles and snowshoes, and rents and sells new and used climbing gear, as well as backcountry ski gear.

Winter Sports
★ **Royal Gorge**   SKIING
(☑530-426-3871; www.royalgorge.com; 9411 Pahatsi Rd, off I-80 exit Soda Springs/Norden, Soda Springs; adult/youth 13-22yr $32/25; ⊘9am-5pm during snow season; 🅿🐾) Nordic-skiing aficionados won't want to pass up a spin around North America's largest cross-country resort (now

operated by Sugar Bowl), with its mind-boggling 125 miles of groomed track crisscrossing 6000 acres of terrain. It has great skating lanes and diagonal stride tracks and also welcomes telemark skiers and snowshoers.

Group lessons are offered a few times daily, with ski camps for kids aged five to 12 (reservations recommended). For a twist, catch some air at the on-site Sierra Snowkite Center (www.sierrasnowkite.com).

Northstar California   SNOW SPORTS
(Map p428; ☑530-562-1010; www.northstarcalifornia.com; 5001 Northstar Dr, off Hwy 267; adult/child 5-12yr/youth 13-18yr $130/77/107; ☺8am-4pm; ☝) An easy 7 miles south of I-80, this hugely popular resort has great intermediate terrain as well as long black runs. Northstar's relatively sheltered location makes it the second-best choice after Homewood (p442) when it's snowing, and the eight terrain parks and pipes are top-ranked. Advanced and expert skiers can look for tree-skiing challenges on the back of the mountain.

Sugar Bowl   SNOW SPORTS
(☑530-426-9000; www.sugarbowl.com; 629 Sugar Bowl Rd, off Donner Pass Rd, Norden; adult/child 6-12yr/youth 13-22yr $85/35/76; ☺9am-4pm; ☝) Cofounded by Walt Disney in 1939, this is one of the Sierra's oldest ski resorts and a miniature Squaw Valley in terms of variety of terrain, including plenty of exhilarating gullies and chutes. Views are stellar on sunny days, but conditions go downhill pretty quickly, so to speak, during stormy weather.

The resort is 4 miles southeast of I-80 (exit Soda Springs/Norden). Stats: 13 lifts, 1500 vertical feet, 103 runs.

Boreal   SNOW SPORTS
(☑530-426-3666; www.rideboreal.com; 19659 Boreal Ridge Rd, off I-80 exit Castle Peak/Boreal Ridge Rd; adult/child 5-12yr/youth 13-17yr $64/34/54, night skiing adult/child $30/25, tubing $35; ☺9am-9pm; ☝) Fun for newbies and intermediate skiers, Boreal is traditionally the first resort to open each year in the Tahoe area. For boarders, there are five terrain parks including a competition-level 450ft superpipe. Boreal is the only North Tahoe downhill resort besides Squaw that offers night skiing. Stats: seven lifts, 500 vertical feet, 33 runs.

Soda Springs   SNOW SPORTS
(☑530-426-3901; www.skisodasprings.com; 10244 Soda Springs Rd, off I-80 exit Soda Springs/Norden, Soda Springs; adult/child under 18yr $43/35, snowmobiling $16, tubing $35; ☺10am-4pm Thu-Mon,

daily during holidays; ☝) This cute little resort is a winner with kids, who can snow-tube, ride around in pint-sized snowmobiles, or learn to ski and snowboard. Stats: two lifts, 650 vertical feet, 15 runs.

Donner Ski Ranch   SNOW SPORTS
(☑530-426-3635; www.donnerskiranch.com; 19320 Donner Pass Rd, Norden; adult/child 7-12yr/youth 13-17yr $69/29/59; ☺9am-4pm; ☝) Generations of skiers have enjoyed this itty-bitty family-owned resort. It's a great place to teach your kids how to ski, or for beginners to build skills. Prices drop after 12:30pm. It's 3.5 miles southeast of I-80 exit Soda Springs/Norden. Stats: six lifts, 750 vertical feet, 52 runs.

Tahoe Donner   SNOW SPORTS
(☑530-587-9444; www.tahoedonner.com; 11603 Snowpeak Way, off I-80 exit Donner Pass Rd; adult/child 7-12yr/youth 13-17yr $48/25/45; ☺9am-4pm; ☝) Small, low-key and low-tech, Tahoe Donner is a darling resort with family-friendly beginner and intermediate runs only. Stats: five lifts, 600 vertical feet, 14 runs.

Clair Tappaan Lodge   SKIING
(☑530-426-3632; http://clairtappaanlodge.com; adult/child under 12yr $9/5; ☺9am-5pm; ☝) You can ski right out the door if you're staying at this rustic mountain lodge near Donner Summit. Its 7 miles of groomed and tracked trails are great for beginner and intermediate skiers, and connect to miles of backcountry skiing. Stop by the lodge for ski and snowshoe rentals, and value-priced ski lessons at all skill levels (sign-up 9am daily).

Beaches & Water Sports

Warmer than Lake Tahoe, tree-lined Donner Lake (p447) is great for swimming, boating, fishing (license required), water-skiing and windsurfing.

West End Beach   SWIMMING, WATER SPORTS
(☑530-582-7720; www.tdrpd.com; off Donner Pass Rd; adult/child 2-17yr $4/3; ☝) This Donner Lake (p447) beach is popular with families for its roped-off swimming area, snack stand, volleyball nets, and kayak, paddleboat and SUP rentals.

Tributary Whitewater Tours   RAFTING
(☑530-346-6812; www.whitewatertours.com; half-day trip per adult/child 7-17yr $69/62; ☝) From roughly mid-May through September, this long-running outfitter operates a 7-mile, half-day rafting run on the Truckee River over Class III-plus rapids that will thrill kids and their nervous parents alike.

LAKE TAHOE TRUCKEE & DONNER LAKE

Hiking & Climbing

Truckee is a great base for treks in the **Tahoe National Forest** (Map p428), especially around **Donner Summit**. One popular 5-mile hike reaches the summit of 8243ft **Mt Judah** for awesome views of Donner Lake (p447) and the surrounding peaks. A longer, more strenuous ridge-crest hike (part of the **Pacific Crest Trail**) links **Donner Pass** to Squaw Valley (15 miles each way), skirting the base of prominent peaks, but you'll need two cars for this shuttle hike.

Donner Summit is also a major rock-climbing mecca, with over 300 traditional and sport-climbing routes. To learn the ropes, so to speak, take a class with **Alpine Skills International** (☑530-582-9170; www.alpineskills.com; 11400 Donner Pass Rd).

☞ Tours

Tahoe Adventure Company   ADVENTURE
(☑530-913-9212; www.tahoeadventurecompany.com; 7010 N Lake Blvd; tours per person from $55) A great option for guided Sierra adventures. Staff know the backcountry inside out and can customize any outing to your interest and skill level, from kayaking, hiking, mountain biking and rock climbing to any combination thereof. They also offer full-moon snowshoe tours, SUP lessons and guided lake paddles.

🛏 Sleeping

A few dependable midrange chain motels and hotels are found off I-80 exits, plus there's a great hostel (p450) behind the train station.

★ Redlight   HOSTEL $
(☑530-536-0005; www.redlighttruckee.com; 10101 West River St; dm $30, d from $70; 🛜) The name pays tribute to this hostel's 19th-century incarnation as a brothel. With a mix of dorms beds, doubles and even a suite with kitchenette, this is a great option for travelers on a budget. Communal areas are decked out in brocade and red drapes, and there's a good shared kitchen, board games and even a dry sauna.

Donner Memorial
State Park Campground   CAMPGROUND $
(Map p428; ☑530-582-7894, reservations 800-444-7275; www.reserveamerica.com; tent & RV sites $35; ⊘late May–late Sep) Brace yourself to camp near Donner Lake (p447): this family-oriented campground has 138 campsites with flush toilets and hot pay showers.

USFS Campgrounds   CAMPGROUND $
(Map p428; ☑518-885-3639; www.recreation.gov; campsites $17-48; 🛜) Conveniently located along Hwy 89 (though with street noise) are three minimally developed riverside camping areas within a few minutes' drive of each other: Granite Flat, Goose Meadow and Silver Creek. All have potable water and vault toilets.

★ Cedar House
Sport Hotel   BOUTIQUE HOTEL $$
(Map p428; ☑530-582-5655; www.cedarhousesporthotel.com; 10918 Brockway Rd; r $170-295, pet fee $50; 🅿🛜@🐾🛜) ✔ This chic, environmentally conscious contemporary lodge aims at getting folks out into nature. It boasts countertops made from recycled paper, 'rain chains' that redistribute water from the green roof garden, low-flow plumbing and in-room recycling. However, it doesn't skimp on plush robes, sexy platform beds with pillow-top mattresses, flat-screen TVs or the outdoor hot tub. It also houses Stella (p451) dining room.

Guided tours and multisport outdoor adventures can be arranged in-house.

Truckee Hotel   HISTORIC HOTEL $$
(☑530-587-4444; www.truckeehotel.com; 10007 Bridge St; r $79-229; 🛜) Tucked behind an atmospheric four-story redbrick streetfront arcade, Truckee's most historic abode has welcomed weary travelers since 1873. A recent remodel has updated the carpets and furniture to genteel Victorian-infused modern luxury, and there's regular live music in its restaurant Moody's Bistro & Lounge (p451). Parking available across the street. Expect some train noise and no elevator.

Truckee Donner Lodge   HOTEL $$
(☑530-582-9999; www.truckeedonnerlodge.com; 10527 Cold Stream Rd, off I-80 exit Donner Pass Rd; r $84-204; ✳🛜🛜) Just west of Hwy 89, this ex–Holiday Inn property gives you easy driving access to area ski resorts, shaving time off your morning commute to the slopes. No-nonsense, spacious hotel rooms come with microwaves and mini-refrigerators, and some have gas fireplaces. The hot-and-cold continental breakfast bar is complimentary.

River Street Inn   B&B $$
(☑530-550-9290; www.riverstreetinntruckee.com; 10009 E River St; r $145-220; 🛜) On the far side of the tracks, this sweet 1885 Victorian inn in Truckee's historic downtown has 11 rooms that blend nostalgic touches like claw-foot

tubs with down comforters, but have few amenities other than TVs. Mingle with other guests over breakfast in the lounge. Bring earplugs to dull the occasional train noise.

Hotel Truckee-Tahoe

HOTEL $$

(Map p428; ☑530-587-4525; www.hoteltruckee tahoe.com; 11331 Brockway Rd; r $189-229, pet fee $50; ❄@☎☎☎) Forget about retro ski-lodge kitsch as you cozy up inside these crisp, earth-toned and down-to-earth hotel rooms that abound in sunny, natural woods. Sink back onto the feather-topped mattresses, refresh yourself with spa-quality bath amenities or hit the seasonal outdoor heated pool by the hot tub.

✖ Eating & Drinking

Coffeebar

CAFE $

(☑530-587-2000; www.coffeebartruckee.com; 10120 Jiboom St; items $3-9; ☺6am-6pm Sun-Thu, to 7pm Fri & Sat; ☎) ❂ This beatnik, bare-bones industrial coffee shop serves Italian gelato, delectable pastries and home-brewed kombucha. Go for tantalizing breakfast crepes and overstuffed panini on herbed focaccia bread, or for a jolt of organic espresso or flavored tea lattes.

Squeeze In

DINER $

(www.squeezein.com; 10060 Donner Pass Rd; mains $8-15; ☺7am-2pm; ☝) Across from the Amtrak station, this snug locals' favorite dishes up breakfasts big enough to feed a lumberjack. Over 60 varieties of humongous omelets – along with burgers, burritos and big salads – are served in the funky space crammed with silly tchotchkes and colorful handwritten notes on the walls.

★ Moody's Bistro & Lounge

CALIFORNIAN $$

(☑530-587-8688; www.moodysbistro.com; 10007 Bridge St; mains lunch $12-18, dinner $13-32; ☺11:30am-9:30pm) ❂ With its sophisticated supper-club looks and live jazz (Thursday to Saturday evenings), this gourmet restaurant in the Truckee Hotel (p450) oozes urbane flair. Only fresh, organic and locally grown ingredients make it into the chef's perfectly pitched concoctions like pork loin with peach barbecue sauce, roasted beets with shaved fennel or pan-roasted Arctic char.

★ Stella

CALIFORNIAN $$$

(Map p428; ☑530-582-5665; www.cedarhouse sporthotel.com; 10918 Brockway Rd; mains $28-59; ☺5:30-8:30pm Wed-Sun) ❂ Housed at the trendy Cedar House Sport Hotel (p450), this modern mountain-lodge dining room ele-

vates Truckee's eating scene with Californian flair, harmonizing Asian and Mediterranean influences on its seasonal menu of housemade pastas, grilled meats and pan-roasted seafood. Bonuses: veggies grown on-site, housemade artisan bread and a killer wine list.

Fifty Fifty Brewing Co

BREWERY

(Map p428; www.fiftyfiftybrewing.com; 11197 Brockway Rd; ☺11:30am-9pm Sun-Thu, to 9:30pm Fri & Sat) Inhale the aroma of toasting grains at this brewpub south of downtown, near the Hwy 267 intersection. Sip the popular Donner Party Porter or Eclipse barrel-aged imperial stout while noshing a huge plate of nachos or other pub grub.

❶ Information

Truckee Donner Chamber of Commerce

(☑530-587-2757; www.truckee.com; 10065 Donner Pass Rd; computer access per 15min $3; ☺9am-6pm; ☎) Inside the Amtrak train depot; free walking-tour maps and wi-fi.

USFS Truckee District Ranger Station

(☑530-587-3558; www.fs.usda.gov/tahoe; 10811 Stockrest Springs Rd, off I-80 exit 188; ☺8am-5pm Mon-Sat, Mon-Fri winter) Tahoe National Forest information.

❶ Getting There & Around

Truckee straddles the I-80 and is connected to the lakeshore via Hwy 89 to Tahoe City or Hwy 267 to Kings Beach. The main drag through downtown Truckee is Donner Pass Rd, where you'll find the **Amtrak Depot** (☑800-872-7245; www.amtrak.com; 10065 Donner Pass Rd) and metered on-street parking. Brockway Rd begins south of the river, connecting over to Hwy 267.

Though the Truckee Tahoe Airport has no commercial air service, **North Lake Tahoe Express** (☑866-216-5222; www.northlaketahoeexpress. com; per person to Truckee $49) shuttles to the closest airport at Reno. Buses make several runs daily from 3:30am to midnight, serving multiple northern and western shore towns and **Northstar** (p449) and **Squaw Valley** (p446) ski resorts. Make reservations in advance.

Greyhound (☑800-231-2222; www.greyhound. com) has twice-daily buses to Reno ($22, one hour), Sacramento ($51, 2½ hours) and San Francisco ($45, six hours). Greyhound buses stop at the train depot, as do Amtrak Thruway buses and the daily California Zephyr train to Reno ($16, 1½ hours), Sacramento ($41, 4½ hours) and Emeryville/San Francisco ($47, 6½ hours).

Truckee Transit (☑530-587-7451; www. laketahoetransit.com; single/day pass $2.50/5) links the Amtrak depot with Donner

Lake hourly from 9am to 5pm Monday through Saturday. For Tahoe City and other towns on the lake's north, west or east shores, hop on the **Tahoe Area Rapid Transit** (p443) bus at the train depot. During ski season, additional buses run to many area ski resorts.

LAKE TAHOE NORTHERN SHORE

Northeast of Tahoe City, Hwy 28 cruises through a string of cute, low-key towns, many fronting superb sandy beaches, with reasonably priced roadside motels and hotels all crowded together along the lakeshore. Oozing old-fashioned charm, the north shore is a blissful escape from the teeming crowds of South Lake Tahoe, Tahoe City and Truckee, but still puts you within easy reach of winter ski resorts and snow parks, and summertime swimming, kayaking, hiking trails and more.

The **North Lake Tahoe Visitors' Bureau** (☎800-468-2463; www.gotahoenorth.com) can help get you oriented, although the closest walk-in office is at Incline Village, NV.

Tahoe Vista

Pretty little Tahoe Vista has more **public beaches** (www.northtahoeparks.com) than any other lakeshore town. Sandy strands along Hwy 28 include small but popular **Moon Dunes Beach**, with picnic tables and fire pits opposite the Rustic Cottages (p452); **North Tahoe Beach** (Map p428; 7860 N Lake Blvd), near the Hwy 267 intersection, with picnic facilities, barbecue grills and beach-volleyball courts; and **Tahoe Vista Recreation Area** (7010 N Lake Blvd; parking $10), a locals' favorite with a small grassy area and marina and the **Tahoe Adventure Company** (☎530-913-9212; www.tahoeadventurecompany.com; 7010 N Lake Blvd; activities $15-80) renting kayaks and SUP gear.

Away from all the maddening crowds, **North Tahoe Regional Park** (Map p428; ☎530-546-4212; www.northtahoeparks.com; 6600 Donner Rd, off National Ave; per car $5; ☉7am-9pm Jun-Aug, to 7pm Sep & Oct, to 5pm Nov-May; ℗ 🐾) offers forested hiking and mountain-biking trails, an 18-hole disc-golf course, a children's playground and tennis courts lit up for night play. In winter a sledding hill (rentals available) and ungroomed cross-country ski and snowshoe tracks beckon.

🛌 Sleeping

★ Cedar Glen Lodge　　CABIN $$
(☎530-546-4281; www.tahoecedarglen.com; 6589 N Lake Blvd; r, ste & cottages $139-350, pet fee $30; ◙🐾🛜🏊🐕) Completely renovated and upgraded, these gorgeous cabins and rustic-themed lodge rooms across from the beach have pine paneling, new mattresses and kitchenettes or full kitchens. Kids go nuts over all the freebies, from Ping-Pong tables, a horseshoe pit and volleyball to an outdoor swimming pool, putting green and toasty fire pit.

Franciscan Lakeside Lodge　　CABIN $$
(☎530-546-6300; www.franciscanlodge.com; 6944 N Lake Blvd; cabins $109-399; ℗🐾🛜🏊) Spend the day on a private sandy beach or in the outdoor pool, then light the barbecue grill after sunset – ah, now that's relaxation. All of the simple cabins, cottages and suites have kitchenettes. Lakeside lodgings have better beach access and views, but roomier cabins near the back of the complex tend to be quieter and will appeal to families.

Firelite Lodge　　MOTEL $$
(☎530-546-7222; www.tahoelodge.com; 7035 N Lake Blvd; r $79-154; 🛜🏊) Upgraded with thick walls, soundproofed windows, and kitchenettes and gas fireplaces in every room, the family-run Firelite is a good-value stay in a prime walkable location, with the Tahoe Vista Recreation Area (p452) right across the street. The upstairs king-bed rooms have perfect lake-view balconies. Outside amenities include bikes to rent and a hot tub.

Rustic Cottages　　CABIN $$
(☎530-546-3523; www.rusticcottages.com; 7449 N Lake Blvd; cottages $109-244; 🛜🐕) These cottages consist of a cluster of about 20 little storybook houses in the pines, with name tags fashioned from hand saws. They sport beautiful wrought-iron beds and a bevy of amenities. Most cabins have full kitchens, and some have gas or real wood-burning fireplaces.

Other perks: waffles and homemade muffins at breakfast, and free sleds and snowshoes to borrow in winter.

🍴 Eating & Drinking

★ Old Post Office Cafe　　AMERICAN $
(☎530-546-3205; 5245 N Lake Blvd; mains $8-12; ☉6:30am-2pm; 🐕) Head west of town toward Carnelian Bay, where this always-packed, cheery wooden shack (never, in fact, a post office) serves scrumptious breakfasts:

buttery potatoes, eggs Benedict, biscuits with gravy, fluffy omelets with lotsa fillings and fresh-fruit smoothies. Waits for a table get long on summer and winter weekends, so roll up early.

Gar Woods Grill & Pier   BAR
([✓]530-546-3366; www.garwoods.com; 5000 N Lake Blvd; ⊙11:30am-11:30pm) A shoreline hot spot, Gar Woods pays tribute to the era of classic wooden boats. Don't show up for the lackadaisical grill fare, but instead to slurp a Wet Woody cocktail while watching the sun set over the lake. Be prepared to duke it out for a table on the no-reservations side of the beachfront deck out back.

Kings Beach

The utilitarian character of fetchingly picturesque Kings Beach lies in its smattering of back-to-basics retro motels all lined up along the highway (and belies the fact that the town has some of the area's best restaurants). This is one of the more ethnically diverse lakeshore communities, with a large Latino population, many of whom work in the tourism industry around Lake Tahoe.

Activities

Adrift Tahoe   OUTDOORS
([✓]530-546-1112; www.standuppaddletahoe.com; 8338 N Lake Blvd; rentals per hour $25-50, per day from $80; ▣) At **Kings Beach State Recreation Area** (Map p428; [✓]530-583-3074; www.parks.ca.gov; off Hwy 28; per car $10; ⊙6am-10pm; [P][▣][☀]), Adrift Tahoe handles kayak, outrigger canoe and SUP rentals, and offers private lessons and tours.

North Tahoe Event Center   HEALTH & FITNESS
(http://northtahoeevents.com; 8318 N Lake Blvd) Hosts jazzercise, yoga and other classes.

Old Brockway Golf Course   GOLF
([✓]530-546-9909; www.oldbrockwaygolf.com; 400 Brassie Ave, cnr Hwys 267 & 28; green fees $35-60, club/cart rental from $25/20) Just inland from the lake, the 1920s Old Brockway Golf Course runs along pine-bordered fairways where Hollywood celebs once swung their clubs.

Sleeping

★Hostel Tahoe   HOSTEL $
([✓]530-546-3266; www.hosteltahoe.com; 8931 N Lake Blvd; dm/d/q $33/60/80; [@][⊚]) ⌁ Minutes from Northstar (p449) and the beach,

this former motel has private rooms and single-sex dorms with hand-painted murals and gauzy hanging textiles. A separate common building is the pièce de résistance, sunlight bathes the fireplace living room and a well-equipped honor kitchen stocks coffee, tea and food staples. Free loaner bikes, and breakfast included on Saturday and Sunday.

Eating & Drinking

Log Cabin Caffe   DINER $
([✓]530-546-7109; www.logcabinbreakfast.com; 8692 N Lake Blvd; mains $8-16; ⊙7am-2pm) Come early (especially on weekends) to join the queue for the North Shore's best breakfast. Eggs Benedict, whole-wheat pancakes with hot fresh fruit and cranberry-orange waffles are just a few highlights from the huge menu. Tip: call ahead to put your name on the waiting list. It sells ice cream out back in summer.

Char-Pit   FAST FOOD $
(www.charpit.com; 8732 N Lake Blvd; items $3-12; ⊙11am-9pm; ▣) No gimmicks at this 1960s fast-food stand, which grills juicy burgers and St Louis–style baby back ribs, and also fries up crispy onion rings and breaded mozzarella sticks. Somebody call an ambulance!

Lanza's   ITALIAN $$
([✓]530-546-2434; www.lanzastahoe.com; 7739 N Lake Blvd; mains $12-23; ⊙5-10pm, bar from 4:30pm) Next to the Safeway supermarket stands this beloved Italian trattoria where a tantalizing aroma of garlic, rosemary and 'secret' spices perfumes the air. Dinners, though undoubtedly not the tastiest you've ever had, are hugely filling and include salad and bread. Look for the owner's sepia-colored family photos in the entranceway.

Jason's Beachside Grille   BAR
(www.jasonsbeachsidegrille.com; 8338 N Lake Blvd; ⊙11am-10pm) Looking for the party around sundown? Hit this waterfront deck with a schooner of microbrew. Never mind the unexciting American fare (dinner mains $13 to $25), like smoked chicken pasta, alongside an overflowing salad bar. On colder days, red-velvet sofas orbiting a sunken fireplace are the coziest, but in summer it's all about sunset views.

Grid Bar & Grill   PUB
(www.thegridbarandgrill.com; 8545 N Lake Blvd; ⊙11am-2am) This locals' dive bar looks rough around the edges, but happy hours are supercheap and you can catch live music, from

bluegrass to punk, DJs, dancing or karaoke, or trivia nights.

❶ Getting There & Around

Tahoe Area Rapid Transit (p443) buses between Tahoe City and Incline Village make stops in Tahoe Vista, Kings Beach and Crystal Bay hourly from approximately 6am until 6pm daily. Another TART route connects Crystal Bay and Kings Beach with the **Northstar** (p449) resort every hour or so from 8am until 5pm daily; in winter this bus continues to Truckee (between May and November, you'll have to detour via Tahoe City first).

Crystal Bay (Nevada)

Crossing into Nevada, the neon starts to flash and old-school gambling palaces pant after your hard-earned cash. Though currently closed, historic Cal-Neva Resort literally straddles the California–Nevada border and has a colorful history involving ghosts, mobsters and Frank Sinatra, who once owned the joint. Ask about the guided secret tunnel tours if it ever reopens. **Crystal Bay Casino** (Map p428; ☑ 775-833-6333; www.crystal baycasino.com; 14 Hwy 28; ℗) is open though, and there you can try your luck at the gambling tables or catch a live-music show.

For a breath of pine-scented air, flee the smoky casinos for the steep 1-mile hike up paved Forest Service Rd 1601 to Stateline Lookout. Sunset views over Lake Tahoe and the mountains are all around. A nature trail loops around the site of the former fire lookout tower – nowadays there's a stone observation platform. To find the trailhead, drive up Reservoir Rd, just east of the Tahoe Biltmore parking lot, then take a right onto Lakeview Ave and follow it uphill just over a half-mile to the (usually locked) iron gate on your left.

🛏 Sleeping & Eating

Tahoe Biltmore Lodge & Casino　　　　　　　　　CASINO HOTEL $
(Map p428; ☑ 800-245-8667; www.tahoebiltmore. com; 5 Hwy 28; r $84-129; 🛜🏊) An old-school lodge and casino that has definitely seen better days.

Cafe Biltmore　　　　　　　　　　　　AMERICAN $
(Map p428; 5 Hwy 28; mains $8-15; ⊙7am-9pm) With floral carpet and a mirrored ceiling, this meat-heavy joint is visually bizarre enough to merit a peek.

LAKE TAHOE EASTERN SHORE (NEVADA)

Lake Tahoe's eastern shore lies entirely within Nevada. Much of it is relatively undeveloped thanks to George Whittell Jr, an eccentric San Franciscan playboy who once owned a lot of this land, including 27 miles of shoreline. Upon his death in 1969, it was sold off to a private investor, who later wheeled and dealed most of it to the USFS and Nevada State Parks. And lucky it was, because today the eastern shore offers some of Tahoe's best scenery and outdoor diversion.

Incline Village

One of Lake Tahoe's ritziest communities, Incline Village is the gateway to **Diamond Peak** (Map p428; ☑ 775-832-1177; www.diamond peak.com; 1210 Ski Way, off Tahoe Blvd/Hwy 28; adult/child 7-12yr/youth 13-23yr $74/29/54; ⊙9am-4pm; 🚡) and **Mt Rose** (Map p428; ☑ 775-849-0704; http://skirose.com; 22222 Mt Rose Hwy/Hwy 431, Reno; adult/child 0-5yr/youth 6-15yr $60/20/30; ⊙9am-4pm) ski resorts. The latter is a 12-mile drive northeast via Hwy 431 (Mt Rose Hwy). During summer, the nearby **Mt Rose Wilderness** (Map p428; www.fs.usda.gov/ltbmu) offers miles of unspoiled terrain, including a strenuous 10-mile round-trip to the summit of majestic **Mt Rose** (10,776ft). The trail starts from the deceptively named Mt Rose Summit parking lot, 9 miles uphill from Incline Village. For a more mellow meadow stroll that even young kids can handle, pull over a mile or so earlier at wildflower-strewn **Tahoe Meadows** (Map p428; Mt Rose Hwy; 🚻). Stay on the nature loop trails to avoid trampling the fragile meadows; leashed dogs are allowed.

In summer, you can also visit George Whittell's mansion, **Thunderbird Lodge** (Map p428; ☑ 800-468-2463; http://thunderbird tahoe.org; adult/child 6-12yr from $39/19; ⊙Tue-Sat mid-May–mid-Oct; 🚻), where he spent summers with his pet lion, Bill.

🛏 Sleeping

Hyatt Regency Lake Tahoe　　　　　　RESORT $$$
(Map p428; ☑ 775-832-1234; https://laketahoe. regency.hyatt.com; 111 Country Club Dr; r Sun-Thu/ Fri & Sat from $199/379, ste & cottages Sun-Thu/ Fri & Sat from $319/629; 🅿🐾@🛜🏊) Decorated like an arts-and-crafts-style mountain lodge, every room and lakeside cottage here looks lavish, and the spa is even bigger than the

casino. In summer you can sprawl on a private lakefront beach or in winter let the heated outdoor swimming lagoon warm you up after a day on the slopes.

🍴 Eating & Drinking

Austin's   AMERICAN $
(Map p428; www.austinstahoe.com; 120 Country Club Dr; mains $9-17; ⊙11am-9pm; 🚗🐕) A hearty welcome for the whole family is what you'll find at this wood-cabin diner with an outdoor deck. Buttermilk fries with jalapeño dipping sauce, chicken-fried steak, classic meatloaf, burgers, huge salad bowls and sandwiches will fill you up – and so will mountain-sized martinis.

Bite   CALIFORNIAN $$
(☎775-831-1000; www.bitetahoe.com; 907 Tahoe Blvd; shared plates $8-19; ⊙5-10pm, closed Wed Oct-May; 🚗) Don't let the strip-mall location stop you from rocking this creative, eclectic tapas and wine bar. Mix light, seasonal, veggie-friendly dishes with modern takes on rib-sticking comfort food like honeyed baby back ribs or green-chili mac 'n' cheese. An après-ski crowd turns up for happy hour.

Lone Eagle Grille   COCKTAIL BAR
(Map p428; https://laketahoe.regency.hyatt.com; 111 Country Club Dr; ⊙11:30am-10pm Sun-Thu, to 11pm Fri & Sat) At the Hyatt Regency's (p454) many-hearthed cocktail lounge, sip a divine orange-flavored margarita, then head outside for sunset and to hang out by the beach fire pit.

Lake Tahoe-Nevada State Park

Back on the lake, heading south, is **Lake Tahoe-Nevada State Park** (Map p428; ☎775-831-0494; www.parks.nv.gov; per car $7-12; 🅿🐕), which has beaches, lakes and miles of trails. Just 3 miles south of Incline Village is beautiful **Sand Harbor** (Map p428; ☎775-831-0494; www.parks.nv.gov/parks/sand-harbor; 2005 Hwy 28; per car $7-12), where two sand spits have formed a shallow bay with brilliant, warm turquoise water and white, boulder-strewn beaches. It gets very busy here, especially during July and August, when the **Lake Tahoe Shakespeare Festival** (☎800-747-4697; www.laketahoeshakespeare.com; ⊙Jul & Aug) is underway.

At the park's southern end, just north of the Hwy 50/Hwy 28 junction, **Spooner**

THE RENO ARCH

Be sure to check out the iconic **Reno Arch** (cnr Virginia St & Commercial Row), a fabulously retro neon sign spanning Virginia St at the intersection of Commercial Row, denoting the epicenter of 'casino central' and proclaiming Reno to be 'The Biggest Little City in the World.' First built in 1926, the arch has had a number of incarnations in different locations downtown. Its slogan was chosen by competition in 1929, and has held tight, despite attempts to change it: proud locals love that Reno remains the 'biggest little city' to this day.

Lake (Map p428; ☎775-749-5980; www.parks.nv.gov; per car $7-10) is popular for catch-and-release fishing, picnicking, nature walks, backcountry camping and cross-country skiing. Spooner Lake is also the start of the famous 13-mile **Flume Trail** (Map p428), a holy grail for experienced mountain bikers. From the trail's end near Incline Village you can either backtrack 10 miles along the narrow, twisting shoulder of Hwy 28 or board a shuttle bus. Arrange shuttles and rent bikes by the trailhead inside the park at **Flume Trail Bikes** (Map p428; ☎775-298-2501; http://flumetrailtahoe.com; 1115 Tunnel Creek Rd; mountain-bike rental per day $39-100, shuttle $15, state park entrance $2).

RENO (NEVADA)

Reno has a compact clutch of big casinos in the shadow of the Sierra Nevada. It has a reputation for being a 'poor man's Vegas,' but while in some ways that cap fits, we're here to set the record straight: Reno is oh, so much more. Beyond the garish downtown, with its photoworthy mid-century modern architecture, neon signs and alpine-fed Truckee River, sprawls a city of parks and pretty houses inhabited by a friendly bunch eager to welcome you.

Stealing a piece of California's tech-pie, the gargantuan Tesla Gigafactory will open its doors here in 2020, bringing plenty of cashed-up youngsters to town, and Reno is ready: the transformation of the formerly gritty Midtown District continues, injecting a dose of funky new bars, top-notch restaurants and vibrant arts spaces into Reno's already unique and eclectic mix.

If you like pleasant surprises or just go for the underdog, chances are you'll love Reno.

◉ Sights

★**National Automobile Museum** MUSEUM
(☑775-333-9300; www.automuseum.org; 10 S Lake St; adult/child 6-18yr $10/4; ☺9:30am-5:30pm Mon-Sat, 10am-4pm Sun) Stylized street scenes illustrate a century's worth of automobile history at this engaging car museum. The collection is enormous and impressive, with one-of-a-kind vehicles – including James Dean's 1949 Mercury from *Rebel Without a Cause,* a 1938 Phantom Corsair and a 24-karat gold-plated DeLorean – and rotating exhibits with all kinds of souped-up and fabulously retro rides.

Nevada Museum of Art MUSEUM
(☑775-329-3333; www.nevadaart.org; 160 W Liberty St; adult/child 6-12yr $10/1; ☺10am-5pm Wed & Fri-Sun, to 8pm Thu) In a sparkling building inspired by the geological formations of the Black Rock Desert north of town, a floating staircase leads to galleries showcasing temporary exhibits and eclectic collections on the American West, labor and contemporary landscape photography. In 2016 the museum opened its $6.2-million Sky Room function area. Visitors are free to explore and enjoy the space – essentially a fabulous rooftop penthouse and patio with killer views – providing it's not in use.

Fleischmann Planetarium & Science Center MUSEUM
(☑775-784-4811; http://planetarium.unr.nevada.edu; 1664 N Virginia St; planetarium adult/child under 12yr $8/6; ☺noon-8pm Mon-Thu, to 9pm Fri, 10am-9pm Sat, to 6pm Sun; ▣) Pop into this flying-saucer-shaped building at the University of Nevada for a window on the universe during star shows and feature presentations.

Nevada Historical Society Museum MUSEUM
(☑775-688-1190; www.nvdtca.org/historicalsociety; 1650 N Virginia St; adult/child under 17yr $5/free; ☺10am-4:30pm Tue-Sat) Within the main campus of the University of Nevada, the state's oldest museum includes permanent exhibits on neon signs, local American Indian culture and the presence of the federal government.

Circus Circus CASINO
(☑775-329-0711; www.circusreno.com; 500 N Sierra St; ☺24hr; ▣) The most family-friendly of Reno's casinos, Circus Circus has free circus acts to entertain kids beneath a giant, candy-striped big top, which also harbors a gazillion carnival and video games that look awfully similar to slot machines.

Silver Legacy CASINO
(☑775-329-4777; www.silverlegacyreno.com; 407 N Virginia St; ☺24hr) A Victorian-themed place, the Silver Legacy is easily recognized by its white landmark dome, where a giant mock mining rig periodically erupts into a fairly tame sound-and-light spectacle. The casino's hotel tower is usually lit emerald green at night and looks like something out of *The Wizard of Oz.*

Eldorado CASINO
(☑775-786-5700; www.eldoradoreno.com; 345 N Virginia St; ☺24hr) Right downtown, near the Reno Arch, the Eldorado has a kitschy Fountain of Fortune that probably has Italian sculptor Bernini spinning in his grave.

Harrah's CASINO
(☑775-786-3232; www.harrahsreno.com; 219 N Center St; ☺24hr) Founded by Nevada gambling pioneer William Harrah in 1946, Harrah's is still one of the biggest and most popular casinos in town.

★**Atlantis** CASINO
(☑775-825-4700; www.atlantiscasino.com; 3800 S Virginia St; ☺24hr) Looking like it's straight out of a 1970s B-grade flick on the outside, Atlantis is all fun on the inside, modeled on the legendary underwater city, with a mirrored ceiling and tropical flourishes like indoor waterfalls and palm trees. It's one of Reno's most popular offerings, though not downtown.

GREAT BALLS OF FIRE!

For a week in August during the **Burning Man** (www.burningman.com; entry $425; ☺Aug) festival, 'Burners' from around the world descend on the Black Rock Desert to build the temporary Black Rock City, only to tear it all down again and set fire to an effigy of man. In between, there's peace, love, music, art, nakedness, drugs, sex and frivolity in a safe space where attendees uphold the principles of the festival.

🏃 Activities

While gamblers feed their addictions indoors, countless others relish Reno's outdoor activities, from river floats and kayaking to mountain biking, climbing and skiing.

Reno is under an hour's drive from Lake Tahoe ski resorts – most hotels and casinos offer stay-and-ski packages.

For information on regional hiking and mountain-biking trails, including the Mt Rose summit trail and Tahoe-Pyramid Bikeway, download the *Truckee Meadows Trails Guide* (www.washoecounty.us/parks/trails/trail_challenge.php).

Truckee River Whitewater Park   OUTDOORS
(www.reno.gov; Wingfield Park) Mere steps from the casinos, the park's class II and III rapids are gentle enough for kids riding inner tubes, yet sufficiently challenging for professional freestyle kayakers. Two courses wrap around Wingfield Park, a small river island that hosts free concerts in summertime. Tahoe Whitewater Tours (p457) and Sierra Adventures (p457) offer kayak trips and lessons.

Tahoe Whitewater Tours   OUTDOORS
(☑ 775-787-5000; www.gowhitewater.com; 400 Island Ave; 2hr kayak rental/tour from $48/68) Tahoe Whitewater Tours rents tubes and kayaks and leads guided tours.

Sierra Adventures   OUTDOORS
(☑ 866-323-8928, 775-323-8928; www.wildsierra.com; Truckee River Lane; kayak rental from $22) This affable outfitter offers tons of adventure: kayaking, tubing, mountain biking, skiing, horseback riding and snowmobiling.

👉 Tours

Historic Reno Preservation Society   WALKING
(☑ 775-747-4478; www.historicreno.org; suggested donation $10) Dig deeper with a walking or biking tour of Reno that highlights subjects including architecture, politics and literary history. Check the website for the exhaustive list of tours available.

🎉 Festivals & Events

Hot August Nights   CULTURAL
(www.hotaugustnights.net; ⊙ Aug) Catch the *American Graffiti* vibe during this celebration of hot rods and rock and roll in early August held over separate dates and various locations around Reno and Virginia City. Hotel rates skyrocket.

PYRAMID LAKE

Pyramid Lake is a stunning stand-alone sight, with shores lined with beaches and eye-catching tufa formations. This piercingly blue expanse in an otherwise-barren landscape is 25 miles north of Reno on the Paiute Indian Reservation. Iconic pyramid-like Anaho Island, nearer its east side, is a bird sanctuary for American white pelicans.

Permits for camping on the beach on the west side of the lake and fishing are available online, at outdoor suppliers and CVS drugstore locations in Reno, and at the **ranger station** (☑ 775-476-1155; http://plpt.nsn.us/rangers; 2500 Lakeview Dr, Sutcliffe; ⊙ 9am-1pm & 2-6pm Thu-Mon) east of SR445 in Sutcliffe.

Tour de Nez   SPORTS
(www.tourdenez.com; ⊙ Jul) Called the 'coolest bike race in America,' the Tour de Nez brings together pro and amateur cyclists for five days of races and partying in July.

Reno River Festival   SPORTS
(www.renoriverfestival.com; ⊙ May) The world's top freestyle kayakers compete in a mad paddling dash through Whitewater Park in mid-May. Free music concerts as well.

🛌 Sleeping

Reno has a wide range of accommodations, from budget motels to boutique hotels and decadent casino suites. Room rates in smoky casino towers can sometimes seem ridiculously inexpensive – this is to get as many people through the doors as possible. Many casinos also whack on a resort fee to your bill. Reno's prices are generally higher than in other parts of the state, especially on weekends.

Mt Rose Campground   CAMPGROUND $
(Map p428; ☑ 877-444-6777; www.recreation.gov; Mt Rose Hwy/Hwy 431; RV & tent sites $20-50; ⊙ mid-Jun–Sep; P ☀) Reserve your spot a minimum of four days in advance for this gorgeous and popular high-altitude (9300ft!) campsite overlooking Lake Tahoe. It's located within the Humboldt-Toiyabe National Forest, 28 miles from downtown Reno. Reservations can be made via the website.

Sands Regency
HOTEL **$**

(📞775-348-2200; www.sandsregency.com; 345 N Arlington Ave; r from $49 Sun-Thu, from $89 Fri & Sat; 🅿❄🛜🏊🐾) The Sands Regency has some of the largest standard digs in town. Its rooms are decked out in a cheerful tropical palette of upbeat blues, reds and greens – a visual relief from typical motel decor. Empress Tower rooms are best. The 17th-floor gym and Jacuzzi are perfectly positioned to capture the drop-dead panoramic mountain views, and an outdoor pool opens in summer.

Peppermill
CASINO HOTEL **$$**

(📞775-826-2121; www.peppermillreno.com; 2707 S Virginia St; r from $69 Sun-Thu, from $149 Fri & Sat; 🅿❄@🛜🏊) 🍴 With a dash of Vegas-style opulence, the ever-popular Peppermill boasts Tuscan-themed suites in its newest 600-room tower, and plush remodeled rooms throughout the rest of the property. The two sparkling pools (one indoors) are dreamy, with a full spa on hand. Geothermal energy powers the resort's hot water and heat. The nightly resort fee is $20.

Renaissance Reno Downtown
HOTEL **$$**

(📞775-682-3900;www.marriott.com/hotels/travel/rnobr-renaissance-reno-downtown-hotel; 1 Lake St; r from $149; 🅿🛜🏊) Formerly the boutique Siena hotel, this property joined the Renaissance group in 2017 and at the time of writing was undergoing an extensive transformation. Renovated, oversized guest rooms will follow a contemporary theme using tones and textures that complement its fabulous riverside position, moments from downtown. With the best rooftop pool in town, this is a smart alternative to casino hotels.

🍴 Eating

Reno's dining scene is coming of age, finally going beyond the cheap casino buffets and ubiquitous old-school diners. Many downtown restaurants are open around the clock, or at least until the wee hours. The Midtown District has an impressive selection of new restaurants across a wide genre of cuisine.

★ Gold 'n Silver Inn
DINER **$**

(📞775-323-2696; www.goldnsilverreno.com; 790 W 4th St; mains $6-20; ⊘24hr) A Reno institution for over 50 years, this slightly divey but superfriendly 24-hour diner has a huge menu of homestyle American favorites such as meatloaf, plated dinners, all-day breakfasts and burgers, not to mention seriously incredible caramel milkshakes.

Pho 777
VIETNAMESE **$**

(📞775-323-7777; 102 E 2nd St; mains $6-8; ⊘10am-9pm) A no-frills Vietnamese noodle shop just off the casino strip that serves up bowls and bowls of steamy soup.

Peg's Glorified Ham & Eggs
DINER **$**

(www.eatatpegs.com; 420 S Sierra St; mains $7-16; ⊘6:30am-2pm; 👶) Locally regarded as having the best breakfast in town, Peg's offers tasty grill food that's not too greasy.

★ Old Granite Street Eatery
AMERICAN **$$**

(📞775-622-3222; www.oldgranitestreeteatery.com; 243 S Sierra St; dinner mains $12-29; ⊘11am-10pm Mon-Thu, to 11pm Fri, 10am-11pm Sat, to 3pm Sun; 🍴) A lovely well-lit place for organic and local comfort food, old-school artisanal cocktails and craft beers, this antique-strewn hot spot enchants diners with its stately wooden bar, water served in old liquor bottles and lengthy seasonal menu. Forgot to make a reservation? Check out the iconic rooster and pig murals and wait at a communal table fashioned from a barn door.

Silver Peak Restaurant & Brewery
PUB FOOD **$$**

(📞775-324-1864; www.silverpeakbrewery.com; 124 Wonder St; dinner mains $15-26; ⊘restaurant 11am-10pm Sun-Thu, to 11pm Fri & Sat, pub open 1hr later; 👶) Casual and pretense-free, this place hums with the chatter of happy locals settling in for a night of microbrews and great eats, from pizza with barbecue chicken to filet mignon.

★ Wild River Grille
GRILL **$$**

(📞775-847-455; www.wildrivergrille.com; 17 S Virginia St; mains lunch $11-16, dinner $21-37; ⊘11am-9pm; 🍴) At the Wild River Grille you'll love the smart-casual dining and the varied menu of creative cuisine, from the Gruyère croquettes to the lobster ravioli, but most of all the wonderful patio overlooking the lovely Truckee River: it's also the best spot in town for a drink on a balmy summer's evening and a great place to take a date.

🍷 Drinking & Nightlife

Reno is a fun place with plenty going on, including regular monthly pub crawls, the only gay bars in Nevada outside Las Vegas and an emerging arts scene.

★ Imperial Bar & Lounge
BAR

(📞775-324-6399; www.imperialbarandlounge.com; 150 N Arlington Ave; ⊘11am-2am Fri & Sat, to 10pm Sun-Thu) A classy bar inhabiting a relic of the past – this building was once an old bank, and in the middle of the wood floor you can see cement where the vault once stood. Sandwiches and pizzas go with 16 beers on tap and a buzzing weekend scene.

Chapel Tavern   COCKTAIL BAR
(☑ 775-324-2244; www.chapeltavern.com; 1099 S Virginia St; ☉ 2pm-2am Mon-Wed, to 4am Thu-Sun) Midtown's cocktail mecca makes its own infusions – try the bourbon with fig – and a seasonal drinks menu attracts year-round interest to its antler-adorned bar and outdoor patio. DJs keep it jamming on Friday and Saturday, and patrons comprise a diverse age mix.

Jungle   CAFE, WINE BAR
(☑ 775-329-4484; www.thejunglereno.com; 246 W 1st St; ☉ coffee 6am-midnight, wine 3pm-midnight Mon-Thu, 3pm-2am Fri, noon-2am Sat, noon-midnight Sun; ☎) A side-by-side coffee shop and wine bar with a cool mosaic floor and riverside patio all rolled into one. The wine bar has weekly tastings, while the cafe serves breakfast bagels and lunchtime sandwiches ($6 to $8) and puts on diverse music shows.

☆ Entertainment

The free weekly *Reno News & Review* (www.newsreview.com/reno/home) is your best source for listings.

Knitting Factory   LIVE MUSIC
(☑ 775-323-5648; http://re.knittingfactory.com; 211 N Virginia St) This midsized music venue books mainstream and indie favorites.

❶ Information

Galena Creek Visitor Center (☑ 775-849-4948; www.galenacreekvisitorcenter.org; 18250 Mt Rose Hwy; ☉ 9am-6pm Tue-Sun) Check in with this center when you arrive at the Galena Creek Recreation Area for the latest conditions and friendly advice.

Reno-Sparks Convention & Visitors Authority Visitor Center (☑ 775-682-3800; www.visitrenotahoe.com; 135 N Sierra St; ☉ 9am-6pm) Stop by this conveniently located center when you get to town for the latest on what's on, where and when.

❶ Getting There & Away

About 5 miles southeast of downtown, the **Reno-Tahoe International Airport** (RNO; www.renoairport.com; ☎) is served by most major airlines, with connections throughout the US to international routes.

The **North Lake Tahoe Express** (☑ 866-216-5222; www.northlaketahoeexpress.com; 1 way $49) operates a shuttle (six to eight daily, 3:30am to midnight) to and from the airport to multiple North Shore Lake Tahoe locations including Truckee, Squaw Valley and Incline Village. Reserve in advance.

The **South Tahoe Airporter** (☑ 866-898-2463; www.southtahoeairporter.com; adult/child 1 way $29.75/16.75, round-trip $53/30.25) operates several daily shuttle buses from the airport to Stateline casinos; the journey takes from 75 minutes to two hours.

RTC Washoe (☑ 775-348-0400; www.rtcwashoe.com) operates six wi-fi-equipped RTC Intercity buses per day from Monday to Friday to Carson City ($5, one hour), which loosely connect to BlueGo buses – operated by **Tahoe Transportation District** (☑ 775-589-5500; www.tahoetransportation.org) – to the Stateline Transit Center in South Lake Tahoe (adult/child $4/2 with RTC Intercity transfer, one hour).

Greyhound (☑ 800-231-2222; www.greyhound.com) offers up to five direct buses a day to Reno from San Francisco (from $8, from five hours): book in advance for these lowest fares.

Discount bus company **Megabus** (www.megabus.com) has two daily departures to San Francisco (from $15, 4½ hours) via Sacramento.

The **Amtrak** (☑ 800-872-7245; www.amtrak.com) *California Zephyr* train makes one daily departure from Emeryville/San Francisco ($52, 6¾ hours) to Reno, onwards to Chicago (from $122, 44¾ hours): a shared sleeper berth will set you back $467. Up to three other daily services depart Emeryville/San Francisco for Sacramento, connecting with a bus service to Reno ($60, from 6½ hours).

❶ Getting Around

It's easy to get around Reno on foot, but parts of downtown beyond the 24-hour casino area can be sketchy after dark. Exercise caution when walking along Ralston St, between W 4th and 5th Sts, especially at night.

Casino hotels usually offer frequent free airport shuttles for their guests (and generally don't ask to see reservations – just saying...).

The local **RTC Washoe** (p459) RTC Ride buses blanket the city, and most routes converge at the RTC 4th St station downtown (between Lake St and Evans Ave). Useful routes include the RTC Rapid line for S Virginia St, 11 for Sparks and 19 for the airport.

The Sierra Spirit bus (50¢) loops around all major downtown landmarks – including the casinos and the university – every 15 minutes from 7am to 7pm.

Yosemite & the Sierra Nevada

Best Places to Eat

➜ Evergreen Lodge (p478)

➜ Lakefront Restaurant
(p506)

➜ Majestic Yosemite Dining
Room (p478)

➜ Erick Schat's Bakkerÿ
(p513)

➜ Mono Inn (p501)

➜ Fork & Love (p485)

Best Places to Sleep

➜ Sequoia High Sierra Camp
(p490)

➜ Majestic Yosemite Hotel
(p475)

➜ Rush Creek Lodge (p478)

➜ Yosemite Bug Rustic
Mountain Resort (p481)

➜ Inn at Benton Hot Springs
(p514)

➜ Hotel Charlotte (p485)

Why Go?

An outdoor-adventurer's wonderland, the Sierra Nevada is a year-round pageant of snow sports, white-water rafting, hiking, cycling and rock climbing. Skiers and snowboarders blaze through hushed pine-tree slopes, and wilderness seekers come to escape the stresses of modern civilization.

With fierce granite mountains standing watch over high-altitude lakes, the eastern spine of California is a formidable but exquisite topographical barrier enclosing magnificent natural landscapes. And interspersed between its river canyons and 14,000ft peaks are the decomposing ghost towns left behind by California's early white settlers, bubbling natural hot springs and Native American tribes that still call it home.

In the majestic national parks of Yosemite and Sequoia & Kings Canyon, visitors will be humbled by the groves of solemn giant sequoias, ancient rock formations and valleys, and the ever-present opportunity to see bears and other wildlife.

When to Go

Yosemite National Park

May & Jun The Yosemite waterfalls are gushing and spectacular in spring.

Jul & Aug Head for the mountains for wilderness adventures and glorious sunshine.

Dec–Mar Take a wintertime romp through snowy forests.

YOSEMITE NATIONAL PARK

The jaw-dropping head-turner of America's national parks, and a Unesco World Heritage site, Yosemite (yo-*sem*-it-ee) garners the devotion of all who enter. From the waterfall-striped granite walls buttressing emerald-green Yosemite Valley to the skyscraping giant sequoias catapulting into the air at Mariposa Grove, the place inspires a sense of awe and reverence – four million visitors wend their way to the country's third-oldest national park annually. But lift your eyes above the crowds and you'll feel your heart instantly moved by unrivalled splendors: the haughty profile of Half Dome, the hulking presence of El Capitan, the drenching mists of Yosemite Falls, the gemstone lakes of the high country's subalpine wilderness and Hetch Hetchy's pristine pathways.

History

The Ahwahneechee, a group of Miwok and Paiute peoples, lived in the Yosemite area for around 4000 years before a group of pioneers, most likely led by legendary explorer Joseph Rutherford Walker, came through in 1833. During the gold-rush era, conflict between the miners and native tribes escalated to the point where a military expedition (the Mariposa Battalion) was dispatched in 1851 to punish the Ahwahneechee, eventually forcing the capitulation of Chief Tenaya and his tribe.

Tales of thunderous waterfalls and towering stone columns followed the Mariposa Battalion out of Yosemite and soon spread into the public's awareness. In 1855 San Francisco entrepreneur James Hutchings organized the first tourist party to the valley. Published accounts of his trip, in which he extolled the area's untarnished beauty, prompted others to follow, and it wasn't long before inns and roads began springing up. Alarmed by this development, conservationists petitioned Congress to protect the area – with success. In 1864 President Abraham Lincoln signed the Yosemite Grant, which eventually ceded Yosemite Valley and the Mariposa Grove of Giant Sequoias to California as a state park. This landmark decision, along with the pioneering efforts of conservationist John Muir, led to a congressional act in 1890 creating Yosemite National Park; this, in turn, helped pave the way for the national-park system that was established in 1916.

Yosemite's popularity as a tourist destination continued to soar throughout the 20th century and, by the mid-1970s, traffic and congestion draped the valley in a smoggy haze. The General Management Plan (GMP), developed in 1980 to alleviate this and other problems, ran into numerous challenges and delays. Despite many improvements, and the need to preserve the natural beauty that draws visitors to Yosemite in the first place, the plan still hasn't been fully implemented.

◉ Sights

There are four main entrances to the park: South Entrance (Hwy 41), Arch Rock (Hwy 140), Big Oak Flat (Hwy 120 W) and Tioga Pass (Hwy 120 E). Hwy 120 traverses the park as Tioga Rd, connecting Yosemite Valley with the Eastern Sierra.

Visitor activity is concentrated in Yosemite Valley, especially in Yosemite Village, which has the main visitor center, a post office, a museum, cateries and other services. Half Dome Village is another hub. Notably less busy, Tuolumne (too-*ahl*-uh-*mee*) Meadows, toward the eastern end of Tioga Rd, primarily draws hikers, backpackers and climbers. Wawona, the park's southern focal point, also has good infrastructure. In the northwestern corner, Hetch Hetchy, which has no services at all, receives the smallest number of visitors.

◉ Yosemite Valley

The park's crown jewel, spectacular meadow-carpeted Yosemite Valley stretches 7 miles long, bisected by the rippling Merced River and hemmed in by some of the most majestic chunks of granite anywhere on earth. The most famous are, of course, the monumental 7569ft **El Capitan** (El Cap), one of the world's largest monoliths and a magnet for rock climbers, and 8842ft **Half Dome**, the park's spiritual centerpiece – its rounded granite pate forms an unmistakable silhouette. You'll have great views of both from **Valley View** on the valley floor, but for the classic photo op, head up Hwy 41 to **Tunnel View**, which boasts a new viewing area. With a little sweat you'll have even better postcard panoramas – sans the crowds – from **Inspiration Point**. The trail (2.6-mile round-trip) starts at the tunnel.

Yosemite's waterfalls mesmerize even the most jaded traveler, especially when the spring runoff turns them into thunderous cataracts. **Yosemite Falls** is considered the

Yosemite & the Sierra Nevada Highlights

1 Yosemite National Park
(p461) Marveling at the waterfall gush in spring.

2 Mammoth Mountain (p504) Whooshing down the wintertime heights of this snow-draped mountain.

3 Sequoia & Kings Canyon National Parks (p485) Gazing heavenward through the celestial sequoia canopies.

4 Bodie State Historic Park (p497) Ambling around this evocative ghost town.

5 Mono Lake (p501) Canoeing or kayaking amid the lake's haunting tufa.

0   25 miles
0   50 km

NEVADA

Reno (45mi)

CARSON CITY

Incline Village
Tahoe City
Lake Tahoe
South Lake Tahoe
El Dorado National Forest

American River

Markleeville
Topaz Lake
Walker
Grover Hot Springs State Park
Monitor Pass (8314ft) (closed in winter)
Ebbetts Pass (8730th) (closed in winter)
Lake Alpine
Sonora Pass (9624ft) (closed in winter)
Mokelumne River
Bear Valley
Stanislaus River
Calaveras Big Trees State Park
Dodge Ridge

Arnold
Murphys
Sonora

Sierra

Stanislaus National Forest
Groveland

Midpines
El Portal

Yosemite Village
Yosemite National Park **1**

Tioga Pass (9946ft) (closed in winter)

Ansel Adams Wilderness

Hoover Wilderness

Bodie State Historic Park

Bridgeport

Humboldt-Toiyabe National Forest

Lee Vining
Mono Lake **5**

June Lake

Devils Postpile

Mammoth Mountain **2**
Mammoth Lakes
Crowley

Inyo National Forest

Inyo National Forest

7 Benton

Inyo National Forest
White Mountain (14252ft) ▲

Humboldt-Toiyabe National Forest

Tuolumne River

Walker Lake

6 Devils Postpile National Monument (p513) Viewing this bizarre volcanic formation.

7 Benton Hot Springs (p514) Soaking your troubles away at these hot springs.

8 Manzanar National Historic Site (p515) Visiting the museum and site of one of the darkest events in US history.

Yosemite National Park

⊙ Top Sights
1	Mariposa Grove	C7

⊙ Sights
2	Bridalveil Fall	C5
3	Chilnualna Falls	C7
4	Dewey Point Lookout	C5
5	Inspiration Point	B5
6	Mariposa Grove Museum	C7
7	McGurk Meadow	C5
8	Nevada Fall	D5
9	Olmsted Point	D4
10	Parsons Memorial Lodge	E4
11	Pioneer Yosemite History Center	C7
12	Tueeulala Falls	B3
13	Tunnel View	C5
14	Valley View	C5
15	Vernal Fall	C5
16	Wapama Falls	B3
17	Yosemite Falls	C5

⊕ Activities, Courses & Tours
18	Badger Pass	C5
	Badger Pass Cross-Country Center & Ski School	(see 18)
19	Ostrander Ski Hut	C6
20	Yosemite Ski School	C6
21	Yosemite Stables Wawona	C7

⊟ Sleeping
22	Bridalveil Creek Campground	C6
23	Crane Flat Campground	B5
24	Dimond O Campground	A4
25	Evergreen Lodge Resort	A4
26	Hodgdon Meadow Campground	A4
27	May Lake High Sierra Camp	D4
28	Porcupine Flat Campground	C4
29	Sunrise High Sierra Camp	D4
30	Tamarack Flat Campground	B5
31	Wawona Campground	C7
32	Wawona Hotel	C7
	White Wolf Campground	(see 33)
33	White Wolf Lodge	C4
34	Yosemite Creek Campground	C4

⊗ Eating
	Wawona Hotel Dining Room	(see 32)

tallest in North America, dropping 2425ft in three tiers. A slick wheelchair-accessible trail leads to the bottom of this cascade or, if you prefer solitude and different perspectives, you can also clamber up the **Yosemite Falls Trail**, which puts you atop the falls after a grueling 3.4 miles. No less impressive is nearby **Bridalveil Fall** and others scattered throughout the valley.

Any aspiring Ansel Adams should lug their camera gear along the 1-mile paved trail to **Mirror Lake** (Yosemite Valley) early or late in the day to catch the ever-shifting reflection of Half Dome in the still waters. The lake all but dries up by late summer.

South of here, where the Merced River courses around two small islands, lies **Happy Isles**, a popular area for picnics, swimming and strolls. It also marks the start of the **John Muir Trail** and **Mist Trail** to several waterfalls and Half Dome.

Yosemite Museum   MUSEUM
(www.nps.gov/yose; 9037 Village Dr, Yosemite Village; ⊙ 9am-5pm summer, 10am-4pm rest of year, often closed noon-1pm) 🅿 FREE The Yosemite Museum has Miwok and Paiute artifacts, including woven baskets, beaded buckskin dresses and dance capes made from feathers. Native American cultural demonstrators engage visitors with traditional basket weaving, tool making and crafts. There's also an **art gallery** with paintings and photographs from the museum's permanent collection. Behind the museum, a self-guided **interpretive trail** winds past the reconstructed 1870s **Indian Village of Ahwahnee**, with pounding stones, an acorn granary, a ceremonial roundhouse and a conical bark house.

Majestic Yosemite Hotel   HISTORIC BUILDING
About a quarter-mile east of Yosemite Village, the former Ahwahnee Hotel is a graceful blend of rustic mountain retreat and elegant mansion dating back to 1927. You don't need to be a guest to have a gawk and a wander. Built from local granite, pine and cedar, the building is splendidly decorated with leaded glass, sculpted tiles, Native American rugs and Turkish kilims. You can enjoy a meal in the baronial dining room or a casual drink in the piano bar.

Around Christmas, the hotel hosts the **Bracebridge Dinner** (☏ 888-413-8869; www.bracebridgedinners.com), a combination of banquet and Renaissance fair. Book early.

Yosemite Valley

YOSEMITE & THE SIERRA NEVADA YOSEMITE NATIONAL PARK

Nature Center at Happy Isles   MUSEUM
(www.nps.gov/yose; ⊘ 9am-5pm late May-Sep; 🚻)
🏴 An aging but still fun hands-on nature
museum, the Nature Center has displays explaining the differences between the park's
various pinecones, rocks, animal tracks and
(everyone's favorite subject) scat. Out back,
don't miss an exhibit on the 1996 rockfall,
when an 80,000-ton slab plunged 2000ft to
the nearby valley floor, killing a man and
felling about 1000 trees. The center is off
Southside Dr in Yosemite Valley.

⊙ Glacier Point

If you drove, the views from 7214ft **Glacier
Point** might make you feel like you cheated
– superstar sights present themselves to you
with you making hardly any physical effort.
A quick mosey up from the parking lot and
you'll find the entire eastern Yosemite Valley
spread out before you, from **Yosemite Falls**
to **Half Dome**, as well as the distant peaks

that ring Tuolumne Meadows. Half Dome
looms practically at eye level, and if you look
closely you can spot hikers on its summit.

To the left of Half Dome lies the glacially carved **Tenaya Canyon**, and to its right
are the wavy white ribbons of **Nevada and
Vernal Falls**. On the valley floor, the Merced
River snakes through green meadows and
groves of trees. Sidle up to the railing, hold
on tight and peer 3200ft straight down at
Half Dome Village. **Basket Dome** and
North Dome rise to the north of the valley,
and **Liberty Cap** and the **Clark Range** can
be seen to the right of Half Dome.

Almost from the park's inception, Glacier
Point has been a popular destination. It used
to be that getting up here was a major undertaking. That changed once the Four Mile
Trail opened in 1872. A wagon road to the
point was completed in 1882, and the current Glacier Point Rd was built in 1936.

At the tip of the point is **Overhanging
Rock**, a huge granite slab protruding from
the cliff edge like an outstretched tongue,
defying gravity and once providing a scenic
stage for daredevil extroverts. Through the
years, many famous photos have been taken
of folks performing handstands, high kicks
and other wacky stunts on the rock. The
precipice is now off-limits.

⊙ Tioga Road
& Tuolumne Meadows

Tioga Rd (or Hwy 120 E), the only road
through the park, travels through 56 miles
of superb high country at elevations ranging from 6200ft at Crane Flat to 9945ft at
Tioga Pass. Heavy snowfall keeps it closed
from about November until May. Beautiful
views await after many a bend in the road,
the most impressive being **Olmsted Point**
(🚻), where you can gawp all the way down
Tenaya Canyon to Half Dome. Above the
canyon's eastern side looms the aptly named
9926ft **Clouds Rest**. Continuing east on Tioga Rd soon drops you at **Tenaya Lake**, a
placid blue basin framed by pines and granite cliffs.

Beyond here, about 55 miles from Yosemite Valley, 8600ft **Tuolumne Meadows** is
the largest subalpine meadow in the Sierra.
It provides a dazzling contrast to the valley,
with its lush open fields, clear blue lakes,
ragged granite peaks and domes, and cooler temperatures. If you come during July or
August, you'll find a painter's palette of wildflowers decorating the shaggy meadows.

Yosemite Valley

Tuolumne is far less crowded than the valley, though the area around the campground, lodge store and visitor center does get busy, especially on weekends. Some hiking trails, such as the one to **Dog Lake**, are also well traveled. Remember that the altitude makes breathing a lot harder than in the valley, and nights can get nippy, so pack warm clothes.

The main meadow is about 2.5 miles long and lies on the northern side of Tioga Rd between **Lembert Dome** (Map p498) and **Pothole Dome** (Map p498). The 200ft scramble to the top of the latter – preferably at sunset – gives you great views of the meadow. An interpretive trail leads from the stables to muddy **Soda Springs** (Map p498), where carbonated water bubbles up in red-tinted pools. The nearby **Parsons Memorial Lodge** (Map p498) has a few displays.

Hikers and climbers will find a paradise of options around Tuolumne Meadows, which is also the gateway to the High Sierra camps.

The Tuolumne Meadows Tour & Hikers' Bus makes the trip along Tioga Rd once daily in each direction, and can be used for one-way hikes. There's also a free Tuolumne Meadows Shuttle, which travels between the Tuolumne Meadows Lodge and Olmsted Point, including a stop at Tenaya Lake.

◉ Hetch Hetchy

In the park's northwestern corner, Hetch Hetchy, which is Miwok for 'place of tall grass,' gets the least amount of traffic yet sports waterfalls and granite cliffs that rival its famous counterparts in Yosemite Valley. The main difference is that Hetch Hetchy Valley is now filled with water, following a long political and environmental battle in the early 20th century. It's a lovely, quiet spot and well worth the 40-mile drive from Yosemite Valley, especially if you're tired of the avalanche of humanity rolling through that area. The 2013 Rim Fire charred a huge section of the forest in this region, but its beauty has not been significantly diminished.

The 8-mile-long **Hetch Hetchy Reservoir**, its placid surface reflecting clouds and cliffs, stretches behind O'Shaughnessy Dam, site of a parking lot and trailheads. An easy 5.4-mile (round-trip) trail leads to the spectacular **Tueeulala** (*twee*-lala) and **Wapama Falls**, which each plummet more than 1000ft over fractured granite walls on the north shore of the reservoir. **Hetch Hetchy Dome** rises up in the distance. This hike is best in spring, when temperatures are moderate and wildflowers poke out everywhere. Keep an eye out for rattlesnakes and the occasional bear, especially in summer.

There are bathrooms but no other visitor services at Hetch Hetchy. The road is open only during daylight hours; specifics are posted at the Evergreen Rd turnoff.

◉ Wawona

Wawona, about 27 miles south of Yosemite Valley, is the park's historical center, home to its first headquarters (supervised by Captain AE Wood on the site of the Wawona Campground) and its first tourist facilities.

★ Mariposa Grove
FOREST

With their massive stature and multi-millennium maturity, the chunky high-rise sequoias of Mariposa Grove will make you feel rather insignificant. The largest grove of giant sequoias in the park, Mariposa is home to approximately 500 mature trees spread over 250 acres. Walking trails wind through this very popular grove; you can usually have a more solitary experience if you come during the early evening in summer or anytime outside of summer.

Closed to visitors since the start of a major restoration project in July 2015, at the time of writing the grove was scheduled to reopen in fall 2017. Visitors will benefit from new trails, including accessible boardwalks, and the removal of most of the parking lot, gift shop, tram tours and grove roads should translate to less traffic congestion and a more natural visitor experience. Another multimillion-dollar grant from the Yosemite Conservancy is funding the building of a new trail, scheduled to open in 2018, from the South Entrance to Mariposa Grove.

On your right as you enter the lower grove, the **Fallen Monarch** may be familiar to you from an iconic 1899 photo of the US 6th Cavalry – and their horses – posed on the tree's length. Its exposed roots illustrate the sequoias' shallow but diffuse life-support system.

Walk a half-mile up to the 1800-year-old **Grizzly Giant**, a bloated beast of a tree with branches that are bigger in circumference than most of the pine trees in this forest. The walk-through **California Tunnel Tree** is close by, and the favored spot for 'I visited the tall forest' photos. Incredibly, this tree continues to survive, even though its heart was hacked out back in 1895.

In the upper grove, the more famous **Fallen Wawona Tunnel Tree**, however, fell over in a heap in 1969 – its 10ft-high hole was gouged from a fire scar in 1881. Other notable specimens include the **Telescope Tree** and the **Clothespin Tree**. It's about a mile round-trip from the Fallen Wawona Tunnel Tree to the wide-open overlook at **Wawona Point** (6810ft), which takes in the entire area.

Depending on your energy level, you could spend half an hour or a few hours exploring the forest. Between the new shuttle stop and the Wawona Tunnel Tree in the upper grove, the elevation gain is about 1000ft, but the trail is gentle.

In summer, and during weekends and holidays, parking at the grove is limited to visitors with accessible placards; others must take the free shuttle bus from the South Entrance unless they arrive outside of the to-be-determined shuttle hours. It takes at least an hour to drive from Yosemite Valley to the grove shuttle at the South Entrance. Snowfall closes Mariposa Grove Rd to cars from about November to April, but you can always hike, ski or snowshoe in (2 miles, 500ft of elevation gain) and experience it during its quiet hibernation.

Mariposa Museum & History Center
MUSEUM

(☏209-966-2924; www.mariposamuseum.com; 5119 Jessie St; adult/child $5/free; ◎10am-4pm; ♿) Mariposa's past comes alive, well, as much as possible, considering the fairly fusty objects displayed in this museum. Menus, logbooks, train tickets, photos etc are organized in small diorama-style rooms to tell the stories of specific historical epochs or people. Some gems, like actual gold-miners' letters, can be found if you have the time.

Several period buildings and a Yosemite Miwok bark house can be visited on the museum grounds.

Pioneer Yosemite History Center
HISTORIC BUILDING

(☏209-372-0200; www.nps.gov/yose; Wawona; rides adult/child $5/4; ◎24hr, rides Wed-Sun Jun-Sep; P♿) FREE Off Wawona Rd, about 6 miles north of Mariposa Grove, you can take in the manicured grounds of the elegant Big Trees Lodge and cross a covered bridge to this rustic center, where some of the park's oldest buildings were relocated. It also features stagecoaches that brought early tourists to Yosemite, and offers short horse-drawn **stagecoach rides** in summer.

IMPOSSIBLE TIOGA PASS

Hwy 120, the main route into Yosemite National Park from the Eastern Sierra, climbs through Tioga Pass, the highest pass in the Sierra at 9945ft. On most maps of California, you'll find a parenthetical remark – 'closed in winter' – printed next to the pass. While true, this statement is also misleading. Tioga Rd is usually closed from the first heavy snowfall in October until May, June or even July! If you're planning a trip through Tioga Pass in spring, you're likely to be out of luck. According to official park policy, the earliest date the road will be plowed is 15 April, yet the pass has been open in April only once since 1980. Other mountain roads further north, such as Hwys 108, 4 and 88/89, may also be closed due to heavy snow, albeit only temporarily. Call ☏ 800-427-7623 for road and weather conditions.

🏃 Activities

Hiking

Over 800 miles of hiking trails cater to hikers of all abilities. Take an easy half-mile stroll on the valley floor; venture out all day on a quest for viewpoints, waterfalls and lakes; or go camping in the remote outer reaches of the backcountry.

Some of the park's most popular hikes start right in Yosemite Valley, including to the top of Half Dome (17 miles round-trip), the most famous of all. It follows a section of the John Muir Trail and is strenuous, difficult and best tackled in two days with an overnight in Little Yosemite Valley. Reaching the top can only be done after rangers have installed fixed cables. Depending on snow conditions, this may occur as early as late May or as late as July, and the cables usually come down in mid-October. To whittle down the cables' notorious human logjams, the park now requires permits for day hikers, but the route is still nerve-racking as hikers must 'share the road.' The less ambitious or physically fit will still have a ball following the same trail as far as **Vernal Falls** (2.6 miles round-trip), the top of **Nevada Fall** (6.5 miles round-trip) or idyllic Little Yosemite Valley (8 miles round-trip). The Four Mile Trail (9.2 miles round-trip) to Glacier Point is a strenuous but satisfying climb to a glorious viewpoint.

Along Glacier Point Rd, **Sentinel Dome** (2.2 miles round-trip) is an easy hike to the crown of a commanding granite dome. And one of the most scenic hikes in the park, the **Panorama Trail** (8.5 miles one way), descends to the valley (joining the John Muir and Mist Trails) with nonstop views, including Half Dome and Illilouette Fall.

If you've got kids in tow, easy destinations include Mirror Lake (p465) (2 miles round-trip, or 4.5 miles via the **Tenaya Canyon Loop**) in the valley, the **McGurk Meadow** (1.6 miles round-trip) trail on Glacier Point Rd, which has a historic log cabin to romp around in, and the trails meandering beneath the big trees of Mariposa Grove (p469) in Wawona.

The Wawona area also has one of the park's prettiest (and often overlooked) hikes to **Chilnualna Falls** (8.6 miles round-trip). Best done between April and June, it follows a cascading creek to the top of the dramatic overlook falls, starting gently, then hitting you with some grinding switchbacks before sort of leveling out again.

The highest concentration of hikes lies in the high country of **Tuolumne Meadows**, which is only accessible in summer. A popular choice here is the hike to **Dog Lake** (2.8 miles round-trip), but it gets busy. You can also hike along a relatively flat part of the John Muir Trail into lovely **Lyell Canyon** (17.6 miles round-trip), following the Lyell Fork of the Tuolumne River.

Backpacks, tents and other equipment can be rented from the Yosemite Mountaineering School (p470). The school also offers two-day Learn to Backpack trips for novices, and all-inclusive three- and four-day guided backpacking trips ($375 to $500 per person), which are great for inexperienced and solo travelers. In summer the school operates a branch from Tuolumne Meadows.

Rock Climbing

With its sheer spires, polished domes and soaring monoliths, Yosemite is rock-climbing nirvana. The main climbing season runs from April to October. Most climbers, including some legendary stars, stay at Camp 4 (p475) near El Capitan, especially in spring and fall. In summer another base camp springs up at Tuolumne Meadows Campground (p476). Climbers looking for partners post notices on bulletin boards at either campground.

Yosemite Mountaineering School (☏ 209-372-8344; www.travelyosemite.com; Half Dome

Village; ⊘ Apr-Oct) offers top-flight instruction for novice to advanced rock hounds, plus guided climbs and equipment rental. All-day group classes for beginners are $148 per person.

The meadow across from El Capitan and the northeastern end of Tenaya Lake (off Tioga Rd) are good for watching climbers dangle from granite (you need binoculars for a really good view). Look for the haul bags first – they're bigger, more colorful and move around more than the climbers, making them easier to spot. As part of the excellent 'Ask a Climber' program, climbing rangers set up telescopes at El Capitan Bridge from 11am to 3pm (mid-May through mid-October) and answer visitors' questions.

Cycling
Mountain biking isn't permitted within the park, but cycling along the 12 miles of paved trails is a popular and environmentally friendly way of exploring the valley. It's also the fastest way to get around when valley traffic is at a standstill. Many families bring bicycles, and you'll often find kids doing laps through the campgrounds. Hard-core cyclists brave the skinny shoulders and serious altitude changes of the trans-Sierra Tioga Rd. Bike rentals are available at **Yosemite Valley Lodge** and **Half Dome Village** (per hour/day $12.50/30.50; ⊘ 9am-6pm Mar-Oct).

Swimming
On a hot summer day, nothing beats a dip in the gentle Merced River, though if chilly water doesn't float your boat, you can always pay to play in the scenic outdoor swimming pools at **Half Dome Village** (adult/child $5/4; ⊘ end May-Sep) and **Yosemite Valley Lodge** (adult/child $5/4; ♿). With a sandy beach, Tenaya Lake is a frigid but interesting option, though White Wolf's Harden Lake warms up to a balmy temperature by midsummer.

Horseback Riding
The park's concessionaire runs guided trips to such scenic locales as Mirror Lake and Chilnualna Falls from Wawona's **Big Trees Lodge Stable** (🖉 209-375-6502; www.travelyosemite.com; ⊘ 7am-5pm Jun-Sep) and **Yosemite Valley Stable** (🖉 209-372-8348; www.travelyosemite.com). The season runs from May to October, although this varies slightly by location. No experience is needed, but reservations are advised, especially at Yosemite Valley Stable. Some mounts are

horses, but most likely you'll be riding a sure-footed mule.

Rafting
From around late May to July, floating along the Merced River from Stoneman Meadow, near Half Dome Village, to Sentinel Bridge is a leisurely way to soak up Yosemite Valley views. Four-person **raft rentals** (🖉 20 9-372-4386; per person $30; ⊘ late May-late Jul) for the 3-mile trip are available from the concessionaire in Half Dome Village and include equipment and a shuttle ride back to the rental kiosk. Children must be over 50lb. Or bring your own raft and pay $5 to shuttle back.

River rats are also attracted to the fierce **Tuolumne River**, a classic class IV run that plunges and thunders through boulder gardens and cascades. Outfitters **OARS** (🖉 20 9-736-4677, 800-346-6277; www.oars.com) and Groveland-based **Sierra Mac** (🖉 20 9-591-8027, 800-457-2580; www.sierramac.com; 27890 Hwy 120) offer guided trips.

Winter Sports
The white coat of winter opens up a different set of things to do, as the valley becomes a quiet, frosty world of snow-draped evergreens, ice-coated lakes and vivid vistas of gleaming white mountains sparkling against blue skies. Winter tends to arrive in full force by mid-November and peter out in early April.

Cross-country skiers can explore 350 miles of skiable trails and roads, including 90 miles of marked trails and 25 miles of machine-groomed track near the Yosemite Ski & Snowboard Area (p471). The scenic but grueling trail to Glacier Point (21 miles round-trip) also starts from here. More trails are at Crane Flat and Mariposa Grove. The ungroomed trails can also be explored with snowshoes.

A free shuttle bus connects the valley and the Yosemite Ski & Snowboard Area. Roads in the valley are plowed, and Hwys 41, 120 and 140 are usually kept open, conditions permitting. Tioga Rd (Hwy 120 E), however, closes with the first snowfall. Be sure to bring snow chains with you, as prices for them double once you hit the foothills.

Yosemite Ski & Snowboard Area
SNOW SPORTS
(🖉 209-372-8430; www.travelyosemite.com; lift ticket adult/child $47/29; ⊘ 9am-4pm mid-Dec–Mar) Most of the action converges on one of California's oldest ski resorts, about 22 miles

YOSEMITE THROUGHOUT THE YEAR

January

Short days and freezing temperatures mostly empty out the parks, and ice-quiet solitude has never looked so stunning. Skiing and other snow sports reign supreme.

A TASTE OF YOSEMITE

At the **Majestic Yosemite Hotel** (p475), meet top chefs from around the country as they lead cooking demonstrations and offer behind-the-scenes kitchen tours in January and February. It's all topped off by a sumptuous gala dinner.

February

Daytime temperatures gradually begin to inch up the thermometer as the days get longer. The ski and snowboarding season hits its stride and the long Presidents' Day weekend brings out the snow hounds.

HORSETAIL FALL

For two weeks at the end of the month, this thin, seasonal cascade becomes Yosemite's most photographed attraction. When the sun sets on clear evenings, the flow lights up like a river of fire.

March

When it's sunny, Yosemite Valley can top out at almost 60°F (15°C), though ice forms in the evenings. Spring feels like it's creeping closer at lower elevations.

YOSEMITE SPRINGFEST

Yosemite Ski & Snowboard Area (www.travelyosemite.com) hosts this winter carnival on the last weekend of each ski season, usually in late March or early April. Events include slalom racing, costume contests, obstacle courses, a barbecue and snow sculpting.

April

Don't forgo the tire chains – there's still the possibility of snowstorms during winter's last gasp. But by the end of the month, the dogwoods start to bloom and the waterfalls begin awakening.

FISHING SEASON BEGINS

Anglers froth at the mouth counting the days until the last Saturday of the month. Why? It's the kickoff date of the fishing season, and the trout are just waiting to bite (www.wildlife.ca.gov).

May

Things really start stirring on Memorial Day weekend, when flocks of vacationers flood the area and the spring snowmelt courses through park waterfalls. Chilly nights punctuate the occasional 70°F (21°C) day.

WATERFALL SEASON

For falls fanatics, the warmer weather means one thing: cascades gushing off the hook. Yosemite's most famous attractions demonstrate their vigor, and seasonal flows like Hetch Hetchy's **Tueeulala Falls** (p468), and Silver Strand Falls and Sentinel Falls in Yosemite Valley briefly come to life.

June

The high country has begun to thaw, and the summer visitor influx begins. It's the best time to explore trails below 8000ft, though you'll want snow gear to hike much higher.

TIOGA ROAD OPENS

Though it varies year to year, by now this crucial trans-Sierra highway is usually plowed and open. The Eastern Sierra suddenly feels a little closer, and hikers feel that itch to strike the trail.

July

Snow has usually receded from the higher elevations, though mosquitoes often wait to greet you there. At exposed lower ground, summer heat may leave you wilting at midday.

BADWATER ULTRAMARATHON

About 30 years ago someone came up with a preposterous idea: why not run a race (www.badwater.com) between the highest and lowest points in the continental US? Over 60 hours, runners attempt a nonstop course from Death Valley (35 miles southeast of Lone Pine) to Whitney Portal.

August

Temperatures in Yosemite Valley and the lower areas of Sequoia and Kings Canyon keep rising, making an escape to the higher altitudes a refreshing relief.

TUOLUMNE MEADOWS POETRY FESTIVAL

A poetry festival on the grass in Tuolumne Meadows – how can you beat that? Wildflowers and words take center stage during a weekend of workshops and readings.

September

The summer heat begins to fizzle as the month progresses, giving way to brisk days and frigid evenings. The crowds recede and waterfalls are at a trickle.

YOSEMITE FACELIFT

The biggest volunteer event of the year – in Yosemite or any other national park – sees climbers and other grateful souls arrive for a major cleanup (www.yosemiteclimbing.org) at the end of the season. The result? Over 100,000lb of garbage removed.

October

The weather's hit and miss, with either Sierra Nevada sunshine or bucketfuls of chilling rain. Mountain businesses wind up their season and diehards take one last hike before the first snowflakes appear.

AUTUMN FOLIAGE

Fall colors light up the Sierra Nevada and leaf-peeping photographers joyride looking for the best shot. Black oaks blaze dramatically in the undulating foothills, but it's the stands of aspen that steal the show as they flame gold under blue high-elevation sky.

November

Deep snow shuts Tioga Rd and – ta-da! – it's the unofficial start of winter. The Thanksgiving holiday reels in families, and backcountry campers tune up their cross-country skis.

December

Vacationers inundate the resorts during the week between Christmas and New Year's Day, though otherwise the parks remain frosted and solitary. Think snowshoe hikes and hot chocolate.

BRACEBRIDGE DINNER

Held at the Majestic Yosemite Hotel, this traditional **Christmas pageant** (p466) is part feast and part Renaissance fair. Guests indulge in a multicourse meal while being entertained by more than 100 actors in 17th-century costume.

MANDATORY HALF DOME PERMITS

To stem lengthy lines (and increasingly dangerous conditions) on the vertiginous cables of Half Dome, the park now requires that all day hikers obtain an advance permit to climb the cables. There are currently three ways to do this, though check www.nps.gov/yose/planyourvisit/hdpermits.htm for the latest information. Rangers check permits at the base of the cables.

Preseason permit lottery (www.recreation.gov) Lottery applications ($10) for the 300 daily spots must be completed in March, with confirmation notification sent in mid-April; an additional fee of $10 per person confirms the permit. Applications can include up to six people and seven alternate dates.

Daily lottery Approximately 50 additional permits are distributed by lottery two days before each hiking date. Apply online or by phone (✆877-444-6777) between midnight and 1pm Pacific Time; notification is available late that same evening. It's easier to score weekday permits.

Backpackers Those with Yosemite-issued wilderness permits that *reasonably include* Half Dome can request Half Dome permits (from $12.50 per person) without going through the lottery process. Backpackers with wilderness permits from a National Forest or another park can use that permit to climb the cables.

from the valley on Glacier Point Rd. The gentle slopes are perfect for families and beginner skiers and snowboarders. There are five chairlifts, 800 vertical feet and 10 runs, a full-service lodge and equipment rental ($27 to $37 for a full set of gear).

The excellent **Yosemite Ski & Snowboard Area School** (www.travelyosemite.com), where generations of novices have learned how to get down a hill safely, offers group lessons (from $47).

Ostrander Ski Hut　　　　　SKIING
(✆209-379-5161; www.yosemiteconservancy.org) More experienced skiers can trek 10 miles out to this popular hut on Ostrander Lake, operated by Yosemite Conservancy. The hut is staffed all winter and open to backcountry skiers and snowshoers for $35 to $55 per person, per night, on a lottery basis. See the website for details.

Half Dome Village Ice Skating Rink　SKATING
(2½hr session adult/child $10/9.50, skate rental $4; ⊗noon-2:30pm, 3:30-6pm & 7-9:30pm Mon-Fri, 8:30-11am, noon-2:30pm, 3:30-6pm & 7-9:30pm Sat & Sun Nov-Mar; ⊕) A delightful winter activity is taking a spin on the outdoor rink, where you'll be skating under the watchful eye of Half Dome.

☞ Tours

The nonprofit **Yosemite Conservancy** (✆209-379-2317; www.yosemiteconservancy.org) has scheduled tours of all kinds, plus custom trips.

First-timers often appreciate the year-round, two-hour **Valley Floor Tour** (✆209-372-1240; www.travelyosemite.com; adult/child $35/25; ⊗year-round; ⊕), which covers the valley's highlights.

For other options, stop at the tour and activity desks at **Yosemite Valley Lodge** (✆209-372-1240; ⊗7:30am-7pm), Half Dome Village or Yosemite Village, call ✆209-372-4386 or check www.travelyosemite.com.

🛏 Sleeping

Competition for campsites is fierce from May to September, when arriving without a reservation and hoping for the best is tantamount to getting someone to lug your Barcalounger up Half Dome. Even first-come, first-served campgrounds tend to fill by noon, especially on weekends and around holidays. Campsites can be reserved up to five months in advance. Reservations become available from 7am PST on the 15th of every month in one-month blocks, and often sell out within minutes.

Without a booking, your only chance is to hightail it to an open first-come, first-served campground or proceed to one of four campground-reservation offices in Yosemite Valley, Wawona, Big Oak Flat and Tuolumne Meadows (the latter three are only open seasonally). Try to get there before they open at 8am (the Yosemite Valley office may open at 7:30am in summer), put your name on a waiting list and then hope for a cancellation or early departure. Return when the ranger tells you to (usually 3pm) and if you hear your name, consider yourself very lucky indeed.

All campgrounds have flush toilets, except for Tamarack Flat, Yosemite Creek and Porcupine Flat, which have vault toilets and no potable water. Those at higher elevations get chilly at night, even in summer, so pack accordingly. The Yosemite Mountaineering School (p470) rents camping gear.

If you hold a wilderness permit, you may spend the nights before and after your trip in the backpacker campgrounds at Tuolumne Meadows, Hetch Hetchy, White Wolf and behind North Pines in Yosemite Valley. The cost is $5 per person, per night, and reservations aren't necessary.

Opening dates for seasonal campgrounds vary according to the weather.

🛏 Yosemite Valley

Camp 4 CAMPGROUND $
(www.nps.gov/yose; shared tent sites per person $6; ☺year-round) Walk-in campground at 4000ft, popular with climbers and entwined in climbing history; sites are shared.

North Pines Campground CAMPGROUND $
(tent & RV sites $26; ☺Apr-Oct; 🐾) Within walking distance of some of the valley's most popular trailheads, North Pines (4000ft) has 81 sites near Mirror Lake; reservations required. Can feel crowded and cramped with recreational vehicles (RVs).

Upper Pines Campground CAMPGROUND $
(www.nps.gov/yose; tent & RV sites $26; ☺year-round; 🐾) Busy, busy, busy – and big (238 sites, 4000ft); reservations required mid-March through November. Sites are fairly small and close to one another.

Lower Pines Campground CAMPGROUND $
(www.nps.gov/yose; tent & RV sites $26; ☺ Apr-Oct; 🐾) Jam-packed and noisy, with 60 sites at 4000ft; reservations required.

Housekeeping Camp CABIN $$
(www.travelyosemite.com; Southside Dr; q $112; ☺Apr-Oct) This cluster of 266 cabins, each walled by concrete on three sides and lidded by a canvas roof, is crammed and noisy, but the setting along the Merced River has its merits. Each unit sleeps six and has electricity, light, a table and chairs, and a covered patio with picnic tables. Laundry and shower facilities are open to guests and non-guests.

Half Dome Village CABIN $$
(☑ reservations 888-413-8869; www.travelyosemite. com; tent cabins from $143, r from $260, cabins with shared/private bath from $170/225; ☺ daily mid-Mar–late Nov, Sat & Sun early Jan–mid-Mar; 🅿☺🐾📶🍴) Founded in 1899 as summertime Camp Curry, Half Dome Village has hundreds of units squished together beneath towering evergreens. The canvas cabins (heated or unheated) are basically glorified tents, so for more comfort, quiet and privacy get one of the cozy wood cabins, which have vintage posters. There are 18 motel-style rooms in Stoneman House, including a loft suite that sleeps six.

Cabin 819, with its fireplace, sofa bed and king-sized bed, is probably the most luxurious of the bunch. The village is off Southside Dr.

★ Majestic Yosemite Hotel HISTORIC HOTEL $$$
(☑ reservations 888-413-8869; www.travelyosemite. com; 1 Ahwahnee Dr; r/ste from $480/590; 🅿☺@📶🍴) The crème de la crème of Yosemite's lodging, this sumptuous historic property (formerly called the Ahwahnee) dazzles with soaring ceilings and atmospheric lounges with mammoth stone fireplaces. Classic rooms have inspiring views of Glacier Point and (partial) Half Dome. Cottages are scattered on the immaculately trimmed lawn next to the hotel. For high season and holidays, book a year in advance.

Suite 332 has a fireplace, a chandelier and incredible panoramic views.

The Majestic is the gold standard for upscale lodges, but even if you're not staying here you can still soak up the ambience during afternoon tea, a drink in the bar or a gourmet meal.

Yosemite Valley Lodge MOTEL $$$
(☑ reservations 888-413-8869; www.travelyosemite. com; 9006 Yosemite Lodge Dr; r from $260; 🅿☺@📶🍴) 🏊 Situated a short walk from Yosemite Falls, this large complex contains a wide range of eateries, a lively bar, a big pool and other handy amenities. The rooms, spread out over 15 buildings, feel somewhat lodge like, with rustic wooden furniture and striking nature photography. All have cable TV, telephone, fridge and coffeemaker, and great patio or balcony panoramas.

🛏 Tioga Road & Tuolumne Meadows

Tuolumne Meadows Campground
CAMPGROUND $

(Map p498; www.nps.gov/yose; Tioga Rd; tent & RV sites $26; ⊙ Jul-Sep; 🐾) Biggest campground in the park (8600ft), with 304 fairly well-spaced sites; half of these can be reserved.

Porcupine Flat Campground
CAMPGROUND $

(www.nps.gov/yose; tent & RV sites $12; ⊙ Jul-mid-Oct; 🐾) Primitive 52-site area at 8100ft; some sites near the road.

Tamarack Flat Campground
CAMPGROUND $

(Old Big Oak Flat Rd; tent sites $12; ⊙ late Jun-Sep; 🐾) Quiet and primitive (pit toilets only) at 6315ft; the 52 tent sites are a rough 3-mile drive off Tioga Rd. Despite its relatively secluded location, you'll need to show up early to snag a spot, especially on weekends. Bring plenty of water.

White Wolf Campground
CAMPGROUND $

(www.nps.gov/yose; tent & RV sites $18; ⊙ Jul-early Sep; 🐾) Attractive setting at 8000ft, but the 74 sites are fairly boxed in.

Yosemite Creek Campground
CAMPGROUND $

(www.nps.gov/yose; tent sites $12; ⊙ Jul-early Sep; 🐾) The most secluded and quiet campground (7659ft) in the park, reached via a rough 4.5-mile road. There are 75 first-come, first-served primitive sites (no potable water).

Tuolumne Meadows Lodge
CABIN $$

(Map p498; ☎ reservations 888-413-8869; www.travelyosemite.com; tent cabins $137; ⊙ mid-Jun–mid-Sep) Set amid the magnificent high country, about 50 miles from Yosemite Valley off Tioga Rd, this option attracts hikers to its 69 canvas tent cabins with two or four beds each, a wood-burning stove and candles (no electricity). Breakfast and dinner are available (surcharge applies; dinner reservations required). A fork of the Tuolumne River runs through the property.

White Wolf Lodge
CABIN $$

(www.travelyosemite.com; White Wolf Rd; tent cabins without bath $140, cabins $170; ⊙ Jun–mid-Sep) This complex enjoys its own little world a mile up a spur road, away from the hubbub and traffic of Hwy 120 and Yosemite Valley. There are 24 spartan four-bedded tent cabins without electricity and four very-in-demand hard-walled cabins that feel like rustic motel rooms. The generator cuts out at 11pm, so you'll need a flashlight until early morning.

There's also a dining room with somewhat-overpriced fare and a tiny counter-service store.

WILDERNESS PERMITS FOR OVERNIGHT CAMPING

Shedding the high-season crowds is easiest in Yosemite's backcountry wilderness. Start by identifying a route that matches your schedule, skill and fitness level. Then secure a wilderness permit (www.nps.gov/yose/planyourvisit/wpres.htm), which is mandatory for overnight trips. The advance-reservation fee is $5, plus there's a fee of $5 per person; walk-ins are free. To prevent tent cities sprouting in the woods, a quota system limits the number of people leaving from each trailhead each day. For trips between mid-May and September, 60% of the quota may be reserved by fax (209-372-0739), phone (☎ 209-372-0740) or mail (PO Box 545, Yosemite National Park, CA 95389) from 26 weeks to two days before your trip. Faxes received between noon (the previous day) and 7:30am (the first morning you can reserve) get first priority.

The remainder are distributed by the office closest to the trailhead on a first-come, first-served basis (beginning at 11am one day before your planned hike) at Yosemite Valley Wilderness Center, Tuolumne Meadows Wilderness Center, the information stations at Wawona and Big Oak Flat, and the Hetch Hetchy Entrance Station. Hikers who turn up at the wilderness center nearest the trailhead get priority over those at another wilderness center. For example, if a person who's been waiting for hours in the valley wants the last permit left for Lyell Canyon, the Yosemite Valley Wilderness Center calls the Tuolumne Meadows Wilderness Center to see if any hikers in Tuolumne want it. If a hiker waltzing into the Tuolumne office says 'yes!', they get priority over the person in the valley.

Reservations are not available from October to April, but you'll still need to get a permit by self-registering at the park.

Hetch Hetchy & Big Oak Flat Road

Crane Flat Campground
CAMPGROUND $

(www.nps.gov/yose; Big Oak Flat Rd; tent & RV sites $26; ☺Jun–mid-Oct; 🐾) Large family campground at 6192ft, with 166 sites; reservations required. The **Clark Range overlook hike**, 4 miles out and back, begins from here.

Hodgdon Meadow Campground
CAMPGROUND $

(Tuolumne Grove Rd; tent & RV sites $18-26; ☺year-round; 🐾) Utilitarian and crowded 105-site campground at 4875ft; reservations required mid-April to mid-October.

Dimond O Campground
CAMPGROUND $

(☑877-444-6777; www.recreation.gov; Evergreen Rd; tent & RV sites $24; ☺May-Sep) Away from the valley bustle and 4 miles off Hwy 120 in the Stanislaus National Forest, this reservable United States Forest Service (USFS) campground has 35 forested sites adjacent to the Tuolumne River. Arriving from the west, it's the last campground before the Big Oak Flat Entrance, and a good fallback if you can't get a campsite inside the park.

★Evergreen Lodge
CABIN $$$

(☑209-379-2606; www.evergreenlodge.com; 33160 Evergreen Rd, Groveland; tents $90-125, cabins $180-415; ☺usually closed Jan–mid-Feb; P☺❄@☎🛏) 🏊 Outside Yosemite National Park near the entrance to Hetch Hetchy, this classic, nearly century-old resort consists of lovingly decorated and comfy cabins (each with its own cache of board games) spread among the trees. Accommodations run from rustic to deluxe, and all cabins have private porches without distracting phone or TV. Roughing-it guests can cheat with comfy, prefurnished tents.

Wawona & Glacier Point Road

Bridalveil Creek Campground
CAMPGROUND $

(www.nps.gov/yose; tent & RV sites $18; ☺Jul-early Sep; 🐾) Quieter than the Yosemite Valley campgrounds, with 110 sites at 7200ft.

Wawona Campground
CAMPGROUND $

(www.nps.gov/yose; Wawona; tent & RV sites $26; ☺year-round; 🐾) Idyllic riverside setting at 4000ft with 93 well-spaced sites; reservations required May to September.

Eating

You can find food options for all budgets and palates within the park, from greasy slabs of fast food to swanky cuts of top-notch steak. All carry good vegetarian options. The **Village Store** (Yosemite Village; ☺8am-8pm, to 10pm summer) has the best selection (including health-food items and some organic produce), while stores at Half Dome Village, Wawona, Tuolumne Meadows and the Yosemite Valley Lodge are more limited.

Yosemite Valley Food Court
CAFETERIA $

(Yosemite Valley Lodge, 9006 Yosemite Lodge Dr, Yosemite Valley; mains $5.50-13.50; ☺6:30am-10pm, to 8pm winter; 🖉🕭) This self-service restaurant has several tummy-filling stations serving a large choice of pasta, burgers, pizza and sandwiches, either made to order or served from beneath heat lamps. Proceed to the cashier (lines can be long) and find a table inside or on the patio. At the time of writing it was scheduled to be fully remodeled after the 2017 summer season.

Degnan's Loft
PIZZA $$

(www.travelyosemite.com; Yosemite Village) Above the new Degnan's Kitchen, off Village Dr, the Loft retains its old name but has also received a top-to-bottom remodeling. Kick back and enjoy artisan pizzas, specialty appetizers and desserts, and beer and wine in this space with high-beamed ceilings and a many-sided fireplace.

Meadow Grill
FAST FOOD $

(Half Dome Village; mains $8; ☺11am-5pm Sep-Apr, to 7pm summer) Hot dogs, burgers and a few salads are available on a deck near the parking area. Even when lines are long, the food's served up fairly quickly.

Tuolumne Meadows Grill
FAST FOOD $

(Map p498; Tioga Rd; mains $7-12; ☺8am-5pm mid-Jun–mid-Sep) You can hardly say you've visited Tuolumne without scoffing down a chili burger and a basket of crispy fries in the parking lot in front of the Tuolumne Meadows Grill. The soft-serve ice-cream cones and hearty breakfasts – not to mention the people-watching at the picnic tables – are equally mandatory.

Village Grill
FAST FOOD $

(Yosemite Village; mains $6-13; ☺11am-6pm mid-Mar–Oct; 🖉) Fight the chipmunks for burgers, hot sandwiches, salads and fries alfresco. Expect crowds and lines.

★ **Evergreen Lodge**   AMERICAN $$
(☎ 209-379-2606; www.evergreenlodge.com;
33160 Evergreen Rd; breakfast & lunch $12-18,
dinner $20-34; ⏰ 7-10:30am, noon-3pm & 5-9pm;
🅿 👬) Creative and satisfying, the Ever-
green's restaurant serves some of the best
meals around, with big and delicious break-
fasts, three types of burger (Black Angus
beef, buffalo and veggie) and dinner choices
including rib-eye steak, grilled venison and
vegan tamales.

The homey wooden tavern is a perennial
favorite for evening cocktails, beers on tap
over a game of pool and live music on se-
lect weekends. A general store fills the gaps
with to-go sandwiches, snacks and dreamy
gelato.

**Majestic Yosemite
Dining Room**   CALIFORNIAN $$$
(☎ 209-372-1489; Majestic Yosemite Hotel, 1 Ah-
wahnee Dr, Yosemite Valley; breakfast $7-22.50,
lunch $15-22, dinner $28-46; ⏰ 7-10am, 11:30am-
3pm & 5:30-9pm; 🅿) 🍴 The formal ambience (mind your manners!) may not be for
everybody, but few would not be awed by
the sumptuous decor, soaring beamed ceiling and palatial chandeliers here. The menu
is constantly in flux, but most dishes have
perfect pitch and are beautifully presented.
There's a dress code at dinner, but otherwise
shorts and sneakers are OK.

Sunday brunch (adult/child $45/15; 7am
to 3pm) is amazing. Reservations highly
recommended for brunch and dinner.

🍷 Drinking & Nightlife

No one will mistake Yosemite for nightlife
central, but there are some nice spots to
relax with a cabernet, cocktail or cold beer.
Outside the park, the Yosemite Bug Rustic
Mountain Resort (p481), **Rush Creek Lodge**
(☎ 209-379-2373; www.rushcreeklodge.com;
34001 Hwy 120; @ 🐾 🏊) 🍴 and Evergreen
Lodge (p477) have lively lounges.

Mountain Room Lounge   BAR
(www.travelyosemite.com; Yosemite Valley Lodge,
9006 Yosemite Lodge Dr, Yosemite Valley; ⏰ 4:30-
11pm Mon-Fri, noon-11pm Sat & Sun) Catch up on
the latest sports news while knocking back
draft brews at this large bar that buzzes in
wintertime. The small food menu (mains $9
to $16) features tacos, salads and chili. Order
a s'mores kit (graham crackers, chocolate
squares and marshmallows) to roast in the
open-pit fireplace. Kids welcome until 10pm.

Majestic Bar   BAR
(www.travelyosemite.com; Majestic Yosemite Hotel,
1 Ahwahnee Dr, Yosemite Valley; ⏰ 11am-10pm) The
perfect way to experience the Majestic Yosemite Hotel without dipping too deep into
your pockets; settle in for a drink at this cozy
bar completely remodeled in 2016. Appetizers and light meals ($10.50 to $25) provide
sustenance.

☆ Entertainment

In addition to events at the Yosemite Theater, other activities scheduled year-round include campfire programs, children's photo
walks, twilight strolls, night-sky watching,
ranger talks and slide shows, and the tavern
at the Evergreen Lodge (p477) has live bands
some weekends. Scan the *Yosemite Guide*
for full details.

Yosemite Theater   THEATER
(www.yosemiteconservancy.org/yosemite-theater;
7pm film screenings adult/child $8/4; ⏰ 9:30am-
4:30pm; 👬) Behind the Yosemite Valley Visitor Center (p479), this theater screens two
films: Ken Burns' *Yosemite: A Gathering of
Spirit*, a celebration of the Yosemite Grant's
150th anniversary, and the painfully dramatic but beautifully photographed *Spirit
of Yosemite*. The movies alternate, starting every half-hour between 9:30am and
4:30pm (from noon on Sunday), and offer a
free, air-conditioned respite from the summer heat.

In the evening, take your pick from a rotating selection of films. Actor Lee Stetson
portrays the fascinating life and philosophy of John Muir, and park ranger Shelton
Johnson re-creates the experiences of a buffalo soldier. Other films explore search-and-
rescue missions and rock climbing in the
park. There are also special children's shows.

ℹ Information

Yosemite's entrance fee is $30 per vehicle or $15
for those on a bicycle or on foot and is valid for
seven consecutive days. Passes are sold (you
can use cash, checks, traveler's checks or cred-
it/debit cards) at the various entrance stations,
as well as at visitor centers in Oakhurst, Groveland, Mariposa and Lee Vining. Upon entering the
park, you'll receive a National Park Service (NPS)
map and a copy of the seasonal *Yosemite Guide*
newspaper, which includes an activity schedule
and current opening hours of all facilities. The
official NPS website (www.nps.gov/yose) has the
most comprehensive and current information.

For recorded park information, campground availability, and road and weather conditions, call ☑209-372-0200.

The park has a bare-bones **dog kennel** (☑209-372-8326; www.travelyosemite.com; Yosemite Valley Stable; per dog per day $9.50; ☺late May-early Sep), at which dogs are kept in outdoor cages (no food is allowed, due to wildlife concerns) and stay unattended. No overnight stays are allowed. You must provide a written copy of vet immunization records. Reservations are strongly recommended.

A-frame Building (☑209-372-0409; Yosemite Ski & Snowboard Area; ☺9am-4pm winter) In winter, wilderness permits are available by self-registration at the A-frame Building, where the first-aid station and ski patrol are also situated. Rangers usually staff the office from 8am to 5pm.

Big Oak Flat Information Station (☑209-372-0200; ☺8am-5pm late May-Oct) Has a wilderness permit desk.

Tuolumne Meadows Visitor Center (Map p498; ☑209-372-0263; ☺9am-6pm Jun-Sep) Information desk, bookstore and small exhibits on the area's wildlife and history.

Tuolumne Meadows Wilderness Center (Map p498; ☑209-372-0309; ☺8am-5pm Jun-Sep) Issues wilderness permits.

Wawona Visitor Center (☑209-375-9531; Wawona; ☺8:30am-5pm May-Oct) Located off Wawona Rd in the historic studio of artist Thomas Hills; has information and issues wilderness permits.

Yosemite Valley Visitor Center (☑209-372-0200; 9035 Village Dr, Yosemite Village; ☺9am-5pm; ⟐) Park's busiest information desk. Shares space with bookstore run by Yosemite Conservancy and part of the museum complex in the center of Yosemite Village.

Yosemite Valley Wilderness Center (☑209-372-0745; Yosemite Village; ☺8am-5pm May-Oct) Wilderness permits, maps and backcountry advice.

DANGERS & ANNOYANCES

Yosemite is prime black-bear habitat. Follow park rules on proper food storage and utilize bear-proof food lockers when parked overnight. Mosquitoes can be pesky in summer, so bug spray's not a bad idea. And please don't feed those squirrels. They may look cute but they've got a nasty bite.

INTERNET ACCESS

Yosemite Valley Lodge (p475), **Majestic Yosemite Hotel** (p475) and **Half Dome Village** (p475) offer free wi-fi to guests.

Half Dome Village Lounge (Half Dome Village) Next to the food pavilion; free wi-fi.

Mariposa County Public Library (☑209-372-4552; 58 Cedar Ct, Girls Club Bldg, Yosemite Valley; ☺9am-noon Mon & Tue, to 1pm Wed & Thu; ☎) Free internet terminals and wi-fi.

MEDICAL SERVICES

Yosemite Medical Clinic (☑209-372-4637; 9000 Ahwahnee Dr, Yosemite Village; ☺9am-7pm daily late-May–Sep, to 5pm Mon-Fri late Sep-late May) A 24-hour emergency service is available.

MONEY

Stores in Yosemite Village, Half Dome Village and Wawona all have ATMs, as do the **Yosemite Valley Lodge** (p475) and the **Majestic Yosemite Hotel** (p475).

POST

The main **post office** (9017 Village Dr; ☺8:30am-5pm Mon-Fri, 10am-noon Sat) is in Yosemite Village, but **Wawona** (☑209-375-6574; 1 Forest Dr; ☺9am-5pm Mon-Fri) and the **Yosemite Valley Lodge** (9006 Yosemite Lodge Dr; ☺12:30-2:45pm Mon-Fri) also have year-round services. A seasonal branch operates in **Tuolumne Meadows** (☑209-372-8236; ☺9am-5pm Mon-Fri, to noon Sat, closed mid-Sep–mid-Jun).

TELEPHONE

There are payphones at every developed location throughout the park. Cell-phone reception is sketchy, depending on your location: AT&T and Verizon have the only coverage and both are best in the Yosemite Village area near the visitor center.

❶ Getting There & Away

CAR & MOTORCYCLE

Yosemite is accessible year-round from the west (via Hwys 120 W and 140) and south (Hwy 41), and in summer also from the east (via Hwy 120 E). Roads are plowed in winter, but snow chains may be required at any time. In 2006 a mammoth rockslide buried part of Hwy 140, 6 miles west of the park; traffic there is restricted to vehicles under 45ft. Big Oak Flat Rd was closed for several months after a 'slide', really of an entire hillside, in February 2017.

Gas up year-round at Wawona inside the park (you'll pay dearly), at El Portal on Hwy 140 just outside its western boundary or Lee Vining at the junction of Hwys 120 and 395 outside the park in the east. In summer, gas is also sold at Crane Flat; the gas station in Tuolumne Meadows is now closed.

PUBLIC TRANSPORTATION

Yosemite is one of the few national parks that can easily be reached by public transportation. **Greyhound** buses and **Amtrak** trains serve

Merced, west of the park, where they are met by buses operated by the **Yosemite Area Regional Transportation System** (YARTS; ☑ 877-989-2787; www.yarts.com), and you can buy Amtrak tickets that include the YARTS segment all the way into the park. Buses travel to Yosemite Valley along Hwy 140 several times daily year-round, stopping along the way.

In summer (roughly June through September), another YARTS route runs from Mammoth Lakes along Hwy 395 to Yosemite Valley via Hwy 120. One-way tickets to Yosemite Valley are $13 ($9 child and senior, three hours) from Merced and $18 ($15 child and senior, 3½ hours) from Mammoth Lakes, less if boarding in between.

YARTS fares include the park-entrance fee, making them a super bargain, and drivers accept credit cards.

🛈 Getting Around

BICYCLE

Bicycling is an ideal way to take in Yosemite Valley. You can rent a wide-handled cruiser (per hour/day $11.50/32) or a bike with an attached child trailer (per hour/day $19/59) at the **Yosemite Valley Lodge** (p471) or **Half Dome Village** (p471). Strollers and wheelchairs are also rented here.

CAR

Roadside signs with red bears mark the many spots where bears have been hit by motorists, so think before you hit the accelerator, and follow the pokey posted speed limits. Valley visitors are advised to park and take advantage of the Yosemite Valley Shuttle Bus. Even so, traffic in the valley can feel like rush hour in LA.

Glacier Point and Tioga Rds are closed in winter.

Village Garage (☑ 209-372-8320; Tecoya Rd; ☻ 8am-5pm) provides emergency repairs and even gasoline when you're in an absolute fix.

PUBLIC TRANSPORTATION

The free, air-conditioned **Yosemite Valley Shuttle Bus** (www.nps.gov/yose) is a comfortable and efficient way of traveling around the park. Buses operate year-round at frequent intervals and stop at 21 numbered locations, including parking lots, campgrounds, trailheads and lodges. For a route map, see the *Yosemite Guide*.

Free buses also operate between Yosemite Valley and the Yosemite Ski & Snowboard Area (winter only). The **Tuolumne Meadows Shuttle** (1 way adult/child 5-12yr $9/4.50; ☻ 7am-7pm Jun-mid Sep) runs between Tuolumne Lodge and Olmsted Point in Tuolumne Meadows (usually mid-June to early September), and the **El Capitan Shuttle** runs a summertime valley loop from Yosemite Village to El Capitan.

Two fee-based hikers' buses also travel from Yosemite Valley. For trailheads along Tioga Rd, catch the **Tuolumne Meadows Hikers' Bus** (☑ 209-372-1240; www.travelyosemite.com), which runs once daily in each direction. Fares depend on distance traveled; the trip to Tuolumne Meadows costs $14.50/23 one way/round-trip. The **Glacier Point Hikers' Bus** (☑ 888-413-8869; 1 way/return $25/49; ☻ mid-May–Oct) is good for hikers as well as for people reluctant to drive up the long, windy road themselves. Reservations are required.

YOSEMITE GATEWAYS

Fish Camp

Fish Camp, just south of Yosemite on Hwy 41, is more of a bend in the road, but it does have some good lodging options as well as the ever-popular **Sugar Pine Railroad** (☑ 559-683-7273; www.ymsprr.com; 56001 Hwy 41; rides adult/child $24/12; ☻ approximately Mar-Oct; 👪).

🛏 Sleeping & Eating

Summerdale Campground   CAMPGROUND $
(www.fs.usda.gov; tent & RV sites $30; ☻ May-Sep; 🐾) The closest campground to Yosemite, Summerdale is a pleasant spot along Big Creek, with 28 well-dispersed sites in a grassy meadow with shade trees.

White Chief Mountain Lodge   MOTEL $$
(☑ 209-742-7777; www.whitechiefmountainlodge.com; 7776 White Chief Mountain Rd; r $159-179; ☻ Apr-Oct; 🐾) The cheapest and most basic option in Fish Camp, this 1950s-era motel has simple kitchenette rooms with uninspiring furnishings. It's located a few hundred yards east of Hwy 41; watch for the sign and go up the wooded country road. An on-site restaurant with dreary decor usually serves breakfast and dinner in summer.

Big Creek Inn B&B   B&B $$$
(☑ 559-641-2828; www.bigcreekinn.com; 1221 Hwy 41; r $259-299; 🐾) Each of the three white-palette rooms has peaceful creek views and a private balcony, and two have gas fireplaces. From the comfortable rooms or the back patio you can often spot deer and beavers, or hummingbirds lining up at the patio feeder. Amenities include in-room DVD/Blu-ray players and a large movie library, kitchenette use and big soaking tubs with bath salts.

★**Narrow Gauge Inn** AMERICAN $$$
(☑559-683-7720; 48571 Hwy 41; mains $18-35;
☻5-9pm late Apr-Oct) Excellent food and
knockout views make the dining experience
at the Narrow Gauge Inn one of the finest
in the Yosemite region. The dinners are cre-
atively prepared, the lodge-like atmosphere
is casual but elegant, and the windows look
out on lush mountain vistas.

Cozy up to the fireplace on colder eve-
nings or warm yourself up at the small Buf-
falo Bar, perfect for a cocktail or a glass of
wine. Reservations recommended.

Oakhurst

Although only about 16 miles south of Yo-
semite's southern entrance (and the Maripo-
sa Grove), at the junction of Hwys 41 and 49,
Oakhurst feels worlds away from the park's
natural majesty. It's the most quotidian of
Yosemite's gateway towns: think strip malls
and fast-food joints. For park-goers it func-
tions primarily as a service town and is your
last chance to stock up on reasonably priced
groceries, gasoline and camping supplies.

🛏 Sleeping & Eating

★**Sierra Sky Ranch** LODGE $$
(☑559-683-8040; www.sierraskyranch.com;
50552 Road 632; r $199-279; ❇☎❄🐾) This
1875 former ranch encompasses 14 attractive
acres. The homespun rooms are phone-free
and pet friendly, with double doors that open
onto shady verandas. The rambling and
beautiful old lodge features a **restaurant**
(☑559-658-2644; dinner mains $28-35; ☻5-9pm
Wed-Sun), a rustic saloon and loads of comfortable lounging areas. A major renovation
following new ownership in 2015 upgraded
the room furnishings and public spaces.

With a storied history including previous
uses as a tuberculosis hospital and a bordello,
the ranch counts such past guests as Marilyn
Monroe and John Wayne. Many swear that
it's cheerfully haunted by former residents.

Hounds Tooth Inn B&B $$
(☑559-642-6600; www.houndstoothinn.com;
42071 Hwy 41; r $180-230; ❇☎) A few miles
north of Oakhurst, this gorgeous garden
B&B is swimming in rosebushes and Vic-
torianesque charm. Its 12 airy rooms and
two cottages, some with spas and fireplac-
es, have a slight English-manor-house feel.
Complimentary wine and hot drinks are
available in the afternoon.

Château du Sureau BOUTIQUE HOTEL $$$
(☑559-683-6860; www.chateaudusureau.com;
48688 Victoria Lane; r $420-645, 2-bedroom villas
$2950; ❇@☎❄🐾) Never in a billion years
would you expect to find a place like this in
Oakhurst. A luxe and discreet full-service
European-style hotel and world-class spa,
this serene destination property boasts an
exceptional level of service.

★**Erna's
Elderberry House** CALIFORNIAN, FRENCH $$$
(☑559-683-6860; www.chateaudusureau.com/
ernas-elderberry-house-restaurant; Château du
Sureau, 48688 Victoria Lane; prix-fixe dinner $75-
112, Sun brunch mains $18-24, tasting menu $68;
☻dinner daily, plus 11am-1pm Sun; 🖉) With wall
tapestries, oil paintings and ornate chande-
liers, the Californian-French restaurant at
Château du Sureau (p481) could be a castle.
But you don't have to be royalty to eat here
(and the service is notably unstuffy), only
willing to shell out for dishes like fois-gras
parfait, truffle gnocchi and Pacific halibut,
wonderfully presented and enhanced with
locally sourced herbs and vegetables.

Merced River Canyon

The approach to Yosemite via Hwy 140 is
one of the most scenic routes to the park, es-
pecially the section that meanders through
Merced River Canyon. Right outside the
Arch Rock entrance, and primarily inhab-
ited by park employees, **El Portal** makes a
convenient Yosemite base.

The canyon is a top spot for **river rafting**,
with many miles of class III and IV rapids.
(Age minimums vary with water levels.)
Outfitters include OARS (p471), a worldwide
rafting operator with a solid reputation.

🛏 Sleeping & Eating

★**Yosemite Bug
Rustic Mountain Resort** HOSTEL, CABIN $
(☑209-966-6666; www.yosemitebug.com; 6979
Hwy 140, Midpines; dm $30, tent cabins from $65,
r with/without bath from $165/95; 🅿☺@☎) 🖉
This folksy oasis is tucked away on a forest-
ed hillside about 25 miles west of Yosemite.
A wide range of accommodations types lines
the narrow ridges; some require more walk-
ing from parking areas and bathrooms than
others. The June Bug Cafe (p484) is highly
recommended. Also available are yoga les-
sons, massages and a spa with hot tub.

California Wildlife

Unique creatures great and small inhabit the land, sky and waters of California's diverse ecosystems. Visit them at the ocean or in the forest, or just scan the skies.

1. Elephant seal
Equipped with a trunk-like nose, the enormous males noisily battle for dominance on the beach.

2. Black bear
The name is misleading, as bear fur can be shades of brown, black, cinnamon or tawny blonde.

3. California condor
A 10ft wingspan is the hallmark of these endangered carrion scavengers. Captive breeding has increased the population, though lead bullet poisoning remains its biggest threat.

4. Gray whale
Dramatic breaches and the puffs of water spouts mark the passage of these school-bus-sized mammals. Pods of whales migrate yearly between Mexico and Alaska, with peak viewing between December and April.

5. California sea lion
With dog-like faces and oversized flippers, vocal sea lions typically haul out in large social groups. The crowd-pleasing colony at San Francisco's Pier 39 mysteriously appeared soon after the 1989 Loma Prieta earthquake.

6. Mule deer
Ubiquitous throughout the state, mule deer are recognizable by their ample ears and black foreheads. Bucks wear forked antler racks.

7. Desert tortoise
Able to live for over half a century, these high desert reptiles burrow underground to survive extreme heat and cold.

8. Hawk
Frequently seen riding the thermal currents on windy ridges, a dozen types of hawks can be found in California. These speedy birds of prey are known for their keen eyesight and strong talons.

9. Mountain lion
Also known as cougars, panthers or pumas, these territorial big cats primarily stalk and feed on deer. They hunt from dusk to dawn, and can sprint at up to 50 miles per hour.

10. Banana slug
Tread carefully along the forest floor so you don't slip on these large and squishy bright yellow specimens.

11. Monarch butterfly
These orange and black beauties flutter thousands of miles to complete their annual migration.

12. Elk
Three subspecies of elk roam the state, with majestic males parading chandeliers of velvety antlers, and bugling dramatically during the fall rutting season.

3

6

9

12

SIERRA VISTA SCENIC BYWAY

Set entirely within Sierra National Forest, this scenic route follows USFS roads in a 100-mile loop that takes you from 3000ft to nearly 7000ft. Along the way are dramatic vistas, excellent fishing, and camping almost anywhere you like (dispersed camping is allowed in most areas). It's a great way for car campers – and curious day trippers – to lose themselves within the mountains.

From its start in **North Fork**, the route takes a half-day to complete, emerging on Hwy 41 a few miles north of **Oakhurst**. Open from June to November, the road is paved most of the way, but it's narrow and laced with curves. See www.fs.usda.gov for a map and information on sights and the best overlooks.

★**June Bug Cafe**　　　　CALIFORNIAN $$
(☏206-966-6666; www.yosemitebug.com/cafe.html; Yosemite Bug Rustic Mountain Resort, 6979 Hwy 140, Midpines; mains $8-22; ⏰7-10am, 11am-2pm & 6-9pm; ☛🍴) Guests of all ages and backgrounds at the Yosemite Bug resort (p481) convene at this friendly cafe to share stories and delicious, freshly prepared meals, beer and wine in the evenings, and live music some nights. More than a half-dozen healthy and hearty dishes are on the whiteboard menu and served cafeteria-style.

Mariposa

About halfway between Merced and Yosemite Valley, Mariposa (Spanish for 'butterfly') is the largest and most interesting town near Yosemite National Park. Established as a mining and railroad town during the gold rush, it has the oldest courthouse in continuous use (since 1854) west of the Mississippi, loads of Old West pioneer character and a couple of good museums dedicated to the area's history.

Rock hounds should drive to the Mariposa County Fairgrounds, 2 miles south of town on Hwy 49, to see the 13lb 'Fricot Nugget' – the largest crystallized gold specimen from the California gold-rush era – and other gems and machinery at the **California State Mining & Mineral Museum** (☏209-742-7625; www.parks.ca.gov/?page_id=588;

5005 Fairgrounds Rd; adult/under 13yr $4/free; ⏰10am-5pm Thu-Sun May-Sep, to 4pm Oct-Apr). An exhibit on glow-in-the-dark minerals is also very cool.

🛏 Sleeping & Eating

River Rock Inn　　　　MOTEL $$
(☏209-966-5793; 4993 7th St; r $135-179; ✳🛜🍴) Updated kitchenette rooms are done up in artsy earth tones at this inn that claims to be the oldest motel in town. It features a courtyard deck and a small cafe serving breakfast to guests. It's a block removed from Hwy 140 on a quiet side street.

Mariposa Hotel Inn　　　HISTORIC HOTEL $$
(☏209-966-7500; www.mariposahotelinn.com; 5029 Hwy 140; r $149-169; ✳🛜) This creaky 1901 building has six king or queen rooms with quilts and period-style furniture, and a corridor crammed with old town photos and newspaper clippings. Room 6 has an original claw-foot tub. Hummingbirds love the flowery back patio where breakfast is served.

★**Happy Burger**　　　　DINER $
(☏209-966-2719; www.happyburgerdiner.com; Hwy 140, cnr 12th St; mains $8-14; ⏰5:30am-9pm; 🛜☛✳🍴) Burgers, fries and shakes served with a heavy dose of nostalgic Americana. Happy Burger, decorated with old LP album covers, and boasting the largest menu in the Sierra, offers one of the cheaper meals in town. Besides burgers, there are sandwiches, Mexican food, salads and a ton of sinful ice-cream desserts. Free computer terminal inside and a 'doggy dining area' outdoors.

You can call and order in advance and pick up your food at the restaurant's to-go window.

Sugar Pine Cafe　　　　AMERICAN $
(☏209-742-7793; www.sugarpinecafe.com; 5038 Hwy 140; mains breakfast $6-9, dinner $7-21; ⏰7am-8:30pm Tue-Sat, to 3pm Sun & Mon) Gussied up with chrome soda-counter stools and red circular booths, this 1940s-era diner serves yummy breakfast items, hot or cold sandwiches, and burgers on whole-wheat buns. Dinner fare is pure comfort food like spaghetti and meatballs, and pork chops.

Savoury's　　　　AMERICAN $$
(☏209-966-7677; 5034 Hwy 140; mains $17-35; ⏰5-9:30pm, closed Wed winter; ☛) Upscale yet casual Savoury's is the best restaurant in town. Black lacquered tables and contemporary art create tranquil window

dressing for dishes like wild-mushroom ravioli, Cajun-spiced New York steak with pan-seared onions, and crab cakes with cilantro-lime aioli.

ℹ Information

Mariposa County Visitor Center (☎ 209-966-7081; cnr Hwys 140 & 49; ⊙ 8:30am-5:30pm; 🛜) Helpful staff and racks of brochures; public restrooms.

ℹ Getting There & Away

YARTS (☎ 209-388-9589, 877-989-2787; www.yarts.com) buses run year-round along Hwy 140 into Yosemite Valley ($6 one way, 1¾ hours), stopping at the Mariposa visitor center. Tickets include admission to Yosemite.

Groveland

From the Big Oak Flat entrance to Yosemite, it's 22 miles to Groveland, an adorable town with restored gold-rush-era buildings and lots of visitor services.

About 15 miles east of Groveland, in the Stanislaus National Forest, **Rainbow Pool** (www.fs.usda.gov/stanislaus) is a popular swimming hole with a small cascade; it's signed on the south side of Hwy 120.

🛏 Sleeping & Eating

★**Hotel Charlotte** BOUTIQUE HOTEL **$$** (☎ 209-962-6455; www.hotelcharlotte.com; 18736 Main St; r $149-249; ❇@🛜❄) Casually sophisticated and designed with a mix of vintage flair and contemporary conveniences, the Charlotte is the nicest spot in Groveland. Some of the rooms have beautifully restored claw-footed bathtubs, and the owners, a husband-and-wife team, work diligently to help guests with their Yosemite stay. A sophisticated bistro (p485) and bar serves a creative small-plates menu.

The owners also have six three-bedroom vacation rentals in the nearby gated community of Pine Mountain Lake.

★**Blackberry Inn Bed & Breakfast** B&B **$$$** (☎ 209-962-4663; www.blackberry-inn.com; 7567 Hamilton Station Loop; r $205-295; ⊙ mid-Mar–Oct; ❇@🛜) On a rural road right off Hwy 120, this stunningly converted house and newer wing offer 10 sumptuous rooms showcasing stained-glass scenes of Yosemite, soaking tubs and electric fireplaces that give off real heat or just cozy ambience. Its *big* breakfasts can be delivered to your room

or patio so you can spy on the hummingbirds. Two-night minimum stay.

Cocina Michoacana MEXICAN **$** (☎ 209-962-6651; 18730 Main St; mains $9-14; ⊙ 10am-10pm) Quick and friendly service and large servings of tasty Mexican fare make this the most popular restaurant with Groveland locals. The chicken mole is especially recommended and there's a good selection of Mexican beers.

★**Fork & Love Restaurant** MODERN AMERICAN **$$** (www.forkandlove.com; 18736 Main St; mains $17-28; ⊙ 6-9pm Thu-Sat, 9am-1pm Sun Mar-Nov) 🌿 Scarce in these parts, 'local, organic and sustainable' is done right at this rustically refined restaurant in a historic saloon space in the Hotel Charlotte (p485). The small plates, as well as the mains, like pork spatzle, carne masala (black Angus beef with homemade masala sauce) and artichoke fried rice, are innovative and best enjoyed by sharing.

🍷 Drinking & Nightlife

★**Iron Door Grill & Saloon** BAR (☎ 209-962-6244; www.iron-door-saloon.com; 18761 Main St; ⊙ restaurant 7am-10pm, bar 11am-2am, shorter hours winter) Claiming to be the oldest bar in the state, the Iron Door is a dusty, atmospheric place, with swinging doors, a giant bar, high ceilings, mounted animal heads and hundreds of dollar bills tacked to the ceiling. There's live music summer-weekend nights, and the adjacent, more contemporary dining room serves good steaks, ribs and pasta dishes (mains $9.50 to $25).

Also hosts open-mike and karaoke nights.

SEQUOIA & KINGS CANYON NATIONAL PARKS

The twin parks of Sequoia and Kings Canyon dazzle with superlatives, though they're often overshadowed by Yosemite, their smaller neighbor to the north (a three-hour drive away). With towering forests of giant sequoias containing some of the largest trees in the world, and the mighty Kings River careening through the depths of Kings Canyon, one of the deepest chasms in the country, the parks are lesser-visited jewels where it's easier to find quiet and solitude.

Throw in opportunities for caving, rock climbing and backcountry hiking through granite-carved Sierra landscapes, and backdoor access to 14,494ft Mt Whitney – the tallest peak in the lower 48 states – and you have all the ingredients for two of the best parks in the country.

The two **parks** (Map p488; ☑ 559-565-3341; www.nps.gov/seki; 7-day entry per car $30; [P][🚻]) 🌿, though distinct, are operated as one unit with a single admission fee; for 24-hour recorded information, including road conditions, call the number listed or visit the parks' comprehensive website. At either entrance station (Big Stump or Ash Mountain), you'll receive an NPS map and a copy of the parks' *Guide* newspaper, with information on seasonal activities, camping and special programs, including those in the surrounding national forests and the **Giant Sequoia National Monument** (Map p488; www.fs.usda.gov). It's easy enough to explore sections of both parks in a single day.

History

In 1890 Sequoia became the second national park in the USA (after Yellowstone). A few days later, the 4 sq miles around Grant Grove were declared General Grant National Park and, in 1940, absorbed into the newly created Kings Canyon National Park. In 2000, to protect additional sequoia groves, vast tracts of land in the surrounding national forest became the Giant Sequoia National Monument.

ⓘ Dangers & Annoyances

➡ Air pollution wafting up from the Sequoia Central Valley and Kings Canyon often thwarts long-range visibility, and people with respiratory problems should check with a visitor center about current pollution levels.

➡ Black bears are common and proper food storage is always required.

➡ Heed park instructions on wildlife procedures.

Kings Canyon National Park

With a dramatic cleft deeper than the Grand Canyon, Kings Canyon offers true adventure to those who crave seemingly endless trails, rushing streams and gargantuan rock formations. The camping, backcountry exploring and climbing here are all superb. **Big Stump Entrance** (Map p488;

Hwy 180), not far from Grant Grove Village, is Kings Canyon National Park's only entrance station.

◉ Sights & Activities

Kings Canyon National Park has two developed areas with markets, lodging, showers and visitor information. **Grant Grove Village** is only 4 miles past Big Stump Entrance (in the park's west), while **Cedar Grove Village**, with a simple lodge and snack bar, is 31 miles east at the bottom of the canyon. The two are separated by the Giant Sequoia National Monument and are linked by Kings Canyon Scenic Byway (Hwy 180).

General Grant Grove   FOREST
(Map p488; [P][🚻]) This sequoia grove off Generals Hwy is nothing short of astounding. The paved half-mile **General Grant Tree Trail** is an interpretive walk that visits a number of mature sequoias, including the 27-story **General Grant Tree**. This giant holds triple honors as the world's second-largest living tree, a memorial to US soldiers killed in war, and the nation's official Christmas tree since 1926. The nearby **Fallen Monarch**, a massive, fire-hollowed trunk you can walk through, has been cabin, hotel, saloon and stables.

To escape the bustling crowds, follow the more secluded 1.5-mile **North Grove Loop**, which passes wildflower patches and bubbling creeks as it gently winds underneath a canopy of stately sequoias, evergreen pines and aromatic incense cedars.

The magnificence of this ancient sequoia grove was nationally recognized in 1890 when Congress first designated it General Grant National Park. It took another half-century for this tiny parcel to be absorbed into the much larger Kings Canyon National Park, established in 1940 to prevent damming of the Kings River.

Panoramic Point   VIEWPOINT
(Map p488) For a breathtaking view of Kings Canyon, head 2.3 miles up narrow, steep and winding Panoramic Point Rd (trailers and RVs aren't recommended), which branches off Hwy 180. Follow a short paved trail uphill from the parking lot to the viewpoint, where precipitous canyons and the snow-capped peaks of the Great Western Divide unfold below you. Snow closes the road to vehicles during winter, when it becomes a cross-country ski and snowshoe route.

OVERNIGHT BACKPACKING

For overnight backcountry trips you'll need a wilderness permit (per group $15), which is subject to a quota system in summer; outside the quota season, permits are free and available by self-registration. About 75% of spaces can be reserved, while the rest are available in person on a first-come, first-served basis. Reservations can be made from March 1 until two weeks before your trip. For details, see www.nps.gov/seki/planyourvisit/wilderness_permits.htm. There's also a dedicated wilderness desk at the **Lodgepole Visitor Center** (p495).

All ranger stations and visitor centers carry topo maps and hiking guides. Note that you need to store your food in park-approved bear-proof canisters, which can be rented at markets and visitor centers (from $5 per trip).

From Grant Grove's visitor center, follow the paved side road east, turning left after 0.1 miles, then right at the John Muir Lodge.

Redwood Canyon
FOREST

(Map p488) Over 15,000 sequoias cluster in Redwood Canyon, making it one of the world's largest groves of these giant trees. In an almost-forgotten corner of the park, this secluded forest lets you revel in the grandeur of the trees away from the crowds while you hike mostly moderate trails. What you won't find here, however, are any of California's coast-redwood trees – that's what early pioneers mistook these giant sequoias for, hence the erroneous name.

The trailheads are at the end of a 2-mile bumpy dirt road (closed in winter) that starts across from the Hume Lake/Quail Flat signed intersection on the Generals Hwy, just over 5 miles southeast of Grant Grove Village. It's a good spot for a picnic before heading out on a hike.

Cedar Grove
FOREST

(Map p488) Cedar Grove is the last outpost of civilization before you reach the rugged grandeur of the Sierra Nevada backcountry. A popular day hike climbs 4 miles one way to roaring Mist Falls (p487) from Road's End; continue uphill alongside the river 2.5 more miles to **Paradise Valley**. A favorite of birders, an easy 1.5-mile nature trail loops around **Zumwalt Meadow**, just west of Road's End. Watch for rattlesnakes, black bears and mule deer.

Mist Falls
WATERFALL

(Map p488) One of the most popular destinations for a day hike from the Cedar Grove area of Kings Canyon, Mist Falls is a fairly Edenic spot, with massive boulders and interesting rock formations. It's ideal for a picnic and a rest before you turn back or venture higher into the backcountry.

🛏 Sleeping & Eating

Accommodations (and pay showers) are offered in Grant Grove and Cedar Grove Villages. Unless otherwise stated, all campsites are first-come, first-served. Apart from the campsites, facilities in Cedar Grove Village don't start operating until mid-May.

Potential campers should keep in mind that there are great free, uncrowded and undeveloped campgrounds off Big Meadows Rd in the Sequoia National Forest. They're some of the only empty campsites in the Sierra Nevada during peak summer season. Free roadside camping is also allowed in the forest, but no campfires are allowed without a permit (available from the Grant Grove Visitor Center).

🛏 Grant Grove

Crystal Springs Campground CAMPGROUND $
(www.nps.gov/seki; tent & RV sites $18; ⊙mid-May–Sep; 🅿) At the smallest campground in the Grant Grove area, off Generals Hwy, a few dozen wooded, well-spaced sites are generally very quiet.

Princess Campground CAMPGROUND $
(Map p488; www.fs.usda.gov; Hwy 180; tent & RV sites $25-27; ⊙late May-late Sep; 🅿) Just off the scenic byway and only a few miles from Hume Lake, here almost 90 reservable sites border a pretty meadow, with sequoia stumps at the registration area. It's especially popular with RVs. Reservations essential.

Azalea Campground CAMPGROUND $
(www.nps.gov/seki; tent & RV sites $18; ⊙year-round; 🅿) Among stands of evergreens, the nicest of the 110 sites at this busy campground border a green meadow. It's off

Sequoia & Kings Canyon National Parks

Generals Hwy; General Grant Grove (p486) is a short walk downhill.

Sunset Campground CAMPGROUND $
(www.nps.gov/seki; Generals Hwy; tent & RV sites $22; ⊙ mid-May–early Sep; 🐾) Grant Grove's biggest campground is a five-minute walk from the village and has more than 150 shady sites set among evergreen trees. Ranger campfire programs in summer.

Hume Lake Campground CAMPGROUND $
(Map p488; www.fs.usda.gov; Hume Lake Rd; tent & RV sites $22; ⊙ mid-May–mid-Sep; 🐾) Almost always full yet still managing a laid-back atmosphere, this campground operated by California Land Management offers almost 75 relatively uncrowded, shady campsites, a handful with lake views. It's on the lake's northern shore. Reservations highly recommended.

Grant Grove Cabins CABIN $$
(☎ 866-807-3598; www.visitsequoia.com; Grant Grove Village; cabins $78-148; ⊙ some cabins Apr-Oct only) Set amid towering sugar pines, the accommodations here include aging tent-top shacks, rustic camp cabins with electricity and outdoor wood-burning stoves, and heated duplexes (a few wheelchair accessible) with private bathrooms and double beds. Number 9 is the lone hard-sided, free-standing 'Honeymoon Cabin' with a queen bed, and it books up fast.

John Muir Lodge LODGE $$
(☎ 866-807-3598; www.visitsequoia.com; Grant Grove Village; r from $225; 🅿🐾📶) An atmospheric building hung with historical black-and-white photographs, this is a place to lay your head and still feel like you're in the forest. Wide porches have rocking chairs, and homespun rooms, completely renovated a couple of years ago, contain rough-hewn wooden furniture and patchwork bedspreads. On chilly nights, cozy up to the big stone fireplace with a board game.

Grant Grove Market MARKET $
(Grant Grove Village; ⊙ 8am-9pm late May-early Sep, shorter hours Apr-late May & early Sep-Oct) This small grocery store has firewood, camping supplies and packaged food, with a small selection of fruit and veggies, as well as pizza by the slice (plus an ATM).

🛏 Cedar Grove

Cedar Grove's **Sentinel** (www.nps.gov/seki; Hwy 180, Cedar Grove Village; tent & RV sites $18; ⊙ late Apr–mid-Nov; 🅿🐾) campground, next

Sequoia & Kings Canyon National Parks

to the village area, is open whenever Hwy 180 is open; **Sheep Creek** (Map p488; www. nps.gov/seki; Hwy 180, Cedar Grove Village; tent & RV sites $18; ☺ late May–mid-Sep), **Canyon View** (www.nps.gov/seki; Hwy 180; tent sites $40; ☺ late May–Sep) (tent only) and **Moraine** (Map p488; www.nps.gov/seki; Hwy 180; tent & RV sites $18; ☺ late May & early Jul-early Sep) are opened as overflow when needed. These campgrounds are usually the last to fill up on busy summer weekends and are also good bets early and late in the season thanks to their comparatively low elevation (4600ft). All have flush toilets. Other facilities in the village don't start operating until mid-May.

★ **Sequoia High Sierra Camp**   CABIN $$
(Map p488; ☎866-654-2877; www.sequoiahigh sierracamp.com; tent cabins without bath incl all meals adult/child $250/150; ☺mid-Jun–mid-Sep) A mile's hike deep into the Sequoia National Forest, this off-the-grid, all-inclusive resort is nirvana for those who don't think luxury camping is an oxymoron. Canvas bungalows are spiffed up with pillow-top mattresses, feather pillows and cozy wool rugs. Restrooms and a shower house are shared. Reservations are required, and there's usually a two-night minimum stay.

Cedar Grove Lodge   LODGE $$
(☎559-565-3096; www.visitsequoia.com; 86724 Hwy 180, Cedar Grove Village; r from $130; ☺mid-May–

mid-Oct; P✆❄�♠) The only indoor sleeping option in the canyon, this riverside lodge offers 21 unexciting motel-style rooms. A recent remodel has updated some of the frumpy decor. Three ground-floor rooms with shady furnished patios have spiffy river views and kitchenettes. All rooms have phone and TV.

Cedar Grove Snack Bar   AMERICAN $
(Hwy 180, Cedar Grove Village; mains $6-15; ☺ 7:30-10:30am, 11:30am-2:30pm & 5-8pm mid-May–mid-Oct; ☏♠) This basic counter-service grill dishes up hot meals and cold deli sandwiches. Dine outside on the riverside deck. In summer barbecue gets smoked all afternoon long through dinnertime.

ℹ Information

Cedar Grove Visitor Center (☎559-565-3793; Hwy 180, Cedar Grove Village; ☺9am-5pm late May-late Sep) Small, seasonal visitor center in Cedar Grove Village selling books and maps.

Kings Canyon Visitor Center (Map p488; ☎559-565-4307; Hwy 180, Grant Grove Village; ☺9am-5pm) The park's main facility in Grant Grove Village; open year-round with a bookstore and gift shop inside.

Road's End Wilderness Permit Station (Map p488; ☺ usually 7am-3:45pm late May-late Sep) Dispenses wilderness permits, rents bear canisters and sells a few trail guides and maps. It's 6 miles east of Cedar Grove Village, at the end of Hwy 180.

❶ Getting There & Away

BUS

An option in summer only is to use **Big Trees Transit** (☑ 800-325-7433; www.bigtreestransit. com; round-trip incl park entry fee $15; ☺ late May-early Sep) to travel between Fresno and Grant Grove ($15 round-trip, 2½ hours) in Kings Canyon.

CAR & MOTORCYCLE

From the west, Kings Canyon Scenic Byway (Hwy 180) travels 53 miles east from Fresno to the Big Stump Entrance. Coming from the south, you're in for a long 46-mile drive through Sequoia National Park along sinuous Generals Hwy. Budget about two hours' driving time from the Ash Mountain Entrance to Grant Grove Village. The road to Cedar Grove Village is only open from around April or May until the first snowfall.

Sequoia National Park

Picture unzipping your tent flap and crawling out into a 'front yard' of trees as high as a 20-story building and as old as the Bible. Brew some coffee as you plan your day in this extraordinary park with its soul-sustaining forests and gigantic peaks soaring above 12,000ft.

◉ Sights

Nearly all of the park's star attractions are conveniently lined up along the Generals Hwy, which starts at the Ash Mountain Entrance and continues north into Kings Canyon. Tourist activity concentrates in the Giant Forest area and in Lodgepole Village, which has the most facilities, including a visitor center and market. The road to remote Mineral King veers off Hwy 198 in the town of Three Rivers, just south of the park's Ash Mountain Entrance.

Giant Forest   FOREST

(Map p488) Hugging the trees is a daunting prospect in this 3-sq-mile grove protecting the park's most gargantuan specimens. Among them is the world's biggest tree, the **General Sherman** (Map p488; 🏛), rocketing 275ft into the sky. Pay your respects via a short descent from the Wolverton Rd parking lot, or join the Congress Trail, a paved 2-mile pathway that takes in General Sherman, the Washington Tree (the world's second-biggest sequoia) and the see-through Telescope Tree. The 5-mile Trail of the Sequoias helps you lose the crowds.

The top destination in the park, Giant Forest was named by John Muir in 1875. At one point over 300 buildings, including campgrounds and a lodge, encroached upon the sequoias' delicate root systems. In 1997, recognizing this adverse impact, the park began to remove structures and resite parking lots. It also introduced a convenient, free seasonal visitor shuttle, significantly cutting traffic congestion and reducing the potential harm to these majestic trees.

Giant Forest Museum   MUSEUM

(Map p488; ☑ 559-565-4480; www.nps.gov/seki; cnr Generals Hwy & Crescent Meadow Rd; ☺ 9am-4:30pm; 🅿🚻) 🎟 FREE For a primer on the intriguing ecology and history of giant sequoias, this pint-sized modern museum will entertain both kids and adults. Hands-on exhibits teach about the life stages of these big trees, which can live for over 3000 years, and the fire cycle that releases their seeds and allows them to sprout on bare soil. The museum is housed in a historic 1920s building designed by Gilbert Stanley Underwood, famed architect of the Majestic Yosemite (formerly Ahwahnee) Hotel.

The museum is crushed with visitors in summer. To avoid parking headaches, take the free in-park shuttle bus. You can also try the information desk here when the Lodgepole Visitor Center is closed in winter.

Mineral King   HISTORIC SITE

(Map p488; Mineral King Rd) A scenic subalpine valley at 7500ft, Mineral King is Sequoia's backpacking mecca and a good place to find solitude. Gorgeous and gigantic, its glacially

BUFFALO SOLDIERS

Beginning in 1899, US Army infantry and cavalry troops drawn from well-respected, though segregated, African American regiments of 'Buffalo Soldiers' were sent to patrol the Sierra Nevada's new national parks. In Sequoia National Park and what was then General Grant National Park, the troops impressively built roads, created a trail system and set a high precedent as stewards of the land. These first park rangers were commanded by Captain (later Colonel) Charles Young, who at the time was the army's only African American captain. In 1903 he became the first African American acting superintendent of a US national park.

sculpted valley is ringed by massive mountains, including the jagged 12,343ft Sawtooth Peak. The area is reached via Mineral King Rd – a slinky, steep and narrow 25-mile road not suitable for RVs or speed demons; it's usually open from late May through October. Plan on spending the night unless you don't mind driving three hours round-trip.

Hiking anywhere from here involves a steep climb out of the valley along strenuous trails, so be aware of the altitude, even on short hikes. Enjoyable day hikes go to Crystal, Monarch, Mosquito and Eagle Lakes. For long trips, locals recommend the Little Five Lakes and, further along the High Sierra Trail, Kaweah Gap, surrounded by Black Kaweah, Mt Stewart and Eagle Scout Peak – all above 12,000ft.

In spring and early summer, hordes of hungry marmots terrorize parked cars at Mineral King, chewing on radiator hoses, belts and wiring to get the salt they crave after their winter hibernation. If you're thinking of going hiking during that time, you'd be well advised to protect your car by wrapping the underside with a diaper-like tarp – apparently, the marmots have learned to get around the previously recommended chicken wire.

From the 1860s to the 1890s, Mineral King witnessed heavy silver mining and lumber activity. There are remnants of shafts and stamp mills, though it takes some exploring to find them. A proposal by the Walt Disney Corporation to develop the area into a massive ski resort was thwarted when Congress annexed it to make it part of the national park in 1978. The website of the Mineral King Preservation Society (www.mineralking.org) has all kinds of info on the area, including its rustic and still-occupied historic mining cabins.

Activities

With an average elevation of about 2000ft, the foothills in the park's south are much drier and warmer than the rest of the park. Hiking here is best in spring, when the air is still cool and wildflowers put on a colorful show. Summers are buggy and muggy, but fall again brings moderate temperatures and lush foliage.

HIKING IN SEQUOIA & KINGS CANYON NATIONAL PARKS

NAME	REGION	DESCRIPTION	DIFFICULTY
Mist Falls	Cedar Grove	partly shaded forest & granite hike to a gushing waterfall	moderate
Rae Lakes Loop	Cedar Grove	passes a chain of jewel-like lakes in the heart of the Sierra Nevada high country	difficult
Zumwalt Meadow Loop	Cedar Grove	flat, meadow boardwalk loop traces the Kings River beside canyon walls	easy
Marble Falls	Foothills	lower-elevation hike parallels a river canyon to a thundering cascade	moderate
Big Trees Trail	Giant Forest	paved, kid-friendly interpretive trail circling a sequoia-bordered forest meadow	easy
Crescent Meadow Loop	Giant Forest	beautiful subalpine meadow ringed by giant sequoias & summer wildflowers	easy
General Sherman Tree to Moro Rock	Giant Forest	huge sequoias, peaceful meadows & the pinnacle of Moro Rock	moderate
High Sierra Trail to Bearpaw Meadow	Giant Forest	gorgeous sequoia-grove & canyon-view hike crossing mountain streams	difficult
Moro Rock	Giant Forest	steep granite dome ascent for panoramic peak & canyon views	easy
General Grant Tree Trail	Grant Grove	paved interpretive loop through a giant-sequoia grove	easy
Tokopah Falls	Lodgepole	one of Sequoia's largest, most easily accessed scenic waterfalls	easy
Monarch Lakes	Mineral King	high-country hike to two alpine lakes at base of Sawtooth Peak	difficult

Swimming holes abound along the Marble Fork of the Kaweah River, especially near Potwisha Campground. Be careful, though – the currents can be deadly, especially when the river is swollen from the spring runoff.

🛏 Sleeping & Eating

Wuksachi Lodge (p494) is the only accommodation in the main section of the park proper. Two other lodges are in the adjoining Sequoia National Forest, and Grant Grove Village in Kings Canyon has a couple of options. Three Rivers, just outside the Ash Mountain Entrance, has the widest choice of accommodations. Otherwise, camping is the highly recommended way to go.

🛏 Generals Highway

A handful of campgrounds line the highway and rarely fill up, although space may get tight on holiday weekends. Those in the foothills area in the south of the park are best in spring and fall when the higher elevations are still chilly, but they get hot and buggy in summer. Unless noted, sites are available on a first-come, first-served basis. Free dispersed camping is possible in the Giant Sequoia National Monument (p486). Stop by a visitor center or ranger station for details or a fire permit. Lodgepole Village (p495) and Stony Creek Lodge (p494) have pay showers.

Stony Creek Campground CAMPGROUND $
(Map p488; www.fs.usda.gov; Generals Hwy; tent & RV sites $24; ☉mid-May–late Sep; 🐾) A mile north of the national-park boundary near Stony Creek Lodge, this forest campground operated by California Land Management fills with families in summer. Its nearly 50 sites are spacious and shady.

Lodgepole Campground CAMPGROUND $
(Map p488; www.nps.gov/seki; Lodgepole Rd; tent & RV sites $22; ☉late Apr–Nov; 🐾) Closest to the Giant Forest area, with over 200 closely packed sites, this place fills quickly because of its proximity to Kaweah River swimming holes and Lodgepole Village amenities. The 16 walk-in sites are more private. Reservations

DURATION	ROUND-TRIP DISTANCE	ELEVATION CHANGE	FEATURES	FACILITIES
3-5hr	8 miles	+800ft	view; waterfall	restrooms; drinking water; ranger station
5 days	40 miles	+7000ft	wildlife-watching; view; waterfall	restrooms; drinking water; ranger station; backcountry campsite
1hr	1.5 miles	+100ft	wildlife-watching; view; great for families	
3-4hr	7 miles	+2000ft	view; waterfall	restrooms; drinking water
45min	1.2 miles	+100ft	wildlife-watching; great for families	restrooms; drinking water; transportation to trailhead
1hr	1.6 miles	+200ft	wildlife-watching; great for families	restrooms; drinking water; transportation to trailhead
2½-4hr	6 miles	+1600ft	wildlife-watching; view; rock climbing	restrooms; drinking water; transportation to trailhead
2 days	22 miles	+2200ft	wildlife-watching; view	restrooms; drinking water; ranger station; backcountry campsite
40min	0.5 miles	+300ft	view; great for families; rock climbing	transportation to trailhead
30min	0.5 miles	+100ft	view; great for families	restrooms; drinking water
2hr	3.5 miles	+500ft	wildlife-watching; view; great for families; waterfall	restrooms; drinking water; transportation to trailhead
4-6hr	8.5 miles	+2700ft	wildlife-watching; view	restrooms; drinking water; backcountry campsite; swimming

YOSEMITE & THE SIERRA NEVADA SEQUOIA NATIONAL PARK

> **DON'T MISS**
>
> ## CRYSTAL CAVE
>
> Discovered in 1918 by two parks employees who were going fishing, this unique **cave** (www.explorecrystalcave.com; Crystal Cave Rd; tours adult/child/youth from $16/5/8; ⊙May-Sep; P ⚃) was carved by an underground river and has marble formations estimated to be 10,000 years old. Stalactites hang like daggers from the cave ceiling, and milky-white marble formations take the shape of ethereal curtains, domes, columns and shields. The cave is also a unique biodiverse habitat for spiders, bats and tiny aquatic insects that are found nowhere else on earth.
>
> Tickets for the 50-minute introductory tour are only sold online in advance or, during October and November, at the Giant Forest Museum and Foothills Visitor Center, not at the cave. Bring a jacket.

available (and strongly recommended) from late May through late September.

Potwisha Campground CAMPGROUND $
(Map p488; www.nps.gov/seki; Generals Hwy; tent & RV sites $22; ⊙year-round; ⚃) Popular campground with decent shade near swimming spots on the Kaweah River. It's 3 miles northeast of the Ash Mountain Entrance, with 42 sites. Reservations (highly recommended) taken May through September.

Dorst Creek Campground CAMPGROUND $
(Map p488; www.nps.gov/seki; Generals Hwy; tent & RV sites $22; ⊙mid-Jun–early Sep; ⚃) Big and busy campground with more than 200 sites. The quieter back sites are for tents only, while the front loops can fill with RVs. It's about 7 miles northwest of Wuksachi Village. No reservations accepted.

Buckeye Flat Campground CAMPGROUND $
(Map p488; www.nps.gov/seki; tent sites $22; ⊙late Mar-late Sep; ⚃) This tent-only campground is off Generals Hwy in an open stand of oaks, about 6 miles northeast of the Ash Mountain Entrance, down a winding road that's off-limits to RVs and trailers. Reservations accepted (and strongly advised) between late May and late September.

Stony Creek Lodge LODGE $$
(Map p488; ☑reservations 559-565-3388, reservations 877-828-1440; www.sequoia-kingscanyon.

com; 65569 Generals Hwy; r $179-199; ⊙mid-May–early Oct; ☎) About halfway between Grant Grove Village and Giant Forest, this wood-and-stone lodge has a big river-rock fireplace in its lobby and a dozen aging motel rooms with telephones and TVs. Laundry facilities and coin-operated showers are available for nonguests.

Wuksachi Lodge LODGE $$
(Map p488; ☑information 866-807-3598, reservations 317-324-0753; www.visitsequoia.com; 64740 Wuksachi Way; r $215-290; P ⊙ ☎ ⚃) Built in 1999, Wuksachi Lodge is the park's most upscale option. But don't get too excited: the wood-paneled atrium lobby has an inviting stone fireplace and forest views, but the motel-style rooms are fairly generic, with coffeemakers, minifridges, oak furniture and thin walls. The location near Lodgepole Village, however, can't be beat, and staff members are friendly and accommodating.

Rooms, many of which were renovated in the winter and spring of 2017, are spread out over three three-story buildings a short walk from the lobby and restaurant and from each building's respective parking lot. If you have a lot of gear, it's best to ask for help lugging things to your room.

🛏 Backcountry

Bearpaw High Sierra Camp CABIN $$
(Map p488; ☑reservations 317-324-0753; www.visitsequoia.com; per person incl breakfast & dinner $175; ⊙usually mid-Jun–mid-Sep) An 11.3-mile hike east of Crescent Meadow on the High Sierra Trail, this canvas-tent village at 7800ft is ideal for exploring the backcountry without lugging your own gear. Rates include showers, dinner and breakfast, as well as bedding and towels. Bookings start at 7am PST every January 2 and places sell out almost immediately, though you can always check for last-minute cancellations.

🛏 Mineral King

Mineral King's two pretty campgrounds, **Atwell Mill** (Map p488; www.nps.gov/seki; Mineral King Rd; tent sites $12; ⊙late May-late Oct; ⚃) and **Cold Springs** (Map p488; www.nps.gov/seki; Mineral King Rd; tent sites $12; ⊙late May-late Oct; ⚃), often fill up on summer weekends. Pay showers are available at the rustic **Silver City Mountain Resort** (Map p488; ☑559-561-3223; www.silvercityresort.com; Mineral King Rd; cabins with/without bath from

$175/110, chalets from $250; ☺ late May-late Oct; 🕿), the only food-and-lodging option anywhere near these parts.

Three Rivers

Named for the nearby convergence of three Kaweah River forks, Three Rivers is a friendly small town populated mostly by retirees and artsy newcomers. The town's main drag, Sierra Dr (Hwy 198), is sparsely lined with motels, eateries and shops.

Sequoia Village Inn CABIN, COTTAGE $$
(Map p488; ☎559-561-3652; www.sequoiavillageinn. com; 45971 Sierra Dr; d $155-319; ❄🕿🌊🐕) These 10 cottages, cabins and chalets (most with kitchens and the rest with kitchenettes) border the park and are great for families or groups. Most have outdoor woodsy decks and BBQs; the largest can sleep 12 people.

Buckeye Tree Lodge MOTEL $$
(Map p488; ☎559-561-5900; www.buckeyetree lodge.com; 46000 Sierra Dr; d $159; ❄🕿🌊🐕) 🖋 Sit out on your grassy back patio or perch on the balcony and watch the river ease through a maze of boulders. Fairly generic motel rooms, one with a kitchenette, feel airy. The outdoor picnic area has BBQ grills.

ℹ Information

Foothills Visitor Center (Map p488; ☎559-565-4212; 47050 Generals Hwy; ☺8am-4:30pm) Just past the Ash Mountain Entrance; a good place to stop, get your bearings and check out campground availability further up the road.

Lodgepole Village This complex includes grocery store, gift shop, snack bar, visitor center, and coin-operated showers and laundry facilities.

Lodgepole Visitor Center (☎559-565-4436; Lodgepole Village; ☺7am-5pm late Apr-early Oct, to 7pm peak season) Often less than helpful or informative; non-NPS staff members sell books and maps, and rangers issue wilderness permits. Off the Generals Hwy.

Mineral King Ranger Station (Map p488; ☎559-565-3768; Mineral King Rd; ☺8am-4pm late May-late Sep) Almost 24 miles east of Three Rivers; small, seasonal ranger station issuing wilderness permits, renting bear canisters and selling a few books and maps.

ℹ Getting There & Around

BUS

Sequoia Shuttle (☎877-287-4453; www. sequoiashuttle.com; ☺late May-late Sep) buses run five times daily between Visalia and the Giant Forest Museum ($15, 2½ hours) via Three Rivers; reservations required. Cost includes park admission fee.

CAR & MOTORCYCLE

Hwy 198 runs north from Visalia through Three Rivers past Mineral King Rd to the Ash Mountain Entrance. Beyond here the road continues as the Generals Hwy, a narrow and windy road snaking all the way into Kings Canyon National Park, where it joins the Kings Canyon Scenic Byway (Hwy 180) near the western Big Stump Entrance. Vehicles over 22ft long may have trouble negotiating the steep road with its many hairpin curves. Budget about one hour to drive from the entrance to the Giant Forest/Lodgepole area and another hour from there to Grant Grove Village in Kings Canyon.

There are no gas stations in the park.

EASTERN SIERRA

Cloud-dappled hills and sun-streaked mountaintops dabbed with snow typify the landscape of the Eastern Sierra, where slashing peaks – many over 14,000ft – rush abruptly upward from the arid expanses of the Great Basin and Mojave Deserts. It's a dramatic juxtaposition that makes for a potent cocktail of scenery. Pine forests, lush meadows, ice-blue lakes, simmering hot springs and glacier-gouged canyons are only some of the beautiful sights you'll find in this region.

The Eastern Sierra Scenic Byway, officially known as Hwy 395, runs the entire length of the range. Turnoffs dead-ending at the foot of the mountains deliver you to pristine wilderness and countless trails, including the famous Pacific Crest Trail, John Muir Trail and main Mt Whitney Trail. The most important portals are the towns of Bridgeport, Mammoth Lakes, Bishop and Lone Pine. Note that in winter, when traffic thins, many facilities are closed.

ℹ Information

Check out www.thesierraweb.com for area events and links to local visitor information, and *Sierra Wave* (www.sierrawave.net) for regional news.

ℹ Getting There & Around

The Eastern Sierra is easiest to explore under your own steam. Keep in mind that mountain roads close in winter, as do most of the passes that take you over the Sierras from east to west.

BUS

Eastern Sierra Transit Authority (☑800-922-1930, 760-872-1901; www.estransit.com) buses make a round-trip between Lone Pine and Reno ($59, six hours) on Monday, Tuesday, Thursday and Friday, stopping at all Hwy 395 towns in between. Fares depend on distance, and reservations are recommended. There's also an express bus between Mammoth and Bishop ($7, one hour, three times daily) that operates Monday to Friday.

In summer, connect to Yosemite via **YARTS bus** (p480) in Mammoth Lakes or Lee Vining.

Mono Lake Region

Bridgeport

Barely three blocks long, set amid an open high valley and in view of the peaks of Sawtooth Ridge, Bridgeport flaunts classic Western flair with charming old storefronts and a homey ambience. Most everything shuts down or cuts back its hours for the brutal winters, but the rest of the year the town is a magnet for anglers, hikers, climbers and hot-spring devotees.

◉ Sights & Activities

Mono County Courthouse   HISTORIC BUILDING
(cnr Main & School Sts; ☺9am-5pm Mon-Fri) The gavel has been dropped since 1880 at this courthouse, an all-white italianate dreamboat surrounded by a gracious lawn and a wrought-iron fence. On the street behind it, look for the Old County Jail, a spartan facility fashioned with iron latticework doors and stone walls 2ft thick. Unlucky inmates overnighted in its six cells from 1883 until 1964.

Mono County Museum   MUSEUM
(☑760-932-5281; www.monocomuseum.org; Emigrant St; adult/child $2/1; ☺9am-4pm Tue-Sat Jun–Sep) In an 1880 schoolhouse, this museum has mining artifacts on display from all the local ghost towns, plus a room of fine Paiute baskets.

★ Travertine Hot Spring   HOT SPRINGS
(Map p498) FREE A bit south of town, head here to watch a panoramic Sierra sunset from three hot pools set amid impressive rock formations. To get here, turn east on Jack Sawyer Rd just before the ranger station, then follow the dirt road uphill for about 1 mile.

Ken's Sporting Goods   FISHING
(☑760-932-7707; www.kenssport.com; 258 Main St; ☺7am-7pm Mon-Thu, to 8pm Fri & Sat mid-Apr–Oct, 9am-4pm rest of year) Stop by Ken's for information and fishing gear. If you're trolling for trout, try the Bridgeport Reservoir and the East Walker River.

🛏 Sleeping & Eating

Redwood Motel   MOTEL $
(☑760-932-7060; www.redwoodmotel.net; 425 Main St; d $89-99; ☺Apr-Nov; ❀🐾📶🐕) A bucking bronco, an ox in a Hawaiian shirt and other wacky farm-animal sculptures provide a cheerful welcome at this little kitchenette motel. Rooms are homey and simply furnished, and your dog-friendly host is super helpful in dispensing local-area tips.

Bodie Victorian Hotel   HISTORIC HOTEL $
(☑760-616-1977; www.bodievictorianhotel.com; 85 Main St; r $60-125; ☺May-Oct; ❀📶) To experience an 1800s boarding house in all its rickety glory, try a room in this building transplanted from the abandoned mining town of Bodie (p497). It can feel rundown despite the great-great-grandmother-style antiques, bold Victorian wallpaper and striking bordello accoutrements. If no one's here, poke your head into the Sportsmens Bar & Grill next door to rustle up an employee.

❶ Information

Bridgeport Ranger Station & Visitor Center (Map p498; ☑760-932-7070; www.fs.usda. gov/htnf; Hwy 395; ☺8am-4:30pm daily Jun–mid-Sep, 8am-12:30pm & 1-4:30pm Mon-Fri mid-May–May) The local office for maps, information on the Humboldt-Toiyabe Forest (Map p498; www.fs.usda.gov) (in both California and Nevada) and Hoover Wilderness (Map p498; www.fs.usda.gov) permits.

Twin Lakes

Eager anglers line the shoreline of Twin Lakes, a gorgeous duo of basins cradled by the fittingly named Sawtooth Ridge. The area's famous for its fishing – especially since some lucky guy bagged the state's largest ever brown trout here in 1987 (it weighed in at a hefty 26lb). Lower Twin is quieter, while Upper Twin allows boating and waterskiing. Other activities include mountain biking and, of course, hiking in the Hoover Wilderness Area and on into the eastern, lake-riddled reaches of Yosemite National Park.

The main trailhead is at the end of Twin Lakes Rd just past Annett's Mono Village; weekly overnight parking is $10 per vehicle. From here, hikers can set off along Robinson Creek for adventures in the stunning **Hoover Wilderness** and overnight backpacking trips (wilderness permit required from the Bridgeport Ranger Station & Visitor Center (p496)) into northeastern Yosemite. The day hike to lovely **Barney Lake** (8 miles round-trip) takes in magnificent views of jagged granite spires in **Little Slide Canyon** – where rock climbers detour to scale a fierce wall called the Incredible Hulk – and steep boulder rockslides on the ridge to the north.

For a hike with great views of Twin Lakes, go south from Annett's on the **Horse Creek trail**, which soon leads to the cascades of **Horsetail Falls**. It continues up to skirt the wilderness boundary and then descends back to Twin Lakes on the **Cattle Creek trail**. Loop back along the lake for 7.5 miles in total. In *Dharma Bums*, Beat author Jack Kerouac describes an ascent he made from Horse Creek Canyon to nearby Matterhorn Peak (12,300ft) with poet Gary Snyder.

A stroll down a hillside brings you to the out-of-the-way (though it can still get crowded) **Buckeye Hot Spring** (Map p498). Water emerges piping hot and cools as it trickles down into several rock pools right by the side of lively Buckeye Creek, which is handy for taking a cooling dip. One pool is partially tucked into a small cave made from a rock overhang. Clothing is optional.

USFS campgrounds (☑800-444-7275; www.recreation.gov; tent & RV sites $17-22; ☺late Apr–Sep) in the Humboldt-Toiyabe National Forest are generally open from late April to early October. You can also set up tents for free in undeveloped spots along both sides of nearby Buckeye Creek.

Buckeye Campground (Map p498; tent & RV sites $18; ☺May–mid-Oct), west of Bridgeport and north of Twin Lakes in the Humboldt-Toiyabe National Forest, has tables, fire grates and toilets, but you'll need to bring or treat water. Take Twin Lakes Rd from Bridgeport for 7 miles before turning right onto Buckeye Rd. It's another 3 miles and then left at a fork to reach the campground.

Bodie State Historic Park

At **Bodie State Historic Park** (Map p498; ☑760-647-6445; www.parks.ca.gov/bodie; Hwy 270; adult/child $8/4; ☺9am-6pm mid-Mar–Oct, to 4pm Nov–mid-Mar; [P] [🐾]), a gold-rush ghost town is preserved in a state of 'arrested decay.' Weathered buildings sit frozen in time on a dusty, windswept plain. To get there, head east for 13 miles (the last three unpaved) on Hwy 270, about 7 miles south of Bridgeport. The access road is often closed by snow in winter.

WILDERNESS PERMITS FOR THE EASTERN SIERRA

➡ Free wilderness permits for overnight camping are required year-round in the Ansel Adams, John Muir, Golden Trout and Hoover Wilderness areas.

➡ For the first three areas, trailhead quotas are in effect from May to October; about 60% of the quota may be reserved online at www.recreation.gov for a $5 fee (per person).

➡ From November to April, you can pick up permits at most ranger stations. If you find a station closed, look for self-issue permits outside the office.

➡ Wilderness permits for the Inyo National Forest can be picked up in Lone Pine, Bishop, Mammoth Lakes or its Mono Basin ranger stations.

➡ For information, call the **Inyo National Forest Wilderness Permit Office** (p514) in Bishop.

➡ Yosemite's Tuolumne Meadows Wilderness Center can also issue permits for trips from Saddlebag Lake.

➡ Permits for the Hoover Wilderness that depart from the Humboldt-Toiyabe National Forest (seasonal quotas on some trails) are issued at the **Bridgeport Ranger Station & Visitor Center** (p496).

➡ The forums on High Sierra Topix (www.highsierratopix.com) are an excellent resource for planning trips.

Mono Lake Area

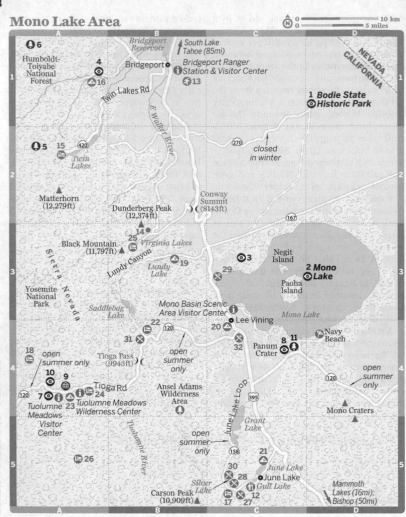

Gold was first discovered here in 1859, and within 20 years the place grew from a rough mining camp to an even rougher boomtown with a population of 10,000 and a reputation for unbridled lawlessness. Fights and murders took place almost daily, the violence no doubt fueled by liquor dispensed in the town's 65 saloons, some of which did double duty as brothels, gambling halls or opium dens. The hills disgorged some $35 million worth of gold and silver in the 1870s and '80s, but when production plummeted, so did the population, and eventually the town was abandoned to the elements.

Peering through the windows of the 200 weather-beaten buildings, you'll see stocked stores, furnished homes, a schoolhouse with desks and books, and workshops filled with tools. The jail is still there, as are the fire station, churches, a bank vault and many other buildings.

The former Miners' Union Hall now houses a museum and visitor center. Rangers conduct free general tours. In summer, they also offer tours of the landscape and the cemetery; call for details. The second Saturday of August is **Friends of Bodie Day** (www.bodiefoundation.org), with

Mono Lake Area

stagecoach rides, history presentations and lots of devotees in period costumes.

Lee Vining

Hwy 395 skirts the western bank of Mono Lake, rolling into the gateway town of Lee Vining, where you can eat, sleep, gas up (for a pretty penny) and catch Hwy 120 to Yosemite National Park when the road's open. A superb base for exploring Mono Lake, Lee Vining is only 12 miles (about a 30-minute drive) from Yosemite's Tioga Pass entrance. **Lee Vining Canyon** is a popular location for **ice climbing**.

The **Upside-Down House** (Map p498; www.monobasinhistory.org; 129 Mattly Ave; donation $2; ⊙10am-4pm Thu-Mon late May–early Oct), a kooky tourist attraction created by silent-film actress Nellie Bly O'Bryan, is worth a quick look. Originally situated along Tioga Rd, it now resides in a park in front of the tiny **Mono Basin Historical Society Museum**. To find it, turn east on 1st St and go one block to Mattley Ave.

🛏 Sleeping

Lodging rates drop when Tioga Pass is closed. Psst, campers: **Mono Vista RV Park** (Map p498; ☑760-647-6401; www.monovistarv park.net; 57 Beaver Lane; tent/RV sites $27/35; ⊙9am-6pm Apr-Oct) has the closest pay showers to Tuolumne Meadows. Most of the options in town are fairly ordinary, but the Tioga Pass Resort (p499) is in an extraordinary setting, way up Hwy 120 near Yosemite. Mammoth Lakes, with an abundance of accommodations, is only 31 miles south.

El Mono Motel   MOTEL **$**
(☑760-647-6310; www.elmonomotel.com; cnr Hwy 395 & 3rd St; r $75-99; ⊙mid-May–Oct; 🛜) Grab a board game or soak up some mountain sunshine in this friendly, flower-ringed place attached to an excellent cafe (p500). In operation since 1927, it's often booked solid, and each of its 11 simple rooms (a few share bathrooms) is unique, decorated with vibrant and colorful art and fabrics.

★**Tioga Pass Resort**   CABIN **$$**
(Map p498; www.tiogapassresort.com; Hwy 120; d $145, cabins $180-280; ⊙Jun-Sep) Situated at a whopping 9550ft and only 2 miles east of Tioga Pass, this is as close to a Yosemite experience as you can get without staying in the park. Founded in 1914, this high-country resort attracts a fiercely loyal clientele to its quiet, comfortable, woodsy cabins (most with full kitchen) beside Lee Vining Creek. Walk-ins can sometimes snag a cancellation.

The thimble-sized **cafe** (mains lunch $10-11.50, dinner $22; ⊙7am-9pm Jun-Sep; 🍴) serves excellent fare all day at a few tables and a broken horseshoe counter, with a house pastry chef concocting dozens of freshly made desserts.

At the time of writing, record winter snowfall had caused the resort to close temporarily. Check the website for updates.

Yosemite Gateway Motel   MOTEL **$$**

(📞760-647-6467; www.yosemitegatewaymotel.com; 51340 Hwy 395; r $159-229; ❄️🛜) Think vistas. This is the only motel on the eastern side of the highway, and the views of Mono Lake and surroundings from some of the rooms are phenomenal. The somewhat-tired rooms have comfortable beds with thick duvets and big bathrooms.

Murphey's Motel   MOTEL **$$**

(📞760-647-6316; www.murpheysyosemite.com; 51493 Hwy 395; r $80-150; ❄️🛜🐾) At the northern end of town, this large, two-story, log-cabin-style place offers comfy rooms with all mod cons. It's one of the few hotels in Lee Vining open year-round. A little cafe serving pastries and espresso drinks is attached.

Eating

Latte Da Coffee Cafe   CAFE **$**

(cnr Hwy 395 & 3rd St; sandwiches $6; ⏰7am-8pm; 🛜) Located at the El Mono Motel (p499), this cafe is a charming spot for sandwiches, scones and excellent espresso drinks. The cozy wood-floored interior is bested by the front porch and tiny backyard garden.

⭐ **Whoa Nellie Deli**   AMERICAN **$$**

(Map p498; 📞760-647-1088; www.whoanelliedeli.com; Tioga Gas Mart, 22 Vista Point Rd; mains $9-19; ⏰6:30am-8:30pm late Apr-Oct; 🐾) Years after its famed chef moved on to Toomey's (p506) at Mammoth Lakes, this Mobil-gas-station restaurant off Hwy 120 is still, surprisingly, a damn good place to eat. Stop in for delicious burgers, fish tacos, wild-buffalo meatloaf and other tasty morsels, and live bands some nights.

EBBETTS PASS SCENIC BYWAY

For outdoor fanatics, a scenic 61-mile section of Hwys 4 and 89 called the Ebbetts Pass Scenic Byway (www.scenic4.org) is a road trip through paradise. Heading northeast from **Arnold**, gaze up at the giant sequoias of **Calaveras Big Trees State Park** (p419) and in winter stop at the family-friendly ski resort of **Bear Valley** (📞209-753-2301; www.bear-valley.com; 2280 Hwy 207, Bear Valley; ski-lift ticket adult/6-12yr/13-19yr $79/32/68; ⏰hours vary end Nov-May; 🐾). Nearby is the **Bear Valley Adventure Company** (📞209-753-2834; www.bearvalleyxc.com; 1 Bear Valley Rd, Bear Valley; ⏰hours vary; 🐾), a one-stop shop for other outdoor adventures in the area. Continuing east, the stunningly beautiful **Lake Alpine** is skirted by slabs of granite, has several great beaches, and boasts excellent water sports, fishing and hiking. A handful of campgrounds line the lakefront, as well as the rustic **Lake Alpine Resort** (📞209-753-6350; www.lakealpineresort.com; 4000 Hwy 4, Bear Valley; tent cabins $70-80, cabins with kitchenette or kitchen $170-280; ⏰May-Oct; 🅿️❄️🐾).

The next stretch is the most dramatic, when the narrow highway continues past picturesque **Mosquito Lake** and the **Pacific Grade Summit** (8060ft) before slaloming through historic Hermit Valley and finally winding up and over the 8730ft summit of **Ebbetts Pass**. North on Hwy 89 and just west of **Markleeville**, you can visit the two developed pools and seasonal campground at **Grover Hot Springs State Park** (📞530-694-2249, 530-694-2248; www.parks.ca.gov; 3415 Hot Springs Rd, Markleeville; pool adult/child $10/5; ⏰hours vary; 🐾). It's worth returning to Markleeville for dinner at the **Stone Fly** (📞530-694-9999; www.stoneflyrestaurant.com; 14821 Hwy 89, Markleeville; mains $15-24; ⏰5-9pm Fri-Sun) restaurant.

The relatively little-known **Hope Valley Wildlife Area** (📞916-358-2900; www.wildlife.ca.gov; 🅿️) 🆓, a gorgeous reserve of meadows, streams and forests ringed by high Sierra peaks, is not far northwest of Markleeville. **Sorensen's Resort** (📞800-423-9949, 530-694-2203; www.sorensensresort.com; 14255 Hwy 88, Hope Valley; r $145-210, cabins $145-325; 🅿️❄️🐾), with a variable collection of cabins and rooms, makes an excellent base camp.

From San Francisco, it's a three-hour drive east to Arnold, via Hwy 108 and Hwy 49. Ebbetts Pass closes after the first major snowfall and doesn't reopen until June, but Hwy 4 is usually plowed from the west as far as Bear Valley.

VIRGINIA LAKES

South of Bridgeport, Hwy 395 gradually arrives at its highest point, Conway Summit (8143ft), where you'll be whipping out your camera to capture the awe-inspiring panorama of Mono Lake, backed by the Mono Craters, and June and Mammoth Mountains.

Also at the top is the turnout for **Virginia Lakes Road**, which parallels Virginia Creek for about 6 miles to a cluster of lakes flanked by Dunderberg Peak (12,374ft) and Black Mountain (11,797ft). A trailhead at the end of the road gives access to the Hoover Wilderness Area and the **Pacific Crest Trail**. The trail continues down Cold Canyon through to Yosemite National Park. With a car shuttle, the excellent 10.5-mile hike to **Green Creek** visits a bevy of perfect lakes; an extra mile (each way) takes you to windswept – check out the mammoth tree blowdown! – **Summit Lake** at the Yosemite border. Check with the folks at the Virginia Lakes Resort, opened in 1923, for maps and tips about specific trails.

Nearby, **Virginia Lakes Pack Outfit** (Map p498; ☑ 760-937-0326; www.virginialakes. com; half-/full-day rides $90/150) offers horseback-riding trips.

★**Mono Inn** AMERICAN $$$
(Map p498; ☑ 760-647-6581; www.themonoinn. com; 55620 Hwy 395; mains $20-38; ☺ 5-9pm Tue-Sat, to 8pm Sun Apr–mid-Nov) A restored 1922 lodge owned by the family of photographer Ansel Adams, this elegant yet casual lakefront restaurant makes everything from scratch and has correspondingly delectable views. Stop in for the occasional live band on the creekside terrace. It's located about 5 miles north of Lee Vining.

Mono Lake

North America's second-oldest lake is a quiet and mysterious expanse of deep blue water whose glassy surface reflects jagged Sierra peaks, young volcanic cones and the unearthly tufa (too-fah) towers that make the lake so distinctive. Jutting from the water like drip sand castles, tufas form when calcium bubbles up from subterranean springs and combines with carbonate in the alkaline lake waters.

In *Roughing It*, Mark Twain described **Mono Lake** (Map p498; www.monolake.org) as California's 'dead sea.' Hardly. The brackish water teems with buzzing alkali flies and brine shrimp, both considered delicacies by dozens of migratory bird species that return here year after year. So do about 85% of the state's nesting population of California gulls, which take over the lake's volcanic islands from April to August. Mono Lake has also been at the heart of an environmental controversy, lasting decades, that involves the diversion of the lake's freshwater feeder streams to Los Angeles' drinking-water supply.

◎ Sights & Activities

South Tufa NATURE RESERVE
(Map p498; adult/child $3/free) Tufa spires ring Mono Lake, but the biggest grove is on the southern rim, with a mile-long interpretive trail. Ask about ranger-led tours at the Mono Basin Scenic Area Visitor Center (p502). To get to the reserve, head south from Lee Vining on Hwy 395 for 6 miles, then east on Hwy 120 for 5 miles to the dirt road leading to a parking lot.

Navy Beach BEACH
The best place for swimming in Mono Lake is at Navy Beach. It's also the best place to put in canoes or kayaks.

Panum Crater NATURAL FEATURE
(Map p498) Rising above southern shore of Mono Lake, Panum Crater is the youngest (about 640 years old), smallest and most accessible of the craters that string south toward Mammoth Mountain. A panoramic trail circles the crater rim (about 30 to 45 minutes), and a short but steep 'plug trail' puts you at the crater's core. A dirt road leads to the trailhead from Hwy 120, about 3 miles east of the junction with Hwy 395.

Black Point Fissures NATURAL FEATURE
(Map p498) On the north shore of Mono Lake are the Black Point Fissures, narrow crags that opened when a lava mass cooled and contracted about 13,000 years ago. Access is from three places: east of Mono Lake County Park, from the western shore off Hwy 395, or south off Hwy 167. Check at the Mono Basin Scenic Area Visitor Center (p502) for specific directions.

YOSEMITE & THE SIERRA NEVADA MONO LAKE REGION

LUNDY LAKE

After Conway Summit, Hwy 395 twists down steeply into the Mono Basin. Before reaching Mono Lake, Lundy Lake Rd meanders west of the highway for about 5 miles to Lundy Lake. This is a gorgeous spot, especially in spring, when wildflowers carpet the canyon along Mill Creek, or in fall when the landscape is brightened by colorful foliage. Before reaching the lake, the road skirts first-come, first-served **Lundy Canyon Campground** (Map p498; tent & RV sites $16; ☺ late Apr-Oct; ❀), with vault toilets; there's water available, but it must be boiled or treated. At the end of the lake, there's a ramshackle resort on the site of an 1880s mining town, plus a small store and boat rentals.

Past the resort, a dirt road leads into Lundy Canyon; after 2 miles, it dead-ends at the trailhead for the Hoover Wilderness Area. A fantastic 1.5-mile hike follows Mill Creek to the 200ft-high **Lundy Falls**. Industrious beavers define the landscape along the trail, with gnawed aspens scattered on the ground and a number of huge dams barricading the creek. Ambitious types can continue on via Lundy Pass to **Saddlebag Lake** and the **Twenty Lakes Basin**, though the final climb out of the canyon uses a very steep talus chute.

ⓘ Information

Mono Basin Scenic Area Visitor Center (Map p498; ☑ 760-647-3044; www.fs.usda.gov/inyo; 1 Visitor Center Dr; ☺ generally 8am-5pm Apr-Nov; ❀) Half a mile north of Lee Vining, this center has maps, interpretive displays, Inyo National Forest wilderness permits, bear-canister rentals, a bookstore and a 20-minute movie about Mono Lake.

June Lake Loop

Under the shadow of massive Carson Peak (10,909ft), the stunning 16-mile June Lake Loop (Hwy 158) meanders through a picture-perfect horseshoe canyon, past the relaxed resort town of **June Lake** and four sparkling, fish-rich lakes: Grant, Silver, Gull and June. It's especially scenic in fall, when the basin is ablaze with golden aspens. Catch the loop a few miles south of Lee Vining.

🏃 Activities

June Lake is backed by the Ansel Adams Wilderness area, which runs into Yosemite National Park. Hiking and horse-riding trips into the backcountry are the equal of any in the Sierra Nevada.

June Mountain Ski Area   SKIING
(Map p498; ☑ 888-586-3686, 24hr snow info 760-934-2224; www.junemountain.com; lift tickets adult/13-18yr & senior/under 13yr $72/48/free; ☺ 8:30am-4pm; ❀) Winter fun concentrates in this area, which is smaller and less crowded than nearby Mammoth Mountain (p504) – Mammoth lift passes can be used here – and perfect for beginner and intermediate skiers. Some 35 trails crisscross 500 acres of

terrain served by seven lifts, including two high-speed quads. Boarders can get their adrenaline flowing at three terrain parks with a kick-ass super pipe.

Ernie's Tackle & Ski Shop   SPORTS & OUTDOORS
(☑ 760-648-7756; 2604 Hwy 158; ☺ 6am-7pm) One of the most established outfitters in June Lake village.

🛌 Sleeping & Eating

June Lake Campground   CAMPGROUND $
(☑ 800-444-7275; www.recreation.gov; tent & RV sites $22; ☺ mid-Apr–Oct; ❀) On the June Lake shoreline and a short walk from town. Accepts reservations.

Oh! Ridge Campground   CAMPGROUND $
(Map p498; ☑ 800-444-7275; www.recreation.gov; tent & RV sites $27; ☺ mid-Apr–Oct; ❀) Large open-air campground popular with families because of its access to a swimming beach on June Lake. Accepts reservations.

June Lake Motel   MOTEL $$
(☑ 760-648-7547; www.junelakemotel.com; 2716 Hwy 158; r with kitchenette/kitchen $115/165; ❀@🛜❀) Enormous rooms – most with full kitchens – catch delicious mountain breezes and sport attractive light-wood furniture. There's a fish-cleaning sink and barbecues.

Silver Lake Resort   CABIN $$
(Map p498; ☑ 760-648-7525; www.silverlakeresort.net; 6957 Hwy 158; cabins $131-212; ☺ late Apr–mid-Oct) Across the road from Silver Lake and astride Alger Creek, this sweet cabin compound opened in 1916 and has a duck pond and boat rentals in addition to almost 20 rustic cabins with full kitchens. Its tiny

old-time **cafe** (mains $8-11; ⊙7am-2pm; P) displays the requisite antique winter-sports equipment and serves diner fare like burgers, sandwiches and grilled chicken; it's most popular for excellent big breakfasts.

Double Eagle Resort & Spa   RESORT $$$
(Map p498; ✓760-648-7004; www.doubleeagle. com; 5587 Hwy 158; r $249, cabins $369; ✿❄❅) A swanky spot for these parts, Double Eagle has sleek two-bedroom log cabins and balconied hotel rooms that lack no comfort. Worries disappear at the elegant spa, and there's a heated indoor pool and a fully equipped gym. The **restaurant** (mains $15-35; ⊙7:30am-9pm) exudes rustic elegance, with cozy booths, a high ceiling and a huge fireplace.

★**Ohanas 395**   FOOD TRUCK $
(www.ohanas395.com; 131 S Crawford Ave; mains $8-14; ⊙11:30am-6:30pm Mon & Wed-Sat, noon-5pm Sun) Check out this food truck parked at **June Lake Brewing** (www.junelakebrewing. com; 131 S Crawford Ave; ⊙11am-8pm Wed-Mon, to 9pm Fri & Sat; ❅), serving wait-worthy 'Hawaiian soul food' with a dash of Mexican fusion. Try the kalua pig or naan tacos (the Korean beef brisket and the portobello mushroom are favorites), a classic plate lunch or an ahi *poke* (raw-fish salad) bowl.

Tiger Bar   AMERICAN ❅❅
(✓760-648-7551; www.tigerbarcafe.com; 2620 Hwy 158; mains $9-20; ⊙8am-10pm) After a day on the slopes or trails, people gather at the long bar or around the pool table of this no-nonsense, no-attitude place, around in some form or another since 1932. The kitchen feeds all appetites, with burgers, salads, tacos and other tasty grub, including homemade fries; there are fresh-baked pies for dessert.

Carson Peak Inn   AMERICAN $$$
(Map p498; ✓760-648-7575; Hwy 158, btwn Gull & Silver Lakes; meals $24-40; ⊙5-10pm, shorter hours winter) Inside a cozy house with a fireplace, this restaurant is much beloved for its tasty old-time indulgences, such as fried chicken, pan-fried trout and chopped sirloin steak. Portion sizes can be ordered for regular or 'hearty' appetites.

Mammoth Lakes

Mammoth Lakes is a small mountain-resort town endowed with larger-than-life scenery – active outdoorsy folks worship at the base of its dizzying 11,053ft Mammoth Mountain. Long-lasting powder clings to these slopes, and when the snow finally fades, the area's an outdoor wonderland of mountain-bike trails, excellent fishing, endless alpine hiking and blissful hidden spots for hot-spring soaking. The Eastern Sierra's commercial hub and a four-season resort, outdoorsy Mammoth is backed by a ridgeline of jutting peaks, ringed by clusters of crystalline alpine lakes and enshrouded by the dense Inyo National Forest.

⊙ Sights

★**Earthquake Fault**   NATURAL FEATURE
(Map p509) On Minaret Rd, about 1 mile west of the Mammoth Scenic Loop, detour to gape at Earthquake Fault, a sinuous fissure half a mile long gouging a crevice up to 20ft deep into the earth. Ice and snow often linger at the bottom until late summer, and Native Americans and early settlers used it to store perishable food.

Mammoth Museum   MUSEUM
(Map p505; ✓760-934-6918; www.mammoth museum.org; 5489 Sherwin Creek Rd; suggested donation $5; ⊙10am-6pm mid-May–Sep; ❅) For a walk down memory lane, stop by this little museum inside the historic Hayden log cabin, with photographs and artifacts from its heyday as a hunting and fishing lodge.

🏃 Activities

The excellent website of the **Mammoth Lakes Trail System** (www.mammothtrails. org) contains a comprehensive guide to local hiking, biking and cross-country ski trails, with maps and information on services available.

McGee Creek Pack Station   HORSEBACK RIDING
(✓800-854-7407, 760-935-4324; www.mcgeecreek packstation.com; McGee Creek Rd; half-/full-day rides $80/140; ❅) Whether it's backcountry multiday packing trips or hour-long rides on nearby trails, the owners of this company offer decades of experience and knowledge.

Rock Creek Pack Station   HORSEBACK RIDING
(✓760-872-8331; www.rockcreekpackstation.com; Rock Creek Rd; half-/full-day ride $90/140; ❅) Old, experienced hands run this backcountry packing company high up in the Rock Creek wilderness. Short of dressage, nearly every equine activity, as well as hiking and fishing trips, is on offer.

Caldera Kayaks
KAYAKING

(☑760-935-1691; www.calderakayak.com) Caldera Kayaks has single ($30 for a half-day) and double kayaks ($50) for use on Crowley Lake.

Skiing & Snowboarding

Mammoth Mountain (Map p509; ☑800-626-6684, 760-934-2571, 24hr snow report 888-766-9778; www.mammothmountain.com; adult/13-18yr/7-12yr $125/98/35; ♿) is one of California's premier ski resorts. There's free cross-country skiing along the more than 300 miles of ungroomed trails in town and in the Inyo National Forest. Pick up a free map at the Mammoth Lakes Welcome Center (p507) or head to **Tamarack Cross-Country Ski Center** (☑760-934-2442; www.tamaracklodge.com/xc-ski-center; 163 Twin Lakes Rd; all-day trail pass incl equipment adult/child/senior $58/52/29; ⊙8:30am-5pm).

Hiking

Mammoth Lakes rubs up against the **Ansel Adams Wilderness** (Map p509; www.fs.usda.gov) and **John Muir Wilderness** (Map p509; www.fs.usda.gov) areas, both laced with fabulous trails leading to shimmering lakes, rugged peaks and hidden canyons. Major trailheads leave from the Mammoth Lakes Basin, Reds Meadow and Agnew Meadows; the latter two are accessible only by shuttle. **Shadow Lake** is a stunning 7-mile day hike from Agnew Meadows, and **Crystal Lake** makes a worthy 2.5-mile round-trip trek from Lake George in the Lakes Basin.

From various spots along the Reds Meadow area, long-distance backpackers with wilderness permits and bear canisters can easily jump onto the **John Muir Trail** (to Yosemite to the north and Mt Whitney to the south) and the **Pacific Crest Trail** (fancy walking to Mexico or Canada?).

Cycling & Mountain Biking

Stop at the Mammoth Lakes Welcome Center (p507) for a free biking map with area route descriptions.

Mammoth Mountain
Bike Park
MOUNTAIN BIKING

(Map p509; ☑800-626-6684; www.mammothmountain.com; day pass adult/7-12yr $45/24; ⊙9am-4:30pm Jun-Sep) Come summer, Mammoth Mountain morphs into the massive Mammoth Mountain Bike Park, with more than 80 miles of well-kept single-track trails. Several other trails traverse the surrounding forest. In general, Mammoth-style riding translates into plenty of hills and soft, sandy shoulders, which are best navigated with big, knobby tires.

But you don't need wheels (or a medic) to ride the vertiginous **gondola** (Map p509; ☑800-626-6684; www.mammothmountain.com; adult/13-18yr/5-12yr $29/24/12; ⊙hours vary; P♿) to the apex of the mountain, where there's a cafe and an interpretive center with scopes pointing toward the nearby peaks. And for kids 12 and under, a $40 Adventure Pass buys unlimited day access to a zip line, climbing wall, bungee trampoline and child's bike-park area.

When the park's open, it runs a free mountain-bike **shuttle** (9am to 5:30pm) from the Village area to the Main Lodge. Shuttles depart every 30 minutes, and mountain bikers with paid mountain passes get priority over pedestrians.

Lakes Basin Path
CYCLING

One of Mammoth's fantastic multi-use paths, the 5.3-mile Lakes Basin Path begins at the southwestern corner of Lake Mary and Minaret Rds and heads uphill (1000ft, at a 5% to 10% grade) to Horseshoe Lake, skirting lovely lakes and accessing open views of the Sherwin Range. For a one-way ride, use the free Lakes Basin Trolley, which tows a 12-bicycle trailer.

Fishing & Boating

From the last Saturday in April, the dozens of lakes that give the town its name lure in fly- and trout fishers from near and far. California fishing licenses ($15/47 for a one-day license for California residents/nonresidents) are available at sporting-goods stores throughout town. For equipment and advice, head to **Troutfitter** (Map p505; ☑760-924-3676; www.thetroutfitter.com; 2987 Main St; ⊙8am-4pm) or **Rick's Sports Center** (Map p505; ☑760-934-3416; 3241 Main St; ⊙6am-8pm).

🛌 Sleeping

Mammoth B&Bs and inns rarely sell out midweek, when rates tend to be lower. During ski season, reservations are recommended at weekends and essential during holidays. Many properties offer ski-and-stay packages. Condo rentals often work out cheaper for groups.

The Mammoth Lakes Welcome Center (p507) has a full list of campgrounds, dispersed free camping locations (don't forget to pick up a free but mandatory fire permit) and public showers.

Mammoth Lakes

Mammoth Lakes

Davison Street Guest House HOSTEL $
(Map p505; ☏760-924-2188; www.mammoth-guest.
com; 19 Davison St; dm $35-45, d $75-125; ☜) A
charming and interesting five-room A-frame
chalet hostel on a quiet residential street, this
place has a stocked kitchen, plus mountain
views from the living room (with fireplace)
or sundeck. There's a nifty electronic self-
registration system when the manager isn't
around. Fills with long-distance backpackers
in June and July.

Mammoth Creek Inn INN $$
(Map p505; ☏760-934-6162; www.mammothcreek
inn.com; 663 Old Mammoth Rd; r $139-149, with
kitchen $199-209; @☜☷) It's amenities galore
at this pretty inn at the end of a commercial
strip, with down comforters and fluffy terry
robes, as well as a sauna, a hot tub and a
fun pool-table loft. The best rooms overlook
the majestic Sherwin Mountains, and some
have full kitchens and can sleep up to six.

Austria Hof Lodge
LODGE $$

(Map p505; ☑760-934-2764; www.austriahof.com; 924 Canyon Blvd; r $109-215; ☎) Close to Canyon Lodge, rooms here have modern knotty-pine furniture, thick down duvets and DVD players. Ski lockers and a sundeck hot tub make winter stays here even sweeter. The lodge restaurant (dinner mains $25 to $40) serves meaty gourmet German fare in a muraled cellar dining room.

Alpenhof Lodge
HOTEL $$

(Map p505; ☑760-934-6330; www.alpenhof-lodge.com; 6080 Minaret Rd; r $99-199; @☎☎) A snowball's toss from the Village, this Euro-flavored inn has updated lodge rooms with tasteful accent walls and ski racks, plus more luxurious accommodations with gas fireplaces or kitchens. The basement houses the Clocktower Cellar (p507).

✗ Eating

Good Life Café
CALIFORNIAN, MEXICAN $

(Map p505; ☑760-934-1734; www.mammothgoodlifecafe.com; 126 Old Mammoth Rd; mains $8-17; ☺6:30am-8:30pm; ☑) Healthy food, generously filled veggie wraps and big bowls of salad make this a perennially popular place. It's been around for over 20 years and the diner-style decor is showing its age. A few tables on the front patio facing the parking lot are great for a long brunch on a warm day.

Stellar Brew
CAFE $

(Map p505; www.stellarbrewnaturalcafe.com; 3280 Main St; salads & sandwiches $5.50-10; ☺5:30am-5pm; ☎☑☎) ✐ Proudly locavore and mostly organic, Stellar entices you to settle into a comfy sofa for your daily dose of locally roasted coffee, homemade granola, breakfast burritos and scrumptious vegan (and some gluten-free) pastries.

Base Camp Café
AMERICAN $

(Map p505; www.basecampcafe.com; 3325 Main St; mains $7-15; ☺7:30am-3pm Sun-Fri, to 9pm Sat; ☎☑) Fuel up with a bracing dose of organic tea or coffee and a filling breakfast, or comfort food like Tex-Mex jalapeño-onion straws, turkey chili in a bread bowl and pesto-chicken fajitas. Decorated with various backpacking gear and beer mats, the bathroom has a comical photo display of backcountry outhouses.

Sierra Sundance Whole Foods
HEALTH FOOD $

(Map p505; 26 Old Mammoth Rd; ☺9am-7pm Mon-Sat, to 5pm Sun; ☑) Stock up on organic produce, free-range meats and healthy bulk foods at this large store and deli.

Toomey's
AMERICAN $$

(Map p505; ☑760-924-4408; www.toomeyscatering.com; 6085 Minaret Rd; mains $12-33; ☺7am-9pm; ☑) Since 2012, Toomey's chef, once of legendary Whoa Nellie Deli (p500) in Lee Vining, has been preparing his eclectic menu of wild-buffalo meatloaf, seafood jambalaya and lobster *taquitos* (filled, rolled and fried tortillas) with mango salsa. The central location's perfect for grabbing a to-go breakfast or a sit-down dinner near the Village Gondola.

Stove
AMERICAN $

(Map p505; www.thestoverestaurantmammoth.com; 644 Old Mammoth Rd; breakfast items $6-13, lunch mains $10-13; ☺6:30am-2pm) Great coffee and carbs; try the cinnamon-bread French toast and fresh-baked fruit pies. Excellent soups, salads and sandwiches for lunch.

Lakefront Restaurant
AMERICAN $$$

(☑760-934-2442; www.lakefrontmammoth.com; 163 Twin Lakes Rd; mains $30-70; ☺5-9:30pm, plus 11am-2pm summer, closed Tue & Wed fall & spring) The most atmospheric and romantic (and pricey) restaurant in Mammoth, this intimate dining room at Tamarack Lodge overlooks the lovely Twin Lakes. The chef crafts delights like halibut and pan-seared duck accompanied by creative seasonal vegetable sides, and the staff is superbly friendly. Reservations recommended.

Petra's Bistro & Wine Bar
CALIFORNIAN $$$

(Map p505; ☑760-934-3500; www.petrasbistro.com; 6080 Minaret Rd; mains $23-36; ☺5-9:30pm Tue-Sun) Settle in for seasonal cuisine and wines recommended by the staff sommeliers. In wintertime the best seats in the house are the cozy fireside couches. Start the evening with a cheese course, and choose from 36 wines available by the glass (250 by the bottle) or from the excellent cocktail menu. Reservations recommended.

Mammoth Rock Brasserie
AMERICAN $$$

(Map p505; ☑760-934-4200; 3029 Chateau Rd; mains $19-34; ☺5:30-9pm Mon-Thu, to 10pm Fri-Sun) The classically trained French chef at this swanky brasserie at Mammoth Rock 'n' Bowl serves tasty small plates and meaty main courses like elk medallions and pork mignon. Breathtaking views of the Sherwin Range are available from the 2nd-floor dining room.

Drinking & Nightlife

Clocktower Cellar
PUB

(Map p505; www.clocktowercellar.com; 6080 Minaret Rd; ☻4-11pm) In winter especially, locals throng this dive bar–pub in the basement of the Alpenhof Lodge (p506). The ceiling is tiled with a swirl of bottle caps, and the bar has 150 whiskeys, about 30 beers on tap and about 50 bottled varieties.

Mammoth Brewing Company
BREWERY

(Map p505; ☑760-934-7141; www.mammoth brewingco.com; 18 Lake Mary Rd; ☻10am-9:30pm Sun-Thu, to 10:30pm Fri & Sat) You be the judge whether beer is brewed best at high altitude. Boasting the highest West Coast brewery, at 8000ft, Mammoth Brewing Company offers more than a dozen brews on tap (flights $5 to $7) – including special seasonal varieties not found elsewhere. Tasty bar food's available, and you can pick up some IPA 395 or Double Nut Brown to go.

Shopping

Gear heads will find no shortage of shops staffed by passionate young enthusiasts indulging their own outdoor adventures on days off. Most sell ski and snowboard equipment, with great sales in low season. In-town shops, especially for equipment rentals, are usually cheaper than those at Mammoth Mountain.

Footloose
SPORTS & OUTDOORS

(Map p505; ☑760-934-2400; www.footloose sports.com; 3043 Main St; ☻8am-8pm) Full range of footwear and seasonal equipment; local biking info and rentals.

Mammoth Mountaineering Supply
SPORTS & OUTDOORS

(Map p505; ☑760-934-4191; www.mammothgear. com; 361 Old Mammoth Rd; ☻8am-8pm) Offers friendly advice, topo maps and all-season equipment rentals.

Wave Rave
SPORTS & OUTDOORS

(Map p505; ☑760-934-2471; www.waverave snowboardshop.com; 3203 Main St; ☻7:30am-9pm Sun-Thu, to 10pm Fri & Sat, shorter hours low season) Snowboarders worship here. In summer it rents stand-up paddleboards and electric bikes.

Information

The **Mammoth Lakes Welcome Center** (Map p505; ☑760-924-5500, 888-466-2666; www. visitmammoth.com; 2510 Hwy 203; ☻9am-

5pm) and the **Mammoth Lakes Ranger Station** (Map p505; ☑760-924-5500; www.fs.usda. gov/inyo; ☻9am-5pm) share a building on the northern side of Hwy 203. This one-stop information center issues wilderness permits and rents bear canisters, helps find accommodations and campgrounds, and provides road- and trail-condition updates. From May to October, when trail quotas are in effect, walk-in wilderness permits are released at 11am the day before, though numbers are given to those lined up at 8am; permits are self-issue the rest of the year.

The following are locations where you can purchase lift tickets to Mammoth Mountain:
➡ **Canyon Lodge** (Map p505; 1000 Canyon Blvd)
➡ **Eagle Lodge** (Map p505; 4000 Majestic Pines Dr)
➡ **Main Lodge** (Map p509; 1001 Minaret Rd)
➡ **Mill Cafe** (Map p509; 1 Minaret Rd)
➡ **The Village** (Map p505; 72 Canyon Blvd)

Getting There & Away

AIR

Mammoth Yosemite Airport (MMH; www. visitmammoth.com/fly-mammoth-lakes; 1300 Airport Rd) has nonstop flights to San Francisco and Denver, operating winter through to spring on **United** (www.united.com). **Alaska Airlines** (www.alaskaair.com) runs year-round service to Los Angeles and ski-season service to San Diego. All flights are about an hour.

Taxis meet incoming flights, some lodgings provide free transfers and Mammoth Express buses (run by Eastern Sierra Transit; one way $3.50) ply the route to Mammoth Lakes. **Mammoth Taxi** (☑760-934-8294; www.mammoth-taxi.com) does airport runs as well as hiker shuttles throughout the Sierra.

BUS

Mammoth is a snap to navigate by public transportation year-round. In summer, **YARTS** (☑877-989-2787; www.yarts.com) runs buses to and from Yosemite Valley, and the **Eastern Sierra Transit Authority** (p496) has year-round service along Hwy 395, north to Reno, NV, and south to Lone Pine.

Getting Around

Within Mammoth Lakes, a year-round system of free and frequent **bus shuttles** – operated by the **Eastern Sierra Transit Authority** (p496) – connects the whole town with the Mammoth Mountain lodges; in summer, routes with bicycle trailers service the **Lakes Basin Path** (p504) and **Mammoth Mountain Bike Park** (p504). Check the website for details on routes and schedules.

YOSEMITE & THE SIERRA NEVADA MAMMOTH LAKES

The **Reds Meadow/Devils Postpile shuttle** (Map p505) (adult/child $7/4, season pass $35) provides public transportation to Reds Meadow and the **Devils Postpile National Monument** (p513). From 9am to 5pm it runs nearly every 20 minutes, departing from just under the base of the gondola in the Village.

Around Mammoth Lakes

Reds Meadow

One of the beautiful and varied landscapes near Mammoth Lakes is the Reds Meadow Valley, west of Mammoth Mountain. Drive on Hwy 203 as far as Minaret Vista for eye-popping views (best at sunset) of the Ritter Range, the serrated Minarets and the remote reaches of Yosemite National Park.

The road to Reds Meadow is only accessible from about June until September, weather permitting. To minimize impact when it's open, the road is closed to private vehicles beyond Minaret Vista unless you are camping, have lodge reservations or are disabled, in which case you must pay a $10 fee per car. Otherwise you must use a mandatory shuttle bus ($7/4 adult/child). The bus leaves from a lot in front of the Adventure Center (next to the mammoth statue) approximately every 30 minutes between 7:15am and 7pm (last bus out leaves Reds Meadow at 7:45pm), and you must buy tickets inside before joining the queue. There are also three direct departures from the Village (on Canyon Blvd, under the gondola) before 9am, plus the option of using the free mountain-bike shuttle between the Village and the Adventure Center. The bus stops at trailheads, viewpoints and campgrounds before completing the one-way trip to Reds Meadow (45 minutes to an hour).

The valley road provides access to six campgrounds along the San Joaquin River. Tranquil, willow-shaded **Minaret Falls Campground** (www.fs.usda.gov; tent & RV sites $22; 🐾) is a popular fishing spot where the best riverside sites have views of the namesake cascade.

Hot Creek Geological Site

For a graphic view of the area's geothermal power, journey just south of Mammoth Lakes to where chilly Mammoth Creek blends with hot springs and continues its journey as **Hot Creek** (www.fs.usda.gov/inyo; Hot Creek Hatchery Rd; ⊙ sunrise-sunset) **FREE**. It eventually enters a series of steaming, bubbling cauldrons, with water shimmering in shades of blue and green reminiscent of the tropics. In 2006 a significant increase in geothermal activity began sending violent geysers of boiling water into the air, so swimming is strictly prohibited.

To reach the site, turn off Hwy 395 about 5 miles south of Mammoth Lakes and follow signs to the Hot Creek Fish Hatchery. From here it's another 2 miles on gravel road to the parking area, and a short hike down to the canyon and creek.

Convict Lake

One of the area's prettiest lakes, **Convict Lake** has emerald water embraced by massive peaks. A hike along the gentle trail skirting the lake, through aspen and cottonwood trees, is great if you're still adjusting to the altitude. A trailhead on the southeastern shore gives access to Genevieve, Edith, Dorothy and Mildred Lakes in the John Muir Wilderness. To reach the lake, turn south from Hwy 395 on Convict Lake Rd (across from the Mammoth airport) and go 2 miles.

In 1871 Convict Lake was the site of a bloody shoot-out between a band of escaped convicts and a posse that had given chase. The posse leader, Sheriff Robert Morrison, was killed during the gunfight and the tallest peak, Mt Morrison (12,268ft), was later named in his honor. The bad guys got away, only to be apprehended later near Bishop.

McGee Creek

Eight miles south of Mammoth Lakes, off Hwy 395, McGee Creek Rd rises into the mountains and dead-ends in a dramatic aspen-lined canyon, a particularly beautiful spot for autumn foliage. From here, the **McGee Pass Trail** enters the John Muir Wilderness, with day hikes to **Steelhead Lake** (10 miles round-trip) via an easy walk to subtle **Horsetail Falls** (4 miles round-trip).

On the drive up, the McGee Creek Pack Station (p503) offers trail rides. Spacious **McGee Creek Campground** (www.fs.usda. gov; McGee Creek Rd; tent & RV sites $23; ⊙ late Apr-Oct; 🐾) has 28 reservable sites at 7600ft,

See Mammoth Lakes Map (p505)

with sun-shaded picnic tables along the creek and stunning mountain vistas.

Don't miss the coffee and home-baked goodies at the cute **East Side Bake Shop** (☎760-914-2696; www.facebook.com/EastSide BakeShop; 1561 Crowley Lake Dr; mains $8-15; ⊙6:30am-3pm Wed, Thu & Sun, to 9pm Fri & Sat, shorter hours winter); check its calendar for fun local music at weekends.

Rock Creek

South off Hwy 395 and roughly equidistant between Mammoth Lakes and Bishop, Rock Creek Rd travels 11 miles into some of the dreamiest landscapes in the Sierra. At road's end, the Mosquito Flat trailhead into the **Little Lakes Valley** (part of the John Muir Wilderness) clocks in at a whopping 10,300ft of elevation. Mountaintops seem to be everywhere, with the 13,000ft peaks of Bear Creek Spire, Mt Dade, Mt Abbot and

Mt Mills bursting out along the southwestern horizon and lush canyon meadows popping with scores of clear blue lakes. Ecstatic hikers and climbers fan out to explore – an excellent day-hike destination is the second of the **Gem Lakes** (7 miles round-trip), a lovely aquamarine bowl and five-star lunch spot.

A dozen popular **USFS campgrounds** (☎877-444-6777; www.recreation.gov; tent & RV sites $22; ⊙late May-Sep; 🐾) line Rock Creek Rd; most are along Rock Creek and a few are reservable. In wintertime there's a Sno-park 7 miles in, and during summer the Rock Creek Pack Station (p503) offers trail rides from its location just before the trailhead.

The area is deservedly popular, and trailhead parking can be challenging; be prepared to trek an extra half-mile from the overflow lot.

...indy Lake (p502) **2.** John Muir Trail (p504) **3.** Little Lakes
...ey (p509)

Best Hikes of the Sierra Nevada

Packed with ancient granite peaks, icy-blue lakes and serpentine stream meadows, the Sierra Nevada beckons mountain worshippers. Though the sights may look lovely from the car, you need to stop, smell and touch to really experience the landscape. And once you witness its burning alpenglow, you'll understand why Sierra Club cofounder John Muir called it the 'Range of Light.'

Lundy Canyon

In the Hoover Wilderness west of Mono Lake, ambitious beavers gnaw and stack stands of leafy aspens, and frothy waterfalls draw you deeper and deeper into this stunning and solitary canyon.

John Muir Trail

Load up that pack and connect the dots from the heart of Yosemite to the pinnacle of Mt Whitney, the highest peak in the contiguous USA. This 200-plus-mile trek goes step by step up and over six passes topping 11,000ft. Cross chilly rivers and streams between bumper-to-bumper Yosemite Valley, the roadless backcountry of Sequoia and Kings Canyon and the oxygen-scarce summit of Mt Whitney.

Little Lakes Valley

Marvel at this perfect chain of alpine lakes nestled between snow-tipped summits. With the Sierra's highest trailhead, there's no need to earn your elevation here.

Yosemite High Sierra Camps

Tour Yosemite's high country without a bulging backpack and share the sights with pudgy whistling marmots. Highlights include overnights at pristine May Lake, the waterfalls of Glen Auli and lake-studded Vogelsang.

Bishop

The second-largest town in the Eastern Sierra, Bishop is about two hours from Yosemite's Tioga Pass entrance. A major recreation hub, Bishop offers access to excellent fishing in nearby lakes, climbing in the Buttermilks just west of town, and hiking in the John Muir Wilderness via Bishop Creek Canyon and the Rock Creek drainage. The area is especially lovely in fall, when dropping temperatures cloak aspen, willow and cottonwood in myriad glowing shades.

The earliest inhabitants of the Owens Valley were Paiute and Shoshone Native Americans, who today live on four reservations. White settlers came on the scene in the 1860s and began raising cattle to sell to nearby mining settlements.

◉ Sights

★ Laws Railroad Museum & Historic Site
MUSEUM

(☑760-873-5950; www.lawsmuseum.org; Silver Canyon Rd; donation $5; ◷10am-4pm; ♿) Railroad and Old West aficionados should make a detour off Hwy 6 to this museum. It recreates the village of Laws, an important stop on the route of the *Slim Princess*, a narrow-gauge train that hauled freight and passengers across the Owens Valley for nearly 80 years. You'll see the original 1883 train depot, a post office, a schoolhouse and other rickety old buildings. Many contain funky and eclectic displays (dolls, fire equipment, antique stoves etc) from the pioneer days.

Mountain Light Gallery
GALLERY

(☑760-873-7700; www.mountainlight.com; 106 S Main St; ◷10am-5pm Mon-Sat, 11am-4pm Sun) FREE To see the Sierra on display in all its majesty, pop into this gallery, housed in the historic Monument Bank building, which features the stunning outdoor images of the late Galen Rowell. An accomplished mountaineer and a *National Geographic* photographer, Rowell produced work that bursts with color, and his High Sierra photographs are some of the best in existence.

Besides the stunning fine-art prints that are for sale, the gallery sells a good selection of books on the Sierras and mountaineering in general.

Owens Valley Paiute Shoshone Cultural Center
CULTURAL CENTER

(☑760-873-8844; www.bishoppaiutetribe.com/cultural-center.html; 2300 W Line St; ◷10am-5pm Tue-Sat) FREE A mile west of Hwy 395, this underutilized tribal cultural center and museum, run by the local Paiute Shoshone tribe, includes exhibits on local basketry, tools and the use of medical herbs; behind the building is an interpretive native-plant walk.

Activities

In the summer, fishing is good in the high-altitude lakes of **Bishop Creek Canyon** (west of town along Hwy 168). Other fine spots include the scenic, twisty and down-right magical **Owens River** (northeast) and the **Pleasant Valley Reservoir** (Pleasant Valley Rd, north of town).

Climbing

Bishop is prime bouldering and rock-climbing territory, with terrain to match any level of experience and any climbing style. The main areas are the granite **Buttermilk Country**, nearly 8 miles west of town on Buttermilk Rd, and the stark **Volcanic Tablelands** and **Owens River Valley** (Happy and Sad Boulders) to the north. The tablelands are also a wellspring of Native American petroglyphs – tread lightly.

Hiking

Hikers will want to head to the high country by following Line St (Hwy 168) west along Bishop Creek Canyon, past Buttermilk Country and on to several lakes. Trailheads lead into the John Muir Wilderness and on into Kings Canyon National Park. Check with the White Mountain information station (p514) for suggestions, maps and wilderness permits for overnight stays.

Swimming

Keough's Hot Springs
SWIMMING

(Map p488; ☑760-872-4670; www.keoughshotsprings.com; 800 Keough Hot Springs Rd; adult/child 3-12yr/child under 2yr $12/7/4; ◷11am-7pm Wed-Fri & Mon, 9am-8pm Sat & Sun, longer hours Jun-Aug; ♿) About 8 miles south of Bishop, this historic institutional-green outdoor pool (dating from 1919) is filled with bath-warm water from local mineral springs and doused with spray at one end. A smaller and sheltered 104°F (40°C) soaking pool sits beside it. Camping and tent cabins are also available.

DEVIL'S POSTPILE

The most fascinating attraction in Reds Meadow is the surreal volcanic formation of **Devils Postpile National Monument** (Map p509; ☑760-934-2289; www.nps.gov/depo; shuttle day pass adult/child $7/4; ⊙ late May–Oct). The 60ft curtains of near-vertical, six-sided basalt columns formed when rivers of molten lava slowed, cooled and cracked with perplexing symmetry. This honeycomb design is best appreciated from atop the columns, reached by a short trail. The columns are an easy half-mile hike from the Devils Postpile Ranger Station.

From the monument, a 2.5-mile hike passing through fire-scarred forest leads to the spectacular **Rainbow Falls** (Map p509), where the San Joaquin River gushes over a 101ft basalt cliff. Chances of actually seeing a rainbow forming in the billowing mist are greatest at midday. The falls can also be reached via an easy 1.5-mile walk from the Reds Meadow area, which has a cafe, a store, the **Reds Meadow campground** (Map p509; tent & RV sites $22; ☀) and a pack station. Shuttle services run to the Reds Meadow area in season.

🛏 Sleeping

Bishop is loaded with economically priced motels, mostly chains. The majority are located on or just off Main St. A couple of campgrounds at the foot of the Volcanic Tablelands just to the north of town are open year-round.

USFS Campgrounds CAMPGROUND $
(www.recreation.gov; tent & RV sites $23; ⊙ May–Sep; ☀) For a scenic night, stretch out your sleeping bag beneath the stars. The closest USFS campgrounds, all but one first-come, first-served, are between 9 miles and 15 miles west of town on Bishop Creek along Hwy 168, at elevations between 7500ft and 9000ft.

Hostel California HOSTEL $
(☑760-399-6316; www.hostelbishop.com; 213 Academy Ave; dm $28-39, d $70, 6-person r $170; ☀🛜) A rambling, historic Victorian house located in the center of town, this hostel packs in dusty long-distance backpackers during June and July, with a more varied mix of hikers, anglers, climbers and international travelers the rest of the year. Visitors love the full kitchen, laundry-time loaner clothes, and bicycles, as well as the communal outdoors-loving atmosphere. Adults only.

Owner Matt Meyers, an avid climber, is an excellent source of information. Showers for nonguests are available for $5.

★ Bishop Creekside Inn MOTEL $$
(☑760-872-3044; www.bishopcreeksideinn.com; 725 N Main St; r $130-209, ste $140-230; ☀@🛜☀) Bishop's most upscale lodging,

with an enviable location alongside Bishop Creek, underwent a full-scale renovation completed in summer 2017. Woodsy art and Western-style leather armchairs outfit rooms that come with marble bathrooms (with walk-in glass showers), roomy armchairs, Keurig coffeemakers and thick duvet bedding. Whistling Trout, the hotel's new restaurant, was set to open in fall 2017 at the time of writing.

Joseph House Inn Bed & Breakfast B&B $$
(☑760-872-3389; www.josephhouseinn.com; 376 W Yaney St; r $153-188; ☀🛜☀) This beautifully restored ranch-style home with a patio overlooking a tranquil 3-acre garden has six nicely furnished rooms, some with fireplaces, all with TV. Guests enjoy a complimentary gourmet breakfast and afternoon wine.

🍴 Eating

★ Erick Schat's Bakkery BAKERY $
(☑760-873-7156; www.erickschatsbakery.com; 763 N Main St; sandwiches $6-9; ⊙6am-6pm Sun-Thu, to 7pm Fri; 🛗) A deservedly hyped tourist mecca filled to the rafters with racks of fresh bread, Schat's has been making its signature sheepherder bread and other baked goodies since 1938. Some of the desserts, including the crispy cookies and bear claws, are addictive, and call for repeated trips while in town. Also has a popular sandwich bar and outdoor tables.

Great Basin Bakery BAKERY, CAFE $
(☑760-873-9828; www.greatbasinbakerybishop.com; 275d S Main St; salads & sandwiches $5-8; ⊙6am-4pm Mon-Sat, from 6:30am Sun; 🛜🗷) 🌿 In the southern part of town, this excellent

DON'T MISS

BENTON HOT SPRINGS

Soak in your own hot-springs tub and snooze beneath the moonlight at **The Inn at Benton Hot Springs** (☑866-466-2824, 760-933-2287; www.historicbentonhotsprings.com; Hwy 120, Benton; tent & RV sites for 2 people $40-50, d with/without bath $129/109; ✳ 🛰 📶), a small, historic resort in a 150-year-old former silver-mining town nestled in the White Mountains. Choose from nine well-spaced campsites with private tubs or themed, antique-filled B&B rooms with semiprivate tubs. Daytime dips ($10 per person per hour) are available. Reservations essential.

The inn is reachable from Mono Lake via Hwy 120 (in summer), Mammoth Lakes by way of Benton Crossing Rd, or Bishop via Hwy 6; the first two options are undulating drives with sweeping red-rock vistas that glow at sunset, and all take approximately one hour. An Eastern Sierra Transit Authority bus connects Bishop and Benton ($6, one hour) on Tuesday and Friday, stopping right at the resort.

If you have time, ask for directions to the Volcanic Tablelands petroglyphs off Hwy 6, where ancient drawings decorate scenic rock walls.

mom-and-pop bakery serves locally roasted coffee, breakfast sandwiches on freshly baked bagels with local eggs, homemade soups and lots of delectable baked goods (with vegan and gluten-free options). Enter from Lagoon St.

Back Alley AMERICAN $$
(www.thebackalleybowlandgrill.com; 649 N Main St; mains $15-24; ⊙11:30am-10pm, to 9pm Sun) Tucked off the main drag, behind Yamatani's Restaurant, this busy bowling-alley bar and grill (with bowling-pin carpeting!) earns the locals' affection with huge portions of fresh fish, rib-eye steak and burgers. Specials come with loads of sides and the homemade desserts are surprisingly good amid the tattered Tiki-meets-televisions surf decor.

❶ Information

Bishop Area Visitors Bureau (☑760-873-8405; www.bishopvisitor.com; 690 N Main St; ⊙10am-5pm Mon-Fri, to 4pm Sat & Sun; 📶) Helpful staff with information on accommodations and activities in Bishop and the surrounding region.

Inyo National Forest Wilderness Permit Office (☑760-873-2483; www.fs.usda.gov/inyo; 351 Pacau Lane, suite 200) Offices for Inyo National Forest staff and wilderness-permit office.

White Mountain Public Lands Information Station (☑760-873-2500; www.fs.usda.gov/inyo; 798 N Main St; ⊙8am-5pm daily May-Oct, Mon-Fri Nov-Apr) Wilderness permits, trail and campground information for the entire area.

Public showers are available in town at **Wash Tub** (☑760-873-6627; 236 N Warren St; ⊙9am-6pm Mon-Fri, 8am-10pm Sat & Sun; 📶).

Big Pine

This blink-and-you-missed-it town has a few motels and basic eateries. It mainly functions as a launchpad for the **Ancient Bristlecone Pine Forest** (☑760-873-2500; www.fs.usda.gov/inyo; ⊙usually mid-May–Nov; 🅿 ♿) 🖉 and to the granite **Palisades** in the John Muir Wilderness, a rugged cluster of peaks including six above 14,000ft. Stretching beneath the pinnacles is **Palisades Glacier**, the southernmost in the USA and the largest in the Sierra Nevada.

To get to the trailhead, turn onto Glacier Lodge Rd (Crocker Ave in town), which follows trout-rich Big Pine Creek up Big Pine Canyon, 10 miles west into a bowl-shaped valley. The strenuous 9-mile hike to Palisades Glacier via the North Fork Trail skirts several lakes – turned a milky turquoise color by glacial runoff – and a stone cabin built by horror-film actor Lon Chaney in 1925.

Glacier Lodge (Map p488; ☑760-938-2837; www.glacierlodge395.com; tent sites $25, RV sites $35, cabins $160-190; ⊙mid-Apr–mid-Nov; 📶) is a bunch of rustic cabins with kitchens, as well as a campground. Though the original building no longer exists, it was one of the earliest Sierra getaways when built in 1917. Two-night minimum stay.

Independence

This sleepy highway town has been a county seat since 1866, but it's on the map because of its proximity to the Manzanar National Historic Site (p515) south of town and to wilderness trails in the Sierra Nevada.

West of town via Onion Valley Rd (Market St in town), pretty **Onion Valley** harbors the trailhead for the **Kearsage Pass** (9.4 miles round-trip), an old Paiute trade route. This is also the quickest east-side access to the **Pacific Crest Trail** and Kings Canyon National Park.

Fans of **Mary Austin** (1868–1934), renowned author of *The Land of Little Rain* and vocal foe of the desertification of the Owens Valley, can follow signs leading to her former house at 253 Market St.

◎ Sights

★Manzanar National
Historic Site
HISTORIC SITE
(Map p488; ☑760-878-2194; www.nps.gov/manz; 5001 Hwy 395; ◎9am-5:30pm Apr–mid-Oct, 10am-4:30pm mid-Oct–Mar; Ⓟ♿) ✦FREE A stark wooden guard tower alerts drivers to one of US history's darkest chapters, which unfolded on a barren, windy sweep of land some 5 miles south of Independence. Little remains of the infamous war concentration camp, a dusty square mile where more than 10,000 people of Japanese ancestry were corralled during WWII. The camp's lone remaining building, the former high-school auditorium, houses a superb interpretive center. A visit is one of California's historical highlights and should not be missed.

Watch the 20-minute documentary, then explore the thought-provoking exhibits chronicling the stories of the families that languished here yet built a vibrant community. Afterward, take a self-guided 3.2-mile driving tour around the grounds, which includes a recreated mess hall and barracks, vestiges of buildings and gardens, and the haunting camp cemetery.

Eastern California Museum
MUSEUM
(☑760-878-0364; www.inyocounty.us/ecmsite; 155 N Grant St; donation requested; ◎10am-5pm; Ⓟ♿) This museum contains one of the most complete collections of Paiute and Shoshone baskets in the country, as well as artifacts from the Manzanar National Historic Site (p515) and historic photographs of primitively equipped local rock climbers scaling Sierra peaks, including Mt Whitney.

🛏 Sleeping

USFS Campgrounds
CAMPGROUND $
(www.fs.usda.gov; tent & RV sites $18; ◎approx May-Sep; ☗) There are three USFS campgrounds alongside Independence Creek, including one at the Kearsage Pass trailhead. Reservations available at www.recreation.gov.

Mt Williamson Motel & Base Camp
CABIN $
(☑760-878-2121; www.mtwilliamsonmotel.com; 515 S Edwards St; r $85-95, ste $125; ❋ 🐾 🐕) A low-key hiker favorite, Mt Williamson has cute cabins with flat-screen TVs, calico bedspreads, tea kettles and arresting prints of the local bighorn sheep, all nestled among fruit trees. Ask about the hiker packages that include trailhead transportation. Full breakfast included mid-June to October.

🍴 Eating

Owens Valley
Growers Co-op
SUPERMARKET, CAFE $
(☑760-915-0091; 149 S Edwards St; mains $8; ◎cafe 5-7pm Fri, supermarket hours vary; 🐾🖊) The cafe, serving locally grown produce and other products, is open for Friday-night dinners; an outdoor farmers market is held at the same time from late May to September. Lunch and dinner other days of the week are a possibility.

Still Life Cafe
FRENCH $$
(☑760-878-2555; 135 S Edward St; lunch $9-16, dinner $16-24; ◎11am-3pm & 6-9:30pm Wed-Mon) Fairly upscale and unexpected in such a flyspeck town, the Still Life Cafe prepares escargot, steak au poivre and other French bistro faves and serves them with Gallic charm in this dimly lit, eclectically decorated dining room.

Lone Pine

A tiny town, Lone Pine is the gateway to big things, most notably Mt Whitney, the loftiest peak in the contiguous USA, and Hollywood. In the 1920s cinematographers discovered that the nearby Alabama Hills were a picture-perfect movie set for Westerns, and stars from Gary Cooper to Gregory Peck could often be spotted swaggering about town.

◎ Sights

★Alabama Hills
NATURAL FEATURE
The warm colors and rounded contours of the Alabama Hills, located on Whitney Portal Rd, stand in contrast to the jagged, snowy Sierras just behind. The setting for countless ride-'em-out movies, the popular *Lone Ranger* TV series and, more recently,

rts of *Iron Man* (Jon Favreau, 2008) and
lentin Tarantino's *Django Unchained*
(2012), the stunning orange rock formations
are a beautiful place to experience sunrise
or sunset.

You can drive, walk or mountain bike
along dirt roads rambling through the boulders, and along Tuttle and Lone Pine Creeks.
A number of graceful rock arches are within easy hiking distance of the roads. Head
west on Whitney Portal Rd and either turn
left at Tuttle Creek Rd, after a half-mile, or
north on Movie Flat Rd, after about 3 miles.
Following the latter route, the road eventually turns into Moffat Ranch Rd and brings
you back to Hwy 395, only 3½ miles south
of Manzanar National Historic Site (p515).
The websites of the Lone Pine Chamber of
Commerce (p518) and the Museum of Western Film History (p516) have excellent movie-location maps.

Mt Whitney MOUNTAIN
(Map p488; www.fs.usda.gov/inyo) West of Lone
Pine, the jagged incisors of the Sierra surge
skyward in all their raw and fierce glory.
Cradled by scores of smaller pinnacles, Mt
Whitney is a bit hard to pick out from Hwy
395, so, for the best views, take a drive along
Whitney Portal Rd through the Alabama
Hills (p515).

As you get a fix on this majestic megalith,
remember that the country's lowest point is
only 80 miles (as the crow flies) east of here:
Badwater in Death Valley. Climbing to Mt
Whitney's summit (p517) is among the most
popular hikes in the entire country.

Museum of Western Film History MUSEUM
(☑ 760-876-9909; www.museumofwesternfilm
history.org; 701 S Main St; adult/under 12yr $5/
free; ⊙10am-6pm Mon-Wed, to 7pm Thu-Sat, to
4pm Sun Apr-Oct, 10am-5pm Mon-Sat, to 4pm Sun
Nov-Mar; P ♿) More than 400 movies, not to
mention numerous commercials (mostly for
rugged SUVs and Jeeps), have been shot in
the area, and this museum contains exhibits
of paraphernalia from locally set films. One
of the most fascinating pieces in the collection is the 1928 Lincoln camera car, acquired
in 2016 – the mounted cameras caught the
action while cars drove alongside galloping
horses. The museum's theater screens a well-made film about the history of Westerns
shot in the Alabama Hills (p515).

The museum hosts a film festival – geared
to Westerns, of course – on the first weekend
in October.

🛏 Sleeping

★ **Alabama Hills Bureau
of Land Management** CAMPGROUND
(Alabama Hills) **FREE** You can't go wrong
with free camping amid some of the most
striking scenery in the Sierras. Pull off onto
any of the dirt roads to find a private spot
behind a rock formation with snowcapped
mountains towering above. Of course, services are nonexistent, but for those you can
head into Lone Pine, a short drive away.

★ **Whitney Portal
Hostel & Hotel** HOSTEL, MOTEL $
(☑ 760-876-0030; www.whitneyportalstore.com;
238 S Main St; dm/d $25/85; ❄🖧🛜🍴) A popular launchpad for Mt Whitney trips and a
locus of posthike washups (public showers
are available), the Whitney has the cheapest
beds in town – reserve dorms months ahead
for July and August. There's no common
space, just well-maintained single-sex bunk-bed rooms, though amenities include towels, TVs, in-room kitchenettes and stocked
coffeemakers.

The majority of the establishment consists of plush, modern motel rooms, and
many look towards Whitney and its neighbors. The ground-floor general store (p517)
is an excellent place to stock up on basic
gear and food supplies.

Tuttle Creek CAMPGROUND $
(Horseshoe Meadows Rd; tent & RV sites $5; 🐕)
Off Whitney Portal Rd, this first-come, first-served Bureau of Land Management campground has 83 primitive sites with panoramic 'pinch-me!' views of the Sierras, the White
Mountains and the rosy Alabama Hills
(p515). There's not much shade, though.

Lone Pine Campground CAMPGROUND $
(Map p488; www.fs.usda.gov; Whitney Portal Rd;
tent & RV sites $22; ⊙mid-Apr–Oct; 🐕) About
midway between Lone Pine and Whitney
Portal, this popular creekside USFS campground (elevation 6000ft) offers vault toilets
and potable water.

Dow Hotel & Dow Villa Motel HOTEL, MOTEL $$
(☑ 760-876-5521; www.dowvillamotel.com; 310 S
Main St; hotel r with/without bath from $89/70, motel r $117-158; P❄🖧@🛜🌀🛜) John Wayne
and Errol Flynn are among the stars who
have stayed at this venerable hotel. Built in
1922, the place has been restored but retains
much of its rustic charm. The rooms in the
newer motel section have air-con and are

more comfortable and bright, but also more generic.

Eating

Alabama Hills Cafe
DINER $

(☑760-876-4675; 111 W Post St; mains $8-14; ☺7am-2pm; 🛜🖊🧒) At everyone's favorite breakfast joint, the portions are big, the bread is fresh baked, and the hearty soups, sandwiches and fruit pies make lunch an attractive option too. You can also plan your drive through the Alabama Hills (p515) with the help of the map on the menu.

Lone Pine Smokehouse
BARBECUE $

(☑760-876-4433; www.lonepinesmokehouse.com; 325 S Main St; sandwiches $9; ☺noon-8pm Mon, to 9pm Thu-Sun; 🐾) The quality seems to be hit or miss – the beef brisket and pulled pork are most consistent – at this friendly Texas-style-barbecue place. And, despite the Western-themed facade, the dining room is utterly unadorned. It's best to grab an outdoor table on a sunny day (dogs allowed).

Lone Star Bistro
SANDWICHES $

(107 N Main St; sandwiches $5-8; ☺6am-7pm Tue-Sun, to noon Mon; 🛜) You can satisfy most of your needs at this mash-up of a gift shop, deli, ice-cream parlor and cafe. Soups, pastries and hiking fare to go are also offered.

Seasons
AMERICAN $$

(☑760-876-8927; 206 N Main St; mains $17-30; ☺5-9pm daily Apr-Oct, Tue-Sun Nov-Mar) Seasons has everything you fantasized about the last time you choked down freeze-dried rations. Sautéed trout, roasted duck, filet mignon and plates of carb-replenishing pasta will revitalize your appetite, and nice and naughty desserts will leave you purring. Reservations recommended.

🛍 Shopping

★ Whitney Portal Store
FOOD & DRINKS

(Map p488; ☑760-876-0030; www.whitneyportal store.com; ☺hours vary May-Oct; 🛜) Food, beer, souvenirs and excellent advice from the friendly staff make this *the* (only) place to

---

HIKING MT WHITNEY

The mystique of 14,505ft **Mt Whitney** (p516) captures the imagination, and conquering its hulking bulk becomes a sort of obsession for many. The main **Mt Whitney Trail** (the easiest and busiest one) leaves from Whitney Portal, about 13 miles west of Lone Pine via Whitney Portal Rd (closed in winter), and climbs about 6000ft over 11 miles. It's a superstrenuous, really, really long walk that'll wear out even experienced mountaineers, but it doesn't require technical skills if attempted in summer or early fall. Earlier or later in the season, you'll likely need an ice axe and crampons, and to overnight.

Many people in good physical condition make it to the top, although only superbly conditioned, previously acclimatized hikers should attempt this as a day hike. Breathing becomes difficult at these elevations and altitude sickness is a common problem. Rangers recommend spending a night camping at the trailhead and another at one of the two camps along the route: **Outpost Camp** at 3.5 miles or **Trail Camp** at 6 miles up the trail.

When you pick up your permit and pack-out kits (hikers must pack out their poop) at the **Eastern Sierra Interagency Visitor Center** (p518) in Lone Pine, get the latest info on weather and trail conditions. Near the trailhead, the **Whitney Portal Store** (p517) sells groceries and snacks. It also has public showers ($5) and a cafe with enormous burgers and pancakes. The message board on its website is a good starting point for Whitney research.

The biggest obstacle in getting to the peak may be to obtain a **wilderness permit**, which is required for all overnight trips and for day hikes past Lone Pine Lake (about 2.8 miles from the trailhead). A quota system limits daily access to 60 overnight and 100 day hikers from May to October. Because of the huge demand, permits are distributed via the online **Mt Whitney lottery** (www.fs.usda.gov/inyo; per group $6, plus per person $15), with applications accepted from February to mid-March.

Want to avoid the hassle of getting a permit for the main Mt Whitney Trail? Consider ascending this popular pinnacle from the west, using the **backdoor route** from Sequoia & Kings Canyon National Parks. It takes about six days from Crescent Meadow via the High Sierra Trail to the John Muir Trail – with no Whitney Zone permit required – and wilderness permits are much easier to secure.

NAMING THE ALABAMA HILLS

Wouldn't the Alabama Hills to the west of Lone Pine have more suitably been named the 'California Hills'? So why Alabama? It turns out that a group of miners digging in these hills during the Civil War years were supporters of the Confederacy and chose the moniker in honor of the CSS *Alabama*, which was wreaking havoc on Union ships.

visit before and/or after your hike up Mt Whitney. It sits just a few yards from the trailhead and is only open during the peak hiking season.

Elevation   SPORTS & OUTDOORS
(☑ 760-876-4560; www.sierraelevation.com; 150 S Main St, cnr Whitney Portal Rd; ☉ call for hours)

Rents bear canisters and crampons, and sells hiking, backpacking and climbing gear.

Lone Pine Sporting Goods   SPORTS & OUTDOORS
(☑ 760-876-5365; 220 S Main St; ☉ call for hours) Sells camping gear, clothing, fishing licenses (cash only) and maps.

ℹ Information

Eastern Sierra Interagency Visitor Center
(☑ 760-876-6222; www.fs.fed.us/r5/inyo; cnr Hwys 395 & 136; ☉ 8am-5pm) USFS information center for the Sierra Nevada, Death Valley and Mt Whitney; about 1.5 miles south of town.

Lone Pine Chamber of Commerce (☑ 760-876-4444; www.lonepinechamber.org; 120 S Main St; ☉ 8:30am-4:30pm Mon-Fri) Housed in a historic building with loads of brochures and friendly and helpful staff.

Understand Northern California

Northern California Today

The drought may be over, but water – and climate change – remain deeply concerning for Northern Californians. Scientists expect the region to perpetually suffer from periods of excessive rain and extreme drought, threatening the water supply, devastating agricultural production and wreaking havoc on wildlife. Meanwhile, the cost of living has skyrocketed and the state has essentially declared war on President Donald Trump (with a small movement for secession billowing after the 2016 election). Good thing voters legalized recreational pot as of January 1, 2018.

Best on Film

Vertigo (1958) Alfred Hitchcock's noir thriller, set in SF and San Juan Batista.
Dirty Harry (1971) Clint Eastwood as an SFPD inspector, investigating murder.
Mrs Doubtfire (1993) Robin Williams hilariously disguises himself as an SF nanny.
Milk (2008) Sean Penn gives an Oscar-winning performance as gay-rights activist and SF icon Harvey Milk.

Best in Print

Grapes of Wrath (John Steinbeck; 1939) Written in Monte Serreno, about a poor Oklahoma family seeking better times in California.
Tales of the City (Armistead Maupin; 1978) First novel in a series exploring alternative lifestyles and underground culture in 1970s SF.
The Call of the Wild (Jack London; 1903) SF native's tale of dog from Santa Clara Valley forced to relocate to the Klondike.

Best in Music

American Beauty (The Grateful Dead; 1970) SF was the birthplace of jam-band pioneers Jerry Garcia and Bob Weir.
Dookie (Green Day; 1994) The album that put these East Bay punk rockers on the map.
In a Major Way (E-40; 1995) Major label debut of the King of Bay Area rap.

NorCal in a Nutshell

The story of California has always been a story of water. At the time of research, Governor Jerry Brown had just declared an end to the 'drought state of emergency' that had essentially become a way of life in NorCal over the last four years, though the warning remains in place for a few still-parched counties. It was an unusual deluge of rain and snow in early 2017 that mostly ended the drought, though that extreme weather had repercussions of its own: reservoirs and rivers overflowed and thousands of people had to be evacuated from San Jose, Orville and Salinas. Between 2012 and 2016, those same rivers and reservoirs had sunk dangerously low, and large swaths of the agricultural Central Valley had gone unplanted. Food prices had soared and farmers were forced to slaughter their cattle because they had nothing to feed them.

By most accounts, Californians handled the worst drought on record rather well, taking shorter showers and flushing less to comply with an ordered 25% cut in urban water use. And despite sizeable setbacks in the agricultural industry, the state's economy went right on thriving. In 2015 California's $2.46 trillion GDP surpassed that of France, rendering it the world's sixth-largest economy. In an attempt to protect the state's productivity and also an enormous population of undocumented immigrants, lawmakers in 2017 introduced legislation that would make California the nation's first sanctuary state, meaning that law enforcement couldn't arrest or detain anyone over immigration violations. The move seemed part of California's larger effort to defy its arch nemesis, President Donald Trump, who promptly accused California of being 'out of control' but didn't explain how.

In some ways the California of today is very much under control, with a reasonably balanced budget and low crime rates relative to previous decades. And while fuddy-duddies might argue that relaxing marijuana laws will incite chaos, in Northern California those old things have been ignored for as long as anyone can remember. There is one aspect of life, however, that has become wildly intractable: the cost of living. In the Bay Area and beyond, rents and home prices have soared, camps of homeless people are expanding and commutes to desirable cities are lengthening. The legislature has attempted to address the state's housing woes by introducing more than 100 bills on the issue, but in 2017 the outlook for reform remained dim. Northern California may be an achingly beautiful place to visit, but for the vast majority of residents, it's an increasingly difficult place to afford.

Roots of Environmentalism

Californians originally kick-started the world's conservation movement in the midst of the 19th-century's industrial revolution, with laws curbing industrial dumping, and protections for pristine wildernesses that helped establish the national parks system. In the 1970s, the modern-day environmental movement was born, when then-President Nixon established the Environmental Protection Agency, following an oil spill off the Santa Barbara coast. Today Northern Californians continue to lead the nation with new ideas about sustainable food and low-impact lifestyles – often with smug self-satisfaction. In late 2016 Cali voters approved the first statewide ban on plastic bags in the nation, and it should come as no surprise that NorCal has the country's highest demand for hybrid vehicles.

Fast Companies, Slow Food

The technology boom has changed the cultural DNA of Northern California, with cutting-edge biotech research, online social media juggernauts such as Facebook and Twitter, and of course Google. Tech gazillionaires have driven up housing prices in San Francisco (and beyond), transforming the city and surrounding areas into bedroom communities for Silicon Valley. Longtime locals aren't pleased, and blame the giant tech shuttlebuses – which everyone calls the 'Google Bus' – for the city's gentrification.

If talking tech is straying into dangerous social territory, change the subject to food. Northern Californians are obsessed by what they eat, fetishizing seasonal foods such as heirloom peaches and heritage cuts of pork the way a bodybuilder worships protein supplements. But nowhere else in America can lay claim to such incredible bounty. Even in urban San Francisco, farmers markets offer still-warm-from-the-sun fruit, picked that very morning. 'Locavore' eating began here, and after you've gotten your own taste, chances are you too will be asking the provenance of your fried green tomatoes.

POPULATION: **15.38 MILLION**

PROPORTION OF US GDP: **13.64%/$2.45 TRILLION (NUMBERS FOR WHOLE OF CALIFORNIA)**

ESTIMATED ANNUAL REVENUE FROM MEDICAL MARIJUANA SALES: **$2.4 BILLION (NUMBER FOR ALL OF CALIFORNIA)**

if California were 100 people

39 would be Hispanic
38 would be Caucasian
15 would be Asian
6 would be African American
2 would be American Indian

belief systems

(% of population)

32 Protestant   3 Jewish   2 Buddhist

28 Roman Catholic   27 None   8 Other

population per sq mile

California   San Francisco   Los Angeles

 ≈ 250 people

History

When European explorers arrived in the 16th century, over 100,000 Native Americans called this land home. Spanish conquistadors, and priests determined to convert the natives, marched through in search of a fabled 'city of gold' before establishing Catholic missions and *presidios* (military forts). After winning independence from Spain, Mexico briefly ruled the land, but got trounced by the fledgling USA, just before gold's discovery in 1848. Immigrant waves of star-struck dreamers haven't stopped washing up on these shores ever since.

Before the Ghosts

In some Central Californian Native American communities, mothers-in-law were traditionally so revered that you dared not speak to yours, and obeyed her without question.

Speaking some 100 distinct languages, Native Californians mostly lived in small communities and a few migrated with the seasons. Their diet was largely dependent on acorn meal, supplemented by small game, such as rabbit and deer, and fish and shellfish. They were skilled craftspeople, making earthenware pots, fishing nets, bows, arrows and spears with chipped-stone points. Many tribes developed a knack for weaving baskets of local grasses and plant fibers, decorating them with geometric designs – some baskets were so tightly woven that they could even hold water.

Northern coastal fishing communities, such as Ohlone, Miwok and Pomo, built subterranean roundhouses and sweat lodges, where they held ceremonies, told stories and gambled for fun. Northern hunting communities, including the Hupa, Karok and Wiyot, constructed big houses and redwood dugout canoes, while the Modoc lived in summer tepees and winter dugouts; all chased salmon during their seasonal runs. Kumeyaay and Chumash villages dotted the central coast, where tribespeople fished and paddled canoes.

When English sea captain Sir Francis Drake harbored briefly in 1579 on Miwok land north of San Francisco, the English were taken to be the dead returned from the afterworld, and shamans saw the arrival as a warning of apocalypse. The omens weren't far wrong: within a century of the 1769 arrival of Spanish colonists, Northern California's indigenous

TIMELINE	130,000 BC	1542–43 AD	1769
	New evidence shows signs of ancient humans living in California more than a hundred thousand years before humans were previously thought to exist in the Americas.	Juan Rodríguez Cabrillo becomes the first European explorer to navigate the California coast. His journey ends in the Channel Islands, when a gangrenous wound kills him.	Franciscan friar Junípero Serra and Captain Gaspar de Portolá lead a Spanish expedition to establish missions, rounding up Native Americans as converts and conscripted labor.

population was diminished to 20,000 by European diseases, conscripted labor, violence and famine.

Spain's Mission Impossible

When 18th-century Russian and English trappers began trading valuable otter pelts along the California coast, Spain concocted a plan for colonization. For the glory of God and the tax coffers of Spain, missions would be built across the state. This 'Sacred Expedition' was approved by Spain's quixotic visitor general, José de Gálvez of Mexico, who was full of grand schemes – including controlling Sonora province with a trained army of apes.

Almost immediately after Spain's missionizing plan was approved in 1769, it began to fail. When Franciscan friar Junípero Serra and Captain Gaspar de Portolá made the overland journey to establish Mission San Diego de Alcalá in 1769, only half the sailors on their supply ships survived. Portolá had heard of a fabled cove to the north but, failing to recognize Monterey Bay in the fog, he gave up and turned back.

Portolá reported to Gálvez that if the Russians or English wanted California, they were welcome to it. But Serra wouldn't give up, and secured support to set up *presidios* (military posts) alongside missions. When soldiers weren't paid regularly, they looted and pillaged local communities. Clergy objected to this treatment of potential converts, but still relied on soldiers to round up conscripts to build missions. In exchange for their forced labor, Native Californians were allowed one meal a day and a place in God's kingdom – which came much sooner than expected, due to diseases such as smallpox and syphilis that the Spanish brought.

It's no surprise that California's indigenous tribes often rebelled against the Spanish colonists. However, the missions did achieve modest success at farming and just barely managed to become self-sufficient. But as a way of colonizing California and converting the indigenous people to Christianity, the colonists were abject failures. The Spanish population remained small, foreign intruders were not greatly deterred and, ultimately, more Native Californians died than were converted.

California Under Mexico

Spain wasn't sorry to lose California to Mexico in the 1810–21 Mexican War for Independence. As long as missions had the best grazing land, *rancheros* (ranchers) couldn't compete in the growing market for cowhides and tallow (for use in soap). Yet Spanish, Mexican and American settlers who intermarried with Native Americans were now a sizable constituency, and together these 'Californios' convinced Mexico to secularize the missions in 1834.

Traces of a Native American culture dating from the 1st century remain at Chumash Painted Cave State Historic Park, which features the most elaborate indigenous rock designs outside of the deserts of the Southwest.

1821	1846	1848	1848
Mexican independence ends Spanish colonization of California. Mexico inherits 21 missions in various states of disrepair, along with unruly Californio cowboys and a decimated Native American population.	Sierra Nevada blizzards strand the Donner Party of settlers, some of whom avoid starvation by eating their dead companions. Five women and two men snowshoe 100 miles for help.	Treaty of Guadalupe Hidalgo is signed by the US and Mexico, ending the Mexican-American War. America pays $15 million for 10 states including California.	Gold is discovered at Sutter's Mill in Coloma, California, spurring the gold rush and subsequently decimating the local Native American population.

Californios quickly snapped up deeds to privatized mission property. Only a few dozen of them were literate, so boundary disputes were settled with muscle, not paper. By law, half the lands were supposed to go to Native Californians who worked at the missions, but few actually received their entitlements.

Through marriage and mergers, by 1846 most of the land and wealth in California was held by just 46 *ranchero* families. The average *rancho* (ranch) was now 16,000 acres, having grown from cramped shanties to elegant haciendas where women were supposedly confined to quarters at night. But *rancheras* (ranch women) weren't so easily bossed around: women owned some Californian ranches, rode horses as hard as men and caused romantic scandals worthy of *telenovelas* (soap operas).

Meanwhile, land fever and dreams of westward migration swept America, and settlers from the east began walking across the continent to California. There was no easy route. Some arrived via the dangerous and hot Santa Fe and Old Spanish Trails into the dusty backwater that was Los Angeles. Most came via the straighter Oregon and California Trails, arriving at Sutter's Fort in Sacramento, but this necessitated crossing the Sierra Nevada, which you had to time just right, lest you get trapped by snow – as happened to the infamous Donner Party, tragically stranded at the summit, near Truckee, and forced into cannibalism to survive.

Despite distance and terrain, the US saw potential in California, but when US President Andrew Jackson offered financially strapped Mexico $500,000 for the territory, the offer was tersely rejected. After the USA annexed the Mexican territory of Texas in 1845, Mexico broke off diplomatic relations and ordered all foreigners without proper papers to be deported from California. The Mexican-American War was declared in 1846 and lasted two years, with very little fighting in California. Hostilities ended with the Treaty of Guadalupe Hidalgo, which ceded California and the present-day Southwest to the USA. The timing was fortuitous: a few weeks after the US took possession of California, gold was discovered.

In her bestselling book *The Joy Luck Club*, Amy Tan weaves the stories of four Chinese-born women and their American-born daughters into a textured history of immigration and aspiration in San Francisco's Chinatown.

Eureka!

The gold rush began with a bluff. Real-estate speculator, lapsed Mormon and tabloid publisher Sam Brannan was looking to unload some California swampland in 1848 when he heard rumors of gold flakes found near Sutter's Mill, 120 miles east of San Francisco in the Sierra Nevada foothills. Figuring this news should sell some newspapers and raise real-estate values, Brannan published the rumor as fact. Initially the story didn't generate excitement so Brannan ran another story, this time verified by Mormon employees at Sutter's Mill who had sworn him

1850	1851	1869	1882
With hopes of solid-gold tax revenues, the US dubs California the 31st state. When miners find tax loopholes, SoCal ranchers are left carrying the tax burden, creating early north–south rivalries.	The discovery of gold in Australia means cheering in the streets of Melbourne and panic in the streets of San Francisco, as the price of California gold plummets.	On May 10, the 'Golden Spike' is nailed in place at Promontory, UT, completing the first transcontinental railroad connecting California to the East Coast.	The US Chinese Exclusion Act suspends new immigration from China, denies citizenship to those already in the country and sanctions racially targeted laws that stay on the books until 1943.

to secrecy. Brannan kept his word by running through San Francisco's streets, brandishing gold entrusted to him as tithes for the Mormon church, shouting, 'Gold on the American River!'

Newspapers around the world ran stories of 'gold mountains' near San Francisco, and by 1850, the year California was fast-tracked for admission to become the 31st US state, California's non-native population had ballooned from 15,000 to 93,000. Early arrivals from across the country and around the world panned for gold side by side, slept in close quarters, drank locally made wine and ate wok-fired Chinese food; when they struck it rich, they ordered 'Hangtown Fry' (an omelet with bacon and oysters).

California's motto 'Eureka' translates from Greek to mean 'I have found it' in English. The motto appears on the state seal.

With each wave of new arrivals, profits dropped and gold became harder to find. In 1848 each prospector earned an average of about $300,000 in today's terms; by 1849, earnings were less than half that, and by 1865 they had dipped to $35,000. When surface gold became scarce, miners picked, shoveled and dynamited through mountains. The work was grueling and dangerous; the cost of living in cold, filthy mining camps was sky-high; and with few doctors around, injuries often proved lethal. With only one woman for every 400 men in some camps, many turned to paid company, booze and opium for consolation.

Vigilantes & Robber Barons

Prospectors who did best arrived early and got out quick; those who stayed too long either lost fortunes searching for the next nugget or became targets for resentment. Successful Peruvians and Chileans were harassed and denied renewals to their mining claims, and most left California by 1855. Native American laborers who helped the forty-niners strike it rich were denied the right to hold claims. Also at the receiving end of hostilities were the Chinese, the most populous minority group in California by 1860. Frozen out of mining claims, many Chinese opened service-based businesses that survived when mining ventures went bust. Meanwhile, criminal wrongdoing was sometimes hastily pinned on Australians – starting in 1851, San Francisco's self-appointed Committee of Vigilance tried, convicted, lynched and deported the 'Sydney Ducks' gang, so when another gold rush began in Australia that same year, many were ready to head home.

Inter-ethnic rivalries obscured the real competitive threat posed not by fellow miners or service workers, but by those who controlled the means of production: California's 'robber barons.' These speculators hoarded the capital and industrial machinery necessary for deep-mining operations. As mining became industrialized, fewer miners were needed, and jobless prospectors turned their anger toward a convenient target: Chinese workers, who by 1860 had become, after Mexicans, the

1906	1927	1933	1934
An earthquake strikes the coast of NorCal, setting off fires in San Francisco that rage for days and level three-quarters of the city. Survivors immediately begin reconstruction.	After a year of tinkering, San Francisco inventor Philo Farnsworth transmits the first successful TV broadcast of...a straight line.	The birth of the Central Valley Project, which created dams and canals throughout Central California from the 1930s to the 1970s and forever changed Northern California geography and wildlife migration.	A longshoremen's strike ends with 34 San Francisco strikers shot and 40 gassed or beaten by police. After mass funeral processions and city-wide strikes, shipping magnates meet union demands.

second-most populous group in California. Discriminatory Californian laws restricting housing, employment and citizenship for anyone born in China were reinforced in the 1882 US Chinese Exclusion Act, which remained law until 1943.

Laws limiting work options for Chinese arrivals served the needs of robber barons, who needed cheap labor to build railroads to their claims and reach East Coast markets. To blast tunnels through the Sierra Nevada, workers were lowered down sheer mountain faces in wicker baskets, planted lit sticks of dynamite in rock crevices, then urgently tugged the rope to be hoisted out of harm's way. Those who survived the day's work were confined to bunkhouses under armed guard in cold, remote mountain regions. With little other choice of legitimate employment, an estimated 12,000 Chinese laborers blasted through the Sierra Nevada, meeting the westbound end of the railroad in 1869.

Oil & Water

During the American Civil War (1861–65), California couldn't rely on food shipments from the East Coast, and started growing its own. California recruited Midwestern homesteaders to farm the Central Valley, with shameless propaganda. 'Acres of Untaken Government Land...for a Million Farmers...Health and Wealth without Cyclones or Blizzards,' trumpeted one California-boosting poster, neglecting to mention earthquakes or ongoing land disputes with *rancheros* and Native Californians. It worked: more than 120,000 homesteaders came to California in the 1870s and '80s.

These homesteaders soon discovered that California's gold rush had left the land badly scarred. Hills had been stripped bare, vegetation wiped out, streams silted up and mercury washed into water supplies. Cholera spread through the open sewers in camps and claimed many lives. Because mining claims leased by the US government had been granted significant tax exemptions, there were insufficient public funds for clean-up programs or public water works.

Frustrated farmers south of Big Sur voted to secede from California in 1859, but appeals for secession were shelved during the Civil War. In 1884 Southern Californians passed a pioneering law preventing dumping into California's rivers and, with the support of budding agribusiness and real-estate concerns, passed bond measures to build aqueducts and dams that made large-scale farming and real-estate development possible. By the 20th century, the lower one-third of the state took two-thirds of available water supplies, inspiring Northern California's own calls for secession.

While Southern California was urbanizing following the discovery of oil, Northern Californians – who had witnessed firsthand the

California was named after a fictional island paradise ruled by women and populated with griffins (fantastical lion-eagle hybrids) in a 16th-century romance novel.

1941	1942	1957	1967
Counties in Northern California and Southwestern Oregon begin making plans to secede and form the State of Jefferson. Plans are halted when Japan bombs Pearl Harbor	Executive Order 9066 sends 120,000 Japanese Americans to internment camps. The Japanese American Citizens' League files lawsuits, providing legal support for the 1964 Civil Rights Act.	At the height of McCarthyism, City Lights in San Francisco wins a landmark ruling against book-banning over the publication of Allen Ginsberg's *Howl*.	The Summer of Love kicks off on January 14 at the Human Be-In in Golden Gate Park with blown conch shells and brain cells and draft cards used as rolling papers.

environmental devastation of mining and logging – were jump-starting the nation's first conservation movement. Sierra Nevada naturalist, lyrical writer and San Francisco Bay Area farmer John Muir founded the Sierra Club in 1892, and became California's greatest environmental champion. Pipelines and dams – including Hetch Hetchy Reservoir in Yosemite, which still supplies Bay Area water – were constructed to provide water to communities in California's deserts and coastal cities, despite Muir's strenuous objections. In drought-prone California, tensions still regularly come to a boil between land developers and conservationists.

Reforming the Wild West

When the great earthquake and fire hit San Francisco in 1906, it signaled change for California. With public funds for citywide water mains and fire hydrants siphoned off by corrupt political bosses, there was only one functioning water source in San Francisco. When the smoke lifted, one thing was clear: it was time for the Wild West to change its ways.

While San Francisco was rebuilt at a rate of 15 buildings per day, political reformers got to work on improving city, state and national policies, one plank at a time. Californians concerned about public health and the trafficking of women pushed for passage of the 1914 Red Light Abatement Act, which shut down brothels statewide. Mexico's revolution from 1910 to 1921 brought a new wave of migrants and revolutionary ideas, including ethnic pride and worker solidarity. As California's ports grew, in 1934 longshoremen's unions coordinated a historic 83-day strike along the entire West Coast, which forced concessions for safer working conditions and fair pay.

At the height of the Depression in 1935, some 200,000 farming families fleeing the drought-plagued Dust Bowl in Texas and Oklahoma arrived in California, where they found scant pay and deplorable working conditions. California's artists alerted America to the migrants' plight, and the nation rallied around Dorothea Lange's haunting documentary photos of famine-struck families and John Steinbeck's harrowing fictionalized account in his 1939 novel *The Grapes of Wrath*. The book was widely banned and Steinbeck was accused of harboring Communist sympathies, but he still won both the Pulitzer and Nobel Prizes for his masterwork. The public support he generated for farm workers helped launch the United Farm Workers union.

California's workforce permanently changed in WWII, when women and African Americans were recruited for wartime industries and Mexican workers were brought in to fill labor shortages. Contracts in military communications and aviation attracted an international elite of engineers, who would launch California's high-tech industry. Within a decade after WWII, California's population grew by 40%, surpassing 13 million.

The grizzly bear was designated the state animal in 1953 and emblazoned on the state flag and seal, but the last sighting of a grizzly in California happened in 1924, in Sequoia National Park.

1969	1976	1977	1989
Native American activists symbolically reclaim Alcatraz as native land until ousted by the FBI in 1971. Public support for protesters strengthens self-rule concessions for Native American tribes.	In the 'Judgment of Paris,' a blind wine-tasting competition, Napa Valley wines beat out French ones and California's Wine Country finds its place on the map.	San Francisco Supervisor Harvey Milk becomes the first openly gay man elected to California public office. Milk sponsors a gay-rights bill before being murdered by political opponent Dan White in 1978.	On October 17, the Loma Prieta earthquake hits 6.9 on the Richter scale near Santa Cruz, destroying a two-level section of Interstate 880 and resulting in 63 deaths and almost 4000 injuries.

NORTHERN CALIFORNIA'S FIGHT FOR CIVIL RIGHTS

Before the 1963 march on Washington, DC, the Civil Rights movement was well under way in California. When 120,000 Japanese Americans along the West Coast were ordered into internment camps by President Roosevelt in 1942, the San Francisco–based Japanese American Citizens' League immediately filed suits that eventually made their way to the Supreme Court. These lawsuits established groundbreaking civil rights legal precedents; in 1992 internees received reparations and an official letter of apology for internment signed by George W Bush.

Adopting the nonviolent resistance practices of Mahatma Gandhi and Martin Luther King Jr, labor leaders César Chávez and Dolores Huerta formed United Farm Workers in 1962 to champion the rights of underrepresented immigrant laborers. While civil-rights leaders marched on Washington, Chávez and Californian grape pickers marched on Sacramento, bringing the issue of fair wages and the health risks of pesticides to the nation's attention. When Bobby Kennedy was sent to investigate, he sided with Chávez, bringing Latinos into the US political fold.

The Seeds of Counterculture

It's only fitting that San Francisco sits at the far left edge of the country, mirroring the city's political inclinations. WWII sailors discharged in San Francisco for insubordination and homosexuality found themselves at home in North Beach's bebop jazz clubs, bohemian coffeehouses and City Lights bookstore. San Francisco was home to free speech and free spirits, and soon everyone who was anyone was getting arrested: Beat poet Lawrence Ferlinghetti for publishing Allen Ginsberg's epic poem *Howl*, comedian Lenny Bruce for uttering the F-word onstage, and Carol Doda for becoming the first stripper to go topless.

When the CIA made the mistake of using writer and willing test subject Ken Kesey to test psychoactive drugs intended to create the ultimate soldier, it inadvertently kicked off the psychedelic era. At the January 14, 1967 Human Be-In at Golden Gate Park, trip-master Timothy Leary urged a crowd of 20,000 hippies to dream a new American dream and 'turn on, tune in, drop out.' When Flower Power faded, other Bay Area rebellions grew in its place: Black Power, Gay Pride and medical marijuana clubs.

Geeking Out

When Silicon Valley introduced the first personal computer in 1968, advertisements breathlessly gushed that Hewlett-Packard's 'light' (40lb) machine could 'take on roots of a fifth-degree polynomial, Bessel functions, elliptic integrals and regression analysis' – all for just $4900

Roman Polanski's film *Chinatown* (1974) is the fictionalized yet accurate account of the brutal water wars waged to build San Francisco and Los Angeles. For the real story of how LA swindled Eastern Sierra farmers, read *Cadillac Desert: The American West and Its Disappearing Water*, by Marc Reisner (1986).

1996	2000	2003	2004
Proposition 215 (aka the Compassionate Use Act of 1996) passes by voter-led initiative, legalizing the medical use of cannabis; pot smoke begins to appear on the afternoon breeze in San Francisco.	The Nasdaq crashes, ending the dot-com era. Traditional industries gloat over the burst bubble, until knock-on effects lead to a devalued dollar and New York Stock Exchange slide beginning in 2002.	Republican Arnold Schwarzenegger (aka 'The Governator') is elected governor of California. Schwarzenegger breaks party ranks on environmental issues and wins re-election in 2007.	Google's IPO raises a historic $1.67 billion at $85 per share. Share prices have since increased over 900%, and the company's worth now exceeds $498 billion.

(nearly $35,000 today). Consumers didn't know quite what to do with computers, but in his 1969 *Whole Earth Catalog*, author (and former LSD tester for the CIA) Stewart Brand explained that the technology governments used to run countries could empower ordinary people. Hoping to bring computer power to the people, Steve Jobs and Steve Wozniak, both in their 20s at the time, introduced the Apple II at the 1977 West Coast Computer Faire, with unfathomable memory (4KB of RAM) and microprocessor speed (1MHz).

Still, the question remained: what would ordinary people do with all that computing power? By the mid-1990s an entire dot-com industry boomed in Silicon Valley with online start-ups, and suddenly people were getting everything – their mail, news, politics, pet food and, yes, sex – online. But when dot-com profits weren't forthcoming, venture-capital funding dried up and fortunes in stock-options disappeared when the dot-com bubble burst and the Nasdaq plummeted on March 10, 2000. Overnight, 26-year-old vice-presidents and Bay Area service-sector employees alike found themselves jobless. But as online users continued to look for useful information – and one another – search engines and social media boomed. The Bay Area real-estate market boomed in parallel, with companies such as Google, Twitter, AirBnB and LinkedIn and their employees grabbing up housing and office space. It was only in 2017 that the long-surging tech market began showing signs of slowing.

California's biotech industry has been nothing to sneeze at, either. In 1976 an upstart company called Genentech was founded in the San Francisco Bay Area, and quickly got to work cloning human insulin and introducing the Hepatitis B vaccine. In 2004 California voters approved a $3 billion bond measure for stem-cell research. By 2008 California had become the USA's biggest funder of stem-cell research, as well as the focus of Nasdaq's new Biotechnology Index, and by 2014 the Bay Area was home to 1377 life science and biotech companies reporting revenues of $4.1 billion and employing more than 140,000 people.

In 2015, with hefty contributions by the tech, biotech and aerospace industries, California generated a collective income of $2.46 trillion and surpassed the GDP of France to become the world's sixth-largest economy.

California is America's top technology hub, accounting for one-third of all US venture capital, half of biotech employment and half of all FDA-approved medical therapies since 1985.

To read more about the garage-workshop culture of Silicon Valley go to www.folklore.org, which covers the crashes and personality clashes that made geek history.

HISTORY GEEKING OUT

2008	2008	2013	2016
California voters pass Proposition 8, defining legal marriage as between a man and a woman. Courts eventually rule the law unconstitutional, and same-sex marriages resume in 2013.	California voters approve the sale of bonds to fund California's High-Speed Rail Project, which by 2029 will link San Francisco and Los Angeles in under three hours.	The eastern span of the Bay Bridge opens, after 24 years of planning and construction, sparked by the 1989 Loma Prieta earthquake. It cost $6 billion, the state's costliest-ever public-works project.	California voters approve Proposition 64, legalizing the use of recreational marijuana and creating the largest market for pot products in the US.

The Way of Life

Believe (most of) what you've heard – Northern Californians are a different breed. Typically they espouse a live-and-let-live sensibility, which explains how ultra-left hippies and ultra-right libertarians coexist throughout the region. And although it may seem absurd to ponder the similarities between young tech execs from Silicon Valley and grizzled old lumberjacks from the far north, both pride themselves on fiercely independent thinking, the linchpin of NorCal culture.

Regional Identities

In the Bay Area the politics are liberal and the people are generally open-minded, with a strong sense of social justice and a passionate devotion to the outdoors. Over the years, the tech boom has caused a wild rise in real-estate prices, changing the demographics of many San Francisco neighborhoods, which are starting to resemble the demographics of overwhelmingly wealthy and white Marin County, just over the Golden Gate Bridge. Both have a tremendous sense of self-satisfied civic pride. San Francisco, despite its all-embracing image, lately suffers from a loss of diversity. The East Bay and Alameda County, which include Oakland and Berkeley, have more ethnic diversity and middle-class blending, but because of unaffordable real-estate prices in San Francisco, these counties are also seeing prices climb.

Far north of San Francisco, it's a different scene altogether. The counties of Mendocino, Humboldt and Del Norte are where people go to get away from other people, making for a small, self-selecting population. There aren't a lot of people in the far north – and there's not a lot of money either. At least not legal money.

Despite the fact that medical marijuana is legal in California, and recreational weed will be as of January 2018, the remote woods of the far north still harbor enormous illegal marijuana farms, bringing with them an underground culture of growers and itinerant pickers. Some are on the up and up, growing 'medicine' (or 'flowers') for legal urban cannabis clubs, but since pot remains against federal law, even if legal by state law, the DEA flies in every year and destroys many farms (it doesn't usually seize the land, just the pot). Other operations are shadier, fly-by-nighters run by drug cartels, which set up for a season on public land that gets trashed by the grow. This pot goes out of the state. When in the far north, don't ever jump fences marked 'private property', lest you hear rifle fire.

The state's more progressive liberals also live up north, and have fostered a strong and innovative culture of sustainability. (If you spot a beat-up old diesel Mercedes-Benz chugging along the highway, chances are it's running on biodiesel or recycled French-fry grease.) This faction is firmly entrenched against another sizable voting bloc: the conservative contingent in the northeast, who are still largely dependent on logging and mining.

The Central Coast, with its smaller pockets of population, starts below left-of-center Santa Cruz, and stretches all the way south to the laid-back, liberal college town of San Luis Obispo. Along the way, Hwy 1 winds past

California is defined as a 'minority majority' state, with no ethnic population in the majority. In March 2014, Latinos surpassed non-Hispanic whites as the state's largest ethnic group, comprising 39% of the population.

working-class Monterey, made famous in John Steinbeck's novels; the bohemian Big Sur coast; the conservative upper-crust villages of Carmel-by-the-Sea; and Cambria, where the 'newly wed and nearly dead' have multimillion-dollar homes.

The Central Valley is the most socially conservative part of the state, with a largely agricultural economy. This is the land of cowboys, farmers, fruit barons and migrant workers – but as the prices of the coastal cities have continued to rise, it is also a new frontier for the creative class. The identity of the region is also dramatically impacted by the presence of a Latino workforce that harvests the vast agricultural plains. Highway billboards warn you to get right with God, and AM radio plays mariachi music.

The foothills of the Sierra Nevada include the small towns of the Gold Country, which are socially conservative; many locals are retirees. Further east, the high mountains of the Sierra have fewer towns because of winter's deep snows. Locals in the high mountains likewise skew conservative, but they are offset by the hordes of Bay Area families who have weekend houses in the areas around Lake Tahoe and Truckee, where skiing and hiking are the major draws.

Lifestyle

Creativity, imagination and intellectualism are defining characteristics of Northern Californians, who are proud of their 'green' reputation and sensitive to environmental issues. On the whole, Californians have zoomed ahead of the national energy-use curve, buying more hybrid, fuel-efficient and electric cars than any other state. In recent years, electric-vehicle charging stations have been added to airports, businesses, freeway rest stops and parking lots across the state, which has become the world's top electric-vehicle market. In addition, California voters enacted the nation's first statewide plastic bag ban in 2016, and San Francisco has set the goal of 'zero waste' by 2020, going beyond mere recycling to city-wide composting of leftover food scraps.

With a median household income of $64,500, few Californians can afford a beachfront dream house. Many people rent their homes, as buying

Southern California is totally known for its surfer drawl, but Northern California, too, has its own mix of idiosyncratic slang. The most iconic examples? 'Hella' and 'hecka,' which are technically defined by linguists as intensifiers.

After President Trump threatened to defund NASA's Earth Science division, including some satellites that track climate change, California Governor Jerry Brown said this: 'If Trump turns off the satellites, California will launch its own damn satellite.'

WHO'S UP IN THAT TREE?

Although many people in Northern California are active defenders of the environment, few demonstrate the zeal of Julia Butterfly Hill, who protested the deforestation of Northern California's redwood forests by climbing into a 180ft tree near Scotia on December 10, 1997. And then she stayed there. Hill's tree, a 1500-year-old coast redwood that she named 'Luna,' was under threat from the Pacific Lumber Company. In an astonishing act of civil disobedience, Hill lived on a 6ft-by-6ft platform, weathering cold, rain and persistent harassment from lumberjacks, for 738 days – over two full years.

Hill's actions captured the nation's imagination, and she became both the face of radical environmental action and a punch line for late-night talk-show hosts. In the end, Luna was spared, and a $50,000 deal was brokered with the Pacific Lumber Company. Not that the campaign to protect old-growth redwood is over – a proposition to widen and straighten Hwy 101 by CalTrans threatened to bring chainsaws to over 40 trees in Richardson Grove State Park until, in 2014, courts ruled that the state highway agency hadn't followed the law in its assessment of impacts on the trees.

In 2016 the redwoods were facing a new enemy – climate change, and more specifically, drought. A recent study predicted that in a worst-case scenario, a hot and dry future, the coastal redwood forest range could decrease by 79%. In response, the California Department of Parks and Recreation partnered with the Save the Redwoods League in a commitment to restore 10,000 acres of redwood forests over the next five years.

THE WAY OF LIFE THE HOMELESS

MARRIAGE EQUALITY: RIGHTS FOR ALL

Forty thousand Californians were already registered as domestic partners when, on Valentine's Day weekend in 2004, San Francisco Mayor Gavin Newsom issued marriage licenses to same-sex couples. This was in defiance of a statewide same-sex marriage ban, making San Francisco the first place in America to legally recognize gay marriage. City Hall remained open all weekend, and couples waited in the rain for hours in lines that snaked around the block, while other lovestruck San Franciscans arrived with umbrellas, trays of cookies and champagne, and musical instruments to serenade the waiting couples.

In the subsequent month, 4000 same-sex couples married, until courts blocked the issuance of any more licenses, pending legislative review. In November of that same year, the California Supreme Court deemed that the mayor hadn't possessed the authority to bypass state law, and voided the marriages. Subsequent lawsuits were brought by the couples whose marriages had been voided, and in May 2008 the state Supreme Court overturned the statewide ban, deeming it unconstitutional. For six months, couples once again came from around the world to marry in California, until in November 2008 voters passed – by slim margins (48% to 52%) – Proposition 8, which amended the state's constitution to prohibit same-sex marriage. This left those couples who held legally binding marriage certificates in legal limbo.

Meanwhile, over a dozen other states had begun to allow same-sex marriage, either by court decision, state legislation or popular vote. Then, in 2013, the US Supreme Court overturned Proposition 8, and maintained the validity of the licenses issued prior to the ban. Now some legally married couples hold two licenses: one from 2004 and one from 2008. In June 2015, the US Supreme Court struck down same-sex marriage bans across the nation, ruling that same-sex marriage is a legal right. You heard it first in San Francisco.

has become prohibitive in recent years: 18 of the 25 most expensive US housing markets are in California. Almost half of all Californians reside in cities, but much of the other half lives in the suburbs, where the cost of living is just as high, if not higher; Marin County and Santa Cruz are among the most costly places to live in America. San Francisco consistently tops national quality-of-life indices, and is right behind New York City and Honolulu as one of the nation's most expensive cities.

In 2002, Sacramento was cited by Time magazine and the Civil Rights Project at Harvard University as America's most diverse and integrated city. According to the Sacramento Bee, this still held true 10 years later.

Among adult Californians, one in four lives alone, and almost 50% are unmarried. Of those who are currently married, 33% won't be in 10 years. Increasingly, Californians are shacking up: the number of unmarried cohabiting couples has increased 40% since 1990.

Politically, Northern California is among the most liberal places in the US, particularly in the coastal areas. In the 2016 election voters overwhelmingly rejected Donald Trump, who lost the state by more than four million votes. Post-election, no state was more vocal about its dissatisfaction with the outcome.

Self-help, fitness and body modification are major industries throughout California, successfully marketed since the 1970s as 'lite' versions of religious experience – all the agony and ecstasy of the major religious brands, without those heavy commandments. Exercise and good food help keep Californians among the fittest in the nation. Yet over 758,607 Californians are apparently ill enough to merit prescriptions for medical marijuana.

The Homeless

Homelessness is not part of the California dream, but it is a reality for at least 118,142 Californians. In recent years, cities such as San Francisco and Sacramento have seen an uptick of 3%, according to the Department of Housing and Urban Development, and nearly half of the nation's 'unsheltered' homeless are living on the streets of California. With the additional impact of the housing boom and changing demographics of San Francisco, some suggest that the numbers are actually much higher. The sheer visibility of homeless people in Northern California, particularly in San Francisco, is a shock for many visitors.

Understanding the causes and demographics of Northern California's homeless is not easy. Some are teens who have run away or been kicked out by their families, but the largest contingent of homeless Californians are US military veterans. Some say the problem started in the 1960s, when Ronald Reagan slashed funding to mental-health facilities, drug-rehab programs and low-income housing programs, both as governor of California and later as president. Over the following decades this left few options for many Californians suffering from mental illness and drug addiction.

Also standing in line at homeless shelters and food banks are the working poor, unable to cover rent and expenses on minimum-wage salaries, despite recent increases to the latter. Rather than addressing the underlying causes of homelessness, some California cities have criminalized loitering, panhandling and even sitting on sidewalks, further marginalizing the homeless.

The bottom line is nobody knows how to address the issue, and until they do, panhandlers will be part of the experience of visiting Northern California cities – especially San Francisco. Whether you offer money or food is obviously up to you, but in general a polite 'no, thank you' will suffice if you'd rather not.

Sports

California has more professional sports teams than any other state, and loyalties to local NFL football, NBA basketball and major-league baseball teams run deep. Still, San Francisco doesn't necessarily have the sports nuts in large numbers like other American cities. That said, people in the Bay Area do get worked up before a big game – just go ahead and try to find tickets to see the San Francisco 49ers. After a dizzying season in 2010, the San Francisco Giants won the baseball World Series and transformed San Francisco's typically apathetic population into rabid fans in orange and black; they swarmed the streets again in 2012 and 2014, after two more World Series wins.

California is the only state that has hosted both the Summer and Winter Olympics.

Although studies have found that Californians are less likely to be couch potatoes than other Americans, when one Californian team plays another, the streets are deserted, bars are full, and all eyes are glued to the tube. The biggest grudge matches are between the San Francisco Giants and the LA Dodgers, the Oakland A's and Anaheim's Angels and the San Francisco 49ers and the Oakland Raiders, though the Raiders recently announced a future move to Las Vegas. The team will remain at the Oakland's Coliseum in 2017 and possibly 2018, before heading to a new stadium in Vegas. Oakland fans are far more pleased these days with their Golden State Warriors, who won the 2015 and 2017 NBA championships.

To see small but dedicated crowds of hometown fans (and easily score cheaper tickets), watch pro men's or women's (WNBA) basketball in Sacramento, or pro hockey or soccer in San Jose. Or catch minor league baseball teams up and down the state, especially the winning San Jose Giants.

Surfing is the coastal spectator sport of choice, with waves reaching 100ft at the annual Mavericks competition near Half Moon Bay.

Except for championship play-offs, the regular season for major-league baseball runs from April to September, soccer from April to October, WNBA basketball from late May to mid-September, NFL football from September to early January, NHL ice hockey from October to March, and NBA basketball from November to April.

Music & the Arts

You'll be sitting in a San Francisco *taqueria* minding your own business when suddenly a posse of mariachis arrives and breaks into a brassy ballad. *This* is the essence of Northern California's relationship with the arts: deeply woven into everyday life, unexpected and unavoidable. Northern California has been a bastion for creative thinkers, artists, contrarians and crackpots since its beginning. Expect to encounter the thriving culture they've created: broadly independent, highly spirited and marching to its own beat.

Music

The essential sounds of Northern California would be a schizophrenic playlist. It would lead with a track from Summer of Love icons such as Jefferson Airplane, Janis Joplin or the Grateful Dead, include a few choice cuts from twanging, heartbroken country heroes from the Central Valley, and eventually make its way to the distinctive thump of the East Bay's 'hyphy' hip-hop movement. You'd also have to have a sample of haute folk nuevo acts such as Joanna Newsom and a couple of lilting *norteño* ballads, which dominate the region's AM radio, and round things out with the San Francisco Symphony, now one of the nation's most exciting orchestral bodies, under the baton of Michael Tilson Thomas.

San Francisco is where most of the musical action happens. But even outside the city, you'll find fantastic outdoor festivals and spunky music scenes in college towns such as Arcata and Chico. Look for events listings online and also at coffeehouses, where bulletin boards often have posters for upcoming out-of-town events as diverse as the Queer Music Festival and Reggae on the River.

Golden Oldies

The guy crooning in the corner of the taco shop represents one of California's longest musical traditions – Mexican folk music. This sound arrived even before the gold rush introduced Western bluegrass, bawdy dance-hall ragtime and Chinese classical music and is still an essential sound of the region. Still, by the turn of the 20th century, opera had become California's favorite sound. San Francisco alone had 20 concert and opera halls before the 1906 earthquake literally brought down the houses. Among San Francisco's first public buildings to be completed was the War Memorial Opera House, now home to the second-largest US opera company after New York's Metropolitan. Although the San Francisco Opera still rolls out the same chestnuts that entertained fans after the quake, today its program includes a number of visionary modern works, including recent premieres *The Bonesetter's Daughter,* with a libretto written by Bay Area author Amy Tan, and *Dolores Claiborne,* adapted from the story by Stephen King.

When the 1906 earthquake hit San Francisco, the visiting Metropolitan Opera lost all its costumes, and tenor Enrico Caruso was thrown from his bed. Caruso never returned, but the Met played free shows in the rubble-choked streets.

It Don't Mean a Thing...

Swing – imported from black neighborhoods in the East and dance halls of the South – swept Northern California in the 1930s and '40s. Big bands packed houses in the Bay Area and Western Swing (the country kind) filled Central Valley dance halls. Swing's arty edge flourished on the stages of San Francisco's underground, integrated jazz clubs. These scenes might sound like estranged cousins, but swing's essential feel – lilting, often up-tempo rhythmic underpinnings – was the colorblind common thread.

Still, the era swung in two distinctly segregated ways in Northern California: the African American communities that arrived via the 'Great Migration' to work in the Bay Area's WWII shipping and manufacturing industries, and satin-clad Western Swing outfits that modeled themselves after Texas fiddler Bob Wills. While both San Francisco and Oakland fostered working-class blues scenes throughout the 1940s and '50s, championed by guitarists Pee Wee Crayton from Texas and Oklahoma-born Lowell Fulson, the most happening scene was in San Francisco's Fillmore district, known as the 'Harlem of the West' – which is rumored to have hosted the only gig where jazz icons Charlie Parker and Louis Armstrong ever played together. By marrying Western Swing and a rural working-class aesthetic, the Central Valley minted the Bakersfield Sound, a hard-edged, honky-tonk genre that would see the rise of Buck Owens and Merle Haggard.

While Beat poets riffed over improvised bass-lines and audiences snapped their fingers along in San Francisco's North Beach neighborhood, the cool West Coast Jazz movement emerged from the 1950s, with champions in trumpeter Chet Baker and pianist Dave Brubeck. In the 1950s and '60s, doo-wop, rhythm and blues, and soul music were all in steady rotation at nightclubs in San Francisco, while the nexus of pop music became firmly established in the studios of Los Angeles.

The Monterey Jazz Festival is among the longest-running jazz festivals in the world and has been swinging along on the Central Coast since 1958. Its organizers have included pianist Dave Brubeck and actor, former Carmel mayor (and occasional composer) Clint Eastwood. It is held annually at the end of September.

The San Francisco Sound & Summer of Love

No tune captures the psychedelic San Francisco sound better than the brilliant, twisted, totally bizarre trip of Jefferson Airplane's musical take of Lewis Carroll's *Alice's Adventures in Wonderland*, 'White Rabbit.' After the building waves of musical rebellion manifested in the form of a sassy, sultry, salty singer named Janis Joplin, all ears were on San Francisco during the '60s. The Grateful Dead would emerge as the most enduring Bay Area ambassadors, but they were only a sliver of the scene. A seething, psychedelic mess of musical exploration, sexual liberation and mind-altering expression, it was a sound presented in vivid Technicolor by groups such as Moby Grape, Quicksilver Messenger Service and Santana. This movement was cranked up to 11 during 1967, when the Summer of Love brought 10,000 pilgrims to San Francisco's Haight-Ashbury neighborhood. Golden Gate Park's 'Human Be-In' in January of that year kicked things off with a free-form festival of good vibes, LSD and live music. At the end of the '60s, Sly and the Family Stone – a funky, interracial group lead by the so-called 'Black Prince of Woodstock', Sly Stone – perfectly captured the all-embracing, edgy, revolutionary spirit of the times with their hit 'I Want to Take You Higher.'

Wider social tensions, civic unrest and an increasingly volatile discourse on the Civil Rights movement later boiled over and changed the vanguard players of San Francisco's sound, and many musicians instrumental in the Summer of Love entered a period of decline hastened by over-exposure and overdoses. Those who survived cleaned up and cashed out (lookin' at you, Mr Santana), though the Grateful Dead soldiered on until Jerry Garcia's passing in a Marin County rehabilitation clinic in 1995.

Alternative NorCal

Forget the '80s, the spandex, the commercial synth pop and hair metal. While these trends wafted north from LA like a noxious cloud of Aqua

PUNKS OF THE NORTH

In the 1970s, when American airwaves were jammed with commercial arena rock, California rock critics like Lester Bangs and Greil Marcus formed the cultural front line to fight back. Sick of the prepackaged anthems, teenagers across the US and Northern California plugged secondhand guitars into crappy, distorted amplifiers and articulated their fury with three chords and unvarnished rage. Punk was born.

San Francisco's punk scene was arty and absurdist, in rare form with Dead Kennedy's singer (and future San Francisco mayoral candidate) Jello Biafra howling 'Holiday in Cambodia.' The Avengers opened for the Sex Pistols' 1978 San Francisco show, which Sid Vicious celebrated with an OD in the Haight that broke up the band.

In the mid-'90s a fresh wave of influential punks grew out of all-ages, DIY venues like Berkeley's (now defunct) Gillman Street Project, including bands such as Operation Ivy and Rancid. Of these, none had more sustained success than the Berkeley trio Green Day, who churned out catchy pop-punk hooks about suburban doldrums, masturbation and teen ennui. While Green Day grew into arena-sized audiences through the next decade, their 2004 LP *American Idiot* was a mainstream success with Bay Area ideals: its songs derided war, capitalism and conservative politics.

Net hair spray, Northern California's music scene slumbered. Aside from a couple of marginal mainstream acts, such as Huey Lewis & the News, Tesla and MC Hammer, Northern California was relatively quiet and its influence relatively minor. But there's something in the cultural DNA of Northern California that delights in swimming against the stream, so when the cultural backlash against mainstream movements began in earnest with college radio, late-night MTV programming and the emergence of arty, post-punk underground, Northern California was back in the action.

As so-called 'alternative music' found larger and larger audiences, well-packaged Bay Area folk rockers such as Counting Crows, Chris Isaak and 4 Non Blondes crossed over and enjoyed a moment of Top 40 success. Still, the most interesting music of the '90s was produced by a group of quietly influential, genre-bending groups such as Jawbreaker, Pavement, Primus and Faith No More.

The dot-com boom was the death knell of San Francisco's underground music in the 2000s; escalating rents were bankrolled by venture-capital firms, and artists watched their venues and rehearsal spaces transformed into offices, sushi restaurants and boutiques. In better news, indie electronic music project Tycho, led by San Franciscan (and former Sactown resident) Scott Hansen, was nominated in 2016 for a Grammy.

Over the last decade, Northern California's music has flourished across the bay in Oakland, where there are plucky scenes of underground rock and hip-hop. Further afield, unlikely musical centers have flourished – Nevada City is home to harp-playing indie darling Joanna Newsom.

In 2016, 36 people were tragically killed in a fire that broke out at a concert being held in an unsafe Oakland warehouse called Ghost Ship.

Rap & Hip-Hop Rhythms

Los Angeles' Compton neighborhood was the epicenter of the West Coast rap and hip-hop movements throughout the 1980s and '90s, but Northern California maintained a healthy grassroots hip-hop scene in the heart of the black-power movement in Oakland. One of the primary figures of West Coast rap, Tupac Shakur, spent his high-school years on the not-so-mean streets of Marin County. It wasn't until the 1990s that the Bay Area sound came into its own with the 'hyphy movement.' Like the Bay Area's punk and rock movements, its roots were also contrarian – a reaction against the increasing commercialization of hip-hop. Its most enduring and influential players were underground Oakland artists such as Keak Da Sneak, Mac Dre and E-40.

Also from Oakland, Michael Franti & Spearhead blended hip-hop with funk, reggae, folk, jazz and rock stylings into messages for social justice and peace in 2010's *The Sound of Sunshine*. Meanwhile, Korn from Bakersfield combined hip-hop with rap and metal to popularize 'nu metal.'

Architecture

There's more to Northern California than bungalows and boardwalks, and buildings here have often adapted imported styles to the climate and available materials – just look at the fog-resistant redwood-shingle houses in Mendocino. But after a century-plus of grafting on inspired influences and eccentric details as the mood strikes, the element of the unexpected is everywhere: tiled Maya deco facades in Oakland, English thatched roofs in Carmel, chinoiserie streetlamps in San Francisco. California's architecture was postmodern before the word even existed.

Oddball California Architecture

Hearst Castle, San Simeon

Tor House, Carmel-by-the-Sea

Sea Ranch Chapel, Sea Ranch

Winchester Mystery House, San Jose

Spanish Missions & Victorian Queens

The first Spanish missions were built around courtyards, using materials that Native Californians and colonists found on hand: adobe, limestone and grass. Many missions crumbled into disrepair as the church's influence waned, but the style remained practical for the climate. Early California settlers later adapted it into the *rancho* (ranch) adobe style, as in the San Carlos Borroméo de Carmelo Mission in Monterey.

Once the mid-19th-century gold rush was on, Northern California's nouveau riche imported materials to construct grand mansions matching European fashions, and raised the stakes with ornamental excess. Many millionaires favored the gilded Queen Anne style. Outrageous examples of Victorian architecture, including 'Painted Ladies' and 'gingerbread' houses, can be found in such Northern California towns as San Francisco, Ferndale and Eureka.

Art Deco & Arts & Crafts

Like much of the rest of the state, simplicity was the hallmark of Northern California's arts-and-crafts style. Influenced by both Japanese design principles and England's arts-and-crafts movement, its woodwork and handmade touches marked a deliberate departure from the Industrial Revolution. SoCal architects Charles and Henry Greene and Bernard Maybeck popularized the versatile one-story bungalow in Northern California, which became trendy at the turn of the 20th century. Today you'll spot these bungalows all over Sacramento and Berkeley with their overhanging eaves, terraces and sleeping porches, harmonizing indoors and outdoors.

In 1915, newspaper magnate William Randolph Hearst commissioned California's first licensed female architect, Julia Morgan, to build his Hearst Castle. The commission would take decades to complete.

California was cosmopolitan from the start, and couldn't be limited to any one set of international influences. In the 1920s, the international art-deco style took elements from the ancient world – Mayan glyphs, Egyptian pillars, Babylonian ziggurats – and flattened them into modern motifs to cap stark facades and outline streamlined skyscrapers, most notably in downtown Oakland and Sacramento. Streamline moderne kept decoration to a minimum and mimicked the aerodynamic look of ocean liners and airplanes, as seen at San Francisco's Maritime Museum at Fisherman's Wharf.

Postmodern Evolutions

True to its mythic nature, California can't help wanting to embellish the facts a little, veering away from strict high modernism to add unlikely postmodern shapes to the local landscape. Following in the footsteps of Southern California buildings like Richard Meier's Getty Center, and

In the North Coast community of Sea Ranch, buildings are subject to rigorous zoning guidelines that require simple timber-frame structures clad in wooden siding or shingles and a harmonious relationship with the surroundings.

Frank Gehry's Walt Disney Concert Hall in Los Angeles, San Francisco has become home to a brave new crop of buildings in the new millennium.

San Francisco's brand of postmodernism is emblematic in Pritzker Prize–winning architects that magnify and mimic California's great outdoors, especially in Golden Gate Park. Swiss architects Herzog & de Meuron clad the MH de Young Memorial Museum in copper, which will eventually oxidize green to match its park setting. Nearby, Renzo Piano literally raised the roof on sustainable design at the LEED platinum-certified California Academy of Sciences, capped by a living garden.

Visual Arts & Theater

Although the earliest European artists were trained cartographers accompanying Western explorers, their images of California as an island show more imagination than scientific rigor. This exaggerated, mythologizing tendency of depicting California continued throughout the gold-rush era, as Western artists alternated between caricatures of Wild West debauchery and manifest-destiny propaganda that urged pioneers to settle in the golden West. The completion of the Transcontinental Railroad in 1869 brought an influx of romantic painters, who produced epic California wilderness landscapes. In the early 1900s, homegrown colonies of California impressionist plein-air painters emerged, particularly at Carmel-by-the-Sea.

With the invention of photography, the improbable truth of California's landscape and its inhabitants was revealed. Pirkle Jones saw expressive potential in California landscape photography after WWII, while San Francisco native Ansel Adams' sublime photographs had already started doing justice to Yosemite. Adams founded Group f/64 with Edward Weston from Carmel and Imogen Cunningham in San Francisco. Berkeley-based Dorothea Lange turned her unflinching lens on the plight of Californian migrant workers in the Great Depression and Japanese Americans forced to enter internment camps in WWII, producing poignant documentary photos.

As the postwar American West became crisscrossed with freeways and divided into planned communities, Californian painters captured the abstract forms of manufactured landscapes on canvas. In San Francisco Richard Diebenkorn and David Park became leading proponents of Bay Area Figurative Art, while San Francisco sculptor Richard Serra captured urban aesthetics in massive, rusting monoliths resembling ship prows and industrial Stonehenges. San Francisco also developed its own brand of pop art, with the rough-and-ready-made 1950s Beat collage, 1960s psychedelic Fillmore posters, earthy '70s funk and beautiful-mess punk, and '80s graffiti and skate culture. This tradition remains alive at the Fillmore Auditorium, which distributes show posters after most of its concerts.

The contemporary art scene in Northern California is a blend of all these influences, informed by the international community and augmented by muralist-led social commentary. There's also an obsessive dedication to craft and a new-media milieu pierced by Silicon Valley's cutting-edge technology. To see California-made art at its most experimental, check out independent NorCal art spaces in San Francisco's Mission District and the laboratory-like galleries of SoMa's Yerba Buena Arts District. The Yerba Buena Center for the Arts is at the center of it all, and has excellent modern-art programs.

San Francisco's priorities have been obvious since the great earthquake of 1906, when survivors were entertained in tents set up amid the smoldering ruins, and its famous theaters were rebuilt well before City Hall. Major productions destined for the lights of Broadway and London premiere at the American Conservatory Theater, and San Francisco's answer to Edinburgh is the annual SF Fringe Festival at the Exit Theatre. The Magic Theatre gained a national reputation in the 1970s, when Sam Shepard was the theater's resident playwright, and still today it premieres innovative California playwrights. Across the Bay, the Berkeley Repertory Theatre has launched acclaimed productions based on such unlikely subjects as the rise and fall of Jim Jones' People's Temple.

Film in San Francisco

Although San Francisco can't hold a candle to the cinematic clout of its neighbor to the south, the city hosts a number of internationally renowned film festivals. The annual San Francisco International Film Festival, held each spring, is the oldest continuously running film festival in the Americas and the city also hosts several other notable film festivals each year, including the Asian American Film Festival in March and the International LGBTQ Film Festival in June as part of the city's Pride Month. Film fans who come at other times of the year should look into UC Berkeley's Pacific Film Archive.

The Bay Area is also home to some notable film houses, including animation giant Pixar and George Lucas' Skywalker Ranch.

By the Book

For a traveler, there's much to love about Northern California's duo of great early literary icons, Jack London and Mark Twain. After all, it was Twain whose thoughts on travel are just so quotable: 'The World is a book, and those who do not travel read only a page.' Both men were avid adventurers, vivid storytellers and iconic literary stylists.

Frogs and Wolves

Long before Huck Finn, Twain got his break with a story called *The Celebrated Jumping Frog of Calaveras County*, which he wrote while living in a cabin in the California foothills. Every year the central event of Twain's story still sees the competition of little green contestants at the Calaveras County Fair in Angels Camp. Jack London was also a restless vagabond. Born in San Francisco, London shipped in and out of the ports of Oakland, which informed seafaring stories and adventure novels such as *White Fang, The Call of the Wild* and *The Sea-Wolf*. London's old neighborhood isn't the turf of salty dogs any more; the waterfront area in Oakland is now a dining and entertainment district that bears his name.

Beatniks

A generation later came the Beats, a collection of poets, novelists and alternative thinkers who populated San Francisco's North Beach neighborhood. The cast of characters who drifted in and out of the scene are household names in American literature: Jack Kerouac, Allen Ginsberg and Lawrence Ferlinghetti. Ferlinghetti's City Lights bookstore published many of the generation's most definitive titles, including Ginsberg's *Howl and Other Poems*, which won a landmark 1957 obscenity case during the oppressive era of McCarthyism.

Modern Mythmakers

Timeless, rare Ansel Adams photographs are paired with excerpts from canonical Californian writers, such as Jack Kerouac and Joan Didion, in *California: With Classic California Writings*, edited by Andrea Gray Stillman.

More recently, a number of Northern California authors have enjoyed attention on the international stage. Chinese American novelist Amy Tan's *Joy Luck Club* was a celebrated work about the dynamics of families in San Francisco's Chinatown. Writer, editor and publisher Dave Eggers was a Pulitzer Prize finalist for his 2000 memoir *A Heartbreaking Work of Staggering Genius*, and two literary ventures have earned national attention: a literary magazine *The Believer* and a nonprofit literary advocacy program, 826 Valencia, which is named for its Mission District address.

Some of the most eloquent modern writing on Northern California, the Summer of Love, the Central Valley and the California political circus is by the hand of Sacramento native essayist Joan Didion. Didion's *White Album* is a collection of essays that goes deep into the psyche of California in the late '60s, and discussion of the Central Valley in *Where I Was From* takes a thoughtful look at Ronald Reagan's governor mansion, water wars and the odysseys of California's mythmakers.

The Land & Wildlife

Northern California has stunning landscapes. Its Mediterranean climate – characterized by dry summers and mild, wet winters with snow only at high elevations – makes it an easy year-round destination. Though the north is more sparsely populated than the south, together they comprise the largest population of any US state, and have the nation's highest projected growth rate. This puts tremendous strain on the natural environment, which is under constant threat from logging, drought, water diversion and urban sprawl.

Lay of the Land

The third-largest state after Alaska and Texas, California covers more than 155,000 sq miles, making it larger than 85 of the world's smallest nations. California is bordered to the north by Oregon, the east by Nevada and Arizona, the south by Mexico, and the west by 3427 miles of Pacific coastline.

Geology & Earthquakes

As a whole, California is a complex geologic landscape formed from fragments of rock and earth crust scraped together as the North American continent drifted westward over hundreds of millions of years. Northern California has crumpled coastal ranges, the downward bowing Central Valley and the still-rising Sierra Nevada; all provide evidence of the gigantic forces exerted as the continental and ocean plates crushed together.

Everything changed about 25 million years ago, when the ocean plates stopped colliding and instead started sliding against each other, creating the massive San Andreas Fault, which today moves an average of two inches per year. Because this contact zone doesn't slide smoothly, but catches and slips irregularly, it rattles California with an ongoing succession of tremors and earthquakes.

The San Andreas Fault is where the Pacific Plate (which runs under the Pacific Ocean floor and much of California's coastline) meets the continental North American Plate. The fault runs for over 650 miles and has spawned numerous smaller faults that extend toward the shoreline. Earthquakes are common, although most are too small or too remote to be detected without sensors. Fear not: small earthquakes are good news, evidence that the plates are moving along their paths, rather than storing kinetic energy and later causing bigger quakes.

The state's most famous earthquake, in 1906, measured 7.8 on the Richter scale and demolished San Francisco, leaving more than 3000 people dead. Walk the Earthquake Trail at Point Reyes National Seashore for an up-close lesson in plate tectonics: a broken fence line reveals how the 1906 quake moved the earth nearly 20ft in under a minute. The Bay Area made headlines again in 1989, when the Loma Prieta earthquake (6.9) caused a section of the Bay Bridge to collapse, and in 2014 when the South Napa earthquake (6.0) caused an estimated $300 million in damage and loss.

According to the US Geological Survey, the odds of a magnitude 6.7 or greater earthquake hitting California in the next 30 years are 99.7%.

The Coast to the Central Valley

Much of Northern California's coast is fronted by rugged coastal mountains that capture winter's water-laden storms and block passage of summertime fog, except at the Golden Gate, where fog slips inland over San Francisco Bay. San Francisco divides the Coast Ranges roughly in half. The foggy North Coast remains sparsely populated, while the Central Coast and lower regions of the Bay Area have a balmier climate and many more people.

Over 120 inches of rain fall each year in the northernmost reaches of the Coast Ranges and, in some places, persistent summer fog contributes another 12 inches of precipitation. Nutrient-rich soils and abundant moisture foster forests of giant trees, including stands of towering redwoods growing as far south as Big Sur and north all the way to the Oregon border, where their habitat abruptly stops. Because of this unique arrangement of mountains and weather, the most reliably sunny time to visit the North Coast is in the fall, when moisture (in the form of fog) isn't being sucked in by the blisteringly hot Central Valley's rising air currents.

On their eastern flanks, the Coast Ranges subside into gently rolling hills that give way to the sprawling Central Valley. Once an inland sea, this flat inland basin is now an agricultural powerhouse producing about half of America's fruits, nuts and vegetables, valued at over $17 billion a year. Its bounty is evident when driving through the region – large fields of edibles stretch horizon to horizon. The productivity of the region is a modern agricultural feat: about 450 miles long and 50 miles wide, the Central Valley gets about as much rainfall as a desert, but receives huge volumes of water running off the Sierra Nevada (drought conditions between 2012 and 2017 notwithstanding). Before the arrival of Europeans the valley was a natural wonderland – a region of vast marshes, flocks of geese that blackened the sky, and grasslands carpeted with countless flowers and plants where millions of antelopes, elk and grizzly bears grazed. Virtually this entire landscape has been plowed and replaced with alien weeds (including agricultural crops) and livestock.

Browse over 1200 aerial photos covering almost every mile of California's gorgeously rugged coastline, from Oregon to the Mexican border, at www.california coastline.org.

Mountain Highs

Bordering the Central Valley on its eastern side looms California's most prominent topographic feature: the world-famous ridges of the Sierra Nevada mountain range. At 400 miles long and 50 miles wide, this is not only one of the largest mountain ranges in the world, it is also home to vast wilderness areas and 13 peaks over 14,000ft. The entire 150-mile region from Sonora Pass south to Mt Whitney lies mostly above 9000ft and is known as the High Sierra; this is a stunning and remote landscape of glaciers, sculpted granite peaks and lonely canyons. It's beautiful to see from a distance, but difficult to access, and crossing it posed the greatest challenge to settlers attempting to reach California in the 1800s.

The soaring Sierra Nevada captures wintertime storm systems and drains them of their water, with most precipitation at over 5000ft falling as snow. Snowfalls average 38ft at mid-elevations on the west slope, making the Sierras a premier skiing and winter-sports destination. During the 2017 ski season, the region saw record snowfall, with more than 500in blanketing Squaw Valley, Kirkwood, Heavenly, Northstar, Mammoth and other ski resorts, in some cases burying ski lifts and ski patrol shacks. The snowpack eventually flows into 11 major river systems down the west slope, and several on the east slope,

California claims both the highest point in contiguous US (Mt Whitney, 14,497ft) and the lowest elevation in North America (Badwater, Death Valley, 282ft below sea level) – plus they're only 90 miles apart, as the condor flies.

providing the vast majority of water for agriculture in the Central Valley and meeting the needs of major metropolitan areas from San Francisco to Los Angeles.

Most of the Sierra Nevada is cloaked in dense conifer forests, with stands of oak in the lower foothills and chaparral zones. Twenty-three species of conifer occur in the Sierra Nevada, ranging from the stately incense cedars of the western foothills to tiny wind-sculpted white-bark and foxtail pines at 12,000ft. In between, mid-elevation forests are home to massive Douglas firs, ponderosa, sugar and jeffrey pines, and biggest of all, the giant sequoia.

At its northern end the Sierra Nevada lowers in elevation and merges imperceptibly into the southern tip of the volcanic Cascade Mountains that continue north into Oregon and Washington. This wet mountainous region extends westward to the coast through a tangle of ancient and geologically complex ranges that are sparsely populated and also heavily cloaked with conifer forests.

National & State Parks

The majority of Californians rank outdoor recreation as vital to their quality of life, and the number of preserved lands has steadily grown due to important pieces of legislation passed since the 1960s, including the landmark 1976 California Coastal Act, which saved the coastline from further development. Today, California State Parks (www. parks.ca.gov) protects nearly a third of the state's coastline, along with redwood forests, mountain lakes, desert canyons, waterfalls, wildlife preserves and historical sites.

In 2011, federal and state budget shortfalls and chronic underfunding caused the State of California to announced that it planned to close 70 state parks – about 25% of the system. Horrified environmentalists, nonprofit organizations and park advocates scrambled to help, tracking down $20 million for the parks, and in his 2014 budget Governor Jerry Brown allocated $40 million for the estimated backlog of $1 billion in overdue maintenance. Meanwhile, the California Parks Forward Commission was created to make recommendations and set a new direction for the parks and a 'transformation team' was assembled to implement reform. Miraculously, all of California's 279 state parks remain open.

Over the past couple of years, California State Parks has taken steps to improve the visitor experience and secure funds more quickly and easily, adding automated and smartphone payment systems, speeding up revenue collection, and contracting a new reservation system, which was rolled out in 2017. Alongside Save the Redwoods League, the park system has launched a project to come to the rescue of redwood forests imperiled by climate change and other threats in both state and national parks, committing to restoring 10,000 acres over the next five years. These efforts are appealing to nature-lovers but protecting the wilderness is also in line with California's economic interests, since recreational tourism consistently outpaces competing 'resource extraction' industries, such as mining and logging.

Unfortunately, some of Northern California's parks are also being loved to death. Overcrowding severely impacts the environment, and it's increasingly difficult to balance public access with the principles of conservation. If possible, try visiting big-name parks such as Yosemite in the shoulder seasons (not the summer) to avoid the biggest crowds. Alternatively, lesser-known natural areas managed by the National Park Service (www.nps.gov/state/ca) may go relatively untouched most

THE LAND & WILDLIFE NATIONAL & STATE PARKS

Pick up one of the excellent *California Natural History Guides* published by the University of California Press (www.ucpress. edu), which are compact enough to carry in a day pack.

California's Top Parks

Point Reyes National Seashore

Redwood National & State Parks

Yosemite National Park

Sequoia and Kings Canyon National Parks

Lassen Volcanic National Park

of the year, which means you won't have to reserve permits, campsites or accommodations months in advance.

There are 18 national forests in California run by the US Forest Service (USFS; www.fs.fed.us/r5), including lands around Mt Whitney, Mt Shasta and Big Bear Lake, and many other areas worth exploring. National wildlife refuges (NWR), favored by bird-watchers, are managed by the US Fish & Wildlife Service (USFWS; www.fws.gov/refuges). More wilderness tracts are overseen by the Bureau of Land Management (BLM; www.blm.gov/ca/st/en.html).

Northern California Water

Understanding California geography demands an understanding of how water moves – both physically and politically. Spring through fall are dry; almost all of the precipitation falls in the winter, when weather off the Pacific zips across the state, then gets hung up on the ridges of the Sierra Nevada, where snowstorms can last for days and dump up to 10ft of snow at a time. Come spring, all that snow begins to melt and drains down the river courses that support white-water rafting, through irrigation systems that provide water for California's famous crops, and through giant aqueducts and webs of pipes that provide fresh water to the densely populated urban Bay Area. Water has a profound effect on all aspects of culture in Northern California. Lately water has been an especially hot topic, with the state's worst drought in history beginning in 2011 and coming to an end 2017, thanks to dramatic floods that have taken out bridges, damaged highways and caused large-scale evacuations all over Northern California.

Moving through the inland territory of the region, you'll almost certainly encounter one or both of the region's two major rivers, the Sacramento and the San Joaquin. These are the aquatic highways into which so many other river systems feed – rivers such as the Kern, which runs through Bakersfield; the Tuolumne, which rushes through Yosemite's High Country; and the American, which crosses the Gold Country. For these rivers, the end of the line is the San Francisco Bay, where 65% of the fresh water in all California drains into the Pacific. In the far north, another six rivers are popular for recreation – the Trinity, Smith, Klamath, Mad, Eel and Van Duzen.

Lakes are likewise a major draw for travelers. Lake Tahoe, the second-deepest lake in the US, and Clear Lake, north of Wine Country, are two of the region's most popular natural lakes, but reservoirs, such as Shasta Lake and Whiskeytown Lake, are also hugely popular destinations for recreation.

Northern California's water policies have major environmental, political and social consequences. An example is Hetch Hetchy Reservoir, in Yosemite National Park. Once a deep natural gorge described by California's greatest environmental champion John Muir as 'one of nature's rarest and most precious mountain temples,' Hetch Hetchy was dammed and flooded in 1923 to create a pristine source of water for the city of San Francisco. (Some say Muir died of heartbreak when Congress approved the construction project in 1914.) Lately a small, but vocal, minority has called for the draining of the reservoir to restore Hetch Hetchy Valley to its natural state. Opponents argue that not only is the valley's pristine state now irretrievable, but that un-damming it would undermine San Francisco's supply of clean water. Voters agreed, and with 77% of the vote, soundly defeated a 2012 ballot measure to tear down the dam.

The San Francisco airport introduced green 'hydration stations' at its state-of-the-art terminal to decrease waste from bottled water. The stations came with a snappy slogan, offering a drink from the 'pristine Sierra snowmelt.'

CALIFORNIA'S CAP & TRADE

In October 2011 California lawmakers adopted a cap-and-trade system for air emissions, in order to help the state achieve its ambitious goals to reduce greenhouse gas by 2020 and become a leader in climate policy. The complex market system fixes a price on heat-trapping pollution by California's dirtiest industries – coal, oil and manufacturing – and allows them to trade carbon credits. Beginning in 2012, the state's largest carbon emitters were required by law to meet the caps or buy credits.

The program, originally endorsed by former governor Arnold Schwarzenegger, has struggled with a series of legal challenges and at times faced low demand in the face of uncertainty about the future. Still, the system has raised a few hundred million dollars every year, a third of which was allocated by Governor Jerry Brown to finance California's high-speed rail, which by 2029 will connect San Francisco and Los Angeles in under three hours. At the time of research, a state senator had just proposed legislation that would revamp the cap-and-trade program, clearing up its legal issues while establishing one of the highest prices in the world for carbon dioxide.

To pass, the new measure would have to obtain a two-thirds majority approval in both California's State Assembly and Senate, where in 2017 Democrats held a slim super-majority.

Conserving California

Although California is in many ways a success story, development and growth have come at great environmental cost. Starting in 1849, gold-rush miners tore apart the land in their frenzied quest for the 'big strike,' ultimately sending more than 1.5 billion tons of debris, and uncalculated amounts of poisonous mercury, downstream into the Central Valley where rivers and streams became clogged and polluted.

Water, or the lack thereof, has long been at the heart of California's epic environmental struggles and catastrophes. The diversion of water to LA has contributed to the destruction of Owens Lake and its fertile wetlands, and to the degradation of Mono Lake. Statewide, the damming of rivers and capture of water for houses and farms has destroyed countless salmon runs and drained marshlands. The Central Valley, for example, today resembles a dust bowl, and its underground aquifer is in poor shape.

Altered and compromised habitats, both land and water, make easy targets for invasive species, including highly aggressive ones that wreak havoc on California's economy and ecosystems. In San Francisco Bay, one of the most important estuaries in the world, there are now over 230 alien species choking the aquatic ecosystem, and in some areas they already comprise as much as 95% of the total biomass.

Although air quality in California has improved markedly in past decades, it's still among the worst in the country. Auto exhaust and fine particulates generated by the wearing down of vehicle tires, along with industrial emissions, are the chief culprits. An even greater health hazard is ozone, the principal ingredient in smog, which makes sunny days around the Central Valley look hazy.

But there's hope. Low-emission vehicles are becoming the most sought-after cars in the state, and rapidly rising fuel costs are keeping more gas-guzzling SUVs off the road. Californians voted recently to ban plastic bags and also to fund construction of solar-power plants. There's even talk of harnessing the tremendous tidal flows of the Pacific to generate more 'clean' energy. By law California's utilities must

In 2006 the world's tallest tree was discovered in Redwood National Park (its location is being kept secret). It's named Hyperion and stands at a whopping 379.3ft tall.

get 33% of their energy from renewable resources by 2020, the most ambitious target yet set by any US state.

Also, some of the most visionary sustainability practices in the world are unfolding throughout Northern California. The wine regions north of San Francisco are the greenest in the world, maximizing their water and energy usage and pioneering techniques that have all but eliminated the use of pesticides. The city government of Arcata has world-leading sustainability practices. The city purchased tracts of forest land to protect the integrity of its water supply and developed a revolutionary marsh-based sewer treatment system. Built on a solid waste, the marsh processes wastewater through a series of oxidation ponds and wetlands that also serve as a wildlife sanctuary. Additionally, citizens in towns of the far north, such as McCloud and Shasta, have brought landmark civic actions to protect their natural resources. In 2009 they blocked multinational Nestlé from tapping the Shasta watershed for a water-bottling facility.

Wild Things

Although the staggering numbers of animals that greeted the first European settlers are now extinct, you'll still see wildlife thriving in Northern California, provided you go to the right places at the right times of year. During your travels, you're likely to spot at least a few iconic species, such as coyotes, bobcats and eagles. Unfortunately, some of these are but shadow populations, hovering at the edge of survival, marginalized by the burgeoning human population.

Whales & Other Marine Mammals

Peak mating season for northern elephant seals along the Pacific coast just happens to coincide with Valentine's Day (February 14).

Spend even one day along Northern California's coast and you'll get a crash course in marine wildlife – from the gulls overhead (and eyeing your picnic) to tide pools of starfish. Still, the king of the Northern California coast is much, much bigger: the magnificent gray whale. Gray whales migrate in growing numbers along California's coast, and visitors to coastal bluffs in the north should scan the horizons for their clouds of spray. Adult whales live up to 70 years, are longer than a city bus and can weigh up to 40 tons, making quite a splash when they dive below or leap out of the water.

In summer the whales feed in the Arctic waters between Alaska and Siberia. In the fall they move south down the Pacific coast of Canada and the USA to sheltered lagoons in the Gulf of California, by the Mexican state of Baja California. During this 6000-mile migration, the whales pass by California between December and April. Traveling night and day at a clip of about 3mph, this is thought to be the longest migration of any mammal. (Sooty shearwaters, seabirds that resemble a dark gray seagull, hold the record for the longest migration of anything in the animal kingdom, and they also can be seen in Northern California.)

The best way to see whales is by getting right out on the water. During the season of their migration, visitors can depart from many cities along the North Coast on whale-watching expeditions, which often last two hours. These have no guarantees, but visitors can ask the boat operators about recent sightings to get an idea of what to expect.

Even if you don't spot the big guys, you'll likely see other charming little creatures, including playful sea otters and harbor seals. These species especially like to crowd around public piers and protected bays. Since the 1989 earthquake, the air of San Francisco's Pier 39 has been filled by the distinct sound (and distinct odor) of barking sea lions, much to the delight of ogling tourists. Another place to see wild pinnipeds is Point Lobos State Natural Reserve near Monterey.

Almost hunted to extinction by the late 19th century, northern elephant seals have made a remarkable comeback along California's coast. Año Nuevo State Park, north of Santa Cruz, is a major breeding ground for northern elephant seals. But California's biggest elephant seal colony is found at Piedras Blancas near Hearst Castle, south of Big Sur. There's a smaller rookery at Point Reyes National Seashore.

Mountain Kings

There's some irony in the fact that California's most symbolic animal is the grizzly bear. The brown beast that graces the state flag is long gone. Extirpated in the early 1900s, grizzlies once roamed California's beaches and grasslands in large numbers, eating everything from whale carcasses to acorns. Grizzlies were particularly abundant in the Central Valley, but retreated upslope into the mountains as they were hunted out. There's occasionally chatter from conservationists about reintroducing the grizzly population to California, but it seems unlikely.

All that remains now are the grizzlies' relatively diminutive cousins, black bears, which typically weigh under 400lb. These burly omnivores feed on berries, nuts, roots, grasses, insects, eggs, small mammals and fish, but can become a nuisance around campgrounds and mountain cabins where food is not stored properly. Remember the old adage that 'a fed bear is a dead bear' – people invite the destruction of these beautiful animals by carelessly leaving food unattended in their cars and at campsites. It's a wonderful complement to a trip in the woods to see a black bear foraging in a high mountain meadow, but sadly they're most often seen scrounging around in the campground dumpster.

Northern California's other fearsome mammal is the mountain lion. Sometimes called cougars, they hunt throughout the mountains and forests of Northern California, especially in areas teeming with deer. Solitary lions, which can grow to 8ft in length and weigh 175lb, are formidable predators, but they are very, very seldom seen. Although they incite a panic in many urbanites (and you'll see warning signs at many trailheads), these large cats are very skittish and attacks on humans are extremely rare. Most human encounters have occurred where encroachment has pushed hungry lions to their limits – for example, at the boundaries between wilderness and rapidly developing suburbs.

Feathered Friends & Butterflies

Northern California lies on major migratory routes for over 350 species of birds, which either pass through the state or linger through the winter. This is one of the top birding destinations in North America. Witness, for example, the congregation of one million ducks, geese and swans at the Klamath Basin National Wildlife Refuges every November. During winter, these waterbirds head south into the refuges of the Central Valley, another area to observe huge numbers of native and migratory species.

Year-round you can see birds at California's beaches, estuaries and bays, where herons, cormorants, shorebirds and gulls gather at places such as Point Reyes National Seashore and the shores near Redwood National and State Parks. Monarch butterflies are gorgeous orange creatures that follow long-distance migration patterns in search of milkweed, their only source of food. They winter in California by the

California's mountain forests are home to an estimated 25,000 to 35,000 black bears, whose fur actually ranges in color from black to dark brown, cinnamon or even blond.

The Audubon Society's free California chapter website (http://ca.audubon.org) has helpful birding checklists, a newsy blog, and descriptions of key species and important birding areas statewide.

THE LAND & WILDLIFE WILD THINGS

WILDFLOWER WATCHING

The famous 'golden hills' of California are actually the result of European grasses drying up in preparation for the long dry summer. Originally, before these invasive species took root, the hills of California remained green year-round with native bunch grass. Other plants have adapted to long periods of almost no rain by growing prolifically during California's mild wet winters, springing to life with the first rains of autumn and blooming as early as January. As snows melt later at higher elevations in the Sierra Nevada, Yosemite National Park's Tuolumne Meadows is a prime spot for wildflower walks and photography, with peak blooms usually in late June or early July.

tens of thousands, mostly on the Central Coast, including at Santa Cruz, Pacific Grove and Pismo Beach.

As you drive along the Big Sur coast, look skyward to spot endangered California condors, which also soar over inland Pinnacles National Monument. Condors are the largest flying birds in the hemisphere, with a wingspan that can reach 9ft. They're easy to mistake with the wobbly, and common, turkey vulture, who are also frequent guests above the shorelines. You can tell the difference by their coasting pattern: turkey vultures are poorly balanced and seem to soar drunkenly, whereas condors glide much more smoothly. Also keep an eye out for regal bald eagles, which can be seen in the Sierra Nevada and along the North Coast.

Survival Guide

Directory A–Z

Accommodations

➡ Budget-conscious accommodations include campgrounds, hostels and motels, but midrange properties generally offer better value.

➡ At midrange motels and hotels, expect clean, comfortable and decent-sized double rooms with private bathroom and amenities including cable TV, direct-dial telephone, a coffeemaker and perhaps a microwave and minifridge.

➡ Top-end lodgings offer more amenities, and perhaps a scenic location, designer decor and/or a historical building. Pools, fitness rooms, business centers, full-service restaurants and bars are standard.

➡ In Northern California, where it rarely gets hot, air-con is not often provided; ask when you book. Some accommodations offer online computer terminals for guests, sometimes for an additional fee; others offer only wi-fi.

➡ When wireless internet access is offered, there may be a fee, especially for in-room access. Look for free wi-fi hot spots in hotel public areas, such as the lobby or poolside.

➡ Many lodgings are now exclusively nonsmoking. Where they still exist, smoking rooms are seldom renovated and are tucked away in less-desirable locations. Expect a hefty 'cleaning fee' ($100 or more) if you light up in designated nonsmoking rooms.

Rates & Reservations

➡ Reservations are recommended for weekend and holiday travel year-round, and every day during high season.

➡ Generally, midweek rates are lower, except in hotels geared toward weekday business travelers. Unless noted, rates do not include taxes, which exceed 10%.

➡ If you plan to arrive late in the evening, call ahead on the day of your stay. Hotels overbook, but if you've guaranteed the reservation with your credit card, the hotel should accommodate you.

➡ Discount cards and auto-club membership (AARP or AAA) may yield an additional 10% off standard rates at participating hotels and motels.

➡ Look for free ad magazines with hotel and motel discount coupons at gas stations, highway rest areas, tourist offices and online at HotelCoupons (http://hotelcoupons.com).

➡ Bargaining may be possible for walk-in guests without reservations, especially during off-peak times.

Hotels & Motels

➡ Rooms are often priced by the size and number of beds, rather than number of occupants. Those with a double or queen-size bed usually cost the same for one or two people; rooms with a king-size bed or two double beds cost more.

➡ In America, a double room means double occupancy – as in two people, *not* two beds; you must specifically request two beds.

➡ There is often a surcharge for the third and fourth person, but children under a certain age (this varies) may stay free. Cribs or roll-away cots sometimes cost extra.

➡ Beware that suites or 'junior suites' may simply be oversized rooms; ask about

---

BOOK YOUR STAY ONLINE

For more accommodations reviews by Lonely Planet authors, check out http://lonelyplanet.com/hotels/. You'll find independent reviews, as well as recommendations on the best places to stay. Best of all, you can book online.

the layout when booking. Proper suites have two (or more) rooms, separated by doors.

➡ Recently renovated or larger rooms, or those with views, usually cost more. Descriptors like 'oceanfront' and 'ocean view' are too liberally used; rooms described as such may require a periscope to spot the surf.

➡ You can reserve chains by calling their central-reservations line, but to learn about specific amenities and promotions, call the property directly.

➡ If you arrive without reservations, ask to see a room before paying, especially at motels.

➡ Rates may include breakfast, which could be just a stale doughnut and wimpy coffee, an all-you-can-eat buffet, or anything in between.

B&Bs

If you want an atmospheric or perhaps romantic alternative to impersonal motels and hotels, bed-and-breakfast inns typically inhabit fine old Victorian houses or other heritage buildings, bedecked with floral wallpaper and antique furnishings. People who find privacy may find them too intimate.

Rates often include a home-cooked breakfast, but occasionally breakfast is *not* included (never mind what 'B&B' suggests). Amenities

vary widely. Rooms with TV and telephone are the exception; the cheapest rooms may share bathrooms. Standards are high at places certified by the California Association of Boutique & Breakfast Inns (www.cabbi.com).

Most B&Bs require advance reservations, although some will accommodate the occasional drop-in guest. Minimum stay requirements are common, especially on weekends and in high season.

Camping & Holiday Parks

In California, camping is much more than just a cheap way to spend the night. The best campsites offer moonlit ocean views by the beach, cushioned spots under pine trees next to an alpine lake,

or stargazing in desert sand dunes. The state park system has a variety of campsites. To reserve, check out www.reservecalifornia.com.

BOOKING SERVICES

For camping, the booking service Hipcamp (www.hipcamp.com) offers reviews, photographs, real-time availability and reservations at NorCal campgrounds.

Hostels

Northern California has over a dozen hostels affiliated with **Hostelling International USA** (☏ 240-650-2100; www.hiusa.org). Dorms in HI hostels are typically gender-segregated; alcohol and smoking are prohibited. HI-USA membership cards (adult/senior per year $28/18, under-18s free) get the holder every third night for free.

There are scores of independent hostels, particularly in coastal cities. They generally have more relaxed rules, often no curfew and frequent parties and activities. Some hostels include a light breakfast, arrange tours or offer pick-ups at transportation hubs. No two are alike, but facilities typically include mixed dorms, semiprivate rooms with shared bathrooms, communal kitchens, lockers, internet access, laundry and TV lounges. The latest amenity is a lockable cabinet with electrical outlet, so you can charge electronics while they're stored; ask when you book.

Some hostels say they only accept international visitors (basically to keep out homeless locals), but Americans who look like travelers (eg you're in possession of a plane ticket) may be admitted, especially during slow periods.

Dorm-bed rates average $25 to $55 per night, including tax. Reservations are always recommended, especially in high season. Most accept reservations online or by phone. Online booking services sometimes offer lower rates.

Customs Regulations

Each person over 21 years is allowed to bring 1L of liquor and 200 cigarettes duty-free into the USA. Non-US citizens are allowed to bring $100 worth of duty-free gifts. If you're carrying over $10,000 in US and foreign cash, traveler's checks or money orders, you must declare the excess amount – undeclared sums in excess of $10,000 may be subject to confiscation.

Discount Cards

'America the Beautiful' Annual Pass (12-month pass $80) Admits four adults and all children under 16 years for free to all national parks and federal recreational lands (eg USFS, BLM) for 12 months from the date of purchase. US citizens and permanent residents aged 62 years and older are eligible for a lifetime Senior Pass ($10), which grants free entry and 50% off some recreational-use fees such as camping.

International Student Identity & Youth Travel Cards (12-month card $25) Offers savings on airline fares, travel insurance and local attractions for full-time students (ISIC) and for nonstudents under 26 years of age (IYTC). Cards are issued by student unions, hosteling organizations and youth-oriented budget travel agencies.

Senior Discounts People over the age of 65 (sometimes 55, 60 or 62) often qualify for the same discounts as students; any ID showing your birth date should suffice as proof.

Go San Francisco Card (one-day pass adult/child three to 12 years from $65/49) Covers museums, bicycle rental and bay cruises. You've got to do a lot of sightseeing over multiple days to make the pass pay off. For discounts, buy online.

Student Advantage Card (12-month card $22.50) For international and US students, offers 15% savings on Amtrak trains and 20% on Greyhound buses, plus discounts of 10% to 20% on some rental cars and shopping.

Electricity

Type A
120V/60Hz

Food & Drink

➡ Lunch is generally served between 11:30am and 2:30pm, and dinner between 5pm and 9pm daily, though some restaurants stay open later, especially on Friday and Saturday nights.

➡ If breakfast is served, it's usually between 7:30am and 10:30am; some diners and coffee shops keep serving breakfast into the afternoon, or all day. Weekend brunch is a laid-back affair, usually available from 11am until 3pm on Saturdays and Sundays.

➡ Like all things Northern Californian, restaurant etiquette tends to be informal. Only a handful of restaurants require more than a dressy shirt, slacks and decent shoes.

PRACTICALITIES

Newspapers San Francisco Chronicle (www.sfgate.com), San Jose Mercury News (www.mercurynews.com), Sacramento Bee (www.sacbee.com), East Bay Times (www.eastbaytimes.com).

Radio National Public Radio (NPR), lower end of FM dial.

Smoking Generally prohibited inside restaurants and public buildings, including airports, shopping malls and train and bus stations; at hotels, you must request a smoking room (some hotels are entirely nonsmoking).

TV PBS (public broadcasting); cable: CNN (news), ESPN (sports), HBO (movies), Weather Channel

Videos & DVDs NTSC standard (incompatible with PAL or SECAM); DVDs coded region 1 (USA & Canada only)

Weights & Measures The imperial system is used.

➡ Tipping 15% to 20% above the pre-tax total is expected anywhere you receive table service.

➡ Smoking is illegal indoors. Some restaurants have patios or sidewalk tables where smoking is tolerated (ask first or look around for ashtrays), but don't expect your neighbors to be happy about secondhand smoke.

➡ You can bring your own wine to most restaurants, but expect a 'corkage' fee of $15 to $30. Lunch rarely includes booze, though a glass of wine or beer, while not common everywhere, is socially acceptable.

➡ If you ask the kitchen to divide a plate between two (or more) people, there may be a small split-plate surcharge.

➡ Vegetarians, vegans and travelers with food allergies are in luck – many restaurants are used to catering to specific dietary needs.

Health

➡ Medical treatment in the USA is of the highest caliber, but the expense could kill you.

➡ Many health-care professionals demand payment at time of service, especially from out-of-towners or international visitors.

➡ For medical emergencies, call 911 or go to the nearest 24-hour hospital emergency room (ER).

➡ For non-emergency medical treatment, phone around to find a doctor who will accept your insurance.

➡ **https://www.cdc.gov** Centers for Disease Control and Prevention is the federal agency that conducts and supports health promotion, prevention and preparedness activities in the United States.

➡ **San Francisco City Clinic** (☏415-487-5500; www.sfcityclinic.org; 356 7th St; ⊙8am-4pm Mon, Wed & Fri, 1-6pm Tue, 1-4pm Thu) Contact this organization about sexually transmitted diseases, emergency contraception or post-exposure prevention of HIV.

➡ Some health-insurance policies require you to get pre-authorization for non-emergency medical treatment before seeking help.

➡ Overseas visitors with travel health-insurance policies may need to contact a call center for an assessment by phone before getting medical treatment.

The tap water is safe to drink.

Hypothermia

➡ Skiers and hikers will find that temperatures in the mountains and desert can quickly drop below freezing, especially during winter. Even a sudden spring shower or high winds can lower your body temperature dangerously fast.

➡ Instead of cotton, wear synthetic or woolen clothing that retains warmth even when wet. Carry waterproof layers (eg Gore-Tex jacket, plastic poncho, rain pants) and high-energy, easily digestible snacks such as chocolate, nuts and dried fruit.

➡ Symptoms of hypothermia include exhaustion, numbness, shivering, stumbling, slurred speech, dizzy spells, muscle cramps and irrational or even violent behavior.

➡ To treat mild hypothermia, get out of bad weather and change into dry, warm clothing. Drink hot liquids (no caffeine or alcohol) and snack on high-calorie food.

➡ For more advanced hypothermia, seek immediate medical attention. Do not rub victims, who must be handled gently.

Insurance

Getting travel insurance to cover theft, loss and medical problems is highly recommended. Some policies do not cover 'risky' activities such as scuba diving, motorcycling and skiing: read the fine print! Make sure the policy at least covers hospital stays and an emergency flight home.

Paying for your airline ticket or rental car with a credit card may provide limited travel accident insurance. If you already have private health insurance, or a homeowner's or renter's policy, find out what those policies cover and only get supplemental insurance. If you have prepaid a large portion of your vacation, trip cancellation insurance may be a worthwhile expense.

Worldwide travel insurance is available at www.lonelyplanet.com/travel-insurance. You can buy, extend and claim online anytime – even if you're already on the road.

Internet Access

➡ Internet cafes typically charge $8 to $15 per hour for online access.

➡ With branches in most cities and towns, FedEx offers internet access at self-service computer workstations (50¢ to 75¢ per minute) and sometimes free wi-fi, plus digital-photo printing and CD-burning stations.

➡ Plenty of accommodations, cafes, restaurants and bars provide wireless access; some have online computer kiosks. There may be a charge for either.

➡ Wi-fi hot spots (free or fee-based) can be found at major airports; many hotels, motels and coffee shops (eg Starbucks); and some tourist information centers, campgrounds (eg KOA), stores (eg Apple), bars and restaurants (including fast-food chains such as McDonald's).

➡ Public libraries have internet terminals, although online time may be limited, advance sign-up may be required and a nominal fee for out-of-network visitors may apply. Libraries also increasingly have free wi-fi access.

Legal Matters
Drugs & Alcohol

➡ In California, it is now legal to use, possess and share cannabis, as well as grow it at home, but it's still illegal to smoke and drive a vehicle. Possession of any other drug is a felony punishable by lengthy jail time. For foreigners, conviction of any drug offense is grounds for deportation.

➡ Police can make roadside sobriety checks to assess if you've been drinking or using drugs. If you fail, they'll require you to take a breath, urine or blood test to determine if your blood-alcohol is over the legal limit (0.08%). Refusing to be tested is treated as failing the test.

➡ Penalties for driving under the influence (DUI) can include license suspension, fines and jail time.

➡ It's illegal to carry open containers of alcohol inside vehicles. Unless they're full and sealed, store them in the trunk.

➡ Consuming alcohol anywhere other than at private residences or licensed premises is illegal, which puts most parks and beaches off-limits (although many campgrounds allow it).

➡ Bars, clubs and liquor stores often ask for photo ID as proof of age.

Police & Security

➡ For police, fire and ambulance emergencies, dial 911. For non-emergency police assistance, call directory assistance (411) for the number of the nearest local police station.

➡ If you're stopped by the police, be courteous. Don't get out of the car unless asked. Keep your hands where the officer can see them (eg on the steering wheel). You have the right to refuse a search of your possessions or vehicle. Simply say, 'I do not consent to a search.'

➡ There is no system of paying fines on the spot. Attempting to do so may result in attempted-bribery charges.

➡ For traffic violations, the ticketing officer will explain your options. Most matters can be handled by mail.

➡ If you are arrested, you have the right to remain silent and are presumed innocent until proven guilty. Everyone has the right to make one phone call. Immediately ask to see a lawyer. If you don't have one, one will be appointed to you free of charge. Foreign travelers should call their embassy or consulate.

➡ Due to security concerns over terrorism, never leave your bags unattended, especially not at airports, bus stations or train stations.

➡ Carrying Mace or cayenne-pepper spray is legal in California, as long as the spray bottle contains no more than 2.5oz of active product. Federal law prohibits it from being carried on planes.

➡ In cases of sexual assault, rape-crisis center and hospital staff can advocate on your behalf and act as a liaison to community services, including the police. Telephone books have listings of local crisis centers, or call the 24-hour **National Sexual Assault Hotline** (RAINN; ☎800-656-4673; www.rainn.org).

LGBT+ Travelers

Northern California is a magnet for lesbian, gay, bisexual and transgender travelers. Hot spots include San Francisco's Castro District, along with Guerneville and Calistoga, both in Wine Country. Same-sex marriage is legal in California. Despite widespread tolerance, homophobic bigotry still exists. In small towns, especially away from the coast, tolerance often comes down to 'don't ask, don't tell.'

Resources

Damron (www.damron.com) Classic, advertiser-driven gay travel guides and 'Gay Scout' mobile app.

Gay & Lesbian National Hotline (http://www.glbthotline.org/hotline.html; 888-843-4564) For counseling and referrals of any kind.

Out Traveler (www.outtraveler. com) Free online magazine with travel tips, destination guides and hotel reviews.

Purple Roofs (www.purpleroofs. com) Online directory of LGBTQ accommodations.

Money

ATMs

➡ ATMs are available 24/7 at most banks, shopping malls, airports, and grocery and convenience stores.

➡ Expect a surcharge of $3 to $4 per transaction, in addition to fees from your home bank.

➡ Most ATMs are connected to international networks and offer decent foreign-exchange rates.

➡ Withdrawing cash from an ATM using a credit card incurs hefty fees and high interest rates.

Cash

Most people do not carry large amounts of cash for everyday use, relying instead on credit cards, ATMs and debit cards. Some businesses refuse bills over $20.

Credit Cards

Major credit cards are almost universally accepted. You'll need one to rent a car, book a room or buy tickets over the phone. Visa, MasterCard and American Express are the most widely accepted.

Exchange Rates

Australia	A$1	$0.75
Canada	C$1	$0.74
Europe	€1	$1.12
Japan	¥100	$0.89
Mexico	MXN10	$0.54
New Zealand	NZ$	$0.70
UK	£1	$1.30

For current exchange rates see www.xe.com.

Moneychangers

➡ You can exchange money at major airports, some banks and all currency-exchange offices such as American Express (www. americanexpress.com) or Travelex (www.travelex. com). Always inquire about rates and fees.

➡ Outside cities, exchanging money may be impossible. Carry sufficient cash and/or a credit card.

Taxes

➡ The California state sales tax of 7.25% is added to the price of most goods and services

➡ Gasoline is heavily and increasingly taxed in California; by July 2019 drivers will be paying 58.3¢ on the gallon, plus another 18.4¢ in federal tax.

➡ Local and city sales taxes may add up to 1.5% more.

➡ Hotel taxes vary statewide, but currently average at around 12%. In San Francisco, it's 14%.

Tipping

Tipping is *not* optional. Only withhold tips in cases of outrageously bad service.

Airport skycaps & hotel bellhops $2 per bag

Bartenders Minimum $1 per drink

Concierges Up to $20 for securing last-minute restaurant reservations, sold-out show tickets etc

Housekeeping $2 to $4 daily

Parking valets At least $2

Restaurant/room-service waiters, hairdressers, massage therapists 15% to 20%

Taxi Drivers 10% to 15% of metered fare

Traveler's Cheques

➡ Traveler's checks have pretty much fallen out of use.

➡ Larger restaurants, hotels and department stores will often accept traveler's checks (in US dollars only),

but small businesses, markets and fast-food chains may refuse them.

➡ Visa and American Express are the most widely accepted issuers of traveler's checks.

Opening Hours

Standard opening hours:

Banks 9am to 5pm Monday to Thursday, to 6pm Friday, some 9am to 12:30pm Saturday

Bars 5pm to 2am daily (to midnight in rural areas)

Business hours (general) 9am to 5pm Monday to Friday

Nightclubs 9pm to 2am Thursday to Saturday

Post offices 9am to 5pm Monday to Friday, some 9am to noon Saturday

Restaurants 7am to 10:30am, 11:30am to 2:30pm and 5pm to 9:30pm daily, some later Friday and Saturday

Shops 10am to 6pm or 7pm Monday to Saturday, noon to 5pm Sunday (malls open later)

Post

➡ The US Postal Service is inexpensive and reliable.

➡ For sending important letters or packages, also consider FedEx or UPS.

Public Holidays

On national holidays, banks, schools and government offices (including post offices) are closed, and transportation, museums and other services operate on a Sunday schedule. Holidays falling on a weekend are usually observed the following Monday.

New Year's Day January 1

Martin Luther King Jr Day Third Monday in January

Presidents' Day Third Monday in February

Caesar Chavez Day March 31

Memorial Day Last Monday in May

Independence Day July 4

Labor Day First Monday in September

Columbus Day Second Monday in October

Veterans' Day November 11

Thanksgiving Day Fourth Thursday in November

Christmas Day December 25

School Holidays

➡ Colleges take a one- or two-week 'spring break' around Easter, sometime in March or April. Some hotels and resorts, especially on the coast and in the mountains, increase their rates during this time.

➡ Summer vacations run from early June to late August, making July and August the busiest travel months.

Safe Travel
Earthquakes

Earthquakes happen all the time, but most are so tiny they are detectable only by sensitive seismological instruments. If you're caught in a serious shaker:

➡ If indoors, get under a desk or table or stand in a doorway.

➡ Protect your head and stay clear of windows, mirrors or anything that might fall.

➡ Don't head for elevators or go running into the street.

➡ If you're in a shopping mall or large public building, expect the alarm and/or sprinkler systems to come on.

➡ If outdoors, get away from buildings, trees and power lines.

➡ If you're driving, pull over to the side of the road away from bridges, overpasses and power lines. Stay inside the car until the shaking stops.

➡ If you're on a sidewalk near buildings, duck into a doorway to protect yourself from falling bricks, glass and debris.

➡ Prepare for aftershocks.

➡ Turn on the radio and listen for bulletins.

➡ Use the telephone only if absolutely necessary.

Riptides

If you find yourself being carried offshore by a dangerous ocean current called a riptide, the important thing is to just keep afloat. Don't panic or try to swim against the current, as this will quickly exhaust you. Instead, swim parallel to the shoreline and once the current stops pulling you out, swim back to shore.

Wildlife

➡ Never feed or approach any wild animal, not even harmless-looking critters – it causes them to lose their innate fear of humans, which in turn makes them dangerously aggressive. Many birds and mammals, including deer and rodents such as squirrels, carry serious diseases that can be transmitted to humans through a bite.

➡ Disturbing or harassing specially protected species, including many marine mammals such as whales, dolphins and seals, is a crime, subject to enormous fines.

➡ Black bears are often attracted to campgrounds, where they may find food, trash and any other scented items left out on picnic tables or stashed in tents and cars. Always use bear-proof containers where they are provided. For more bear-country travel tips, visit the **SierraWild website** (http://sierrawild.gov/bears).

➡ If you encounter a black bear in the wild, don't run. Stay together, keeping small children next to you and picking up little ones. Keep back at least 100yd. If the bear starts moving toward you, back away slowly off-trail and let it pass by, being careful not to block any of the bear's escape routes or to get caught between a mother and her cubs. Sometimes a black bear will 'bluff charge' to test your dominance. Stand your ground by making yourself look as big as possible (eg waving your arms above your head) and shouting menacingly.

➡ Mountain lion attacks on humans are rare, but can be deadly. If you encounter a mountain lion stay calm, pick up small children, face the animal and retreat slowly. Make yourself appear larger by raising your arms or grabbing a stick. If the lion becomes menacing, shout or throw rocks at it. If attacked, fight back aggressively.

➡ Snakes and spiders are common throughout California, not just in wilderness areas. Always look inside your shoes before putting them back on outdoors, especially when camping. Snake bites are rare, but occur most often when a snake is stepped on or provoked (eg picked up or poked with a stick). Antivenom is available at most hospitals.

Telephone
Cell Phones

Foreign GSM multiband phones will work in the USA. Prepaid cell phones are widely available. Coverage can be spotty in remote areas.

➡ You'll need a multiband GSM phone in order to make calls in the US.

➡ SIM cards are sold at telecommunications and electronics stores. These stores also sell inexpensive prepaid phones.

➡ You can rent a cell phone at San Francisco airport from TripTel (www.triptel.com); pricing plans vary, but typically are expensive.

Payphones & Phonecards

➡ Where payphones still exist, they are usually coin-operated, although some may only accept credit cards (eg in national parks).

➡ Local calls usually cost 50¢ minimum.

➡ For long-distance calls, you're usually better off buying a prepaid phonecard, sold at convenience stores, supermarkets, newsstands and electronics stores.

Phone Codes

➡ US phone numbers consist of a three-digit area code followed by a seven-digit local number.

➡ When dialing a number within the same area code, use the seven-digit number.

➡ If you are calling outside your area code, dial 1 plus the area code plus the phone number.

➡ Toll-free numbers begin with 800, 855, 866, 877 or 888 and must be preceded by 1.

➡ For direct international calls, dial 011, plus the country code, plus the city code (without the initial '0'), plus the local phone number.

➡ For international call assistance, dial 00 – but if the operator places the call it will be very expensive.

➡ If you're calling from abroad, the US country code is 1 – the same as Canada, but beware international rates apply between the two countries.

Time

Pacific Standard Time (UTC minus eight hours). Clocks are set one hour ahead during Daylight Saving Time (DST), from the second Sunday in March until the first Sunday in November.

Toilets

Public toilets are common, free and in most cases well-maintained. In an effort to bolster transgender rights, Governor Jerry Brown signed legislation requiring restrooms for single users to be designated all-gender in 2016.

Tourist Information

➡ For pre-trip planning, peruse the information-packed website of the California Travel & Tourism Commission (www.visitcalifornia.com).

➡ The California Travel & Tourism Commission operates nearly 20 California Welcome Centers (www.visitcwc.com) around the state, where staff dispense maps and brochures and help find accommodations.

➡ Almost every city and town has a local visitor center or a chamber of commerce where you can pick up maps, brochures and information.

Travelers with Disabilities

Northern California is reasonably well-equipped for travelers with disabilities.

Mobility & Accessibility

➡ Most intersections have dropped curbs and sometimes audible crossing signals.

➡ The Americans with Disabilities Act (ADA) requires public buildings built after 1993 to be wheelchair-accessible, including restrooms.

➡ Motels and hotels built after 1993 must have at least one ADA-compliant accessible room; state your specific needs when making reservations.

➡ For nonpublic buildings built prior to 1993, including hotels, restaurants, museums and theaters, there are no accessibility guarantees; call ahead to find out what to expect.

➡ Most national and many state parks and some other outdoor recreation areas offer paved or boardwalk-style nature trails accessible by wheelchairs.

➡ US citizens and permanent residents with a permanent disability qualify for a free lifetime 'America the Beautiful' Access Pass (http://store.usgs.gov/pass/access.html), which waives entry fees to all national parks and federal recreational lands and offers 50% discounts on some recreation fees (eg camping).

➡ California State Parks' disabled discount pass ($3.50) entitles those with permanent disabilities to 50% off day-use parking and camping fees; for an application, go to www.parks.ca.gov.

Communications

➡ Telephone companies provide relay operators (dial 711) for the hearing impaired.

➡ Many banks provide ATM instructions in braille.

Helpful Resources

A Wheelchair Rider's Guide to the California Coast (www.wheelingcalscoast.org) Free accessibility information covering beaches, parks and trails, plus a downloadable PDF guide to the San Francisco Bay Area coast.

Access Northern California (www.accessnca.org) Extensive links to accessible-travel resources, including outdoor recreation opportunities, lodgings, tours and transportation.

Access San Francisco Guide (www.sftravel.com) Search the city's official tourism site for this free, downloadable PDF guide – dated, but useful.

Access Santa Cruz County (www.scaccessguide.com) Free online accessible-travel guide for visiting Santa Cruz and around, including restaurants, lodging, beaches, parks and outdoor recreation.

Accessible Travel (http://lptravel.to/AccessibleTravel) Download Lonely Planet's free Accessible Travel guide.

California State Parks (http://access.parks.ca.gov) Searchable online map and database of accessible features at state parks.

Flying Wheels Travel (☑507-451-5005; www.flyingwheelstravel.com) Full-service travel agency for travelers with disabilities, mobility issues and chronic illnesses.

Transportation

➡ All major airlines, Greyhound buses and Amtrak trains can accommodate people with disabilities, usually with 48 hours' advance notice.

➡ Major car-rental agencies offer hand-controlled vehicles and vans with wheelchair lifts at no extra charge, but you must reserve these well in advance.

➡ For wheelchair-accessible van rentals, try **Wheelchair Getaways** (☑800-642-2042; www.wheelchairgetaways.com) in San Francisco, or **Mobility Works** (☑877-275-4915; www.mobilityworks.com) in San Francisco, Oakland, San Jose, Sacramento, Fresno and Chico.

➡ Local buses, trains and subways usually have wheelchair lifts.

➡ Seeing-eye dogs are permitted to accompany passengers on public transportation.

➡ Taxi companies should have at least one wheelchair-accessible van, but you'll need to call ahead.

Visas

Visa information is highly subject to change. Double-check current visa requirements *before* coming to the USA on the State Department's US Visa website (https://travel.state.gov/content/visas/en.html).

➡ Currently, under the US Visa Waiver Program (VWP), visas are not required for citizens of 38 countries for stays of up to 90 days (no extensions), as long as your passport meets current US standards. See the website of US Customs & Border Protection (https://travel.state.gov/content/visas/en/visit/visa-waiver-program.html).

➡ Citizens of VWP countries must still register online with the Electronic System for Travel Authorization (ESTA; https://esta.cbp.dhs.gov) at least 72 hours before travel. Once approved, ESTA registration ($14) is valid up to two years or your passport's expiration date, whichever comes first.

➡ For most Canadian citizens traveling with Canadian passports that meet current US standards, a visa for short-term visits (usually up to six months) and ESTA registration aren't required.

➡ Citizens from all other non-VWP countries, or whose passports don't meet US standards, should apply for visas in their home country. The process costs a nonrefundable $160, involves a personal interview and can take several weeks. Apply as early as possible.

Volunteering

Casual drop-in volunteer opportunities are most common in cities, where you can socialize with locals while helping out nonprofit organizations. Browse upcoming projects and sign up online with local organizations such as San Francisco's One Brick (www.onebrick.org) or HandsOn Bay Area (www.handsonbayarea.org). For more opportunities, check local alternative weekly newspapers and Craigslist (www.craigslist.org).

Helpful Resources

California Volunteers (www.californiavolunteers.org) State-run volunteer directory and matching service, with links to national service days and long-term programs.

Habitat for Humanity (www.habitat.org) Nonprofit organization that helps build homes for impoverished families across California; has day, weekend and week-long projects.

Idealist (www.idealist.org) Free searchable database that includes both short- and long-term volunteer opportunities.

Sierra Club (www.sierraclub.org) Day or weekend projects and longer volunteer vacations (including for families) that focus on environmental conservation (annual membership $25).

Wilderness Volunteers (www.wildernessvolunteers.org) Week-long trips that help maintain national parks, preserves, forests, seashores and other wilderness conservation and outdoor recreation areas.

Worldwide Opportunities on Organic Farms (https://wwoofusa.org) Long-term volunteering opportunities on local organic farms (annual membership from $30).

Transportation

GETTING THERE & AWAY

Getting to Northern California by air, bus, car or train is easy, but not always cheap. Flights, tours and train tickets can be booked online at www.lonelyplanet.com/bookings.

GETTING AROUND

A car is a nuisance in San Francisco, but a necessity everywhere else in Northern California.

Car Essential for travel at your own pace. Drive on the right. For highway information, contact Caltrans (www.dot.ca.gov).

Train Amtrak serves many cities in Northern California; uses connecting bus services from main train routes to lesser destinations. Read schedules carefully; look for bus icons to determine which routes are served by bus, not train.

Bus Greyhound serves major California cities, with limited service on the coast. Other companies, notably around San Francisco, serve the suburbs and parts of Wine Country.

Air Because of the state's size, consider flying between some cities (you'll need a rental car when you arrive in secondary cities and towns).

Air

Several major US carriers fly within Northern California, including low-cost Southwest. Flights are often operated by regional subsidiaries, such as Alaska Airlines/Horizon Air, American Eagle, Delta Connection and United Express.

Bicycle

Although bicycle is a nonpolluting 'green' way to travel, the distances involved in cycling around Northern California demand a high level of fitness and make it hard to cover much ground. Forget the mountains in winter.

Davis, San Francisco, San Luis Obispo, Santa Barbara and Santa Cruz are among California's most bike-friendly communities, as rated by the League of American Bicyclists (www.bikeleague.org).

A couple of helpful resources:

Adventure Cycling Association (www.adventurecycling.org) Online resource for purchasing bicycle-friendly maps and long-distance route guides.

California Bicycle Coalition (http://calbike.org) Links to cycling route maps, events, safety tips, laws, bike-sharing programs and community nonprofit bicycle shops.

CLIMATE CHANGE & TRAVEL

Every form of transport that relies on carbon-based fuel generates CO_2, the main cause of human-induced climate change. Modern travel is dependent on airplanes, which might use less fuel per kilometer per person than most cars but travel much greater distances. The altitude at which aircraft emit gases (including CO_2) and particles also contributes to their climate change impact. Many websites offer 'carbon calculators' that allow people to estimate the carbon emissions generated by their journey and, for those who wish to do so, to offset the impact of the greenhouse gases emitted with contributions to portfolios of climate-friendly initiatives throughout the world. Lonely Planet offsets the carbon footprint of all staff and author travel.

Road Rules

→ Cycling is allowed on all roads – and some freeways where there's no suitable alternative; mandatory exits are clearly marked.

→ Some cities, including San Francisco, Oakland and Sacramento, have designated bicycle lanes, but urban biking is not for the fainthearted.

→ Cyclists must follow the same road rules as vehicles. Don't expect drivers to always yield right of way.

→ Bike helmets are mandatory for riders under 18 years old.

→ Ensure you have proper lights and reflective gear, especially if riding at night or in fog.

Rental & Purchase

→ You can rent bikes by the hour, day or week in most cities and major towns.

→ Rentals start at around $10 per day for beach cruisers and up to $45 or more for mountain bikes; ask about multiday and weekly discounts.

→ Most rental companies require a big credit-card security deposit.

→ To buy or sell used bikes, check online bulletin boards such as Craigslist (www. craigslist.org) – but beware of scams.

Transporting Bicycles

→ Greyhound transports bicycles as luggage (surcharge from $30), provided the bicycle is disassembled and placed in a rigid container (boxes are available at a cost at some terminals).

→ Amtrak's *Capitol Corridor* and *San Joaquin* trains have onboard bike racks; space is more limited aboard the latter and is first-come, first-served.

→ On Amtrak trains without racks, bikes must be put in a box then checked as luggage. Not all stations or trains offer checked-baggage service.

→ Bicycles may be transported on many local trains (ie CalTrain and BART), sometimes only during off-peak, noncommuter hours; for rules, check the railroad's website.

→ Some urban and suburban buses have first-come, first-served pull-down racks for two bikes, but beware of theft in certain San Francisco neighborhoods, notably the Mission.

Boat

In San Francisco Bay, regular ferry routes operate between San Francisco and Sausalito, Larkspur, Tiburon, Angel Island, Oakland, Alameda and Vallejo.

Bus

Greyhound (www.greyhound. com) buses are an economical way to travel between major cities and points along the coast, but won't get you off the beaten path or to national parks. Frequency varies, but main routes have service several times daily.

Greyhound buses are usually clean, comfortable and reliable. The best seats are near the front, away from the bathroom. Limited on-board amenities include freezing air-con (bring a sweater) and slightly reclining seats; select buses have electrical outlets and wi-fi. Long-distance buses stop for meal breaks and driver changes.

Bus stations are typically dreary places, often in dodgy areas. If you arrive at night, take a taxi into town or directly to your lodgings. In small towns where there's no station, know exactly where and when the bus arrives, be obvious as you flag it down, and pay the driver with exact change.

Costs

→ Save money by purchasing tickets seven to 14 days in advance, and by traveling Monday through Thursday.

→ Discounts (on unrestricted fares only) are available for seniors over 62 (5% off), students with a Student Advantage Card (10%) and children aged two to 16 (20%). Tots under two ride free without their own seat.

→ Special promotional discounts are often available on the Greyhound website, but come with restrictions and blackout periods.

Tickets & Reservations

It's easy to buy tickets online with a credit card, then pick them up (bring photo ID) at the terminal. You can also reserve a seat online, over the phone or in person from a ticket agent then pay at the station. Greyhound-terminal ticket agents also accept debit cards, traveler's checks (in US dollars) and cash.

Most boarding is first-come, first-served. Buying tickets in advance does not guarantee you a seat on any particular bus unless you also purchase priority boarding ($5), available only at some terminals. Otherwise, arrive at least one hour before the scheduled departure to secure a spot in the line; allow extra time at weekends.

Travelers with disabilities who need special assistance should call 800-752-4841 (TDD/TTY 800-345-3109) at least 48 hours before traveling. Wheelchairs are accepted as checked baggage, and guide dogs are allowed on board.

Car, Motorcycle & Recreational Vehicle (RV)

For flexibility and convenience, you'll probably want a car, but rental rates and gas prices can eat up a good chunk of your trip budget.

Automobile Associations

For 24-hour emergency road-side assistance, free maps and discounts on lodgings, attractions, entertainment, car rentals and more, consider joining an auto club.

Driver's License

➡ Visitors may legally drive a car in California for up to 12 months with their home driver's license.

➡ If you're from overseas, an International Driving Permit (IDP) will have more credibility with traffic police and simplify the car-rental process, especially if your license doesn't have a photo or isn't in English.

➡ To drive a motorcycle, you'll need a valid US-state motorcycle license or a specially endorsed IDP.

➡ International automobile associations can issue IDPs, valid for one year, for a fee. Always carry your home license with the IDP.

Fuel

➡ Gas stations in Northern California, nearly all of which are self-service, are ubiquitous near cities, but not in national parks and sparsely populated mountain areas.

➡ Gas is sold in gallons (one US gallon equals 3.78L). At press time, the cost for mid-grade fuel hovered around $3 a gallon.

Insurance

California law requires a minimum of $15,000 liability insurance for all vehicles. When renting a car, check your auto-insurance policy from home or your travel-insurance policy to see if you're already covered. If not, expect to pay about $10 to $20 per day, depending on coverage maximums. Sometimes the minimum liability insurance is included in the rate, but to protect your assets, make sure you have appropriate coverage.

Insurance against damage to the car itself, called Collision Damage Waiver (CDW) or Loss Damage Waiver (LDW), costs another $10 to $15 per day; you may be required to pay the first $100 to $500 – or more – for repairs (this is called the 'deductible'; ask if your specific policy has one). Some credit cards cover this, provided you charge the entire cost of the rental to the card. If there's an accident you may have to pay the rental-car company first, then seek reimbursement from the credit-card company. Carefully check your card's policy before renting.

Parking

➡ Parking is usually plentiful and free in small towns and rural areas, but scarce and expensive in cities.

➡ You can use coins (eg quarters) in municipal parking meters, and sometimes credit or debit cards.

➡ Expect to pay $30 to $50 to park overnight in a garage.

➡ When parking on the street, read all posted regulations and restrictions, and pay attention to colored curbs, or you may be ticketed or towed – which costs a fortune in San Francisco. Red curbs mean no parking or stopping; yellow have posted restrictions, usually limited to loading by commercial vehicles; green have posted time limits; white zones are for loading and unloading only; blue curbs are exclusively for disabled parking and require a placard.

Rental

CARS

To rent, you'll typically need to be at least 25 years old, hold a valid driver's license and have a major credit card, *not* a check or debit card. A few companies may rent to drivers under 25 (but over 21) for hefty surcharges. If you don't have a credit card, you may be able to make a large cash deposit instead.

With advance reservations, you can often get an economy-size vehicle with unlimited mileage from around $30 per day, plus insurance, taxes and fees, which typically double the rate. Weekend and weekly rates are usually more economical. Airport locations may have cheaper rates but higher fees. City-center branches may offer free pickups and drop-offs.

FURTHER AFIELD: LOS ANGELES & LAS VEGAS

For muscle beaches, celebrity sightings and camera-ready wackiness, head south from San Francisco on coastal Hwy 1 to Los Angeles. It'll take 12 hours depending on traffic and how often you stop. A quicker jaunt is less-scenic Hwy 101 (nine hours); the fastest route is boring inland I-5, which takes about six hours.

Las Vegas, NV, is a nine-hour nonstop drive from San Francisco. Cross the Bay Bridge to I-580 east, then take I-5 south; veer off towards Hwy 99 south (at exit 278), to Hwy 58 east, then take I-15 the last 160 miles. A slower, gloriously scenic option is to go east through Yosemite National Park on Hwy 120 (summer only; verify by calling 800-427-7623), then south on Hwy 395, east on Hwy 190 through Death Valley National Park, then south on Hwy 95 straight into Sin City.

Rental rates generally include unlimited mileage, but expect surcharges for additional drivers and one-way rentals. Some companies let you pre-pay your last tank of gas; this is rarely a good deal, as prices are higher than at gas stations and you'd need to bring the car back almost empty. Child or infant safety seats are compulsory (reserve when booking); they're sometimes free, or $10 per day (with a capped maximum of about $65).

If you'd like to minimize your carbon footprint, some car-rental companies offer 'green' fleets of hybrid or biofueled rental cars, but they're in short supply. Reserve well ahead and expect to pay more for these models – but you'll save on gasoline.

MOTORCYCLES

Motorcycle rentals and insurance are not cheap, especially if you've got your eye on a Harley. Depending on models, renting a motorcycle costs $100 to $200 per day, plus taxes and fees. Discounts may be available for multiday and weekly rentals. Security deposits range from $1000 to $3000 (credit card required).

RVS

It's easy to find campgrounds throughout Northern California with electricity and water hookups for RVs, but in big cities RVs are a nuisance, since there are few places to park or plug them in. RVs are cumbersome to drive and they burn fuel at an alarming rate (you only get a measly seven to 13 miles per gallon). But they do solve transportation, accommodation and cooking needs in one fell swoop. Even so, there are many places in national and state parks and in the mountains that RVs can't go. Book RV rentals as far ahead as possible. Rental costs vary by size and model, but expect to pay over $100 per day. Rates often don't include mileage, taxes, vehicle-prep fees and

bedding or kitchen kits. If pets are even allowed, expect a surcharge.

Road Conditions & Hazards

For up-to-date highway conditions in Northern California, including road closures and construction updates, dial 800-427-7623 or visit www.dot.ca.gov. For Nevada highways, call 877-687-6237 or check www.nvroads.com.

In mountain areas where winter driving is an issue, tire chains and snow tires may be required on two-wheel-drive vehicles. Four-wheel-drive vehicles with snow tires are usually excluded. The speed limit with chains is 25mph. Ideally, carry your own chains and learn how to use them before you hit the road. Otherwise, you can buy chains (but not cheaply) on the highway, at gas stations or in nearby towns; the best prices are at automotive stores. State-regulated chain installers operate on major highways, such as I-80 or US-50; expect to pay $30 for installation, $20 for removal (note that it's far easier to remove than install them; consider paying only for installation). In rural areas, you're on your own. Most car-rental companies don't permit the use of chains, and also prohibit driving off-road.

In rural areas, livestock sometimes graze next to unfenced roads. These areas are typically signed as 'Open Range,' with the silhouette of a steer. Where deer and other wild animals frequently appear roadside, you'll see signs with the silhouette of a leaping deer. Take these signs seriously, particularly at night.

In coastal areas thick fog may impede driving – slow down and if it's too soupy, get off the road. Along coastal cliffs and in the mountains, watch for falling rocks, mudslides and avalanches that could damage or disable your car.

Road Rules

➡ Drive on the right-hand side of the road.

➡ Talking or texting on a cell phone without a hands-free device is illegal – even when stopped at a light.

➡ The use of seatbelts is required for drivers, front-seat passengers and children under age 16. Drivers are responsible for compliance.

➡ Any child under age eight must be buckled up in the back in a child or infant safety seat, unless they're over 4ft 9in tall.

➡ All motorcyclists must wear a helmet. Scooters are not allowed on freeways.

➡ High-occupancy vehicle (HOV) lanes marked with a diamond symbol are reserved for cars with multiple occupants (minimum two or three, depending on the road), sometimes only during morning and afternoon rush hours.

➡ Unless otherwise posted, the speed limit is 65mph on freeways, 55mph on two-lane undivided highways, 35mph on major city streets and 25mph in business and residential districts and near schools.

➡ It's forbidden to pass a school bus – from either direction – when its red lights are flashing.

➡ Except where a sign says that it's illegal to do so, turning right at red lights, after coming to a full stop, is permitted; intersecting traffic has the right of way. Likewise, turning left on red between two intersecting one-way streets is also permitted, unless otherwise indicated.

➡ At four-way stop signs, cars proceed in the order they arrived. If two cars arrive simultaneously, the one on the right has the right of way. When in doubt, politely wave the other driver ahead.

→ When emergency vehicles (ie police, fire or ambulance) approach from either direction, carefully pull over to the side of the road.

→ California has strict anti-littering laws; throwing trash from a vehicle may incur a $1000 fine.

→ Driving under the influence of alcohol or drugs is illegal.

→ It's illegal to carry open containers of alcohol inside a vehicle – even empty ones. Unless containers are full and still sealed, store them in the trunk.

Local Transportation

Bus, Cable Car & Streetcar

→ Almost all cities and larger towns have reliable local bus systems (average $1 to $3 per ride). Outside of major metro areas, they may provide only limited evening and weekend service.

→ San Francisco's extensive Municipal Railway (MUNI) network includes not only buses and trains, but also historic streetcars and those famous cable cars.

Train

To get around the San Francisco Bay Area, hop aboard Bay Area Rapid Transit (BART) or Caltrain. Sacramento and San Jose also have limited light-rail systems.

Taxi

→ Taxis are metered, with flag-drop fees of $2.50 to $3.50 to start, plus $2 to $3 per mile. Credit cards may be accepted; check before embarking.

→ Taxis may charge extra for baggage (but not in San Francisco) and/or airport pickups.

→ Drivers expect a 10% to 15% tip, rounded up to the next dollar.

→ Taxis cruise the busiest areas in large cities, but elsewhere you may need to phone for one.

→ For quickest service in San Francisco, download the Flywheel app for smartphones, which dispatches the nearest taxi.

Train

Amtrak (www.amtrak.com) runs comfortable, if occasionally tardy, trains and buses to major California cities and limited towns. At some stations Thruway buses provide onward connections – or replace trains (read schedules carefully). Smoking is prohibited on board.

Amtrak routes within California:

→ **California Zephyr** Daily service from Emeryville (near San Francisco) via Davis and Sacramento to Truckee (near Lake Tahoe) and Reno, NV.

→ **Capitol Corridor** Links San Francisco's East Bay (including Oakland, Emeryville and Berkeley) and San Jose with Davis and Sacramento several times daily. Thruway buses connect west to San Francisco, north to Auburn in the Gold Country and east to Truckee and Reno, NV. Transfer to BART trains in Richmond for faster rush-hour connections to San Francisco from Sacramento.

→ **Coast Starlight** Chugs north–south almost the entire length of the state. Daily stops include LA, Santa Barbara, San Luis Obispo, Paso Robles, Salinas, San Jose, Oakland, Emeryville, Davis, Sacramento, Chico, Redding and Dunsmuir.

→ **San Joaquin** Several daily trains with on-board wi-fi between Bakersfield and Oakland or Sacramento. Thruway bus connections include San Francisco, LA, Palm Springs and Yosemite National Park.

Tickets

Purchase tickets at train stations, by phone or on-line. Fares depend on day of travel, advance booking, route, seating etc. Fares may increase during peak travel times (eg summer). Round-trip tickets cost the same as two one-way tickets.

Usually seniors over 62 and students with an ISIC or Student Advantage Card receive a 15% discount. Up to two children, aged two to 12, accompanied by an adult, get 50% off. AAA members save 10%. Special promotions can become available any time: check Amtrak's website.

Reservations

Reservations can be made from 11 months in advance to day of departure. In summer and around holidays, trains sell out, so book tickets as early as possible. The cheapest coach fares are usually for unreserved seats; business-class fares come with guaranteed seats.

Travelers with disabilities who need special assistance, wheelchair space, transfer seats or accessible accommodations should call 800-872-7245 (TDD/TTY 800-523-6590), and also inquire about discounted fares when booking.

Train Passes

Amtrak's California Rail Pass costs $159 ($80 for children aged two to 12). The pass is valid on all trains (except certain long-distance routes) and most connecting Thruway buses for seven days of travel within a 21-day period. Passholders must make advance reservations for each leg of travel and obtain hard-copy tickets prior to boarding.

Behind the Scenes

SEND US YOUR FEEDBACK

We love to hear from travelers – your comments keep us on our toes and help make our books better. Our well-traveled team reads every word on what you loved or loathed about this book. Although we cannot reply individually to your submissions, we always guarantee that your feedback goes straight to the appropriate authors, in time for the next edition. Each person who sends us information is thanked in the next edition – the most useful submissions are rewarded with a selection of digital PDF chapters.

Visit **lonelyplanet.com/contact** to submit your updates and suggestions or to ask for help. Our award-winning website also features inspirational travel stories, news and discussions.

Note: We may edit, reproduce and incorporate your comments in Lonely Planet products such as guidebooks, websites and digital products, so let us know if you don't want your comments reproduced or your name acknowledged. For a copy of our privacy policy visit lonelyplanet.com/privacy.

AUTHOR THANKS

Helena Smith

Many thanks to everyone who offered warm hospitality in the Gold Country and Lake Tahoe, most especially Naomi Terry for keeping us company, and Anna and her family for hospitality and local expertise. King was a great road-trip buddy, and so was Art Terry, who drove and DJ'd me round California, and made every exploration a joy.

Brett Atkinson

Thanks to everyone who made my exploration of California's Central Coast so enjoyable, especially Christina Glynn in Santa Cruz. In Santa Cruz thanks also to Margaret Leonard for travel inspiration beyond the borders of Monterey Bay. The staff at the region's visitor centers were all uniformly helpful, and at Lonely Planet, huge thanks to Cliff Wilkinson for the opportunity to return to Big Sur.

Alison Bing

Thanks to Cliff Wilkinson, Sarah Sung, Lisa Park, DeeAnn Budney, PT Tenenbaum, and above all, Marco Flavio Marinucci, for making a Muni bus ride into the adventure of a lifetime.

Celeste Brash

Thanks to my Aunt Kem and Uncle Ken for Susanville roots, Gerad in Mt Shasta City for great beer and info, countless friends and family for tips and suggestions, and my husband and kids for being the best people to come home to. Last but not least, big love to the glorious state of California, where my heart will always live.

Nate Cavalieri

Many thanks to my partner Florence, who is always game for a last-minute road trip to Bakersfield. Thanks to Cliff, Daniel, Jane, Diane and the staff at Lonely Planet for all the support, and to my colleague Alison Bing, who inspired me to get back in the travel-writing game after a long and ill-advised hiatus.

Michael Grosberg

Thanks especially to Carly, Rosie and Booney for keeping the home fires burning, and Carly especially for sharing her experiences as a forest ranger in Mammoth Lakes and Mono Lake all those years ago. Thanks also to Peter Bartelme of Yosemite Conservancy, Lisa Cesaro from Aramark, Joe Juszkiewicz at Rush Creek Lodge, Lauren Burke in Mammoth, Tawni Thompson in Bishop and Julie Wright for help in Sequoia.

Ashley Harrell

Thanks to my coauthors and editors for their diligence and support, the kind people all over Wine Country for their time and recommendations, David Roth and Andy Wright for their endless amusement, Amy Benziger for letting me trash her apartment, Shane Henegan for his glorious Airstream, Paul Stockamore for David Applebaum, Adele Fox for being the best Gumpy, Anne Murphy for sharing her ranch and wise/hilarious opinions, and Andy Lavender for his innumerable contributions and unrelenting care.

Josephine Quintero

Thanks to Cliff Wilkinson for the opportunity of researching this fabulous region of California. Also to my road trip buddy Robin Chapman and my good local resident pals who invaluably assisted me: Janice Crowe and Linda Sinclair. Also thanks to the helpful folk in the various visitor centers and, last but not least, those at the SPP help desk for helping me when I had a serious technical glitch!

John A Vlahides

Thanks to destination editor Clifton Wilkinson and my coauthor Alison Bing, with whom it's always lovely to work. And most of all, thanks to you, dear reader – you make my life so joyful and I'm grateful for the honor of being your guide through the cool grey city of love.

ACKNOWLEDGEMENTS

Climate map data adapted from Peel MC, Finlayson BL & McMahon TA (2007) 'Updated World Map of the Köppen-Geiger Climate Classification', Hydrology and Earth System Sciences, 11, 1633¬44.

Illustration pp72-73 by Michael Weldon.

Cover photograph: paddleboarding, Lake Tahoe, topseller/Shutterstock.

BEHIND THE SCENES

THIS BOOK

This 3rd edition of *Northern California* was researched and written by Helena Smith, Brett Atkinson, Sara Benson, Alison Bing, Celeste Brash, Nate Cavalieri, Michael Grosberg, Ashley Harrell, Josephine Quintero and John A Vlahides. The previous edition was researched and written by John A Vlahides, Sara Benson, Alison Bing, Celeste Brash, Tienlon Ho and Beth Kohn. This guidebook was produced by the following:

Destination Editors Clifton Wilkinson, Sarah Stocking

Product Editors Will Allen, Kate Mathews, Rachel Rawling

Senior Cartographer Alison Lyall

Assisting Cartographer Mick Garrett

Assisting Editors Sarah Bailey, Andrew Bain, Judith Bamber, Katie Connolly, Andrea Dobbin, Carly Hall, Kellie Langdon, Jodie Martire, Charlotte Orr, Gabrielle Stefanos

Book Designer Mazzy Prinsep

Cover Image Researcher Naomi Parker

Thanks to Sasha Drew, Shona Gray, Alexander Hall, John Malone, Anne Mason, Virginia Moreno, Wibowo Rusli, Erin Thiem, Dennis van IJpen, Tony Wheeler

Index

INDEX S

Map Legend

Sights
- Beach
- Bird Sanctuary
- Buddhist
- Castle/Palace
- Christian
- Confucian
- Hindu
- Islamic
- Jain
- Jewish
- Monument
- Museum/Gallery/Historic Building
- Ruin
- Shinto
- Sikh
- Taoist
- Winery/Vineyard
- Zoo/Wildlife Sanctuary
- Other Sight

Activities, Courses & Tours
- Bodysurfing
- Diving
- Canoeing/Kayaking
- Course/Tour
- Sento Hot Baths/Onsen
- Skiing
- Snorkeling
- Surfing
- Swimming/Pool
- Walking
- Windsurfing
- Other Activity

Sleeping
- Sleeping
- Camping
- Hut/Shelter

Eating
- Eating

Drinking & Nightlife
- Drinking & Nightlife
- Cafe

Entertainment
- Entertainment

Shopping
- Shopping

Information
- Bank
- Embassy/Consulate
- Hospital/Medical
- Internet
- Police
- Post Office
- Telephone
- Toilet
- Tourist Information
- Other Information

Geographic
- Beach
- Gate
- Hut/Shelter
- Lighthouse
- Lookout
- Mountain/Volcano
- Oasis
- Park
- Pass
- Picnic Area
- Waterfall

Population
- Capital (National)
- Capital (State/Province)
- City/Large Town
- Town/Village

Transport
- Airport
- BART station
- Border crossing
- Boston T station
- Bus
- Cable car/Funicular
- Cycling
- Ferry
- Metro/Muni station
- Monorail
- Parking
- Petrol station
- Subway/SkyTrain station
- Taxi
- Train station/Railway
- Tram
- Underground station
- Other Transport

Routes
- Tollway
- Freeway
- Primary
- Secondary
- Tertiary
- Lane
- Unsealed road
- Road under construction
- Plaza/Mall
- Steps
- Tunnel
- Pedestrian overpass
- Walking Tour
- Walking Tour detour
- Path/Walking Trail

Boundaries
- International
- State/Province
- Disputed
- Regional/Suburb
- Marine Park
- Cliff
- Wall

Hydrography
- River, Creek
- Intermittent River
- Canal
- Water
- Dry/Salt/Intermittent Lake
- Reef

Areas
- Airport/Runway
- Beach/Desert
- Cemetery (Christian)
- Cemetery (Other)
- Glacier
- Mudflat
- Park/Forest
- Sight (Building)
- Sportsground
- Swamp/Mangrove

Note: Not all symbols displayed above appear on the maps in this book

Celeste Brash

Northern Mountains Like many California natives, Celeste now lives in Portland, Oregon. She arrived, however, after 15 years in French Polynesia, a year and a half in Southeast Asia and a stint teaching English as a second language (in an American accent) in Brighton, England – among other things. She's been writing guidebooks for Lonely Planet since 2005 and her travel articles have appeared in publications from *BBC Travel* to *National Geographic*. She's currently writing a book about her five years on a remote pearl farm in the Tuamotu Atolls.

Nate Cavalieri

Sacramento & the Central Valley Nate is a writer and musician based in Oakland, California, and has authored over a dozen titles for Lonely Planet including guides to California, the Caribbean and Latin America. He also married his obsessive interest in cycling and travel as an author of Lonely Planet's *Epic Bike Rides of the World*. In other loosely professional pursuits, he's cycled across China and Southern Africa as a guide with Tour d'Afrique, played third chair percussion in an Orlando theme park and accompanied modern dance classes. He's fortunate to make his living writing about things he loves: music, travel and social justice.

Michael Grosberg

Yosemite & the Sierra Nevada Michael has worked on over 45 Lonely Planet guidebooks. Whether covering Myanmar or New Jersey, each project has added to his rich and complicated psyche and taken years from his (still?) relatively young life. Prior to his freelance writing career, other international work included development on the island of Rota in the western Pacific, writing about political violence and helping train newly elected government representatives in South Africa, and teaching in Ecuador. He has a Masters in Comparative Literature, and taught literature and writing as an adjunct professor at several New York colleges.

Ashley Harrell

Napa & Sonoma Wine Country After a brief stint selling day-spa coupons door-to-door in South Florida, Ashley decided she'd rather be a writer. She went to journalism grad school, convinced a newspaper to hire her, and starting covering wildlife, crime and tourism, sometimes all in the same story. Fueling her zest for storytelling and the unknown, she traveled widely and moved often, from a tiny NYC apartment to a vast California ranch to a jungle cabin in Costa Rica, where she started writing for Lonely Planet. From there her travels became more exotic and farther-flung, and she still laughs when paychecks arrive.

Josephine Quintero

North Coast & Redwoods Josephine first got her taste of not-so-serious travel when she slung a guitar on her back and traveled through Europe and Israel in the early '70s. In the mid '70s Josephine moved to the US and launched her journalism degree as assistant editor for a wine-and-lifestyle magazine in the Napa Valley. This was followed, ironically, with a move to 'dry' Kuwait, where she was editor of the *Kuwaiti Digest* for six years until August 1, 1990 – the day Iraq invaded. After six weeks as a hostage and escape to Turkey, Josephine moved to the relaxed shores of Andalucia in southern Spain where she initially earned a crust as a ghostwriter, mainly on autobiographies for Marbella-based crooks and minor celebrities. Throughout this time, Josephine wrote regularly for in-flight magazines. She also writes short stories and has had some minor publishing success.

John A Vlahides

San Francisco (Nob Hill, Russian Hill & Fillmore; The Castro & Noe Valley; The Marina, Fisherman's Wharf & the Piers) John has been a cook in a Parisian bordello, a luxury-hotel concierge, a television host, a safety monitor in a sex club and a French–English interpreter, and he is one of Lonely Planet's most experienced and prolific guidebook authors. A native New Yorker living in San Francisco, John has contributed to 18 Lonely Planet guidebooks since 2003. He also cohosted the TV series *Lonely Planet: Roads Less Travelled*.

OUR STORY

A beat-up old car, a few dollars in the pocket and a sense of adventure. In 1972 that's all Tony and Maureen Wheeler needed for the trip of a lifetime – across Europe and Asia overland to Australia. It took several months, and at the end – broke but inspired – they sat at their kitchen table writing and stapling together their first travel guide, *Across Asia on the Cheap*. Within a week they'd sold 1500 copies. Lonely Planet was born.

Today, Lonely Planet has offices in Franklin, London, Melbourne, Oakland, Dublin, Beijing and Delhi, with more than 600 staff and writers. We share Tony's belief that 'a great guidebook should do three things: inform, educate and amuse'.

OUR WRITERS

Helena Smith

Curator, Lake Tahoe, Gold Country Helena is an award-winning writer and photographer covering travel, outdoors and food, and has written guidebooks on destinations from Fiji to northern Norway. Helena is from Scotland but was partly brought up in Malawi, so Africa always feels like home. She also enjoys global travel in her multicultural home area of Hackney and wrote, photographed and published *Inside Hackney,* the first guide to the borough (https://insidehackney. com). Her 1000-word autobiography won a *Vogue* annual writing contest, and she's a winner of the *Independent on Sunday* travel-writing competition.

Brett Atkinson

Central Coast Brett is based in Auckland, New Zealand, but frequently on the road for Lonely Planet. He's a full-time travel and food writer specializing in adventure travel, unusual destinations and surprising angles on more well-known destinations. Craft beer and street food are Brett's favorite reasons to explore places. He is featured regularly on the Lonely Planet website and in newspapers, magazines and websites across New Zealand and Australia. Since becoming a Lonely Planet author in 2005, Brett has covered areas as diverse as Vietnam, Sri Lanka, the Czech Republic, New Zealand, Morocco, California and the South Pacific.

Sara Benson

Marin County & the Bay Area After graduating from college in Chicago, Sara jumped on a plane to California with one suitcase and just $100 in her pocket. Today she makes her home in Oakland. She also spent three years living in Japan. She has worked as a teacher, a journalist, a nurse and a national park ranger. The author of more than 70 travel and non-fiction books, Sara's writing has featured in national and international newspapers and magazines. She has written for Lonely Planet guides covering Peru, Japan, Malaysia, Las Vegas, California, Southwest USA, Canada, Australia and Hawaii, as well as several other Lonely Planet titles.

Alison Bing

San Francisco (Downtown, Civic Center & SoMa; Golden Gate Park & the Avenues; North Beach & Chinatown; The Haight & Hayes Valley; The Mission & Potrero Hill) Over 10 guidebooks and 20 years in San Francisco, author Alison Bing has spent more time on Alcatraz than some inmates, become an aficionado of drag and burritos, and willfully ignored Muni signs warning that safety requires avoiding unnecessary conversation.

OVER PAGE | MORE WRITERS

31901062826096

Published by Lonely Planet Global Limited
CRN 554153
3rd edition – March 2018
ISBN 978 1 78657 361 2
© Lonely Planet 2018   Photographs © as indicated 2018
10 9 8 7 6 5 4 3 2 1
Printed in China